$\mathcal{F}$LIGHT AND $\mathcal{F}$LYING

A CHRONOLOGY

$\mathcal{F}$LIGHT AND $\mathcal{F}$LYING

A CHRONOLOGY

➤ ➤ ➤

David Baker

Facts On File®

AN INFOBASE HOLDINGS COMPANY

Flight and Flying: A Chronology

Facts On File, Inc.
460 Park Avenue South
New York NY 10016

Library of Congress Cataloging-in-Publication Data
Baker, David, 1944–
    Flight and flying : a chronology / David Baker.
        p.   cm.
    Includes bibliographical references and index.
    ISBN 0-8160-1854-5
    1. Aeronautics—History—Chronology.   I. Title.
TL515.B23   1993
629.13'009—dc20   92-31491

Facts On File books are available at special discounts when purchased in bulk quantities for businesses, associations, institutions or sales promotions. Please call our Special Sales Department in New York at 212/683-2244 or dial 800/322-8755.

Text design by Ron Monteleone
Jacket design by Soloway Mitchell Design Associates
Composition and manufacturing by the Maple-Vail Book Manufacturing Group
Printed in the United States of America

10 9 8 7 6 5 4 3 2 1

This book is printed on acid-free paper.

➢ ➢ ➢

To old fliers,
bold fliers and aspirants everywhere

CONTENTS

INTRODUCTION

This book is a detailed and anecdotal chronology of aviation and as such provides a record of achievement in almost 90 years of powered flight. It also includes a survey of developments in lighter-than-air flying beginning with the first hot-air balloons of the late 18th century and the dirigibles of the late 19th century. It does not, however, purport to assemble a complete record of every event associated with flying. To do that would render the book impossibly large. Nor does it include every aircraft or air event that might be mentioned. What it does do is provide for the reader a general survey of aviation history drawing upon events that have in some measurable way contributed to the development of flight and flying.

Because aircraft have played a major role in almost every war this century, a chronology of aviation will obviously have to include many events associated with those conflicts. But this book is not a chronology of conflict itself, nor does it try to cover every activity of air warfare. The reader will note an emphasis on World War I and World War II simply because so many activities in each conflict played an important part in the development of military aviation. Similarly, the expansion of civil aviation in the 1920s and 1930s may appear to concentrate disproportionately on record-breaking flights. The reason for that is contained within the pioneering work done by so many aviators in that period.

The history of aviation is replete with many lessons for politicians and industrialists today. It also has lessons for those who work in the industry and for those who work in other fields but commit interest and spare time to a thorough study of flight. The book has been written with all of these groups in mind because history itself has shown where wrong decisions have had catastrophic results and because these lessons are important for legislators and decision-makers of today and tomorrow. There have been many changes that have both helped and hindered an industry that frequently stands as a national leader in export currency. For so important and vital an employer, there must be a proper sense of direction, and that can only be determined with clarity when past lessons are transformed into working models for the future.

A word about why this book has been written in the way it has may be in order. Most chronologies list numerous events in cryptic style, devoting barely a line to each activity. This chronology is different. Each event is dealt with at some length to ensure a qualified explanation for why the event is important and in a manner that allows the reader to understand the implication for the individual or the activity.

Much thought has gone into style and format. Military ranks, places, company names and other words subject to change through time are written in the form correct on the date to which they apply. Care has gone into relating one event to another so that a researcher may identify, through the index, development of a particular aircraft, project or research program. Some forms of presentation may be at variance with other reference sources. For instance, Messerschmitt aircraft are prefixed ''Bf'' or ''Me'' according to when they were allocated a service identification.

There are also differences from many highly respected references regarding the date or time of a particular event. Wherever possible, the author has used primary sources for reference and avoided as far as possible secondary sources, since these are frequently found to be in error. In several other chronologies, errors have been perpetuated through the continuous use of incorrect information from previously published sources. It is hoped that this has been prevented here.

The NASA Space Shuttle has been relegated to a companion volume on rockets, missiles and spacecraft because the author does not consider it an aircraft. The only qualifying criteria for the shuttle is that it has wings and can glide during its descent through the atmosphere. But it is primarily a spacecraft and cannot fly without first being sent on its way to space, unlike a sailplane that exists to fly in the earth's atmosphere. For this reason, rocket-powered research aircraft are included, as are details of the development of the X-30 hydrogen-burning, air-breathing, research aircraft.

FLIGHT AND FLYING: A CHRONOLOGY

850 B.C. Although the event was first recorded in writing in chronicles dated as late as 1516 (A.D.) in a manuscript titled "The British King he tried to Fly," one of the earliest attempts at flight involved the legendary King Bladud, who is reputed to have devised wings that he attached to his arms for an attempted gliding descent. Reputedly attempting to fly from the Temple of Apollo, he fell ingloriously to his death. The story is not confirmed as a real event but may have some basis in historical fact. Many attempts of this kind are recorded throughout the centuries and may have originated soon after the first man-made structures were built in the earliest civilizations.

200 B.C. The Chinese general Han Hsin used a large kite to measure the approximate distance to enemy fortifications, providing his engineers with information they needed to dig a tunnel under the walls and enter the citadel by a subterranean route. A rope whose length was marked at intervals was attached to the kite and, by measuring the amount of rope played out, this provided the information about the distance from General Han's camp to the inside of the walled fortress. For at least 1,000 years thereafter, the Chinese used kites for observation, sending intrepid observers in baskets high above battlegrounds and enemy camps. Kites were also useful as signaling devices, communicating in code to friendly troops many miles away.

A.D. 852 In one of the first documented attempts at flying, the Moorish savant Armen Firmin survived a perilous descent in a voluminous cloak attached to his back. Although he was unable to fly in the manner he had attempted, the large folds of his mantle prevented the leap from taking his life, enough air being caught in the cape to sufficiently retard his descent and allow him to survive the hair-raising leap to fame. The event took place in Spain and was probably the first recorded incident where the concept of a parachute, albeit primitive, was demonstrated. There are also unsubstantiated records of enormous "cloaks" being used to decelerate intrepid escapees from the walls of besieged castles.

875 In what may conceivably have been the first successful attempt at gliding, Abbas ibn-Firnas leaped from a tower in Spain and "flew to a considerable distance as if he had been a bird." Ibn-Firnas is reported by contemporary writers to have built wings to which he attached feathers in simulated bird flight. The feathers would have done nothing for him, but the wings may have inadvertently provided sufficient lift to give the Moor a limited flight as he glided to the ground. It is just as likely, however, that the reports were prejudiced and that the event was embellished for his contemporary readers.

1000 After centuries of using kites for aerial signaling and for lifting manned observation baskets, the Chinese began devising better lifting surfaces for greater efficiency and weight-lifting capacity in the 10th century. The surfaces of a basic kite are inefficient because they are flat and do not generate lift in still air.

This was understood by the Chinese centuries before it was observed by European aeronauts. Not until George Cayley in the 19th century would such wisdom be chronicled elsewhere.

1010 Eilmer, a monk from Malmesbury, England, is reputed to have put together a series of attachments for his body that enabled him to fly from great heights. Special wings attached to his hands and feet are believed to have provided lift that enabled him to glide some considerable distance. Although not reported until the 19th century, accounts tell of Eilmer jumping from a tall tower and "gliding" a distance of more than 600 ft. There are no precise dates for Eilmer, but scholars believe he was born in 980 and died in 1066.

1250 Roger Bacon, a Franciscan monk, scientist and mathematician and a prolific writer, wrote *Of the Marvellous Powers of Art and Nature* and sought to refute assertions of alchemists that magical powers transcend logic. He was sure that man would learn to fly and that he himself would develop unmanned devices that could be propelled through the air. Because he was unable to appreciate that lift would be crucial to sustained flight, he believed human flight would happen when "flapping" machines were developed.

1452 April 15 Leonardo da Vinci was born at Vinci near Florence, Italy of unmarried parents. He designed several flying devices, most notable being a series of ornithopters, including a man-carrying flying machine that presumed to work by the wings flapping up and down like a bird. There is no evidence to suggest that Leonardo actually built and flew his ingenious contraptions, and evidence suggests that most designs were a collection of contemporary concepts from other inventors. Ornithopters undoubtedly existed in concept well before da Vinci's time and his flapping-wing machine had been preceded by the tireless efforts of aeronauts over the preceding centuries. Da Vinci's work is, however, the first eloquent expression of early concepts in defined shapes and artistic representation, which may have been the limit of his originality in the field of flight. Leonardo died in 1519.

1460 In what may have been the depiction of an early toy ornithopter, a painted panel by an unknown artist shows the Christ child seated on the knee of Mary and holding a device shaped like a spinning top with four short rotor blades and a length of string wound around the bobbin. If attached to a central shaft and appropriately shaped, the rotors would whirl around and generate lift like similar toys today. This predates the ornithopter designs depicted in the drawings of Leonardo da Vinci and confirms that the concept was well developed by the time da Vinci exploited the idea.

1540 June 20 From the tower of a cathedral in Viseu, Portugal, João Torto was reported by contemporaries to have tried an ingenious way of reaching the adjacent St. Matthews Field by air when he attached a set of double wings to his body and leaped over the parapet. The wings were made from iron hoops with cloth lining and covered with calico. Torto donned a helmet in the form of an eagle's head complete with open beak. Unfortunately, but predictably, Torto crashed onto a roof below the tower and died from his injuries within a few days.

1600   In 1700 Paolo Guidotti (1560–1629) was recorded as having made, a century earlier, what was at that time the longest recorded glide in history, a distance of more than 1,000 ft. from the top of a tall building in Lucca, Italy. With wings made of whalebone and feathers, springs were attached to give the wings curvature like that of a bird, an idea brought about by visual comparison rather than the knowledge that camber improves lift at low speed. The validity of the claim is suspect.

1640   A boy of 10 was reputedly propelled through the air a distance equal to the length "of a barn" by a flying device built by the marquis of Worcester, England, an event recorded by Edward Somerset, the second marquis, in his book *A Century of Inventions* published during 1663. The event is supposed to have taken place in a barn "on an Hay-Moor" at Vauxhall. It is possible a car suspended from a cable was used to evaluate different shapes of flying machine, but there is no known way that the event could have actually taken place as recorded by chroniclers. It does serve, however, as further proof of continuing efforts to achieve sustained manned flight.

1650   Salomon Idler of Cannstatt (1610–1670) made a dramatic attempt to fly when he leaped from a tower onto a wooden bridge on which a mattress had been placed. Fitted with iron wings covered with feathers, Idler broke the bridge on impact and killed a group of hens nesting underneath. A cobbler by trade, Idler fled to Oberhausen to escape the wrath of the chicken owner and smashed his wings to pieces in efforts to escape liability.

1655   Robert Hook designed flying models and constructed a module that "sustained itself in the air," in reality suspended by a system of hooks and springs attached to overhead beams, in an effort to calculate the forces required to achieve free flight. Hook came to the revolutionary view that muscle power alone was not capable of achieving sustained flight and that some mechanical contraption would be essential if man were ever to fly. This contradicted popular opinion and did little to stem the ever ready flow of volunteers willing to leap from high places under their own power.

1670   One of the most delightfully romantic contraptions conceived for sustained flight was designed by Father Francesco Lana, the 17th-century Italian prophet of manned flight. His device comprised a small boat suspended by four copper spheres, each 20 ft. in diameter. Lana speculated that being lighter than the surrounding air, an airless container would rise from the ground and fly. With two balloons on either side of the boat, a small sail would provide direction control. What Lana failed to grasp was that the paper-thin vacuum spheres would collapse under atmospheric pressure and that the vessels themselves would serve as sails without the need of canvas. The device was never built.

1678 December 12   An issue of the French magazine *Journal des Scavans* reported the activities of the would-be French aeronaut named Besnier who "flew down from a stool, then a table, afterward from a window and finally from a garrett, from which he passed across houses in the neighborhood." To achieve this remarkable sequence of flights, Besnier was reputed to have attached oblong taffeta frames at each end of two long rods. With a rod held over each shoulder, the forward sections attached to the hands, the rear section to the feet, the operator would pull strings and alternately open and shut concertina strips like window blinds to generate a flapping motion. The shape of this strange device was etched in a wooden panel that hung outside an inn owned by a member of the Besnier family.

1680 April 3   Several flights are reported to have been attempted by daring inventors in the Russian empire, one of the more implausible being the attempt made by a Polish peasant using a rigid airframe supporting wings made of mica. The peasant had apparently received a subsidy from the local authorities that had to be refunded when the attempt failed. The event is reported as having taken place near Moscow, and the peasant was severely beaten for having failed.

1687   In further recorded evidence of the early development of parachutes, de la Loubère's *History of Siam* speaks of what may have been the first parachute descent in the true sense. There is evidence that an athlete was fitted with two huge umbrella-like canopies attached to his waist by two thongs. The king of Siam was witness to the attempt when the athlete flung himself into the air from a tall building and made a successful descent to the ground supported by these canopies.

1709 August 8   The first recorded ascent by a balloon took place when a model hot-air device lifted from the floor of a building at the Casa da India, Terreiro do Paco, Portugal. The balloon was invented by the 24-year-old, Brazilian-born Father Bartolomeu de Gusmao. The Jesuit priest had traveled through Peru and may have picked up the idea for his balloon from ancient legends recording hot-air ballooning 2,000 years earlier. Peru's Nazca Desert is criss-crossed with geometric markings that can be seen properly only from a balloon or a powered airplane. Trials in 1975 with a balloon made from cotton woven to a pattern found in a prehistoric grave proved that pre-Inca Peruvians could have made hot-air balloons from local materials and flown them.

1709   Johannes Ludovicus Hanneman published a book asserting that "we have had no examples or experimental evidence to show that any man has ever flown successfully." It was the first recorded sentiment about flying that approached reality. By the 18th century, pioneers were disillusioned by frequent failure, and the awakening reality of early modern science revealed major problems for would-be aeronauts. From now on, a more systematic application of scientific laws and logic would slowly overwhelm the exhibitionists and dabblers, replacing impossible devices with increasingly plausible design concepts.

1749   During the late 18th century, western scientists turned increasingly to the kite as a tool for practical research into a wide variety of atmospheric phenomena. In 1749 the Scottish astronomer Alexander Wilson raised a series of kites carrying thermometers in a scientific attempt to measure air temperature at various altitudes. In 1752 the American Benjamin Franklin flew a kite during a thunderstorm in an attempt to explore and characterize electricity.

1764   Great Britain's King George III received a request from Melchior Bauer of Saxony for £500 to fund development of a flying machine incorporating wings with a fixed dihedral. It was one of the earliest turning points in aeronautics, where flapping wing designs gave way to fixed wings with camber to generate lift. Flappers were still used, however, to provide forward motion, much in the way a bird was thought by Bauer to propel itself through the air. He was refused the donation and went from England to Prussia, where he asked the same favor of Frederick the Great, only to receive a similar reply. He was branded an idiot, told he was insane and sent packing.

1772   Although not officially recorded until eight years later, an attempt was made to fly from the top of the Tour Guinette in France in a wicker gondola supported by a small canopy and with wings for lift. The wings spanned less than 20 ft., and the canopy measured only 8 ft. by 6 ft. The attempt was a failure, and the contraption and occupant plunged to the ground, with the contraption breaking up as it fell.

1781   An advanced form of glider was built by an Austrian, Karl Friedrich Meerwein (1737–1810), who designed his flying machine using calculations of lift, mass and drag. The glider was constructed in such a manner that it could carry a pilot. The wings were ellipsoidal in shape, and the pilot could control the up and down movement of the elliptical wings, providing, so it is claimed, a minimal degree of ''propulsion.'' The peculiar-looking flying machine is believed to have been flown in Austria on at least two occasions. Meerwein's interest was aroused by rumors of hotter-than-air balloon experiments in France, and he wrote a book discussing his ideas for winged flying machines.

1782 November   The Frenchman, Joseph Montgolfier, began experiments with small balloons made of silk and inflated by hot air. He proposed the use of this ''superhuman means'' to deliver troops on Gibraltar and take the rock from the British. By means of a bag inflated with heat from burning straw, said Montgolfier, ''it will be possible to introduce into Gibraltar an entire Army, which, borne by the wind, will enter right above the heads of the English.'' The first experiments were carried out at Avignon.

1783 April 25   Joseph and Etienne Montgolfier flew the first balloon capable of carrying the weight of a man. From small experimental models, the Montgolfier brothers developed the 35-ft. balloon they launched from Annonay, France, which was calculated as being able to lift 450 lb. A small fire of paper, straw and wood burned below the neck of the envelope, providing the hot air that carried the balloon 1,000 ft. into the French skies. The balloon landed about 1,000 yd. from its launch point and provided both information and encouragement for the Montgolfiers to continue their experiments.

1783 June 5   The Montgolfier brothers first flew the developed version of their balloon at Annonay. This was a much larger balloon than those flown previously, measuring 121 ft. 5 in. in circumference and 137 ft. 9 in. in height. The hot air for the envelope was produced by a small fire and caused the balloon to rise to a height of 6,000 ft. This flight was unmanned as there were still fears about what might happen to people once they rose above the ground into the unknown; one of the questions yet to be answered was whether there would be sufficient air to breathe.

1783 August 27   Jacques Alexandre César Charles flew the first balloon filled with gas rather than fire-heated air. Using hydrogen produced by pouring 498 lb. of sulfuric acid on 1,000 lb. of iron, Charles's first balloon had a diameter of 12 ft. The apparatus was taken to the Champs de Mars, Paris, where its strange appearance caused some panic among local people. There it was launched on a 45-minute flight, coming down near the town of Gonesse 6 mi. away. It was attacked with guns and pitchforks and destroyed

The Montgolfier brothers made history in 1783 with the world's first recorded ascent of a hot-air balloon.

by the people of Gonesse, who thought it was a monster fallen from the sky and tied it to the tail of a terrified horse. The powerful smell of the sulfurated hydrogen must have helped this theory gain credence.

1783 September 19   A 41-ft.-high Montgolfière carried out the first ascent with live passengers at the Court of Versailles. The passengers carried on this flight were a duck, a cockerel and a sheep, secured in a reed cage suspended beneath the balloon envelope. The balloon reached a height of 1,700 ft. during its eight-minute flight, landing safely 2 mi. from the Court in the forest of Vaucresson. The occupants were none the worse for their experience, and their flight helped pave the way for a manned ascent, having helped dispel the worst fears about man's ability to survive in the sky.

1783 October 15   François Pilatre de Rozier made the first manned flight in a hot air balloon, thus becoming the world's first aeronaut. The balloon was a Montgolfière suspended on cables, with a fire of straw suspended beneath the fabric envelope providing the hot air. The first flight was winched out to about 82 ft., but over the next few days, the altitude was increased until de Rozier and others had made flights to 6,500 ft. These tethered test flights answered many questions about the balloon's lifting performance but also demonstrated the potential usefulness of this amazing 18th-century contraption.

1783 November 4   The first officially credited balloon flight in England took place when a 5-ft.-diameter sphere filled with hydrogen was launched privately in London and without the attention of the public. The balloon created considerable consternation when it suddenly floated over Highgate and landed at Waltham Abbey. The balloon's designer was a 31-year-old Italian sailor, Count Francesco Zambeccari. While serving as a mercenary with the Spanish fleet against the Moors, Zambeccari had gotten into trouble with the Inquisition and fled to England, where he recruited the artificial flowermaker Michael Biaggini to make the small balloons.

1783 November 21   François Pilatre de Rozier and the Marquis d'Arlandes made the first untethered balloon flight, becoming the first pilot and passenger to make a journey by air. The balloon was 82 ft. high and 78 ft. 8 in. in diameter. A straw fire produced the hot air and could be fueled by the crew in flight to extend the time aloft. The 25-minute flight began in the gardens of the Chateau de la Muette in the Bois de Bologne. The balloon drifted with the wind across Paris, at a height of about 1,000 ft. and made a safe landing at the Butte aux Cailles near Fontainebleau, a distance of about 5.5 mi., visible proof that balloons could travel distances with passengers and observers.

1783 November 21   In a letter to Sir Joseph Banks, Benjamin Franklin pointed out the value of balloons for lifting besieged people from captive towns and cities and for moving spies under cover of darkness. Balloons could, said Franklin, also be used to observe and survey enemy fortifications, to transmit signals to friendly forces and to coordinate the collective efforts of several military units over great distances. In general, it was civilian more than military personnel who foresaw the potential use and advantages of balloons for military activity.

1783 November 25   The first major public demonstration of a hydrogen balloon in England took place at the Artillery Ground, Moorfields, when Count Francesco Zambeccari organized the unmanned ascent of a 10-ft.-diameter sphere made of oiled silk. The balloon had been exhibited for several days at the Lyceum in the Strand, London, and a large crowd gathered to see it fly. The balloon was carried southwest of London by a stiff breeze, coming down not far from the south coast after traveling 50 mi. A local farmer retrieved it and put the balloon on show for a penny a look.

1783 December 1   Jacques Alexandre César Charles and a Monsieur Robert became the first men to make a free flight in a hydrogen balloon. The flight began at Les Tuileries, Paris before a large crowd and covered more than 20 mi. before landing at Nesles, where it was regarded with awe and astonishment but not attacked as had happened after earlier flights. The balloon envelope was 27 ft. 6 in. in diameter and was made of closely woven taffeta.

1783   Sebastian Lenormand demonstrated the use of one of the world's first aerodynamic braking devices—or parachutes—at Montpellier, France. He jumped from an observation tower suspended beneath a conical canopy that filled with air and arrested his rate of descent. Although modern parachutes are flexible devices easily packaged into a small space, Lenormand's device was rigidly braced and retained its shape.

1784 January 16   Recognizing the long-term military advantages of balloons and aerial devices, Benjamin Franklin asserted in a letter to Jan Ingenhousz, "Ten Thousand Men descending from the Clouds might not in many places do an infinite deal of mischief before a Force could be brought together to repel them."

Moreover, he affirms, "Five Thousand balloons capable of raising two men each, could not cost more than Five Ships of the Line; and where is the Prince who can [not] afford so to cover his country." It would be Guyton de Morveau who would promote the military use of balloons after the French Revolution.

1784 January 19   The largest manned Montgolfière to ascend to date was constructed at Lyons and measured 138 ft. in height and 108 ft. in diameter. Seven people were carried in the balcony surrounding the base of the balloon's envelope. Even carrying this weight, the balloon managed to attain a height of more than 3,000 ft. The crew of this flight included one Montgolfier, Pilatre de Rozier and the Prince de Ligne. Such feats strengthened public acceptance of flight as a safe pursuit and popularized ballooning as a sport. The manufacture and operation of a balloon this size was no mean feat and gave the Montgolfière the potential for carrying useful loads as a practical means of aerial navigation.

1784 February 25   The first balloon flight made in Italy took place from the grounds of a villa owned by Chevalier Paul Andreani near Milan and used a modified Montgolfière hot-air design built by the brothers Charles and Augustin Gerli. The fire brazier was suspended beneath the envelope, and the car was suspended from the hoop supporting the heat source. This was the first such design of its type and would become standard on hydrogen balloons. The balloon had a horizontal diameter of 72 ft. and carried a crew of three. Charles and Augustin Gerli were accompanied by Chevalier Paul Andreani on this first 20-min. flight, during which they attained a height of more than 1,000 ft.

1784 February 25   In the first attempt to control the direction of balloon flight, which otherwise is governed by the direction of the wind, the Academy of Dijon allowed Guitton de Morveau and Monsieur Bertrand to experiment with its balloon. The craft was fitted with a main sail and a rudder in the manner of a ship to allow it use of the wind to steer it through the air. Two large oars were also fitted as a means of propulsion for small maneuvers or calm days. On the first journey, the equipment had no effect on their course except that the sail caused the balloon to gyrate. One more flight on June 12 was no more successful.

1784 March 2   At the Champs De Mars in Paris, the great French pioneer aeronaut Jean-Pierre Blanchard made his first flight with a novel balloon design in which a parachute was fitted between the car and the envelope. Blanchard hoped that in the event of a punctured balloon he could open the parachute and descend safely in his car, which had wings that he assumed would help him navigate. Planning to carry a Benedictine monk named Pesch, he was assailed by a frenetic youth named Dupont de Chambon, who drew a sword and wounded Blanchard in the arm and cut the rigging and wings before he could be restrained. A short flight was made later—without the youth.

1784 April 15   According to an unconfirmed report, the first manned balloon flight in Ireland was made by a Mr. Rosseau, accompanied by an unidentified boy. Contemporary press records state the journey lasted two hours, but the take-off point and the place of landing have not been identified. If true, this flight would make Ireland the third country in which a manned balloon ascent was successfully completed.

1784 April 28   One of the most advanced experiments of its day was the demonstration of the first self-propelled model helicopter by a Monsieur Launoy and a Monsieur Bienvenu at the Académie des Sciences, Paris. A shaft, on which were mounted two four-bladed rotors, ran through a bearing in the center of the bow. The bow-string was looped around the shaft. The bow was then held, and the shaft was rotated to wind the bow-string around it. This tensioned the bow, which, as soon as it was released, unwound the bow-string and rotated the shaft. This drove the rotors and produced lift.

1784 May 20   The first women to make an ascent in a balloon—the Marchioness de Montalembert, the Countess de Montalembert, the Countess de Podenas and Mademoiselle de Lagarde—did so in a tethered Montgolfière from the Faubourg St. Antoine. There is no confirmed report of the height to which they ascended, and there appears to have been no other occupant of the car.

1784 June 4   The first woman to make a free flight in a balloon was Mademoiselle Thible, who ascended in a Montgolfière hot-air balloon named *Le Gustave* and was accompanied by a Monsieur Fleurant, who was in charge of the balloon. They reached an altitude of about 8,500 ft. during a flight that lasted about 45 min. The ascent took place at Lyon, south of Paris, before the king of Sweden, in whose honor the balloon had been named.

1784 June 23   Pilâtre de Rozier carried a chemist named Proust on a record-breaking flight to a height of 11,700 ft. They took off from Versailles before the king of Sweden and the French royal family in a balloon called *Marie Antoinette*. The flight ended after about 45 min. in a field at Luzarche nearly 40 miles away. This was a remarkable performance for the day and marked the level of progress that had been achieved with hot-air balloons evolved from the basic Montgolfière design, which on so many occasions had proved successful and moderately reliable.

1784 July 15   In an attempt to develop a control system to govern the climbing and descending of their balloon, Monsieur Robert and the Duc de Chartres flew a cigar-shaped balloon at St. Cloud that was fitted with a ballonet (a little balloon) inside the main envelope. The ballonet could be emptied entirely or filled with atmospheric air, and it was the presence of this variable weight that was intended to control the balloon, making it ascend when the ballonet was empty and descend when it was full. The craft was also fitted with oars and a rudder intended to enable the balloon to maneuver. The success of these devices was minimal due to the bad weather.

1784 July 18   The first partial success in directing the flight of a balloon was claimed by Jean-Pierre Blanchard, who ascended from Rouen, France in a gas balloon, the control car, or gondola, of which was equipped with four wings and a rudder. The wings were capable of an oar-like motion by which the balloon could be "rowed" through the air, or they could be deployed in the manner of sails, to provide a method of steering the craft. With flapping wings "which I agitated with great force," Blanchard succeeded in turning the balloon, which landed 6 km (3.6 mi.) from Paris, but little else was achieved and he failed to get the credit for what he considered a major contribution to ballooning. Blanchard made his last albeit brief ascent, in France from Bordeaux on July 26 before packing up and leaving for England where there was little competition from other balloonists.

1784 August 25   The son of a Scottish minister, James Tytler, made the first manned balloon hop in England when his hot-air device made a brief but uncontrolled ascent with Tytler in the basket to an altitude of a few hundred feet. His Montgolfière was 40 ft. high and 30 ft. in diameter and carried a large furnace. A

flight attempt on August 7 had been aborted when the contraption caught fire. A major drawback with Tytler's balloon was that the neck opening was almost as great as the diameter of the balloon, which allowed it to draw in unheated air. A third attempt on September 1 was also a failure, and some reports claim the car of Tytler's balloon was broken to pieces by an impatient crowd.

1784 September 15   The first significant hydrogen balloon flight in the United Kingdom was made by Vincenzo Lunardi of Lucca, a member of the Italian embassy staff. He flew a Charles gas balloon, so named because of the development work of gas balloon pioneer Jacques A. C. Charles. The flight began from the Honourable Artillery Company's training ground at Moorfields in London. During the course of his 2-hr. 15-min. flight he landed momentarily in North Mimms parish on the site of what is now Welham Green village in Hertfordshire. Here, his cat, which had accompanied Lunardi on the flight, was landed. Lunardi then jettisoned the balloon's ballast and took to the air again, eventually landing for the last time at Standon Green End near Ware in Hertfordshire, a total journey of 25 mi.

1784 September 19   M. Robert and M. Hulin began a 6-hr. 40-min. flight from the Jardin des Tuileries in Paris in an attempt to demonstrate how balloons might be controlled in the air by means of external appendages. Their balloon gondola was fitted with large parasol-like devices, which could be opened and closed. The idea was that by using these "parasols," the air surrounding the balloon could be either drawn in or pushed away. The aeronauts reckoned that the pulls and pushes would cause a reaction in the opposite direction, thus directing the balloon's course. No discernible change of course is recorded as having resulted from their efforts.

1784 October 4   The first English aeronaut, and the first British subject to make a controlled flight within the United Kingdom, was James Sadler who went aloft in his Montgolfière from the city of Oxford. Sadler ascended to a height of almost 4,000 ft. before coming to earth between Islip and Woodeaton, about 4 mi. away. He was a daring inventor and succeeded in modifying the basic Montgolfière with several innovative and helpful changes that improved the maneuverability of the balloon. On his first flight, his balloon was modified so that the fire could be controlled more efficiently than usual and shut off altogether if necessary.

1784 October 16   French balloonist Jean-Pierre Blanchard made his first ascent in England with John Sheldon (who put up the money for the flight). Their box-shaped car carried a variety of scientific instruments and a basket of pigeons; but the instruments remained aboard only as long as it took Blanchard to realize they hampered lift, whereupon they were thrown overboard. The ascent took place from Lochees Military Academy, Chelsea, and the balloon sped west from London across Chiswick, Twickenham and on to Sunbury, where Sheldon disembarked, before flying on to touch ground at Romsey more than 70 miles from where it set off.

1784   Monsieur Gérard, a French inventor, designed and built an ornithopter, a vehicle in which a wing-flapping mechanism powered by a gunpowder-fuel engine would provide lift and propulsion. It is certain that flight was never achieved by the machine. The idea that manned, powered flight in heavier-than-air craft could be achieved only by emulating bird flight was one that remained popular until the Wright brothers' success at Kitty Hawk in 1903.

1785 January 7 French balloonist pioneer Jean-Pierre Blanchard and an American, Dr. John Jeffries, made an aerial crossing of the English Channel in the first overseas flight. The gas balloon was initially equipped with four oar-like wings to help propel the craft; but as effective control devices they were useless, and Blanchard disposed of them to lighten the load shortly after leaving Dover. In the end, everything that could be jettisoned was thrown out except for a bottle of brandy and a packet of letters, which constituted the first airmail delivery in history. They landed in the Forêt de Felmores, 12 mi. from the coast, after a flight of little more than 2 hr. and a journey of 40 mi.

1785 June 15 In the world's first air disaster, the famous balloonists Pilatre de Rozier and Jules Romain were killed in an attempt to cross the English Channel from France to England. Romain had built a remarkably advanced craft combining a spherical, 33-ft.-diameter hydrogen balloon of the Charlière type tethered above a cylindrical hot-air balloon of the Montgolfière design only 24 ft. high and 12 ft. in diameter. The fire gallery for creating hot air was suspended below the Montgolfière, but lines around the exterior of the cylinder were connected to the hydrogen sphere above. The pair took off at 7:15 A.M., but at 5,000 ft.. the hydrogen was ignited by static electricity and they crashed to earth. This led to the development of static-free balloon fabric. The venture was sponsored by the Comte de Provence, and Rozier's friend the Marquis de la Maisonfort had pleaded unsuccessfully to be taken aboard in place of Romain.

1785 June 29 Letitia Anne Sage was the first woman to make a free balloon flight in the United Kingdom, from St. Georges fields in London. Vincenzo Lunardi had arranged a flight on which he intended Sage, George Biggin and Col. Hastings to accompany him. Inadvertently, Sage also posed one of aviation's first weight and balance problems, as by her own admission she weighed in excess of 200 lb. Lunardi and Col. Hastings, unwilling to embarrass their large passenger, stepped out of the basket, thus reducing the weight to an amount the balloon could lift. The flight ended 10 mi. away at Harrow in Middlesex, where the boys of the famous Harrow school had to rescue Biggin and Sage from an angry farmer upon whose property they had landed.

1785 August 25 Modest results in steering the course of a balloon were obtained in experiments carried out by Messieurs Alban and Vallet, directors of the Javel factory in France. Their balloon was fitted with two large propeller devices similar in construction to the blades of a windmill. These were hand turned, which severely limited their power output, but due to their size it is conceivable that they were able to move a sufficient quantity of air to affect the balloon's course in calm conditions. A lightweight engine might have brought success to the experiment, but as yet none was available. The tests ended September 20.

1785 Following his successes in France and England, Jean-Pierre Blanchard carried out many ascents from several countries throughout Europe. Experimenting with unique combinations of equipment and keeping up a major effort as propagandist for and promoter of balloon flight, he did more than any other balloonist to generate a sense of awareness that a new age of aerial navigation had arrived. During the year, Blanchard made the first aerial ascents in Germany, Holland and Belgium.

1786 June 17 French balloonist Testu Brissy set out from Paris on a gas-balloon flight. He descended initially at Montmorency, a small provincial town in France, where a crowd tried to drag the balloon down by its anchor rope to punish Brissy for a crime of which he was innocent. In the ensuing struggle, the oars of his craft were broken, and fearing for his safety, Brissy cut the anchoring line and dropped his ballast. The balloon climbed to about 4,500 ft. and Brissy was forced to fly for 3 hr. in the middle of a thunderstorm. After a total flight time of 11 hr. he landed again only 6 mi. from Paris.

1787 Blanchard began experiments with parachutes as a means of providing aeronauts with a safe device for making emergency descents from balloons. Unlike earlier experiments with aerodynamic braking systems, the Blanchard canopies were not held open by a rigid structure. Instead they were unbraced cloth discs that were opened and filled with air by the action of their descent, exactly as a modern parachute functions. The first experimental descent was made by a dog, who survived the experience. This success was followed by further drops of increasingly heavier weights.

1788 Blanchard carried out the first aerial ascents from Switzerland. When vertical lift did not occur, throwing caution aside, he dispensed with the car beneath the balloon and hung onto four cords without support. Thus lightened, the balloon slowly ascended.

1789 Blanchard made the first aerial ascents in Poland and Bohemia using Montgolfière balloons rather than the hydrogen balloons he had come to favor. He would return to the hydrogen type later. These European hops brought Blanchard great renown at a time when impatient onlookers expected thrill and would attack the aspiring aeronaut if he did not put his life at risk quick enough! Most spectators came to see the balloonist plunge to his death, and only a few were sufficiently inspired to be genuinely intrigued by the ballooning itself.

1793 January 9 Blanchard made the first balloon flight in the United States. The French pioneer had arrived in America after escaping from the Austrian government, which had arrested him at Kufstein in the Tyrol and charged him with spreading propaganda about the French Revolution. Blanchard's 45th balloon flight began in Philadelphia, Pennsylvania and lasted 46 min. before ending in Gloucester County, New Jersey, a flying distance of 15 mi.

1794 April 2 The world's first air force, the Aerostatic Corps of the Artillery Service was formed in France following a demonstration ascent from the gardens of the Chalais-Meudon on the outskirts of Paris in the hydrogen balloon *L'Entreprenant,* the first used for military tests. Two scientists, Charles Coutelle and Nicolas Conté, were recruited by the Committee of Public Safety to develop the apparatus. Conté was appointed to direct workshops and training facilities at Meudon, and Coutelle was given the rank of captain and appointed to head the corps' first company and a second one set up on June 23. Almost at once, they were dispatched to join the army at Maubeuge.

1794 June 26 The first time a man-carrying balloon played a decisive role in winning a battle was when the Aerostatic Corps of the French Artillery Service used its hydrogen balloon *L'Entreprenant* at the battle of Fleurus to pass messages to the ground while the French Republican Army faced the Austrians. Passing written messages along a thin cord linking the balloon with the ground, Coutelle sent Gen. Morlot information about the effect of French tactical moves on the ground, the first occasion a battle was conducted from the air. Believing the French forces to have signed a pact with the devil and that *L'Entreprenant* was a supernatural object, the Austrians' confidence was broken and they were eventually beaten. The Aerostiers conducted a victory parade into

Brussels, where their balloon remained before being exhibited at Liège.

1794 October 31 The National School for Aerostationing was founded at Meudon by the French government and put under the direction of Nicolas Conté. A number of balloons were designed and built, and their names reflected the revolutionary fervor of the day by characterizing popular themes: *Martial, Emule, Céleste, Industrieux, Intrépide, Précurseur, Svelte, Vétéran* and *Agile.* The school was responsible for developing balloon-handling practices as well as for teaching operating fundamentals and developing a cadre of military balloonists that would satisfy the increasing demand for this new form of reconnaissance.

1796 In the first of a series of experiments that were to lead to his being regarded as the father of aerodynamics, Englishman Sir George Cayley built a bow-powered model helicopter very similar to a small toy flying top from China. Cayley put four feathers at each end of a short rod and powered the device with a bow and string mechanism made from whalebone. Each set of feathers was inclined in opposite directions and the tiny device powered itself into the air. Cayley pioneered the use of propellers yet abandoned this line of research until, near the end of his life, he built a larger model with metal rotors.

1797 October 21 André Jacques Garnerin made the world's first completely successful manned parachute descent from an aerial device when he jumped from a balloon over the plain of Mousseaux. The parachute was attached to the balloon by a line running from the center of the fixed canopy, and Garnerin stood in a cylinder that hung below the canopy for the descent, rather than being bodily attached to it by a harness in the modern manner. His flight began in the Parc Monceau near Paris, and he was taken up to an altitude of more than 1,000 feet, from where he jumped.

1797 October 30 The fee-paying public who attended balloon ascents wanted more showmanship than the mere drama of men and women risking their lives provided, and balloonists were required to add novel features to their spectaculars and satisfy the audience by creating unique events. In an amazing public spectacle, Testu Brissy, aeronaut turned showman, made a balloon flight while seated on a horse. A platform surrounded by a lightweight balustrade was suspended below the gas-bag, on which horse and rider stood completely untethered. The flight was completed successfully with no injuries to either party.

1799 February 18 Upon returning from the Egyptian campaign, Napoleon disbanded the Aerostatic Corps of the Artillery Service, terminating the services of the world's first military air force after five years. N. J. Conté had accompanied the dispatch of balloons and troops to the Egyptian campaign in 1797, but the equipment was captured and destroyed by the British at Aboukir in 1798. The balloon facilities at Meudon, France had run out of money, and Napoleon had a bitter hatred of balloons and their protagonists, believing his own military instincts to be sufficient for battles and wars in which he would engage.

1799 The first design for an aeroplane as we know it today—with fixed wings, cruciform tail unit and a propulsion system—began to emerge when Sir George Cayley engraved on a silver disc the basic outline of a biplane. His was the first design to address the problems of heavier-than-air flight in a practical manner, with provision for control of the craft in its pitch and yaw axis. Many of the aircraft built in later years did not achieve this level of sophistication. Where Cayley failed was in suggesting a

series of paddles as a means of propulsion, a legacy from former ideas that were equally implausible.

1802 November 25 The dangers facing the early hot-air balloonists were tragically demonstrated when aeronaut Monsieur Olivari was killed during a flight that started from Orléans, France. The fuel intended for the balloon's furnace was stowed in the galley area around the base of the balloon, where it was exposed to the heat of the fire. The stored fuel caught fire while the balloon was in flight. Olivari was faced with a terrible choice—one that was to face many pioneer aviators before the general acceptance of parachutes in the 1920s—to jump or to burn. He jumped and was killed.

1802 André Jacques Garnerin made the first successful parachute jump in England from a balloon that carried him 10,000 ft. into the air from St. George's Parade, London. The event was watched by, among others, the painter Robert Cocking, who was an ardent follower of balloonists and their antics, and was reported upon by Sir George Cayley in his 1810 discourse *Aerial Navigation.* Garnerin nearly came to a disastrous end when his parachute swayed violently from side to side due to turbulence at altitude, but he landed safely but bruised in a field near St. Pancras. The Duke of York was one of the first on the scene. At a later date, Garnerin's wife and niece also made parachute descents.

1803 July 18 The first balloon flight conducted expressly for the purpose of scientific research ascended from Hamburg, Germany with Etienne Gaspard Robertson and a German music teacher named Loest. Robertson claimed the balloon reached a height of 23,526 ft. carrying simple scientific experiments provided by the French Academy. Robertson was prone to gross exaggeration, and because his balloon was probably incapable of reaching a height of more than 10,000 ft., it is doubtful he got anywhere near the altitude he claimed.

1804 June 30 Under the auspices of the French Academy, J. B. Biot and J. L. Gay-Lussac began the first in a series of ascents for the purpose of taking atmospheric measurements with a flight from the Conservatoire des Arts et Métiers in the Rue St. Martin. They were unable to exceed an altitude of 13,000 ft. and obtained results that showed conclusively that Etienne Robertson could not have achieved the altitude he claimed the year before.

1804 October 3 Three Italians, a Count Zambeccari, a Signor Andreoli and a Signor Grassetti, made a night balloon flight from Bologna. They experienced the extreme cold of night flying at altitude and eventually came down in the Adriatic Sea, close to some fishing vessels. The fishermen sailed away from the terrifying object that had landed among them, and the three balloonists were saved only after several hours adrift, when the navigator of a passing ship recognized their balloon for what it was and rescued them. Count Zambeccari continued his flights only to be killed when his gas balloon caught fire in 1812.

1804 December 1 Sir George Cayley described for the first time in his notebook a model glider that displayed the flying configuration of a heavier-than-air machine. It had a large-area kite wing attached one-third of the way along the fuselage and had cruciform tail surfaces attached to the fuselage by a universal joint mounted behind the wing. The nose was weighted to keep the model in trim. Cayley was certainly aware of the advantage in a high-aspect-ratio wing, so it is curious that he gave his flying model such a peculiarly inefficient form of lifting device as a kite wing.

Fantasy, fiction and surrealism converged to create a montage of the improbable in this flying machine contrived in 1805.

1804 December 16 To celebrate the coronation of Napoleon, André Jacques Garnerin decorated a giant hydrogen balloon bearing an inscription in gold along with several hanging lanterns and an enormous gilded crown and set it loose from the gates of Nôtre Dame. The balloon was a wonder to behold and completely stole the show as it drifted into the night sky. Next morning it swept low over Rome, barely missing the dome of St. Peter's and the Vatican. In its flight over Rome, part of the gilded crown fell off and dropped onto the tomb of Nero, which was considered by the French to be a bad omen. The balloon came down in Lake Bracciano, and it was held in the Vatican until the French retrieved it in 1814.

1806 April 7 Monsieur Mosment, a French aeronaut, was killed in a tragic accident when he fell from his balloon during a flight from Lille. Instead of making the flight in a gondola or basket hung below the balloon envelope as was the normal practice, Mosment had constructed a simple platform beneath his balloon. He had begun the flight freestanding on this platform but lost his balance, after the balloon had climbed some distance, and fell to his death.

1808 July 24 The first man known without doubt to have abandoned a damaged balloon and saved his life with a parachute was aeronaut R. Jordarki Kuparento when his craft caught fire and he was able to make a safe descent. He had been making a flight in a Montgolfière hot-air balloon over Poland when his craft caught fire while flying over Warsaw. The type of parachute device he employed in his escape is not recorded.

1809 Jacob Degen, a German-Swiss engineer, claimed to have achieved flight by using an ornithopter supported by a small hy-

drogen balloon. The ornithopter could not make an unassisted sustained flight with its externally braced wings flapped by the pilots arms, and after several unsuccessful attempts at flying with the ornithopter alone, Degen suspended the machine beneath a hydrogen balloon to provide the extra lift. In a public appearance of the machine at the Champ de Mars in Paris, Degen failed to achieve his intended flight and was beaten and mocked by the crowd.

1809 George Cayley continued his experiments with heavier-than-air craft when he progressed from test models to his first full-size glider, which had a wing area of 200 sq. ft. The aircraft followed the successful pattern that he had developed in his model experiments and was successfully flown across Brompton Dale, a valley in Yorkshire close to Cayley's manor house, Brompton Hall. All the flights with this glider were carried out without a pilot. Cayley did not record these events in his notebook but reported on the principles involved in articles published by *Nicholson's Journal of Natural Philosophy, Chemistry and the Arts.*

1811 November 10 The first Danish citizen to carry out a balloon flight was Johan Peter Colding from the drill ground at the Rosenberg Castle in Denmark. Colding had been invested with the Order of Knighthood of the Danish Flag Name more than two years earlier and began his balloon experiments by sending up small balloons carrying animals attached to "parachutes." Colding pioneered the use of small balloons for carrying messages across tracts of water that usually hindered the conveyance of mail. The first man to make an ascent from Danish territory was the Belgian Etienne Robertson who went up from Copenhagen on October 1, 1806.

1818 The German-Swiss engineer Jacob Degen, who had been beaten by a Parisian crowd when his ornithopter demonstration had failed (1809), built a model helicopter with contra-rotating rotors. Powered by a clockwork motor, it was the first self-sustaining model to be produced since Launoy and Bienvenu's bow-powered device in 1784. The design was an advanced one, in which each contra-rotating rotor canceled out the torque force produced by the other, thus eliminating one of the major problems of rotary-winged flight. It is not known if the model flew.

1819 July 7 Madame Blanchard, the 40-year-old widow of the French pioneer balloonist Jean-Pierre Blanchard, was killed when a hydrogen balloon flight over Paris went tragically wrong. A ring of fireworks had been suspended beneath the basket of her balloon as part of a display at the Tivoli gardens. Spectators were stunned by the beauty of fireworks and lanterns drifting to earth on miniature parachutes until a stray spark ignited the hydrogen in the balloon envelope. The burning balloon hit the roof of a house in the Rue de Provence, and tipped Blanchard into the street below.

1819 The first parachute descent recorded in America was performed by Louis Charles Guille. Guille jumped at about 8,000 ft. from a hydrogen balloon and landed at New Bushwick, Long Island, N.Y. Even though such demonstrations proved the value of parachutes as emergency life-saving devices at this early stage in the development of aviation, it was to be over 100 years before a parachute was officially recommended or adopted for either civilian or military fliers.

1821 July 19 Charles Green made his first ascent in his revolutionary coal-gas balloon named *George IV Royal Coronation Balloon.* (Heated coal emits a toxic gas that is captured and stored under pressure for use as a lifting agent.) The balloon was the first to use coal gas, and Green would become famous as the arch exponent of the fuel, claiming greater ease of handling, less cost (coal gas cost less than one-third the price of hydrogen) and reduced leakage. Because coal gas was almost eight times as heavy, a balloon of given displacement weighed more and had less lifting capacity. This influenced the size of balloons, which grew rapidly throughout the 19th century as increasing numbers of people used coal gas types.

1824 May 25 A British balloonist named Thomas Harris was killed in an unfortunate accident with a hydrogen balloon. Shortly after ascending from the Eagle Tavern, City Road, London, his balloon was seen plunging to earth at Beddington Park, Croydon, the hydrogen having been inadvertently released from the envelope. It was reported that Harris opened the vent valve too much, but this is implausible. It is more likely that Harris had tied the vent line to the basket and that as the gas slowly escaped and the envelope reduced in size it would cause the line to stretch further and release more gas. Harris died instantly, though his passenger, an 18-year-old girl named Stocks, escaped with injuries.

1824 August 13 The Native American chief Waschisabe made the first aerial ascent by a Native American as a passenger of Dupois Delcourt's balloon "flotilla" at Montjean, France.

1824 November 7 Dupois Delcourt flew his aerial "flotilla" at Montjean, France again. This remarkable craft had one large and four small gas-bags and resembled a small fleet of balloons, hence the name.

1825 Monsieur Morgat, in an attempt to outdo the showmanship of rival aeronaut Testu Brissy, made a flight in a hydrogen balloon from Paris while seated on a stag named Zéphire. In the same way that Brissy had been seated on a horse (1797), the stag stood completely untethered on a platform suspended beneath the gas-bag. In order to draw crowds to their events and fund the high cost of ballooning, aeronauts were always devising fantastic and spectacular events such as this.

1827 The eccentric English schoolmaster and inventor George Pocock built kites big enough to lift his children off the ground. He also attached a pair to his carriage by which, he claimed, he was pulled the 40 mi. between Bristol and Marlborough, Wiltshire at 20 MPH. This *char-volant* (from the French words for chariot and kite) was reportedly demonstrated to King George IV at Ascot races. Pocock also devised a method of pulling a pony-trailor behind the kite-drawn carriage so that the pony could pull the carriage if the wind dropped; apparently he did not understand that if a pony was carried, the kites were an unnecessary complication!

1828 A helicopter with contra-rotating blades was designed by Vittorio Sarti, an Italian engineer, but never built. Although models had proven the viability of the rotary-winged approach to flight, the problem of developing a lightweight powerplant proved the major stumbling block in its development.

1836 November 7 The first long-distance flight made from England began when a hydrogen balloon, named the *Royal Vauxhall* (because the flight began at Vauxhall Gardens in London), carried Charles Green, the balloonist, Robert Holland, member of Parliament, and Monck Mason, the Irish flute player and opera patron, nonstop to the Duchy of Nassau. Copper floats carried by the huge (70,000 cu. ft.) balloon to provide buoyancy in case it came down in the English Channel were dumped over France. The balloon covered 480 miles in 18 hr., and the trio were treated like heroes by the people of Weilburg, a town near their landing place.

1837 July 24 An English painter and parachute inventor, Robert Cocking, plunged to his death while trying out a radical new parachute design after being released from a huge balloon, called the *Nassau* (formerly the *Royal Vauxhall*) and piloted by Green, at a height of about 5,000 ft. Cocking had seen the 1802 descent by Garnerin, where wild oscillations threatened disaster. Cocking persuaded the owners of the *Nassau* to pay for construction of a 33-ft. diameter, funnel-shaped parachute weighing 223 lb. and made from light timber spars in the form of an inverted cone, a decision first proposed by Cayley after watching Garnerin. The design was acceptable, but construction was flawed, and Cocking, aged 61, paid with his life.

1839 April 27 The American balloonist John Wise made his first flight with a balloon equipped to deflate on landing. The envelope was made with a detachable panel from which a line ran down to the basket. The "ripping panel" could be pulled loose the instant the basket touched earth, preventing the envelope filling with air and dragging basket and passengers along the ground. Although this ingenious device made landing a lot safer and more uneventful than the common practice of deploying a grappling hook, it was a long time before the ripping panel became a standard feature.

1842 A working model of a steam-powered helicopter was built by English engineer W. H. Phillips. Steam pipes were set into the rotor blades, and the rotor was powered by steam pressure released through nozzles at the rotor blade tips. This was a remarkable achievement but lacked a proper control system. The theory of rotary-winged flight was receiving attention from engineers all over the world, but it was to be another century before the development of a working three-axis control system would allow for the mechanical adjustment of not only the pitch of the individual blades but also the tilt of the entire rotor disc.

1843 July 16 A child had an incredibly lucky escape when he was caught by the belt in the landing hook of an empty balloon belonging to a M. Kirsch. The balloon had broken free from its moorings at Nantes, France and was trailing its landing hook on the end of a rope. The child, whose name has not been recorded, was carried out to sea at a height of about 1,000 ft. The balloon and its unwilling passenger made a gentle landing little more than a mile away on the island of Gloriette. The child was uninjured.

1843 Patents were issued on the design of a steam-powered, passenger-carrying airplane designed by English engineer William Samuel Henson, who was born in 1812. The Aerial Steam Carriage, or Ariel as it was known, was to form the backbone of the prospective Henson's Aerial Steamship Company. The detailed drawings that accompanied the patent application showed a further move toward the modern configuration of an airplane. It was a large monoplane with a span of 150 ft. and a tail combining control functions of elevators and rudder. Power was to be provided by a 30 HP-steam engine driving two sets of six-bladed propellers. Cayley dismissed the idea, asserting steam engines were too heavy to power a flying machine.

1845 The first model airplane powered by a steam engine was built by two English engineers, William Samuel Henson and John Stringfellow (1799–1883). It was a scale model of Henson's "Aerial Steam Carriage" design and had a wing span of 20 ft. and a wing area of 62.9 sq. ft. The tiny steam engine drove twin pusher propellers, and the take-off was assisted by an angled launching ramp. Even with this assistance, the model was not able to maintain flight due to the low power and high weight of its engine. Tests with the airplane continued for two years, and its lack of success discouraged Henson who, after marrying, emigrated to the United States in 1848.

1848 Stringfellow tested a model airplane fitted with a modified steam engine based on the unsuccessful trials made with the Henson model beginning in 1845. The airplane had a span of 10 ft. 6 in. and a wing area of 12 sq. ft., with a scalloped trailing edge believed to improve stability. The device was launched along a wire at Chard in Somerset, near Bala Down where the Henson-Stringfellow tests of 1845–47 took place, but there is no evidence that it was capable of true flight.

1849 June During the siege of Venice, the Austrians attempted the first recorded incident of pilotless aerial bombing. They attached 30-lb. bombs to time switches connected to small Montgolfière balloons and hoped winds would carry the balloons across to the enemy, but the air currents caused many of the 200 balloons thus launched to drift back in the direction from whence they had come. Almost no damage was done to the enemy by those that did manage to make it. The lack of directional flight control was a serious drawback with hot-air balloons and kept alive the spirits of aeronauts intent on achieving heavier-than-air flight.

1849 The first person in the world to fly in a heavier-than-air aircraft was a 10-year-old boy who made a tethered flight in a triplane glider designed and built by Cayley at Brompton Hall, near Scarborough, England. The glider was launched into the air on the end of a rope pulled by people running downhill. When the glider passed over the heads of the runners, the rope automatically released from a hook on the aircraft. Flights of only a few yards were achieved. The name of the boy who made the flight was not recorded, but as Cayley had no children, it was most likely the son of a servant.

1850 September The French aeronaut Monsieur Gall was killed when he was unexpectedly pulled into the air by his hydrogen balloon. He had intended to fly while seated on a horse suspended beneath the gas-bag in a harness, unlike the previous flights with animals where the mount stood on a platform. Due to a misunderstanding, the harness was not secured, and Gall was carried aloft while holding onto the balloon. He eventually lost his grip, fell into a vineyard and was killed. Many stunt flights ended in tragedy, and this led to a macabre fascination among the public for such events.

1851 M. E. Godard, the French aeronaut famous for his bizarre and spectacular balloon flights, made one of his most remarkable trips, on a flight that began at the Paris Hippodrome in a passenger-carrying gas balloon. What made the flight so unusual was the accommodation Godard provided for his guests. Rather than a gondola or basket, as was the normal practice, Godard suspended a comfortable, fully furnished house beneath the gas envelope. The house had been built for this purpose and was made as light as possible.

1852 September 24 The world's first powered, manned dirigible flew for the first time. Designed and built by Frenchman Henri Giffard, the power was supplied by a 3-HP steam engine driving an 11-ft. diameter three-bladed propeller. A small steam engine was a manageable weight in a dirigible. The controls, engine and crew were suspended beneath an elliptical, 88,000 cu. ft. capacity coal-gas envelope. The entire assembly was 144 ft. long. The

flight from the Paris Hippodrome to Trappes lasted 3 hr. 25 min. and covered 17 mi. at an average speed of 5 MPH. This was a major breakthrough; at last man could choose his course in the air.

1852 Cayley published the description of a modern airplane that had it been noted at the time, possessed all the elementary characteristics of heavier-than-air flying machines. The glider had a monoplane configuration with a large, bat-like wing beneath which hung an aerial car, the entire assembly being very rigid and liberally equipped with rigging. There appears to be some development since the boy-carrying glider of 1849, and Cayley appears to have gone to considerable length to strengthen the structure for man-carrying flight. A technical review of the design was published by Cayley in the *Mechanics Magazine,* September 25, 1852.

1853 The first man to fly in a heavier-than-air device is believed to have been Sir George Cayley's coachman, propelled into the air downhill in a full-size glider designed and built by Cayley. The design of the flying machine is not known in detail, although it was probably a biplane and possibly even a triplane built on information developed from his 1852 design. Tests took place sometime after August 25 when he noted that the machine had been built and weighed but not tested. The coachman reportedly protested that he had been employed to drive horses and not to fly!

1853 A French aeronautical designer, Michel Loup, put together the first seriously practical airplane configuration and suggested an airplane made in the shape of a bird with a rigid fuselage. It would be powered by two propellers, one set into each wing, and it had a tricycle undercarriage with which it would run along the ground before reaching flying speed. It is not certain if Loup really appreciated the purpose of the undercarriage or if it was merely a mechanism for the airplane to stand on while motionless. It did, nevertheless, establish a realistic approach to airplane design in France.

1853 Louis Charles Letur became the first person to pilot a heavier-than-air machine when he tested for the first time his parachute-glider carried into the air by a balloon. Comprising a large, umbrella-like device beneath which sat the pilot, it had two large wing-like oars with which Letur thought the pilot could row himself down to the ground. In reality, the oars probably maintained lateral stability while the canopy retarded the rate of descent, but it was not successful. Letur was killed when the balloon dragged him through trees near Tottenham, England as he was trying to land.

1856 The author of *L'Empire de l'Air,* L. P. Mouillard, designed, built and attempted to fly a model glider. This and several other attempted models were to prove incapable of flight. Although the basic formula of weight, thrust, lift and drag had been explained by Sir George Cayley in England, they had not been widely circulated, and there were still a great many inventors and designers who did not understand the fundamental physics of flight. Consequently most of the designs for aircraft in this period were completely unaerodynamic.

1856 Viscount Carlingford designed a monoplane with wings and tail in the form of a bird, the common configuration for aerial machines of the day, and suggested it would fly if equipped with a propeller in the nose. There is little evidence to suggest he actually built the device, but at least the frame was put together in the form of either a kite or a glider. Carlingford tested this so-called aerial chariot in Ireland, but little is known about the success of the contraption, which probably comprised a kite-like object held against the wind.

1857 December 15 Dubbed the Father of Aeronautics by his peers and properly recognized for having laid the foundation of aviation science only decades after his death, Sir George Cayley died at his home at Brompton Manor at age 83. Inspired by the Montgolfier brothers, Cayley never lost faith in his belief that man would fly heavier-than-air machines one day.

1857 French Navy officer Félix du Temple de la Croix began experiments with model aircraft that were to lead him to the brink of success. His first models were powered by clockwork motors and flew well. Thus encouraged, du Temple began flights in 1858 using miniature steam engines. In model form, a steam engine was sufficiently powerful and light to enable such a craft to work, but when scaled up to man-carrying proportions, the power-to-weight ratio was incapable of sustained flight. Nevertheless, de la Croix's models probably made the first sustained flights with heavier-than-air devices.

1857 A former sea captain and amateur aspiring aeronaut, Jean-Marie le Bris, attempted to make a flight in a glider he built resembling an albatross. As a seaman, le Bris had frequently admired the soaring flight of the great sea bird and made his glider in its image. With a body in the shape of a canoe, it had narrow, arching wings each 23 ft. long with a lifting surface of 215 sq. ft. Equipped with pulleys and cables for control, the device was launched down a slope on a horse-drawn cart before being released for flight. The trial was not particularly successful—le Bris broke his leg—but he persisted with the design for more than 10 years without result.

1858 March 29 Two men named Brown and Dean made the first balloon flight in Australia in a hydrogen balloon named the *Australasian.* The flight began in Cremorne Gardens, Melbourne. On the whole, Australians were much more enthusiastic about the development of aviation than Europeans were, and they recognized even at this early stage that aviation, once fully developed and available, would solve many problems of distance and isolation peculiar to their continent. As evidenced by newspaper and magazine articles testifying to this view, some Australians also felt that aerial navigation would become just as important for the future development of nations as seapower had been for the expansion of empires.

1861 June 9 Two members of the First Rhode Island Regiment, James Allen and Dr. William H. Helme, made the first U.S. Army trial captive balloon ascent. On April 15 President Abraham Lincoln called for troops to support the Union cause, and on April 19 Allen and Helme carried two of Allen's balloons from Providence, Rhode Island to Washington, D.C. For several decades, American balloon enthusiasts had been experimenting with the use of balloons for military reconnaissance duties but with little idea of the optimum application for surveillance. There were reports that one of the two balloons was moved to Harper's Ferry, but this remains unsubstantiated. Allen left the army in July 1861 following the loss of both balloons but rejoined in March 1862 as head of the Balloon Corps.

1861 June 18 Thaddeus S. C. Lowe transmitted the first telegraphic message ever sent from a balloon during tests at the Columbia Armory, Washington, D.C. The tests were funded by a $250 grant from the War Department. A wire was connected from a key in the balloon to a line between the War Office and the Alexandria telegraph office with a spur line going straight to the White House. Convinced of the balloon's use in the two-month-old civil war, balloon advocate Lowe was brought to Washington by Murat Halstead, editor of the Cincinnati *Commercial,* where he met President Lincoln on June 11. Lowe had made his first trial flight for a projected Atlantic crossing on April 20, 1861—just a week after hostilities began—between Cincinnati and Unionville, S.C., but he had been allowed to return via Louisville, Kentucky.

1861 July 24 Thaddeus Lowe made the first free balloon ascent for the Union Army when he went up at Fort Corcoran to observe whether victorious Confederate forces were marching on Washington. He was able to confirm that no such force was approaching. Lowe had lost out to balloonist John Wise in a bid for construction of an army balloon, submitted June 26, 1861. However, when Wise failed to show up at Gen. Irvin McDowell's headquarters to support the latter's march on Virginia, Lowe was ordered July 17 to join McDowell's Army of the Potomac. As Lowe was inflating his balloon, Wise arrived and was sent forward to join McDowell, but his balloon was damaged en route. Lowe went forward in his place, only to meet up with McDowell's men returning to Arlington from their defeat at Bull Run.

1861 July 31 John La Mountain made the first successful aerial reconnaissance of the Civil War when he ascended in his balloon *Atlantic* over Hampton, Virginia. He had been sent from New York to the assistance of Maj. Gen. Benjamin F. Butler at Fort Monroe and ascended to a height of 1,400 ft., from where he spotted two previously unknown Confederate camps. La Mountain had been involved with balloons before war broke out, and he quickly volunteered his services along with other balloonists, including Thaddeus Lowe. His letters were ignored until June 5 when Maj. Gen. Butler, commander of the War Department of Virginia, offered La Mountain the job of aerial observer.

1861 August 3 La Mountain became the first balloonist to use boats for aerial operations in a military conflict. Using the Union tug *Fanny,* he ascended from its deck to a height of 2,000 ft. to conduct aerial reconnaissance of Confederate forces, gaining vital information about their positions and strength. Later, the tug *Adriatic* was also pressed into similar service.

1861 September 24 Thaddeus Lowe made the first use of aerial telegraphy on the battlefield to signal from his balloon, *Union,* to help target enemy artillery fire on Confederate forces at Falls Church. The first military balloon of Lowe's design had been completed in August, and it had a volume of 25,000 cu. ft. It was the first balloon anywhere to incorporate design changes made directly to assist its military potential. Lowe added a spreader-hoop below the primary hoop to keep the lines connecting the observation car to the envelope out of the way of observers leaning over the side. This helped their view and their ability to move around the car.

1861 October 1 Lowe created the first air arm in the U.S. armed forces, the American Army Balloon Corps. One of the first trained aeronauts in the United States and a staunch believer in the potential of aviation, Lowe remained a civilian and was given the title of chief aeronaut of the Army of the Potomac under Gen. McClellan. The formation initially consisted of 50 men and five balloons, and they were tasked with providing a long-range reconnaissance platform and supplying accurate direction of fire for the artillery.

1861 October 4 Following his transfer to the Army of the Potomac in July, La Mountain began a series of free ascents from the Cloud's Mill headquarters of Brig. Gen. W. B. Franklin with his balloon *Saratoga*. La Mountain's practice was to ascend into prevailing easterly winds to drift toward the Confederate lines, then jettison ballast and rise into the westerlies at higher altitude to bring him back to the Union lines when his mission was over. On one occasion, October 18, he came down into the German Brigade under Brig. Gen. Louis Blenker and received a volley of rifle fire. *Saratoga* was lost November 16 when winds tore it from its moorings, leaving only the older, smaller *Atlantic*.

1861 November The USS *G. W. Parke Curtis* was pressed into service and adapted as the world's first aircraft carrier. Converted from a coal barge, the *Curtis* was fitted with a flat deck for handling and launching balloons, several winches for deploying the balloons and large hydrogen cylinders in the hold for inflating the balloons. The conversion and deployment was carried out under the direction of Chief Aeronaut Lowe. As part of Gen. McClellan's Army of the Potomac, the *Curtis* was used to transport and tow observation balloons along the Potomac River.

1862 February 19 John La Mountain was dismissed from the service of the Union Army following a confrontation with Thaddeus Lowe, who sought to discredit him. Lowe had impressed Union commanders with his organizational skills and used favor to eliminate people who he believed could challenge his own ambitions, which were to dominate balloon activities in the Union Army. Lowe unjustly persuaded the Army that La Mountain was incompetent and had both La Mountain and John Wise dismissed.

1862 May 31 During the Battle of Fair Oaks, the American Army Balloon Corps' hydrogen balloon *Intrepid* saw service as a reconnaissance, observation and artillery spotting platform. Although military strategists acknowledged that balloons provided unique advantages unavailable elsewhere, they refused to accept that they could, by themselves, alter the outcome of a conflict.

1862 December 11 A U.S. Army balloon was used successfully as an observation and warning platform during the crossing of the Rappahannock River. The great value of this new information source in such tactical movements was the ability to keep the field commander in touch with the positions of his forward

Flying machines like this steam-powered helicopter of 1862 were contemplated by inventors and fiction writers alike.

units, and in preventing outflanking and surprise maneuvers by the opposition from seriously endangering the advance. It was the speed with which the reconnaisance information could be passed back and acted upon that made a great difference to the conduct of the land battle.

1863 April 30 The American Army Balloon Corps saw action during the battle of Chancellorsville where several balloons were used for observation and artillery direction between this date and May 5. The entire battle area could be covered in depth by the use of strategically located balloons at differing altitudes. The reports of reinforcements and rear echelon maneuvers from a high balloon could be added to the immediate tactical assessments of a lower balloon covering the battlefield to give the field commander an overall picture of the enemy dispositions, allowing him to plan the most effective counter to the enemy's strategy.

1863 June The U.S. Army Balloon Corps was disbanded, leaving a void in military aeronautics that would last for 30 years. It was administered first by the Topographic Engineers from the first ascent by James Allen on June 19, 1861, and on March 31, 1862, it was put under the control of the Quartermaster. On May 25, 1862, it was put under the command of the Chief Topographic Engineer of General McClellan's staff. It was returned to the Quartermaster after the Peninsula Campaign, and then on April 7, 1863, it was transferred to the Corps of Engineers under Capt. Cyrus B. Comstock, chief engineer of the Army of the Potomac, before command passed to Brig. Gen. Gouverneur K. Warren shortly before the Balloon Corps was disbanded.

1863 October 4 One of the largest balloons of the 19th century made its first flight from the Champ de Mars in Paris when the brothers Louis and Jules Godard ascended for a flight lasting several hours. In what may have been the first commission for a device designed for aerial land mapping, Gaspard Félix Tournachon had the Godard family design and build his *Le Géant*. It was 197 ft. high with a capacity of 212,000 cu. ft. and a lifting payload of almost 5 tons. The basket was 13 ft. by 8 ft. and could accommodate special wheels below the floor. Tournachon hoped to stimulate experiments leading to powered heavier-than-air flight, about which he wrote much during the year.

1864 June Maj. Gen. Benjamin F. Butler, commander of the Union Army of the James, ordered engineer Edward W. Serrell to research the prospect of aircraft being developed for aerial reconnaissance. Serrell was told about a helicopter device that had been proposed to Gen. Ormsby M. Mitchell in November 1861. This tin toy mounted a 4-in. fan capable of lifting it to a height of 100 ft. Serrell designed a 52-ft.-long machine with four lifting fans and two propulsion fans driven by a steam boiler. Wealthy oilmen paid for construction of a 32-ft. sheet-iron screw capable of lifting 500 lb., and Bennett & Risley of New York were contracted to build the steam engine. It was never finished.

1864 During the War of the Triple Alliance (1864–70), the forces of Brazil, Argentina and Uruguay fought Paraguay. The Brazilian Marquis de Caxais used balloons for reconnaissance and as platforms for gun-spotting during the conflict. The Brazilians were to occupy Paraguay until 1876.

1864 Possibly influenced by the inventions of Gustave de Ponton, of the French Société d'Aviation, who was a prolific inventor and potential aeronaut, M. Nadar made engravings to show his concept of a rotary-winged flying machine utilizing coaxial motors and umbrella-shaped parachutes. De Ponton built small toys powered by electric motors, and Nadar appears to have taken the idea a stage further without the practicalities that made the toys achieve some level of success. Drawings and engravings began to appear in profusion, and in a period when nobody knew for sure which configuration of flying machine would be the most successful, anything looked like a potential favorite.

1865   After two years of work, the French engineer Charles le Louvrie put the finishing touches on a refined design for a reaction motor that was sound in principle although Louvrie lacked the more vital physical data essential for an efficient design. The device was to be propelled by gasoline or some form of hydrocarbon exhausting through twin tail pipes. Just as there were many different views on the most efficient shape of an aircraft, propulsion engineers were exploring all forms of power in the hope of finding an effective method of moving an airframe through the air.

1866 June 27   The first meeting of the Aeronautical Society of Great Britain, recently formed in London, heard a paper from the respected marine engineer Francis Herbert Wenham about airfoils and lifting surfaces. In this paper, he extended the findings of Cayley and concluded that a cambered wing generated more lift than a flat surface and that most of the lift generated came from the forward portion of the wing when set at an appropriate incidence. Wenham had wide interests in science and engineering, and his paper, ''Aerial Locomotion,'' was to become a classic in the manner of Cayley's three-part discourse *On Aerial Navigation* published in 1809.

1867   The design of a reaction-powered, delta-wing aircraft was patented by two Englishmen, J. W. Butler and E. Edwards. The patent covered a specific form of delta aircraft powered through the air by a reaction motor burning a mixture of gas and oil or by the action of compressed steam causing a reaction for forward flight. Butler and Edwards also patented a biplane airframe propelled by a giant, four-bladed propeller spun by tip-jets exhausting compressed steam.

1868 June   The Aeronautical Society of Great Britain staged its first exhibition at Crystal Palace, London. The quest for a successful, lightweight aircraft powerplant was displayed in the many model engines powered by steam, oil, gas and guncotton. Although all had drawbacks of weight, size, power output or, in the case of one of the oil engines, extreme vibration, the exhibit proved that strenuous efforts were being made all over Europe to solve the problems of heavier-than-air flight, even in the face of official indifference and public ridicule.

1868   British patent no. 392 was issued to M. P. W. Boulton for an aircraft control concept based on gas-jet reaction control and movable surfaces like stabilizers attached to the side of the fuselage. This was the first recorded instance of a control concept integrating separate aerodynamic surfaces to maintain stable and directional flight by reacting against air pressure. Boulton proposed the use of a pendulum to automatically operate the flaps when the aircraft rolled, lateral control being maintained by the up and down movement of these surfaces. Boulton also suggested the idea that a pilot could manually control the movement of these surfaces to change flight direction.

1870 July 19   As the Franco-Prussian War began, the Prussian Army formed two Luftschiffer detachments organized by the British balloonist Henry Coxwell, from whom the Germans had ordered balloons. Coxwell had demonstrated the use of balloons for bombing during demonstrations conducted in Berlin during 1848–49. The Luftschiffer detachments comprised a balloon and 20

men each, but they were disbanded several months later when the two detachments were immobilized through the lack of a hydrogen generator. One balloon was taken to the outskirts of Paris, but unable to inflate it, the Germans had to take it back unused.

1870 September 17   Four army balloons were sent into the air at the Battle of Valenton, the first French balloons to be used for military service during the Franco-Prussian War. Two private balloons were also sent up from Montmartre and Montsouris, but little came of their efforts to spy on the enemy. Later, when Paris was encircled, the balloonists suggested to the head of the post office that they use their balloons to carry mail in and out of the city to maintain contact with the provisional government at Tours.

1870 September 23   Accepting an offer to help shift messages between the besieged city of Paris and the government of Tours, postal officials loaded the balloon called *Le Neptune* (which had a leaky, old gas-bag) before it shot off into the air at high speed from the Place St. Pierre in Montmartre. Dropping propaganda cards on the Germans who had effectively cut off all ground access to Paris, balloonist Jules Duruof sped through the sky with 227 lb. of mail that he delivered at the Chateau de Craconville, 3 mi. from Evreux, 3 hr. 15 min. later.

1870 November 24   The first night flight takes place when *L'Archimède* leaves the Orléans station and flies to Castelze in Holland. A second flight that night, with *La Ville d'Orléans*, carried a balloonist and his passenger 1,950 miles to Konigsberg, Norway in 14 hr. 40 min. at an average speed of 133 MPH. Daylight flights had been stopped November 18 after rumors circulated that Prussian guns outside Paris could shoot down balloons as low as 3,500 ft.

1870   A model ornithopter was successfully flown by Gustave Trouve, using a novel form of propulsion involving revolver cartridges fired into a tube. The action of the discharge pushed movable wings into the down position while springs reversed the action and brought them back up, followed immediately by the firing of a second cartridge to begin another cycle. The model was surmounted by a canopy, but as only 12 cartridges were carried, the flight performance was strictly limited. Nevertheless, Trouve managed flights of 200 ft. from a mid-air launch and even drew plans for a scaled-up version. The mechanical complexity would have added so much weight that large, man-carrying machines would have been impossible.

1870   British patent no. 1469 was issued to Richard Harte for his designs related to the control of aircraft in flight. As an improvement on the work of M. P. W. Boulton in 1868, Harte proposed the use of flaps on the wing trailing edge for directional control and for stability. These foreshadowed the use of ailerons for lateral control but operated in a different manner. Harte suggested these control surfaces could be used together as elevators or separately to make the aircraft turn. He also suggested they could be used to counteract the torque of a rotating propeller.

1870   One of the giants of aeronautical application was the Frenchman Alphonse Pénaud, who studied Cayley and applied to working models many of the early writings of that extraordinary Englishman. The first was the application of the twisted rubber band to miniature flying machines, a development exploited throughout the world ever since. All children (and those children at heart) have Pénaud to thank for countless hours of pleasure ''flying'' toy airplanes powered by rubber bands. He also built a small helicopter with contrarotating rotors that inspired manufacturers to take up the device as an early toy for air-minded children—and others!

1871 January 28 The last balloon to leave Paris during the Prussian siege took off with orders for the French fleet to bring food and supplies to replenish the French capital, an armistice having been signed. The flight of the *General Cambronne* ended a period of almost exactly 5 months during which the advantages of balloons were put to efficient use. In that period, 58 balloons on one-way trips successfully departed Paris and reached the outside world carrying a total 102 people, 5 dogs, 400 pigeons and 2.5 million items of correspondence weighing a total of almost 10 tons. In addition to these, 8 balloons (12%) failed to make it out successfully. For their efforts, each balloonist was presented with a special medal.

1871 August 18 Alphonse Pénaud achieved the first flight of an inherently stable airplane when his Planophore was flown 131 ft. in 11 sec. before the Société de Navigation Aérienne in the Tuileries Gardens, Paris. The model had a wing span of only 18 in. and a wing area of 76 sq. in. with a small rubber band driving an 8-in. propeller in the tail. The center of gravity was just behind the center of pressure, and the model obtained lateral stability through pronounced dihedral at the wing tips. The tail was in a diamond shape, also with tip dihedral. By this act, Pénaud revitalized the study of aerodynamics, resurrected the works of Cayley and stimulated serious effort toward sustained heavier-than-air flight with an inherently stable flying machine.

1871 The world's first wind tunnel was built by F. H. Wenham in collaboration with John Browning for the Aeronautical Society of Great Britain. Wenham was also the first scientist to investigate and deduce the properties of lift and lift distribution from a cambered airfoil section wing, although others had earlier calculated the beneficial effects of a cambered wing. He tested and proved his theories by building and flying a series of gliders with great success. As with all of the great pioneers of the day, Wenham was hampered by the lack of an efficient, lightweight engine; except for that, there is a reasonable chance that his experiments would have ultimately proved successful.

1872 February 2 In what may have been the only attempt to employ a group of people on the task of rowing a balloon through the air, the cylindrically shaped airship designed and built by Dupoy de Lome made its first flight from the Fort Neuf in Vincennes, France. Originally commissioned to build a balloon that would reach the besieged city of Paris, de Lome finished his balloon too late for that duty. It was 118 ft. long with a diameter of almost 49 ft. and carried a car that held eight "rowers." On its first flight, it reached a height of 3,350 ft. and a maximum speed of 6 MPH, its designer unaware that a steam engine would weigh less than eight rowers!

1872 A 50m-long dirigible was successfully demonstrated by Austrian Paul Hanlein. This machine was a major breakthrough but suffered from several design drawbacks. The dirigible was powered by a 5-HP (3.7 kW) Lenoir engine that was fueled by hydrogen from the envelope. The airship literally consumed itself as it flew. This put a severe limitation on range and payload capabilities for the craft, but as an experimental machine, it substantiated several theories regarding powered flight and broke new ground in aeronautics. Hanlein made a number of tethered flights in the airship, but no free flights are recorded.

1874 October 16 In France, a Commission on Communications was set up with balloon, telegraph and pigeon sections. The balloon section was headed by Col. Laussedat of the Corps of Engineers, who had as his deputy one of the most prominent early figures in French aeronautical history, Capt. Charles Renard. Born on November 23, 1847, Renard studied at the Ecole Polytechnique in 1868 and chose a military career with the engineers. Like Alphonse Pénaud, Renard appreciated that heavier-than-air flight was the key to aerial navigation but sought to experiment first with balloons. During the early 1870s, Renard experimented unsuccessfully with a ten-wing glider.

1874 By using a launching ramp to gather speed, Félix du Temple de la Croix, a French Navy officer, made a short hop, rather than a true flight, in his bird-like monoplane aircraft at Brest in France, thus becoming the first person to leave the ground in a powered aircraft. The aircraft proved incapable of sustained flight and would have been unable to accelerate sufficiently to achieve even short hops if du Temple had attempted to take off under his own power from level ground. Power came from a small steam engine driving a multi-blade propeller. This installation was to prove too heavy and too weak to maintain sufficient airspeed for flight.

1875 April 15 Beginning at precisely 11:32 A.M., the balloon *Zenith* ascended carrying Gaston Tissandier, the physicist Joseph Croce-Spinelli and Henri Sivel in an attempt to establish an altitude record. They had individual breathing tubes fed by separate bladders of air and oxygen. Reaching almost 23,000 ft., they began to use the oxygen and dropped ballast. Shortly thereafter, they became ill and descended before dropping more ballast and climbing to more than 26,000 ft. In the rarefied air, Tissandier passed out twice and woke from the second faint to find his colleagues dead on the floor of the basket. *Zenith* returned to earth, and Tissandier survived.

1875 Thomas Moy, an ardent engineer and patent agent, successfully "flew" a steam-powered flying machine at the Great Exhibition Hall and Park, Crystal Palace, London with his Aerial Steamer, the product of ten years of devoted research into the problems of powered flight. Hurtling round a circular track, the 120-lb. flying machine was powered by a 3-HP steam engine, which eventually allowed sufficient lift under its wings to lift it a mere 6 in. into the air before it clattered down to the rails again. This was the peak of Moy's achievements, and nothing else developed from his labors.

1876 The firm Otto and Lantgen produced an efficient four-stroke internal combustion engine whose development would provide the route by which aerodynamicists could finally obtain the technology for manned, heavier-than-air flight. Having been manufacturing piston engines at their factory in Deutz, Germany since 1867, they improved their original engine and designed the first compression engine on the four-stroke principle. The engine produced about 4 HP, more than most steam engines but too little for efficient use in flying machines.

1876 Developing the theory of rotary-winged flight, American J. B. Ward produced the designs for a flying machine combining the concept of a helicopter and an air-cushion vehicle (hovercraft). The rotary wing was intended for use close to the ground, where it could push air against the ground and therefore reap the lift advantages of increased pressure, or "ground effect." The craft was never built and its potential not developed, but it is the earliest known combination of aeronautic concepts for an air-cushion vehicle.

1876 Alphonse Pénaud patented a design for an amphibious aircraft, a veritable monster calculated to weigh 2,640 lb. and achieve a flying speed of 60 MPH. Pénaud put into this design all the characteristics he deemed necessary in a flying machine for powered flight. It had two tractor engines, counter-rotating propellers, curved wings of an elliptical shape, a retractable undercarriage with shock absorbers, movable surfaces on the wings acting like speed brakes, instruments giving altitude, direction and time and two seats for a pilot and his passenger. The wing area was large, and the fuselage was shaped like a boat.

1877 May 27 A major milestone in Japanese aviation history was accomplished with the first flight of a military balloon. The Japanese took flying very seriously, and with several islands and many mountainous areas across their territory, they understood the advantages of aerial navigation. The first balloon, developed jointly by the army and the navy in cooperation with Tokyo University, had a capacity of 14,000 cu. ft. and was inflated with coal gas. Inspiration for this may have been delivered by the American Rufus Wells when he went to Japan to demonstrate ballooning.

1877 The Établissement Aérostatique Militaire of France was founded at Meudon with the purpose of training military aeronauts and developing the military applications of dirigibles and balloons. The world's first military aviation establishment had been set up at Meudon in 1794 and disbanded by Napoleon in 1799. This new establishment took over the whole spectrum of aviation activities, no longer just aeronaut training but also the manufacture and development of balloons and airships, technical training and maintenance.

1878 August 23 Captain J. L. B. Templer of the Middlesex Militia and Capt. H. P. Lee of the Royal Engineers flew the coal-gas hydrogen balloon *Pioneer,* the first British government-funded aviation project. *Pioneer* was constructed at a total cost of 71 pounds and had a capacity of 10,000 cu. ft. Although Capt. Templer was the first British air commander—his own balloon, *Crusader,* was the first balloon used by the British army in trials during 1879—he was not the first British military aeronaut. Capt. F. Beaumont and Lt. G. E. Grover of the Royal Engineers had been attached to the Union Army as aeronauts during the American Civil War.

1879 July 31 Canadians Richard Cowan, Charles Page and Charles Grimley made the first balloon flight in Canada. They took off from Montreal in a hydrogen balloon. It is not recorded where the flight ended or how long the journey lasted, but interest in aviation was spreading rapidly. Entrepreneurs traveled around the globe to raise money by performing feats of daring and providing exhibitions that attracted local interest and inspired efforts by inventors and engineers.

1879 Frenchman Victor Tatin (1843–1913) successfully flew a model aircraft powered by a compressed-air motor. The design incorporated a monoplane wing with a span of 6 ft. 2 in., two tractor propellers, each with four blades, and a tricycle undercarriage. The compressed air was housed in the barrel-shaped fuselage, and the model was attached to a pole. The little model flew a distance of about 50 ft. and did much to popularize the monoplane configuration, which had been absent from most aeronautical designs for about 40 years.

1880 June 24 The first British military use of a manned balloon was at the army maneuvers held at Aldershot, Hampshire. A balloon detachment was tasked with the reconnaissance and artillery direction of the assembled forces. The results from these field trials convinced the army of the practical value of the balloon as

a reconnaissance platform and led to the introduction of a Balloon Section of the Royal Engineers in 1889 with proper funding and equipment.

1883 October 8 Designed and built by Tissandier, the first electrically powered airship made its first flight from Auteuil to Saint-Germain, both in France. The power for the Siemens electric motor came from 24 bichromate of potash batteries. Batteries were lighter than the gas cylinders needed for compressed gas motors, and the electric motors of the day were lighter than alternative motors. The powerplant was still limited by the use of heavy cells that needed replacement after practically every flight. Although this weight severely limited the range of these airships, the batteries provided a useful source of power for airships.

1884 August 9 The first fully controllable dirigible, *La France,* was flown for the first time by Capt. Charles Rénard and Lt. Arthur Krebs of the French Corps of Engineers. The flight followed a circular 5-mile course, returning safely to its point of departure, the Factory at Chalais-Meudon, after 23 minutes. The airship was 165 ft. long with a diameter of 27 ft. and a capacity of 66,000 cu. ft. A silk-covered bamboo car was slung beneath the envelope. With a length of 108 ft. and a width of 4 ft. 6 in., the car was more than two-thirds the length of the envelope. It was initially fitted with 882-lb. chlorochromic batteries designed by Rénard driving a 7.5-HP motor, replaced later with a more advanced Gramme motor delivering 9 HP driving a 23-ft. diameter, four-bladed propeller.

1884 November 6 In Italy, the Balloon Section (Sezione Aerostatica) of the army was established, marking the formal inauguration of military air units in that country. It was attached to the 3(o) Regimento Genio and would be supplemented on July 17, 1910, by the formation of the first Italian military aircraft unit, the Battaglione Specialisti.

1884 December 19 A balloon detachment accompanied a British military expedition to Bechuanaland (now Botswana) under Capt. H. Elsdale and Lt. Trollope. The detachment had three balloons, the first in Africa, and the commanding officer of the force, Gen. Sir Charles Warren made several ascents to see the lay of the land for himself. Although they were strongly favored by the officers, there was little for the balloons to do. Elsdale did much to garner support for the use of balloons in military operations and lost no opportunity to promote their use.

1884 I. Golubev piloted a 46-ft., steam-engined monoplane on a short hop from an inclined ramp. The aircraft was designed and built by Alexander Fedorovich Mozhaiski, a Russian engineer. Mozhaiski's machine was incapable of accelerating unaided. Steam engines light enough to fit aircraft did not produce sufficient power to accelerate. The layout of the aircraft was completely conventional, with monoplane wings and tail, and fuselage and engines fitted in the manner of a normal modern aircraft. A 20-HP steam engine powered the front tractor propeller and a 10-HP engine drove two pusher propellers mounted in the center section of each of the rectangular wings.

1885 February 15 A balloon detachment left Britain for the Sudan under the command of Maj. J. L. B. Templer assisted by Lt. Mackenzie. It was unable to play a significant role in the conflict due to lack of adequate support equipment; a major problem was getting hydrogen to remote areas, which hampered the use of balloons and reduced their operational readiness. But Mackenzie remained airborne throughout a march between Suakin and Tofrik, his balloon tethered at a height of about 750 ft. from the middle of the column. He remained aloft for 7 hr., watching for signs of imminent attack and observing the road ahead.

1888 August 12   The first aerial device to be successfully flown with a gasoline engine was a small balloon designed and built by Dr. Karl Wolfert. It was fitted with a Daimler single-cylinder gasoline engine and flown by a young mechanic called Michael. The flight took place at Daimler's Seelberg facility in Germany. The engine delivered 2 HP, and the balloon had a volume of 8,750 cu. ft. Further flights were made from Cannstadt and Ulm. The engine's very lower power output made the balloon uncontrollable in all but the lightest breeze, and attaching the engine directly to the envelope of the hydrogen-filled balloon made the risk of fire very high.

1888   The French balloon section at Chalais-Meudon was given more prominent status when it was renamed the Military Ballooning Directorate with Maj. Charles Rénard appointed as its director. He had designed a dirigible named *Général Meusnier* in 1885 which was to be powered by an 8-cylinder 100-HP motor. Development had proven difficult, but now Rénard got stronger encouragement to complete the airship. Further calculation, moreover, showed Rénard that his dirigible would be unstable, and he had to redesign it. Rénard had a dislike of the media and never achieved just recognition for his work. In 1898 Samuel P. Langley visited him and declared, "If I had come sooner I could have saved twenty years of work."

1889   A British balloon section participated for the first time in army maneuvers at Aldershot, England. At the end of activities, a balloon headed the parade led by Maj. Elsdale, who had replaced Capt. Lee as head of the balloon detachments at Woolwich Arsenal, London. Elsdale was succeeded as head of the balloon detachment in Bechuanaland by Maj. C. M. Watson. Watson succeeded in getting Aldershot officially named as the home of the Balloon Detachment. In 1890 it was also to become the home of the Balloon Section of the Royal Engineers.

1889   Otto Lilienthal, the great German aero-theorist, published a book titled *Birdflight as the Basis of Aviation* that explored the dynamics of bird flight, the wing structure of birds and the methods he concluded were the mechanisms for avian propulsion. Lilienthal published tables of lift calculations derived from wings with varying camber. Lilienthal had been born in the Pomeranian village of Ankam in 1848. During boyhood, he carried out primitive aeronautical experiments with his brother Gustav at night to escape ridicule. He later studied at the Technical Academy in Potsdam.

1890 October 1   The U.S. Congress authorized the Army Signal Corps responsibility for collecting and transmitting information for the army. The Chief Signal Officer, Brig. Gen. Adolphus V. Greely, interpreted this to include all forms of aeronautical devices capable of supporting that broad objective, and in 1892 a balloon section was established in the Signal Corps. In 1891 Lt. William A. Glassford was sent to Europe to study the latest developments in ballooning. In 1893 Glassford demonstrated a small French balloon called *General Myer* at the Chicago World's Fair, during which the first balloon-to-ground telephone calls were made.

1890 October 9   The French electrical engineer Clement Ader achieved the first powered flight from level ground with a pilotless, steam-driven contraption called the *Eole*. The flight at the Château Pereire, Armainvilliers near Gretz covered a distance of

165 ft., and the *Eole* rose 8 in. The *Eole* was bat-winged monoplane with a span of 49 ft. and total weight of 653 lb., including the pilot. The most important aspect of the *Eole* was the lightweight steam engine the boiler for which was directly in front of the pilot's seat. Designed by Ader, the engine developed almost 20 HP to drive a single tractor propeller. Ader followed early aeronautical tests with a tethered kite in 1873 and began work on the *Eole* in 1882. Ader never claimed *Eole*'s hop as a flight, but he did see it as a prelude to manned flying.

1891 April 29   The first flight in Japan of a heavier-than-air flying device took place when the amazing Japanese inventor Chuhachi Ninomiya successfully propelled a rubberband-powered model airplane a distance of 33 ft. These tests and rehearsals for bolder objectives led Ninomiya to build a larger model powered by a clockwork motor driving a tractor propeller. This too was successful, and plans were drawn up for a manned flying machine for which the inventor sought financial subsidy from the Imperial Japanese Army. The army was not convinced and denied Ninomiya the funds that may have brought him ultimate success.

1891 October   Octave Chanute published the first in a series of 27 papers about aerodynamics and the science of flight. Collectively, the writings would be published three years later as *Progress in Flying Machines*. This work added to Lilienthal's writings about the status of contemporary research. Born in Paris in 1832, Chanute emigrated with his parents to America in 1838, and after schooling in New York he became a successful civil engineer. He settled in Chicago with his wife and family in 1890 and set up his own engineering firm. He is considered to be the world's first great aviation historian.

1891   Otto Lilienthal carried out tests with his first successful glider from Dertwitz, Germany, near the Magdeburg railway station. Lilienthal had been experimenting with gliders since 1889, the year he turned theory into practice and built his first heavier-than-air flying machine. It was unsuccessful, as was a second design, built in 1890; the second design had tail surfaces that marginally improved its aerodynamics. Thus began an intensive series of gliding tests in which Lilienthal would shift his body around the center of mass (the center of the wing) to maintain control of direction, an important step toward effective flight control.

1891   The Balloon School and Factory, the maintenance, support and training element of the Balloon Section of the Royal Engineers, was moved to a new establishment at Farnborough, Hampshire, which was to become one of the great centers of British aviation. Farnborough would become famous for aeronautical science and engineering and transform the individual achievements of entrepreneurs and inventors into technically advanced flying machines. The place name has become synonomous around the world for aeronautical excellence.

1892 February 3   In what is probably the first bomber contract for a heavier-than-air flying machine, the French Ministry of War awarded Clement Ader a 650,000 franc contract to build a version of his *Eole* capable of carrying 165 lb. in bombs. Ader worked up his *Avion II* design, which was to be powered by an improved version of the already remarkable engine utilized for the *Eole* in 1890. This new engine was used later by Gabriel Voisin with compressed air for lecture purposes. The *Avion II* was never completed, and after renegotiating the contract, Ader set to work on *Avion III*, which would be tested in October 1897.

1892 Samuel Pierpont Langley, an American physicist, began designing and building steam-powered model aircraft from which he would develop ideas for a man-carrying machine. Born in 1834, Langley was the first well-known American pioneer of heavier-than-air flight, although he pursued scientifically questionable design configurations that never produced the desired results. Langley was a great mathematician and astronomer and eventually became the secretary of the Smithsonian Institution, a position from which he gained acceptability in excess of his accomplishments.

1893 May A strange multiplane flying machine, designed by Englishman Horatio Phillips, was tested on a circular track at Harrow. Looking more like a venetian blind than an airplane, the model had a wingspan of 19 ft. and each lifting surface had a chord of only 1.5 in., giving a total surface area of only 140 sq. ft. across all 60 wings. The device was powered by a steam engine driving a 6 ft. 5 in. propeller and was made to run along a circular track with a diameter of 103 ft. It clattered along at 40 MPH, and although the rear lifted into the air, the front wheels never left the track. Phillips had worked on multiplane configurations from 1884 to 1893 and was to build a larger machine in 1907, said by him to be capable of lifting 385 lb.

1893 August 1 The International Conference on Aerial Navigation opened as part of the World Columbian Exposition in Chicago. A committee had been formed the previous year with a reluctant Chanute as chairman. For much of the week, cranks, geniuses and would-be aeronauts paraded their views. Among the more worthwhile developments first announced at the conference was the Australian Lawrence Hargrave's cellular wing.

1893 November 16 After putting together three steam-powered model airplanes that failed to provide sufficient lift for free flight, Langley took his *Aerodrome No. 4* to a houseboat on the Potomac River about 30 miles south of Washington. Nine flight attempts were carried out before Langley abandoned the idea on November 16. Power was marginal, and slight breezes destabilized the model, which had a lightweight steam engine on an airframe with a lifting area of 14 sq. ft.

1894 January 27 Captain B. F. S. Baden-Powell (the brother of the first Chief Boy Scout) made a kite ascent from Pirbright Army Camp, England in what appears to have been the first use

This multiwinged flying machine from 1893 represents the bizarre product of an outrageous imagination frequently seen in the last century.

of man-carrying kites outside China. Stringing together a row of several monoplane kites in addition to the more familiar box-kite, Baden-Powell obtained sufficient lift to ascend to several hundred feet. The feat excited interest from the military in the use of kites for observation to replace the technically complex gas balloons and the attendant support equipment they required.

1894 July 31 Hiram Maxim, inventor of the Maxim machine gun, briefly "flew" his amazing 8,000 lb. biplane. Powered by two 180-HP steam engines, each driving a 17 ft. 9 in. diameter propeller, the craft careened along on four cast iron wheels at 42 MPH for 600 ft. before leaving the ground. The giant contraption was 200 ft. long with a wingspan of 107 ft. and supported a platform 40 ft. long for the light steam engine and three people. The outer wing panels had pronounced dihedral, and single fore and aft elevators contributed to a combined lifting area of 4,000 sq. ft. Built in Baldwyns Park, Kent, England, the machine was set upon a steel rail and, because it was considered a test rig for demonstrating lift, restrained from "flying" more than a few inches by two wooden guard rails. The first two runs were unsuccessful, but on the third run, the machine lifted off and broke through one of the guard rails only to collapse back down.

1894 November 12 Far from the centers of aeronautical experimentation, Lawrence Hargrave of Sydney, Australia was lifted 16 ft. into the air by four box-kites attached to each other in a row to provide one continuous biplane surface, a forerunner of the familiar configuration for early powered flying machines. The magnanimous Hargrave refused to patent his designs, believing people everywhere should pool their knowledge for universal progress. Hargrave had first built a monoplane glider based on Lilienthal's work, but it crashed in June 1894, and Hargrave turned to box-kite, or cellular, configurations, which he had been tinkering with for more than a year.

1894 Lilienthal began serious design tests with his gliders after finding suitable slopes at the Rhinower Hills, 6 mi. northwest of Berlin. Some hills were 164 ft. high, and Lilienthal would launch himself into the air from halfway up, achieving flight distances of more than 1,000 ft. Before this, he had built an artificial hill near his home from which flights in excess of 100 ft. were achieved. Among his distinguished visitors was Samuel Pierpont Langley, then secretary of the Smithsonian Institution.

1895 May 9 Alexander Graham Bell served as official timekeeper for a series of flight attempts with Langley's *Aerodrome No. 5* steam-powered glider from the banks of the Potomac. Much of the design for this glider is credited to Augustus Moore Herring, who joined Langley in December 1894 after the latter became aware of his work on Lilienthal-type gliders he had subtly modified for improved performance. In three attempts this day, the most successful was "the nearest approximation to horizontal flight of any attempts," according to Langley. The small, powered glider achieved a speed of almost 40 MPH after accelerating down an incline.

1895 American industrialist and businessman James Means made an impressive contribution to the development of aeronautics by accurately and meticulously chronicling writings on aviation from all over the world in the first of a series of three books called the *Aeronautical Annual*. Successive volumes were published in 1896 and 1897. His books were to be a source of great inspiration to several pioneers, and Wilbur and Orville Wright in particular would testify to the value they placed upon his books. When he made sufficient money to support his family, he retired to devote all his time to recording the achievements of aviation pioneers.

1895 A suitable successor to Sir George Cayley and a contemporary peer of Lilienthal, the Englishman Percy Sinclair Pilcher from Yorkshire, built and flew his first glider, the *Bat*. After building the *Bat* without horizontal tail surfaces, Pilcher visited Lilienthal to question the necessity for such improvements. After tests at Cardross in Scotland proved his glider still would not work properly, Pilcher modified his glider to convert the single vertical fin into a conventional tailplane, as Lilienthal said would be necessary. The *Bat* had an empty weight of 45 lb. and a wing area of 150 sq. ft.

1895 A patent was granted to Count Ferdinand von Zeppelin for his method of rigid airship construction. His system was to enclose the gas bags in a cloth-covered metal frame, with cars slung beneath the frame for crew and engines. This general approach to the problem was to become the accepted method of airship construction worldwide.

1895 Using tethered gliders, Irish professor George Francis Fitzgerald attempted several flights using aircraft similar in design to those of Otto Lilienthal. Despite the airworthy appearance of these machines, the experiments were unsuccessful. Unfortunately, no record of Fitzgerald's designs survive, so the exact cause of his failure is unknown. But his is a typical example of the increasingly scientific approach to aeronautical research based on the respected work of men like Cayley and Lilienthal, thanks to the distribution of technical papers and scientific debate among aeronautical groups throughout Europe.

1896 May 6 The first successful flight of Langley's steam-powered model *Aerodrome No. 5* took place from a modified houseboat on the Potomac when assistants launched the monoplane, which weighed a mere 26 lb., at 3:05 P.M. Captured on film, this was the world's first flight of a powered, heavier-than-air machine to be photographed. The *No. 5* slid off its launching rail 20 ft. above the Potomac and dipped slightly before rising and beginning the first of a series of gentle curves to the right, settling on the water 425 ft. behind the houseboat after flying a total distance of 3,300 ft. at almost 25 MPH.

1896 June 22 While researching his book *Progress in Flying Machines*, Octave Chanute arrived at Miller, Indiana to begin flight trials with man-carrying gliders. Chanute had recruited the services of A. M. Herring, William Avery, the Russian emigré William Paul Butusov and James Ricketts to act as test pilots while he directed operations and refined the gliders, many of which were based on Lilienthal's designs. Within a week, Herring was making flights in excess of 100 ft. from the slopes of the sand dunes. Now 64, Chanute was unable to fly the gliders.

1896 August 9 Otto Lilienthal crashed in his *No. 11* glider while flying from the Rhinower Hill range. In clear weather with calm winds, a sudden gust brought his glider to a standstill. Lilienthal threw his body forward over the wing and tried to dive back down to gain speed, but the glider stalled, the starboard wing fell, and the machine spun to the ground. Lilienthal broke his back and was taken to the Bergmann Clinic where he died the next day. Lilienthal had made approximately 2,500 flights with his various gliders and was convinced that powered flight would one day be practical.

1896 Percy Pilcher built the last, and most successful, of his four gliders, which he called the *Hawk*. It was equipped with the world's first sprung undercarriage and flew successfully during the summer months. The *Hawk* had been built in Glasgow, Scotland, but because Pilcher moved south to join Hiram Maxim, the first flight took place from Eynsford in Kent, England. The *Hawk* had a span of 23 ft. 4 in. and a wing area of 180 sq. ft. and weighed only 50 lb. empty and 195 lb. with Pilcher aboard, chest and shoulders protruding above the wing. Two wheels attached to struts near the wing's leading edge were attached to stiff springs.

1896 Pilcher took out patent no. 9144 for a powered, heavier-than-air flying machine that, he calculated, would require a 4-HP-engine driving a single tractor propeller for a horizontal flying speed of 30 MPH. The airframe was to be a development of his *Hawk* glider built during the winter of 1895–96, and the device was to become airborne by running downhill. Pilcher began design work in 1897 on a modified version of the *Hawk* to accommodate an engine and propeller weighing a mere 43.5 lb., which, added to the all-up weight of the *Hawk* of 195 lb., would achieve the necessary performance. Correspondence with Chanute in the United States convinced him to abandon the monoplane and begin work on a biplane.

1897 July 11 The Swedish adventurer Salomon August Andrée, with fellow balloonists Nils Strindberg and Knut Fraenkel, set off from Spitsbergen in an attempt to reach the North Pole by air, an expedition funded by the king of Sweden and Alfred Nobel, among others. The balloon had a volume of 170,000 cu. ft., special valves to counter the effects of ice and snow and three drag ropes, each 1,100 ft. long. Named *Ormen* (eagle), the balloon took off at 1:46 P.M. amid anxious concern from millions around the world who heard of the attempt through newspapers. The skeletons of the three men were found in 1933 only 280 mi. from Spitsbergen. The *Ormen* was apparently brought down by snow.

1897 October 12 Clement Ader made the first flight attempt with his *Avion III* steam-powered flying machine on a specially prepared circular track at a military camp at Satory near Versailles. With a span of almost 56 ft. and an all-up weight of 880 lb., the machine was powered by two 20-HP steam engines, finely machined and assembled, driving two propellers. The first flight attempt was unsuccessful, and *Avion III* remained firmly attached to the rails. Having already spent 650,000 francs, the military withdrew its support, although Ader later claimed that *Avion III* had flown almost 1,000 ft.

1897 November 2 The first flight of the world's first rigid metal airship took place at Schoneberg on the outskirts of Berlin. Designed by the Austrian engineer David Schwartz, who had worked on the idea for four years, the airship was 45 ft. 11 in. deep and 39 ft. 5 in. wide, had a length of 157 ft. 6 in. and held 130,000 cu. ft. of gas. The internal structure comprised aluminum tubing covered with aluminum sheet 0.08 inch thick. Schwartz died suddenly in January 1897, but his wife carried on preparations. An incompetent team of ground handlers released the airship for flight in winds too high for safety. The airship was destroyed, but the petrified pilot lived.

1898 March 25 Intrigued by the albeit limited success of Samuel Langley's steam-powered model gliders, Theodore Roosevelt, then assistant secretary of the navy, recommended that two officers with "scientific attainment and practical ability" be appointed to investigate the flying machine and evaluate its military potential.

1898 March 31 As a result of recommendations from Theodore Roosevelt, Samuel Langley and Charles D. Walcott of the U.S. Coast and Geological Survey met and discussed the possibility of a military airplane funded by the government. Langley claimed

Clement Ader preparing his Avion III *steam-powered flying machine of 1897. He came close to making the first powered flight.*

he needed at least $50,000 to complete development of a flying machine, and Walcott offered to introduce the idea to Pres. McKinley. Two days later, Langley reiterated his belief that a modified version of his *Aerodrome No. 5* or its companion *No. 6* could be developed into a useful flying machine for "land and naval warfare." In return, Langley wanted a free hand as to how he spent the money.

1898 April 29   Following a demonstration at the Smithsonian Institution before a presidential advisory panel composed of Alexander Graham Bell and representatives of the army, the navy and the president, Langley received unfunded support to develop his steam-powered models into man-carrying war machines. It was hoped these could be ready to fight the Spanish, as war with that country had been declared on April 24. It would be the end of the year before Langley received notice that funds had been appropriated by the Board of Ordnance and Fortification, the authority responsible for military research and development.

1898 May 31   The army balloon *General Myer* was shipped from New York to Tampa, Fla., at the outbreak of the Spanish-American War. Under the command of Lt. Col. Joseph E. Maxfield of the Signal Corps, with three officers and 24 enlisted men, the unit was dispatched to Santiago, Cuba, where it arrived June 22. Three ascents were made June 30 to spy on Spanish naval preparations in the harbor at Santiago. On July 1, an ascent during the Battle of San Juan Hill at a point only 2,000 ft. from the Spanish lines revealed a second trail affording access to the enemy from two directions. The balloon was rendered unserviceable by enemy rifle fire but it had proved its worth.

1898 September 18   Alberto Santos-Dumont, a native of Brazil, made the first flight in his *No. 1* airship from the Jardin d'Acclimation in Paris. Powered by a de Dion-Bouton automobile engine, it was a cylindrical balloon 82 ft. long and 11 ft. 6 in. in diameter with a capacity of 6,360 cu. ft. The son of a wealthy coffee plantation owner, Santos-Dumont arrived in Paris during 1897 and began work on a powered airship, or dirigible, with which he hoped to develop long distance flight. His *No. 1* ended its first flight snagged tenaciously by a tree's branches.

1898 October 10   Augustus Herring achieved free flight in a biplane glider fitted with a twin-cylinder, compressed-air engine

capable of driving a dual propeller arrangement, one pusher and one tractor. Having first worked for Langley, then Chanute, Herring struck out on his own with the financial help of Matthias Arnot and built a flying machine weighing only 88 lb. with a wingspan of 18 ft. The flight took place near Herring's home at St. Joseph, Mich., a small port on the shores of Lake Michigan. Herring started the engine, lifted the biplane up on his shoulders and ran forward into a 20-MPH wind. He sailed about 50 ft. across the sand during 30 sec. before landing.

1898 October 22   Convinced that he had made the world's first powered flight, Herring sought to repeat his success of October 10 and made a second attempt to fly in his biplane glider powered by a twin-cylinder, compressed-air engine. Several witnesses were on hand when Herring faced into a 26-MPH wind and started the engine. Running forward, he lifted a few feet into the air and sailed very slowly forward at a ground rate not much above walking speed. He came down after flying 73 ft. in 10 sec. during which, a reporter for the Niles (Mich.) *Mirror* would note, his "feet almost grazed the ground."

1898 November 3   Langley ordered a 12-HP internal combustion engine intended to power the *Great Aerodrome*, a man-carrying development of the earlier steam-powered models. Langley hoped the *Great Aerodrome* would be accepted as a military flying machine, but he had, as yet, received no financial support. On advice from Robert Thurston of Cornell Univ., Langley employed a student named Charles Manly to help design and build the *Great Aerodrome*. Manly was just completing his studies in electrical and mechanical engineering when he was recruited. As the designing continued, Langley visited Europe and gathered several innovative ideas for control mechanisms.

1898 December 11   Langley was officially informed by Lt. Lewis of the Board of Ordnance and Fortification that he had been granted funds to develop his military flying machine, the *Great Aerodrome*, outside the auspices of the Smithsonian Institution. Under the agreement, Langley would get a $25,000 advance, with a further $25,000 made available subject to satisfactory progress. There was to be no publicity, but Langley could spend the money as he saw fit and was free to announce any test results he obtained.

1898   The Aéro Club de France was formed and would, as a body, influence the development of early European aviation. By offering prizes and sponsoring flying events, the club fostered early aviation and brought it to the attention of the disbelieving public. The club also served as a stimulus for research and development and provided a forum for debate and the exchange of ideas. At this period, aeronautical science was eagerly pursued with the usual excitement at the practical demonstration of ideas, and the club distributed theories and findings from a wide range of potential aeronauts.

1899 May 30   Wilbur Wright sent a letter to the Smithsonian Institution requesting information about flying and aeronautics, asserting that he had been "interested in the problems of mechanical and human flight ever since as a boy I constructed a number of bats of various sizes after the style of Cayley's and Penaud's machines." Wilbur received four pamphlets and a list of other writings. Born in Dayton, Ohio on April 16, 1867, Wilbur was the son of a United Brethren church bishop. His brother Orville was born on August 19, 1871, and the two developed a bicycle sale and manufacturing business that would finance their experiments with gliders. Orville ran the bicycle shop, and Wilbur went to work on a model.

1899 July 21   Wilbur Wright described to his brother Orville a novel method of flight control for gliders and powered flying machines. By warping the tips of the wings down and up, he mused, it would be possible to respectively add and subtract lift to the airfoil. If the wings were warped in different directions on opposing tips, the wing would bank to left or right, thereby providing an effective method of lateral control in the air. If this were done deliberately, the glider would bank to port or starboard on demand.

1899 July 27   Wilbur Wright completed the assembly of a model glider that demonstrated the wing-warping control concept described to Orville six days earlier. With line and pulley linkages, the glider had a wingspan of 5 ft. and a chord of 13 in. with a horizontal tail fore and aft. The wing-warping was controlled by lines attached to the tips and held by an operator on the ground so that the glider was, in fact, a tethered kite held against the air for tests in stability and control. Without publicity, the brothers tried it out on a field near their home with only schoolboys as witnesses. It worked reasonably well.

1899 August   Having conducted their first practical experiments in aeronautical science by conceiving, designing and building an experimental glider to test the wing-warping method of flight control, the Wright brothers began an intensive period of study and calculation to design a full-size, man-carrying glider. For the rest of 1899 and most of 1900, the brothers worked with information from technical papers and published sources, especially descriptions of Lilienthal's airfoil sections, to develop data on pressures, weight distribution and construction.

1899 September 30   During a gliding demonstration for students on the grounds of the estate owned by Lord Braye at Stamford Hall near Market Harborough, England, Percy Pilcher crashed from a height of about 30 ft. and died two days later without recovering consciousness. Delayed by wind and rain during the morning, Pilcher took his glider up twice without success before the fatal launch. Weakened by water-soaked bamboo, the tail collapsed, and nosed into the ground. Pilcher had originally planned to power the *Hawk*, but attempts at forming a company to fund it canceled that plan.

1899   Langley organized development of the *Great Aerodrome*, paid for by a first grant of $25,000 from the U.S. Army. With his assistant, Charles Manly, Langley resumed tests with *Aerodromes No. 5* and *No. 6* and with a ⅛th-scale model of the full-size machine. Load tests were carried out on full-size wings at the Smithsonian, but Langley had recurring problems getting his lightweight engine from the maker, Stephen M. Balzer of New York. On December 18, following an inspection of progress, Langley received the second half of the $50,000 authorized in December 1898.

1900 May 13   A year after first seeking help from the Smithsonian, Wilbur Wright wrote to the great American pioneer Octave Chanute, telling him, ''I have been trying to arrange my affairs in such a way that I can devote my entire life for a few months to experiments in this field.'' Wilbur stated his belief in the spread of aeronautical knowledge, asserting that ''the problem is too great for one man alone and unaided to solve in secret.''

1900 July 2   From its floating hangar at Lake Constance near Friedrichshafen, Germany, Count von Zeppelin's LZ 1 dirigible made its first flight, remaining in the air for approximately 20 min. powered by two Daimler engines each rated at 16 HP. A lattice girder structure covered in cotton cloth enclosed 16 balloons of rubberized cloth containing 400,000 cu. ft. of hydrogen. The LZ 1 was 420 ft. long and 36 ft. 6 in. in diameter. On its first flight, it ascended to a height of 1,300 ft. and traveled less than 4 mi. Its limited power made control difficult. A funding subscription to develop the LZ 1 had been formed in late 1896, and a limited company was founded two years later with capitalization of 400,000 marks.

1900 September 13   Wilbur Wright arrived at Kitty Hawk, N.C., a small isolated community on the narrow barrier beach between the Atlantic Ocean and Albemarle Sound. The Wrights came for steady, onshore wind in which to fly their glider. Orville arrived on the twenty-eighth, and the brothers lodged with the Tate family until October 4 when they erected a tent. Their glider had a span of 17 ft., a chord of 5 ft. and an area of 165 sq. ft. An 18-in. section in the center of the lower wing was left open for the pilot. Curved to a depth of 2.5 in., the wing had a camber of 1 in 21. The wings were joined together by five sets of braced interplane struts. A single, movable foreplane was attached in front.

1900 October 23   Wilbur and Orville Wright broke camp at Kitty Hawk, having spent most of the month testing their glider to determine its flying and handling qualities, which, in general, were good. Most of the time the glider was ''flown'' as a kite, with the wing-warping operated from the ground. When they were able to get sufficient wind for gliding, they accomplished flights of up to 400 ft. at speeds of almost 30 MPH. Armed with results and calculations from these brief trials, the Wrights returned to Dayton, Ohio to continue with their bicycle business and design a new and improved glider, which they were convinced would move them closer to powered flight.

1900 November 16   Wilbur Wright sent a letter to Chanute to report progress with the first season of glider trials at Kitty Hawk and to explain in detail the exact construction of the machine and the aeronautical theory he employed to design it. It also revealed to Chanute that the Wrights failed to appreciate important aspects of construction, namely that smooth surfaces are a vital part of efficient flight. Chanute was greatly impressed with their standard of manufacture and in the neatness and simplicity of their fixtures for rigging and control.

1901 June 19   Charles Manly coordinated activity on the Potomac for the first in a series of flight trials with a one-quarter scale model of Langley's *Great Aerodrome* powered by a 1.5-HP naphtha engine built by Balzer of New York. The model had been ready for a year, but delays with the engine held up tests. In four flight attempts from the same houseboat Langley had used for his earlier *Aerodrome* steam-powered glider flights, the machine proved woefully underpowered, with its pitifully small engine, and achieved a best distance of 350 ft. before landing on the water.

1901 June 26   In a historic encounter, Octave Chanute called upon the Wright brothers at their home in Dayton, Ohio to meet them and discuss progress made since their glider tests at Kitty Hawk. Wilbur had wanted to obtain an anemometer and wrote to Chanute asking for his help, whereupon the old patron replied by inviting himself to the Wrights'. Chanute was so impressed he offered helpers and money and suggested the Wrights take one of his gliders to Kitty Hawk for tests. They declined his offers and remained steadfast in their determination to pursue their own course.

1901 July 11 Wilbur and Orville Wright arrived back at Kitty Hawk with their new glider for a season of trials at Kill Devil Hill dunes, 4 mi. south of Kitty Hawk. The 1901 glider had a wingspan of 22 ft. and a chord of 7 ft. with 290 sq. ft. of wing area. It had a larger forward elevator and a weight of 98 lb. Their new glider had a wing camber of 1 in 12, conforming to Lilienthal's tables of wing camber.

1901 July 27 The Wright brothers began the 1901 testing season using their new glider. Against advice from Orville and helpers, Wilbur attempted to make a flight without first having tried it with ballast. At first the new glider refused to lift into the air, but after nine attempts with different settings of controls and pilot, Wilbur finally made a glide of 100 ft. before stalling at a height of 30 ft. Instead of the glider spinning to the ground, its design by chance incorporated a corrective lifting surface in the forward elevator that, when tipped forward as the glider was pitched up, allowed it to settle its nose down again and glide to earth. This led the Wrights to explore the phenomenon in later tests.

1901 July 31 The world's first record altitude balloon flight, confirmed by scientific instruments carried aloft, was set by Prof. Berson and Prof. Suring of the Prussian Meteorological Institute when they reached a height of 35,435 ft. Berson and Suring began high altitude attempts in 1893, and the balloonists used oxygen cylinders with simple breathing tubes, despite which they were prone to lose consciousness. Berson and Suring had ascended on December 4, 1894, to a height of 30,000 ft. in a balloon called *Phoenix*, which had a capacity of 92,000 cu. ft. For their confirmed record, Berson and Suring used the *Preussen*, which had a capacity of 300,000 cu. ft. Several companies provided equipment for these scientific ascents, including Bosch with instruments for atmospheric physics such as a device for measuring the precise temperature of the air and equipment to study moisture, pressure and temperature gradients.

1901 August 4 Octave Chanute arrived at the Wright brothers' camp at Kill Devil Hill and photographed their flight tests with the 1901 glider. A tendency to stall led to a change of wing camber from 1 in 12 to 1 in 19 in efforts to alter the center of pressure under different lifting conditions. Chanute recorded success with a more responsive control system as the glider achieved flights up to 389 ft. and speeds of almost 30 MPH. Without Chanute's camera, many of the important tests carried out by the Wrights this year would have gone unrecorded as they redefined principles of aeronautical science expressed by earlier pioneers and scientists.

1901 August 9 Wilbur Wright experienced what may have been his first defined spin. In flight tests with the glider from the dunes at Kill Devil Hill, Wilbur attempted to turn in the air and experienced a port wing stall while the starboard wing was high and still turning. Although banked to the left, the glider slewed to the right and spun in, a reaction similar to the spin that killed Percy Pilcher. Fortunately, Wilbur was not that high up, and the glider collapsed into the sand. After deliberation, they took to the air again five days later and wrote to Chanute telling him of the problem.

1901 August 14 Gustav Whitehead, a Bavarian who emigrated to America, claimed he flew a powered aircraft of his own design at Bridgeport, Conn. The aircraft was said to have flown 880 ft. on its first flight, making a second flight later that day. During the flight, Whitehead reportedly steered around trees in his path. A 20-HP acetylene engine powered the aircraft while a 10-HP engine drove the wheels. The device had the appearance of a large bat, and its design was aerodynamically flawed. It has been frequently reported by historians as a potential candidate for the honor of first powered flight, but there is no confirmed evidence to suggest that it accomplished anything other than a loud noise.

1901 August 20 The Wright brothers left Kitty Hawk, N.C., at the end of their second season of testing gliders and returned to Dayton, having moved beyond the simple dynamics of lifting flight to explore the complexities of turns and maneuvers in the air. They were beginning to extend the frontiers of human knowledge as they challenged the conclusions of men like Lilienthal through direct experimentation, which enabled them to correct tables of air pressure and its effect on lifting surfaces. This was important for their eventual success with powered flying machines.

1901 September 18 At the invitation of Chanute, Wilbur Wright addressed the Western Society of Engineers in Chicago with a 10,000-word paper titled "Some Aeronautical Experiments." He entered into considerable detail about the dynamics of flying gliders and about corrections to previously accepted conclusions from earlier theoreticians and experimenters by showing that failures with these early attempts proved the figures were wrong.

1901 October 19 Alberto Santos-Dumont won the Deutsch de la Meurthe prize of 125,000 francs for being the first person to take off in a balloon from St. Cloud, fly to and around the Eiffel Tower in Paris and return to St. Cloud within 30 minutes, a distance of 6.8 mi. The purse was established in 1900 by the gasoline magnate Henri Deutsch de la Meurthe. Santos-Dumont's *No. 6* was 108 ft. long with a capacity of 21,965 cu. ft. and was powered by a 12-HP Buchet water-cooled engine. He took off at 2:42 P.M. in light winds and flew within 165 ft. of the Eiffel Tower, returning with just 27 sec. to spare! Half the prize money was given to the poor of Paris, and half he gave to his helpers at St. Cloud. The government of Brazil gave him a further 125,000 francs and a special medal.

1901 November The Wright brothers began to develop methods of carrying out basic research on airfoils and lifting surfaces, first by attaching small-scale wings to a horizontal bicycle wheel rotated at high speed and then by attaching stub wings to a bicycle driven as fast as possible. These methods of observing the reaction of lifting surfaces to airflow were inaccurate, and the Wrights decided to build a wind tunnel 18 in. long. This was quickly replaced by a larger one 6 ft. long by 16 in. square and operated by a gas engine. These tests were completed at the end of the year.

1902 January 17 In letters published in the April 1 issue of the journal *American Inventor*, Gustav Whitehead made wild claims to having carried out the world's first flight with a powered amphibian aircraft, when he supposedly took off and flew 7 mi. over Long Island Sound. His amphibious vehicle was reported as 16.5 ft. long with a wing area of 450 sq. ft. and two propellers 6 ft. in diameter driven by a single 40-HP kerosene engine. The craft weighed 800 lb., and Whitehead claimed to have flown it to a height of 200 ft. and made turns and maneuvers in the air. There were no reliable witnesses, and the evidence is overwhelmingly against the claims of the inventor.

1902 September 20 On August 28, Wilbur and Orville Wright arrived at Kill Devil Hill for a third season of glider trials with a much larger and improved flying machine developed as a result of wind tunnel tests in Dayton. The new glider had a wingspan of just over 32 ft., a chord of 5 ft. and a camber of 1 in 24. With higher aspect ratio and an area of 305 ft., only 5% more than the 1901 glider, it was expected to have better lift and control characteristics. The forward elevator was shaped more like an airfoil and its area reduced. Two 6 ft. by 1 ft. vertical fins were spaced close together on the forward elevation in efforts to counteract spin during turns. It also had a cleverly designed hip cradle to help the pilot shift his weight around the top of the lower wing and improve the handling and control input. On this first flight this day, Wilbur overreacted to a gust of wind and instinctively responded as if he were flying the 1901 glider with the old control's system, which would inadvertently induce a spin in this case. Saved from stalling by the forward elevator generating lift, he slipped to the ground and was uninjured. This and following flights showed the new vertical fins were causing tailspin, and flying stopped while a solution was worked out.

1902 October 8 The flight of the modified 1902 Wright glider demonstrated for the first time a fully controllable flying machine. The two vertical fins had been modified into a single rudder, its movement linked to the wing-warping mechanism in a successful attempt thought up by Orville to prevent the dangerous side slip and tailspin. By the close of their third season on Oct. 28, the Wrights had perfected wing-warping and elevator and rudder control, thereby demonstrating every essential aspect of a fully controllable airplane. They had conducted several hundred demonstrations, including landings with the glider in strong crosswinds. When brought to a virtual standstill by strong wind, the glider was under perfect control and stable throughout turns and maneuvers. The Wrights were convinced that their next step should be to prepare a powered glider for 1903.

1902 November 13 The Lebaudy-Julliot I semi-rigid dirigible made its first flight from Moisson, France as the world's first fully controllable airship. Employed by sugar barons Pierre and Paul Lebaudy to build a dirigible for long distance flights, the French engineer Henri Julliot built a semi-rigid airship 187 ft. long and 32 ft. in diameter with a capacity of 80,000 cu. ft. and a boat-shaped car slung beneath a 70 ft. by 20 ft. keel on 19-ft. vertical steel rods. The 16-ft. long car carried a 40-HP Daimler water-cooled engine driving two 9-ft. propellers that provide a speed of up to 25 MPH.

1902 December Unable to find a manufacturer who could fabricate an engine to their exacting specifications, the Wright brothers talked to Charlie Taylor about the design of a lightweight four-stroke engine with sufficient power to deliver 8 HP of useful energy. When completed, the engine weighed 180 lb. and delivered 12 HP at 1,025 RPM with 2.5 HP lost through the transmission—just enough to power a flying machine based on their 1902 glider. Taylor, who looked after the bicycle business while they were in Kitty Hawk, machined parts of the new engine.

1903 February The French aeronautical magazine, *L'Aérophile*, published detailed information and illustrations of the Wright biplane concept, based on the lecture by Wilbur Wright on September 18, 1901, at Chicago. The French artillery officer Ferdinand Ferber had obtained the text of that lecture from Samuel Langley. In that lecture, Wright described the methods he and his brother were using for controlled gliding flight. Ferber switched from studying Lilienthal's work to studying the Wright biplane concept and can be credited with directly introducing the biplane to Europe.

1903 February The Wright brothers began development of propellers for their 1903 powered flying machine. With no theory or references to work from (nobody had yet produced a propeller

with the efficiency their flying machine would need to get off the ground) and after several calculations, they prepared a simple propeller from a solid piece of wood. The following month, they fashioned two more propellers from three laminations of spruce, wrapping the tips in cloth and glue to prevent them delaminating. Each propeller was 8.5 ft. long and a masterpiece of contouring to very precise calculation. When finished, they were tested as having 66% efficiency, which was within 1% of earlier calculations.

1903 March 23 The Wright brothers filed a patent request for a powered flying machine based on the second (modified) version of their 1902 glider successfully tested at Kill Devil Hill. The patent issue was a prudent move but would bring the Wrights into confrontation more than once with enthusiastic pioneers and entrepreneurs.

1903 June 23 Santos-Dumont exemplified the new image of the commuting aeronaut by getting in his balloon at Neuilly-St.-James and flying to his house on the corner of the Champs Elysées and Rue Washington, tying it up outside while he went indoors for coffee! This eccentric dandy would frequently commute between his balloon factory and his favorite restaurants in the center of Paris using a small (9,217 cu. ft.) balloon with which he moved through the skies at very low altitude, trail rope dragging on the ground.

1903 June 24 Wilbur Wright gave his second address to the Western Society of Engineers in Chicago and described in great detail the work conducted during 1902. The Wrights failed to include any mention of their attempts to fly a powered machine in order to dampen enthusiasm for their work and reduce the risk of unwanted visitors and spectators during the 1903 season at Kitty Hawk. Nevertheless, they were rapidly becoming the center of attention in the aviation world, especially to men like Ferber who wanted to sell Wright biplane gliders in France.

1903 August 8 The first successful flight of the quarter-scale model of the *Great Aerodrome* designed by Samuel Langley took place on the Potomac. Launched from the houseboat specially equipped to support the full-size machine then being made ready for manned flight, the model was launched at 9:30 A.M. and flew straight out for 350 ft. before banking round and flying a farther 1,000 ft. It had been in the air for about 27 sec. and qualified, for Langley and his assistant Manly, the basic design of the full-size machine.

1903 August 18 Carl Jatho became the first German to "fly" through the air in a powered, heavier-than-air machine when he made a running hop for a distance claimed to be 59 ft. His strange machine had two wings of unequal span, the upper wing much narrower than the lower, and it was powered by a 9-HP gasoline engine. The device had no control surfaces, and its design showed little appreciation of the finer points of aerodynamics. The flight took place on the Vahrenwalder Heide near Hanover and was said to have been repeated during the following October, this time for 200 ft.

1903 September 25 Wilbur and Orville Wright arrived at Kitty Hawk to await the arrival of their 1903 flying machine, which was to be sent down separately from their workshop in Dayton, Ohio. Storms had battered the coastline, and the shed containing their 1902 glider had been almost blown apart. It took three days to repair the damage, although, miraculously, the glider was unharmed.

1903 September 28   The Wright brothers began flight trials with glider tests using the 1902 machine at Kitty Hawk, N.C. and familiarized themselves with control mechanisms they had successfully modified the previous year. They made 75 flights in perfect weather, one for just over 30 sec. in duration. Moreover, they fine-tuned flight control, "hovering" in the strong wind for almost 27 sec. before coming to earth only 50 ft. away from the take-off point. This demonstrated a level of controllability unmatched by any previous aeronaut, vital for powered flight and augured well for the stability of the 1903 design, the Wright Flyer.

1903 October 7   The first attempt was made to fly Langley's full size *Great Aerodrome* with Charles M. Manly at the controls. The 54 ft. long machine was a dual monoplane (one wing behind the other) with a total of 1,040 sq. ft. and a span of 48 ft. A single gasoline engine delivered 52 HP and powered two propellers, one on each side of the fuselage just behind the trailing edge of the forward wing. The pilot sat behind this assembly, and the entire assembly weighed 730 lb., including pilot. Propelled along a rail attached to a houseboat on the shore of the Potomac, the *Great Aerodrome* plunged into the river, Manly escaping wet but unhurt.

1903 October 9   The Wright Flyer was taken in crates to Kill Devil Hill, the boat *Lou Willis* that brought it having docked at Kitty Hawk the previous day. The powered flying machine had a larger wing than used in any Wright glider, with a span of 40 ft. 4 in. and a chord of 6.5 ft. giving a total area of 510 sq. ft. The biplane had a wing camber of 1 in 20. The Flyer was 21 ft. 1 in. in length and had two contra-rotating 8.5-ft. propellers driven by the 12-HP Wright engine.The Flyer weighed 610 lb. empty or 750 lb. with one of the brothers aboard. Since arriving September 25, Wilbur and Orville had busied themselves putting up a shed 44 ft. by 16 ft. to house the Flyer alongside the refurbished shed for their 1902 glider.

1903 November 5   The Wright brothers finished assembling their powered Flyer and ran up its engine for the first time. Never before had all the separate parts of the powered flying machine been together in a complete airplane because their bicycle workshop in Dayton where it was made was too small to allow complete assembly. When the engine misfired and spluttered, vibrations bent a propeller shaft, and George Spratt, an assistant, left to send both shafts back to the bicycle shop with a note for Charles Taylor to straighten the bent shaft and strengthen each of them. The shafts were back at Kill Devil Hill November 17 and installed that afternoon.

1903 November 28   The Wright brothers tested the engine on their powered Flyer in the newly constructed shed and again engine misfires caused vibrations that cracked a propeller shaft. Orville left for Dayton on November 30 to fashion solid ones from high-grade steel in the bicycle workshop. He arrived back with the new shafts December 11, and they were installed the morning after. During his journey, Orville had learned about Langley's unsuccessful attempt at manned flight with the *Great Aerodrome*.

1903 December 8   Manly made the second attempt to fly Langley's full-size *Great Aerodrome*. The machine was again launched from a catapult on the roof of a houseboat on the Potomac River. The rear wing caught in the launching gear, and the *Aerodrome* fell tail first into the river. This time the damage was severe, but Manly was uninjured. This second failure caused the U.S. government to reexamine the aircraft and its prospects of flight, and official backing for the project was withdrawn when the cost of eventual success was judged to be too high.

1903 December 14   The Wright Flyer was taken from its shed and put on a 60-ft. track inclined slightly downhill on the slopes of a dune. Made ready for its first flight, the brothers tossed a coin, and Wilbur won the honor of riding it through the air for the first time. As it rattled down the track and became airborne, Wilbur pulled back too hard on the forward elevator, bringing the nose up sharp and causing the Flyer to stall after reaching a height of 15 ft. It came down to the sand after traveling 60 ft. in little more than 3 sec., doing minor damage.

1903 December 17   The world's first manned, sustained, controlled, powered flight in a heavier-than-air machine was achieved by Orville Wright at the controls of the Wright Flyer in a 27-MPH wind. Orville Wright's first flight at Kill Devil Hill, Kitty Hawk, N.C. took place at 10:35 A.M., lasted about 12 sec. and covered 120 ft. The second flight was made by Orville's brother Wilbur and took place at 11:20 A.M. covering a distance of 175 ft. in approximately 12 sec. About 30 minutes later, Orville made the third flight, covering just over 200 ft in 15 sec., and at noon Wilbur made the fourth flight of the day, flying just over 200 ft. in 15 seconds. Witnesses to the flight were lumberman W. D. Brinkley, lifesavers John Daniels, Will Dough and Adam Etheridge and teenager Johnny Moore.

1903 December 19   The Wright brothers packed up and left Kill Devil Hill to return to Dayton, Ohio for Christmas. The Flyer was crated up for shipment back to the bicycle shop. The Wrights received two telegrams, one asking for pictures to publish in a women's magazine and one from the *New York World* offering exclusive rights to the story. Other messages requested details for publication, and one from Octave Chanute read simply: "Pleased at your success. When ready to make [details] public, please advise me." Wilbur and Orville's sister Lorin released information to the press as arranged.

1904 January   Capt. Ferdinand Ferber delivered a lecture at the Palais de la Bourse in Paris, where an enthusiastic 23-year-old architecture student by the name of Gabriel Voisin approached him and proclaimed his devotion to solving the problems of flight. Born in 1880, Gabriel Voisin and his brother Charles had been carrying out experiments with biplane gliders since 1898. After a year he resumed glider tests in 1903 before addressing the problems of powered flight. Voisin would become a practical but controversial pillar of European aviation.

1904 April   Gabriel Voisin was hired by Ernest Archdeacon, a wealthy Paris lawyer, to apply his knowledge of gliders to the construction of a glider styled after the Wright 1902 machine. It had wing camber, a fixed forward lifting surface and a vertical tail. Ferber's switch from the Lilienthal-type design to the Wright concept influenced Voisin, who applied the Wright specifications to his glider for Archdeacon. It had no means of control and no attempt at wing warping, and although it glided, it was not a successful flying machine.

1904 May 23   The Wright brothers made the first flight attempt with Flyer II, which was 80 lb. heavier than Flyer I of 1903, with a 1 in 25 wing camber and a rebored 16-HP engine. The Wrights now used a field at Huffman Prairie, 8 mi. outside Dayton, which gave them the opportunity for sustained activity in both development and testing. No longer would they have to trudge the 500 miles to Kitty Hawk for one spell of flying each year. The first attempt to get Flyer II into the air ended when it slithered off the track. Further attempts were made later that week after journalists who had gathered for a spectacle dwindled and vanished, much to the delight of the Wrights.

On December 17, 1903, Orville Wright became the first man to fly in a powered heavier-than-air flying machine. Courtesy of American Aviation Society.

1904 August 3 In a dirigible named *California Arrow*, Thomas Scott Baldwin carried out the first circular flight by an airship in America. It was powered by a converted motorcycle engine built and dispatched by Glenn Curtiss. Baldwin was an acrobat and set up a balloon factory in San Francisco in early 1904. After the earthquake and fire of 1906, he moved to Hammondsport, N.Y. and struck up an association with Curtiss, who by that time was the primary source of engines for American balloonists, from which came a love for flying. (Curtiss had made a considerable name for himself as a motorcycle record breaker; on January 24, 1907, he would become the fastest man on earth with a speed of 137 MPH.)

1904 September 7 The Wright brothers made the first assisted start using a specially constructed derrick in the rented field at Huffman Prairie to give their airplane flying speed. It was a tee-pee-shaped structure of four poles. A line ran from the aircraft at the base of the derrick, forward to a pulley at the front of the track, back to the base of the poles and up to a mass of 600 lb. weights. When the weights were dropped, it pulled the Flyer along the track with a force of 300 lb.

1904 September 15 Wilbur Wright made the first controlled turn in the air with a powered flying machine when attempting to perform a complete circle. He only managed half a circle, but it was the first real accomplishment with the Flyer II, which had been compromised on performance due to the high altitude and reduced air pressure of Huffman Prairie. The Wright brothers were now making all their flight tests at Huffman Prairie because

it was close to the bicycle shop where the airplanes were built. Kitty Hawk was more than 800 ft. lower than Dayton, which, with the marginal performance of the basic design, made a significant difference.

1904 September 20 Wilbur Wright made the first complete circle in the air during the afternoon while piloting the Flyer II at Huffman Prairie, Ohio. Wilbur remained in the air 1 min. 36 sec. and travelled a distance of 4,000 ft. His flight was observed by Amos T. Root, the subsequent report being the first recorded eyewitness account of a powered airplane in flight. Earlier flights had not been recorded by independent witnesses.

1904 October 23 Lt. Col. John P. Capper, a member of the British Aeronautical Society and a balloon expert, visited the Wright brothers to examine pictures of the Flyer and accounts of their powered flights. Capper enthused over the potential use of such a machine for the British Army and asked the Wrights to prepare a proposal for the sale of a flying machine to the British government. The Wrights submitted a plan for a two-seat machine with a range of 50 miles and proposed a financial plan that would give them £500 for every mile in the longest flight achieved during trials. The British vacillated, saying the performance was too uncertain.

1904 October The Aéro Club de France (French Air Club) announced details of several prizes offered to European aviators or aviators flying European aircraft. One, known as the Coupe Ernest Archdeacon (Ernest Archdeacon Cup), consisted of two separate awards: a silver trophy worth 2,000 francs donated by Archdeacon to the first pilot to fly a distance of at least 25 m (82 ft.) and a cash prize of 1,500 francs to the first pilot to fly a distance of more than 100 m (328 ft.). The Aéro Club also offered 1,500 francs to the first pilot to fly more than 100 m. Henry Deutsche de la Meurthe and Ernest Archdeacon put up 50,000 francs for the Grand Prix d'Aviation Deutsch-Archdeacon award to the first person to cover a circular distance of 1 km (3,281 ft.).

1904 October   The first full-size aircraft to feature ailerons as a control surface was the glider designed and built by Robert Esnault-Pelterie. Esnault-Pelterie had attempted to make an exact copy of the Wright glider but failed to satisfactorily duplicate the wing-warping control concept. His first glider, finished in April 1904, was a flop, and he resorted to the use of a completely separate surface for roll control, thus being the first person to use ailerons on the outboard sections of wings. The Frenchman was later to become famous for his REP series of powered monoplanes, particularly the REP 2-bis.

1904 November 9   Wilbur Wright accomplished the first manned airplane flight lasting more than 5 min., exceeding that time by 4 sec. He remained airborne during four complete circuits of the field at Huffman Prairie, covering 2.75 mi., and came down only when the engine showed signs of stress. Orville duplicated this accomplishment on December 1.

1904 December 9   The Wright brothers discontinued trials with their Flyer II after completing 105 tests and 80 brief flights since they began flying the new machine in May. Unlike Flyer I, which had made just four flights on December 17, 1903, before it was discarded, Flyer II would be broken down and cannibalized, only its engine parts going into the new model for 1905. The brothers were concerned about stability problems in turns and resolved to concentrate on this during the following year in a concerted effort to develop a truly practical flying machine for long distance flights.

1905 January 3   In efforts to interest the U.S. government in the use of airplanes for military scouting duties, Wilbur Wright spoke with his congressman, Rep. Robert M. Nevin, who asked him to prepare a letter for submission to the secretary of war that he, Nevin, would deliver and endorse. The letter never reached Nevin but went straight to the Board of Ordnance and Fortification, which, in 1898, had voted $50,000 for Langley's unsuccessful *Great Aerodrome* project. For the time being, the army declined the offer.

1905 March 10   The French lawyer and aspiring aeronaut Ernest Archdeacon sent a letter to the Wright brothers in Dayton, Ohio challenging them to prove the validity of their claims, which he asserted to be "so remarkable, even, that they give rise to a certain incredulity in my country." This marks the beginning of a bitter contest between the Wrights and European aeronauts, who copied many of their designs but were reluctant to accept the progress the two bicycle makers had achieved without the evidence of their own eyes. Archdeacon affirmed his willingness to go to Dayton "to see your machines (but) only if I am allowed to see them functioning; unless you think fit to come to France to show us what you have done."

1905 May 27   Capt. Ferdinand Ferber successfully carried out a motorized glide of about 330 ft. at Chalais-Meudon, France with his newly adopted *No. 6-bis* biplane configuration designed after discussions with Octave Chanute. The launch mechanism was an ingenious inclined cable suspended between three towers. The total weight of the motorized glider was 550 lb., and a modicum

of lift given to it by the extra speed provided by the motor was calculated to convert the glide from a flight angle of 1 in 5 to 1 in 7. In 1903 Ferber had attached a 6-HP Buchet motor driving two counter-rotating, coaxial propellers to his *No. 5* biplane glider. News of his work reached Charles Renard, who brought him to Chalais-Meudon from where he developed his *No. 6-bis*.

1905 June 6   Towed by a motorboat, Gabriel Voisin achieved a brief take-off on the Seine River in Paris while testing the Voisin-Archdeacon float glider. Archdeacon had commissioned Voisin to build the glider, which was mounted on floats and built like a large box kite with a smaller box kite mounted on booms behind it to form the tail plane. The aircraft applied Lawrence Hargrave's box kite principles, although pitch control was provided by a forward, Wright-type elevator mounted on booms. The pilot sat upright on a chair mounted between the floats, just forward of the main plane. The box kite approach to making wings was to become popular with a number of early manufacturers.

1905 June 18   Gabriel Voisin carried out the first flight attempt with the Blériot II float glider on the Seine in Paris. It was similar to the Voisin-Archdeacon biplane glider first flown earlier in June, except that the upper wing had a greater span than the lower and the top wing had a shorter span than the Archdeacon glider. From a towed start, it went out of control after a few seconds of flight. The Voisin-Archdeacon glider was also flown on this date but without much success. Blériot later approached Voisin to assemble an elliptical-winged floatplane, which would be called the Blériot III.

1905 June 23   The Wright Flyer III was taken into the air for the first time at Huffman Prairie by Orville Wright, who tried out the new control system. Powered by an engine that now delivered about 18 HP, the Flyer III had a wingspan of 40 ft. 6 in., a reduced wing area of 503 sq. ft., a camber of 1 in 20 and an elevator area increased from 50 to 84 sq. ft. For this flight, a semicircular vane called a "blinker" was installed between the two horizontal elevator surfaces in an effort to increase vertical stability. It was not a satisfactory modification and was removed after the first flight, which ended heavily, breaking four wing ribs.

1905 October 5   On its longest flight to date, the Wright Flyer III with Wilbur Wright at the controls covers 24.2 mi. in 38 min. 3 sec. around the field at Huffman Prairie. On Flyer III, the wing warping and rudder controls were separate, unlike in earlier Wright aircraft where they were combined into a single control, and it was capable of full maneuverability without the drawbacks of the earlier control design. The engine was now delivering more than 20 HP, twice the power of the Flyer I, and could run for longer periods. The first flight exceeding 30 minutes had been made by Orville Wright on October 4 when he remained in the air for 33 min. 17 sec., flying a distance of 21 mi.

1905 October 14   The Fédération Aéronautique Internationale (FAI) was established in France as an official body to ratify records and set standards in aviation, work it has continued down to the present day. A truly international organization, it has acted as an information pool, in which member countries could share the technical advances made in aviation to the benefit of all. As technology has advanced, the FAI has also acted as consultant on matters of legislation arising from those advances.

1905 October 16   Wilbur Wright carried out the last flight of the 1905 season with the Flyer III, now considerably modified from its first configuration. Flying tests had displayed the need to extend the position of the forward elevators twice as far in front of the wings as they were at the beginning of the season, with the vertical rudder moved 3 ft. farther back to considerably extend the length of the aircraft. The Flyer had made 50 flights, bringing to 134 the number of powered ascents the two brothers had made since December 17, 1903; the longest of these was the 38 min. flight achieved on October 5. It would be three years before Orville and Wilbur Wright flew again—with a completely revised design.

1905 November 30 The Aero Club of America was founded to act as a central body of information for the development and support of American aviation. Interest in the science of aeronautics and the technology of flying machines was still confined very much to the small community of enthusiasts. The government was reluctant to support further research because it had already put money into ventures with little or no hope of success. Even the Wright brothers, with their extensive flight program, had been unable to provide a protracted record of achievement. There was no alternative but to form organizations that could represent common interests.

1905 December 30 The Wright brothers signed a contract for one million francs with Frenchman Arnold Fordyce for the sale of a powered flying machine capable of flying a nonstop distance of 31 mi. It was to be demonstrated before August 1, 1906. Fordyce had been sent by Ferdinand Ferber who intended to work a deal for the flying machine by selling it, at a profit, to the French government. When a contingent of French government officials came to Dayton in April 1906 to change the agreement by seeking exclusivity for one year, the idea was dropped. In October 1906, the Wrights received 25,000 francs (then about $5,000) for their trouble, the first money they earned from flying.

1906 January 13 The first air exhibition of the Aero Club of America opened for eight days in the Sixty-ninth Regiment Armory in New York City and gathered together for the first time a collection of aspiring, and successful, aeronauts. The Wrights were asked to send the motor that powered their 1903 flying machine but could only salvage the crankshaft and flywheel. Langley's steam-powered gliders were there as were Augustus Herring's propellers, which, because of his association with Langley and Chanute, gave him greater credibility than his performance deserved.

1906 January 17 Count von Zeppelin's second airship, LZ 2, made its first flight from Lake Constance, but after ascending to a height of 1,500 ft., strong winds forced it to put down at Kissleg for the night. The airship was wrecked in a storm that tore it to pieces. Similar to LZ 1 but incorporating several modifications and more powerful engines delivering 85 HP, the airship had been completed in October 1905. A flight attempt November 30 had to be aborted when it was blown across the lake only to be brought back to the safety of its hangar.

1906 March 3 Trajan Vuia, a Romanian, made a hop in his *No. 1* monoplane, an aircraft with novel features. The tractor layout was supported by an undercarriage with pneumatic tires, real innovations at the time. The 25-HP Serpollet carbolic acid gas engine drove a 7 ft. 2.5 in. diameter, two-bladed propeller and was mounted next to the pilot's seat in the balloon car-like, four-wheel chassis suspended beneath the 22 ft. 11.5 in.-span wing. There was no tail plane except for a rudder attached to the rear of the chassis. The longest flight achieved by the *No. 1* is believed to have been about 79 ft. (24 m). The French pioneer Victor Tatin assisted Vuia in the construction of the *No. 1*.

1906 May Gabriel Voisin carried out unsuccessful tests with the Blériot III floatplane, which was powered by a 24-HP Antoinette engine driving two propellers. Built at a small works at Billancourt on the Seine River near Paris, the airplane had ellipsoidal wings and tail of equal dimensions for a total lifting surface of 646 sq. ft. It was later modified by replacing the main ellipsoidal wing with a Wright-type box configuration. In this form, and known as the Blériot IV, it was tried out during October but again failed to lift. Shortly after this Blériot was bought out by Voisin, and the partnership was severed.

1906 July 18 The Brazilian aviator Alberto Santos-Dumont registered his name as a competitor for the Ernest Archdeacon Cup and for the French Aero Club cash prize of 1,500 francs, which would go to the first person to take off from the ground and fly more than 100 m (328 ft.). Santos-Dumont designed a cellular biplane called the *14-bis* with a wing span of 37.7 ft., a lifting area of 560 sq. ft. and a 24-HP Antoinette engine. It was called the *14-bis* because Santos-Dumont planned to carry it into the air slung beneath his *No. 14* airship. He would conduct initial flight tests after dropping the *14-bis* from the balloon after which he would attempt to win the Aero Club prize by taking off from the ground.

1906 September 12 The Danish inventor Jacob C. Ellehammer made a flight of 138 ft. in his semi-biplane powered by an 18-HP 3-cylinder engine. His aircraft flew around a circular track, while tethered to a pole in the center. His engines were the product of good design and assembly, but the aircraft was never capable of controlled flight. Although some have claimed he should be given credit for having made the first airplane flight in Europe, his attempts to get off the ground were little more than frantic leaps by a machine incapable of sustained flight through the air.

1906 September 13 After a series of abortive attempts at getting into the air that began on August 21, Alberto Santos-Dumont in his *14-bis* biplane made what is considered by most historians to be the first powered flight by a European aircraft. The flight took place at the polo ground in the Bois de Bológne, Paris and, although not measured precisely, was variously estimated by witnesses to have covered between 4 m (13 ft.) and 7 m (23 ft.). The *14-bis* had pronounced dihedral and a box-like tail unit forward of the wings. Power was provided by a 50-HP Antoinette engine (the original 24-HP Antoinette being found to have insufficient power) driving an aluminum propeller 8 ft. 2 in. in diameter. The covered fuselage supported a place for the pilot to stand, and the machine weighed 661 lb.

1906 October 9 The first flight took place with Count von Zeppelin's third airship, the LZ 3, which had been funded through a state lottery sanctioned by the king of Württemberg. Stabilizing wings were attached for stability in the pitch axis and an attempt to reduce the pitching, or wallowing, motion noticed with the first two designs. It did much to encourage popular support for the airship, and the army eventually took it over under the designation Z 1. Subsequently, Z became the prefix for German army airships, while German navy airships were given the prefix L.

1906 October 23 Alberto Santos-Dumont won the 2,000 franc Ernest Archdeacon Cup trophy in his *14-bis* biplane when he became the first European to exceed a distance of 25 m (82 ft.) in the air with a flight of approximately 60 m (197 ft.) at 4:45 P.M. The precise distance he flew was never measured accurately, but it inspired a torrent of passionate nationalistic fervor that only served to harden French hearts against the achievements of the Wrights. Although Santos-Dumont was a Brazilian, he had made

France his home, and he did achieve the record on French soil using a French engine.

1906 November 12   In his *14-bis* biplane, Alberto Santos-Dumont won the 1,500 franc Ernest Archdeacon cash prize and the French Aero Club prize of 1,500 francs when he completed a distance of 220 m (722 ft.) in 21 sec. at an average speed of 25.06 MPH. This was also the first record ratified by the Fédération Aéronautique Internationale (FAI) formed in October 1905. Control of the *14-bis* was effected through a body harness attached by wires to two octagonal ailerons mounted in the outer bay of the mainplanes between each wing. The pilot leaned to the right or left to keep the machine on an even keel. Control in pitch came from tilting the entire forward box-kite assembly up or down by the use of a wheel in the cockpit.

1906 November 19   No longer patronized by the Chalais-Meudon, which he had left in June, French aviator Ferdinand Ferber saw his immediate hopes of powered flight dashed when his *No. 8* was destroyed on the ground by a storm. Ferber had accepted a position with up-and-coming manufacturer Levavasseur, who had built him a 25-HP motor that was attached to *No. 8*. Ferber was to help design the Antoinette I, but he constructed another machine designated *No. 9*, similar to *No. 8*, and flew perfectly at Issy-les-Moulineaux on July 25, 1908.

1907 February 17   Gabriel and Charles Voisin completed construction of the first land biplane built for a customer. A flight attempt on March 3 was unsuccessful, and the machine never flew. Built for Henry Kapferer, a member of the French Aero Club and an advocate of Wright designs, the biplane was powered by a Bouchet motor that was incapable of providing the necessary speed for take-off. The Voisins adopted Wright-type wings with a Hargrave box-kite tail and forward, horizontal elevators. This was the first development of the classic pusher biplane layout where the engine is mounted on the rear of a short fuselage with tail surfaces on booms extending from the trailing edge of the wings. This marked the first serious efforts by the Voisin brothers to manufacture airplanes for paying customers.

1907 March 16   Built for Leon Delagrange and piloted by Charles Voisin, the Voisin-Delagrange biplane made its first flight at 11:00 A.M. from Bagatelle, France, achieving a height of 13 ft. and a distance of 260 ft. Additional flights followed, and Delagrange took over his biplane on October 31 with plans to fly it from Issy-les-Moulineaux, which he did for the first time two days later, achieving a distance of 150 ft. On his second attempt, November 5, he stalled and crashed, destroying the biplane. In design it was similar to the biplane built for Henry Kapferer.

1907 April 5   Louis Blériot made a brief flight of almost 20 ft. in an aircraft of his own design, the tail-first, pusher engined Blériot Type V monoplane. He was to make only four flights in this craft before it crashed and was destroyed. This was Blériot's first excursion into the dizzy realm of inventor, designer and test pilot combined, predicated by his departure from association with the Voisin brothers. Blériot was convinced the monoplane had a better future than the biplane and set about designing a series of airplanes that by the end of the year brought Blériot credit for establishing a classic tractor style, the first of which would be the Type VII.

1907 July 11   The Blériot Type VI Libellule made its first flight, achieving a distance of about 80 ft. The aircraft was designed by Louis Peyret and had a tandem wing design similar to that of the Langley Aerodrome, featuring the first cantilever wings to be used

on an airplane. Roll control was by wingtip ailerons. In flights that continued into August, it left the ground 11 times and on six of these flights achieved a distance of over 328 ft. In September, Blériot modified the Type VI to carry a 50-HP, 16-cylinder Antoinette engine. On the 11th flight, Blériot crashed and almost lost his life.

1907 July   After 20 years of important experiments with airfoil sections, during which he accurately defined the way a wing creates lift, Horatio Phillips flew his Multiplane for approximately 500 ft. at Streatham in London. With its 224 narrow chord wings in four separate vertical stacks, this aircraft thus achieved the distinction of becoming the first manned powered aircraft to fly in the United Kingdom but was never officially credited as such. Phillips had patented the airfoil section he used on his aircraft and had done a great deal of research into the forces acting on a wing in flight. His aircraft had four rectangular frames that held the wings and a 20-HP engine driving a single propeller.

1907 August 1   The U.S. Army set up an aeronautical division in the office of the chief signals officer to take responsibility for "all matters pertaining to military ballooning, air machines, and all kindred subjects." The division consisted of just three men: Capt. Charles de Forrest Chandler, Cpl. Edward Ward and Pvt. Joseph E. Barrett, although Barrett soon left the Army. The Signal Corps used this opportunity to extend its activity with balloons and to carry out radio experiments. A dirigible was acquired in 1908, and some officers were trained as airship pilots.

1907 September 10   The first flight of the British Army *Airship No. 1*, more popularly known as *Nulli Secundus*, took place with Col. John Capper of the Royal Engineers as pilot, Samuel F. Cody as engineer and Capt. W. A. de C. King, the adjutant of the British Army Balloon School, as observer. A 50-HP Antoinette engine drove two propellers. *Nulli Secundus* was 122 ft. long and 26 ft. in diameter, had a capacity of 55,000 cu. ft. and had been built at the Army Balloon Factory, South Farnborough, England. It was flown from Aldershot to the Crystal Palace outside London in 3 hr. 25 min., a distance of 50 mi., on October 5.

1907 September 19   The first helicopter to lift a man from the ground was the Breguet-Richet helicopter built by the Breguet brothers at Douai, France. The flight was not a free, controlled event, however, as the machine had to be steadied from the ground by men using long poles. The machine was powered by a 40-HP

Powered by French engines, British Army Airship No. 1 (Nulli Secundus) *made its first flight in 1907.*

Antoinette gasoline engine. The tests included one flight in which the machine rose too quickly for the handlers and was damaged when it crash-landed in a field. Four rotors in stacked pairs of eight blades were mounted on each end of a cross-shaped frame, making four sets of rotors in all. The engine was mounted in the middle. The date of this event is sometimes given as August 24.

1907 September 30 The Voisin-Farman I flew for the first time. Flown by Henri Farman, the aircraft was to prove very successful, making about 20 true flights at Issy-les-Moulineaux before November 23. On November 9, the flight lasted 1 min. 14 sec. and covered 3,379 ft. The aircraft was a classic pusher biplane. The box-kite tail surfaces were mounted on spars that ran aft from the trailing edge of the wing. Between these spars, the engine and propeller turned, fixed to the rear end of the short nacelle-type fuselage. A combination elevator and fore plane was mounted at the front of the fuselage. The undercarriage consisted of two main wheels mounted below the fuselage and two tail planes, one under each fin of the box-kite tail.

1907 October 1 The inventor and scientist Dr. Alexander Graham Bell, among others, formed the Aerial Experiment Association (AEA) ''for the purpose of constructing a practical aerodrome, driven by its own motive power and carrying a man.'' Other prominent members included Lt. Thomas Etholen Selfridge of the U.S. Army Signal Corps, F. W. Baldwin, J. A. D. McCurdy and Glenn Curtiss, the motorcyclist-turned-aviator who founded the Curtiss Aircraft Company. The AEA amassed data on all forms of aerial flight, including kites, balloons, hang gliders and engines. It was dissolved by prior arrangement on March 31, 1909, to release the members for their individual ventures.

1907 October 26 Henri Farman, flying the Farman-Voisin I biplane, set a Fédération Aéronautique Internationale world aircraft distance record of 2,530 ft. in 52.6 sec. In doing so, Farman won the Archdeacon trophy and gained great prestige for himself and the plane's builders, the Voisin brothers. Three days earlier, Farman had achieved a flight distance of 610 ft. in just over 15 sec., winning a prize of 200 francs, and on October 25, he flew for 656 ft. Despite the awards, it should be noted that the 52.6 sec. flight was not as long as the best Wright brothers' flight on the day they first took a powered machine into the air almost four years earlier.

1907 November 9 Flying the Voisin biplane that had given him the FAI world distance record on October 26, 1907, Henri Farman became the first person in Europe to fly a distance in excess of 3,281 ft. (1 km). Farman remained airborne for 1 min. 14 sec. and flew a total distance of 3,380 ft., almost making a complete circle in the process. In not achieving a complete circle in the air, Farman just failed to qualify for the Grand Prix d'Aviation Deutsch-Archdeacon prize set up in October 1904.

1907 November 10 The Blériot Type VII was flown for the first time at Issy-les-Moulineaux by Louis Blériot. It was the first of the classic tractor monoplane designs that would become familiar in the European skies. Surprisingly, Blériot designed the Type VII to be inherently unstable for better maneuverability and powered the machine with a 50-HP Antoinette engine. Six flights were achieved with this aircraft, the longest over 1,600 ft., before it crashed on December 18. The externally braced monoplane wing used wing warping for roll control instead of ailerons, something that was to remain a feature of Blériot's aircraft.

1907 November 13 The world's first entirely free flight in a manned helicopter was made by Paul Cornu in his twin-rotor

machine at Lisieux, France. The flight lasted about 20 sec. and took the helicopter to a height of about 1 ft. The helicopter was developed from a model Cornu had built in 1906, powered by a 2-HP Buchet engine that had been reduced in weight from 31 lb. to 15 lb. to bring the all up weight of the model down to an acceptable 28 lb. The full-size helicopter was powered by a 24-HP Antoinette gasoline engine that drove two 19 ft. 8.25 in. diameter rotors via a belt drive system.

1907 November 16 French pioneer Robert Esnault-Pelterie flew for 1,968 ft. in his REP I monoplane. The airplane had a tapered wing and adopted the Wright brothers' style of wing warping for flight control. However, the design gave poor stability, and the design concept was not a success, although several flights were made before the end of the year. Learning well from the mistakes made with REP No. 1, Esnault-Pelterie went on to develop a reliable family of monoplanes. His expertise, however, was with engines—an immaculate little 25-HP, seven-cylinder, fan engine powered his No. 2 machine.

1907 December 6 Lt. Thomas E. Selfridge flew a powered, man-carrying kite that carried him 168 ft. into the air for 7 min. at Baddeck, Nova Scotia. The tetrahedral kite was designed by Alexander Graham Bell and was powered by a Curtiss engine in a project sanctioned by the Aerial Experiment Association, of which all three men were founding members. Lt. Selfridge had visited Bell at Baddeck during the previous spring and so impressed the inventor that Bell sought permission from U.S. Pres. Theodore Roosevelt to have himself assigned as official test observer. Shortly after the flight, Lt. Selfridge turned his hand to heavier-than-air machines and designed *Red Wing*, which first flew on March 12, 1908.

1907 December 23 The chief signals officer of the U.S. Army, Brig. Gen. James Allen, issued specification no. 486, the first military aircraft specification for which commercial tenders were invited. The airplane had to fly at a speed of at least 36 MPH, carry two people with a combined weight of 350 lb., perform a nonstop flight of 125 mi. and be easily transportable. It arose from a meeting Wilbur and Orville Wright had with Lt. Frank P. Lahm, who persuaded members of the Board of Ordnance and Fortification to reexamine the opportunities for a military airplane. The specification was written around the capabilities of the Wright Flyer and though published for bids to conform to army requirements, only the Wrights were expected to respond by the closing date of February 1, 1908.

1907 In France, Louis and Laurent Séguin began work on what was to become one of the most famous and important lightweight gasoline engines of its day. Intended from conception as a power source for aircraft, their work resulted in the Gnôme rotary engine. (A rotary engine is one in which the cylinders rotate with the crankshaft, whereas a radial engine is one in which stationary cylinders are placed radially around the propeller shaft.) The Gnôme rotary was used first in Paulhan's Voisin biplane in June 1909. Tens of thousands were made in various marks into the 1920s.

1908 January 13 The first officially accredited circular flight exceeding 1 km (3,281 ft.) in Europe was flown by Henri Farman in a modified Voisin-Farman I biplane. This achievement won for Farman the Grand Prix d'Aviation Deutsch-Archdeacon prize of 50,000 francs set up in 1904. The Voisin flying machine was powered by a 50-HP Antoinette engine driving a single propeller. The conditions for the prize were that the airplane should fly around a point .5 km (1,640.5 ft.) from the starting point and

An airship at Croydon, site of one of London's first airports, before World War I.

return, passing in both directions through two posts set 164 ft. apart. The flight lasted 1 min. 28 sec., the turn being effected by rudder control since the Voisin lacked proper lateral control surfaces.

1908 January 29 The Imperial All-Russia Aero Club was founded and raised money through public subscription by imperial decree. Unlike their counterparts in other European countries, aspiring Russian aeronauts were not given the financial rewards of prizes or trophies for spectacular feats or competitions, and there were no government departments seriously interested in promoting aviation. Despite this, several names had begun to emerge already. Igor Sikorski was working on helicopter models, Oleg Antonov was learning the science of aeronautics by flying gliders, and Nikolai Zhukovski was writing papers on the science of flight.

1908 February 1 The deadline for bids on a military airplane specification issued by the U.S. Army on December 23, 1907, arrived with only 22 feasible propositions out of 41 applicants. [Only three sent deposit checks against 10% of the bid.] The Wrights submitted (as previously arranged) a proposal priced at $25,000 for an airplane to be delivered within 200 days. Augustus Herring submitted a proposal priced at $20,000 for an airplane within 180 days, and J. F. Scott of Chicago priced his design at $1,000 for an airplane within 185 days. Scott withdrew voluntarily, but the army issued contracts to the Wrights and Herring. Despite numerous contract completion extensions, the army never did see the Herring flying machine. The Wright airplane was delivered.

1908 February 8 Designed by Léon Levavasseur, the *Gastambide-Mengin I* tapered monoplane made its first flight piloted by the mechanic Boyer from the flying ground at Bagatelle, France. It was to do for the monoplane what the Farman did for the biplane, establishing a strong line of successful airplanes called Antoinette, after the Société Antoinette engine firm run by Levavasseur. Powered by a 50-HP Antoinette engine driving a two-bladed metal propeller, the airplane had no control surfaces and stood on four main wheels. Its best flight took it a distance of 492 ft. but it crashed on February 14 and had to be rebuilt as the *Gastambide-Mengin II*.

1908 February 24 The chief signal officer of the U.S. Army, Gen. James Allen, awarded a contract to Thomas Baldwin for

Signal Corps *Dirigible Balloon No. 1*, in the same month that the Wright brothers and Augustus Herring were each contracted for a powered, heavier-than-air flying machine. Slowly, the U.S. Army was getting air-minded and wanted to explore the military potential of both types of flying devices. The dirigible was built at Hammondsport, N.Y., and Glenn Curtiss provided the motor (as he had for most American balloons) while Thomas Selfridge supplied the propeller.

1908 March 12 The first flight of the first airplane built by the U.S. Aerial Experiment Association took place when Thomas Baldwin flew the *Red Wing* (Aerodrome No. 1) designed by Lt. Thomas E. Selfridge 318 ft. 11 in. and ended in a crash landing. The aircraft was a biplane with a movable forward elevator and a fixed tail stabilizer with a rudder. The *Red Wing* (so called from its red silk wings) had no lateral control and used skids to take off from ice. Some people still claim this was the first airplane flight in the United States, and it was cited in legal battles over patent rights between the Wrights and Curtiss. A second flight of about 120 ft. was made by Thomas E. Selfridge, confirming the need for effective lateral control.

1908 March 14 Henri Farman made the first flight in his modified Voisin-Farman I-bis, the biplane built by the Voisin brothers that he first flew on September 30, 1907. It served him well until May 1909. The I-bis was powered for its first flight only by a 50-HP, eight-cylinder Renault engine, which was subsequently replaced by an Antoinette engine of similar power. Farman rigged the wings of his Voisin, giving it dihedral, and fitted a smaller box-tail unit to improve performance as well as add curtains between the wings on either side of the pilot. He also re-covered the wings and tail with rubberized linen in place of the varnished silk fitted by Voisin.

1908 March The Wright brothers signed an agreement for European marketing of the Wright Flyer, and La Compagnie Générale de Navigation Aérienne was formed with capital of 700,000 francs. Hart Berg, the American salesman with offices in Paris for selling U.S. inventions, had organized the deal whereby Wilbur and Orville Wright would get the majority of the stock, royalties on flying machines sold in Europe and cash sums when demonstration flights in France had been completed. It was agreed that Wilbur would carry out the demonstration flights in France while Orville tested the two-man Flyer for the U.S. Army.

1908 May 3 Léon Delagrange crashed in his Voisin-Delagrange II, which he had ordered from the Voisin brothers following the crash of his first Voisin in November 1907. Delagrange fitted it with the same modifications Farman made to his biplane, and following the crash, a few additional changes were made, including the addition of the side curtains, which qualified it to be renamed Voisin-Delagrange III. In July, extra curtains were fitted to the outer portion of the wings, enclosing the struts that held the two wings together at four locations instead of two. It was with this machine that Delagrange continually challenged Farman throughout the year.

1908 May 6 Wilbur Wright took to the air for the first time since October 16, 1905, when he last flew the Flyer III at Huffman Prairie, near Dayton, Ohio. This time, the Wright brothers were back at Kill Devil Hill, Kitty Hawk, having last flown there on December 17, 1903, the day of the first four powered flights. Now they were testing the modified Flyer III prepared for the U.S. Army trials, and Wilbur flew it into the air without a launching derrick for a distance of 1,008 ft. in 22 sec. Known as the Type A, the Flyer had a span of 41 ft., a chord of 6.5 ft., a length of 31 ft., an elevator area of 70 sq. ft. and a wing area of 510 sq. ft. Powered by a 30-HP Wright engine, it was capable of 40 MPH.

1908 May 14 Dayton, Ohio mechanic Charles Furnas became the first passenger to fly in a powered, heavier-than-air flying machine when he was taken for a ride lasting 22.6 sec. at Kill Devil Hill, Kitty Hawk, N.C. With Wilbur Wright at the controls of the modified 1905 Flyer, the flight took place at 8:00 A.M. in a southwest wind. A second flight with Furnas aboard was piloted by Orville Wright and lasted 4 min. It is uncertain whether Furnas was sent to Kitty Hawk by the Wrights or whether he made his own way, but his presence was essential to demonstrate the capability of the modified Flyer.

1908 May 18 Thomas Baldwin made the first flight in his *White Wing* (Aerodrome No. 2), the second airplane designed and built by the U.S. Aerial Experiment Association, and carried out the first flight in the United States in an airplane equipped with wheels. It was also the first airplane in the world to fly with a tricycle undercarriage, where the machine is balanced on two main wheels and single nose wheel. The first flight covered a distance of 279 ft. and attained a height of 10 ft. and was followed by three more flights during the day; on one, Glenn Curtiss flew for 1,017 ft. On May 19, Lt. Selfridge became the first U.S. Army officer to fly solo in a mechanically powered, heavier-than-air flying machine. J. A. D. McCurdy crashed *White Wing* on May 23 after flying 549 ft.

1908 May 24 The first flight by a powered aircraft in Italy took place when Delagrange demonstrated his 50-HP Voisin at the start of a series of demonstrations held in Rome, Milan and Turin, which inspired young army officers to take up flying. Lt. Alessandro Pecori Giraldi became the first member of the Italian army to receive his pilot's brevet on September 12, 1909.

1908 May 29 The first passenger to fly in a heavier-than-air aircraft in Europe was Ernest Archdeacon, who was flown by Henri Farman in his Voisin-Farman I-bis biplane at Ghent, Belgium. This came only 23 days after the Wright Flyer had successfully taken the world's first passenger into the air at Kitty Hawk, and showed the rate of progress under way in Europe just as Wilbur had arrived in Paris to show off the modified Wright Flyer to European enthusiasts and to support the marketing program for Wright airplanes.

1908 May 30 Léon Delagrange became the first European aviator flying a European aircraft to remain aloft for more than one-quarter hour. Flying his Voisin-Delagrange III at Issy-les-Moulineaux, Delagrange flew 12 km 75 m (7 mi. 2646 ft.) in 15 min. 25 sec., but this did not constitute the official record because appropriate observers were not on hand. Instead, his rival Henri Farman took the honor on July 6, 1908, when he remained in the air over Issy in his Voisin-Farman I for 20 min. 20 sec. For this, Farman received the French Armengaud prize of 10,000 francs, which had been put up for the first aviator to remain airborne for more than 15 min.

1908 June 8 British aviator Alliott Verdon Roe made his first independent flight in the Roe I biplane by hopping off the ground 2 to 3 ft. at Brooklands, England. This biplane was based on the design of a model that had won a *Daily Mail* flying model competition held at Alexandra Park and was originally towed into the air by racing cars, since its 9-HP J. A. P. engine was not powerful enough to propel it into the air. The Roe I was a canard

biplane of wire-braced wood built for £75 in April 1907 and only became airborne when A. V. Roe installed a 24-HP Antoinette engine. Roe I had a span of 30 ft., a length of 23 ft. and a maximum weight, with pilot, of 650 lb.

1908 June 8 Esnault-Pelterie carried out extensive changes to his REP No. 2 monoplane (built in 1907) and made his first flight in it, reputedly covering a distance of 3,900 ft. at more than 50 MPH. His No. 2 now had a span of 28 ft. and a 30-HP, air-cooled, 7-cylinder engine driving a four-bladed propeller. Major modifications included increased surface area in the tail and the addition of small elevators on the fuselage near the engine. The wings had pronounced anhedral and adopted downward wing warping for lateral control, but the machine was inherently unstable and few enthusiasts rated it highly.

1908 June 10 The United States Aeronautical Society was established in New York for the dissemination and publication of engineering and technical performance information for the benefit of all. The formation of societies such as this had an encouraging and accelerating effect on the development of aviation in America, serving as a forum for discussion and debate among enthusiasts and entrepreneurs.

1908 June 17 Louis Blériot made the first flight in his No. VIII, a tractor monoplane powered by a 50-HP Antoinette engine. It had an enclosed fuselage that would later be changed to an open trellis-type characteristic of his later monoplanes. When first flown, the No. VIII had a wingspan of 36 ft., but this was reduced to 28 ft. It made several flights at Issy-les-Moulineaux, France by June 29 and then began flying from Toury, where it carried the first flaps fitted to a powered flying machine, attached in efforts to increase lift at slow speed. In this form, it was known as the Blériot VIII-bis and on July 6 flew for 8 min. 24 sec.

1908 June 18 Monoplane designer Robert Esnault-Pelterie set out on a short test flight with his REP No. 2 and crashed, ending his career as pilot of his own innovative designs. After forgetting to trim back the engine, he had been thrown against the fuel tank while trying to land at full speed. Unconscious, he was revived by a local farmer but suffered from shock and concussion. From this point on, Esnault-Pelterie would fly only as a passenger for fear some involuntary movement occasioned by fear would cause him to crash again with dire consequences.

1908 June 20 The zeppelin LZ 4, the fourth type built by Count von Zeppelin's factory on the shores of Lake Constance, made its first trial flight successfully. The LZ 4 was 446 ft. long with a diameter of 43 ft. and a capacity of 519,000 cu. ft. Each engine delivered 105 HP that gave the dirigible a top speed of 30 MPH. A special shaft allowed access from one of the gondolas slung beneath the envelope to an observation post on top, a position that in wartime could carry a machine gun post. Two gondolas supported 10 crew members, of which 6 were engineers. The first flight was followed by one of 2 hours on June 23, and von Zeppelin put plans together for a flight across the Swiss-German border.

1908 June 20 Curtiss carried out the first flight of the third airplane built by the Aerial Experiment Association (AEA), called *June Bug* (Aerodrome No. 3). *June Bug* had a span of 42 ft. 6 in., a wing area of 370 sq. ft. and a maximum weight of 615 lb. This was the first airplane financed and flown by Curtiss, although it reflected little of the flare for performance his designs would have when he went into business on his own.

1908 June 28 Danish pioneer aviator J. C. H. Ellehammer made the first aircraft flight in Germany when he flew his No. IV biplane at Kiel. (Notwithstanding the earlier efforts of Karl Jatho in his powered hang glider, indigenous German aviation only began when Hans Grade first flew his Ellehammer-inspired triplane at Magdeburg in October, making him the first German pilot.) Ellehammer eventually moved into the field of rotary-winged flight and began experiments with various powered helicopters of his own design.

1908 July 1 Count von Zeppelin set off on a flight from Lake Constance near Friedrichshafen, Germany across the Swiss border to Zurich and back in the LZ 4 first flown on June 20. As was noted at the time, more than any other event, this demonstrated the awesome war capabilities of a machine that could roam across national boundaries at will. As the giant silver airship droned slowly across the towns and villages of southern Germany and Switzerland, it gathered spectators in the thousands and brought hysteria to fever pitch when the celebrations for this event and the Count's 70th birthday began several days later.

1908 July 4 Glenn Curtiss won the first part of a trophy issued by the *Scientific American* magazine for the first U.S. citizen to make a public flight in a heavier-than-air aircraft over a measured course of 1 km (3,281 ft.). He flew his aircraft *June Bug* a distance of 1.5 km (5,090 ft.) in a time of 102.2 sec., an average speed of 34 MPH. The trophy had been established to stimulate American inventiveness and redress the imbalance that threatened to set in if European progress in aviation continued unanswered. Although European aviators were not yet achieving the results the Wrights had obtained, there were more of them and progress was becoming rapid.

1908 July 8 The first woman to fly in a heavier-than-air aircraft and the first woman passenger of a powered airplane was Madame Thérèse Peltier, when she accompanied Léon Delagrange on a 500 ft. flight in a Voisin biplane at Turin, Italy. She also became the first woman to fly solo, but because she did not continue flying, she was never considered a qualified pilot. These aerial exploits were designed to gather popular support for individual pilots, and the stunts and circus tricks so common in the early days of ballooning were to become standard for powered airplanes also.

1908 July 22 The first flight of the *Gastambide-Mengin II*, otherwise known as the *Antoinette II,* took place at Issy-les-Moulineaux, France piloted by an Antoinette employee, Welferinger. Essentially a rebuilt version of the *Gastambide-Mengin I*, which made its first flight on February 8, 1908, but crashed 10 days later, the *Antoinette II* had improved flying control surfaces with triangular ailerons, twin rudders and elevators. Robert Gastambide, one of two employees of Société Antoinette for whom the original version had been built, was taken up by Welferinger on August 20.

1908 July The brilliant American journalist Frederick W. Wile was employed by a British newspaper to penetrate German airship activities, including those of the Zeppelin company, to determine the level of war planning then under way and publish the story. He met with a German government adviser who, believing him to represent interests that wished to purchase a Zeppelin, attempted to impress him with the capabilities of the airship by letting him in on a plan, should war come, to send 350,000 troops from the coast of France to England in 30 min. The adviser claimed that they would "conclude no peace until a German Army had occupied London."

1908 August 4 Count von Zeppelin took the LZ 4 on a 24-hr. flight from Lake Constance, down the Rhine to Basel, then to Strasbourg and Mainz and back to Stuttgart, a total nonstop distance of 435 mi. All along its advertised path, crowds waved and shouted as the Zeppelin moved silently overhead. Known as the "grand tour," it was a successful attempt to demonstrate the performance capabilities of the latest airship. On the return leg, engine trouble altered plans to return to Friedrichshafen, and the LZ 4 headed for Stuttgart with the intention of landing near the Daimler works, where its two 105-HP engines were built, but a storm carried it into electrical wires where it exploded, without loss of life.

1908 August 8 Wilbur Wright made his first flight in Europe by flying the Wright Flyer A from the racetrack at Hunaudières, 5 mi. south of Le Mans, France. Watched by a small crowd of men and women, Wright kept the Flyer in the air for precisely 1 min. 45 sec. at up to 40 MPH and stunned watchers by performing the first banked turns under perfect control ever seen in Europe. European flyers had difficulty making turns because lateral stability was poor, and turns like that made by Farman for the Grand Prix d'Aviation in November 1907 were wide side-slips made by applying rudder. Wright made nine flights of up to 8 min. duration, the last on August 13 before returning to America.

1908 August 12 Controlled by Thomas Baldwin and Glenn Curtiss, the Signal Corps' *Dirigible Balloon No. 1,* the first Army dirigible, began flight trials at Fort Meyer near Washington, D.C. after delivery on July 20. Known as SC-1 (Signal Corps No. 1) it was shaped like an elongated sausage, 96 ft. long with a volume of 20,000 cu. ft. and an endurance of 2 hr. with two people on board. The SC-1 was powered by a 25-HP four-cylinder Curtiss in-line engine, and the car for the two-man crew was 66 ft. long and 2 ft. 6 in. wide. On August 14, it maintained an average speed of almost 20 MPH and remained in the air for a record 2 hr. 10 min. on Aug. 15. Thomas Selfridge, Frank P. Lahm and Benjamin D. Foulois, all lieutenants in the Signal Corps Aeronautical Division, were trained to fly SC-1.

1908 August 20 The Wright Flyer built for flight trials before the U.S. Army arrived at Fort Myer eight days ahead of schedule. It was assembled by August 25 prior to several days of testing to perfect engine adjustments. The specification required a speed of 40 MPH achievement of which would guarantee the quoted contract price of $25,000. The Wright brothers would receive an additional $2,500 for every 1 MPH above specification, or default by the same amount for every increment of 1 MPH below 40 MPH. Before flight trials began, tests to check transportability, another stipulation, began.

1908 August 21 Wilbur Wright began flying demonstrations of his Flyer A from the artillery ground known as Camp d'Auvers, 7 mi. east of Le Mans, France, having moved from the Hunaudières race course. The move was necessary because the restricted area of Hunaudières made it necessary to carry out repeated turns, confusing accurate distance measurement and diminishing accurate performance estimates. The *Flyer* made its last ascent from the race course on August 13, and two days later the flying machine was towed to Camp d'Auvers by automobile.

1908 August 21 The first turn in the air performed by a monoplane was carried out by *Antoinette II,* first flown at Issy-les-Moulineaux on July 22, 1908. Originally known as the *Gastambide-Mengin I,* it had been rebuilt as the *Antoinette II* following an accident after four hop flights at Bagatelle five months earlier. This turn lasted 1 min. 36 sec.

Lt. Thomas E. Selfridge (left), U.S. Army, and Orville Wright prepare for a flight from Fort Myer, September 1908.

The Wright Flyer passing over the West Gate of Arlington National Cemetery, Arlington, Va., September 3, 1908.

1908 September 3 Orville Wright began flight trials in the Wright Flyer built for the U.S. Army contract issued in February. The first flight, before a crowd of about 500 gathered to witness this very first public flight in America by a Wright brother, took place at Fort Myer, Washington, D.C. and lasted 1 min. 11 sec. It greatly impressed the throng and did much to promote awareness of aviation and its potential value before politicians and planners in the nation's capital.

1908 September 5 The Goupy I, a French design, was the first full-size powered triplane to fly, albeit for a brief hop. The aircraft was conventional in layout, having a tail-wheel undercarriage and a tractor engine mounted on a fuselage that ran the length of the machine. The tail plane was of a box-kite type, reminiscent of that used on Voisin biplanes. The three mainplanes were joined at the tips by a solid panel, also giving the appearance of an oversize box kite. The two lower planes were joined to the fuselage with the top plane on struts above, a layout that became standard for both triplanes and biplanes.

1908 September 9 Orville Wright almost doubled the time aloft record of 29 min. 54 sec. achieved by Leon Delagrange of France when he stayed aloft in the Army Flyer for 57 min. 25 sec. and, later in the day, for 1 hr. 2.5 min. Late in the afternoon, Lt. Frank P. Lahm was taken for a ride lasting 6 min. 24 sec., becoming the first army officer to ride as a passenger in an airplane. Three days later, Maj. Squier, the acting chief signal officer, was taken aloft as a passenger for a flight lasting 9 min. 6 sec., establishing a new two-man endurance record.

1908 September 17 Veteran flyer Lt. Thomas E. Selfridge became the first person to be killed in a powered airplane when he

died of wounds sustained in a crash while flying as a passenger with Orville Wright in the Flyer A at Fort Myer, Washington, D.C. during U.S. Army trials. The flight began just after 5:00 P.M. The accident occurred when a propeller broke and severed control wires, causing the Flyer to plunge to the ground. Selfridge died at 8:10 P.M. shortly after an operation on the base of his skull. Orville was hospitalized until October 31 and spent several weeks on crutches.

1908 September 17 Lt. George C. Sweet and Naval Constructor William McEntee were official U.S. Navy observers during the trials with the Wright Flyer at Fort Myer and prepared a report for Rear Admiral W. S. Cowles, chief of the bureau of equipment. On December 2, Cowles submitted this report to the secretary of the navy, recommending aircraft for scouting and observation duty and outlining a suitable specification. The report also examined the effect of airplanes on naval action in war and recommended that airplanes be purchased for the Navy and personnel be trained.

1908 September 21 Wilbur Wright made one of the first significant long distance endurance flights in Europe when he flew the Wright Flyer he was demonstrating from Camp d'Auvers for a distance of 41.4 miles. The flight lasted 1 hr. 31 sec., by far the longest flight to date. The longest previous European flight was 30 min. 27 sec., flown by Farman three days earlier. Finding it all too easy to outpace the competition, Wilbur Wright did not join the friendly rivalry between Delagrange and Farman that characterized European flight throughout the year.

1908 September 25 The first multiple fatality air accident, in which four people lost their lives, occurred at Moulins in France. The French dirigible *République* lost a propeller, which, still spinning, ripped into the gas bag. The sudden loss of gas caused the airship to fall from about 400 ft., and the crew of four was killed on impact. *République* had made its maiden flight from Moisson on June 24 and was taken over by the French Army for whom it had been built. It had a length of 215 ft., a diameter of 33.8 ft. and a volume of 114,773 cu. ft. and was powered by a 75-HP Panhard-Levassor engine.

1908 September 29 American S. F. Cody became the first pilot to fly a British-made machine from English soil. He flew a dis-

The wreck of the world's first fatal, powered airplane accident, in which U.S. Army Lt. Selfridge lost his life, September 17, 1908.

tance of 234 ft. in the British Army *Aeroplane No. 1*. Construction of this airplane began at the end of 1907 and was carried out by Cody, who was the Royal Engineers' kite instructor at the Army Balloon Factory, Farnborough. The No. 1 borrowed much from the Wright machine but had unique features, including main wheels, an extra rudder above the wings and ailerons for lateral control. It had a span of 52 ft., a wing area of 790 sq. ft. and a fully loaded weight of 2,540 lb. with a 50-HP Antoinette engine giving a maximum speed of 40 MPH.

1908 October 7   Mrs. Hart Berg, wife of the American sales representative for the company formed to sell Wright Flyers in Europe made a flight with Wilbur Wright and inadvertently started a fashion craze. To conform with Edwardian modesty, Mr. Berg had tied a cord around the bottom of Mrs. Berg's dress to prevent it flapping around her during the brief, 2-minute flight. After landing, she took a few steps without remembering to untie the cord. A photograph of her immediately triggered the hobble-skirt fashion that rocked Paris.

1908 October 8   The first Englishmen to fly as passengers in a heavier-than-air, powered aircraft were taken up on demonstration flights by Wilbur Wright in the Wright Flyer at Camp d'Auvers in France. The first, Mr. Griffith Brewer, was followed by Hon. Charles Rolls, cofounder of Rolls-Royce, Mr. F. H. Butler, founder of the Aero Club of Great Britain and Major B. F. S. Baden-Powell, the secretary of the Aeronautical Society of Great Britain. Just as France had been shocked into action by the sight of the Wright Flyer, so too were other European countries joining the race for aerial supremacy encouraged by prizes.

1908 October 9   The Antoinette IV monoplane, the first in a series of aerodynamically refined monoplane designs, made its first flight and reflected every nuance of Levavasseur's artistic flair for matching design with aerodynamics. It was powered by a 50-HP engine with modest dihedral on thick, elliptical wings with an area of 322.9 sq. ft. This was increased to 538.2 sq. ft. and the first flight with the bigger wing took place on February 19, 1909, at Mourmelon.

1908 October 16   Samuel Cody made a flight of 27 sec. when piloting the British Army *Aeroplane No. 1* from Farnborough, England. He covered a total distance of 1,390 ft. and reached a

height of 30 ft. before coming down with a bump and partly wrecking the frail machine. Only two days earlier he had landed after reaching a height of 10 ft. for fear of the height! In September 1909, Cody flew 40 miles in 1 hr. 3 min. around Laffan's Plain near Farnborough.

1908 October 30   With an eye on the Michelin Cup, Henri Farman carried out a cross-country flight of nearly 17 mi. between Camp de Chalons and the outskirts of Reims in about 20 min. with his Voisin biplane at a speed of 45 MPH and a height of 130 ft. The Michelin Cup carried a cash prize of 20,000 francs, which would be awarded to the person who, by December 31, had made the longest flight of the year. The cup itself, valued at 10,000 francs, would be awarded to the Aero Club in which the lucky recipient was a member. Wilbur Wright was a favorite contender, although he was watching closely the increasing flight times of Farman, Delagrange and Blériot.

1908 October   During the month, the *Daily Mail*, a London newspaper, offered a prize of £1,000 to the first person to cross the English Channel. Wilbur Wright was offered an extra £1,000 if he would try for the record, but fearing inclement weather, he declined. Being an American, Wilbur Wright was unaware of the political significance in being the first person to break the isolation from Europe that England believed had saved it from invasion for almost 900 years. With German territorial aspirations on the rise, a quick hop from France to England would stir new fears of attack from continental adversaries.

1908 October   Louis Blériot made the first heavier-than-air aircraft flight in Romania when he flew his monoplane at Bucharest. Blériot was the first to threaten the early lead gained by the Voisin brothers in European aviation. Six Voisin biplanes were flying, and their exploits at the hands of such pilots as Henri Farman and Delagrange were making the name Voisin synonymous with powered flight in Europe. Blériot's experiments with his prototypes were developing into a far superior aircraft that would soon be world famous.

1908 November 26   Henri Farman made the first successful flight with his modified Voisin biplane. It included changes he put into effect to increase its performance and enhance his chances at winning the Michelin Cup for the longest flight of the year. He achieved a speed of 50 MPH and was able to demonstrate improved handling. The modifications began when Farman ordered a third wing from Voisin, 23 ft. in length, to be fitted between the two existing wings. After trying the airplane in this configuration on November 24, he found it rolled too easily; so a horizontal tail surface was added to restore the center of pressure, and the two existing wings were reduced to the same span as the new wing to convert his biplane into a triplane.

1908 December 4   The Englishman J. T. C. Moore-Brabazon (later Lord Tara of Brabazon) made a flight of 1,350 ft. in a Voisin biplane at Issy-les-Moulineaux in France while learning to fly. Moore-Brabazon became one of the guiding lights of early British aviation and was issued the first British pilot's license, then called an aviator's certificate. He had ordered his machine from the Voisin brothers and made several hops testing it while learning how to control a flying machine in the air.

1908 December 6   The first flight of the *Silver Dart* (Aerodrome No. 4) built by the Aerial Experiment Association, occurred with Canadian J. A. D. McCurdy at the controls. It was more successful than the earlier *June Bug* and early in 1909 was taken to Baddeck, Nova Scotia, where on February 23 it became the first airplane flown in Canada. The *Silver Dart* had a span of 49 ft. and a wing area of 420 sq ft. with a gross weight of 860 lb. The airplane took the form of a biplane with no rear stabilizer and a propeller driven by chain and sprocket instead of direct drive, and it was powered by a 50-HP, water-cooled, V-8, Curtiss engine.

1908 December 24 The world's first aeronautical exhibition opened in Paris when the French president inaugurated the second half of the Annual Automobile Salon at the Grand Palais. Exhibiting Ader's Avion III as its centerpiece, the "First Aeronautical Salon" included airplanes on static display from Voisin, Farman, Blériot, Antoinette and REP.

1908 December 31 Wilbur Wright made the first flight in history to exceed 2 hr. and took the Michelin Cup for the longest flight of 1908. Flying his Flyer A at Camp d'Auvers, France, he remained aloft for 2 hr. 20 min. 23 sec. traveling a distance of about 99 mi. at 33 MPH. The day began with a flight during the morning that lasted 42 min. before a broken fuel line cut short his attempt. The record flight began at 2:00 P.M., and in freezing weather following a light fall of snow. During the flights that began August 8, Wilbur had logged about 26 total hours in the air in France.

1908 H. G. Wells' novel *The War in the Air* was published, commenting upon the vulnerability to air attack of civilian populations in towns and cities one thought impregnable or too far removed from battle to suffer the consequences of war. In his autobiography, Wells later said that the civilian can no longer regard war "as a vivid spectacle in which his participation is that of a paying spectator at a cricket or baseball match." His novel did much to alert the man in the street to the effects of aerial bombardment, while at higher levels of political debate, there was growing concern about the use of aviation for military purposes.

1908 During the year, aviation had made amazing progress, largely at the hands of Wilbur and Orville Wright. The duration record stood at 2 hr. 20 min. 23 sec., achieved by Wilbur Wright in the Wright Flyer A at Champ d'Auvers, France on December 31. The longest flight by a European pilot during 1908 lasted 44 min. 31 sec. and was achieved by Henri Farman in his modified Voisin at Bouy on October 2. This was the last year the Wright brothers held such a wide performance lead and the last year they were to hold all records for powered airplanes. During the year, the first fatality from a powered airplane accident was recorded, and the first flights were achieved in the following countries (chronologically): Italy, Belgium, England, Holland, Scotland and Germany.

1909 January 2 The first issue of the world's oldest continuously running aviation weekly appeared when the British magazine *Flight—A Journal devoted to the Interests, Practice, and Progress of Aerial Locomotion and Transport* was published in London at a price of 1 pence. As a weekly covering all aspects of aviation and eventually space technology as well, its most enduring British competitor was to be *The Aeroplane,* which appeared in 1912 and ran continuously until 1962 when it metamorphosed into a journal covering civil aviation only.

1909 January 14 Wilbur Wright, his brother Orville and sister Katharine, who had just arrived from America, moved to Pau in the south of France after completing flying demonstrations at Camp d'Auvers. While there, he made 60 flights at Pont-Long, many of which involved flying lessons for the three trainees that his

marketing contract required him to train: Count Charles de Lambert, Capt. Paul Lucas-Girardville and Paul Tissandier. The last flights were carried out on March 20, by which time the three trainees had each made solo flights of around 20 min.

1909 January 19 Gabriel Voisin began work on Henri Farman's second flying machine, ordered the previous month after Farman agreed to sell his No. 1 Voisin to an Austrian syndicate that wanted to fly it in air shows planned for Vienna and Budapest. Meanwhile, J. T. C. Moore-Brabazon visited Gabriel Voisin and persuaded him to sell the machine ordered by Farman. Left without a new machine, Farman had to fly a rebuilt machine for a while, and to pilots of the day, the absence of a flying machine for any significant period could lose them valuable prize money and prestige, the latter frequently seen as more important. Infuriated, he refused to fly a Voisin biplane again.

1909 January 23 One of the most significant and successful aircraft of its day, the Blériot XI, made its first flight. The prototype was powered by a 30-HP REP engine, but this was soon replaced by the much lighter and more efficient 25-HP Anzani, three-cylinder, air-cooled, semi-radial engine. In this form, the Blériot XI was sold throughout Europe and became one of the first designs to be mass produced. Blériot's experimental designs had led him away from the biplane, which was easier to construct with the materials and technology available at the time, and made him an advocate of the monoplane, which was both lighter and caused less drag.

1909 February 17 Col. H. S. Massey of the Bengal Lancers and Stephen A. Marples, a consulting engineer, held a meeting of aviators and enthusiasts at the Carlton Hotel, London to announce the establishment of the Air League of the British Empire. Both men were immediately voted in as honorary secretaries and given an office in Staple Inn, High Holborn, London. Although it had absolutely no official standing, the league quickly set about deciding national air boundaries and discussing how commercial aviation should be organized. At one meeting presided over by Rudyard Kipling, the league debated freedom of the air. In the 1930s it instituted Empire Air Day.

1909 February 23 Canadian J. A. McCurdy made the first powered airplane flight in Canada when he flew the *Silver Dart* at Baddeck, Nova Scotia. This was the fourth and last airplane built by the Aerial Experiment Association, formed largely at the behest of Alexander Graham Bell. Later in the year, the first Canadian military demonstrations of airplanes were carried out by McCurdy and F. W. Baldwin with the *Silver Dart* and the Baddeck No. 1 biplanes, that event taking place between August 2 and 13. Both airplanes were wrecked in flying accidents.

1909 February Wilbur Wright and Eustace Short of Short Brothers Ltd., England, signed an agreement to allow Short to build six Wright Flyers under license in Great Britain for a total cost of £8,400; all had been ordered by members of the Aero Club. This was the first such license agreement signed for aircraft production, and made the Wright Flyer the first aircraft to enter series production. Short Brothers Ltd. had registered their company in November 1908 with £600 capital, the three directors being the Short brothers Oswald, Horace and Eustace.

1909 March 2 The Aeronautical Society of New York and Glenn Curtiss made public that the former had ordered from the latter a biplane that would be known as the *Golden Flyer,* or the *Gold Bug.* The arrangement had been made in January 1909 but was not officially acknowledged before Curtiss left the Aerial Exper-

Curtiss developed the airplane in the configuration that was to transform it from a curiosity into a practical machine.

iment Association, which had been established in October 1907. The Aeronautical Society paid $5,000 for the biplane, which was excluded from negotiations then under way between Curtiss and Augustus Herring about setting up an airplane manufacturing company later the same month. The biplane got its name from the gold tint of the varnished fabric and not from any affiliation to the AEA's *June Bug* or *Silver Dart*.

1909 March 19   Glenn Curtiss and Augustus M. Herring incorporated the Herring-Curtiss company with capitalization of $360,000. Herring was to be the vice-president and director and Curtiss would be vice-president and general manager. County court judge Monroe M. Wheeler was officially appointed president. Curtiss put the G. H. Curtiss Manufacturing Co. into the new firm, and Herring put in patents that would, he said, help them develop new airplanes. Thomas Baldwin and Courtlandt Field Bishop, president of the Aero Club of America, were directors of the new company.

1909 March 19   The first British Aero Show opened at Olympia, London and attracted 11 airplanes, including seven biplanes and two monoplanes. Several engine manufacturers were represented. One of the most interesting exhibits was the first showing in Britain of the Gnôme rotary engine designed by Sequin, which would come to play an important part in the development of aviation. Engine developments were fast becoming as important as aerodynamic design. Reliable, powerful engines were becoming the key to long and successful flights.

1909 April 1   Wilbur Wright arrived in Rome to deliver a Flyer to the Aeronautical Society of Rome for the sum of $10,000, the parts for the machine having been sent in crates from Dayton. The Flyer used for demonstrations in France was left with the

Musée des Arts et Métiers in Paris. Two days later, Wilbur was presented to King Victor Emmanuel, and flight trials with the Flyer began on April 15. Wilbur (with Orville and Katharine, who had joined him in Rome during the second week) left at the end of the month for the United States via Paris and London.

1909 April 21   At a meeting of the British National Defence Association, Lord Montagu of Beaulieu dramatically articulated the effect on London of a fleet of airships carrying bombs and high explosives. He described how centers of civilian activity would be hit, such as post offices, telephone exchanges, government offices and centers of administration. As the heart of a worldwide empire, said Lord Montagu, London was a special target for enemy air forces. He believed that defenses then existing would be powerless to intervene and that the country should begin to plan for such an eventuality.

1909 April 24   The first photograph taken from an airplane in flight was snapped by a cameraman taken into the air by Wilbur Wright from the field at Centocelle, Italy, where he had been carrying out flight demonstrations since April 15. The primary purpose of these flights was to demonstrate the machine ordered by the Aeronautical Society of Rome and to give instruction to Lt. Calderara and another student from the Italian Army. Some historians claim Wilbur Wright carried a photographer during the many flights he made from Camp d'Auvers, but there is no proof to show that a photograph was taken.

1909 April 30   J. T. C. Moore-Brabazon made his first tentative hops in England while flying a Voisin biplane (originally ordered from Voisin by Henri Farman in December 1908) at Leysdown on the Isle of Sheppey for a distance of 456 ft. Longer flights were made during the next two days, the best being 1,500 ft.

1909 May 13 The Flugmaschine Wright Gesellschaft was set up to handle the construction of Wright flying machines in Germany, with a franchise to sell not only in Germany but also in Luxembourg, Turkey, Sweden, Norway and Denmark. The Wright brothers received 200,000 marks in cash and a 10% royalty on every machine sold. Orville arrived in Berlin August 19, 1909, to begin flying demonstrations at Tempelhof, which got under way August 31. Demonstrations of the performance and maneuverability inherent in the Wright Flyer thrilled the crowds that on some days swelled to more than 200,000 people.

1909 May 14 Samuel Cody made the first powered airplane flight of more than one mile in Britain. He flew the British Army *Aeroplane No. 1* from Laffans Planin to Danger Hill in Hampshire at an average height of 30 ft. Later that afternoon, the Prince of Wales asked if Cody could repeat the flight. Unfortunately, during the flight, Cody was forced to turn quickly to avoid some troops in his path, and smashed the tail of *No. 1* against an embankment. The aircraft was rebuilt at Farnborough with design changes to improve the performance.

1909 May 20 Paul Tissandier set the only officially recognized FAI speed record for a Wright biplane when he covered a distance of 57.5 km (33.2 mi) in 1 hr. 2 min. at an average speed of 54.8 km/hr. (34.05 MPH). This machine was known as the Model A (France) and was powered by a 35-HP, 4-cylinder Wright engine built by the French company Bariguand et Marre. This record did not exceed the unratified achievements of the Wright brothers, who undoubtedly achieved speeds considerably in excess of the record established on this particular day witnessed by FAI officials.

1909 May 26 Lt. Frank S. Lahm and Lt. B. D. Foulois became the first army pilots of a U.S. Army dirigible when they took to the air from Fort Omaha in the Signal Corps *Dirigible Balloon No. 1* designed and built by Thomas S. Baldwin. This first flight lasted only 9 min., because of a fracture in the fuel supply line to the engine, but a later flight on May 31 was more successful. In the contract, Baldwin had been required to train two pilots. Three student officers later qualified as airship pilots, but they were relieved from the aeronautics division on October 29, 1909.

1909 June 17 Frederick Handley Page formed the firm of Handley Page Ltd., the first British company set up exclusively to design and manufacture powered airplanes. The company had a subscription of 500 pounds and authorized capital of £10,000; 500 shares were owned by Handley Page, his brother Arthur and engineers Francis Dalton and W. G. Magdalen. Premises were at Creekmouth near Barking, England. Handley Page had exhibited gliders made by one José Weiss at the 1909 Olympia Aero Show. In time, the company produced an outstanding series of airplanes, including the O/400 long-range bomber of World War I, the Halifax bomber of World War II and the Victor strategic nuclear bomber.

1909 June 26 Glenn Curtiss carried out a spectacular demonstration flight in the *Golden Flyer* built for the Aeronautical Society of New York, performing the first circle in the air seen by New Yorkers before an estimated 5,000 spectators in Morris Park. Curtiss was bent on getting the 1909 *Scientific American* trophy for the first person to fly 25 km (15.5 mi.) or more in the United States as measured by a committee. Curtiss had won the 1908 trophy for the first 1 km (3,281 ft.) flight from a rolling start (the Wright planes at that time still were launched from rails).

1909 June 28 The Breguet I made its first flight from La Brayelle near Douai, France. Originally designated Breguet IV, it was

the first of the famous tractor biplanes that would ultimately evolve into the bombers of the French Air Service in World War I. Unusual for its steel tube construction, the Breguet was the first fixed-wing product of Louis and Jacques Breguet, brothers who had previously dabbled in helicopter designs. The brothers were descended from a family of clock and instrument makers. They exhibited the engineless shell of their Breguet I (then designated Breguet IV) at Olympia, London in March 1909.

1909 June 29 In opening demonstration flights before the U.S. Army at Fort Myer, Virginia, Orville Wright made the first flight with the new Wright A built to replace the one destroyed in September 1908. Skidding off the launching rail, the Flyer was damaged, and in later flights during the same day, it was unable to remain airborne for lengthy periods. On July 2, Orville smashed into a thorn tree, ripped the fabric and returned to Dayton the next day to make repairs and bring new cloth. The new Flyer had a modified forward skid design and separate control handles for wing warping and rudder actuation. It had a 13 gal. fuel tank providing an endurance of 3.5 hr.

1909 June The first occupant of a powered airplane known to have smoked in flight was Hubert Latham. While piloting his Antoinette monoplane, in the face of a 45-MPH slipstream, he managed to roll a cigarette, light it and smoke it! The flight began at Châlons, France and, if nothing else, proved the increasing confidence of the aviator in his equipment!

1909 July 13 If the brief hops made by Alliott Verdon Roe on June 8, 1908, are discounted (as some would say they should be), the first flight made by an Englishman in an English airplane took place when Roe flew his Roe I triplane for the first time at Lea Marshes in Essex. He flew only 100 ft.; but on July 23, he extended the distance to some 900 ft. off the ground. The triplane was powered by a 9-HP JAP engine, later changed for a similar engine delivering 20-HP. It had three 20-ft. span wings and three horizontal tail sections fixed to a covered fuselage with triangular cross section.

1909 July 19 In an attempt to win the *Daily Mail* prize of £1,000, Hubert Latham—an English-educated Frenchman—attempted unsuccessfully to fly across the English Channel. His attempt was made in an Antoinette monoplane designed by Leon Levavasseur and powered by a 50-HP, V-8, water-cooled, Antoinette engine that drove a two-bladed propeller. The flight started at Sangatte near Calais, but after covering only 7 mi., the engine started to run rough and then failed altogether. He glided down from about 1,000 ft. and landed gently on a calm sea; his plane floated and when picked up by the boat *Harpoon*, he was found calmly smoking a cigarette.

1909 July 25 Louis Blériot made the first crossing of the English Channel in a powered airplane to win the *Daily Mail* prize of £1,000. The aircraft he used was a Blériot XI monoplane powered by a 25-HP three-cylinder, Anzani engine. Blériot took off from Baraques near Calais, France at 4:41 A.M., and landed on Northfall Meadow by Dover Castle at 5:17 A.M., a flight of just 36 min. over a distance of 23.5 mi. at an average speed of 39 MPH. Blériot had flown with his leg in plaster from a recent flying accident, and the landing near Dover was heavy, his airplane ending up nose down on the cliff top.

1909 July 27 Latham made a second attempt to fly across the English Channel, this time in an Antoinette VII with a 50-HP Antoinette V-8 engine. Once again, Latham was forced to ditch in the channel when his engine failed only 1 mi. from the English

A Blériot monoplane close to the design used by Louis Blériot to cross the English Channel on July 25, 1909.

coast. He was quickly rescued. He had cut his face on glass from his broken goggles but was otherwise uninjured. The flight was intended to better Blériot's time across the channel and was remarkable in the fact that it was the maiden flight of this particular aircraft. Latham continued flying and set records for height and distance in later aircraft. Following a series of problems during initial trials with the new Flyer from June 29, Orville Wright carried out the final demonstration of the Wright Flyer for the U.S. Army at Fort Myer, Va. The final demonstration flight was set to carry out speed trials that would determine by how much more or less the Wrights would get the agreed contract price of $25,000. A vast crowd gathered to see Orville clock speeds up to 42.5 MPH, which meant the brothers would get an extra $5,000—$2,500 for every 1 MPH above the 40 MPH specified by the contract awarded in February 1908.

1909 July   The first powered aircraft flight in Russia was made at Odessa by van den Schkrouff in a Voisin biplane. Voisin aircraft were to be sold in some numbers to Russia partly to equip the embryonic Russian Air Service. Later, Cattaneo and Legagneux would make flights from Moscow and St. Petersburg. Aviation had been slow in coming to Russia, although the Imperial All-Russia Aero Club had been in existence for approximately 18 months and had served to stimulate national interest and attract pioneers from other European countries.

1909 August 2   The U.S. Army formally accepted delivery of its first airplane, the Wright Flyer, which had been tested in July 1909. Unfortunately, the airplane was damaged in an accident

November 5, and the pilots assigned to it were transferred for various reasons. In February 1910, Lt. Foulois flew it, in a series of short flights, to Fort Sam Houston, Texas, where it spent the winter months. Foulois had not received proper training when Orville Wright trained the army pilots during July, so he received what became the first correspondence course in flying, from the Wright brothers. In May 1911, the War Department restored the Flyer and retired it to the Smithsonian Institution.

1909 August 14   The first woman passenger to fly in a powered airplane in Great Britain was the wife of Samuel F. Cody. Mrs. Cody was taken for a 3-mi. flight from the Royal Engineers Balloon Factory at Farnborough in Cody's British Army *Aeroplane No. 1*. This aircraft had been much modified from its original form, and now had a 60-HP ENV model-F engine and ailerons mounted halfway between the wings in the middle of the outermost four interplane struts. Cody had gained sufficient experience with the aircraft to feel able to take passengers, of whom Mrs. Cody was only the second. The first that day had been Col. J. E. Capper, the superintendent of the Balloon Factory.

1909 August 18   Papers were served on Glenn Curtiss and the Herring-Curtiss Co. that sought to prevent them from using their airplanes for exhibitions or public flying displays. The Wright brothers claimed patent infringement of control devices, wing warping in particular, and cited the presence of Augustus Herring at the glider trials during 1902 at which they claimed he ''stole'' design secrets. To prevent litigation inhibiting the development of aeronautics, the president of the Aero Club of America unsuccessfully sought to raise a fund in 1908 to buy out the Wright patents.

1909 August 22 The world's first international aviation meeting began at Reims, France; 38 participants registered, though only 23 actually flew. Hubert Latham established the first speed record over 100 km (62 mi.) by flying an Antoinette in 1 hr. 28 min. 17 sec. at an average speed of 42 MPH. Latham also established the altitude record at 508.5 ft. American Glenn Curtiss set the outright speed record of 47.09 MPH but his was not ratified as an official record. Henri Farman secured the distance and duration records for a closed circuit of 112.5 mi. in 3 hr. 4 min. 56.4 sec. and made the first flight with two passengers for a distance of six mi. The meeting ended August 29.

1909 August 28 Organized by James Gordon Bennett, wealthy newspaper magnate, owner of the *New York Herald* and the man who sent H. M. Stanley to look for Dr. Livingstone in Africa, the first Gordon Bennett Aviation Cup race held on the Plain of Bétheny near Reims, France is won by Glenn Curtiss. The first organized air race anywhere, it drew 100,000 spectators. In the *Golden Flyer* powered by a 50-HP Curtiss engine, Curtiss achieved a speed of 46.9 MPH, followed by Louis Blériot with a speed of 46.8 MPH and Hubert Latham at 42.5 MPH. The second Gordon Bennett race, in 1910, was won by Englishman Claude Grahame-White; the third in 1911 was won by American Charles T. Weymann; the fourth in 1912 was won by Frenchman Jules Védrines; and the fifth, the last before World War I, was won by another Frenchman, Maurice Prévost.

1909 August 29 At the end of a two-day flight from Lake Constance during which he traveled a total distance of more than 400 mi., Count von Zeppelin made a spectacular flight in his dirigible *LZ 5* over the city of Berlin. More than 100,000 people were on hand as the airship came gently to earth in the presence of Orville and Katharine Wright and the German royal family. Von Zeppelin descended from his airship and met the Wrights in a historic confrontation: The first man to fly a powered heavier-than-air flying machine and the first man to successfully develop the rigid airship, machines that would vie for supremacy in a war only five year away.

1909 September 8–20 The Società Italiana di Aviazione sponsored a major air fair in Brescia. Louis Blériot and Glenn Curtiss were present, as was Lt. Mario Calderara, who had been taught to fly by Wilbur Wright. His machine had been purchased by the Club Aviatori di Roma and supplied by the Wrights. A highlight of the meet was a flying competition around Brescia which was won by Curtiss. It was with Curtiss that the poet, politician and airman Gabriele D'Annunzio first flew in a plane.

1909 September 22 Ferdinand Ferber, a long-time friend of the Wright brothers, died when the Voisin biplane he was flying nosed over and he was crushed by the mass of the engine. Ferber had been trying to land at Boulogne and was moving fast along the ground when he struck a ditch and overturned. It was the first fatality in a Voisin, but aviation was taking its toll. Only one person died in 1907, three died in 1908, and 29 died in 1910. Ferber had popularized flying in France more than anyone else. He had published many articles, he was primarily responsible for the French government industrial cooperation mission to the United States in 1906, and he had stimulated wide public support for flying.

1909 September 26–October 3 The first major aviation meeting in Germany opened at Johannisthal, Berlin. It proclaimed to

attract the "foremost aviators in the world." It had been stimulated by the successful exhibition of flying put on by Orville Wright since he arrived in Germany the preceding month and by the flight of Zeppelin's *LZ 6* on August 29. Orville Wright decided not to participate in the show, however, leaving Hubert Latham's 6-mi. cross-country flight the main attraction. Germany was becoming increasingly air-minded, and great public excitement was generated by these events.

1909 September 28 Wilbur Wright and Glenn Curtiss made flights at the Hudson-Fulton Celebration in New York City marking the 300th anniversary of the voyage up the Hudson River by Henry Hudson's ship, *Half Moon*, and the 102d anniversary of the first commercial steamship, Robert Fulton's *North River Steam Boat* (also known as the *Clermont*). Wright was offered $15,000 for a 10-mi. flight and Curtiss was offered $5,000 for a 20 mi. flight. Curtiss' flight began at 7:00 A.M. from Governors Island and lasted only a few minutes, but Wright took off at 10:00 A.M. and flew around the Statue of Liberty accompanied by blasts from the passenger liner *Lusitania* slowly creeping out to sea. His takeoff had been signalled to the ship by Guglielmo Marconi with his primitive wireless set. This was the last public flight made by one of the Wrights.

1909 September The French military purchased their first airplanes, two Farman biplanes powered by 50-HP Gnôme rotaries, two Wright biplanes with 30-HP Wright-Bariquand engines and a Blériot with a 25-HP LaManche-Anzani engine. They were delivered to the Corps of Engineers and had been purchased as a result of interest shown by Gen. Roques, director of engineering, who had been inspired by recent cross-country flights to consider the military applications of airplanes. He set up a commission to look at the best available designs for possible military use and purchased the five airplanes to carry out tests. In August, the Artillery Aviation Establishment had been formed, and Maj. Estienne received 200,000 francs from the government to buy airplanes for artillery spotting.

1909 October 2 German Crown Prince Friedrich Wilhelm, son of the kaiser, was given a short flight at comparatively low altitude by Orville Wright from the Bornstedt drill ground at Potsdam, about 20 mi. from Berlin. The crown prince presented Orville with a diamond-studded pin carrying the letter "W," which the prince said could just as well stand for Wright as Wilhelm. Orville had just begun training a student from the German Wright company named Paul Engelhard. On another flight this day, Orville achieved an altitude of 1,600 ft. exceeding the 508 ft. record set by Hubert Latham at Reims during the August 22–29 meeting.

1909 October 5 The first German air show, the Internationale Luftschiffahrt-Ausstellung (International Airship Exhibition), opened in Frankfurt with a scheduled week of flying getting under way two days later. Airships, balloons and aircraft were on display, and several foreign participants appeared with their flying machines. The slow start to German aviation was apparent when, despite bad weather, French aviators swept the field and claimed all the prizes.

1909 October 15 The first aviation meeting in England opened at Doncaster. Because a similar meeting in Blackpool was scheduled for only three days later, only nine airplanes took part, including five Blériot monoplanes. One participant's airplane was destroyed by its pilot's vanity; while draped casually across his monoplane in what he considered a suitable pose for photographers, the fuselage split under his weight, and he ended up on the grass. Two other pilots crashed their airplanes in full view of the crowd, but walked away unhurt; and Samuel Cody nosed over on a patch of sand and cut his forehead. The only notable feats were achieved by Delagrange, who got up to almost 50 MPH in his Gnôme-powered Blériot, and the Frenchman Sommer, who flew for almost 30 mi. in 20 circuits of the field.

1909 October 16 With capitalization of 3 million marks, the world's first airline company, Deutsche Luftschiffahrt Gesellschaft (DELAG), was formed. It was partly subscribed by the Hamburg-Amerika shipping line (HAPAG), which arranged bookings and flight reservations. The airline was slow to get under way and for a while was essentially a charter service until 1917 when routine flights were scheduled. Between March 1912 and November 1913, however, DELAG flew 19,100 passengers on 881 flights covering a total distance of 65,000 mi. Eventually, the outbreak of war in Europe put an end to these activities; DELAG was disbanded and another use was found for Count von Zeppelin's airships.

1909 October 18–24 The Blackpool Race Meeting, the second aviation meeting in England, began with three Voisin biplanes, flown by Rougier, Singer and Fournier, a 50-HP Henri Farman, flown by Farman and Paulhan, two Blériot monoplanes, flown by Leblanc and Parkinson, an Antoinette, flown by Hubert Latham, and the Roe I triplane, flown by A. V. Roe. In addition, three unnamed monoplanes and a small biplane took part. Only five airplanes flew, and Latham established a reputation for flying in a very gusty wind. Farman made a flight of almost 48 mi. in 1 hr. 32 min. 17 sec. at an average speed of 31 MPH.

1909 October 24 The first qualified woman pilot in the world, Madame la Baronne de la Roche (Elsie Deroche), a balloonist and showwoman of some repute, made a flight around the parade ground at Chalons, France, completing two circuits for a distance of about 4 mi. Deroche made good progress in strong gusty weather and earned the applause of onlookers. She learned to fly on Voisin aircraft and received her aviator's certificate at Chalons in France after training by the Voisin instructor, M. Chateau.

1909 October 30 J. T. C. Moore-Brabazon won the *Daily Mail* prize of £1,000 by becoming the first Englishman to fly an English airplane for a circular flight of at least 1 mi. The event took place at Shellbeach in a machine Moore-Brabazon built as a direct copy of the Wright biplane. In that respect, it cannot be said to have been a British flying machine, as it even used the Wright derrick-launch method for launching the airplane. It is, however, notable for having introduced the excellently designed and built 60-HP Green engine, which Gustavus Green had developed in his bicycle works during 1908. The flight lasted 2 min. 36 sec. The total distance being about 1.5 mi.

1909 November 2 Flight training with Wilbur Wright as tutor to two U.S. Army officers, stipulated in their February 1908 contract, was completed at College Park, Md. A special field near the state agricultural college had been assigned, and the training began there October 8. Lt. Frederick Humphreys had been the first to go solo on October 26 after a total instruction time of 3 hr. 4 min. 7 sec., followed later the same day by Lt. Frank P. Lahm after 3 hr. 7 min. 38 sec. Lt. Benjamin Foulois, who had assumed he would be one of the two trainees, had been sent instead to an aeronautical congress in Paris but returned in time to receive a few lessons, which was just as well—Lt. Humphreys was sent back to the cavalry for having given a woman an unauthorized joy ride! On November 3 Lt. Lahm carried his first passenger Lt. George C. Sweet, USN.

1909 November 3 Henri Farman made the first flight to exceed 4 hr. remaining airborne for 4 hr. 17 min. 53 sec. from Camp de Chalons in a flight officially observed by the French Aero Club. Farman flew a total distance of 150 mi., 13 mi. of which was flown after sunset. Farman had carried out a long-distance flight of 1 hr. 16 min. 35 sec. with a passenger aboard two days earlier in tests preparatory to going for the world record.

1909 November 14 A British government report on military aviation in foreign countries showed that Germany was preparing airships for war should hostilities break out. Claiming that trials had already taken place in Germany with airships equipped to carry bombs, and that German artillery officers were working on the problems of air defense, it went on to state that German literature had appeared calling for the "invasion of England in airships." This was the first of five annual reports on military aviation to appear before World War I broke out in August 1914.

1909 November 15 M. Metrot took off in a Voisin from Algiers. Although the flight only lasted a few seconds and the biplane flew only a few hundred feet it was the first flight to take place in Africa and preceded several more that were conducted by Metrot for much greater distances. The 1909–10 period saw many European aeronauts use the early Voisin biplane for first flights and record-breaking attempts. The Voisin name had already been merged with other famous marquees.

1909 November 22 The Wright company was incorporated with a capital stock of $1 million and paid-in value of $200,000 and offices on Fifth Avenue in New York City. Wilbur Wright was president, and Orville began as vice-president but became president when Wilbur died in 1912. At first, space was rented in Dayton until the company could acquire premises large enough to manufacture the Wright flying machines. The brothers each received a cash payment of $100,000 and received a 10% royalty on every order, as well as one-third of the stock. Orville sold his share in 1915, and a year later the company bought the Simplex Automobile Co. In September 1916, the Wright Co. and the Glenn L. Martin Co. merged to form the Wright-Martin Corp. of New York.

1909 November 29 The Etrich-Taube monoplane made its first flight at Wiener-Neustadt in Austria, the first native-designed aircraft to fly there. Originally dubbed Praterspatz, the aircraft got its name Taube (Dove) from the shape of its wings and was to prove very reliable, being built in large numbers for both civil and military operators, mostly in Austria and Germany. As a monoplane, it helped establish a distinctive line of scouting airplanes designed and built by Dr. Igor Etrich in Austria and by Rumpler Flugzeug-Werke GmbH in Germany. The first Taube was capable of 43 MPH and flew distances of almost 3 mi.

1909 December 5 George Taylor made the first manned glider flight in Australia in a glider of his own design. He made a total of 29 flights at Narrabeen Beach in New South Wales. Taylor had a wide variety of interests and skills and made a living from being a poet, artist, inventor and journalist. His wife, Florence Taylor, was to become the world's first woman glider pilot when she flew his aircraft later in the month.

1909 December 9 American Dr. Henry W. Walden made the first flight with his triplane known as the Walden III. It was powered by a three-cylinder, 22-HP Anzani engine and took off from Mineola, Long Island, N.Y. Walden also designed a monoplane during 1909 that had the shape of a Curtiss biplane without the upper wing. It was powered by a single pusher engine and carried a tricycle undercarriage. Dr. Walden is remembered for this achievement and for designing and building the first American monoplane. Although Blériot was making a name for the monoplane in Europe, the biplane was firmly established as the design concept preferred by American inventors.

1909 December 9 A racing driver, Colin Defries, was reported to have made a flight of 5.5 sec. in a Wright-type biplane at Victoria Park, Sydney. Although some consider this the first flight on the Australian continent, the distinction was contested by two other claimants. Fred Constance was reported to have remained aloft for more that 5 min. in a Blériot on March 17, 1910, and escapologist Harry Houdini (his real name was Ehrich Weiss) was known to have flown a Voisin biplane three times from Diggers Rest, Victoria, on March 18, 1910. Houdini is generally considered to have made the first significant flight in Australia because his maximum distance of 2 mi. far exceeded the distances reported to have been flown by Defries and Constance.

1909 December 15 The Wright brothers concluded two days of patent rights infringement hearings before Judge Hazel in contest with Glenn Curtiss and the Herring-Curtiss Co. They were represented by Harry Toulmin, who had visited the Wrights in 1904, and Curtiss was represented by Emerson Newell in what was the first litigation action in the history of powered flight. Judge Hazel reached a liberal interpretation of the Wright control mechanisms that were the point in contest, and on January 3, 1910, ordered Curtiss to stop making airplanes and flying them in public displays. Curtiss appealed, and the judgment was overturned on June 14, 1910.

1909 December The first airplane designed and built by Englishman Geoffrey de Havilland made its one and only flight when it was run downhill into the wind at Seven Barrows near Newbury, Wiltshire. Called the *De Havilland Biplane No. 1,* the plane weighed 850 lb. and was powered by a 45-HP, 4-cylinder engine designed by de Havilland and built to his specification by the Iris Motor Co. of Willesden, London. De Havilland's wife sewed on the cotton covering of the wings and control surfaces. Shortly after take-off, de Havilland pulled the nose up too sharply, which caused the wings to fail, and it crashed.

1909 In London, Fred T. Jane compiled and produced the first edition of *Jane's All the World's Airships,* naming all the principal airships and aircraft of the day. This publication soon became an annual and its title changed to *All the World's Aircraft.* Still published as an annual today, it is considered the standard reference work regarding world aircraft, airships and engines. Jane had established his reputation by providing compilations of the world's warships. When the publishing house passed into other hands after World War II, Jane's references covered a broad spectrum of general military subjects.

1909 During the year, records began to tumble with considerable speed, and progress in aviation was making noticeable strides forward. At the end of the year, the world duration record was held by Henri Farman, in his 50-HP Gnôme-powered Farman biplane, at 4 hr. 17 min. 53 sec., almost twice the record for 1908 and an all the more remarkable achievement because no other pilot had remained in the air for even three consecutive hours. Farman also held the closed-circuit distance record at 145 mi. Both records were achieved at Chalons, France. Hubert Latham held the altitude record, at 1,485 ft., achieved in his Antoinette monoplane. The official speed record was held by Ferber in a Voisin at 32 MPH. During the year, three people had been killed in powered airplanes compared with one in 1908. First

flights were made in (chronologically) Canada, Austria, Russia, Sweden, Hungary, Romania, Algeria, Turkey, Egypt, South Africa, Ireland, Portugal and Mexico.

1910 January 10–20 The Aero Club of California staged the first aviation meeting in the United States at Dominque Field, Los Angeles. During the meeting, the spot-landing prize was won by Charles F. Willard, a pilot who was to become famous as one of the first American barnstormers. More than 25,000 people were reported to have attended the show. Several non-American participants showed up, and Frenchman Louis Paulhan became the first non-U.S. citizen to fly in the United States. This emphasized the progress Europeans had achieved in the preceding year, the first full year since the Wright machines stunned Europe. Louis Paulhan walked off with a total $20,000 in prize money.

1910 January 19 Lt. Paul Beck became the first man to "bomb" objects on the ground from a powered airplane when he dropped sandbags representing dummy bombs at the air show in Los Angeles from an aircraft piloted by Louis Paulhan. This experiment proved the lethal potential of the airplane, which was not lost on the military planners of the day. Although it was to be many years before the full awesome destructive power of that potential was to be realized, the seed was sown in many minds.

1910 January 20 On the last day of the first aviation meet in Los Angeles, Frenchman Louis Paulhan won the endurance prize of $10,000 with a flight lasting 1 hr. 49 min., during which the aviator flew an estimated distance of 64 mi. As spectators took to the roads and byways on horses, bicycles and motorcycles following Paulhan on his cross-country jaunt, great cheers would go up as he chugged over groups of people waving him on. When he finally returned after his marathon flight, the milling throng seized him from his airplane and carried him off, shoulder high.

1910 January Alliott Verdon Row formed the firm of A. V. Roe and Co. with the help of his brother H. V. Roe. They negotiated work space in the Brownsfield Mills, Manchester, a famous textile town in England. The first product was the Roe II triplane exhibited at the second Olympia Aero Show beginning March 11. It was similar to the Roe I first flown in June 1909 but with a 35-HP Green engine. With the prefix "Avro," airplanes built by this company would include some of the most famous in the annals of aviation, including the Avro 504 trainer, the Avro Lancaster bomber of World War II and the Avro Vulcan strategic nuclear bomber.

1910 February 15 King Edward VII bestowed the prefix "Royal" on Britain's Aero Club and elevated it to a prestigious level from where it would attract many aeronauts and would-be plane makers. It established a headquarters at 166 Piccadilly, and there was a clubhouse at Shelbeach, near Sheppey, where the flying took place. A flying field had been established there in 1909, visited by the Wright brothers. It was at Shelbeach that Shorts set up a shed to build the six Wright flying machines, the first substantial order for Wright Flyers. London became the place to host distinguished guests, but Shelbeach was where the work was done.

1910 February 19 Sir George White, with his brother Samuel and his son G. Stanley, formed four airplane companies: the Bristol Aeroplane Co. Ltd., the Bristol Aviation Co. Ltd., the British and Colonial Aeroplane Co. Ltd., and the British and Colonial Aviation Co. Ltd. He began trading with the third of these four, capitalized with £25,000 and registered at offices in Clare Street, Bristol. The other three were given just £100 each. Factory space

A. V. Roe designed a succession of successful airplanes. One of the most notable of these was his famous Triplane.

was leased from Bristol Tramways Co., offices at Filton House being provided in late 1911. Using the prefix "Bristol," the company would produce a fine stable of airplanes, including the Bristol Scout of World War I, the Bristol Bulldog fighter, the Bristol Beaufighter of World War II and the Bristol Britannia and Freighter passenger and military cargo airplanes.

1910 March 11–19 The London Olympia Aero Show opened with exhibits from leading aeronauts, aviators and manufacturers of the day. Alliott Verdon Roe showed his Roe II triplane, although it had not yet flown, and the prince and princess of Wales attended, receiving enthusiastic welcome from all the exhibitors who wanted their particular products patronized by the royal presence. Thirty airplanes and 45 engines were shown, including the first Blackburn monoplane, the Handley Page Bluebird monoplane (not yet finished) and the Bristol Zodiac biplane, which was essentially a license-built version of the Voisin type built for Henri Farman.

1910 March 27 The Cannes air show opened on the Mediterranean coast with the spectacular crash of Léon Molon when he smashed his airplane to pieces after doing only seven circuits. He walked away without major injury. The Russian Prince Nicholas Popoff flew across to the Lerin Islands in a Wright biplane, a journey that took him just over 18 min. The Grand Duchess Anastasia of Mecklenburg was there to congratulate Popoff on his return.

1910 March 28 The first flight of Henri Fabre's Hydroavion, the first powered seaplane in the world, took place at La Mède harbor, Martigues, France. The hydroplane flew for about 1,600 ft. at a maximum height of 7 ft. The Hydroavion was powered by a 50-HP Gnôme engine and comprised a tail at the front with a single float and a wing with dihedral, a single float under each tip. At speed, the floats generated lift on the upper surface of the water. The Hydroavion has the added distinction of being the first airplane to carry four working engines.

1910 April 28 Louis Paulhan won the *Daily Mail* newspaper prize of £10,000 offered to the first person to fly the 185 mi. between London and Manchester, England within 24 hr. Englishman Claude Grahame-White, who had learned to fly in November 1909 made an unsuccessful attempt April 24. Paulhan set off in his Farman biplane at 5:21 P.M. on April 27 followed by Claude Grahame-White in another Farman at 6:29 P.M. By 7:43 P.M. Paulhan had reached the halfway point, a town called Nuneaton, guided along the way by a specially commissioned train containing Paulhan's wife and Henri Farman himself. Paulhan landed for a night's rest with only 56 mi. to go. Grahame-White landed at the town of Roade with 123 miles to go. Paulhan took off again at 4:16 A.M. on the 28 and reached Manchester at precisely 5:32 A.M.

1910 April Englishman A. Rawlinson became the first pilot to be forced down by the action of another aircraft. At the Meeting d'Aviation Nice, held April 10–25, Rawlinson was flying his new Farman biplane over the sea, close to the water, when another Farman, piloted by the Russian pioneer Michel Effimov, passed within feet of him, so close that the turbulence from his slipstream pushed Rawlinson's aircraft into the sea. Fortunately, the English pilot was not seriously hurt. The organizers of the meeting severely reprimanded Effimov and fined him 100 francs for his lack of consideration and manners! Nonetheless, he managed to gather $15,150 in prize money.

1910 May 29   Glenn Curtiss won a $10,000 prize for being the first person to fly between Albany, N.Y., and New York City, a distance of 135 mi., in 2 hr. 32 min. The prize had been offered by the *World* newspaper, and the contestant was allowed to make one refueling stop, which Curtiss did at Poughkeepsie. He also landed outside the city limits before taking off on the final leg, for Governors Island. Curtiss used the Hudson Flyer for this attempt, an airplane very similar to the one he used for the Reims meeting in France in August 1909, modified to carry flotation gear in case he came down on water. The span of the upper wing was increased to lift the additional weight.

1910 June 2   Englishman C. S. Rolls made the first two-way non-stop flight between England and France when he took off from Dover at 6:30 P.M., dropped a letter addressed to the Aero Club of France over Sangatte and returned to Dover by 8:06 P.M. Rolls had received his first Wright biplane from Shorts in October 1909. This was the first of six production Wright biplanes built by Shorts in England. Rolls took several prizes for flights from Shelbeach, England in his first Wright Flyer before giving it to the Royal Engineers Balloon Company and collecting the Flyer he used for the England-France-England flight.

1910 June 6   English Capt. Bertram Dickson set a new duration record for a flight with a passenger when he kept his Henri Farman biplane airborne at Anjou, France for two hours. The Farman design was beginning to outsell most of its rivals as its reputation for speed, endurance and, above all, reliability was reinforced by flights such as this. The basic pattern of the pusher biplane with strut-mounted tail planes and forward elevator surface was to be copied by a number of European manufacturers, derived as it was from the Voisin layout.

1910 June 9   French Army Lt. Fequant, with Capt. Marconnet as a passenger, took off from Châlons, France at 4:30 A.M. and landed 2 hr. 40 min. later at Vincennes, 90 mi. away. During the flight, Marconnet took a number of photographs with a hand-held camera in efforts to show the potential application to military purposes of airplanes used in support of ground forces. From this point on, military cross-country flights in France increased, and maneuvers held in Picardy during September 1910 vindicated the use of airplanes for reconnaissance and message-carrying.

1910 June 15   The world's youngest flyer, 15-year-old Marcel Hanriot, got his pilot's brevet, no. 15. His father was Ren Hanriot, the famous Darracq racing driver who first exhibited an airplane design at the 1907 Paris Salon de l'Aéronautique. Powered by a 50-HP Buchet engine, it was a single-seat monoplane with a wingspan of 31 ft. 2 in. Hanriot opened a school at Bétheny near Reims and then developed other monoplanes with the help of his son and another racing driver, Louis Wagner. Hanriot developed a small family of capable fighters during World War I.

1910 June 17   The Vlaici I parasol monoplane makes its first flight in Romania, a day still celebrated in that country as National Aviation Day. The aircraft was designed and built by Ouvert Vlaici, a Romanian engineer, and was a canard monoplane with two shaft-driven propellers mounted near the wing tips powered by a single 50-HP Gnôme rotary engine. The aircraft was reported to have flown well and was purchased by the Romanian

government. Two years later, a newer design won Vlaici a prize for landing in the smallest circle (spot landing) and for dropping fake bombs on marked ground targets. Vlaici was killed in late 1912 when his airplane crashed.

1910 June 19   The Zeppelin LZ 7, designed for passenger-carrying work, made its first flight, after which it was delivered to Duesseldorf where, on the 24th, it carried 32 passengers into the air for a flight to Essen, Bochum and Dortmund before returning to Duesseldorf. Along the way, passengers dropped greeting cards on the places they passed over. The LZ 7 *(Deutschland)* was 485 ft. long with a diameter of 45.9 ft. and a volume of 681,600 cu. ft. Powered by three 120-HP Daimler engines, it could lift 7.5 tons (U.S.) and had a maximum speed of 37 MPH. It was destroyed on June 28 when rain forced it down on trees that smashed the rear section. It was replaced by LZ 8 in March 1911.

1910 June 19   Lt. C. G. Colmore of the Royal Navy became the first naval officer in the world to begin flying lessons when he ascended in a Short biplane, the S.26. The airplane had been built for Frank McClean as a Short derivative of the Farman biplane and was powered by a 40-HP Green engine. Colmore remained in the air for 20 min. flying a distance of 11 mi. and completed his tests for a pilot's certificate (no. 15) the following day, receiving it from the Royal Aero Club on June 21. Colmore had learned to fly as a private citizen. As a naval officer, his association with Short was especially interesting since that company became one of the world's great seaplane manufacturers.

1910 June 24   The first flight of the Roe III triplane took place at Brooklands, England following taxiing trials that began three days before. By July 4, A. V. Roe had managed to make a flight lasting 11 min., getting up to 25 min. on July 9. The airplane was essentially identical to the Roe II that crashed on April 17, 1910, shortly after its first flight. The Roe III had a 35-HP engine built by either JAP or Green. The second pair of four Roe III machines built went to the United States, No. 3 crashing at Boston, Mass. on September 8 and No. 4 crashing on September 15 after delivery to the Harvard Aeronautical Society.

1910 June 30   During a flight over Lake Keuka at Hammondsport, N.Y., Glenn Curtiss dropped lead darts from a height of about 50 ft. and dropped dummy bombs on to a phantom battleship the outline of which was marked with buoys on the surface. His mission was to demonstrate the practical uses of airplanes in war, hopefully to stimulate sales to the military and expand the production orders. Curtiss used a modified biplane similar to the Hudson Flyer he had flown between Albany and New York City in May 1910. Also during June, Curtiss became the first American to put down on water, but his floatplane had insufficient power to take off again with the added weight of the canoe he had strapped on for insurance!

1910 July 4   The training of German army officer pilots began at the Flieger Kommando Doberiz flying school under the tutelage of Simon Brunnhuber, who had been the chauffeur of airplane-maker Dr. Walter Huth from the Albatros Werke, a manufacturer that had recently been set up in Germany. Huth had Brunnhuber taught to fly and then gave his Farman biplane and the services of the newly qualified chauffeur to the school. By March 1911, Brunnhuber had taught 10 German pilots to fly. The flying school had little money and had to borrow a small tent to house the Farman and later a Sommer biplane. Flying was prohibited if an exercise ground nearby was being used for training cavalry because the noise frightened the horses.

1910 July 7 Belgian military aviation was founded with a plan to develop flying schools and to procure airplanes for scouting, reconnaissance, gun targeting and general observation. The first Belgian military pilots were trained by the chevalier de Lamine. He had been training on Farmans for several months and helped the Belgian authorities set up the first squadron several months later.

1910 July 10 The French aviator Léon Morane became the first pilot to officially crack the 100 km/hr. barrier when he flew his modified Blériot XI powered by an 80-HP Gnôme, Gamma rotary engine to an average speed of 106.59 km/hr. (66.23 MPH). The FAI-recognized record was established over a 5 km (3.1 mi.) circuit in 2 min. 49 sec. and was established at the second Reims Flying Week. The aircraft had a wing span of 29 ft. 2 in., a length of 25 ft. 1 in. and a wing area of 161.5 sq. ft. It had a take-off weight of about 667 lb.

1910 July 11 The Bournemouth air show opened in England with participants from the continent and the United Kingdom. All week the flyers aimed for prizes ranging from £25 to £1,000. The greatest altitude was achieved by L. Morane in a Blériot monoplane at 4,107 ft., and the longest flight went to Grahame-White, who flew his Farman for more than 90 mi. in 2 hr. 34 min. 56 sec. L. Morane achieved the fastest lap, showing a speed of 56.6 MPH. As an indication of its impact, Gnôme-powered machines won £6,915 in prizes, whereas all other French engines won £785 and all British engines won £150.

1910 July 12 Hon. Charles Stewart Rolls, a cofounder of the Rolls Royce Co., lost his life while flying at the Bournemouth aviation show, becoming the first Englishman to lose his life while flying a powered airplane. A passionate aeronaut with an unbounding enthusiasm for flying he had trained many army officers to fly. He was flying a Wright biplane in a competition to land within a 100 ft. diameter circle with the engine switched off during the approach. High winds and difficult turns attempted without power got Rolls into a steep descent from which he had insufficient altitude to recover. In attempting to arrest the descent rate, he overstressed the tail in a turn, causing it to fail.

1910 July 16 Australian John R. Duigan made the first flight in his aircraft at Mia Mia, Victoria, becoming the first Australian to ascend in an Australian-designed-and-built airplane. A resident of Melbourne, Duigan had designed the aircraft by reference to photographs of a Wright Flyer. He had no other knowledge of the design and assembly sequence and received no formal advice on how to fly the machine. He put together written reports of how to fly and promptly applied them to the Wright design. On his first flight, Duigan managed to fly a distance of only 24 ft. but on October 6, he covered a total distance of 590 ft. at a height of about 12 ft.

1910 July 17 The formal beginning of a military aircraft section of the Italian Army was marked by the establishment of the Battalion of Specialists (Battaglione Specialisti) of the Aviation Section (Sezione Aviazione). It replaced the Autonomous Brigade of Specialists (Brigata Specialisti Autonome), which had been formed on September 23, 1909. The first flying school was at Centocelle near Rome followed by others at Bovolenta, Cameri, Cortile, Malpensa, Pordenone and Salussola. The first flight by a powered aircraft in Italy had taken place on May 24, 1908, when Delagrange demonstrated his 50-HP Voisin. On his own initiative, Lt. Alessandro Pecori Giraldi became the first member of the Italian military to receive his pilot's brevet on September 12, 1909. In an effort to encourage military support for flying,

the War Minister General Spingardi was taken for a flight in a Farman biplane on August 2, 1910. By the end of 1910, 31 pilots had qualified for their brevets.

1910 July 24 August Euler patented an invention for a machine gun fitted to the front of a lattice-section fuselage with pusher engine in such a manner that the gun was aimed by pointing the aircraft at the target. His patent anticipated by several years the appearance of forward-firing, fixed machine guns that would characterize fighter aircraft from 1915 and should not be confused with later patents for synchronized guns designed to fire through the arc of a revolving propeller.

1910 July 26 Capt. G. W. P. Dawes became the first British Army officer to be awarded an aviator's certificate in England, when he qualified for certificate no. 17 on a Humber monoplane at Wolverhampton. The growing number of self-financed, trained pilots in the armed services were to become the backbone staff of the British air units when they were formed. At this time, Capt. John Fulton had been put in charge of facilities at Larkhill, Salisbury Plain, where many army officers learned to fly.

1910 July 30 The Curtiss Exhibition Co. was formed in a marketing bid to attract customers to Curtiss airplanes and to stimulate awareness of the Curtiss products. The company also controlled the activities of the Curtiss flying schools, thereby providing a service for new airplane buyers. The company stood to make a lot of money from the increasing number of displays and air shows where daredevil flying was beginning to become a key attraction.

1910 July 30 The Bristol Boxkite made its first flight from Larkhill, Salisbury Plain piloted by a Frenchman called Edmond. He had persuaded the directors of the British and Colonial Aeroplane Co. Ltd. to abandon their first product called the Zodiac, shown at Olympia in March 1910, and build a direct copy of the latest Henri Farman biplane. Though dubbed the Boxkite, this derogatory title belied its efficiency of design and performance. The first two Boxkites were hurriedly sent up to Lanark in Scotland where an air show was about to begin.

1910 July Reputed to have been the first British woman to fly solo in a powered airplane, Miss Edith Maude Cook lost her life while attempting a parachute descent from a balloon at Coventry, England. Under the show name of Miss Spencer Kavanagh, Cook made theatrical displays out of aerial feats before packed crowds and is believed to have flown solo for the first time early in the year at the Grahame-White flying school at Pau in the French Pyrénées. Cook had certainly flown as a passenger in several airplanes and had carried out many parachute jumps performing her act before astonished spectators. On her fatal last jump, the canopy failed to open properly.

1910 August 6–13 An international aviation meeting opened at Lanark, Scotland, drawing a wide range of flyers and airplanes. In all, 22 competitors assembled, and there were six British machines. Samuel Cody brought along a new biplane, and the Bristol Boxkite made a short appearance, taking a prize for the slowest flight while remaining airborne. It is interesting to note that the positions of the start, finish and judging lines were placed on the converted race course without any attention to the fact that flyers like to take off and land heading into wind! Midweek, a record crowd of 50,000 exceeded the previous best for attendance at a British air show.

1910 August 10 Claude Grahame-White attempted to fly the first airmail in the world to be carried on a powered airplane when he took off from Squires Gate near Blackpool, England, heading for Southport. His attempt failed as his little Blériot monoplane was severely battered by the bad weather along his route, and Grahame-White was forced to land. The mail continued to its destination by more conventional means. Airmail deliveries would eventually become one of the most commonly exploited peacetime applications of aviation, a service that would await the development of airplanes capable of reliable, long distance flight.

1910 August 20 The first U.S. Army experiments with firing a rifle from a airplane took place when Lt. Jacob Earl Fickel conducted firing trials from a Curtiss biplane piloted by Curtiss himself. He shot at a 3 ft. by 5 ft. target set up on the Sheepshead Bay race track, New York City, and scored two hits on four passes. The experiment had been proposed by Maj. Samuel Reber of the Signal Corps. The War Department was so interested in the result that it sent Lt. Fickel to the Remington Arms Co. in Bridgeport, Conn. to assist in designing a special rifle sight to compensate for the motion of travel in the air. The following month further air trials were conducted with an automatic pistol.

1910 August 27 During a series of experiments, J. A. D. McCurdy fitted a radio transmitter-receiver to his Curtiss biplane. These trials proved successful, with McCurdy able to transmit and receive messages while airborne. The equipment was only able to use Morse code, but the practical advantages of observers aboard an airplane being able to make an instantaneous report were obvious and followed the lead shown by balloonists who had pioneered air-to-ground communication in the 19th century.

1910 September 2 Blanche Scott, the first woman known to have made a flight in the United States, took off briefly and, reportedly, by accident. Scott had been taking lessons in the basic flying controls of a powered airplane from Glenn Curtiss himself, who was concerned that a fatality involving a woman would taint aviation and set back progress in aeronautics for decades. He carried out several taxi runs along the ground with her until, responding to an unexpected gust of wind, the airplane by accident or contrived manipulation lifted from the ground and reached a height of 40 ft. before Blanche Scott brought it gently back to earth. Curtiss never again took a woman into an airplane with the purpose of giving her flying instructions.

1910 September 3–13 The Harvard Aeronautical School hosted an international gathering of aviators for a 10-day air show. With $100,000 in prize money, the main attraction was a $10,000 prize for the fastest flyer around the Boston Light. A large group of enthusiasts and dignitaries from surrounding towns and cities attended, including Pres. Taft. The event was held in glorious weather with lots of sideshows to keep the crowds amused, including about 170 egg bombs hurled at targets, one intended target being a car carrying spectators.

1910 September 8 An accident took place at Wiener-Neustadt, Austria during which two airplanes were reported to have collided in midair, resulting in both crashing to earth, though without a fatality. If true, this would qualify as the first midair collision; but little evidence supports the contention. Two brothers by the name of Warchalowski were flying Autobiplanes, developed copies of the Henri Farman biplane. Reports indicate that one airplane got into the effect of slipstream from the second airplane, causing it to lose control. The ensuing maneuvers to avoid each other brought them both to earth, one pilot breaking a leg.

1910 September 10 The first controlled, sustained flight made by Geoffrey de Havilland took place when he flew his No. 2

biplane for about 1,300 ft. at Seven Barrows, Berkshire, England. It was styled on the Farman biplane, which in turn was a refined and much modified adaptation of an early Voisin design. The No. 2 had a 45-HP engine reconstructed from parts recovered from the first biplane built and flown by de Havilland in 1909 but wrecked when it crashed on its first flight. De Havilland had become airborne briefly while rolling downhill, a performance not usually credited as being a recognized flight.

1910 September 11 Flying a Farman biplane, the actor turned air-enthusiast Robert Loraine made the first crossing from the British Isles to Ireland by flying from Holyhead on Anglesey (an island off the north coast of Wales) to the Irish shore at a point near Baily Lighthouse on the north margin of Dublin Bay. Loraine had crash-landed his Farman at Holyhead during a flying meeting at Blackpool and, with only 10 hr. of solo flying time, decided to head for Ireland without rescue boats or any other arrangements. At 4,000 ft. and within 20 mi. of land, his Gnôme rotary stopped, only to start again when he had glided down to a height of only 1,500 ft. He eventually came down on the water, within 60 ft. of land.

1910 September 11 The first flight of the Paulhan biplane took place at St.-Cyr, France. It was a remarkable and bewildering design with an open girder for the single main spar of each wing, which supported curved ribs covered with fabric. Designed as a two-seat pusher powered by a 50-HP Gnôme engine, the biplane had a maximum speed of about 50 MPH. Paulhan's fame in winning the London-Manchester race on April 28 helped establish his reputation in England, and Paulhan's agent, George Holt Thomas, persuaded the War Office to buy one of his biplanes for tests. It was delivered to the Balloon Factory at Farnborough on February 16, 1911.

1910 September 15 During a two-month intensive investigation by a German military commission into the possible use of airplanes in war Hptm. de le Roi flew a Farman biplane 12 mi. between Doberitz and Bornstedter Field in 20 min. at a height of about 500 ft. Gen. Ludendorff got his first flight during the commission's investigation into flying when he was flown by de la Roi. The German Army decided to purchase seven airplanes at a total cost of 150,000 marks, and it was also decided to subsidize the costs of DELAG, the German company attempting to open up passenger services with Zeppelin airships, by contributing funds.

1910 September 16 Discounting the flight of Blanche Scott on September 2, the first official flight by a woman in a powered airplane took place when Bessica Raiche got a few feet off the ground on her first solo flight. She had built her airplane from bamboo and imported Chinese silk held together with piano wire at her house in New York. As she progressed with her flying, her efforts came to the attention of the Aeronautical Society, which awarded her a diamond-studded pin engraved with the words "The First Woman Aviator of America." Later, she gave up flying and became a successful physician.

1910 September 26 A key, if somewhat minor, event marking increased U.S. Navy interest in aviation took place when Capt. W. I. Chambers was appointed as the U.S. Navy representative for all correspondence about airplanes and flying received from the general public and congressmen. Chambers remained in this role for three years as the navy developed its awareness of the role aviation could play in its activities and helped develop the organization through which command and control of air elements would evolve. Two navy officers had been present at the army trials in 1908 involving the Wright flyer Model A, but little genuine enthusiasm had been expressed outside the few committed navy protagonists. That attitude was now changing to a more positive awareness.

1910 September 30 Ongoing tests with wireless sets in airplanes at Larkhill, England resulted in the first successful transmission across a distance of 1 mi. Throughout September, Lt. Robert Loraine had been preparing for army maneuvers on Salisbury Plain in Bristol Boxkite No. 8 accompanied by Capt. Bertram Dickson in Boxkite No. 9. Equipped with a Thorne-Baker wireless transmitter, Loraine successfully transmitted to a receiver on Lark Hill for a distance of just over 1 mi. The maneuvers had begun September 21 and were attended by Gen. Sir John French, Lord Kitchener, Lord Roberts and Winston S. Churchill.

1910 September The definitive A. V. Roe triplane, the Roe IV, was completed and flown several times by Hubert Oxley and C. Howard Pixton. Only one was built, but it was reconstructed 50 years later as a replica for the highly acclaimed film *Those Magnificent Men in Their Flying Machines*. It was the archetypical pre-World War I flying machine and, powered by a 35-HP Green engine, made a delightful sight above the pastoral countryside of rural England. Roe reverted to wing warping and fitted a circular wheel as a control column. The aircraft had a predilection for dumping its pilots in the local sewage farm, which inspired a similar fate for characters in the 1960s film.

1910 September Large-scale military maneuvers took place in Picardy, France in which airplanes and dirigibles were used for the first time. The Second Army Corps had two Farmans, one Sommer and one Blériot and the Ninth Army Corps had two Farmans, one Wright and one Blériot. Despite high winds that kept the dirigibles grounded and unfavorable countryside affording little opportunity for emergency descent, the airplane was deemed indispensible to modern warfare. Charged with reporting on their performance, Col. Hirschauer claimed that they "went beyond what was demanded of them, beyond any hopes that could have been conceived." The pilots expressed surprise that no one had thought to arm the airplanes. After the maneuvers, the army promptly ordered 40 more Blériots and Farmans in equal number.

1910 October 1 Louis Blériot opened the Hendon Aerodrome in London to the general public. Another Frenchman, Louis Paulhan, had taken off from a field at Hendon at the start of his prize-winning flight between London and Manchester on April 27, 1910. Several companies had hangars at Hendon, including Blériot, who stocked them with monoplanes of the type he had used to cross the English Channel in July 1909, and Grahame-White, who transferred his flying school there from Pau in France. Increasingly, Hendon would be the "London Aerodrome" of pre-World War I flying for national and international aviators in England.

1910 October 10 Capt. Bertram Dickson and a Frenchman named Thomas collided in the first confirmed midair collision between two powered, piloted airplanes. (See also 1910 Sept. 8.) Dickson was flying a Henry Farman at an aviation meeting in Milan, Italy when Thomas accidentally flew his Antoinette monoplane down onto the top wing of the Farman. Entangled, both airplanes collapsed to the ground. Thomas escaped uninjured, but Dickson was severely hurt and remained crippled for the rest of his life.

1910 October 10 In an attempt to resolve a dispute about the responsibility for military aviation in France, war minister Gen.

Brun imposed a decree that stipulated all balloon and heavier-than-air aviation conducted by the army was to fall under the authority of a general officer to be appointed permanent inspector of military aeronautics. There had been fierce debate between the engineers and the artillery corps about who should have supreme responsibility. The Corps of Engineers at Chalais-Meudon went ahead with technical problems affecting aviation, while the artillery unit at the newly formed aviation establishment, Vincennes, under Maj. Estienne developed operational techniques for reconnaissance, spotting and bombing.

1910 October 14 The English aviator Grahame-White made a spectacular appearance in Executive St., Washington, D.C., alongside the White House when he flew in from Benning Racing Trace and landed on the road, pedestrians having been cleared to the sidewalks and traffic halted. Grahame-White had been invited to visit Gen. Allen, U.S. Army chief signal officer, while he and American aviator Clifford B. Harmon were conducting flying displays at Benning. The Englishman decided to take up the offer and fly in to land close by the Executive Office Building, which, as a leading magazine of the day said, paralyzed "for a period of at least an hour the whole administrative service of the United States, both civil and military."

1910 October 15–22 At the annual Paris Air Show the Voisin brothers displayed the first airplane to be equipped with a gun installed as part of the fuselage. They had developed their 1910 Tourist biplane into a Type Militaire, not exclusively for the purpose of reconnaissance but also for attacking targets on the ground and other airplanes in the sky carrying out observation duties. The biplane had an extra wheel projecting forward and down from the nose, abandoned the side curtains characteristic of the 1909 model to increase pilots' field of vision and adopted aileron control. It was powered by a 100-HP Gnôme rotary engine and had the first metal propeller fitted to an airplane. Attached prominently in the nose was a "mitrailleuse," a French machine gun.

1910 October 22–30 A major air show at Belmont Park, New York included contestants from the United States, England and France. In all, 27 leading fliers came to show off their airplanes and their flying skills. Prizes totalled $72,300, with a $10,000 prize for the first flight around the Statue of Liberty. It was also the venue for the second Gordon Bennett Trophy, the first held in the United States, on October 29. Throughout the week, weather kept fliers fighting for control of their machines in the air, let alone records. Bands played in attempts to placate bored spectators.

1910 October 22 One of the leading figures in British aviation history and the founder of two great manufacturing companies (Sopwith and Hawker) made his first flight in a powered airplane. Thomas ("Tommy") Octave Murdoch Sopwith had bought a monoplane from the Howard T. Wright company (not connected with the Wright brothers) for £630 and taken it to Brooklands where he flew for about 1,000 ft. before pulling it up too sharply and stalling at a height of 40 ft. Damage caused by the crash landing was repaired, and Sopwith took off again on November 4, gradually feeling his way into straight-line hops, longer flights, then turns in the air. Witnesses said he made the fastest progress of anyone observed at Brooklands, and he received his pilot's certificate (no. 31) on November 22.

1910 October 22 A distinct French air force was brought a step closer with the formation of the Inspection Permanente de l'Aéronautique headed by Gen. Roques. Before this date, aviation had been divided between the engineers and the artillery.

Now it was considered sufficiently advanced to become an independent arm. The army already had about 30 airplanes on hand—15 Farmans and five Wright biplanes, with four Sommer, four Blériot and two Antoinette monoplanes—with 61 still on order but not delivered.

1910 October 28 The world flight record for distance in a closed circuit was increased to 289.38 mi. by a French aviator named Tabuteau. The flight took place at the French town of Etampes and was made in a Maurice Farman biplane. This flight signaled the end of the two-year supremacy of Wright aircraft in the record books, and they were never to regain their lead. However, it testifies to the advanced nature of the Wright biplane that with only minimal change and modification it was able to remain a credible performer against improved European types at a time when progress in performance was being made by leaps and bounds.

1910 October 29 At the second Gordon Bennett Trophy race, held at Belmont Park, New York, Frenchman Alfred Leblanc seized the first FAI-recognized record outside France when he recorded an average speed of 109.756 km/hr. (68.2 MPH) over a 5 km (3.1 mi.) course in 2 min. 44.78 sec. Leblanc was flying his Blériot XI-bis powered by a 100-HP Gnôme Double Oméga rotary engine. The record stood for less than six months before Leblanc broke it on April 12, 1911, with a speed of 111.81 km/hr. (69.47 MPH) at Pau, France flying the same airplane.

1910 October 29 At the week-long Belmont Park, New York air show, the second Gordon Bennett Trophy race included teams representing America, England and France competing for speed and distance prizes. Each country had three named participants. England's team included Claude Grahame-White, flying a Blériot monoplane powered by a 100-HP Gnôme rotary, the most powerful yet flown. He went around the 62.14 mi. circuit in 1 hr. 1 min. 4 sec. American John B. Moissant took second place, flying a Blériot monoplane powered by a 50-HP engine in a time of 1 hr. 57 min. 44 sec. Englishman Alec Ogilvie took third place in his British-built Wright biplane, taking 2 hr. 6 min. 36 sec.

1910 October 30 The climax to the Belmont, New York air show took place when flyers competed for the fastest time to the Statue of Liberty and back, a distance of 34 mi. The quickest time completed was by John B. Moissant, flying for the American team in a Blériot monoplane that he purchased from Frenchman Alfred Leblanc after ploughing into Clifford Harmon's biplane while taxiing. Consequently, he took off after the official start-time deadline of 4:00 P.M., when Grahame-White had put up the fastest time. Grahame-White contested Moissant's time on the basis that he took off late. After examining the case for two years, the Fédération Aéronautique Internationale awarded victory to the Englishman, including the $10,000 prize money plus interest!

1910 October One of the most impressive exhibits at the Paris Air Show was the little biplane of Gaston and René Caudron, who had set up a factory earlier in the year at Romiotte on the Seine. For their first biplane, they tested several design configurations, including wing-warping mechanism and ailerons set between the wings similar to those characteristic of Curtiss airplanes and seaplanes. The biplane was powered by a 25-HP Anzani engine and is believed to have carried a passenger into the air. It made the first night flight over Paris in February 1911. Caudron would produce a wide range of military airplanes during World War I.

1910 November 14 Civilian Eugene B. Ely piloted the first powered airplane to take off from the deck of the cruiser USS *Birmingham*. The *Birmingham* had been fitted with wooden planking 83 ft. long and 24 ft. wide, and the ship was motionless off Hampton Roads, Va., when Ely took off in a Curtiss pusher

Development of the airship was to continue apace with heavier-than-air machines for several decades.

biplane at precisely 3:16 P.M. The instant he left, the *Birmingham* sent the radio message "Ely's just gone." As the Curtiss fought for flying speed, it dipped toward the sea, clipping the water with its propeller, but Ely gained a proper flying altitude and landed at Willoughby Spit just over 3.5 mi. away.

1910 November 15   The first production order for a British airplane was signed by the British and Colonial Aeroplane Co. Ltd. The order for eight Boxkites was negotiated between the British manufacturer and the Russian attaché in Paris, William Rebikoff. These airplanes were modified from the standard design and had enlarged rudders and fuel tanks. The first three machines (Nos. 17–19) were powered by 50-HP Gnôme rotaries, and the remainder had 70-HP Gnômes, as agreed by the contract.

1910 November 26   The first Henri Farman biplane ordered by the British War Office was handed over to the British authorities at Chalons, France. It was purchased for £1,008 with an additional 10 pounds paid for instruments telling speed and altitude. Known as the Type Militaire, the Farman III was powered by a 50-HP Gnôme rotary engine and carried the serial number F1. It was one of the earliest airplanes purchased for the British Army and was part of a select group that within a few months would also include the Bristol Boxkite and the Paulhan biplane. The airplane was first flown from the Balloon Factory at Farnborough, on October 4.

1910 December 10   The Romanian air-enthusiast Henry Coanda was reported to have made a single hop into the air, but there is no substantial evidence, and the design of his flying machine leaves the fact in considerable doubt. The fuselage resembled that of a Antoinette monoplane but with sesquiplane wings. He designed a large fan attached to the front of a 50-HP Clerget engine. The fan and part of the engine were enclosed by a cylinder through which air was forced back from the fan blades across the fuselage. In theory, the airplane would fly forward as a reaction to the expelled mass of air accelerated through the fan. Although Coanda's engine has been hailed by some as the first "jet" engine, the principles of operation are totally dissimilar.

1910 December 18   Thomas Sopwith, who had made his first flight as recently as October 22, carried off the Baron de Forest prize of £4,000 for making the longest straight-line flight from England into continental Europe during 1910. Sopwith carried 20 gal. of gasoline, sufficient for 6 hr. of flying, and a flask of hot meat extract. Sopwith left Eastchurch at 8:16 A.M. and flew his Howard-Wright biplane east for Dover, crossing the coast shortly after 9:00 A.M. Facing strong winds and total cloud cover, Sopwith came down near the Belgian town of Beaumont, 9 mi. from the French frontier, having flown 177 mi. in 3 hr. 40 min.

1910 December 20   A revolutionary airplane, and one that was specifically designed to possess inherent stability, the Dunne D.5 was tested in flight at Eastchurch, England by Lt. J. W. Dunne, an invalided Boer War veteran of the British Army Wiltshire Regiment. Dunne had built a powered airplane and made spasmodic hops in it beginning on November 16, 1908. The D.5 was developed by the Blair Atholl Aeroplane Syndicate Ltd. of London, which had been formed by the marquis of Tullibardine. It was built by Short Brothers and comprised a tailless biplane with swept wings supporting a 60-HP ENV F engine behind the center-section of the lower wing. This resulted in a "flying-wing" airplane just over 20 ft. long and with a span of 46 ft. Its flight test was watched by several observers, one of whom was Orville Wright.

1910 December 30   Maurice Tabuteau won the 1910 International Michelin Cup for making the longest flight of the year when he flew his Maurice Farman biplane with Renault engine a distance of 365 mi. in 7 hr. 48 min. 31 sec. The Maurice Farman was similar to the Henri Farman but was influenced by the design developed by Maurice from the original Voisin concept. A relatively close second in the cup contest was P. M. Bournique and his REP with a flight of 330 mi. in 6 hr. 30 min.

1910 December 31   Samuel F. Cody won the British Empire Michelin Cup and £500 prize money for the British citizen making the longest flight of the year in a British airplane. Cody used a biplane developed from the British Army *Aeroplane No. 1*-type delivered in September 1908. Cody's strongest competitor was Thomas Sopwith, who flew a Howard-Wright until the fuel tank ran dry at 4 hr. 7 min. 17 sec. while circling Brooklands. Alec Ogilvie had also put up a credible time of just under 4 hr. in his Short-Wright, but Cody covered 185.5 miles in 4 hr. 47 min. on Laffan's Plain. Cody, an Anglo-American Irishman raised in Texas, came to England in 1896 where he stayed to become a British citizen.

1910   An increase in air-mindedness across France resulted in significant progress for French military aviation. In the second half of the year, two flying schools were opened, one under Lt. Cammerman at Châlons, the other under Gen. Philippe Féquant at Vincennes. By the end of the year, 52 army and six navy pilots had graduated, with the first being sent back into the schools as instructors. At this time, a military pilots license was granted by the same qualifying criteria as that stipulated by the Aero Club of France, that is, three 5-km closed circuit flights and a controlled landing.

1910   At the end of the year, six years after the first powered flight, the world duration record stood at 8 hr. 12 min. 47 sec., achieved by Henri Farman in his Farman biplane powered by a 100-HP Gnôme engine. The closed circuit distance record of 363.34 mi. was claimed by Tabuteau in his Maurice-Farman biplane with Renault engine, and the altitude record stood at 10,746 ft. set by G. Legagneux in a Gnôme-powered Blériot. During the year, the duration record had doubled, the closed circuit record had more than doubled, and the altitude record had increased five-fold. Also during 1910, the first flights took place (chronologically) in Australia, Argentina, Brazil, Cuba, Spain, Switzerland, Transvaal (South Africa), Chile, Norway, Indochina, India and Japan. A total of 29 people had been killed in flying accidents during 1910, up from 3 in 1909 and 1 in 1908 when the first aviation fatality was recorded.

1911 January 6   A crowd of 750,000 people gathered at the Calcutta Maidan, India to watch Henri Jullerot fly Bristol Boxkite No. 12. It was the largest group of spectators gathered together for a single aviation event prior to World War I. Bristol Boxkite No. 12 was one of two Boxkites that had upper-wing extensions for military activities, although that role was primarily at the suggestion of the British and Colonial Aeroplane Co. Ltd. Supervised by Farnall Thurstan, the India tour was a sales tour designed to procure orders. By this time, Boxkites were in production at the rate of eight each month.

1911 January 15   Live bombs were dropped from an airplane for the first time by Lt. Myron Crissy of the U.S. Coast Artillery Corps and Phillip Parmelee flying a Wright biplane at the Tanforan Race Track near San Francisco, Calif. Lt. Paul W. Beck had been ordered to study military aviation in January 1910, and he designed a timed bomb-release gear tested January 19, 1910,

The Bristol Boxkite of 1910, forerunner of a distinguished line of British aircraft.

when he dropped dummy bombs from a Farman piloted by Louis Paulhan. Crissy and Parmalee used this gear to drop the live bombs, demonstrating that 36-lb bombs could be made to fall within a 20-ft. circle from a height of 1,500 ft.

1911 January 17 In a special agreement with the owners, Coronado Beach Co., Glenn Curtiss established an aviation school on North Island, San Diego. Under the terms, Curtiss could use portions of the island as an airfield for up to three years or until such time as the owners needed it. Curtiss invited the U.S. Army to send pilots there, and on November 29, 1910, and in January 1911, Lts. Paul Beck, John C. Walker Jr. and S. E. M. Kelly were sent to Curtiss for instruction. In November 1912, Lt. Geiger arrived to command a signal corps school and a detachment of eight men. With him were Lts. Goodier, Mcleary, Brereton and Park, and signal corps aircraft S.C. Nos. 2, 6 and 8 were sent from College Park to formally establish the Signal Corps School on December 8, 1912.

1911 January 18 At 11:01 A.M. Eugene B. Ely made the first landing by an aircraft on a ship when he flew his Curtiss pusher biplane from Selfridge Field near San Francisco to a specially prepared wooden deck on the stern of the armored cruiser USS *Pennsylvania,* which was anchored in San Francisco Bay under the command of Capt. C. F. Pond. The landing planks were 119 ft. long, but Ely used only 30 ft. in coming to a stop. At precisely 11:58 A.M., he took off again to return to Selfridge Field, thus becoming the first pilot to first land and then take off from the deck of a ship.

1911 January 19 The German war minister, Gen. von Herringen, completed a report to the kaiser on the military pilot training program. Von Herringen endorsed expansion of the flying unit at Doberitz, to 14 officers and eight airplanes, which included three Farman biplanes, two Albatros-Farman biplanes, one Sommer biplane, one Aviatik biplane and one Etrich-Rumpler Taube. Flying training was given to both pilots and observers, but new tests were included in the flying program for an aviator's certificate. From now on, a cross-country flight of 1 hr. at an average height of 164 ft. would be mandatory, as would an unpowered glide from 330 ft. to the ground.

1911 January 26 Curtiss carried out a successful flight with his "hydro-aeroplane," later known as a seaplane, developed to encourage U.S. Navy support for aviation. A main float 5 ft. long and 6 ft. wide was attached directly under the lower wing of the biplane, with a smaller float forward and a tiny hydrovane at the

extreme forward position, placed so as to prevent the front of the airplane digging into the water as it accelerated. Curtiss thought the wide, main float would provide auxiliary lift while pushing the wave either side of the pusher propeller. The biplane was very similar in appearance to the Curtiss-Herring No. 1 used at Reims in 1909. The tests took place at North Island, San Diego.

1911 February 1 Curtiss performed the first tests with a modified arrangement of floats used with the hydro-airplane first tested successfully January 26, 1911. Using the same biplane, Curtiss removed the three original floats and replaced the center one with a main float 12 ft. long, 2 ft. wide and 1 ft. deep. In addition, small floats were attached on trailing struts below each lower wing tip for stability. Thus began the design evolution leading to the classic seaplane configuration. A second machine was built in which the engine was mounted in front driving a tractor propeller, the pilot was positioned where the engine had been and the forward elevator was eliminated.

1911 February 1 Summoned by George V, Thomas Sopwith (the first British airman to be summoned to his king) took off from the town of Datchet and flew to Windsor Castle in his Howard-Wright biplane. Edward VII had died in May 1910, and the new king was determined to understand as much as possible about aviation and how it might affect the country. Having taken the Baron de Forest prize on December 18, 1910, Sopwith was a natural choice to tell him.

1911 February 11 An important pioneer in developing aviation in New Zealand, Vivian C. Walsh piloted a Howard-Wright biplane on what is generally considered the first flight in New Zealand by a powered airplane. Walsh and his brother Leo had assembled the plane at their home in Auckland using parts shipped from England by the Howard-Wright company and a 60-HP ENV engine, a configuration similar to that used by Thomas Sopwith for his first flight in October 1910 and for a subsequent tour of the United States. In 1914 Walsh became the first New Zealander to fly a seaplane.

1911 February 12 The first wartime use of a powered airplane took place when American Charles Hamilton working for the Mexican rebels flew 20 mi. from El Paso, Tex. to the besieged town of Ciudad Juarez in Mexico where troops were holed up by the rebel leader Orozco. An agreement had been reached with the rebels that they would not fire on Hamilton's Curtiss pusher biplane, but when the garrison saw his airplane approach at a height of 1,000 ft., they ran for cover, appearing again when he circled without firing on them or dropping bombs. They waved to him to land, but he carried out his reconnaissance mission and returned to El Paso to deliver his report.

1911 February 17 In a demonstration of operational flexibility, Curtiss flew a tractor-engined hydro-airplane to the cruiser USS *Pennsylvania* at anchor alongside North Island, San Diego and was winched aboard by crane. The *Pennsylvania* had been used for the first deck-on/deck-off operations the previous month. The hydro-airplane used for this demonstration was the second machine of this type built by Curtiss. It had no forward elevator but carried the single 12-ft. pontoon-type central float employed for its first flight on February 1. The pusher engine had been converted to tractor operation by fixing it to the front of the biplane, and spray deflectors were attached to the forward section of the float.

1911 February 18 The first successful airmail delivery was accomplished in India by the Frenchman Henri Pequet when he flew a Humber biplane a distance of 5 mi. across the Jumna River, a tributary of the Ganges, between Allahabad and Naini Junction to deliver 6,500 letters as part of events associated with the Universal Postal Exhibition then taking place at Allahabad. A regular delivery was set up on February 22, franked with the stamp "first Aerial Post, U. P. Exhibition, Allahabad, 1911." The regular service was run by Pequet and the English Army Capt. W. G. Windham.

1911 February 21 A new 1910 Wright Type B Flyer owned by *Collier's* magazine publisher Robert F. Collier arrived at San Antonio, Tex. on rent to the U.S. Army for $1.00 per month to supplement the aging Wright biplane first accepted on August 2, 1909. The older Wright aircraft had been rebuilt after a crash November 5, 1909, and in August 1910, Cpl. Glen Madole and the army's first civilian mechanic, Oliver G. Simmons, attached a makeshift tricycle landing gear to the skids that was similar to the new Type B. Flying started February 22 under instructions from Phillip O. Parmelee on loan to the army from the Wright Company. Flying was suspended February 27 when the air detachment moved to Fort McIntosh at Laredo, Tex., close to the Mexican border.

1911 February 25 Glenn Curtiss successfully flew the first amphibian, named *Triad,* at North Island, San Diego. Developed from his hydro-airplane first flown January 26, the *Triad* featured retractable main wheels either side of the main float beneath the lower wing. A single nose wheel was added at the front of the main float, and two small outrigger floats were retained for stability. The main wheels folded forward and up to lie alongside the float for water operation but could be manually lowered to allow the airplane to climb up a ramp onto land. Curtiss restored the pusher configuration with the pilot in front and a forward elevator for pitch control. He achieved another first this day by taking up the first passenger in a seaplane.

1911 March 1 Four Royal Navy officers began flight training with the full approval of the British Admiralty and with the generosity of Francis K. McClean, who offered the use of two Short S.28 and S.29 biplanes. George Cockburn of the Royal Aero Club trained the four lieutenants, C. R. Samson, A. M. Longmore and R. Gregory with Lt. E. L. Gerrard from the Royal Marine Artillery.

1911 March 3 With Capt. Benjamin D. Foulois navigating a course and Phillip Parmelee at the controls, the Wright Type B on loan from Robert F. Collier made an unofficial U.S. cross-country record when it flew from Laredo to Eagle Pass, Tex. It flew the 106 mi. in 2 hr. 10 min. with the flyers dropping messages to troop detachments en route. During the return flight two days later, one of the two airmen accidentally released the engine cam lever, stopping the engine. The airplane came down in the Rio Grande River, damaging the ribs and tearing fabric after it turned turtle in 4 ft. of water. The crew was uninjured. Spotted by a cowboy who raised the alarm, the Wright was returned to San Antonio by rail.

1911 March 4 The U.S. Congress appropriated $125,000 for the U.S. Army aeronautics program with authorization for a further $100,000. Chief Signal Officer James Allen ordered three additional airplanes from Wright and two from Curtiss. To date, the army had received only the one Wright biplane accepted August 2, 1909, and one Wright Type B leased by publisher Robert F. Collier in early 1911. The army also planned flying schools and set aside funding needs for better facilities. In the same appropriation bill, Congress appropriated $25,000 for the U.S. Navy aeronautics program, to be handled by the Bureau of Navigation.

1911 March 12 The 7th Company, Coast Artillery Corps, of the U.S. Army was installed with an aviation unit, becoming the first element of the California Air National Guard. Money was not allocated for the purchase of airplanes and National Guard members frequently raised the funds to buy their own airplanes. During the 1920s, most Guard aircraft were assigned to Army observation units and funds became available. In the 1930s, the ANG expanded so that every State in the Union had its own unit. The wealth of flying experience acquired by the peacetime reservists was put to good use when America went to war against Japan and Germany in 1941. Many Air Guard pilots served as instructors in the USAAF, President Roosevelt having inducted the Guard into active service on August 27, 1940. A decade later, 27 ANG combat wings served in the Korean War and today the Air National Guard is a fully integrated part of the USAF and operates modern combat airplanes such as the F-16.

1911 March 13 U.S. Army *Aeroplane No. 2* was ordered from Curtiss and delivered the same month. It was a single-seat Curtiss Model D with a span of 33 ft. 4 in., a length of 25.75 ft. and a height of almost 7.5 ft. Powered by a 60-HP pusher motor built by Curtiss, it could attain a speed of 55 MPH and weighed 950 lb. packed for shipping. It cost $5,000 and was used for several years until, like all pushers, it was grounded in February 1914. The airplane was eventually refurbished and put back to its original condition before delivery to the Air & Space Museum in Washington, D.C., where it is today.

1911 March 14 The British War Office placed an order for four Bristol Boxkites in the military configuration, the first British Army order for this airplane. The military model had extensions to the upper wings, increasing the span from 34.5 ft. to either 47 ft. 8 in. or to 46 ft. 6 in. The first two Boxkites on this order were fitted with 50-HP Gnôme engines, and the second pair had 60-HP Renault engines. Four more were ordered by the War Office, two to be powered by 50-HP Gnômes, and two supplied as spare airframes without engines. Thus was the Bristol Boxkite launched on a profitable production line until 1914.

1911 March 16 The first certificate of airworthiness awarded to an airplane in Britain was signed by Mervyn O'Gorman, superintendent of the Balloon Factory at Farnborough, covering the Farman III Type Militaire purchased by the British Army during the second half of 1910. After initial trials in England, it had been damaged and then repaired by Geoffrey de Havilland. Following tests and minor modifications, it was the recipient of certificate no. 1. O'Gorman testified that it had been carried out "with a 14 stone [196 lb.] passenger." The Farman III was used many times until retirement in 1912, after which it was used for ground based instruction.

1911 March 17 U.S. Navy Lt. John Rodgers reported to the Wright Co. at Dayton, Ohio for flying instructions. On March 9, the Wrights had offered to train one Navy pilot if that service bought a Wright flying machine at a cost of $5,000. The conditional offer was later replaced by one that provided unconditional free training for one would-be Navy pilot.

1911 March 23 An incredible feat of performance and capacity was reportedly carried out when a single airplane carried 11 people into the air. The event took place in France and involved Louis Breguet in one of his early biplanes. To achieve this feat, he packed seven boys and three adult passengers into the forward section of his airplane and staggered a few feet into the air, hardly qualifying for the achievement announced by the headlines! Next day, Roger Sommer did a similar thing, carrying 12 passengers for 2,600 ft. Exaggerated though they were, these flights did stimulate awareness that, with additional power and lifting capacity, airplanes would serve well for passenger and cargo transport.

1911 March Claude Grahame-White and Harry Harper coauthored a book called *The Aeroplane, Past, Present and Future* in which they compiled what they believed to be a definitive listing of all successful pilots up to that date. Out of 729 names, France had 387, England 128, Germany 46, Italy 38, Russia 37 and the United States 31; the rest of the world made up the balance. Of the total, 361 had used biplanes, 302 had used monoplanes, and 66 had used aircraft of ''unusual'' design. Of the biplanes, the Henri Farman was the most popular type, 135 aviators using that type; the Voisin, with 59 pilots, was the next most common. Of the monoplanes, the Blériot had 158 pilots compared with 47 flying the Antoinette. Only 39 pilots were flying Wright machines, and the Valkyrie monoplane and the Bristol Boxkite had 7 and 16 pilots respectively.

1911 April 11 The formation of the first U.S. Army flying school at College Park, Md. (near Washington, D.C.) was authorized as part of a plan to move the center of army aviation from Fort Sam Houston in Texas. Though the move took place during June and July, on May 10 Lt. G. E. M. Kelly crashed and was killed—the first fatality in flying training, the commanding officer of Fort Sam Houston banned further flying from his base. No further training flights took place until the flying facilities had been moved. During the winter months, the flyers would move from the D.C. area to Augusta, Ga.

1911 April 12 Pierre Prier made the first nonstop flight from London to Paris in a Blériot monoplane powered by a 50-HP Gnôme rotary engine. It began from the Hendon airfield just north of London, where Prier was chief flying instructor at the Blériot school. Prier flew north from Hendon, headed south for Chatham and Canterbury, crossed the coast at Dover and reached France over Calais, flying thence across Boulogne, Abbéville and Beauvais and landing at Issy-les-Moulineaux 3 hr. 56 min. later. He averaged 62 MPH over 230 mi.

1911 April 27 The U.S. Army Signal Corps at Fort Sam Houston accepted its second official airplane, the *S.C. No. 2,* known as the Curtiss IV Model D Military. It had a wingspan of 30 ft., a length of 29 ft. 3 in. and a height of 7 ft. 10 in. with a weight of 700 lb. It was powered by a 70-HP, 8-cylinder, water-cooled engine driving a single pusher propeller behind the wing's center-section. Designed with a tricycle landing gear, the airplane was a distinct improvement over the *S.C. No. 1* Wright biplane delivered with skids and only provisionally modified to have a strap-on tricycle undercarriage; *S.C. No. 3,* a Wright Type B with the elevator moved to the rear and wheels attached to the skids, was also accepted by the army this day.

1911 May 4 The U.S. War Department approved a suggestion that *S.C. No. 1* (the Wright Flyer accepted by the army August 2, 1909) be put at the disposal of the Smithsonian Institution for exhibition purposes following refurbishment. Secretary Walcott of the Smithsonian accepted the airplane on October 20, 1911. The army had wanted to have the airplane refurbished for continued service use, but the Wrights advised against this due to its dated design and condition.

1911 May 5 The first indigenous Japanese airplane was flown on its maiden flight by its designer and builder, Sanji Narahara. He made a creditable flight of approximately 197 ft. before coming down to earth. This was the second airplane he had built, but his first to fly. It was powered by a 50-HP Gnôme, testament to the universal popularity this exciting new type of engine had achieved by mid-1911. The first flight in Japan had taken place in a Henri Farman, flown by Y. Tokugawa on December 19, 1910, at Tokyo.

1911 May 8 A French pilot by the name of See carried out his first flight of the Voisin Canard (Duck), so-named because, like the *14-bis* of Santos-Dumont, it was a tail-first design. It had been designed in 1910. The flight began at 6:00 A.M., and for almost 10 min., things went well, until it suddenly pitched forward spilling See onto the roof of a nearby factory, to his disgust and embarrassment!

1911 May 21 The French minister of war, Berteaux, was killed when he was hit by the propeller of a monoplane flown by Emile Louis Train on the opening day of the Paris-Madrid air race in which 29 entrants were to participate. Train took off from a field closely packed with an estimated 300,000 people, but when his engine cut, he descended directly into a crowd of dignataries that included the minister of war. The propeller struck several people and also injured the French prime minister, Monis. Pressed by the unruly crowd, the Horse Guards had been unable to prevent the VIPs from being pushed onto the field itself.

1911 May 26 The second Voisin Canard, a machine ordered by Prince Bibesco, the sporting French millionaire, made its first flight from the Seine at Billancourt, France. Fitted with four floats it was introduced to army officials as a possible machine for military duties. The first Canard had been flown in February 1911, and the second attracted the interest of the French Navy, who ordered one after a demonstration October 10. The Russians ordered two machines of this type also. It was never a great success for Voisin, however, and he turned his attention increasingly toward land-based planes.

1911 May Important trials took place at Hendon, England in front of a powerful and distinguished group of officials including Prime Minister Asquith, future prime ministers David Lloyd George and Winston Churchill, Minister for War Lord Haldane and Under-Secretary for War Col. J. E. B. Seely. Gustav Hamel flew his Blériot 35 mi. to Farnborough in 40 min. with a dispatch that took 55 min. to send by telegraph. He returned in 30 min., beating a return telegraph message. Also, M. Hubert and C. C. Paterson flew two army officers in search of troops deployed in the countryside between St. Albans and Hendon; their positions were located on maps and reported. This display was a major turning point in government plans for military airplanes.

1911 June 8 The first in a line of historically significant airplanes, the Santos Experimental No. 1 was taken into the air for the first time at Farnborough. Designed by Geoffrey de Havilland, the S.E. 1 was so named because it bore more than superficial resemblance to the *14-bis* of Brazilian Santos-Dumont, although the initial letters would quickly come to stand for Scouting Experimental. A tail-first pusher biplane, it was powered by a 60-HP ENV engine and had a relatively large wing span of 38.5 ft. and a fuselage length of 29 ft. It evolved into the S.E. 5 of World War I fame.

1911 June 18 The Circuit of Europe air races began in Vincennes outside Paris and involved point-to-point flights through

France, Belgium, Holland and England, connecting specific towns or cities as start and finish points for prizes worth as much as 18,300 pounds. The 43 contestants received a tumultuous send-off at 6:00 A.M. when more than 500,000 people restrained by more than 6,000 policemen clapped and cheered in pouring rain. Only nine finished the full set of races, ending back where they began July 7. Lt. de Vaisseau Conneau won in a Blériot, followed by Roland Garros in another Blériot, Vidart in a Deperdussin and Vedrines in a Morane Saulnier.

1911 June 19 The third Wright biplane ordered by the U.S. Army Signal Corps was delivered to College Park and became *S.C. No. 4.* Training was complicated by the fact that the control system comprised two elevator levers, one for each pilot, but only a single-wing warping-rudder lever. Because this was located between the two side-by-side seats, trainees necessarily became right-handed or left-handed pilots. The situation was alleviated when in 1912 the aircraft were retrofitted with a complete set of dual controls. *S.C. No. 5,* a Burgess-Wright, so-called because it was built by the W. Starling Burgess Company, completed acceptance tests October 10, 1911, and *S.C. No. 6,* a second Curtiss pusher, was delivered July 27, 1911.

1911 June 27 As spectators watched in amazement, Lincoln Beachey flew his Curtiss pusher biplane over Horseshoe Falls, the most spectacular of the Niagara Falls. After passing under the International Bridge, Beachey continued down the gorge in a display of flying that held 50,000 people spellbound for more than 6 min. For his daring flight, Beachey received the sum of $5,000 and a permanent place in the annals of aerial showmanship. As he was to boast through advertising literature, "The Silent Reaper and I shook hands."

1911 June 30 The Curtiss A-1 seaplane was tested for the first time by Glenn Curtiss. The next day he flew with Lt. T. G. Ellyson from Lake Keuka, Hammondsport, N.Y. for a 5-min. flight at 6:50 P.M. Ellyson made two solo flights later that evening. The A-1 was the first U.S. Navy airplane and was a Model E biplane with a span of 35 ft. 4 in., a length of 25.75 ft. and a height of 8 ft. It was powered by a 50-HP Curtiss engine and cost $5,500. A more powerful, 75-HP, V-8 engine was installed later. By October 16, 1914, it had made 60 flights totaling 285 hr. On July 3, Ellyson made the first navy night flight, landing on water at Hammondsport.

1911 July 1 American aviator C. Weymann won the third Gordon-Bennett International Contest at Eastchurch, England with a phenomenal speed of 78 MPH, completing the 25-lap (94-mi.) circuit in 1 hr. 11 min. 36 sec. in his Nieuport powered by a 100-HP Gnôme rotary engine. Second place went to A. Leblanc, who had acquitted himself well at the previous year's Gordon-Bennett race in New York and who put up an average speed of 75 MPH in 1 hr. 13 min. 40 sec. with his 100-HP Blériot. The only American airplane in the contest was a Wright biplane flown by Englishman Alec Ogilvie, who completed the circuit in 1 hr. 49 min. at an average speed of 51 MPH, which included one stop to refuel.

1911 July 4 Horatio Barber carried a box of Osram electric light bulbs from Shoreham, England to grass lawns at Hove, Sussex for Page & Miles Ltd. in what is believed to have been the first commercial carriage of aerial cargo in England. The airplane he used was a Valkyrie B built by Aerial Syndicate Ltd., a company set up during early 1909. It was a two-seat canard monoplane with a span of 31 ft. and a length of 26 ft., powered by a 50-HP Gnôme engine that provided a top speed of 70 MPH. The

Valkyrie B had been developed as a racing machine from the Valkyrie A first flown in 1910. Horatio Barber formed his company at Salisbury Plain but moved later to Hendon.

1911 July 13 Curtiss delivered his second airplane for the U.S. Navy. Known as the A-2, it was dispatched as a land-based plane but was designed to operate as a seaplane by replacing the wheeled tricycle undercarriage with a central float. The A-2 was later modified to become the first Curtiss flying boat. A flying boat is different from a seaplane in that its fuselage is shaped like the hull of a boat and rests in the water, whereas a seaplane rests on a central float or pontoon. The A-2 was modified by encasing the single strut-mounted float with a fairing, thereby making it an integral part of the fuselage so that the whole machine rested on the water.

1911 July 20 Count von Zeppelin's first major success with passenger-carrying airships began with the successful introduction of the LZ 10 Schwaben into service with the Deutsche Luftschiffahrts A.G. (DELAG), the German airship company. Commanded by Hugo Eckener, the LZ 10 carried 4,354 passengers a total distance of 16,980 mi. in 224 flights until the airship was destroyed by fire on June 28, 1912 (without loss of life). Its sister ship the LZ 11, *Victoria Louise,* joined the LZ 10 in early 1912, and together these airships did much to advance the concept of lighter-than-air passenger travel.

1911 July 22 The *Daily Mail* round-Britain air race began. Entrants were required to fly from Brooklands to Hendon and thence to Edinburgh (Scotland) via Harrogate and Newcastle. From Edinburgh, they had to fly to Bristol in the southwest of England via Stirling, Glasgow and Manchester. From Bristol, they would fly to Exeter, Salisbury Plain, Brighton and back to Brooklands, a distance of 1,010 mi. in five days with 13 compulsory stops. A total of 28 entrants started the race, but only two machines were able to complete the course in the specified time. Lt. de Vaisseau Conneau in a Blériot monoplane won with a total flying time of 22 hr. 29 min. 26 sec. and at an average airborne speed of 50 MPH.

1911 August 2 Drama critic Harriet Quimby became the first American woman to be awarded a pilot's license. Several other woman before her had made flights either with an instructor or solo. Blanche Scott and Dr. Bessica Raiche had flown several times before Harriet Quimby, but neither had gone on to obtain a certificate. A team member of Matilde Moissant and coperformer in a flying circus show operated by the Moissant brothers, Quimby became well known for her aerobatics and daring antics. Women pilots brought an added excitement to air shows, and people flocked to see the (then) astonishing spectacle.

1911 August 18 The British F.E.2 biplane made its first flight from Farnborough, England piloted by its designer, Geoffrey de Havilland. (F.E. stood for Farman [type] Experimental.) The F.E.2 was a completely different design concept from the F.E.1, which was built originally as the de Havilland Biplane No. 2, with the forward elevator moved to the rear position to form a biplane tail arrangement and rudder. The F.E.2 was a singularly unique design and bore no relationship to the more famous F.E.2a, b, c and h series of World War I fame. It crashed in February 1914.

1911 August 19 British naval officer Comdr. Charles R. Samson set a new British endurance record of 4 hr. 58 min. 30 sec. Flying the Short S.38 biplane with special tanks allowing sufficient fuel for more than 4 hr. flying, Samson's watch stopped during the flight, and he circled round and round as the time at

5-min. intervals was displayed to him on a chalk board from the ground. He could have remained in the air longer, but conditions were excessively bumpy and he came down for safety reasons. Two days earlier, Lts. Gerrard and Lushington had remained aloft for 4 hr. 13 min., returning only when their fuel ran out.

1911 August 22–29 During Italian Army maneuvers, airplanes were used extensively for reconnaissance and patrol duties. This was the first time airplanes had been used for this purpose in Italy. ''Red'' team had three airplanes under the command of Capt. Carlo Piazza, and the ''Blue'' team had four airplanes. The maneuvers took place in Monferrato and were under the overall command of Tenente Gen. Pollio. The use of airplanes in maneuvers did much to encourage their wider application in the Italian Army and helped develop operational techniques valuable during the Italo-Turkish war that began during September.

1911 August 29 The first British woman flier to receive a pilot's certificate was granted Royal Aero Club license no.122 after qualifying at Brooklands in a Farman biplane. Hilda B. Hewlett and French aviator Blondeau owned the Hewlett & Blondeau Flying School at Brooklands and the airplane that Blondeau taught Hewlett to fly in. None of the other British woman pilots took qualifying trials for a license.

1911 September 7 Lt. T. G. Ellyson carried out the first flight trials with a wire-assisted launch technique for the Curtiss A-1 Seaplane. Running through a groove in the center of the main float, a taut wire just beneath the water's surface held the airplane straight and true as it accelerated into the air. The low power of contemporary engines restricted operations to the calmest available water; the wire launch aid helped keep the seaplane on course. Later, tests were carried out using an adapted version of the compressed-air torpedo launcher, then coming into use with the U.S. Navy, to hurl the seaplane into the air.

1911 September 9 Gustav Hamel carried the first bag of official airmail in England in his Blériot monoplane between Hendon and Windsor, covering the 19 mi. in 10 min. at an average speed of more than 105 MPH, aided by a strong tail wind. The general post office sold special envelopes and cards in London for the air service that was inaugurated to commemorate the coronation of King George V, delivery between Hendon and Royal Farm, Windsor having been entrusted to pilots from the Blériot and Claude Grahame-White schools at Hendon. The special service terminated September 26 after 1,015 lb. of mail had been delivered.

1911 September 11 Samuel Cody completed a designated 125-mi., cross-country course around Laffan's Plain, England in 3 hr. 7 min. to win the British Michelin Cup No. 2 and a prize of £400. This was the first of the Cup No. 2 races, entrants for which had until October 15 to attempt the course. No contestants challenged Cody before the closing date. The original British Michelin Cup was now known as the British Michelin Cup No. 1 to distinguish it from the new one.

1911 September 17 The first transcontinental flight across the United States began from Sheepshead Bay, New York when Calbraith Perry Rodgers set off on his Wright B biplane, the *Vin Fiz Flyer,* in pursuit of a $50,000 prize for the first person to reach the Pacific coast in 30 days or less but also no later than October 10. The prize was put up by newspaper owner William Hearst in October 1910, and it took 11 months for a competitor to come forward. Rodgers arrived at Long Beach, Calif. on December 10, too late for the money. Along the way, he flew 4,321 mi. in 84 days, of which only 3 days 10 hr. 4 min. was actual flying time.

He had 70 crash-landings out of 82 legs flown and rebuilt the biplane each time, and only a single strut and rudder from of the original machine completed the whole journey.

1911 September 18 The first airplane to fly with two engines and three propellers took off from Eastchurch, England, with Frank McClean at the controls of the Short S.39 Triple-Twin biplane. Although other planes had flown with two engines, this was the first to have three propellers and the first to have a combined pusher-tractor arrangement. The nacelle carried two people with a single, 50-HP Gnôme at the back driving a pusher and a single 50-HP Gnôme in front chain-driving two propellers that rotated in opposite directions to reduce torque. The S.39 had a span of 34 ft., a length of 45 ft. and a maximum speed of 55 MPH. The triple-twin design led to the Tandem Twin concept with single propellers in front and back.

1911 September 19 Studies in aerial photography began at College Park, Md. when an aerial photograph of the flying school was taken from a height of 600 ft. using an unmodified commercial Graflex camera. Later photographs from heights of between 1,500 ft. and 2,000 ft. revealed topographic features of the ground below, adding value to the use of pictures for observation by showing the potential application of mapping duties by air. These pictures were used several years later by the editor of the *Army Navy Register* when the chief signal officer was attempting to encourage broad service support for aerial photography and reconnaissance.

1911 September 23 Veteran aviator Earle L. Ovington became the first American pilot to officially carry mail in the United States when he received a sack containing 640 letters and 1,280 postcards weighing 10 lb. and flew them 3 mi. from Nassau Boulevard, N.Y. to Mineola. This flight drew a reported crowd of 10,000 and made newspaper headlines. On the underside of his wings were the words ''Ovington. U.S. Mail Aeroplane No.1.'' Over the next week, Ovington and his Queen monoplane conveyed a total of 3,993 letters and 1,062 circulars.

1911 September 26 United States Army Lt. Thomas deWitt Milling carried two passengers in a Burgess-Wright biplane for 1 hr. 54 min. 42.6 sec., a new world record. The Burgess-Wright was a license-built Wright Flyer B or C model, designated by the company as Burgess Models F and J, respectively. Lt. Milling had joined the flying group at the signal corps in May and learned to fly at the Wright Flying School in Dayton, receiving his pilot's certificate in July. During World War I, Milling became chief of staff of the air corps.

1911 October 8–November 28 The first major competition was held to select military airplanes for the French army at Montcornet near Reims. The objective was to stimulate manufacturers in their design of military airplanes, specifically a three-seat reconnaissance airplane carrying pilot, copilot and observer. Although 43 manufacturers signed up with 140 airplanes, only 31 manufacturers actually showed up. Nine planes passed preliminary tests, and the army ordered a total of 20. First prize went to a 100-HP Nieuport monoplane, and 10 were purchased at 40,000 francs each; second prize went to a 140-HP Breguet biplane, of which six were ordered, and third prize went to a 100-HP Deperdussin monoplane, of which four were bought.

1911 October 11 The U.S. Army flying school at College Park, Md. began the first military trials of a bombsight and dropping device designed by Riley E. Scott, formerly of the U.S. Coast Artillery. Scott and his telescope-like device were carried into the air by Capt. Thomas Milling in a Wright B along with a set of tables for calculating drop times from a height of 400 ft. Two 18-lb. bombs were carried; on the first try, they missed the 4 ft. by 5 ft. target by 62 ft., then by 32 ft. But by the end of the day, Scott got his bombs within 10 ft. of the target.

1911 October 13 The Italian Army dispatched the first military airplane unit ever sent to a theater of war. Five qualified pilots and six reserve pilots together with two Blériots, three Nieuports, two Farmans, two Etrichs and nine hangars of the Sezione Aviazione formed July 17, 1910, and left Naples for Tripoli, Libya aboard two ships, the *Enrichetta* and the *Sannio.* They had been ordered to North Africa to assist Italian Army units against Turkish forces. The five qualified pilots were Capt. Paolo Piazza, Capt. Riccardo Moiza, Lt. Leopoldo De Rada, Lt. Ugo De Rossi and 2d Lt. Giulio Gavotti. They arrived in Tripoli October 15 where they had to transship airplanes and supplies across a mile of sea on barges and rafts.

1911 October 17 United States Navy Capt. W. I. Chambers wrote to Glenn Curtiss and discussed his ideas for improved propulsion systems for airplanes. Outlining his ideas regarding oil, diesel and turbine engines, he went on to suggest the use of reaction motors that would make practical use of engines that at high velocity expelled atomized particles combusted in a special chamber. This was a direct reference to the physical principles of jet engines, and Chambers suggested that Curtiss should begin development of such a system, asserting that "the aircraft manufacturer who gets in with it first is going to do wonders."

1911 October 17 The first Schutte-Lanz airship, the SL 1, made its first flight before being handed over to the German Army. The Luftschiffbau Schutte-Lanz company had been formed in 1909 at Mannheim-Rheinau by Johann Schutte from Danzig. A successful boat builder, Prof. Schutte designed his airships to be built from wood rather than the steel girder assemblies selected by von Zeppelin. The SL 1 had a capacity of 688,637 cu. ft. and its exterior lines were meticulously designed for optimum streamlining, with a triangular shaped keel running the length of the airship, inside the hull.

1911 October 17 Zee Yee Lee was awarded Royal Aero Club pilot's certificate no.148 after qualifying on a Bristol Boxkite at Salisbury Plain, England. He was the first Chinese national to receive a pilot's license and put the training to good use. Upon returning to Peking (Beijing), he established and became chief instructor at the Nanyuen Military Flying School.

1911 October 23 Capt. Paolo Piazza took off on the first military mission with a powered airplane—a Blériot monoplane (Type XI)—by a participating combatant from Tripoli at 6:19 A.M. He flew five miles to Azizia to spy on Turkish forces and returned by 7:20 A.M. to report he had sighted 150 to 200 men. (The first known reconnaissance flight during a conflict took place on February 12, 1911.)

1911 October 29 Samuel F. Cody won the British Michelin Cup for the longest flight around a closed circuit at Laffan's Plain, England. This year the cup had a minimum qualifying distance of 250 miles, and no other aviator managed even to reach this distance. In his biplane, Cody flew a distance of 261.46 mi. in 5 hr. 15 min., which was also a British endurance record. The cup had a closing date this year of October 31, an indication that race organizers were becoming aware of their responsibilities to prevent flyers from pressing on in wintry conditions.

1911 November 1 Italian pilot 2d Lt. Giulio Gavotti dropped the first bombs dropped in hostile action. The bombs were released on ground targets in the North African campaign against Turkish forces occupying Libya. Four 4.4-lb. Cipelli bombs were dropped, one on Ain Zara and three on the Tagiura oasis. Outraged Turks publicly decried this action, and Prime Minister Giolitti was required to explain why such an act had been allowed. Despite the protests, the Italian aviators continued to bomb targets with hand grenades dropped both from airplanes and from airships.

1911 November 14 Sub-Lt. F. E. T. Hewlett of the Royal Navy received the Royal Aero Club's pilot certificate no.156 after having been coached by his mother, an accomplishment believed to be unique not only in the Royal Navy but in any of the world's naval air services. Early in 1911, Mrs. Hewlett had been the second British woman to pilot an airplane, and shortly thereafter she had flown to a garden party held by the publisher and politician Lord Northcliffe (who was concerned about the progress of German military aviation) to lend her support for aeronautical causes.

1911 November 18 The first British seaplane to leave the water, albeit briefly, and the first seaplane to take off from British waters took to the air at the hands of Royal Navy Comdr. Oliver Schwann from Barrow-in-Furness, Scotland. The airplane, the first of six Avro Type Ds, powered by a 35-HP Green engine, had been fitted with floats after Schwann bought the airplane for £700 from A. V. Roe. The next design initiative after the Roe IV triplane, its wheels were removed and floats designed by Schwann were fitted in their place. The first flight was a brief one, and from 20 ft., the biplane fell back into the water and was damaged. Trials resumed in April 1912.

1911 November 28 Along with one Wright biplane, one Wright-Burgess and two Curtiss pushers, five officers and 20 men left College Park, Md. by train for Augusta, Ga. to take up quarters in their newly appointed winter aviation school. The site of the Augusta school was centered on Barnes Farm, rented by the quartermaster for $15 a month. Officers were quartered in a nearby hotel, and the enlisted men occupied a nine-room house on the farm. Canvas tents protected the airplanes, and sheds served as repair shops with vehicles, horses and mules kept in barns.

1911 December 1 In an attempt to win the Mortimer Singer award (including £500 cash) for the army and the navy pilots who flew the greatest distance with a passenger before March 31, 1912, Lt. A. M. Longmore, Royal Navy, flew a distance of 172 mi. with a passenger in a specially modified Short S.27 biplane. The record flight accomplished by a British Army pilot was achieved on February 14, 1912, in a Nieuport.

1911 December 4 Piloted by Geoffrey de Havilland, the first B.E.1 tractor biplane took off at the Army Aircraft Factory (renamed from the Balloon Factory on April 26, 1911), Farnborough, England. It was the first in a long line of superficially similar B.E. reconnaissance biplanes that would see service up to and throughout World War I. Although the B.E. stood for Blériot Experimental, the French aviator had no hand in the planes design. Blériot was believed to have been the father of the tractor airplane just as Farman was considered the father of the pusher airplane and Voisin the father of the canard (tail-first) airplane.

1911 December 11 A Wright B biplane was shipped from the United States to the U.S. Army base on the Philippines along with Cpl. Vernon Burge and Pvt. Kenneth L. Kintzel four months after Gen. James Allen, chief signal officer, recommended the establishment of an airplane station on the islands. Five more mechanics were picked up in Manila, and at Fort William Mc-Kinley the quartermaster built a hangar for two airplanes at the edge of the polo field. In September 1911, Lt. Col. William A. Glassford, chief signal officer of the Philippines Department, pressed for two airplanes and one aviator, but resources would not stretch that far. Lt. Frank P. Lahm was sent out and on March 12, 1912, opened the Philippine Air School.

1911 December 15 In what may be the first use of antiaircraft fire against airplanes in combat, Turkish forces in Libya used field artillery at maximum gun elevation against Italian aviators operating from Tripoli. The Italians were carrying out photographic reconnaissance of enemy forces and dropping propaganda leaflets and bombs on the enemy.

1911 December 20 Using a Curtiss A-1 pusher seaplane piloted by Lt. Towers, special experiments in radio communication were carried out at Annapolis, Md. by Ens. C. H. Maddox. The tests involved a drum attached to the Curtiss that carried a long antenna unreeled in flight for radio transmission tests. The antenna was found to be totally unsatisfactory, and the signal was too weak for the useful transmission of information military forces might need in wartime.

1911 The great American pilot and pioneer of U.S. naval aviation Eugene B. Ely, was killed in a flying accident. His outstanding contributions to the development of naval aviation during 1910 and 1911 were recognized when, in 1933, he was posthumously awarded the Distinguished Flying Cross. The only monetary benefit he received in recognition for his outstanding contributions was $500 provided by the U.S. Aeronautical Reserve. Ely is remembered most for having made the first flight of a powered airplane from the deck of a warship and for having carried out the first landing on a ship.

1911 During the year, the absolute endurance record had been raised by the French aviator Fournier when he flew his Farman biplane for 11 hr. 1 min. 29.5 sec. at Buc, France. The closed-circuit distance record stood at 449 mi. achieved by A. Gobe in a Nieuport, also at Buc, and Roland Garros flew to a height of 12,828 ft. in his Blériot monoplane with a Gnôme engine. The official speed record was held by E. Nieuport on a Nieuport monoplane at 82.73 MPH.

During 1911, France produced 1,350 airplanes, 1,400 engines and 8,000 propellers and licensed 350 civilian pilots. Most of its products were exported including some to Germany, whose army had, by year's end, 37 airplanes and 30 pilot officers. During 1911, a total 43 people were killed from flying or died from injuries sustained in a crash compared with 24 in 1910, more than the cumulative total up to the end of 1910 when fatalities stood at 33. During the year, first flights were carried out in (chronologically) New Zealand, Peru, China, Madagascar, Korea and the Philippines, bringing to 39 the number of countries where a powered, piloted airplane flight had taken place.

1912 January 10 Glenn Curtiss made the first trials of the world's first flying-boat, the Curtiss Flying Boat No. 1. This was a development of the highly successful series of Curtiss seaplanes, with a long hull mounted under the mainplanes instead of the single float. The engine was situated in the hull forward of the wings and drove two outrigger propellers mounted on the interplane struts through a chain drive system. The crew of two had side-by-side seats in a cockpit aft of the wings, and the tailplane was mounted on spars. The 60-HP, Curtiss, V-8 engine was not

strong enough to get the No. 1 airborne, but the craft did prove that such a development was practical and encouraged Curtiss to continue his research.

1912 January 10 A Short S.38 biplane was flown off wooden planking on the fore-gun turret of the Royal Navy warship HMS *Africa,* the first British airplane flown by a British pilot to take off from a British warship. The S.38 had been flown from Eastchurch to the Isle of Grain by Comdr. Charles R. Samson and then loaded onto a coal lighter from which it was hoisted to the specially constructed deck for the flight. Samson only just cleared the bow of the ship before climbing away to a height of 300 ft. on the flight back to Eastchurch. These tests were part of concerted efforts to raise support for naval aviation in Great Britain.

1912 January 10 The German War Office set up separate training programs for pilots and observers of reconnaissance airplanes operated by the army. Observers no longer needed to get their pilot's license as well as certificates of proficiency in observation from the air. However, they had to be schooled in tactics and to be in a position to make subjective judgments about what they saw and to understand the maneuvers by land forces on the ground below. Germany was worried that France appeared to have a lead in the observation field.

1912 January 20 Glenn Martin delivered a sack of mail by air, taking it from Dominguez Field, Los Angeles to the official postmaster at nearby Compton. The Los Angeles *Tribune* proclaimed, ''Pacific Aerial Delivery Route Number 1 Opened by Glenn Martin.'' Glenn Martin had worked repairing automobiles until news of the Wright brothers tempted him to build a primitive biplane in a rented church. He made hops in this biplane during 1909 and gradually eased his way into air shows and competitions.

1912 January 27 Glenn Curtiss was awarded the first Robert J. Collier trophy at a banquet held by the Aero Club of America in recognition of ''the greatest achievement in aviation in America, the value of which has been demonstrated by use during the preceding year.'' The annual award was established in 1912 by Robert J. Collier, the owner of *Collier's* magazine and a strong supporter of aviation. Given to the leading aeronautical figure of the year, it would be won again in 1913 by Curtiss for his work on the development of seaplanes. This was the only time the same person would receive the trophy in two consecutive years.

Glenn Martin, a pioneer of American aviation, at the wheel of his biplane.

1912 January 31   The first person to be wounded in the air suffered injury from ground fire during a flight in North Africa. Capt. Montu of the Civilian Aviator's Fleet (Flottiglia Aviatori Civili), comprising Italian civilian volunteer pilots, in Tobruk was being piloted by a Mr. Rossi on a bombing mission to an enemy camp at Emme Dauer when he was hit and wounded by Turkish gunfire. Two other military pilots were flying with the civilian aviators, and members from the 1st Squadriglia in Tripoli were there in Henri Farman biplanes. Colonial peacekeeping exercises were rapidly proving the worth of airplanes for aerial reconnaissance.

1912 January   The German General Staff decided to organize operational flying squadrons for military aviation with the aim of having the organization in operation by October 1, 1912. The plan was to establish an instruction school by April 1 and to set up two airfields, one at Metz and the other at Strasbourg. Between April and June, five field flying squadrons were to be established with four airplanes each located at Cologne, Trier, New-Breisach, Saarburg and Metz. The kaiser personally interceded to speed things up and expand the air service and he introduced a plan whereby Germany would have 120 military planes in 20 squadrons.

1912 February 1   Geoffrey de Havilland flew the first B.E.2 from Farnborough, England to Laffan's Plain and back. Following quickly on the B.E.1, the B.E.2 would be adopted as the basis for a long family of Royal Flying Corps scouting and reconnaissance airplanes. The B.E.2 initially had a 60-HP Renault engine and an airframe that was almost identical to its numerical predecessor. It was soon a popular airplane, and in May, de Havilland converted it temporarily into an amphibian, fitting it with a combination of wheels and floats.

1912 February 4   Notwithstanding the increasing awareness instilled in larger numbers of ordinary people that flight required specially designed flying machines, a 33-year-old Austrian tailor by the name of Franz Reichelt jumped from the Eiffel Tower in Paris wearing nothing more than a large cloak. He attempted to fly to the ground from the first platform at a height of 190 ft. His parachute-like device did little to retard his fall, and 5 sec. after jumping from a table placed alongside the rail, he struck the ground and was killed.

1912 February 8   Following discussions with officers from College Park and consultations with Orville Wright on September 11, 1911, the U.S. Signal Corps issued a new specification for two different types of airplane. The single-seat Speed Scout was to be used for strategic reconnaissance, have a 100-mi. radius of operation, a speed of 65 MPH and a 3-hr. endurance. The two-seat Scout was for tactical reconnaissance with a 4-hr. endurance with a speed of 38–45 MPH, depending upon load (up to 600 lb.). Both airplanes had to have ploughed field take-off and landing capability and the ability to glide from 1,000 ft. with a dead engine.

1912 February 14   Lt. B. H. Barrington-Kennett of the British Army, Royal Engineers, won the Mortimer Singer prize of £500 offered to a British Army pilot who could fly the greatest distance before March 31, 1912. Since the flight achieved this day was the longest to that date, it qualified for the prize. To get the prize, Lt. Barrington-Kennett flew 249.5 mi. in a Nieuport monoplane at Salisbury Plain. (See also Dec 1, 1911.)

1912 February 19   One of the most successful pre-World War I airship operations began with the first flight of the Zeppelin LZ 11, *Victoria Louise,* and its introduction into service with the German airship company DELAG. Before the start of World War I, it carried 9,783 people on 489 flights a total distance of 33,755 mi. in 981 hr. of flying time with an average cruising speed of 34.4 MPH. On August 1, 1914, it was handed over to the navy as a training airship for new crews. It was destroyed on October 8, 1915.

1912 February 22   The Fokker Aviatik G.m.b.H. company was entered in the trade register at Berlin with a quoted capital of 20,000 marks. Born in Holland on April 6, 1890, Anthony Herman Gerard Fokker was brought up in Haarlem, the Netherlands and moved to Germany where he developed a passion for aviation before designing his first airplane—the Spider No. 1—in late 1910, in which he carried out a few unspectacular hops. It was followed by a second machine, and Fokker received his pilot's certificate in Spider No.2 on May 16, 1911. Fokker was establishing an expanding reputation for himself at Johannisthal, the mecca of German aviators.

1912 February 22   The first FAI-certified airspeed record in excess of 100 MPH was achieved by Jules Védrines in his Deperdussin powered by a 140-HP Gnôme Double Gamma. The aircraft flew a measured distance of 10 km (6.2 mi.) in 3 min. 43.2 sec. at an average speed of 161.29 km/hr. (100.22 MPH). Védrines broke this record on February 29 and again on March 1, March 2, July 13 and September 9, 1912, setting a record speed of 174.1 km/hr. (108.18 MPH) for the year on the latter date. In doing this, he achieved the greatest number of consecutive absolute FAI-ratified speed records broken by one man; all of these records were set in Deperdussin airplanes.

1912 March 1   Capt. Albert Berry made the first parachute descent from a powered airplane in America when he jumped from a Benoist aircraft that was being flown by the company pilot, Anthony Jannus. The aircraft was flying at a height of 1,500 ft. over Jefferson Barracks in St Louis, Mo., and Berry used a static line parachute. The expanded popularity of flying made parachutes an attractive prospect for passengers and pilots, although little had been done to advance the design of such devices since they had first appeared for use with balloons.

1912 March 11   The secretary of the navy authorized expenditure of "not more than $50" for developing models of helicopter designs proposed by F. E. Nelson of the USS *West Virginia.* The navy's view was that airplanes would have important roles to play when power and performance provided the speed and range to carry out useful duties safely. Nelson, was interested in accelerating that process and sought to encourage development of vertical take-off and landing flying machines, circumventing the need for using planking over gun turrets for long take-off runs.

1912 March 19   The first of the U.S. Signal Corps Scout series capable of meeting a specification issued February 8, 1912, the *S.C. No. 8,* was delivered to Augusta, Ga., by Curtiss pilot Charles F. Walsh. It finally passed all tests at College Park, Md., in May with Lincoln Beachey at the controls. Five more airplanes had been ordered by this time. Three, two from Wright and one from Burgess-Curtiss, were in the Scout category, and two more from the Wright Co. were Speed Scout-class airplanes.

1912 March 29   A law was passed in France formally organizing the military aviation forces into seven companies of balloons and dirigibles, ten "aeronautical" sections of airplanes and one of engineers with their associated equipment and personnel. During the first half of the year, five escadrilles (squadrons) of six airplanes each were established: H.F.1 at Châlons with Henry Farmans, M.F.2 at the de Buc school with Maurice Farmans, B.L.3 at Pau with Blériots, D.4 at Saint-Cyr with Deperdussins and M.F.5 at Saint-Cyr. On July 14 the new aeronautics flag was presented to the aviation forces at Longchamp by President Fallières of France.

1912 March   The British government completed final plans for a thorough overhaul and administrative reorganization of the army and navy aviation groups. A Royal Flying Corps was to be formed, with seven squadrons of 12 airplanes each, staffed by 13 officer pilots and 13 noncommissioned officers. Civilians were to be encouraged to learn to fly and apply for commissions. Serving officers who paid for their own training at a civilian school where they would learn basics would, upon entering a central flying school for advanced instruction, be awarded 75 pounds toward their costs for the elementary lessons. Much of the plan was put together by Col. J. E. B. Seely, under-secretary for war.

1912 April 1   Officers and men at the U.S. Signal Corps' winter aviation school at Augusta, Ga. broke camp and left for College Park, Md. Since arriving at Augusta at the end of November 1911, flights had been carried out on only 58 of the 124 days they were stationed there due to bad weather and other difficulties. Classroom instruction had begun December 11, and all officers attended weekday morning instruction in technical and operational matters. On the course, it was determined that flights at a height of about 5,000 ft. rendered airplanes safe from ground-based small arms fire; it was also determined that 5,000 ft. was the maximum altitude for good reconnaissance.

1912 April 12   In Britain, a white paper was published giving details of the government plan to form a Royal Flying Corps to replace the Air Battalion, Royal Engineers, within which it would become the military wing. The new army expenditure estimates on aviation showed an increase from £131,000 in 1911 to £322,000 in 1912—(still far short of the £880,000 spent by France)—and that 36 new airplanes had been ordered to supplement the 16 already owned by the army. The new RFC would control both land and maritime aviation, the latter through the naval wing, a move universally viewed as a built-in recipe for disaster.

1912 April 13   After a false start on March 15, the French engineer F. Denhaut made a series of successful flights from the Seine River with a new type of flying boat that improved upon the hull design of Glenn Curtiss and that Curtiss would build on and utilize in his own later designs for flying boats and seaplanes. The Denhaut design created a full fuselage hull in which the tail was supported by an upswept rear end and the entire undersurface was stepped for ease in ''unsticking'' the hull from the water. The firm of Donnet and Lévêque, one of whose directors was Lt. de Vaisseau Conneau, took up the design of this small, two-seat biplane with a 50-HP Gnôme rotary and set up manufacturing facilities at Quay de Seine, Argenteuil.

1912 April 16   American aviator Harriet Quimby, the first American woman aviator to receive a pilot's license, became the first woman to fly an airplane from England to France across the English Channel. She flew from Dover to the beach at Hardelot, France at an altitude of between 1,000 ft. and 2,000 ft. and an average speed of 60 MPH. Quimby had ordered a new Blériot, and it was in this machine, powered by a 50-HP Gnôme rotary, that she carried out the flight. Fearing for her safety, Gustav Hamel (who had tested her plane) had offered to don her colorful mauve flying clothes, make the flight for her and land on the

French side at a remote location where she could take over the airplane and claim the achievement.

1912 April 20   Requirements for the rating of military aviator were published in a report by the U.S. secretary of war to the House of Representatives. The new rating had been announced by the U.S. War Department in *Bulletin No. 2* on February 23, 1912. Applicants had to be commissioned army officers, demonstrate their ability to reach an altitude of 2,500 ft., fly in a 15-MPH headwind, carry a passenger to a height of 500 ft., make a dead-stick landing within 150 ft. of a designated spot and conduct a 20-mi. cross-country flight at an average altitude of 1,500 ft. The first military aviator certificates were awarded to Capt. Charles deForest Chandler and Lts. H. H. Arnold and Thomas deWitt Milling on July 5, 1912.

1912 April 21   Fearing that German aviation was flagging behind that of France, Prince Henry of Prussia, brother of the German kaiser, called for a public subscription to raise money for a major program of aviation, mostly military. Appealing to national pride and patriotism, the fund had raised 7.5 million marks within six months, most of which came from industry. As a result of this, technical developments were funded, and prizes were given for aero-engine competitions that attracted no fewer than 44 contending designs, reduced to 19 after the application of qualifying tests.

1912 May 1   Wilfred Parke flew the Avro Type F, the first airplane with a fully-enclosed cabin for the pilot, for the first time from Brooklands Aerodrome, Byfleet, England. The Type F was Avro's first attempt at an airplane that could afford full-weather protection and was the first of its kind in the world. It had a five-cylinder, 35-HP, radial engine, which gave the plane a top speed of 65 MPH. The Type F flew successfully several times before it was damaged beyond repair on September 13, 1912. Its engine is held today at the Science Museum, London, and the rudder is at the Royal Aero Club, London.

1912 May 13   Britain's Royal Flying Corps officially came into existence one calendar month after assent by Royal Warrant. The RFC was divided into five sections: the central flying school at Salisbury Plain; the military wing; the naval wing; the reserve; and the Army Aircraft Factory, Farnborough. Also No. 1 Squadron was formed from the old No. 1 (Airship) Company, No. 2 Squadron from a group of pilots at Farnborough and No. 3

A Bristol Fighter of No. 1 Squadron, Royal Flying Corps, showing off the twin Lewis guns of this robust aircraft.

Squadron from No. 2 (Aeroplane) Company of the air battalion. The naval wing would be separated from the RFC and become the Royal Naval Air Service on July 1, 1914, and the RFC itself would be superseded by the Royal Air Force (RAF) on April 1, 1918.

1912 May 22 The first U.S. Marine aviator, 1st Lt. Alfred A. Cunningham, was assigned to flight instruction at Annapolis. He soloed on August 1, 1912, after 2 hrs. 40 min. flying instruction and became naval aviator no. 5. Lt. Cunningham was followed by 1st Lt. Bernard L. Smith and 1st Lt. William M. McIlvain later the same year and by 1st. Lt. Francis T. Evans in June 1915. 1st Lt. Roy S. Geiger reported to Lt. Comdr. Henry C. Mustin at Pensacola on March 31, 1916, and these five men formed the Marine aviator corps until the United States entered the war with Germany in 1917. All made outstanding contributions to the development of Marine aviation, and Lt. Geiger served with distinction in two world wars.

1912 May 28 Capt. Charles deForest Chandler, commanding officer of the U.S. Signal Corps Aviation School at College Park, Md. received War Department form no. 395 AGO, dated February 2, 1912, which was the first document on U.S. aviation medicine. It dictated that ''all candidates for aviation only shall be subject to a vigorous physical examination to determine their fitness for duty.'' Hitherto, no fitness examination had been required; but Capt. Chandler promptly carried out the new instructions and had all officers on duty and students medically examined. All were found satisfactory for flying duties.

1912 May 30 At 3:15 A.M. stricken with typhoid fever, Wilbur Wright died. His father, Bishop Wright, wrote in his diary: ''An unfailing intellect, imperturbable temper, great self-reliance and as great modesty, pursuing it steadily, he lived and died.'' Two weeks earlier, of the quest for powered flight, Wilbur had written: ''The problem was so vast and manysided that no-one could hope to win unless he possessed unusual ability to grasp the essential points, and to ignore the nonessentials . . . Those who failed for lack of time had already used more time than was necessary; those who failed for lack of money had already spent more money than was necessary; and those who were cut off by accident had previously enjoyed as many lucky escapes as could reasonably be expected.''

1912 June 1 Lt. Hans E. Dons became the first Norwegian to make a flight in a powered airplane in Norway. A submarine officer, Lt. Dons flew a German Start airplane from Horten across Aslo Fjord to Fredrikstad. The Norwegian parliament was suitably impressed and allocated $2,160 for expenses to send four officers to learn to fly in Paris.

1912 June 7 Capt. Charles de Forest Chandler of the U.S. Signal Corps became the first man to carry a machine gun into the air and fire it while the airplane was in flight. Named for its inventor, Col. Isaac N. Lewis of the U.S. Coast Artillery, the low recoil Lewis gun weighed 25 lb. 6 oz. and fired standard rifle ammunition from a 50-round drum adjusted at rates of between 300 and 700 shots/min. Chandler took an early model up in a Wright Model B biplane flown by Lt. Milling, held it against the footrest of the passenger position and fired down toward the ground. Milling flew over a 6-ft. by 7-ft. cheesecloth target three times at 250 ft., and Chandler scored five hits among several near misses.

1912 June 8 The first Aerial Derby around London, sponsored by the *Daily Mail,* was won by T. O. M. Sopwith. Attracting

45,000 spectators, the race was flown around an 81-mi. route starting and finishing at Hendon, with various landmarks on the outskirts of the city as turn points. Although Sopwith completed the course in 1 hr. 23 min. 8.4 sec., Gustav Hamel was declared the winner because Sopwith was believed to have flown inside, rather than outside, one of the markers. After an appeal, the decision was reversed, and Sopwith got the prize. Subsequent derbies were won by Gustav Hamel on September 20, 1913, and by Brock, on June 6, 1914.

1912 June 26 Marking a significant commitment to maritime aviation that would characterize Japanese military flying for 33 years, the Naval Aeronautical Research Committee was established in Japan. The first airplanes purchased for the facilities the committee intended to fund were a single Farman and one Curtiss hydro-airplane. These were flown for the first time by Lts. Kaneko and Kano on November 2, 1912, just a few weeks after the first naval air station opened.

1912 June George Holt Thomas registered the Aircraft Manufacturing Co. Ltd. in England with capital of £14,700. It was more popularly known as the Aircraft Co. in advertisements, or simply Airco. Thomas had acquired the British manufacturing rights for biplanes designed by the Farman brothers in 1911 and for some time was content to build under license. Geoffrey de Havilland joined Airco as chief designer in June 1914, and Airco airplanes were known as D. H. designs until de Havilland formed his own company in 1920.

1912 July 1 The Aviation Battalion of the Italian Army was officially formed under the command of Lt. Col. Vittorio Cordero di Montezemolo. He was to have command of 44 officers, 23 noncommissioned officers and 278 men. Balloons and airships were to remain under the Battaglione Specialisti with 40 officers, 894 petty officers and men, seven civilians and 83 horses. A study of military aviation and its applications prepared by Maj. Giulio Douhet of the Italian General Staff at this time has become a classic text on basic principles and recommendations for an independent air force. Douhet's requirements for airplanes, squadrons and personnel were to stimulate the development of many European air arms.

1912 July 4 The first truly indigenous Sopwith design made its first flight at the hands of Thomas Sopwith. Known as the Sopwith Three-Seater Tractor Biplane, it had Wright-design wings and camber with a streamlined fuselage. It borrowed features from the Burgess-Wright biplane Sopwith had purchased in America during 1911 but was powered by a 70 HP-Gnôme engine driving a 9.5-ft. propeller. The biplane crashed on July 12 but was rebuilt and used later for armament practice at Eastchurch.

1912 July 26 The French inspection permanente de l'aéronautique issued instructions for all military airplanes to display an insignia comprising three concentric circles to aid identification. The 1 m (3.28 ft.) diameter outer circle would be red; next would be a 70-cm (27.5 in.) diameter white ring; and the blue center would be 40 cm (15.7 in.) in diameter. In addition, stripes were to be applied to the rudder, with blue forward followed by white then red. Military airplanes were to bear a letter indicating the manufacturer 30 cm (11.8 in.) tall on both sides of the rudder followed by a serial number 15 cm (5.9 in.) tall.

1912 August 4 In collecting a new Breguet tractor biplane from Douai, France, W. B. Rhodes-Moorhouse, his wife and a friend became the first three people to cross the English Channel in one airplane. They took off from Douai at 6:30 A.M. and flew via

Arras and Boulogne, France to Dungeness, England and then across to a small village near Ashford where they came down in bad weather, crash landing and damaging the Breguet. Rhodes-Moorhouse had learned to fly on a Blériot monoplane and had no experience with biplanes.

1912 August 10 Englishman Francis K. McClean became the first pilot to fly under bridges spanning the Thames River when he took off from Harty Ferry, Eastchurch in Short biplane S.33. He flew up the Thames under each bridge, with the exception of Tower Bridge, where he flew between the footbridge at the top of twin towers and the road span below. Fitted with pontoons, his biplane landed on the water between Westminster and Chelsea Bridges. Permission had originally been granted for Lt. de Conneau to fly from Boulogne and carry out this stunt, but when engine trouble kept him in France, McClean took off at 6:30 A.M. and 90 min. later had satisfied the gathering newsmen. His machine was returned to Eastchurch by road.

1912 August 24 The second appropriation for U.S. military aviation was made with approval for the sum of $100,000. Out of this, four new airplanes would be purchased, and by the end of fiscal year 1913 (June 30, 1913), the Signal Corps was expected to have at least 22, possibly 24, airplanes. It was calculated that annual maintenance costs for each airplane would be $2,500. The FY 1913 sum was $25,000 less than the appropriation for FY 1912, but the larger figure had included funds for 15 new aircraft.

1912 August 28 Three French aviation groups were formed as increasing numbers of military leaders grew concerned at progress being made in Germany toward long-range military airplanes. Groupe I was based at Versailles under the command of Lt. Col. Bouttieaux, Groupe II at Reims under Lt. Col. Breton and Groupe III at Lyon under Lt. Col. Estienne. Lt. Col. Voyer was appointed director of aeronautical material from his headquarters at Chalais, Mendon.

1912 August The Military Aeroplane Competition was held at Larkhill, Salisbury Plain with the object of testing by several competitive trials the performance and resilience of a wide range of flying machines. From England and abroad, 31 entries registered for trials that tested climb rate, gliding ability, fuel consumption, range, speed, landing performance, quick take-off, rough weather performance and rapid assembly. Of the total, only 20 flew, of which all but two were foreign. Samuel F. Cody's biplane powered by a 120-HP Austro-Daimler engine was the overall winner, but the B.E.2 used by Geoffrey de Havilland to ferry officials about was very well liked. The competition was considered an assessment of current airplanes, and no orders were placed as a result.

1912 August In efforts by the protagonists of military aviation to demonstrate the potential use of airplanes as replacements for artillery, Lt. Gaubert of the French Army dropped bombs on ground targets with remarkable accuracy. Twelve bombs out of 15 dropped from a height of 656 ft. landed within a circle 65 ft. 7 in. in diameter and eight out of 15 released from a height of 2,625 ft. landed within a rectangular target 394 ft. by 131 ft. Gaubert used a primitive bomb sight, and the results encouraged further studies by the French War Department.

1912 August The U.S. Army accepted the first of six Burgess H biplane trainers, the first tractor-engined airplanes to enter service with the Signal Corps. The boat builders W. Starling Burgess Co. of Marblehead, Mass. built Curtiss-type pusher seaplanes

in 1910, then put together license-built Wright biplanes and in 1912 came out with designs of their own. Essentially land planes, they were converted to seaplane use by removing the wheels and attaching pontoon floats to the forward skids.

1912 September 6 Capt. Patrick Hamilton and Lt. Wyness-Stuart of the Royal Flying Corps lost their lives when the Deperdussin monoplane they were flying broke up in the air and crashed at Graveley, near Welwyn. The Deperdussin had a 60-HP Anzani engine and had been bought for the army in January. Four days later, Lts. E. Hotchkiss and C. A. Bettington lost their lives when their Bristol-Coanda monoplane plummeted to the ground, fabric ripped from the starboard wing. Romanian engineer Henri Coanda designed the monoplanes built by Bristol. There had been an unjustified suspicion that monoplanes were unsafe, and these two accidents resulted in a ban issued September 14 by Col. Seely, secretary of state for war, on monoplane-flying in the RFC. It was reversed after only five months when technical studies showed monoplanes to be no more dangerous than biplanes.

1912 September 8–12 The German Kaiser Maneuver afforded the German General Staff the opportunity to make determinations about the strength and future requirements of military flying units. As a result of using airplanes in a simulated combat operation with ground troops, cavalry and lancers, the general staff drew plans for 34 Feldflieger Abteilungen (field flying sections), 8 Etappen Flugzeugparke (army aeroplane parks) and locations for 13 Festungsflieger Abteilungen (fortified flying units) for the defense of Cologne, Mainz, Diedenhofen, Metz, Strassburg, Germersheim, New-Breisach, Breslau, Posen, Thorn, Graudenz, Lotzen and Koenigsberg. All this was completed by April 1, 1914.

1912 September 9 The fourth Gordon Bennett air race was held at Chicago because the American aviator Charles T. Weymann had won the previous year and the rules stipulated that the winning country should be the next host. Unfortunately, it was not to be an American victory this time, and the event was a shadow of the 1911 event. All foreign entrants with the exception of France withdrew for different reasons, nobody could be persuaded to put up prize money, and only 1,500 spectators turned up. The three French pilots flew monoplanes—Jules Védrines and M. Prévost flew Deperdussins and André Frey flew a Hanriot. Védrines won with an average speed of 108.18 MPH. No American entry flew although two had been expected.

1912 September 12 Belgian aviators Lt. Nelis and 2d Lt. Stellingwerf carried out air-to-ground firing trials at the Sant Job't Goor airfield with a Lewis machine gun mounted to a Farman F.20, the first biplane built entirely in Belgium. A representative of the American Lewis company arranged to bring one of the new machine guns for the Military Aviation School to test. Intending ground tests only, Commandant Mathieu threatened a court martial when the two aviators attached a Lewis to a Farman and shot to pieces a white sheet that had been placed on the ground! Mathieu and Stellingwerf took the Lewis to England and showed it to the British army, who adopted it for service use.

1912 September 19 Less than two months after its first flight, the Zeppelin airship LZ 13 *Hansa,* operated by the DELAG (German airship company), made the first international flight conducted by a lighter-than-air flying machine. Carrying von Zeppelin and Hugo Eckener, the LZ 13 left Hamburg, Germany and flew to Copenhagen, Denmark to change passengers before flying on to Malmo in Sweden. From there, it returned to Hamburg, completing a total distance of 435 mi. The LZ 13 was taken over by the German army when war broke out in August

The passenger-carrying German airship Hansa *of 1912 was used until 1916 for training air crews.*

1914, and was housed at Duesseldorf before the navy took it over and used it to train airship crews.

1912 September 26 On the closing day of the first Russian competition (which began September 2) to select a military airplane, Igor Sikorsky demonstrated the S.6A tractor biplane before observers and judges at the Moscow Aeronautics Exhibition. Sikorsky had been appointed to head the Russo-Baltic Waggon Factory (RBVZ), and the S.6 with a 100-HP Argus engine was the first airplane chosen for the RBVZ workers to build. It competed against the Sikorsky S.7, a Farman biplane and a Nieuport monoplane during tests held during July and August in St. Petersburg. The head of the RBVZ, Michael V. Shivlowski, had already asked Sikorsky to design a four-engined airplane with a covered cockpit.

1912 October 1 The first major attempt at restructuring German army aviation units got under way. Extra funds were requested and approved for the expansion and improvement of flying units. It was the first step in the remodeling of German military aviation into what would become the German air service. A special budget was requested by the army from the Reichskanzler (Reichs chancellor), and the kaiser approved funds for the sustained enlargement of military aviation. Four Prussian flying battalions and one Bavarian battalion were established.

1912 October 12 Samuel F. Cody won the British Empire Michelin Trophy No. 2 three days before the closing date for 1912. He flew his *Cathedral* biplane fitted with a 100-HP, in-line, Green engine a distance of about 220 mi. around a marked circuit of 186 mi. in 3 hr. 23 min. at an average speed of 64 MPH. The extra mileage was performed when he lost his way and flew too far south. Only the 185 mi. were credited, so the average speed was logged at 55 MPH. Cody won the contest

because nobody else challenged him, so the victory was a hollow one.

1912 October 13 People in the south of England reported having seen a giant German airship in the skies above Sheerness, starting off a wave of concern about the nation's vulnerability to attack from the air. Later examination of its records shows that the German navy's first airship, the Zeppelin LZ 14 (navy number L 1) had made its first flight on October 7 and that it was running up long endurance trials before being commissioned on October 17. On October 13, it was on a 30-hr. flight and may have used Sheerness, the site of the Royal Flying Corps' Naval Wing activity, as a mock military reconnaissance objective.

1912 October 24 Harry G. Hawker won the British Michelin Trophy No. 1, awarded to the British pilot who remained airborne the longest in a British airplane. He flew a Sopwith-Wright biplane, which was extensively modified by Thomas Sopwith from the Howard Wright biplane design he had used during an American tour in 1911. Powered by a 40-HP A.B.C. engine, the single-seat pusher remained in the air for 8 hr. 23 min., securing for Hawker not only the cup and a cash prize of 500 pounds but the British endurance record as well. Hawker had received his Aero Club flying certificate on September 17 after learning to fly at the Sopwith school where he also began a lifelong association with Sopwith.

1912 November 5–13 The first use of airplanes in the United States to direct artillery fire took place in a series of tests in which U.S. Signal Corps airplanes were used to locate targets, provide range and direction to the battery, report on hits per target and provide any necessary corrections. Radio telephony was used to communicate information to the ground, and tests were conducted with an alternative method using handwritten notes dropped over the side as well as a smoke signal method that proved unsuitable. Three officers and eight enlisted men had been sent from College Park, Md. to Fort Riley, Kans., where they conducted aerial observation and artillery support trials.

1912 November 12   The U.S. Navy made the first successful catapult launch of an aircraft from a ship in the Washington Navy Yard. The aircraft was the navy's first seaplane, the Curtiss A-3, and was flown by Lt. Theodore G. Ellyson. The 75-HP, V-8 Curtiss engine was boosted by a powerful compressed air catapult built at the Naval Gun Factory, Washington Navy Yard to plans drawn up by Capt. W. I. Chambers. An attempt to launch the A-3 had been made July 31, but crosswinds caught the seaplane half way along the catapult and tossed it into the Anacostia River without injury to the pilot.

1912 November 18   The U.S. Signal Corps College Park aviation school closed for the winter, the Curtiss airplanes and personnel being sent to the Glenn Curtiss flying school at San Diego while the Wright pilots and planes went to Augusta, Ga. San Diego would become the first permanent home for U.S. Army aviation. By this time, College Park had eight airplanes, eight sheds, 14 flying officers, 39 enlisted men and one civilian mechanic. In all, the Signal Corps had nine airplanes, one of which was in the Philippines. Legislation was introduced May 6, 1913, to buy College Park grounds, but the chief signal officer recommended that the site be given up, and it was, when the lease expired on June 30, 1913.

1912 November 22   The first production airplane built by Thomas Sopwith, the Three-Seater Tractor Biplane first flown in July, was delivered to the British Admiralty by Harry Hawker, having been purchased for 900 pounds by Comdr. Oliver Swann. (Swann had to pay for it out of his own account and claim the 900 pounds as expenses.) Sopwith was eager to shift from sporting flyer to airplane builder, and he appointed his first draughtsman on October 21. By the end of 1912, he had set up the Sopwith Aviation Co. in a disused skating rink at Kingston, Surrey, purchased with money from the sale of the Tractor Biplane. The first major product was Bat Boat flying boat using a hull designed and built by the Saunders Co.

1912 November 27   The U.S. Signal Corps received its first flying boat, the two-seater Curtiss F-Boat. The first of three delivered to the army was actually known as an E-Boat and had a composite hull, but the second and third models had mahogany hulls and were designated F-Boats. Modifications to later models also included a strut from the front engine bearers to the forward fuselage to inhibit forward movement of the engine so that in the event of a crash, the pilot would not be crushed. Seating was a side-by-side arrangement. Many changes were made to the F-Boats during their life, and no two models were exactly the same.

1912 December 5   At the banquet to celebrate the achievements of aviators in the fourth Gordon Bennett Aviation Cup held at Chicago, Jacques Schneider formally announced a special contest to be known as La Coupe d'Aviation Maritime Jacques Schneider, or the Schneider Trophy. Born in January 1879, Jacques Schneider was a wealthy coal baron. Excited by Wilbur Wright's flying in France during 1908, he received his pilot's license in 1911. The trophy would be given each year to the Aero Club that put up the best time across a 150-mi. course. It would be worth £1,000 annually. If any country succeeded in winning the trophy in three out of five years, they would keep it and the contest would end.

1912 December 8   The U.S. Signal Corps established an aviation school at North Island, San Diego, Calif. and paid Glenn

Curtiss $25 per month to sublease some land for that purpose. Quarters comprised an old barn, a shed, a canvas hangar and a lean-to. Officers lived in San Diego, and enlisted men were quartered at Fort Rosecrans. An old motorboat was used to transport men back and forth. The army had airplanes S.C. Nos. 2, 6 and 8, and shortly after establishment the army's first flying boat, *S.C. No. 15* arrived. This airplane was fitted with an early version of the Sperry automatic pilot for flight tests that began February 17, 1913.

1912 December 18   French aviator Roland Garros became the first pilot to bridge two continents in a single flight when he flew his Blériot monoplane from Tunis to Trapani, Sicily, half-way across the Mediterranean from North Africa to Europe. The distance of 177 mi. was over water all the way, and a week after this feat, Garros flew on to Rome, a further 745 mi., half of that over water too. It was from Tunis on December 11 that Garros had achieved the world altitude record of 18,406 ft., which he attained while competing with Georges Legagneux, one of the early Voisin flyers.

1912   The first naval vessel to be commissioned for service use as an airplane-carrying warship was HMS *Hermes,* a British light cruiser that was converted to carry two seaplanes late in the year. Winston Churchill ordered special trials to be held with a folding-wing seaplane, and tests were carried out by Comdr. Charles Samson. The Royal Navy was giving considerable attention to the use of airplanes in war and seriously considered the seaplane not only for reconnaissance but also for torpedo dropping. When war with Germany broke out in August 1914, the English Channel steamers *Empress, Engadine* and *Riviera* were similarly converted.

1912   At the end of the year, the flight duration record was held by the French aeronaut Fornay in a Maurice-Farman biplane powered by a Renault engine. He remained aloft for 13 hr. 22 min., more than 2 hr. longer than the previous record a year before. The record was made at Etampes, as was the distance in a closed circuit held by the same pilot on the same airplane at 631.5 mi. The speed record of 108.18 MPH had been set on September 9. During the year, France produced 1,425 airplanes, 2,217 engines and 8,000 propellers, the Aero Club awarding licences to 469 civilian pilots. For the first time, a British aviator got into the annual record books. Lt. B. H. Barrington-Kennett, adjutant of the RFC, carried a passenger 249 mi. 840 yd. around a closed circuit. The record distance in a straight line was said to be the 217 mi. set by Sgt. Feierstein of the French army with Lt. van den Vaero as passenger in a Blériot monoplane on December 26.

1913 January 1   The U.S. chief signal officer issued new specifications for military airplanes. Among them was the requirement to have the bottom of the fuselage of every scout airplane covered with a chrome steel sheet 0.075 in. thick as protection against small arms fire from the ground. Moreover, there was to be space for instruments and a radio. The airplane engine had to be subjected to a 6-hr. test at the Bureau of Standards in Washington, D.C., and the airplane had to be capable of a 2,000 ft. climb in 10 min. carrying a payload of at least 450 lb. Minimum and maximum speeds were required to be 38 MPH and 55 MPH, respectively and the it had to be possible to assemble the airplane from a crated condition within one hour.

1913 January 1   The two-seat Burgess Model I twin-float seaplane made its first flight powered by a 60-HP Sturtevant engine. The W. Starling Burgess Co. was a boat builder with facilities at

Marblehead, Mass. It began constructing airplanes in 1910 and turned its hand to floatplanes in 1912. The Model I was the first to fly, followed by the Model K on April 16, 1913. The U.S. Navy selected this during May and designated it the D-I, then changed that to the AB-6. The Model H was also purchased as the D-2 (AB-7). It was during 1913 that Burgess severed its connections with the Wright Co., whose airplanes it had been building, and employed the English designer Capt. John W. Dunne, who devised a series of tailless airplanes.

1913 February 8 Russian pilot N. de Sakoff became the first pilot shot down in combat when his airplane was hit by ground fire following a bombing run on the walls of Fort Bezhani during the First Balkan War. De Sakoff who was flying for the Greeks, came down near the small town of Preveza, on the coast north of the Aegean island of Levkas, secured the assistance of Greek locals to repair the damage and resumed his return flight to base. De Sakoff carried six small bombs on the bottom wing of his biplane, attached by lines to his feet. Gently lowering them over the side, he flicked free the slip knot that held the bombs, allowing them to fall to the ground.

1913 February 13 At the second British Aero Show, which opened at Olympia in London, the world's first airplane specifically designed to carry a gun was displayed for the first time. Called the *Destroyer* and built by Vickers, Sons & Maxim, it was officially called the Experimental Fighting Biplane No. 1 (E.F.B.1) and arose from a concept for marrying a 37-mm cannon with a biplane. The E.F.B.1 crashed on its first flight and was replaced by the E.F.B.2 with a more powerful 100-HP Monosoupape Gnôme. In this form, the airplane began tests in October 1913. The E.F.B.2 was the direct ancestor of the Vickers F.B.5 Gunbus, which would serve with distinction in the Royal Flying Corps during World War I.

1913 February 17 Tests with an automatic pilot designed by Sperry began with flight trials of the device installed in Signal Corps airplane no. 15, the first U.S. Army flying boat, at the U.S. Signal Corps flying school on North Island, San Diego. Next day the pilot, Capt. Lewis E. Goodier, crashed the flying boat and sustained a fractured skull. The Curtiss flying boat was rebuilt but crashed a second time on April 8, after which it was written off. The automatic stabilization device was taken to Hammondsport for further development and as finally devised consisted of a double set of gyroscopes controlling ailerons and rudder.

1913 March 2 After two days of traveling from Augusta, Ga. in 11 rail cars, Capt. Charles Chandler, four officers, 21 enlisted men and 5 airplanes arrived at Texas City to support maneuvers near the Mexican border in a show of force following the seizure of power in Mexico by Gen. Victoriano Huerta. Flying began several days later after the equipment had been unpacked and the airplanes assembled. Two more officers from a Palm Beach, Fla. flying school also arrived at Texas City with their airplane, and Capt. Frederick B. Hennessy from the Washington, D.C. Aviation Section chose a suitable campsite close to the waterfront so that floatplanes could also be used.

1913 March 2 The third appropriation bill for U.S. military aviation was approved for the sum of $125,000. In testimony supporting the request, the chief signal officer pointed out that for the 22 airplanes on hand by the end of FY 1914 there were only 14 officers and that because each airplane was a two-seater there would be a shortfall of 30 officers. This did not impress the Congress, who voted to limit to 30 the total number of officers

assigned to aviation duty. It did, however, authorize increasing aviation officers' pay by 35%.

1913 March 5 The first operational unit of the U.S. Signal Corps, Aeronautical Division, was formed as the 1st Aero Squadron under Capt. Charles Chandler. The 1st Aero Squadron was formed at Texas City, Tex. and came under the 2d Infantry Division. It was instructed to patrol the Mexican border to repel troop incursions into the United States, although no combat flying took place because hostilities did not break out beween the United States and Mexico. Nevertheless, the pilot officers complained vigorously of what they considered bad management when they failed to get facilities and logistical support from Washington, D.C. As a result they got the reputation of being undisciplined prima donnas, a complaint that would sour relations between foot soldiers and flyers.

1913 March 31 Two German army majors, Canter and Boehme, successfully flew a long-distance, cross-country flight of 370 mi. from Jueterbog to Luebeck via Kustrin and Stettin in 6 hr. 9 min. A duration record for Germany, this flight was an important demonstration of long-range reconnaissance potential. This led to a special military exercise in the use of airplanes for surveillance over extended distances, and the training of pilots and observers was accelerated. The instruction course now lasted between five and seven months, much less than had previously been the case.

1913 April 1 The British newspaper the *Daily Mail* offered a prize of £10,000 to the first person to fly the Atlantic Ocean. The rules stipulated that contestants depart from a position on the territory of the United States, Canada or Newfoundland and reach Great Britain or Ireland no more than 72 hr. later. Several airplane manufacturers, pilots and enthusiasts became involved, including Curtiss and Cody. The attempt was thwarted by international affairs and abandoned when war broke out in Europe August 3, 1914. Had it not been for that, the Atlantic may have been bridged at least five years before it finally was in 1919.

1913 April 16 The first Schneider Trophy contest for seaplanes was flown over 28 laps of a 6.2 mi. course at Monaco, ending a two-week program of competition flying. French pilot Maurice Prévost won the race in a Deperdussin monoplane powered by a 160-HP, Gnôme rotary engine in an attributed time of 3 hr. 48 min. 22 sec., and official average speed of 45.75 MPH. This included one extra hour spent taking off again and reflying the last lap at the insistence of officials who pointed out that, by alighting on the water 1,600 ft. short and taxiing across the finish line, he had violated the rules. Actual flight time was 2 hr. 50 min. 47 sec. at 61 MPH.

1913 April 16 In France, a decree was issued modifying the organization of military aviation. The escadrilles and groups would henceforth come under the control of army corps commanders in whose region the unit was stationed. Conflict had arisen between those in the army who saw military aviation as merely extending the activities of the ground forces and those who wanted a more independent role for airplanes. This debate was common to all air-faring nations, but no other air units had to put up with such heated contention as the military air arms of France.

1913 April 17 The plucky aviator Gustav Hamel made a nonstop flight from England into the heart of Germany to demonstrate the vulnerability of Britain to aerial assault. Contrived by Great Britain's Imperial Air Fleet Committee formed in February 1913 and newspaper magnate Lord Northcliffe, the event was supported by the London *Standard,* which contributed to the purchase of a two-seat Blériot powered by a 80-HP Gnôme engine. With Frank Dupree as passenger, Hamel flew the Blériot 340 mi. between Dover and Cologne across four countries in 4 hr. 18 min.

1913 May 10   The first aerial bombing conducted in the Western Hemisphere took place when French-born American Didier Masson and Thomas J. Dean, working for the revolutionary Pancho Villa, dropped bombs on a Mexican federal gunboat in Guaymas Bay in the Gulf of California. The Masson bomb was a pipe 18-in. long and 3 in. in diameter with a cap on each end. The nose cap contained a rod, the internal end of which was close to a detonator. The bomb was held on course by vanes and set off when the rod was pushed into the top of the detonator on impact. Special racks with eight bombs packed with dynamite were loaded beneath the airplane. Masson also carried a crude bombsight that Dean used to align the target.

1913 May 13   The first four-engined airplane, the Bolshoi Baltiski (Grand Baltic One) Type B made its maiden flight in Russia. Designed by Igor Sikorsky and built by the Russo-Baltic Waggon Factory (RBVZ), it originated as a giant twin-engined biplane with a span of about 90 ft. and a fuselage 65 ft. long. Powered by two 100-HP Argus engines, it made its first flight during March 1913. The airplane was underpowered, so Sikorsky redesigned it and added two more engines behind the existing pair, each pair driving a single set of pusher propellers. The giant airplane had an enclosed fuselage and a large cabin at the front with glass windows for the crew. It had twin fins and rudders and stood upon a set of wheels under the lower wing.

1913 May 27   Belgian aviators Lts. Soumoy and Moulin carried out impressive reconnaissance flights in front of Belgian King Albert during large scale military maneuvers at Beverloo. In Farman F.20 biplanes, the two aviators did stunning work in support of the military maneuvers and convinced the Belgian army to organize four reconnaissance squadrons, each with four airplanes. Two such units were ready by August 1913 for maneuvers carried out between the Maas and Sambre. For eight days, the airplanes flew back and forth on mock reconnaissance sorties and helped evolve tactics that would be used in the early stages of World War I.

1913 May 30   The French-born American pilot Didier Masson flew his Martin pusher biplane to drop bombs on the Mexican gunboat *Guerrero* from a height of 2,500 ft. Accompanied by Mexican observer, Capt. Joaquin Alcalde, Masson was flying as a mercenary for the rebel armies in Mexico. His pusher was a modified version of a Martin biplane powered by a 75-HP Curtiss engine.

1913 June 10   The French aviator Marcel Brindejonc des Moulinais gave a breathtaking foretaste of what aviation could do for travel when he flew from Paris to Berlin and on to Warsaw (Poland) beween dawn and dusk. Competing for the Pommeroy Cup, awarded to the aviator completing the longest distance between sunrise and sunset, Brindejonc had breakfast in Paris, lunch in Berlin and dinner in Warsaw! He flew on to St. Petersburg in Russia, then crossed the Baltic to Stockholm before going on to Copenhagen, The Hague and Paris by July 2. He had covered 3,100 mi. in 22 days, making only seven landings.

1913 June 15   Easing of political tension between Mexico and the United States resulted in the withdrawal of the 1st Aero Squadron from the border area back to North Island, San Diego, leaving a small detachment of two airplanes, three pilots and 26

men in case of trouble. Deployed in March, this had been the first official U.S. military operation involving airplanes on patrols aimed at monitoring possible insurgency activity from Mexican forces. This group would re-form in April 1914 and return to Mexico for direct involvement in repulsing the rebel leader Pancho Villa.

1913 June 20   In the first fatality in U.S. naval aviation, Ens. W. D. Billingsley was thrown from the pilot seat of the second Wright C-H seaplane, numbered B-2, at a height of 1,600 ft. in turbulent air over Annapolis, Md. His passenger, Lt. J. H. Towers stayed with the airplane and sustained injuries when it hit the water. The Wright seaplane was a modified conversion of the Type B land plane driving two pusher propellers through chains connected to a 60-HP Wright engine. The navy had ordered three from Orville Wright after Wilbur's death in 1912. The performance of these airplanes was seriously impeded by the dated design and configuration of the Wright models.

1913 June 21   The first parachute descent made by a woman from a powered airplane occurred when the American parachutist Georgia "Tiny" Broadwick, who was only 18 years old at the time, descended to Griffith Field, Los Angeles. Pioneer aviator and manufacturer Glenn Martin flew her to 1,000 ft., from where Broadwick jumped, deploying an 11 lb. (5 kg) silk parachute immediately after she left the airplane. Her descent and landing were normal and should have indicated the practicality of the parachute even at this early stage in its development. Sadly, its potential as a life-saving device was to remain unexploited for nearly a decade.

1913 June 23   The first large airplane designed exclusively as a bomber made its first flight in Russia. Known as the Russki Vityaz *(Russian Knight)*, it was designed by Igor Sikorsky and built by the RBVZ. It was essentially a redesigned variant of the Bolshoi Baltiski first flown during May 1913, with four 100-HP Argus engines mounted to the lower wing, each driving tractor propellers. It had a wingspan of 105 ft. and a gross weight of 12,130 lb. with a top speed of 62 MPH. It had a crew of seven and could lift 1,540 lb. The Russki Vityaz was lost with all crew in a freak accident during the 1913 military trials when the Gnôme rotary on a Moller II pusher biplane tore loose and hit the giant bomber.

1913 June 29   Lt. Harold Geiger and about 12 enlisted men left the United States for Hawaii where they set up a U.S. Army flying school with two airplanes—a Curtiss E two-seater and a Curtiss G tractor biplane. The unit arrived at Honolulu July 13 and went to Schofield Barracks; the flying school was eventually set up on Fort Kamemeha. The first flight with the Curtiss E was made on August 8, 1913, and the Curtiss G took to the air on August 28. Violent winds prevented much flying, and the officers were reluctant to risk the airplanes on operational training activities. On November 25, they were packed up in storage, and although brought out for a while in 1914, the unit was eventually returned to the United States.

1913 July 1   An aviation division equipped with Farman F.22 biplanes and based at Soesterberg was established by the Royal Netherlands Army. Dutch interest in aeronautics had begun as early as 1886 when a special balloon unit was formed for artillery observation and gun spotting. In 1911, airplanes were integrated with army exercises in an attempt to quantify the value of powered flying machines in military operations. (The naval aviation arm was founded on August 18, 1917.)

1913 July 8 One of the most complex and exacting set of rules for a context was satisfactorily followed by the English aviator Harry Hawker when he won the Mortimer Singer prize and £500 for an all-British amphibian. Using the Sopwith Bat Boat, Hawker had to execute six return flights between a point on land and a point on water, alighting at each point before resuming his journey, the entire sequence to be completed within 5 hr. On one flight, the amphibian had to reach a height of 1,500 ft. and at least 750 ft. on the others. Watched by members of the Royal Aero Club, Hawker accomplished all requirements.

1913 July 15 Franz Schneider, an airplane designer with the German firm of Luft-Verkehrs Gesellschaft M.L.H. (L.V.G.), patented the design for a gun-synchronizing gear that would enable the gunner to fire through the moving propeller arc of an airplane in flight without shattering the blades. Schneider had designed a gun mechanism in 1912 that would fire through the hollow propeller shaft, but the synchronizing gear allowed the gunner to fire forward without the complexity of an integral engine-gun system. At the end of 1914, Schneider designed the L.V.G. EI monoplane, the first German airplane fitted with a fixed, synchronized gun for the pilot and a manual machine gun on a ring mounting for the observer.

1913 July The German airplane manufacturing company of Pfalz Flugzeug-Werke was established and financed by the Bavarian government to ensure some measure of control over the companies building military airplanes for the army. The Eversbusch brothers Alfred, Walter and Ernst ran the Pfalz factory at Speyer am Rhein and produced the first airplane, a pusher biplane fitted with a 100-HP Rapp engine. Then the brothers got a manufacturing license for the Morane-Saulnier monoplanes, which, with Oberursel engines, became the AI and AII, used for reconnaissance work when war broke out in August 1914.

1913 August 7 In a modified version of his Cathedral biplane with which he won the 1912 Military Trials at Laffan's Plain, England in 1912, Samuel F. Cody and his passenger W. H. B. Evans were killed when the front spar on the lower wing of his Hydro-biplane broke at a height of 200 ft. and they were thrown out of the airplane. Built for Cody to compete in the *Daily Mail* £5,000 round-Britain seaplane race, the airplane was the biggest of Cody's designs, with a span of 59.5 ft., a length of 40.75 ft. and a wing area of 770 sq. ft. It was powered by a 100-HP Green engine and had a single, four-step float with two outriggers under the inboard interplane struts.

1913 August 16 The first major British seaplane competition was sponsored by the *Daily Mail* newspaper for a flight around Britain by a British airplane starting and finishing at Southampton. Four aircraft were entered for the 1,540 mi. round-trip, that had to be completed within 72 hrs. The only starter was Harry Hawker, who crash-landed his Sopwith biplane at Dublin after completing only 1,043 mi. in about 22 hr. For his effort he received £1,000 in compensation.

1913 August 20 French aviator Adolphe Pégoud carried out the first parachute descent ever made whereby the parachute was deployed before the pilot left the airplane. Flying a very old and un-airworthy Blériot monoplane powered by a five-cylinder, Anzani engine, Pégoud took off and staggered to an altitude of 700 ft. attached to a special parachute designed to be deployed from a box. Pégoud shut down the motor, pushed the stick forward and deployed the parachute. When safely inflated, it pulled him away from the Blériot and deposited him in tree tops while the airplane gently glided down to a perfect landing. The device proved impractical and was never developed.

1913 August 23 Léon Letort carried out the first nonstop flight between Paris and Berlin when he flew his Morane-Saulnier monoplane fitted with an 80-HP Le Rhône engine the 560 mi. between the two capitals in 8 hr. His attempt had been preceded in August 1912 by the first Paris-Berlin flight made in only two stages when Edmond Audemars had flown his Blériot monoplane along that route. The Le Rhône used by Letort had seven cylinders and was beginning to topple the monopoly on rotary engines held by Gnôme. Letort did not live to savor his victory and was killed shortly after this flight when an engine crushed him beneath his airplane.

1913 August 30 American inventor Lawrence B. Sperry successfully demonstrated the first gyroscopic automatic stabilizing device for powered airplanes when Lt. Patrick N. L. Bellinger piloted a U.S. Navy flying boat designated C-2 and relinquished full control to the autopilot. Basically an early production Curtiss flying boat with increased span on the upper wing, the C-2 was stabilized in pitch and yaw while the pilot flew hands-off for extended periods. The navy was interested in devising ways an airplane could be flown automatically while the pilot attended to other duties, such as operating reconnaissance cameras for instance.

1913 September 2 Flying a Blériot monoplane from the Juvisy airfield, Adolphe Pégoud became the first pilot known to have flown his airplane in sustained inverted flight. Instead of rolling his wings over until the airplane was upside down, he pulled up in a half-loop until the Blériot was inverted, remaining thus for several minutes. Then Pégoud completed the loop to return his airplane to a wings-level, head-up attitude. Pégoud had prepared for the flight by having his airplane mounted on a trestle upside down, allowing him to experience the sensation before the attempt.

1913 September 7 Affronted by the reports in French newspapers that the Paris-Berlin nonstop flight made by Léon Letort on August 23, 1913, demonstrated the superior state of French aviation, Alfred Friedrich flew from Berlin to Paris in a Taube built by Igor Etrich and powered by a 100-HP Mercedes engine. Friedrich was on his way to London, and the Paris stop was in answer to popular conceptions throughout Europe about French aviation. Germany was increasingly aware of the importance of aviation for extending national prestige across international boundaries and encouraged its pilots to use every opportunity for making news headlines in this way.

1913 September 9 The Zeppelin LZ 18, the largest airship built before the start of World War I, made its first flight. Bearing the German navy designation L 2, it was 518 ft. long and 54.5 ft. in diameter, had a volume of 935,500 cu. ft. and was powered by four 180-HP, Maybach, six-cylinder motors giving it a top speed of 49 MPH. It had a cruising range of 652 mi. and could lift just over 12 tons. Delivered to the Johannisthal airfield outside Berlin on September 20, it made nine test flights for the navy before plunging to the ground in flames, killing 28 people on October 17, 1913. Count von Zeppelin became discouraged in airships and turned his personal attention to large airplanes.

1913 September 9 Lt. Petr Nikolaevich Nesterov of the Imperial Russian Army became the first pilot to fly his airplane in an uninterrupted loop when he took off from Syretzk aerodrome and flew his Nieuport Type IV monoplane in what until then had been thought an impossible maneuver. The Nieuport was powered by a 70-HP, Gnôme rotary engine and had been one of several built at the Dux factories in Moscow in a license deal arranged with the parent firm in France. Nesterov was severely disciplined for having carried out what was thought to have been a foolish maneuver. The pilot became one of Russia's leading aces during World War I, and a town was subsequently named for him.

1913 September 18 One of the most successful British airplanes ever built made its first flight when the prototype Avro 504 was flown for the first time. Construction had begun during April, and the completed airplane was taken to Brooklands for its initial flight trials. Evolved from the Avro 500, first flown in 1912, the 504 was initially powered by a 80-HP Gnôme rotary. On September 20, 1913, it took fourth place in the second British Aerial Derby when F. P. Raynham averaged 66.5 MPH around 94.5 mi. course in 1 hr. 26 min. 1 sec. By the end of World War I in 1918, more than 8,300 504s had been built and the type would serve on in many air forces and in numerous civilian roles well into the 1930s.

1913 September 23 The French aviator Roland Garros became the first pilot to cross the Mediterranean Sea nonstop when he flew from a beach location at Fréjus near the French seaside town of St. Raphaël 500 miles across the sea to the French naval base at Bizerte, Tunisia on the coast of North Africa. Garros left Fréjus in his Morane Saulnier monoplane just after dawn and 7 hr. 53 min. later arrived in Africa with just enough fuel for 12 min. of flying. He landed 37 mi. from where he planned, missing Tunis. Garros wore a rubber tire round his waist for buoyancy and carried a red cloth tied to a fishing rod to wave at passing ships in case he ditched in the Mediterranean.

1913 September 29 The fifth Gordon Bennett race was run from Bétheny airfield near Reims, France with four contenders, of whom three were French and one was Belgian. Emile Védrines, brother of the 1912 cup winner, was there, but the speed winner was Maurice Prévost who became the first pilot to officially exceed 200 km/hr. with an FAI-acknowledged run averaging 203.85 km/hr. (126.7 MPH). All contenders flew Deperdussin monoplanes except Védrines, who elected to use a monoplane designed by Alfred Ponnier, formerly of the Hanriot airplane works but now an independent constructor. The one would-be American entrant, Norman Price, was too late to enter. The great benefactor of French aviation, Armand Deperdussin, president of the Aéro Club de France, Knight of the Legion of Honor, on whose airfield the race was run had been arrested August 5 for fraud. This was the last of the famous Gordon Bennett air races before World War I; the next took place in 1920.

1913 October 7 The U.S. navy secretary appointed Capt. W. I. Chambers to head a board of inquiry about the future of naval aviation. The board published its conclusions after two weeks and made a number of important recommendations: Naval aviation should be expanded and integrated into standard fleet practices as quickly as possible; Pensacola, Fla. should be made the navy air training center; a program of operational tests within the fleet should be instituted in order to develop standard operating procedures for aviation in the fleet environment; and $1.3 million should be appropriated for the coming year.

1913 October 13 An aerial derby around Manhattan Island was held as stimulus to American aviation. Sponsored by the Aeronautical Society, a splinter group from the Aero Club of America, it was financed with $2,250 in prize money from the *New York Times* newspaper. Five contenders flew the course, which began at Oakwood Heights and took them around Manhattan and back to Staten Island. More than 4,000 people watched the race in a powerful west wind as one by one the aviators flew out. William S. Luckey won in his Curtiss pusher, putting up a time of 53 min. 6 sec., with Charles F. Niles, in another Curtiss, taking second place in 55 min. 5 sec.

1913 October 15 Germany spent 300,000 marks on competitions aimed at significantly improving long-distance flight records. Prizes were awarded for the best flights up to October 31. Incentive prizes were awarded for a flight of 1,000 km (621 mi.) in a single day. Pilots Schlegel, Caspar, Thelen, Dastner, Geyer and Stiefvatter all exceeded the 1,000 km target. This was a major encouragement to proponents of military aviation and spurred airplane manufacturers to develop more efficient machines, thus securing greater laurels for their designs—and more orders.

1913 November 6 The British Michelin Cup No. 1 was won by R. H. Carr when he flew 315 mi. in a Grahame-White Charabanc to claim the £500 prize. Rules this year stipulated a continuous flight back and forth between Brooklands and Hendon with a compulsory stop of 5 min. at the end of each third journey. Qualification required a minimum flight distance of 300 mi. between 7:00 A.M. and 1 hr. after sunset. Harry Hawker made an attempt on October 31 but became ill after 11 laps and 220 mi.

1913 November 18 The best attempt to claim the British Michelin Cup No. 2 was carried out when Harry Hawker flew his Sopwith biplane a distance of 265 mi. in 5 hr., 32 mi. short of the qualifying distance of 297 mi., around a cross-country circuit. Contestants were required to compete by November 30. The only other contender, R. H. Carr, battled against fierce and gusty winds to fly a mere 140 mi. in 5 hr. 10 min. at an average speed of 27 MPH. A second attempt was made by Hawker on November 27, but fog turned him back. The cup was left unclaimed when the expiration date came and went without further improvements on performance.

1913 November 24 Lincoln Beachey stunned crowds in California when he looped his airplane over San Diego Bay, capping a reputation as America's greatest aerial exhibitionist. Beachey had been born in 1887 and operated small airships for Thomas Baldwin before moving on to Curtiss pushers and gaining his aviator's certificate in 1911. His most breathtaking speciality was to cut his engine at 5,000 ft. and dive headlong toward the ground, pulling out at the last minute to execute a perfect landing. He also made a display out of racing his airplane against cars, most notably against American automobile ace Barney Oldfield.

1913 December 4 Although the 1st Aero Squadron of the U.S. Signal Corps had been functioning since March when they were part of the forces dispatched to Texas City, the army formally prescribed for the first time on this date the provisional organization. Consisting of 20 officers, 90 men, eight airplanes and some tractors and motorcycles, it was officially approved by the chief signal officer on January 7, 1914. The squadron was commanded by Capt. Arthur S. Cowan with Lt. Roy C. Kirtland as adjutant and supply officer. The first company was under Lt. Benjamin D. Foulois and included Lts. George A. Dodd, William C. F. Nicholson, Joseph C. Morrow Jr., Fred Seydel and Douglas B. Netherwood with four Burgess tractor airplanes; the second company was under Lt. Walter R. Taliaferro, with Lts. Lewis E. Goodier Jr., Hollis LeR. Muller, Robert H. Willis Jr.,

Joseph E. Carberry, Henry B. Post, and Edgerly with four Curtiss airplanes.

1913 December 11 The Sikorsky Ilya Muromets made its first flight at Komendantski airfield outside St. Petersburg but stalled and crashed-landed, incurring damage that took five days to repair. Named after a 10th-century hero of Russian folklore, the I.M., as it became known, was designed from the combined experience of the Bolshoi Baltiski and the Russki Vityaz to be the largest airplane built by the RBVZ. It had a wing span of 113 ft., a fuselage length of 67 ft. and four 100-HP Argus tractor engines. Designed as a passenger-carrying airplane, it had a promenade deck on top of the enclosed cabin area and a rounded, glass-fronted nose.

1913 December North Island, San Diego, Calif. was designated by the U.S. Signal Corps as the army aviation school. Aeronautics, meteorology and their attendant secondary subjects were to be taught by a staff of assigned instructors consisting of 20 officers. There was to be an experimental element to the school that was to investigate new applications and equipment for military aviation, to include, initially, bombing and bomb sights, the detection of minefields and the potential military uses of parachutes. Ground training would supplement flying training, and visiting scientists from the Smithsonian Institution would be assigned to various classes.

1913 During the year, the French aviator Fournier extended the world duration for a piloted, powered airplane to 13 hr. 22 min. at Etampes in a Maurice-Farman biplane powered by a Renault engine. For distance in a closed circuit, A. Séguin took the record in his Henri Farman powered by a Gnôme rotary engine when he remained airborne for 634 mi. between Paris and Bordeaux and back on October 13. Letort took the straight-line distance record of 568 mi. from Paris to Berlin in his Morane-Saulnier with a Le Rhône engine. The altitude record went to G. Legagneux in a Nieuport, again powered by a Le Rhône, when, carrying oxygen, he reached 20,014 ft. on December 28 at St. Raphaël in the south of France. Speeds had increased to the record 127 MPH achieved by Prévost September 29, and engine power was increasing toward the 200 HP mark.

1913 In the first decade of powered flight with winged airplanes, remarkable progress had followed in the wake of the Wright brothers. But it was the end of an age. It was the last full year of peace, and from now on, airplanes would fight each other in aerial battles that would be but a prelude to an era of sophisticated war machines. Aviation had blossomed to enormous proportions between 1911 and 1913; the greatest progress and advancement had been made in France. In 1911 France produced 1,350 airplanes and 1,400 engines; in 1912 it produced 1,425 airplanes and 2,217 engines; and in 1913, it produced 1,148 landplanes, 146 seaplanes and 2,440 engines—in three years, 4,069 airplanes and 6,057 engines.

1914 January 1 The world's first scheduled airplane passenger service operated by an airline company—the Airboat Line—began at 10:00 A.M. when Anthony Jannus flew his first passenger from St. Petersburg to Tampa, Fla. The aircraft was a two-seat Benoist Type XIV flying boat of the Benoist Co. powered by a 75-HP Roberts or a 70-HP Sturtevant, six-cylinder, in-line engine driving a pusher propeller. The fare for the 22-mile over-water flight was $5 with a surcharge if the passenger weighed more than 200 lbs. The service made two trips every day but closed after only a few months of running because it was uneconomic.

The Airboat Line carried 1,205 passengers and flew 11,000 mi., and only 18 flights were cancelled due to bad weather.

1914 January 7 The first of two mandatory U.S. Signal Corps orders relating to aviation at the San Diego flight school was issued as general order no. 1. It stipulated that "officers, enlisted men and civilians on duty at this school will under no circumstances give out for publication any information concerning the work of the school. Such information as is considered proper for publication will be given out by the Commanding Officer." General order no. 2, issued January 15, 1914, required everyone connected with the school to wear a protective flying helmet and a leather flying coat over land or flotation jackets over water.

1914 January 20 The U.S. Navy moved its aviation unit from Annapolis, Md. to Pensacola, Fla. This was the first U.S. naval air station to be established and was intended to form the center of naval aviation training, a role that it fulfills to the present day. The initial complement of the school consisted of nine officers and 23 enlisted men to operate and maintain seven aircraft, and the unit was commanded by Lt. J. H. Towers.

1914 January The Chinese Army Air Arm was formed with the establishment of the first Chinese flying school at Nan Yuan. The school used as its initial equipment several Caudron biplanes that had been ordered from the French in 1913. Army personnel were carefully selected for flying instruction and were trained by a staff headed by American pilot Art Lym. Several American and European pilots had visited China since the first flight in that country during February 1911, but very little indigenous industry was developing and all the airplanes flown in China were of foreign origin.

1914 February 12 Igor Sikorsky piloted the Ilya Muromets four-engined biplane to a height of almost 1,000 ft. carrying 15 passengers and Sikorsky's dog, Shkalik. The total payload lifted by the giant airplane was about 3,000 lb., a significant performance for the period and one that duly impressed Czar Nicholas II when he inspected the machine at the Krasnoye Selo military parade later in the year. The czar was shown around the airplane by Igor Sikorsky, who had adorned the rounded nose of the airplane with the motif of the Russian Imperial eagle. Nicholas II ordered it to be built for the Imperial Russian Air Service as a long-range bomber.

1914 February 14 An official American nonstop duration and distance record was made when Lt. Townsend Dodd and Sgt. Herbert Marcus flew the U.S. Signal Corps Burgess H tractor biplane *(S.C. No. 26)* 244.8 mi. in 4 hr. 43 min. Although established as a record for two people in one airplane, it also exceeded the previous single-seat record. The flight took place from the Signal Corps aviation school at North Island, San Diego. Two days later Lts. Joseph E. Carberry and Walter R. Taliaferro established a new U.S. Army altitude record of 8,800 ft. in airplane *S.C. No. 23*.

1914 February 23 Glenn L. Martin demonstrated his new patented parachute at the U.S. Army aviation school at North Island, San Diego. The pack-type parachute was far ahead of anything else and significantly in advance of Army purchases (it was 1917 before the Signal Corps took serious steps to equip its pilots with the safety device). Accompanied by Lt. Hollin Muller and Charles Broadwick, Martin ascended to a height of 1,150 ft., at which point Broadwick jumped to execute a perfect descent. Tests were completed by September, and the army was invited to purchase parachutes, each one of which would be demonstrated by Broadwick. There is no record that any were bought.

1914 February 23 The Bristol Scout A biplane was delivered to Larkhill, England for its first flight, piloted by H. R. Busteed. Designed by Frank Barnwell, the Scout was a converted monoplane originally designed for Bristol by Henri Coanda. The fuselage had been built by Bristol as part of a bid by the British company to build Caproni airplanes under license. Barnwell adapted the redundant Coanda fuselage and married it to biplane wings, producing an airplane capable of high-speed scouting duties with a top speed of around 100 MPH. Although the Royal Flying Corps equipped several squadrons with the type, it was not a favorite with pilots, and by August 1916 it was struck off the operational list.

1914 March 16 The fifth British Aero show was opened at Olympia, London by H M King George V, king of England. Of the 25 complete airplanes on display, nine were seaplanes, floatplanes or flying boats. Sopwith showed off a Gunbus and soon received an order from Greece for six fitted with machine guns. Supermarine showed off the P.B.1 flying boat designed by Noel Pemberton Billing who in 1912 set up a boat building site at Woolston, Southampton. He chose the word ''Supermarine'' as his telegraphic address since it was the antonym for ''submarine'' and epitomized his dream of flying over the water instead of through it. The only British monoplane at the show was the Blackburn I, first flown in August 1913.

1914 March 23 The Royal Siamese Flying Corps was created by the chief of the Siamese general staff, the prince of Piscnoulok, on the return of three Royal Siamese Army Engineers from France with a favorable report on the potential for military flying machines. While in France, the three men had received flying training, and they brought eight French aircraft back to Siam to form the core of the fledgling service. This was one of the first serious attempts in the Far East after China to equip armies with flying machines.

1914 April 17 Riley E. Scott began official U.S. Army tests with his bombsight and dropping mechanism first tried on October 10, 1911. Preparations had been under way since June 1913 when the Ordnance Department agreed to manufacture special bombs. Scott arrived at North Island April 7, 1914, and the first test involved a Burgess-Wright tractor piloted by Lt. Townsend Dodd. A large number of tests with 15-lb. dummy bombs were made from between 900 ft. and 2,000 ft. This first series of tests ended when the airplane was ordered to Galveston, Tex. to be replaced by a Martin biplane suitably modified.

1914 April 20 Howard Pixton won the Schneider Trophy seaplane race for Britain flying a Sopwith Tabloid around the 28-lap Monaco course in 2 hr. 13 sec. at an average speed of 86.78 MPH. Pixton flew a special, single-seat Tabloid with floats and a 100-HP Gnôme Monosoupape rotary engine. Entrants from France, Germany, Britain, Switzerland and the United States registered for the race, but the Americans did not fly. Second place went to the Swiss Ernest Burri in an FBA (Franco-British Aviation Co.) flying boat. He alighted once and completed the course in 3 hr. 24 min., the only other contender to go the full distance. Pixton completed an extra two laps to average 86.6 MPH over 300 km (186.4 mi.), a new seaplane record.

1914 April 21 By decree of the French Ministry of War, the Directorate of Military Aeronautics was set up under the direction of Gen. Bernard. The Permanent Inspectorate of Aeronautics had

been abolished on February 12, 1914, and separate technical inspectorates were instituted for aerostation and aviation. On February 21, the Directorate of Aeronautic Materiel was abolished, and each of its sevices became autonomous under separate titles: the central aerostation materiel establishment, the laboratory of aerology and telephotography, the aviation manufacture service, the aeronautical laboratory at Chalais-Meudon and the aviation laboratory at Vincennes.

1914 April 21 The first news movie shot from the air was filmed by a cameraman from Warwick Bioscope Chronicle Film, England. He was taken up by B. C. Hucks at 11:00 A.M., 30 min. after King George, aboard his royal yacht, HMS *Victoria and Albert,* left Dover to cross the English Channel for Calais, France. Hucks flew down to within 400 ft. of the yacht and its escorts, circling Calais as the boats berthed, before landing at the local airfield to receive a bouquet from the mayor as the first Englishman to land at the town. With the exposed film strapped to the passenger seat, Hucks sped back alone, landing at Hendon at 2:35 P.M., covering the 125 mi. in 1 hr. 50 min. The film was rushed to Charing Cross Road, London, where it was developed and taken to the Coliseum moving picture theater by 4:45 P.M., in time for the 5:20 P.M. news.

1914 April 25 The U.S. Navy carried out its first operational airplane mission when Lt. (jg) P. N. L. Bellinger flew the AB-3 flying boat on a visual reconnaissance mission of the city of Vera Cruz, Mexico and of possible mine fields in the harbor area. This activity was repeated on April 28 when Lt. Bellinger and Ens. W. D. LaMont photographed the harbor from their Curtiss AB-3. This was essential to intelligence data about possible troop activity in the town and mines that could threaten U.S. warships if a landing was necessary.

1914 April Anthony Fokker tested his M.5, progenitor of the German fighter that would dominate the Western Front in World War I between mid-1915 and mid-1916. There were two versions; the M.5L (suffix ''lang,'' or long) had a longer wing span than the M.5K (''kurz,'' or short), which was the first to fly equipped with a 50-HP Gnôme rotary. Stimulus for the design of the M.5 series came from the French Morane-Saulnier monoplanes, which had greatly impressed Fokker from the time he saw the machine used by Léon Letort to fly from Paris to Berlin in July 1913. Fokker went to Paris and by early 1914 had purchased cheap a Morane-Saulnier that he returned to Germany and copied.

1914 May 2 Piloted by Lt. (jg) P. N. L. Bellinger and carrying Ens. W. D. LaMont, the Curtiss AB-3 flying boat from the warship USS *Mississippi* flew the first U.S. Navy mission in support of ground operations. Asked by the marines to locate attacking Mexican troops near the U.S. camp at Tejar, the two aviators flew on a reconnaissance sortie to help direct ground fire. This was the first use of U.S. military airplanes in a coordinated air-ground operation involving naval forces offshore. It was to serve as a further reminder to the secretary of the navy that aviation had an important part to play in combat support.

1914 May 6 Ground fire hit the Curtiss AH-3 seaplane, flown by Lt. (jg) P. N. L. Bellinger with Lt. (jg) R. C. Saufley as observer, as they flew across the Mexican town of Vera Cruz on a reconnaissance flight. This was the first time a U.S. military airplane had been hit by rifle fire, although the damage done was slight and the airplane safely made it back to the USS *Mississippi.* By May 19, the need for reconnaissance activity had diminished to the point that the aviators could stand down prior to returning to their base at Pensacola, Fla. These displays of aerial support endorsed the formation of the office of naval aeronautics in the operations division under the secretary of the navy.

1914 May 9   H. Newell made the first parachute descent from a powered airplane over Britain when he jumped from a Grahame-White Charabanc 2,000 ft. over Hendon. The plane was flown by R. H. Carr accompanied by F. W. Gooden, who was seated on the lower wing, and Newell was seated in a rope sling seat attached to the port undercarriage and was holding his parachute rolled up in his lap. The 40-lb. parachute was 26 ft. in diameter unfurled, and it was the product of a series of experiments Newell had made from towers and balloons. Newell was encouraged to jump by a push from Gooden's foot, making a gentle descent to the fields below which took 2 min. 22 sec.

1914 May 15   Canada's first passenger to travel by air between cities did so by flying from Toronto to Hamilton in a Curtiss flying boat named the *Sunfish*. The pilot of the historic flight was Theodore Macaulay, who made the return flight during the same day. The name of the passenger on these flights is not known.

1914 May 17   A series of grueling cross-country air races involving 26 German contestants began in Germany, watched by Capt. W. Henderson of the British Royal Navy and Lt. Col. A. Russell of the British Army. Known as the Prince Henry Circuit, it involved a circuit with stages totaling more than 6,000 mi. to be completed in six days. When four airmen were killed, the Germans considered they had lost their lives in action and the race continued with added fury. The British observers were impressed with the German enthusiasm for flying and with the large numbers of applicants for flying lessons.

1914 May 23   Celebrated British aviator Gustav Hamel disappeared over the English Channel and was presumed drowned. The son of a well-known English surgeon, Hamel gained his flying license in France on February 3, 1911. He had gone to Paris to collect a new Morane-Saulnier racing monoplane with an 80-HP Gnôme Monosoupape engine, which he intended to enter in the Aerial Derby. Hamel left Hardelot at 12:15 P.M. after flying up from Villacoublay and stopping for breakfast at Crotoy. The Royal Navy sent a flotilla of ships to search for him, but nothing was ever found.

1914 May 25   The first fatal collision between two machines of the Royal Flying Corps resulted in the death of Capt. E. V. Anderson and his passenger Air Mechanic Carter when their Sopwith three-seater biplane was accidentally rammed by Lt. C. W. Wilson in another Sopwith of the same type. Wilson was returning from Brooklands and descending to land at Farnborough when he struck the other Sopwith, which was climbing away from the airfield on a familiarization flight. Wilson escaped with bruises and a broken jaw. Both machines and all three airmen were from No. 5 Squadron, RFC.

1914 May 28   Glenn Curtiss successfully flew the refurbished Langley *Aerodrome* for a distance of approximately 150 ft. at Keuka Lake, Hammondsport, N.Y. The *Aerodrome* had made its first flight attempts in 1903 from a converted houseboat on the Potomac. Several innovative improvements had been applied, including some that were patent designs from the Wright brothers. When the *Aerodrome* made a second short flight on June 5, 1914, Lorin Wright, Orville's brother, infiltrated the Curtiss camp and gathered evidence for a court hearing on Curtiss' patent infringements.

1914 June 1   An aviation department was set up in the German War Ministry with a view to expanding military aviation by mobilizing large numbers of reconnaissance and bombing airplanes should hostilities break out. The department examined German industry and in one of the first major studies of air expansion plans laid down procedures and channels of supply for materials and men in the event of war. The German High Command was convinced that aviation would play a leading, perhaps decisive, role in modern war. It used the department to draw up a schedule of requirements, including the need for more airplanes.

1914 June 4   The first fatal accident to a British seaplane resulted in the death of Lt. T. S. Cresswell and Comdr. A. Rice of the Royal Navy. Ascending from the Calshot Air Station the Short S.128 seaplane they were flying flew over a motorboat on Southampton Water where Short's test pilot Gordon Bell and Lt. Spencer Grey were watching the flight. At a height of just over 200 ft., the seaplane appeared to break up in the air and plummet to the sea, killing both occupants. Some witnesses said they believed that the seaplane stalled and that the wings folded up as the structural limits were exceeded.

1914 June 6   Armored airplane prototypes were displayed to French Gen. J. J. C. Joffre. The prototypes included a new Voisin powered by a 100-HP Canton-Unne engine and carrying a 37-mm gun. Other armored airplanes displayed included a parasol-winged Morane-Saulnier and a Blériot-Gouin. There was resistance to seeing the airplane as anything other than a scouting machine, as witnessed by the condescending comments of the high command upon receiving a report on July 2 from Capt. Jean Faure on the tests of the cannon-armed Voisin: "Very interesting work which shows that the officer that conceived it has a spirit of research that deserves to be encouraged, but one that smacks much more of Jules Verne than of reality."

1914 June 6   W. L. Brock became the first American to win a major British aviation competition when, flying a Morane-Saulnier monoplane with an 80-HP Rhône rotary, he came in first in the third *Daily Mail* Aerial Derby, winning £300 prize money. His time of 1 hr. 18 min. 54 sec. around the 94.5 mi. Hendon course produced an average speed of 71.9 MPH. R. H. Carr came in second in a Henri Farman biplane, averaging 53.2 MPH in 1 hr. 46 min. 27 sec. Of 21 machines entered in the race, only 11 started in a repeat of appalling weather that had postponed it for two weeks. The fastest airplane in the race was the Schneider Trophy-winning Tabloid fitted out as a landplane and, but for weather forcing it down, it would have won.

1914 June 8   The U.S. Army's chief signal officer, Gen. George P. Scriven, requested permission of the adjutant general to hold a competition "for the development of a suitable military aeroplane for service use, purchasing the machine making the highest number of points . . . the competition to be held at San Diego, Calif." Approval was granted June 15, and Gen. Scriven announced the competition on July 1. The specification called for a tractor biplane capable of being assembled from crates in two hours by four mechanics with maximum/minimum flying speeds of at least 70/40 MPH. Entries were to be filed by September 1, 1914, with airplanes delivered by October 20; 12 companies indicated they would compete.

1914 June 12   The first Curtiss tractor, a biplane known as the Model G, was accepted by the U.S. Army. Two had been ordered in 1913 at a cost of $5,500 after interest in the design of such a type had been expressed the previous year. The first, designated the *S.C. 21*, was a two-seat biplane with a 41-ft. wingspan and a length of 25 ft. fitted with floats for operations in Hawaii. With a 75-HP Curtiss Model O engine driving a three-blade propeller, the airplane had a top speed of 53 MPH. The second machine, designated *S.C. 22,* had shorter wings with a four-wheel undercarriage and a 90-HP engine.

1914 June 17 Igor Sikorsky and Capt. Prussis of the Imperial Russian Army made a remarkable long distance flight in the prototype Sikorsky Ilya Muromets. The airplane had been powered originally by four 100-HP Argus engines, but for this flight, it was equipped with two different powerplants. It had two 140-HP Argus engines inboard and two 132-HP Argus engines outboard. It made a flight between its base at St. Petersburg and the city of Kiev, a distance of approximately 750 mi. In honor of this feat, the prototype Ilya Muromets was given the name *Kievski.* It made its return flight to St. Petersburg on June 29, with just one stop, in a flying time of 10 hr. 30 min.

1914 June 18 The four-engined Sikorsky Ilya Muromets Type A made a sustained endurance flight of 6 hr. 3 min. carrying seven people, including the pilot, on an impressive demonstration of its potential range as a military airplane for either bombing duties or as a transport airplane. The Type A was fitted with four 150-HP Salmson radial engines from France because the usual supply of Argus engines from Germany had been cut off due to the worsening political climate. The efficiency and reliability of the French engines, however, was suspect, and refurbished Argus motors were preferred to new Salmsons.

1914 June 20 In one of the last great British pre-World War I aerial sporting contests, the American aviator W. L. Brock won the London-to-Manchester air race in his Morane-Saulnier monoplane powered by a 80-HP Gnôme rotary engine. The course was a round-trip flight to Manchester from Hendon, just outside London, with a mandatory stop each way at Birmingham. Out of eight starters, only three finished, and Brock won easily with a time of 4 hr. 42 min. 26 sec. at an average speed of 69 MPH. Englishmen R. H. Carr in a Morane-Saulnier monoplane and J. Alcock in a Farman were second and third. Brock won prizes worth £650, including one from the Anglo-American Oil Company.

1914 June 22 Naming ceremonies were held for the Curtiss flying boat *America,* which had been designed and built for the trans-Atlantic crossing aimed at obtaining the £10,000 prize ($50,000) announced in 1913 by the British newspaper the *Daily Mail.* Funded by wealthy store owner Rodman Wanamaker, the Model H twin-engined flying boat was designed by Curtiss, and an order for two was placed in December 1913. It was powered by two (later three) 90-HP engines, had a length of 37.5 ft. and a wing span of 74 ft. and could fly at 65 MPH for 1,100 mi. The planned Newfoundland-Portugal route was to go via Fayal and San Miguel in the Azores, but war intervened.

1914 June 23 The naval wing of Britain's Royal Flying Corps became the Royal Naval Air Service when the Admiralty withdrew the personnel and equipment from the wing to use as the basis of the new service and announced the formation of the Air Department (of the Admiralty), the central air office, the Royal Naval flying school and the Royal Naval air stations. From this date, the central flying school would be operated by the War Office, and Eastchurch would become the RNAS flying school. The Admiralty had never supported the amalgamated form of the British air services, and there were many disagreements with the War Office over several major policy decisions.

1914 June Late in the month, Oblt. Hermann Kastner of the 3rd Air Battalion at Cologne, Germany flew one of the new Fokker M.5L monoplanes that had been ordered as a military trainer. The longer-span M.5L had been selected over the shorter-span M.5K (both now fitted with the 80-HP Oberursel rotary engine) because it was deemed to have better flying qualities. The M.5K, however, would be the direct predecessor to the E-series monoplane fighters of 1915–16. Shortly after Kastner's flight, another officer flew it and crashed, possibly due to an unfamiliarity with monoplanes. Fokker was ordered to convert some M.5Ls into two-seat trainers.

1914 June With a capital of £20,000, English airplane manufacturer Robert Blackburn formed the Blackburn Aeroplane and Motor Co. Ltd. and set up shop at the Olympia works in Leeds. To handle seaplanes, Blackburn occupied premises in the village of Brough just outside the city. (Legend asserts the deciding factor lay in the quality of beer at the local inn!) The Brough plant was requisitioned by the government during World War I, and most production work during this period was on license building other designs than those originating within the company.

1914 July 4 William Edward Boeing got his first flight when a visiting aerial showman agreed to take him up from a field near Seattle, Wash. (Boeing had first tried to be taken up in 1910 by offering Louis Paulhan money to fly him as a passenger.) Boeing was heir to a large Washington timber business and put up a shed on the shores of Lake Union in Seattle so that, together with his naval friend Conrad Westervelt, he could disassemble a Martin biplane and learn how airplanes were put together. He then started building his own airplane to challenge the Curtiss hold on naval aviation.

1914 July 4 In the wake of a worsening political position in Europe, the German Transport Inspectorate ordered 220 airplanes from German manufacturers in an attempt to quickly expand the military inventory. Albatros received orders for 42 planes, LVG for 40, Aviatik 30, AEG and Gotha 30 each and DFW and Rumpler 18 each. These orders resulted in massive subcontracts to materials suppliers who exploited the situation and raised prices by the end of the year by as much as 100%; the airplane manufacturers were left with massive losses because they had agreed with the government to freeze prices at prewar levels.

1914 July 11 The last major international air race prior to the start of World War I was won by American W. L. Brock when he flew his Morane-Saulnier monoplane from Hendon, England to Buc, France and back. Fourteen entrants from Great Britain, the United States, France, Germany and Switzerland assembled at Hendon, seven contestants started the race, and three finished. Brock took 7 hr. 3 min. 6 sec. to fly the 508.5 mi. distance, almost 60 mi. of which was over water, at an average speed of 71.5 MPH. Roland Garros took 8 hr. 28 min. 37 sec. in an identical airplane, but third place man Eugène Reneaux in a Maurice-Farman took 26 hr. 55 min. due to a night stop in Boulogne.

1914 July 11 The last international endurance record before the outbreak of World War I was achieved by the German pilot R. Bohm when he kept an Albatros B.I tractor biplane powered by a 100-HP Mercedes in-line engine in the air for more than 24 hr. His epic flight lasted 24 hr. 12 min., adding almost 11 hr. to the previous record, and took place from the Johannisthal airfield outside Berlin. The Albatros factory produced the three-bay biplane designed by Ernst Heinkel earlier in the year. It had a span of 47.5 ft. and a length of 26 ft. with a maximum speed of 62 MPH and a design range of 400 mi.

1914 July 14 The last altitude record claimed prior to the start of World War I was achieved by the German pilot H. Oelerich when he attained a height of 26,780 ft. in a DFW B.I, powered by a 100-HP Mercedes in-line engine, from Leipzig-Lindenthal in Germany. The DFW monoplanes and biplanes were well known in the period 1912–14 as reliable and sturdy workhorses. The B.I had a span of 45 ft. 10 in. and a length of 27.5 ft. and had a maximum speed of 75 MPH, and they were used during the Balkan War of 1912–13. Oelerich's remarkable altitude record underscored the extent to which French domination of aviation was being overtaken by Germany.

1914 July 18 The U.S. Congress passed H.R.5304, to create the Aviation Section of the U.S. Signal Corps. It was to have a strength of 60 officers and 260 enlisted men over and above those allotted to the Signal Corps, with Lt. Col. Samuel Reber, head of the Aeronautical Division since October 20, 1913, in command. Col. Reber ran both organizations until Capt. George S. Gibbs became acting chief of the aeronautical division. The Aviation Section was to be responsible for operational activities involving balloons, airships and powered airplanes belonging to the army, and it was authorized to recruit only unmarried officers. Debate in Congress included discussion about whether aviation should remain under the Signal Corps or constitute a completely new corps.

1914 July 27 The first torpedo drop from a powered airplane in Britain took place at Calshot. Short Brothers' test pilot Gordon Bell dropped the 14-in. 810-lb. torpedo from a specially adapted 160-HP Gnôme-powered Short seaplane, the S.121. The drop was made after dark, and a magnesium flare attached to the torpedo enabled it to be found when it came to rest at the end of its test run. Comdr. A. M. Longmore of the Royal Navy piloted the S.121 next day and became the first serving officer to drop the torpedo. The first torpedo drop was made in Italy during February 1914 by Gen. Alessandro Guidoni from a monoplane floatplane built by Pateras Pescara and powered by two 200-HP Gnôme rotaries. Sopwith had also carried out tests earlier in the year with a torpedo-carrying Type C floatplane.

1914 July 28 Lt. V. D. Herbster and Lt. B. L. Smith of the U.S. Army issued a report on trials they had completed in the use of airplanes for dropping bombs and other munitions. The trials were carried out at the Indian Head Proving Grounds in Maryland. Several targets were attacked on both land and water, the average dropping height being about 1,000 ft. Live and dummy rounds were dropped by both pilots, and the report examined their findings in detail. Fearing it would suck funds from traditional arms and munitions, there was opposition in some military circles to the use of airplanes, but politicians were more concerned about the expansion of foreign air forces and the potential threat they could pose.

1914 July 29 The British Royal Naval Air Service issued an instruction to its units on the role it should henceforth adopt and gave the first declaration ever made that airplanes should fight airplanes in the sky in addition to reconnaissance or scouting duties. Based upon intelligence reports about possible German incursions in the event of war, the RNAS gave the defense of British skies as the primary role of its airplanes, secondary to reconnaissance. Units at Eastchurch had been practicing air-to-air combat with each other and had worked out defensive formations as well as tactics for attack, and they were better prepared for war than the Royal Flying Corps.

1914 July 30 The North Sea separating England from Scandinavia and the Low Countries was crossed for the first time by an aircraft when Lt. Tryggve Gran, a Norwegian, flew his Blériot monoplane from Norway to England. Flights across the open seas proved the capabilities of powered airplanes, and these were not lost on the politicians and military leaders throughout Europe, now locked on a collision course with all-out war. For its part, the United States believed its greatest threat came from Mexico and Central America, and there was little encouragement to understand the military use of aerial bombardment in the way it was perceived in Europe.

1914 July 31 The Swiss Fliegertruppe was formed and became the basis of the present day Swiss Air Force. Its initial base was at Buedenfeld, and on formation, the truppe boasted one Swiss and three French monoplanes as its front-line strength. Switzerland would maintain its neutrality throughout World War I, but the gathering clouds of conflict sharpened the concern felt by political and military leaders that Switzerland should be in a position to defend its borders.

1914 July 31 On the eve of Germany's attack on France, Britain's Royal Flying Corps and the Royal Naval Air Service had about 113 airplanes and seaplanes on strength plus six airships, but only a small number were fully operational and deployed in squadrons. The RFC had 33 airplanes with squadrons 2, 3 and 4; squadrons 1 and 5 had none, although that situation would change. There were 12 airplane makers in Britain, of which three were specialized in seaplanes. Orders outstanding accounted for 15 airplanes and 34 seaplanes for the RNAS, and with existing production facilities, the industry could turn out about 100 airplanes each year.

Just over 11½ years after the first powered flight in America by Orville Wright on December 3, 1903, the first great age of pioneer aviation was about to end. From this point on, airplane performance would be dominated by research and development toward bigger, better and more powerful combat planes. By the end of the month, the world duration record stood at 24 hr. 12 min., and the altitude record stood at 26,780 ft., both achieved by German aviators. The closed circuit distance record was held by the French aviator A. Sequin, who flew 634 mi. from Paris to Bordeaux and back, and the straight-line record went to the Frenchman Letort with his 568-mi. flight from Paris to Berlin. The closed-circuit speed record stood at 127 MPH, taken by M. Prévost in a Deperdussin with a 160-HP Gnôme.

1914 August 1 German mobilization was ordered at 6:30 P.M., signaling the start of World War I with the invasion of France followed by Luxembourg and Belgium on August 2. The Germans had about 230 airplanes in 30 Prussian and three Bavarian field flying sections (Feldflieger Abteilungen) and 10 garrison defense sections (Festungsflieger Abteilungen). The navy had very few serviceable seaplanes. The army had 10 rigid airships of the Zeppelin and Schutte-Lanz types and two rigid or semi-rigid types. In addition, there were 16 kite balloons and a number of free balloons, and the navy had one serviceable airship and one nearing completion. The Austro-Hungarians had 36 airplanes, one dirigible and 10 balloons. By comparison, France had about 126 airplanes in 23 escadrilles (squadrons) and six airships, Belgium had 37 pilots and fewer airplanes, and Russia had 145 airplanes in squadron service, 12 airships and 46 kite balloons.

1914 August 3 When the German Army attacked Belgium and Germany declared war on France, several French Dorand biplanes (DO.1s) with 90-HP Anzani engines were awaiting delivery to Russia but were diverted into the new Escadrille DO.22, the first unit to be set up in France due to the war. The DO.1 was a strange-looking biplane, with a rear stagger to the upper wing and a pilot's cockpit behind the trailing edge of the upper wing. The airplane was not a success, and the unit soon re-equipped with Maurice-Farman biplanes.

1914 August 4   Failing to receive a reply to a message from the prime minister requiring assurances from Germany that that country would respect Belgian neutrality, the British government declared war on Germany at 11:00 P.M. From the Home Office, R. McKenna issued a proclamation forbidding the use of civilian airplanes for any aerial journey inside Great Britain. He stated: "I prohibit the navigation of aircraft of every class and description over the whole area of the United Kingdom, and over the whole of the coastline thereof and territorial waters adjacent thereto . . . This order shall not apply to Naval or Military aircraft." It was to be the end of civil aviation for almost five years.

1914 August 6   The first attempt at aerial bombing from a German airship took place when army Zeppelin Z VI (factory designation LZ 21) made an unsuccessful run to the French town of Liege, carrying eight artillery shells as bombs weighing a total of 440 lb. As it descended through 5,200 ft., it was hit by ground fire, damaging the rear gas bags and causing the airship to turn for home. Jettisoning all loose equipment, it continued to lose altitude and came down heavily in woods near Bonn. Zeppelin Z VI was 485 ft. long and 54.5 ft. in diameter and had a volume of 738,500 cu. ft. It had made its first flight on November 10, 1913.

1914 August 8   The first French air casualty of World War I was the observer on a reconnaissance flight piloted by Sadi Lecointe. A German rifleman hit and wounded the observer. Although observers would soon carry small arms and rifles into the air as defense against other airplanes and as means of attacking enemy reconnaissance planes, there was little defense against ground fire, and although powered airplanes were faster than airships, they frequently had a ground speed little more than that of a galloping horse, especially so when flying into a strong head wind. At low altitudes (under 500 ft.), they were easy prey for eagle-eyed snipers.

1914 August 8   Britain's Royal Naval Air Service ordered coastal patrols to begin immediately off the entire British east coast region from Kinnaird's Head, Aberdeenshire, Scotland down as far as Dungeness on the south coast of England between Dover and Hastings to look out for ships of the Imperial German Navy and to scout for incoming enemy airships. But after the Germans invaded Belgium, there was fear of a concentrated attack by aircraft, and the order was changed to concentrate the patrols between the Humber River, dividing Yorkshire and Lincolnshire on the east coast, and the Thames River.

1914 August 10   Britain's only armed nonrigid airship, the *Astra Torres* (Naval Airship No. 3) began patrols over the English Channel to search for signs of German warships, airships or airplanes. The airship had one Hotchkiss machine gun and was accompanied on these patrols by an unarmed rigid airship of German origin, the *Parseval* (Naval Airship No. 4), soon to be joined by Nos. 5, 6 and 7. Whereas the average patrol time for an airplane was 3 hr., these airships could remain on search for 12 hr., clearly displaying an operational advantage.

1914 August 12   The first German air casualty of World War I was Oberleutnant Reinhold Jahnow of the German Air Service. He was hit and killed by ground fire over Malmédy in Belgium while carrying out a reconnaissance flight. The Germans were

developing a strong force of observation and reconnaissance airplanes, and casualties would soon become a daily statistic.

1914 August 13   The first British airplane to reach French soil after mobilization was a BE2a, serial number 327, flown by Capt. F. F. Waldron and Air Mechanic Skerritt of No. 2 Sqdn. RFC commanded by Maj. C. J. Burke. They set off from Dover in the vanguard of airplanes from No. 2 Sqdn. as well as those from Nos. 3 and 4 Sqdn. and landed at Amiens in France early in the morning. Airplanes from these three squadrons had arrived at Dover by the previous evening, and Lt. Col. F. H. Sykes from RFC headquarters got there at midnight and ordered all pilots to be ready for take-off at 6:00 A.M. No. 5 Sqdn. arrived in France two days later.

1914 August 17   The German navy Zeppelin airship L 3 was sent out on the first long airship flight of World War I. Konteradmiral Franz Hipper, commander of the Naval Airship Division, ordered L 3 out to patrol the Skagerrak off Denmark in search of British warships rumored to have arrived in those waters. L 3 flew 300 mi. north but found nothing. The L 3 (Zeppelin LZ 24) had first flown in May 1914 and was based at Fuhlsbuttel. It was 518 ft. long and 48.5 ft. in diameter and had a volume of 794,500 cu. ft. It was powered by three 210-HP engines that provided a top speed of 47 MPH.

1914 August 17–23   A second series of U.S. Army tests with the Riley Scott bombsight and dropping gear took place. A Martin biplane *(S.C. No. 31)* was used to drop 30 dummy and live explosive bombs, grenades and a standard 3-in. artillery shell on a 100 ft. diameter target from between 1,000 ft. and 2,000 ft. altitude. Measurements were made showing that a 15-lb. bomb made a 4-ft. diameter crater 1 ft. deep and that a 50-lb. bomb made a crater 10 ft. in diameter and 4 ft. deep. Participating officers recommended the purchase of five bomb-aiming sets, but senior officers disallowed the request, citing the airplane's primary role of reconnaissance.

1914 August 19   The first reconnaissance patrols of World War I carried out by the British Royal Flying Corps took place when Capt. P. B. Joubert de la Ferte in a Blériot monoplane from No. 3 Sqdn. and Lt. G. W. Mapplebeck of No. 4 Sqdn. in a BE2a took off from Maubeuge, France at 9:30 A.M. to patrol the countryside across the border in Belgium. Expected to remain together, they lost each other. Mapplebeck wandered over Brussels without recognizing the Belgian capital, but he eventually found his way down to Le Cateau from where he returned to Maubeuge at 12:00 noon. De la Ferte lost his way completely and landed at Tournay to get directions, got lost again and landed at Courtrai. He made it back to Maubeuge by 5:30 P.M.

1914 August 19   The French army airship *Fleurus,* one of six in military service at the start of the war, became the first dirigible to enter German airspace when it flew up the Saar River and as far as Treves during a night reconnaissance mission. The French were not hindered by blackout because the threat of nighttime aerial attack had not yet materialized. Night flying had its drawbacks, however. Aware of the infamous zeppelins, friendly fire had been directed at the French airship *Conté* for 10 min. on August 9 as it passed near Lunéville, and it had difficulty returning to base. On August 24, the *Dupuy de Lôme* was riddled with bullets at Reims despite forewarning of its approach.

1914 August 20   The Michelin brothers, Edouard and Andre, offered to turn their entire factory capacity over to the production of aircraft for the French Ministry of War as part of their contribution to the national war effort. The offer was accepted, and in November they were contracted to build 100 Brequet BU3 aircraft, which were designated BUM to denote their Michelin manufacture. The war inspired astonishing acts of patriotism such as the Michelins, but many middle-men began to make excessive profits out of arranged deals whereby supplies necessary to build the airplanes were suddenly priced out of all proportion to their market value.

1914 August 22 The first British airplane brought down by enemy action fell to earth in Belgium as a result of German infantry fire. The airplane, an Avro 504 piloted by Lt. W. Waterfall and carrying an observer, Lt. C. G. G. Bayly, belonged to No. 5 Sqdn. This unit had been conducting tests with machine guns on their airplanes, and on the very day Waterfall and Bayly were shot down, another British airman, Maj. J. T. B. McCudden, reported a German airplane over their airfield. Capt. Longcroft took off in a Farman biplane with a machine gun in hot pursuit of it—but without success. The wreckage of the Avro 504 is believed to have been the instrument through which the Germans first became aware the British had landed on the continent.

1914 August 22 The first deep reconnaissance patrol of the war began when the Schutte-Lanz airship SL 2 moved into Russian territory on a two-day flight that would log a total distance of 865 mi. and perform a straight-line distance penetration of almost 300 mi. Of the duration, only 24 hr. was spent in the air. The findings on Russian troop movements and concentrations were reported back to the Austrians at Przemsyl. The SL 2 was based at Liegnitz, and its survival on such a perilous mission was due entirely to the effort its crew took to keep the airship well away from ground fire.

1914 August 25 The first aerial engagements between airplanes of the British and German air units took place. Three BE2a biplanes of No. 2 Squadron RFC forced down a German two-seater by bearing down upon it from above, and Lts. H. D. Harvey-Kelly and W. H. C. Mansfield landed nearby and gave chase on foot to the occupants who bolted for the nearest wood. Trophies were taken from the German airplane, and it was then burned before the RFC pilots returned to base. A second German two-seater was forced to land and was captured near Le Quesnoy along with its crew.

1914 August 26 The Czarist High Command of the Imperial Russian Army issued an instruction that two Ilya Muromets, four-engine, biplane bombers were to be taken to the northwest front and given evaluation trials. During the previous month, the giant airplanes had carried out their first tests as bombers and early forms of bomb-aiming instruments had been devised. However, the use of untrained aircrew operating these complex airplanes in action gave evaluation results that were disappointing, and by mid-October, the two bombers were withdrawn and orders for 32 cancelled. Grand Duke Nikolai Nikolayevich was able to restore faith in the airplane when he returned to active duty and used RBVZ technicians as crew.

1914 August 26 A two-seat biplane piloted by Baron Lt. von Rosenthal, one of three Austrian planes flying over the Russian town of Sholkiv, was the first airplane to be destroyed by ramming in mid-air during World War I. A Morane-Saulnier Type M monoplane piloted by the famous Russion pilot Petr Nikolaevich Nesterov of the Eleventh Corps Air Squadron chased the Austrian biplane and rammed it; both pilots were killed. Nesterov was buried with full military honors and, the town of Sholkiv

was renamed in his honor. Nesterov had achieved fame in September 1913, by being the first to loop a Nieuport.

1914 August 30 Paris came under aerial bombardment for the first time when a German single-seat Taube monoplane piloted by Lt. Ferdinand von Hiddessen dropped several small bombs on the Quai de Valmy, killing or injuring several people. General confusion was caused, and not since the blockade of Paris began in 1870 during the Franco-Prussian war had Parisians been given a taste of military combat. The bombing attack was of little military significance but achieved poignancy when Gen. Joseph Galliéni, a former marine officer during the siege of 1870, was appointed governor of Paris to coordinate defenses as the German armies bore down upon the French capital.

1914 August In the first month of World War I, the beliefs on the part of the Germans that rigid airships would deal a deadly blow to Britain, and on the part of the British that German raiders would create havoc in the streets, was found to be inflated exaggeration. Of the 10 German army airships theoretically on strength, only six were operational when war broke out and four were disabled by the end of the month. Z V was lost August 25 when it was brought down by ground fire at Tannenberg, Z VI was lost August 6 (see entry), and Z VII and Z VIII were also brought down by gunfire.

1914 September 2 France was saved from military collapse by a reconnaissance mission conducted by Cpl. Louis Breguet flying one of his biplanes and carrying an observer named Watteau. Contrary to the von Schlieffen plan, Gen. von Klück was observed wheeling around toward the southeast of Paris and not heading for an encircling movement to the northwest as expected. In a daring maneuver to overwhelm the British corps and catch the retreating French, von Klück exposed his left flank. The report was disbelieved by the French command, but next day Lts. Prot and Hugel confirmed it and Capt. Bellinger, commander of the air section of the Sixth Army, took the information to the British, who accepted the word of the aviators. Gen. Joffre was briefed and so began preparations for the Battle of the Marne that halted the German advance on Paris.

1914 September 3 The British Royal Naval Air Service was given a measure of responsibility for the defense of the British Isles in a move predicated by Lord Kitchener, the secretary of state for war, and Winston S. Churchill, first sea lord, when it was decided that the Admiralty would defend the land mass of England, Scotland, Wales and Northern Ireland. Because the Admiralty had gained control over the naval air units formerly embraced by the naval wing of the RFC prior to late June 1914, the RNAS would be responsible for helping defend British territory from attack.

1914 September 22 The first major attack by British airplanes on German positions was carried out by the Royal Naval Air Service when it sent four airplanes to bomb airship sheds at Düsseldorf and Cologne, two in each city. The airplanes were based at Antwerp under the command of Sqdn. Cdr. E. L. Gerrard, who had arived at Ostend for just this sort of mission on September 3. Of the four airplanes, only one, flown by Lt. Collet, found its target. Diving down on the sheds from a height of 6,000 ft., he flew through mist from 1,900 ft. to a bombing height of 400 ft. and dropped one 20-lb. bomb too short, while the other three hit the sheds but failed to explode.

1914 September 27 The first French bombing groups were formed with the direct purpose of attacking enemy positions and tactical targets behind the lines. Developed at the instigation of bombing advocate Commandant Barès, the director of aeronautics, the first Groupe de Bombardement was set up on paper, although it would be two months before the equipment and support facilities were available for use. Escadrilles VB.1, 2 and 3 would form the first bombing group, and three more such groups would be set up by February 1915.

1914 September Maj. Gen. Siegert formed the first German strategic bombing unit under the code name of Ostend Carrier Pigeon Flight *(Brieftauben Abteilung Ostende)*. With the objective of bombing England, the unit was housed for mobility in railway carriages; but the absence of long-range airplanes with sufficient power to carry out significant raids across the English Channel and the North Sea kept it occupied with Belgian and French targets on the continent for most of the time until it was moved to the Eastern Front in the spring of 1915.

1914 September The First Aero Squadron of the U.S. Army reformed at San Diego, Calif. under the command of Capt. Benjamin Foulois. The new unit was larger than had been previously authorized with a strength of 16 officers and 77 enlisted men operating eight airplanes. These changes were to develop into a standard structure for U.S. Army squadrons as the fledgling force grew in size. Under Captain Foulois, the First Aero Squadron represented the sum total of U.S. tactical air power, a situation that would not change until America's entry into the First World War.

1914 October 5 The first airplane to be shot down by a French airplane in flight crashed to earth when a Voisin flown by Sgt. Joseph Frantz and Cpl. Quenault of the French Air Service attacked a German two-seat Aviatik biplane flown by Feldwebel Willhelm Schlichting with Oblt. Fritz von Zangen as observer. The Voisin belonged to V.24, a unit with whom Frantz and Quenault had served since joining the French air service together. The V.24 ex-artillery commander, Capt. Faure, allowed Frantz

and Quenault to fly the armed airplane after Gabriel Voisin adapted six Hotchkiss machine guns and delivered them to V.24 at Mezières, 160 mi. from Paris on August 19.

1914 October 8 Spenser Grey, a squadron commander in the Royal Naval Air Service, bombed the main railway station at Cologne, and Flt. Lt. F. L. G. Marix bombed airship sheds at Düsseldorf. Their base at Antwerp was under fire from German artillery when they took off, Spenser Grey at 1:20 P.M. and Marix at 1:30 P.M. each in a Sopwith Tabloid. Marix hit the airship sheds from a height of 600 ft., and the roof fell in within 30 sec. as flames erupted 500 ft. into the air from gas cells in Zeppelin LZ 25. Heavy rifle and gunfire hit the Tabloid, and on the way back Marix had to land 20 mi. short of Antwerp, completing the return journey on a bicycle. Spenser Grey returned at 4:45 P.M. At 6:00 P.M. a general evacuation to Ostend was ordered.

1914 October 8 The first war plan of France's general headquarters helped provide a foundation for the enlargement of the air service. From 23 escadrilles at the start of the war, eight had been added already; but the new plan envisaged a total of 65 by January 1915. There were to be 16 bomber units, 16 reconnaissance and pursuit units and 30 observation squadrons each with six airplanes and three cavalry units for four airplanes each. Cavalry units would use airplanes to assist with reconnaissance duties. The 384 planes would have to be maintained in serviceable order and losses replaced so a production rate capable of replacing 50% of this force each month was essential.

1914 October 20 Only two manufacturers responded to a competition for new airplanes, as requested June 8, 1914, by the U.S. Army chief signal officer Gen. George P. Scriven, and delivered airplanes for scrutiny by the deadline. Although 12 companies had indicated their intention of sending airplanes, only Curtiss and Martin showed up. The competition was called off because of the lack of competitive bids, but tests of the Curtiss and Martin airplanes were held as scheduled between October 23

In France, Voisin set the style for a successful line of tricycle aircraft; this Voisin 10 was built during World War I.

and November 8, 1914. The review board set up to judge the competition had included Capts. Benjamin D. Foulois and George A. Dodd, Lts. Walter R. Taliaferro, Thomas DeWitt Milling and Joseph E. Carberry and a civilian engineer, Grover Loening.

1914 October 25 The French general Bernard was replaced as director of aeronautics by Gen. Hirschauer, who in 1912 had been permanent inspector of aeronautics. Better management of production techniques had its impact, with output increasing from 100 airframes in October to 137 in November, 192 in December, 262 in January 1915 and 431 in March. By March 1915, the number of escadrilles had increased to 53, with 130 line officers, 500 pilots, 240 observers and 4,650 enlisted men, even with 15% of airplane output being diverted to France's allies, in equal numbers of planes going to England and Russia.

1914 October In response to concern about the practicality and safety of a rear-engine design, the U.S. Signal Corps placed an order for eight Curtiss JN-2 and two JN-3 tractor biplanes. Curtiss had recruited British airplane designer B. Douglas Thomas from Avro to produce the Model J and the Model N, two very similar tractor biplanes differing mainly in the airfoil sections adopted for the wing design. With the best attributes combined in a third design, the JN series, type designation began with JN-2, which had equal-span wings, and JN-3, with a longer span upper wing. The initials JN became the unofficial "Jenny," as all subsequent JN types were known.

1914 October The Caproni Ca.1 made its inaugural flight, the first in a long line of successful heavy bombers that the Italian Royal Army Air Service would use with good effect when Italy entered the war on the Allied side on May 24, 1915. The Ca.1 had three engines, two 80-HP Gnôme rotaries set on the lower wing each side of the fuselage and one 100-HP Gnôme driving a pusher propeller set at the rear of the short fuselage nacelle, in line with the trailing edge of the wings, which spanned almost 73 ft. Twin booms were attached to the two main engine enclosures supporting a horizontal tail unit and triple fins. The Ca.1 was 35 ft. 9 in. long and weighed 6,600 lb.

1914 October Flying a Curtiss flying boat powered by a 90-HP engine, Sub. Lt. H. Cutler of the Royal Navy made a successful reconnaissance flight along the Rufiji River in German East Africa (now Tanzania) and discovered the whereabouts of the German cruiser *Koenigsberg*, which was subsequently attacked by naval forces and sunk (July 11, 1915). The Curtiss had been bought by a South African mining prospector in efforts to use aerial reconnaissance for observing the location of potential mining areas.

1914 October The first production models of the Fokker M.8 monoplane (developed from the M.5 first flown in April 1914) reached German units and were given the military designation Fokker A.I. These had a wingspan of 31 ft. 5 in. and length of 23 ft. 11 in., and were powered by 80-HP Oberussel engines. It was a shoulder-wing monoplane with increased wing area over its predecessor and a fuselage 40% wider to permit two people to squeeze into the cockpit side by side. Two squadrons of six airplanes each, Field Flying Sections (or units) 40 and 41, were formed to operate the M.8, with which they were exclusively equipped until late 1915. Other units too received the successful monoplane, and it became the first major success for Fokker.

1914 November 21 Three unarmed Avro 504A biplanes, each powered by a single 80-HP Gnôme rotary engine and each carrying four 20-lb. bombs, made a successful attack on the Zep-

pelin sheds at Friedrichshafen from a base at Belfort near the Franco-Swiss border, after a flight of 120 mi. across German air space. Four 504A's were prepared but one, piloted by Flt. Sub/-Lt. Cannon failed to start. The other three, piloted by Sqdn. Comdr. E. F. Briggs, Flt. Lt. S. V. Sippe and Flt. Comdr. J. T. Babington followed the Rhine River at 5,000 ft., flew over Lake Constance at 10 ft., ascended to 1,200 ft. and dropped their bombs after diving to 700 ft. A total 11 bombs were dropped in the target area, and massive explosions ripped the sheds. Briggs was shot down and taken prisoner, but the others returned.

1914 November 25 Brig. Gen. William Crozier, U.S. Army Ordnance Corps, suggested to the U.S. Army chief signal officer that consideration be given to mounting offensive machine guns on Signal Corps airplanes. The two available guns were the 29-lb. air-cooled automatic 0.30-in. caliber 1909 machine rifle and the 36-lb. water-cooled Vickers. One of each was shipped to the aviation school at North Island, San Diego, Calif. for trials with an officer from the Benecia Arsenal. During September, Gen. George P. Scriven and Lt. Col. J. E. Hoffer of the Ordnance Department had examined a recoilless gun at the New London Ship and Engine Co., Groton, Conn. With a length of 10 ft. and a weight of 155.35 lb., it was considered too heavy for airplane use.

1914 November 29 To decentralize their operations, squadrons of the British Royal Flying Corps were organized into wings of two squadrons each, the first such formation in any air arm: Nos. 2 and 4 Squadrons were in the First Wing, commanded by Lt. Col. H. M. Trenchard, who had arrived in France November 18; the Second Wing comprised Nos. 5 and 6 Squadrons and was commanded by Lt. Col. C. J. Burke. On December 25, the British Expeditionary Force was divided into two armies. The First Wing went with the First Army under Sir Douglas Haig, and the Second Wing went to the Second Army under Sir Horace Smith-Dorrien.

1914 November The first Russian woman known to have served as a pilot for the Imperial Russian Air Service joined the first Field Air Squadron as a reconnaissance pilot. Princess Eugenie Mikhailovna Shakhovskaya had trained to fly at Johannisthal, near Berlin, Germany and had gained her aviator's certificate on August 16, 1911. Returning to Russia, she pleaded with Czar Nicholas II to be allowed to fly as a military pilot when war broke out and was duly permitted to enter military training school from where she graduated and joined the reconnaissance unit.

1914 November The first two Curtiss H.4 Small America flying boats were delivered to the Royal Naval Air Service in England, following an effective Admiralty lobbying exercise by John Porte, who was to have attempted the Atlantic crossing planned for the Curtiss Model H America before war broke out. Porte returned to his native England, joined the Royal Naval Air Service and helped develop flying boat operations. Eventually, the Royal Naval Air Service would order an additional 62 production airplanes, of which eight were built in Britain. The H.4 had twin 90-HP Curtiss engines when delivered but were fitted by the British with either 100-HP Anzani or 130-HP Clerget engines.

1914 December 4 The first seaplane unit formed by the German navy officially came into existence under the designation See Flieger Abteilung 1 (Seaplane Unit No. 1) and began operations from Zeebrugge, Belgium two days later with three officers, 55 other ranks and two seaplanes. In all, the German navy had little more than 20 seaplanes, but there was increasing emphasis on their value for coastal patrol, reconnaissance and bombing.

The mainstay of the seaplane force was the operating range of Friedrichshafen machines, which, at this stage of war, were little more than unarmed observation airplanes with little or no armament and able to carry only a bomb or two.

1914 December 8 While serving with Field Flying Section 13, future German air ace Oswald Boelcke received a new Fokker M.8 monoplane, identified in military service as the Fokker A.I, from the distribution center at Rethel. Only a handful were in existence at this time, but Boelcke's enthusiasm for the agile little airplane had been fired by a machine of this type flown into Boelcke's base at Pontfaverger by Lt. Otto Parschau on November 11. Although used for occasional patrol duties, Boelcke's usual mount at this time was the Albatros B.II reconnaissance biplane.

1914 December 8 The No. 9 Squadron, Royal Flying Corps, was organized as a wireless unit responsible for supplying airplanes equipped with wireless communication equipment to whichever army unit required the service. The headquarters were at St. Omer in France, but it soon became apparent that no centralized wireless unit could effectively serve the needs of the entire army, so steps were taken to use St. Omer as a distribution center for wireless units set up in every Royal Flying Corps squadron. Because of this, No. 9 Squadron was disbanded in April 1915 and withdrawn to England where it reformed as a home wireless school. By July 1, 1916, 306 of the 410 Royal Flying Corps airplanes on strength would be equipped with wireless sets.

1914 December 10 The Eskadra Vozdushnykh Korablei (E.V.K.), or Squadron of Flying Ships of the Imperial Russian Army, was set up as a bombing force operating Sikorsky Ilya Muromets four-engine biplane bombers under the command of the newly promoted Maj. Gen. M. V. Shidlovski. The squadron was equipped with training schools, weather stations, photo-laboratories, an antiaircraft battery and 1,350 personnel. Ilya Muromets bombers completed at the RBVZ factory were flight tested by the squadron before operational use.

1914 December 11 General headquarters of the British Expeditionary Force in France decreed that airplanes of the Royal Flying Corps carry roundels in red, white and blue on the wings and the fuselage for national identification. Since October 19, 1914, the Union Jack had been painted on Royal Flying Corps airplanes. Unfortunately, the Cross of St. George predominated and was easily confused at a distance with the Cross Patee (the Maltese Cross), which had been used on German airplanes since the first few weeks of war. The French had used roundels on military airplanes since July 1912, with blue in the center. Adopting the same colors, the British reversed this and had red in the center, blue on the outer ring. Small Union Jacks appeared on the rudder, but these were replaced by vertical flashes beginning May 16, 1915, with blue at the front and red at the rear as in the French style.

1914 December 11 British patent no. 17385 was lodged for a Vickers-Challenger gun deflector that would place a wedge ''between the gun and the propeller which rotates in synchronism with the propeller and serves to deflect bullets when the propeller blades are in the line of fire.'' Other patents had already been lodged with the patent office in London relating to devices similar to the device patented by Franz Schneider in 1913. Similar work was also under investigation by Warrant Officer F. W. Scarff based on designs prepared by the Polish immigrant Lt. Comdr. V. V. Dibovski.

1914 December 14 Voisin bombers of the first Groupe de Bombardement formed during November 1914, the first independent bombing force to operate on the Western Front, made their first raid against the railway station at Freiburg in daylight and repeated the exercise five days later. The three squadrons attached to the bombing group were specifically controlled as a tactical and strategic bombing force and were not at the general disposal of army commanders.

1914 December 16 Successful tests were carried out with a two-way radio between a U.S. Army Burgess-Wright pusher biplane and a ground transceiver. The Burgess-Wright used for this activity was one of the early biplanes purchased for the Signal Corps and was of little operational use, best suited to research and development activity. The interest in radio communication arose when it was recognized that real-time transmission of information from an observer in the air to the ground was a significant advantage over a verbal report made several hours after the observation.

1914 December 17 The British Admiralty issued an instruction that all Royal Naval Air Service airplanes would carry a red circle with a white center on the wings for national identification. Prior to that, in an instruction of October 26, 1914, the Admiralty ordered the Union Jack to be painted on the underside of Royal Naval Air Service airplane wings. Recognizing that this was too close for comfort to the German cross, the roundels were introduced. By late 1915, further instructions had stipulated a blue-white-red insignia similar to that adopted by the Royal Flying Corps, in the diameter ratio of 5:3:1.

1914 December 21 The first successful air raid by German airplanes on British territorial waters took place when a Friedrichshafen FF 29 (No. 203) of Sea Flying Section No. 1 at Zeebrugge, Belgium raided the English coast at Dover and dropped two bombs in the sea at 1:00 P.M. near Admiralty Pier. It frightened the locals but caused no injury, and the seaplane made it back to base without challenge. An earlier attempt by Field Flying Section No. 9 to attack England on October 25 was made when a lone Gotha Taube got almost as far as Dover. The Germans claimed it as a success and the crew (Lts. Caspar and Roos) were feted in the German press.

1914 December 21 The first night bombing raid was carried out by Comdr. C. R. Samson flying a Maurice-Farman Shorthorn pusher biplane powered by a 130-HP Canton-Unne engine. The Shorthorn (serial no. 1241) carried 18 16-lb. bombs, which it dropped on German artillery batteries at Ostend, Belgium. In all, this airplane carried out 120 flying hr. of duty on the Western Front before being packed and sent to the Dardanelles in 1915. The Shorthorn had a speed of just over 60 MPH but could remain in the air for 3¾ hr., giving it the ability to hit targets more than 100 mi. from base.

1914 December 24 The first bomb to drop on English soil was released by a lone Friedrichshafen FF 29 seaplane (No. 204) operating from the Sea Flying Section No. 1 at Zeebrugge. After approaching Dover at 5,000 ft., it dropped a single, 22-lb. bomb at 10:45 A.M. into the garden of auctioneer Thomas A. Terson, breaking windows in his house and causing £40 worth of damage. The bomb made a crater 10 ft. in diameter and 4 ft. deep, and the FF 29 was pursued unsuccessfully by a Wright seaplane from Eastchurch and a Bristol TB 8 scout. The slow climbing speed of these airplanes made it impossible to overtake the intruder.

1914 December 25 In what was the first successful seaplane-carrier operation, HMS *Empress*, HMS *Engadine* and HMS *Riviera* launched a force of seven Short seaplanes from a position at sea 12 mi. north of Helgoland Island off the German northwest coast. These converted cross-channel steamers sailed from Harwich with an escort to protect them from attack. The Short seaplanes failed to find the airship sheds at Cuxhaven they went to attack but dropped their bombs on the Kiel canal. Three found their way back to the ships, but three landed on the water near Norderney and were picked up by a German E-class submarine; one was rescued by Dutch fishermen after descending prematurely near the boats.

1914 December 25 The first air attack on London was carried out by Oblt. Stephan Prondzynski and his observer, von Frankenburg, flying in a Friedrichshafen FF 29 (No. 203) from Sea Flying Section No. 1 at Zeebrugge, Belgium. The presence of this airplane was alerted at 12:20 P.M while it was flying at 7,000 ft., and fire from the ground was so enthusiastic that telephone lines were shot away! Descending to 4,000 ft., the FF 29 flew up the Thames River and dropped several bombs in the dock area before several British airplanes began to converge in pursuit. The raider escaped, but the observer was wounded by gunfire after the seaplane put down off the Belgian coast so the crew could find out where they were.

1914 December 28 The specification for a large, long-range patrol bomber designated Type O was issued by the British Admiralty based on a proposal from the Handley Page Co. The search for such an airplane had been stimulated by a signal from Comdr. C. R. Samson of the Royal Naval Air Service during the evacuation of Antwerp in October when he called for "a bloody paralyser [of an aeroplane] to stop the Hun in his tracks!" The specification was the basis for a contract for four prototypes of what would become the 0/100 and the 0/400, each capable of carrying six 100-lb. bombs, achieving a top speed of 65 MPH and climbing to 3,000 ft. in 10 min.

1915 January 10 Responding to pressure from the army and the navy and to December attacks on Freiburg by French bombers with civilian casualties, Admiral Hugo von Pohl, chief of the general staff, instructed the commander-in-chief of the German High Seas Fleet that airships could bomb military targets in London and other English cities so long as they were not likely to incur civilian casualties. The relationship between the English and German royal families made the kaiser reluctant to involve ordinary citizens in a conflict he believed was a dispute between governments. The fine distinction would soon disappear.

1915 January 19 The first German airship raid on England began when navy Zeppelins L 3 and L 4 left Fühlsbüttel for the Humber estuary on England's northeast coast at 11:00 A.M. and L 6 left Nordholz with Peter Strasser, chief of the German Naval Airship Division, on board at 9:38 A.M. heading for the Thames estuary. L 6 had to turn back with engine trouble, but L 3 reached the coast of Norfolk, 70 mi. south of the Humber, at 8:50 P.M. and dropped bombs on Yarmouth. L 4 crossed the Norfolk coast at 9:30 P.M. and dropped bombs at the villages of Sheringham and Snettisham and the town of Kings Lynn. L 3 landed at Fühlsbüttel at 9:40 A.M. followed by L 4 at 9:47 A.M. Four people had been killed and 16 injured, and damage was 7,740 pounds.

1915 January 22 Col. D. C. Shanks, inspector general, began his annual inspection of the First Aero Squadron, U.S. Signal Corps, and concluded January 26 with a recommendation that observers be sent to Europe to report firsthand on the developing

use of airplanes for war. He also recommended that new barracks be set up on North Island, San Diego and complimented the squadron on its progress with better types of airplane. Citing the recently secured two-man U.S. altitude record of 11,690 ft., achieved January 5, Col. Shanks supported the move to completely replace all pusher airplanes with tractor biplanes, a transition that had been almost completed.

1915 February 6 The prototype Sikorsky S.16 two-seat biplane scout was completed at the RBVZ factory in St. Petersburg. Powered by an 80-HP Gnôme rotary, the airplane was underpowered for its intended role as a reconnaissance and escort fighter for the giant Ilya Muromets four-engine bombers. It had been designed to have the 110-HP Le Rhône, but shortages prevented the use of that engine. After two more had been built in March, evaluation in flying units led to an order for 18 by September, but by then it was obsolete.

1915 February 12 A German imperial order was issued that broadened the opportunities for army and navy airships and airplanes to attack England's cities if they contained supply dumps, military facilities, barracks, oil or gasoline dumps or docks. Previous instructions from the kaiser ordered only military targets be attacked. The army general staff interpreted the order to mean it could now attack the eastern reaches of London, although the kaiser prohibited attacks on "residential areas of London, or above all on royal palaces." This was the signal for a strategic plan code-named FILM FETWA for mass zeppelin attacks on London.

1915 February 15 The first sustained large-scale bombing operation got under way when the giant Russian Ilya Muromets bombers operated by the E.V.K. under Maj. Gen. M. V. Shidlovski began attacks on targets in East Prussia. With astonishing hit scores of up to 90% (defined as the percentage of bombs dropped that hit the designated targets), the bombers struck the towns of Neidenburg, Soldau and Willenberg using special high-definition bombsights designed by Prof. G. A. Botezat with his assistants Tolmachev and Harf and Capts. Ivanov and Shuravchenko. They destroyed the German seaplane base at Angern Lake, Courland and the headquarters of the German commander in chief of the Eastern Front, Oberstgeneral von Below despite heavy ground fire and fighter attacks. It would be 20 mon. before the first Ilya Muromets was shot down.

1915 March 2 The first aerial photographic camera specifically designed for use by British Royal Flying Corps observation airplanes was used for the first time by Lts. J. T. C. Moore-Brabazon and Campbell over enemy trench positions. The camera used was known as the type A and had been developed by these two officers in collaboration with the Thornton-Pickard Manufacturing Co. The camera comprised a conical box with a fixed lens recessed at the front and photographic plates at the back. This successful operation led to special photographic sections being set up in every squadron to develop prints and distribute the pictures to field commanders.

1915 March 3 On its last working day, the 63rd U.S. Congress passed a resolution prepared by the Smithsonian Institution that would lead to the formation of the National Advisory Committee for Aeronautics, NACA, to "supervise and direct the scientific study of the problems of flight, with a view to their practical solution." The House Committee on Naval Affairs attached the charter as a supplement to the 1915 naval appropriations bill, and Congress appropriated $5,000 for the first year. NACA was ill-defined by charter, had no teeth and was set up in the hope of

In the American Civil War, the observation balloon became a useful observation platform. It advanced to this World War I design.

catching up with European aviation by emulating the British Advisory Committee for Aeronautics constituted on April 30, 1909.

1915 March 4   Congress approved a FY 1916 appropriation bill of $300,000 for U.S. Army aviation. In the same period, naval aeronautics appropriation was to be $1,000,000, and beginning with the start of the fiscal year, an Office of Naval Aeronautics was set up, a clear indication of the importance now placed on this new arm of the service. The annual average number of personnel attached to naval aviation was also raised to 48 officers and 96 men from the navy and 12 officers and 24 men from the marines. The U.S. Army had requested $1,006,300, quoting appropriations for aviation in Germany ($45 million), Russia ($22.5 million), France ($12.8 million), Austria ($3 million), Britain ($1.08 million) and Italy ($0.8 million).

1915 March 10   At 7:30 A.M., the battle of Neuve Chapelle began when the British First Army began its attack on German positions, a battle based for the first time on hundreds of aerial reconnaissance photographs. About 1,500 maps of the German trench positions drawn to a scale of 1:8,000 were distributed to army corps units providing for the first time a complete intelligence picture of enemy positions and fortifications before an assault. Royal Flying Corps observation airplanes flew 7,500 ft. above the village as the attack began and reported German movements. During the three-day battle, RFC airplanes with makeshift bomb racks attacked German positions and supply dumps in the area of Lille, Menin and Courtrai.

1915 March 12   A Burgess H biplane (No. 28) set a world endurance record for a pilot and two passengers by remaining in the air for 7 hr. 5 min. With extra fuel tanks and special attention to the engine, student pilot Quincy B. Jones flew the airplane to the new record duration. This particular airplane had been modified by Grover C. Loening at San Diego, where the army training school was located. The fuselage and 70-HP Renault engine were retained, but substantial changes were made to the wings, providing aileron control instead of wing warping.

1915 March 18   The leading Russian air ace of World War I, Alexander Alexandrovich Kazakov, brought down his first airplane not far from the village of Guzov. Kazakov began flying training at Sevastapol at the end of 1914 and devised a method of bringing down enemy airplanes by attaching an anchor to a

long steel cable dangled beneath the fuselage. He was attempting to use this device on his first victim this day, an Albatros, when it jammed and he resorted to ramming the enemy airplane with his undercarriage. His official score of 17 airplanes shot down does not include 15 victories while flying for the British Royal Air Force against communists in Russia between August 1918 and July 1919.

1915 March 22   The term naval aviator (still in use today) was adopted for U.S. Navy officer pilots to replace the identification navy air pilot in official terminology. From the 1930s, the term naval aviation pilot was used to refer to noncommissioned aviators. The U.S. Navy was taking note of the increasing importance Royal Navy air operations were assuming in the war against German forces in Europe, and they were scaling up their resources and commitments.

1915 April 1   With a Hotchkiss machine gun firing through the propeller arc, French pilot Lt. Roland Garros with Escadrille M.S.23 shot down a German two-seat Albatros observation airplane carrying Gefreiter (Lance-Corporal) August Spacholz and Lt. Walter Grosskopf. In March the gun had been mounted on top of the nose section of a Morane-Saulnier Type N and then on a Type L when the N was damaged. Bullets were prevented from shattering the armored two-blade propeller by steel plates attached to the blades, forming wedges that were intended to deflect projectiles that otherwise strike the rear face of the blade.

1915 April 11   The Zeppelin V.G.O.I (Versuchs Gotha Ost I) three-engine bomber made its first flight at Menzell. In a change of technology from airships to giant bombers, Count von Zeppelin controlled the design by Prof. Baumann, Gustav Klein and Helmut Hirth of a flying machine with a wingspan of 138.5 ft., a length of 78 ft. 9 in. and a height of 21 ft. 8 in. powered by three 240-HP Maybach engines (two pusher and one tractor). Each engine nacelle carried a forward-mounted gun position. With a loaded weight of almost 21,000 lb., the V.G.O.I was about twice the weight of the Russian Ilya Muromets and had a speed of just over 60 MPH. Rebuilt after a crash in December 1915, it served with the Navy as R.M.L.1.

1915 April 13   Two officers of the First Aero Squadron were sent to Brownsville, Tex. with a single Martin T airplane fitted with a 90-HP Curtiss OX engine. The Model T was purchased at the request of Grover Loening, then in charge of engineering at the army aviation school at San Diego, for tractor trainers to replace the outdated Curtiss pushers. The Martin T was to patrol the border with Mexico, and Lts. Thomas Dewitt Milling and Byron Quincy Jones were to look out for guns set up by the insurgent Francisco ''Pancho'' Villa. By this time Villa was already operating three airplanes and employed five American pilots to fly against the U.S. Army.

1915 April 16   As a continuation of catapult tests first carried out November 12, 1912, with C-1, the Curtiss hydro-airplane, a catapult launch from a barge on water was performed by Lt. P. N. L. Bellinger at Pensacola, Fla. The airplane was the Navy AB-2, a Curtiss Navy Type C flying boat which, as C-2 on August 13, 1913, had been used for automatic pilot trials using Sperry equipment. Designed by naval constructor Holden C. Richardson, the catapult was built at the Washington Navy Yard. Following these successful trials, a similar device was cleared for installation on ships.

1915 April 17   The Belgian aviator Fernand Jacquet shot down in the air as the first confirmed victim of the Belgian Air Force when he successfully attacked a German Aviatik over the village of Beerst. Jacquet joined the air force in 1913, but flying was limited due to numerous defects on the Belgian airplanes, so instead of flying, he modified a 100-HP Opel racing car, attached a Lewis gun and charged around behind the German lines attacking cavalry! Jacquet scored seven victories during the war, ran a flying school in the 1920s and joined the resistance movement in World War II. He died in October 1947 and was buried under the oldest tree in Belgium.

1915 April 19 Roland Garros was shot down in his Morane-Saulnier Type L monoplane fitted with the gun deflection gear that had enabled him from the beginning of the month to shoot through the arc of his propeller. An old reserve rifleman guarding a railway station near Courtrai got off the shot that brought Garros to earth near Ingelmunster when a bullet severed his gasoline tank feed line. The airplane was captured intact, and Hptm. Foerster was directed to copy the deflectors and study armored propellers. He in turn called in Anthony Fokker, who was allowed to take away the propeller and a new Parabellum air-cooled machine gun from Garros' Morane.

1915 April 22 Warning of the first gas attack of World War I was given when Capt. L. A. Strange of No. 6 Squadron, Royal Flying Corps, flying northeast of the Belgian town of Ypres saw a yellow-green cloud emerge from the German trenches at 5:00 P.M. and slowly drift toward the French Forty-fifth Division. The Germans released 20 tons of chlorine gas creating a cloud 4 mi. across. Strange was able to observe the French fall dead while, naively unaware of its effects, they succumbed to the poison. Suspicions had been aroused when a German prisoner captured by the French told of the impending use of gas, but adverse winds postponed the attack for seven days from April 15.

1915 April 23 The U.S. National Advisory Committee for Aeronautics, Brig. Gen. George P. Scriven, chief signal officer, in charge, met for the first time in the office of the secretary of state for war. Scriven promptly suggested that NACA should become a lobbying body for more funds for military aviation. Charles D. Walcott was elected chairman of NACA, which was to comprise two members from the War Department, two from the Navy Department, one each from the Smithsonian Institution, the U.S. Weather Bureau and the Bureau of Standards, and up to 5 others.

1915 April 23 U.S. Navy Lt. P. N. L. Bellinger established an American altitude record for seaplanes by flying a Burgess-Dunne AH-10 two-seater to a height of 10,000 ft. from the Pensacola Naval Base, Fla. The Burgess-Dunne AH-10 was a license-built seaplane version of the British Dunne BD two-seat, tailless, pusher biplane. It was fitted with a single 100-HP Curtiss OXX engine which provided a maximum speed of approximately 69 MPH. The unusual-looking airplane had a span of 46.5 ft. and weighed 2,000 lb. loaded. Two seaplane versions of the British airplane were built by Burgess.

1915 April 26 A spirited attack on German supply trains in the railway station at Courtrai won for 2d Lt. W. B. Rhodes-Moorhouse of No. 2 Squadron, Royal Flying Corps, the first Victoria Cross given to an aviator. Britain's highest award for gallantry, the Victoria Cross, was awarded May 22 for an attack in which Rhodes-Moorhouse dropped a 100-lb. bomb from his B.E.2c at a height of only 300 ft. He flew through a hail of machine gun and rifle fire, receiving an intense burst from a gunner in the belfry of Courtrai church. Wounded in the abdomen, he flew on and was again hit in the thigh and one hand. Struggling to reach his own airfield at Merville, he brought his airplane safely back but died the next day.

1915 May 1 Lady des Vouex unveiled a B.E.2c biplane at Farnborough, England. It had been paid for by public donation and had the word OVERSEAS on the side of the fuselage. Organized by the Overseas League, set up to link British families in foreign countries, the voluntary contributions had been encouraged as a means of displaying unity among British people overseas and rallying morale at home. It was the first of many Royal Flying Corps, Royal Naval Air Service and Royal Air Force aircraft to carry "presentation" details, beginning a practice that would be continued in World War II.

1915 May 8 The first nonrigid airships (blimps) procured for the British Royal Naval Air Service were set up at the base for these aircraft at Folkestone. The first was called Sea Scout 1 (S.S.1). By the end of the year, eight airships of this type had been delivered to Folkestone, and a second base at Eastbourne was set up July 6. In all, the RNAS would acquire 36 airships of this type, used for patroling the Dover Straits, the Thames estuary and other deserted waterways and coastal regions where German surface or airborne raiders might try to sneak in undetected. Observation cars comprised B.E.2b or Farman fuselages suspended by cables.

1915 May 13 The first of the German navy's second-generation Zeppelin airships, the L 10, made its first flight. The first generation had a capacity of about 740,000 cu. ft., but L 10, the first of 15 in its class, had a capacity of 1,126,400 cu. ft., a length of 536.5 ft. and a diameter of 61 ft. 4 in. Powered by four 210-HP Maybach engines, L 10 could top 57 MPH and had a carrying capacity of 35,000 lb. It made 28 military flights, of which five were raids on England. It was struck by lightning on September 3, 1915, off Neuwerk Island near Cuxhaven, Germany and destroyed, killing all 19 people on board. It had been commanded by Kptlt. Hirsch.

1915 May 23 Anthony Fokker gave a stunning demonstration of his new E.I monoplane at Stenay, Germany in front of the German crown prince and, among others, Lt. Otto Parschau, one of the first German air aces. The E.I was fitted with an interrupter gear enabling a machine gun to fire through the propeller arc by a device that would prevent the gun firing when a propeller blade was directly in front of the barrel. Developed by Fokker when he was given the propeller blades from Roland Garros' Morane Type N shot down April 19, the gear was fitted to M.5K serial number 216, and from this demonstration, a major production order ensued when it was given the military type designation E.I. Parschau accompanied Fokker on demonstrations to German flying units on how best to use the monoplane in combat.

1915 May 23 Italy declared war on Germany and the Austrian empire. By the next day, the Military Aeronautics Corps (Corpo Aeronautico Militare), set up on January 7, 1915, had three major groups with a total of 75 aircraft, 50 pilots and six observers. Four squadrons with Blériot monoplanes formed the First Group, attached to the Third Army; three squadrons with Nieuports formed the Second Group with the Second Army; and two squadrons of Maurice-Farmans and one of Nieuports formed the Third Group attached to Army headquarters. A separate squadron of Blériot monoplanes was stationed at Venice with three airships, and the Naval Air Service had two airships and 30 airplanes, of which five were Curtiss pushers.

1915 May 26 In the first known incident in which a German observation biplane shot down another airplane in flight, Oblt.

Kastner and his observer Lt. Georg Langhoff attacked a French Voisin pusher reconnaissance biplane so badly that it was forced to land near Douai. The German two-seat Halberstadt C I was a more compact version of the Halberstadt B II but with the observer seated behind the pilot and free to use a ring-mounted machine gun. It was the first attempt to configure crew and defensive armament for optimum efficiency, but the aircraft was still not a fighter; the gun was carried to defend the observer, whose primary job was reconnaissance, and not to initiate an attack on enemy aircraft, which is more properly the role of a fighter. The future German air ace Oswald Boelcke retrieved the gun from the Voisin and attached it to his reconnaissance biplane for practice.

1915 May 31   The first German airship raid on London began when army Zeppelin LZ 38 commanded by Hptm. E. Linnarz crossed the British coastline at 9:42 P.M. LZ 38 dropped 30 small bombs and 90 incendiary devices between Stoke Newington in north London (which it passed at 11:20 P.M.) and Wanstead in northeast London (11:35 P.M.). On the way, it circled south almost as far as the Thames River, laying some bombs close to St. Paul's Cathedral. In all, seven people were killed, 35 were injured, and £18,596 worth of damage was caused. LZ 38 left England on a course almost due east. In frustrated anger, some Londoners attacked shops owned by people believed to be of German origin.

1915 June 1   The Connecticut Aircraft Co. received a contract from the U.S. Navy for the navy's first airship, designated DN-1 for Dirigible Navy No. 1. The $45,646 contract stipulated delivery in late 1915, but not until December 1916 did the airship finally arrive. It was originally fitted with two 140-HP Sturtevant engines, but this weighed the airship down and one engine had to be removed before it could fly. When the Navy airship designation system was formalized in 1917 with the B-series, the DN-1 was retrospectively redesignated an A type, the sole example.

1915 June 1   Brainchild of the British airplane designer Geoffrey de Havilland, the prototype Airco D.H.2 was flown for the first time, the second independent design produced by the Aircraft Manufacturing Co. Ltd. De Havilland had left the Royal Aircraft Factory in May 1914 to design airplanes for Airco, but as a reserve Royal Flying Corps officer, he reported for duty August 4, 1914. Within three months, he was back at Airco designing a twin-boom pusher biplane with an observer in front wielding a 0.303 Lewis machine gun. The D.H.1 appeared in January 1915, but the improved D.H.2 was a greater success and reached squadrons in January 1916.

1915 June 4   The first German navy airship of the Schutte-Lanz type, the SL 3, made its first raid on England. It was the biggest airship built to this date and had a length of 502 ft., a diameter of almost 65 ft. and a volume of 1,143,500 cu. ft. Powered by four 210-HP Maybach motors, the SL 3 had a trials speed of 52 MPH. Made of wood, as were all Schutte-Lanz airships, it rapidly absorbed moisture and could not reach altitudes higher than 6,560 ft. Nevertheless, it dropped bombs on the countryside in England before returning to base.

1915 June 6   Although not the first to be so attacked, a Russian Ilya Muromets four-engine bomber operating against Prussian targets on the Eastern Front was attacked by a large number of German airplanes 40 mi. inside German territory in a remarkable example of the aircraft survivability. Engaged on a long-distance bombing mission, the giant airplane was hit repeatedly with machine gun fire. In spite of severe damage and two engines out of

action, the Ilya Muromets struggled back safely to base. The Russian bomber was building a formidable reputation for itself among friend and foe alike.

1915 June 7   Flt. Sub-Lt. R. A. J. Warneford, flying a Morane-Saulnier Type L monoplane (serial no. 3253), of No. 1 Squadron, Royal Naval Air Service, in France, successfully attacked and destroyed German Army Zeppelin LZ 37 commanded by Oblt. van der Haegen. Warneford spotted LZ 37 in the dark and destroyed it by gliding down from a height of 11,000 ft. and dropping six 20-lb. Hale bombs along its length from 150 ft. at 2:25 A.M. The resulting explosion threw the monoplane upside down and cut the fuel line, but Warneford landed behind enemy lines, repaired the damage and took off again, got lost and landed at Cap Gris Nez on the English Channel. In a bizarre footnote, one of the survivors, airship helmsman Alfred Muhler, crashed through the roof of a nunnery and onto a bed, killing two nuns. Warneford was awarded the Victoria Cross on June 11, 1915, the first for the Royal Naval Air Service.

1915 June 8   Glenn H. Curtiss was awarded patent no. 1,142,754 from the U.S. patent office for the design of a stepped flying boat or seaplane hull or float. Curtiss had pioneered the application of a step in the undersurface of seaplanes, enabling them to "unstick" from the water and reduce drag affecting free flight. The step allowed the seaplane to lift and simultaneously reduce the surface friction area, providing a reduced-area planing surface to aid ascent. Like so many patents of this type, Curtiss was too specific about the design detail to prevent it being circumvented by a simple design innovation.

1915 June 16   Flying a new German Albatros C. I two-seater (serial no. 162/15) with his observer, Lt. Wühlisch, in the rear seat with a machine gun, Lt. Oswald Boelcke engaged five enemy airplanes in separate encounters between 10:20 A.M. and 8:50 P.M. Though he may have damaged some, none were officially recorded as victories. The five engagements, one in the morning and four in the afternoon, were recorded on four separate flights. Boelcke had had an encounter with a Bristol Scout the day before, following two days of flying the new Albatros to get used to the airplane.

1915 June   Anthony Fokker and Lt. Otto Parschau were sent to Douai, on the Western Front, with the demonstration Fokker E.I equipped with an interrupter gear for the forward-firing machine gun. The German army wanted to test the new fighting airplane in the real combat of the Verdun and Arras sectors on the Western Front. More than 40 Fokker E.Is had been ordered, and the new Fokkers were to be issued for escorting unarmed two-seat reconnaissance biplanes.

1915 July 1   Flying one of the new Fokker E.I fighting monoplanes equipped with a forward-firing machine gun, Lt. Kurt Wintgens, one of Germany's earliest but largely unsung aces, shot down a Morane-Saulnier monoplane, his first victory. This airplane was the first to be shot down by the new Fokker E.I, effectively the world's first purpose-built fighter. Wintgens would achieve distinction flying Fokker monoplanes with the Bavarian unit Field Flying Sections F1 67b and 62. On July 1, 1916, he would receive the Ordre Pour le Mérite (established by Frederick the Great in 1740 when French was the language of the Prussian court). Before his death on September 26, 1916, Wintgens would be credited with 18 airplanes shot down.

1915 July 2   Alexander Prokofieff de Seversky was shot down in a two-seat seaplane on his first bombing flight in the Russian

Reconnaissance aircraft like this Albatros C.I formed the majority of military aircraft in service during World War I.

Imperial Naval Air Service. His plane fell into the Gulf of Riga, but the impact detonated a bomb on the seaplane, killing the observer and blowing off Seversky's right leg. A graduate of the Imperial Navy Academy, Seversky went on to shoot down 13 enemy airplanes, becoming Russia's third leading air ace before making his home in America after the Bolsheviks came to power. In 1936, he designed America's first monoplane fighter to feature an enclosed cockpit and retractable undercarriage.

1915 July 4   Lt. Oswald Boelcke was piloting a two-seat Albatros C.I reconnaissance plane when his observer shot down their first victim, a French Morane-Saulnier Type L monoplane flown by Lt. Tetu and Comte Beauvicourt, after a spirited attack that lasted 25 min. In the new Albatros C.I, the observer was situated behind the pilot and had an increased field of fire. In the rear seat, Lt. Wühlisch kept his gun trained on the monoplane as Boelcke held the Albatros within range of its target. In an ironic twist of fate, Comte Beauvicourt fell dead into the grounds of his own estate in France.

1915 July 7   Oswald Boelcke began flying his new Fokker E.I monoplane (serial no. E3/15) with forward-firing machine gun, a type he had first tested on June 24. The new fighter was welcomed by Boelcke, a master tactician and aggressive but prudent combatant who would mold future fighter pilots through careful training and leadership. Boelcke's second aerial victory, his first with the E.I, came on August 19, 1915, when he shot down a Bristol Scout over the Western Front. His third victory was achieved September 9 using a new Fokker E.II (serial no. 37/15), a plane similar to the E.I but with a more powerful 100-HP Oberursel engine.

1915 July 19   The man destined to become the second-highest-scoring French air ace in World War I, Cpl. Georges M. L. J. Guynemer, scored his first aerial victory while flying a two-seat Morane-Saulnier parasol monoplane over Coucy with his gunner, a mechanic named Guerder. They overhauled an Aviatik two-seat observation airplane and closed to within 150 ft., at which point Guerder opened fire, observing splinters flying from the Aviatik. Return fire from the German airplane grazed Guerder's head and a hand as Guynemer flew under the Aviatik for his gunner to fire up from below. The German airplane fell away and burst into flames.

1915 July 20   Vice-Adm. Bachmann, chief of the German naval staff, sought permission from Kaiser Wilhelm II for indiscriminate bombing of London, with the proviso ''on humanitarian grounds that these be made only on week-ends, from Saturday to Monday morning, so that buildings in the City would be unoccupied.'' The excuse was that the commercial heart of London must be destroyed to bring England to her knees and stop the war. The kaiser agreed that henceforth the indiscriminate bombing of civilian targets was justified, except for the royal palaces and historic buildings.

1915 July 25   Maj. Lanoe George Hawker of No. 6 Squadron, Royal Flying Corps, flying a Bristol Scout C (serial no. 1611) biplane fitted with a 80-HP Gnôme rotary engine, downed three German airplanes, an action for which he was awarded the third Victoria Cross given to a British aviator (August 24). The first encounter was a German observation biplane near Ypres, Belgium, which fell away after Hawker fired off a 47-round drum of ammunition from his gun, fixed at a 45° angle to one side of the fuselage. Over Houthoulst Forest, he attacked another and shot it down, followed by another over Hooge, which tipped its observer out as it fell earthward from 11,000 ft.

1915 July 26   The First Aero Squadron left San Diego, Calif. for Fort Sill in Oklahoma for trials at the field artillery school in an effort to perfect army cooperation techniques and observation as well as gun spotting and fire control, in which the airplane crew communicate information about firing accuracy to artillery batteries on the ground. The need for this had been demonstrated in April when two pilots had been sent to Texas for operations with the army against Pancho Villa in Mexico, with poor and uncoordinated results. Army requests for airplane support on the Mexico border, however, once again sent a detachment south before proper tactics could be worked out.

1915 July   In France manufacturers were asked to produce a bomber capable of hitting the German town of Essen, and Brequet successfully produced a derivative of the November 1914 BU3 bomber. Of unequal span, the newer biplane was powered by a 220-HP Renault pusher engine and appeared in October 1915 as a two-seat airplane with a tail supported by four booms attached to the wings. Capable of carrying a 639-lb. bomb load, it had a four-wheel landing gear with two wheels on struts under the nose and two under the wings. To support BU3 operations, the Michelin brothers sought a flying field to set up a special bombing school and found a suitable location but with sticky soil. In January 1916, they built the world's first concrete runway—1,312 ft. long and 65 ft. wide.

1915 August 1   Max Immelmann of the German air unit Field Flying Section 62 under Hptm. Kastner shot down a B.E.2c of No. 2 Squadron, Royal Flying Corps, while flying a Fokker E.I. It was a protracted attack for although the airplane was unarmed, Immelmann's machine gun jammed three times. 2nd Lt. W. Reid was wounded when the B.E.2c crash-landed near Bredières and was taken prisoner. Immelmann had first tried the E.I on July 31, successfully firing 30 rounds at ground targets.

1915 August 11   The U.S. naval observatory asked Eastman Kodak to develop a special aerial reconnaissance camera that could be used from an airplane flying at heights of 3,000 ft. to 6,000 ft. A special high-speed lens would be needed, along with fast film, to capture clearly small objects and features on the ground below. The United States was now far behind similar developments in Great Britain and continental Europe, where the spur to aerial reconnaissance brought about by war had generated enormous developments universally applied to the several air forces involved.

1915 August 12   Flying a Short 184 seaplane, Flt. Comdr. C. H. K. Edmonds of the Royal Naval Air Service fired a torpedo in combat for the first time. A small converted packet boat, *Ben-my-chree* from the Isle of Man had been adapted to carry seaplanes and in such a configuration sailed May 21 for the Dardanelles in the Aegean Sea, arriving at the Gulf of Xeros on June 12. With only 45 min. of fuel and limited to a maximum height of 800 ft., the Short lumbered along to attack a Turkish transport ship off Gallipoli. Edmonds launched his torpedo from a height of 15 ft., 900 ft. from the ship, which had already been crippled by a submarine. Five days later, Edmonds attacked another ship, which he successfully hit and set on fire, leaving it a useless hulk.

1915 August 19   Col. H. M. Trenchard took command of the British Royal Flying Corps in France and Sir David Henderson,

who had gone to France with the first squadrons a year earlier, returned to England to serve on the army council. Trenchard had received his pilot's certificate on August 13, 1912, on a Farman biplane, and then went to the Central Flying School (CFS) for his military flying training. On August 7, 1914, with the temporary rank of Lieutenant Colonel, he was appointed commanding officer of the Royal Flying Corps military wing. Trenchard would become a leading force in the Royal Flying Corps and the Royal Air Force that succeeded it in April 1918.

1915 August   The first Fokker E.III monoplanes began to reach front-line German fighter units. These were an improvement on the E.I and E.II in that the wings spanned 31 ft. 3 in. versus 29 ft. 4.5 in. and gave reduced wing loading, greater maneuverability and better performance. Known by the Fokker type number M.14, the E.III had better synchronizing gear and, from October, a rate of fire that increased from 400 RPM to 600 RPM. The standard E.III had a single machine gun, but some had two, and air ace Max Immelmann wanted a battery of three guns with a more powerful engine. This led to the final version, the E.IV, developed during October and November.

1915 September 7   The first airship to bomb the "square mile" of the city of London killed 18 people and injured 28 in a raid that began around midnight and caused 9,616 pounds worth of damage. The Army Zeppelin LZ 74 commanded by Hptm. Friedrich George and the Army Schutte-Lanz SL 2 commanded by Hptm. Richard von Wobeser dropped bombs on Millwall, Deptford, Greenwich and Woolwich docks and Cheshunt while a single incendiary hit Fenchurch St. Army airship LZ 77 commanded by Hptm. Alfred Horn had set out with George and Wobeser but only raided the east coast.

1915 September 8   The greatest material damage incurred by a single air raid on England during World War I resulted from a raid on London by Navy Zeppelin L 13, commanded by Kptlt. H. Mathy, which included the dropping of the first 660-lb. bomb used in the war. The attack began at about 10:40 P.M. when Mathy dropped a stick of sighting bombs between Euston and Liverpool streets killing 26 and injuring 94. Fires started as a result and caused damage worth 534,287 pounds. Adm. Sir Percy Scott, a practical and antibureaucratic man, was put in charge of London's defenses and quickly recognized that airplanes, not guns, would be most effective in bringing down the raiders.

1915 September 8   Anton Knubel lost his life in an aircraft of his own design and build and that he had covered with a transparent material called "Cellon." As early as May 1912, Hptm. Petrocz von Petroczy had covered an Etrich Taube with transparent "Emmalit" material, and following Knubel's work, several German manufacturers, including Fokker, experimented unsuccessfully with making aircraft virtually invisible in the sky by covering them with "Cellon."

1915 September 13   The Royal Flying Corps carried out the first in a daring series of attempts to land agents behind enemy lines. Capt. T. W. Mulcahy-Morgan of No. 6 Squadron flew a special agent to Courtrai in a B.E.2c, hoping to set him down in a small field near a forest. The pilot collided with a tree, and both men were injured and eventually captured, but friendly locals retrieved carrier pigeons, which the agent would have used to send messages, along with secret, incriminating papers. A successful attempt was made on September 28, establishing a precedent that would expand through World War I and, in time, World War II.

A twin-engined AEG G.II bomber and its crew prepare to take off for a flight over the lines.

1915 September 15 At the start of a tragic series of debilitating accidents, German air ace Rudolf Berthold was shot down in an A.E.G. reconnaissance biplane. Uninjured, he obtained a Fokker E.III in January 1916 but was shot down again after his fifth victory, for which he received the Ordre Pour le Mérite. Fighting with vigor and determination, he increased his score to 28 before his right arm was torn off by gunfire. With special controls, he returned to combat, a flaming sword painted on his airplane. Flying demonically and wracked with pain as his wounds frequently opened in flight, Berthold crashed into a house after his 44th victory. Having survived the war, he met an ignominious end, being bludgeoned and battered by communists before being throttled with his medal ribbon on March 15, 1920.

1915 October 2 The French airship *Alsace* was destroyed during a low-altitude night bombing raid, and its commander, Lt. Cohen, was taken prisoner along with the rest of the crew. The loss dissuaded the army from night bombing raids on nights other than the very darkest. The *Alsace* had been built by the Societé Astra des Constructions Aéronautiques, one of the most successful French airship manufacturing companies. It was one of the first enlarged designs improved from a semi-rigid Spanish airship known as the Torrès Quevedo. It had a length of 295 ft. and a volume of 494,340 cu. ft. and, at the request of Gen. Etienne Joux, was improved by the addition of an antiaircraft machine gun on an upper platform. The *Alsace* could carry 2,866 lb. of bombs at 920 ft. or reach 13,100 ft. unladen.

1915 October 7 The American adventurer and future ace of the Escadrille Lafayette (a squadron of American volunteer aviators anxious to fight against Germany), Gervais Raoul Lufbery was posted to the Escadrille des Bombardements VB.106 to serve as a pilot of two-seat bombing planes. Lufbery had joined Escadrille N.23 in September 1914 to serve as mechanic to his friend

and veteran aviator Marc Pourpe. When Pourpe was killed, Lufbery trained to fly on Maurice-Farman and Voisin biplanes and received his brevet on July 29. Lufbery would remain with VB.106 until beginning his training for single-seat scout airplanes.

1915 October 9 Lts. Herbert A. Dargue and Walter G. Kilner of the U.S. Signal Corps' San Diego flying school carried out the first flight tests preceding development of an airplane radio telegraph transmission service capable of communication across several hundred miles. Lt. Kilner piloted a Curtiss tractor biplane while Lt. Dargue voiced into a dictaphone to record sound levels of the human voice, the wind and the engine. The first successful long-range radio telegraphy tests were carried out in spring 1916, and by early 1917 several sets had been produced.

1915 October 11 U.S. Army aviator Lt. Walter R. Taliaferro was flying a Curtiss J, *S.C. No. 30,* when he attempted a loop at 2,000 ft. but was unable to complete it before striking the water of San Diego Bay with terrific force. Next day his body was found pinned beneath the airplane in 50 ft. of water. The cause of the accident was never officially announced, but the accident prompted aviation training schools to teach aerobatics as a positive form of flying so other pilots could be equipped with professional knowledge regarding the consequences of such maneuvers in the air. On September 17, 1915, Lt. Taliaferro had set a new single-seat U.S. endurance record of 9 hrs. 48 min.

1915 October 15 At the second meeting of the National Advisory Committee for Aeronautics in Washington, D.C. since its inaugural session in April 1915, the secretary was instructed by the committee to inform other federal government departments about NACA conclusions on the state of aviation in the United States and on how they might usefully increase experimental work leading to greater progress with aviation. Such instructions were basically a fudge because nobody could seriously anticipate where aeronautics was going in the United States and how it might be harnessed for greater progress in aviation and the development of the airplane. To the perceptive, NACA served to reinforce fears that America was now lagging far behind England and continental European countries.

1915 November 1 The first air company of the U.S. National Guard was formed under the command of Capt. Raynal C. Bolling and was called the Aviation Detachment, First Battalion, Signal Corps, National Guard, New York. It soon became known as the First Aero Company and had four officers and 40 enlisted men. Because Congress had not appropriated greater funds for military aviation, the Aero Club of America had set up a subscription campaign to raise funds for National Guard air units and on April 15, 1915, had announced an airplane competition for the National Guard and Naval Militia. This was postponed because of the scare caused by the sinking of the *Lusitania*.

1915 November 3 The first take-off by a wheeled landplane from the deck of a ship specially converted to carry seaplanes was made when the Royal Navy flew a Bristol Scout C piloted by Flt. Sub-Lt. H. F. Towler off the *Vindex*, an Isle of Man packet boat converted to carry seven seaplanes. The Bristol Scout had to ditch alongside the *Vindex*, which had no provision for landings. On August 6, 1915, a Sopwith Baby with wheels on its floats had taken off from the *Campania*, a 20,000-ton seaplane carrier converted from a Cunard liner to accommodate up to 10 trolleyed seaplanes on a 200 ft. deck. Not before August 2, 1917, however, would an airplane with wheels successfully land on a ship.

1915 November 5 United States Navy pilot Lt. Comdr. H. C. Mustin made the first catapult launch of a powered airplane from the stern deck of the battleship USS *North Carolina*, at anchor in Pensacola Bay, Fla. This test followed a previous catapult launch from a barge on April 16 and preceded a launch with the ship under way November 6. The Curtiss AB-2 used for the test was the same machine used in the barge experiment. The designation AB-2 indicated by the initial letter *A* that it was built by Curtiss, the first constructor to sell the navy an airplane, and by the letter *B* that it was a flying boat. The number indicated the delivery sequence for the batch AB-1 through AB-5.

1915 November 13 Future German air ace Otto Parschau, the first man to fly the new generation of fighting Fokker monoplanes, issued his test report on the Fokker E.IV, the definitive monoplane of its type. Still using wing warping like its predecessors, it was given an optimistic evaluation. Developed by Fokker as his Type M.15, the E.IV had two machine guns and was powered by a 160-HP Oberursel; but was overweight and quickly eclipsed by Allied fighters that appeared in early 1916. Max Immelmann requested a three-gun E.IV and had a captured 160-HP Le Rhône engine fitted to one also, but this was unsatisfactory, as was the E.IV generally.

1915 November 19–26 The U.S. Army First Aero Squadron made what amounted to its first cross-country migration when it flew its airplanes in several stages from Fort Sill, Okla., which it had occupied since July, to Fort Sam Houston, San Antonio, Tex. The 439 mi. were covered without incident and provided many lessons in the logistical problems of moving airplanes over great distances. The detachment at Brownsville, Tex., which had been sent there in August, joined the main unit at Fort Sill before the end of the year.

1915 December 1 The First Company, Second Aero Squadron, was formally brought into being at San Diego, Calif., having been established on paper May 12, 1915, to operate from the Philippines. The first five officers and 33 men left San Francisco on the U.S. transport ship USS *Sheridan* bound for Manila on January 5, 1916. This was the first element in a plan to establish air bases on the Philippines, Hawaii and the Panama Canal Zone, and funds were requested for these latter activities to be set up during 1916–17. Airplanes for the Philippine squadron (some equipped wth radio transmitters) began to arrive at Fort Mills, Atlanta on March 19, 1916.

1915 December 4 Charles E. J. M. Nungesser, third-highest-scoring French air ace of World War I, received the Légion d'Honneur for shooting down a German airplane over Nomeny. Nungesser had joined the army at the beginning of the war, after returning hastily from Argentina where he had been searching for his uncle while, at the age of 17, building his own airplane. Nungesser received a citation within one month of joining the Second Hussars, and he then received the Médaille Militaire for the heroic capture of a German staff car behind German lines. He joined Escadrille V.B.106 in April 1915, then moved to Escadrille N.65 in November 1915.

1915 December 12 Designated J 1 by the research establishment Junkers and nicknamed *Blechesel* (''tin donkey''), the first all-metal airplane was flown for its inaugural flight by Lt. von Mallinckrodt. A cantilever monoplane, the J 1 was powered by a 120-HP Mercedes engine. This was followed by the more successful J2 in 1916, and a number were built and tested. Much impressed by the unprecedented standard of construction, the Airplane Ministry ordered an armored biplane (for which Junkers involved the servces of Prof. Madelung) known as the Junkers J 4 (J I by the army), which was completed in 1917.

1915 December 17 The prototype Handley Page O/100 bomber (serial no. 1455) made its first flight from Henden, England at 2:00 P.M. powered by two 250-HP Rolls Royce V-12 engines driving four-blade propellers, with Lt. Comdr. J. T. Babington and Lt. Comdr. E. W. Stedman on board. The O-type bomber ordered by the Admiralty in December 1914 was given its numerical designation 100 from its 100-ft. wingspan. It had a length of 62 ft. 10 in. and a maximum loaded weight of 14,000 lb.—a little shorter than the Ilya Muromets but a lot heavier. On the first flight, the O/100 became airborne at 50 MPH.

1915 December 17 A meeting between senior officers of the British and French air units discussed a common bombing policy and coordinated operations involving airplanes of both forces. A close cooperation had already been established between the French and the Royal Naval Air Service via the Admiralty. This meeting confirmed policy that would be directed toward a strategic bombing offensive implemented as and when technical performance of available airplanes allowed. The French requested British bombing sights and ordered some Sopwith 1½ Strutters, with which they were very impressed.

1916 January 1 The German Ostend Carrier Pigeons, which had been formed in September 1914, and the Metz Carrier Pigeons, formed in August 1915, were renamed Combat Squadrons of the High Command (Kampfgeschwader der Obersten Heeresleitung, or Kagohl). Divested of the code names that hid their original purpose of carrying out bombing missions, Ostend Carrier Pigeons became Kagohl 1 and Metz Carrier Pigeons became Kagohl 2. By midyear, the number of squadrons had increased to seven, but without effective long-range bombers, they were denied the opportunity to conduct strategic attacks.

1916 January 12 Max Immelmann and Oswald Boelcke, two of Germany's greatest air aces, received the first awards of the Ordre Pour le Mérite given to airmen for scoring eight confirmed victories over enemy airplanes. A friendly rivalry for highest scores began soon after they achieved their first victories in July and August 1915, respectively. Boelcke would be remembered for his dictates on fighter tactics and squadron organization. Immelmann is forever remembered for exploiting a maneuver known as the "Immelmann turn," in which the airplane is pulled up through a half-loop, then, when inverted, rolled into level flight, flying in the opposite direction to it original course. Beginning in 1917, the award was given only after 16 victories.

1916 January 12 A tally of the U.S. Army aviation showed the Aviation Section, comprising the Aeronautical Division, the San Diego Signal Corps Aviation School, the First Aero Squadron and the First Company, Second Aero Squadron, had 46 officers, 243 enlisted men and 23 airplanes. In the six years since 1909, the Signal Corps had bought 59 airplanes, of which one was in the Smithsonian, 32 had been destroyed or written off and three were out of repair. The Aeronautical Division was temporarily headed by Capt. William Mitchell, who had been appointed to the task on April 3, relieving Capt. George S. Gibbs, and would soon be promoted to major.

1916 January 13 The Curtiss Aeroplane and Motor Corp. was formed, incorporating Burgess and Curtiss of Marblehead, Mass. Thus began the first major American air industrial concern, which during World War I would build 5,221 airplanes and over 5,000 engines in nine factories and employ 18,000 workers. Curtiss had successfully established a nationwide name for his airplanes, which, although capable of good exhibition performance, lagged far behind the combat-tested European products.

1916 January 14 The headquarters of the Royal Flying Corps issued a directive requiring henceforth that reconnaissance airplanes "be escorted by at least three other fighting machines." This resulted from an unprecedented success rate achieved by German Fokker monoplane fighters equipped with forward firing machine guns in shooting down two-seaters, a so-called "Fokker scourge." A typical patrol formation would position an escorting fighter 500 ft. either side of the escorted biplane, with the third escort on rear guard 500 ft. higher. The Fokker would soon meet their match in the British D.H.2 and F.E.2b biplanes with single pusher engines.

1916 January The last nonrigid airships obtained by the Royal Naval Air Service and built in Britain were ordered as N.S.1 to N.S.12, the N.S. standing for North Sea, which was to be their prime patrol area. *N.S.1* was completed in February 1917 and flew 1,500 mi. during a 49.5 hr. flight. Beginning July 1917, the airships were based at East Fortune, but they suffered increasingly from technical problems and could not accompany the Grand Fleet as expected. A typical patrol lasted 24 hr., although after the war *N.S.11* set an endurance record in 1919 of 101 hours, traveling 4,000 mi.

1916 February 9 The first truly successful British tractor-engined fighter, the Sopwith Scout (later called Sopwith Pup) was cleared for flight trials at Sopwith's experimental works in England. Powered by an 80-HP Le Rhône engine, it had a maximum loaded weight of just under 1,300 lb. Production machines would feature a forward-firing Vickers machine gun attached to

the fuselage between the pilot and the engine. Because Sopwith was a navy contractor, the Royal Naval Air Service evaluated the Pup, but when Maj. Gen. Hugh Trenchard received word on its performance, he ordered the airplane for operations in France. The Pup was a delight to fly, was loved by all pilots and would serve as a fighter with the Royal Flying Corps until late 1917 and with the Royal Naval Air Service until the end of 1918.

1916 February 16 Field Marshal Lord French, the British commander-in-chief home forces, assumed control of London's defenses against air attack. He took over air defenses for the rest of England six days later. Home forces command estimated that a minimum of 10 squadrons would be necessary eventually. Maj. T. C. R. Higgins was given command of No. 19 Reserve Aeroplane Squadron, which was to be responsible for London's defenses.

1916 February 18 Italian Caproni bombers made their first air raid on key installations in Serbia. A flight of the biplane bombers attacked the important town of Ljubljana in Slovenia. The Corpo Aeronautico Militare had built up the Caproni force to eight squadrons, and they were used against Austro-Hungarian troops. Other Caproni units were based in France for bombing missions against the German forces on the Western Front.

1916 March 15 Following an attack by Mexican rebel Pancho Villa on New Mexico, Brig. Gen. John J. Pershing was ordered to take a force of 15,000 men to Columbus, N.Mex., while the First Aero Squadron arrived to support ground forces. Capt. Benjamin D. Foulois had just eight airplanes and 94 officers and men, although this would increase to 138 in May. Operations began on March 19 but were a farce. Violent winds and high mountains prevented any reconnaissance patrols and the Curtiss JN biplanes were relegated to mail carrying. Only two airplanes were operational by April 20, several having been lost to friendly fire. The unit remained, however, through early 1917.

1916 March 17 Believing naval power to be an important instrument for Japan's defensive and imperial aspirations, Japan established its naval air corps and equipped it with several European airplanes. Some of the Blériot, Short, Sopwith and Farman airplanes, although designed in France and Britain, were built in Japan. After the war, naval aviation would lag behind developments with army aviation because an air mission from Britain projected the view that airplanes were primarily instruments for army cooperation rather than serving as a force in their own right.

1916 March 24 Oswald Boelcke issued a report on the 160-HP Fokker E.IV monoplane fighter and dismissed the logic of fitting it with three upward-firing machine guns, as Immelmann had requested. Moreover, said Boelcke, the type was slow, unable to make the agile turns characteristic of the lower-powered E.III and prone to failure due to poor manufacturing standards. Failures in the synchronization gear caused Immelmann to shoot his propeller off in December, March and May, causing him to make emergency landings. After getting his E.IV on December 13, 1915, Boelcke, too, shot his propeller off.

1916 March 25 A Bristol Scout C (serial no. 5313) fitted with a Vickers machine gun and a Challenger synchronizing gear, the first British airplane to reach the Royal Flying Corps in France fitted with a gun that would fire through the propeller arc, arrived at No. 12 Squadron. It then went to No. 11 Squadron and in it, on May 15, future air ace Albert Ball had a fight with an Albatros two-seater, having joined the squadron eight days earlier. More widely used, however, would be the Sopwith 1½ Strutter armed with a synchronized Vickers gun and a Lewis gun in the rear cockpit, which appeared on the Western Front about this time.

1916 March 29   The Society of British Aircraft Constructors (SBAC) was registered as a private group of plane makers following an idea put together by George Holt Thomas that British aircraft builders should speak to government and the treasury with a united voice. At the first meeting on April 13, a management committee was formed comprising H. White Smith (British & Colonial Aeroplane Co.), Maj. H. F. Wood (Vickers Ltd.), R. O. Carey (Sopwith Aviation Co.), G. Holt Thomas (Aircraft Manufacturing Co.), Howard T. Wright (J. Samuel Wright & Co.), A. V. Roe (A. V. Roe & Co.), E. B. Parker (Short Bros.), L. Coatalen (Sunbeam Motor Car Co.) and E. W. Petter (Westland Aircraft Works). H. White Smith was voted chairman and Charles V. Allen secretary with offices at St. Stephen's House, Victoria Embankment, London. Today SBAC stands for Society of British Aerospace Companies.

1916 March 30   The secretary of the treasury wrote to the U.S. Navy Department assigning funds for the first of six U.S. Coast Guard officers to receive flight training at Pensacola, Fla. One of these men, Lt. Elmer F. Stone, with Norman Hall, conceived in early 1915 the possibility of using airplanes for reconnainance on Coast Guard activity. A Curtiss F was used for preliminary evaluation in 1915, and Hall went to the Curtiss factory to study engineering in 1916, the year Coast Guard aviation truly began.

1916 April 2   Lt. R. C. Saufley of the U.S. Navy established a record altitude for seaplanes by reaching a height of 16,072 ft. in a Curtiss. On November 30, 1915, Saufley had flown the Curtiss Type AH-8 hydro-airplane, designated AH-14 by the navy, to a height of 11,056 ft., increasing that to 11,975 ft. on December 3 and to 16,010 ft. on March 29, 1916. Saufley was killed when he crashed June 9, 1916, off Pensacola at 8 hr. 51 min. into a long-duration flight attempt in a Type AH-8.

1916 April 6   In what is believed to be the first air-launch of an airplane from the top of another airplane in flight, a Bristol Scout C (serial no. 3028) flown by Flt. Lt. M. J. Day of the Royal Naval Air Service was carried into the air by a Felixstowe Porte Baby flying boat. At a height of about 1,000 ft. over Harwich, the engine of the Bristol Scout was started and it flew away from the Porte Baby. The carrier airplane bore the name of its designer, Sqdn. Comdr. John Porte, and was powered by three 250-HP Rolls Royce engines, two driving tractor propellers and one driving a pusher. With a design based on the Curtiss flying boat America, the Porte Baby had a wing span of 124 ft., a length of 63 ft. and a loaded weight of 18,600 lb.

1916 April 7   Future top Italian air ace Francesco Baracca scored his first victory during a fight with an Austrian Aviatik on reconnaissance duty. Baracca was born in May 1888 and joined the flying school at Reims in April 1912, having spent three years in the Italian cavalry. He was a seasoned pilot by the time Italy declared war on the Central Powers in May 1915. Baracca had his first encounter with an enemy airplane on September 7, 1915, but failed to shoot it down and spent seven frustrating months trying to gain his first victory. Flying a Nieuport 11, Baracca was successful when his unit, the Seventieth Squadron, was ordered up to attack gun-spotting airplanes.

1916 April 20   The first group of volunteer American pilots arrived at the French air base at Luxeuil to commence operations with Escadrille N.124, the Lafayette Americaine. A small group

of American pilots serving with different French squadrons got the idea of forming a special unit of volunteer Americans. William Thaw was instrumental in setting this up through the French authorities while serving with N.65. Responding to objections from the Germans about so flagrant a declaration of neutral America, the unit was renamed Lafayette Escadrille. When it was absorbed into the U.S. Army Air Section as the 103rd Aero Squadron on February 18, 1918, it would have had a total strength of 39 pilots.

1916 April 26   The Russian Central Military Technical Board ordered 80 Anatra D reconnaissance biplanes, which were delivered in time to participate in aerial activity during the summer of 1916. The Anatra Company, Odessa, had designed this biplane early in the year, and despite a bad reputation gained through an earlier, unsuccessful design, the firm received an order for a further 400 in October 1916 and 300 in 1917. Powered by a 100-HP Gnôme engine, the Anatra D had a wing span of 37 ft. 8 in., a length of 25 ft. 3 in. and a gross weight of 1,910 lb.

1916 April 27   The first airplanes to make a bombing attack on a battleship were three German seaplanes based on the converted freighter *Santa Elena*. The battleship *Slava* was on operations in the Gulf of Riga when it was sighted by the seaplanes and attacked. Out of 31 small bombs dropped from the seaplanes, only three hit the battleship, but these incurred sufficient damage for the *Slava* to withdraw for repairs.

1916 May 5   Twenty-four French observation balloons were torn from their winches during a storm on the Western Front. Eighteen observers jumped with parachutes; 11 landed in friendly territory, two were captured by the Germans, two were killed by being dragged along the ground, and two were seriously injured. Before the war, the French had completely abandoned the use of balloons for military purposes, relying instead on airplanes. Capt. Jacques Saconney had encouraged a restoration of ballooning for the military just before the war began, and 10 companies were available by the end of October 1914. This increased rapidly and peaked at 75 companies by spring 1916, and in all, 1,100 French balloons were manufactured during the war.

1916 May 16   Future British air ace and, at 19, one of the youngest fighter pilots of the Western Front, Albert Ball scored the first of 44 aerial victories. His first victim was a two-seat Albatros reconnaissance airplane, which crashed near Givenchy-Beaumont. Ball joined the army when war broke out and transferred to the Royal Flying Corps in January 1916, after learning to fly at Hendon. On B.E.2cs with No. 13 Squadron in France from February 15, he frequently went over the enemy lines looking for enemy airplanes. Ball was moved to No. 11 Squadron on May 7.

1916 May 18   The first combat victory achieved by a member of the Lafayette Escadrille went to Lt. Kiffin Rockwell in a French Nieuport 11 biplane. Referred to as a sesquiplane by its designer, Gustav Delage, the Type 11 evolved from the Type 10, which had a narrow chord lower wing capable of rotating around the single spar, doubling it as a speedbrake for tight turns in fast races. The upper wing of the Nieuport 11 had twice the area of the lower wing and a maximum span of only 24 ft. 9 in. The Type 11 had a total loaded weight of just over 1,000 lb. It was one of the most universally used fighters, bought by the British, Italians and Russians. Rockwell was killed in action on September 23, 1916.

1916 May 22   Le Prieur rockets were used against German Drachen observation balloons for the first time when Nieuport 11

Powered aircraft were considered noisy and impractical by military men, but the observation balloon retained favor with some.

sesquiplanes of the French Air Service Escadrille N.65 went into the attack with spasmodic results. A month later, on June 25, 1916, 100 French and British aircraft took part in a Drachen attack, again with mixed results. Albert Ball was unable to set fire to a balloon he attacked from as close as 50 ft. until he resorted to his 0.303-in. Lewis gun, and the new phosphorous incendiary ammunition that would eventually supersede the Le Prieur rocket. Developed by the French naval lieutenant Y. P. G. Le Prieur, the solid propellant rockets would be electrically fired from up to 10 hollow tubes attached to the outboard interplane struts of biplanes.

1916 May 28 The Sopwith Triplane single-seat fighter was cleared for flight trials. A contemporary of the Sopwith Pup, it could be fitted with either one or two Vickers synchronized machine guns and a 100-HP Clerget rotary engine that provided a top speed of 112 MPH. Fast, highly maneuverable, with three equal length wings spanning 26.5 ft., the triplane was ordered into production on June 7 with deliveries from late 1916. In the first half of 1917, it was to be a formidable opponent until superseded by the Sopwith Camel and the S.E.5.

1916 May 30 The first of the Super-Zeppelin airships, the L 30, became available for operational use by the German navy at Nordholz two days after her first flight at Friedrichshafen. Known in Germany as the Large War Type (Grosskampftype), L 30 had a length of 649.5 ft., a diameter of 78.5 ft. and a capacity of 1,949,600 cu. ft. Powered by six 240-HP Maybach six-cylinder engines, it had a speed of 63 MPH and a carrying capacity of 61,000 lb. L 30 made nine important raids on England and sur-

vived the war, after which it was handed over to the Belgians who, lacking facilities to house it, asked that it be broken up at its base.

1916 May 31 The first use of seaplanes for reconnaissance operations during a major naval engagement occurred when Short Type 184 (serial number 8359) was launched from HMS *Engadine* at 3:08 P.M. during the Battle of Jutland in the North Sea, due west of the Skagerrak between Denmark and Norway. Flt. Lt. F. J. Rutland with G. S. Trewin as observer sent wireless messages to the *Engadine* that due to poor visibility, had to be conducted from low altitude and close to the German warships. At 3:48 P.M., a fuel line broke and Rutland landed on the sea and repaired the line, eventually making it back to the *Engadine* by 4:00 P.M.

1916 May An American pilot serving with the Lafayette Escadrille, Sgt. Maj. E. Cowdin, became the first from that unit, and the first American, to receive France's Military Medal (Médaille Militaire). Cowdin was one of the original seven pilots that made up N.124 when it was called the Lafayette Americaine. Like other pilots of that unit, he flew a single-seat scouting fighter biplane, the Nieuport 11.

1916 May The British prime minister announced that he had sanctioned establishment of an air board headed by Lord Curzon as president to examine the wider needs of the Royal Flying Corps and the Royal Naval Air Service and to coordinate supplies, men and material. This was the first faltering step toward an air ministry, which Parliament objected to as a meaningless bureaucratic step. There was, however, general agreement that the two services should be amalgamated. Although originally together as naval and military wings of the Royal Flying Corps, they had become separate entities in late June 1914 when the Royal Naval Air Service was formed at the behest of the Admiralty and the naval wing disbanded.

1916 June 8 The first public meeting between the National Advisory Committee for Aeronautics executive committee and representatives of the American aviation industry was held in an attempt to reconcile the needs of the consumer with those of the producer. With American aviation falling increasingly behind aviation in Europe and with the increasing probability of America joining the European war, the conflicting interests of the military and industrial profiteers had been compounded by existing bureaucracy, said chairman of the meeting Charles D. Walcott. The mood of cooperation, rather than confrontation, set by the role of the mediator assumed by the NACA began the long process whereby American aero-engine production was in a position to produce the Liberty engine by 1918.

1916 June 9 With an envelope capacity of 170,000 cu. ft. and an endurance of 11 hr., the first of 45 Coastal(C.)-type, nonrigid British airships ordered for the Royal Naval Air Service made its first flight from the airship station at Pembroke. The first Coastal had been ordered in September 1915, but the poor performance and lack of technical excellence in these and other nonrigid types gradually moved the RNAS away from ordering further types. Nevertheless, operating stations were set up at Pulham, Howden, Longside, Mullion and East Fortune.

1916 June 15 The first use of mass air strikes to support large-scale ground operations took place when 37 Caproni and Farman bombers of the Italian Corpo Aeronautica Militare attacked Austro-Hungarian positions north of Asiago. During the attack, 160 bombs and 60,000 steel darts were dropped on ground targets. Five days later, another attack took place on the airfield at Pergine when 34 Capronis and Farmans supported army operations. Aircraft used in these operations had been moved from the Julian Front to the Trentino Front on June 12 as the Italians prepared to take advantage of a major Austro-Hungarian troop withdrawal to help contain a Russian surge in the Brusilov Offensive.

1916 June 17 The first prototype R.E.8 (serial number 796) made its first flight at Farnborough. Designed by the Royal Aircraft Factory as a replacement for the aging B.E.2c reconnaissance biplane, the R.E.8 was equipped from the outset with a forward-firing Vickers gun and a rear-mounted Lewis gun for the observer. The first R.E.8 unit went to France on November 21, 1916. Initial results were not that good, but early losses were more a result of poor training than any inherent design fault, and before the end of the war, more than 4,000 R.E.8s were delivered to the Royal Flying Corps and its successor the Royal Air Force.

1916 June 18 Victor of 17 aerial combats, the German air ace Lt. Max Immelmann was killed at about 10:15 P.M. when his Fokker E.III monoplane crashed after breaking up in the air when the interrupter gear malfunctioned and he shot away his propeller. Immelmann had been fighting an F.E.2b piloted by 2d Lt. G. R. Gubbin with Cpl. J. H. Waller as gunner. Because Immelmann scored most of his later victories over the French town of Lille, he quickly became known as the Eagle of Lille. Already eclipsed by Oswald Boelcke, who by this date had 18 victories, he was Germany's first great air ace, immortalized in the name of the famous Immelmann turn (see 1916 Jan. 12).

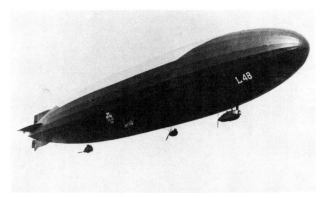

Development of the German airship led to increasingly large and more capable dirigibles, as represented here by Zeppelin L 48.

1916 June 18 The first American volunteer pilot to be shot down while serving with the Lafayette Escadrille (N.124) crashed-landed near Verdun after being attacked by enemy airplanes. H. Clyde Balsley was wounded but returned to his unit some time later. Five days later, on June 23, Victor Emmanual Chapman became the first American volunteer with N.124 to lose his life in action. He too was shot down near Verdun but lost his life in the resulting crash.

1916 June 25 Preparatory to the first Battle of the Somme, aimed at delivering a knock-out blow to German forces, a concentrated air attack on German kite balloons resulted in four being brought down by Le Prieur rockets and a fifth by phosphor bombs invented by Allbright and Wilsons of Birmingham, England. Of the 23 German spotting balloons in the air at 4:00 P.M., 15 were attacked. Three more balloons were brought down by air-to-air rockets next day. Le Prieur rockets were proving effective.

1916 June 29 The first flight of a Boeing airplane took place when William Edward Boeing flew his home-built design put together with the help of his friend Conrad Westervelt. It flew well and stimulated Boeing to move ahead with a seaplane design to compete with Curtiss. Boeing had first flown in a Curtiss seaplane in 1914 but believed he could design and build a better one. On July 15, 1916, Boeing formed the Pacific Aero Products Co. and, with a capital of $100,000, set about the business of building competitive airplanes. Little did he know that his company would become one of the world's biggest manufacturers.

1916 June While trying to escape attack during a bombing raid he was leading on the German station at Angem, the Russian pilot Jan Jozefovich Nagorski looped his Shchetnin M-9 flying boat, the first time a flying boat had conducted such a maneuver. Disbelievingly, his comrades questioned the possibility, and on September 17 Nagorski repeated the maneuver, this time over his own airfield where he twice looped the M-9. His airplane was powered by a 150-HP Canton-Unne pusher engine set high above the center fuselage. The flying boat had a wing span of 52 ft. and a length of 29.5 ft. with a maximum loaded weight of 3,400 lb.

1916 July 1 On the first day of the Battle of the Somme, British and French air patrols flew low over the trenches and over waves of attacking Allied troops to report the units involved. Throughout the day these contact patrols were constantly suffering the explosive concussion of the artillery barrage, "tossed about in the disturbed air like surf-riding corks,'' according to the official history. As contact observers tracked the progress of field units, other airplanes kept up continuous gunnery-spotting patrols. The bombing program had begun June 30 with waves of attacks on rail stations, ammunition dumps and other targets.

1916 July 14 The prototype Bristol M.1 monoplane made its first flight at Filton, near Bristol, England at the hands of Fred P. Raynham. Designed for fast and agile maneuvers, it was one of several single-seat fighters emerging to combat the German Fokker monoplane menace. With a 110-HP Clerget, it had a top speed of 132 MPH, and as a private venture, Bristol hoped for production orders. The Royal Flying Corps said the landing speed of 49 MPH was too high for makeshift flying fields in France, and although several were used in Macedonia and the Middle East, the M.1 never gained the wide application its performance and handling deserved.

1916 July 17 The first phase of the Battle of the Somme ended. It was the first major land battle where airplanes made a significant difference to the running progress of a major offensive involving several million men. The entire attack area had been photographed, observers flew up and down the lines of barbed wire, reporting its condition where artillery had tried to dislodge the wire. German gun batteries had been neutralized by directed, pin-point artillery barrages, and the sky over the enemy lines was controlled by the Allies, who had driven German scouts back. When bad weather stopped flying, the accuracy of the guns fell, and fire control was much less accurate.

1916 July 21 Four German bombers from Field Flying Section 40 attacked the ammunition dump at Audricq, half-way along the Calais-to-St.Omer railway. Reconnaissance by Field Flying Section 6 had located the dump on photographs, and the attack was carried out between 1:00 A.M. and 2:00 A.M. A shed received a direct hit and was set on fire, which was spread as boxed ammunition exploded, igniting ammunition trucks and other sheds. In all, 23 sheds and a mile of railroad track were destroyed as 8,000 tons of ammunition went up. Three people were killed, and 23 injured, and houses were damaged for several miles around.

1916 July 22 The second U.S. Signal Corps flying school was opened at Mineola, later Hazelhurst Field, N.Y., under the command of Lt. Joseph E. Carberry. He was assigned 15 officers and enlisted men and given authorization to hire civilian instructors (known as aero scouts) at $150 per month. Build-up was completed in eight months, and from April 1917, there were about 40 airplanes on strength.

1916 July 23 The second phase of the Battle of the Somme began with a general attack along the entire front following two days of bombardment by heavy artillery. A German air build-up had begun July 14 with the deployment of two new fighter squadrons (Kampfeinsitzer Kommandos). Throughout the second phase, the German air units reorganized and were increasingly concentrated on the Somme. By the beginning of September, a major air offensive was under way, resulting in some of the toughest aerial combats. The Royal Flying Corps kept up a major bombing campaign behind the German lines, terrorizing infantry with low-level sweeps.

1916 July 27 A series of tests in aircraft radio transmission and reception took place beginning with Capt. Clarence C. Culver and Sgt. William C. Ocker in airplane *S.C. No. 50*. Equipped with a 180-watt French transmitter, they sent messages 119 mi. from Santa Monica to San Diego, Calif. Reception was handled

by Dr. R. O. Shelton, assisted at the flying school by Lt. W. A. Robertson. On August 18, two-way messages were sent and received over a distance of 11 mi., and on August 20, this was increased to 20 mi. The first airplane-to-airplane communication was achieved on September 2 between Cpl. A. D. Smith and Lt. Robertson in *S.C. No. 50* and Lt. Herbert A. Dargue in *S.C. No. 51*. The tests ended October 26.

1916 July 30 The American ace Gervais Raoul Lufbery scored his first air victory over Etain on the Western Front two months after joining the Lafayette Escadrille (N.124). Lufbery left V.B.106 (a Voisin bombing unit) during April 1916 for special training as a fighter pilot, and after struggling to master the tiny Nieuport, he was sent to N.124 on May 24, 1916. Lufbery was the first American to receive the British Military Cross, which he was awarded in June 1917. By that time, Lufbery had shot down nine enemy airplanes and was well on the way to his total of 16 confirmed victories, making him third-highest-scoring American ace of World War I.

1916 July 30 The first unit equipped with the British-built B.E.12, single-seat, general purpose biplane arrived in France. No. 19 Squadron, Royal Flying Corps, became the first to operate the variant of the B.E.2 family that was expected to offer a temporary response to expanding German fortunes in the air war, where the psychological effect of the Fokker monoplanes had extracted a temporary advantage for the Germans. Although the B.E.2 had been a useful workhorse for reconnaissance, gun-spotting and, occasionally, fighting, the single-seat version with a 120-HP RAF engine and a synchronized Vickers gun, sometimes a Lewis as well, was seriously outclassed.

1916 August 1 The first issue of America's most influential and long-running aircraft magazine appeared at a price of 5 cents. Called *Aviation and Aeronautical Engineering,* it was the ancestor of today's *Aviation Week & Space Technology* and was published twice a month. In 1917 a second magazine appeared from the same publisher called *Aircraft Journal* and was published weekly. On November 1, 1920, they were merged into the weekly *Aviation and Aircraft Journal,* and in 1947 became *Aviation Week* before finally getting the present title in 1960.

1916 August 2 The first coordinated bombing raid involving No. 3 Wing Royal Naval Air Service using pathfinder techniques that would be refined in World War II was carried out by the British when 10 Caudron G.IV bombers and one Farman escorted by five Sopwith 1½ Strutters attacked the enemy airfield at St. Denis Westrem near Ghent, Belgium. Hugh Trenchard requested the raid to be carried out by No. 3 Wing, which had been formed in May 1916 to carry the air offensive to Germany in strategic raids that would damage her production capacity. One of the Sopwiths fired flares in an early application of ''master bomber'' (pathfinder) tactics where a lead airplane signals the others.

1916 August 2 For the first time, aircraft carriers and seaplane tenders were used in the air defense of England during a night raid by German airships. The carrier *Vindex* with a Bristol Scout D put to sea from Harwich upon reports of approaching zeppelins, while the tender *Brocklesby* set out from Lowestoft with a Sopwith Baby and a Sopwith Schneider. Weighted down by flotation bags that would be used when the Bristol Scout ditched alongside the *Vindex,* Flt. Lt. C. T. Freeman struggled above Zeppelin L 11 and dropped Rankin darts—steel darts containing high explosives—on its hull without effect. Freeman had to ditch prematurely when his engine failed and spent 90 min. on the Bristol's tail before rescue.

One of the more renowned British fighting scouts of World War I, the S.E.5a, with a Lewis gun clearly visible above the wing.

1916 August 6 Future French air ace René Fonck shot down his first aerial victim while flying a Caudron G.IV fitted with a forward-firing machine gun. A German Rumpler was forced to land, and its crew gave themselves up to the French aviator. Fonck began his flight training in February 1915 and joined the Caudrons of Escadrille C.47 in June. He received several citations for gallantry and then had several fights during which he successfully shot down airplanes that fell on the German side of the lines and were, therefore, unconfirmed victories.

1916 August 10 Anticipating a major increase in appropriations for FY 1917, the U.S. Navy dispatched a telegram to Curtiss asking for "a proposition to supply at the earliest date practicable, 30 school hydro-aeroplanes." What emerged was a derivative of the JN-4B, two-seat, landplane trainer fitted with a 100-HP Curtiss OXX engine, a single float under the fuselage and a wingtip float under each pair of outer interplane struts. The N-9 became the standard naval trainer, and deliveries began during November, the first 30 being delivered by February 1916.

1916 August 16 The fourth Zeppelin large bomber made its first flight. It was called the Zeppelin Staaken R.IV, because the V.G.O. works had moved from Manzel to Staaken and because it was the fourth in the new category of Riesenflugzeug, or Giant Airplane ("R"-plane), types. It was the longest serving R-plane of all, and after serving with the Giant Airplane Flying Unit (Riesenflugzeug Abteilungen or Rfa) 500 on the Eastern Front in June 1917, it was sent to the Western Front to supplement Gotha raids on England. The R.IV had a wingspan of 138.5 ft., a length of 76 ft. 1 in. and a height of 22 ft. 3 in. and was powered by two 160-HP Mercedes and four 220-HP Benz engines grouped in two nacelles and in the nose, driving five propellers.

1916 August 23 The first of a series of fighting squadrons (Jagdstaffeln, or Jasta) was set up as part of the major reorganization of German air units in which individual fighting squadrons would operate in needed sectors of the battlefront. With the aim of achieving and maintaining air superiority, they confirmed the value of the reconnaissance airplane and the vital need to protect its day-to-day work. Jasta 1 was formed under the command of Hptm. Zander, and Jasta 2 was formed on August 27 under Hptm. Boelcke (promoted May 22 as the youngest officer of that rank in the Royal Prussian Army). Jastas 1–7 were formed during August, Jastas 8–15 in September and Jastas 16–33 by the end of December 1916.

1916 August 28 Maj. Benjamin D. Foulois reported on the activities of the First Aero Squadron for the period between March 15, 1916, and August during its relocation in support of the Mexican campaign. The squadron had conducted 540 flights totaling 346 flying hours in a total distance of 19,533 miles. Maj. Foulois also advised about the unsatisfactory conditions experienced by the flyers. Poor weather resulted in their flying through rain, hail and snow, while on the ground they suffered from severe cold and bad facilities.

1916 August 29 A special emergency act awarded a massive increase in U.S. military aviation when Congress voted $13.3 million for the Aviation Section of the Signal Corps. Aware of the inefficiency of the U.S. airplanes and the possibility that the United States might find itself involved in the European war, a major expansion program was funded that included $600,000 for new land on which new air bases could be built. Of the total being made available, the National Guard units would be awarded $9.6 million. On March 31, 1916, the FY 1917 appropriation of

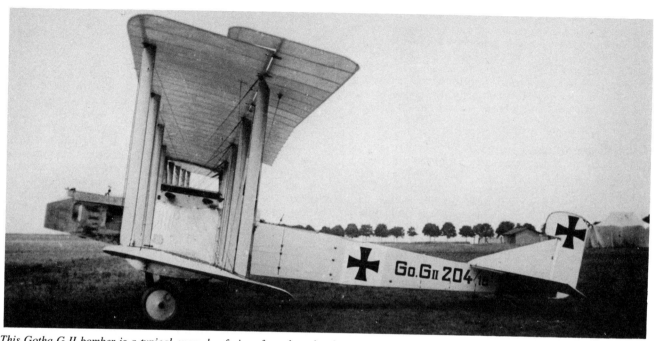

This Gotha G.II bomber is a typical example of aircraft as the role of air power expanded and its use increased in World War I.

$500,000 had been awarded by Congress, and the new, greatly increased sum reflected concerns raised by the poor showing of the First Aero Squadron during the punitive Mexican expedition.

The fiscal year 1917 Naval Appropriation Act was passed and called for a Naval Flying Corps to be staffed by 150 officers and 350 enlisted men and for the establishment of a Naval Reserve Force, including a Naval Flying Corps with surplus graduates from aeronautical schools. Few people now thought America would not enter the European war at some point, and preparations were being put in hand for the deployment of naval aviation forces in operational roles when that need arose.

Responding to encouraging support from congressmen prior to hearings on the FY 1917 budget, the War Department had authorized a total complement of seven Aero Squadrons, each with 12 airplanes. The First, Third, Fourth and Fifth Aero Squadrons would be based in the United States, the Second would be assigned duty in the Philippines, the Sixth would serve in Panama and the Seventh in Hawaii. Although all seven were established by early 1917, only the First would have a full complement of men and airplanes.

1916 August The Albatros D.I single-seat biplane fighter was put through its paces prior to delivery to the German Air Service. With a 160-HP Mercedes engine and two forward-firing machine guns, it was selected for the new fighting squadron (Jasta) but proved inferior to the best of the opposition like the D.H.2. Albatros responded with the D.II, which was better, with improved visibility, and helped restore German air superiority on the Western Front. The first of the D.IIs went to the newly formed fighting squadrons and proved successful, despite misgivings about its projected superiority over other German biplanes then vying as replacements for the obsolete Fokker monoplanes.

1916 August The prototype D.H.4 day bomber and fighter reconnaissance biplane made its first flight at Hendon. Designed by Geoffrey de Havilland and built by Airco, it was a great success with the Royal Flying Corps units, which began receiving the D.H.4 in March 1917, and by the end of the war, 1,449 had

been delivered. The type was equipped with a variety of engines in the 200–400-HP range, providing a maximum speed of up to 140 MPH, a climb rate of 1,350 ft./min. and an endurance of over 3 hr. Three American manufacturers built a total 4,846 D.H.4s, the majority of which ended up forming initial air forces for Latin American countries long after World War I.

1916 September 2 Deliveries began of one of the most famous and effective fighters of World War I, the French Spad S.VII, which had been flown for the first time by M. Bequet in May 1916. Powered initially by a 150-HP Hispano-Suiza 8Ac engine, later models had increasingly powerful engines, including the 200-HP Hispano, and more than 6,000 were built. The stork motif used by Hispano-Suiza for their engines became the insignia for Les Cigognes, the Stork group of squadrons that began with SPA.3 (Spad Attack Squadron No. 3) and eventually included Escadrille SPA.26, 73 and 103. The Société pour Aviation et ses Dérives (SPAD) began life in 1914 when Louis Blériot took over the Société pour les Appareils Deperdussin from Armand Deperdussin, who had been implicated in a financial scandal.

1916 September 3 Early in the morning hours, 2d Lt. William Leefe Robinson of No. 39 Squadron, Royal Flying Corps, based at Suttons Farm, England, successfully attacked and shot down the German Army Schutte-Lanz airship SL 11, the first airship destroyed over England. Commanded by Hptm. W. Schramm, SL 11 was one of 15 airships that set out to raid England. It was attacked by Robinson at about 2:05 A.M. while flying a B.E.2c north of London. Robinson began his attack from 800 ft. raking the side and underside with machine gun fire. Finally, he sprayed ammunition into the underside from 500 ft. below the giant hulk. SL 11 caught fire and fell to earth, ending the myth of the airships' invincibility.

1916 September 6 Future ace and fourth-highest-scoring British pilot, James Thomas Byford McCudden of No. 29 Squadron scored his first aerial victory over the Western Front. Flying a D.H.2 pusher, McCudden pursued a white, German, two-seat, observation biplane at 14,000 ft. and got to within 1,200 ft. before opening up with his single machine gun. Changing gun drums twice, he finally saw the biplane plunge to earth from 4,000 ft., and the kill was confirmed next day. McCudden had joined the Royal Flying Corps in 1913 and was a mechanic when war began. Sent to France on August 13, 1914, he was returned to England in January 1916 to learn to fly, and joined No. 29 Squadron on August 3 after a brief spell with No. 20 Squadron since July 8.

1916 September 6   Tests in aerial refueling between a nonrigid airship and a ship at sea were carried out by the British using Coastal 1 (C.1) and the light cruiser HMS *Canterbury*. These airships were powered by two engines, one with 220 HP and one with 100 HP, providing a top speed of 50 MPH and fuel for a maximum endurance of 24 hr. It would have been useful if these airships could have remained on patrol for longer periods, and tests like this were intended to explore the possibility of making them less dependent on shore bases for their patrols of the Forth, Scotland and of the Humber, the Norfolk coast and Land's End, England.

1916 September 9   The first flight of the Bristol F.2A took place at the hands of Capt. C. A. Hooper. Designed by F. S. Barnwell, the F.2A was the result of a search, begun in March 1916, for a two-seat reconnaissance airplane with good defensive armament. The observer sat close behind the pilot and had a good field of view across the top of the upper wing and back down along the tapered fuselage, with a machine gun on a rotating ring mounting. The fuselage was set between the wings, eliminating the large blind spot below and behind. From the start, it was a promising design, and on August 28, 1916, the first 52 had been ordered.

1916 September 12   The first flight of a radio-controlled airplane took place when a Hewitt-Sperry biplane built as a seaplane by Curtiss, powered by a 40-HP engine, was flown without human control for much of its flight by an automatic pilot designed by Elmer Sperry. Observed by the U.S. Bureau of Ordnance, the airplane was flown with Lt. T. W. Wilkinson and Lawrence Sperry, son of Elmer Sperry, on board. When the airplane took a nose

dive toward a simulated target (as directed from the ground), Sperry took over control and restored normal flight. As a flying bomb, the biplane would be capable of carrying 308 lb. of explosives.

1916 September 14   The first successful combat with air-to-air missiles occurred when Lt. A. M. Walters of No. 60 Squadron RFC shot down an L.V.G. German, two-seat, observation airplane with his Le Prieur rockets that had been attached to the wing struts. The rockets carried no explosive substance but were intended to penetrate the target and set it alight with heat from the hollow case, which they did with dramatic effect. Each Le Prieur rocket comprised a cylindrical case 18 in. long attached to a stick up to 6.2 ft. long inclined 17.5° to the airplane's line of flight. The case burned 200 grams of black powder for propulsion. Born in 1885, Le Prieur served as a naval interpreter in Tokyo where he copied a Voisin glider. He died in 1963 at the age of 77.

1916 September 15   The third phase of the Battle of the Somme opened the waves of British and French ground attack and bombing flights over enemy lines. The new German fighter squadrons were overwhelmed, suffering heavy losses. The Fokker scourge was over, and new British and French airplanes continually harried the enemy. In deteriorating weather, the reconnaissance flights kept up a continual report on enemy movements and artillery batteries, which in turn became new targets for artillery fire, the accuracy of which was reported by air. By mid-October, of all German aircraft on Eastern, Western and Italian fronts, fully one-third were concentrated on the area of the Somme Valley on the Western Front, exceeding the numerical strength of British and French aircraft in this sector.

1916 September 17   Top-scoring ace of Germany's new air arm, Lt. Manfred Freiherr von Richthofen scored his first confirmed aerial victory when he shot down a F.E.2b from No. 11 Squadron, Royal Flying Corps, piloted by 2d Lt. L. B. F. Morris with observer Lt. T. Rees over Villers-Plouich, both of whom were killed. Richthofen believed he had shot down three earlier victims, but lacking confirmation, they could not be attributed to him. Born May 2, 1892, Richthofen joined the Uhlans (Prussian

The German Zeppelin LZ 45 setting out on a bombing raid, typical of many this airship made during 1916.

Oswald Boelcke, probably the greatest exponent of air combat during World War I, commanded one of the first fighting scout squadrons.

light cavalry) in 1912 and transfered to the air service in May 1915. Picked by Boelcke to join Jasta 2 at Lagnicourt, Richthofen had arrived at his new post September 1.

1916 October 11 The U.S. War Department recommended to the U.S. Navy that a joint army-navy aeronautical board be established to coordinate development of airships, dirigibles and balloons for military applications. The secretary of the navy accepted this proposal and thus began a period of productive cooperation that was to last until lighter-than-air craft were phased out of service with U.S. forces in 1948, when the aeronautical board was dissolved.

1916 October 12 No. 3 Wing, Royal Naval Air Service, formed to conduct strategic raids on Germany from Luxeuil, France, carried out its first major bombing raid. The Mauser factory at Oberndorf was attacked by 15 naval bombers and six fighters from the British RNAS and 16 French bombers accompanied by large numbers of fighters. Of the total, six French and three British airplanes were shot down, a casualty level of almost 20%. On October 23, the Thyssen works was attacked by 20 airplanes, and on November 10 the steel works at Volklingen were hit. Two days later, St. Ingert was attacked, and further raids were made on November 24 and 27.

1916 October 12 During the attack on the Mauser works at Oberndorf, the American air ace Norman Prince crashed while returning from flying a protective cover on the bombers. Coming in to land, he hit a high tension cable and sustained injuries from which he died on October 15 after two days in a coma. Prince had sponsored the construction of a racing airplane from the Burgess Co. for the 1912 Gordon Bennett Cup held in Chicago. He

enlisted in the French Air Service in March 1915 and spent almost a year on bombers and Nieuport scouts before joining the Escadrille Lafayette in April 1916.

1916 October 25 Raymond Collishaw scored the first of 60 aerial victories that would make him the top-scoring ace of the Royal Naval Air Service and the third-highest-scoring British pilot. He was born in British Columbia in 1893 and went to sea at the age of 17 before joining Robert Falcon Scott's expedition to the Antarctic. Collishaw transferred to the RNAS in January 1916. He survived the war and went to Russia with No. 47 Squadron, RAF, in Juily 1919 to fight the Bolsheviks and served with distinction in World War II.

1916 October 28 The then-leading German air ace Oswald Boelcke was killed when an airplane being harried by von Richthofen caused Lt. Erwin Boehme and Hptm. Boelcke to turn violently when it cut across their path. The undercarriage of Boehme's Albatros tore the upper wing of Boelcke's airplane and he crashed. Lt. Stephan Kirmaier took over Jasta 2, which eventually bore Boelcke's name. It had taken Boelcke a year to get his first 19 victories, but such was the increased pace of aerial fighting on the Western Front that by the end of the war, Jasta Boelcke would notch up 336 confirmed victories with the loss of 26 of its pilots.

1916 November 18 The third phase of the Battle of the Somme ended with German air units having seized in October a measure of superiority against a backdrop of the world's longest continuously running land battle, which had been going effectively without pause for almost 150 days. The focused ground assaults had channeled German squadron organization and generated new fighting units that were, however, increasingly challenged by better and more capable airplanes developed by the British and the French to reverse the trend set during mid- to late-1916 by the Fokker monoplanes. For their part, the Allies had restructured the way airplanes would be used, clarifying the distinctions between reconnaissance, fighter-escort and bombing.

1916 November 21 The prototype Breguet 14 bomber made its first flight. Designed for a 300-HP in-line engine then on the drawing boards, the authorities were reluctant to believe the engine could be developed to produce this amount of power, and on its inaugural flight, it was powered by a 220-HP Renault engine. It became, however, one of the most effective bombers of World War I, with 250 going to U.S. squadrons; in all, some 8,000 had been built when production ended in 1926. The Breguet 14 had a maximum weight of only 3,400 lb. but could carry a 520-lb. bomb load.

1916 November 23 The highest-scoring Australian to serve with the Royal Flying Corps in World War I, Robert Alexander Little achieved his first victory in a Sopwith Pup when he shot down an Aviatik C I a month after joining No. 8 Squadron, Royal Naval Air Service. Little arrived from Victoria, Australia in July 1915 and learned to fly at Hendon before joining the RNAS unit at Eastchurch in January 1916. Six months later he was sent to Dunkerque, France. Little scored a total 47 victories before he was shot down and killed over England attacking a Gotha bomber.

1916 November 23 Manfred von Richthofen shot down and killed Maj. Lanoe G. Hawker of No. 24 Squadron, Royal Flying Corps, in his 11th aerial victory since his first just over two months earlier. Hawker was a member of the first RFC squadron to be equipped exclusively with fighter airplanes, the D.H.2, introduced on the Western Front during January 1916, and had received a Victoria Cross for attacking three airplanes in one

Upcoming German air ace Manfred von Richthofen chasing Maj. Lanoe Hawker to his death, November 23, 1916.

engagement and in attacking the zeppelin sheds at Gontrode. In a D.H.2, Hawker fought gallantly from 8,000 ft. down to 100 ft. and was finally caught by Richthofen just short of the British lines after the German ace had expended 900 rounds of ammunition.

1916 November 23   The NACA Subcommittee on a Site for Experimental Work and Proving Grounds for Aeronautics recommended 1,650 acres of land at the mouth of the Back River in Hampton, Va., as the location for the first airplane experimental establishment. Trying to stimulate joint NACA-Army liaison, NACA encouraged the army to buy the site and give up a portion to the experimental work, which it did. The main location for army experimental work, however, was to be McCook Field in Dayton, Ohio. In August 1917, the NACA Aviation Experimental Station and Proving Grounds became, simply, Langley Field, in memory of the great aeronautical pioneer Samuel Pierpont Langley.

1916 November 28   One of the boldest German air raids on England took place when Lt. Walther Igles and Deck Officer Paul Brandt flew L.V.G. C.IV (serial no. 275/16) across central London and dropped six 22-lb. bombs from a height of 13,000 ft. This was the first daylight airplane raid on London, and the bombs reached perilously close to the Admiralty, which was the prime target. The raid began at 11:50 A.M., 1 hr. 15 min. after the L.V.G. had taken off from Markiakerke near Ostende in occupied Belgium. The British defenses were inept, and the first order to pursue was not issued until 12:45 P.M. The German raider returned safely to its base.

1917 January 1   Five Royal Naval Air Service aircrew (Lts. H. C. Vereker and Hibbard plus three others) unwittingly delivered a New Year's present to the Germans when they landed their Handley Page 0/100 bomber behind the German lines at Chalandry, near Lâon, France. They had taken off from Manston, England for Villacoublay but ran into cloud, lost direction due to a compass fault and came down to land to ask their way. Before they could take off or burn the airplane, a German infantry patrol arrested them. There is an unconfirmed story that Manfred von Richthofen flew this machine to a height of 10,000 ft. before the kaiser at a later date.

1917 January 6   Impressed by the performance of German airships in bombing raids on England, the psychological effect of

which had been more significant than the material damage caused, a board of U.S. Army and Navy officers recommended to the secretaries of the war and navy departments that the United States design and build a zeppelin-type airship under the authority of the chief constructor of the navy. The suggestion was made that airships of this type were the only aeronautical contraptions that stood a good chance of crossing great oceans on a regular basis.

1917 January 8   The first attempt to arm a U.S. Navy airplane was conducted when the Burgess-Dunne AH-10 biplane fitted with a Benet-Mercie machine gun fired at an altitude of between 100 ft. and 200 ft. above the naval base at Pensacola, Fla. The airplane reacted well to the tests, and the machine gun fired exactly as expected. The AH-10 was a British Dunne tailless biplane built under license in America by the Burgess Co. of Marblehead, Mass. It was powered by a 100-HP Curtiss OXX-2 engine and had a top speed of almost 70 MPH.

1917 January 16   Cavalry Captain Manfred von Richthofen was awarded the Ordre Pour le Mérite for his exploits as a pilot with Jasta (fighting squadron) 2, a week before he was moved to command Jasta 11 at Douai. Jasta 11 had been formed several months earlier but had not as yet scored a single victory. Richthofen had now shot down 16 confirmed airplanes in combat since his first in September 1916, nine of which were pusher biplanes without rear gunners. Within a month of transfer to Jasta 11, he had scored five more victories and stimulated a more aggressive combat attitude in his fellow pilots.

1917 February 11   Lts. Peter and Frohwein of the German Air Service carried out the first successful night combat between airplanes while flying a DFW C.V two seater. The C.V was a reliable, well-built reconnaissance machine used also for observation and photographic patrols. It was powered by a 200-HP, Benz inline engine and carried a rear-mounted flexible machine gun for the observer as well as a forward-firing gun for the pilot. In the vicinity of Malzeville, Peter and Frohwein shot down two enemy bombers as they were attempting to land and made it safely back to their airfield.

1917 February 13   Largely as a result of efforts by the National Advisory Committee for Aeronautics, the U.S. Aircraft Manufacturers Association was formed to control cross-license agreements satisfactory to all patent holders producing aircraft and materials used in their construction. It was accepted by the government that Wright-Martin and Curtiss companies held the basic patents on airplanes and that each of them was to receive $2 million for these patents to be funded by U.S. manufacturers paying $200 per airplane to each of these prime patent holders until the sum had been accumulated. Thereafter, a royalty fee of no more than $25 per airplane was to be paid.

1917 February 16   The prototype Campania built by the Fairey aircraft company made its first flight at the Marine Experimental Depot on the Isle of Grain in Kent, England. The Campania was the first airplane in the world to be designed and built specifically for operation from seaplane carriers at sea. Named after the ship it was built to operate from, an 18,000-ton converted Cunard liner, the Campania had twin floats and was powered by a 250-HP Rolls Royce Eagle Mk.IV; later models had the 260-HP Sunbeam Maori II and were designated the F.22.

1917 February 25   France transferred all army dirigibles to the navy. The increasing participation of aircraft in the war diminished the role of the airship, and increased German submarine activity made their shift in operations a logical step. In June 1916,

An unusually marked Sopwith Camel of 1917, a sprightly but difficult fighter to handle.

Gen. Etienne Joux had been placed in charge of all French army airships with responsibility for improving operational duties. During the war, France had deployed 10 army airships and carried out 63 missions on land targets in the west, losing five airships. There were 28 land missions in 1914, 19 in 1915, 14 in 1916 and 2 in 1917.

1917 February 28 A prototype Sopwith F.1 Camel (serial No. N517) was tested by the Admiralty and delivered to Dunkerque, France for a test with the Royal Naval Air Service on March 1. The design of the new Sopwith fighter had been cleared at the Kingston, England works on December 22, 1916. Conceived as a development of the Sopwith Pup, it was "a fierce little beast"—faster, more agile and more powerful. Powered by a 130-HP Clerget rotary engine, it weighed 1,453 lb. fully loaded and had a wingspan of 28 ft. and a length of 18 ft. 9 in. A total 5,490 Camels were built, of which 2,116 served in France. They shot down 1,294 airplanes from July 1917 through November 1918, a greater total than any other World War I airplane.

1917 February The first operational Royal Naval Air Service unit to fly the Sopwith Triplane, No. 1 Squadron received its first aircraft. It joined the Royal Flying Corps in operations over the Western Front when appeals by Sir Douglas Haig to the British War Office for more squadrons led to the RNAS sharing duty over the battlefield. The Triplane reigned until July 1917 when it was replaced by the Sopwith Camel. Powered by a 130-HP Clerget, the Triplane had a ceiling of 20,000 ft., could achieve 117 MPH at 5,000 ft. and weighed only 1,541 lb. loaded.

1917 March 1 The first production S.E.5 (serial no. A4845) was completed at Farnborough, England. The design of the S.E.5 was completed by H. P. Folland at the Royal Aircraft Factory during June 1916 as a single-seat fighter designed to accommodate the 150-HP Hispano-Suiza engine that had appeared in early 1915 and greatly impressed Lt. Col. H. R. M. Brooke-Popham. The S.E.5 first flew on November 22, 1916, and Capt. Albert

Ball took it up the following day. The first S.E.5 scouts went to No. 56 Squadron and to France, where Ball led the first combat patrol in this type on April 22, 1917. Simultaneously, minor modifications and the use of a 200-HP Hispano-Suiza applied the designation S.E.5a to airplanes thus equipped.

1917 March 6 The first British unit using airplanes fitted with the new Constantinesco machine gun synchronization gear, No. 55 Squadron, Royal Flying Corps, arrived in France for front-line service. Whereas contemporary interrupter gear used weighty cogs and had to be uniquely designed for each type of engine, the Constantinesco gear utilized impulses transmitted through a column of pressurized liquid. It did away with cogs and could be used on any engine. Despite teething troubles, it became an outstanding success, and more than 26,000 sets were produced before the war's end.

1917 March 12 An interservice agreement on aviation planning was submitted to the secretary of war and the secretary of the navy by a board of officers from both services. The agreement described in detail common areas of responsibility for each service and stressed the need for more cooperation between the services in the development of equipment and techniques for flight. It also made special provision for the interservice sharing of all resulting information.

1917 March 16 The first operation raid carried out by the Handley Page 0/100, the first of which had been delivered to the unit in November 1917, was flown during the late evening by No. 3 Wing, Royal Flying Corps. The target was railway yards at Moulins-les-Metz. With reduced fuel, the 0/100 could carry up to 1,800 lb. of bombs and proved a useful and versatile bomber for both tactical and, later, strategic missions against the enemy.

1917 March 21 Prof. A. M. Low demonstrated the first in a series of cruise-type missiles developed under the code name AT (for aerial target) to senior British officers and airplane experts in

Morale received a boost when German airships were brought down over England, as here, with L 32 a mass of twisted steel.

England. It was believed the abbreviation AT would hide the true purpose of the project, which was to develop a successful autopilot for unmanned airplanes packed with explosives and used as flying bombs. Low, an inventor who had demonstrated in 1914 the principles of television, was asked by the British War Office to develop a missile for attacking German airships. Working at Brooklands, Low developed the first auto-controlled AT from the wings and fuselage of a Sopwith Pup.

1917 March 25   One of the greatest fighter pilots of World War I, Lt. Col. William Avery Bishop, scored his first combat victory over an Albatros single-seat fighter while flying a Nieuport. Bishop was born in Ontario, Canada and joined the Royal Flying Corps in March 1915. By May his score is reputed to have reached 20, but questions exist over the validity of his claims. Once Bishop claimed he shot down 25 airplanes in 12 days. Awarded the Victoria Cross for purportedly attacking single-handed an enemy airfield where he shot down three airplanes taking off, his score reached 45 by August 1917. Ordered to the Air Ministry, London, he later set up the Canadian Air Force. He served as an air marshal in World War II and died peacefully in 1956.

1917 March   The first U.S. Navy production contract for airships was awarded to Goodyear for 10 B-series airships. Designated B-1 through B-10, they would each have a capacity of 77,000 cu. ft. and have a length of 160 ft. They would be followed by B-11 through B-14 built by Goodrich, each with a capacity of 80,000 ft. and a length of 167 ft. B-15 and B-16, built by the Connecticut Aircraft Co., had a volume of 75,000 cu. ft. and a length of 156 ft. All 16 airships were delivered to the navy between June 1917 and July 1918. Goodyear eventually built four

more (B-17 through B-20); B-20 which had a capacity of 84,000 cu. ft.

1917 April 4   The British air offensive on the Western Front began five days before the land engagements in the Battle of Arras. More efficient German use of the Albatros and Halberstadt fighters had helped restore German air supremacy, an imbalance partly remedied by the redeployment of the Sopwith Pup and Triplane, soon to be supplemented by the Bristol Fighter. A prime objective in this period was to maintain control of the skies across the German lines for Allied reconnaissance airplanes. Losses were heavy. In the five days April 4–8, 75 British airplanes were shot down along with 105 personnel in addition to 56 airplanes lost through accidents.

1917 April 5   On the first offensive patrol conducted by six Bristol (F.2A) Fighters, flown by No. 48 Sqdn., Royal Flying Corps, four were shot down by von Richthofen and his pilots. Capt. Leefe Robinson was taken prisoner. Only when pilots learned to fly the two-seat Bristol Fighter as they did a single-seater did the success rate go up dramatically and the airplane become effective. Instead of providing a stable flying platform for the rear gunner to fire at the enemy, pilots had to attack aggressively and use the rear gunner only as a supplement. This tactic was adopted from April 30 on, and the Bristol Fighter began to build a reputation that would last throughout the war.

1917 April 6   The United States declared war on Germany and the Austro-Hungarian Empire to become an associated power of the Allies in Europe. In October it would provide loans worth $9.5 billion for the Allies and eventually spend $50 billion in helping win World War I. At the onset, the Aviation Section of the Signal Corps had just 131 officers and 1,087 enlisted men, with 118 airplanes and fewer than 50 trained pilots. The airplanes were best assessed as "trainers," and there were none capable of fighting, bombing or long-range reconnaissance duty. The navy and the Marine Corps had 48 officers, 230 enlisted men, 54 airplanes, 1 airship, 3 balloons and 1 air station.

1917 April 7 A single Sopwith Triplane flown by Flt. Lt. Raymond A. Little of No. 8 Squadron, Royal Naval Air Service, attacked 11 Albatros D.III biplanes of Jasta 11, von Richthofen's unit. Outmaneuvered, the German pilots were forced all over the sky trying to escape the Triplane's guns while unsuccessfully attempting to shoot it down. On April 20, von Richthofen engaged a Triplane and was greatly impressed by its performance. The new Albatros D.V was unable to match it, and Gen. E. W. von Hoeppner claimed it was one of the best Allied fighters. Von Richthofen had already written to staff headquarters urging better fighters to counter the new threat.

1917 April 12 The National Advisory Committee for Aeronautics took an important first step in preparing military officials, Congress and the public for a major expansion of U.S. air strength by recommending an aircraft production program for 3,700 airplanes in 1918, 6,000 in 1919 and 10,000 in 1920. To this date, the United States had produced less than 1,000 airplanes in the 13 years since the Wright brothers' first flight. Of 366 airplanes ordered in 1916, the army had received only 64. Ambitious as it was, the NACA plan would soon be eclipsed by even grander schemes.

1917 April 14 The U.S. Naval Consulting Board recommended that $50,000 be spent on automatically controlled airplanes packed with high explosives and known as flying bombs. Founder of the Sperry Gyroscope Co. Elmer Sperry had been carrying out basic design of such a concept since first approached by Peter C. Hewitt, inventor of the mercury vapor lamp, in April 1915. Secretary of the Navy Josephus Daniels formed a five-man committee that recommended expenditure of $200,000 on the experiments, which Daniels approved in late May 1917.

1917 April 20 Designated DN-1 (Dirigible Nonrigid No. 1) before the U.S. Navy introduced standard classification codes for airships, the navy's first airship flew for the first time. A floating hangar had been built for it at Pensacola, Fla. because it was intended for operation from water in the manner of a seaplane. It had a boat-shaped car suspended from the envelope, which had a capacity of 150,000 cu. ft. In the new system of airship designations, DN-1 became the A-type but made only two more flights, the last on April 29, 1917, due to poor performance.

1917 April 22 In an action that typified the devastating impact that Sopwith Triplanes of the Royal Naval Air Service made on the Western Front, two machines from No. 1 Squadron clashed with 14 German two-seater and single-seat scouts flying toward the Allied lines at 16,000 ft. Flown by Flt. Comdr. R. S. Dallas and Flt. Sub-Lt. T. G. Culling, the Triplanes broke up the formation and shot down three German airplanes before scattering the formation in a 45-minute dogfight that left the Germans in full flight back toward their bases. In the next 13 days, Sopwith Triplanes flew 95 offensive patrols, attacked 175 German airplanes and drove down 16, four of which were destroyed in the air.

1917 April 24 Second-highest-scoring German air ace of World War I, Lt. Ernst Udet, officially became an ace when he was credited with his fifth victory in the air, a Nieuport scout shot down at 7:30 P.M. over Chavigon. Born in Frankfurt on April 26, 1896, Udet learned to fly at the Gustav Otto school and transferred to the air service in June 1915 after having served the army as a dispatch rider since August 1914. His first victory came on March 18, 1916, when he shot down a Farman biplane. His next victory came in October, after he joined Jasta 15. In June 1917, Udet had a fight with French air ace Georges Guynemer, without result.

1917 April 26 The Pacific Aero Products Co. set up by William Boeing on July 15, 1916, was renamed the Boeing Airplane Co. and its headquarters set up on the Heath Shipyard on the Duwamish River, Seattle, Wash. The company had 21 employees and an order for 50 trainers for the navy. The navy order came as a result of tests on the sixth and seventh airplanes built by Boeing, an unusual feature of which was the absence of a fixed horizontal tail surface that the designer said was unnecessary due to the staggered wing configuration.

1917 April 30 A temporary reorganization of German fighter unit operations grouped flights from Jastas 3, 4, 11 and 33 into a temporary grouping (not to be confused with the formation of Jagdgeschwader [Fighter Group] No. 1 at the end of June). This aimed to focus a skies-control policy against Allied reconnaissance airplanes and their protecting fighters. It worked well, and general sweeps of the battle front began when 20 German fighters from Douai patrolled parallel to the lines, leaving smaller units to go down and harry low flyers and strafe the trenches.

1917 April In what became known hereafter as Bloody April, the British lost 139 airplanes in combat, more than in any other month of the war. Air support of the Battle of Arras began April 4 and included the start of a major Allied bombing campaign April 5 simultaneously with a major artillery offensive. Royal Flying Corps squadrons, notably No. 100 Squadron, attacked airfields where German fighters were based. Along the main sector of the front around Arras the RFC had 365 front-line aircraft, of which about 120 were single-seat fighters, and the Germans had 195 aircraft, including almost 100 fighters. In the first five days of the air offensive, the RFC lost 131 aircraft, of which 75 were lost in combat and 56 in accidents. The Germans lost 72 aircraft. Fighting was intense, the leading air ace von Richthofen alone accounting for 18 losses to the RFC. The French, who were less involved, lost 33 aircraft.

1917 May 1 Responding to the mobilization of the U.S. forces for deployment to Europe, plans were laid for the modest expansion of the Aviation Section of the Signal Corps. Relegating air power to a minor role, appropriations of only $10.8 million were allocated for aviation in May and $43.4 million in June; but the aviation plan envisaged by the chief signal officer would provide six additional Aero squadrons, bringing the total to 13, and two additional balloon squadrons supporting an army of 1 million men planned for the European war. Within a few weeks, reports back from Maj. William Mitchell in France and Brig. Gen. Foulois in the United States escalated the plan.

1917 May 7 British air ace Albert Ball was killed when his S.E.5 (serial no. A4850) crashed on the German side of the lines near Lens in the late evening. He had been in a fight involving Lothar von Richthofen, brother of Manfred, but was last seen diving into cloud. A machine gun crew in a church tower claimed to have shot him down, but von Richthofen was probably responsible for the killing shot. Ball had joined No. 56 Squadron, Royal Flying Corps, on April 7, 1917, after serving as a flight instructor

Powered by three engines, this Lloyd triplane bomber crashed on its first flight.

in England for six months. Prior to that he had had a roving commission with No. 60 Squadron, RFC. Ball scored a total 44 victories.

1917 May 7   Edward Mannock, the leading British air ace of World War I, scored his first aerial victory by shooting down a German observation balloon exactly one month after he first began to fly Nieuport scouts with No. 40 Squadron, Royal Flying Corps. Born on May 24, 1887, Mannock joined the Royal Army Medical Corps when war broke out. He transferred to the Royal Engineers and then, inspired by the stories of Capt. Ball, joined the RFC in August 1916, gaining his pilot's certificate a month later. Mannock joined No. 40 Squadron on April 6, one day before his first flight in the Nieuport. By July he had been awarded the Military Cross, promoted to captain and made a flight commander.

1917 May 8   Lt. Hermann Goering of Jasta 28 shot down his fifth aerial victim, the first with this unit, thus becoming an official air ace. Born in 1893, Goering had joined the army in 1912 and in 1915 transferred to the air service. He joined Jasta 5, flying Fokkers in September 1916, and three months later obtained his first confirmed victory. Goering moved from Jasta 28 to Jasta 27 in June 1917 and on July 8, 1918, replaced Oblt W. Reinhard as head of Jagdgeschwader No. 1 when the latter was killed. Goering scored only one victory with JG.1, a Spad shot down on July 18, bringing his total to 22. After the war, he went to Sweden as an airline pilot.

1917 May 14   A Curtiss H-12 Large America flying boat (serial no. 8666) operated by the Royal Naval Air Service became the first American-built aircraft to shoot down another aircraft in World War I when it encountered German Navy Zeppelin L 22. Radio messages from the L 22 had been heard by British listening posts, and the Royal Naval Air Service station at Great Yarmouth was ordered to send a flying boat to intercept. The H-12 found the airship near the Terschelling Light Vessel in the North Sea off

the Dutch coast and set it alight by gunfire. All 21 German crewmen on board were killed.

1917 May 17   The U.S. Navy and the U.S. Army officially adopted a five-pointed white star with a red center on a blue field as the national marking for its airplanes. The blue field was to extend as far as the outer points on the star and the inner circle was to link the inner projections of the star. Prior to this there had been no formal marking for U.S. airplanes, although some navy airplanes had carried an anchor marking to denote their ownership! When U.S. airplanes reached the Western Front in Europe, pilots said the marking could be confused with the German cross, and from February 8, 1918, a tricolor roundel was adopted with red on the outside followed by blue and a white center. The tail striping was applied with red at the leading edge followed by white and blue. The original star marking was reintroduced in August 1919.

1917 May 20   An American built Curtiss H-12 Large America flying boat of the Royal Naval Air Service sank the first German submarine to be successfully attacked by an aircraft. The submarine (once mistakenly thought to be UC36, which actually sank on May 17 or May 18) was found by a Curtiss crewed by Flt. Sub-Lts. Morrish and Boswell while on patrol over the North Sea. The aircraft carried four 100-lb. bombs, which were dropped on the submarine, straddling and sinking it. Further successful attacks on other German submarines followed on July 29, September 22 and September 28, 1917. With a ceiling of 10,800 ft. and an endurance of 6 hr., the H-12 was a valuable and successful airplane for maritime patrol.

1917 May 22   The first government-approved civilian airmail service began when 480 lb. of mail were flown from Turin, Italy to Rome with special postage stamps to mark the occasion. The service ran for a week, and then others were tried, including a service between Brindisi, Italy and Valona, Albania between the end of May and the end of June. On June 28, the Società Industrie Meridionali set up an airmail service between Naples and Palermo. In France an airmail service between Paris and St. Nazaire via Le Mans was started on August 17 using Letord aircraft, and in Britain a communications squadron was formed with two flights of D.H.4s for sending military mail.

1917 May 24　Pres. Woodrow Wilson received a cable from French Prime Minister Alexandre Ribot proposing an expansion of American air power sufficient to ''allow the Allies to win the supremacy of the air.'' Ribot suggested that the Americans build up a corps of 4,500 airplanes, 5,000 pilots and 53,000 mechanics. Moreover, American factories should produce 2,000 airplanes and 4,000 aero engines a month, producing, during the first half of 1918, 16,500 new airplanes and 30,000 engines. An active force of 4,500 airplanes was about equal to the combined totals of British and French air power on the Western Front.

1917 May 25　A daylight offensive against southern England by German bombers opened with an attack on the coast by 21 Gothas from Kagohl 3, comprising Flights 13 and 14 based at St. Denis Westrem, Belgium, and Flights 15 and 16 based at Gontrode. Powered by two 260-HP Mercedes engines providing an operating height of 15,000 ft., the bombers had a decided advantage over the limited performance of defending fighters and each Gotha G.IV could carry up to 1,100 lb. of bombs. Of the 23 Gothas that set out, two turned back, and the Germans claimed one was shot down by British air defense fighters. Of the 77 sorties flown that night, only a handful of British fighters even saw the bombers. Of 95 people killed, 56 were women and children, and total damage amounted to 19,405 pounds.

1917 May 26　The increasing importance of aviation in U.S. plans for the European war was marked by an order from Gen.

John J. Pershing, commander in chief of the American Expeditionary Forces (AEF), assigning Maj. Townsend F. Dodd as the aviation officer on his staff at headquarters. Maj. Dodd's assistant, Lt. Birdseye B. Lewis, went to New York to recruit assistants, one of whom was racing driver Edward V. Rickenbacker. Employed as a chauffeur with the rank of sergeant 1st class, Rickenbacker would soon achieve fame as America's highest-scoring air ace.

1917 May 31　The first aerobatic display by a Russian pilot in a Russian-built airplane took place when Capt. Makarov, commanding officer of the Eleventh Army Squadron, twice looped his aging Anatra D biplane. It was a brave maneuver indeed, for shortages of high quality wood led the Russian airplane builder to make up each wing spar in two pieces, overlapped by only 12 in. at a join held together by glue and tape. The following month, 6 Anatra Ds crashed because of poor quality manufacturing, killing their pilots.

1917 May　The Spad S.XIII, a development of the S.VII and one of the fastest fighter aircraft of World War I, entered service with escadrilles of the French air units. The aircraft was also extremely strong, an attribute that endeared it to the pilots who flew it. S.XIIIs were also operated by the American volunteer pilots with the Lafayette Escadrille and later by American fighter units serving with the American Expeditionary Force. The S.XIII was powered by a 200- or 220-HP Hispano-Suiza that gave it a maximum speed of 135.5 MPH at a height of 10,000 ft. Standard armament consisted of two Vickers machine guns.

1917 May　The U.S. Council of National Defense authorized the Aircraft Production Board, which became the Aircraft Board by act of Congress on October 1, 1917. The board's purpose was

Shorts produced this refined and aesthetically pleasing bomber design incorporating a four-wheeled landing gear.

to advise U.S. military services about the facilities needed for large-scale aircraft production and about the level of human and material resources committed to the build-up. It would help formulate a production plan for the Aviation Section of the Signal Corps, now rapidly expanding into the corps' most organizationally demanding activity.

1917 June 2 In a move to control the many expanding elements of the military aviation build-up under way at the U.S. Signal Corps, the Aviation Section became the Airplane Division, with other divisions formed to coordinate production, engineering and so on. All the separate divisions would be under the overall command of the chief signal officer, Brig Gen. George O. Squier.

1917 June 4 The U.S. Aircraft Production Board and the Joint Technical Board on Aircraft approved the construction of five prototype models of the 8- and 12-cylinder variants of the Liberty engine. The basic principle of the engine's design and layout was conducted by J. G. Vincent of the Packard Motor Co. at the Willard Hotel, Washington, D.C. during the previous week. The Liberty engine was to power airplanes built in the United States under license from Britain and would form the basis of an indigenous American aero-engine manufacturing capability.

1917 June 5 The Gloucestershire Aircraft Co. Ltd. was registered with a capital of 10,000 pounds set up by the Aircraft Manufacturing Co. Ltd. (Airco) to build fuselages and airplanes for the de Havilland-designed aircraft, helping relieve assembly congestion at Airco now that major orders were flowing from the Royal Flying Corps. Airco had 50% of these orders, and A. W. Martyn, managing director of coachbuilders H. H. Martyn & Co. Ltd., had the rest. Making its first flight in June 1921, the first Gloster product, the Mars I racing airplane, was the first in a long line of famous airplanes that would include such types as the Gamecock, Gauntlet, Gladiator, Meteor and Javelin.

1917 June 5 The First Aeronautic Detachment, the first U.S. military unit to arrive in France, landed at Pauillac on the USS *Jupiter.* It comprised seven officers and 122 enlisted men (some of whom were on the USS *Neptune,* which docked at St. Nazaire June 8) commanded by Lt. Kenneth Whiting. After settling in at the French military aviation school at Tours, training began June 25 using Caudron biplanes under French instructors. About 50 men were sent to St. Raphael to be trained as mechanics.

1917 June 7 The infantry attack at the battle of Messines began during the most intensive Allied artillery barrage carried out to date and coordinated air support that would spot for the guns and keep the skies free of German reconnaissance airplanes. The attack was signaled by the detonation of 400 tons of ammonal (a mixture of TNT, ammonium nitrate, and aluminum powder) in specially dug mines beneath the German lines at 3:10 A.M., which rocked Paris and shook London. Primitive radio-detection of enemy airplanes was operated, helping vector fighters to the attack. It had been hoped that Allied fighters could carry radio receivers for in-flight updates on the position of enemy airplanes, but this luxury was denied.

1917 June 8 The first Zeppelin production bomber was delivered to the German Air Service following flight trials at Staaken. Known as the R.VI, it had a wing span of 138 ft. 5 in., a length of 72.5 ft. and a height of 20 ft. 8 in. It was powered by four 260-HP Mercedes engines in two nacelles, driving two pusher and two tractor propellers, plus a 120-HP Mercedes in the fuselage driving a supercharger. The R.VI, of which 18 were built, had an enclosed crew cabin with defensive gun positions in the

wings, the nose and the rear fuselage. It could carry a maximum bomb load of 4,410 lb. for short distances but usually carried about 2,400 lb. or less on flights of up to 10 hr. in duration.

1917 June 10 The battle of Messines on the Western Front ended—Allied troops having advanced more than 2 mi. in the preceding days—and all air support operations were brought to a halt. With numerical superiority assuring command of the skies, the Royal Flying Corps had kept artillery on target and mapped German positions to achieve a major military success for the infantry. In 10 days, 2,233 guns fired more than 2.8 million shells weighing 64,164 tons along a 5.6 mi. front, about 1,500 lb. of high explosives per yard per day for 10 days. The aerial spotters positioned the guns to destroy 268 enemy batteries and 169 gun-pits and to conduct 234 trench bombardments.

1917 June 13 The first German daylight bombing raid on London was carried out by 18 Gothas from Kagohl 3 in an action for which permission had been sought since the beginning of the war and for which its commanding officer, Hptm. Ernst von Brandenburg, was awarded the Ordre Pour le Mérite. None of the Gothas were engaged by defensive fighters on their way to London, and only a few of the 94 airplanes that rose to the attack saw the bombers on their way back, all of which returned safely. Kagohl 3 was building up to four flights of six Gothas each, a force that would be complete by July. The bombing left 162 dead, 432 injured and damage worth £129,498.

At a cabinet meeting in London held a few hours after the raid, Sir William Robertson, chief of the Imperial General Staff, asked cabinet members to approve a major expansion of air power, both for the defense of towns and cities in England as well as for expanding the war effort. There was increasing awareness of the potential for delivering the war to the Germans in their own towns and cities and for using strategic bombing to knock out its industries and material sources. Many regarded this as the only practicable means of breaking the deadlocked trench warfare in France and Flanders and forcing Germany to surrender.

1917 June 14 The prototype Nieuport 28, a radical departure from previous Nieuports, made its first flight. With modest dihedral on the upper wing of a staggered pair, the tail was about the only element in the design reminiscent of the familiar sesquiplane design of the early Nieuports. Unusually for all airplanes, the lower wing carried the ailerons. With an empty weight of 960 lbs., it was the heaviest Nieuport scout to date, though it was 500 lb. lighter than the German Albatros D.III and D.V scouts. Not before early 1918 did the type go into production. Prone to shed fabric from its wings, it was not popular, although the Americans bought 297.

1917 June 26 In a concentration of German air power, the first fighter wing (Jagdgeschwader) was formed from Jastas 4, 6, 10 and 11 by order of the army chief of staff. JG.1 was to be commanded by Manfred von Richthofen, who by this time had scored 56 confirmed aerial victories. With suitable transportation and tents for airplanes, JG.1 was to be a flexible combat wing of four squadrons able to quickly relocate along the front as required. JG.2 and JG.3 would be formed on February 2, 1918, followed by JG.4 on October 14, 1918, only two weeks before the armistice. Because of the mobile nature of these wings and the colorful airplanes they flew, they became known as the Flying Circuses.

1917 June 26 Maj. Raynal C. Bolling, commanding officer of the First Reserve Aero Squadron, New York National Guard, arrived in Liverpool, England with two flying officers, two naval officers, industrial experts, 93 skilled mechanics and factory experts in weapons manufacturing and production to begin a survey of Allied needs and requirements in the fight against Germany. Known as the Bolling Commission, this group arranged for American linen for airplane wings to be supplied to British airplane makers. Maj. Dodd provided liaison between Bolling and the French.

1917 June   The first airplane designed from the outset as a torpedo-carrier for operation from the deck of a ship at sea, the Sopwith Cuckoo, made its first flight at the Isle of Grain, England. Powered by a 200-HP Hispano-Suiza engine, the production Cuckoo appeared in July 1918, and by the end of the war in November 1918, about 90 had been delivered to the Royal Naval Air Service. It was operational aboard HMS *Argus* on October 19, 1918, and the type remained in service until April 1923. It had a loaded weight of 3,883 lb. and cruised at 98 MPH with a single 18-in. torpedo beneath the fuselage.

1917 June   Birdseye B. Lewis formed the Lewis & Vought Corp. along with his old friend Chance M. Vought, who had received his flying license in August 1912. After a period as flying instructor at the Lillie School of Aviation in Chicago, Vought was employed by Curtiss as design engineer before working for the Wright Co. Lewis eventually went to France and was killed, leaving Vought to carry on the aircraft business. In 1922 the company name would be changed to Chance-Vought.

1917 July 2   The British cabinet agreed to a major expansion of air power by increasing the operational strength of the Royal Flying Corps from 108 squadrons to 200 and by a corresponding increase in the strength of the Royal Naval Air Service. Long-range bombing was to be a vital element in this expansion, with 40 strategic bombing squadrons in total. The British commander-in-chief in France, Gen. Sir Douglas Haig, disagreed on the need for long-range strategic bombers. He preferred instead fighters, reconnaissance airplanes and light bombers capable of attacking enemy airfields. He was assured that these other essential duties would not be neglected.

1917 July 4   After an incredible effort by a team of engineers and designers from various U.S. companies, including the designer J. G. Vincent of the Packard Motor Co., the first 8-cylinder version of the Liberty aero-engine was produced and delivered to the National Bureau of Standards in Washington, D.C. The first bench test was conducted on July 23, but unsatisfactory results following the first flight of an airplane equipped with this

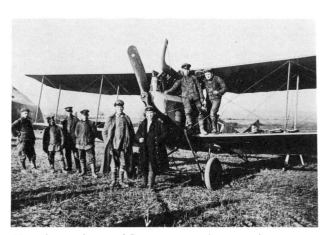

Air and ground crew of German reconnaissance unit Fliegerabteilung (Flying Section) 227 pausing for publicity.

engine on August 20 led to the abandonment of the 8-cylinder model in December 1917. Work then concentrated on the 12-cylinder model because Gen. Pershing wanted more power and that could be obtained only with the bigger engine.

1917 July 6   Manfred von Richthofen was shot down following an engagement with six F.E.2d biplanes from No. 20 Squadron, Royal Flying Corps. Von Richthofen, in his red-colored Albatros D.V., had led a group of pilots from Jasta 11 into the attack on the English biplanes, which formed a defensive circle. More airplanes arrived from both sides until about 40 were involved in the scrap. Capt. D. C. Cunnell and his observer, 2nd Lt. A. E. Woodbridge rendered four German fighters out of control and reported one that fell away. This was von Richthofen who, shot in the head, passed out and came to just 500 ft. from the ground. He was hopitalized until July 25, when he returned to Jagdgeschwader.

1917 July 10   Gen. John J. Pershing, chief of the American Expeditionary Forces, forwarded a plan to Washington known as the General Organization Project, developed jointly by his headquarters and Col. Chauncey Baker, who had been sent to France by the War Department to examine resources and materiel available to the U.S. troops. Under the plan, Pershing recommended a field army of about 1 million men in 20 divisions, with 59 air squadrons, of which 39 were to be observation, 15 pursuit and 5 bombardment.

1917 July 11   British Prime Minister David Lloyd George and South African Lt. Gen. Jan C. Smuts, a member of the Imperial War Cabinet, formed a special cabinet committee to investigate the urgent problem of the German daylight bomber raids on England and the poor state of the U.K. air defenses. The defenses had been unsuccessful in seriously disrupting the high altitude raids, a fact that attracted much bitter comment in the U.K. press and government. Smuts delivered the results of his investigations in two reports in July and August, recommending a single Air Ministry to act as a central authority for all aspects of air warfare, instead of individual systems governed by the army and navy.

1917 July 12   The National Advisory Committee for Aeronautics' subcommittee on patents proposed to the executive committee that a ceiling of $2 million should be placed on cross-licensing agreements between Wright and Curtiss and that royalties for future inventions should be controlled by the Aircraft Manufacturers Association created in February. This sought to remove damaging patent claims that were considered a hindrance to all-out development of aviation in the United States. It recommended the government be able to hand designs from one company over to another with 1% royalty per airframe paid to the original designer.

1917 July 15   Members of the Bolling Commission in Europe, including Col. Bolling himself, arrived in Italy at the express invitation of the government and in an effort to determine whether Italian facilities could add to French airplane production (see July 1917). Italy agreed to train 500 American pilots at the school at Foggia, and the commission placed an order for 500 airplanes and 1,500 aero engines. In addition, 200 Caproni bombers were ordered for delivery to American air units when they reached the front lines. Another contract, signed October 16, 1917, called for 200 touring cars and 1,050 automobile engines for American air units.

1917 July 23   Maj. Benjamin D. Foulois was appointed commanding officer of the Airplane Division of the U.S. Signal Corps.

One of the great figures of early American aviation, Foulois had served in the Aviation Section since its inception and had been responsible for many of the developments in American military aviation. He had already seen active service over Mexico and was a serious-minded, orthodox officer who had converted many previously skeptical colleagues to the practicality of military aviation by his level-headed approach to the subject.

1917 July 23 The first 47 American aviation recruits for flight training arrived in France under the leadership of Capt. James E. Miller. They had been sent on recommendations made by Col. Bolling June 26 that British, French and Italian aviation schools could usefully begin immediate training for U.S. aviation recruits. All received commissions, although 10 were sent to Paris to help build up headquarters. One of these 10 was C. F. Douglas Campbell, who would become the first American air ace. The remaining 37 went to Tours on August 15. Other American recruits arrived at training schools in England and Italy during September 1917.

1917 July 24 Pres. Wilson signed a congressional act that appropriated $640 million for aviation, the largest single-sum voted to date for a single purpose. It endorsed the cable request from French Prime Minister Ribot received at the White House May 26. With the temporary rank of brigadier general, Benjamin D. Foulois had been tasked with formulating a plan for air support of an army of 1 million American soldiers and skirted protests from Pershing's general staff by urging the need for such a program before the House Military Affairs Committee.

1917 July 27 The German Directorate of Aircraft Production sent a message signed by Hptm. Muehlig-Hofmann inviting all German aircraft manufacturers to inspect a captured Sopwith Triplane. The British Triplane had gained an impressive reputation for performance and leading German air aces viewed it as a major threat, especially since the Albatros single-seaters were becoming increasingly outclassed. Believing low-wing loading and agility to be the key to renewed air superiority, it led to a flood of triplane designs from German manufacturers.

1917 July 31 At 3:50 A.M., the main offensive of the Third Battle of Ypres (Passchendaele) began, with 508 British airplanes (of which 230 were single-seaters), 200 French (of which 100 were single-seaters) and 40 Belgian (of which 20 were single-seaters), a total of 748, plus 104 airplanes from the Royal Naval Air Services. The Germans on that sector had approximately 600 airplanes, 200 of which were single-seat fighters. The Battle of Ypres would last until mid-November and witness a major effort by both sides to win aerial supremacy and clear the skies for reconnaissance and bombing missions.

1917 July The Bolling Commission examined the French airplane industry and saw for themselves that its capacity was not fully exploited. An agreement was discussed whereby American machine tools and raw materials would be supplied to the French factories at cost if the French would manufacture large numbers of airplanes for the Americans on the same basis. The state of the American aircraft manufacturing industry gave little hope of gearing up to U.S. Army needs for several years. A step in that direction would be made by license-building British D.H.4 bombers over the next few years.

1917 August 2 Squadron leader E. H. Dunning of the Royal Naval Air Service became the first pilot to land an airplane on the deck of a moving ship when he put a Sopwith Pup down on HMS *Furious.* Designed as a light cruiser, *Furious* was con-

structed to carry a forward deck 228 ft. long instead of an 18-inch gun turret, the first ship built as an aircraft carrier. Dunning flew the Pup along the starboard side of HMS *Furious,* which was steaming at 26 knots into a 21-knot wind, giving an over-deck wind almost equal to the landing speed of the airplane, and side-slipped it onto the planking. Ratings grabbed the Pup and strapped it down. Five days later Dunning was killed when the Pup stalled and crashed into the sea.

1917 August 5 The First Aero Squadron of the Signal Corps left the United States for Europe under the command of Maj. Ralph Royce. The squadron had suffered hardship and operational pressures in the Mexican campaign and in December 1916 had received a warm message of gratitude from Gen. Pershing. During April and May of 1917, the squadron was prepared for foreign service by taking an advanced course in flying and navigation. No flying had been carried out during June and July, but the officers and enlisted men completed a course in infantry drill and rifle practice.

1917 August 7 Noted for the success of its monoplanes in prewar performance competitions and races and for early fighter applications in 1915 and 1916, Morane-Saulnier made the first flight of their AI monoplane. It could be fitted with either a 120-HP Le Rhône rotary or a 160-HP Gnôme Monosoupape, providing a top speed of almost 130 MPH at 6,500 ft., and it was equipped with one or two Vickers guns. Although the type saw only limited service during early 1918, 1,200 were built, of which 51 were supplied to the American Air Service before the end of the war.

1917 August 14 The first order for 100 Handley Page 0/400 bombers was placed for delivery to the Royal Flying Corps. A development of the 0/100, which had been designed and built for the Royal Naval Air Service, the 0/400 was powered by either two 375-HP Rolls Royce Eagle VIIIs, two 284-HP Rolls Royce Eagle IVs, or two 275-HP Sunbeam Maoris. It could carry up to 2,000 lb. of bombs and up to five Lewis guns for defense. The original order was canceled and reestablished at least twice before the first airplanes reached operational service in August 1918.

1917 August 15 The technical staff of the Signal Corps Airplane Division at Dayton, Ohio examined the airframe of a British D.H.4 bomber with a view to mass production by automobile manufacturers. The D.H.4 was adapted for the American Liberty engine. Car makers naively thought it would be simply a matter of converting production lines to building airplanes rather than cars, but the fine tolerances of airplane structures necessitated new skills that took time to acquire. In return, agreements were reached with the British whereby American raw material, especially wood, would be sent from the United States. Without these materials, British airplane production would have floundered during 1918.

1917 August 16 The second and third Fokker Dr.1 Triplanes (serial nos. Fok F.1 102/17 and Fok. F.1 103/17) began flight acceptance tests at Schwerin. Designed by Fokker's Reinhold Platz in response to a call from the German Directorate of Aircraft Production for competitive triplane designs, the first had been sent to Adlershof early in the month for structural tests. The two others were taken to von Richthofen's JG.1 fighter wing at Courtrai for display and demonstration.

1917 August 18 Neutral during World War I, the Dutch became increasingly aware of the importance of aviation to national defense and formed the Royal Netherlands Naval Air Service (Marine Luchtvaartdienst) to complement the army's aviation division established July 1, 1913. Equipment initially comprised a mixture of types, including Martin biplanes from the United States and Friedrichshafen seaplanes from Germany. After the war in Europe, the RNNAS developed its maritime air forces in the Dutch East Indies (now Indonesia) and mixed German Dornier and Focke airplanes with British-built Fairey IIIB seaplanes.

1917 August 19   In a remarkable demonstration of the use of bombers in support of a land campaign, Italian Capronis attacked Austro-Hungarian positions at the beginning of the Eleventh Battle of the Isonzo. The 95 aircraft dropped 23 tons of explosive, and attacks involving more than 200 aircraft were made on the following days. For the balance of the month and the whole of September, around 20 tons of bombs were dropped daily, and thousands of separate projectiles were let loose on the troops and equipment below.

1917 August 22   The last daylight raid on England by German bombers in World War I took place when 10 Gothas attacked the southeast coast killing 12, injuring 27 and causing damage estimated at 17,145 pounds. Fifteen Gothas had started out (five turned back before reaching the English coast), and three were shot down—two by antiaircraft fire and one by a Sopwith Camel. Only four days earlier, nine Gothas out of 28 that set out for England were destroyed when bad weather forced them back, two being shot down and seven crashing in Belgium. These losses could not be sustained, and responding to stiffer air defenses, bombing raids were switched to night attacks, which began late in the evening of September 2.

1917 August 24   In a London meeting of the the Imperial War Cabinet, the British government agreed to form a separate air force independent of direct control by the army or the navy and directed Lt. Gen. Smuts to draw up the necessary legislation that would be presented to parliament for its approval. Called the Air Organization Committee, it put together the structure of a Royal Air Force, an effort greatly assisted by Lt. Gen. Sir David Henderson. It set out everything from the formation of an air council to a scale of pay for servicemen and women. Some, like Sir Douglas Haig, opposed the independence this would give air elements, which he considered subservient to the needs of the army.

1917 August 25   The first 12-cylinder Liberty engine successfully passed a 50-hour bench test, clearing the way for its first use in an airplane, a British built D.H.4, which would take place October 21. It was originally rated at 314 HP, but this increased to 395 HP by the time of the first flight and to 450 HP by May 1918. The engine was efficient and had a high performance for its day. The eight-cylinder model had been abandoned in favor of the high powered model.

1917 August 25   Rear Adm. David W. Taylor, chief of the Bureau of Construction and Repair of the U.S. Navy, conceived the idea of a seaplane that could be delivered to the European war by flying across the Atlantic. Such a flying boat could, he theorized, also be used to attack submarines that threatened trans-Atlantic cargo ships. The result was the Curtiss NC (Navy Curtiss) series, which, it was speculated, would be designed for the new American Liberty engine. Navy engineers G. Conrad Westervelt and Jerome Hunsaker started design work during September, and Curtiss was called to Washington, D.C. Threatened with cancellation at war's end, the NC was revived for the *Daily Mail* trans-Atlantic prize originally announced in 1913.

1917 August 28   Col. William L. Kenly, Seventh Field Artillery, was appointed chief aviation officer, replacing Col. Bolling.

Kenly was soon promoted to the rank of brigadier general and operated from the air service headquarters at Chaumont. Col. William Mitchell had been placed in charge of aviation in the zone of advance, but Kenly would deal with administration, supply of materials and pilots and general schedules and inventories.

1917 August 30   A contract between the United States, represented by Gen. Pershing, and the French government, represented by the civil servant Daniel Vincent, was drawn up calling for the large-scale production of French airplanes that would form the initial equipment of the American air units in France. Under the agreement, France would supply 5,000 airplanes and 8,500 motors with an estimated value of $65 million. Breguet received an order for 1,500 bombers and reconnaissance machines, Spad for 2,000 5.XIII fighters along with 1,500 new Spads or Nieuport 28s. The first 1,000 airplanes and engines were to be delivered by February 1, 1918.

1917 August   The Aviation Section of the U.S. Signal Corps completed plans for the build-up of American military air power to support ground forces in the European war and received approval to begin implementing it. The plan envisaged 345 combat squadrons, 45 construction companies, 81 supply squadrons, 11 repair squadrons and 26 balloon companies. Of that total, 263 combat squadrons were expected to go to Europe by June 30, 1918, with the remainder to be deployed in the United States, Panama and the Pacific. Production fell badly behind, and this plan was never realized.

1917 September 1   Flying a Fokker Dr.1 Triplane, Manfred von Richthofen shot down a British R.E.8 two-seat observation biplane carrying 2d Lt. I. B. C. Madge and 2d Lt. W. Kember, the former surviving and being made a prisoner of war and the latter dying from wounds. Unaware that the approaching triplane was a new German machine and not the more familiar (British) Sopwith Triplane, Madge and Kember allowed von Richthofen to approach to within 200 ft. and fire 20 rounds before the R.E.8 went down, giving him his 60th victory. Richthofen had made a brief flight, his first in the Fokker Triplane, that morning, and his hearty endorsement of the type did much to immortalize an otherwise mediocre airplane.

1917 September 8   The first of a new and more advanced family of Zeppelin airships was commissioned for the German Navy. Known as V-type airships, Zeppelin L 55 had a capacity of 1,977,900 cu. ft., a length of 644 ft. 8 in. and a diameter of 78 ft. 5 in., with a lifting capacity between 85,000 lb. and 89,600 lb. Eleven airships of this type would be built for naval patrol and bombing duties, of which two would be specially modified to have increased capacity.

1917 September 11   The French air ace Georges Guynemer took off on patrol with another pilot, both flying Spad biplanes, and disappeared during a furious air combat with a German biplane over Poelcapelle, Belgium. No German claim was entered regarding that fight, although the Germans did claim two days later that a Lt. Wesimann had shot Guynemer down. No remains of either Guynemer or his airplane were ever found. Guynemer's score stood at 53, making him the second-ranking French air ace of World War I. He had logged 660 flying hours and fought more than 600 combats, been shot down seven times and received 26 citations.

1917 September 14   The prototype Fairey N10 made its first flight from the Isle of Grain, England. The Fairey Aviation Co. Ltd. had been registered in July 1915 on the promise of assembly orders for Short 827 seaplanes. The first airplane to be solely designed by Fairey was the F.2, which appeared in early 1916. The next success was a seaplane called Campania, built specially to operate from the converted liner of the same name. The N10, which had been built to an Admiralty specification for a carrier-based seaplane, was renamed Fairey III and modified into the IIIA, in which form it served with the Royal Naval Air Service and newly created RAF in 1918.

1917 September 18   In an appendix to the General Organization Project forwarded to Washington on July 10, 1917, from Gen. Pershing's headquarters in France, the Service of the Rear Project (SRP) defined what kinds of troops and what sort of equipment would be needed to implement the recommended 1 million-man army for the European war. The American Expeditionary Force took the SRP and added a further 201 squadrons, bringing to 260 the total number of squadrons recommended. Of these, 120 would be for pursuit, 80 would be for observation and 60 for day and night bombardment. Total complement of officers and men would number 125,837 with 4,680 operational combat airplanes and 144 balloons.

1917 September 21   Lt. Erich Lowenhardt shot down his fifth aerial victim, an observation balloon, and by doing so became a German air ace. Lowenhardt would score 53 victories—46 airplanes and seven balloons—in little more than 12 months to rank third among German air aces. On August 10, 1918, his airplane collided with that of Lt. Wentz. Both were wearing parachutes, but Lowenhardt's failed to open and he fell to his death. Lowenhardt was only 21 when he died and had joined Jasta 10 of JG.1 in July 1917.

1917 September 21   After initial balloon barrages against low-flying aircraft had been set up by respective armies in Germany and Italy earlier in the year, the British attempted to raise balloons in a trial from Richmond Park near London, but when high winds tore them loose, Air Mechanics H. E. James and W. J. Pegge hung onto handling lines and were carried aloft. James fell to his death in the park from a height of 1,000 ft. while Pegge crawled into the rigging and fell to earth over Croydon, 15 mi. away. The first successful London barrage was completed during October.

1917 September 23   Flying Fokker Dr.1 Triplane (serial no. Fok. F.1 102/17), German air ace Werner Voss, age 20, was killed during one of the most outstanding aerial combats of World War I. Voss began by attacking a lone S.E.5a, which attracted an Albatros to assist plus six S.E.5as of No. 56 Squadron, Royal Flying Corps, led by Capt. McCudden, leaving the two Germans fighting seven enemy airplanes. Albatros fighters, Spads and Camels joined the fray. No mean combatant himself, 2d Lt. A. P. F. Rhys-Davids in an S.E.5a was on the third drum of his Lewis gun before Voss was overwhelmed. The Triplane began a shallow dive and stalled at 1,000 ft. Arguably the finest German fighter pilot, Voss had scored a total 48 victories in only 10 months.

1917 September 28   The first Zeppelin-Staaken bombers raided London. Withdrawn from the Eastern Front to equip Riesenflugzeug Abteilung 501 at Ghent commanded by Hptm. Richard von Bientivegni, the Staaken R.IV became the only R-plane (Giant Airplane) to operate on both fronts. It set out, along with 25 Gothas, accompanied by a Staaker R.VI-type that, along with 22 Gothas, had to turn back before it reached the target. Not for some months were the authorities aware that this new and imposing class of giant bomber, the largest to fly against England in

The gondola of the German airship L 54 shows the method of its attachment to the main structure supporting the envelope.

both world wars, had been introduced, despite intelligence information that forewarned of their imminent use against Britain.

1917 September   Illustrative of the intense aerial activity under way by Allied reconnaissance and bombing units supporting the Ypres offensive and of the absolute superiority of Allied aviation over German aviation, the British Royal Flying Corps carried out 226 bombing attacks by day and night during the month, dropping 7,886 bombs for a total weight of 135 tons on enemy targets. The Germans dropped 969 bombs on the British. The RFC ranged artillery fire on 9,539 German targets, most of which were gun batteries. Utilizing airplane wireless, the Germans ranged 743 targets. Moreover, the RFC exposed 14,678 photographic plates and sent 346,999 prints to unit and field commanders.

1917 October 1   Official orders were issued to set up a board of U.S. Army officers to examine members of the Lafayette Escadrille who had requested permission to transfer to the air service of the American Expeditionary Force in Europe. These experienced volunteers were to help from the core of Army Air Service squadron as commanders and flight leaders as well as instructors. Eventually, 90 Lafayette veterans were redeployed with the U.S. Army Air Service primarily for the purpose of building up pursuit aviation.

1917 October 11   Responding to incessant day, then night, bombing from airships and manned bombers, the British government authorized reprisal attacks on industrial Germany and formed No. 41 Wing, Royal Flying Corps, under the command of Lt. Col. (later Lord) C. L. N. Newall. The unit was formed at the urging of Gen. Hugh Trenchard backed by Gen. Smuts. Headquarters were at Bainville-sur-Madon, France, and equipment initially comprised about 30 D.H.4 and F.E.2b bombers—a pathetic little force for the task at hand. Later, Handley Page 0/100 bombers would be supplied. The first raid took place on October 17 when 1,792 lb. of bombs was dropped on Saarbruecken, Germany by eight D.H.4s of No. 55 Squadron.

1917 October 18   Col. Duval, head of the French Aeronautical Service at general headquarters set up a new goal for airplanes and escadrilles in a plan approved by Gen. Joffre. There were to be 238 escadrilles with a total 2,870 airplanes, including 30 escadrilles with 15 bombers each. This superseded the French plan of March 15, which set as a goal acquisition of 2,665 airplanes in 189 escadrilles, a level that was achieved by June 1. By this time, the French Air Service was numerically the largest on the Western Front, but the quality of its equipment was poor. On December 7, a new plan was approved for 4,000 operational airplanes by July 1, 1918, comprising 1,500 observation airplanes, 1,500 pursuit planes and 1,000 bombers.

1917 October 20   William George Barker of No. 28 Squadron, Royal Flying Corps, shot down an Albatros D.III single-seat biplane while flying Sopwith Camel serial no. B6313. Flying this aircraft, Barker would be credited with 46 victories, making B6313 the most successful fighter in the RFC or the RAF. Born in Manitoba, Canada, Barker arrived in Europe with the Manitoba Regiment but transferred to the RFC late in 1915. Flying first as an observer, then as a pilot with No. 15 Squadron, he served briefly as a flying instructor before he returned to the front where he was assigned to No. 28 Squadron in late September. His unit went to Italy, where Barker joined No. 66 Squadron in April 1918; he took command of No. 139 Squadron in France in July 1918, finally notching up a total score of 50 aerial victories.

1917 October 20   The Junkers-Fokker Werke A.G. was formed with a capital holding of 6 million marks subscribed equally by Hugo Junkers and Anthony Fokker. Junkers was a brilliant aircraft engineer and designer renowned for his metal monoplanes, but he lacked production experience and the German Inspectorate of Flying (IdFlieg) encouraged a partnership whereby Fokker could manage production of Junkers' designs. Fokker eventually withdrew due to incompatibility. After the war, Junkers would slowly develop his own company, which began, on April 24, 1919, as the Junkers Flugzeugwerke A.G. based at Dessau. It would produce some of the most important German airplanes for the following 26 years.

1917 October 21   The new 12-cylinder, 395-HP, low-compression Liberty engine was installed and flown for the first time in the Curtiss HS-1 prototype. Adapted as a single-engine version of the H-14 flying boat, itself a development of the America series, the HS flying boats would be built by five other manufacturers before remaining orders were canceled when the war ended. Curtiss built 675, and the type soldiered on into the 1930s as a transport flying boat and for short-haul airline use. Developed versions of the HS-1 were slightly bigger, but the type retained its two-seat layout.

1917 October 29   The first British D.H.4 bomber sent to the United States as a prototype for a U.S. model included a 12-cylinder Liberty engine instead of the originally planned eight cylinders. The American D.H.4 was produced by the Standard Aircraft Corp. of Patterson, New Jersey, the Dayton-Wright Co. of Dayton, Ohio, and the Fisher Body Division of General Motors. Together these companies built 4,846 D.H.4s, including 3,227 by the end of the war; orders for an additional 7,502 were canceled at the end of hostilities in Europe. The American D.H.4

became known as the Liberty Plane. Outdated by the time it reached the front, the Libertys needed a lot of work when they arrived in Europe to rectify poor quality work on U.S. production lines. The last D.H.4s were withdrawn from army use as late as 1931.

1917 October 29   Lt. Heinrich Gontermann, known as the Balloon Strafer, received fatal injuries when the Fokker Dr.1 Triplane he was flying (serial no.115/17) suffered structural failure while he was performing aerobatics over his airfield at 1,500 ft. The plane had been delivered to Jasta 15 on October 22, but poor weather kept it grounded until October 28. Gontermann had been a pilot for two years and joined Jasta 5 in late 1916 and Jasta 15 in April 1917. He scored 21 airplanes shot down and 18 balloons. His Triplane failed when the top wing broke up, and the ensuing crash caused terrible facial injuries from which he died the next day.

1917 October 31   Lt. Pastor from Jasta 11, one of the JG.1 units under Manfred von Richthofen, was killed when the Fokker Dr.1 Triplane he was flying (serial no.121/17) suffered structural failure and crashed. Following on Gontermann's accident two days previously, all Fokker Triplanes were immediately grounded, and those pilots affected reverted temporarily to Albatros D.Va and Pfalz D.III scouts. The accidents were investigated November 2 and reported on 13 days later. Instructions for manufacturing and assembly improvements were implemented, and production and flying resumed November 28, 1917.

1917 November 10   Curtiss delivered the first automated "flying bomb" adapted from the N-9 trainer controlled by automatic stabilization equipment. The navy had given Sperry five standard N-9 seaplanes for tests of the automatic equipment, and more than 100 tests were carried out between September and October. Pilots in the airplane controlled only take-offs and landings. The new unmanned N-9 had a span of 25 ft. and a length of 15 ft., could carry a 1,000 lb. load of explosives and was powered by a 100-HP Curtis OX-5 engine. Fully automated tests began November 24 but were repeatedly unsuccessful.

1917 November 12   Gen. Foulois arrived in France to head the U.S. Air Service and took up his position at headquarters in Chaumont, replacing Brig. Gen. Kenly on November 27, who returned to the United States to build up the new office of Director of Military Aeronautics. Kenly would also administer the expansion of army air power and coordinate production and procurement planning. Gen. Foulois made several major administrative changes, among which was the appointment of Col. Bolling to be member of the Joint Army and Navy Aircraft Committee set up to liaise with the Allies and to channel communications between headquarters and Washington, D.C.

1917 November 15   The pilot who would rank second among Italian air aces of World War I, Silvio Scaroni, scored his first aerial victory against an Albatros two-seater, which crashed in flames near Colberstadio. In one remarkable fight on June 25, 1918, Scaroni saw an Albatros he attacked literally disintegrate in front of him; the engine from the plane plummeted straight through a second Albatros, which also crashed to earth. Scaroni scored his final, 26th victory on July 12, 1918, before being shot down. Crash landing in no-mans-land, he spent the rest of the war in a hospital. In 1928 he became air attache in Washington, D.C. and was eventually recalled to Italy, this time to fight against the Allies in World War II.

1917 November 18   The U.S. Navy began patrols off the French coast at Le Croisac with six French Tellier flying boats. Commissioned November 27, the seaplane station was commanded by Lt. W. M. Corry. The flying boats were assigned convoy protection, antisubmarine duties and mine detection. Alphonse Tellier, owner of the factory, had been a boat builder, and it was his boat *La Rapière* that towed Voisin's floatplane on the Seine River, June 6, 1905. Powered by a 200-HP Hispano-Suiza engine, the U.S. Navy airplanes were operated with French serial numbers, only one being sent to the United States for evaluation. Tellier also supplied flying boats to the Russians as well as the British.

1917 November 20 One of the most audacious attempts at breaking entrenched stalemate on the Western Front began when the Allied attack on German forces opened the Battle of Cambrai and started a new phase in air support. Noted as the first major battle to use mass tank assaults, Cambrai saw the use of Allied airplanes for ground attack behind the lines supporting large-scale infantry assaults. Allied losses were as high as 30% of ground attack units. The British had 289 airplanes in the area, of which 134 were single-seat fighters, while the entire German 2d Army, which was deployed along a front from Cambrai to St. Quentin, had a total of 78 airplanes, including 12 fighters.

1917 November 21 The U.S. Army chief signal officer, Brig. Gen. George O. Squier watched a demonstration test of a Curtiss N-9 trainer flown for a distance of seven miles under automatic pilot. With him were Glenn Curtiss, Elmer Sperry and Rear Adm. Ralph A. Earle, who were there to judge the potential military value of pilotless airplanes for the army. Although the navy had already begun trials of unmanned airplanes, the army was only just accepting the concept. Brig. Gen. Squier wrote to the chairman of the Aircraft Board on November 26 advising a go-ahead and appointed a board to monitor progress with the device. Only one board member, Charles F. Kettering, was enthusiastic and received a contract to develop the idea.

1917 November 21 A specially modified V-type Zeppelin airship left Jamboli, Bulgaria with supplies for beleaguered German troops holding out against the British in East Africa. Stretched to a length of 743 ft. by the addition of two gas bags, increasing capacity to 2,419,400 cu. ft. and lifting potential to 114,000 lb., the L 59 carried 311,000 rounds of ammunition, 57,500 machine-gun cartridges, 30 machine guns, 61 sacks of medical supplies and many smaller items. After two days and within 125 mi. of its destination, L 59 was ordered back, the situation on the ground now hopeless. In 95 hr., the L 59 covered 4,200 mi. on the round trip.

1917 November 29 The Air Force Bill received the royal assent at the hand of King George V and was passed into law, creating the Royal Air Force that would replace the Royal Flying Corps and the Royal Naval Air Service, putting into one organization the aviation personnel and flying machines of both services. When the RAF formally came into being on April 1, 1918, a separate corps was set up for the 10,168 personnel from the Women's Army Air Corps, the Women's Royal Naval Service and the Women's Legion, who were transport drivers attached to flying units of the RFC in England. The Women's Royal Air Force was initially run by Chief Superintendent Lady Gertrude Crawford, but she was succeeded a month later by the Hon. Violet Douglas-Pennant.

1917 November 30 The prototype Vickers Vimy made its first flight at the hands of Gordon Bell at Joyce Green, England. Designed as a twin-engined bomber, the Vimy originated in July 1917 when it was suggested that Vickers should develop an airplane that could effectively benefit from surplus Hispano-Suiza engines then becoming available. The result was an impressive airplane with a bomb capacity in excess of 2,000 lb., a wing span of 67 ft. 2 in. and a length of 43.5 ft. Intended for bombing Germany, it did not enter service until October 1918; but it served as a front-line bomber with the RAF until replaced by the Virginia in 1924.

1917 December 3 An official announcement was made that the Lafayette Escadrille of volunteer American pilots gathered together into the unit now designed Escadrille Spa.124, flying Spad fighters, would be integrated into the Air Service of the American Expeditionary Force in France. That just a few battle-hardened aviators could be of much use in passing on valuable combat experience to the flood of American flyers soon on their way to Europe was a vain hope. There was much pride, however, that American representation in World War I had been established long before the Congress declared war.

1917 December 5 An agreement between the United States and Britain was reached whereby the United States would provide 15,000 mechanics for aircraft engineering schools in England, releasing an equivalent number of experienced British technicians for squadrons at the front, where manpower shortages were becoming acute. Because Britain was also short of 26,000 laborers to build airfields and facilities, it was agreed the United States would provide 1,200 bricklayers, 1,000 carpenters and 4,000 laborers. At a meeting of the Inter-Allied Aviation Council in Paris this month, Sir William Weir proposed idle Lancashire cotton mills could turn out bombers for U.S. squadrons. The final agreement on that, signed in January 1918, recognized that such a scheme was impossible due to the very different skills and equipment.

1917 December 21 The composition and structure of the British Air Council, being set up along with the new Royal Air Force, was announced. Against the wishes of Sir Douglas Haig, the C-in-C of British forces in France, Maj. Gen. Sir Hugh Trenchard was being withdrawn from command of the Royal Flying Corps in France to serve under Lt. Gen. Sir David Henderson on the Air Council. Trenchard had served 2½ years as head of the RFC in France and had gained considerable respect from his senior generals and staff, providing appropriate liaison between the fighting units and the bureaucratic chiefs in England.

1917 December The first true American-built fighter, the Orenco B, was ordered, but only two were built. Designed in mid-1917, by Walter Phipps of the aviation department of the Ordnance Engineering Co. of Baldwin, Long Island, it was modeled after the Spad S.VII and had a 160-HP Gnôme Monosoupape rotary engine, which gave it a ceiling in excess of 20,000 ft. It carried wireless, the first such fitting as standard in an American airplane. The Orenco B was followed by the C, of which six were ordered. This model was built as a trainer with an 80-HP engine. The D fighter was powered by a 300-HP Wright-Hispano engine, and 50 were eventually built by Curtiss.

1918 January 5 The new U.S. aviation force plan was approved by the Commander-in-Chief, General Staff following submissions by a committee set up in December with Lt. Col. W. B. Burtt of the Aviation Section and Lt. Col. A. B. Barber of the general staff. It found widely diverging views from Europe about priorities. The British favored a major infantry build-up with aviation when appropriate, the French favored a major American air presence to bomb German lines. A compromise prevailed, and plans were set for a total 190 squadrons of 28,500 men by June 30, 1918, with a total 270 squadrons and 40,500 men by December 31, 1918.

1918 January 15   Col. William Mitchell was appointed chief of air service, First Army Corps, under the command of Gen. Hunter Liggett. Mitchell was also given command of U.S. air units at the front from Gen. Liggett's headquarters. Mitchell assembled his operating staff during February and began an intensive study of French tactics in the air as a basis for American operations. He formed liaison groups to carry information from the front line units to aviators coming up from the training schools.

1918 January 17   Glenn L. Martin received a contract from the U.S. Army for a new bomber expected to improve on the performance of the British D.H.4, which was to be manufactured in quantity under license in America. Martin had set up his own company late in 1917 after leaving the Wright organization. With the designation GMB, for Glenn Martin Bomber, the airplane would be powered by two Liberty engines and was designed by Donald Wills Douglas. It would subsequently be designated the MB-1. The order was in part a mechanism for providing U.S. manufacturing companies with an indigenous airplane to build in addition to the D.H.4. The MB-1 would fly for the first time in August 1918.

1918 January 19   The U.S. School of Aviation Medicine, under the command of Maj. William H. Wilmer of the Signal Corps, began studies and investigations into the physiological effects of aviation. The school was founded at Hazelhurst Field, Mineola, N.Y. Equipment included a low-pressure tank that could simulate the atmosphere up to altitudes of 30,000 ft. to enable the scientists to assess crew performance in the rarified air and to develop safety equipment for air crews. Some of the altitude experiments took place on Pikes Peak, in Colorado, which enabled larger test groups to be monitored over longer periods than in the test tank.

1918 January 26   An agreement signed between Gen. Foulois for the United States and Lord Rothermere for Great Britain ratified a proposal from England that the Handley Page 0/400 should be supplied for 30 American bomber squadrons. Finished parts, including guns and cockpit instrumentation, would be manufactured in Great Britain and completed bombers would be delivered through the Amercian Acceptance Park in England. American airmen would be trained on these airplanes before flying to France.

1918 January 28   The Germans launched their largest night bombing raid against England during World War I, and the Royal Flying Corps night fighters shot down their first Gotha bomber. The raid began when 15 bombers left for England, including two R-planes, one of which turned back along with six Gothas. The rest hit London beginning around 8:30 P.M., and a Gotha G.V was attacked by 2d Lt. C. C. Banks and Capt. G. H. Hackwill of No. 44 Squadron, RFC, each flying a Sopwith Camel, before it crashed in flames at Wickford about 10:10 P.M. The bombers returned to their base; 67 people were killed and 166 injured during the raid.

1918 January 31   The Curtiss R-6 twin-float seaplane became the first U.S.-built airplane to operate overseas with American forces when the First Marine Aeronautic Company, commanded by Capt. F. T. Evans, USMC, arrived at Naval Base 13, Ponta Delgado, in the Azores. They were there to protect convoys from enemy submarines. The R-6 had been developed in early 1917 and was powered by a 360-HP Liberty engine. The R-series was designed to a requirement set forth in 1915 for J- and N-series replacements.

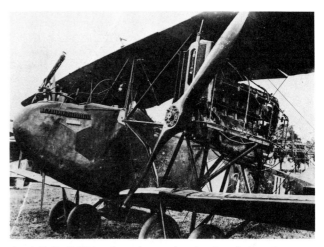

An A.E.G. G.IV bomber, damaged and stripped of engine panels, reveals the results of an air attack by scouts.

1918 January 31   A German fighter competition opened at Adlershof, Berlin, which would decide the next two production airplanes for the German Air Service. Over three days, several manufacturers demonstrated 23 different designs, a week after, Manfred von Richthofen had taken part in flight trials that would decide on one rotary-engined fighter and one with an in-line engine. Fokker won both contracts. The rotary-engined V.13 was ordered as the Fokker D.VI, and the V.11 model was ordered as the D.VII, one of the most potent fighters of its period. Similar in appearance to a biplane version of the Fokker Triplane, only 60 D.VIs were built.

1918 February 1   The British Eighth Brigade began operations this day from its headquarters at Chateau de Froville near Bayon, France. It had been formed December 28, 1917, from the bombing force of the army's Forty-first Wing and was under the command of Brig. Gen. C. L. N. Newall. Until May, No. 55 Squadron, Royal Flying Corps, and No. 16 Squadron, Royal Naval Air Service, conducted day bombing, and No. 100 Squadron, RFC, conducted night operations. They were reinforced by D.H.9s of No. 99 Squadron, RFC, from May 3. The first raid with this squadron took place May 21 when six airplanes bombed the Metz-Sablon triangle.

This Gotha G.Vb carried additional pairs of wheels to prevent damage to the nose if the tail should tip up.

The mid-ships defensive gun positions of a German Gotha G.V bomber.

1918 February 5 Lt. Stephen W. Thompson from Ohio became the first American from the First Aero Squadron and the first American in the uniform of a U.S. airman to shoot down a German airplane. He was sent by Maj. Ralph Royce when the French telephoned for a loan observer to fly back seat in a Breguet bomber on a bombing flight to Saarbruecken. On the return, the Breguet was attacked by three German Albatros D.III fighters, and the French pilot maneuvered into position for attack. Thompson had never fired a machine gun before but succeeded in shooting down one of the fighters, which could not be credited to him as a victory score because he was not officially on board the airplane.

1918 February 15 The busiest period of the war for French aviators concluded. Since December 1, 1917, in just 2½ mon., French aviators carried out 22,518 flights, an average 292 each day, and lost 104 pilots. In this period, 1,400 photographic reconnaissance flights were made, producing 21,328 photographs, an average of 15 pictures per flight. This achievement is all the more creditable given the poor weather at this time of year, but it reflects the intensity of activity in the final year of World War I.

1918 February 16 The largest bomb used during an air raid in World War I was dropped by a Zeppelin-Staaken R.VI (serial no. 39/16) on London during a raid involving five R-type bombers of Riesenflugzeug Abteilungen 501. Accompanied by an R.IV type (serial no. 12/16), which dropped bombs on Beckenham, the R.VI dropped its single 2,205-lb. bomb on the Chelsea Royal Hospital, believing it had hit the docks. Of the other three R.VIs, one turned back with engine trouble before reaching the coast, and the other two bombed the Dover area before returning to base.

1918 February 17 Following the collapse of czarist rule in Russia and the revolution that followed, large-scale bombing operations against German forces were brought to a halt when 30 Ilya Mu-

romets bombers were stacked together and burned on the airfield at Vinnitsa to prevent them falling into the hands of advancing German forces. Production of the giant airplanes had stopped in October 1917. Since February 1915, the bombers had carried out 442 raids, dropping 2,000 bombs, and claimed 40 enemy airplanes shot down by defensive gunners with the loss of only three Muromets. Yet rarely had more than 25 been in operation at any one time.

1918 February 18 The Lafayette Escadrille, formerly the Escadrille Américaine, formally relinquished its affiliation with the French Air Service and became the 103d Aero Squadron. Composed exclusively of American volunteers, the 103rd had a proud history of combat in France and Flanders and was quickly supplemented during February by other combat units, notably the Ninety-fifth and Ninety-fourth Aero squadrons, consolidating American air power, such as it then was, in the Toul sector.

1918 February 21 The U.S. Naval Air Station Bolsena was opened by Ens. W. B. Atwater and was the first commissioned navy base in Italy. For the remainder of the war, the base was used as an acclimatization and training facility to introduce pilots to equipment and procedures in the Mediterranean theater. A variety of aircraft were operated from the base, including the Macchi series of fighter flying boats and several other types of foreign aircraft.

1918 February 21 The first D.H.4s built in the United States were announced as having been completed and ''on their way to France.'' In fact, only one had been completed and was being shipped from Dayton, Ohio, and it was March 15 before it was on a ship leaving Hoboken, N.J. The ship was torpedoed by German submarines. An American-built D.H.4 did not fly for the first time in France before May 17. Production problems prevented the delivery rate from matching optimistic schedules set months before, but despite frustration for the army, few politicians were disturbed or concerned about the matter.

1918 February 25 An Albatros biplane built in Sweden was delivered to Kokkola, Finland, the first airplane to operate from that country. A small force began to build up in succeeding months and reconnaissance and bombing duties were conducted during the civil war. A government manufacturing facility was built in 1920, and several British and French airplanes were constructed there as well as independent designs based on experience with foreign airplanes.

1918 March 1 In preparation for the major German spring offensive and in completion of the targeted objectives of the American Program, the German air units had reached manning targets set in June 1917. The aim of doubling fighter units had been slightly exceeded; there were now 81 Jagdstaffeln instead of 40. The total force included 153 units, or squadrons, of which seven were assigned bombing duties. Production of hardware had not quite kept up with the expectations, and instead of forming 17 new flight units, bringing the total to 200, the Germans had reorganized the existing 183 into 153.

1918 March 1 Paimboeuf, a French nonrigid airship station, was handed over to the control of Lt. Comdr. L. H. Maxfield, U.S. Navy. Along with the airfield, the French also handed over the dirigible Astra-Torres AT-1, which made its first flight under American ownership on March 3. The AT-1 had been the first airship operated by the French Navy. Paimboeuf was where U.S. Navy personnel had been trained by the French Navy in the handling and operation of nonrigid airships since November 1917. The inventory was later increased when the unit at Paimboeuf obtained 11 more dirigibles from the French.

1918 March 2 Lloyd Andrews Hamilton became the first American to receive a commission in the British Royal Flying Corps when he was assigned as lieutenant with No. 3 Squadron in France. Hamilton had reached England in September 1917, where he received flying training and joined the RFC. He transferred to the Seventeenth Aero Squadron, U.S. Air Service (USAS), on June 20, 1918, and was to score 10 official victories

before ground fire brought him down on August 24 a few miles beyond the Allied lines near Langecourt. His grave was discovered in June 1919, and he was reburied with military honors at Bomy, France.

1918 March 4 The man who would become America's leading World War I ace, (then Lt.) Edward Vernon Rickenbacker, joined the Ninety-fourth Aero Squadron at Villeneuve-les-Vertus on the Marne. Rickenbacker was born on October 8, 1890, and quickly became interested in motor racing after a brief career in glass factories, shoe factories and an iron foundry. In 1917 he prepared a racing team for the Sunbeam Motor Co. in England and when the U.S. entered the war, he was arrested in London as a German spy, at which point he changed his name from Reichenbacher! He joined Gen. Pershing's staff as a chauffeur before transferring to the air service in August 1917.

1918 March 4 The prototype D.H.10 Amiens bomber (serial no. C8658) made its first flight with two 230-HP BHP water-cooled engines driving pusher propellers. Performance was under predictions, and the second prototype was fitted with two 360-HP Rolls Royce Eagle VIII engines driving tractor propellers. It was in this configuration that the airplane first flew on April 20, and although 1,295 were ordered, only eight were on strength when the war ended. The D.H.10 had been ordered from Airco as a development of the D.H.3 twin-engined bomber design of 1916, the third airplane designed for Airco by Geoffrey de Havilland.

1918 March 5 The Ninety-fourth Aero Pursuit Squadron arrived on the Western Front in the French sector at Toul, where it joined the Ninety-fifth Aero Pursuit Squadron. These units were amalgamated into the First Pursuit Group in April to counter sorties by large German formations. The squadrons began flying patrols in their Nieuport 28 fighters on March 15 but had no machine guns to fit to their aircraft. When the guns arrived, few pilots could operate them, so intensive training at a French school was necessary before combat operations commenced.

Developed to scout and to fight, the British D.H.2 designed by de Havilland had the engine in the rear and the gun in front.

1918 March 5 The Second Balloon Company became the first U.S. Army balloon unit to commence operations with the American Expeditionary Force in France during World War I. Due to the largely static nature of the ground war, balloons still played an important role in intelligence gathering, particularly reporting any build-up of forces that could give prior warning of an attack.

1918 March 5 The first Curtiss rebuilt Bristol F.2B flown in the United States with a 12-cylinder, 400-HP Liberty engine made its first flight as the USAO-1 (U.S. Army Observation No. 1). The F.2B had been selected in 1917 as suitable for mass production in America with the 300-HP Hispano-Suiza engine, but when the more powerful Liberty engine was installed instead, Bristol warned that the engine was too powerful for the airplane and would cause control problems. Such proved to be the case, and although some were built after the war, production run of 2,000 was canceled.

1918 March 6 Following several failed attempts beginning November 24, 1917, the first successful flight in the U.S. Navy pilotless flying bomb project took place when an unmanned Curtiss N-9 fitted by Sperry for automatic control flew a distance of about 3,000 ft. To prove the airworthiness of the converted Curtiss biplane, Lawrence Sperry had taken it into the air on February 6, 1918, but the following day the N-9 crashed, leaving Sperry unhurt. The catapult used for these flights was inefficient, and a new one was designed later this year by Carl L. Norden, later to become famous for his bomb-aiming devices.

1918 March 7 The largest single force of German R-plane bombers from Riesenflugzeug Abteilungen (Giant Airplane Flying Unit) 501 to raid England attacked—three hit London and two, seemingly lost, dropped bombs at various places in southeast England. One R-plane was the sole R.V built (serial no. 13/15); with five 240-HP Maybach engines, it was the most powerful of the R-planes before the Benz-powered Staaken R.XVI built by Aviatik in 1918. Built in 1916, R.V was accepted for duty September 29, 1917, and carried out its first mission against harbor installations at Calais on January 25, 1918, but was repeatedly dogged by engine transmission trouble.

1918 March 9 The first American air casualty in World War I was Capt. James E. Miller who lost his life in a French Spad while flying a practice patrol across the German lines. Miller had been trained to fly at the Signal Corps Aviation School along with the then-Maj. Bolling of the First Aero Company, New York National Guard, under Capt. J. E. Carberry. Capt. Miller had been sent to France in July 1917 to help with the American build-up and initial training program before being appointed to command the Ninety-fifth Aero Squadron. Miller went out on patrol with Majors Johnson and Harmon in the vicinity of Reims but fell to the guns of a German airplane, coming down near a forest at Craonne.

1918 March 10 The all metal Junkers J9 (D.I in service) made its first flight. The aircraft was a cantilever monoplane fighter powered by a single 185-HP BMW engine. Renowned for its metal airplanes, Junkers built only 41 of the single-seat aircraft before the armistice, and very few of these ever reached the front. The Junkers J9 was entered at the third fighter trials held at Adlershof October 15–31 but was not considered to have good handling characteristics. A two-seat reconnaissance version was designed, of which 47 had been built by the end of the war.

1918 March 10 The giant Navy Zeppelin airship L 59, which had made an abortive attempt to relieve German troops in German East Africa during November 1917, dropped what may be the heaviest bomb load ever dropped from a dirigible. In a night raid on Naples, the L 59 carried 14,000 lb. of bombs that were reportedly dropped from a height of 12,000 ft. on steel plants, gas works and a naval base. The airship had crossed the Adriatic from Scutari to Manfredonia under the command of Kptlt. Ludwig Bockholt, who had successfully persuaded the German naval staff to convert it for bomb carrying.

1918 March 11 A scheduled mail service operated by the German military opened with a service linking Vienna, Austria with Central Powers-occupied Kiev via Krakow, Lvov and Proskurov. It was under the direction of the former pilot A. R. von Marwil. Using a Hansa-Brandenburg C-1, the mail comprised military dispatches and a few civilian letters and packages. The C-1 had been used operationally during mid-1916 and remained a stalwart reconnaissance airplane throughout the war. It had been designed by Ernst Heinkel from the Hansa und Brandenburgische Flugzeugwerke and was built under license by Phönix and Ufag from the Austro-Hungarian flying service.

1918 March 11 The first member of a U.S. Air Service squadron credited with an aerial combat victory was Lt. Paul F. Baer of the 103rd Aero Squadron when he shot down a German airplane in the Reims sector. Baer scored a second kill five days later. The 103rd had been formed around the American volunteer pilots who had flown in the Lafayette Escadrille, of which Baer had been a member. The first victory scored by an American in a U.S. Army uniform had been Lt. Stephan W. Thompson on February 5, 1918, but he had been flying with a French unit.

1918 March 12 The first strategic bombing raid on Coblenz, Germany was performed by 9 D.H.9s from No. 55 Squadron, RFC, from a height of 13,000 ft. One bomb fell on a barracks, killing four soldiers and wounding 12. In addition, five civilians were killed and 49 wounded.

1918 March 17 Maj. John W. F. M. Huffer took command of the Ninety-fourth Aero Squadron, the first U.S. air unit to see action on the Western Front. Huffer was born in Paris of American parents and joined the French air service on January 1, 1916, joining Escadrille N.65 in April that year. He got his commission as a major with the Aviation Section, U.S. Army Signal Corps, on November 7, 1917. By war's end he would score a total of seven confirmed victories, four while serving with the French.

1918 March 19 Led by Maj. Gervais Raoul Lufbery, Lts. Douglas Campbell and Edward Rickenbacker made the first aerial patrol conducted by pilots of the Ninety-fourth Aero Squadron. It had been preceded March 15 by a patrol of three Spads along the Marne River between Epernay and Chalons to practice on the Allied side of the lines. When Maj. Lufbery's flight crossed the trenches, they encountered antiaircraft fire, an experience that the seasoned veteran of the Lafayette Escadrille wanted his young pilots to taste before aerial combat began in earnest.

1918 March 20 The U.S. Navy scored its first aerial victory over an enemy seaplane during a reconnaissance flight along the German coast by a formation of British-based flying boats. The formation was attacked by several German seaplanes, which were beaten off without loss to the American formation. During the fight, Ens. Stephan Potter shot down one of the seaplanes, becoming the first U.S. naval aviator to do so.

1918 March 20 By order of the Inspectorate of Military Aviation (Inspektion der Fliegertruppen), the national marking applied to all German airplanes was to change from the Cross Patee (Maltese Cross), which had been used since the beginning of the war. From April 15, 1918, German airplanes were to carry the Greek Cross (the Balkankreuze), which had straight, parallel sides instead of the curved sides of the former style. Airplanes at the front were crudely repainted with the Greek Cross, and the underlying, factory-finished Cross Patee frequently showed through.

1918 March 21   The March Offensive, Germany's hope for a crushing defeat of the Allies before American soldiers arrived in sufficient numbers to make a significant difference, began at 4:45 A.M. along a 54-mile front. There were 68 German divisions poised to attack, 56 of them in the front lines. The total German air strength, which had increased 60% in the previous 12 months, stood at 3,668 airplanes against the Allies' 4,500. Within a week, the ground assault had been halted, but bitter fighting continued in the air.

1918 March 21   The Curtiss Model 16 HA Dunkirk Fighter seaplane designed by Capt. B. L. Smith of the U.S. Marine Corps made its first flight at Port Washington, Long Island powered by a 12-cylinder, 400-HP Liberty engine. Designed by Capt. Smith specifically to wrest air superiority for the Allies in the Dunkirk-Calais area in Europe, its armament consisted of four machine guns. With a span of 36 ft. and a length of 30.75 ft., the HA had carried a single main float beneath the nose and forward fuselage, with separate outrigger floats beneath each set of outer interplane struts.

1918 March 22   1st Lt. Field E. Kindley was commissioned in the U.S. Air Service and went to serve with the 148th Aero Squadron. Kindley had joined the air service in May 1917 and received his flight training in England during the fall. He scored 12 credited victories while serving with the 148th Aero Squadron. He shared the honor of being the squadron's top-scoring pilot with Capt. Elliott White Springs. Promoted to captain on February 24, 1919, he was killed in an airplane crash in Texas on February 3, 1920.

1918 March 24   A major increase in the tempo of air combat over the Western Front resulted in major losses for the German Air Service. Allied air opposition to the March Offensive had been stunted during the initial waves of attack, but there was a sudden reversal as German air units found increasingly stiff opposition; the Royal Flying Corps alone claimed to have shot down 42 German airplanes this day.

1918 March 25   U.S. Navy Ens. John F. McNamara carried out the first attack by an American naval aviator on a German submarine at sea. McNamara was flying out of the naval air station at Portland, England, and Admiral Sims reported his attack as "highly successful." The secretary of the navy commended Ens. McNamara for this action, asserting it to be a "valiant and earnest effort."

1918 March 27   The U.S. Naval Aircraft Factory completed its first airplane, a Curtiss H-16 twin-engined flying boat (serial no. A-1049). The naval aircraft factory had been established at the Philadelphia Navy Yard in 1917 and was to supplement airplane production. The H-16s were built concurrently with four navy-designed N-1 pusher biplanes. The last of the H-model designs, the H-16 was built in greater numbers than any other Curtiss twin-engined flying boat; the parent design company produced 184 in addition to 150 built by the naval aircraft factory.

1918 March 27   American air ace Lt. James Norman Hall shot down two enemy airplanes in the closing days of his tenure with

the 103rd Aero Squadron. Two days later he took skills and experience obtained from the former Lafayette Escadrille to the Ninety-fourth Aero Squadron when he joined that unit as a flight commander. Hall had joined the war in May 1915, volunteering for service in the British army. He returned to the United States seven months later to look after his ailing father. He joined the French Air Service on October 11, 1916, and the Lafayette Escadrille in June 1917. Although usually credited with having shot down five airplanes, records can be found for only four before he was shot down and captured on May 17, 1918.

1918 March 27   In a demonstration of supreme bravery and resolute commitment, Canadian pilot 2d Lt. A. McLeod, No. 2 Squadron, Royal Flying Corps, saved his life and that of his observer, Lt. A. W. Hammond, after shooting down three Fokker Dr.1 Triplanes in his Armstrong Whitworth F.K.8. Set upon by eight Dr.1s, McLeod received five wounds and Hammond six wounds before the rear cockpit floor of their biplane was shot away. Then the fuel tank caught fire, and to keep the flames fanned away from Hammond, McLeod climbed out on to the port lower wing and side-slipped the biplane to a crash landing in no-man's-land between the lines. Badly injured, he then got Hammond out of the airplane before collapsing. Both men were awarded the Victoria Cross.

1918 March 28   Brainchild of John K. Northrop, the Loughead F-1 twin-engined flying boat took to the air for the first time at Santa Barbara Bay, Los Angeles with Allan Loughead at the controls. Northrop began working for the Loughead Co. in 1916 and quickly showed talent by working up a hull for what became the F-1. Underfunded, the company owned by Loughead and Anthony Stadlman tried to take advantage of the boom in airplane orders. The F-1 was taken on a nonstop flight to San Diego, a distance of 211 mi., in 3 hr. 1 min., but a recently awarded order to Curtiss for the HS-2L flying boat denied Loughead the privilege of a navy order.

1918 March 31   The German Reichstag informed the German High Command that it wished it to prepare a policy document through which the Allies could be encouraged, via a third party, to discuss a moratorium on the bombing of towns and cities in respective countries. The effect on morale of Allied bombing raids on southwest Germany seriously worried the German government. In February 1918, the Spanish government had passed to the British a message from Germany that Germany was prepared to discuss a halt to the bombing of towns and cities. Military advisers were reluctant to give up this option, although the British said they would respond favorably to any such move.

1918 March   The U.S. Navy began coastal patrols with two airships purchased from the French and named Astra-Torres AT-1 and Zodiac-Vedette VZ-3. These were the first in a series of foreign-built airships procured by the navy, which included six British airships and an Italian airship. The U.S. airship building program was slow to fill the needs of the navy, and these foreign airships would allow coastal patrols to go ahead as planned.

1918 March   The U.S. Army placed orders for 5,000 Loening M-8 monoplanes. The armistice canceled these, but the navy eventually acquired 56. Having worked for the Wright brothers, the army flying school and the Sturtevant Aeroplane Co., Grover C. Loening took a radical step when he designed a monoplane with a span of 32 ft. 9 in., a length of 24 ft. and a 300-HP Hispano-Suiza. Novel for its day, it featured a radiator buried in the engine under-cowling. The first flight took place in August.

Second from foreground, the Albatros of Manfred von Richthofen was painted partly in red.

1918 April 1 The Royal Flying Corps and the Royal Naval Air Service officially ceased to exist, replaced by the Royal Air Force. Since being formed on July 1, 1914, the RNAS had built to a strength of 55,066 officers and men with 2,949 airplanes and 103 airships operating through 126 stations in England and abroad.

1918 April 7 The First Corps Observation Group, under the command of Col. William Mitchell, made its first patrol, led by Maj. Ralph Royce, and thus became the first American squadron to go into action in Europe. The First Aero Squadron had become the nucleus for the First Corps Observation Group with Spad XI biplanes. Maj. Royce was awarded a citation and the Croix de Guèrre by an appreciative French Army general staff.

1918 April 9 The Radio Section of the U.S. Air Service came into being, an outgrowth of radio communications activity formerly handled by the Technical Section of the air service that had begun operations August 1917. Studies of British, French and Italian equipment preceded a $1 million order for French radio sets. By the end of the war, 1,688 radio sets had been installed on airplanes operated by the air service for radio liaison with the artillery. In an order issued September 10, 1918, the chief signal officer of the AEF was made responsible for all radio communications affecting land and air forces, and on October 2, 1918, the Signal Section assumed responsibility for air service radio training.

1918 April 13 The Andean mountain range in South America was crossed for the first time by air. Argentinian Army pilot Teniente Luis C. Candelaria flew a French Morane-Saulnier parasol monoplane from Zapala on the Negro River in Argentina to Cunco in Chile, a distance of approximately 100 mi. During the flight, the intrepid aviator reached an altitude of 13,000 ft. above sea level to clear the mountains and descend safely on the other side of the Chilean border.

1918 April 14 Sir Hugh Trenchard was officially succeeded as chief of the air staff in London by Maj. Gen. Sir Frederick Sykes, although Trenchard had privately resigned March 19 following a disagreement with Lord Rothermere, the secretary of state for the RAF. The news was withheld until the RAF had been formed April 1. Sir David Henderson resigned on the grounds that he could not work with Sykes, and on April 25 Lord Rothermere resigned and was replaced by Sir William Weir. Weir's job on the air council as director-general of aircraft production was given to Sir Arthur Duckham.

1918 April 14 Lts. Douglas Campbell and Alan Winslow became the first U.S. pilots to shoot down enemy airplanes while operating under the American flag and with a U.S. aero squadron. Assigned to the sector controlled by the French Eighth Army, the Ninety-fourth Aero Squadron flew operations from the Toul airfield to replace French escadrilles that had been moved to other areas. Campbell and Winslow got airborne in their Nieuport 28s when two German Pfalz biplanes appeared over Toul. In the air for less than five minutes, Campbell shot down the first, and Winslow shot down the second.

1918 April 18 To meet the threat of the new German Jagdgeschwader fighter wings, the French formed two air divisions, self-governing mobile formations that could move at short notice to any area of the front to provide reinforcements. Each division comprised two groups. One had 12 escadrilles of Spad fighters and nine escadrilles of Breguet XIV day bombers. The other had 12 escadrilles of Spads and six Breguet day bombers. In total, and in theory, each division could put 39 escadrilles, almost 600 airplanes, under a single unified authority. The fighters cleared the skies of enemy airplanes so the bombers could hit enemy airfields and installations.

1918 April 21 Manfred von Richthofen, with 80 confirmed victories the highest-scoring German fighter pilot of World War I, was killed during a dogfight over Sailly-le-Sec. Although credited with the victory, Canadian Capt. A. R. Brown of No. 209 Squadron, RAF, may not have shot him down because Richthofen was flying low over the Fifty-third Australian Field Artillery in pursuit of a Sopwith Camel flown by 2d Lt. W. R. May at the time, and they claim to have hit the aircraft with machine gun and rifle fire. Richthofen was buried April 22 with full military honors in the French village of Bertangles, but on November 20,

Lt. Strey of the German Air Service pilots his Albatros, a type favored by all Germany's leading airmen.

German Albatros scouts conducting a mass takeoff from a semipermanent airfield on the Western Front.

1925, his body was moved to a special grave at Invaliden, Germany. In 1937, the flat gravestone was replaced at a special Nazi ceremony.

1918 April 23   Lt. Paul F. Baer of the 103rd Aero Squadron became the first fighter ace of the U.S. Air Service when he shot down his fifth enemy aircraft. This was followed by more victories on May 8, when he shot down two German airplanes in six patrols, and one on May 21. The next day (May 22), after scoring another victory, he was himself shot down and taken prisoner for the duration of the war, an event that conceivably prevented him from becoming a candidate for lead ace, such was the caliber of his flying and fighting skills. Baer scored a total of nine victories, was awarded the Distinguished Service Cross, the Légion d'Honneur and the Croix de Guèrre. Baer survived the war and died September 12, 1930.

1918 April 25   Belgian air ace Willy Coppens de Houthulst shot down his first victim over the Belgian lines between Ramscapelle and Sluype. Coppens was posted to fighter Escadrille No. 1 at Les Moeres airfield in July 1917, entering his first aerial conflict on the twenty-first. Coppens scored a total of 37 victories before a crash landing on October 14 led to an amputated leg. He kept flying until the Germans once again invaded Belgium in May 1940 and then retired to Switzerland after the Belgian surrender.

1918 April 29   Edward "Eddie" Rickenbacker scored his first air victory with the Ninety-fourth Aero Squadron almost two months after joining it. It was the third combat victim successfully claimed by the Ninety-fourth, the first having fallen to fellow pilot Lt. Douglas Campbell more than two weeks earlier. The two aviators began a friendly rivalry for scores, Rickenbacker becoming an ace with his fifth victory on May 28, and Campbell following suit on May 31.

1918 May 6   The U.S. Army issued instructions for the numerical identification of individual airplanes within respective aero squadron flying units. Insignia designed by individual pilots were permitted so long as the pilot had been at the front for one calendar month or had received a citation for distinguished service. Moreover, the First Aero Squadron was given permission to paint a small stars and stripes flag on the fuselage of their airplanes in recognition of their service in Mexico.

1918 May 7   American airman James Norman Hall was shot down by antiaircraft fire that hit his engine after fabric began tearing loose from the upper wing of his Nieuport 28 while diving after an Albatros fighter. He came down near Pagny-sur-Moselle and was taken prisoner by the Germans. Hall was repatriated to the United States on March 10, 1919, his total score being 4 victories. Hall had served little more than six weeks with the Ninety-fourth Aero Squadron before he was shot down and captured. He was to achieve fame later for chronicling the exploits of the Lafayette Escadrille and for numerous other literary works including *Mutiny on the Bounty.*

1918 May 8   The British aviator and future ace, J. Ira T. Jones of No. 74 Squadron, RAF, shot down his first aerial victim, a two-seat reconnaissance biplane. Jones had joined his squadron during March after 10 months in England for pilot training. His service career began when he joined the Territorial Army in 1913. Tired of waiting to be called up, Jones joined the Royal Flying Corps in April 1915. Attached to No. 10 Squadron, RFC, as a first class air mechanic, he flew as an observer before leaving to become a pilot. Jones scored 37 victories in 3 months, driven to avenge the death of air ace Mick Mannock who was killed on July 26. He was recalled to service in 1939 and spent the second war training fighter pilots. Jones died in 1960 after falling off a ladder.

1918 May 9   French air ace René Fonck became the first fighter pilot to shoot down six airplanes in one day, achieving all six victories within three hours. Airborne at 4:00 P.M. with two fellow pilots, Fonck attacked a two-seat reconnaissance airplane protected by two fighters. Within 45 sec., he had shot them down, the wreckage of all three falling within a 1,300 ft. circle. After returning to refuel, Fonck took off again at 5:30 P.M. and shot down a two-seater from below. Then nine fighters came by, and Fonck shot down two before racing back to the lines.

1918 May 13   The British Air Council informed the War Cabinet that it wanted to form an Independent Force from appropriate RAF squadrons. The force would be autonomous and under the command of Maj. Gen. Hugh Trenchard, operating under the authority of the Air Ministry rather than field commanders. The Independent Force was to carry out long-range bombing missions against towns and cities in Germany where the war effort was supported by industrial production, munitions or supply. Sir William Weir cautioned that the French would object to an Independent Force and prefer instead an inter-Allied bombing command, which they did; but the proposal was accepted.

1918 May 15   The Aerial Mail Service of the U.S. Post Office Department began with an appropriation of $100,000 and used Curtiss Standard J and JN aircraft provided by the War Department for a daily service, except Sunday, between Washington and New York. The service itself was operated by the War Department. Flight time from New York to Washington was 2 hr. 50 min., but 20 min. less the other way due to winds, with a single stop in Philadelphia. Initial costs were 24 cents per letter, but when it was realized this was more than it cost, the price dropped to 16 cents on July 15. Cost per ton-mile of mail was $5.35 with an average 7.75 tons carried each month. Routes from New York to San Francisco and from Boston to Key West were set up along with many feeders in the following year.

1918 May 18   The first daylight air raid on Cologne by British airplanes since October 1914 was carried out by six D.H.4s from No. 55 Squadron, RAF, led by Capt. F. Williams. It took 2½ hr. to reach the city, and bombs were dropped from 14,500 ft.

Serious damage was done to 38 buildings, 40 people were killed, and about 100 were injured. A collapse in the city's air raid warning system resulted in complete surprise for the bombers. Two German fighters were shot down. Following this raid, questions were raised in the Reichstag, and the German government was pressed to discuss with the Allies a moratorium on strategic bombing.

1918 May 19 Maj. Gervais Raoul Lufbery was killed when the rear gunner in a German two-seater set his Nieuport on fire. Choosing to jump rather than burn to death, he fell to a flower garden in the village of Maron, and by the time the American troops reached the area, French peasants had covered his body with petals. After serving an administrative role following his commission with the U.S. Air Service in November 1917, Lufbery transferred to the Ninety-fifth Aero Squadron in April 1918. Lufbery's final score was 16.

1918 May 19 The German Air Service made its last raid on England when a force of 38 twin-engined Gothas, three Zeppelin-Staaken R-planes (the R.V and an R.VI) and two Rumpler C.VII weather observation airplanes set out for England with almost 32,100 lb. of high explosives, including the third 2,205 lb. bomb to be dropped on London. Of the total 43 airplanes that set out, 34 reached England, and 18 Gothas and one R-type got through the London defenses, killing 49 and injuring 177 people. In all German airplane raids combined, 857 people had been killed, 2,058 had been injured, and damage had totalled £1,434,526.

1918 May 20 In reply to concerns that the 260-squadron U.S. Army Aviation Service would not be operational by June 30, 1919, Gen. Pershing somewhat unrealistically reaffirmed his intention to work toward that complement. The plan had been developed under the General Organization Project forwarded to Washington on June 10, 1917, and augmented by the Service of the Rear Project update of September 18. However, the War Department had informed the AEF that it did not believe such a force was possible, given prevailing production accomplishments in the preceding months. Gen. Pershing adjusted the distribution of roles to include 60 night bombardment squadrons, 41 day bombardment squadrons, 80 biplane pursuit squadrons and 40 monoplane pursuit squadrons, with 15 corps and 24 army observation squadrons.

1918 May 21 Pres. Woodrow Wilson authorized the transfer of U.S. military aviation away from the Signal Corps and into two separate agencies under the secretary of war that were recognized by the War Department as constituting an air service in its own right. The Bureau of Aircraft Production would oversee airplane production and manufacture. John D. Ryan, formerly of the Equipment Division, would remain in charge. The Bureau of Military Aeronautics, responsible for training and manpower, was placed under the command of Maj. Gen. William L. Kenly, who had recently returned from France.

1918 May 22 The prototype Handley Page V/1500, the biggest bomber built by Britain during World War I (serial no. B9463), made its first straight flight at Clutterhouse Farm, Cricklewood. The V/1500 was developed in great secrecy after the first German daylight airplane raids on London during June 1917 as a reprisal bomber to hit German cities. Powered by four 375-HP Rolls Royce Eagle engines, which gave it a maximum speed of 97 MPH, the V/1500 could carry a 7,500-lb. bomb load. Only six were delivered by the end of the war, and they did not see operational use in the conflict.

1918 May 24 Military aviation in Russia underwent a reorganization when the All-Russian Air Board was replaced by the new Chief Directorate of the Workers and Peasants Military Air Fleet (Glavoce Upravlenie-Raboche-Krestyanskogo Vozdushnogo Flota).

1918 May 24 Italian Caproni Ca.5 biplanes attacked the enemy airfield at Pordenone, Italy, which had been taken by the Austro-Hungarians. The Ca.5 was a development of the Ca.3 series and could carry 1,190 lb. of bombs. It had a maximum take-off weight of 11,700 lb. and a top speed of 95 MPH at low altitude. Few Ca.5 biplane bombers were built, although they began to supplement the more popular Ca.3 during the second half of 1918.

1918 May 29 Maj. Gen. Mason M. Patrick was appointed chief of air service to the American Expeditionary Force in place of Brig. Gen. Foulois, who was made chief of the air service to the First Army. Gen. Pershing made these appointments to break the deadlock that threatened the efficiency of the fledgling air service when young air-minded officers like Foulois, Mitchell and Bolling frequently disagreed. The immediate solution was to appoint Patrick, an older experienced officer, to calm the arguments and make some sense of the organization, which Patrick accomplished with skill.

1918 May 29 John D. Ryan was named as the first director of the newly created U.S. Bureau of Aircraft Production. The new Bureau had been formed from the Equipment Division of the U.S. Signal Corps and was given "full and exclusive jurisdiction and control over the production of aeroplanes, engines and aircraft equipment." Ryan was an industrialist of some repute and was also head of the civilian Aircraft Board, a fact that promoted understanding and efficient communication between the two agencies.

1918 June 1 One of the most famous American aviators of World War I, Elliott White Springs got his first confirmed air victory while flying an S.E.5a with No. 85 Squadron, RAF. Springs received preliminary flight training during studies at Princeton University, then went to England in July 1917 to learn combat flying. He joined No. 85 Squadron in May 1918 and went to France. After a crash on June 27 and subsequent hopitalization, he joined the 148th Aero Squadron. On August 3, he shot down his fifth victim and became the unit's first ace. He finished the war with a score of 16. He later became a successful businessman and wrote the famous book *War Birds* about flying in the 1914–18 war.

1918 June 3 With two colleagues from the Ninety-fifth Aero Squadron, 1st Lt. Sumner Sewell attacked a formation of six enemy fighters and then fought them all alone when the guns of his two colleagues jammed and they were forced to retire. Sewell kept the fight going, and after 15 min. he shot one of the German fighters down in flames. For this action and for coming to the rescue of a lone Allied observation airplane on September 18, when he fought off six enemy predators and shot one down before escorting the two-seater home, he was awarded the Distinguished Service Cross. Sewell had joined the air service in August 1917 and scored seven victories in all.

1918 June 4 A garish color scheme introduced for the Fleet Air Arm of the Royal Air Force originated in an action this day. Four Felixstowe F.2A flying boats and one Curtiss H-12 were involved in a fight with 14 German seaplanes in the North Sea separating northern England from Europe. Although six enemy seaplanes were shot down, two F.2As were forced to alight on the water due to fuel blockages, highlighting the difficulty of spotting gray-colored airplanes against a cold gray sea. The dazzle color schemes introduced for the hulls of British flying boats to make them stand out on water was the very antithesis of camouflage.

1918 June 5   Capt. Douglas Campbell was wounded by gunfire from a two-seat Rumpler German observation airplane and forced to land, putting an end to his career in World War I after scoring six victories. An explosive bullet apparently hit his airplane 2 in. behind the cockpit, wounding Campbell with the fragments. He was invalided back to the U.S.A. and returned to rejoin the Ninety-fourth Aero Squadron shortly after the armistice. After the war, he built a career with Pan American Grace Airways and became vice president of it in 1939, adding the title general manager in 1953. Campbell died in December 1990 at the age of 94.

1918 June 6   The Independent Force of the Royal Air Force officially came into being under the command of Maj. Gen. Hugh M. Trenchard. It comprised the two wings of Eighth Brigade—the Forty-first with Nos. 55, 99 and 104 Squadrons for day attacks and the Eighty-third with Nos. 100 and 216 Squadron for night bombing—and an intelligence unit that provided information on gas manufacturing plants, industrial facilities, factories, war munitions supply lines and so on. The independent force's mission was to conduct a "sustained and continuous attack on one large [industrial] center after another" and to "attack as many large industrial centers" as could be reached by existing bombers. Trenchard formally had taken tactical command of the Independent Force of the Royal Air Force. The commanding officer of Eighth Brigade had been constructing airfields for some weeks, and Maj. Gen. Cyril Newall had been putting in place the administrative essentials prior to the arrival of men and equipment that would support the expansion of the Eighth Brigade's two wings.

1918 June 8   The commanding general of the German Army Air Service (Kommandierenden General der Luftstreitkrafte, or Kogenluft) sent Gen. Ludendorff a program of expansion that covered the period July 1, 1918, to April 1, 1919, in the belief that the war would last at least that long. On top of the America Program expansion, it aimed for a qualitative improvement in airplanes and an increase from 38 to 60 in the number of Schlachtstaffeln (battle sections), formed into 10 new Schlacht-geschwadern (battle squadrons). In addition, the number of Flieger Abteilungen (aviation units) was increased from 37 to 80, each with nine airplanes, for carrying out reconnaissance duty even under heavy enemy attack.

1918 June 17   Frank Leaman Baylies, the highest-scoring U.S. airman to serve his air service exclusively with French forces, was killed in action when a Spad he was flying was attacked by four Fokker Triplanes over the lines between Crèvecoeur and Lassigny. Baylies volunteered for the Automobile Sanitary Section, U.S. Army, and served as a driver at Verdun, the Argonne and in Serbia before he joined the French Aviation Service in May 1917. On November 17 he joined Escadrille SPA.73 and a month later the famous Escadrille SPA.3. Baylies scored his first of 12 victories on February 18, 1918.

1918 June 19   The top Italian air ace, Maj. Francesco Baracca, was killed during a ground strafing mission flown from the 91a Squadron. Baracca had scored 34 victories in 22 months and had been ordered to carry out ground attacks with two colleagues. Flying a Spad, they flew up and down the lines at little more than 100 ft., spraying the ground with machine gun fire. Baracca appeared to vanish, but after the Austrian forces had retreated, his body was found in the burned-out airplane, a single bullet through his forehead.

1918 June 19   Under pressure from the Allied Supreme War Council, Gen. Pershing recommended a buildup in the American Expeditionary Force to 3 million men in 66 divisions by May 1919, including an increase in the number of planned operational air squadrons from 260 to 358 by July 1919. The total was to include 147 pursuit squadrons, 110 squadrons for day and night bombardment in equal numbers and 49 corps and 52 army observation squadrons. Needless to say, there was little realism in these increasingly inflated projections.

1918 June   The second German fighter competition was held at Adlershof, Berlin to select two airplanes for production, one with a water-cooled engine and one with an air-cooled engine. German airplane manufacturers demonstrated 37 airplanes of 31 different types, five of which had alternative engines. Fokker was again chosen to produce front-line fighters. The air-cooled contract went to Fokker for his V.26 parasol monoplane with a 110-HP Le Rhône rotary engine, and the water-cooled design chosen was the Pfalz D.XIIf. The Pfalz was disliked from the outset, and the Fokker planes suffered from poor workmanship once more, when the wings on the E.V began to fail.

1918 June   The largest airplane designed during World War I—an all-metal monoplane flying boat powered by four 1,000-HP diesel engines—was proposed by the German manufacturer Junkers. The 262.5-ft. upper wing of a sesquiplane configuration would have been supported above the 124 ft. 8 in. fuselage and the lower wing by a series of N-shaped struts. This giant R-plane would have had a tailspan of 39 ft. 4 in., a height of 29 ft. 6 in. and a loaded weight of 105,840 lb. It was put forward for the German Navy, but wartime priorities prevented it being ordered in even prototype form. Nevertheless, it was a portent of things to come from Prof. Junkers.

1918 July 1   The first flight of the large Zeppelin L 70, first of a planned new class for the German Navy, occurred at Friedrichshafen. It had a length of 693 ft. 11 in., a diameter of 78 ft. 5 in. and a capacity of 2,195,800 cu. ft. The airship had a useful lift of 97,100 lb. and was powered by seven 245-HP Maybach engines driving six propellers. In trials, L 70 had a top speed of 81 MPH, the fastest of all Zeppelin's wartime airships. It was to have been followed by several other models of this class. Only one other, the L 71, was finished, and this was lengthened to 743 ft. 2 in. with a capacity of 2,418,700 cu. ft. and a load lift of 112,700 lb. but had only six engines. It was surrendered to the British.

1918 July 9   The fourth-highest-scoring British air ace of World War I, Maj. James Byford McCudden, was killed when he side-slipped into the ground while trying to turn back to his airfield after the engine of his S.E.5a cut out. McCudden had taken off from Auxi-le-Château to fly to his new command, No. 60 Squadron, RAF. His last of 57 aerial victories had been scored February 26, 1918, a two-seat Hannover Cl-III. McCudden had joined No. 56 Squadron as a flight commander in August 1917 and between March and July 1918 conducted an instructional tour in England before leaving for France and his new command.

1918 July 14   Lt. Quentin Roosevelt, the son of former U.S. president Theodore Roosevelt, was killed when he engaged and was shot down by a German airplane well behind enemy lines. Lt. Roosevelt was buried with honors at Chambry on the Marne by German soldiers, his grave being found after the war. A German airman dropped a message to the Americans informing them that he had been killed, a not uncommon occurrence. Lt. Roosevelt joined the Ninety-fifth Aero Squadron on June 17, but he

An early example of a famous line of fighting aircraft, the Sopwith 1½ Strutter, bearing its maker's name on the fuselage.

had already scored his first and only victory July 10, when he shot down a German airplane several miles behind the enemy lines.

1918 July 17   Four Italian S.I.A. 9B single-engined bombers, the most powerful single-engined airplanes in operation anywhere, carried out a successful bombing raid on the Austro-Hungarian naval base at Pola. A subsidiary of Fiat, the Società Italiana Aviazione (S.I.A.) developed the 7B in 1917 as a conventional two-seat biplane with a 260-HP Fiat engine. The 9B appeared in late 1917 with a 700-HP engine, and 62 airplanes of this type were eventually built, serving with Italy's 1a "San Marco" Squadron and the 103a and 161a Naval Squadrons. The 9b could carry a bomb load of 770 lb.

1918 July 19   The first piloted flight of the Kettering Bug was carried out by the Army following an order placed on January 25 for 25 pilotless airplanes. This first flight lasted six min. and two more piloted flights were conducted before the first attempt at unmanned, automatic flight. The Kettering Bug biplane was tiny, with a wing span of 15 ft., dihedral of 10°, a length of 12.5 ft. and a launch weight of 525 lb. It was powered by a 35–45-HP engine and had a top speed of 120 MPH with a warload (explosives) of 180 lb.

1918 July 24   Capt. James A. Meissner was appointed to command the 147th Aero Squadron, having scored a total four victories against enemy airplanes while serving with the Ninety-fourth Aero Squadron, which he had joined on March 17, 1918. Meissner left Cornell University to go to war and went to France to learn to be an aviator after volunteering for the air service. Meissner

scored four more victories with the 147th. In 1919 he left the air service and set up the Alabama National Guard.

1918 July 26   Maj. Edward Mannock, top scoring British air ace of World War I, was killed. Mannock first served with No. 40 Squadron, Royal Flying Corps, and then with No. 74 Squadron between the end of March and June 1918 before taking command of No. 85 Squadron on July 5. On the day of his death, he shared with Lt. D. C. Ingalls the credit for shooting down a Junkers CL-1 monoplane at 5:30 A.M. before swooping low over Pacaut Wood and catching machine gun fire that set his fuel tank on fire. Racing back toward the British lines, his S.E.5a suddenly turned away in a long glide before exploding in a ball of fire. Although frequently credited with 73 victories, Mannock is known to have actually shot down 61 aircraft of which 9 are shared with other pilots. His body was never retrieved.

1918 July 30   The 107 officers and 654 enlisted men of the first three U.S. Marine Corps aviation squadrons (designated A, B and C) of the First Aviation Force, arrived at Brest, France aboard the USS *De Kalb*. Squadrons A and B were based near Calais and Dunkerque, with Squadron C at La Fresne to be joined October 5 by Squadron D. The first British built D.H.4 aircraft arrived in September. Because of delays, some pilots flew with Nos. 217 and 218 Squadrons, RAF, until their own equipment arrived. The first all-marine combat mission took place on October 14, by which time the four squadrons had been redesignated 7, 8, 9 and 10.

1918 August 1   Lead elements of the British North Russian Expeditionary Force, including both land and air units, arrived at

Archangel with RAF Fairey Campania seaplanes aboard HMS *Nairana*. During the next several weeks and months, these seaplanes were employed on strafing and bombing missions against Bolshevik (Red Army) forces, which had been formed by the Workers' Party on February 23, 1918. Other airplanes involved were D.H.4 medium bombers, R.E.8s, the Sopwith 1½ Strutter and some Nieuport 17 scouts, the latter forming a special Slavo-British squadron commanded by the Russian air ace Kazakov. The British force comprised 13,000 officers and men, of whom 300 were with the Royal Air Force. Activity included a drive up the River Dvina with seaplanes based on lakes when weather permitted, with the ultimate objective of linking with White Russian forces driving from the east. This was unrealistic, and by 1919 that objective had been abandoned.

1918 August 2   Following a period of intensive development, the Siemens-Schuckert gliding bomb (Torpedogleiter) was carried into the air by Zeppelin airship L 35 and launched for a successful flight of approximately 4.5 mi. The gliding bomb was 24 ft. 3 in. in length and had a weight of approximately 1.1 ton. It had been developed during 1915 and mirrored similar studies and tests under way in the United States and Britain. Many models and tests with biplane configurations were completed before the large, 1.1-ton monoplane type. The gliding bomb was never used operationally.

1918 August 3   Military representatives from France, Britain, the United States and Italy signed a draft resolution for presentation to the Supreme War Council calling for an Inter-Allied Bombing Air Force, which would be under the command of the Allied commander-in-chief in France. France had been the moving force behind the resolution, fearing that Britain's Independent Force for strategic bombing of Germany would run counter to the principal aim of coordinating all Allied initiatives in a common drive against the enemy. It was agreed in October that Trenchard should command the Inter-Allied Air Force, but the war ended before it could be mobilized. Meanwhile, Britain's Independent Force continued operations.

1918 August 5   Five German Navy zeppelins set out on the last raid on England during World War I. Among them was the L 70, commanded by Kptlt. von Lossnitzer and with Flugkapitän Peter Strasser, chief of the naval airship division, on board. They crossed the North Sea at more than 16,000 ft. and ran into defensive opposition from fighters that succeeded in shooting down the L 70 with the loss of all on board. Between 1915 and 1918, 202 German airship sorties reached Britain out of 277 that set out. The 202 airship sorties resulted in the deaths of 557 people with 1,358 injured and damage caused worth £1,527,585. British casualties from aircraft and airship raids on England included 1,414 dead and 3,416 injured.

1918 August 5   The first American night patrol of the war took place when a Felixstowe F.2A flying boat crewed by Ens. Ashton W. Hawkins and Lt. George F. Lawrence took off on patrol from RAF Killinghome, England in foul weather at 10:30 P.M. to search for Zeppelin airships reported to have approached the coast. The flight terminated at South Shields without result at 5:30 A.M., the airplane having almost run out of fuel.

1918 August 8   The British offensive at Amiens, France, opened at 4:20 A.M. with an artillery barrage followed by a forward roll of tanks and infantry supported by air units that, on this one day, carried out 205 bombing attacks dropping 24,000 lb. of high explosives. Along a 25-mile front, the British and French had about 1,904 airplanes, of which 988 were single-seat fighters. Of the

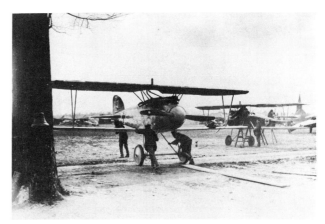

Ground crew wheeling out a German Albatros scout at an airfield on the Western Front.

total, the RAF had 800 aircraft under Gen. Sir Henry Rawlinson's Fourth Army; by the end of the day, 94 had been either shot down or irreparably damaged. The Germans had 365 airplanes, of which only 140 were fighters. Taken completely by surprise, German aircrews suffered heavy losses and were temporarily overwhelmed by numbers, from which they were to partially recover by the end of the month.

1918 August 9   Propaganda leaflets were dropped over Vienna, Austria by seven Italian S.V.A.5 and one S.V.A.9 biplanes from San Pelagio, Italy. Although airplane designers Savoia and Verduzio developed the S.V.A.5 for Fiat as a single-seat scout, it was more effective in a reconnaissance role. Powered by a 220-HP SPA in-line engine, it had a range of 600 mi., although an additional 66-gal. fuel tank was provided for the leaflet flight. They left just before 6:00 A.M. and after 3 hrs. 20 min. arrived over Vienna to drop the propaganda messages and take pictures before flying home. One S.V.A.5 flown by Lt. Guiseppe Sarti had to land at Wiener Neustadt because of engine trouble, but the rest got back safely, having flown 620 mi. in 6 hr. 50 min.

1918 August 9   The first of four RAF squadrons sent to join and augment the existing five squadrons of the Independent Force arrived in France. No. 97 Squadron brought its Handley Page 0/100s and carried out its first operational night mission late on the evening of August 19 against the Metz-Sablon rail yards. No. 215 Squadron arrived August 19 with its 0/100s and began its first night raid on August 23. No. 115 Squadron, with 0/100 bombers, and No. 110 Squadron, with D.H.9s, arrived August 31, the latter carrying out its first raid on September 16 against factories at Mannheim. No. 115 Squadron first sent eight 0/100s to bomb the Metz-Sablon rail triangle late on September 16 although two had to turn back.

1918 August 10   Third-highest-scoring German fighter pilot of World War I, Lt. Erich Lowenhardt was killed when the wheels of a Fokker D.VII flown by Lt. Wentz of Jasta 11 collided with the wing of his own Fokker D.VII, causing it to crash. Born in 1897, Lowenhardt went to the eastern front with an infantry regiment when war broke out, was wounded at Lodz, fought at Tannenberg and joined the air service in 1917. He was posted to JG.1, serving with Jasta 10 from July 1917, and by September 21 had shot down five enemy aircraft. Following a slow period, his scoring picked up in March 1918 with five victories, but his best month was July, when he added 16 to his score, reaching a final total of 53.

A Pfalz D.III of Jagdstaffel 15, one of Germany's better but less popularized scout aircraft of World War I.

1918 August 10   Maj. William Thaw was appointed to command the Third Pursuit Group, comprising the Twenty-eighth, Ninety-third, 103d and 213th Aero Squadrons. Via the French Foreign Legion, Thaw joined the French Air Service on December 24, 1914. He served with Escadrille C.42 between April 1915 and March 1916, before helping form the Escadrille Américaine the following month. Thaw was the only member of what became the Lafayette Escadrille to serve throughout its life. He received his commission as a major in the U.S. Air Service on January 26, 1918, and became commanding officer of the 103rd Aero Squadron when that unit was formed from the dissolved Lafayette Escadrille. Thaw scored a total of five victories.

1918 August 12   Lt. Lothar von Richthofen shot down his 40th and last victim. He had been with Jasta 11 of JG.1 since becoming a fighter pilot in March 1917. Personally encouraged to fly by his brother, the famous Manfred von Richthofen, Lothar had served with the army since just before the war began in 1914. Manfred tutored Lothar well. In only 19 months, he scored all his 40 victories, a total equal to that of the first great German air ace, Oswald Boelcke. Lothar survived the war but was killed July 4, 1922, when an airplane he was flying from Hamburg to Berlin crashed into electrical cables.

1918 August 12   The U.S. Post Office took over management of the experimental airmail service from the War Department, which had been operating the service since May 15, using specially built airplanes provided by the Standard Aircraft Corp. The post office had received $100,000 and gave out tenders for five airplanes on February 21, 1918. It was suggested the army could provide interim airplanes, which they did for the inauguration of the service on May 15. The first route was from New York to Washington, D.C., via Philadelphia, using Curtiss JN-4H train-ing aircraft. Early in 1919, the Post Office took over 100 ex-Army surplus D.H.4Ms, with Liberty engines, 12 Handley Pages and 12 Glenn L. Martin airplanes.

1918 August 13   Lt. Lloyd Hamilton of the Seventeenth Aero Squadron led a remarkable, low-level bombing raid on a German airfield at Varssenaer, Belgium, about 30 mi. behind the German lines. After hitting the airfield with bombs, destroying hangars, he shot up five enemy airplanes parked conveniently in a row, strafing them from 20 ft. above the grass until they burned. Not content with that, Hamilton flew headlong toward the château where the German aircrew were billeted, spraying machine-gun fire through the windows and killing 26 inside. For this action, he was awarded the Distinguished Service Cross.

1918 August 15   The first flight of the LUSAC-11 (Lepère United States Army Combat) fighter designed by Capt. Georges Lepère for the Engineering Division of the Bureau of Aircraft Production was made at McCook Field, Dayton, Ohio with the French test pilot Lt. de Marmier at the controls. Capt. Lepère had been part of the French Aeronautical Mission to the United States during 1917 and had been asked to design a two-seat escort fighter that could be built in the United States. Powered by a Liberty engine, the LUSAC-11 had four machine guns and a top speed of 133 MPH. Peace cut projected orders of several thousand, and only 30 were built, of which two reached Europe.

1918 August 15   Third-highest-scoring French air ace, Charles E. J. M. Nungesser, scored his 43rd and last victory of the war. He had already received the U.S. Distinguished Service Cross, the British Military Cross, the Croix de Guèrre from France, Belgium and Portugal and many other awards from several countries. After the war, Nungesser formed a flying school at Orly, near Paris, and flew a Hanriot HD-1 carrying a gruesome wartime insignia he had painted on his fighter—a skull and crossbones with coffin set on a heart-shaped motif. Nungesser frequently barnstormed around the United States and was killed on May 8, 1927, during an attempted crossing of the Atlantic.

1918 September 12 2d Lt. Frank Luke Jr., the second-top-scoring American air ace of World War I, began a meteoric series of aerial victories by shooting down a German observation balloon over Marieulles. Luke had joined the air service as a private in September 1917 but received flying training beginning in November at Rockwell Field, San Diego. He sailed for France in March 1918 and was eventually posted to the Twenty-seventh Aero Squadron of the First Pursuit Group. Luke struck up a close friendship with Lt. Joseph Fritz Wehner from the Twenty-seventh, and the two soon worked out a routine of close cooperation in the air.

1918 August 16 The chief of air service of the American Expeditionary Force submitted the last air service sizing plan before the end of World War I; approved next day, it called for a total force of 202 squadrons, comprising 60 pursuit squadrons, 14 day bombardment and 27 night bombardment squadrons, and 49 corps and 52 army observation squadrons. It followed the 358-squadron plan submitted by Gen. Pershing on June 19, 1918, but this had been over-ambitious. It would, however, call for 145,983 officers and men and 20,052 aircraft with 31,250 engines by June 30, 1919. When the war ended November 11, 1918, the air service had 45 squadrons, of which 20 were pursuit units, six were day bombardment and one was exclusively night bombardment.

1918 August 17 Inspired by successful operations of the Second Balloon Squadron, the American Expeditionary Force first deployed overseas in December 1917, approved a plan for expanding the projected 69 balloon companies into an organization of 133 balloon companies by the end of FY 1919 (June 30, 1919). According to the schedule, 70 companies should have been in the field by November 1, 1918. In fact, only 35 had arrived by that date. Of these, 12 were at artillery firing centers, six were with armies on the way to the zone of advance, and 17 were with the First and Second Armies at the front.

1918 August 17 The Martin MB-1 bomber made its first flight. The bomber was the first of 10 ordered by the U.S. Army Air Service. With a wing span of 71 ft. 5 in. and a length of 44 ft. 10 in., the MB-1 was powered by two 400-HP Liberty 12A piston engines and had a top speed of 105 MPH. It was equipped with five defensive machine guns and could carry 1,040 lb. of bombs. The first four were built as observation airplanes, the next three were built as bombers, the following one had special long-range tanks, the next was fitted with a cannon in the nose, and the last was modified as an enclosed passenger airplane.

1918 August 23 Acceptance tests on the new parasol Fokker monoplane, the E.V, were suspended following a spate of accidents with structural failure to the wing. JG.1 received its first Fokkers in early August, and several days later Lt. Hans Rolff was killed when the wing failed. Then a pilot from Jagdstaffel 19 was killed when the wing broke in two pieces, and a third pilot died a few days later in a similar accident. The crash investigation suspended delivery of the new fighter until the end of September when several design changes had been stipulated and implemented. The aircraft reappeared as the D.VIII, the E category having been abolished.

1918 August 24 Lt. Lloyd Andrews Hamilton of the Seventeenth Aero Squadron was killed by ground fire near Langecourt just after shooting down his 10th victim, an observation balloon. Hamilton was the first American officer to serve with the Royal Flying Corps, having arrived in England during September 1917. He served with No. 3 Squadron, RFC, and also gained the distinction of being the first American from the first group that had trained in England to bring down an enemy airplane. His grave was found in June 1919, and Hamilton was reburied with full military honors at Bomy, France.

1918 August 29 A Handley Page 0/400 (serial no. C9681) arrived at Ramleh, Palestine, from England after a flight that began May 28 and included several stops before putting down at Heliopolis, Egypt on August 8. It had been requested by T. E. Lawrence (Lawrence of Arabia), who was busily engaged in getting Bedouin support against the Turks. He had already received two Bristol F.2Bs for communication and transport and wanted the heavy bomber to impress the Bedouins, which it duly did when No. 1 Squadron, Australian Flying Corps, at Ramleh used it in the September 19 Battle of Nablus and hit targets.

1918 September 6 Lt. Wolfram von Richthofen, cousin of Manfred and Lothar von Richthofen, scored his fifth aerial victory, becoming an air ace. Thus was the name Richthofen established as the only family to produce three air aces. Unlike his cousins, Wolfram was only an average fighter pilot, lacking both the hunting instinct of Manfred and the flying skills of Lothar. His score reached eight, bringing to 128 the total number of Allied airplanes shot down by the von Richthofen family. Wolfram served as the last commander of the Condor Legion during the Spanish Civil War and commanded the Stuka dive bombers that opened the attack on Warsaw, September 1, 1939.

1918 September 7 The German Admiralty met to consider proposals for a fleet of large Zeppelins to succeed the L 70 class, the first of which had made its first flight July 1. L 72 and subsequent airships were to have capacity increased to 2,418,700 cu. ft. by the addition of one gas bag, and cruise at a height of 26,000 ft. with six engines. Five smaller, existing airships were to be increased to the same capacity by February 1919. In addition, a new Zeppelin with a capacity of 3,813,480 cu. ft. was to be ordered. Called the L 100, it was to have had a length of 780 ft. 10 in. and a diameter of 96 ft. 6 in.; the order was canceled on October 6.

1918 September 12 The U.S. First Army under Gen. John J. Pershing attacked German forces along the St. Mihiel salient as an autonomous American assault supported by 1,480 American, French, Italian and Portuguese airplanes under the central authority of Col. William Mitchell. The St. Mihiel salient had been held by the Germans since late 1914, but within four days, the Americans had cleared the area, taking 15,000 prisoners.

The sixth-highest-scoring American air ace, Lt. David Endicott Putnam was killed when, along with a colleague, he went to the aid of a reconnaissance airplane under attack from eight German fighters. Putnam was flying back from an engagement with 15 enemy airplanes, one of which he had shot down. The second combat proved fatal, and Putnam was killed by two bullets through the heart. Putnam scored the first of his 13 victories on January 19, 1918. He had joined the Lafayette Escadrille in December 1917 but flew with the 139th Aero Squadron from July.

1918 September 15 American air ace 2d Lt. William T. Badham scored the first victory of the five that made him one of the few flyers to become an ace in a two-seat observation airplane. Badham flew with a French observation squadron as a volunteer pilot between February and May 1918, joining the Ninety-first

In efforts to carry even greater bomb loads, giant bombers like this German Staaken R.XIVa were built, albeit in small numbers.

Aero Squadron at the end of the month. Badham scored all five victories within six weeks and remained with the Ninety-first until January 1919, at which date he was transferred to the Army of Occupation.

1918 September 15   The biggest Zeppelin-Staaken to see operational duty made its first bombing raid from the Giant Airplane Flying Unit base, Rfa 500, at Morville when R.45 went to attack Le Havre. The Staaken R.XIV had a wing span of 138 ft. 5 in., a wing area of 3,594 sq. ft. and a length of 73 ft. 10 in. It was powered by five 245-HP Maybach engines, four in twin wing nacelles and one in the nose, providing a maximum speed of 84 MPH and a ceiling of just under 14,800 ft. The Staaken R.XIV weighed 22,050 lb. empty and 31,421 lb. loaded. It had a range of 800 mi. with 2,200 lb. of bombs. Two other Staaken R.XIVs saw action before the end of the war. R.45 was badly damaged when it returned from its first raid and never saw action again. F.43 saw some action in France but was shot down in flames by a Sopwith Camel of No. 151 Squadron, RAF. R.44 was broken up at Cologne in 1919.

1918 September 18   Lt. Joseph Fritz Wehner, a native of Boston, Mass., was killed defending his friend and colleague Lt. Frank Luke Jr. after having scored six aerial victories in just four days with the Twenty-seventh Aero Squadron. Wehner joined the air service in June 1917 and was commissioned in January 1918. During training at Issoudun, he met Frank Luke, and they struck up a friendship that continued when they were both assigned to the Twenty-seventh. Wehner liked to defend Luke's rear while the latter pressed home the attack and may have helped his friend acquire more victories that he otherwise would have achieved. All told, Wehner shot down five balloons and one airplane.

1918 September 20   U.S. Navy Lt. (jg) David S. Ingalls scored his fifth air combat victory and thus became the first, and only, U.S. naval aviator to become an ace during World War I. He was serving with No. 213 Squadron, Royal Air Force. Ingalls shot down his sixth and last airplane, a two-seat Rumpler observation plane, on September 24, 1918. The British awarded Ingalls the Distinguished Flying Cross, the United States gave him the Distinguished Service medal, and the French awarded him the Légion d'Honneur. Ingalls served as a commander in World War II with distinction and became a rear admiral in the U.S. Naval Reserve.

1918 September 22   American pilot Lt. George A. Vaughan of the Seventeenth Aero Squadron led a formation of four airplanes to attack 18 German fighters about to dive on five Allied airplanes. Vaughan shot down two of the enemy, the other three in his flight accounting for two more. For this and for a lone attack on September 28, where he shot down a reconnaissance airplane protected by 7 Fokker D.VIIs, Vaughan was bestowed with the Distinguished Service Cross. Vaughan scored a total 13 victories during the war.

1918 September 23   Maj. Gen. Hugh Trenchard received a letter from Marshal Foch informing him of a plan to conduct an offensive by French and U.S. troops from Verdun to the Suippes River and requesting support from the Independent Force. When the offensive began on Sept. 26 at 5:00 A.M., Trenchard's squadrons carried out seven separate raids during the day and that night, dropping 31,500 lb. of bombs on rail marshaling yards in the Metz-Sablon, Mezières, Ars, Audon-le-Roman and Thionville areas as well as against Frescaty airfield. Weather prevented raids on following nights.

1918 September 25   Capt. Edward V. Rickenbacker took over command of the Ninety-fourth Aero Squadron from Maj. Kenneth Marr. Since becoming an air ace at the end of May, Rickenbacker had been hospitalized during July and August with an ear infection, but in the last two weeks of September, he scored six victories. In October he shot down 14 more, of which four were balloons, for a final score of 26. Rickenbacker had a distinguished business career after the war and in World War II carried out several special missions to Britain, North Africa, the Middle East, Russia and the Far East for the secretary of state for war. Rickenbacker served as chairman of Eastern Airlines in the 1950s and died in 1973.

1918 September 26   Second-highest-scoring German air ace Oblt. Ernest Udet shot down his last victims, two D.H.4s, bringing his final score to 62. From Jasta 37, with whom he scored his seventh through twentieth victories, he moved to Jasta 11 in March, 1918, and Jasta 4 in May. Udet scored 20 victories during August and went on leave, returning to get his last two victories on the same day, both D.H.4s from a U.S. squadron. Udet developed a high regard for British pilots and the "chivalry" he believed they exhibited in the air. After the war he became an exhibition pilot before joining the Luftwaffe.

1918 September 26   French air ace René Fonck of SPA.103 had a remarkable day's fighting, shooting down six German airplanes by dusk, the second time he had accomplished such a feat. Taking off from the airfield near Chalons, Fonck attacked five Fokkers over Somme-py and shot two down. Then over Suippe, he tore the wings off a German two-seater with machine gun fire and sent that crashing to earth. During the afternoon, he was one of four planes shot up by eight German fighters soon joined by five more. Fonck gunned down a Fokker harrying a pilot colleague and then shot down two more before returning for home. Had his gun not jammed, he may have got two more.

1918 September 27   The last great push of World War I began simultaneously along the Western Front with British, French, Belgian and U.S. armies pushing against the so-called Hindenburg Line, a shield of entrenched positions the Germans believed to be an impregnable barrier. A total of 1,058 British airplanes took part, supplemented by French, Belgian and U.S. squadrons. Fierce resistance from German air units led to phenomenal performances. During the week ending September 19, JG.2 had shot down 81 Allied airplanes for the loss of two of their own. During

September, Jasta Boelcke (originally Jasta 2) claimed 46 victories for the loss of two men, one-half the victories it had claimed since August 1916.

1918 September 29   American air ace Frank Luke Jr., credited with 18 victories, was killed resisting capture. Brooding over the loss of his friend Lt. Wehner, Luke took leave in Paris, returned early and went looking for a fight in the air on September 26. Next day he went missing and was reprimanded the next day; he later took off without permission to shoot down a balloon. Absent again that night—he went visiting a French squadron—Luke was grounded when he returned on the morning of the twenty-ninth. Ignoring the order, he took off in his Spad and shot down three balloons after having been wounded from return fire before strafing German troops in Murvaux and being forced to land. Defending himself with his pistol, he was gunned down.

1918 September 30   The first of 10 C-series U.S. Navy non-rigid airships made its first flight. With a capacity of 181,000 cu. ft. and a length of 192 ft., the C series was developed for coastal patrol work and convoy escort. In 1919 a C-series blimp became the first airship to be refueled from a surface ship at sea. Others in the series attempted to beat the Curtiss NC flying boats across the Atlantic Ocean in May 1919, and the C-7 was the first, in 1921, to fly with helium instead of hydrogen.

1918 October 2   The Kettering Bug pilotless airplane being developed by Charles F. Kettering made its first successful unmanned flight test, albeit for only nine seconds. Beginning September 13, three unsuccessful attempts preceded this, and on October 4 the Bug flew 45 min. in wide circles for a total distance of 60 mi and crashed at Xenia, Ohio, about 25 mi. from the start point. A young airman, Henry H. Arnold was nearby and identified as the "pilot" to hide from local bystanders the true nature of the secret project.

1918 October 4   The U.S. Air Service mounted two major bombing attacks on enemy forces. During the morning, the Ninety-sixth Aero Squadron sent its Breguet bombers to Dun-sur-Meuse and created havoc in the town, starting several fires. On the return leg, they were jumped by 15 enemy fighters, which tussled with the larger biplanes for 20 min., bringing down only one machine whose occupants were able to escape back to the Allied lines. In the afternoon, another formation from the Ninety-sixth was intercepted by 30 German fighters on the way back from raiding Landres-St. George with 500 lb. of bombs. Spads from the Second Pursuit Group joined in and shot down 11 while the bombers shot down two enemy fighters without loss.

1918 October 4   The first of four Curtiss NC flying boats, the NC-1, made its first flight. Designed by a Navy-Curtiss team to fly across the Atlantic in stages and avoid the dangers of surface transportation and the submarine threat, NC-1 was powered by three 360-HP Liberty tractor engines; but tests showed it had insufficient power to cross the Atlantic, so a fourth engine was added as a tandem partner to the center engine in its nacelle above the fuselage. The NC was 68 ft. 3 in. in length, had a wing span of 126 ft. and an endurance of almost 15 hr. On November 27, NC-1 would get airborne with a record total of 53 people on board at once.

1918 October 6   Two American pilots in a D.H.4 biplane from the Fiftieth Aero Squadron flew supplies to the beleaguered 307th Battalion, U.S. Army, when it was surrounded by German troops on the Western Front. First Lt. H. E. Goettler and 2nd Lt. E. R. Bleckley were awarded the U.S. Congressional Medal of Honor

for the valiant effort under heavy ground fire. The batallion was able to use the supplies to hold off for another day and to fight their way out into the open, eventually regaining the American lines.

1918 October 15   American air ace Lt. Howard Clayton Knotts was shot down about three weeks after scoring his sixth, and final, victory in the air; nevertheless, he was to more than double the number of German airplanes he destroyed. While on a train carrying him to the rear, he managed to set fire to and destroy seven Fokker fighters being carried back for repair and came close to being executed on the spot! Knotts had joined the Aviation Section soon after America entered the war and flew Sopwith Camels with the Seventeenth Aero Squadron from August 16, 1918. After the war, Knotts made a distinguished name for himself in aviation law; he died in 1942.

1918 October 15   The third German fighter airplane competition trials were held at Adlershof, and a preference had been stipulated for the BMW.IIIa engine to power both types to be selected. Nine types were presented for inspection, including designs from Fokker, L.V.G., Junkers, Rumpler, Zeppelin, Roland and Pfalz. The competition ended October 31, and inspectors were believed to have favored the Fokker V.29, an in-line engine version of the V.26 that had been ordered as the E.V, and the Rumpler D.I. The war ended, however, before either type could be ordered into production.

1918 October 17   The longest flight in the series of unmanned tests with a modified Curtiss N-9 "flying bomb" carried out by the U.S. Navy took place. Programmed for a flight of approximately 8 mi., the N-9 chase-plane pilot had to physically help launch the unmanned modified pilotless N-9 from its launch rail before running to his airplane and taking off. By the time he got into the air, the flying bomb was out of sight. Its distance regulator malfunctioned, and the device was last seen heading east for the ocean.

1918 October 20   Air operations in support of an offensive known as the Battle of Vittorio Veneto began with massed air raids by 199 Italian bombers (including 112 Pomilio PE types), 26 S.A.M.L. two-seat biplanes and some Caproni Ca.4 triplanes. The Austrian Sixth Army faced the Italian Eighth Army along the Piave River, but French, British and U.S. units helped reverse the initiative and captured 300,000 Austrian prisoners on November 4. The Pomilio PE was fast and highly effective as a reconnaissance airplane and was a great success. The Ca.4 triplane had a 98-ft. wing span, a length of 43 ft., three 270-HP Isotta-Fraschini engines and a maximum bomb load of 3,190 lb.

1918 October 27   Flying Sopwith Snipe E8102, Canadian air ace William Barker shot down a white-painted German two-seater but was jumped by a Fokker D.VII, which he promptly shot down too. In the scramble he fell into a formation of 15 German fighters, two of which he drove down, and became momentarily unconscious after receiving a thigh wound. Recovering to find himself with a bleeding leg, he fought fiercely and shot down a second D.VII but was hit in the arm, losing consciousness once more. Recovering a second time and believing his fate doomed, he attempted to ram another Fokker but shot it up, bringing his final score to 50 enemy aircraft in 12 months. Barker was awarded the Victoria Cross for this action, the 19th and last awarded to a British airman during World War I.

1918 October 27   By extraordinary bad luck, the airplane carrying Capt. Hamilton Coolidge of the Ninety-fourth Aero Squadron was hit by the shell from an antiaircraft cannon, which instantly destroyed it, killing Coolidge in the process. Coolidge had spent the first half of 1918 flying about 20 flights a day as commander of a training squadron at Issoudun before joining the Ninety-fourth on June 16. His eight victories included five airplanes and three balloons. Coolidge was awarded the Distinguished Service Cross for diving straight into a pack of six German fighters mauling two Allied observation machines, an act of heroism that resulted in his death.

1918 October 28   Socialist and communist revolutionaries in Germany seized control of the naval airship fleet. On November 9, the airships were hung on steel frame racks in their sheds, deflated and abandoned to await the fate dictated by an Allied investigating commission. The airship crews remained loyal to the German Navy and refused to join the insurrectionists. It was an ignominious end to a once-proud fleet of airships, the world's first strategic bombing force.

1918 October 29   The last navy "flying bomb" unmanned Curtiss N-9 biplane was prematurely destroyed when fuel carried in its tanks shifted to the rear under the acceleration of launch from a canted rail, stalling the engine before it could get airborne. Fearing a runaway similar to the previous flight October 17, the ground crew had loaded only 2 gal. of fuel so the N-9 could be recovered and reused. Unfortunately, there was insufficient fuel to cover the outlet pipe to the engine when the biplane was propelled down the launch rail, and it collapsed in a crumpled heap. This did little to dampen enthusiasm for the concept, and research work continued.

1918 November 1   France's top-scoring air ace, officially the highest scoring fighter pilot of the Allied air forces and second only to Manfred von Richthofen in total victories during the war, René Paul Fonck scored his 75th and last aerial victory by shooting down a German airplane dropping propaganda leaflets. Fonck had averaged almost three combat victories a month for the 27 months of air combat since his first victory in August 1916. From Escadrille C.47, he moved to Groupe de Combat N. 12, the famous "Cigognes" (Stork) group of fighter escadrilles, in April 1917, joining SPA.103 under the command of Capt. d'Harcourt where he remained through the end of the war.

1918 November 2   The U.S. Bureau of Ordnance ordered five "flying bombs" from Wittenman-Lewis based on pilotless airplanes. The navy sustained research on this concept with Carl Norden, former employee of Sperry and famous later for the Norden bombsight, and Hannibal Ford, also from Sperry. Comdr. B. B. McCormick ran the project. Two pilotless airplanes were fitted with Sperry controls and three with Norden controls. The first successful flight took place in March 1919.

1918 November 10   The last major raid carried out by the Independent Force under Maj. Gen. Hugh Trenchard was conducted by No. 55 Squadron, RAF, when 11 D.H.4s attacked rail yards at Ehrang and Deutz works at Cologne. Twelve bombers set out, but one failed to find a target. The last raid of all took place on the night of November 10–11 when two Handley Page 0/400s from No. 216 Squadron attacked the Metz-Sablon rail yard and Frescaty airfield. Five people were killed at Metz and seven injured by bombs that fell on the main street of the town. Since June 6, 1917, when the Independent Force was formed, it had carried out 239 raids and dropped 550 tons of bombs, of which 160 tons had been dropped by day. Of the total bombs dropped, 40% were directed against enemy airfields.

1918 November 11   World War I ended with a ceasefire brought into effect by an armistice signed on November 6 by Mathias Erzberger for the Central Powers and the French general Foch for the Allies, in a railway carriage in the forest of Compiègne. For more than four years and three months, the sound of gunfire had never ceased along the Western Front for a single day; at 11:00 A.M. a quiet settled upon the land such as had not been heard since August 1914. In that time, aviation had come of age. Performance had not changed much, but the importance of aerial conflict to the armies in the field was now a measurable certainty. In four years, the major combatant powers had collectively built more than 200,000 airplanes, of which more than 120,000 had been destroyed in combat, in accidents and in bombing attacks.

At the end of hostilities in World War I, the U.S. Air Service had 45 combat squadrons at the front with a total of 740 airplanes, of which only 547 were available for use, together with 767 pilots, 481 observers and 23 aerial gunners. The U.S. Air Service had conducted 150 bombing raids and dropped 140 tons of bombs. Total losses included 237 airmen, 289 airplanes and 48 balloons. Victory scores were credited against 781 enemy airplanes and 73 balloons. The French had provided the Americans with 4,879 airplanes; the British had supplied 283; the Italians had provided 19. In addition, American factories had turned out 1,433. Of the total, 3,261 airplanes were supplied to the front line, with 3,073 going to the training schools and the balance in reserve.

The Balloon Section of the American Expeditionary Force had a total of 35 companies, 446 officers (of which 230 were commissioned in the sir service) and 6,365 soldiers. In all, 5,866 ascensions had been made lasting a total of 6,832 hr. Balloons were attacked by enemy airplanes on 89 occasions—35 were burned or destroyed by airplanes, 12 were destroyed by enemy ground fire and one was blown over the lines. On 116 occasions, observers jumped from their baskets, parachutes operating on every incident although one was destroyed by burning fragments of the balloon. In all, 12,018 shell bursts were reported, 11,856 enemy airplanes sighted, 2,649 enemy balloons reported ascending, enemy batteries reported firing 400 times, enemy infantry seen 22 times, enemy road and rail traffic reported 1,113 times, fires and flares reported 2,941 times, and explosions reported 597 times.

The U.S. Navy had a total 2,107 airplanes (of which 1,865 were seaplanes) and 215 kite and free balloons on hand, with 6,760 officers and 30,693 men in naval aviation. The U.S. Marine Corps had 282 officers and 2,100 men employed in aviation, and the First Aviation Force had conducted 57 missions, dropping 33,932 lb. of bombs. Of these totals, 570 airplanes and 18,000 officers and men had been sent abroad in support of American participation in World War I. In total, U.S. naval aviators flew 4,314 patrols, escorted 477 convoys and dropped 126,206 lb. of bombs. Unlike the army, the navy obtained the majority of its airplanes from American manufacturers: of the total 2,705 airplanes procured to this date, only 142 reconnaissance types had been purchased in Italy. Of the rest, 1,144 were combat airplanes, 1,084 were delivered to training schools, and 335 were experimental types or former army airplanes.

At the end of hostilities in World War I, the British had 22,171 airplanes and 37,702 aero engines on strength with the Royal Air Force, the most powerful military air force in the world. Of this total, the RAF had approximately 3,300 airplanes and seaplanes and 103 airships at first-line strength in 108 operational squadrons. There were 291,175 officers and men serving with the RAF in all theaters of war at home and abroad. In the four years of war, the Royal Flying Corps, the Royal Naval Air Service and the RAF lost 6,166 killed, 7,245 wounded and 3,212 missing or interned. Total aircraft production during 1914–18 had been 55,093 airframes and 41,034 engines, with an additional 3,051 airplanes and 16,897 engines purchased abroad. Labor employed on airplane and aero-engine assembly totaled 347,112 in October 1918, of which 159,586 were women and boys.

The French Air Service had approximately 11,840 airplanes on hand, of which the first-line strength accounted for 4,511. On the Western Front, there were 3,437 front-line airplanes in 258 escadrilles comprising 126 observation, 80 pursuit and 52 bomber squadrons. There were 16 escadrilles serving in home defense and coastal defense duties with 148 airplanes, training schools had 3,000 airplanes, and there were 300 front-line airplanes in overseas escadrilles. The French Air Service comprised approximately 90,000 men, and naval aviation had an additional 11,000 men and 1,200 airplanes. In all, France had lost 5,533 men killed or wounded out of 16,458 pilots and 2,000 observers trained. Photographic reconnaissance was an important activity of the French Air Service, and the annual totals for photographs reflect the growth in importance: 48,000 pictures were taken by the end of 1915, 293,000 in 1916, 474,000 in 1917 and 675,000 in 1918. Total production during 1914–18 had been 67,982 airframes and 85,317 engines. Production during 1918 alone had been 34,224 airframes and 40,308 engines. The French had 186,000 employees engaged in airplane and aero-engine manufacture.

At war's end, Italy had 68 operational squadrons, 20 of which were fighter units. The Italian Naval Air Service comprised 9 fighter squadrons and 37 reconnaissance squadrons. Italy had built 20,000 airframes and 38,000 engines between 1914 and 1918.

Germany had about 20,000 aircraft with a front line strength of 2,709 serving with 284 aviation units (Fliegen Abteilungen) and sections (Staffeln). Of the army airplanes in front-line strength, between 1,134 and 1,296 were single-seat fighters, 162 were twin-engine bombers and six were R-type heavy bombers. The rest were two-seat reconnaissance airplanes. The Germans employed about 100,000 people in the aircraft production industry. Total production between 1914 and 1918 included 47,637 airframes and 40,449 aero engines. The German Air Service had about 4,500 officers and men, and during the four years of war had lost 8,212 killed or missing and 7,350 wounded. It had lost 3,128 airplanes, 546 balloons and 26 airships.

German naval aviation had made tremendous strides since naval engineer Karl Loew received the first German flying certificate on March 10, 1911. At the end of the war, naval aviation included 16,122 personnel, of which 2,116 were on flying duty. The navy had 1,478 airplanes made up of 673 front-line and 334 training seaplanes, 112 basic training and 11 experimental floatplanes and 191 front-line and 157 training landplanes. Some of the biggest airplanes built during World War I were designed as seaplanes and flying boats, including the giant Dorniers.

By the end of World War I, the German Naval Airship Division had taken possession of 61 Zeppelins (the first two were destroyed before the war), eight Shutte-Lanz, three Parseval and one Gross-Basenach. Only 10 Zeppelins out of a total 73 airships of all makes survived, and one, Zeppelin L 72, was completed after the war and handed over to the French as the Dixmude. It crashed December 21, 1923. The airship division trained about 50 crews, of which 389 members, about 40%, were killed; 17 airships were destroyed along with their entire crews.

At the end of World War I, the total German civilian and military casualties for all British and French air raids on German territory between 1915 and November 11, 1918, were 746 killed and 1,843 injured with material damage estimated at approximately £1,200,000. Far more effective was the damage to the German will to continue the war. The raids induced a political will to seek a ban on bombing of towns and cities, but the war ended before neutral intermediaries like Switzerland could effectively put together a satisfactory proposal, although the Allies expressed a willingness to begin talks about such an undertaking.

1918 November 11 On the day Germany stopped fighting, Hugo Junkers instructed his work force to stop activity on all military projects and to attend instead to the full design of an all-metal passenger transport, which would appear in 1919 as the F.13, the world's first all-metal civilian airplane. Capable of carrying six people, it was to lead directly to the W.33 and W.34 general purpose aircraft first produced in 1926 and which would serve for a limited period as light bombers with the new Luftwaffe during the mid-1930s.

1918 November 12 The U.S. Army Air Service had 78,333 personnel on strength, of whom 58,090 were in France, 20,072 were in England and 171 were in Italy. Of the 20,072 categorized as being in England, 574 were serving as mechanics in RAF squadrons on the Western Front. Of the 58,090 in France, 582 were attached to the British or the French armies, 24,512 were in the American Zone and 32,996 were in training or flying schools. The 25 U.S. Army air training schools had processed 1,674 pilots and 851 observers, with 1,402 pilots and 769 observers having been sent to the front. Between November 11 and January 1, 1919, 675 pilots and 357 observers would graduate from these schools, indicative of their rapidly increased efficiency.

1918 November 15 A Handley Page V/1500 heavy bomber lifted 40 passengers into the air, a total load of 6,022 lb., from Cricklewood, England for a short trip around the airfield. A party of 28 journalists being shown around by Frederick Handley Page had arrived, and he unexpectedly offered them and 12 employees a trip in the giant bomber, during the course of which they reached a height of 6,500 ft. This was the largest number of people lifted in one airplane, a record that was eclipsed 12 days later when the Curtiss NC-1 and its two-man crew carried 51 passengers aloft in the United States.

1918 November 15 The British press announced the reopening of the *Daily Mail* trans-Atlantic challenge with a prize of £10,000, first set on April 1, 1913, and still unclaimed. The Royal Aero Club was made responsible for adjudicating the challengers, who had to make the crossing within 72 hours of beginning. The challenge had been boosted by the addition of £1,000 from businessman Lawrence Philips in July 1918, and it was increased by an additional £2,200 from the Ardath Tobacco Co. at the end of April 1919, bringing the total to £13,200.

1918 November 27 The Dayton, Ohio team developing the Kettering Bug pilotless flying bomb was closed down by the U.S. Army. Following a successful unmanned test October 2, Lt. Col. Bion J. Arnold, in charge of the project, had ordered 75 more, in addition to the 25 originally ordered, and anticipated orders for up to 100,000 at a unit cost of $400. Henry H. Arnold had been sent to France to instruct the Allies in the potential of the flying bomb. When work on the program stopped, four Bugs had been finished, 11 were partially built, and five airframes had been constructed. Tests with these continued under the personal direction of B. J. Arnold.

1918 November 29 A Handley Page 0/400 (serial no. C9700) began a mail route survey flight from Palestine to India. Carrying Maj. Gen. W. G. H. Salmond, General Officer Commanding, RAF Middle East, it reached Delhi on December 12 after eight stops. Fuel, stores and provisions had been stockpiled along the route. The crew comprised Brig. Gen. A. E. Borton as captain, Capt. Ross Smith as copilot, with Sgts. J. M. Bennett and W. H. Shiers. The 0/400 arrived in Calcutta on December 17, and during February 1919 it carried out policing duties on the North West Frontier before being destroyed on the ground in a storm.

1918 December 1 Acting with full authority of Lenin, Nikolai E. Zhukovsky, a professor at the Moscow Higher Technical School, founded the Central Aerodynamics and Hydrodynamics Institute (TsAGI). Zhukovsky spent all his time establishing what became the most famous aeronautical institute in the Soviet Union and is frequently referred to as the father of Soviet aviation. One of his main assistants in setting up this institute was Andrei Nikolayevich Tupolev, who turned his hand increasingly to the design of new airplanes and was to start work soon on his first product, the ANT.1, which made its appearance in 1922.

1918 December 4 Four Curtiss JN-4 two-seat biplanes began a flight across the continental United States, flying from San Diego, Calif. to Jacksonville, Fla. in 18 days to complete the first crossing of the United States by army airplanes. Maj. Albert D. Smith, director of training at Rockwell Field, led Lts. H. D. McLean, Robert S. Worthington and Albert F. Pyle, each carrying a single passenger; in addition to the pilots, there were a flight surgeon, a photographer and two mechanics. A fifth airplane flown by Lt. Bruce Johnson came down in fog on the very first day and wrecked his airplane trying to take off again. The rest made it to El Paso on the seventh, Houston on the eleventh, New Orleans on the fourteenth, Montgomery on the sixteenth and Jacksonville on the eighteenth.

1918 December 12 The U.S. Navy airship C-1, first in the C series of 10 airships, became the first airship to release for free flight an airplane attached beneath the envelope. Piloted by Lt. A. W. Redfield, commanding the Fifty-second Aero Squadron at Mineola, N.Y., the Curtiss JN-4 was flown successfully back down to the ground after being released by the airship commander, Lt. George Crompton, dirigible officer at the Rockaway Naval Air Station. Tests were being conducted to see if airplanes could be used in conjunction with airships, as either extended reconnaissance "eyes" or as defensive fighters for the vulnerable blimps.

1918 December 13 The first direct air flight between England and British India began when the third prototype Handley Page V/1500 took off from Martlesham Heath in Suffolk with Maj. A. S. C. MacLaren as pilot, Capt. Robert Hally as copilot and Sgts. Smith, Crockett and Brown as crew members; Brig. Gen. N. D. K. McEwan went along as a passenger. The plane flew in several stages to Otranto, Italy, picking up nine passengers for Malta before making the 1,050-mi., nonstop flight to Mersa Matruh in Egypt. Then it was on to Baghdad, across the north coast of the Persian Gulf and by several stops to Karachi on January 16, 1919, having flown more than 6,000 mi.

1918 December 14 The English Electric Company Ltd. was incorporated, by amalgamating several British electrical and power production equipment manufacturers, with 5 million pounds in capital and headquarters in London. Companies absorbed by E. E. included the United Electric Car Works, which had manufactured airplanes under license, and the Phoenix Dynamo Manufacturing Co., which had built Short seaplanes. The first English Electric airplane, the *Wren*, flew in 1923, but recession and poor defense contracts kept E. E. away from airplanes until subcontracting work in World War II. Their most famous products, the Canberra jet bomber and the Lightning jet interceptor, would not be manufactured until the 1940s and 1950s.

1918 December 16 Stationed on continental Europe, No. 18 Squadron, RAF, began routine communications flights moving mail between Marquise, France and the German city of Cologne via Maisoncelle, Belgium. A second service operated by No. 110

Squadron from Hesdin, France began May 5, 1919. The service was extended March 1, 1919, to include a cross-channel flight from Hawkinge, England, and during the summer the stop at Maisoncelle was cancelled. These flights served the British forces of Occupation and ended on August 23, 1919. In all, the two RAF squadrons flew 1,842 trips, carrying more than 90 tons of mail with 96% efficiency before the service was handed over to Air Transport & Travel.

1918 December 23 Brig. Gen. William Mitchell issued a *Provisional Manual of Operations of Air Service Units* based on his study of observation, bombardment and pursuit tactics in Europe before the armistice. It compiled a series of bulletins written during several engagements and campaigns and reflected analytical evaluation of how combat aviation could be made more effective and organizationally sound. Brig. Gen. Mitchell hoped that "these articles . . . [would] serve as a valuable guide in the organization and cooperation of future Air Service units." Not before World War II would its recommendations be implemented.

1919 January 2 Australian Capt. Andrew Lang and 19-year-old Canadian Lt. A. W. Blowes, RAF, successfully flew a D.H.9 fitted with the first production 430-HP Napier Lion engine to a record height of 30,500 ft. in England. At that height, the fuel pumps froze up, and the engine stopped. The crew wore specially heated suits to protect against the cold, which reached a record low of −38°F. The "Sidcot" suits they wore had been developed by Capt. Sidney Cotton of the Royal Flying Corps several years earlier.

1919 January 8 At the instruction of August Euler, recently made the head of the the Reich Aviation Office (Reichsluftamt), the Allegemeine Elektrizitats Gesellschaft (A.E.G.) was awarded a license for the first post-war German airline. Called the German Air Transport Agency (Deutsche Luft Reederei, or D.L.R.), it had been formed during 1917 to deliver mail for the military forces and was now a fully licensed passenger and light cargo operator. The first service opened February 5 between Berlin and Weimar, a distance of about 120 mi., using A.E.G. biplanes. A Hamburg-Berlin service opened March 1, followed by a Berlin-Brunswick-Hanover-Gelsenkirchen service April 15. DLR abruptly ceased operations August 1 due to a gas shortage, after having carried 1,574 passengers.

1919 January 8 A military airmail service opened for an experimental period between Zurich and Bern in Switzerland and was extended to Lausanne on February 1. It was planned to begin a public mail service May 1, but poor weather kept the aircraft grounded until May 5. Passengers were carried from June, and at the end of October, when it closed, the service had carried 246 people and 20,348 military dispatches. The aircraft used were Swiss-built Haefeli DH 3 biplanes designed by A. Haefeli in 1916 and that first flew on June 25, 1917. The DH 3 biplane had a wing span of 41 ft., a length of 26 ft. 5 in., and a loaded weight of 2,292 lb. and had a top speed of 90 MPH powered by a 150-HP Hispano-Suiza engine.

1919 January 10 No. 2 (Communications) Squadron of the RAF began regular passenger and mail services between London and Paris, primarily as a rapid communications link between the British government and the peace conference at Versailles. Modified D.H.4s, with enclosed accommodation for two passengers behind the pilot's cockpit, were used for ferrying diplomats and politicians as well as documents and mail in support of the discussions on a final settlement of the armistice.

1919 January 11 Public announcements in Britain defined major changes in the administration of civil and military aviation. Maj. Gen. Trenchard was appointed chief of the air staff, Winston S. Churchill succeeded Lord Weir as secretary of state for air, Maj. Gen. J. E. B. Seely became under-secretary and Maj. Gen. Sir Frederick Sykes was made controller general of civil aviation in the United Kingdom.

1919 January 21 Maj. Theodore C. Macauley, commander of Taliaferro Field near Fort Worth, Tex., began what the U.S. Army hailed as the first ''round-trip'' across the United States when he departed with his mechanic, Pvt. Staley, in a modified D.H.4 equipped to carry an extra 56 gal. of gas and 10 gal. of oil. They reached Baton Rouge on the twenty-third and Arcadia, Fla. on the twenty-fourth. Forced to make an emergency landing at Lake Okeechobee on the twenty-fifth, they damaged their airplane near Americus, Ga. A replacement airplane was similarly damaged on Feb. 2, and a JN-4H was finally employed to carry Maj. Macauley to West Point, N.Y., from where he left in a D.H.4 to fly back to Taliaferro, arriving Feb. 17.

1919 January A three-man board recommended continued development of the U.S. Army Air Service flying bomb project, and Lt. Col. Bion J. Arnold set up the tests at Carlstrom Field near Arcadia, Fla. He was replaced as head of the test program by the former artillery officer Lt. Col. Guy L. Gearhart, and on August 29 he received instructions to send 12 Kettering Bugs to Carlstrom. Gearhart was to collect performance data and report on the viability of the project and any future requirements for additional tests.

1919 January The pre-war aviator Vedrines amazed onlookers by landing his Caudron G.3 on the top of the Galeries Lafayette department store, located alongside the Seine River in Paris. The first of several peacetime exploits for which the slow-flying G.3 was admirably suited, it was used in the same month by Madame de Laroche to attain an altitude of 12,795 ft. In September the aviator Maicon flew his G.3 under a bridge on the Bar River at Nice, and in April 1921 Adrienne Bolland crossed the Andes in his G.3, flying from Tamarindos, Argentina to Santiago, Chile and reaching a maximum height en route of 13,780 ft. A Caudron G.3 is today preserved on display at the RAF Museum, Hendon, England.

1919 January The largest airplane ever flown with a single propeller, and carrying the largest propeller ever used on an airplane, conducted test flights in Germany. Built by Linke Hoffman of Breslau, the R.II had a wingspan of 138 ft. 4 in., a length of 66 ft. 8 in. and was powered by four 260-HP Mercedes D.IVa engines arranged in two pairs in the nose. They were linked to a single propeller with a diameter of 22 ft. 8 in., which revolved via gear train at 545 RPM, providing a maximum speed of just over 81 MPH.

1919 February 1 Aircraft Transport & Travel Ltd. organized a special relief service at the request of the Belgian government whereby RAF D.H.9s flown by civilian pilots would carry food and woollen clothing to war victims in Belgium. The service ran from Hawkinge, near Folkestone, across the English Channel to Ghent in Belgium. Seven aircraft (serial nos. D628, D1197, D1206, D1213, D1214, D1217 and H4275) were used, and each aircraft had an AT&T sticker on the side to identify it.

1919 February 8 The Farman brothers made what they claimed, and others have erroneously endorsed, to be the first scheduled international flight in Europe when a Farman F.60 Goliath piloted by M. Lucien Bossoutrot carried a token load of military passengers between Toussus le Noble airfield outside Paris, France and Kenley in southern England. On more substantive ground is the flight made between Paris and Brussels, Belgium on February 10 when a Caudron C.23 carried five journalists on a prescheduled test flight for a regular weekly service that commenced March 22. The journey took 2 hr. 50 min. After the third flight on April 6, the passengers were examined by a customs official for the first time.

1919 February 13 The first postwar French commercial service was established on a route from Paris to Lille for the carriage of food and clothing to France's northern departments. The French government was concerned about the poor state of the roads and the decimated rail networks in the northeast after more than four years of war. France and Belgium were the only countries so affected, and aviation was a logical means of transporting both people and cargo over the devastated terrain. Consequently, air travel in France was given a boost by the necessities of restoring a normal way of life.

1919 February 21 A major step toward an indigenous American combat plane design and manufacturing capability was made with the first flight of the Thomas-Morse MB-3 Tommy piloted by Frank H. Burnside from an airfield at Ithaca, N.Y. A single-seat, biplane fighter powered by a 300-HP Wright H engine (basically, a license-built Hispano-Suiza Model H), the MB-3 was not a good fighter plane. Overpowered and suffering from vibration, Thomas-Morse built 50, and the army air service requested competitive bids on an order for 200 more, for which Boeing and Curtiss entered competitive prices against Thomas-Morse.

1919 February The prototype Siemens-Schuckert D.VI single-seater fighter was completed and tested. The German Imperial Air Service had ordered the type in 1918 due to the great promise of the design. As tested, the D.VI would have been the fastest fighter aircraft to enter service in Germany had it been built in time. Powered by a 160-HP Siemens-Halske Sh IIIa engine, the prototype recorded a maximum speed of 137.5 MPH. The D.VI was a parasol monoplane development of the earlier biplane D.IV, which was considered by the few pilots who flew it as being superior in performance to any other German fighter of the war.

1919 March 1 The largest airplane built during World War I carried out its first taxi tests after emerging from its hangar at the Siemens-Schuckert Dynamowerke. The SSW R.VIII was the last R-plane from this company, which had been building large bombers since 1914. The R.VIII had a wingspan of 157 ft. 6 in., a length of 70 ft. 10 in. and a maximum weight of 35,060 lb. Powered by six 300-HP Basse & Selve engines in pairs in the fuselage driving two tractor and two pusher propellers in two interplane nacelles, it would have had a maximum speed of 78 MPH, a ceiling of 13,124 ft. and a range of 559 miles. The R.VIII was damaged before its first flight, and the project was canceled June 26, 1919.

1919 March 1 In violaton of British law prohibiting civil flying, Sir Woodman Burbidge, the managing director of Harrods Ltd., the famous London department store, flew from Hendon to Brussels for a business meeting. This may have been the first international charter flight carried out between Britain and the continent of Europe. Not before May would civil flying be legally restored, although there is nothing to suggest that this was the only clandestine journey of the period.

1919 March 3   The first international U.S. airmail service was flown between Seattle, Wash. and Victoria, British Columbia, by the Hubbard Air Service flying a Boeing CL-4S floatplane. This first flight carried only a token quantity of mail, as it was part of a route survey program, but the service was contracted and became regular after October 14, 1920. This first flight was made by Eddie Hubbard and William Boeing. The airmail service was to prove a lucrative business for sharp-witted entrepreneurs.

1919 March 9   U.S. Navy Lt. Comdr. E. O. McDonnell made the first successful flight from a gun turret platform on a U.S. navy battleship. The USS *Texas* was anchored in Guantánamo Bay, Cuba for the test, and a platform devised to allow capital ships to operate aircraft without sacrificing any of their armament supported a Sopwith Camel single-seat fighter. The Camel took off successfully and demonstrated both the platform and the operational application of a shipboard fighter.

1919 March 10   Brig. Gen. William Mitchell was appointed as director of military aeronautics under the director of the air service. Mitchell replaced Maj. Gen. W. L. Kenly in the post. During his stay in Europe and with his observations and interpretations of what air power could become under strong and committed leadership, Mitchell was determined to campaign for political support and for strong army and navy endorsement of aviation as a major military force.

1919 March 13   The British air estimates were announced by Under-Secretary of State for Air, Maj. Gen. Seely. Reflecting the mood of disarmament that followed World War I, whereas Parliament had been asked to approve an aviation budget of £188 million for the last year of the war, aviation funds for the first year of peace were a mere £40 million, plus £26.5 million for contract termination costs. Gen. Seely predicted the decimation of the RAF and said personnel levels would fall below 200,000 versus 291,175 in November 1918.

1919 March   The prototype Airco D.H.16 civilian transport biplane made its first flight at Hendon powered by a 320-HP Rolls Royce Eagle. Basically a converted D.H.9, the D.H.16 could carry four passengers in facing pairs inside a glazed cabin behind the open pilot's cockpit. It entered service with Aircraft Transport and Travel Ltd. in May 1919. Although only nine were built, the type was used to inaugurate a London-Paris air route, to carry passengers for the River Plate Aviation Co. in Buenos Aries and to fly a Croydon-Amsterdam service for KLM, the Royal Dutch Air Line.

1919 March   The Australian government offered a prize of £A10,000 to the first Australian airmen to fly a British airplane between Britain and Australia in less than 30 days. Several attempts were prepared, including Lt. H. J. L. Hinkler with his Sopwith Dove, Lt. Charles Kingsford Smith, Lt. Vlademar Rendle, C. Maddocks and L. Booker in a Blackburn Kangaroo and Lt. R. J. P. Parer and Lt. J. C. McIntosh in an F.E.2b powered by a 200-HP Beardmore engine. Few airplanes of the day had the endurance and reliability to risk on a continuing sequence of flights totaling more than 11,000 mi. with the only spares available en route being those carried along.

1919 April 6   The first international customs service was inaugurated at Brussels where plane passenger baggage was inspected for the first time. The rapid development of civil air routes transformed the management of passenger flights from the ad hoc activity it had been before the war to an increasingly bureaucratized series of scheduled events. This was frequently at variance to the informal approach taken by the majority of pilots and air crew, who were for the most part redundant military aviators discarded in their tens of thousands by the governments of the former combatant powers.

1919 April 10   A 30-day, 190,000-mi. tour of 88 cities in 45 U.S. states began when three air circuses organized for the U.S. Government Victory Loan campaign got on the road. Playing one-night stands, the three groups were under the command of Maj. Ora M. Balinger, and each consisted of about 22 officers, 50 enlisted men and 18 airplanes supported by nine baggage cars, three sleepers and a dining car. Daily shows usually began around 1:30 P.M. local time, with acrobatics, exhibition events, mock dogfights and a free ride for the largest loan subscriber. Cities were "attacked" with pasteboard bombs, and speeches were made.

1919 April 12   Seeking every opportunity to exploit the recently concluded world war to stimulate an awareness of the role air power had played in defeating the Germans, an air show was held at Kelly Field, San Antonio, Tex. depicting "the horrors of war, as carried out by the Huns." The scenario was a town attacked by artillery and bombed by airplanes and occupied by the Germans, who were then driven out as U.S. airplanes won dogfights with "German" airplanes. Under the general title of "War Swept France," the show was a lurid attempt to encourage airmindedness.

1919 April 13   Visually similar to its military ancestor, the prototype Vickers Vimy Commercial made its first flight at Joyce Green, England with Stan Cockerell at the controls. Known as the Vickers Monocoque during design, the Commercial had a large bulbous fuselage able to carry 10 passengers in leather chairs or wicker seats or up to 2,500 lb. of freight in a space of 300 cu. ft. The Vimy Commercial was sold to China, and the Russians and the French each ordered one. An ambulance version was built for the RAF with a nose door for front-loading stretcher cases. The Commercial was one of the first aircraft operated by Imperial Airways.

1919 April 19   The world's first free-fall, pack deployed, parachute descent was made at McCook Field, Dayton, Ohio. Leslie Leroy Irvin used a pack parachute of his own design that he had been developing for the U.S. Army. The Irving Parachute Co., so named due to errors in the reporting of Irvin's name, were to supply the standard aircrew parachute for the major air forces of the world. Aircrew using Irving parachutes in an emergency automatically became members of the Caterpillar Club and were sent membership cards and a gold silkworm caterpillar badge. There are many tens of thousands of members worldwide, and the club is still growing.

1919 April 19   The Aeronautical Commission of the Versailles peace conference declared that "the right of flying over a State from frontier to frontier is recognised subject to safeguard." The safeguard was a provision permitting the country concerned to compel a forced landing on its territory if national interests were deemed to be threatened. What appeared to be a safeguard turned out to be a license for flagrant intervention in the peaceful and commercial pursuits of friendly countries, for the regulation was used many times to impede British aircraft and give succor to the competition by annoying the delayed passengers of British airlines.

1919 April 23   The Blackburn Aeroplane and Motor Co. Ltd. formed a subsidiary, the North Sea Aerial Navigation Co., to run commercial flying services from Soldiers' Field, Roundhay Park,

Leeds, England, using idled *Blackburn Kangaroo* reconnaissance-torpedo aircraft. Characterized by an unusually long nose, the biplane had a wing span of almost 75 ft. and a length of 44 ft.. 2 in. It was powered by two 250-HP Rolls Royce Falcons. The first commercial service was run on May 10 when freight was flown from Gosport to Leeds. A limited freight service was also run to Holland between March 5, 1920 and October 1920.

1919 April 28　An unofficial distance and endurance record for seaplanes was set by a U.S. Navy F5L biplane flying boat flown by Lt. H. B. Grow. The flight lasted 20 hr. 19 min. and covered a total distance of 1,250 mi. The F5L was a development of the British Felixstowe F5 flying boat, which had itself been developed from the Curtiss America, and it was fitted with two 400-HP Liberty engines. This antisubmarine patrol aircraft could be armed with a 1.5-lb. quick-firing cannon, as many as eight machine guns and up to four 230-lb. bombs.

1919 April　The Imperial Japanese Army Air Division was established under Maj. Gen. Ikutaro Inouye. Several Japanese officers had served with the French Air Service during World War I, and in December 1915 the Air Battalion of the Army Transport Command was organized. When Col. Faure brought a French mission to Japan with 63 demonstration pilots, license production of the Spad S.XIII was set up as the standard army fighter, the Nieuport 24C-1 was built as a fighter trainer and the Salmson 2A-2 appeared as a reconnaissance airplane.

1919 April　The first German long-distance flight after World War I was carried out when a Sablatnig P I flew from Berlin to Copenhagen, Denmark, and Stockholm, Sweden. Developed as a two-seat night bomber called the N I, it was developed into a four-passenger cabin transport aircraft called the P I by adding an enclosure behind the pilot that was heated and provided with passenger lighting, the first adaptation of its kind anywhere. The P I was powered by a 200/220-HP Daimler Benz Bx IV in-line engine, which gave a cruising speed of 81 MPH. The biplane had a wing span of 35 ft. 11 in., a length of 27 ft. 8 in. and a loaded weight of 2,579 lb.

1919 April　A D.H.6 piloted by Airco pilot Gerald Gathergood became the first British airplane registered under the air navigation regulations and was given the unusual registration K-100 on special dispensation to permit it to fly during the Easter period. The internationally agreed codes whereby each country had a two-letter symbol had British aircraft carry the letters *G-E* followed by three letters unique to each aircraft. For instance, G-EAAE was civilianized Handley Page 0/400 bomber.

1919 May 1　Banned since August 4, 1914, when Britain declared war on Germany, civil flying officially resumed in Britain with publication of the air navigation regulations requiring all civilian airplanes to be registered, to display the allocated number and nationality marking and to have a certificate of airworthiness. The crew, too, had to have flying certificates. In accordance with the international agreements made this year, each country had a set of letters denoting the nationality of registered airplanes.

1919 May 1　The first British certificate of airworthiness for civilian airplanes and the first civil registration were allocated. Certificate no. 1 was given to Handley Page 0/400 F5414, which bore the civil registration G-EAAF and was the first of 43 planes converted from a military role, six of which were to be exported to China. The first registration under the new international system, soon to be ratified, was D.H.9 C6054 from Aircraft Transport & Travel bearing registration G-EAAA. Piloted by Capt. H.

J. Saint, it took off at 4:30 A.M. carrying newspapers from Hendon to Bournemouth, but one hour later it was wrecked on fog-shrouded Portsdown Hill, north of Portsmouth.

1919 May 8　Three Curtiss flying boats, NC-1, NC-3 and NC-4 took off from the Rockaway Naval Air Station, N.Y. at 10:00 A.M. for a 950-mi. flight to Trepassey, Newfoundland on the first leg of a trans-Atlantic flight attempt. Together known as Seaplane Division One, the NC-1 was commanded by Lt. Comdr. P. N. L. Bellinger, the NC-3 by Comdr. John H. Towers and the NC-4 by Lt. Comdr. A. C. Read. The Atlantic crossing had been seriously pursued since 1913 when the British newspaper *Daily Mail* offered a £10,000, prize for the first flight across. The war prevented that challenge being taken up. The NC flying boats each had four 360-HP Liberty engines in the modified arrangement first applied to NC-1.

1919 May 10　Using a three-seater Avro biplane, A. V. Roe and Co. began the first scheduled airline service in England with a flight connecting Alexander Park, Manchester with Southport and Blackpool. The fare was £4 4s. (4 guineas) for a single journey of under 50 mi. and the flights continued throughout the summer until Sept. 30. By then, 194 flights had taken place out of 222 originally scheduled. A. V. Roe also took on some unscheduled flights during the rail strike of midyear, but when the regular service stopped, it was not repeated by this company.

1919 May 12　Lt. Col. W. Sholto Douglas flew a Handley Page 0/400, dropping bundles of newspapers by parachute during a flight from London to Nottingham, Northampton, Lichfield, Birmingham and back to London at the end of a series of similar flights that began May 1. Flights carried out on May 3, 5, 6, 9 and 11 visited Manchester, Brighton, Eastbourne, Hastings, Carlisle, Dundee, Aberdeen, Montrose, Edinburgh, Preston, Bristol, Exeter, Plymouth, Southampton, Bournemouth, Ryde, Cardiff, Swansea, Norwich, Cromer and Yarmouth. At each place, bundles were dropped in an extraordinary demonstration of aerial delivery.

1919 May 15　The first section of the transcontinental airmail service across the United States was inaugurated between Chicago, Ill., and Cleveland, Ohio by the U.S. Post Office, saving 16 hr. on the New York-Chicago service either by taking the load off the westbound train at Cleveland for onward conveyance by air or connecting with the train to New York on its eastbound run. The New York-Cleveland air link was inaugurated July 1, and on July 31, the San Francisco to Sacramento route was opened. An all-air service from Chicago to New York was running by September 5.

1919 May 16　Having flown up from Rockaway, N.Y., three Curtiss NC flying boats set off from Trepassey Bay, Newfoundland, heading for Horta in the Azores, 1,381 mi. away. It was the longest single leg of the attempted trans-Atlantic crossing. NC-4 made it to Horta and landed at 13:23 GMT, May 17. NC-1 had to come down on the water 100 mi. west of Flores, was lightly damaged and had to be taken in tow by the Greek steamship *Ionia*. When the tow lines broke, the USS *Gridley* took over, but that line broke too and the flying boat sank. After 15 hr. and 1,380 mi., NC-3 landed on the water 45 mi. southwest of Fayal and taxied 200 mi. into the harbor at Horta 52 hrs. after taking off. It was unable to continue the trans-Atlantic attempt.

1919 May 18　English aviators Harry Hawker and Lt. Comdr. K. F. Mackenzie-Grieve took off from St. John's, Newfoundland in an unsuccessful attempt to make a nonstop west-east crossing of the North Atlantic in a Sopwith Atlantic biplane built in six weeks during April and May. It had extra-large fuel tanks, jettisonable undercarriage and an upturned lifeboat doubling as the upper rear fuselage decking. The Atlantic had to ditch next day when the Rolls Royce Eagle overheated, but the Danish ship SS *Mary* picked the crew up 1,000 mi. east of their takeoff point.

1919 May 18 German army captain Helmut Wilberg carried out a study into the aviation requirements of the newly created German National Army (Reichswehr). He defined a need for 1,800 aircraft manned by 9,200 personnel, 8,000 from the army and the rest from the navy, operating out of 16 major air bases. The report was filed by Gen. Hans von Seeckt, ex-chief of staff to Gen. August von Mackensen, away from the prying eyes of the Allies. Von Seeckt secretly plotted to organize military aviation units under innocuous code names that would comply with the terms of the Treaty of Versailles, then in the final stages of preparation for German signature.

1919 May 20 The sole remaining Curtiss flying boat still left in the trans-Atlantic crossing attempt, NC-4, made the 169-mi. hop from Horta to Ponta Delgada, still in the Azores. Lt. Comdr. Read was delayed there by weather and left on the 925-mi. leg to Lisbon, Portugal on May 27, arriving at 8:01 P.M. the same day, having flown 3,425 mi—the first airplane to cross the Atlantic. From there, Lt. Comdr. Read took the NC-4 on to Plymouth, England, adding 500 mi. to the journey for a total flying time of 57 hrs. 16 min. at an average speed of 68.4 MPH. The crew of the NC-4 included Lt. E. F. Stone of the U.S. Coast Guard, Lt. J. L. Breese, Lt. W. K. Hinton and Ens. H. C. Rodd and Ens. E. S. Rhoads of the U. S. Navy.

1919 May 22 A Handley Page V/1500 from No.166 Squadron, RAF, flew a special "figure-8" course from Bircham Newton, England via Birmingham, Southport, Manchester, Lincoln, London, Felixstowe, Great Yarmouth, and Hunstanton in a demonstration of the airplane's capabilities. The RAF had planned to raid Berlin using 3,300-lb. blockbuster bombs carried by the V/1500, but the war ended before that could be undertaken. This demonstration helped qualify the enormous potential of the V/1500. It flew for 11 hr. 33 min. carrying eight people with a takeoff weight of 24,890 lb. and an average speed of 73 MPH.

1919 May 26 The only attempted take-off of the Tarrant Tabor six-engine bomber at Farnborough, England ended in disaster when the giant triplane nosed over as the tail was raised at high speed and the throttles opened on two upper engines. Fatal injuries were sustained by the two crew members on board. Designed by Walter Barling, the Tabor was built by the Tarrant firm of building contractors in a balloon shed at Farnborough. The extended middle wing spanned 131 ft. 3 in., upper and lower wings 98.5 ft., the length was 73 ft. 2 in. and maximum loaded weight was 44,672 lb., including a 4,650-lb. bomb load. Power was provided by six 450-HP Napier Lion engines, four in tandem between the two lower wings and two separate engines between the two upper wings.

1919 May Construction began of the giant E.4/20 four-engine transport aircraft at the Zeppelin-Werke G.m.b.H. at Staaken, Berlin. Under the technical direction of Dr. Ing Adolf Rohrbach, the aircraft was built to carry passengers and cargo between Friedrichshafen and Berlin. It had a wing span of 101 ft. 8 in., and power was provided by four 245-HP Maybach engines. The

A wide range of bombs used by the Royal Flying Corps, from the 1,650-lb. device to a 20-lb. Cooper bomb at right.

The cockpit of the Vickers Vimy, the aircraft in which Alcock and Brown first crossed the Atlantic.

maximum weight was 18,739 lb., and a cruising speed of 124-MPH was calculated. When finally completed in September 1920, the Allied Control Commission suspended flight trials and ordered the aircraft broken up, which was carried out in November 1922.

1919 June 1 The U.S. Army Air Service began patrol operations in California for fire detection and reporting, the first in a series of expanding commitments to the U.S. Forest Service in response to a request from Chief Forester Henry S. Graves. JN-4H airplanes made two daily patrols from March Field, Calif., one going north over Los Angeles National Forest and the other covering the southern end of the Cleveland National Forest; fire patrols began in Oregon during August. During the 1920 season, the air service operated 37 airplanes with 35 officers and 149 enlisted men on fire patrols. They flew nearly 4,000 hr. covering 476,000 mi. over 16 million sq. mi. of forest discovering 818 fires by air.

1919 June 14 British aviators Capt. John Alcock and Lt. Arthur Whitten Brown took off at 1613 GMT from Lester's Field near St. John's, Newfoundland on the first nonstop flight across the Atlantic. They crash-landed 1,890 mi. and 16 hr. 28 min. later, coming down in a bog near Clifden in the west of Ireland at 8:40 A.M. June 15. Alcock and Brown flew a Vickers Vimy modified with fuel capacity expanded from 619 gal. to 1,038 gal., which increased nominal range from 1,880 mi. to 2,440 mi. Shaped like a boat, one tank would provide 600-lb. buoyancy in the event of ditching. At 9:00 P.M. next day, the first mail to cross the Atlantic by air was delivered in London after having been transferred to England by boat.

1919 June 14 In Britain, Handley Page Transport was incorporated with capitalization of £200,000 and George Woods-Humphrey as general manager. This was the fourth British airline to be formed after the war, and it operated in direct competition with Air Transport & Travel set up by George Holt Thomas and run by Sir Sefton Brancker, North Sea Aerial Navigation and Avro. A proving flight had been made on May 1 when a Handley Page 0/400 piloted by Lt. Col. Sholto Douglas flew from Cricklewood to Manchester carrying ten passengers. A weekend service to Bournemouth followed on July 19, and a token load-carrying demonstration on August 25 inaugurated service to

Brussels on the very day that AT&T opened the world's first daily international airline service.

1919 June 15 U.S. Air Service personnel with D.H.-4 airplanes arrived at Fort Bliss, Tex. at the head of a contingent deployed as a result of an attack on government forces in Ciudad Juarez, Mexico by 1,600 men under the Mexican revolutionary Pancho Villa. Stray fire had killed an American soldier and a civilian across the river in Texas. Some 3,600 U.S. troops moved across the border and dispersed the Villistas before returning to the United States. By mid-September there were 104 officers, 491 enlisted men and 67 airplanes from the Eighth, Ninth, Eleventh, Ninetieth and Ninety-sixth Aero Squadrons deployed at Fort Bliss.

1919 June 21 The first London Aerial Derby held since the end of World War I was won by British pilot Gerald Gatherwood flying an Airco D.H.4R powered by a 450-HP Napier Lion engine. Last held in May 1914, the race was run around a 189-mi. circuit of greater London, beginning and ending at Hendon airfield. Gatherwood completed the course at an average speed of 132.3 MPH. This was the first time a British aircraft had won the London Derby, and they were to win the next four annual races. The derby was discontinued in 1923 and replaced by the Beaumont Cup held in France on June 23, 1924.

1919 June 21 The U.S. Navy issued a directive that all its aircraft be henceforth painted in silver on fabric surfaces, the metal and wood areas to be left gray. It was a year before all navy aircraft had been repainted. Since Mar. 15, 1918, navy aircraft had been painted low-visibility gray, and before that some had been painted bright yellow to aid in recognizing the aircraft at a distance. The silver and gray scheme was to remain unchanged until further marking refinements were authorized in 1924.

1919 June 23 Two days after the German Navy scuttled its fleet at Scapa Flow, Scotland, technicians at the German Navy airship bases Nordholz and Wittmundhaven destroyed seven front-line airships, almost all that remained of Germany's once proud Zeppelin fleet. Those destroyed included the L 14, L 41, L 42, L 63 and L 65 at Nordholz and the L 52 and L 56 at Wittmundhaven. At Ahlhorn, Germany, the People's Soviet prevented destruction of the L 64 and L 71. The Zeppelins were destroyed by removing supports beneath their hulls and slackening the suspension cables so that they collapsed under their own weight.

1919 June 25 The first all-metal passenger aircraft, the Junkers F.13 (at first designated J.13), made its first flight. Four passengers could be seated in an enclosed cabin while the crew of two sat ahead of them in an open cockpit. The aircraft was of very advanced design for its time, featuring a cantilever monoplane wing, and was capable of operating from a wheel or ski or float gear. Hugo Junkers had turned his design team to work on an all-metal transport aircraft on the very day the armistice took effect. Eventually more than 300 of the F.13s, were built serving a large number of European airlines. The last was retired from service with Varig (Brazil) in 1948.

1919 June 28 Germany signed the Treaty of Versailles, which stipulated the demobilization of the entire air service. Germany had to hand over 15,000 aircraft and more than 27,000 aero engines to the victorious powers, including examples of the Fokker D.VII, which was specifically requested by the treaty. Germany was prohibited from flying or operating military aircraft for its 100,000 strong German National Army (Reichswehr), which came into being March 6, 1919. The treaty prevented the development of civil aviation for six months from when it went into effect on Jan. 10, 1920. Germany was, however, allowed to operate some naval aircraft to assist with mine clearing.

1919 June 30   As a result of a recruiting drive to enlist more men, at the end of fiscal year 1919, U.S. Army Air Service personnel strength stood at 27,000, of which 5,500 were officers. This was up from a low of 20,000 earlier in the year.

1919 July 2   The British airship R.34 left East Fortune, Scotland at 1:42 P.M. to make the first airship crossing of the Atlantic. Commanded by Maj. G. H. Scott, RAF, it had a crew of 30 and had 70 tanks with 5,880 gal. of fuel in addition to 2,760 gal. of oil and 3 tons of water. The R.34 and its sister ship, the R.33, were 643 ft. long with a diameter of 78 ft. 9 in. and a volume of 1,950,000 cu. ft. Powered by five 250-HP Sunbeam Maori engines, it had a lift of 58,430 lb. in addition to fuel, oil and water and a top speed of 62 MPH. The R.34 arrived at the Roosevelt Flying Field, Mineola, N.Y. on July 6 after 108 hr. 12 min., the first east-west aerial crossing of the Atlantic.

1919 July 3   Designed and built by the Engineering Division of the U.S. Bureau of Aircraft Production, the first of four XB-1As (originally designated USXB-1A) made its first flight at McCook Field, Dayton, Ohio. It was basically a scaled-down Bristol F.2B with a wingspan of 39 ft. 4 in. and a length of 25 ft. 5 in. powered by a 300-HP Wright-Hispano H engine. Dayton-Wright got a contract for 40 XB-1As with 360-HP engines on June 28, 1920. The aircraft were to serve with the Twelfth Observation Squadron and the Thirteenth Attack Squadron in Texas.

1919 July 6   The first person to arrive in the United States by air from Europe was Englishman Flt. Lt. J. E. M. Pritchard, who arrived with the airship R.34, which had entered American skies after leaving Scotland on July 2 to cross the North Atlantic. To organize preparations for the capture and mooring of the large airship, Flt. Lt. Pritchard parachuted onto Long Island, thus becoming the first European to touch American soil without having been carried across by boat. He was, of course, followed within several hours by the complement of the airship itself, which moored at Roosevelt Field, Mineola, N.Y., before returning on July 10 in 75 hours' flying time.

1919 July 11   U.S. Navy appropriations for 1920 were passed providing funds for the modest expansion of naval aviation. Apart from funding an aircraft carrier to be named *Langley* (converted from the collier *Jupiter*) and two seaplane tenders, the navy was to buy two airships, one of which would come from Britain. Designated ZR-2 (*Shenandoah*), it was originally identified by the British as the R.38.

1919 July 13   The British airship R.34 completed the first two-way crossing of the Atlantic and established a new airship distance record of 6,330 mi. when it returned to England after a flight to America that began July 2. The R.34 left New York on July 10 and landed at Pulham, Norfolk little more than 75 hr. later after a trouble-free flight. The only event of note was that a gondola broke loose on the second day out.

1919 July 14   The Fiat B.R. light bomber made the first nonstop flight between Rome, Italy, and Paris, France. The initials stood for Bombardamento Rosatelli; the airplane had been designed toward the end of World War I by Fiat's Ing. Celestino Rosatelli. The Fiat B.R. series would gain prominence in the 1930s and see operational duty in all Europe's wars over the next 25 years.

1919 July 21   The N. V. Nederlandse Vliegtuigenfabriek was set up in Amsterdam, Holland as a holding company for Anthony Fokker's German interests, which effectively provided a legal channel for him to move his assets to his home country. His factory was built at Veere, Zeeland, and after a visit to Holland in early 1919, Fokker convinced the Dutch government to buy vast stocks of his airplanes and engines from the German factory for 5.5 million Dutch florins to finance his new venture. Managers at the German factory hid 220 airplanes and 400 engines, which were shipped to neutral Holland behind the Allies' back using 350 freight cars.

1919 July 24   U.S. Army Lt. Col. Rutherford L. Hartz and Lt. Ernest E. Harmon, plus mechanics Jack Harding and Jerry Dobias, began a flight from Bolling Field, Washington, D.C. around the periphery of the continental United States in a Martin MS-1 bomber. Only 10 MB-1s had been ordered from Martin; the first seven were completed as standard machines, and the last three were experimental. The eighth had special long-range tanks, giving it a range of 1,500 mi. versus the 390 mi. of the standard airplane. In all, the 108-day circuit of the United States logged 9,823 mi. before it ended on November 9 having logged a flying time of 114 hr. 25 min.

1919 July 30   Eight people were carried to a height of 20,013 ft. in the open cockpit of an A.E.G. G.V twin engine biplane. Designed as a bomber the A.E.G. G.V was too late to see service use and some were employed on the Deutsche Luft-Reederei (DLR) earlier in the year, still with their camouflage and markings. Powered by two 260-HP Mercedes D.IVa in-line engines, the G.V had a wingspan of 89.5 ft., a length of 35 ft. 5 in. and a loaded weight of 10,141 lb. A compartment for six passengers was situated immediately behind a partly enclosed cockpit for two pilots, forward of which was a baggage hold in the nose section.

1919 July 31   An extraordinary-looking German flying boat designed by Claudius Dornier made its first flight prior to service trials for the Swiss airline Ad Astra Aero. Known as the Gs I, it was an all-metal parasol monoplane with a wingspan of 68 ft. 11 in. and two tandem-mounted 260-HP Maybach Mb IVa water-cooled engines above the center section. The hull was shallow and supported twin fins and rudders aft with a bulbous section forward and a cabin for six passengers. The pilot sat in an open cockpit. Taken on a publicity tour of Holland and Sweden, the Allied Control Commission ordered it destroyed, and it was broken up on April 25, 1920.

1919 August 7   Capt. Ernest C. Hoy became the first pilot to fly over the Canadian Rockies when he carried mail from Vancouver, British Columbia to Calgary, Alberta in a Curtiss JN-4 biplane. Flying more than 400 mi. across wild and inhospitable terrain, he fought hard to control his biplane against the high winds and gusts flowing through the gorges and between the mountains that his airplane was unable to climb above.

1919 August 19   A Curtiss 18-T flown by Curtiss test pilot Roland Rholfs established a new world speed record of 163 MPH carrying a load of 1,076 lb. The 18-T Wasp had been ordered as a triplane fighter in March, 1918, its companion being the 18-B Hornet biplane; both were powered by a 400-HP engine designed by Charles Kirkham. Therein lay the secret for the Wasp's performance, and the type was frequently referred to as the Curtiss-Kirkham. The engine designed formed the basis for the later Curtiss D-12. The triplane had a wingspan of 31 ft. 10 in., a length of 23 ft. 4 in., a height of 9 ft. 11 in. and a gross weight of 3,050 lb.

1919 August 20   The first passenger airship for the post-war German DELAG line, the Zeppelin LZ 120 *Bodensee* took to the air for the first time. First of two new airships to fly, the *Bodensee* was 429 ft. long and 61 ft. 4 in. in diameter with a volume of 725,713 cu. ft. *Bodensee* was powered by four 260-HP Maybach engines and had a useful load of 22,045 lb. and a top speed of 81 MPH. Scheduled passenger flights began August 24 between Friedrichshafen and Berlin but ended December 1, having carried 2,400 passengers and almost 30 tons of cargo on 103 flights, when LZ 120 was seized by the Allied Control Commission and given to the Italians. It went to Ciampino on July 3, 1921, from where it served as the *Esperia* for several years on long-range trips.

1919 August 25   Laws governing civil aviation entered into force under instruments signed by the major nations during a meeting at The Hague chaired by Sir Sefton Brancker. From this date on, non-military airplanes could fly between countries and enter the air space of others under agreed legislation and rules. This was the first opportunity afforded entrepreneurs and airplane builders, some of whom like George Holt Thomas and his Aircraft Transport and Travel Ltd., formed in 1916, had been waiting years to give people safe and reliable air transport.

1919 August 25   Aircraft Transport and Travel Ltd., the British civilian air passenger company set up by George Holt Thomas, began the first daily commercial airline flight between London and Paris when a D.H.16 (G-EACT) piloted by Maj. C. Patterson carried four passengers from Hownslow to Le Bourget. It had been preceded by a D.H.4 carrying a journalist, some newspapers, pots of cream and several brace of grouse that put down at Le Bourget at 11:40 A.M. and was back at Hownslow just before 1:00 P.M. Frederick Handley Page had sent an 0/400 from Cricklewood, near London, landing at Le Bourget at 9:15 A.M. as advance guard of a scheduled service he planned to run beginning September 2.

1919 August 28   The International Air Traffic Association (IATA) was formed by agreement between airlines from Britain, Denmark, Germany, Holland, Norway and Sweden. The IATA agreement signed by all parties at The Hague, blossomed into a trade association for airlines of many countries around the world. Its name was later changed to the International Air Transport Association. The organization of IATA had been formally agreed August 25 during the meeting at The Hague chaired by Sir Sefton Brancker.

1919 September 10   The third Schneider Trophy seaplane contest—the first since 1914—was held at Bournemouth, England, but poor weather and bad planning led to confusion and the event was declared void. The contest was to run over 10 laps of a 23-mi. course off Bournemouth, but when the winner, Guido Janello of Italy, was accused by the British of not going around every marker in his Savoia S.13, he was disqualified. The decision was reversed by the Royal Aero Club on September 22 but declared void by the Fédération Aéronautique Internationale on October 24, when they asked Italy to hold the 1920 event.

1919 September 19   Curtiss test pilot Roland Rholfs established a new world altitude record of 34,910 ft. flying A Curtiss 18-T. The record was made in the presence of officials from the Aero Club, with government observers and navy representatives on hand.

The attempt began with an ascent from Roosevelt Field, Mineola, N.Y. at 12:06 P.M. and lasted 1 hr. 48 min. The record was achieved with a standard 400-HP Curtiss K-12 engine. Rholfs had broken the French record on July 25.

1919 September 26   Tests began with 12 Kettering Bug flying bombs shipped to Carlstrom, Fla., where Lt. Col. B. J. Arnold was to evaluate their performance. In a series of 14 flights, four were successful, three flying a distance of almost two mi. On the last flight, which was successfully completed October 28, the Bug flew 16 mi. before engine failure brought it down. After reviewing the eight successes out of 36 attempts made between April 1917, and October 1919, the navy believed it was not a viable project, and work stopped. Meanwhile, tests continued with Sperry radio-controlled equipment.

1919 September 29   The Polish Air Force (Polskie Wojska Lotnicze) was formed under the command of Brig. Gen. Macewicz. It included the Kosciuszko Squadron of volunteer U.S. Army Air Service pilots incensed by Soviet Boshevik adventures, veterans of the conflict against the Germans and keen to fight for the Poles. The name came from the Polish patriot Thaddeus Kosciuszko, who fought in the American Revolution before leading his countrymen against Russian imperialism.

1919 September 30   The fifth civilian airline set up by a British organization after the war began operating a temporary service between London and Birmingham. Set up in 1917 by furniture-maker Samuel Waring, the British Aerial Transport Co. (B.A.T.) ran a Koolhoven F.K.26 for this route and for a regular service to Amsterdam that began October 7 carrying 600 lb. of cargo. Dutchman Frederick Koolhoven had been retained by Samuel Waring to set up the technical side of the company, and these flights between the two countries continued at periodic intervals until Koolhoven left B.A.T, in January 1920 and activities came to a halt.

1919 October 7   One of the more outstanding and long-lived international airlines of civil aviation history, KLM (which stands for Koninklijke Luchtvaart Maatschappij voor Nederland an Kolonien or Royal Dutch Airlines for the Netherlands and Colonies) was founded by a group of banking and business interests. Led by Albert Plesman, it began an Amsterdam-London service on May 17, 1920, using a D.H.16 chartered from the British airline Aerial Transport & Travel. In the 1920s, it became a favored operator of Fokker-designed and -built airliners, until the clear superiority of Douglas DC-2 and DC-3 types prevailed in the early 1930s. KLM closed all European flights on August 23, 1939, due to the worsening crisis prior to the German invasion of Poland.

1919 October 8   The First Transcontinental Reliability and Endurance Test from New York to San Francisco began, ending October 31 after it had been extended to include a return race. This air race, sponsored by the U.S. Army Air Service, required participants to cross the United States in a minimum of 22 stages, each stage limited to the distance achieved with only 2½ gal. of fuel on board. In reality, it required up to 40 stages and a mad dash at maximum speed. There were 74 entries, though only 63 reached the starting post. Best overall performance was from preacher Belvin Maynard, who completed the 5,400 mi. round trip in 9 days 4 hrs. 25 min. 12 sec. flying a D.H.4 named *Greyhound*. Five pilots flew ex-German Air Service Fokker D.VII fighters. In all, there were 54 accidents, and nine pilots were killed.

1919 October 11 The first meal service aboard an airliner in flight was provided by Handley Page Transport when the crew issued luncheon baskets in return for a payment of 3 shillings (now about 9 cents) on the London-Brussels Service. Handley Page had started the regular flight to Brussels on September 22, with mail service being added September 29. Eventually, these converted 0/400 bombers had the supreme luxury of an early Marconi airborne radio-telephone.

1919 October 14 The International Air Convention met and signed agreements related to the marking for civilian airplanes, a set of standards based on the British air navigation rules published in London on May 1, 1919. Out of 13 nations that met, only the United States and Japan abstained because they were not yet in a position to agree to the standards and protocols. They did join the agreement later, participating in the first formal, international arrangement for the movement of airplanes from one country to another.

1919 October 21 The first attempt to fly between England and Australia began when Capt. G. C. Mathews and Sgt. T. Kay in a Sopwith Wallaby (G-EAKS) powered by a 374-HP Rolls Royce Eagle VIII left Hownslow at 11:44 A.M. The first part of the flight to Austria, proceeded uneventfully; from then on, their journey was anything but peaceful. Held prisoner in Yugoslavia, they were later snowbound in Belgrade. They cracked a cylinder at Istanbul and were held on the ground by torrential rain at Aleppo, Syria. Finally they crashed at Grokgak on the island of Bali, then part of the Dutch East Indies, on April 17, 1920, almost six months after they left London, and within a thousand miles of their goal.

1919 October 31 The progress of flying and public use of air transport was reflected in figures covering the first six months of authorized post-war civil aviation in Britain. In that period, 4,000 hr. of flying had been logged, during which 52,000 passengers had been carried; 374 pilots and 258 ground engineers had been licensed; and 241 planes had been given certificates of airworthiness. Only 10 people had been injured and two killed in the same period. There were 92 airfields licensed for civilian flying, and 10 major cities had begun negotiations for airfields.

1919 October The Fokker F.II enclosed cabin, cantilever, monoplane transport aircraft make its first flight at Schwerin with Adolph Parge at the controls. Without military orders, Fokker was forced to turn to commercial airplanes and with the F.II began a line of high-wing monoplane transport aircraft that was to characterize the marque for 20 years. The F.II was powered by a 185-HP BMW providing a top speed of 93 MPH. It had a wingspan of 56.7 ft. and a length of 33.9 ft. with a maximum weight of 4,180 lb.

1919 October The first Vickers Viking biplane amphibian made its first flight, inaugurating a periodic excursion by this British manufacturer into maritime aviation. The Viking evolved into the Vulture and the Vanellus, all three carrying the lower wing on the upper fuselage with biplane tail surfaces and a pusher engine. The Viking was a modest success and saw service in many parts of the world, including a London to Paris service that began on the Thames River and ended on the Seine River just 2½ hrs. later—a better time than the journey between city centers takes today!

1919 November 10 The first airmail service contracted in Britain began between London and Paris, following an award of the franchise to Air Transport & Travel. The charge was 2 shillings

6 pence, of which 2 shillings went to AT&T. It was a bad time to begin the service as the public was not taken with the novelty and there was little advantage in time over conventional delivery routes. Moreover, poor winter weather hampered flying, and the service was unable to demonstrate regularity. Emergency landing fields were identified every 20 mi. with four on the English coast and five on the French side of the English Channel. In southern England, railway stations at Redhill, Tonbridge, Ashford and Edenbridge had their names painted on the roofs for identification.

1919 November 12 Responding to a prize offered by the Australian government for the first Australian crew to fly between England and Australia in a continuous series of stages totaling less than 30 days, brothers Capt. Ross Smith and Lt. Keith McPherson Smith, with Sgts. W. H. Shiers and J. M. Bennett, left Hownslow, near London, at 9:10 A.M. Planning to break the journey into 24 stages, their Vickers Vimy (G-EAOU) carried 619 gal. of fuel, 48 gal. of oil and 12 gal. of water, with 800 lb. of spares, tools and equipment. With crew aboard, this gave a gross weight of 13,000 lb., about 500 lb. lighter than the Vimy used by Alcock and Brown to cross the Atlantic in June.

1919 November 14 A Handley Page V/1500 took off from Mitchel Field, Mineola, N.Y. at 7:00 A.M. to carry 1,000 lb. of parcels to Chicago for the American Express Co. The giant airplane landed on a racecourse at Cleveland, Ohio in the mistaken belief it was the Martin factory where arrangements had been made to refuel. The wing tips were sheared off during the landing and the parcels continued by rail. The V/1500 was in the United States trying for the trans-Atlantic record and when Alcock and Brown made their successful flight, was diverted to commercial demonstrations.

1919 November 16 Capt. H. N. Wrigley and Lt. A. W. Murphy of the Royal Australian Air Force became the first aviators to fly across Australia when they flew a B.E.2e from Melbourne, New South Wales to Darwin in the Northern Territory, a journey of almost 2,000 mi. in an airplane with a design range of less than 300 mi. Wrigley and Murphy made the trip specifically to prepare to welcome Australian aviators Capt. Ross Smith and Lt. Keith Smith flying to Port Darwin from London.

1919 November 21 Conversion of the collier *Jupiter* as a U.S. Navy "fly-on/fly-off" aircraft carrier was modified to include provision for stowage of airplanes and special facilities for the repair of airplane damage or mechanical breakdown. In addition, catapults were to be included on both the fore and aft decks. The *Jupiter* would have two folding smoke stacks, no islands protruding above the deck line but a bridge immediately below the deck and behind two forward-firing, 5-in guns. The original conversion was finished July 5, 1919.

1919 November 29 In what was to be the first air route linking French West Africa to Europe, two Levy GL40 seaplanes took off from St. Raphael, France, piloted by Lt. Comdr. Lefranc and Sub. Lt. Montrelay. The GL40 had been designed by a company formed in 1915 by the French banker Léon-Georges Levy. The GL40, their first airplane, was powered by a single 300-HP Renault 12 Fe engine. The GL40 flown by Sub. Lt. Montrelay was forced to land on the water off Morocco. Lt. Lefranc pressed on and reached Dakar (now the capital of Senegal) on January 25, 1920.

1919 December 1 The DELAG airship line's sole Zeppelin, the LZ 120 *Bodensee,* was laid up for the winter due to oil shortages in Germany. Since operations began August 24, the *Bodensee*

had carried 4,050 people on 103 trips between the Zeppelin facility at Staaken near Berlin and Friedrichshafen, making each one-way journey of 376 mi. in a single day. In 1921, the Allied Control Commission demanded that Germany hand over the *Bodensee* and its sister ship the *Nordstern,* which was being built for northern routes. The *Bodensee* was handed over to the Italian army, which renamed it *Esperia,* and the *Nordstern* was handed to the French.

1919 December 1   The Wright-Martin Corp. was liquidated and its New Brunswick, N.J. plant sold to the Mack Truck Co. What was left was reorganized into the Wright Aeronautical Corp. and production carried out from a small plant at Paterson, N.J. Wright-Martin had been formed in September 1916 when the Wright Co. merged with the Glenn L. Martin Co. Although Glenn Martin withdrew a year later, during the war Wright-Martin built 5,816 Hispano-Suiza engines and about 50 airplanes. The company would become part of the Curtiss-Wright Corp. in 1929.

1919 December 2   First in a line of purpose-built Handley Page airliners based on experience with converted 0/400 and V/1500 bombers, the W.8 made its first flight for 20 minutes with 20-year-old test pilot Robert Bager at the controls. The W.8 was powered by two 450-HP Napier Lion engines and could carry 16 passengers 500 mi. at 90 MPH, although the Air Ministry insisted that to lighten the load and increase the safety margin on the journey for safety only 12 seats should be fitted. The W.8 could reach 18,000 ft. It had cane seats adjacent to circular windows with their own curtains, wall-to-wall carpets, electric candelabra and a toilet.

1919 December 10   At 3:00 A.M. local time, Capts. Ross Smith and Keith Smith arrived at Port Darwin, Australia, a distance of 11,340 mi. from Hownslow after flying 135 hr. 55 min. at an average speed of 83 MPH. They won the £A10,000 prize for being the first Australians to fly directly between Great Britain and Australia. Their route took them via Lyons, Pisa, Cairo, Damascus, Ramaadie, Basra, Karachi, Delhi, Allahabad, Akyab, Rangoon (Yangon), Bangkok, Singora, Singapore, Sourabaya and Bima. An 11-stage celebration flight from Darwin to Melbourne began at 10:23 A.M. on December 13 and ended February 25, where, after 14,350 miles. in 188 hr. 20 min. flying time, their Vickers Vimy was handed over to Australia. It resides today on display at the Adelaide airport, where it arrived March 23, 1920.

1919 December 18   The U.S. Joint Army and Navy Board recommended a division of responsibilities for army and navy aviation based upon earlier analysis by the aeronautical board. The board had suggested to the general staff that army airplanes should conduct offensive and defensive operations with army units, leaving the navy to operate coastal patrol, reconnaissance and convoy protection. The joint board, however, stated that the army should command all operations where the navy was faced with overwhelming superiority of force in a conflict and that the navy should command all army (and aviation) elements if it held the advantage. War Secretary Newton D. Baker and Navy Secretary Josephus Daniels approved the scheme.

1919 December 19   The first Paris Aeronautical Exposition to take place since World War I opened with many European companies displaying their airplanes and aeronautical products. Although almost all of the airplanes on display were derived from World War I types, some, such as the British Westland Limousine, were specially designed as enclosed transport biplanes for small numbers of passengers. With massive cutbacks in aviation subsidies from governments across Europe, there were too many

products and too few customers. The exposition made this point self-evident.

1919   During the year, the U.S. Navy issued procurement orders for three D-class airships from Goodyear and two from Goodrich, each with a length of 198 ft. and a volume of 189,000 cu. ft. Goodyear also built two commercial airships which were subsequently purchased by the navy. One, an E-series airship, was powered by a single 150-HP Thomas engine and carried two crew members, while the F-series airship was powered by a 120-HP Union engine and carried a crew of three. The commercial airships each had a length of 162 ft. and a volume of 95,000 cu. ft. Goodyear quickly established, and was to maintain, a monopoly on nonrigid airship production for the U.S. Navy.

1920 January 20   The FAI announced the recommencement of ratifying official airplane records, which had been suspended during the 1914–18 war. Examination of anomalies brought a change in rules for speed record attempts. Rather than taking speed across a fixed distance in one direction, two runs in each direction would have to be made in the future. This would eliminate bias due to winds and by averaging speed across a 1-km (3,281 ft.) distance would produce a better and more accurate indication of an aircraft's actual capability.

1920 January 24   The first contender for a Cairo-Cape Town challenge issued by the *Daily Mail*—£10,000 for the first to carry out the flight successfully—got away from Brooklands, England at 11:30 A.M. Carrying Capts. F. C. G. Broome and S. Cockerell, Sgt. Maj. J. Wyatt and C. Corby, the prototype Vickers Vimy (G-EAAV) was powered by two 350-HP Eagle VII engines. The *Times* newspaper had sponsored the entry under Lord Northcliffe and sent along an observer, Dr. P. Chalmers Mitchell. For four weeks, the Vimy Commercial flew south before crashing in Tanganyika on February 27. No one was hurt.

1920 January 24   The French aviator Maj. Joseph Vuilleman began a pioneering flight between Paris, France and Dakar, Senegal via Algiers and Timbuktu. After more than a year of preparation, during which gasoline and spare parts had been prepositioned along the route, five aircraft left Paris, but only three reached Algeria. Maj. Vuilleman and his passenger Lt. Challus, flying a Breguet XVI Bn 2 were the only ones to reach Dakar, arriving on March 31. In 1938 the then-Gen. Vuilleman became chief of the French air force.

1920 January   In an attempt to put down Mohammed bin Abdullah, a mullah who had proclaimed himself the divine Mahdi and set about raiding pro-British tribes in British Somaliland (now northern Somalia), the RAF dispatched a squadron of D.H.9 bombers commanded by Gp. Capt. R. Gordon with wing Comdr. Frederick Bowhill. Winston Churchill arranged the operation through Sir Hugh Trenchard, and within days the "Mad Mullah," as the British called him, had been driven out of British Somaliland into Ethiopia, where he died. This "aerial policing" job did much to influence British policy on the use of airplanes versus ground forces.

1920 January   The first passenger transport flights were set up in Russia using a few of the giant Sikorsky Ilya Muromets bombers left over from the war. The two routes opened went from Sarapyl to Yekaterinburg and from Moscow to Kharkov. Only the year before, Prof. Nikolai Zhukovski had proposed the creation of a large transport airplane for the vast Russian hinterland. Work started on a giant triplane under the control of the Commission for Heavy

Aircraft (Kommissiya po Tiayeloi Aviatsia), but it was not to appear for two years.

1920 February 4   Aiming to take the £10,000 *Daily Mail* prize for the first crew to fly an airplane from Cairo to Cape Town, Wing Comdr. Pierre van Ryneveld, Flt. Lt. C. J. Quinton Brand, Flt. Sgt. E. F. Newman and W. F. Sherratt left Brooklands, England at 7:30 A.M. on the first leg of the journey in Vickers Vimy G-UABA. Provided by the South African government and using a South African registration, the Vimy, named *Silver Train,* reached Turin, Italy during the afternoon and from there flew nonstop across the Mediterranean to Sollum, reaching Cairo by the evening of February 8.

1920 February 5   The Royal Air Force College was opened at Cranwell, in Lincolnshire. The college was set up to train young RAF officers for the peacetime role of policing the far-flung empire and for creating the nucleus of a national air defense force.

1920 February 7   Piloting a Nieuport-Delage 29V, French aviator Sadi Lacointe became the first pilot to set a new FAI world speed record after World War I. He reached a measured speed of 275.862 km/hr. (171.141 MPH) along a 1 km (3,280 ft.) course. The Nieuport-Delage 29V had been designed in 1918 and was powered by a single 280-HP Hispano-Suiza V8 in-line engine. The biplane had a wingspan of 19 ft. 10 in. a length of 20 ft. 5 in. and a gross weight of 1,838 lb. The basic aircraft had been tested prior to the end of hostilities but failed to enter operational service before the end of the war.

1920 February 10   Carrying the same crewmembers that flew from Booklands, England on February 4 on the first leg of the Cairo-Cape Town flight attempt, the South African Vickers Vimy G-UABA left Cairo at 1:36 P.M. They were hoping to reach Khartoum, 1,000 mi. south, but 530 mi. out they crash-landed at Korosko, Egypt among boulders. The two engines were transferred to a British Vimy of the RAF, and a second attempt began from Heliopolis at 6:45 A.M. February 22. The South African government offered a D.H.9 after the RAF crashed at Bulawayo (in Zimbabwe) March 6, and 13 days later it left Bulawayo. It arrived at Wynberg Aerodrome, Cape Town at 4:40 P.M. March 20, the crew having flown 7,500 mi. in 4 days 13 hr. 30 min. of flying time.

1920 March 1   The National Advisory Committee for Aeronautics spurred development of a new civil aviation policy in the United States when it recommended competitions to stimulate private development for air transport and formation of a Bureau of Aeronautics in the Commerce Department. NACA also wanted more money for army and navy aviation and urged expansion of research facilities, including its own at the Langley Memorial Aeronautical Laboratory. Moreover, it urged the use of air links for delivery of the mail.

1920 March 1   In efforts to reestablish German military aviation, several special offices were set up by Gen. Hans von Seeckt in the Troop Office (Truppenamt). Operating under a code name, the Air Organization and Training Office (commanded by Capt. Helmut Wilberg) would collect as much information as it could on military aviation. The T3, or Foreign Armies Department, was to collect and file intelligence information about foreign air forces and their relative strength. The development of aeronautical technology in other countries would be studied by the Air Technical Office, and the Air Armament Economics Office would examine foreign air industries.

1920 March 11   The new British under-secretary of state for air, Maj. H. C. Tryon, announced a government budget for aviation in 1920–21 of less than £15 million plus £8 million on war debts for canceled contracts. It would necessitate, he said, a cut in RAF personnel from the present 182,000 to about 28,000 during the coming year, from a peak of almost 300,000 at the end of the war. The Women's Royal Air Force was being disbanded. The former under-secretary for air, Maj. Gen. J. E. B. Seely, believed that "the air industry in this country is dying; it is withering away. . . .''

1920 March 15   Established in Britain to buy a stock of idled aircraft left over from the war, the Aircraft Disposal Co. Ltd. took over 10,000 airplanes, thousands of engines and hundreds of thousands of items of ancillary equipment and components worth almost £6 million. The company was a syndicate operating through the British airplane-maker Handley Page, whose aim was to bring all airplanes and equipment up to standard for sale throughout the world. It paid £1 million for the lot and would pay the government half of all profits on sales. It was one of the biggest aviation auctions of all time.

1920 March 23   To avoid excess profit taxes imposed for having been extraordinarily successful in building airplanes for the war effort, the British and Colonial Aeroplane Co. was dissolved, its creditors paid in full and its assets transferred to the Bristol Aeroplane Co. Ltd. Unlike many of its less astute contemporaries, the board always sought ways around the law to stay in business and to avoid draconian penalties from a government frantic to claw back additional revenue for a virtually bankrupt nation.

1920 March 29   The French airline, Cie des Grands Express Aériens (CGEA), began operation of the Farman F.60 Goliath on its regular service between Le Bourget, just outside Paris, and Croydon, near London. The F.60 was designed by Farman Bros. at the end of World War I as a two-seat night bomber. With a wingspan of 86 ft. 10 in., a length of 47 ft. and a gross weight of 12,786 lb. the F.60 powered by two 260-HP Salmson CM.9 radial engines mounted in the lower wing. Several variants were developed, and the type played a central role in the development of European air transport through the 1920s.

1920 March 29   Located about 10 mi. due south of the City of London, England, Waddon Airport at Croydon was used for the first time as London's airport. Until this date, Hownslow had been considered the capital's main airport. Situated 12 mi. west of the city Hownslow would again become London's prime army airport (albeit briefly) after World War II when Heathrow replaced Croydon.

1920 March   The uncertain state of postwar aviation industries led to many failures and bankrupt companies. Wishing to use its manufacturing and production equipment for car bodies and general engineering work, the Birmingham Small Arms Co. Ltd. (BSA) acquired control of the British airplane manufacturer Airco. Airco's Founder Sir George Holt Thomas reflected that there was no prospect of annual orders of £100,000, the sum needed to keep the aviation side together each year and resigned from chairmanship of the company.

1920 April 23   The French airline Cie Franco Roumaine de Navigation Aérienne was formed to open routes to eastern Europe. A route from Paris to Strasbourg began operations September 20, continuing to Prague in October and on to Warsaw in mid-1921. Flights from Paris to Budapest were running via Strasbourg, Prague and Vienna by May 1922, and the leg from Budapest to Bucharest was added in September. The final section to Istanbul began operating October 3, 1922. Flights up to 1923 used single engine airplanes, but three-engine Caudron C.61s were introduced between Strasbourg and Paris on September 2.

1920 April 25 The Kosciuszko Squadron, six American veterans of the U.S. Army Air Service serving as volunteer pilots with Polish armed forces, attacked Bolshevik cavalry and supply trains as the Polish Army cut deep into the Ukraine to establish a Russo-Polish border that would give Poland areas it traditionally claimed. Cedric Fauntleroy was in charge of four air units of the nascent Polish air arm and helped support the army's drive in capturing the Russian city of Kiev. An armistice was signed by the Russians on October 12, 1920 and the squadron disbanded after the Treaty of Riga in May 1921.

1920 April 30 The British shipping line S. Instone & Co. took over their first Vickers-built Vimy Commercial, developed from the famous Vimy bomber. The company recognized the impact aviation would have on general transport and travel and chose a most popular adaptation of the World War I airplane. Vimy Commercial registered G-EASI was the 41st of this type ordered, following an order for 40 from China, most of which remained in crates after delivery. Named *City of London,* G-EASI served Instone for five years and by April 1924, had flown 108,000 miles before it was absorbed by Imperial Airways and scrapped in 1926.

1920 May 26 In a remarkable feat of aerobatic nonsense, the French pilot Fronval flew 1,111 consecutive loops in one flight in a Morane-Saulnier Type A1, registration F-ABAO. The A1 had been developed toward the end of World War I as a high-performance monoplane. One version had a recorded top speed of 134 MPH, which was exceptionally high for its time. Ex-World War I fighter pilot and air ace Charles Nungesser flew one on aerobatic displays around France with registration marking F-NUNG.

1920 May 28 The first Lewis & Vought VE-7 (Vought Experimental No. 7) was delivered to the U.S. Navy. Designed during late 1917, the first VE-7 flew February 12, 1918. Orders for the VE-7 totaled 1,014, 14 of which were to be built by Vought, the rest in equal numbers by the Springfield Aircraft Corp. and the Sturtevant Aeroplane Co. When the war ended, all non-Vought orders were canceled, but in a change of heart the navy, much impressed with the VE-7 ordered a further 60 from Vought and an additional 69 from the Naval Aircraft Factory. Never again was the U.S. Navy without a Vought-designed aircraft in the inventory.

1920 June 4 The U.S. Army Reorganization Bill was passed by Congress, authorizing an army air arm with 1,516 officers and 16,000 men. This dashed the hopes of campaigners like Foulois and Mitchell for an independent military air arm on the lines of Britain's RAF. Immediately after the armistice, 13,000 airplanes and 40,000 aero engines had been canceled, leaving 2,000 airplanes and fewer than 30,000 engines on order. By the end of the month, there were only 155 regular officers and 8,428 men still serving in the air service, a total reduction of more than 180,000 men and $300 million worth of orders in less than 18 months.

1920 June 7 The U.S. Army ordered 20 GAX (Ground Attack Experimental) triplanes from Boeing as the Model 10, an order later reduced to 10 before the first was delivered in May 1921.

Designed by I. M. Laddon at the Engineering Division, McCook Field, and originally known as the GA-1, the GAX was a twin-engined triplane with gunners' positions in the front of each pusher engine nacelle mounted on the center wing. It had a span of 65.5 ft. and a length of 33 ft. 7 in. with a gross weight of 9,740 lb. and a range of 160 mi. With two 435-HP Liberty pusher engines, it was the only triplane to see service with the U.S. Army air forces.

1920 June 9 King George V opened the Imperial War Museum in London. Its large range of aeronautical exhibits of wartime aircraft included many from the Royal Flying Corps, the Royal Naval Air Service and the RAF as well as captured German airplanes such as the Gotha bomber and the metal Junkers monoplane. There was even a Norman-Thompson flying boat floating on an artificial pond. The museum did much to rally awareness of aviation in war and its importance in the recent conflict.

1920 June 11 A 5-ft. atmospheric wind tunnel (AWT) was brought into operational use at the NACA Langley Memorial Aeronautical Laboratory in Virginia. Costing $38,000, it comprised a 5-ft. diameter, closed-throat test section with a maximum 89 MPH wind driven by a single fan powered by a 200-HP electric motor. Development had been authorized Oct. 6, 1917, to provide engineers firsthand experience with wind tunnels.

1920 June 22 Flying a Sopwith Pup fighter purchased from Britain, Lt. T. Kuwahara became the first Japanese pilot to successfully take off from the modified decking of a Japanese ship under way. A special ramp had been fitted to the foredeck of the seaplane tender *Wakamiya,* and the Pup was flown off into a head wind as the added speed of the ship provided a good supplementary flying speed for the difficult take-off. The Japanese were convinced that naval aviation was an important asset for their military capabilities.

1920 July 1 The first intra-African air service began flying passengers between Kinshasa and N'Gombé in what is now Zaire. The Belgian air service SNETA opened the Ligne Aérienne Roi Albert with a Lévy-Lepen flying boat powered by a 300-HP engine with capacity for two passengers and the pilot. Service was limited until a leg from N'Gombé to Lisala was added on March 3, 1921. Four months later, service extended in stages between Kinshasa and Kisangani, a total distance of 800 mi.

1920 July 1 The German Zeppelin L 71 arrived at Pulham, England, piloted by Capt. Heine and with 22 personnel on board. It had left Alhorn, Germany the previous day against a modest head wind and for most of the morning circled around Norwich, England before coming down at Pulham. Believing it could build airships for intercontinental transport throughout the British empire, Vickers wanted to buy the L 71 as a pattern for future developments. There was general consensus that airships held much promise for large-scale passenger work.

1920 July 3 The RAF held its first pageant at Hendon, site of so many famous prewar aviation meetings, races and flying schools. Conceived as a fund-raising event for the RAF Memorial Fund, it attracted 40,000 people who clogged roads for several miles around; even Minister for War and Air Winston Churchill was forced to abandon his car and walk in to the display. The pageant would become an annual event known as the RAF Display from 1925, including mock attacks, and set-piece reconstructions of events, and be a major recruiting tool for young, air-minded enthusiasts. The last event was held in 1937, and the display was absorbed into Empire Air Day events held around England.

1920 July 12   The first postwar International Aero Exhibition opened at Olympia, London with stands filled by all the British manufacturers trying to find markets for what was in reality a surfeit of products. The only design that showed a marked advance over the wood and canvas airplanes of World War I was the single-seat Short Swallow with a metal monocoque fuselage and metal covered wings.

1920 July 19   The first truly streamlined British airship, and the last planned during World War I, made its first flight from the Vickers plant at Barrow, Scotland. Designed by Barnes Wallis, who had been working for Vickers before the war began in 1914, the R.80 had a length of 534 ft., a diameter of 70 ft. and a volume of 1,250,000 cu. ft. Powered by four 230-HP Wolseley-Maybach motors, it had a top speed of 65 MPH and a useful load of 37,480 lb. American airship crews waiting to take over the R.38 designated by the U.S. Navy ZR-2, were trained on the R.80 before its last flight to Pulham, England on September 20, 1921.

1920 July 20   With $40,000 to build an airplane specially designed to fly across the United States nonstop, wealthy sportsman David R. Davis teamed with Donald W. Douglas to set up the Davis-Douglas Co. Using Davis' money, Douglas was to design the airplane from a room in the back of a barber shop on Pico Boulevard in Los Angeles. Born in April 1892, Douglas graduated from Annapolis in aeronautical engineering, attended MIT and then joined the Connecticut Aircraft Co. in 1915 before working as chief engineer for the Glenn Martin Co. where he designed the MB-1 and its transport and naval derivatives. In March 1920, he resigned from Martin and went to California, seeking an opportunity to set up his own business.

1920 July 25   Four U.S. Army Air Service D.H.4B biplanes took off from Mitchel Field, New York, on the first leg of the round-trip flight to Fort Davis on the Nome River, Alaska. Seeking to establish a direct route to the Far East, should the military necessity arise, Brig. Gen. William Mitchell had planned the route, which carried the planes across Lake Erie, Michigan, Wisconsin, Minnesota, North Dakota, Saskatchewan, Alberta, British Columbia, and Wrangell, Alaska. After 40 days and 4,502 mi. the airplanes landed at Fort Davis. They departed on August 31 and were back at Mitchel Field on October 20.

1920 July   The French operator Cie des Grands Express Aériens (CGEA) began using the Farman F.50P twin-engine, biplane, passenger-carrying version of the Type F.50-B.N.2 bomber designed at the end of World War I. The aircraft had an enclosed cabin section for four or five passengers aft of a two-seat open cockpit for the crew. The aircraft had a wingspan of 73 ft. 4 in., a length of 39 ft. 4 in. and a loaded weight of 6,856 lb. Powered by two 275-HP Lorraine-Dietrich 8Bd water-cooled engines, the F.50P operated on the Paris-London and Paris-Amsterdam routes without incident.

1920 August 3   The British government Civil Aircraft Competition began at Martlesham. Prizes totaling £64,000 were put up for winning entrants as a stimulus for the development of new and safer forms of commercial aviation for domestic and foreign markets. The competition had been announced August 14, 1919, and provided three categories: single-engine aircraft, twin-engine passenger airliners and amphibians and flying boats. Handley Page and Westland took the prize money for winning entries.

1920 August 18   The first of five Wittenman-Lewis unmanned flying bombs built for the U.S. Navy crashed after a flight of only 450 ft. On a second attempt in November, the unmanned airplane flew around and around in circles for 20 min. The third flight took place on April 25, 1921, but this, too, ended in failure after a mere two min. Ten flying bombs had been built by the Naval Aircraft Factory, Philadelphia, but the general lack of success resulted in cancellation of these efforts in 1922.

1920 September 3   The Martin MB-2 made its first test flight following a U.S. Army order for 20 placed in June. The MB-2 is essentially an MB-1 with large wings strengthened to lift more weight in weapons and fuel. Nacelles for the two 410-HP Liberty engines, the same as the MB-1, were lowered from a midwing position to the lower wing and four main wheels replaced by two wheels with mudguards. The MB-2 could lift a maximum bomb load of 3,000 lb. but a typical load would be 1,262 lb. allowing a range of 558 mi. Although its rated ceiling was 8,500 ft. fitted with a supercharger, one MB-2 reached a height of 25,600 ft. on December 8, 1921.

1920 September 8   The U.S. transcontinental airmail route was completed with the opening of the final Sacramento-Salt Lake City-Omaha stages. The first stages, Washington-Philadelphia-New York, had opened with Curtiss JN-4s on May 15, 1918. The next stage was opened between Chicago and Cleveland on May 15, 1919, followed by the New York-Cleveland run July 1 and the San Francisco-Sacramento stage July 31; direct New York-Chicago flights began in September 1919. The Chicago-Omaha stage opened May 15, 1920, leaving only the 1,650 mi. haul between Sacramento and Omaha.

1920 September 11   The Sopwith Aviation and Engineering Co. Ltd. went into voluntary liquidation and Tommy Sopwith sold his 2,000-acre estate, Horsley Towers, in Surrey, England. Management of the company had been so well conducted that it had almost £280,000 left after liabilities, but without orders the business could not continue. On November 15, the H. G. Hawker Engineering Co. Ltd. was set up with capital of 20,000 pounds and T. O. M. Sopwith, H. G. Hawker, F. Sigrist and V. W. Eyre as directors. The line would continue until Hawker Engineering became the founding company for Hawker Siddeley Aviation in 1974.

1920 September 14   The close proximity of domestic dwellings to the increasingly busy centers of commercial air activity created new problems for the populace typified by a complaint issued by residents in Kilburn, London. They reported Handley Page airliners flying so low over the chimney pots that propeller wash blew soot down the chimneys and onto the innocents sitting in their front parlors at tea, completely ruining the meal. At least one wag stretched credibility when he claimed it was no longer safe to stand up on the top deck of a tramcar for fear of being mowed down by whirling propellers!

1920 September 20   At the San Andrea Naval Air Station, Italy, the Schneider Trophy race was held with only one entrant turning up to fly the 20.04-mi. course. Nevertheless, Lt. Luigi Bologna in a Savoia S.12 seaplane powered by a 550-HP Ansaldo water-cooled engine flew around the course for 10 laps in 2 hr. 10 min. Four other Italian flying boats had entered the race, but they dropped out to technical problems, leaving Bologna to take the race unchallenged.

1920 September 25   Just three days before the Gordon Bennett Aviation Cup race, for which it had been specifically designed, the Dayton-Wright RB monoplane powered by a 250-HP Hall-Scott L-6a engine, put up a creditable performance at Étampes,

France by flying one lap of the 100-km (62 mi.) course at 165 MPH. Designed and built in America with the help of Orville Wright, the RB was built of plywood and balsa wood and had unusual features for the time, such as a manually retractable undercarriage, and enclosed cockpit and leading and trailing edge wing flaps. The RB had a wingspan of 21 ft. 2 in., a length of 22 ft. 8 in. and a gross weight of 1,800 lb. On race day, September 28, the RB had to retire with a jammed leading edge flap.

1920 September 28   The first Gordon Bennett Aviation Cup race held since 1913 was won by Sadi Lecointe at Etampes, France. Powered by a 320-HP Hispano-Suiza engine, the Nieuport 29V flown by Lecointe completed the 186.45-mile closed circuit at an average speed of 168.7 MPH. Bernard de Romanet came in second with a speed of 112.8 MPH. Under the rules laid down by race founder James Gordon Bennett, the annual contest would be won outright by the country that came in first on three consecutive races. Because France had won in 1912 and 1913, it retained the cup, and the Gordon Bennett races came to an end.

1920 September   The de Havilland Aircraft Co. Ltd. was formed in England by Geoffrey de Havilland. He left Airco after its airplane manufacturing business stopped when BSA took over control of the company in March 1920. Some money was put in by Holt Thomas, but de Havilland was director and chief designer. It was decided to concentrate on the civil market, which, although in a risky state, was likely to generate more orders than the government, with its steadily declining budgets for military aviation.

1920 October 1   The personal strength of the RAF had been reduced to a total force level of 26,664, comprising 2,802 officers and 23,862 men—less than 10% its wartime strength. The

British government had decided that a war in Europe was impossible for the next 10 years, and it examined the possibility of uniting army, navy, and air force procurement under a common defense executive. Air Marshall Sir Hugh Trenchard argued for a strong and independent RAF, citing the time needed to build strength and asserting that war could come without warning.

1920 October 7–17   The first trans-Canada proving flight began from Halifax, Nova Scotia and ended 10 days later in Vancouver—a distance of 3,265 mi. in a flying time of 45 hr. It began when Maj. B. D. Hobbs and Col. R. Leckie of the Canadian Air Force flew a Fairey seaplane to St. John River and then to Riviere du Loup in a HS2L flying boat. There they picked up an engineer named Heath and flew an F3 flying boat to Ottawa, where they collected Capt. G. O. Johnson and flew on to Winnipeg. From there, Capt. C. W. Cudamore flew to Calgary in a D.H.9A, where Capt. G. A. Thompson changed to a different D.H.9A and flew on to Vancouver.

1920 October 14   The first U.S. international airline service and the first regularly scheduled air service linking Seattle, Wash. with Victoria, British Columbia began, using a Boeing B-1 flying boat operated by Hubbard Air Services. Eddie Hubbard and William Boeing had set up the route during 1919, selecting the optimum course across Puget Sound for the 80-mi. flight to Canadian territory.

1920 October 14   The U.S. Navy commenced a series of bombing tests against disused ships to observe and measure the value of air power against naval forces at sea. Brig. Gen. William Mitchell campaigned as spokesman for the pro-bomber lobby who, having seen the impact of air warfare on the enemy in World War I, worried about the lack of enthusiasm in America for a

The French Nieuport Co. produced many scout designs that were purchased by the U.S. Army Air Service.

strong and capable air force. To determine the validity of Mitchell's assertions, attacks were launched against the obsolete battleship USS *Indiana* and continued through November 4 in Tangier Sound, Chesapeake Bay.

1920 October 20   French aeronaut Sadi Lecointe became the first man to officially break the 300 km/hr. speed barrier when he flew his Nieuport 29V(bis) for 1 km (3,280 ft.) at an FAI-ratified average speed of 302.529 km/hr. (178.98 MPH). His aircraft had been modified from the configuration in which he claimed the first FAI speed record after World War I, and it now had a 320-HP Hispano-Suiza 42 in-line engine. The aircraft also had a different wing, with a span of 19 ft. 8 in.; the plane's length of 20 ft. 4 in. and weight of 2,064 lb. was the same.

1920 October 30   The U.S. Marine Corps commandant approved a plan for organization of Marine aviation elements, which had been disbanded in February 1919 but were to be reinstated with provision for 1,020 personnel and permanent aviation bases at Quantico, Va., Parris Island, N.C., and San Diego. There were to be four squadrons with two flights each, but in 1921 there were only 43 pilots, down from 67 in 1920. Marine aviation was the only U.S. military service to experience combat between the two world wars: in Haiti from March 1919 through August 1934 and in Nicaragua from 1927 through 1933.

1920 November 4   The French pilot Bernard de Romanet increased the world air speed record to 192.01 MPH flying the Spad XXbis 6 which had evolved from the basic Spad XX first built as a two-seat biplane fighter in 1918. The Spad XX had a wingspan of 31 ft. 10 in., a length of 24 ft. and a gross weight of 2,888 lb. Powered by a 300-HP Hispano 8 Fbc engine, it was developed into several long-range versions that appeared during the closing months of 1919.

1920 November 16   The first Australian national airline was registered as the Queensland and Northern Territory Aerial Services Ltd. (Qantas) by Lts. Hudson Fysh and P. J. McGinnis. It was formed for a variety of air transport roles, including air taxi services between remote areas, fee-paying joy rides and regularly scheduled airline operations. Fysh and McGinnis had been commissioned by the Australian government in June 1919 to survey a route from Longreach, Queensland to Darwin, Northern Territory. The company's first headquarters were at Winton, Queensland, and its first chairman was Sir Fergus McMaster. The headquarters moved later to Longreach. The first scheduled operations began September 2, 1922, with flights between Charleville and Cloncurry, Queensland.

1920 November 24   A distinctly odd-looking flying boat, the Dornier Do.Cs II Delphin I made its first flight. Of all-metal construction, it had a thick wing attached to the top of the hull section. The hull tapered vertically upward at the nose to meet the 185-HP BMW IIIa water-cooled engine, which was mounted on top. Sponsons were attached each side of the lower hull, which was clear of the water aft of the mid-wing position. A cabin was provided for six people in the hull. Later versions incorporated a boat-like bow protruding forward of the engine position, and several aircraft of this type survived in use into the 1930s. A typical Delphin had a wingspan of 56 ft., a length of 39 ft. 4 in. and a loaded weight of 4,850 lb.

1920 November 25   Capt. Corliss S. Mosely of the U.S. Army Air Service won the first Pulitzer Trophy closed-circuit air race at Mitchel Field, Long Island, N.Y., flying a specially prepared and equipped Verville-Packard 600 biplane. The competition for the Pulitzer Trophy, set up by newspaper owners Ralph, Joseph Jr. and Herbert Pulitzer, was flown over a triangular course around the field. The controlled performance requirements for the contestants stipulated a maximum landing speed of 75 MPH indicative of a low stalling speed. This was not a particularly difficult requirement for the day but demonstrated control at low speed and superior technical performance was an important condition encouraged by the rules.

1920 December 12   The prototype Blériot-Spad 33 passenger aircraft made its first flight powered by a 230-HP Salmson Z.9 water-cooled radial engine. It would become one of the most popular French transport airplanes of the early 1920s and made routine flights between Paris and London beginning in 1921. Several developments of this type appeared during the decade with modifications and improvments culminating in the Spad 126. The Spad 33 had a wingspan of 38 ft. 3 in., a length of 29 ft. 9 in. and a loaded weight of 4,545 lb. with a maximum payload of 1,455 lb. A cabin for four passengers was provided between the wings, and the pilot sat behind in an open cockpit.

1920 December 14   The first fatalities on a regularly scheduled British airline service resulted from the crash of a Handley Page 0/11 (a converted 0/400 bomber) taking off from Cricklewood, England for Paris. R. Bager, the pilot, and two passengers were killed, but three passengers and the mechanic, J. H. Williams, got out. Concussed, Williams wandered off and, suffering loss of memory but obsessed with a commitment to get to Paris, took the Underground to Victoria Station, London, caught a train to Dover and from there went by boat to Calais and on to Paris where he was found in a dazed and thoroughly confused state!

1920 December 24   In hopes of acquiring a good light bomber and ground attack aircraft, the U.S. Army Air Service ordered the Gallaudet DB-1 metal monoplane bomber which appeared in December 1921. Designed as a light bomber, it was powered by a 700-HP Engineering Division W-1A water-cooled engine. It was grossly overweight and when it was observed the control system buckled the metal skin, only one of the two ordered was built. The bomber was inspired by the metal monoplanes from Europe, principally Junkers and Dornier.

1921 January 1   The British cabinet announced £60,000 in subsidies for British companies flying approved civil air transport routes, payment to be made every three months providing certain operating criteria had been met. For instance, payment of 25% of the gross revenue would be made only if within that period the airline had made two-way flights to its advertised destination on a minimum of 45 days. This was an attempt to help subsidize the low cash returns from air transport operations and keep alive the British civil aviation industry.

1921 January 17   A state commission was set up in Russia by order of Lenin and charged with responsibility for establishing civil aviation. This was later to result in the formation of the Chief Administration of the Civil Air Fleet (Glavvozdukhoflot). It began mail flights using Ilya Muromets aircraft on May 1, 1921. It was also decided that discussions would be held with foreign governments regarding cooperation with their respective civil air operations. This would later lead to the Soviet-German agreement whereby German pilots were trained in the Soviet Union.

1921 January 21   The first triple-triplane aircraft, and the first passenger-carrying aircraft designed to carry more than 100 people that actually got off the ground, was launched at Lake Maggiore, Italy. The Caproni Ca.60 had three sets of 98 ft. 5 in.

wings placed at intervals along the top of a 76 ft. long, boat-like hull. Powered by eight 400-HP Liberty engines, four in the forward mid-wing driving three tractor propellers and four in the rear midwing driving pushers, the Ca.60 was built to carry 150 people 410 mi. at 68 MPH. After flotation tests on March 4, a flight was attempted but ended in failure when the 55,000 lb. flying boat nosed into the lake.

1921 January 27   The British rigid airship R.34 was destroyed when it struck a fog-shrouded hill on the Yorkshire Wolds, knocking out one of four engines. More than 300 people helped man-handle the dirigible and moor it to the ground. Increasingly gusty winds bumped and scraped its hull, which eventually pushed one of the cars through the envelope and broke the nose off. This was a bad event for protagonists of airship travel on long, intercontinental routes.

1921 January 29   The Paris Agreement was reached, confirming a prohibition on all German civil aircraft manufacture for three months after the Inter-Allied Aviation Inspection Committee confirmed that Germany had handed over all aircraft and equipment demanded by the Treaty of Versailles. This confirmation was granted February 9, 1922, permitting civil aircraft construction to resume May 5, 1922. On April 24, 1922, a meeting of the Ambassadors' Conference would determine performance restrictions for nonmilitary German aircraft built after that date.

1921 January   Brig. Gen. William Mitchell testified before the U.S. House of Representatives' Appropriations Committee that air forces could ''sink any ship in existence today.'' He appealed for the opportunity to demonstrate this but was rebuffed by the secretary of the navy, who offered to stand, bare-headed, on the deck of any ship under attack in the sure belief that his life would not be in any danger. Mitchell was given his chance to bomb some redundant ships, but the secretary of the navy was not pressed to honor his offer!

1921 January   Believing Britain to be preeminent in naval aviation, the Japanese requested that a delegation from the United Kingdom visit them and lay the foundations for an expansion of Japan's nascent naval air arm. Although the French had been active in the area, the Japanese wanted British airplanes and ordered Avro 504s, F.5 flying boats and 50 Gloster Sparrowhawks.

1921 February 12   The U.S. Army Air Service established the first in an expanding series of airways—routes safely surveyed by the army for civilian and commercial users linking towns and cities by air—by leasing land between Washington and Dayton, Ohio to facilitate a stopover. When Gen. Mason M. Patrick became chief of the air service in October, he expanded the airways concept and developed a nationwide system of air stations and routes. The air service published a description of all airfields and facilities beginning March 1, 1923. Scheduled air service flights along the airway began in 1922 with a D.H.-4B4; in four years service had covered 1.2 million mi. on 671 scheduled flights carrying 1,200 passengers and 31 tons of freight.

1921 February 22   In an attempt to show the advantages of airmail over the railways, a demonstration high-speed run was staged across the United States when two pilots took off from New York heading for San Francisco and two pilots took off from San Francisco heading for New York. Planning to fly through the night, only one of the two westbound aircraft got as far as Chicago and then had to abandon the attempt due to bad weather. Of the two eastbound aircraft, one crashed in Nevada, killing the

pilot, but the second made it all the way to New York in a time of 33 hr. 20 min.

1921 February 24   The Davis-Douglas Cloudster made its first flight carrying Eric Springer and David Davis for 30 min. Built to fly nonstop across the continental United States, the Cloudster, having been designed in the back of a barber shop, had been built in the loft of the Koll Planing Mill in the center of Los Angeles. Powered by a single 400-HP Liberty engine, the Cloudster carried two fuel tanks with a combined capacity of 660 gal. and a 50 gal. oil tank; these provided a range of 2,800 mi. It had a wingspan of 55 ft. 11 in. and a length of 36 ft. 9 in. with a gross weight of 9,600 lb. The Cloudster never did make a trancontinental, nonstop flight.

1921 February 28   Faced with fierce competition from the continent, Handley Page and Instone Air Lines suspended services to Paris. On March 2, the secretary of state for air, Winston Churchill, set up a Cross-Channel Subsidies Committee under Lord Londonderry, which organized government aid to help private operators, and Handley Page and Winston resumed service on March 19. Ironically, it had been Churchill who emphasized in 1919 that British operators should not expect government subsidies, despite government help for European companies. When flights resumed, fares were lowered to match those of French operators, which were subsidized by the government, although the Air Ministry set a maximum of £88,200 on its damage liability.

1921 March 1   A measure of how fully and how quickly the British implemented the policy of using air power in a policing role was provided in the summary report of active squadrons of the RAF and their assignments. Of 28 fully equipped squadrons, six were in Egypt and Palestine, five in Iraq, eight in India, one in Germany, one at Malta and three in Ireland; three were operating with the navy; and one was on training course in England. Of the 28, no fewer than 21 were on policing duties abroad while four were in England.

1921 March 9   To save his company from collapse when partners diverted to automobiles and other engineering applications, Charles R. Fairey put the Fairey Aviation Co. Ltd. into voluntary liquidation and set up Fairey Aviation Ltd. with 100 pounds in 100 shares. Fairey had formed his first company in 1915 and gained a creditable reputation with several good seaplane and flying boat designs, including the Campania and the Fairey III series.

1921 March 17   The first U.S. Marine airmen to serve in the Pacific arrived on Guam with responsibility for supporting U.S. land and sea forces in the region. There, 10 pilots and 90 enlisted men operated seaplanes on reconnaissance duty as Flight L, Fourth Squadron, for 10 years. They were sent on temporary assignment to China in 1927 when civil war threatened American citizens in Shanghai, Peiping (now Beijing) and other large cities in China.

1921 March   The Curtiss CT-1 monoplane made its first flight and was powered by twin 350-HP Curtiss D-12 engines. Unusual for its time, the low-wing monoplane was designed as a revolutionary torpedo-plane with a span of 65 ft. a length of 52 ft. and a gross weight of 11,208 lb.; it's crew consisted of pilot, navigator and gunner. Twin fins and rudders and a biplane tail were carried on the ends of two, horizontal, tubular booms, each side converging at the tailplane. The CT-1 could carry one 1,446-lb. torpedo, but only one was built out of an order for nine because production was canceled by the navy.

1921 March   The British air estimates for 1921–22 announced in the House of Commons showed a modest increase over the preceding year. The government proposed to spend £16.9 million on aviation, an increase of £2 million over the current year, which would permit the addition of five extra squadrons. A small allocation had been made for a Territorial Air Force, which it was hoped could help supplement the full-time force while reducing general expenditure.

1921 April 1   The Australian Air Force was formed with a nucleus of 20 officers and 120 men. It was created out of the Australian Air Corps, which had been formed in 1919, which had in turn been based on the Australian Flying Corps founded in 1913. From August 13, 1921, it was known as the Royal Australian Air Force (RAAF). Not for some time would the RAAF gather strength to match the aspirations of its leaders. When war broke out with Germany in 1939, the RAAF had less than 250 airplanes and fewer then 3,500 personnel. As of 1992, it has 22,600 personnel and 270 aircraft.

1921 April 14   Continuing the evolving series of postwar, high-wing, passenger monoplanes that would bring so much renown to the company during the late 1920s, Fokker delivered the first of several F.III airliners to the Dutch airline KLM. Based on the F.II, it was a five-seater powered by a 230-HP Siddeley Puma engine. An interesting feature of its design was that the pilot sat on the port side of the engine rather than behind it.

1921 April 14   The Davis-Douglas Co. received its first military contract when the U.S. Navy ordered three single-seat DT-1 biplanes equipped with twin floats for use as a torpedo-bomber. It was designed in response to a technical specification issued on February 1 and was powered by a 400-HP Liberty engine. Put together in the Goodyear hangar at Los Angeles, the first one appeared in October. After the first plane, it was decided to develop a twin-seater, and deliveries of a production order for 66 DT-2s began in 1922. The last DT-2 retired from the navy in November 1928.

1921 April   The only H-series observation airship built for the U.S. Navy was completed by Goodyear and delivered along with the first of the J-series patrol airships. The H-1 was 95 ft. long with a volume of 35,000 cu. ft. and a single 50-HP Lawrence radial pusher engine. The H-1 had a relatively short life, being destroyed by fire on August 31, 1921. The J-1 was accepted by the navy. The J series were 196 ft. long with a volume of 210,000 cu. ft. The U.S. Army eventually obtained some J-series airships. Some were inflated with helium instead of hydrogen.

1921 May 6   A trade agreement was concluded between Germany and Russia under which economic and technical cooperation in military aviation could begin. A year later, the Rapallo Treaty was signed (April 16, 1922); among other items, this allowed for German aviators to be taught in the Soviet Union outside the restraints of the Versailles treaty. Gen. von Seeckt played a major role in this agreement, which also repealed war reparations and encouraged trade.

1921 June 8   The U.S. Army School of Aviation Medicine began tests with pressurized cabins of standard production airplanes to investigate the possibility of introducing this concept on aircraft. For tests, a D.H.4 was fitted with an enclosed cabin section for high altitude trials. An initial flight was carried out by Lt. Harold R. Harris at Wright Field, Ohio. Physiological data was sought to help medical evaluation of the effect on the body of pressurized atmospheres, and engineering information helped

technicians study the possibility of designing pressure cabins for production aircraft.

1921 June 8   The first Desert Air Mail flight from Cairo, Egypt to Baghdad, Iraq, was started by the British using D.H.9As of Nos. 30 and 47 Squadron, RAF. To define the route, a convoy drove between the two locations, leaving a trail that was followed from the air. When winds blew out the tracks, a large plow was dragged across the desert by a tractor that stopped every 15 to 30 mi. to prescribe a circle into which a pile of rocks was placed with a number indicating suitable landing spots. Thus marked, the track survived for several years, although restoration was needed at the end of 1922 and 1923. In this way, pilots navigated the 900 miles between Cairo and Baghdad.

1921 June 21   Bombing tests organized against ships in tests requested by Brig. Gen. William Mitchell began off the Virginia Capes. In the first test, an old German submarine, U-117, was sunk by 12 bombs dropped from three U.S. Navy Curtiss F-5L flying boats flying at 1,100 ft. Another attack on June 29 against the ex-U.S. battleship *Iowa* without a crew and controlled by radio signals from shore, began when the ship was located by radar within 1 hr. 57 min. in a 25,600 sq. mi. area. The flying boats dropped 80 dummy bombs and scored two direct hits. The navy participated along with the army and the marine corps in additional attacks on July 13, 18 and 20.

1921 June 29   The first aviation unit of the National Guard to get U.S. government approval was the 104th Observation Squadron of Maryland. Four more were to get federal sanction this year followed by two in 1922, four in 1923, three in 1924, one in 1925 and one in 1926. After World War I, the War Department had declined to organize special aviation squadrons in the National Guard, but so much interest was generated that it reversed its decision and allowed each guard division one aero squadron, a balloon company and a photographic section. To gain federal approval, each Guard aero squadron had to be inspected by the USAAS.

1921 June   The U.S. Army Air Service reported that in the first six months of this year, 69 men were killed and 27 badly injured in 330 crashes. Peacetime training casualties were more than 10% of the 900 pilots and observers on strength. This reflected the poor standard of equipment available to army aviators. Of the total inventory of airplanes, about 1,500 were the Curtiss NJ-4, 1,100 were the British-designed D.H.4 observation aircraft, less than 180 were S.E.5 scouts, and 12 were relatively "modern" Martin MB-2 bombers.

The total number of enlisted men in the U.S. Army Air Service was approximately 11,000, but Secretary of War John W. Weeks slimmed this to 10,300 in a new target ceiling for military aviation. In September 1921, the air service reached a record low of 7,160 enlisted men as many paid the government to release them from service (as they were entitled to do in peacetime). The total, however, increased to just over 9,500 by April 1922 as a result of a recruiting campaign that had resumed in the previous September. In June 1922, Congress reduced total U.S. Army authorization and gave aviation a limit of 8,500. It was to remain within a few hundred of that figure for the next four years, the number in June 1926 being 8,342.

1921 July 1   U.S. Army serial number designation was introduced and remains in use today. From this date, the serial number would bear the last two digits of the fiscal year in which the procurement was made, followed by the sequence in which the order was allocated. For instance, 22-1776 would indicate the

1,776th aircraft procured in 1922. Prior to this date, beginning 1909, army airplanes carried sequential numbers and reached 68592 before changing to the fiscal year allocation.

1921 July 12   Veteran British aviator Harry Hawker was killed when the Nieuport Goshawk he was flying faltered during a climb out of Hendon airfield and crashed. Medical examination led physicians to believe that Hawker had suffered a hemorrhage and that he had tried to get back down on the ground. The king sent a message of condolence, asserting "The nation had lost one of its most distinguished airmen." Sopwith had met Hawker in 1912 and the two had built up a remarkably successful wartime aircraft manufacturing business before Hawker gave his name to the Hawker Co. when Sopwith was forced to close down as a result of cancelled orders.

1921 July 13   U.S. Army bombing attacks on navy ship targets as part of the army-navy test to determine the vulnerability of naval vessels to aerial attack began with 12 S.E.5 fighters strafing the ex-German destroyer G-102 drifting 100 mi. east of Langley Field, Va. The fighters dropped 25-lb. antipersonnel bombs in a simulated deck-clearing exercise. Then 16 Martin MB-2 bombers, each carrying six 300-lb. bombs, attacked. The G-102 was sunk in just 19 min., after 44 bombs had been dropped from a height of 1,500 ft.

1921 July 16   The only air race ever held between Oxford and Cambridge universities in England took place around a course beginning at Hendon and going on to Hertford and then Epping before returning to Hendon—a total distance of 129 mi. Each team had three S.E.5as. Cambridge aviators R. K. Muir, H. A. Francis and W. S. Philcox won the first three places, with the fastest lap recorded at 118.55 MPH. Only two of the Oxford airplanes completed the course.

1921 July 18   In the fourth of a series of five army-navy bombing attacks on shipping to test the vulnerability of surface vessels to air attacks, the 5,100-ton, ex-German light cruiser *Frankfurt* was attacked in 10 bomb drops, or rounds. Each aircraft was limited to a 300-lb. bomb load for the first six rounds, but the hull remained intact and the load was increased to 600 lb. for the last four rounds. On the seventh, the navy attacked with 560-lb. bombs that failed to sink the ship. Then a flight of Martin bombers from Langley Field appeared and dropped fourteen 600-lb. bombs, sinking the *Frankfurt* in just 35 min.

1921 July 21   On the second day of joint service bombing tests against the 22,500-ton ex-German battleship *Ostfriesland,* eight Martin MB-2 bombers each dropped two 1,100-lb. bombs from 2,500 ft. between 12:18 P.M. and 12:31 P.M. all scoring direct hits. Seven more bombers then arrived, each with a single 2,000-lb. bomb. By 12:40 P.M. the battleship had been sunk. U.S. Secretary of War Weeks and Navy Secretary Edwin Denby along with Gens. Pershing and Charles T. Menoher and a host of reporters watched from the USS *Henderson.* The first attacks had been conducted the day before, when 52 600-lb. bombs had been dropped from 1,500 ft. without effect.

1921 July 29   Brig. Gen. William Mitchell led a force of 17 Martin bombers, a Handley Page 0/400 and a Caproni bomber in a mock raid on New York. They approached, flying north in a *V* formation before changing to a battleline, passing the Battery at 8,000 ft. to simulate a bombing run on lower Manhattan. Mitchell estimated the city had been "virtually destroyed" by 21 tons of high explosive, gas and incendiary bombs. Several days later, Mitchell repeated the "destruction" of U.S. cities by attacking Philadelphia, Wilmington, Baltimore and Annapolis, Md., home of the U.S. Naval Academy. Mitchell sent reports to his chief, Gen. Menoher, urging revision of national defense "at once."

The huge triplane Caproni Ca. 42 on duty with the Royal Naval Air Service.

1921 July 31 The Swiss aviator François Durafour initiated what would become a specialized skill for rescuing stranded mountaineers, explorers and skiers by becoming the first pilot to land on a mountain. Durafour flew his Caudron G.3, fitted with skis, onto the col of the Du Dowe, the western slope of Mont Blanc, at an altitude of 14,000 ft. When light aviation developed during the 1950s with more powerful engines, the skills were further developed, and in June 1969, Henri Giraud landed his Piper P.A.18 on the top of Mont Blanc at an altitude of 15,770 ft.

1921 July After David Davis pulled out from the Davis-Douglas Co., Donald Douglas formed the Douglas Co. with a loan of $15,000 secured by 10 California businessmen led by Harry Chandler, publisher of the *Los Angeles Times*. Douglas had a navy contract for three DT-1 torpedo-bombers, and when, after the first, the second and third were modified into a DT-2 configuration, he moved production to a plant in Santa Monica. The first airplane, the DT-1, had been built in the Goodyear hangar in Los Angeles, but more space was needed.

1921 July A Maj. von Niedermayer from the Reichswehr discussed with the aircraft manufacturer Junkers the possibility of cooperation with the Russian Defense Ministry on pilot training in Russia and the construction of an assembly plant for German military aircraft. Junkers was favorable to this because it offered the opportunity of orders where none could be expected on the domestic market because of prohibitions imposed by the Versailles Treaty. To avoid confrontation with the other Allies, the Russian operation would have to be conducted in utmost secrecy.

1921 August 10 The U.S. Navy Bureau of Aeronautics was established under the direction of Rear Adm. William A. Moffett, who remained in charge until he was killed in the Akron disaster of 1933. The bureau had responsibility for ''all that relates to designing, building, fitting out and repairing Naval and Marine Corps aircraft.'' The bureau was also to prepare planning and operational recommendations for the chief of naval operations, thus elevating the stature of aviation within the U.S. Navy. It would also help schedule familiarization and training requirements and interact with other military aviation bureaus.

1921 August 11 The fifth Schneider Trophy seaplane race was held at Venice, Italy. To encourage only serious participants, a 5,000-franc deposit had to be paid to the organizers, refundable only in the event the entrant actually took part in the race of 16 laps around a 15.29 mi. circuit. Out of 17 entrants, 16 Italian and 1 French, only 3 Italian seaplanes finished the course. The race was won by Giovanni de Briganti in a Macchi M.7 powered by a 250-HP Isotta-Fraschini at an average speed of 117.859 MPH.

1921 August 24 In the worst airship disaster thus far, 44 people lost their lives when the British dirigible R.38 was destroyed during routine operations off the coast of Yorkshire, England. The R.38 had been built at the Royal Airship Works, Cardington and made its first flight on June 23. Despite protests that the light frame made the airship dangerous, it was sold to the U.S. Navy as the ZR-2 but made only four flights. On the evening it was destroyed, the R.38 had been approaching the city of Hull when a hard-over position on the rudder induced stresses, causing the airship to buckle. A fire started by electric sparks engulfed the airship; of the 44 killed, 16 were Americans.

1921 August 31 The first production Vickers Vernon, the first troop-carrier designed for the RAF, was delivered by the British manufacturer. The Vernon entered service with No. 45 Squadron at Hinaidi early in 1922 and remained in front-line service for six years before it was replaced by the Victoria. As a descendant of the Vimy bomber, the Vernon was similar to the Vimy Commercial, but it had two 450-HP Napier Lion engines rather than two 200-HP Hispano-Suiza engines, a gross weight of 12,500 lb. versus 9,120 lb., an endurance of 4 hr. (or 320 mi.) and a ceiling of 11,700 ft. versus 9,500 ft. and could carry 12 troops.

1921 September 1 A squadron of D.H.4B biplanes from the First Provisional Air Brigade was ordered to Charleston, W. Va., to stand by in case it was needed to suppress a violent civil uprising in Mingo County. The United Mine Workers of America were threatening to march on Mingo from their camps in the mountains of Logan County. The airplanes were equipped with machine guns and ammunition, and bombs arrived by rail. Several airplanes were wrecked in landing or take-off accidents, and some were blown off course by storms. Foot patrols quieted the miners, and order was restored by September 5.

1921 September 23 Sustained day and night bombing trials using Martin MB-2 bombers against fixed ground and sea targets began a directed assault on the decommissioned U.S. warship *Alabama* moored in Chesapeake Bay. Throughout the day D.H.4 and Martin bombers dropped 25-lb. and 100-lb. phosphor bombs and 50-lb. fragmentation bombs. The attack continued during the night, using flares for sighting, and on through the next day, using machine guns and antipersonnel bombs in a wave of attacks aimed at practicing various techniques. Following a day's respite, the old warship was sunk by 2,000-lb. high-explosive bombs on September 26.

1921 September 26 French aviator Sadi Lecointe became the first man to officially break the 200-MPH barrier for powered flight when he piloted his Nieuport-Delage sesquiplane to an average speed of 330.275 km/hr. (205.82 MPH) along a 1-km (3,281 ft.) course, which he flew in 10.9 sec. The aircraft was powered by a 320-HP Hispano-Suiza 42 engine. This speed record stood for almost a year until Lecointe raised it to 341.232 km/hr. on September 21, 1922.

1921 September The Antarctic explorer Sir Ernest Shackleton took a specially adapted two-seat Avro Baby seaplane, known as the Type 554, on his expedition to the South Pole. It was powered by a 80-HP Le Rhône rotary engine and carried an extended-span upper wing rigged with tubular steel struts instead of wires. The individual interplane struts were replaced with a pair of N-shaped struts. The Type 554 sailed with Shackleton on the *Quest,* but the ship put in at Rio de Janeiro, Brazil, instead of Cape Town, South Africa, where spares had been stacked. The Baby was never used, and after Shackleton died aboard ship on January 5, 1922, it was returned to England on September 16, 1922.

1921 October 5 Maj. Gen. Mason M. Patrick was appointed chief of the army air service when Gen. Menoher resigned over a leaked report to the press September 13 that highlighted strong differences between him and Brig. Gen. William Mitchell. Having been chief of the air service attached to the American Expeditionary Force in France during the war, Maj. Gen. Patrick brought considerable experience to the role. Patrick had to preside over a reduction of the air service while at the same time mollifying both those who opposed strong military air forces and those who were clamoring for an independent air force and trying to prevent both groups from rocking the boat and angering Congress.

1921 October The first practical application of independent air power began with the British decision to replace British Army and Indian Army ground troops in Iraq with RAF squadrons tasked to carry out airborne policing duties against warring tribes. It proved highly effective, and RAF strength was increased to eight squadrons. Air Vice Marshal Sir John Salmond took over control of the area, setting the standard for military operational procedures and tactics that would form the basis of British air-policing throughout the Middle East for almost two decades.

1921 November 3 A Curtiss CR biplane, the second of two being built for the U.S. Navy in the second Pulitzer Trophy Race, broke the world closed-circuit speed record by flying at 176.7 MPH as a private entry by Curtiss piloted by Bert Acosta. Both army and navy entries withdrew, so Curtiss used the second CR, designated CR-2 in 1922. It had a 425-HP Curtiss CD-12 operating on a 50-50 Benzol-gasoline mixture. Designed by Mike Thurston and Henry Routh, the CR had a wingspan of 22 ft. 8 in., a length of 21 ft. and a height of 8 ft. 4.5 in. with special streamlining around protruberances. On November 19, 1921, it reached a speed of 197.8 MPH.

1921 November 12 The first in-flight refueling of one airplane by another took place when Wesley May stepped out of the cockpit of a Curtiss "Jennie" into the cockpit of another with a can of gasoline strapped to his back. With two biplanes in very close formation, May clambered onto the wing of his own airplane, then across to the wing of a second "Jennie" and refueled the airplane from the can. Although impractical as a method of extending an airplane's range, the idea took off and spurred development of hose-linked tanks in separate aircraft.

1921 November 21 At the Washington Conference opened by Pres. Warren G. Harding, Secretary of State Charles Evans Hughes proposed that the United States, Britain and Japan should scrap most of their warship fleets, refrain from building new warships for 10 years, totally prohibit the construction of submarines and limit the size of British and American aircraft carriers to 80,000 tons and to 48,000 tons for Japan. The British agreed, but Japan did not and revoked the Anglo-Japanese Treaty (1902) in favor of an "Agreement for Preservation of Peace in the Pacific." This permitted the continued development of aircraft carriers while limiting the construction of conventional ships.

1921 November 21 The first product of what would become a famous, and extremely important, French airplane manufacturer made its appearance when the Dewoitine D1 took to the air for the first time. Designed by Emile Dewoitine at the new plant at Toulouse, France, the D1 was a parasol monoplane of light metal construction using the new metal alloy duralumin and had fabric covered wings. It was powered by a 300-HP in-line Hispano-Suiza engine giving a top speed of 156 MPH, a ceiling of almost 28,000 ft. and a surprisingly low landing speed of 50 MPH. Dewoitine was liquidated in 1928, but the Société des Avions Dewoitine was set up in Switzerland and then moved back to France as the Société Aéronautique Francaise.

1921 December 4 The first regularly scheduled airline services in Australia began with six Bristol Tourer biplanes operated by Western Australian Airways. The Tourer was basically a Bristol Fighter with provision for two passengers where the observer would have been seated in the F.2B configuration. The Tourers sent to Australia had enclosed coupe hoods leaving the pilot exposed, as most preferred. Maj. Norman Brearley purchased the Tourers in September and opened regular services from Geraldton to Carnarvon, Onslow, Roebourne, Port Hedland, Broome and Derby.

1921 December 7 A report issued by NACA proposed a national U.S. airline for transcontinental travel and a weather service to back up the scheduling and movement of air traffic. NACA believed effective weather reports were "indispensable to the success and safety of air navigation" and that an efficient meteorological service was vital for the entire country and its approaches. NACA was also concerned about the lack of stability in the American airplane industry caused by reduced government spending after the war.

1921 December 15 The U.S. Circuit Court of Appeals found in favor of Glenn Curtiss that he was the inventor of the flying boat, beginning the end of massive litigation and counter-litigation action on patents from the Wright and Wright-Martin controversies. Earlier this year, Glenn Curtiss had retired from aviation, leaving his company to ride the wave of canceled contracts and depressed prices caused by massive government sell-offs at low prices. Curtiss retired to Florida, where he made a fortune in real estate.

1921 December 19 At the behest of Maj. Gen. Patrick, Brig. Gen. Mitchell went to France for the start of a three-month tour of Europe in which he was to learn about progress in European aviation and study the structure of European military air forces. To some extent, by openly challenging military and political authority about the need for large bombing forces, Mitchell had become an embarrassment, and the chief of the air service wanted him kept out of harm's way. Most political and military leaders saw airplanes as adjuncts to land and sea forces, but Mitchell saw them as capable of independently challenging the enemy on land and at sea and worthy of a unique and separate role.

1921 December The German-Swedish combination Junkers-Larsen offered the U.S. Army a corrugated metal monoplane heavily armed for ground attack duties. Called the JL-12, it had a wingspan of 49 ft., a length of 33 ft. and a 420-HP Liberty 12 engine. It featured 28 Thompson 0.45-caliber machine guns installed in the lower fuselage, 12 pointing slightly forward, 6 pointing straight down and 10 pointing to the rear. With a combined fusilade of bullets, it epitomized the ground attack role. It received negative reports from pilots, however.

1921 One of the most notable prophets of air power and a theoretical architect of strategic bombing, the Italian Giulio Douhet (1869–1930) published *The Command of the Air*. In it, he explained his ideas about the use of aircraft in war. Douhet started from the premise that air warfare eliminated the distinction between combatants and noncombatants and claimed that total war from the air would envelop nonmilitary personnel in towns and cities far behind the front lines. Douhet believed that successful campaigns on the ground alone would no longer be possible because air power would play an instrumental, if not decisive, role in all-out war. He said that warring nations should use air power to strike deep at the heart of civilian conurbations and centers of industrial production to demoralize the population and destroy its capacity to produce weapons.

1921 Alexander Lippisch, the German inventor of tailless airplanes, designed his first swept-wing tailless glider. Built by Gottlob Espenlaub, the Lippisch-Espenlaub E2 was the first of more than 50 such designs that would emerge in the next 30 years. Lippisch had been inspired in September 1909, when as a boy of 14 in Berlin he witnessed the remarkable flying performances of Orville Wright. Lippisch's E2 was a distinctly unimpressive flying machine but provided him with the encouragement to perfect his tailless designs. In 1924 Lippisch was appointed director of the aeronautical department of the Rhön-Rossitten-Gesellschaft Company.

1921 The Avions-Caudron C.61 six-passenger biplane made its appearance. With seating for eight passengers and two crew, the C.61 was large, with a wingspan of 79 ft. 2 in., a length of 45 ft. 11 in. and a loaded weight of 7,672 lb. Powered by three 180-HP Hispano-Suiza 8Ab water-cooled engines, some C.61s had a separate nose wheel to prevent damage to the forward engine on landing. The crew sat forward of a cargo hold, which was forward of the enclosed passenger compartment. At least 12 production aircraft of this type were built, some serving the Belgrade-Bucharest route in 1923.

1922 January 9 At its 14th annual banquet, members of the Aero Club of America decided to commercialize their interests and form the National Aeronautic Association (NAA). The existing Aero Club headquarters in New York was closed and a new headquarters opened in Washington, D.C. In January 1923, the NAA was recognized by the FAI as its sole U.S. representative, and it remains so to this day.

1922 February 6 The Treaty of Washington (or the Five Power Naval Treaty) was signed by Britain, France, Italy, Japan and the United States. The United States and Britain were allowed aircraft carriers of up to 135,000 tons, and Japan would restrict her carriers to a maximum 81,000 tons. Moreover, new carriers would be limited to a maximum displacement of 27,000 tons, or two carriers of 33,000 tons each if the total tonnage within those limits was not exceeded by all vessels of that type. Because it allowed the conversion of capital ships, the U.S. Navy sought permission from Congress to adapt the battle cruisers *Lexington* and *Saratoga*.

1922 February The first flight of the Simplex-Arnoux tailless racer took place. Designed by René Arnoux, the biplane made 12 successful flights between February and April until it crashed, killing the pilot, a man named Fetu. Arnoux had designed tailless airplanes before World War I and now, with the help of French air ace Félix Madon, developed his concepts further. A tailless monoplane built for the 1922 Coupe Deutsche race crashed on September 24 with Madon at the controls, who luckily escaped injury. The Simplex-Arnoux had a large ''plank'' wing and a small rudder and was powered by a 320-HP Hispano-Suiza engine providing a top speed of 236 MPH.

1922 February Eager for orders, Curtiss underbid the Martin company on 50 MB-2 bombers, designated NBS-1 (Night Bomber Short-distance 1) quoted at $17,490 each for a total price of $874,500. Curtiss lost $300,000 on the deal. (Since Martin quoted a total price of $1,196,250 for 50, Curtiss could have bid high enough to turn a profit on the deal and still have beaten the Martin quote.) Lowe, Willard and Fowler, or L.W.F., and Aeromarine got orders for 35 and 25 respectively; their bids were even lower than Curtiss, and both companies eventually closed down through insolvency.

1922 March 15 The German aircraft manufacturer Junkers and Sondergruppe R signed a contract to build an airframe and engine construction and assembly plant at Fili near Moscow. A holding company, the Gesellschaft zur Foerderung gewerblisher Unternehmugen (Gefu), was set up with offices in Berlin and Moscow. With a working capital of 75 million Reichsmarks, it administered the flow of materials and workers. Andrei Tupolev was brought in by the Soviets to work with the Germans on adapting manufacturing standards to the needs of Russia.

1922 March 20 The CV-1 *Langley,* America's first aircraft carrier, was commissioned into the U.S. Navy at Norfolk, Va. under the command of Comdr. Kenneth Whiting. The *Langley* had a flight deck 533 ft. 9 in. long and 63 ft. 11 in. wide and had been converted from the collier *Jupiter. Langley* joined the Pacific fleet in November 1924 and was converted to a seaplane tender in October 1936, serving in the Atlantic for six months in 1939 before going to the West Pacific in September of that year. *Langley* served in Australian and Indonesian waters during World War II but was sunk after being struck by five bombs in February 1942.

1922 March 26 One of the first small commercial transport aircraft built based upon experience from passenger flying and the requirements of airline operators, made its first flight from Edgware, near London. Designed after consultation with Daimler Hire Ltd., Instone Air Line Ltd. and the Air Council, de Havilland produced the 10-seat passenger D.H.34, which, with a top speed of 128 MPH and a cruising speed of 105 MPH had a range of 365 mi.

1922 March 30 The first attempt to fly across the South Atlantic between Portugal and Brazil began when a Fairey IIID flown by Comdr. Sacadura Cabral and Capt. Gago Coutinho left Lisbon at 7:00 A.M. for a 703-mi. flight to Las Palmas, Canary Islands. They reached Grand Canary island in 8 hr. 37 min. They flew on to Punta de Gando, the other side of the island in 21 min. on April 2 and from there to São Vincente, Cape Verde Islands, on April 5, flying the 849 mi. in 10 hr. 43 min. Following delays through bad weather, the Fairey IIID flew 170 mi. to São Tiago on April 17 and the next day to the Rocks of St. Peter and St. Paul, where, after 908 mi. in 11 hr. 21 min., they put down with less than 1 gal. of fuel. Caught in heavy seas, the IIID sank. Coutinho and Cabral persisted in their effort, arriving at Rio de Janeiro June 17 in a replacement aircraft of the same type, having travelled 4,367 nm (5,025 mi.) in a flight time of 60 hr. 14 min.

1922 March The Loening PA-1 biplane, the first American fighter equipped with an air-cooled radial engine, made its first flight. Ordered in 1921, only one of two ordered was ever built due to lack of performance with the prototype. It had a wingspan of 28 ft., a length of 19 ft. 9 in. and a gross weight of 2,463 lb. and was powered by a single Wright R-1454 engine delivering 350 HP. The PA-1 was also the only American aircraft to bear the U.S. Army designation for Pursuit Air-cooled, that distinction not being indicated for other air-cooled types.

1922 April 7 The first air collision between two airliners occurred when a Farman Goliath of the French airline Cie des Grands Express Aeriens, registration F-GEAD, crashed head-on with a D.H.18A, registration G-EAWO, owned by Daimler Hire Ltd. The aircraft collided over the Thieulloy-St. Antoine road, France, killing all seven people on board the two planes. Both aircraft had been using the road as a route marker in bad weather and poor visibility. The D.H.18A was piloted by R. E. Duke and only five days earlier had inaugurated the Croydon-Paris service by Daimler Hire Ltd.

1922 April 16 At the signing of the Russo-German Treaty of Rapallo, talks immediately began on using Soviet territory to train German pilots for a new military air force. This resulted in a special pilot and aircrew training school set up at Lipetsk on the Voronezh River, 225 mi. southeast of Moscow, its purpose camouflaged when the Soviets stationed one of their military air units at the same site. Installations were built up during 1924, and in 1925 the first training courses for fighter pilots began. At first there were 30, then 200 and, by 1930, 300 Germans on each course.

1922 April 25 Known as the Stout ST-1, the first all-metal airplane designed for the U.S. Navy made its first flight piloted by Eddie Stinson. Designed by Stout Engineering Laboratory as a torpedo-carrying attack plane, it had two 300-HP Packard V-1237 engines, twin rudders and a conventional landing gear. With a wing span of 60 ft. and a length of 37 ft., the ST-1 had a gross weight of 9,817 lb. and a range of 385 mi. It cost $162,000 to build, but the aircraft had inadequate longitudinal stability and crashed on its 14th flight.

1922 April The *Roma,* the world's largest semirigid airship, was destroyed by fire after a test run at Langley Field in Virginia. With a length of 410 ft., a volume of 1,200,000 cu. ft. and a crew of 18, the airship had a range of 2,796 mi. and was powered by six engines. It had been designed by Usuelli in Italy and designated the T-34 when it emerged from the Government Airships Factory. It was sold to the U.S. Army in 1921 for $195,000. The fire that destroyed it was caused by the nose buckling at the end of a high-speed run.

1922 May 1 The German-Russian Airline Deutsche-Russische Luftverkehr-Gessellschaft, (or Deruluft) opened a scheduled route between Koenigsberg and Moscow, a distance of approximately 745 mi. A Fokker F.III, registered RR4, began services between Koenigsberg, East Prussia and Moscow, each flight lasting more than 10 hr. The airline had been formed on November 11, 1921, and led to a major increase in air travel. German airlines had expanded under the Air Transport Agency set up on January 8, 1919. The first route between Berlin and Weimar, was followed by a second between Dessau and Weimar in 1920. The Russian link was the most ambitious to date.

1922 May 5 Under constraints imposed by ambassadors representing the victorious powers of World War I, Germany was allowed to resume development of civil aircraft. To ensure they could not be adapted for offensive military purposes, speed was to be limited to 106 MPH, range to 186 mi., service ceiling to 13,124 ft. endurance to 2.5 hr. and payload to 1,323 lb. Ironically, German firms such as Heinkel and Caspar had been building military aircraft in kit form for assembly in another country, the U.S. Navy taking over some airplanes this way in 1923.

1922 May 24 Capt. Norman Macmillan, Maj. W. Blake and Lt. Col. L. E. Broome set off from Croydon, near London, England, in a D.H.9 purchased from the Aircraft Disposal Co., hoping to fly around the world. They planned to change to a Fairey III seaplane at Calcutta and to a Canadian D.H.9 at Alaska. They were then to have picked up a Canadian F.3 at New York for the last lap across the Atlantic. In reality, they only got as far as Chittagong (now in Bangladesh), where the Fairey III they had flown from Calcutta sank after its floats became waterlogged.

1922 May First shown at the Paris Air Show in 1921, the Breguet 19 made its first flight with a Renault engine; in production aircraft the Renault was replaced by a 375-HP Lorraine and then a 450-HP engine of the same make. Designed as a replacement to the highly successful Breguet 14 of World War I, it was produced as a reconnaissance airplane or a bomber. In the latter role, it had a range of 435 mi. and a top speed of 112 MPH. The Breguet was supplied to 14 countries, claiming many records before it was finally withdrawn from service in the early 1940s.

1922 May The first Naval Aircraft Factory TS-1 carrier-based biplane fighter for the U.S. Navy was delivered by Curtiss. The company had won an order for 34 at the low-bidder price of

$9,569 for the first nine and $9,975 for the remaining 25. Designed by Jerome C. Hunsacker of the U.S. Navy Bureau of Aeronautics, the TS-1 was specifically designed for service aboard the USS *Langley,* although it drew its designation from Turret Scout when a precursor concept would have operated from wooden platforms on warship gun turrets. It was the first production fighter powered by the new air-cooled, Lawrence J-1 radial engine, which provided a top speed of 131 MPH.

1922 June 6 In an astonishing burst of activity, the U.S. Navy established seven world records for Class C seaplanes. Douglas DT-2s set a 500 km (310.6 mi.) speed record at 72 MPH and a distance and a duration record of 205.2 mi. and 2 hr. 45 min. 9 sec. with a 1,000 kg (2,205 lb.) load. Curtiss F-5Ls seized a distance and a duration record of 575.75 mi. and 10 hr. 23 min. 58 sec. with 250 kg. (551 lb.) load and a distance and a duration record of 466 mi. and 7 hr. 35 min. 54 sec. with a 500 kg (1,102 lb.) load.

1922 June 7 Continuing the record-breaking activity begun the day before, the U.S. Navy broke eight new world marks for Class C seaplanes. Douglas DT-2s got an altitude record of 10,850 ft. while carrying 250 kg (551 lb.) and an absolute altitude record of 13,898 ft. Curtiss F-5Ls set a record altitude of 8,438 ft. carrying a 500 kg (1,103 lb.) load, an altitude record of 7,979 ft. carrying a 1,000 kg (2,205 lb.) load, a duration record with a 1,500 kg (3,307 lb.) load of 2 hr. 18 min. and an altitude record of 5,682 ft. with that load and a duration record of 51 min. and an altitude record of 4,885 ft. while carrying a 2,000 kg (4,409 lb.) load.

1922 June 12 A Douglas DT-2 flown by Lt. (jg) M. A. Schur, U.S. Navy, took three world records at San Diego, Calif. for Class C seaplanes. The DT-2 achieved a duration record of 11 hr. 16 min. 59 sec., a distance record of 792.25 mi. and a speed record across 1,000 km (621.4 mi.) of 70.49 MPH. A day later, Navy Lt. R. A. Ofstie, flying a Curtiss TS-1, set two Class C seaplane speed records for 100 km (62.1 mi.) and 200 km (124.8 mi.) of 121.95 MPH and 121.14 MPH respectively, ending a remarkable period of seven days beginning June 6 where U.S. Navy pilots broke 20 world records.

1922 June 12 Capt. Albert W. Stevens of the U.S. Army Air Service took an oxygen flask with him when he jumped from 24,000 ft. after carrying out photographic duties over Dayton, Ohio. The force of the initial descent tore loose the 11-lb. oxygen bottle strapped to his leg, but he caught it and took a draft of air before it fell away for good. In strong winds and turbulent air, the parachute rocked and tossed about, almost making Capt. Stevens airsick. An unofficial competition had developed over parachute descents from the greatest height and others sought thrills by opening their parachutes after standing on the top wing of a biplane.

1922 June 19 Using converted World War I D.H.4 day bombers, Capt. Burdette S. Wright began the U.S. Army Model Airway service—four flights each week between Bolling Field, Anacostia, D.C. and McCook Field, Dayton, Ohio. Introduced to carry U.S. Army traffic between the eastern seaboard and the Midwest, winter schedules commenced on December 4, linking Long Island, N.Y., with San Antonio, Tex. Four years later the service stretched as far as Los Angeles, Calif., and although several hundred military passengers were carried, the service primarily existed to convey mail and packages until it was superseded by private airlines.

1922 July 1 Plans to convert the USS *Lexington* and the USS *Saratoga* from battle cruisers to aircraft carriers were approved by Congress to avoid scrapping them as required by the January 1922 Treaty of Washington. The largest warships afloat until the *Midway* class at the end of World War II, they were each 830 ft. long, with a beam of 105.5 ft. and a flight deck of 875 ft., and displaced 39,000 tons. Characterized by a single large smokestack from the 16 steam boilers, the *Lexington* was sunk May 8, 1942, and the *Saratoga* was sunk by the atomic bomb in the tests at Bikini Atoll.

1922 July 29 The first of 200 Thomas-Morse MB-3A fighters built by Boeing was delivered to the USAAS. A derivative of the Thomas Morse MB-3, the 3A had radiators moved from below the upper wing to either side of the fuselage. Thomas-Morse had quoted $1.926 million, whereas Boeing offered 200 airplanes of this type for $1.488 million, with bids from Dayton-Wright and Curtiss falling in between. Boeing got the order in April 1921, the largest single order for one type of airplane until 1937, and the American taxpayer saved money. It was the first major production order for the first indigenous American fighter, all 200 being delivered by December 27, 1922.

1922 August 12 The Schneider Trophy seaplane race was won by Henri Baird flying a Supermarine Sea Lion II (registration G-EBAH) for Britain at an average speed of 145.721 MPH. The course was 13 laps of a 17.7 mi. left-hand circuit off Naples, Italy and was contested by British and Italian airplanes, the lone French entrant having pulled out with engine trouble. The Sea Lion had been designed by R. J. Mitchell, who had joined Supermarine in 1916. Baird's winning average was a phenomenal 27.8 MPH faster than the winner of the 1921 race, and he finished 2 min. ahead of second-place-man Alessandro Passaleva in a Savoia S.51 powered by a 300-HP Hispano-Suiza.

1922 August 22 The Vickers Victoria (serial no. J6860) military transport made its first flight, taking off from Brooklands, England with Stan Cockerell at the controls. Designed to a contract dated June 8, 1920, calling for an airplane capable of lifting 25 soldiers and equipment 400 mi. in four hours, with a maximum range of 700 mi., the Victoria emerged from design studies then underway at Vickers for a long-range bomber known as the Virginia.

1922 September 4 The first U.S. transcontinental flight within a 24-hr. period was performed by Lt. James H. Doolittle. He flew a USAAS D.H.4B from Pablo Beach, Fla. to Rockwell Field, San Diego in a flying time of 21 hr. 20 min., covering the 2,163 mi. at an average speed of 101 MPH. Lt. Doolittle stopped at Kelly Field, Tex. for 1 hr. 15 min. to refuel, arriving at Rockwell Field 22 hr. 35 min. after taking off from Florida. The British-designed D.H.4 was proving a useful airplane for several record-breaking flights carried out by pilots of the army air service.

1922 September 20 French aviator Sadi Lecointe became the first pilot to establish an official speed record in excess of 200 MPH. Flying a derivative of the Nieuport-Delage 29, Lecointe set a speed record of 205.2 MPH, raising this to 211.89 MPH the following day. It had taken less than a decade to push the world speed record from 100 to 200 MPH, and it would take less than 8 years to reach 300 MPH and 11 years to push the official record through the 400-MPH barrier. In America, R-series racing aircraft adapted from standard high-performance airplanes would soon push speeds well beyond 200 MPH in efforts to increase the performance of operational types.

1922 September 27 The first simulated mass attack by U.S. Navy attack planes carrying torpedos took place when 18 Naval

The Vickers Virginia with experimental defensive gun position on top of the upper wing center-section.

Aircraft Factory PT-1 biplanes released 17. Mk.VII Model 1 torpedoes against the USS *Arkansas* and two other battleships at full speed. The PT-1s of Torpedo and Bombing Plane Squadron One attacked the ships from port and starboard at 500 to 1,000 yd. and scored eight hits, demonstrating launch techniques and accuracy of drop. The PT-1 first flew in July 1921. It had the fuselage of the Curtiss R-6 twin-float seaplane and the wings of the HS-series biplane flying boat and was powered by a 400-HP Liberty 12 engine.

1922 October 14 Curtiss Model 23, R-6 racing biplanes won first and second places for the army at the third Pulitzer Trophy Race, Detroit, with navy CR-2 and CR-1 biplanes placing third and fourth. The R-6 was developed from the CR, which had won the 1921 Pulitzer as a company entry. The army ordered nine new R-6 versions with 460-HP Curtiss D-12s, smaller and faster than the CR with radiators in the upper wing, helping streamline the cowling area. Lt. Russell Maughan piloted the winning airplane at 205.8 MPH, followed by Lt. Lester J. Maitland at 198.8 MPH, Lt. H. J. Brow at 193 MPH and Lt. A. J. Williams at 187 MPH.

1922 October 16 The Royal Aero Club opened glider trials at a place called Itford on the Sussex Hills, England in response to a £1,000 prize offered by the *Daily Mail* for the longest flight carried out by a glider during the month. The German glider pilot Hentzen had remained aloft for two hr. during trials in the Rhoen mountains the previous year, and the sport was rapidly claiming respectability and the serious attentions of airplane builders. The event ran until October 21 and was won by the Frenchman Alexis Maneyrol in a glider designed by M. Peyret that remained aloft for 3 hr. 21 min. 7 sec.

1922 October 17 Lt. V. C. Griffin, U.S. Navy, flew a Vought VE-7SF off the deck of the USS *Langley* at anchor in the York River, the first time a U.S. Navy aircraft had taken off from the deck of a carrier. Developed during World War I by the Lewis & Vought Corp., the VE-7 was a spirited attempt to produce an indigenous American trainer but was modeled on the D.H.4. Powered by a 180-HP Wright-Hispano engine, the army took 14, and the navy purchased 128 from Vought and NAF factories. The landplane version was fitted with flotation gear designed by the British in World War I, the first U.S. aircraft to be so equipped.

1922 October 18 The second of two Curtiss R-6 racers, the one that won the 1922 Pulitzer Trophy Race on October 14, was flown by Brig. Gen. William B. Mitchell to a new world straight-line speed record of 222.96 MPH. The R-6 had a wingspan of 19 ft., a length of 18 ft. 11 in., a height of 7 ft. 11 in. and a gross weight of 1,950 lb. With a measured top speed of 236 MPH, it was more than 50 MPH faster than the CR type designed by Curtiss for the 1921 Pulitzer. The R-6 had a range of 283 mi., and with a high-gloss paint finish, it looked every inch a racer.

1922 October 19 The U.S. Navy took delivery of the first production Douglas DT-2 floatplane. Powered by a 400-HP Liberty engine, 87 DT-2s were built, including seven under license in Norway—the first foreign license production order for Douglas. The type established numerous records, including altitude and distance, on one flight June 12, 1923, remaining airborne for 11 hr. 16 min. 59 sec. and flying a distance of 792.25 mi. Six days after the first delivery to the navy, the U.S. Army inquired about the DT-2 and this design formed the basis for the Douglas World Cruiser of 1923–24.

1922 October 20 Lt. H. R. Harris of the USAAS became the first American to abandon his airplane in flight and live to tell

the tale, when he jumped out of a disabled Loening PW-A single-seat, high-wing monoplane and came to earth by parachute from a height of 2,000 ft. Developed from the Loening M-8 Kitten, the PW-2 was powered by a 320-HP Wright-Hispano in-line engine. It had a span of 39 ft. 8 in. and a length of 24 ft. 1 in., was constructed of wood and fabric and had been designed in 1920 by Grover C. Loening. The prototype had been ordered in January 1921, and although several were built, it lacked maneuverability and proved unsatisfactory.

1922 October 23 The first reversible-pitch propeller was demonstrated by the American Propeller Co. as a means of improving the theoretical effectiveness of the propeller for helping the performance of aircraft in steep descent and after landing. By reversing pitch, the propeller would induce a braking moment, helping cut landing distances and improve operating and handling in the air.

1922 October 23 Ernst Udet, Heinz Pohl, Erich Scheuermann and Hans Herrmann formed the Udet-Flugzeugbau with capital of 100,000 Reichsmarks. They would design and build light airplanes, beginning with construction of the Udet U-1 light sports and training airplane, the first of which had made its first flight on May 12. Later, the U-5, four-seat, light transport aircraft would be developed in 1923 followed by the U-11 Condor, a four-engine, shoulder-wing monoplane capable of carrying eight passengers. The investment necessary for large aircraft of this type forced the company into a takeover by the Bayerische-Flugzeugwerke A.G. (BFW) in 1926.

1922 October 26 An Aeromarine 39-B piloted by Lt. Comdr. Geofrey DeChevalier became the first U.S. Navy airplane to land on an aircraft carrier when it touched down on the USS *Langley*. The Aeromarine 39-B had been developed from the 39-A, ordered by the navy in 1917 from the Aeromarine Plane and Motor Co. of Keyport, N.J. The 39-B had a wingspan of 47 ft., a length of 30 ft. 4 in. and a gross weight of 2,505 MPH. Fitted with a 100-HP Curtiss OXX-6 engine, it had a top speed of 73 MPH.

1922 November 6 The prototype Dornier Do.J flew for the first time. Known as the Wal, the Do.J was a highly successful flying boat, more than 300 of which were eventually built. To circumvent the restrictions imposed on German aircraft manufacture, Dornier set up an Italian company, Societè di Costruzioni Meccaniche di Pisa, with a plant at Marina di Pisa. Dornier airplanes were built there under license until production began in Germany, at Friedrichshafen, in 1932. License-built production was authorized in Spain, Holland and Japan.

1922 November 11 The French Peugeot engineer Etienne Oehmichen flew his helicopter No. 2 for the first time. Powered by a 120-HP Le Rhône rotary engine, it was driven by four twin-blade rotors, one at each corner of a cruciform framework made of tubular steel. In addition, five conventional propellers were to provide lateral stability (one in the nose was for steering), and two more propellers operated as pushers for forward motion. Though it seems incredible that the contraption flew at all, the No. 2 made more than a thousand test flights.

1922 November 11 The second U.S. Army Air Service pilot in three weeks to be saved by parachute, 1st Lt. Frank B. Tyndall floated to earth after the wings came off the Thomas-Morse MB-3A he was testing at Seattle. As a result of this, the USAAS issued orders requiring army pilots and passengers not to fly without parachutes. (The lack of parachutes made it impossible to implement this order for some time.) To date, one-third of air service fatalities had been attributable to the absence of a parachute. Because of the new instruction, miles flown per fatality increased from 73,631 to 297,375 between 1920 and 1925.

1922 November 24   The Vickers Virginia prototype (serial no. J6856) made its first flight from Brooklands with Stan Cockerell at the controls. Developed in response to a British Air Ministry requirement for a long-distance bombing airplane, the Virginia had an extended Vimy wing with a span of 87 ft. 8 in. and a length of 62 ft. 3 in. With a top speed of 108 MPH and a range of 985 mi., the Virginia could lift a 3,000-lb. bomb load, usually made up from 112-lb. bombs. Virginias began replacing Vimys at the end of 1924, and 124 were built before production ceased in December 1932. The type was replaced by the Handley Page Heyford from 1933 on.

1922 November 28   The Fairey Flycatcher, the first British airplane built with special strengthening for catapult launches from the decks of aircraft carriers, made its first flight. Robust, rugged and tough, the British fighter entered service with the Royal Navy in 1923 and remained as a front-line aircraft for more than a decade. It was powered by a single 400-HP Armstrong-Siddeley Jaguar radial engine and had a top speed of 133 MPH, an initial climb rate of 1,090 ft./min. and a range of 263 mi. The Flycatcher was armed with two Vickers machine guns and could carry four 20-lb. bombs.

1922 November 29   Two U.S. Navy D.H.4Bs piloted by Lts. Ben J. Wyatt and George T. Owen arrived in San Diego, Calif., having completed a transcontinental round-trip of the United States that began October 14. From Tucson, Ariz., they flew to New Orleans, La., Pensacola, Fla., Washington, D.C., Dayton, Ohio, Salt Lake City, Utah and San Francisco, Calif. The 7,000-mi. trip took 90 flying hr. over 46 days. Hold-ups were due to bad weather, bad gasoline, mechanical problems and the complete lack of any navigational aids.

1922 December 1   Occupying hangar space rented from the local authorities at Warnemünde, the Ernst Heinkel Flugzeugwerke was set up to design and build airplanes. In 1911, at the age of 24, Ernst Heinkel had joined the Luft-Verkehrs Gesellschaft (LVG) and designed their first production airplane, the tractor B.I biplane. He joined the Albatros-Werke G.m.b.H. in the spring of 1913 and then moved on to join Igor Etrich as chief designer in a new venture that was eventually acquired by a wealthy Austrian and renamed the Hansa und Brandenburgische Flugzeugwerke G.m.b.H. It was there that Heinkel became famous for his landplane and seaplane designs, which were to have been built under license when the company folded in 1919.

1922 December 18   The first helicopter ordered by the U.S. Army lifted into the air for the first time at the Technical Section, McCook Field and rose 6 ft. from the ground, remaining airborne for 1 min. 42 sec. It had been made by a Russian engineer emigre named De Bothezat who started to build the helicopter under the watchful eye of the Army Air Service at Dayton. His machine had four six-bladed, variable-pitch rotors mounted at the ends of two beams 65 ft. 7.5 in. in length forming a cross. The rotor axes were inclined slightly inward. Two conventional propellers were provided as well as two small propellers above the gearbox. It weighed 3,550 lb. and was powered by a 220-HP engine. On January 19, 1923, it lifted two people 4 ft., and on April 17, it lifted four people, but the army lost interest in the venture.

1922 December 27   The *Hosho* became the world's first purposely built aircraft carrier to be commissioned, when it was commissioned into the Imperial Japanese Navy. With a displacement of 7,470 tons, the *Hosho* was laid down in 1919 and had a long and accomplished life, surviving World War II to be decommissioned after the Japanese surrender. Japan was an early proponent of the use of air power at sea and modeled its plans on British naval aviation, carefully studying technical and operational developments in England that provided a broad and capable naval air service during and after World War I.

1922 December 31   The first German aircraft to land on British soil after World War I touched down at Lympne on the southeast coast of England. It was a Dornier Do.C III Komet operated by Deutsche Luft-Reederei and powered by a 185-HP BMW IIIa inline engine. Essentially a landplane version of the Dornier Do.Cs II Delphin flying boat, the aircraft had been designed and flown for the first time in 1921. An enclosed cabin for four passengers was situated behind the open pilot's cockpit. The Komet had a wingspan of 55 ft. 9 in. and a length of 31 ft. 2 in. with a loaded weight of 4,519 lb. and a cruising speed of 81 MPH. Several aircraft of this type were supplied to the Soviet Union.

1923 January 2   In London, England, a committee chaired by Sir Herbert Hambling was set up by the air minister, Sir Samuel Hoare, to "advise on the best method of subsidizing air transport for the future." For almost four years, British airline operators had been losing money, despite government aid, and competition from the European continent and forecasts gave a bleak view of profits. The government was advised by Sir Hambling's committee that some form of subsidy was vital to Britain's civil aviation industry, such as it was. This resulted in discussions with the four existing operators and the formation on March 31, 1924, of Imperial Airways Ltd.

1923 January 9   The Spanish engineer and inventor Juan de la Cierva flew his C.4 autogyro for the first time from a field near Madrid. Cierva had been working on autogyro and helicopter designs for two years, but none of his inventions were a success. The C.4 had four rotating blades designed to provide lift. With a fuselage modeled on that of a Hanriot biplane, the C.4 had a 110-HP Le Rhône rotary engine and by the end of January had flown 2.5 mi.

1923 January 23   The Handley Page W.8b was ordered by the British Air Ministry as a potential replacement night bomber for the D.H.10 and the Vickers Vimy, a lighter equivalent for the Vickers Virginia. It first flew in October 1923 and was ordered into production as the Hyderabad, joining the RAF in December 1925. The Hyderabad carried a crew of four, three defensive Lewis guns in nose, dorsal and ventral position and a bomb load of up to 1,100 lb. With a wingspan of 75 ft., a length of 59 ft. 2 in. and a gross weight of 13,590 lb., it was powered by two 454-HP Napier Lion engines. The Hyderabad continued to serve until 1934.

1923 January   The first of two prototype Curtiss XPW-8 fighters took to the air competing for a production order with the Boeing XPW-9 then in construction. A twin-bay biplane powered by a 440-HP Curtiss D-12, the XPW-8 had a top speed of 160 MPH and two 0.30 in. machine guns or one 0.50 in. and one 0.30 in. machine gun. Heavier than the Boeing contender, the XPW-8 had wing-mounted radiators vulnerable to bullets in combat. Curtiss was furious at the competition from Boeing but got an order for 25 in return for a bid at a U.S. cross-country marathon flight inspired by Brig. Gen. Mitchell.

1923 February 3   The Soviet Council of the People's Commissariat (Sovnarkom) approved plans for expansion of Soviet civil aviation under the auspices of the Red Air Fleet, which was to control procedures and operations. This date is officially considered to be the start of Soviet civil aviation. The following month, the Enterprise for Friends of the Air Fleet (the ODVF) was formed along with a company called Dobrolet formed from state organizations and commercial interests. Regularly scheduled flights between Moscow and Nizhny Novgorod (later known as Gorky, until 1991) began July 15, 1923.

1923 February 21   To more effectively use the backlog of aero engines left over from World War I production orders, the U.S. Navy Bureau of Aeronautics stipulated that no engine over two years old was to be repaired. Any engine that needed overhaul would be changed for a new replacement engine. Thus free of obsolescent engines, aircraft would benefit from the new generation of aero engines then in development. This had a positive effect on the development of naval aviation in the United States.

1923 March 1   A Mitsubishi 1MF1 biplane fighter was flown off the deck of the aircraft carrier *Hosho* by 1st Lt. Shun-Ichi Kira, the first Imperial Japanese Navy pilot to carry out this feat. The Mitsubishi Internal Combustion Engine Manufacturing Co. had employed Herbert Smith and seven engineers from Sopwith in February 1921 to design a new Japanese fighter. The 1MF1 emerged in October 1921 with a span of 30.5 ft. a length of 22 ft. and a gross weight of 2,513 lb., and with a top speed of 140 MPH and a duration of 2.5 hr. British test pilot Capt. Jordon had flown the 1MF1 off the *Hosho* several days earlier.

1923 March 5   The great aeronautical pioneer Igor Sikorsky set up the Sikorsky Aero Engineering Corp. in the United States with the financial help of several important leading figures of the day, including the composer Sergey Rachmaninoff. Sikorsky had left Russia in 1917 when revolution threatened his work and his life. After traveling to America, he became destitute and almost starved to death before developing his aircraft interests. From now on, Sikorsky was to concentrate on the development of rotary-winged aircraft.

1923 March 6   The ODVF, the Enterprise for Friends of the Air Fleet, was established in a program aimed at getting Russian citizens air minded. Through *Pravda,* air events were publicized, air shows set up and exhibitions organized. People were given joy rides, children were taught to make model airplanes, and an aviation paper called *Samolyot* was published. Soviet workers were told it was patriotic to support aviation, and the air force grew from the several flying schools that sprang up across the country and fostered among the public an enthusiasm and commitment for aviation hard to find in other, less autocratic societies.

1923 March 17   The U.S. secretary of state for war, John W. Weeks, appointed a board headed by Maj. Gen. William Lassiter, assistant chief of staff for operations and training, to evaluate a plan put forward by Gen. Patrick that said that air preparedness by the United States should concentrate on pursuit and bombardment and the ability of the United States to respond quickly to an emergency. Gen. Patrick proposed a peacetime force of 4,000 officers and 25,000 enlisted men with 2,500 air cadets. There should, he said, be 1,680 operational combat planes, 11 airships and 24 balloons. For emergency, the United States should be able to mobilize 12,880 officers, 109,712 enlisted men, 5,194 airplanes, 24 airships and 104 balloons.

1923 March 23   As a part of the reconstruction of the Italian armed forces after World War I, the Regia Aeronautica was formed as the first Italian independent air arm. Following a period of

demobilization, the Italians moved from crisis to crisis until the fascists came to power and turned the monarchy into a figurehead. Strong military forces were implicit within Mussolini's new autocracy, and military aviation received considerable funds. An early mainstay of the new air arm was the Ansaldo A.300/4 general-purpose biplane.

1923 March   The prototype Fairey Fawn took to the air and would eventually become the first day bomber designed after World War I to serve with the RAF. With a span of 49 ft. 11 in. and a length of 32 ft. 1 in., the Fawn had a top speed of 114 MPH and a range of 650 mi. It carried one forward-firing Vickers gun, a single aft-firing Lewis and a 460-lb. bomb load. When production ceased in 1926, 70 had been built, seeing service with six of the 12 home-based day bomber squadrons until the last Fawn was withdrawn in September 1929.

1923 April 9   Equipped with HS-2L aircraft, airline operations opened between New Orleans and Pilottown, La., at the mouth of the Mississippi. Known as the Gulf Coast Air Line Inc., it ferried foreign mail 80 mi. between New Orleans and the ships at Pilottown that plied the Gulf of Mexico between the United States and South America, Cuba and other islands in the Caribbean. Operated by Merrill K. Riddick, it was, along with Hubbard's airline, the only overseas airmail operation of its kind in the United States prior to Pan American international airmail operations beginning 1927.

1923 April 16   Lts. Oakley G. Kelly and John A. Macready took off from Wilbur Wright Field, Ohio in one of two Fokker T-2 monoplanes owned by the USAAS to fly a distance of 2,516.55 mi. over a measured course. They landed back at Wright Field after 36 hr. 4 min. 34 sec., thus achieving, on April 17, a new world distance record. Designated T-2, the Fokker was powered by a Liberty engine purchased from the Dutch aircraft manufacturer and had a wingspan of 79 ft. 8 in. with a length of 49 ft. 1 in. and a gross weight of 10,750 lb. It had a fuel capacity increased from 130 gal. to 725 gal. by the use of additional tanks in the wings and fuselage and extra capacity for oil and water. Lt. Kelly had been trying for a transcontinental hop since his first aborted attempt October 5, 1922.

1923 April 29   The first Boeing fighter, the Model 15, designated XPW-9, made its first flight at Camp Lewis, Wash. piloted by Frank Tyndall. Heavily influenced by the Fokker D.VII and especially its welded steel tubing employed by Reinhold Platz, Fokker's chief engineer, the Model 15 had similar construction. Powered by a 435-HP Curtiss D-12, the XPW-9 prototype had a top speed of 161 MPH and carried one 0.50-in. or two 0.30-in. machine guns and up to 244 lb. of bombs. The Army ordered 114 production XPW-9s which were delivered between October 1925 and May 1928, and the Navy took 43 and applied designations in the FB series.

1923 April   The U.S. Army inspected a German aircraft designed and built in Switzerland by Dornier. Known as the Falke, it was an all-metal cantilever monoplane radical in design and construction for this period. It had clean lines, a Wright H-3 engine that gave a top speed of 162 MPH and two synchronized machine guns; but it was too radical a design concept to generate confidence from the conservative military team that examined it at McCook Field in Dayton. Fearing the wings might fall off without bracing, they rejected it.

1923 May 3   USAAS Fokker T-2 pilots Lts. Oakley G. Kelly and John A. Macready completed the first nonstop flight across the United States in 26 hr. 50 min. 38.4 sec. The route they flew from Roosevelt Field, Long Island, N.Y. took them over Dayton, Ohio, Indianapolis, Ind., St. Louis, Mo., Kansas City, Kans., Tucumcari, N.M., and Wickenburg, Ariz. The flight began at 12:36 P.M. ET, May 2, and they landed at Rockwell Field, San Diego, Calif. at 12:26 P.M. PT on May 3. Their T-2 was powered by a 375-HP Liberty engine. The aircraft is preserved at the National Air & Space Museum in Washington, D.C., where it can be seen today.

1923 May 5   Powered by a 300-HP Hispano-Suiza engine, the Fokker D.XI sesquiplane fighter took to the air for the first time. It had been developed from an earlier Fokker known as the D.IX, which was designed from the D.VII of World War I fame. The USAAS purchased a D.IX and designated it PW-6. The D.XI had a wingspan of 38 ft., a length of 22 ft. and a gross weight of 2,755 lb. In 1925 the D.XI was used in Russia to clandestinely train German pilots. The USAAS ordered three D.XIs, each powered by a 435-HP Curtiss D-12 engine, which it designated the PW-7.

1923 May 7   The first British fighter of all-metal construction to enter service with the RAF, the Armstrong Whitworth Siskin III, made its first flight. A development of the Siskin II, it was powered by a 325-HP Armstrong Siddeley Jaguar III engine, which provided a top speed of 134 MPH and a service ceiling of 20,500 ft., and was armed with twin synchronized Vickers guns. The Siskin III entered service in May 1924, the first post-World War I British fighter. The RAF bought 62 Siskin IIIs and about 400 of the IIIAs, powered by a 450-HP Jaguar IV engine. This latter version served with the RAF for almost a decade.

1923 May 9   The Blériot-Aéronautique test-flew its Blériot 115 two-bay biplane for the first time. The 115 was an eight-passenger transport aircraft powered by four 180-HP Hispano-Suiza 8Ac water-cooled engines, two mounted on the upper surface of the lower wing and two on top of the upper wing center section. In

1924 the 115 was modified to carry 10 passengers on the Paris-London route. The 115 had a wingspan of 82 ft., a length of 47 ft. 5 in. and a loaded weight of up to 11,243 lb. including a 1,763 lb. payload. A developed version, the Blériot 155, could carry 17 passengers, but only two 155s were built.

1923 May 23   The Société Anonyme Belge d'Exploitation de la Navigation Aérienne (SABENA) was formed. By the end of 1924, services were in operation from Brussels to Amsterdam and to Strasbourg and Basle. The airline used early de Havilland biplanes as well as Breguet and Farman Goliaths. A primary objective of the new company was to consolidate air communications in the Belgian Congo (now Zaire), and during 1926 and 1927, a 1,422-mi. route was set up between Boma and Elisabethville (Lubumbashi) via Leopoldville (Kinshasa).

1923 May 26   An agreement was reached between the chief of the USAAS and the chief of the U.S. Navy Bureau of Aeronautics that cooperation over specifications for aircraft equipment would have mutual benefits for the military air services, industry and budget planners. An interservice standardization committee met for the first time at McCook Field and continued a series of annual meetings until 1937. The Naval Bureau of Aeronautics representative at the first meeting was Lt. R. S. Barnaby.

1923 May 29   Reuben Fleet formed the Consolidated Aircraft Corp. of Buffalo, N.Y. Fleet had left the Gallaudet Aircraft Corp., where he had served as chairman and managing director. He bought the entire stock of airplane designs from Gallaudet and then successfully negotiated a similar deal with Dayton-Wright when its owner, General Motors, closed it down. Consolidated produced the PT-1 trainer from the Dayton-Wright TW-3 and built 171 for the Army Air Service. Consolidated would achieve fame for the B-24 Liberator of World War II and, after merging with Vultee in March 1943, produce the B-36 and two Century-series fighters.

One of the better and more robust French bombers late in World War I, the Breguet 14B2 with Michelin bomb racks.

1923 May   The first flight took place of one of the first two post-World War I RAF fighters, the Gloster Grebe. Powered by a 400-HP Armstrong Siddeley Jaguar IV engine, the Grebe could reach a speed of 152 MPH and a height of 23,000 ft. With two Vickers machine guns, it had a loaded weight of 2,614 lb. The RAF purchased 129 Grebes, and the type entered service in October 1924, five months after its contemporary, the Siskin III. A Grebe was the first fighter to achieve terminal velocity of 240 MPH in a dive.

1923 June 14   With a population of less than 1.5 million, the small country of New Zealand became one of the few countries of its size to set up a military air arm, the New Zealand Permanent Air Force. It also established the New Zealand Territorial Air Force, both organizations merging to become the Royal New Zealand Air Force (RNZAF), which was constituted on April 1, 1937. Fifty years later, it had 102 aircraft, of which 46 were front-line combat types, such as the MDC A-4, and 4,200 personnel.

1923 June 24   The U.S. War Department issued instructions to the army air service to obtain complete data on the Fokker F.V transport and the Douglas Cloudster with a view to selecting one for a mass flight around the world. The Fokker F.V was designed as an eight-passenger airliner, an advance on the F.III but a step back from the F.IV, which was considered too big for the needs of the prevailing market. On July 5, Douglas submitted plans for a specially modified version of the DT-2 rather than the Cloudster, now three years old, quoting a price of $23,721 and delivery within 45 days, targets which Fokker could not match.

1923 June 26   The British Prime Minister Stanley Baldwin, announced plans for a Home Defense Air Force in addition to existing RAF responsibilities. The aim was to equip 52 squadrons by adding 34 to the existing total capable of repulsing air attack by the strongest air force within striking distance of Britain. The government also said it was keen to conclude agreements limiting air power by an agreement to the Five Power Naval Treaty of 1922. This did not, however, affect the "10-year rule," whereby the British government believed a conflict in Europe was not possible within at least a decade and that there would therefore be plenty of time to re-arm should crises arise. (This was established as cabinet office policy on August 15, 1919.)

1923 June 27   The first practical demonstration of in-flight refueling took place between two D.H.4Bs flown by Lt. Lowell H. Smith and Lt. John P. Richter of the USAAS as they were unsuccessfully attempting to break the endurance record set on April 16–17. One aircraft was equipped with a hose that could be lowered to a receptacle in the upper wing center-section of a second D.H.4B flying below and behind. A simple shutoff valve prevented gasoline flow when the hose was disconnected. Trials took place to develop the technique, and it was a success from the outset, opening several new and unique possibilities for long-duration flight.

1923 June   The U.S. Army's TC-1 helium nonrigid airship is destroyed by fire. Ordered as replacement for the C- and D-series hydrogen types, the TC-1 had a length of 195 ft. 9 in., a diameter of 44.5 ft. and a volume of 200,600 cu. ft. Airships of this type were built to varying sizes and normally carried a maximum crew of seven; five of the first 10 were built by Goodyear. The army received a total of 14 TC-series airships, the largest of which had a length of 233 ft., a volume of 360,000 cu. ft. and a crew of eight. The last TC was withdrawn from service in 1944.

1923 July 18   The Vickers Vanguard commercial transport, a derivative of the Virginia I, made its first flight from Brooklands, England. Ordered by Instone Air Line as a 23-seat airliner, the Vanguard had the unmistakable appearance of the Victoria troop transporter, which first flew in August 1922. The Vanguard had a slightly greater wingspan than the Victoria and was powered by two 468-HP Napier Lion engines. As the biggest civil transport aircraft of its day, the Vanguard drew strong interest from Europe and America, but nothing came of the negotiations for potential sales and only the one (bearing both military serial no. J6924 and civil registration G-EBCP) was ever built.

1923 July 30   De Havilland's D.H.50, a successor to the D.H.9C, won first prize at the International Air Traffic Competitions in Sweden, flown by A. J. Cobham. The plane had made its first flight at the hands of H. S. Broad only four days before it was flown to Göteborg, Sweden for the event. Cobham would carve an enduring reputation for the D.H.50 by using it to set several long-distance records. The D.H.50 was unusual in that the enclosed fuselage compartment for four passengers was placed forward between the wings, and the open pilot's cockpit was to the rear.

1923 July   The British aircraft carrier HMS *Hermes* was completed at Devonport, England. With a displacement of 10,850 tons, it was the first purpose-built aircraft carrier to be laid down, after an order for her construction was issued in October 1917. (The Japanese carrier *Hosho* was laid down after the *Hermes* but was launched first.) *Hermes* could carry 25 aircraft, but this was reduced to 15 following a refit in 1933. Hermes had a length of 600 ft., a beam of 70.25 ft. and a draught of 21.5 ft. She carried 850 crew and at various times served in home, Mediterranean and Far East waters. She was sunk off Sri Lanka (Ceylon) in action against the Japanese on April 9, 1942.

1923 August 1   Maj. Gen. Mason M. Patrick, chief of the U.S. Army Air Service, approved an around-the-world flight and ordered a prototype Douglas World Cruiser, derived from the DT-2 torpedo bomber, for the purpose. The DWC would have a 60-gal. tank in the upper wings, a 62-gal. tank in each lower wing root, a 150-gal. tank behind the engine, a 160-gal. tank underneath the cockpit and a 150-gal. tank below the rear seat. This would provide a maximum range of 2,200 mi. with the standard 420-HP Liberty engine. Following tests with the prototype, final approval for the flight was granted November 19, and Douglas got a contract for four DWCs on November 23.

1923 August 21   Four days of night flying tests on the 920-mi. Chicago-Cheyenne leg of the transcontinental airmail route began for the purpose of evaluating a lighting system newly installed between the two cities. Some 289 flashing gas beacons had been set up to guide the night flyers with five terminal and 34 emergency landing strips set up with beacons, lights and markers. Seventeen mail planes were equipped with luminous instruments, lights and parachute flares. As a result of these improvements, regularly scheduled night airmail flights began July 1, 1924. The westbound time was set at 34 hr., 20 min. and the eastbound time at 29 hr., 15 min.

1923 August 22   Designed by American Walter Barling for the Engineering Division and built by Witteman-Lewis, the giant XNBL-1 triplane took to the air for the first time, piloted by Lt. H. R. Harris. Powered by six 420-HP Liberty engines in four nacelles between the two lower wings, the two inner nacelles each carried two engines in tandem, the rear two driving pusher propellers. The experimental bomber had a wingspan of 120 ft., a length of 65 ft., a height of 27 ft., four rudders in a biplane tail, 10 wheels, a crew of six and up to seven defensive gun positions. It had a range of 170 mi. with 5,500 lb. of bombs and a maximum weight of 42,569 lb. Only one was built for tests, and that one was abandoned in 1925.

1923 August 23 The I-1 (Il-400), the first independent design from Nikolai Nikolayevich Polikarpov, made its first flight. Polikarpov had worked at the RBVZ on the Ilya Muromets and later became chief engineer at the GAZ-1 plant. In 1922 he designed a 35 ft. 5 in.-span monoplane with a length of 23 ft. 11 in. powered by a 400-HP Liberty engine, which was designated M-5. Difficult to fly, the I-1 nevertheless provided valuable design and manufacturing experience for Polikarpov, who would achieve wide respect for his fighter aircraft designs in the years up to World War II.

1923 August 28 Lt. Lowell H. Smith and Lt. John P. Richter landed after remaining aloft in a D.H.4B for 37 hr. 15 min. 14 sec. over San Diego. To achieve this record, their plane had to be refueled 15 times in midair by a second D.H.4B via a hose through which gasoline flowed into a tank on the upper wing center-section. The aircraft achieved a new refueled flight duration record and a closed-circuit flight distance record of 3,293 mi. The implications for military operations across very great distances were profound, although the technique would not be widely exploited until after World War II.

1923 September 4 The U.S. Navy airship ZR-1 made its first flight at Lakehurst, N.J. with 23 people on board. Named *Shenandoah*, the ZR-1 was the first U.S. airship to use helium gas, which is safer than hydrogen. Designed by the U.S. Navy Bureau of Aeronautics, it was built at the Naval Aircraft Facory in Philadelphia. Fabricated sections were trucked to Lakehurst for assembly at the only hangar capable of holding the airship. *Shenandoah* was 680 ft. long with a volume of 2,115,000 cu. ft. and was based on the Zeppelin L 49 that came down in France during October 1917. Powered by six 300-HP Packard engines, it made 57 flights before a storm destroyed it on September 23, 1925.

1923 September 5 Brig. Gen. William Mitchell was again assigned to use air power to demonstrate the destruction of warships when he was directed by his chief, Maj. Gen. Patrick, to attack the decommissioned battleships *New Jersey* and *Virginia* at anchor, starting with an attack from 10,000 ft. By the end of the day, both ships had been sunk, although dud bombs and faulty rack release gear failed to sink the *New Jersey* until persistent effort finally breached the hull. Nevertheless, there was still a great deal of skepticism about the use of bombers for this kind of operation. Next month Mitchell got married and began a lengthy honeymoon coupled with a tour of the Pacific and the Far East. His chief had diplomatically kept him as far away from Washington, D.C., as possible in the two years since the successful aerial sinking of the *Alabama* on September 26, 1921.

1923 September 9 The first of two Curtiss Model 32s, designated R2C-1 by the U.S. Navy, made its first flight prior to the fourth Pulitzer race for which it had been designed. Building on experience with the CR, the navy winner of the 1921 Pulitzer, and the army R-6, winner of the 1922 Pulitzer, the R2C-1 biplane had its upper wing lowered to the fuselage so that the pilot looked over the upper surface. It was powered by a 507-HP Curtiss D-12A providing a top speed of 266 MPH. With a span of 22 ft. and a length of 19 ft. 8.5 in., the R2C-1 had a gross weight of 2,071 lb.

1923 September 15 Flying a D.H.50, Alan Cobham picked up mail from the United States that had been landed at Plymouth, England by the SS *Manchuria,* and flew it to Birmingham. This was the first demonstration of a series of test flights to pioneer an airmail route on behalf of the Air Ministry and the General Post Office. Four passengers accompanied Cobham, but the weather was bad and the flight took more than four hours. The test series lasted a month, and plans for regular service were abandoned.

1923 September 23 The prototype Fokker D.XIII sesquiplane made its first flight powered by a 450-HP Napier Lion engine. Designed hurriedly so as to provide pilots at the secret German flying school at Lipetsk in the USSR with a high performance aircraft, it was the fastest fighter in the world, with a top speed of 171 MPH. The Germans ordered, via the Soviet Union, 50 D.XIIIs and 50 of the earlier D.XIs, very similar but powered by a 300-HP Hispano-Suiza. In Britain, engines in need of repair were often delivered to Napier after which they were returned direct to Moscow.

1923 September 28 The seventh Schneider Trophy seaplane race was held at Cowes, Isle of Wight, England for the first time and attracted a major U.S. contingent, including three U.S. Navy entrants. The race consisted of five laps around a 37.2 nm left-hand course. A Curtiss CR-3 flown by Lt. David Rittenhouse came in first with an average speed of 177.374 MPH, and Lt. Rutledge Irvine brought the second CR-3 home at 173.35 MPH followed by British aviator Henri Biard in the Supermarine Sea Lion III, which had won the 1922 event, at 157.17 MPH. The French and Italian entries either failed to compete or to finish.

1923 October 6 Lt. Alford J. Williams, U.S. Navy, flying a Curtiss R2C-1, won the 1923 Pulitzer air race, setting 100-km (62.1 mi.) and 200-km (124.2 mi.) records at averages of 243.812 MPH and 243.673 MPH respectively. Lt. H. J. Brow came in second with other navy pilots taking the third and fourth positions. The first four were all faster than the 1922 winning time flown by the U.S. Army. After the race, the army bought Brow's R2C-1 from the Navy for a token price of $1.00 and designated it R-8. It crashed on September 2, 1924, just before the Pulitzer race for that year.

1923 October 30 Lacointe raised the world altitude record to 36,565 ft. while flying a considerably modified Nieuport 29 designated ND 40 R. It had extended-span wings for extra lift and several modifications to the engine allowing reliable operation at extreme altitudes. The aircraft was fitted with a supercharger. It was later fitted with floats and used to capture the seaplane altitude record also. In a spate of altitude attempts, the record had doubled in little more than a decade.

1923 October First in a long line of successful Russian aircraft, the ANT-1 designed by Andrei Nikolayevich Tupolev made its first flight powered by a 35-HP six-cylinder Anzani radial engine. Flown by Ye. I. Pogosski and N. I. Petrov, the ANT-1 incorporated duralumin in certain sections of the aircraft that had been designed by Tupolev for the specific purpose of testing new standardized preformed structures using this metal. Born on September 10, 1888, Tupolev studied engineering under Nikolai Zhukovsky but had been arrested for Bolshevik interests before the revolution.

1923 November 2 One of two Curtiss 32 R2C-1 biplanes flown by Lt. Brow became the first aircraft to officially exceed 400 km/hr. when Brow achieved an average of 417.59 km/hr. (259.48 MPH) over a measured 3 km (1.864 mi.) course at Mitchel Field,

Long Island, N.Y. Two days later, Lt. Williams achieved a new world absolute speed record of 417.59 km/hr. (266.19 MPH) in four flights over the same course. It would stand for more than a year, before being broken on December 11, 1924.

1923 December 23 The Italian pilot Maj. Vasco Magrini carried out the first successful flight of an airplane powered by a ducted-fan engine. Driven by an 80-HP Gnôme rotary engine at 1,150 RPM, the monoplane was flown from the Campi di Marte, Florence. The airplane was designed and built by the Italian enginer Antonio Mattioni on principles first worked out in 1910. Further development work led to more flights later in the year. Caproni picked up the research and Dr. Ing. (Doctor of Engineering) Luigi Stipa of the Aviation Ministry Studies Department designed and built a two-seat, ducted-fan aircraft in 1932.

1923 The origins of Soviet research into tailless airplane designs can be traced to the work of Boris Ivanovich Chyeranovskii who built and tested an unpowered flying wing called the BICh-1 with flight control surfaces combining the functions of elevators and ailerons. Chyeranovskii was to build more tailless airplanes than any one else in the USSR, or the rest of the world. The BICh-1 had a thick wing and resulted from studies at the Zhukovskii Academy in 1922 when he first proposed the concept. His BICh-2 completed in 1924 is reputed to have made 27 flights. The first powered machine would fly in 1926.

1923 Perhaps the strangest aircraft to emerge during the year was the Farman F.121 Jabiru. The fuselage was 44 ft. 10 in. in length and of both metal and wood construction with flat, slab sides and a fuselage depth at the nose of about 10 ft. The nose was rounded but flat on top and bottom with wrap-around windows in front. The wing was attached to the top of the forward fuselage and had a span of 62 ft. 4 in. with sawed off tips. It was powered by four Hispano-Suiza 8Ac engines mounted in tandem in two nacelles, each attached to the wing and the fuselage by struts. The cabin held seats for eight people. A later version designated F-4X had one engine on top of the nose and one under each wing and carried only six passengers.

1923 A major aircraft project visualized by Prof. Hugo Junkers would have had the capacity to fly 100 passengers and 10 crew in a single aircraft. Junkers had for several years dreamed of building flying wings capable of carrying between 100 and 1,000 people in a single hop across the Atlantic. His latest concept was for an airliner with a wingspan of 262 ft. 5 in., a chord of 32 ft. 9 in., a design weight of almost 80,000 lb. and a speed of 124 MPH. Known as the J1000, this project never materialized but reflects the forward thinking of this great German aircraft designer.

1924 January 1 The Focke-Wulf Flugzeugbau A.G. was formed by Heinrich Focke, George Wulf and Werner Naumann at Bremen. Focke and Wulf had been working together on airplane designs for more than 10 years, and although few people outside Germany had heard of them, they soon built a solid reputation. Wulf died in 1927, but the company increased its output and by World War II was a major force in German aeronautics. Their most notable products were the Fw 190 fighter and the Fw 200 Condor.

1924 February 8 Deigned by the Russian aircraft designers V. L. Aleksandrov and V. V. Kalinin, the AK 1 made its first flight powered by a 160-HP Salmson Rb.9 water-cooled radial engine. This aircraft was used in the inaugural flight along the route between Moscow and Kazan, stopping at Nizhny Novgorod. The

AK 1 monoplane had been designed in 1923 with a wingspan of 49 ft., a length of 36 ft. and a loaded weight of 3,637 lb. Like most Soviet aircraft, the aircraft was designed to be flown with either wheels or skis.

1924 February 19 As if to goad the new Labour government into accepting commitments for a strong home defense force made during 1923, Sir Samuel Hoare, the former minister of air, publicly compared Britain's near-total air demobilization to the French by citing the 1,000 front-line combat aircraft held by the French as against barely 100 operated by the RAF. The aircraft industry in Britain had been worried that the Labour ministers might cut aviation expenditures as they implied they might by questioning the premise that a strong air defense force was practical.

1924 March 7 The British air estimates were released showing a planned expenditure of £14.8 million for 1924–25, the first for the new Labour government. There had been fears that the "expansion" program of 1923 would be rescinded by the new government, but confidence in industry was high that the Labour ministers would honor prior commitments. In fact, the government put more money into research than had their predecessors.

1924 March 31 Imperial Airways Ltd. was formed in Britain from the four existing independent British airlines: Handley Page Transport Ltd., formed June 14, 1919; Daimler Air Hire Ltd., a subsidiary of the BSA-Daimler organization and formed on June 7, 1919; British Marine Air Navigation Co. Ltd., founded March 23, 1923, by Hubert Scott-Paine of Supermarine; and Instone Air Line Ltd., formed in December 1921 from the Instone Aerial Transport Dept. Rt. Hon. Sir Eric Campbell Geddes became the first chairman, and offices were established at Wolseley House, Piccadilly, London. It had capitalization of £1 million, and would receive a subsidy of £1 million over 10 years.

1924 April 1 The Royal Canadian Air Force (RCAF) was formed by royal assent of King George V. It had previously been known as the Canadian Air Force. An aviation corps had been formed in September 1914, and although 13,345 Canadians served with the British RFC and RNAS during World War I, there was no concerted attempt to form an independent air force until 1918. After the war, and with the approval of the British government, the first two squadrons of the new Canadian Air Force were formed late in November 1918.

1924 April 4 Four Douglas World Cruisers equipped with floats left Sand Point, Wash. for Prince Rupert, British Columbia, Canada, on the first official leg of their flight around the world sponsored by the USAAS. The first DWC *(Seattle)* (serial no. 23-1229) carried Maj. Frederick L. Martin and Staff Sgt. Alva L. Harvey. *Chicago* (23-1230) carried Lts. Lowell Smith and Leslie Arnold, the third *Boston* (23-1231), carried Lt. Leigh Wade and Staff Sgt. Henry H. Ogden, the fourth *New Orleans* (23-1232), carried Lt. Erik Nelson and Lt. John Harding. The race to beat other countries to the first flight to circumnavigate the globe had been at the instigation of Gen. Patrick.

1924 April 6 Two officers from the Royal Australian Air Force, Wing Comdr. S. J. Goble and Flt. Lt. I. E. McIntyre, began an 8,568-mi. trip around the Australia coastline in a Fairey IIID (serial no. A10.3). The flight was completed May 19 in 90 hr. of flying time for an average speed of about 94 MPH. (The IIID had first flown in August 1920, representing the latest in a line that began with the N10 of 1917.) The Australian government ordered six IIIDs, the first of which had been delivered August 12, 1921.

The Douglas World Cruiser Chicago, *one of four such aircraft that set off April 4, 1924, for a flight around the world.*

1924 April 14 The first FAI distance record for helicopters was given to Étienne Oehmichen for a flight of 1,180 ft. with his No. 2 aircraft comprising four rotors and eight propellers. On April 17, the record was increased to 1,722 ft. On May 4, Oehmichen increased his distance to more than a mile and remained in the air for 14 min., completing the first 1 km (3,281 ft.) closed-circuit helicopter record in 7 min. 40 sec. Oehmichen continued with his helicopter tests and developed other designs before the German occupation of France in 1940 put an end to his work.

1924 April 26 Three British aviators, Sqdn. Ldr. A. S. C. MacLaren, Flying Officer J. Plenderleith and Sgt. Andrews, set off for Tokyo from Karachi in their Vickers Vulture II (G-EBHO), having left England during the third week of March in an attempt to fly around the world. They came down 380 mi. out of Karachi and after several repairs made it to Tokyo. They were finally forced to abandon the attempt just beyond Kamchatka when, after coming down on water, the Vulture was destroyed in strong seas, the crew having made it to shore.

1924 April 28 Britain's Imperial Airways opened its first scheduled service flying from London to Paris, just four weeks after it was formed. The London-Brussels-Cologne service began May 3, and an onward extension of the London-Paris flight opened as a summer service on June 17 with flights to Basle and Zurich. Bearing witness to British intransigence and complete lack of international civil air-mindedness, in 1934 Imperial Airways had exactly the same number of routes and was flying a route mileage actually less than the four companies that formed Imperial Airways flew collectively in 1923. Had German and French air routes not been eliminated by the 1939–45 war, Britain's strong presence in international air travel would have expired anyway in the early 1940s.

1924 April The prototype of one of the most famous inter-war civil aircraft, the Fokker F.VII, took to the air for the first time. Ordered in December 1923 by the Dutch airline KLM, the F.VII was designed as a successor to the F.III. Powered by a 360-HP Rolls Royce Eagle engine, it had a span of 72 ft. 2 in., a length of 47 ft. 8 in. and a gross weight of 8,140 lb. Built to carry eight passengers, it was designed for range, compromising with a top speed of 97 MPH. It was during the design of this aircraft that the Dutch drew plans for a publicity flight from the Netherlands to their territories in the Far East (what is today Indonesia).

1924 May 4 In a fitting demonstration of airlift capacity anticipated for the RAF by the new Vickers Victoria, one of two prototypes helped lift British soldiers to an uprising at Kirkuk, 150 mi. north of Baghdad. Although each of two Vernons had a standard carrying capacity of 2,000 lb. or 12 men, the Victoria could lift twice that amount, or up to 20 fully equipped soldiers. For this flight, however, a total of 66 men were carried in the three RAF aircraft supplemented the following day by an additional 79 men. By train and a forced march, it would have taken five days to reach Kirkuk.

1924 May 24 Three Douglas World Cruisers *(Chicago, Boston* and *New Orleans)* out of four that set off around the world April 4 arrived in Yokohama, Japan, having flown from Sand Point, Wash. via Prince Rupert, Canada and across Alaska via Sitka, Cordova and Chignik. From Yokohama, they flew on to Korea, China, Hong Kong, Indo-China, Thailand, Burma and Calcutta, India, where floats were attached for the flight to Paris. (The fourth DWC, *Seattle,* had been destroyed in a crash near Dutch Harbor, Alaska, but the crew reached safety after 10 days in a blizzard.)

1924 May 25 The opening route of a major expansion of Soviet civil aviation into the Ukraine was inaugurated with a flight from Kharkov to Kiev, via Poltava, by the newly formed airline Ukrvodzdukhput. Other routes added at the same time opened air services between Kharkov, Poltava, Yelisavetgrad and Odessa. The airline had been formed with capitalization of 550,000 rubles provided by a number of banks and industrial concerns run by the government. The first aircraft employed by this airline were two Dornier Komet IIs, each powered by a 260-HP Rolls Royce Falcon engine and capable of carrying six or seven passengers.

1924 May 26 Piloted by N. I. Petrov, the Tupolev ANT-2 made its first flight. Designed as a light, high-wing, transport aircraft, the ANT-2 had a wingspan of 32 ft. 9 in. and a length of 24 ft. 7 in. The first Soviet all-metal aircraft, it was powered by a 100-HP Bristol Lucifer engine. The design was reminiscent of the Junkers corrugated metal aircraft and afforded room for two seats facing each other in the enclosed fuselage beneath the wing. The pilot sat in an exposed cockpit between the leading edge of the wing and the engine. Although successful, the ANT-2 was never produced in quantity.

1924 May The first of two Curtiss Model 36 twin-engined bombers ordered was delivered to the USAAC as the XNBS-4. Designed as a night bomber to replace the NBS-1, it was powered by two 435-HP Liberty 12 engines, carried a crew of four, had a wingspan of 90 ft. 2 in., a length of 46 ft. 5 in., and a gross weight of 13,795 lb. and was capable of carrying a 2,100-lb. bomb load. Maximum range was just over 600 mi. at a cruising speed of 83 MPH. The aircraft was not ordered into production, but Curtiss incorporated much of the design into their Model 52, ordered as the B-2.

1924 June 23 A Curtiss PW-8 of the USAAS, piloted by Lt. Russell Maughan, carried out the first coast-to-coast flight across the United States between dawn and dusk in a Curtiss PW-8. The flight began at Mitchel Field, N.Y. at 2:58 A.M. and ended at San Francisco, a distance of 2,670 mi. flown in 21 hr. 48 min. Lt. Maughan made five refueling stops but just beat dusk by the time he landed at Crissy Field, San Francisco, Calif. despite losing time to strong headwinds, thunderstorms, fog and a broken gas valve that held him up at McCook Field while it was repaired. Representative of the new breed of fighters entering service, the Curtiss PW-8 had a top speed of 168 MPH.

1924 June 23 The first aircraft to emerge from the recently formed Focke-Wulf Flugzeugbau A.G. made its first flight. Known simply as the A 16, it was powered by a 75-HP Siemens & Halske Sh 11 air-cooled radial engine. The wing, with a span of 45 ft. 7 in., had been designed for good stability at high angles of attack. The fuselage, with a length of 27 ft. 11 in., was slab-sided, deep and fitted out to carry a total four people. Several versions appeared, including one with a 135-HP Mercedes D.II in-line engine and a total of 23 A 16s were built. Deutsche Luft Hansa used the A 16 until the late 1920s.

1924 June 23 The first Beaumont Cup (Coupe Commodore Louis D. Beaumont) race was held in Istres, near Marseilles, France. Named after an American industrialist who had taken French nationality, it was a speed contest held over six laps of a 50-km circuit with the winner having to exceed 290 km/hr. (180 MPH) to qualify for the prize. The winner was Frenchman Sadi Lecointe, flying his Nieuport-Delage 42 powered by a 570-HP Hispano-Suiza engine at an average speed of 197.5 MPH. The second and last Beaumont Cup race was won by Lecointe in the same aircraft on October 18, 1925, at an average speed of 194.2 MPH.

1924 July 1 The first regularly scheduled night airmail service got under way between New York and San Francisco, with 14 stops along the way, employing changes of pilot at Cleveland, Chicago, Omaha, Cheyenne, Salt Lake City and Reno. The flight utilized the route-marking beacons set up between Chicago and Cheyenne during 1923. Wesley L. Smith began the westbound flight, and Claire K. Vance opened the eastbound route. Westerly flights would last 34 hr. 20 min., and easterly flights took only 29 hr. 15 min. Even these times were two or three days quicker than the best surface time. The lighting system was extended from Cheyenne to Rock Springs, Wyo. and from Chicago to Cleveland during the year.

1924 July 1 At the start of FY 1925, the U.S. Army Air Service had run down to almost the lowest level it would reach between the wars, with a total 1,364 airplanes on strength, of which only 754 were in commission. This total included 78 pursuit aircraft, 59 bombers, eight attack aircraft and 457 observation types; the balance was made up of training and general purposes machines. Concern about the poor state of U.S. defenses was becoming more audible.

1924 July 9 The first recorded flight of a live bull took place when champion breeder Nico V was flown from Rotterdam, Holland to Paris, France. The bull was carried by KLM in a Fokker F.III transport aircraft. Although passengers were the mainstay of early airline flight, as airplanes increased in size and capacity, the movement of live animals by air became a common occurrence. It was not so typical, however, of air freight in 1924!

1924 July 15 The British cabinet approved a recommendation made by Sir Hugh Trenchard and Vice Adm. Sir Roger Keyes, deputy chief of the naval staff, that the Naval Air Arm of the RAF should be handed to the Admiralty and renamed Fleet Air Arm, as it had been unofficially called for several years. Since the merging of the Royal Flying Corps and the Royal Naval Air Service in 1918, the RAF had imposed a control on the navy's air elements that prevented British naval aviation from getting the same priorities afforded to its counterparts, such as U.S. naval aviation. This resulted in a bitter controversy over who should have control of the maritime air forces, the RAF or the Royal Navy.

1924 August 8 The U.S. Navy airship *Shenandoah* demonstrated at-sea operations by mooring to the USS *Patoka* while the

Patoka was underway. The *Patoka* had been fitted with a mooring mast to receive the tiedown boom on the airship. The airship remained attached to the ship until the following day while various maneuvers were carried out along the eastern seaboard. The *Shenandoah* participated in a naval exercise later in the month when it was used to locate an "enemy" force 300 mi. away at sea.

1924 August 29 Capt. E. J. Jones landed D.H.50A G-AUAB (Australian serial) at Melbourne, Australia after a 7,658-mi. flight around the country that began on August 7. With Jones were Col. H. C. Brinsmead, director of civil aviation for Australia, and Mr. Buchanan, an aircraft inspector. The D.H.50A completed the first circumnavigation of Australia. They spent almost 77 hr. in the air over Australia inspecting planned air routes and surveyed new sites for landing strips. The D.H.50 was one of nine built at Edgeware, England for Australia and was pressed into service for war duty in November 1942. It was powered by a Pratt & Whitney Wasp C radial engine.

1924 August Designed by Ing. (Engineer) Alessandro Marchetti, chief designer of the Società Idrovolanti Alta Italia (S.I.A.I.) since 1922, the twin-hull Savoia-Marchetti S.55 flying boat made its first flight. The monoplane wing had a span of 78 ft. 9 in. and supported on struts above the center section two 400-HP Lorraine-Dietrich engines built under license by Issota-Fraschini. Back to back, they each drove a pusher and a tractor propeller assembly. The thick wing incorporated the cockpit in the center leading edge. Twin booms and rudders supported the horizontal tail. The S.55 had a length of 54 ft. 1 in. Bombs could be suspended beneath the center section, and it had a range of 1,245 mi.

1924 September 12 The Fokker D.XII single-seat biplane fighter (a development of the D.XI) made its first flight. It was precursor to the D.XIII, of which only 50 were ever built. These aircraft went to Russia for German pilots to learn how to fly fast combat planes. Powered by a 450-HP Napier Lion engine, the D.XIII had a top speed of 160 MPH and set several records in 1925. As a link in the training channels for German pilots prohibited from military flying by the Treaty of Versailles, it was a valuable aircraft.

1924 September 28 Two Douglas World Cruisers (*Chicago* and *New Orleans*) returned to Seattle, Wash., having flown a total distance around the world of 26,503 mi. Flying time totaled 371 hr. 7 min at an average speed of 78 MPH. Three DWCs had flown from Calcutta to Paris via the Middle East where their wheels were changed for floats. The third DWC (*Boston*) had ditched after leaving Orkney, north of Scotland, but the crew was picked up and joined the others in Washington, D.C. for a hero's welcome. From Washington, again with wheels on, it was a relatively simple matter to cross the continent.

1924 October 1 A single-engine Fokker F.VII (registration H-NACC), flown by Thomassen ā Thuessinak van der Hoop, Lt. van Weerden-Poelman and van den Broecke, took off from Schiphol Airport, Amsterdam on a marathon journey to Batavia in the Dutch East Indies (now Indonesia). They only got as far as Philippopolis in Bulgaria due to mechanical trouble, but a new engine was sent out and they resumed the journey on November 3, finally reaching Batavia on November 24. The crew returned on the steamship *Patria*, arriving back at Schiphol to a tumultuous reception on December 18.

1924 October 4 The all-conquering Curtiss R-6 racing aircraft that dominated the Pulitzer Trophy races of 1922 and 1923 could

An airship experiment in carrying a Sopwith Camel escort fighter, here attached to British airship R.23.

manage only second place when Henry H. Mills flew his Verville-Sperry R-3 into first place for the 1924 event held at Dayton, Ohio. With a speed of 216.5 MPH, Mills was 27 MPH slower than the 1923 winner; the Curtiss R-6s were now relatively old and showing their age by a reduced performance.

1924 October 12 The German Zeppelin LZ 126 left Friedrichshafen for delivery to the United States as part of agreed upon reparations in the Treaty of Versailles. With Dr. Hugo Eckener on board, the airship arrived at Lakehurst, N.J. after a flight of 81 hr. Specially built for the U.S. Navy, it had a length of 658 ft., a diameter of 90.5 ft. and a volume of 2,472,000 cu. ft, and it was powered by five 400-HP Maybach engines. As the ZR-3, later *Los Angeles,* it flew 331 flights, accumulating 5,368 flying hours before retirement in 1932.

1924 October 16 The French test pilot Fernand Lasne ended an astonishing period of intensive record-breaking that began August 29. In a 48-day period, Lasne broke 16 aviation records flying his Nieuport-Delage 42 modified to achieve speed and distance performance. The N.D.42 was built as a high altitude fighter, but under the civil registration F-AHDQ, and outfitted with extra fuel tanks for endurance, it did much to broadcast the capabilities of Nieuport-Delage. The basic airplane had a wingspan of 39 ft. 4 in., a length of 24 ft. 7 in. and a gross weight of 3,986 lb. with a top speed of 165 MPH.

1924 October 17 A certificate of airworthiness was granted to the Fairey IIID (Fairey number F.576) ordered by Real Daylight Balata Estates Ltd. of British Guiana (now Guyana) for one of the first medical air ambulance roles on the North or South American continents. Balata used the aircraft (registration G-EBKE) to ferry fever victims from the plantations and the mining camps to the hospital at Georgetown. The service was suspended and the Fairey IIID returned to England in March 1928. It was scrapped a year later.

1924 October 23 Demonstrating its effectiveness as a delivery system for aerial dispatches, a Sperry Messenger was dropped

from the U.S. Army TC-1 airship and flew to a safe landing. The Sperry Messenger was designed by Alfred de Verville at the Engineering Division, McCook Field and was the smallest airplane ever used by the U.S. Army. With a wingspan of just 20 ft., the Messenger had a length of 17 ft. 6 in. and a height of 6 ft. 9 in. and weighed only 862 lb. fully loaded. Sperry built 42 Messengers for the army, and several were used for various experimental duties.

1924 October 25 After the 1925 Schneider Trophy race was canceled because of a lack of international competition, the U.S. Navy staged a spectacular series of flights to thrill the public and showcase naval aviation, in the course of which 17 seaplane records for speed were broken. It was a great day for Curtiss—the CR-3 took four world speed records, including absolute speed for seaplanes at 188.078 MPH. The PN-7, as the Naval Aircraft Factory called its modified Curtiss F-5L, seized 13 records for speed with loads, distance and duration.

1924 October The Gloster Grebe entered service with No. 25 Squadron, RAF, one of the first British post-World War I fighters to enter RAF service. The Grebe, and its contemporary the Armstrong Whitworth Siskin III, replaced the Sopwith Snipe, which first entered service in September 1918. When introduced, the Grebe was the fastest British fighter in service; it was used in airship drop tests during 1926 and remained in frontline service until replaced by the Siskin IIIA in 1929.

1924 November 4 At the annual review of the Italian Regia Aeronautica (Italian air force), a demonstration took place of the Fiat C.R.1 (designed by Celestino Rosatelli), the first Italian-designed fighter to enter service. It had an unusual appearance—the lower wing had a greater span, at 29 ft. 4 in., than the upper wing—and it was powered by a 300-HP Hispano engine. Production models had a Issota Fraschini engine that provided a top speed of 168 MPH. In 1925 the C.R.1 entered service with the first of eight squadrons to operate the type and was also used by aerobatic teams before it was retired in 1937.

1924 November 10 Alan Cobham, Arthur Buller Elliott and Air Vice Marshal Sir W. Sefton Brancker, the British director of civil aviation, began a route marking flight to Rangoon, Burma in D.H.50 G-EBFO. With a view to exploring possible routes for Imperial Airways to set up scheduled services to the Far East, the D.H.50 flew 17,600 mi. on a round-trip that ended back at Croydon, England on March 18, 1925. The four-month tour included 220 hr. of flying time at an average speed of 80 MPH, but the object of the journey was route-planning rather than speed.

1924 November 11 The first night catapult launch from a ship took place when Lt. Dixie Kiefer took off from the USS *California* at anchor in San Diego harbor. The launch took place at 9:46 P.M. and was carried out in the full glare of searchlights illuminating the water 3,000 ft. ahead of the ship. This demonstration confirmed the ability of ship-launched seaplanes to assist naval operations at sea day or night.

1924 November 17 The USS *Langley* became the first operational aircraft carrier with the U.S. Navy, being made flagship of Aircraft Squadrons, Battle Fleet, on December 1. The first aircraft from VF Squadron 2—the first naval air unit to train for combined carrier operations—landed on the *Langley*'s deck off San Diego on January 22, 1925. This date also marked the beginning of full operations with the Battle Fleet.

1924 November 24 With implications for the eventual rearmament of Germany and the effect that would have on stimulating the aircraft industry, Germany's Gen. Ludwig Wurtzbacher placed the supply system staff (Nachschubstab) in charge of surveying national industries with a view to ascertaining their suitability for arms production. Because the Weimar government forbade activity of this kind, the staff was to proceed in utmost secrecy as they prepared a blueprint for 63 Army divisions with associated air support. By mid-1925 this ambitious objective had been cut to 21 divisions.

1924 December 5 A wide range of progressive airplane designs at the International Aero Exhibition at the Grand Palais in Paris revealed a French and German preference for duralumin in the construction of airplanes. The British were still building airplanes out of wood and employing much the same techniques they had in World War I, and the Continental methods of construction were distinctly superior. The only British plane with a steel-tube fuselage was the Armstrong Whitworth Siskin V, and it had wooden wings.

1924 December 5 Deliveries to the U.S. Navy of the Boeing NB-series single-float seaplane began with the first of 42 production aircraft ordered. Developed as a trainer, the first production NB-1 was powered by a 200-HP Lawrence engine; a second batch of 30 was powered with the 180-HP Wright-Hispano E-4 water-cooled, in-line engine. Like the NB-1, these NB-2s were capable of being converted to landplane use with wheels. The NB-series served throughout the decade as a primary and gunnery trainer.

1924 December 11 Chief Adjutant Florentin Bonnet established a new world speed record for landplanes of 448.133 km/hr. (278.45 MPH) at Istres, France. He was flying a French-designed Bernard V.2 powered by a 620-HP 12-cylinder, water-cooled engine. This landplane record would stand for more than nine years until broken on September 3, 1932, by the American pilot James A. Doolittle. However, the absolute world air speed record would be broken by a Macchi M.52 seaplane on November 4, 1927.

1924 December 12 A Spanish Army pilot flew a Cierva autogyro from Quatro Vientros airfield to the town of Getafe, a distance of approximately 7 mi. He used a much-modified Cierva C.4 developed from the type first flown on January 9, 1923. This was the longest flight to date of an autogyro and the first cross-country flight achieved by a rotary-winged aircraft. Cierva had developed the autogyro through two additional model numbers, and plans were already being made to bring the autogyro to Britain's Royal Aircraft Establishment at Farnborough for detailed engineering and flight tests.

1924 December 13 The Naval Aircraft Factory NM-1 all-metal airplane made its first flight. Powered by a 325-HP Packard 1A-1237 engine, it was designed to provide a type model for use with the U.S. Navy and the U.S. Marine Corps. Only one (serial number A6450) was built, but it represented a new concept for aircraft design and construction. The British had discovered that aircraft operated at sea had a shorter life than their land-based counterparts, with wood being especially vulnerable to sea water. The NAF examined other methods of construction and built the NM-1 as the prototype of a new generation of metal airplanes for carriers.

1924 December 15 A Sperry Messenger piloted by Lt. Clyde Finter successfully hooked up to a boom cradle on the U.S. Army training blimp TC-3 in the first demonstration of a technique that would be developed later for trials with the rigid airships *Akron* and *Macon* using Curtiss fighters. Attaching fighters to airships increased the fighters' patrol area because the airship could carry them beyond their own range. The fighters could also protect the airship if it was attacked.

1924 December Capt. Geoffrey T. R. Hill carried out the first flight of his tailless monoplane glider. Designed to study unanticipated spins and how to either avoid them altogether or regain control if a spin was experienced—an average 50 lives a year were being lost in the RAF due to spins—Capt. Hill's glider had a wingspan of 45 ft. and a center-section chord of 9 ft. 2 in. The pilot was seated in a cradle beneath the center section just above two small wheels and a rear-facing ski. Two rudders, each at approximately mid-span, would double as air brakes.

1924 Soviet military aviation was reorganized under two new administrations covering military and naval aviation as two separate divisions. The existing Red Air Fleet became the Soviet Air Force (Voenno Vozdushinye Sily, or VVS), and naval aviation was formed into the Soviet Naval and Fleet-Air Force (Voenno Vozdushinye Sily-Voenno Morskogo Flota, or VVS-VMF). The VVS was structured later with separate commands for frontal, fighter/air defense, transport and long-range aviation units. Some facilities were shared by both VVS and VVS-VMF groups.

1925 January 3 The fastest day bomber of its time, the Fairey Fox made its first flight piloted by Norman Macmillan at Hendon. A demonstration in October so greatly impressed Air Vice Marshal Sir Hugh Trenchard that he ordered 28 for the RAF; delivery began August 1926. The Fox was designed around the 480-HP Curtiss D-12 engine, which C. R. Fairey had seen on a visit to the United States in 1923. With a sea-level top speed of 156 MPH, it was 41 MPH faster than the existing day bomber, the Fairey Fawn, and only financial constraints prevented more than one RAF squadron, No. 12, receiving the type. The Fox was replaced by the Hawker Hart in 1931.

1925 February 2 Pres. Calvin Coolidge signed the Kelly Bill, which made into law the Contract Air Mail Act passed by Congress. It approved the transfer of regional airmail service routes from the post office to private ventures. Contract airmail (CAM) routes would be fixed designated by number. The first five contracts were let on October 7, 1925, and these fed into the government airmail service, which was still operating transcontinental flights. The first routes to be flown operationally were CAM-6 and CAM-7, secured by the Ford Motor Co. and inaugurated on February 15, 1926.

1925 February 19   The British air estimates were published revealing a Labour government plan to spend a total £19.1 million in the year 1925–26. The RAF had about 54 operational squadrons and was increasing the number equipped for home defense purposes; there were 18 already. Nevertheless, only two new squadrons were to be added in the next year and beyond that the government was concerned that it should not appear to be arming for a war that, politically, was not considered a possibility.

1925 February 22   Geoffrey de Havilland took off in his newly built D.H.60 Moth G-EBKT, heralding a new age of light aviation. More than 65 years later, its descendant, the Tiger Moth, is still lovingly cherished at many flying clubs around the world. The D.H.60 formed the inventory of five government-funded flying clubs in Britain and was campaigned for by the director of civil aviation, Sir Sefton Brancker.

1925 February 25   The Douglas Co. received a contract for 75 observation biplanes (O-25) based on the XO-2 first flown by Eric Springer toward the end of 1924 at the Wilshire Boulevard plant in Los Angeles. This type was to prove highly successful, 879 being delivered between 1924 and 1936, including 108 that served with foreign air forces. Some versions had enclosed cockpits, and floatplane versions were developed. For a while, the Douglas observation aircraft were in competition with the Packard-powered Curtiss O-1 type, but when Packard ran into engine troubles, orders for the Liberty-powered O-2 increased.

1925 February   The last wooden biplane fighter to enter service with the RAF, the Gloster Gamecock, made its first flight. Similar to the Grebe, it had a 425-HP Bristol Jupiter VI and entered service in March 1926. With a top speed of 155 MPH, it was barely fast enough to catch the Fairey Fox day bomber, but it was a good airplane to fly, remaining with the RAF until the Bulldog replaced it in 1931. The Gamecock had a wingspan of 29 ft. 9 in. and a length of 19 ft. 8 in. with a gross weight of 2,863 lb.

1925 March 1   Ryan Airlines began the first regularly scheduled passenger airline service flown within the mainland United States. At first, the airline used Standard J biplanes. These two-seat biplanes originated in the Standard SJ, ordered into production in 1917 to supplement the JN-4 trainer. The service ran between Los Angeles and San Diego, but when demand overtook the capacity of the J biplanes to serve the need, a Douglas Cloudster was introduced. It was the first use of this large (for the time) airliner on a relatively short, scheduled journey.

1925 March 2   A U.S. Navy exercise called Fleet Problem V was the first to involve aircraft carrier operations. The USS *Langley* was only used for forward scouting of the "Black Fleet" ships toward Guadeloupe, but the demonstration convinced Commander-in-Chief Adm. R. E. Coontz that the *Lexington* and the *Saratoga* must be prepared for duty with all speed and, moreover, that all ships should be equipped with seaplane catapult launching gear and aircraft recovery equipment.

1925 March 7   Curtiss received an order for 15 Model 34A biplane fighters, which become the first to employ the initial *P* to designate the pursuit category of army aircraft. The Model 34A, or the P-1 Hawk, was the series production version of the XPW-8B, a development of the XPW-8 first flown in January 1923. The P-1 was powered by a 435-HP Curtiss V-1150 engine and used the same tubular steel fuselage and wood wing construction as its precursor. It was armed with one 0.50-in. and one 0.30-in. machine gun. In all, 98 P-1-series fighters were built for the army.

1925 March 10   One of the most outstanding flying boats of its day and a stunning demonstration of the skills of aircraft designer R. J. Michell, the Supermarine Southampton made its first flight with Henri Biard at the controls. Evolved from the Supermarine Swan, which first flew on March 25, 1924, the Southampton was powered by two 502-HP Napier Lion V engines placed midway between the wings and had three rudders and a single horizontal tailplane. The type joined No. 480 Coastal Reconnaissance Flight in August and remained in service for 12 years, longer than any other flying boat before the Sunderland.

1925 March 12   The first flight of the Fokker F.VIIa powered by a 400-HP Packard Liberty engine signaled the beginning of a series of modifications and improvements to the basic F.VII, which would culminate in the three-engine F.VIIa-3m. The undercarriage was simplified and the engine attachments were changed so that several different air- or water-cooled engines in the range of 350 HP to 525 HP could be fitted at the owner's preference. The prototype was taken to America for demonstration, and Fokker built a second machine for the Ford Reliability Tour aimed at demonstrating superior performance. Fokker eventually built 42 of the F.VIIa, and the type was built under license in several European countries.

1925 March   Recognizing the need for a new generation of fighters, reconnaissance aircraft and torpedo-bombers for the aircraft carriers USS *Lexington* and the USS *Saratoga,* the U.S. Navy asked for designs to equip the new ships. Curtiss put up the F6C fighter, Vought proposed the O2U scout aircraft, and Martin designed the T3M torpedo-bomber. With the navy's already expanding commitment to aviation, all three types would see extensive duty at sea. This re-equipment program formed the core for the expansion of U.S. Navy interests in military aviation and helped prepare it for new carrier battle group doctrine.

1925 April 1   In the Soviet Union, an order was signed to purge the air forces of all obsolete and foreign aircraft so that eventually there would be only Soviet-designed aircraft. This signaled the expansion of government funding of Soviet aviation and encouraged numerous designers and engineers to concentrate on new designs dictated by state requirements. The use of aviation as an adjunct to military operations was highly regarded by the Red Army generals, and a major commitment was made to build up the air defense umbrella.

1925 April 3   Henry Ford began his private express air service between Detroit and Chicago using a single-engine, six-passenger, Ford 2-AT high-wing monoplane. The Stout Metal Airplane Co., run by Bill Stout, produced the 2-AT in 1924. The 2-AT was powered by a single Liberty engine and designed specifically for mail-carrying duties. Ford opened the 260-mi. run for the purpose of commuting between his facilities, and the service was not available commercially. Ford bought the Stout company on July 31, opened a second route between Detroit and Cleveland

and tasked its designers with a multiengine transport aircraft for longer routes.

1925 April 15 The U.S. Navy began a program of daily flights to altitudes of 10,000 ft. from the Anacostia Naval Air Station in Washington, D.C. The main purpose of these flights was to obtain weather data and to test upper-air sounding equipment that collected information that could be used to forecast weather. When the effectiveness of the service was demonstrated, flights to 15,000 ft. were ordered, seven days a week, year-round. This was the beginning of a navy air weather advisory service that forms an important part of seaborne operations.

1925 May 1 The Air Corps of the Imperial Japanese Army was established under the overall command of Lt. Gen. Kinichi Yasumitsu of the Koku Hombu Air Headquarters. It comprised 500 aircraft, many in a dated and unserviceable condition, with a personnel strength of 3,700 officers and men. Formerly an air division, the corps would expand as a combat support element but with some degree of autonomy for tactical operations. Like most air-minded powers, Japan considered military aircraft an adjunct to ground forces rather than an independent force.

1925 May 2 The Douglas C-1 biplane made its first flight at Santa Monica, Calif. and during the month completed trials at McCook Field. Ordered by the army, the C-1 had many characteristics first employed on the Douglas World Cruiser and the O-series observation aircraft. The C-1 had a 435-HP Liberty V-1650-1 water-cooled engine with side-by-side seating for two just forward of the wing leading edge. Although only 26 were built, the type saw wide use and lasted until the mid-1930s as a general transport aircraft. One was used in 1929 for flight refueling tests.

1925 May 10 The Armstrong Whitworth Atlas, the first airplane designed from the outset as an Army Co-operation-type for the RAF, made its first flight. Powered by a 450-HP Armstrong Siddeley Jaguar IVC, the role for which it was designed encapsulated many of the diverse roles performed by reconnaissance aircraft of World War I: gun spotting, signaling, light bombing duties and so on. The first Atlas squadron became operational with the type in October 1927. Of 446 Atlases built, 175 were trainers, and the type continued to serve the RAF until the mid-1930s.

1925 May 15 The world's first three-engine, all-metal transport aircraft entered service with the Swedish airline AB Aerotransport. Built by Junkers and designated G.23, it was the culmination of a concerted effort by Junkers to develop the metal trimotor concept, and it epitomized the low-wing monoplane layout that would characterize airliner design from this date on. The G.23 was built in Sweden to avoid protests over restrictions on German airplane production imposed by the Treaty of Versailles. The Swedish airline operated the aircraft on the Malmo-Hamburg-Amsterdam route. Development of this aircraft gave Junkers the experience that would later manifest itself in the Ju-52/3m.

1925 May 21 Arguably the first American airline, National Air Transport (NAT) was incorporated in Delaware with Howard E. Coffin, vice president of the Hudson Motor Co., as chairman of the board and Clement M. Keys, previously a financial editor of the *Wall Street Journal,* as chairman of the executive committee. Keys had raised money from several big investors to give NAT an unprecedented authorized starting capital of $10 million, and NAT thus became the first U.S. company formed expressly for

the single purpose of operating as an airline. It was awarded a contract airmail route (CAM 3) on October 7, 1925.

1925 May 25 Two Dornier Wal flying boats (N24 and N25) were used by the Arctic explorer Roald Amundsen in an attempt to reach the North Pole. He planned to fly both N24 and N25 to the pole, transfer the excess fuel from one flying boat to the other and use that to carry everyone to Alaska. Amundsen and two crew took off in N24 at 5:00 P.M. from Spitsbergen, 760 mi. from the North Pole. The three crew members of N25 included the financial backer, Leif Dietrichsen. Both aircraft came down with engine trouble about 3 mi. apart and 150 mi. short of the North Pole. In an attempt to fly back to Spitsbergen with all six men aboard, N25 came down a second time, and the men had to be rescued by a Norwegian boat.

1925 May Anthony Fokker visited his Netherlands Aircraft Manufacturing Co. in the United States, which had been set up in New York during 1921, to survey opportunities for a new market in long-range airliners he believed would emerge in America. Attracted by the Ford Reliability Tour, set up by Henry Ford to attract potential designs for passenger services, Fokker dispatched messages to Holland ordering the design of an airplane he was convinced would fulfill Ford's requirements. This would emerge as the trimotor version of the F.VII airliner.

1925 June 10 A mass flight of Polikarpov R-1 and R-2 biplanes led by M. M. Gromov with M. A. Volkovoinov left Moscow for Peking, China. The R-1 and R-2 had evolved from the D.H.4 and D.H.9A supplied by Britain during World War I, and with little modification were placed in mass production at Soviet aircraft factories. A total of 2,860 R-1 and R-2 were eventually built, the first known mass production aircraft for the Soviet Union. The flight of Polikarpovs arrived in Peking about a month after their journey began.

1925 June 15 A regularly scheduled air service between Berlin and Moscow began when Deutsche Aero Lloyd offered a service between Berlin and Königsberg, in East Prussia, to link with the Deruluft service between Königsberg and Moscow. The Königsberg-Moscow service had been stepped up in 1923 to four flights each week. On July 1, 1924, it was increased to daily flights between the two cities. Operational experience with this international flight would help Deruluft develop internal civil air routes between major Soviet cities.

A popular postwar barnstorming aircraft, a D.H.4 bomber of No. 27 Squadron, Royal Flying Corps (RFC), in the Pas de Calais region.

The D.H.9, workhorse for American stunt flyers and barnstormers in the years after World War I.

1925 July 1 In attempts to speed the transcontinental U.S. air-mail service and save a day between two major centers of commerce, night service opened between New York and Chicago with times averaging 9 hr. 15 min. westbound and 8 hr. 30 min. east-bound. Major improvements and extensions to the night lighting system begun in 1922 were continued with an airway system installed as far west as San Francisco by the end of the year. Within the next five years, fully lighted airways would reach from New York as far south as Atlanta, from Salt Lake City down to Los Angeles and from Chicago all the way to Miami.

1925 July 7 The Boeing Model 40 made its first flight as a purpose-built mail-plane capable of carrying 500 lb. of mail and four passengers. The enclosed cabin area was forward of the open cockpit for the pilot, and because it could carry a mixed passenger-freight consignment, it was a more versatile airplane than its prime competitor, the Douglas DAM-1. The latter plane, a development of the O-2, had just begun flight trials. The Model 40 lost out to Douglas, but the design was used again when the U.S. Post Office turned airmail over to private operators in 1927.

1925 July 13 Western Air Express was incorporated in California with car sales dealer Harris M. ("Pop") Hanshue as president and with the specific purpose of developing air transport services between Los Angeles, Las Vegas and Salt Lake City. Incensed by the selection of San Francisco as the western terminus for the transcontinental airmail route, Harry Chandler and James A. Talbot incorporated WAE, and from May 23, 1926, the freighting service began carrying passengers, 209 people being flown during 1926.

1925 August 18 Increased interest in the use of aircraft to link islands in the Caribbean resulted in the first survey flight from Barranquilla, Colombia via various staging points in Central America to Havana, Cuba, where it arrived September 19. Two leased Dornier Wal flying boats made the trip, which continued up to Palm Beach, Fla., hoping to get a license to open air routes

throughout the region. The Colombian airline SCADTA (Sociedad Colombo-Alemana de Transportés Aereos) financed the survey flight, for which the Dornier flying boats were well suited.

1925 August 26 In a record that would stand until Feb. 24, 1983, Farman Parker of Anderson, Ind. became the world's youngest pilot to fly solo. Born on January 9, 1912, he soloed at the age of 13 yr. 7 mon. 17 days and two days later flew across to Battle Creek, Mich., where he passed his flying tests and was awarded FAI license no. 6334. His ambition was to fly around America championing the cause of aviation and showing how easy it was to fly.

1925 August The first of nine Curtiss F6C-1 was delivered to the U.S. Navy following an order placed in March. The type was a navy version of the Curtiss P-1 Hawk delivered to the U.S. Army beginning March 7. It had a 400-HP Curtiss D-12 engine, with strengthened airframe and an arrester hook for carrier operations. Models F6C-1 through F6C-3 had in-line engines, but the 31 F6C-4s delivered from February 1927 were the first with 410-HP Pratt & Whitney R-1340 radial engines. Though lighter and better to fly than its predecessors, the F6C-4 was already outdated, and only one squadron was equipped with it.

1925 September 1 A new world record for seaplanes was achieved when a U.S. Naval Aircraft Factory PN-9 piloted by Comdr. John P. Rodgers flew from San Francisco toward Hawaii, alighting on the sea with mechanical trouble after 1,841 mi., only 559 mi. short of its destination. Fashioning sails from the PN-9's wing fabric, Comdr. Rodgers' crew sailed all the way to Hawaii, where they were towed into port by a submarine. The airborne distance achieved was accepted as a new seaplane record.

1925 September 3 The U.S. Navy airship *Shenandoah* was wrecked over an Ohio pasture with the loss of 14 lives when it was ordered into the air by the fleet commander against the advice of its captain, Lt. Comdr. Zachary Lansdowne. Severe squalls and high gusts tore the airship apart, and of the 43 on board, only 26 escaped. Lt. Comdr. Lansdowne was one of those killed. The forward section of the airship containing seven men in an underslung gondola broke loose and spent an hour violently tossed around the sky before it touched down 12 mi. away. Lt. Col. William Mitchell issued a statement to the press citing ''incompetency, criminal neglect and almost treasonable administration of the National Defense by the Navy and War Departments.''

1925 September 4   The Fokker F.VIIa-3m trimotor transport aircraft made its first flight at 4:30 P.M. from Schiphol airport, Amsterdam, only two months after design work got under way at the urgent instruction of Anthony Fokker. Seeking an economic transport for the American market and a competitive aircraft to display at the Ford Reliability Tour, Fokker designers added two engines to the single-engine D.VIIa. With three 240-HP Wright Whirlwind engines, it had a wingspan of 63 ft. 5 in. and a length of 47 ft. 1 in. and a gross weight of 8,800 lb. The F.VIIa-3 was to become one of the most popular of the new trimotor generation.

1925 September 5   For the first time, aircraft were used in a mass evacuation of civilians from a war zone when an assortment of 27 different aircraft types airlifted 67 British citizens from the area around Sulaimaniya in northern Iraq. They were taken to the relative safety of the town of Kirkuk. The same aircraft were then used to drop supplies to British Army units and to fly in additional soldiers to help quell an uprising instigated by local rebels.

1925 September 12   With the agreement of U.S. Pres. Coolidge, banker Dwight W. Morrow was ordered by the War Department to conduct an investigation of air power. The first public meeting was held September 21, and the committee heard testimony from 99 witnesses before it compiled its report. When Lt. Col. Mitchell testified, he called for an air force of 2,600 frontline aircraft with only 50% in reserve units and 25,000 officers and men. Already holding an investigation of U.S. air power, a House committee headed by Florian Lampert was examining the Lassiter report, authorized by Secretary of War Weeks on March 17, 1923.

1925 September 16   In America, the Fokker Aircraft Corp. was set up at Hasbrouck Heights, New Jersey, taking over the Atlantic Aircraft Corp. Fokker had set up the Netherlands Aircraft Manufacturing Co. of Amsterdam in New York during 1921. Managed by R. B. C. Noorduyn, it operated as a sales organization, and Fokker was eager to compete directly with Ford, who had bought out the Stout Metal Airplane Co. Fokker's reputation rested in no mean measure on the formidable, but probably overexaggerated, reputation of the D.VII single-seat fighter of 1918.

1925 October 7   The first five contract airmail routes were let: CAM 1 (New York-Boston) to Colonial, with service inaugurated June 18, 1926; CAM 2 (St. Louis-Chicago) to Robertson, inaugurated April 15, 1926; CAM 3 (Chicago-Dallas) to National Air Transport, inaugurated May 12, 1926; CAM 4 (Los Angeles-Salt Lake City) to Western Air Express, inaugurated April 17, 1926; and CAM 5 (Pasco, Wash.-Elko, Nev.) to Varney, inaugurated April 6, 1926.

1925 October 12   The last Pulitzer air race was held at Long Island, N.Y., where the first had been run on November 25, 1920. The U.S. Army and Navy teamed up to buy three Curtiss R3C-1 biplanes, each powered by a 500-HP Curtiss V-1400 engine. Two R3C-1s were entered, and both swept the field, with

Based on the German Zeppelin L 33, the British airship R.33 was built during 1918–19.

army Lt. Cyrus Bettis coming in first at 248.99 MPH followed by Lt. Alford J. Williams of the navy at 241.7 MPH. Leo Dawson came in third in a Curtiss P-1 with a speed of 169.9 MPH. The National Aeronautic Association, which had organized the Pulitzers, decided not to hold any more races when regional organizers disagreed over policy.

1925 October 15   A D.H.53 Humming Bird single-engine monoplane was carried into the air at Pulham, England attached to a trapeze on the underside of British airship R.33. At 3,800 ft., Sqdn. Ldr. R. de Haga Haig took a ladder down into the cockpit, and the Humming Bird was released for free flight. Haig dived toward the ground before starting the engine, flying two loops and rehooking onto the trapeze. On October 28, turbulence created by the airship's bulk prevented a successful hook-up after a free flight, and the D.H.53 had to make an emergency landing. Another, successful, separation, free flight and hook-up was carried out on December 4.

1925 October 28   The court-martial of Lt. Col. William Mitchell began, arising from his open and public criticism of U.S. military leaders for what he considered an outmoded lack of concern for air power and its potential value to the national defense. Having stimulated valuable tests in aerial bombing, Mitchell had openly vilified decisions about the role aircraft would play in future armed conflict. He was critical of the lack of clear-cut plans for coastal defense, although he praised the navy for basing air power on carriers at sea as part of battle fleets. When the court-martial ended December 17, Mitchell was suspended without pay for five years, commuted by Pres. Coolidge to half-pay ($397.67 per month) for that period. There was only one vote for acquittal, Maj. Gen. Douglas MacArthur.

1925 October   The Huff-Daland XLB-1 light bomber made its first flight powered by a 750-HP Packard 2A-2540 engine. Designed and developed as a replacement for the NBS-1, the XLB-1 had been ordered in 1923 and carried two crew side-by-side in the forward cockpit and a gunner near the single tail. With a wingspan of 66 ft. 6 in and a length of 46 ft. 2 in., it had a gross weight of 10,346 lb. and carried a 290-gal. fuel load, which gave it a range of 940 mi. Ten LB-1 bombers, called Pegasus, were ordered in November. These precursor bomber designs were to lead to the Keystone range of bombers ordered in the late 1920s.

1925 November 2 Capt. Geoffrey T. R. Hill began powered trials with the Pterodactyl, a manned tailless flying machine built during 1924 to study spin characteristics in an attempt to develop an aerodynamic configuration that would be tolerant to spin. A light Cherub engine driving a pusher propeller powered the small machine, and in flight tests over the next several weeks, it proved remarkably stable and would not stall, even at 45° incidence. Hill had designed the Pterodactyl as a concept demonstrator and went on to begin work on a biplane version.

1925 November 16 A survey flight for new Imperial Airways routes to Cape Town, South Africa got under way when Alan Cobham, his engineer A. B. Elliott and photographer B. W. G. Emmott flew a D.H.50J from Edgeware, England to Paris on the first leg of the round-trip journey. Going by way of Greece, Egypt and the Sudan, they reached Livingstone, Northern Rhodesia (now Zambia) on January 29, 1926, and Cape Town on February 17. On the return journey, 1,000 Africans were made to tramp up and down the airstrip in N'dola, Northern Rhodesia to pack the dirt into an acceptably firm landing run. The D.H.50J returned to England on March 13, 1926.

1925 November 26 The Tupolev ANT-4 (TB-1) made its first flight, lasting 7 min. with A. I. Tomashyevskii at the controls. The giant monoplane had been inspired by Junkers' all-metal monoplane designs during joint activities in the USSR between the German aircraft designer and Soviet production facilities. With a wingspan of 94 ft. 2 in., a length of 59 ft. and a gross weight of up to 16,535 lb., the ANT-4 was powered by two 450-HP Napier Lion engines or two 730-HP BMW VI engines. The TB-1 could carry a 6,615 lb. bomb load for up to 2.5 hr. or a 2,205 lb. bomb load for 9 hr. As the first in a long line of large metal monoplanes, it was one of the most important aircraft to appear from the Soviet Union.

1925 November 30 Set up on September 12, the Morrow board investigation into the state of U.S. military air readiness reported its findings and disagreed with proponents of air power, believing their claims to be overstated. The board believed that air policy should follow the national defense policy and not direct it. Moreover, it believed that "the next war may well start in the air but in all probability will wind up, as the last one did, in the mud." It called for an air force that could act alone on a mission separate from army support and proposed that the air service should become an air corps.

1925 December 1 The first Boeing FB-1 was delivered to the U.S. Navy following a contract placed in December 1924 for a navy version of the PW-9, which had been developed for the army as a fighter. The 43 FB types built for the navy and the Marine Corps were variously equipped with arrester hooks and Curtiss, Wright or Packard engines, and some could exchange wheels for floats. The last one, an FB-5 delivered in January 1927, was equipped with a 520-HP Packard 2A-1500 engine and had a top speed of 175 MPH.

1925 December 14 The Lampert Committee, set up by authorization of the U.S. House of Representatives in the spring of 1924, issued its final report on recommendations for the future of U.S. military aviation. The committee had received testimony from the maverick army air service colonel, William Mitchell, and issued its findings only three days before the court-martial pronounced him guilty of insubordination. It did, however, concur with much of what Mitchell said and recommended an independent air force within the structure of a unified Defense Department.

1925 December 24 The newly formed aero-engine manufacturer Pratt & Whitney unveiled the first Wasp 9-cylinder radial engine. With a rated output of 425 HP, it was more powerful than the Liberty engine, yet weighed only half as much. The Wasp was developed into an engine delivering 600 HP and led to several new engine projects that held preeminence in aero-engine design and production until the introduction of the gas turbine superseded the piston engine as an economic means of power for high-output engines. The manufacturer, however, remains a world leader in aircraft engines.

1926 January 6 An amalgamation of Junkers-Luftverkehr and Deutscher Aero Lloyd formed the German national airline, Deutsche Luft Hansa (DLH, known as Lufthansa from Jan. 1, 1934). Aero Lloyd had succeeded the first German airline, Deustche Luft Reederei (DLR). Junkers had formed its own airline to promote the Junkers F 13, which had at first been confiscated by the Inter-Allied Aeronautical Commission of Control. Relenting in February 1920, they permitted the use of this aircraft for airline operations. The German government owned 37.5% of Luft Hansa shares when it opened for business under its director, Erhard Milch.

1926 January 8 The only semirigid airship built in the United States, the RS-1 from Goodyear, made its first flight. Assembled at Scott Field with a combined Army-Goodyear team, it had been delivered from the manufacturer during late 1925. The RS-1 was a helium airship, carried a crew of 10, had a length of 282 ft. and a volume of 719,000 lb. and could lift a useful load of 15,740 lb. It was initially powered by four 202-HP Liberty engines, derated and geared down, driving a single propeller shaft. In 1927 the Liberty engines were changed for two 400-HP Packard 2A-1500 engines.

1926 January 18 American businessman, industrialist and philanthropist Daniel Guggenheim became one of the more prominent tangible promoters of commercial aviation through the Daniel Guggenheim Fund. Set up with $2.5 million to expand the airmindedness of Americans across the continent, it supported numerous projects involving science and engineering in the pursuit of aeronautical excellence, and it promoted the development of civil aviation for passenger transportation and the expansion of air freight services.

1926 January 22 Flying Dornier Wal flying boat M-MWAL (named *Plus Ultra*) built in Spain, Maj. Franco and his crew of three took off on the first leg of a trans-Atlantic crossing intending to demonstrate an air route between Europe and South America. They left Palos de Moguer, near Huelva (the port from which Christopher Columbus had departed for America), and landed at the Canary Islands. From there they flew to Cape Verde and on to Pernambuco (now Recife), before reaching Rio de Janeiro on February 10. The 6,258-mi. journey had been completed in 59.5 hr. of flying time for an average speed of about 105 MPH.

1926 January 26 A secret company, the Statistische Gesellschaft (Stega), or Statistics Company, was set up by the German Army Ordnance Office and would be run by Geheimrat (secret councillor) Dr. von Borsig to retrieve and collate relevant information about potential German munitions production. The army wanted German firms to contribute funds secretly to begin the process of rearmament, but industry had few resources to do this. The few German aircraft companies that existed outside the country were contacted and advised to begin design studies for military aircraft that would form the core of a major, rapid rearmament program.

1926 January   The first production Vickers Victoria (serial no. J7921) made its first flight following an extensive series of trials with the two prototype aircraft that had lasted three years. Modeled after the Vickers Virginia Mk.VII, the Victoria III entered service first with No. 70 Squadron, RAF, in Mesopotamia (Iraq) at the beginning of a service life extending well into the 1930s. A developed version of the Victoria, the Vickers Valentia, would remain in service until 1941! The Victoria had a wingspan of 87 ft. 4 in., a length of 59 ft. 6 in. a gross weight of 17,760 lb. and capacity for 22 troops plus a crew of two for a range of 800 mi. It was powered by two 570-HP Napier Lion XI engines.

1926 February 1   Demoted to his permanent grade of colonel in March 1925, William Mitchell resigned from the U.S. Army after having been found guilty by court-martial of gross insubordination by indiscriminately accusing defense chiefs of mismanaging the defense of America. His main focus of concern was the apparent lack of awareness among strategists that Japan posed a serious military threat to America and that Japan's conquest of Asia would provide the raw materials to conduct a war based on air power at sea. He also warned that Germany would rise again and that America would have to fight once more on European soil. It is probably a mistake to ascribe all these prophecies to Mitchell himself, who appears to have been a voice for many unwilling to speak out.

1926 February 15   The Ford Motor Co. became the first U.S. private air carrier to operate a contract airmail (CAM) route. Ford began operations with CAM-6 between Detroit and Chicago and CAM-7 between Detroit and Cleveland. At first, only mail was carried, but experience with operating the route resulted in the inauguration of passenger service starting in August 1926.

1926 March 1   Four Fairey IIIDs set out from Heliopolis, Egypt on the first RAF long-distance formation flight to Cape Town, South Africa and back. They reached Cape Town and began the return flight on April 19. Three more Fairey IIIDs had been stationed at critical points along the route in case one of the four should run into trouble, which they did not. They arrived back at Cairo on May 27 and from there flew on to Lee-on-Solent, England, arriving to an airborne escort of flying boats on June 21. The four aircraft had covered 13,900 mi.

1926 March 16   Capt. F. L. Barnard of Imperial Airways took an Armstrong Whitworth Argosy into the air for the first time. Designed to conform to an Imperial Airways decision that future airliners must be multi-engined, the Argosy had three 385-HP Jaguar engines, two supported midway between the wings and the third in the nose. The Argosy had a wingspan of 90 ft. 8 in. and a length of 65 ft. 10 in., with a gross weight of 18,000 lb. and a capacity for carrying up to 20 passengers in single file either side of an aisle, with adequate toilet facilities and an opening window for each passenger. It was large for its day, and the Argosy did much to stimulate Imperial Airways's European routes.

1926 March 19   The Fairey IIIF, a completely updated and improved version of the Fairey IIID, made its first flight. It was designed as a general-purpose aircraft for the RAF and as a reconnaissance aircraft for the Fleet Air Arm. The IIIF was the final version of a line that began with the Fairey N10 in 1917. It was powered by a Napier Lion VA engine and had a top speed of 120 MPH with a range of 400 miles. The IIIF made a number of record-breaking long distance flights from which it gave the Fairey company experience to develop the Long Range Monoplane.

An enduring evergreen of aviation, the Avro 504 emerged in 1910 and endured long after World War I ended in 1918.

1926 March 24   The Cierva Autogyro Co. Ltd. was formed in England, with Avro building the autogyros at their Hamble, Southampton works. Don Juan de la Cierva was a keen advocate of the autogyro, and the association with Avro was based on utilization of their highly successful Type 504 airframe for what was known as the Avro 575 autogyro. The British Air Ministry ordered a Cierva C.8 type in 1927, which was based on the Avro 504N powered by a Lynx engine. Autogyro flights were to gain attention more for their novelty than for their practical application.

1926 March 25   The Messerschmitt Flugzeugbau G.m.b.H. was formed by Willie Messerschmitt, a graduate of Munich Technical High School and already an experienced designer of light aircraft and sailplanes. The company had an order for M18 light transport aircraft for the newly formed domestic airline Nordbayerische Verkehrsflung G.m.b.H. On September 8, 1927, Messerschmitt merged with the Bayerische Flugzeugwerke A.G. (BFW), which had been formed on July 30, 1926, to help the financially bankrupt Udet Flugzeugbau previously set up in 1922. To deter criticism of using public funds for helping industry, the German government sold its share in BFW and Messerschmitt and bought 12.5% while persuading the rich Strohmeyer-Raulino family to put up the remaining 87.5%.

1926 April 6   One of the great pioneering airlines of its day, the German state airline Deutsche Luft Hansa AG, began flight operations when a Dornier Komet II airliner flew the Berlin-Zurich route via Halle, Erfurt and Stuttgart. The result of a merger of Deutsche Aero Lloyd and Junkers Luftverkehr in January, the airline was to introduce the world's first night passenger services using Junkers G.24 aircraft between Berlin and Königsberg on May 1 and began extending its European services by opening a route to Stockholm on May 3. The G.24 was a development of the G.23, the world's first metal trimotor airliner. Most were powered by three 280/310-HP Junkers engines.

1926 April 6   After the passage of the Kelly Bill, which allowed airmail contracts to be awarded to private operators (formerly the exclusive preserve of the U.S. Post Office), U.S. commercial airmail services burgeoned. The second to be awarded was CAM-5 flown between Elko, Nev. and Pasco, Wash. via Boise, Idaho. The company to operate this first service was Varney Air Lines, renamed Continental Air Lines in 1937. Mail planes were already a specific market for aircraft manufacturers and the release of contract opportunities helped spur this development, each CAM number indicating a specified route and not necessarily the order of contract award.

1926 April 21 The U.S. secretary of the navy ordered all trainee officers at the U.S. Naval Academy at Annapolis to receive 25 hr. of flying instruction as standard training. This was a critically important step in U.S. naval aviation because it developed a strong sense of awareness that air units were a necessary and vital component of the sea war.

1926 April The third airmail delivery service granted a license to operate segments of the transcontinental airmail route operated by the U.S. Post Office began operations when the Robertson Aircraft Corp. started flying the CAM-2 route between St. Louis and Chicago. Robertson was the first of several small companies that would merge to form American Airlines in 1934, one of the largest operators in the United States.

1926 May 5 The Wright F3W-1 Apache, a single-seat experimental fighter, flew for the first time with a 450-HP air-cooled Wright P-1 radial engine. Built by the Wright Aeronautical Co., the Apache had a wingspan of 27 ft. 4 in., a length of 22 ft. and a gross weight of 2,128 lb. It was used by the navy to test the 420-HP Pratt & Whitney Wasp, the competitor to the Wright radial. Only one Apache was ever built, but the Wasp trials led to orders for the F2B, a derivative of the Boeing FB-4 powered by this engine and a long and productive use for the radial in many airplanes.

1926 May 9 The first flight to the North Pole and back was carried out by Lt. Comdr. Richard E. Byrd and Floyd Bennett in a TA-1 named *Josephine Ford,* the prototype Fokker F.VII converted to a 3m three engine configuration by Atlantic Aircraft. It was fitted with special fuel tanks increasing the capacity to 615 gal. and the range to almost 2,200 mi. They took off from Spitsbergen at 1:30 A.M. carrying a hand-cranked shortwave radio, a sled, rubber boat, tent, tools, axes, knives and food for 10 weeks. Eight hr. later they arrived at the pole and circled it several times to take measurements of their position. They returned to Spitsbergen at 4:30 P.M. after 15 hr. and 1,600 mi.

1926 May 11 The first airship flight across the North Pole and the first flight to completely cross the ice cap began when the dirigible *Norge* left Kings Bay, Spitsbergen, at 8:55 A.M. carrying the Norwegian explorer Roald Amundsen. Built in Italy, the airship carried 13 crewmembers under Capt. Umberto Nobile. The project was financially supported by the American Lincoln Ellsworth. When the *Norge* reached the North Pole at 2:00 A.M. May 12, the crew dropped American, Norwegian and Italian flags. Battling against fog, ice and high winds, they came down at Teller, Alaska at 7:15 A.M. on May 14, having flown 3,417 mi. in 70 hr. 40 min. at an average speed of 48 MPH.

1926 May 15 American ethnographer Mathew Stirling and his pilot, American-born Hans Hoyte of Dutch descent, began the first aerial surveys of New Guinea in a Breguet BR.14 seaplane powered by a 400-HP Liberty engine. Having flown through previously unknown gorges and along riverbeds, they set down on the quiet waters of a broad stream and wandered off to explore. Alerted by fresh footprints in the mud and alarmed by wailing noises and the sight of 30 natives in six canoes bearing down upon their aircraft, the two men bolted and took off at full throttle as arrows pierced the fabric of their aircraft. The pictures they took opened a new world for anthropologists to explore.

1926 May 21 The Paris Aviation Treaty permitted Germany to begin building aircraft without restriction on performance, thus allowing for serious planning for a new German air force. By this time Heinkel had produced a range of small aircraft for sale overseas, and the HD 17 was designed as a two-seat version of the Fokker D.XIII purchased in 1923. It was powered by a Napier Lion engine and thus was Britain unwittingly involved in the restoration of German air power.

1926 May Gerhard Fieseler acquired a shareholding in the German light aircraft manufacturer Raab-Katzenstein-Flugzeugwerke G.m.b.H. This company had been formed in November 1925, and it was natural that the future aircraft builder would want to get closely involved with it, for he was a foremost aerobatic pilot of international renown. Fieseler bought out the sailplane builder, Segel-Flugzeugbau-Kassel in April 1930. Two years later he changed the name to Fieseler-Flugzeugbau and thus originated one of the most famous German aircraft manufacturers of the 1930s.

1926 June 6 The final elements of a special Alaskan aerial survey expedition left Seattle, Wash. bound for Alaska. Under the command of Lt. B. H. Wyatt, the expedition had three Loening amphibious aircraft, a barge and the tender USS *Gannet.* Commissioned by the U.S. Department of the Interior, it was the first major photographic mapping operation carried out by American military aviators. The work lasted through September, by which time the aerial mapping of much of Alaska was completed.

1926 June 11 The Ford 4-AT Tri-Motor made its first flight. Powered by three 200-HP Wright J-4 engines with accommodation for 11 passengers, the 4-AT originated in the Stout Metal Airplane Co.'s 2-AT of 1924 (Ford bought Stout in 1925) and "borrowed" many ideas and concepts from the Fokker F.VIIa-3m trimotor as well. So popular was the American rush to emulate Europe and develop airlines that Bill Stout left and bought Ford Tri-Motors to start his own passenger-carrying business!

1926 June 30 The last order for a World War I-type wood and canvas U.S. military aircraft was issued when Vought was asked to build 20 single-seat FU-1 biplanes for the U.S. Navy. A direct descendant of the Vought VE-7 first flown on February 12, 1918, the FU-1 was built as a catapult-launched floatplane fighter powered by a 220-HP Wright J-5 radial engine. With two fixed forward-firing 0.30-in. machine guns and a top speed of only 122 MPH, it was hopelessly outclassed and served only a year with navy unit VF-2B before reassignment to a utility and training role in 1928 with the military designation FU-2.

1926 June 30 Just over three months after he returned from a four-month route-proving flight from England to South Africa and back, British aviator Alan Cobham took off from the River Medway at the start of a similar exercise to Australia. Flying the same D.H.50J G-EBFO, Cobham reached Melbourne, Australia on August 15, left for England on August 29 and was back on October 1, making a grand return by landing on the Thames in the heart of London. The only casualty was a passenger, A. B. Elliott, who was killed when the plane was fired upon by Bedouin tribesmen between Baghdad and Basra on the flight out. The D.H. 50J used by Cobham had flown a total 62,000 mi. on route-proving flights for Imperial Airways and would continue to fly until it crashed on March 1, 1932, in western Australia.

1926 June The Martin T3M-1 torpedo-bomber made its first flight. One of the new generation aircraft designed for the new carriers *Lexington* and *Saratoga,* the T3M-1 was a much-modified version of the Curtiss SC-2 landplane, 35 of which had been built by Martin for the navy as the T2M. It had the same wings as the SC-2, with a 575-HP Wright T-3B radial engine and a welded fuselage framework. The pilot and torpedoman were installed in front of the wing with a gunner at the back of the fuselage near the tail. Floats and wheels were interchangeable, and the last 100 of 124 purchased for the navy had 710-HP in-line Packard 3A-2500 engines.

1926 July 1   The Royal Swedish Air Force (Kungl Svenska Flygvapnet) was officially formed. The new force could trace its origins back to 1911 when single military and naval aircraft had been presented to the nation. The Field Telegraph Aviation Co. (Falttelegrafkarens Flygkompani) had been formed in 1914 and represented Sweden's only military air organization until the formation of the Flygvapnet. Two military flying schools had been formed to support the unit, one at Axvall and the other at Oscar Fredricksborg. By the early 1990s, the Svenska Flygvapnet (the "Royal" was dropped in 1974) had 8,000 personnel and 440 combat aircraft.

1926 July 1   The first night-landing aboard an aircraft carrier was conducted when Flt. Lt. Boyce flew a Blackburn Dart (serial no. N9804) onto the deck of HMS *Furious*. The Dart appeared in 1921 and entered service with the Fleet Air Arm in 1923, remaining in use for more than a decade. With a wingspan of 45 ft. 6 in a length of 35 ft. 4 in. and powered by a 450-HP Napier Lion engine, the single-seat torpedo-carrier had a maximum speed of 107 MPH and a range of 285 mi. A twin-float seaplane version was built, and some had a second cockpit with dual controls for training purposes.

1926 July 2   Drawing on recommendations from the Morrow, Lassiter and Lampert reviews, the Air Corps Act drafted by the War Department, was passed, changing the name of the U.S. Army Air Service (USAAS) to the U.S. Army Air Corps (USAAC). Congress moved to enact legislation that would accept many of the recommendations made by the Morrow board, especially to realign the air force as a "striking arm rather than an auxiliary service." Having failed to achieve the goals of the 1920 Army Reorganization Act, there was, however, satisfaction over a five-year expansion program that would begin July 1, 1927. It envisaged a goal of 1,800 aircraft and 16,650 personnel by June 30, 1932, from the present level of 9,644 personnel and 1,254 airplanes.

1926 July 6   To celebrate the 150th anniversary of the Declaration of Independence, the Philadelphia Rapid Transit Service was inaugurated with the first service between the Philadelphia Navy yard and Hoover Field, Washington, D.C. The service ended on November 30, but in that five-month period, the service carried a total 3,695 passengers on 613 out of a scheduled 688 flights. Contrary to the convention, airmail was carried as and when passenger space permitted on the Philadelphia-Washington (CAM 13) and Philadelphia-Norfolk (CAM 15) routes.

1926 July 15   Two French aviators, Capt. L. Gririer and Lt. Dordilly, established a new world distance record by flying nonstop from Villacoublay, France to Omsk, USSR. The flight began July 14 and covered a distance of 2,930 mi. The aircraft used was a specially prepared Breguet BR.19 two-seat biplane powered by a single 450-HP Lorraine engine that gave the BR.19 a maximum speed of 141 MPH. It was long-distance flights such as this that attracted foreign orders for the aircraft and made it one of the most successful aircraft of its type. Many examples were still in service at the outbreak of World War II.

1926 July 16   The first U.S. assistant secretary of war for air was appointed. F. Trubee Davison would assume responsibility at the highest level for organization of the the expansion program embodied in the Air Corps Act of July 2. The act, and the new office in the War Department ensured that military aviation would get a better deal in the next decade than it had in the eight years since World War I. Edward P. Warner had been sworn in July 10 as the first assistant secretary of the navy for aeronautics.

1926 July 24   On a proving flight to explore the possibility of opening up a direct airline route between Berlin and Peking, two Deutsch Luft Hansa Junkers G.24 monoplanes left Berlin. With registrations D-901 and D-903, they reached the Chinese capital on August 30 after having flown across Siberia. The two aircraft set off on the return journey September 8 and arrived back in Berlin October 26. The G 24 was a development of the Junkers G.23 and had a wingspan of 98 ft. 1 in., a length of 51 ft. 6 in. and a loaded weight of 14,330 lb. It had a range of more than 800 mi. and a cruising speed of 113 MPH.

1926 July 28   A tiny biplane built by the Cox-Klemin Aircraft Corp. in College Point, Long Island, N.Y. became the first aircraft to emerge from a submarine after it surfaced, take off, land again and be returned to the submarine before it submerged. The U.S. Navy submarine S-1 was commanded by Lt. C. B. Momsen and the Cox-Klemin XS-1 was flown by Lt. D. C. Allen. Impressed with the tiny Sperry Messenger, the Navy had the Army Engineering Division design a single-seat scouting seaplane with a wingspan of 18 ft., a length of 18 ft. 2 in. and a gross weight of 1,030 lb. Six were ordered from Cox-Klemin and six from Martin.

1926 August 9   During U.S. Navy tests to determine the rate at which aircraft can operate from carriers at sea, pilots of VF-1 conduct 127 landings on the USS *Langley*. These tests were vital for battle procedures necessary for fleet operations in wartime. When the *Langley* ran into heavy mist, the need to get aircraft back on the carrier deck was accelerated, and in that increased urgency, 12 aircraft landed in just 21 min., an effective display of efficiency that did much to convince the general staff of the potential applications of naval aviation in wartime.

1926 August 17   The Short S.5 Singapore I flying boat made its first flight with John Lankester Parker at the controls and three passengers, including Eustace Short. The Singapore was designed as an all-metal version of the N.3 Cromarty, which appeared in 1921. The Singapore I was powered by two Rolls Royce Condor III engines and had a wingspan of 93 ft., a length of 64 ft. (extended later to 65 ft. 6 in.), a gross weight of 20,000 lb. and a range of 900 mi. Maximum speed was 132 MPH. The Singapore I was the first in a long line of Singapore developments that would emerge during the next 10 years.

1926 August   The U.S. Army Air Corps established the Air Corps Training Center at San Antonio, Tex. under the command of Brig. Gen. Frank P. Lahm; the center included the School of Aviation Medicine. Training activities were now to be carried out by a unified school covering basic and advanced training. This improved efficiency and helped the tutors select pilots for higher levels of flying and responsibility. This was to lead to dedication of Randolph Field as the headquarters of the Air Corps Training Center on June 20, 1930, with advanced training at nearby Kelly Field.

1926 August   An enlarged version of the Huff-Daland LB-1 appeared, designated XHB-1 powered by the same 787-HP Packard

2A-2540 in-line engine. It was bigger, with a wingspan of 84 ft. 7 in. (versus 66.5 ft.), a length of 59 ft. 7 in. (versus 46 ft. 2 in.) and a gross weight of 16,838 lb. (versus 12,415 lb.). Unofficially dubbed Cyclops, it was the only USAAC aircraft to bear the heavy bomber (HB) designation. Built to carry four people, it had two fixed Browning guns in the wings and could carry over 4,000 lb. in bombs. By this time, the army had stipulated a twin-engine layout for bombers, and this was the last single-engined aircraft of its type ordered by the army.

1926 September 20   The top-scoring French air ace of World War I, René Fonck, attempted to take off on a trans-Atlantic crossing using a Sikorsky S.35 twinmotor. Fonck had met Sikorsky when Fonck visited Roosevelt Field, Long Island, N.Y. He chose the S.35 because of the redundancy of its three engines but tests were hurried, including those on a jettisonable undercarriage. Nevertheless, with almost 3,000 gal. of fuel on board, he began the take-off run at 5:00 A.M. but the undercarriage collapsed. The S.35 burst into flames, and although Fonck and his copilot got out, two other crewmembers were killed.

1926 September 30   The first de Havilland trimotor transport aircraft, the D.H.66 Hercules (G-BMW), made its first flight from Edgeware, England piloted by H. S. Broad. Designed to a specification issued by Imperial Airways Ltd. for mail flights between India and Egypt, the D.H.66 was powered by three 420-HP Bristol Jupiter VI engines. It had a wingspan of 79 ft., 6 in. a length of 55 ft. 6 in. and a maximum weight of 15,660 lb., including two crewmembers, seven passengers and 465 cu. ft. of freight. Its name was chosen by E. F. Hope-Jones of Eton College, near Windsor, from selections submitted by readers of *Meccano Magazine*.

1926 September 30   The prototype Dornier Do.R Super Wal made its first flight. Basically an enlarged version of the Do.J Wal, which had appeared in late 1922, the Do.R was powered by two 650-HP Rolls Royce Condor engines. The Wal had proven a popular flying boat and helped German designers continue development of modern airplanes by circumventing the Treaty of Versailles. The Super Wal was similarly successful, but relatively few twin-engine versions were built, the four-engine version appearing in September 1928.

1926 October 10   In efforts to stimulate continued interest in aviation by organizing speed competitions, the U.S. National Aeronautic Association staged the National Air Race in an effort to fill the gap left by the end of the Pulitzer races, the last of which had been held on October 12, 1925. The 1926 event was won at a speed of 180.5 MPH by George Cuddihy flying a Boeing FB-3 powered by a 600-HP Packard 2A-1500. National Air Races were held on the same day each year, the last taking place on October 10, 1929. By this time the U.S. Army and Navy had lost interest in specialized high-speed racing aircraft. Without the stimulus of the military participation, support for the races evaporated.

1926 October 15   The logistics and supply organization of the new U.S. Army Air Corps was rationalized and given a central command base at Dayton, Ohio, with McCook Field named as the headquarters of the Materiel Division under Brig. Gen. William E. Gillmore. The intention behind this change was to produce a more efficient and streamlined supply organization within the expanding service. Within a year, the Materiel Division headquarters had moved to a new and modern plant at Wright Field, Ohio, where it remained.

1926 October 21   A Gloster Grebe piloted by Flying Off. R. L. Ragg, RAF, was successfully released from under the British airship R.33 after it took off from Pulham, England. As part of the airship development program, the test was designed to demonstrate the use of aircraft for reconnaissance patrols from airships operating far beyond the range of small aircraft. A second Grebe flown by Flg. Off. C. Mackenzie-Richards was also released and flew down to Cardington after a minor problem starting the engine.

1926 November 2   The Vought O2U Corsair made its first flight fitted with the new 450-HP Pratt & Whitney R-1340-88 Wasp radial engine and was the first navy aircraft to be designed around this engine. Developed from experience on the U0 and F0 series of observation aircraft, which in turn were derivatives of the highly successful VE-7 series, the 02U had interchangeable wheels and float assemblies. The Corsair was one of the most successful navy observation aircraft of its time, with 621 02Us and 03Us delivered between 1926 and 1935.

1926 November 3   The Boeing Model 69, derivative of the Boeing FB-series, made its first flight as a private venture and was tested by the U.S. Navy, which denigrated the XF2B-1. It was powered by a 425-HP Pratt & Whitney R-1340B. The model 69 had evolved from the Model 66, a USAAC fighter that was to take to the air for the first time in July 1927. The Model 69 had a wingspan of 30 ft. 1 in., a length of 23 ft., an empty weight of 1,984 lb. and a gross weight of 2,805 lb. With a maximum speed of 154 MPH, it had a range of 330 mi. and a service ceiling of 21,500 ft. The Navy ordered 32 F2B-1s in March 1927.

1926 November 13   The ninth Schneider Trophy seaplane race, held at Hampton Roads, Va., was won by Maj. Mario de Bernardi from Italy flying a Macchi M.39 powered by a 800-HP Fiat AS.2. His winning speed of 246.496 MPH was a little more than 15 MPH faster than second-place man, Lt. Christian Frank Schilt, U.S. Marine Corps, flying a Curtiss R3C-2 A6979 powered by a 565-HP Curtiss V-1400 at 231.36 MPH. Two others, both from Italy, finished in third and fourth positions. The course comprised seven laps of a left-hand circuit off Norfolk Naval Air Station.

1926 November 14   The first airline created for the specific purpose of carrying parcels was incorporated as National Air Transport with the participation of the American Railway Express Co. Two special contracts were signed with the airline on the Chicago-Dallas and Chicago-New York routes, but there were delays in getting mail contracts to subsidize the airline, which prevented these being honored. However, the first air express service opened Sept. 1, 1927, between Chicago and Dallas.

1926 November 15   The first lightplane flight from England to India began when T. Neville Stack in D.H.60 Moth G-EBMO and Bernard S. Leete in D.H.60 Moth G-EBKU took off from Croydon, England. The D.H.60s they each flew were modified into single-seaters with extra fuel tanks in the space usually occupied by the front seat. They arrived at Karachi after flying 5,540 mi. in 54 days, landing January 8, 1927. These were the first Moths to reach India, and much joyriding took place at several cities in India before G-EBKU crashed at Calcutta in July. The Moth was rapidly becoming the most popular lightplane of its day.

1926 November   In the first use of an airplane to commit a criminal act in the United States, bombs were dropped in Williamson Co., Ill. during a feud between rival prohibition gangs. The aircraft was flown by members of the Shelton gang, and their target was a farmhouse that housed the alcohol stocks and stills of the rival Birger gang. The three bombs dropped in the raid were manufactured by the Shelton gang but were poorly made and failed to explode.

1926 December 10   A conference financed by the Daniel Guggenheim Fund for the Promotion of Aeronautics was held at NACA in Washington, D.C. The conference lasted two days and included representatives from the Massachusetts Institute of Technology, the California Institute of Technology, New York University, and the universities of Michigan and Washington. The aims of the conference were to compare educational techniques, to coordinate research work at the institutions to avoid duplication and to develop guidelines for specialist courses in aeronautical education.

1926 December 13   Rear Adm. J. M. Reeves, Commanding Aircraft Squadrons, battle fleet, reported on the success achieved with the first dive-bombing activities carried out during fleet gunnery competitions. Dives at 45° angles from 2,500 ft. were flown by Curtiss F6C-2 fighters down to a height of 400 ft. where 25-lb. fragmentation bombs were dropped. The pilots of VF-2 led by Lt. Comdr. F. D. Wagner scored 19 hits with 45 bombs on 100-ft. by 145-ft. targets. Two navy fighter and three navy observation squadrons took part along with one marine squadron. Practice envisaged deck attacks, antipersonnel attacks and attacks on light ships and submarines.

1926 December 13   The Lockheed Aircraft Co. was incorporated by Allan Loughead with the express purpose of designing and manufacturing a high-speed cabin monoplane capable of carrying a pilot and four passengers. Brick-and-tile manufacturer Fred E. Keeler bought a 51% share for $2,550. Having worked for the Loughead Aircraft Manufacturing Co. before it went into liquidation in 1921, Jack Northrop left Douglas and joined Allan Loughead once more to design the Lockheed 1. He suggested the name Vega, and Loughead agreed. What resulted was to be one of the most famous airplanes of the 1920s.

1926 December 18   The opening of the first Imperial Airways desert airmail service was marked by the flight of D.H.66 Hercules G-EBMY that left Croydon, England for Heliopolis, Egypt piloted by Capt. C. F. Wolley Dod. Also on board were Sir Sefton Brancker, air commodore, Mrs. J. G. Weier and Capt. T. A. Gladstone. The RAF operated the Cairo-Baghdad airmail service between 1920 and 1925, but Imperial Airways took over the service for an annual fee of £500,000 for five years, extending it to a fortnightly Cairo-Karachi service. Until 1928, Imperial Airways flights terminated at Basra to avoid difficult terrain along the Persian Gulf.

1926 December 21   Established as a goodwill tour of Central and South America, five amphibious USAAC A0-1 biplanes took off from Kelly Field, Tex. on the first leg of a circumcontinental flight. The A0-1 was a converted Fokker (Atlantic) C.V-C powered by a 500-HP Hispano-Suiza engine and originally intended for reconnaissance and light bombing. The mission flew through Mexico, Central America and Colombia and hugged the west coast of Ecuador, Peru and Chile before crossing to Argentina and flying north to Asunción, Paraguay, then south again to Montevideo, Uruguay and then following the coast north through Brazil, French Guiana, Dutch Guiana (Suriname), British Guiana (Guyana), Venezuela and up through the West Indian islands to Cuba and across to Florida. The flight ended at Bolling Field, Washington, D.C. on May 2, 1927.

1926 December 26   The De Havilland Hercules G-EBMX left England on the first leg of a survey flight to India, carrying the British air minister and his wife, Sir Samuel and Lady Maude Hoare, and piloted by Capt. F. L. Barnard. Also on board were Sir Geofffrey Salmond and C. L. Bullock of the British air ministry. They reached Karachi on January 6 and Delhi two days later after flying 62 hr. 27 min. since leaving England. The return leg began February 7, 1928, and took 32 hr. 50 min. of flying time. The Hercules had been named *City of Delhi* by Lady Irwin, the wife of the viceroy, during its stay at Delhi.

1926 December   The Belgian airline Sabena took delivery of the only aircraft it would operate designed and built in Belgium, the SABCA S-2. Built by the Société Anonyme Belge de Constructions Aéronautiques, it had a wingspan of 47 ft. 11 in., a length of 32 ft. and a loaded weight of 4,409 lb. and was powered by a 240-HP Armstrong Siddeley Puma in-line engine. Although the S-2 was specifically designed for use in the Belgian Congo, there is no record of this aircraft ever having operated in Africa as intended.

1926   The last commercial aircraft built by the Albatros-Flugzeugwerke G.m.b.H. appeared. The L.73 was a biplane powered by two 240-HP BMW IV in-line engines and carried eight passengers in an enclosed cabin. Albatros began its post-World War I aircraft program with the L.58, designed in 1919, a single-engine monoplane used by airlines in Germany and the USSR. Then came three single-engine biplanes (L.72) in 1926, two of which were operated by the publishers of *Berliner Zeitung am Mittag*.

1926   The first transport aircraft produced by the Danish-registered company of Rohrbach-Metall-Flugzeugbau, set up to avoid restrictions on the production of German aircraft, appeared as the Ro VIII Roland and was flight-tested at Staaken. Powered by three 230-HP BMW IV 6-cylinder in-line engines, the Ro VIII had a wingspan of 86 ft. 3 in., a length of 52 ft. 10 in., and a loaded weight of 15,763 lb. These aircraft, and the Roland II derivative, continued to operate until 1936.

1926   Dr. Edmund Rumpler, the Austrian builder of World War I Taube monoplane scout aircraft designed by Igor Etrich, conceived a giant flying boat for intercontinental flight. Comprising a giant wing, spanning 289 ft. and 8 ft. thick, supporting 10 1,000-HP pusher engines set in the trailing edge, the flying boat was to have had two giant hulls supporting a horizontal tail with twin fins and rudders as extensions of each hull. The crew would sit in the forward wing center-section. With 65 tons of fuel carried in the two hulls, the flying boat would have carried 135 passengers in luxurious six-berth cabins at 185 MPH. Needless to say, it was never built!

1927 January 15   The Boeing Aircraft Co. won the U.S. Post Office airmail contract covering the route between San Francisco and Chicago. What is unusual about the granting of this contract is that Boeing was a manufacturer and not an operator. To fulfil the terms of the contract requirements, Boeing quickly formed an airline company, Boeing Air Transport, to operate the route. This company would merge later with several other small American operators, becoming United Air Lines on July 1, 1931.

1927 January 27   The XT2D-1 (BuNo A7051), the first twin-engine aircraft built by Douglas, made its first flight powered by two Wright P-2 engines but was subsequently reengined with two 525-HP Wright R-1750 radials. The design originated at the Naval Aircraft Factory, which wanted an improved torpedo-bomber to replace the Curtiss CS-1 and the Martin SC-1. The Douglas XT2D-1 was a multi-purpose aircraft and an order for 30 was eventually placed, its designation being changed later to P2D. With optional floats or wheels, the aircraft was an attempt to package several patrol, bombing and torpedo attack functions into one, but it mostly served as a floatplane torpedo-bomber.

1927 February 28 The first contract was placed for A-category attack aircraft when Curtiss was asked to build the first batch of 76 A-3s. The A-3 was a derivative of the two-seat O-1 Falcon built for the U.S. Army Air Corps. The Falcon had been purchased by the army in 1925 as an observation aircraft and light bomber. Powered by a 435-HP Curtiss V-1150, the A-3 was developed from the O-1B and had a single 0.30-in. machine gun in each lower wing in addition to the two 0.30-in. guns in the nose. It could also carry 200-lb. bomb loads.

1927 February Having produced two single-engine bombers for the U.S. Army, the LB-1 and the HB-1, Huff-Daland produced a twin-engined development known as the LB-5 Pirate. Huff-Daland became the Keystone Aircraft Corp. this month, and it was under that name that the 10 LB-5 and LB-5A (twin tail) types appeared. The LB-5 was based on the single-engine LB-1 and had two 420-HP Liberty V-1650-3 engines, a wingspan of 67 ft., a length of 44 ft. 8 in. and a range of 435 mi. with a 2,312-lb. bomb load.

1927 March 2 The private venture Boeing Model 74 made its first flight powered by a 425-HP Pratt & Whitney R-1340-80. It was tested by the U.S. Navy and given the designation XF3B-1 before being returned to Boeing for modifications. When it reappeared, the aircraft was slightly bigger, with a slight sweepback on the upper wing and all-metal tail. The navy liked it and ordered 73, the first production model of which was delivered in August 1928 and served aboard the *Langley, Lexington* and *Saratoga* until 1932.

1927 March 12 The prototype Fokker F.VIII, registered H-NADU, made its first flight. Designed to KLM requirements for a larger transport aircraft than the F.VII, it was basically similar to its numerical predecessor with two 480-HP Gnôme Rhône 9-cylinder, air-cooled rotary engines and seating for between 10 and 24 passengers, depending upon the variant. The aircraft was bigger than the F.VII, with a wingspan of 75 ft. 5 in, a length of 54 ft. 11 in. and a loaded weight of 12,566 lb. One Fokker F.VIII is known to have remained operational in the Netherlands on photographic survey work until destroyed by bombing on May 10, 1940.

1927 March 14 The Aviation Corp. of America (AVCO), headed by Juan Trippe, formed Pan American Airways to qualify for a contract for airmail deliveries from the post office and established the route between Key West, Fla. and Havana, Cuba as the first of several routes it would acquire. Capital was acquired primarily from the Atlantic Coast Line and the Florida & East Coast Line, which served Miami. Other investors included Rockefeller, Vanderbilt, Harriman, Fairchild, Hoyt and Lehman. The first operation with a borrowed Fairchild floatplane began October 19, 1927.

1927 March 26 The prototype Handley Page Hinaidi (serial number J7745) made its first flight at Martlesham Heath, England with Sqdn. Ldr. T. H. England at the controls. The prototype Hinaidi was an early Hyderabad fitted with Gnôme-Rhône Jupiter engines instead of the usual Napier Lions. Production aircraft were basically improved Hyderabads and had two 440-HP Bristol

Jupiter VIII engines with a top speed of 122 MPH, a range of 850 mi. and an improved bomb load of 1,448 lb. It began to replace the Hyderabad in RAF service from October 1929 and was finally declared obsolete in 1937.

1927 March 27 Young American airmail pilot Charles A. Lindbergh registered his entry in the Raymond Orteig challenge for the first man to cross the Atlantic Ocean solo. The challenge, and a $25,000 prize, had been issued in 1920, but no one had so far been successful in making the flight. Born on February 4, 1902, Lindbergh learned to fly in 1923 while a member of the U.S. Army Air Service Reserve. He had 2,000 hr. of flying time and successfully enlisted backers from St. Louis to buy a Ryan M-1 monoplane.

1927 March The Westland Wapiti made its first flight and was tested at Martlesham Heath, England for its role as a two-seat, general-purpose aicraft for the RAF. More than 500 Wapitis were built for the RAF and the Auxiliary Air Force, with many serving in a variety of roles in the Middle East. Powered by either a 480-HP Bristol Jupiter VII or a 500-HP XFa engine, it had been designed as a replacement for the D.H.9A and incorporated as many parts from that aircraft as possible. It continued to serve the RAF until the early 1940s.

1927 April 20 The Daniel Guggenheim Fund for the Promotion of Aeronautics announced the Safe Aircraft Competition with a prize of $100,000 to the design team displaying ''a real advance in safety flying [sic].'' This inspired James A. McDonnell Jr. to team with James Cowling and Constantine Zakhartchenko to form the company J. S. McDonnell Junior and Associates. McDonnell would resign from this company in 1928, and via employment with first the Airtransport Engineering Corp. and then the Great Lakes Aircraft Corp., he would find work as chief engineer for landplanes with the Glenn L. Martin Co.

1927 April 28 The first flight of the modified Ryan M-1 Brougham converted for Charles Lindbergh's attempt to fly solo across the Atlantic took place. Built as a four-seat tourer, the modified M-1 was given the designation NYP (New York-Paris) and included several additional fuel tanks for the long flight across open water. The single pilot seat was moved toward the rear of the cockpit and a special periscope installed, the only means by which Lindbergh could get a view forward due to the bulk of the additional installations.

1927 April Elements of Marine Air Flight L., Fourth Squadron, were sent from their base on Guam to Shanghai where they were to disperse into China and help quell a civil uprising that threatened foreigners. Marine air reinforcements from San Diego added men and planes, and in May separate units were formed as Fighting Squadron 6-M, Observation Squadron 10-M and Scouting Squadron 1-M. Between May 1927 and November 1928, the Marines flew a total of 3,818 reconnaissance missions around the Tientsin area.

1927 May 1 Imperial Airways introduced a first-class service on its route between London and Paris. Known as the ''Silver Wing'' service, it operated only on the Armstrong Whitworth Argosy, which had been a highly successful airliner since its introduction with Imperial Airways in July 1926. A round-trip London-Paris Silver Wing ticket cost £9 and included steward and bar service on the 2 hr. 30 min. flight. The Handley Page airliners operated the second-class service, costing £7 10s for the 2 hr. 50 min. flight.

1927 May 4 The first of three Boeing TB-1 torpedo bombers made its first flight. Designed by the navy, the TB-1s were the last aircraft built by Boeing before World War II to someone else's design. With a single 770-HP Packard 1A-2500 in-line engine, the TB-1 had a 53 ft. wingspan and a length of 42 ft. 7 in. with a gross weight of 10,703 lb. The design of this large aircraft had been greatly influence by the Martin T3M and was mounted on twin floats with both scout and torpedo-bomber versions.

1927 May 8 The World War I French air ace Charles Nungesser and his copilot Albert Coli disappeared without a trace during an attempt to fly the Atlantic Ocean from east to west. Their Levasseur P.L.8, a two-seat biplane, had been extensively modified with the addition of fuel tanks and a jettisonable undercarriage to reduce drag. It was powered by a 450-HP Lorraine and had a top speed of about 120 MPH. No wreckage was ever satisfactorily identified as belonging to the aircraft.

1927 May 17 Powered by a 490-HP Bristol Jupiter VIIF, the prototype Bristol Type 105 Bulldog single-seat fighter made its first flight. Designed to an air ministry specification issued in 1926, the Bulldog won a competitive fly-off, and 372 were eventually ordered for the RAF, 59 of which were two-seat trainers. The Bulldog had a top speed of 174 MPH and a climb time of 14.5 min. to 20,000 ft. Fitted with twin synchronized Vickers guns, it could also carry four 20-lb. bombs. The Bulldog became one of the more famous British fighters of the 1930s, being replaced from 1937 by the Gloster Gladiator.

1927 May 20 Charles Lindbergh took off from Roosevelt Field, N.Y. to become the first person to fly solo across the Atlantic and in so doing establish a new long-distance record. His Ryan NYP was named *Spirit of St. Louis* in honor of the Missouri businessmen who backed his venture. It was powered by a 237-HP Wright J-5C Whirlwind 9-cylinder radial providing a top speed of 124 MPH. Laden with 450 gal. of fuel, the Ryan monoplane almost struck trees and power cables as it struggled for height after taking off from Roosevelt Field. After struggling against violent winds, ice, poor visibility and tiredness, Lindbergh was only 3 mi. off course when he made landfall and landed safely at Le Bourget, Paris, 33 hr. 30 min. 28 sec. later after a flight of 3,590 miles at an average speed of 107 MPH.

1927 May 20 A specially modified Hawker Horsley two-seat biplane bomber took off from RAF Cranwell, England with Flt.

Preserved in the Smithsonian's National Air and Space Museum: the Ryan monoplane used by Lindbergh to cross the Atlantic, May 21, 1927.

Lts. C. R. Carr and L. E. M. Gillman in an attempt to fly nonstop to India. Fuel capacity had been increased from 276 gal. to 1,320 gal., which increased takeoff weight from 9,000 lb. to 14,000 lb. After 34 hr. of flying time and 3,420 mi., the crew brought the Horsley down in the Straits of Hormuz at the neck of the Persian Gulf, landing on what they believed to be flat sand but which proved to be water; the aircraft was destroyed, but they escaped unhurt.

1927 May The first French aircraft carrier, the *Bearn,* was completed. Laid down as a *Normandie*-class warship in January 1914, it was launched in April 1920, and work began in August 1923 to convert it to a carrier. With a displacement of 27,950 tons, the *Bearn* was 598 ft. long with a deck beam of 115 ft. 4 in. The carrier operated with the French Navy between 1927 and 1939, when it became an aircraft transporter. In 1940 it was laid up but was reintroduced as a transporter in 1945. Three years later it became a training ship and then a submarine depot ship, before it was finally scrapped in 1967, the longest-lived carrier of all.

1927 June 7 Only two weeks after Charles Lindbergh flew the Atlantic solo for the first time, Americans Clarence C. Chamberlain and Charles A. Levin flew a Bellanca Columbia from Roosevelt Field, N.Y. to Eisleben, Germany. They flew a total distance of 3,911 mi., and bad weather over England forced them up to 20,000 ft.—quite a feat without oxygen. Chamberlain and Levin broke the existing nonstop distance record with this flight. (It is interesting to note that Lindbergh had initially expected to fly the Bellanca to Europe but changed to the Ryan monoplane instead.)

1927 June 15 The world's first intercontinental charter flight began when American millionaire W. van Lear Black hired a Fokker F.VIIa (H-NADP) named *Baltimore Sun* with Bristol Jupiter engines from the Dutch national airline, KLM. Commanded by Capt. G. J. Geysendorffer with J. B. Scholte and K. A. O. Weber as crew and Leo Bayline along as Black's valet, they flew 9,120 mi. in 86 hrs. 27 min. over 13 days between Amsterdam, Holland and Jakarta, Dutch West Indies (now Indonesia). The return journey was made in 14 days, covering 9,590 mi. in a flying time of 97 hr. completed July 23.

1927 June 28 The first trans-Pacific crossing between North America and the Hawaiian Islands began when Lts. Lester J. Maitland and Albert Hegenberger took off from Oakland, California at the start of a 2,407-mi. flight to Honolulu. Flying the first Fokker C-2 of three ordered by the USAAC after the Ford Reliability Tour, their aircraft had a special wing with extended tips that increased span from 63 ft. 6 in. to 71 ft. 2 in. Basically a Fokker F-VIIa-3m, it had provision for eight passengers and was powered by a 220-HP Wright J-5 engine. Named *Bird of Paradise*, the C-2 covered the distance in 25 hr. 50 min. aided by directional beacons, one in Maui, the other in San Francisco. Tired and hungry when they landed, the crew had failed to find chicken, soup and coffee stowed aboard before the flight.

1927 June 29 Comdr. Richard E. Byrd took off from Roosevelt Field, N.Y. with Lt. Neville, Bert Acosta and Bernt Balchen in an attempt to make the first direct crossing from the United States to continental Europe, but Lindbergh beat them as they were preparing for the flight. They did almost get to the destination, landing in the water off Ver-sur-Mer in France. They flew a Fokker F.VIIB-3m, which was the latest and ultimately proved to be the most popular Fokker trimotor. It had been developed as the Fokker C-2 for the U.S. Army Air Corps.

1927 June 30   The U.S. Marine Corps placed an initial order for two prototype XF8C-1 fighter-bomber biplanes. Essentially an A-3 Falcon attack plane fitted with a 432-HP Pratt & Whitney R-1340B radial engine rather than the Curtiss V-1150 Conquerer, the type first flew in November 1927 and was introduced in early 1928, all 31 ordered being delivered by February. Known in the navy as the OC-1 or the OC-2, the F8C had a wingspan of 38 ft., a length of 27 ft. 11 in., a height of 11 ft. 8 in. and a gross weight of 4,191 lb. The OC had two forward-firing 0.30-in. guns in the lower wing and a single 0.30-in. gun on a Scarff ring mounting for the observer.

1927 June 30   The U.S. Navy ordered 17 Curtiss F7C-1 single-seat biplane fighters, the first Curtiss aircraft specially designed for carrier-based work rather than being an adapted landplane. Flown first on February 28, 1927, under private ownership, it had a wingspan of 32 ft. 8 in. and a length of 22 ft. 2 in. The F7C-1 was powered by a 450-HP Pratt & Whitney R-1340B; climb time was 2.6 min. to 5,000 ft. with a top speed of 155.5 MPH and an operational range of 355 mi. The F7C had been designed around the radial when the navy found it difficult to maintain in-line engines at sea.

1927 July 1   The U.S. Post Office handed over authority for the lighted airway system to the Department of Commerce. The system to this date included 405 rotating, gas-fired illumination beacons, 100 electric emergency beacon lights, 89 emergency landing fields fully equipped for night landings and 17 air stations for scheduled landings. In less than 10 years, the post office had carried over 300 million letters by air and flown 15 million air mi. for the loss of 43 pilots in 200 crashes with a further 37 seriously injured. This singular achievement profoundly marked the ascent of U.S. commercial aviation, positioning it for supremacy over European aviation.

1927 July 1   Boeing Air Transport began its airmail charter operation on the Chicago to San Francisco route. A subsidiary of the Boeing Airplane Co., it had a fleet of 24 Boeing Model 40 aircraft, the last of which had been delivered June 30. (The first flight of the type was May 20.) The aircraft was powered by a single 420-HP Pratt & Whitney Wasp radial. It could carry 1,200 lb. of mail. The Model 40 had a wingspan of 44 ft. 2 in. and a length of 33 ft. 2 in. with a maximum weight of 6,000 lb., a cruising speed of 105 MPH, a ceiling of 14,500 ft. and a range of 650 mi.

1927 July 4   The first of a celebrated line of Lockheed Vega types made its first flight from a site now part of the Los Angeles International Airport with Edward "Eddie" A. Bellande at the controls. Designed by Jack Northrop, the Vega was of wood construction with a monocoque fuselage and the cantilever wing concept favored by several American aircraft builders following the success of the Fokker types of World War I. The first Vega was sold to George Hearst Jr., at a loss, for the Dole Race from Oakland, Calif. to Hawaii. The Vega was a high-wing monoplane with a span of 41 ft., a length of 27 ft. 6 in. and a 225-HP Wright Whirlwind.

1927 July 17   Nicaraguan rebels besieging the U.S. Marine Corps garrison at Ocotal were attacked by five Marine Corps D.H.4B light bombers operating under the new close tactical support doctrine. Close support dive-bombing and strafing missions were flown against the rebels' positions and were successful in forcing them to withdraw. The aircraft were led by Maj. Ross Rowell, USMC, and the action was pressed home without loss.

1927 July 30   The world's first two-seat autogyro, the Cierva C.6D, made its first flight with a passenger, the aircraft's designer Don Juan de la Cierva. All Cierva's previous designs were single-seaters, but the additional seat gave the autogyro a potential for commercial applications that the others did not have. The C.6D had made its first flight the previous day when it ascended at Hamble, England piloted by F. T. Courtny, who was also responsible for taking Cierva up on the first two-seat autogyro flight.

1927 July   The Huff-Daland (renamed the Keystone Aircraft Corp.) LB-1 began flight trials for the U.S. Army. Ordered in November 1925, it had a gross weight of 12,415 lb. and carried up to 350 gal. of fuel. This provided a range of 430 mi. with a 2,750-lb. bomb load. Called *Pegasus,* the type was powered by a Packard 2A-2540 rated at 787-HP and could carry four crew-members, one more than the prototype. However, because the army had decided to adopt twin-engine designs for bombers, the LB-1 was no longer a candidate for production.

1927 July   The propeller research tunnel (PRT) was declared operational at the NACA Langley Memorial Aeronautical Laboratory. Comprising a 20-ft. diameter open-throat chamber, the PRT enabled researchers to carry out accurate, full-scale tests on propellers, landing gear, tail surfaces and large-size model wings. A single 27-ft. diameter fan driven by two 1,000-HP diesel motors provided a maximum wind speed of 110 MPH. The diesel engines were changed for electric motors in 1933, and the PRT continued in operation until dismantled in 1950 to provide space for the transonic pressure tunnel (TPT).

1927 August 10   The Soviet aircraft designer N. N. Polikarpov presented a report entitled *The Maneuverability of the High-Powered Fighter* to a meeting at the Technical Council of Aviatrust. Polikarpov was one of the first designers of his generation to tackle the problem posed by increasing engine power: namely, that greater weights resulted in a more sluggish design that ran counter to the principle of maneuverability and agility. The report was examined by members of the TsAGI (Central Aerodynamics and Hydrodynamics Institute) and the VVS (air force) and led to production of a radial-engined fighter, the I-6, which was drawn up in late 1928.

1927 August 17   Art Goebel and Bill Davis in a monoplane built by the Travel Air company and named *Woolaroc* landed safely in Hawaii after a 2,439-mi. flight from Oakland, Calif., winning the $25,000 first prize in the Dole Race. Sponsored by Hawaii Pineapple Co. owner James D. Dole, the race was entered by eight contestants, only four of whom started. Jack Frost and Gordon Scott in the first Lockheed Vega and Augy Pedlar and Mildred Doran in their Buhl biplane *Miss Doran* disappeared and were never seen again. Martin Jensen and Paul Schluter in their Breeze monoplane *Aloha* won the $10,000 second prize.

1927 August 27   Sqdn. Ldr. H. J. (Bert) Hinkler left Croydon airfield, London at 5:27 A.M. flying the prototype Avro 581 Avian (G-EBOV) equipped with a special long-range fuel tank that would keep him airborne all the way to Riga, Latvia. Designed by Roy Chadwick, the 581A Avian had a wingspan of 28 ft. (reduced from the 32-ft. wingspan when it first flew in 1926), a length of 24 ft., 6 in., loaded weight of 1,580 lb. and a maximum speed of 70 MPH. Powered by an 85-HP A. D. C. Cirrus II engine, it landed at Riga after almost 11 hr., having covered 1,200 mi. in the longest light aircraft flight to date.

1927 September 1   The first flight of a light aircraft between London, England and Cape Town, South Africa began when Flt.

Lt. R. R. Bentley took off from Croydon in a D.H.60X Moth (G-EBSO) named *Dorys* and powered by a Cirrus engine. After 27 days, Bentley arrived in Cape Town, having covered 8,300 mi. Bentley won the Air Force Cross for this achievement and was to make two more round-trip flights by 1929, logging a total 51,652 mi. Performances such as this helped immortalize the Moth as the best general purpose light aircraft of its day.

1927 September 12   The first successful flight after Canadian Transcontinental Airways received the Canadian government's first commercial airmail contract was made by Capt. Quigley (former founder of the Dominion Aerial Exploration Co.). Flying an HS2L, he carried 500 lb. of mail 330 mi. down the St. Lawrence River from Montreal to Rimouski via Three Rivers. (The first attempt, three days earlier, failed when the Vickers Vanessa being used for the attempt was unable to get off the ground.) The return flight was successfully accomplished September 16 followed by seven more flights during the fall.

1927 September 26   The British pilot Flt. Lt. S. N. Webster won the tenth Schneider Trophy seaplane race held this year at Venice, Italy. He averaged 281.655 MPH around the seven laps of a 50 km (31.07 mi.) left-hand course flying Supermarine S.5 N220 powered by an 875-HP Napier Lion VIIB engine. Designed by Supermarine's R. J. Mitchell, Webster's S.5 was one of three entered by Britain, in addition to three Gloster IVs designed by H. P. Folland and a Short-Bristow Crusader designed by W. G. Carter. This was the greatest number of entries ever mounted by one country. The Americans declined to enter. The S.5 (N219) flown by Flt. Lt. O. E. Worsley was the only other entry to finish, at 273.07 MPH, making the race outcome an outright win for Britain.

1927 September   The army began flight trials with the Curtiss XB-2, a bomber design based on the earlier XNBS-4. Only one prototype was ordered, and, redundant to needs, it was destroyed in December after only 59 hr. of flying time. The XB-2 had a wingspan of 90 ft., a length of 47 ft. 6 in. a wing area of 1,499 sq. ft. and a gross weight of 16,344 lb. Powered by two 600-HP Curtiss GV-1570 Conquerer engines, it had a top speed of 130 MPH and a service ceiling of 16,140 ft. The XB-2 carried a maximum bomb load of 4,000 lb., although standard mission load was 2,500 lb., a crew of five and three defensive gun positions.

1927 October 12   The headquarters of the U.S. Army Air Corps Materiel Division and Engineering Section was established at Wright Field. The 45,000-acre site near Dayton, Ohio was to become the administrative and technical center of the USAAC and most of the experimental programs in military aviation were carried out there before the end of World War II, when such activities were dispersed to other locations.

1927 October 14   Two British aviators, Capt. W. N. Lancaster and his sponsor Mrs. Keith Miller as passenger, set off from Croydon, England with the intention of reaching Australia, which they eventually did on March 19, 1928, after 32 flying days. They were in the second Avro 594 Avian (G-EBTU, *Red Rose*), powered by a hand-made 90-HP Avro Alpha engine. This constituted the first flight between England and Australia attempted by a light aircraft, although Bert Hinkler got there first after leaving England February 7, 1928. It was also the first flight between the two countries with a woman passenger on board. The 594 Avian had a wingspan of 28 ft., a length of 24 ft. 3 in., an all-up weight of 1,467 lb. and a range of 325 mi.

1927 October 15   Capt. Dieudonné Costes and Lt. Comdr. Joseph Le Brix completed the first nonstop crossing of the South Atlantic when they landed at Natal, Brazil after having flown 2,215 mi. in 19 hr. 50 min. They took off from St. Louis, Senegal in Africa the previous day in a specially modified Breguet 19 single-engine, two-seat biplane. It was named *Nungesser-Coli* after the two famous French airmen who had disappeared during an attempted flight across the Atlantic. This flight was part of a journey around the world that took six months, although the Pacific was crossed by ship.

1927 October 17   Leading four superbly finished, metal-hulled, Supermarine Southampton flying boats, Grp. Capt. H. M. Cave-Brown-Cave set out from England for a 14-month tour of the Far East to reconnoiter new flying boat bases, give crews experience in operating far from Britain, survey new routes for Imperial Airways and generally show the flag. In December 1928, their task completed, the RAF Far East Flight disbanded, and the four Southamptons (one had been replaced) formed No. 205 Squadron based at Seletar, Singapore, effective January 8, 1929. In 14 months, the flying boats had flown 27,000 mi., each aircraft logging almost 352 flying hr. at an average speed of 80 MPH.

1927 October 19   The first air service operated by the recently formed Pan American Airways began across the 90 mi. of water between Key West, Fla. and Havana, Cuba. The aircraft used was a Fairchild seaplane, but on October 28, operations got under way with the first of five Fokker F.VIIA-3m monoplane transport aircraft flown by Hugh Wells and Ed Musick. The aircraft carried 772 lb. of airmail, but Pan American was more interested in passenger traffic and would quickly develop other overwater routes out of the United States.

1927 November 17   Alan Cobham took off from the Thames River in a Short Singapore (G-EBUP) at the start of a survey of Africa for Imperial Airways. During the 23,000 mi. journey that ended back in England May 31, 1928, the Singapore carried Sir Alan and Lady Cobham, H. V. Worrall, the pilot, F. Green and C. E. Conway, crew, and C. R. Bonnett, cameraman, via Malta, the Nile, the Great Lakes, Durban and Cape Town. They discovered and charted 50 potential flying boat landing areas and covered the distance in 330 flying hr. The Singapore had high-compression Condor engines and several modifications.

1927 November 27   Texas Air Transport began using Pitcairn Mailwing single-seat biplanes, becoming the first carrier to operate this purpose-built aircraft designed from the outset for airmail. Powered by a Wright Whirlwind radial engine, it had a top speed of 136 MPH and a welded tubular steel fuselage and wooden wings. Pitcairn Aviation received the first airmail contract for this aircraft on January 28, 1927, but the service would not start before May 1928, leaving Texas Air Transport the first to use the Mailwing.

1927 December 13   After six years as head of American military aviation, most recently as chief of the U.S. Army Air Corps since its formation in July 1926, Maj. Gen. Mason M. Patrick retired and was replaced (from December 14) by Maj. Gen. J. E. Fechet. Maj. Gen. Patrick had fought hard to keep the fledgling air service viable and as independent a force as possible within the severe budgetary limits imposed upon it. The gradually improving condition of America's military aviation was due in large measure to the unflagging efforts of Patrick.

1927 December 29   Douglas received an order for 25 Naval Aircraft Factory PN patrol flying boats, to be delivered beginning in the spring of 1929. Douglas improved the basic PN, and the modified aircraft was designated PD-1; similarly modified planes built by Martin were designated PM-1 and PM-2; and those built by Keystone were designated PK-1. The most notable achievement of the navy's PN-series had been the flight between San Francisco Bay and Hawaii on September 1, 1925. Several PD-1 types were used as trainers, the last being struck off charge on March 31, 1939.

1927 December 31 The Cessna Aircraft Co. was incorporated in Omaha, Nebr. after the partnership of Clyde V. Cessna and Victor Roos was dissolved when Roos sold his share of the Cessna-Roos Aircraft Co., formed September 8, 1927, to Cessna. Roos had previously been a partner in the Bellanca-Roos Aircraft Co. Born in 1879, Cessna designed his first aircraft in 1910 after watching a Frenchman fly a Bleriot Type XI at Oklahoma City. The former motor mechanic designed and built wings for a copied Bleriot fuselage and then taught himself to fly. Cessna built a further 14 aircraft before teaming in 1925 with Walter Beech and Lloyd Stearman as the Travel Air Manufacturing Co. but left the company in 1927 to concentrate on his own designs. By 1990 the Cessna Aircraft Co. had produced almost 180,000 aircraft, extending its range from light aircraft to carriers and executive jobs.

1928 January 1 The Polish National Aviation Co. (Państwowe Zaklady Lotnicze, or PZL) was established as the state-nationalized aircraft design and manufacturing company. Several European manufacturers helped build the Polish aviation industry before it was tested in war during four weeks in September 1939. The first aircraft it produced was the PZL L.2 high-wing reconnaissance monoplane powered by a 220-HP Wright J-5 Whirlwind and built under license by Skoda. The predilection for British engines continued, the P.5 having a 120-HP Gypsy, the P.6 and P.7 having a 485-HP Bristol Jupiter and the P.11 a 645-HP Bristol Mercury.

1928 January 5 At a meeting in Paris, the FAI debated the need for a change in the rules governing the annual Schneider Trophy race for seaplanes and unanimously judged that the event should be held in alternate years rather than annually as had been the tradition since the first contest in 1913. The technical development of new airframes required longer intervals between contests. The rules were also changed so that the winner of three races out of five successive contests would gain possession of the trophy.

1928 January 6 Pilot Lt. C. F. Schilt, USMC, landed a Vought O2U-1 Corsair in the street of a Nicaraguan village to rescue wounded officers and men. Ten flights were made over three days to the village of Quilahi, and during this period, 18 servicemen were rescued by the two-seat aircraft that frequently came under fire. For this remarkable feat of daring, Lt. Schilt was awarded the Medal of Honor. The Corsair had been designed to carry wheels or a single float with outrigger stabilizers under each wing.

1928 January 7 The Polikarpov U-2 prototype piloted by M. M. Gromov made its first flight in the Soviet Union. It was the first in a long line of derivatives and variants that would maintain this single-engine biplane in service for more than 60 years. With a range of engines, wheels, floats, skis and pontoons, the U-2 was developed as a general-purpose aircraft and served as a crop duster, air ambulance, light transport, gun spotter, light bomber, ground attack aircraft, aerial survey plane, reconnaissance aircraft and aerial broadcast platform. Some estimates on production

claim 41,000 U-2s were built for the Soviet Union and neighboring countries.

1928 January 30 Delivery of the first of 32 Boeing F2B-1 carrier-based biplane fighters ordered in March 1927, was made. The first operational units to take charge of this aircraft were VF-1B and VB-2B on the USS *Saratoga*. Almost exactly the same size and weight as the XF2B-1, the F2B-1 had either one 0.50-in. machine gun and one 0.30-in., or two 0.30-in. machine guns. It had a top speed of 158 MPH at sea level and a range of 317 mi. with an absolute ceiling of 22,300 ft. Although a bomber squadron, VB-2B became famous for its Three Sea Hawks team whereby three F2B-1 aircraft were tied together by cord for aerobatic displays.

1928 January 31 Imperial Airways advertised a pleasure trip scheduled to begin this day, a flight that constituted one of the first attempts at organized air tours. Passengers would have been carried in an Armstrong Whitworth Argosy from London to France, Spain, North Africa, Italy, back to France and home to London. The price of £456 15s included meals, sightseeing, fine hotels and a guide. Due to the economic depression, this event did not take place.

1928 February 3 The Boeing F3B-1 naval fighter made its first flight. It was the first production model of the precursor XF3B-1, which first had flown on March 2, 1927. Developed as a privately funded initiative, the model 74 was designed originally as a multi-capability naval fighter-bomber able to operate with floats or fixed undercarriage. Returned to Boeing in November 1927, it was redesigned as the F3B-1 with an enlarged wing and duralumin covering on flight control surfaces. The Navy ordered 73 F3Bs, all of which were operational by the end of 1928 but which had a service life of only four years.

1928 February 7 Bert Hinkler took off from Croydon near London at 6:48 A.M. flying the Avro 581E Avian prototype (G-EBOV) on the first leg of a flight to Australia. (The suffix E denoted several modifications, including rounded wing tips first used by Mrs. Elliot-Lynn during altitude flights the previous October.) Hinkler flew via Rome, Malta, Tobruk, Ramleh, Basra, Jask, Karachi, Cawnpore, Calcutta, Rangoon, Victoria Point, Singapore, Bandoeng and Bima. He landed in Darwin, Australia on February 22, having flown 11,005 mi. in a flying time of 128 hr. over less than 16 days. His flight was the second between England and Australia carried out by a light aircraft, although despite having set off after Lancaster and Miller, he arrived before them and is credited with the first successful England-Australia lightplane flight.

1928 February 12 Lady Heath (formerly Mrs. Elliott-Lynn), the first woman to fly solo from Cape Town, South Africa to London took off in an Avro Avian for the long flight north. The Anglo-Irish pilot arrived at Cairo on April 3, and when the RAF would not grant her permission to cross the Mediterranean alone, she flew via Heliopolis and Benghazi to Tripoli where Mussolini provided a seaplane escort. Lady Heath reached Paris on the morning of May 17 and flew to Croydon, England that afternoon.

1928 February 14 The first Short S.8 Calcutta flying boat (registration no. G-EBVG) flew from the Medway River, England with J. Lankester Parker as the pilot, Maj. Herbert G. Brackley as copilot and Eustace Short, his son Francis and George Cotton as crewmembers. This British flying boat was the first stressed skin design to enter commercial service. It had been built on instructions from the Air Council as a development of the Short

Singapore for Imperial Airways and was powered by three 540-HP Bristol Jupiter XIF engines or three 840-HP Armstrong Siddeley Tiger VI engines. With performance similar to the Singapore, it conformed to the airline safety requirement for three engines.

1928 February 27   The first U.S. naval aviator, Comdr. T. G. Ellyson, was killed when a Loening OL amphibian he was flying crashed at night in Chesapeake Bay while on a flight from Norfolk, Va. to Annapolis, Md. With him were Lt. Comdr. Hugo Schmidt and Lt. Rodgers Ransehausen, who were also killed. The OL had a single float faired into the underside of the fuselage and was powered by a 475-HP Packard 1A-2500 radial engine. The wings were almost identical to the wings of the D.H.4 but had improved efficiency. The Loening company merged with Keystone Aircraft Corp., which was eventually acquired by the Curtiss-Wright Corp.

1928 February 28   The Consolidated Aircraft Co. of Buffalo, N.Y. received a contract to build one XPY-1 flying boat designed by the U.S. Naval Aircraft Factory. It was completed in January 1929, but Martin underbid Consolidated and received the production contract in June 1929. The XPY-1 was the first monoplane ordered for the navy, with a 100 ft. wingspan, a length of 61 ft. 9 in., a gross weight of 13,734 lb. and a range of up to 2,620 mi. and a cruising speed of 110 MPH. Powered by two 450-HP Pratt & Whitney R-1340-38 radial engines set below the parasol wing and a third engine on struts above the center-section on the prototype only, the XPY-1 introduced features embodied later in the famous PBY Catalina.

1928 March 1   An airmail route between France and Chile was opened with a fast sea link between Dakar, Senegal and Natal, Brazil. To stimulate traffic, Latécoère produced a range of monoplane mail carriers to service the route, the most successful of which were the Laté 17, 25 and 26. Almost 100 aircraft of these types were operational along the mail route, sections of which were run by Cia Aeropostal Brasileira and Cia Aeroposta Argentine. The development of this route began in 1925 and helped stimulate the expansion of aviation in South America with strong European connections.

1928 March 5   The all-metal Beardmore Inflexible made its first flight at Martlesham Heath, England. It was the aircraft with the greatest wingspan—157 ft. 6 in.—built and flown in Britain before the Bristol Type 167, Brabazon I, took off on September 4, 1949. Designed on the principle of all-metal construction and skinning pioneered by Dr. Adolph Rohrbach in Germany, the Inflexible had a length of 75 ft. 6 in. and an all-up weight of 37,000 lb. and had been contracted to the Scottish engineering firm run by William Beardmore. Powered by three 650-HP Rolls Royce Condor II engines, the Inflexible was registered G-EBNG but given the RAF serial no. J7557. Flown at the 1928 Hendon RAF Display, it was dismantled in 1930.

1928 March 9   On what was to become the first round-trip flight between London and Cape Town, South Africa flown by a woman, the English aviatrix Lady Mary Bailey took off from Croydon. She reached Cairo on March 19 and was permitted to continue only because she was to be accompanied from Khartoum to Lake Victoria by Lt. R. R. Bentley (who had flown north from Johannesburg with Lady Heath) in a D.H. 60 Moth. Lady Bailey crashed at Tabora, Tanganyika (now Tanzania) but carried on with a replacement aircraft supplied by the South African Air Force, reaching Cape Town on April 30. Lady Bailey arrived back in England on May 12.

1928 March 30   The FAI-ratified world speed record was pushed through 300 MPH for the first time. Flying a specially adapted Macchi M-52bis seaplane, Italian Maj. Mario de Bernardi achieved a speed of 512.69 km/hr. (318.64 MPH). This was an increase of 20.81 MPH over his previous record run, in a standard Macchi M-52, of 297.83 MPH (479.21 km/hr.) achieved on November 4, 1927. It had taken just eight years to double the world speed record, but it would take 17 years for it to double again.

1928 March   Deutsche Luft Hansa introduced the Junkers G.31 trimotor monoplane on its Hamburg-Amsterdam-London and Berlin-Danzig-Königsberg routes. The aircraft had first appeared in 1926 and was developed from the G.24 but was a little bigger and had seating for 15 passengers. Powered by three 450-HP Gnôme-Rhône Jupiter radial engines, the G.31 had a cruising speed of 106 MPH and a range of about 600 mi. Aircraft of this type were used throughout Europe during the first half of the 1930s in Germany and between Germany and Holland, Austria, Denmark and Sweden.

1928 April 12   A Junkers W.33 floatplane named *Bremen* took off from Baldonnel, Ireland at the start of the first east-west non-stop crossing of the North Atlantic by aircraft. The W.33 belonged to Deutsche Luft-Hansa and was piloted by Capt. Hermann Kohl, the airline's director of night flying. The other crewmembers were Baron Gunther von Hunefeld from Luft-Hansa and Irishman Comdr. J. Fitzmaurice. The aircraft landed safely at Greenly Island, Labrador the next day after 37 flying hr.

1928 April 15   The Australian explorer George Hubert Wilkins and his pilot Carl Ben Eielson took off from Elson Lagoon, Alaska in the third Lockheed Vega, specially modified and fitted with wooden skis, on the initial leg of an east-west trans-Arctic flight. After 20 hr. 20 min., flying half-way around the Arctic Circle, they landed at Dead Man's Island, Greenland in swirling snow and a 70 MPH wind. Only 5 mi. short of their pre-planned destination, they took off when the storm abated and (completed the 2,200 mi. from Elson Lagoon. This flight did much to publicize the capabilities of the rugged Lockheed Vega.

1928 April 17   Novice aviatrix Amelia Earhart became the first woman to cross the Atlantic by air when she flew as a passenger in a Fokker F.VIIB-3m/W, the floatplane version of the famous Ford Tri-Motor, with three 300-HP Wright Whirlwind engines. The aircraft was flown by Wilmer Stultz and Lou Gordon. Named *Friendship,* it was originally assigned to Richard E. Byrd's Antarctic expedition but was replaced by a Ford Trimotor. The Atlantic crossing began at Trepassey, Newfoundland and ended at the port of Barry in southern Wales.

1928 May 1   Founder of the famous seaplane races that bore his name, Jacques Schneider died at the ultimely age of 49 at Beaulieu-sur-Mer, outside Nice in southern France. Conceived as a stimulus to conventional seaplane development, the Schneider races nevertheless made their greatest mark on advances in engine power and technology, horsepower growing 10-fold in the 15 years since the first race was held only a few miles from where Schneider died, poor and unrecognized by the popular press.

1928 May 1   Pitcairn Aviation started regular operations on civil airmail (CAM) route 19 flying mail between New York and Atlanta using Pitcairn PA-5 Mailwing single-seat biplanes. Seven months later the airline began operating the Atlanta-Miami route (CAM 25) previously flown by Florida Airways as CAM 10 before it expired. Pitcairn had been formed on September 15, 1927, as a combination aircraft manufacturer and airline service company. On January 17, 1930, it became known as Eastern Air Transport Inc. The New York-Atlanta route was extended to Boston, and beginning in August 1930, passengers were carried for the first time in Curtiss Condor biplanes.

1928 May 16　A major new business initiative from Clement Keys established Transcontinental Air Transport with $5 million capital and shareholders including Curtiss, Wright Aeronautical Corp., the Pennsylvania Railroad and St. Louis businessmen. It was the first major airline to be formed with the specific purpose of carrying passengers rather than mail or freight. Charles Lindbergh helped pioneer new routes west, and a committee was established to select multi-engined aircraft. A weather reporting line 150 mi. wide spanned the continent with 50 stations across the United States. Ford Tri-Motor monoplanes were selected until Curtiss Condor biplanes could be purchased.

1928 May 17　The first permanent Flying Doctor service began when Capt. A. H. Affleck flew the modified D.H.50A, G-AUER, to Julia Creek, Australia. (This plane, ex-G-EBIW, had been granted a certificate of air worthiness on May 28, 1924, and was the first of its type to enter service in a British Commonwealth country.) First used by QANTAS and named *Hermes,* it was renamed *Victory* in May 1928, when it had been refurbished, re-rigged, given a strengthened undercarriage and adapted to carry two stretchers. The same aircraft had been used to carry out the first, unofficial Flying Doctor flight in August 1927.

1928 May 23　The Italian semirigid airship *Italia,* sister ship to the *Norge,* left Kings Bay, Norway with Gen. Umberto Nobile and 14 crew members for an Arctic survey flight from which she never returned. *Norge* had arrived in Norway three weeks earlier and conducted a 60-hour flight beginning May 15, during which the airship covered 2,400 mi. around Franz Josef Land, Severnaya Zemlya and Novaya Zemlya. The last flight moved up the northeast coast of Greenland and, after 12 hr. headed for the North Pole, which was reached at 12:20 A.M. on May 24. High winds brought the airship down on the return journey, killing six as it hit the ice. One of the remaining nine died, but the others were rescued.

1928 May 31　The Australian ex-RFC pilot Capt. Charles Kingsford-Smith and his copilot Charles Ulm took off from Oakland, Calif. in a Fokker F.VIIB-3m, VH-USU, named *Southern Cross,* for a flight across the Pacific between America and Australia. They arrived at Honolulu at 12:15 P.M. on June 1, logging 2,400 mi. in just over 27 hr., and two days later flew on to Suva, Fiji, landing there after a flight of 3,200 mi. in less than 35 hr. despite rain, high wind and violent storms. The final leg to Australia began June 8 and ended at Brisbane next day completing 83 hr. 38 min. flying time. The aircraft had been named after the Australian town in which funds were raised to finance the venture.

1928 June 11　The world's first rocket-powered aircraft took to the air for a 35-sec. flight when the German aviator Fritz Stamer piloted an Ente glider propelled by two 44-lb.-thrust solid propellant rocket motors provided by Alexander Sander. Approached by ardent rocket proponents Fritz von Opel and Max Valier, Alexander Lippisch of the Forschungsinstitut, Rhön-Rossiten Gesellschaft (the Rhön-Rossiten Research Institute Company), supplied the Ente, which he had designed. A second flight was made with two 55-lb.-thrust rockets, this time lasting 70 sec. for a ground distance of 4,000 ft., which also included a full turn. This work would lead to the Me 163 rocket-powered interceptor, the prototype of which first flew in July 1941.

1928 June 18　A contract was placed with Martin for the XT5M-1 dive-bomber, which was to compete with the XT2N-1 ordered from the U.S. Naval Aircraft Factory. It was powered by a 525-HP Pratt & Whitney R-1690-22 radial providing a top speed of 134 MPH and a climb time of 7.8 min. to 5,000 ft. The specification demanded a 1,000-lb. bomb load. With metal fuselage and wing structure, the XT5M-1 was the first aircraft designed to pull out of a dive with a 1,000-lb. warload. The XT5M-1 had a wingspan of 41 ft. and a length of 28 ft. 9 in. and would be ordered into production as the BM-1 (the *T* in XT5M-1 for torpedo bomber, having been changed to *B* for bomber).

1928 June 18　A French Latham 47-02 biplane flying boat powered by two 600-HP engines left Cherbourg, France for Norway at the start of a rescue attempt aimed at locating and recovering the crew of the Italian semirigid airship *Italia* that crashed on the ice returning from the North Pole May 24. At Bergen, the polar explorer Roald Amundsen joined the aircraft, and it set out on a search before vanishing without trace. Three months later a wing float was washed up, but nothing else was ever found, either of the aircraft or its crew, including Amundsen.

1928 June 20　Oklahoma City Airline came into operation and began flying services on the route between Oklahoma City and Tulsa. It had been formed by the brothers Thomas and Paul Braniff, and in 1930 the company was renamed Braniff Airways, becoming Braniff International in 1948. In 1967 Braniff absorbed the South American airline Panagra (Pan American Grace Airways). Braniff ceased operating on May 12, 1982.

1928 June 25　The Boeing Model 83 biplane, the last from this company in which wood was used for the wing frame and the last biplane built by Boeing, made its first flight and was subsequently tested for the U.S. Navy as the XF4B-1 carrier-based fighter-bomber. A companion design, the Model 89, designed for the army was also ordered by the navy as the second XF4B-1. Powered by a 500-HP Pratt & Whitney R-1340B engine, the XF4B-1 had a wingspan of 30 ft., a length of 20 ft. 7 in., a top speed of 169 MPH and a range of 520 mi. It was armed with one 0.50-in. and one 0.30-in. machine gun or two 0.30-in. guns, plus the option of a 120-lb. bomb load.

1928 June　One of the most famous British aircraft of the period, the prototype Hawker Hart (serial no. J9052) two-seat light day bomber made its first flight and was subsequently evaluated with competitors from Fairey and Avro. The Hart was found to be fast and nimble, RAF fighters being unable to catch them. Powered by a 510-HP or 525-HP Rolls Royce Kestrel, the Hart had a top speed of 184 MPH, a climb time of 8 min. to 10,000 ft. and a range of 470 mi. It was armed with one forward-firing Vickers gun and a Lewis in the rear cockpit with provision for a 500-lb. bomb load. About 460 Hart bombers were built for the RAF, and some served until 1939.

1928 August 7　One of the most successful designs of the day, the first Curtiss Model 50 Robin, took to the air. Subject to a wide variety of variants and derivatives, a typical Robin had a wingspan of 41 ft. and a length of 25 ft. 8 in. with a 185-HP engine. In all, 769 were built, and several examples are still flying today. With its high-wing monoplane configuration and fixed landing gear, it was rugged, adaptable and popular. The Robin had a gross weight of 2,440 lb., a cruising speed of 84 MPH and a service ceiling of between 10,200 ft. and 13,000 ft., depending on type. It had a top speed of up to 120 MPH and a range of up to 480 mi.

1928 August 8 Designed to seize the world distance record for France, the Couzinet 10-01 named *Arc-en-Ciel* (Rainbow) was destroyed during a test flight. Designed by René Couzinet and built by the Société des Avions René Couzinet, the aircraft was a three-engine monoplane of unusual appearance that led to further design concepts that merged in the early 1930s as the Couzinet 70 and 71. These aircraft had a wingspan of 98 ft. 5 in. and a length of 53 ft. Powered by three 650-HP Hispano-Suiza 12Nb 12-cylinder, V, water-cooled engines, they had a range of 4,225 mi.

1928 August 18 An aborted attempt to fly from North America to Stockholm via Greenland began with the first leg from the United States to Cochrane, Ontario. Flying a modified, single-engine, Stinson SM-1 Detroiter, ex-World War I aviators Bert Hassell and Parker Kramer set out for Greenland on August 20. Heading northeast along the wild, deserted countryside of Quebec Province and then across the Davis Strait separating Baffin Island from Greenland, they finally came down on the ice short of their destination after more than 20 hr. in the air. Unable to take off, they were rescued by Eskimos on September 2.

1928 August 20 Arthur Goebel and Harry J. Tucker flew a Lockheed Vega 5 from Mines Field, Los Angeles to Curtiss Field, New York in the first nonstop east-west crossing of the United States. Named *Yankee Doodle,* this Vega was the first of the series, powered by a Pratt & Whitney Wasp radial engine. Goebel and Tucker took off August 19 and flew the full distance in 18 hr. 58 min., with Tucker periodically refilling the fuel tanks from five-gallon drums and a hand pump. On October 24, Tucker began the 24 hr. 51 min. flight back to California with pilot Charles Collyer, becoming the first passenger, in the first aircraft, to fly both ways across the continent.

1928 August The Boeing Model 80 unequal span biplane powered by three 410-HP Pratt & Whitney Wasp radials, later changed to three 525-HP Pratt & Whitney Hornet radial engines, made its first flight. Designed to support expanding traffic in Boeing Air Transport airline operations, the Model 80 had an upper wingspan of 80 ft. and a 56 ft. 6 in. fuselage capable of carrying 12 passengers and a flight stewardess trained as a nurse. This was the first time female attendants were assigned, starting a trend to which all airlines would eventually subscribe. The Model 80 had a maximum weight of 17,500 lb., a cruising speed of 125 MPH and a range of 460 mi.

1928 September 15 The first four-engine Dornier Do. R Super Wal took to the air, two years after the first Super Wal (with two engines), had made its first flight. The four-engine version carried 19 passengers, although one was completed with provision for 29. Deutsche Luft Hansa bought six, one of which was powered by two 650-HP Rolls Royce Condor engines, four with four 450-HP Lion engines and four with Jupiter engines. Six more Super Wals were delivered to an Italian airline, and some were built under license in Spain.

1928 September 18 Following a relaxation of airship-building restrictions in Germany, Dr. Hugo von Eckener solicited funds from public subscription for a passenger-carrying dirigible, which was flown for the first time from its assembly base at Friedrichshafen. Designated LZ 127, but named *Graf Zeppelin* on July 8, the airship had a length of 776 ft., a diameter of 100 ft., a displacement of 3,708,040 cu. ft. and a useful load of 160,937 lb. Powered by five 580-HP Maybach engines, it had a maximum speed of 79.5 MPH and a maximum range of almost 7,500 mi.

1928 September 18 Autogyro designer Juan de la Cierva, flying the second of his C.8L machines powered by a 200-HP, 7-cylinder, Armstrong Lynx Ivc radial engine, made the first autogyro crossing of the English Channel between Croydon, near London, and Le Bourget, near Paris. It had a four-bladed rotor diameter of 39 ft. 8 in., a fuselage length of 28 ft. 6 in., a height of 14 ft. 9 in. and a maximum weight of 2,470 lb. With a top speed of 100 MPH, the C.8L could cruise at almost 4,000 ft. and had a range of 255 mi.

1928 October 11 The German airship *Graf Zeppelin* began its first trans-Atlantic crossing, which was accomplished in 4 days 15 hr. 44 min., covering the 6,167 mi. at a little over 55 MPH before landing at Lakehurst, N.J. As it crossed the Atlantic, the airship ran into a violent storm that ripped fabric from control surfaces, but the 20 passengers and 62,000 letters arrived safely in the United States. The *Graf Zeppelin* began its return trip on October 29 and took just 2 days 23 hr. 51 min. to reach Friedrichshafen.

1928 November 7 Construction began at Goodyear-Zeppelin, a subsidiary of the Goodyear Tire & Rubber Company, of the ZRS-4, which, along with ZRS-5, had been authorized by the U.S. Navy in 1926 as a dirigible for scouting and patrol duties. The design was unique in that it incorporated a 60 ft. by 75 ft. hungar space for up to four small escort fighters. Using helium, the ZRS-4, named *Akron,* and its sister ship, the *Macon,* were 785 ft. in length, had a diameter of 133 ft. and a volume of 6,500,000 cu. ft. and carried a crew of 60. Powered by eight 560-HP Maybach engines carried inside the hull, the dirigible had a maximum speed of almost 85 MPH and a range of more than 9,000 mi.

1928 November 14 Piloted by Sqdn. Ldr. A. G. Jones-Williams, who was accompanied by Flt. Lt. F. V. Major, the first Fairey Long Range Monoplane took off from Northolt, near London. Named *Postal* to indicate its role as a research project for long-distance mail and communication duties, the aircraft was designed and built to project the prestige of Britain and the RAF by seizing the long-distance record, which stood at 4,466 mi. achieved by Capt. Arturo Ferrarin and Maj. del Prete in a Savoia S.64. The Monoplane had a wingspan of 82 ft., a length of 48 ft. 6 in. and a height of 12 ft. It was powered by a 570-HP Napier Lion XIA engine.

1928 November 30 Acting on the advice of his brokers, Donald Douglas restructured his very successful aircraft business, the Douglas Co., formed in July 1921, with a $15,000 bank loan into the Douglas Aircraft Co. Inc., with $1 million in shares. Incorporated in Delaware to benefit from favorable tax laws, Douglas kept the old premises in Santa Monica, Calif. and invested $650,000 from the sale of 100,000 public shares in new facilities in Santa Monica, which would support production of the PD-1, the first Douglas flying boat.

1928 November Production orders for the F4B-1 navy fighter-bomber and the P-12 army air corps fighter were placed with Boeing. Both originated with an almost identical design first flown on June 25 as the navy XF4B-1. On November 7, the army placed an order for nine production P-12 fighters based on the Model 102, which was the original Model 89 with minor changes. The first took to the air on April 11, 1929. On November 28, the navy placed its first order for 27 F4B-1 Model 99s (essentially the original XFB-1 Model 83) fighter-bombers. The last of 586 F4B and P-12 types would be delivered in February 1933, an uncommonly lengthy production life. Although officially retired in the late 1930s, a few examples soldiered on into the 1940s.

1928 November The Aeronautical Corporation of America was incorporated as an aircraft manufacturer specializing in light aviation and became, in effect, the first U.S. manufacturer to produce a light airplane for the general public. The first notable success, the single-seat Aeronca C.2 monoplane, was designed by Jean A. Roche from the USAAC with a range of 240 mi. on 8 gal. of fuel. Aeronca produced a valuable air observation/liaison aircraft, the L-3 Grasshopper, which served with the USAAF (U.S. Army Force) from 1942. Later, renamed Aeronca Aircraft Corp., the company produced its most prolific type, the Aeronca 7 Champion, building more than 10,000 between 1946 and 1951.

1928 December 6 Put together by Clement M. Keys as a means of protecting weak companies and capitalizing on their successes, North American Aviation Inc. was formed as a holding company capitalized by shares from publicly quoted firms it owned. Keys was a financier who had once run *The Wall Street Journal* and was now the controlling shareholder in several aircraft companies, including Curtiss, Curtiss-Robertson, Curtiss-Caproni, Wright Aeronautical, Travel Air, North Aircraft Corp. and the Keystone Aircraft Corp.

1928 December 19 The first American rotary-winged aircraft was flown by Harold F. Pitcairn at Willow Grove in Philadelphia. The Ciervo autogyro used for the event had been purchased in Europe and shipped to the United States where Pitcairn used it as the basis for his own experiments. Pitcairn's pioneering work was largely overshadowed by the development rotary-winged aircraft for the army by the Kellet company. Formed in 1929, the Kellet Autogyro Co. would manufacture Cierva autogyros under license.

1928 December 20 The Arctic explorer George Hubert Wilkins and Ben Eielson took off from Deception Island, a volcanic rock near Graham Land, the northernmost tip of Antarctica, in one of two Lockheed Vegas at the start of the first extended survey flight on the Antarctic continent. Their prepared landing strip was hacked from the volcanic tuff, 2,500 ft. long and 40 ft. wide. A preliminary flight had been made October 16, but this first extended survey lasted about 10 hr. and carried Wilkins and Eielson 500 mi. south to Graham Land, at which point they turned to battle their way back against poor weather. The two Vegas were lashed down for the winter as Wilkins sailed for South America.

1928 December 23 In an operation that would not end before February 25, 1929, RAF transport aircraft operated the world's first major airlift when they flew 586 people and 24,193 lb. of baggage from Kabul, Afghanistan to Peshawar, Pakistan a distance of approximately 140 mi. Across rugged terrain flanked by 10,000-ft. mountains, eight Victoria transport aircraft and one Hinaidi from No. 70 Squadron flew 82 missions, lifting civilians from the British Embassy after an uprising against King Amanullah. The aircraft flew a total 28,160 mi. without a single loss of life despite poor flying conditions and only rudimentary landing strips.

1928 December 29 The first flight of the Boeing Model 95 took place. Essentially a developed Model 40, it had a bolted duralumin fuselage length of 31 ft. 11 in. with fabric-covered biplane wings spanning 44 ft. 3 in. Powered by a 525-HP Pratt & Whitney radial engine, 25 Model 95 biplanes were built, 20 of which were operated by Boeing Air Transport, four by Western Air Express and one by National Air Transport. It had a maximum weight of 5,840 lb., a cruising speed of 120 MPH, a service ceiling of 16,000 ft. and a range of 520 mi. The pilot was situ-

ated aft to make room for mail compartments, although one was modified to a two-seat configuration.

1928 December A British engineer who had worked for the Sopwith Aviation Co. Ltd., Herbert Smith, submitted a design for an all-wood biplane that he had been commissioned to prepare for the Mitsubishi Kokuki K.K. (Mitsubishi Aircraft Co. Ltd.) of Japan. Mitsubishi wanted to sell the design to the Japanese Navy but failed and only reintroduced the proposal when the navy ordered two Ka-2 aircraft designed by engineer Hattori. The Smith design was to have been a trainer, with seating for an instructor and up to four pupils. It was designated M-13 by the manufacturer.

1928 Military officials in Germany carried out an assessment of the preparedness of German industry to support an aircraft rearmament program. They concluded that German industry should be able to put out 8,750 aircraft a year by 1929. In the past five years, the Reichswehr budget had doubled, and in 1928–29, expansion of the aircraft industry received almost one-half the money allocated for industrial expansion. Although production figures were greatly optimistic, very large sums of money were now flowing into the secret rearmament program.

1929 January 7 Maj. Carl Spaatz, Capt. Ira C. Eaker and Lt. Elwood Quesada set an unofficial endurance record for refueled aircraft in the second of eight Fokker F.VIIA-3m (serial no. 28-120) trimotors, which had been ordered for the USAAC as the C-2A. This aircraft carried a longer wing, spanning 74 ft. 2 in. versus 63 ft. 6 in. and was powered by three 220-HP Wright R-790 radial engines. Named *Question Mark,* 28-120 used similar air-to-air refuelling techniques as Lts. Smith and Richter first applied in August 1923. They remained in the air for almost six days nine hrs.

1929 January 15 The famous American polar explorer and aviator, Richard Evelyn Byrd made his first flight in the Antarctic. Two weeks later he discovered a mountain range that he named Rockefeller Mountains. Geologists led by Laurence Gould took off in a Fokker monoplane that had been sent to the area by ship to explore the region, and within a week the work had been completed. High winds tore loose the moorings holding down the aircraft, and the party had to walk back to the Little America base camp east of the Bay of Whales where Byrd waited.

1929 January 27 The U.S. Navy exercise Fleet Problem IX ended after four days of activity, during which the two new fleet carriers USS *Lexington* and USS *Saratoga* served with opposing teams in simulated battle exercises. In an attempt to "destroy" the Panama Canal, the "Black Fleet" commander ordered the *Saratoga* to launch an air attack, and 69 aircraft set out on the morning of January 26, their target being canal locks Miraflores and Pedro Miguel. Umpires declared the attack a success. As a result of this exercise and others, tactical units built up around the aircraft carrier started appearing in force organization during the early 1930s.

1929 January 30 The U.S. airline Inter-Island Airways Ltd. was formed to carry passengers among the Hawaiian Islands; service did not begin operations until November 11, when two Sikorsky S-38 flying boats linked Honolulu with the other islands. The airline began flying mail in 1934 and acquired Sikorsky S-43 amphibians before changing its name to Hawaiian Airlines on October 1, 1941. Trans-Pacific Airlines set up in competition on June 9, 1946, and changed its name to Aloha Airlines on February 1, 1959.

Airmen involved in refueling the world record-breaking airplane Question Mark *in January 1929.*

1929 January Built to a British Air Ministry specification (designated F.9/26) for a night fighter armed with two 0.303-in. Vickers guns and with the speed to catch new bombers like the Fairey Fox, the Gloster SS.18 was flown by Howard Saint for the first time. With a top speed of 183 MPH at 10,000 ft., it was exactly 30 MPH faster than the Fox. Designed as a contender to replace the Gamecock and the Siskin in RAF service, the SS.18 was a conventional two-bay biplane, but developments led to the SS.19, and tests with up to six machine guns presaged the day of the fast multi-gun fighter. The SS.19 was eventually ordered into production as the Gloster Gauntlet.

1929 January American inventor Edward Albert Link made the first sale of the initial model for his electro-mechanical flight simulator. The system, which was intended to introduce cost-effective pilot instrument-flying training, later became known as the Link trainer, and was the forerunner of the modern flight simulator. The device was a cockpit with a full suite of flight instruments, situated in a very short fuselage with miniature control surfaces attached to stubby wings and a scaled down tailplane. The simulator was mounted on a set of pivots that allowed a degree of motion in three axes.

1929 February 1 The aviation and air transport operations of Boeing and Pratt & Whitney were merged to form the United Aircraft & Transport Corp. Boeing already owned the Chance Vought company of Long Island, N.Y., and the new United bought the Hamilton Propeller Co., the Stearman Aircraft Co., the Sikorsky Aviation Corp. and Stout Air Services. With capital of $146 million, United was well placed to take on the empire built by Clement Keys, who had formed North American Aviation in 1925 and Transcontinental Air Transport in 1928.

1929 February 4 Henry Adler Berliner and Temple Nach Joyce joined forces to create the Berliner-Joyce Aircraft. Joyce had an engineering degree from Baltimore Technical Institute and from Lehigh University and had enthusiastically participated in flying from an early age. Berliner fought in France during World War I and after leaving the U.S. Army in 1923 worked as sales representative for Morane-Saulnier. The company tried to build aircraft for the navy and produced the first aircraft in the army pursuit-biplane (PB) category, but failure to obtain production orders led to the company shutting up shop in 1934.

1929 March 19 The first Antarctic air-sea rescue search took place when Lt. Comdr. Byrd and pilot Dean Smith with navigator Malcolm Hanson flew off in search of Bernt Balchen, Harold June and Laurence Gould, who had been stranded at the foot of Rockefeller Mountains after landing their Fokker monoplane on March 7. A blizzard damaged their aircraft and prevented them taking off. The rescue mission began from the Little America base on the Ross Ice Shelf.

1929 March 22 Prior to attempting a long-duration record by flying nonstop from England to South Africa, Flt. Lts. Jones-Williams and Major accompanied by D. L. Hollis Williams as observer took off from Cranwell in Lincolnshire, England, on a 1,950-mi. endurance test of the new Fairey Long Range Monoplane. There were few technical problems, the aircraft using 430 gal. of fuel and 15 gal. of oil, which indicated a still-air range of about 5,500 mi. sufficient to break the existing record of 4,466 mi. However, it was judged that Flt. Lt. Major was psychologically unfit for the record attempt, and his place was taken by Flt. Lt. N. H. Jenkins.

1929 March 26 The first all-metal version of the Fairey IIIF, the Mk.III, was flown for the first time powered by a 570-HP Napier Lion XIA engine. The aircraft had wings with corrugated drawn-tube spars and pressed ribs clipped on, with a span of 45 ft. 9 in. and a length of 34 ft. or 35 ft. 6 in. in a three-seat version. The two-seat reconnaissance spotter had a loaded weight of 6,301 lb. and an endurance of up to 4 hr. Of the 622 Fairey IIIFs built, 379 were operated by the Royal Navy, of which 291 were the all-metal Mk.IIIs.

1929 March 30 Imperial Airways inaugurated a weekly passenger service from England to India, part of which would have to be taken by rail. For £130 single fare, the journey originated

A Fokker trimotor being refueled over Burbank, Calif. during a record endurance flight in January 1929.

by Armstrong Whitworth Argosy at Croydon and went to Basle (Switzerland) via Paris (France). The rail trip from Basle to Genoa was necessitated because the Italians refused landing rights to British land-based aircraft. The next leg began at Genoa with Short Calcutta flying boats flying passengers to Rome, Naples, Corfu, Athens, Suda Bay (Crete), Tobruk, Alexandria, Gaza, Rutbah Wells, Baghdad, Basra, Bushire, Lingeh, Jask, Gwadar and Karachi seven days after leaving England. The first flight began when Argosy G-EBLF *City of Glasgow* took off piloted by Capts. A. S. Wilcockson and H. G. Brackley.

1929 April 24   A British attempt on the nonstop distance record of 4,466 mi. began when Flt. Lts. A. G. Jones-Williams and N. H. Jenkins took off from Cranwell in the Fairey Long Range Monoplane (serial no. J9479). They planned to fly from England to South Africa, but delays prevented proper weather conditions being found on that route, so the attempt was made by heading for India. The aircraft landed at Karachi (now in Pakistan), 50 hr. 37 min. after flying 4,130 mi., an insufficient distance to break the record but achieving, nevertheless, the first nonstop flight between England and British India. They were forced by weather to land at Karachi.

1929 May 3   Ancestor of one of the most exciting families of racing aircraft of the 1930s, the first of eight Gee Bee Model A biplanes made its first flight piloted by Zantford Granville from the East Boston Airport, Mass. Established by Granville and his brothers Robert, Mark and Edward, Granville Brothers Aircraft (Gee Bee) was an aircraft repair firm until they built their first unique design. Model A had a wingspan of 29 ft., a length of 20 ft. 7 in. and power from a 118-HP 5-cylinder Kinner K-5 radial engine providing a top speed of 108 MPH. With financial backing from Tate, the dairy producers, Granville Brothers Inc. moved to Springfield Airport.

1929 May 7   The first of the Tupolev ANT-9 all-metal trimotor monoplane transport aircraft made its first flight after having been assembled in Red Square, Moscow to celebrate May Day. Tupolev displayed in this design considerable influence from his experience in the Russian Junkers factory. It was a typical trimotor configuration with corrugated surfaces. Powered by three 230-HP GR Titan engines, the ANT-9 was developed into several variants, some being powered by two 680-HP M-17 engines. The main cabin had seating for nine passengers, with a toilet at the rear and a special baggage compartment.

1929 May 7   The initial attempt by Dornier to enter the world of civil passenger and freight transport with a competitive design got off the ground when the Do.K made its first flight. A conventional high-wing monoplane powered by a 510-HP Siemens-built Bristol Jupiter VI radial engine, the Do.K1 had seating for eight passengers, but poor performance led to the K2 with four 240-HP Gnôme-Rhône Titan radials. The K2 was a poor performer, so the K3 was designed with a cantilever wing and seating for 10. Though it performed better than its predecessors, it failed to attract orders.

1929 May 10   The U.S. secretary of the navy presented the Distinguished Flying Cross to Lt. A. J. Williams recognition of his bravery during a series of experimental flights in March where he performed violent maneuvers to find better ways of testing aircraft and more effective and accurate means of measuring performance. The test program provided an improved base from which to evaluate new aircraft and to develop procedures for safer flying as well as enhanced operational efficiency.

1929 May 31   Martin received an order for 25 PM-1 flying boats (later increased to 30), which were essentially production versions of the Naval Aircraft Factory PN series. Powered by two 575-HP Wright R-1820-64 engines and with a wingspan of 72 ft. 10 in. and a length of 49 ft. 2 in., the PM-1 had a single rudder. Later versions of the PN series would have twin rudders. The PM-1 had a gross weight of 16,117 lb. and a range of about 1,300 mi. with a top speed of 118 MPH. The aircraft were delivered beginning June 1930 and supplemented an order for 25 PD-1 flying boats from Douglas.

1929 May   General Motors Corp. purchased 40% of the Fokker Aircraft Corp. the founding company's U.S. subsidiary. Anthony Fokker owned 20% of the shares and was appointed technical director, and several famous names joined the organization. Edward V. Rickenbacker moved from the Cadillac Works to become vice president for sales. The Fokker Aircraft Corp. became the General Aviation Corp. in May 1930 and continued the downward trend for the Dutch manufacturer's U.S. enterprise brought about by stronger competition from exclusively U.S. companies. A crash in 1931 grounded Fokker aircraft, and on July 10, 1931, Anthony Fokker was ousted from the board of the former Fokker Aircraft Corp.

1929 June 6   In an attempt to demonstrate the performance of the Tupolev ANT-9 trimotor monoplane transport aircraft, M. M. Gromov, Mikheyev and Spirin flew it from Moscow to Odessa and Sevastopol, from there to Kiev and then back to Moscow on June 12 in a dress rehearsal of a European goodwill tour planned for the following month. With eight passengers on board, Gromov flew to Travemünde on July 10 and from there to Berlin, Paris, Rome and Marseilles before landing in England, the first Soviet aircraft to do so. From there, it was back to Paris, then on to Berlin and Warsaw before heading back for Moscow on August 8, having travelled 5,615 mi. in 53 flying hr.

1929 June 14   In efforts to encourage passenger traffic for their expanding international air routes (Imperial Airways [Africa] Ltd. had been formed on June 6), Imperial Airways made the first 30-minute "tea" flight over London. Costing £2 2s, reduced in 1931 to £1 10s, they were carried out by Argosy aircraft and proved novel and at first popular digressions. But they did little to seriously stimulate air travel and were cancelled in 1932.

1929 June 29   The Glenn L. Martin Co. was given a contract for production of nine Consolidated XPY-1 high-wing flying boats, under the designation P3M-1, which utilized a wing identical to that of the XPY-1, designed by Consolidated before Martin underbid that company for a production order. The first Martin flying boat eventually appeared in February 1931. It was powered by two 450-HP Pratt & Whitney R-1340-38 engines in nacelles under the wing, but the P3M-2 had two 525-HP Pratt & Whitney R-1690-32 Hornet engines. Martin also tested a development model as the XP2M-1.

1929 June 29   One of the most historic mergers in aviation history took place when the old rivals Curtiss and Wright joined forces to create the Curtiss-Wright Aeronautical Corp. The merger would never have taken place had the respective companies still been in the hands of their founders, the bitter conflict between the Wright brothers and Glenn Curtiss having been rife and peppered with litigation. Curtiss-Wright became a pillar of the American aviation industry through the post-World War II period, but the corporation was unprepared for peace and the airplane division closed in 1951, its facilities and projects going to North American at that time.

1929 June The U.S. War Department issued a contract for two Fokker X0-27 high-wing monoplanes, the second of which was finished as a potential bomber. The War Department was eager to develop monoplane bomber designs with significantly higher performance than the aging biplanes. Twelve Fokkers were ordered, all completed as observation aircraft. The second X0-27 completed in 1929 and tested in 1930 as the XB-8 bomber had a wingspan of 64 ft., and a length of 47 ft. was powered by two 600-HP Curtiss V-1570-23 engines and had a top speed of 160 MPH with a gross weight of 10,545 lb.

1929 June Selected by the USAAC in preference to competing designs from Curtiss and Boeing, Berliner-Joyce was awarded a contract for one XP-16 two-seat biplane fighter. This aircraft would eventually serve with the USAAC in the early 1930s as the only type given the pursuit-biplane (PB) category. The XP-16 was the last USAAC aircraft with a tail skid, the subsequent YP-16 (later P-16) types having tail wheels. The XP-16 had a wingspan of 34 ft., a length of 28 ft. 5 in., a gross weight of 3,927 lb. and a top speed of 186 MPH at 10,000 ft.

1929 June The first flight of a civilian transport version of the Curtiss B-2 bomber took place. They were called Condor 18s because of their design capacity for carrying 18 passengers. Six were built, but the type failed to gain acceptance, and four ended up carrying passengers at local air circuses. The Condor 18 had a wingspan of 91 ft. 8 in. and a length of 57 ft. 6 in. With a gross weight of 17,900 lb., the Condor was powered by two 625-HP Curtiss GV-1570 engines that provided a cruising speed of 125 MPH and a ceiling of 17,000 ft.

1929 July 7 A 48-hr. coast-to-coast passenger service across the United States was inaugurated by Transcontinental Air Transport, using both air and rail routes, following 17 days of route-proving flights during which 231 passengers were carried a total of 50,000 air mi. The service began in New York where passengers took an overnight Pennsylvania Railroad train to Columbus, Ohio. The following day, Ford Tri-motors were used to fly the passengers to Waynoka, Okla. From there, the Atchison, Topeka and Santa Fe Railroad was used for a second overnight trip to Clovis, N.M. The last stage of the journey was again by Ford Tri-Motor to Glendale, Calif.

1929 July 22 The German national airline Luft Hansa speeded delivery of mail from Germany to America by catapulting a Heinkel He 12 floatplane off the liner SS *Bremen* on its maiden voyage to New York. Carrying mail, the He 12 was launched when the liner was 249 mi. from New York. On the return trip to Germany, the same aircraft was catapulted off the *Bremen* for a similar function near Cherbourg on August 1. On that occasion, the aircraft flew 497 mi. and reached Bremerhaven 24 hr. ahead of the ship.

1929 July 25 The largest aircraft of its day, the Dornier Do.X flying boat began flight tests at Bodensee (Lake Constance). It had been designed by Dornier in 1926 and built at the AG für Dornier-Flugzeuge at Altenrhein, Switzerland. The aircraft had a wingspan of 157 ft., 6 in. which carried 12 525-HP Siemens Jupiter air-cooled engines mounted in tandem in six nacelles and driving six pusher and six tractor propellers. The Do. X had a length of 131 ft. 5 in. and a maximum loaded weight of 114,640 lb. Built to carry up to 72 passengers, with lounge, bar, smoking room, sleeping quarters and a writing room, it never entered airline service.

1929 August 1 Dr. Hugo Eckener commanded the first airship flight to circumnavigate the globe when the flight left Frie-

drichshafen in Germany on the first leg of its historic trip, going first to Lakehurst, N.J., to pick up passengers that included a party headed by newspaper magnate William Randolph Hearst. Back at Friedrichshafen, the formal start of the world trip began August 15 with a direct flight to Tokyo, where it landed four days later. The Tokyo-Los Angeles stage was completed in three days beginning August 23. *Graf Zeppelin* arrived back at Friedrichshafen on September 4, having logged 21,000 mi. in 12 days 12 hr. 20 min. flying time.

1929 August 19 The first metal airship built for the U.S. Navy made its first flight. Designed in 1922 and sold as an idea to the navy in 1926 by the newly formed Aircraft Development Corp. of Detroit, Mich., the ZMC-2 was a 22,600 cu. ft. helium balloon supported by transverse metal frames and longitudinal stiffeners with a thin metal covering forming the outer skin. The 0.08-in. thick metal skin with three million rivets served as a pressure balloon for the inert gas. The airship had a length of 149 ft. 6 in. and operated for exactly 10 years to the day before being retired.

1929 August 20 Lt. A. W. Gorton, U.S. Navy, successfully carried out tests with a modified Vought UO-1 biplane in which the aircraft hooked up to a trapeze suspended from the USS *Los Angeles* over the Lakehurst Naval Air Station. A previous attempt on July 3 failed because the hook on the aircraft designed to engage with the trapeze failed to operate after the pilot had flown the aircraft into contact with the airship. Several successful repeats of the exercise were demonstrated before flying ended for the day.

1929 August 23 With the Soviet registration URSS-300, an ANT-4 (TB-1) twin-engine monoplane took off from Moscow on a public relations mission to New York. Equipped with wheels for the flight via Ormsk, Novosibirsk, Krasnoyarsk and Chita to Kharbarovsk, floats were fitted after its arrival on September 5. Seven days later it took off and flew via Petropavlovsk, Attu, Seward and Sitka to Seattle, Wash. where it arrived October 13. At Seattle, it was fitted with wheels and on October 18 flew to New York, arriving November 1, via San Francisco, Salt Lake City, Chicago and Detroit. Despite numerous engine problems and one forced landing for repairs, the ANT-4 had flown 13,200 mi. in 137 hours.

1929 August 26 The first flight of the largest trimotor transport aircraft built by Fokker, the F.IX, took to the air on its first flight. The prototype (PH-AGA) was handed over to KLM on May 8, 1930, and given the name *Adelaar* (Eagle). The aircraft had been specifically designed for flights to the East Indies and had a more modern appearance than its predecessors. Carrying between four and six passengers on very long routes, it had a range of more than 700 mi. and a cruising speed of around 109 MPH. Powered by two 480/500-HP Gnôme-Rhône Jupiter VI engines, the aircraft could carry up to 18 passengers on short European hops.

1929 August The first public demonstration in the United States of a rotary-winged aircraft took place when the Cierva C.19 Mk.II autogyro (G-AAKY) appeared at the Cleveland Air Races. Powered by a 100-HP Genet Major I radial engine and a four-bladed 30-ft. diameter propeller, it was sold to the Pitcairn Autogyro Co. in Willow Grove, Pa. The Mk.II had a length of 18 ft., a height of 10 ft. and an all-up weight of 1,400 lb. It was stated to have a top speed of 95 MPH, a cruising speed of 70 MPH and a range of 300 mi.

1929 September 7   The eleventh Schneider Trophy contest was held at Calshot, England and was won by Flying Off. H. R. D. Waghorn of Britain in a Supermarine S.6 (serial no. N247) powered by a 1,900-HP Rolls Royce R. The seaplane flew the seven-lap, 50-km (31.07 mi.) course at an average speed of 328.629 MPH. Warrant Off. Dal Molin of Italy came in second in a Macchi M.25R powered by a 1,000-HP Fiat AS.3 at 284.20 MPH, followed by Flt. Lt. D. D'Arcy Greig of Britain in a Supermarine S.5 powered by a 875-HP Napier Lion VIIB at 282.11 MPH, the only other contestant to finish.

1929 September 9   Precursor to one of the most famous British sporting monoplanes of the 1930s, the D.H.80 made its first flight; although formally it had no type name, it was variously called Moth Three, Hawk Moth and Moth Six. Powered by an inverted Gypsy II engine, it was designed to provide a modicum of comfort and better visibility than earlier designs that placed the cylinder heads of the engine directly in the line of view from the pilot's seat. The aircraft was never produced in quantity, but work started on its definitive successor, the D.H.80A Puss Moth, which was to be powered by a Gypsy III.

1929 September 11   Soviet test pilot Mikhail M. Gromov flew the Tupolev ANT-7 for the first time. Basically a scaled down ANT-4 (TB-1), the ANT-7 monoplane had a wingspan of 76 ft. 1 in. and a length of about 50 ft., depending on landplane or seaplane variant. Developed as a long-range escort-fighter/fighter-bomber/penetrating-reconnaissance type, it was powered by two 730-HP BMW VI engines, or two 715-HP M-17Fs. Some of these aircraft continued to see service into the early 1940s.

1929 September 24   Lt. James H. Doolittle carried out the first ''blind flight'' from Mitchel Field, Long Island, N.Y. in a Consolidated NY-2 Husky adapted to carry a Sperry artificial horizon and gyroscope and Kollsman altimeter. The flight from takeoff to landing was made without the pilot being able to see outside the aircraft and served to effectively demonstrate the value of blind flying instruments for night or bad weather use. Notwithstanding the great value of the equipment, the flight required remarkable bravery from the pilot, who might easily have crashed.

1929 September 30   The German automobile manufacturer Fritz von Opel successfully flew a rocket-powered glider 5,000 ft. at a maximum speed of 95 MPH at Frankfurt. Designated Opel-Sander Rak 1, the glider had been designed by a former glider pilot named Hatry and equipped with 16 rockets. After two false runs, the Rak 1 lifted into the air from its launching rail, propelled by a combined thrust of 900 lb. Opel lost heart when later tests ended in a crash, but interest had been sown in others. Before the end of the year, secret German rocket tests were given the official go-ahead.

1929 October 1   A major reorganization of German Army air elements took place and Brig. Gen. Hilmar Ritter von Mittelberger was made head of the Training Inspectorate, a secret organization for the clandestine expansion of military aviation. In 1928 the Reichswehr efficiency specialist Maj. Albert Kesselring proposed a separate aviation inspectorate, but this was turned down because, it was said, such a blatant and obvious violation of the intent behind the Treaty of Versailles would inflame European opinion outside Germany. It was, nevertheless, another step toward the open denunciation of the treaty and its objectives.

1929 October 8   In-flight entertainment for airline passengers began in the U.S. when Transcontinental Air Transport Inc. showed a motion picture on board one of their Ford Tri-Motor monoplane

airliners flying over land at a height of 5,000 ft. A great deal of attention was given to the equipment used in the trial, which resulted in the total weight of the film, projector and accessories being kept to a modest 34 lbs. It set a precedent that has stood the test of time; today, no self-respecting airline would undertake a long-distance flight without at least one in-flight movie.

1929 October 14   The British airship R.101 made its first flight beginning at 11:10 A.M. from the mooring mast at Cardington, near Bedford, England. A companion to the R.100, which would fly two months later, it was soon discovered to be overweight and was modified. After these changes, it had a length of 777 ft., a diameter of 133 ft. and a volume of 5,500,000 cu. ft. and was powered by five 585-HP Beardmore Tornado Diesel engines. It had a useful load of 160,000 lb. and a range of up to 5,000 mi. These two airships had been developed and built with government money to fly as potential passenger carriers throughout the British Empire.

1929 October 18   Designed to carry a small Besson floatplane in a special watertight hangar, the French submarine *Surcouf* was launched. The largest submarine in the world, it had a submerged displacement of 4,820 tons. The specially designed Besson MB 411 floatplane had a monoplane wing with a span of 32 ft. 4 in., a length of 23 ft. and a central strut-mounted float with underwing outriggers. Its hangar was 13 ft. square with a length of 23 ft. and a small crane would lower the floatplane to the water and retrieve it at the end of a flight. After escaping from Brest harbor when the Germans invaded in 1940, *Surcouf* was accidentally rammed and sunk while en route to the Far East by a U.S. merchant ship on February 18, 1942.

1929 October 21   The Dornier Do.X 12-engine flying boat carried 169 people into the air for about 1 hr. over the Bodensee, Switzerland, establishing a world record for the number of people lifted into the air at the same time. The onboard complement was made up of 150 passengers, 10 crew and 9 stowaways who were found after take-off. Usually outfitted for 66 passengers on long-duration flights and up to 100 people on short flights, the Do.X had a cruising speed of 109 MPH and a service ceiling of only 1,377 ft., increased to 1,640 ft. when fitted with 12 600-HP Curtiss Conquerer engines. With these engines and several modifications, range increased from 621 mi. to 1,056 mi.

1929 November 2   A group of women calling themselves the Ninety-Nines met for the first time at Curtiss Field in Valley Stream, Long Island, N.Y. to form an association of female fliers. Their name was derived from the 99 women charter members who founded the organization. Their purpose was to improve opportunities in aviation for women pilots, to lobby for participation in the National Air Races and to campaign for rules admitting women to air races around the world. In time, the Ninety-Nines became international, and almost all women fliers of the 1930s joined the organization.

1929 November 6   The first Junkers G.38 monoplane (D-2000) made its first flight from Dessau. The largest aircraft built up to this date, it had a wingspan of 144 ft. 4 in., an area of 3,229 sq. ft., a maximum chord of 32 ft. 9 in. and a maximum thickness of 5 ft. 7 in. The swept leading edge carried two 400-HP Junkers L 8 and two 800-HP Junkers L 88 engines, and the entire wing was covered in corrugated duralumin sheet. The G.38 had a length of 76 ft. 1 in. and a maximum loaded weight of 52,911 lb. The prototype had accommodation for 30 passengers, but the second could carry 34, and the first was eventually modified to carry the same number.

1929 November 18 Lt. Comdr. R. E. Byrd, Bernt Balchen and Harold June took off from the Antarctic base Little America in a Ford Tri-Motor with the intention of carrying out a reconnaissance prior to attempting a direct flight to the South Pole and back. They located Queen Maud Land, more than halfway to the pole, landed and left supplies that might be needed by the later flight. On the way back, they landed short of Little America and were rescued from thin ice by the Fairchild aircraft from the main base.

1929 November 27 Evelyn Trout of California and Elinor Smith of New York became the first women aviators to refuel an aircraft in midflight when they took off for an attempt at the women's long duration record. The aircraft had been modified by attaching a pipe on the outside with a special receptacle that received a fuel line from a second aircraft. A bunk had also been installed so one pilot could sleep while the other flew the aircraft. The two women remained in the air for 42 hr. and although successfully securing the record, they are better known for their refueling operation that made the record possible.

1929 November 28 Lt. Comdr. Byrd, with Balchen and June, took off from the Antarctic base Little America in a Ford Tri-Motor named *Floyd Bennett*, at 3:29 P.M. to fly to the South Pole and back for the first time. They were forced to jettison extra fuel and food to lighten the aircraft sufficiently to gain the proper altitude. They reached the pole at 1:14 A.M. November 29 and began the journey back, arriving at Little America at 10:08 A.M. The flight had logged a total distance of 1,600 mi. and taken 17 hr. 26 min.

1929 November 30 Keystone received an order for 18 PK-1 production versions of the Naval Aircraft Factory PN series flying boat. With twin rudders and two 575-HP Wright R-1820-64 Cyclone engines, the PK-1 had a range of 1,250 mi. and a top speed of 120 MPH. Similar to other versions built by Douglas and Martin, the PK-1 had a gross weight of 16,534 lb. and a maximum loaded weight of 17,074 lb. The aircraft had a service ceiling of 9,700 ft. and a climb time of 5,000 ft. in 11 min. Twin rudders were also incorporated on 25 Martin PM-2s delivered from June 1931, the PK-1 being delivered from April 1931.

1929 December 6 Leroy Randle Grumman, Leon Swirbul and William Schwendler incorporated the Grumman Aircraft Engineering Corp. with a 11,465 sq. ft. rented plant at Baldwin, N.Y. Grumman had served in the U.S. Navy, gaining his pilot's license in 1918 before becoming a flying instructor at Pensacola and then a test pilot at the League Island Naval Yard on the Delaware River. He joined the Loening Engineering Corp. but left when it merged with Keystone, taking Swirbul and Schwendler with him. Grumman owned 46.7% of the company with a total of six investors providing $81,325. Grumman opened for business January 2, 1930, with 15 employees.

1929 December 15 The Fairey Long Range Monoplane left RAF Cranwell, England for an attempted nonstop flight to South Africa in an effort to beat the world distance record, which stood at 4,912 mi., achieved in September by D. Costes and M. Bellonte in a Breguet XIX A.2. To get an official record, that distance would have to be exceeded by 100 km (62.15 mi.). All hope was dashed when the aircraft flew into a hillside in Tunisia and was destroyed at 18:45 GMT, less than 13 hours after taking off. The barograph showed it had inexplicably descended from a cruising height of 5,000 ft. to 2,300 ft, 160 ft. below the hilltop it struck.

1929 December 16 The second of two British civilian airships, the R.100, made its first flight from Howden, Yorkshire to the

One of the last two great British airships, the R.100, moored at the Cardington mast with Graf Zeppelin *in the background.*

airship mast at Cardington, near Bedford. Unlike its sister ship, the R.101, which had been built at the government airship works in Cardington, R.100 had been built by the Airship Guarantee Co. It had a length of 709 ft., a diameter of 133 ft. and a volume of 5,200,000 cu. ft. and was powered by six 670-HP Rolls Royce Condor IIIB engines. These provided a top speed of 81 MPH (versus 74.5 MPH for the R.101) and a range of 5,000 mi. These were to be the last big airships built in Britain.

1929 December 31 The man often referred to as the ''Father of the Royal Air Force,'' Marshal of the RAF Sir Hugh Trenchard, withdrew from active service and was replaced by Sir John Salmond. Trenchard had been chief of the Air Staff for the previous 11 years and had fought hard against the War Office and the Admiralty to maintain the independence of the RAF. The commanders of the other services were still pressing for the dissolution of the RAF and the return of two separate units under army and navy control, although the success of the RAF in tasks such as policing Iraq had done much to weaken their arguments.

1929 December A 5-ft. Vertical Wind Tunnel (VWT) was set up at the NACA Langley Memorial Aeronautical Laboratory in Virginia to test and investigate the spinning characteristics of aircraft in flight. The tunnel had a maximum wind speed of 80 MPH and comprised an 8-ft. diameter, open-throat structure. One of the primary objectives of the tunnel was to measure the spin characteristics of different aircraft and then work out the procedures necessary for pilots to recover control and land safely.

1929 The first of the Goodyear airships that would later become famous in advertising began construction and would be delivered to the U.S. Navy in 1935 as the G-1, named *Defender*. It had a length of 184 ft., a diameter of 45 ft. and a capacity of 178,000 cu. ft. carrying eight people, including the crew. Powered by two pusher 165-HP Wright engines, it was eventually propelled by 225-HP J-6-7 engines, with which it had a range of 1,175 mi. During the early 1940s, six more G-type airships were built with length increased to 192 ft. and volume to 196,000 cu. ft. and powered by two 220-HP Continental R-670-4 engines.

1930 January 7 Douglas received a contract for two experimental all-metal, high-wing, observation aircraft designed to replace the Douglas observation biplanes, of which 879 would be built between 1924 and 1936. The two XO-31 prototypes resulted in a line of observation monoplanes designated O-31, O-43 and O-46, the last of which was retired in January 1946. The O-31 series had a distinguishable gull wing with a span of 46 ft. 4 in., a length of 33 ft. 5 in. and a 600-HP Curtiss Conquerer V-1670 12-cylinder in-line engine. The Douglas observation monoplanes were the last in the series of army observation types built by this manufacturer.

1930 January 8 The first flight over Mount Kilimanjaro, Kenya took place when the Swiss explorer and photographer Walter Mittelholzer took off from the Serengeti Plain in a Fokker tri-motor transport aircraft powered by three 220-HP Armstrong Siddeley Lynx engines. The crew took the first aerial pictures of Kibo crater 20,000 ft. above sea level, their aircraft reaching that height in freezing air on up-draughts and gusty winds that buffeted their aircraft. After 230 min. of photographing the famous mountain, they flew back to Nairobi.

1930 January 16 British patent no. 347,206 defining a gas turbine for jet propulsion was filed for application by Frank Whittle, then a young RAF officer in an instructors course at the central flying school in Wittering. The idea originated two years earlier while Whittle was a flight cadet at RAF Cranwell, but the Air Ministry turned down the gas turbine as an impractical idea. Whittle was similarly unable to interest industry in the idea, which, after the patent lapsed, was to be resurrected in 1935 when R. D. Williams and I. C. B. Tinling encouraged him to try again.

1930 January 23 Full flight certification was awarded to both landplane and floatplane versions of the Consolidated Fleetster Model 17, a radical step forward in design and manufacturing for a company hitherto involved exclusively in biplanes and flying boats. The Fleetster 17 was a cantilever monoplane with metal monocoque fuselage and a fabric-covered wood wing. Developed during 1929 and flown for the first time in October, the aircraft could carry a load of 1,974 lb. and had a range of 675 mi. and a top cruising speed of 180 MPH. Only four were built.

1930 January 25 American Airways Inc. was formed by bringing together several competitive airlines. These included the Universal Aviation Corp., Colonial Airways Corp. and Southern Air Transport, which together represented the merged interests of 11 separate smaller companies. In addition, American incorporated Interstate and Embry-Riddle. On May 13, 1934, American Airways Inc. became American Airlines Inc. and survives today as one of America's and the world's foremost airlines. During its history, the company has stimulated many production orders and helped subsidize development of several famous airliners.

1930 January 25 Francis C. Chichester arrived in Darwin, Australia five weeks after having left Croydon, England in his D.H.60G Gipsy Moth (G-AAKK) named *Madame Eiijah*. His was the first flight between England and Australia in a Moth and helped increase the already weighty reputation of this little aircraft. (G-AAKK had received its certificate of airworthiness on July 23, 1929.) This was was the first of several epic flights and voyages made by this famous New Zealander. *Madame Elijah* was shipped to New Zealand and a year later fitted with floats for a flight to Australia during which the tiny Norfolk and Lord Howe Islands were successfully used by Chichester for interim stops on his flight.

1930 January 30 First in a new line of Boeing monoplane designs aimed at increasing fighter performance beyond what the company believed was attainable in biplane designs, the Model 202 made its first flight. Identical in design, the Model 205 fol-lowed in February and was assigned to the navy as its first candidate monoplane fighter, and the Model 202 went to the army for trials. As the XP-15, the Model 202 had poor handling characterics, and the army did not place an order. A similar fate befell the navy's XF5B-1 (Model 205). Both types had a parasol wing with a span of 30 ft. 6 in. and a total length of 21 ft. Power was provided by a single Pratt & Whitney SR-1340 radial.

1930 February 23 The Soviet Council of the People's Commissariat (Sovnarkom) in the USSR abolished the council for civil aviation and transferred its activities to the chief inspectorate of the civil air fleet, the GVF. On October 29, 1930, the chief inspectorate of the GVF was abolished, its activities transferred to a new organization, specially created, called the All-Union Enterprise of the Civil Air Fleet, or VOGVF. This came under the authority of the Council for Labor and Defense. Also abolished on October 29 was Dobrolet, an airline company formed on March 17, 1923.

1930 April 29 One of the most famous biplane fighters of its day, the Polikarpov I-5 made its first flight powered by a 450-HP supercharged Jupiter VII radial engine. Designed to have two forward-firing machine guns (increased to four from the tenth aircraft), the I-5 had a wingspan of 33 ft. 7 in., a length of 22 ft. 3 in. and a loaded weight of 2,987 lb. Production machines had a top speed of 173 MPH, a service ceiling of 24,600 ft. and a range of 410 mi. By 1935, when production ceased, about 800 I-5 fighters had been produced, and some remained in service as trainers until the early 1940s.

1930 May 4 The E.15 rocket-powered aircraft flew for the first time at Bremerhaven, Germany. Designed by the Swiss engineer A. Sohldenhoff in cooperation with Gottlob Espenlaub (who along with Alexander Lippisch had formed the small company Weltensegler G.m.b.H. in 1921), the tailless aircraft originated at the behest of Fritz von Opel and Max Valier. It was tested first with a 20-HP Daimler engine, but the solid propellant rockets failed to meet expectations, displaying serious limitations for powered flight. After a crash later in the month, Espenlaub abandoned rockets.

1930 May 5 One of the most famous solo flights ever got under way when Amy Johnson took off from Croydon, England at 7:45 A.M. in her D.H.60G Gipsy Moth (serial no. G-AAAH) called *Jason* to become the first woman to fly solo to Australia. Born 1903 in Hull, England, Amy Johnson studied for a bachelor's degree at Sheffield University, went to work as secretary to a lawyer in London and joined the London Aeroplane Club in 1928, flying solo after only 16 hours. In December 1929, she became the first woman to obtain an aircraft engineer's license in Britain and decided to attempt the solo flight to Australia.

1930 May 6 The Boeing Model 200 Monomail made its first flight. Designed exclusively as a mail-carrier, the aircraft was an all-metal, low-wing monoplane with a partially retractable undercarriage capable of carrying 2,300 lb. With a wingspan of 59 ft. 1 in. and a length of 41 ft. 2 in. the Model 200 had a cruising speed of 135 MPH and a range of 550 mi. Powered by a 575-HP Pratt & Whitney Hornet B radial, the aircraft was followed three months later by the Model 221, which featured a 41 ft. 10 in. fuselage also capable of carrying eight passengers. The Model 200 entered service on Boeing's Air Transport route between San Francisco and Chicago in July 1931.

1930 May 12 Jean Mermoz and two crewmembers named Dabry and Gimie flew nonstop from St. Louis, Senegal, on the west coast of Africa, to Natal, Brazil, arriving May 13. They carried mail for the south trans-Atlantic leg of a mail route that began in Paris, France and ended in Santiago, Chile. The aircraft they used was the first of five Latécoère Laté 28.3s built as mail planes and was the same one used on April 11 and 12 to capture the world closed-circuit distance record for seaplanes (2,677.085 mi.). The aircraft had a wingspan of 63 ft. 1 in. and a length of 44 ft. 9 in. and was powered by a 500-HP Renault 12jb piston engine.

1930 May 13   Amy Johnson arrived at Rangoon, setting down on the football field in her D.H.60G Gypsy Moth en route to Australia. After leaving England, Johnson flew via Vienna to Istanbul, Turkey and from there crossed the 12,000-ft. Taurus mountains to Baghdad, where she ran into violent winds and a sandstorm. Two days later, she reached Karachi, having covered 1,560 miles, two days ahead of the time set by Bert Hinkler in 1928. Problems continued to follow her as she flew the biplane across India and into Southeast Asia. On landing in Rangoon, the Gipsy Moth nosed over and broke the undercarriage, part of the wing and the propeller, but the flight continued after repairs.

1930 May 15   The registered nurse Ellen Church became the first stewardess to serve in flight when she joined the crew of a Boeing Air Transport run between San Francisco and Chicago. Eight nurses had been hired as stewardesses, requirements stipulating a maximum height of 5 ft. 4 in. and a weight of not more than 115 lb. A special jump-seat was attached to the rear of the Boeing Model 80 passenger cabin for use during take-off and landing, and pay was $125 a month for 100 hr. of flying time.

1930 May 19   The German army command issued formal notification of the inventory of air units for Case A, the code for emergency mobilization, for which plans were already being made. In the event that Germany opted for mobilization, one reconnaissance squadron, two fighter squadrons and a single night bomber squadron *would* be placed under the command of the army chief of command, each army higher command and each corps command. This demanded 22 squadrons in all. The order, setting inventory requirements for the period 1931–37, was signed by Lt. Col. Felmy.

1930 May 24   Amy Johnson landed at Port Darwin, Australia at 3:30 P.M., having flown 9,960 mi. from Croydon, England in less than 20 days, only four days off the record established by Bert Hinkler in 1928. After leaving Rangoon on May 14, Amy Johnson had flown to Bangkok, then to Singara, reaching Singapore on May 18. From there she flew 800 mi. to Tjormal, 260 mi. to Surabaya, which she reached on May 20, 900 miles to Atamboea on May 22 and 23 and the final leg of 500 mi. to Port Darwin on May 24. Her Gipsy Moth is preserved in the Science Museum, London, England.

1930 May 30   The first holder of a U.S. Aero Club license, Glenn Curtiss made his last flight when he flew in a civilian Condor from New York celebrating the 20th anniversary of the Albany–New York flight of May 29, 1910. Curtiss had retired in 1921, although he remained on the board of the newly merged Curtiss-Wright group. Ironically, he was still fighting claims in court from the heirs of Augustus Herring and was in New York at the time of this flight to attend hearings for those activities. Curtiss, one of the first great practical American aviation pioneers, died of pulmonary embolism at the age of 52 on July 23, 1930, and was buried at Hammondsport, a short distance from the site of his flights in the *June Bug* in 1908.

1930 May   Mitsubishi completed the first prototype Ka-2, known also as the 4MS1, which was designated K3M1 by the Japanese

Handley Page Hyderabads of No. 99 Squadron, RAF, seen in formation. Note the close proximity of the engines to the fuselage.

navy. Designed by Eng. Hattori, the aircraft was a high-wing parasol monoplane with a span of 51 ft. 9 in. and a metal fuselage with a length of 31 ft. 4 in. As a naval trainer, the aircraft was not well liked and suffered from vibration. Reengined to have a single 340-HP Hitachi Amakaze 11 radial engine and designated K3M2, the aircraft was produced as the Navy Type 90 Crew Trainer Model 1. A further development, the K3M3, was used during World War II as a utility aircraft.

1930 June 12   Designed as a timely replacement for British night bombers like the Virginia, the Hyderabad and the Hinaidi, the prototype Handley Page Heyford (serial no. J9130) made its first flight at Radlett, England with Jim Cordes at the controls. With a wingspan of 75 ft., a length of 58 ft. and a loaded weight of 16,900 lb., the Heyford could carry a 3,500-lb. bomb load. With a maximum speed of 142 MPH, it was 20 MPH faster than the Hinaidi and almost 35 MPH faster than the Virginia and the Hyderabad. Its construction was unusual in that the upper wing was attached to the fuselage, leaving the lower wing close to the ground for easy bomb loading on the center-section; 124 were built. It entered service late in 1933, the last RAF biplane bomber.

1930 June 30   The U.S. Navy Bureau of Aeronautics ordered the Curtiss XF9C-1, which had been designed in response to a specification for a new fighter. To keep the project secret, the navy had not told potential bidders that they wanted the aircraft for stowage aboard airships for reconnaissance or as defense fighters. The manufacturers were told only the maximum size and weight of the desired aircraft, inferring it wanted an aircraft for operation aboard carriers. Unsuccessful contenders were the General Aviation XFA-1 and the Berliner-Joyce XFJ.

1930 July 8   Built to study stability and control problems and to evaluate the aerodynamic effects of different lifting surfaces, a new 7-ft. by 10-ft. atmospheric wind tunnel (AWT) became operational at the Langley Memorial Aeronautical Laboratory, Langley, Va. With a maximum speed of 80 MPH, the tunnel was driven by a fan powered by a 200-HP electric motor and equipped with a floating frame balance that allowed measurement of forces in six axes. The AWT was deactivated in 1946.

1930 July 21   With a first prize of $15,000, the Cirrus All American Flying Derby got under way from Detroit at the start of a 5,541-mi. race to Montreal, New York, Dallas, Los Angeles, Omaha, Chicago and back to Detroit. Ten out of 18 starters finished, and the race was won by the Commandaire Little Rocket at an average of 127.11 MPH. Second was the Gee Bee X Sportster, the first Granville low-wing monoplane design that would set the trend for their future aircraft. It had a wingspan of 25 ft. and a length of 16 ft. 5 in. and power was provided by a supercharged 110-HP Cirrus Hi-Drive in-line engine for a maximum speed of 145 MPH.

1930 July 24 One of the greatest airline conglomerates of all time, Transcontinental and Western Air Inc. (TWA) was incorporated in Delaware with 1 million shares. Formed by merging Transcontinental Air Transport and Western Air Express, TWA was stimulated by the challenging competition from United, which had recently formed, and it was one of the four big carriers that emerged at the beginning of the 1930s. It would retain its position as one of the foremost U.S. airlines until the 1990s.

1930 July 29 The British airship R.100 began a round-trip of the north Atlantic when she slipped her moorings at Cardington, England for a flight to Montreal, Canada. Carrying 55 people, 13 of whom were passengers, the airship reached its destination August 1 in a flight time of 78 hr. 51 min. shortly after surviving a violent thunderstorm that tore covering from the stern. After flying on to Ottawa and Toronto, the R.100 visited the United States and left for England from New York on August 13. The airship arrived back at Cardington in a flying time of 56 hr. 30 min. This was the last commercial flight by the R.100.

1930 August 18 Wolfgang von Gronau set off from Sylt, Germany on the first leg of the first east-west crossing of the North Atlantic by flying boat. Gronau was flying a Dornier Wal similar to the one used by Roald Amundsen in 1926 and plotted a course via Iceland and Greenland. With Gronau were three crewmembers, including a radio operator and a mechanic. After a weather delay of three days at Reykjavik, Iceland, the Wal flew on to Ivigtut on the west coast of Greenland. After fighting their way through thick fog and low clouds, the crew made it to Labrador and from there down the eastern seaboard, arriving in New York on August 26.

1930 September 1 A Breguet XIX named *Point d'Interrogation* (Question Mark) and flown by the French crew of Dieudonné, Costes and Maurice Bellonte made the first successful nonstop, east-west crossing of the North Atlantic between Paris and New York. The Type XIX had appeared during 1921 and had been designed as a replacement for the Breguet 14 bomber of World War I. As a bomber with the French Air Force, it soldiered on until the late 1930s although some foreign operators continued to use aircraft of this type until the 1940s, more than 20 years after it was first shown off at the Paris Salon de l'Aéronautique.

1930 September 1 In an attempt to reinvigorate high-speed aircraft races in America, the first Thompson Trophy competition was held at Chicago. Organized by industrialist Charles E. Thompson from Cleveland, Ohio, the race was won by Charles Holman flying a Laird LC-DW-300 Solution powered by a 470-HP Pratt & Whitney Wasp Jr. at an average speed of 201.9 MPH. Designed and built in four weeks by Matty Laird, the Solution was built around the classic lines of a Curtiss racing biplane but with a radial engine instead of an in-line engine. The Thompson Trophy race was held annually, the last taking place September 2–5, 1939.

1930 October 5 The British airship R.101 crashed into a hillside near Beauvais, France at 2:09 A.M. on the first leg of its first

flight to India, killing 47 of the 54 people on board, including Lord Thompson, Britain's secretary of state for air, and Maj. Gen. Sir Sefton Brancker, director of civil aviation. Overweight and underpowered, the R.101 had already received several modifications and changes since its first flight in October 1929. This disaster shattered British faith in long-distance passenger-carrying airship flight, and the R.101's sistership, the R.100, was scrapped in October 1931.

1930 October 13 The Junkers Ju 52 single-engine cargo aircraft made its first flight. It was a standard Junkers all-metal aircraft with corrugated skin powered by an 800-HP Junkers L 88 engine, soon changed to a 600/755-HP BMW VIIau. The Ju 52 had a span of 95 ft. 2 in., a length of 60 ft. 8 in. and a main cargo hold 21 ft. by 5 ft. 3 in. in width and 6 ft. 3 in. in height, providing a volume of 590 cu. ft. The aircraft was adaptable to use wheels or floats. Some aircraft were converted to carry up to 15 passengers. In 1931 the fifth Ju 52 was taken over by Canadian Airways, and skis were added to its undercarriage inventory.

1930 October 25 Transcontinental and Western Air Inc. (founded July 24) began operations on the first coast-to-coast scheduled airline passenger service across the North American continent. To inaugurate the service, flights departed simultaneously from New York and Los Angeles. The transcontinental flight had a stopover at Kansas City and took 36 hr. using Ford Tri-Motor monoplanes.

1930 October 27 The Curtiss XF9C-1 successfully performed the first hook-up to the airship USS *Los Angeles*, following a series of conventional flight trials that began during March and ended in June. By this time, Curtiss was designing a second prototype that was more effectively designed around the needs of the specification for an airship-home fighter. The new prototype had been veiled from the design team for security reasons. When they learned that a diminutive fighter was wanted not for carrier operation but stowage aboard airships, the privately funded XF9C-2 was given a 438-HP Wright R-975-E3 engine, redesigned landing gear, a new tail and a wing 4 in. higher above the fuselage. It was delivered in September 1931.

1930 October In Poland, the PZL P.7 gull wing, all-metal, monoplane fighter made its first flight powered by a Jupiter VII enclosed by a cowling designed to improve aerodynamic performance. (The cowling was changed in a subsequent version when mechanics found it almost impossible to gain access to the engine.) With a wingspan of 33 ft. 10 in. and a length of 23 ft. 6 in. the P.7a was the first all-metal aircraft to join front-line squadrons anywhere in the world. The Polish Air Force (Lotnictwo Wojskowe) took delivery beginning in late 1931, and more than 100 were still in service at the start of World War II.

1930 November 2 The Dornier Do.X, a 12-engine flying boat, began an inauspicious flight from Germany to the Americas. With two Luft Hansa pilots among the crew, the aircraft left Friedrichshafen and flew to Lisbon, stopping at Amsterdam, Holland and Calshot, England on the way. At Lisbon, repairs had to be effected after fire damaged a wing. At the Canary Islands, the hull was damaged by an aborted take-off attempt before the giant aircraft flew on to Bolama, Cape Verde Island, Fernando de Noronha and Natal. It then flew on to Rio de Janeiro, Antigua and Miami before arriving at New York on August 27, 1931. The Do.X was eventually placed in a Berlin museum where it was destroyed in Allied bombing raids during World War II.

1930 November 5 The Naval Research Laboratory issued a report explaining the experiments and results of two civilian scientists, L. C. Young and L. A. Hyland, involved in studying the use of radio waves for detecting objects in the air. The NRL claimed the two scientists had unwittingly detected an aircraft in the air during experiments to study the directionality of propagated radio beams. This resulted in some limited work to confirm the theory that reflected radio waves received back at the propagation station would detect the presence of aircraft. Thus began research at the NRL into what would eventually become radar.

1930 November 13 The prototype Fokker F.IX trimotor departed from Amsterdam, on the first leg of a journey to the Dutch East Indies (Indonesia). After a total 84 hr. 20 min. of flying time and 13 days later, the aircraft reached Batavia carrying 458 lb. of mail and 26 lb. of cargo. Along the way, it tested short-wave and long-wave radio equipment, evaluating transmission levels and the performance of air-to-ground radio. Only two F.IXs were built, although two modified versions were built by the Czechs. The aircraft had a length of 60 ft. 8 in., a wingspan of 89 ft. and a loaded weight of 19,841 lb. Performance included a maximum speed of 132 MPH and an endurance of 6.5 hr.

1930 November 13 Two Lockheed Vega transport aircraft inaugurated the first scheduled service of the newly formed Braniff Airways, set up exactly 10 days earlier. The first flight linked Tulsa, Okla. to Wichita Falls, Tex. with a stopover at Oklahoma City. Organized by Thomas E. Braniff who, along with brother Paul, had coformed the small Paul R. Braniff Inc. airline in May 1928 embraced a year later by the Universal Aviation Corporation, the new enterprise was likewise a concern set up by the two brothers. Braniff began an expansion program that would lead the airline into a major position as one of the more successful U.S. airlines for more than 50 years.

1930 November 14 The Handley Page H.P.42, one of the last great biplane airliners, made its first flight from Radlett, England. The only other airliner built previously by Handley Page had been the W.8, W.9, and W1.0 series of civilianized 0/400 World War I bombers. The H.P.42 design was based on the V/1500 heavy bomber of 1918. It was built exclusively for Imperial Airways with a corrugated metal skin and fabric flying surfaces and tail section. Powered by four 490-HP Bristol Jupiter XIF engines, the H.P.42 had a cruising speed of around 95 MPH and a range of 500 mi. It had a wingspan of 130 ft., a length of 92 ft. 2 in. and a maximum weight of 28,000 lb.

1930 November 18 The Boeing Model 96, that company's first monoplane design, made its initial flight but found no favor among test pilots, who believed it to handle so badly as to be dangerous. With a semi-monocoque rear fuselage and a high-mounted, externally braced wing spanning 36 ft. 6 in. the XP-9 had a length of 25 ft. 1 in. and a single 600-HP Curtiss SV-1570-15 supercharged engine. Designed to an army specification issued May 24, 1928, for a single-seat fighter, the Model 96 had two 0.30-in. guns and an ordnance load of 244 lb.

1930 November 25 Designed by D. L. Hollis Williams and P. A. Ralli, the team behind the Fairey Long Range Monoplane, the Fairey Night Bomber made its first flight from Harmondsworth, England with Norman MacMillan at the controls. It was later named Hendon and would become the first all metal, low-wing, cantilever monoplane to enter service with the RAF. The first production aircraft did not reach squadrons before November 1936, and the last of 14 were withdrawn from service at the end of 1938. Production aircraft were powered by two 600-HP Rolls Royce Kestrel VI engines, and the Hendon had a wingspan of 101 ft. 9 in., a length of 60 ft. 9 in., a maximum bomb load of 1,660 lb. and a range of 1,360 mi.

1930 November 28 The British chief of naval operations, Adm. W. V. Pratt, announced major policy decisions regarding the integration of sea and air forces in the Royal Navy. Naval aviation was stated and recognized to be an integral element in sea warfare, and carriers were declared important mobile assets for offensive action and long-range engagements of sea, air and land targets. It was decided that naval air stations would be under the authority of fleet commanders while training, and maintenance facilities would be run under shore command.

1930 December 2 Following the crash of the R.101 in France on October 5, 1930, and with faith in the potential use of dirigibles for long-range passenger transport destroyed, the Airship Guarantee Co., Howden, Yorkshire, England was closed. A wholly owned subsidiary of Vickers, the company had been set up in 1923 to build airships for the Atlantic and Far East routes. The demise of Airship Guarantee led to the emergence on March 13, 1931, of a successful, but small, British aircraft manufacturer called Airspeed, which would survive independently for 20 years before being absorbed into de Havilland.

1930 December 22 The revolutionary Tupolev ANT-6 (TB-3) heavy bomber flew for the first time in the USSR with M. M. Gromov at the controls. Designed between 1926 and 1929, the giant ANT-6 was held up while the Red Army evaluated the TB-1 (ANT-4) all-metal monoplane beginning 1926. When the design was finalized, Tupolev was building the huge ANT-14 transport aircraft, and some details converged. With a wingspan of 129 ft. 7 in. and a length of 80 ft., the TB-3 was far ahead of its contemporaries elsewhere. It had four 600-HP Curtiss V-1760 engines, a maximum loaded weight of up to 53,000 lb. on some versions, a bomb load of 4,410 lb. and a range of 600 to 800 mi.

1931 January 6 Gen. Italo Balbo, Italy's air minister, organized and led a flight of 12 Savoia Marchetti S.55 flying boats across the Atlantic between Portuguese Guinea (now Guinea-Bissau) and Natal, Brazil. Of the 12 aircraft that set out, three crashed before reaching their destination. Balboa was a staunch supporter of Italy's fascist regime and planned the flight to display the prowess of his countrymen. The S.55 was a twin-hull, high-wing monoplane first produced in 1925 with a span of 78 ft. 9 in. and a length of 54 ft. 1 in. It was powered by two 400/450-HP Isotta-Fraschini engines.

1931 January 9 A long-standing dispute between the U.S. Army and the U.S. Navy over whose air units were responsible for coastal defense was resolved when Army chief of staff Gen. Douglas MacArthur and chief of naval operations Adm. William V. Pratt reached agreement about the roles and duties of their respective forces. The army was to be responsible for the defense of coastal facilities in the U.S. and at bases overseas. The navy air units would support the fleet and operate under the direct control of the commander in chief, U.S. Fleet.

1931 January 29 Ramsay MacDonald, prime minister of England, issued a statement confirming the willingness of his government to allow the RAF to compete in the 1931 Schneider Trophy seaplane contest if private funds could be obtained to compensate for the cost, a day after Lady Houston, widow of shipowner Sir Robert Houston, offered to fund the British entry. (On September 25, 1929, only 18 days after Britain won the contest for the second time, the Labour government had decided not to fund further participation by the RAF.) Britain only had to win it once again to keep the trophy permanently.

1931 January Based on an R-5 airframe, the Grigorovich TSh-1 appeared as an armored heavy ground attack biplane equipped with grenade dispenser and two synchronized machine guns on a flexible mounting in the rear cockpit. The TSh-1 was not successful, and only three were built. The TSh-2 appeared in late 1931 when 10 were built of this more successful version. The Red Army was eager to develop ground attack roles for armored aircraft, and considerable effort was spent developing aircraft of this type.

1931 March 3 The prototype Fairey Gordon two-seat day bomber made its first flight from Harmondsworth, England piloted by C. S. Staniland. Essentially a reworked Fairey IIIF Mk.V with a 525-HP Armstrong Siddeley Panther IIA engine, the Gordon had a 460-lb. bomb capacity, a top speed of 145 MPH and a range of 600 mi. The first of 160 Gordons went to No. 40 Squadron, RAF, at Upper Heyford, England in April 1931, with the first overseas unit, No. 6 Squadron, getting its Gordons in June 1931, replacing World War I Bristol Fighters. The Gordon remained front-line equipment until late 1938, and some remained in servce with the Fleet Air Arm until 1942, ending a line that began with the IIIA in 1918.

1931 March 9 An unusual-looking aircraft, the Blériot 125 made its first flight in a series of tests that continued into 1933 without resulting in any orders. Designed as a passenger aircraft, it comprised two giant fuselages joined by a wing center-section that carried two tandem 550-HP Hispano-Suiza in-line engines driving a pusher and a tractor propeller each. The two fuselages provided support for a horizontal tail and twin fins and contained seating for six in each fuselage section. The crew of three sat in a cupola on top the middle center-section. With a wingspan of 96 ft. 5 in. and a length of 45 ft. 4 in., the aircraft had a top speed of 137 MPH and a range of 621 mi.

1931 March 13 Airspeed Ltd. was formed in York, England with a capital of £50,000 with A. Hessell Titman and N. S. Norway as joint managing directors and founders. Both men had worked for the Vickers subsidiary, the Airship Guarantee Co., that closed on Dec. 2, 1930. The first product was the A.S.1 Tern, a sailplane with a wingspan of 50 ft., a length of 24 ft. 7 in., a wing area of 201 sq. ft. and a loaded weight of 400 lb. It first flew in August 1931 and on August 24 achieved the first British sailplane distance record of 8.3 mi., later achieving a British sailplane altitude record of 800 ft. Only two were built.

1931 March 25 The first Hawker Fury single-seat interceptor took to the air, the first RAF fighter to exceed 200 MPH in level flight. Developed from the Hawker Hornet and the F.20/27 contender and designed by Sydney Camm, the Fury had a top speed of 207 MPH, more than 30 MPH faster than the Bristol Bulldog that joined the RAF in 1930 and 50 MPH faster than the Siskin that it replaced in service beginning May 1931. It had a wing span of 30 ft., a length of 26 ft. 8 in. and a loaded weight of 3,490 lb. The Fury remained in service until 1939.

1931 March 26 Formed from the Ad Astra Aero AG and the Basle Air Traffic Co., Swissair (Schweizerische Luftverkehr AG) emerged as Switzerland's premier airline. The Ad Astra Aero AG had begun activity in 1919 flying seaplane links between domestic cities, building up a reasonable business but without opportunities to expand and capture larger markets. In the 1930s, Swissair would grow using Lockheed Orion monoplanes and be-

come one of the first airlines outside the United States to buy the DC-2. Privately owned, Swissair built a reputation for quality of service and on-time departure.

1931 March 31 A Fokker trimotor crashed in Kansas during a thunderstorm and began a chain of events that was to destroy future opportunities for Anthony Fokker in the United States. Believing that the aircraft itself was unsafe, the aeronautics branch of the Department of Commerce issued a notice on May 4 grounding all trimotors, the first time the branch had issued such an order. Only when the Department of Commerce admitted that maintenance, and not construction, methods were suspected of causing the crash was Fokker partially vindicated. The ban was lifted, but the airlines panicked and withdrew their Fokkers, TWA burning theirs to ashes.

1931 March 31 The Curtiss XF9C-1 began three months of flight trials at Anacostia prior to airship hook-up tests using the *Los Angeles* and operational trials with the airships *Akron* and *Macon*. The XF9C-1 had a wingspan of 25 ft. 6 in. and a length of 19 ft. 5 in., larger than the specification issued in 1930 demanded but acceptable for trials. Powered by a 420-HP Wright R-975C, the Sparrowhawk, as it was named, had a gross weight of 2,482 lb., a service ceiling of 22,600 ft. and a range of almost 330 mi.

1931 April 9 A production order for the Martin XT5M-1 torpedo bomber was awarded by the U.S. Navy after evaluation of this aircraft along with its competitor, the Naval Aircraft Factory XT2N-1. As the BM-1 in a new category for navy bombers, the biplane had a wingspan of 41 ft., a length of 28 ft. 9 in. and a gross weight of 6,218 lb. and was powered by a 625-HP Pratt & Whitney R-1690-44 engine. The design originated from a 1927 specification for a dive-bomber stressed to carry a 1,000-lb. bomb through a terminal velocity dive and come out intact. Only 32 BM-1s and BM-2s were built, but they set a precedent for bombers of this type.

1931 April 22 Five D.H.60M Moth biplanes landed at Baghdad, Iraq, having flown from Hatfield, England. Bearing Royal Iraqi Air Force markings and piloted by Iraqi aircrew, they each carried a radio set, bomb racks, 10 gal. fuel tanks in addition to the installed tanks, a special drinking tank holding 2 gal. of water and a reconnaissance camera fitted to the nose. The Moths were used by No. 1 Squadron, RIAF, until 1941 when the RAF destroyed them during action.

1931 April 29 Developed from the Model 200 Monomail, the Boeing XB-901 made its first flight powered by two 575-HP Pratt & Whitney R-1860-13 Hornet radial engines. It was Boeing's attempt to use the successful, high-speed, mail-carrying monoplane as the basis for a high-performance replacement bomber for the Keystone biplanes. With a wing-span of 76 ft. 10 in. and a fuselage length of 51 ft. 9 in., the six test aircraft designated Y1B-9A ordered by the USAAC had a top speed of 188 MPH and a range of 540 mi. with a bomb load of 2,260 lb. Although advanced for its day, the Boeing XB-901 was not ordered into production, and Martin got a contract for its XB-907, ordered as the B-10.

1931 May 26 Consolidated received a contract for the XP2Y-1 parasol flying boat using the same 100-ft.-span wing designed for their XPY-1, a production contract for which had gone to Martin in June 1929, who built it as the P3M-1 and P3M-2. In a sesquiplane configuration, and powered by two 575-HP Wright R-1820E radials, a production order was placed by the navy on July 7 for the first of several P2Y versions that joined the navy in 1933. The P2Y had a length of 61 ft. 9 in., a top speed of 139 MPH and a range of 1,180 mi. with a 2,000-lb. bomb load. The last flying boats of this type were withdrawn in 1941.

1931 May 27 Prof. Auguste Picard, the Swiss balloonist, and Dr. Paul Kipfer became the first people to ascend into the stratosphere when they reached a height of 51,775 ft. over Augsburg in Southern Germany. Using a large balloon with a capacity of 498,991 cu. ft. lifting a spherical aluminum gondola supplied with its own oxygen, the two scientists took just 30 min. to reach this record height. As they descended, the balloon drifted into the Tyrolean Alps, where the gondola and envelope remained until they could be retrieved a year later. Nevertheless, experiments measuring the upper atmosphere and cosmic rays from space were recovered intact.

1931 May 27 The first full-size tunnel (FST), a wind tunnel capable of housing full-size aircraft, became operational at the NACA Langley Memorial Aeronautical Laboratory, Langley, Va. and was dedicated during the Sixth Annual Aircraft Engineering Conference. At an initial cost of $900,000, the FST was authorized in February 1929 and could achieve a simulated wind speed of 118 MPH through two fans driven by two 4,000-HP electric motors driving air into a 30-ft. by 60-ft. open-throat test section. It is still in operational use.

On the same day, NACA also began work with NACA Tank No. 1, a device designed to facilitate experiments on airplane hydrodynamics and concentrate on an area of aeronautical research and scientific theory that had hitherto been all but ignored. Authorized in March 1929, the tank cost $649,000 and was 2,060 ft. long by 28 ft. wide and 26 ft. high. A high-speed carriage capable of simulating speeds of 80 MPH across water was installed five years later, and the tank was extended to a length of 2,960 ft. It served NACA, and later NASA, until 1959, when it was turned over to the U.S. Navy.

1931 May The First Provisional Air Division of the USAAC was formed temporarily at Wright Field, Dayton, Ohio under the command of Maj. Gen. B. D. Foulois. The division was made up of a pursuit wing, a bombardment wing, two observation wings, an attack group and a transport group. This experimental unit took personnel and equipment from every tactical training unit in the United States and assembled 1,300 men and 663 aircraft. When the division made its first mass training sortie, 449 aircraft made up the largest mass formation flight conducted to date. The Italians would eclipse this later in the year by flying 894 aircraft on military maneuvers.

1931 June 1 Overcommitted with major development work, the Bayerische Flugzeugwerke A.G. (BFW) filed for bankruptcy with a loss of 600,000 Reichsmark for 1930. Although officially absorbed by BFW in 1928, the Messerschmitt Flugzeugbau retained legal hold on capital and worked with the receiver to add orders for new production machines. This resulted in the bankruptcy being discharged on April 27, 1933. With just 82 employees, BFW began to build back its place in the aviation industry. Aided by Luftwaffe expansion plans, a new company called Messerschmitt G.m.b.H. was formed on July 24, 1936, and on July 11, 1938, changed its name to Messerschmitt A.G., after its chairman and managing director.

1931 June 22 The superior performance of the Hawker Hart light day bomber resulted in the development of the derivative Hart Fighter (which became known as the Demon), of which the first preproduction machine made its maiden flight this day.

The initial production version of the Demon first flew in February 1933 with a 485-HP Rolls Royce Kestrel IIS engine providing a similar performance to the Hart. The Demon joined the RAF in 1934, but from 1936 all aircraft were fitted with a Frazer-Nash hydraulic gun turret in the rear cockpit. Some 234 Demons were delivered to the RAF before the type was retired in 1939.

1931 June 23 With Harold Gatty as his navigator, one-eyed ex-oil driller Wiley Post set off from Roosevelt Field, N.Y. in a Lockheed Vega 5B called *Winnie Mae* to fly around the world. The record for circumnavigation stood at 21 days, set by the German airship *Graf Zeppelin*. The *Winnie Mae* beat this by a handsome margin when Post and Gatty arrived back in New York on July 1, having taken just 8 days 15 hr. 51 min. to cover 15,474 mi. They went via Newfoundland, England, Germany, the USSR, Alaska and Canada. This was but one of many exceptional flights, some of them record-breakers, that gave the Lockheed Vega an important reputation for rugged performance.

1931 June The Ford XB-906 bomber derived from the all-metal Ford trimotor passenger transport, made its first flight, powered by three 500-HP Pratt & Whitney R-1340E radial engines equipped with low-drag cowlings. A special bombardier's seat, and downward facing windows, was placed behind the engine in the nose, and 2,000 lb. of bombs could be carried. The aircraft had a wingspan of 77 ft. 11 in., a length of 51 ft. 6 in. and a gross weight of 14,137 lb. The type was not successful, defensive armament being difficult to operate, and it never entered service.

1931 July 1 Boeing Air Transport, National Air Transport, Pacific Air Transport and Varney Air Lines amalgamated to form United Air Lines. The separate companies would continue to operate under their respective names. (In early 1928, Boeing had bought Pacific Air Transport and merged with Pratt & Whitney to form United Aircraft and Transport Corp.) Along with American Airlines, Eastern Airlines and Transcontinental & Western Air Inc. (TWA), United was to play a major role in the development of 1930s domestic air transport and would hail itself as the "World's Largest Air Transport System."

1931 July 15 Attempting to consolidate its position as one of the major new airline conglomerates emerging in the United States, Eastern Air Transport bought out New York Airways, which had been formed June 1, 1930, as a subsidiary of Pan American Airways. This enabled Eastern to add Atlantic City to its route schedules. Eastern was building a firm business base by concentrating its slow expansion acquisitions on continental routes in the East rather than compete with other airlines developing foreign or over-water services.

1931 July 25 Scotsman Jim Mollison left Sydney, Australia in his D.H.60G Gipsy Moth VH-UFT on a record-breaking attempt to reach England in less time than the 10 days 23 hr. put up by fellow aviator Charles Scott. Mollison made Batavia on the first day out, having flown 1,730 mi., the longest flight in a day made by a light aircraft to date. Mollison reached Singapore on July 26 and Karachi on August 2. He arrived in England August 6, after 8 days 19 hr. 25 min. This set a new record for the England-Australia time in either direction.

1931 July 27 Charles Lindberg and his wife Anne left America in their special Lockheed Sirius on the first leg of a route-proving flight to China. A high performance, low-wing monoplane powered by a 575-HP Wright Cyclone engine, the Sirius had been ordered by Lindberg in 1929. It reached the Northwest Territories on August 2, and from there the Lindberghs went to Japan via

Alaska and Petropavlovsk in the USSR, arriving at Nemuro on August 23. Greeted by a crowd of 10,000, they flew on to Tokyo and from there to Hankow where, on October 2, the plane was damaged while being placed on the Yangtze River by a crane from the carrier HMS *Hermes*. The mission was deemed a great success despite the accident.

1931 July 28 On the first leg of a round-the-world flight in a Bellanca monoplane, American pilots Russell N. Boardman and John Polando established a new world distance flight record by remaining airborne between Floyd Bennett Field, N.Y. and Istanbul, Turkey for a total distance of 5,011 mi. They went on through the USSR, Japan and North America to circle the globe in 81 days through several stages before landing back in New York on October 27.

1931 July 28 Amy Johnson and C. H. G. S. Humphreys, a former ground engineer at the London Aeroplane Club, left Lympne on the southeast coast of England for Tokyo, hoping to bridge the distance between England and Japan in seven days. Powered by a 120-HP Gypsy III, the Puss Moth G-AAZV, named *Jason II*, made it to Tokyo in 8 days 22 hrs. 35 min., a flying time of 79 hr. across the 7,000 mi. journey. The return journey began August 24 when *Jason II* left Osaka but had to return due to bad weather. Four days later a second attempt was launched, and the Puss Moth landed back at Lympne on September 9.

1931 August 5 On a flight sponsored by Transamerica Airlines, Parker Cramer and Canadian Oliver Paquette flew across the Greenland ice cap at a height of 10,000 ft. in their Bellanca Peacemaker monoplane powered by a 225-HP Packard diesel engine. They had flown from Detroit, Mich. and in just 5 hr. reached the east coast of Greenland. They flew on past Iceland and the Faroes, passing over the Shetland Islands north of Scotland before starting on the final leg to Copenhagen, Denmark. They were never heard from again and were never found, probably succumbing to a violent storm over the North Sea. Remains of the aircraft were discovered in September.

1931 August 14 Piloted by M. M. Gromov, the Tupolev ANT-14 large passenger aircraft made its first flight. The largest landplane of its day, the ANT-14 could carry 36 passengers two-abreast on either side of a central aisle, the first time this configuration was possible. With a wingspan of 132 ft. 6 in. and a length of 86 ft. 11 in., the ANT-14 had a maximum weight of 38,646 lb. and could operate across a range of 560 mi. at a cruising speed of 120 MPH. Too big for airline routes of the day, the ANT-14 was used for joyriding and propaganda, carrying a record 40,000 passengers without accident by 1941.

1931 August 29–Sept 7 The Cleveland National Air Races opened. The fastest aircraft at the contest was the Gee Bee Z racer piloted by Lowell Bayles at an average speed of 236.2 MPH; second place finisher was Jimmy Wedell in his Wedell Williams 44, who came in second at 228 MPH. The Gee Bee Z had a wingspan of 23 ft. 6 in. a length of 15 ft. 1 in. and a gross weight of 2,280 lb. Powered by a 535-HP Pratt & Whitney Wasp Jr. 985, the Z had a top speed of 270 MPH. Painted yellow and black with a brown pinstripe, the aircraft brought unprecedented fame to its designers, the Granville brothers, despite a spectacular crash on December 5 in which Bayles was killed going for the world speed record.

1931 August The PZL P.1 fighter, the aircraft that would become the pride of Poland's fighter units made its first flight when the P.11 took to the air powered by a single 515-HP Bristol Jupiter IX.ASb. Production versions of this plane were fitted with the 645-HP Bristol Mercury VI.S2 radial and were known as the P.11c. The P.11c had a wingspan of 35 ft. 2 in. with the famous gull shape designed by Zygmunt Pulawski, a feature of all PZL fighters. With two 7.7-mm guns and racks for light bombs, the aircraft had a top speed of 242 MPH and a range of 435 mi. with a service ceiling of 26,245 ft.

1931 September 1 The second of two Junkers G.38 four-engine monoplane transport aircraft was delivered to Deutsche Luft Hansa. Behind the pilot's cockpit was a buffet and behind that a cabin for 11 passengers, at the back of which was a stairwell leading to two more cabins below and to the rear, which held 11 more people. Behind these was a separate smoking cabin with seats for four; a toilet was also installed in this area. Each side of the fuselage, in the forward section of each wing a single cabin held three passengers with forward-facing windows forming the wing leading edge. The fuselage nose carried two more seats while a second toilet and wash room facilities were also provided.

1931 September 4 Set up by Vincent Bendix of the Bendix Aeronautical Co., the first annual Bendix Trophy race was held. It was a speed race held between Burbank, Calif. and Cleveland, Ohio, a distance of 2,043 mi. The first race was won by James Doolittle in a Laird LC-DW-500 powered by a 535-HP Pratt & Whitney Wasp Jr. at a speed of 233 MPH. Subsequent races were held each year, the last being won by Frank Fuller Jr. in a Seversky Sev-S2 on October 10, 1939, at a speed of 282.1 MPH. The Sev-S2 was almost identical to the USAAC P-35.

1931 September 13 Postponed a day due to bad weather, the 12th Schneider Trophy seaplane contest was held without opposition to Britain's entry. The circuit was seven laps of 31.07-mi. left-hand circuit off the Isle of Wight, England. France and Italy ran out of time to prepare potential contestants, and the United States failed to put up a sponsor. Flt. Lt. J. Boothman flew a Supermarine S.6B (serial no. S1595) around the course at an average speed of 340.08 MPH. Not as sporting as the United States had been when it voluntarily canceled the 1924 contest due to an unopposed fly-past of its entry, now having "won" three contests in succession, Britain retired with the trophy for good.

1931 September 29 Curtiss received a contract for the A-8 Shrike, all-metal, low-wing, attack monoplane that had been developed during 1930 and first flown in June 1931. Five service evaluation YA-8s and eight Y1A-8s were ordered powered by either 600-HP or 675-HP versions of the Curtiss Conqueror V-1570 engines. The 46 production aircraft were known as A-12s. The Shrike became the first American combat aircraft to enter service fitted with lift augmentation devices (slots and flaps) on the wings. They were powered by the 690-HP Wright R-1820-21 Cyclone radial engine, had a wingspan of 44 ft. and a length of 32 ft. 3 in. and could carry a 400-lb. bomb load in addition to five 0.30-in. Browning machine guns.

1931 September 29 Following success in the 1931 Schneider Trophy race, the Supermarine S.6B piloted by Flt. Lt. George Stainforth of the RAF High Speed Flight became the first aircraft to officially exceed 400 MPH in level flight when it flew a measured course off the south coast of England. Officially sanctioned by the FAI at 655.66 km/hr (407.5 MPH), the record also constituted a world air speed record and would stand for more than two years until broken by Lt. Francesco Agello in a Macchi M.52-bis at 681.97 km/hr (423.85 MPH) on April 10, 1934.

1931 September   The Heinkel He 59a, the second of two prototypes, with the registration D-2215, made its first flight. Designed as a large twin-engined attack and reconnaissance aircraft, the first He 59 prototype, the He 59b, flew in January 1932, fitted with floats, and it was in this form that the aircraft was most extensively used during World War II. Painted white, with large red crosses, the He 59 was employed on air-sea rescue duties in the English Channel during the Battle of Britain in 1940. The aircraft had a wingspan of 77 ft. 9 in. and a length of 57 ft. 1 in. and was powered by two 660-HP BMW VI 6,0 ZU 12-cylinder V engines.

1931 October 1   The British Air Ministry issued specification F.7/30 calling for design tenders for a single-seat, four gun, day and night fighter to replace the Bristol Bulldog. The specification had been formed in early 1930 but held back until development of a suitable engine that could guarantee the demanding performance required was assured. Thus began the RAF's prewar transition from biplane to monoplane fighters, epitomized by the Hurricane and the Spitfire. Blackburn, Bristol and Westland put up their contenders, as did Supermarine with its Type 224. Bristol built two: the 123 and the 133. All were unsuccessful, although the specification remained open. Gloster prepared a biplane as a private venture that became the Gladiator, and Hawker unsuccessfully put up a modified Fury. F.7/30 was the specification that would ultimately lead to the Spitfire.

1931 October 3   The first nonstop flight across the Pacific between Japan and North America began when U.S. aviators Hugh Herndon Jr. and Clyde E. Pangborn took off in their Bellanca CH-200 monoplane from Samushiro, about 300 mi. north of Tokyo. After flying time of 41 hr. 31 min., crossing about 5,000 mi. of the Pacific Ocean, they landed at Wenatchee, Wash., which was rapidly becoming a favorite landing spot on trans-Pacific flights.

1931 October 20   Without fuss or publicity, Bert Hinkler quietly left Toronto, Canada on the first of a series of record-breaking flights. He left New York October 27 to fly nonstop from North Beach Airport to Kingston, Jamaica, a distance of 1,472 mi. in just over 18 hrs. On November 9 he flew 700 mi. through driving rain across the Caribbean to Venezuela and flew on across French Guinea arriving at Port Natal on November 26.

1931 October 25   The famous German glider pilot Günther Grönhoff demonstrated the flying qualities and aerobatics of a powered flying wing designed by Alexander Lippisch. Known as the Delta I, it was a further manifestation of Lippisch's preoccupation with tailless aircraft. Flown for the first time as a two-seater powered by a 30-HP Bristol Cherub, the flying wing was not given the certificate of airworthiness because it did not have a tail—which was the whole point of the design! In 1933 Lippisch was able to spend most of his time on tailless designs through the German Research Institute for Glider Flight, or DFS.

1931 October 26   The famous D.H.82 Tiger Moth made its first flight when G-ABRC took to the air from Stag Lane, Edgeware, England. The aircraft was an instant success, and the central flying school and several other Air Ministry training units bought the type. Orders also came in from home and abroad, and production exceeded 8,000 by 1945. Powered at first by a 120-HP D.H. Gipsy Major III engine, the Tiger Moth had a wingspan of 29 ft. 4 in., a length of 23 ft. 11 in. and an all-up weight of 1,825 lb. It served with the RAF and several Commonwealth air arms, and many examples remain in use with flying clubs today and probably will into the next century.

1931 October 27   The Curtiss XF9C-1 conducted the first successful hook-up to the navy airship *Los Angeles* prior to tests with the *Akron* and *Macon,* which effectively served as flying aircraft hangars. The *Akron* was commissioned into service with the navy this day at the start of several trials that would culminate in June 1932 tests with aircraft hooking up in flight to a trapeze carried below the airship. At the end of October, the Navy ordered six Curtiss F9C-2 Sparrowhawks that operated as scouts with the *Akron* until that airship was lost in 1933, whereupon they transferred to the *Macon* until that airship too was destroyed on February 12, 1935.

1931 October 28   The second Fairey Long Range Monoplane (serial no. K 1991) built for the RAF completed a 2,857-mi. proving flight in 31 hr. when it landed at Abu Sueir, Egypt, having flown from RAF Cranwell, England. Carrying an automatic pilot developed at the Royal Aircraft Establishment, Farnborough, the Monoplane carried about 10% more fuel than its predecessor (which had crashed in December 1929), extending the range from 4,800 mi. to approximately 5,550 mi. The aircraft was flown back to England Dec. 15, 1931, but was forced down in fog about 3 mi. from Saffron Walden, Essex, 80 miles from Cranwell.

1931 October 30   The 21-year-old aviatrix Peggy Salaman and 25-year-old A. Gordon Store left Lympne, Kent, England at 11:00 P.M. in Salaman's De Havilland D.H.80A Puss Moth G-ABEH named *Good Hope* for a record-breaking flight to Maitland Aerodrome, Cape Town, South Africa. They reached their destination at 5:40 A.M. on November 5 after a flight lasting 6 days 6 hr. 40 min. En route Salaman and Store were forced down into the bush near Kimberley, but it was an otherwise uneventful flight. They became the first to transport lions by air, when Salaman took two cubs (Juba and Joker) on board between Juba, Sudan, and Kimberley.

1931 November 1   Following a dedication ceremony in June 1930 as America's premier military aviation school, Randolph Field, San Antonio, received its first students. Nearby Kelly Field was retained as the advanced flying school, and these two facilities would remain the only army pilot training schools in the United States until just before World War II, when the increased needs of army aviation dictated an expansion of the training program.

1931 November 2   The first two Marine Corps aviation squadrons assigned to operational aircraft carriers embarked on the USS *Lexington* and the USS *Saratoga.* USMC Squadron VS-15M went to the *Lexington,* and VS-14M went with the *Saratoga.* They would remain carrier-based for approximately three years and gather much experience in seaborne operations and training. They were integrated in the new Aircraft Battle Force organization structure.

1931 November 3   The new U.S. Navy airship, *Akron,* carried a record 207 people into the air, the first time more than 200 had been taken off the ground by a single flying machine. The *Akron* (ZRS-4) had been christened by Mrs. Herbert Hoover on August 8, 1931, and on September 23, the *Akron*'s captain, Charles E. Rosendahl, took the airship into the air for the first time. The *Akron* had a length of 785 ft., a diameter of 133 ft., a volume of 6,500,000 cu. ft. and propulsion from eight 560-HP Maybach VL II 12-cylinder engines.

1931 November 9   The Handley Page H.P.42 biplane airliner *Hanno* inaugurated the England to South Africa service with aircraft of this type by setting out from Croydon destined for Cairo

Several record-breaking flights to Arctic locations were conducted by the Soviet TB-3 before World War II.

via France and other European countries. Eight airliners of this type were built, named *Hannibal, Hadrian, Hanno, Horsa, Heracles, Horatius, Hengist* and *Helena.* Divided by a cargo compartment adjacent the noisy engines, forward and aft passenger compartments seated a total 24 people in relative quiet and comfort. These airliners remained the flagships of Imperial Airways' eastern and South African runs throughout the 1930s, and some carried troops to France in 1940.

1931 November 9   Flying a specially adapted long-range Comper Swift, one of the smallest light planes of the period, C. A. Butler arrived at Darwin, Australia, having flown from Lympne, England in 9 days 2 hr. 20 min. Manufactured by Flt. Lt. Nicholas Comper and by a company that had been founded by him upon his leaving the RAF, the Swift had first flown on May 17, 1930. It had a wingspan of 24 ft. and a length of 17 ft. 8 in., and this particular Swift (G-ABRE) had an all-up weight of 1,160 lb., compared with 985 lb. for a standard machine. Powered by a 75-HP Pobjoy R engine, it had a cruising speed of 120 MPH and a ceiling of 22,000 ft.

1931 November 19   Charles Lindbergh piloted the first passenger-carrying Sikorsky S-40 flying boat when it left Miami for the Canal Zone in Panama on the inaugural flight of Pan American's service with this aircraft via Cuba and Jamaica. Ordered on December 20, 1929, the S-40 amphibian was a generally conservative design but large. With a wingspan of 114 ft., the aircraft was powered by four 575-HP Pratt & Whitney Hornet radial engines and could accommodate 32 passengers in addition to the crew of eight. In a special ceremony held October 12, 1931, Mrs. Herbert Hoover named the first S-40 *American Clipper.*

1931 November 26   Having departed from Port Natal, Brazil, November 25, the first direct west-to-east crossing of the South Atlantic and the first solo flight across that ocean was completed by Bert Hinkler in a D.H.80A Puss Moth. He flew the tiny monoplane from Natal, Brazil to Bathurst (now Banjul), Gambia at the end of a series of flights that began in Toronto on October

20. His aircraft was tossed and buffeted all the way for 22 hr. by winds and storms, and he covered the 1,760 mi. at an average speed of 80 MPH. It was the longest nonstop flight made by a light aircraft to date.

1931 December 3   The first airborne separation of an I-4 parasol-wing fighter from a Tupolev TB-1 bomber took place in tests designed to qualify the concept of two parasitic fighters being carried on the upper surface of the bomber's wing. Conceived by V. S. Vakhmistrov of the Red Air Force Science and Research Institute, the idea proved sound and was developed into a variety of remarkable mated configurations, including one in which a TB-3 carried two biplane fighters on the upper surface of the wing, two monoplane dive bombers slung beneath the lower surface and one suspended from a trapeze below the center fuselage.

1931 December 21   Maj. Gen. Foulois took over command of the U.S. Army Air Corps from Maj. Gen. J. Fechet. He would last barely four years and leave office in a cloud of bitterness not unlike the fate suffered by William Mitchell a few years earlier. Maj. Gen. Foulois had flown with the Wrights and organized the first tactical air unit, the First Aero Squadron at San Diego. He had seen action in France during World War I and for a time was chief of the air service. During May 1931, Foulois was in charge of the provisional air division that carried out aerial demonstrations over major cities.

1931 December 29   The first production Hawker Audax two-seat army cooperation aircraft took to the air for the first time. Adapted from the Hart day bomber, the Audax was powered by a 530-HP Rolls Royce Kestrel IB engine, providing a top speed of 170 MPH and a service ceiling of 21,000 ft. Its dimensions were almost identical to the Hart's and it had two load-carrying panniers with a total capacity of 224 lb. It was equipped with message-collecting hook, which could snatch a small bag from the ground at low altitude. The Audax began service life with No. 4 Squadron, RAF, in February 1932, some remaining operational until 1941.

1931 December 29 Powered by a 575-HP Wright R-1820-E radial engine, the Grumman XFF-1 prototype two-seat navy fighter made its first flight at Anacostia with test pilot Bill McAvoy at the controls. One year later the navy ordered the first batch of 116 FF-1s, dubbed Fiffis, bringing Grumman its first substantial order and the beginning of continuing navy involvement with the company. When the FF-1 entered service in June 1933, it was faster than its contemporaries and featured a retractable undercarriage and a top speed of 207 MPH. It had a wingspan of 34.5 ft. and a length of 24.5 ft. The last FF-1 was retired in June 1942.

1931 The U.S. Navy built the first K-series airship at the Naval Aircraft Factory, utilizing gaseous fuel for two 330-HP Wright J-6-9 engines contained in a ballonet of 51,700 cu. ft. capacity. The airship itself had a volume of 319,900 cu. ft. and a length of 218 ft. with a diameter of 54 ft. The class was favored by the navy and suited its defined role whereby coastal defense was relegated to the army. The navy built several K-series airships, some being enlarged after World War II to a volume of 527,000 cu. ft.

1931 The Taylor Aircraft Co. was formed with head offices at Bradford, Pa. C. Gilbert Taylor was president, and William T. Piper was the secretary and treasurer. The company's first aircraft was the Cub, a two-seat light monoplane with a wingspan of 35 ft. 2 in. and a length of 22.5 ft. and powered by a 35-HP Continental A-40 air-cooled engine. It was the first in a series of Cub designs that were arguable the best known and most widely used light aircraft in the world and that almost by themselves transform light aviation in the United States. When C. G. Taylor set up Taylorcraft in 1936, W. T. Piper bought the Bradford plant and established the Piper Aircraft Corp. in 1937, his son becoming secretary and treasurer.

1931 Aged 16 and 18 years respectively, the German brothers Walter and Reimar Horten began tests with a sailplane known as the Horten I. Consisting of a fabric-covered wooden wing devoid of the usual protruberances such as tailplane and fuselage, aircraft of this type are known as "flying wings" and in theory possess less drag due to the streamlined and dominant lifting surface. The Horten I used ailerons and elevators on the trailing edge of the wing for pitch and roll, while so-called drag rudders were used near the wing tips for yaw control; drag rudders are split-control surfaces operating in unison to slew the aircraft left or right. The Horten brothers would design a wide range of flying-wings during World War II.

1932 January 20 The first England-South Africa airmail run by Imperial Airways began when the H.P.42 *Helena* took off from Croydon, outside London, and began an 11-day flight to Cape Town. This was to be the first through-run of airmail to Cape Town on a regularly scheduled service, extending the service that previously terminated in Central Africa. *Helena* reached Cape Town on February 2, only six days after the first Imperial Airways Cape Town-London airmail flight began using D.H.66 Hercules aircraft. The survey flight for these scheduled services had been conducted in 1931.

1932 January The Northrop Corp. was formed with a 51% shareholding from the Douglas Aircraft Co. Inc. A principal of Lockheed Aircraft Co. since it was formed in December 1926, Jack Northrop had later formed the Avion Corp. with Ken Jay in 1928 to pioneer stressed skin construction. A year later, after Avion's name was changed to Northrop Aircraft Corp., the company became a division of the United Aircraft & Transport Corp. United wanted to consolidate Northrop with Stearman Aircraft in

Kansas, but Jack Northrop resigned to stay in California and set up the Northrop Corp. with his old friend Donald Douglas.

1932 February 5 Chinese and Japanese aircraft met in combat for the first time during carrier-based operations in support of Japanese ground forces in the area of the International Settlement at Shanghai. Trouble around the settlement had escalated quickly into a shooting war, and the Imperial Japanese Navy dispatched the seaplane carrier *Notor*. Recognizing the scale and potential of the engagement, it then committed two carriers, the *Kaga* and the *Hosho,* which provided a total force of 76 aircraft for support operations. It was from the *Hosho* that five aircraft under the command of Lt. Nagamoto Hirabayashi fought nine Chinese pilots. One Chinese aircraft was forced to land, took off again and then crashed.

1932 February 22 The first aircraft to be shot down by Japanese fighters was a Boeing 218 demonstration version of the P-12. Flown by U.S. pilot Robert Short during the Sino-Japanese War, it was attacked by three Nakajima Type 13-2 fighters from the carrier *Kaga* when Short attacked three B1M3 Japanese torpedo bombers. The aircraft were operating in support of Japanese forces around the International Settlement at Shanghai. Short made repeated attacks on the formation, damaging one torpedo bomber and killing its gunner. The three Japanese fighters jointly attacked Short and shot him down.

1932 February 24 The USAAC requested the U.S. Navy to supply them with 25 new Norden Mk XV bomb sights. The sight had achieved impressive results at field trials when it was used by the navy on the target ship *Pittsburgh* during bombing trials in October 1931. The tests demonstrated the sight to be nearly twice as effective as the standard Mk IX used by the USAAC. Trust in the Norden bomb sight would significantly influence the army, swaying it to favor precision daylight bombing raids when U.S. bombers began operating against Germany from England in 1942.

1932 February 25 A major reorganization of Soviet civil aviation began with the administrative grouping of all Soviet civil aviation under the Chief Directorate of the Civil Air Fleet, which had been formed two years earlier. A month later, on March 25, the name of the Soviet Civil Air Fleet was changed to Aeroflot, the name it kept until the collapse of communism in 1991. In 1933 the Communist Party Congress drew up plans for a major expansion of civil aviation as the primary method of transport across the USSR.

1932 February Deutsche Luft Hansa commissioned Heinkel to produce a fast airliner to compete against the Lockheed Orion, which had begun operations on the Zürich-Munich-Vienna route for Swissair. Opting first for a monoplane with a fixed undercarriage, Heinkel's original design was capable of only 177 MPH, versus more than 185 MPH achieved by the Orion. Siegfried and Walter Günter then designed a streamlined monoplane with rectractable undercarriage powered by a single 630-HP BMW VI 6,0 Z 12-cylinder engine. The final design was completed in June 1932, and work commenced on a series production version.

1932 March 20 The airship *Graf Zeppelin* began a series of flights between Germany and Brazil. Several round-trips were planned per year, embarkation being at Friedrichshafen bound for Recife and later to Rio de Janeiro. The trips were organized by the Luftschiffbau Zeppelin G.m.b.H., the Hamburg Sudamerikanische Linie, Deutsche Luft Hansa and the Syndicato Condor.

The first American bomber capable of more than 200 MPH, the Martin B-10 posed a challenge for contemporary fighters.

Regularly scheduled flights between Germany and Brazil got under way in 1933, with 18 trips completed during the year.

1932 March 20   Designed by Martin as the Model 123 and ordered by the army as the XB-907, the precursor to the B-10 light bomber was delivered. Powered by two 600-HP Wright SR-1820-E Cyclone engines, it had a wingspan of 62 ft. 2 in., which was changed later to 70 ft. 7 in. The XB-907 had three open cockpits and three more crew spaces in the fuselage. During the fall, Martin changed the engines to two 675-HP R-1820-19 types and installed a manually operated transparent gun turret in the nose. These improvements increased speed from a credible 197 MPH to a remarkable 207 MPH, making it faster than most contemporary fighters.

1932 March 20   The Boeing Model 248 (XP-936) made its first flight. An all-metal, low-wing monoplane, the XP-936 was designed in response to concerns from the USAAC that fighters were now slower than new bombers and that a substantial increase in performance was essential. The XP-936 proved to have a top speed of 227 MPH at 10,000 ft., a service ceiling of 30,700 ft. and a normal range of 358 mi. With a wingspan of 27 ft., a length of 23 ft. 6 in. and a gross weight of 2,740 lb., it was powered by a 550-HP Pratt & Whitney R-1340-21 cowled radial. The last of the three XP-936 prototypes was delivered in April 1932.

1932 March 23   Flying a Blériot 110, French aviators Lucien Bossoutrot and Maurice Rossi took off for a record closed-circuit distance of 6,587.442 mi. at Oran, Algeria. First flown on May 16, 1930, the Blériot 110 had been designed as a long-range record breaker. With the registration F-ALCC and named *Joseph Le Brix* after the navigator of a Dewoitine D.33 killed while attempting a record, the aircraft had snatched three world records between November 15, 1930, and March 26, 1932, when this

flight ended after a flying time of 76 hr. 34 min. Powered by a 600-HP in-line Hispano-Suiza, the aircraft had a wingspan of 86 ft. 11 in., a length of 47 ft. 9 in. and a maximum take-off weight of 19,378 lb. Range was an estimated 7,830 mi.

1932 March 24   Jim Mollison left Lympne, Kent, England at the start of a record-breaking attempt to fly to South Africa in a D.H.80A Puss Moth (G-ABKG) specially modified as a long-range single seater. The Puss Moth was by now a firm favorite for record-breaking attempts, Peggy Salaman and Gordon Store having also flown one to set the previous record of 6 days 6 hr. 40 mins. starting October 31, 1931. Jim Mollison's time was only 4 days 17 hr. 19 min.

1932 March 25   The Curtiss XF11C-2 biplane made its first flight. It was essentially a civil Hawk II with a 700-HP Wright R-1820 Cyclone modified as a prototype for the bomber-fighter role eagerly sought now by the U.S. Navy. The first order for an F11 precursor was the XF11C-1 ordered April 16, 1932, and delivered in September, followed by a production order for the F11C-2 on October 18. Deliveries would begin in February 1933, later models being designated BF2C. The XF11C-2 had a wingspan of 31.6 in. and a length of 25 ft. and carried two forward-firing Browning 0.30-in. guns and four 116-lb. bombs or one 500-lb. bomb.

1932 March   The last British production variant of the Avro 504, the 504N, finally went out of production, calling a halt to construction of an aircraft designed before World War I and first flown on September 18, 1913. Other 504Ns were built in Belgium through 1937 and during World War II 504Ns were used by the RAF for towing gliders in radar experiments on aircraft made of wood. Thus was the Avro 504 the only aircraft to perform operational duty in both world wars.

1932 April 20 Yet another derivative of the Hawker Hart, the Hart Trainer, made its first flight. Basically a Hart day bomber, the Trainer was little different from its parent except that it had dual controls and no machine gun mounting in the rear cockpit. The type replaced several older trainers in RAF service, and a total of 507 were eventually built; it was not before 1939 that it was replaced by the Harvard and the Miles Master. The aircraft had a cruising speed of 145 MPH, a ceiling of 22,800 ft. and a range of 430 mi.

1932 April 27 Imperial Airways inaugurated the first regularly scheduled passenger service between England and South Africa when D.H.66s extended the previously scheduled run from Croydon, England to Mwanza, Central Africa. The additional stage necessary to complete the England-South Africa service carried passengers from Kisumu, Kenya to Cape Town. Previously the airmail service had stopped at Mwanza, but flights to South Africa left from Kisumu. Six years old, the D.H.66 was still a match for contemporary airliners.

1932 April 28 Charles W. A. Scott arrived in Darwin, Australia, having flown from England in the record time of 8 days 20 hr. 47 min. in his D.H.60M Moth VH-UQA, registered G-ACOA during its stay in England after Scott arrived in it June 5, 1931, having lowered the Australia-England record to 9 days 4 hr. 11 min. in the process. Moth G-ACOA (VH-UQA) flew for four more years before it was destroyed in a crash at Hanworth on August 20, 1936.

1932 April The first flight took place of the Junkers Ju 52/3m, the three-engine version of the Ju 52 all-metal, low-wing monoplane transport aircraft. Most aircraft of this type were powered by the 9-cylinder BMW radial engines, and early versions had the 525/600-HP BMW Hornet. Designed as a 15- to 17-passenger transport aircraft for use as a freighter, glider-tug, ambulance or troop carrier, the 52/3m was also intended to serve as a bomber. More than 4,800 aircraft of this type would be built. The 52/3m had a wingspan of 95 ft. 11 in., a length of 62 ft. (or 63 ft. 8 in. as a floatplane), a cruising speed of 152 MPH and a range of almost 570 mi.

1932 April The Japanese naval staff made crucial decisions regarding the independence of Japanese aircraft manufacturers in an effort to free them from foreign cooperation and especially to encourage the use of domestic rather than foreign manufacturers for naval aircraft. Designed to the 7-Shi specification, Mitsubishi submitted a low-wing monoplane while Nakajima presented a parasol monoplane. Neither was judged to have the necessary requirements, but the Nakajima A4N1 was purchased as a temporary measure. The resulting deficiency led to the 9-Shi specification of February 1934, leading directly to the Mitsubishi A5M.

1932 May 7 The Dornier Do.F, built in Altenrhein by the Swiss Dornier company, made its first flight. A high-wing, metal fuselage monoplane designed as a prototype bomber from the outset, the Do.F was introduced to the world as a freighter and civilian transport aircraft. It had a wingspan of 86 ft. 3 in. and a length of 61 ft. 8 in. and was powered by two 550-HP Siemens Jupiter air-cooled radial engines; production aircraft were fitted with the 600/650-HP Siemens Sh 22B radial. Production during 1933 brought the new designation Do 11C, aircraft with a wingspan of 91 ft. 11 in. The Do 13 bomber of 1933 was developed from the Do.F.

1932 May 15 A Cierva C.19 Mk.III autogyro (G-AAYP) flown by R. A. C. Brie came in second in a 45-mi. air race held at Skegness, Lincolnshire, England. The winning entry, a Spartan Three-seater I (G-ABTT) was flown by Capt. A. G. Store. The race included nine entrants, and the autogyro made it around the course at an average speed of 93 MPH.

1932 May 20 American aviatrix Amelia Earhart took off from Harbor Grace, Newfoundland in a Lockheed Vega 5B, one of 28 aircraft designed to have higher operating weights than the standard Vega. When she landed in Londonderry, Ireland next day after 15 hr. 18 min., Earhart was the first woman to have flown solo across the Atlantic in any direction, and she had done so in record time. Amelia Earhart began her Atlantic crossing with a hop from Teterboro Airport, New Jersey and then took off across the sea in her modified Vega carrying enough fuel for a nonstop range of 3,200 mi.

1932 June 6 The first British monoplane airliner operated by Imperial Airways made its first flight when the Armstrong Whitworth A.W.15 Atlanta, designed by Argosy designers J. Lloyd and F. M. Green, took to the air. Flouting extant theories that low landing speeds needed the greater wing area of a biplane configuration, the Atlanta represented a great step forward in British thinking at a time when the Handley Page and de Havilland biplane airliners were strongly favored. Designed to open passenger routes south of Nairobi, Kenya, the Atlanta had a plywood covered steel construction with a thick-section cantilever wing set on a streamlined fuselage.

1932 June 16 The Lockheed Aircraft Corp. finally closed down, eight months after the receivers were called in to its parent company, the Detroit Aircraft Corp. On June 21, however, investment broker Robert Ellsworth Gross led a consortium that bought the assets and opened a new company under the same name. Work began on a single-engine transport aircraft designed by Lloyd C. Stearman but was switched to a twin-engine concept, the Lockheed Electra. An important part of the design team led by Hall Hibbard and Richard Von Hake was a young engineer whose name would eventually be honored among the great—Clarence L. "Kelly" Johnson, who would design the P-38 Lightning, F-104 Starfighter and the U-2 and SR-71 spy planes.

1932 June 19 The prototype French Dewoitine D.500 made its first flight with test pilot Doret at the controls. It had been purchased by the French government for 870,000 francs and bore the civil registration F-AKCK. When a production order for 57 was placed on November 23, 1933, it became the first all-metal cantilever monoplane to enter service with the Armée de l'Air. The D.500 was powered by a 690-HP Hispano-Suiza 12 Xbrs-1 engine and had a wingspan of 39 ft. 8 in., a length of 25 ft. 3 in. and a maximum takeoff weight of 3,792 lb., increased on later versions to 4,200 lb. Maximum speed was 224 MPH, or 342 MPH in later versions introduced in 1939.

1932 June 29 The first Curtiss F9C-2 successfully hooked up to the airship *Akron*. Developed from the XF9C-1, which flew in March 1931, the Sparrowhawk was an improved version of the prototype with the same basic specification and a 438-HP Wright R-975-E3 radial engine. First flown on April 14, 1932, the first F9C-2 was one of six delivered to the U.S. Navy by September 1932 for use as scouts with the *Akron*. When the *Akron* was destroyed in 1933, flying continued with the *Macon* until this airship too was destroyed two years later. A surviving F9C-2 is preserved in the National Air and Space Museum, Washington, D.C.

1932 June 30 Procurement orders for what would turn out to be the last combat biplanes to serve with American air forces were issued by the U.S. Navy to Curtiss for a prototype XF12C-1 two-seat parasol-wing fighter and to Vought for a XF3U-1 of similar design. Designed with retractable undercarriage, the XF12C-1 was designated XS4C-1 when it was assigned the scout category and XSBC-1 in January 1934 when the navy decided to give it the role of scout-bomber. The XF12C-1 had an enclosed cockpit area aft of the upper wing and wheels designed to fold up into bays behind the engine compartment. With fixed wheels, the Vought XF3U-1 was modified into a scout bomber and assigned the designation XSBU-1.

1932 June 30 At the end of the five-year expansion period authorized by the U.S. Air Corps Act of July 2, 1926, delayed by budget constraints until July 1, 1927, the USAAC had failed to meet the declared targets of 1,650 officers, 15,000 enlisted men and 1,800 operational aircraft. The USAAC had on strength only 1,305 officers, 13,400 enlisted men and a complement of 1,709 aircraft, not all of which were by any stretch of credibility considered operational. Of the 45 squadrons, four were attack, 12 bombardment, 16 pursuit and 13 for observation duties. In addition, there were two airship and two balloon squadrons. In the five years, nine squadrons had been added.

1932 June The first Hall PH-1 flying boats entered service with the U.S. Navy two years after Hall Aluminum received a contract for nine aircraft. Modeled on the Naval Aircraft Factory's PN-7, the Hall XPH-1 was a variant of the PN-11 and had been ordered in December 1927. The PH-1 had biplane wings mounted above the metal hull with power provided by two 750-HP Wright R-1820F-51 engines. The pilot sat in a covered cockpit, and armament comprised four 0.30-in. Lewis guns. Production was reopened in 1936 when the U.S. Coast Guard purchased seven PH-2s for air-sea rescue work.

1932 July 1 New legislation regarding the number of commissioned and noncommissioned aircrew in U.S. naval aviation came into effect. The original act had undergone a series of changes that allowed the secretary of the navy to exercise his judgment on the subject. The bill arose from financial restraints placed on the U.S. Navy, but the amendments allowed the navy to set the figure of noncommissioned aircrew at 20% of the total number of flight crew rather than 30% as had been stipulated in the first draft.

1932 July 21 A Dornier Wal began what would result in the first circumnavigation of the world by flying boat when Wolfgang von Gronau and his crew flew from Germany to Iceland. Accompanied by Gert von Roth, Fritz Albrecht and Franz Hack, von Gronau flew west via Greenland, Montreal, Canada, the Aleutian Islands, Japan, Dutch West Indies (Indonesia), Burma (Myanmar), India, Greece and back to Altenrhein. The complete journey took 111 days.

1932 August 2 Responding to potential competition from a new Boeing 247 monoplane airliner ordered off the drawing board by Boeing Air Transport Services, Transcontinental and Western Air issued a specification calling for an all-metal trimotor capable of carrying 12 passengers 1,800 mi. at 150 MPH. Moreover, to maintain schedules the aircraft would be required to take off on any two engines at any TWA airport, including Albuquerque at almost 5,000 ft. where temperatures reach 100°F. The Boeing 247 would be regarded as the first of the then ''modern'' airliners, while the TWA specification, issued to Consolidated, Curtiss, General Aviation, Martin and Douglas, would result in the DC-1 from Douglas.

1932 August 13 The Gee Bee R-1 Super Sportster made its first flight, piloted by Russell Boardman. Designed for the 1932 racing season, it epitomized the Granville brothers' philosophy of designing the minimum airframe for the maximum size engine. With a wingspan of 25 ft. and a length of 17 ft. 9 in., it had a gross weight of 2,415 lb. in racing trim and carried 160 gal. of fuel. Powered by a 9-cylinder 800-HP Pratt & Whitney Wasp Sr. 1344 radial engine, the R-1 could top 300 MPH, and in September James Doolittle broke the world speed record when he achieved an average 296.287 MPH in an R-1.

1932 August 19 The British aviator Jim Mollison became the first person to fly the Atlantic solo in the east-west direction using a light plane when he landed his D.H.80A Puss Moth named *The Hearts Content* (G-ABXY) at Pennfield Ridge, New Brunswick, Canada. His aircraft was equipped with a 192 gal. tank, which increased the range to 3,600 mi. The flight began August 18 from Portmarnock Strand, north of Dublin, Ireland and was accomplished in a total flying time of 31 hr. 20 min., the longest nonstop flight to date with a light plane. (Jim Mollison and the record-breaking aviatrix Amy Johnson had married on July 29.)

1932 August 24 Amelia Earhart became the first woman to fly nonstop across the North American continent in a flight that began in Los Angeles, and ended in Newark, N.J. after a total flying time of 19 hr. 5 min. across a distance of 2,448 mi. The aircraft used by Earhart (now married to George Palmer Putnam) was a Lockheed Vega 5, rebuilt as a Vega 5B after the aircraft (construction number [c/n] 22) had been damaged shortly after she received it in 1930. The fuselage of another Vega (c/n 68) was used in the rebuild. This Vega 5 was the same plane that Earhart used when she became the first woman to fly solo across the Atlantic in May 1932.

1932 September 20 Transcontinental and Western Air awarded a contract to the Douglas Aircraft Co. for a prototype Douglas Commercial One, later known simple as DC-1. Designing to a specification issued by TWA on August 2, Douglas departed from the stipulated three-engine requirement. TWA's owner General Motors Corp. ordered its other subsidiary, General Aviation, to design a competitor with the stipulated three engines. As the DC-1 prototype was completed first and accepted by TWA, the General Aviation contender was never finished.

1932 September A major step toward reequipping the RAF with modern, monoplane bombers to replace the aging post-World War I designs came with specification B.9/32, which was issued to manufacturers, calling for a twin engine day bomber. Compromised at first by limitations on size and performance conforming to general discussions on bomber limits at the Geneva Disarmament Conference, restrictions were relaxed when these talks were stalled. Through several changes, B.9/32 resulted in the Handley Page Hampden and the Vickers Wellington, both of which reached RAF service in 1938 and would prove remarkably effective nearly 10 years after they were designed.

1932 November 2 A further milestone in the evolution of fast, high-performance fighters for the U.S. Navy was achieved when Grumman was awarded a contract for the XF2F-1 prototype. It evolved during the summer and autumn of 1932 as a smaller and faster development of the FF-1. Powered by a Pratt & Whitney R-1535 Twin Wasp Jr., twin-row, 14-cylinder radial engine, it had a wingspan of 28 ft. 6 in. and a length of 34 ft. 6 in. with a loaded weight of 3,490 lb., 1,187 lb. lighter than its predecessor. The XF2F-1 had a top speed of 229 MPH at 8,400 ft., a climb rate of 3,080 ft./min. and a maximum range of 750 mi.

1932 November 4   The first product of what was to become one of the most famous light aircraft manufacturers in the world made its first flight when the Beech Model 17R Staggerwing took to the air. Set up earlier in the year by Walter Beech and his wife, Ann, the Beech Aircraft Corporation's first design had a backward stagger biplane configuration with a wingspan of 32 ft., a length of 26 ft. 9 in. and a 450-HP Pratt & Whitney R-985-AN-4 Wasp Jr. radial engine providing a speed of 212 MPH and a maximum range of 1,000 mi. With Lloyd Stearman, Beech had formed the Travel Air Manufacturing Co. in 1925; he sold out his share to Curtiss-Wright in 1931. His wife Ann was chairman of Beech through the 1980s and was still chairman emeritus of a company that had sold 49,000 aircraft by 1991.

1932 November 14   In an attempt to break the London-Cape Town record set by her husband, Jim Mollison, Amy Johnson set off from Croydon, England in a D.H.80A Puss Moth (G-ACAB) named *Desert Cloud* at precisely 6:37 A.M. Flying south, she reached Cape Town at 3:31 P.M. on November 18, having covered the 6,200 mi. in a new record elapsed time of 4 days 6 hr. 54 min. On the return leg, Johnson beat her own South Africa-England record leaving Cape Town at 7:00 A.M. on December 11 and arriving in Croydon at 12:05 P.M. with a time of 7 days 7 hr. 5 min.

1932 November 19   A national monument to Wilbur and Orville Wright was dedicated at Kitty Hawk, N.C. on the approximate spot where the world's first officially recognized flight by a powered aircraft carrying a pilot in control of his machine took place. The precise location of sand dunes present when they conducted their experiments had shifted, and an artificial hill was raised upon which to set the simple memorial. It remains a shrine today for lovers of aircraft and aviation history.

1932 November 24   The prototype D.H.84 Dragon 1 made its first flight. Designed originally as a bomber for the Royal Iraqi Air Force, the aircraft set a design configuration for the popular D.H.89 Dragon Rapide via an intermediate design, the D.H.86 of 1934, the first four-engine aircraft from de Havilland. The Dragon 1 had a wingspan of 47 ft. 4 in., a length of 34 ft. 6 in. and two 130-HP D.H. Gipsy Major engines. Cruising speed was 109 MPH and range was 460 mi. with a ceiling of 12,500 ft. The aircraft appeared as a landplane or floatplane, and although primarily a civilian aircraft, it could carry 16 20-lb. bombs, two fixed forward-firing guns and one gun in the cabin.

1932 November 29   The first Northrop aircraft produced since John K. Northrop and Donald W. Douglas joined forces to establish the Northrop Corp. in January 1932 was handed over to explorer Lincoln Ellsworth, who named his Gamma 2B monoplane *Polar Star*. With a wingspan of 48 ft., a length of 29 ft. 9 in. and a loaded weight of 7,000 lb., it was powered by a 500-HP Pratt & Whitney Wasp SD 9-cylinder radial driving a three-bladed propeller. *Polar Star* achieved fame in the Antarctic before it was handed over to the Smithsonian, where it is preserved today in the National Air and Space Museum.

1932 November   The Hawker Osprey two-seat carrier fighter-reconnaissance biplane joined the Fleet Air Arm of the Royal Navy. Yet another product from the Hawker Hart lineage, the Osprey was the first navy aircraft of its class. Equipped with either wheels or floats, it had a folded wingspan of 15 ft. 7 in. and a length, as a seaplane, of 31 ft. 10 in. Toward the end of its life, the Osprey was used for target towing and training activities, but the type was not fully withdrawn until 1940.

1932 December 1   Piloted by Flugkapitän Werner Junck, the prototype Heinkel He 70 made its first flight from Warnemünde to Travemünde airfield. Designed as a low-wing monoplane airliner, it had seats for four passengers in facing pairs, a maximum speed of 224 MPH and a range of 621 mi. at a cruising speed of 208 MPH. The He 70 entered service in June 1934 and was used by the Luftwaffe for high-speed communication. Two-seat bomber and reconnaissance versions were developed in a total production run of 324, only 28 of which were built as commercial aircraft. The He 70 had a wingspan of 48 ft. 6 in., a length of 38 ft. 4 in. and a loaded weight of 7,541 lb.

1932 December 9   Pres. Herbert Hoover signed an executive order abolishing the National Advisory Committee for Aeronautics (NACA) as part of a cost-saving measure to amalgamate overlapping government research organizations. Criticism had been mobilized by William "Billy" Mitchell who had openly lambasted NACA and called for it to be transferred to the army air corps. Seeking budget reduction measures, the president acted on this and subsequent criticism by reversing a prior decision by Congress, following inspection of facilities, to support the aeronautical research organization. Fortunately for NACA, Congress stepped in again during January 1933, and overrode the presidential veto by a unanimous vote.

1932 December   The last of 320 production Lioré et Olivier LeO 20 twin-engine biplane bombers was delivered to the French Aéronautique Militaire. First flown in 1927, the aircraft had a wingspan of 73 ft., a length of 45 ft. 4 in, a maximum takeoff weight of 12,037 lb. and power provided by two 420-HP Gnôme-Rhône 9Ady radial engines. At the outbreak of World War II, 92 LeO 20 bombers were still in service as target tugs and training aircraft. It had a maximum speed of 123 MPH, a service ceiling of 18,900 ft. and a range of 621 mi. Derivatives in the 200 series were used as airliners and a successor, the four-engine LeO 206, appeared in service in 1934.

1932   The Brewster Aeronautical Corp. emerged from an old wagon and cart company formed by James Brewster in 1810. Intent upon changing the flagging fortunes of this Long Island, N.Y. company, the directors attempted to shift it fully into the world of aviation by designing its own aircraft. To keep a cash flow going, Brewster built floats for seaplanes while working on the aircraft that would be its only claim to fame: the F2A Buffalo, the first monoplane fighter to equip a U.S. Navy unit. Its only other product, the SB2A Buccaneer, was a flop, and although 771 were built, none saw combat during World War II.

1933 January 5   Piloted by Capt. L. A. Egglesfield as far as Cairo and by Capt. H. W. C. Alger from there to Cape Town, the first commercial flight between England and South Africa with the Armstrong Whitworth A.W. 15 Atlanta got under way. It arrived in Cape Town on February 14. The Atlanta was the first modern-looking single-wing airliner produced by a British manufacturer and had a wingspan of 90 ft. and a length of 71 ft. 6 in. and was powered by four 340-HP Armstrong Siddeley Serval III engines. The aircraft had a cruising speed of 130 MPH and a nominal range of 400 mi. Five Atlantas were handed over to the Royal Indian Air Force in December 1941 and were used for coastal reconnaissance from a base at Madras.

1933 January 11   Based on results from three Boeing XP-936 prototypes, the USAAC ordered 111 (later 136) P-26A (Boeing Model 266) low-wing monoplane fighters, the first all-metal aircraft to serve in the USAAC. This was also the last U.S. Army fighter to have a nonretractable undercarriage, externally braced wings and open cockpit and the last Boeing fighter ordered into production. The P-26A had a wingspan of 27 ft. 11 in. and a length of 23 ft. 7 in., and power came from a 600-HP Pratt & Whitney R-1340-27 radial engine. Known colloquially as the Peashooter, the P-26A served in front-line units until replaced by the P-35 and P-36 at the end of the decade.

1933 January 13 A French Couzinet 70 transport aircraft of the French flying service Aéropostale, named Arc-en-Ciel (Rainbow) and piloted by Jean Mermoz, began a crossing of the South Atlantic. The overnight flight took place between St. Louis, Senegal, and Natal, Brazil, and was completed in a flying time of 14 hr. 27 mins. After the flight, several modifications were carried out, and the aircraft began operations on the South Atlantic route on May 28, 1934, by which time Aéropostale had become Air France. The service ran once a month beginning July 1934, alternating with a Latécoère 300 flying boat.

1933 January 17 Variously known as the Martin Model 123 and Model 139, the Martin XB-907A was ordered into production for the USAAC and given the designation B-10. It was the army's first all-metal bomber. The XB-907A had already been modified to have an enclosed front gun turret. Production aircraft had covered pilot and rear cockpits, which could now carry a radio operator and a rear gunner equipped with a single 0.30-in. gun. In addition to the nose gun of similar type, a third gun was carried in the ventral position. An extra 130 were ordered in 1934 and 1935. One was used to evacuate people from the Dutch East Indies (Indonesia) to Australia during 1942.

1933 February 6 The Kawanishi E7K1 twin-float biplane made its first flight, powered by a 500-HP Hiro Type 91 12-cylinder, W, water-cooled engine. Designed as a three-seat reconnaissance seaplane, the E7K1 had one fixed forward-firing 7.7-mm Type 92 machine gun and one in a flexible, rear-firing position. It could carry up to four 66-lb. bombs and seated its crew in separate open cockpits. The E7K2 replaced the initial version in late 1938, and these (code-named Alf) were used on convoy escort, reconnaissance and antisubmarine work throughout World War II.

1933 February 8 The first Boeing 247 took to the air and opened a new era in air transport, representing the new age of all-metal monoplane designs. With a wingspan of 74 ft. and a length of 51 ft. 7 in., the Boeing 247 was powered by two 550-HP Pratt & Whitney S1H-1G Wasp radial engines that provided a cruising speed of 189 MPH at 8,000 ft. and a range of 745 mi. Carrying up to 10 passengers, the aircraft had retractable main landing gear, pneumatic deicing boots on the leading edges of the wings, tailplane and fin and carried two crew members and a stewardess. The Boeing 247 entered service with Boeing Air Transport, and others were ordered by United Air Lines.

1933 February 8 A new world unrefuelled distance record was set by RAF pilots Sqdn. Ldr. O. R. Gayford and Flt. Lt. G. E. Nicholetts when they landed their Fairey Long Range Monoplane at Walvis Bay, South Africa. This aircraft was the second Long Range Monoplane built (serial no. K1991) and had a 1,380 gal. fuel capacity and an automatic pilot developed at the Royal Aircraft Establishment, Farnborough. The flight began from RAF Cranwell, England at 7:15 A.M. February 6 and was completed after a nonstop flying time of 57 hr. 25 min., covering the 5,309 mi. at an average speed of 92 MPH. The autopilot failed south of Nigeria, the rest of the flight being flown manually.

1933 February 18 Imperial Airways completed the first 10 million miles of air transport service having demonstrated an ex-

cellent safety record that did much to help bring down the cost of flying insurance. Up to this time, a British traveler would have paid 12 shillings (about 42 cents in 1990 prices) for every £1,000 ($700) of insurance. From March, travelers' premiums were cut to just 1 shilling (3.5 cents) for the same insured value.

1933 February 25 The first U.S. aircraft carrier designed and built as such was launched at Newport News, Va. With a displacement of 14,500 tons, the *Ranger* (CV-4) was intended to carry reconnaissance aircraft along with the battle fleet, and since battleships of the day moved at around 21 knots, speed was abandoned in favor of accommodating as many aircraft as possible. USS *Ranger* could carry up to 80 aircraft, and catapults were installed in 1944. The *Ranger* served throughout World War II and was withdrawn from service in October 1946.

1933 February Several major steps took place in Germany to mobilize the expansion of air power. Four days after Adolf Hitler became chancellor of the Third Reich, with Paul von Hindenburg as president, Hitler appointed Hermann Göring as Reich commissioner for aviation (Reichskommissariat für die Luftfahrt). This served notice on the army and the navy that Hitler wanted a strong military air arm. In a completely unrelated move on February 8, the Air Raid Protection Department (Luftschutzant) was set up with the real purpose of controlling army and navy air activity.

1933 February The British racing driver and former Royal Flying Corps pilot, Capt. Archibald Frazer-Nash, designer of the car that bore his name, and fellow former pilot Capt. Esmond Grattan Thompson received a contract to give an aerial gunner complete protection while allowing rapid gun-laying and target-tracking. In September the Frazer-Nash turret was ordered for flight trials in a Hawker Demon fighter, and early in 1935 the company Nash & Thompson was formed. The Frazer-Nash gun turrets became famous during World War II, and aircraft manufacturers were instructed virtually to design the airframe around the turret.

1933 March 3 The British air estimates for 1933–34 were announced and showed a reduction, albeit by a very small amount, in expenditure on the RAF: a sum of £19,683,600 to fund 75 squadrons. Under pressure from the political realities of the day, Britain had only just abandoned the "10-year rule," whereby it was believed another war in Europe would give 10 years warning, thus providing ample time for rearmament. Britain had only half the front-line air strength of France and now ranked only fifth in world air power; in 1918 she had been supreme. Failure of disarmament talks in Geneva led to gloomy predictions about the future of the peace when Germany remained firm on its international right to have a force equal in strength to its biggest neighbor.

1933 March 4 As a cost cutting measure, Pres. Franklin D. Roosevelt abolished the offices of the assistant secretary of war and the assistant secretary of the navy, aviation posts that were considered superfluous to essential needs and requirements for the two services. Decisions about military aviation now could be taken out of cabinet-level meetings. The offices were reinstated when the United States went to war against Japan in 1941.

1933 March 4 With subsidies from the German government, the Arado Flugzeugwerke G.m.b.H. was formed from an existing company in response to a call for industrial commitments to aircraft manufacture from the new leaders of the Third Reich. Dating back to 1917 the original firm had been acquired by the industrialist Hugo Stinnes in 1921, who expanded into light aircraft design from an existing preoccupation with boats, marine craft and furniture. During World War II, the company would make important contributions to the development of military aviation, most notable of which was the Ar 234 jet bomber first flown June 15, 1943.

1933 March 30 In response to a call for industrial participation in German rearmament only two months after Hitler became chancellor, the old established German locomotive and railway engine firm of Henschel und Sohn became Henschel Flugzeugwerke AG. The company had its works at Schönefeld and employed Friedrich Nicolaus as its senior designer. It would serve the German armament needs most effectively as a manufacturer of other company's designs under license, although it would produce the widest range and the largest number of German guided missiles during World War II.

1933 March The Australian confectioner Sir MacPherson Robertson announced an England-Australia air race in October 1934 to commemorate the 100th anniversary of the state of Victoria; £15,000 in prize money was put up to attract contenders for the 12,300-mi. race. Because the only aircraft then in existence likely to win were American, to insure a British victory, de Havilland offered to build specially designed racing aircraft—the D.H.88 Comet—for £5,000 each if ordered by February 1934. It drew three orders, one each to Jim and Amy Mollison, the racing driver Bernard Rubin and the hotelier A. O. Edwards.

1933 April 3 Two British-built aircraft became the first to fly over the top of Mt. Everest, at 29,802 ft. the highest point of land on earth, and to photograph the summit from above. Flying the prototype Westland Wapiti V modified into a configuration where it became the Wallace (G-ACBR) was Flt. Lt. D. F. McIntyre with photographer S. R. Bonnet. They were accompanied by the Westland PV-3 (serial no. G-ACAZ) piloted by Sqdn. Ldr. Lord Clydesdale and carrying S. L. Blacker. Each aircraft was powered by a single 525-HP Bristol Pegasus I.S3. The Wallace had a length of 34 ft. 2 in. and a span of 46 ft. 5 in., and the PV-3 had a length of 34 ft. 2 in. and a span of 46 ft. 6 in. With electrically heated suits, the crews took off at 8:25 A.M. and spent 15 min. in the vicinity of the summit just above the peak.

1933 April 4 In a flight along the New England coast that began April 3, the USS *Akron,* one of two rigid airships designed to carry parasite aircraft in special hangars, crashed with the loss of 73 lives; only three men escaped. Among the dead was Rear Adm. William A. Moffett, who had headed the U.S. Navy Bureau of Aeronautics since its establishment in 1921. Caught in foul weather and buffeted by a vicious storm, the *Akron*'s tail struck the water and tore loose the aft control surfaces. The airship reared up and smashed into the water again, tail first. The *Akron*'s sister ship, the *Macon,* made her first flight on April 21, 1933.

1933 April 18 Flying an O2U seaplane, U.S. Navy Lts. G. A. Ott and B. A. Van Voorhis carried out the first tests of a device called the plane trap. It consisted of a V-shaped boom device attached to the stern of the battleship USS *Maryland,* permitted by a series of struts to ride at an even depth in the water. To operate the retrieval system, the seaplane would alight and taxi up to the boom that had a receptor designed to snag a ball-shaped probe on the under-fuselage float. This would hold the seaplane steady for hoisting. The plane trap was simple and an immediate success and five U.S. battleships were modified to incorporate it.

1933 April 24 One of the more enduring amphibians of World War II began life as the Grumman XJF-1, which made its first flight at the hands of Paul Hovgard. Ordered into production as the JF-1 and known informally as the Duck, the aircraft had a biplane wing configuration with a span of 39 ft., a fuselage length of 33 ft. and power provided by a 700-HP Pratt & Whitney R-1830-62 14-cylinder radial. The crew of two sat in tandem within a common cockpit. In a production run extending for nine years from early 1934, 645 aircraft were built, and the type saw extensive service as a general utility aircraft throughout World War II; some were still airborne as late as the 1970s.

1933 April 27 German Pres. Paul von Hindenburg established the Air Ministry of the Reich (Reichluftfahrtministerium, or RLM) out of the old Reich Commission for Aviation (Reichskomissariat Für die Luftfahrt) to control all military and civilian aviation in Germany. On May 15, 1933, military aviation was brought under the authority of the air minister, Hermann Göring, while civilian aviation was managed by the secretary of state for aviation, Erhard Milch. From September 1, 1933, military and civilian affairs were combined under Göring with Milch acting as secretary of state for both.

1933 May 22 Following the premature death of Air Chief Marshal Sir Geoffrey Salmond on April 28, ACM Edward L. Ellington assumed the post of chief of the air staff. Sir Geoffrey had taken over the post from his brother, Sir John Salmond, on April 1, 1933; and Sir John, in turn, had succeeded Sir Hugh Trenchard at the beginning of 1930. ACM Ellington would command the RAF through an intensive period of rearmament following the failure of the Disarmament Conference in Geneva. A conservative man at heart, Edward Ellington was every inch the soldier and would adapt more than a little during his tenure, which ended in September 1937, when he was replaced by ACM Sir Cyril L. N. Newall.

1933 May 27 The fixed undercarriage of the Curtiss F11C-2 navy fighter-bomber was replaced by a retractable undercarriage folding into a specially modified bulbous forward fuselage for the XF11C-3, the first of which was delivered to the navy this day. This modification was inspired by success with the retractable undercarriage on the Grumman FF, but the metal wings on the F11C-3, which entered service in October 1934, caused vibration, and the type was withdrawn. At 225 MPH, the F11C-3 was 23 MPH faster than the F11C-2, although its 650-HP Wright R-1820-04 was 50 HP less than that of the R-1820-78 adopted for its predecessor.

1933 June 1 The superior performance of the Boeing 247 twin-engine airliner over the Ford Tri-Motor was demonstrated with crushing effect on the latter when United Air Lines began a coast-to-coast flight time of just under 20 hr. compared with almost 27 hours for the Tri-Motors operated by TWA. When operations from high altitude airstrips exposed shortcomings in the Boeing, variable pitch propellers provided by Hamilton (one of the United's companies) improved take-off runs and climb rates. Yet less than a year later, the DC-2 made its first flight and directly challenged the Boeing 247.

1933 June 2 Flying the first Northrop Gamma completed after the formation of the Northrup Corp., aviator Frank Hawks snatched the coast-to-coast record by flying between Los Angeles and New York in 13 hr. 27 min. at an average speed of 181 MPH. The aircraft had been purchased by Texaco in December 1932 and was operated by Texaco Domestic Sales. Designated Gamma 2A, the machine completed for Frank Hawks was powered by a 785-

HP geared Wright Whirlwind GR-1510 14-cylinder radial engine and had a cockpit for the pilot located behind the wing trailing edge. Frank Hawks used this aircraft to set other records as well, including point-to-point time and distance records. After being sold to Gar Woods, the Gamma 2A was destroyed in a crash in a 1936 air race.

1933 June 12   The Great Lakes XBG-1 biplane, a two-seat Navy dive bomber, began flight trials leading to a competitive fly-off with the Consolidated XB2Y-1, which began its tests September 18, 1933. Both had been ordered June 22, 1932, around a specification demanding carriage of a 1,000-lb. bomb. The Great Lakes contender won, and the production BG-1 entered service powered by a Pratt & Whitney R-1535-64 Wasp radial. With a wingspan of 36 ft. and a length of 28 ft. 9 in., it was succeeded by the B2G-1, which had retractable main landing gear and a belly enclosure for the bomb load.

1933 June 19   Erhard Milch and Col. Walther von Reichenau, representing the German defense minister, presented plans for a combat air force of 600 aircraft and 51 squadrons by the fall of 1935. Of this number, approximately 200 would be bombers. This plan was reviewed by Göring and Werner von Blomberg eight days later and approved. By September, following sharp criticism of the ''conservative'' estimates of defense needs, the two-year production program was almost doubled to just over 1,000 aircraft. It too was soon deemed inadequate, and the famous Rhineland program became effective Jan. 1, 1934.

1933 June 21   The predecessor of one of the most respected stalwarts of the British Fleet Air Arm during World War II, the Supermarine Seagull V, made its first flight. Designed by R. J. Mitchell as a private venture for Supermarine, it was originally based on an earlier family of Seagull seaplanes to which it ultimately bore no real resemblance. Ordered by the Australian government, it was adopted for the Fleet Air Arm following flight trials in 1935. With the name Walrus, it served far and wide, loved for its durability and rugged survivability; 744 were built by Supermarine and Saunders Roe. The Walrus had a wingspan of 45 ft. 10 in. and a length of 37 ft. 3 in., and power was provided by a 775-HP Bristol Pegasus II.

1933 June 22   A special device to retrieve seaplanes with the parent ship under way was successfully tested by the *Maryland*. A cargo net was trailed by the *Maryland* so that the forward end closest the stern was just at water level and the rear was slightly submerged. Navy aviator Lt. G. A. Ott ran his O2U seaplane up onto the net, and a hook on the central pontoon secured the seaplane to the net. Once the seaplane was pulled into position, a conventional hoist was used to raise it to the deck. Later, an alongside retrieval procedure was tested, on this occasion crumpling the wings of the seaplane as it swung sharply into the hull. Nevertheless, the alongside retrieval concept was proven and eventually adopted.

1933 June 22   The first flight of the Tupolev ANT-25 single-engine monoplane took place with M. M. Gromov at the controls. With its cantilever high-aspect ratio wings, the plane was designed and built to set altitude records. Although the aircraft never did achieve significant records, around 20 were eventually built for long-range research flights, among them two long-distance flights between the USSR and North America over the North Pole. The ANT-25 had a wingspan of 111 ft. 6 in. and a length of 44 ft. with power provided by a single 750-HP or 874-HP M-34.

1933 June 22   In flying from Pendine Sands in southern Wales to Bridgeport, Conn., Jim and Amy Mollison became the first married couple to fly the Atlantic. They were taking their specially modified D.H.84 Dragon 1 (G-ACCV) to New York from where they hoped to fly nonstop to Baghdad to set a new distance record. The aircraft turned over on landing and was damaged, and was replaced by a similar type shipped to Canada from England. Several abortive attempts to get it airborne October 3, 1933, frustrated the would-be record-breakers, and it was sold to J. R. Ayling and L. Reid, who flew it to England August 8, 1934, making the first non-stop flight between Canada and Britain.

1933 June   Designed to a specification issued in 1932 for a successor to the French Lioré et Olivier 20 day-and-night bomber, which had been ordered into service during 1926, the Bloch M.B.200 made its first flight. It had a wingspan of 58 ft. 11 in., a length of 40 ft. 9 in. and a maximum takeoff weight of 17,688 lb. Capable of carrying an internal bomb load of only 882 lb., the aircraft was, nevertheless, an important addition to the French bomber force. It entered service in1934, and 208 were built, of which 92 were still in service at the outbreak of the World War II, as were 155 of the much redesigned derivative, the Bloch M.B. 210, of which 253 were built.

1933 July 1   The first Douglas DC-1 twin-engine airliner made its initial flight from Clover Field in Santa Monica, Calif. with Carl Cover and Fred Herman at the controls. TWA ordered 20 and thus began a line of Douglas airliners using the same basic design layout through three successive types (including the DC-2 and DC-3). Some DC-3s continued in regular, scheduled use into the 1990s. With seating for 12 passengers, the original DC-1 had two 690-HP Wright SGR-1820-F radials, but with the more powerful 710-HP F3 model, it had a cruising speed of 190 MPH, a ceiling of 23,000 ft. and a range of 1,000 mi.

1933 July 1   In a demonstration of Italy's technical progress under its fascist rulers, a mass formation flight of 24 Savoia-Marchetti S.55X flying boats led by air minister Gen. Italo Balbo left Rome on the first leg of a flight to America via Iceland. They arrived at their destination, the World's Fair in Chicago on July 15, having flown 6,065 mi. in a flying time of just under 49 hr. The aircraft used for this epic formation flight had a more streamlined structure than predecessors of the same type and were powered by 750-HP Asso engines driving three-bladed metal propellers.

1933 July 4   The Hamburger Flugzeugbau G.m.b.H. was formed as a subsidiary of the Blohm und Voss shipbuilders of Hamburg. Under the directorship of Walther Blohm, the company would become a principal aircraft design and manufacturing organization. Having had experience building aircraft parts under subcontract to Junkers, the firm developed seaplanes, flying boats and tactical reconnaissance aircraft. During the latter half of World War II, most work by Blohm und Voss was on subcontract work for other aircraft builders.

1933 July 9   Flying their Lockheed Sirius built in 1929 and used for the 1931 survey flight of Alaska, the North Pacific and China, Charles Lindbergh and his wife began a major route-proving tour of the North and South Atlantic. Fitted out as a floatplane and with a more powerful 710-HP Cyclone engine, the Lindberghs completed their survey on December 6, after which the Sirius Special was given to the American Museum of Natural History in New York, eventually finding its way to the Smithsonian's National Air and Space Museum in Washington, D.C.

1933 July 15   Pioneer American aviator Wiley Post set off from Floyd Bennett Field, N.Y. on the first solo flight around the world in his Lockheed Vega 5B (registration no. NC105W) *Winnie Mae.* He completed the first leg by making the first nonstop flight to Berlin, arriving 25 hr. 45 min. after take-off. Post pressed on via Moscow, Irkutsk, Khabarovska and Alaska, finally arriving back at New York just 7 days 18 hr. 43 min. after his journey began, despite his having sustained a broken propeller and damaged undercarriage en route. Total flying distance was 15,596 mi., and the time beat his June 1931 circumnavigation when he was accompanied by Harold Gatty.

1933 August 5   French Air Force pilots Lts. Paul Codes and Maurice Rossi began a record-breaking straight-line distance flight between New York and Rayak, Syria, overflying France en route. Named *Joseph Le Brix,* the aircraft they used was the highly successful Blériot 110 monoplane of wooden construction and powered by a 600-HP Hispano-Suiza 12Lb in-line engine. The total distance covered, 5,657 mi., set a new straight-line distance record that remained intact until broken by a Soviet Tupolev ANT-25 in July 1937.

1933 August 8   The U.S. Navy Commander Aircraft, Battle Force, formally requested the installation of variable pitch propellers on seven Boeing F4B fighters for the navy. Tests, which were successfully reported, had been carried out by Fighting Squadron Three on the aircraft carrier *Langley.* Variable pitch has the advantage of "redesigning" the propeller in flight by altering the angle at which the blade is positioned with respect to the air flow. This increases the efficiency of the propeller and allows the pilot to set the pitch angle for optimum effect at a given airspeed. Variable pitch propellers would become an important technical advance for all aircraft.

1933 August 11   Designed and built for the South Atlantic route specified by the French Air Ministry, the Blériot 5190 Santos Dumont made its first flight at Caudebec en Caux, France with Lucien Bossoutrot at the controls. The aircraft was a high-wing monoplane flying boat with a wingspan of 141 ft. 1 in. and a length of 85 ft. 3 in. and was powered by four 650-HP Hispano-Suiza 12Nbr 12-cylinder V engines arranged so that the center engine housing contained a tandem pair with single tractor engines to either side. The first crossing from Dakar, Senegal to Natal, Brazil was made on November 27, 1934. The flight reduced the travel time from Toulouse, France to Buenos Aires, Argentina to 3 days 20 hr.

1933 August 11   Designed essentially as an elliptically shaped flying wing with twin tail booms and a forward crew nacelle, the giant Kalinin K-7 bomber designed by K. A. Kalinin made its first flight from Kharkov in the Soviet Union. With a span of 173 ft. 11 in., a length of 91 ft. 11 in., an empty weight of 53,792 lb. and a maximum emergency overload weight of 102,513 lb., it was powered by six tractor engines in the wing leading edge and a single pusher engine in the wing trailing edge between the booms. The crew of 11 included a gunner in the rear of each tail boom and two gunners in each landing gear gondola slung beneath the wing. As an airliner, the K-7 could have carried 120 people, but the bomber prototype crashed and was destroyed on November 21.

1933 September 4   American aviator James R. Wedell in Wedell-Williams No. 44 (registration no. NR278V) became the first pilot to fly a landplane at an officially credited record speed in excess of 300 MPH when he achieved an average 490.080 km/hr. (304.52 MPH) on a measured 3 km (1.86 mi.) course at Cleveland, Ohio. It had taken less than 10 years to progress from the first landplane speed record achieved in excess of 100 MPH to a speed record in excess of 200 MPH, but it had taken almost 12 years to exceed 300 MPH. In only six more years, Hans Dieterle would break through the 400 MPH landplane barrier with a speed run of almost 464 MPH.

1933 September 7   Lt. Comdr. H. E. Halland, U.S. Navy, of VP-5F commanded a nonstop flight of six Consolidated P2Y-1 flying boats that set off from Norfolk, Va. and landed at Coco Solo in the Panama Canal Zone, the home of VP-5F, next day. With specially installed long-range fuel tanks, the 2,059 mi. were flown to demonstrate long-range deployment and was completed in a time of 25 hr. 20 min. at an average speed of 81 MPH. On January 10, 1934, Lt. Comdr. K. McGinnis of VP-10F took six P2Y-1 flying boats from San Francisco to Pearl Harbor in Hawaii, flying a distance of 2,399 mi. in 24 hr. 35 min. at an average speed of 98 MPH, breaking the world straight-line distance record for seaplanes.

1933 September 11   The Breguet 521 Bizerte flying boat designed and built for the French Navy made its first flight powered by three 800/845-HP Gnône-Rhône 14 Krsd 14-cylinder air-cooled radial engines. With a span of 115 ft. and a length of 66 ft. 7 in., the biplane flying boat was an enlarged version of the Short Calcutta for which Blériot had a manufacturing license. A civilian version, the 530 Saïgon was developed for Air Union and used on its Marseilles-Tunis route, the first flying in May 1934. The Saïgon could accommodate up to 20 passengers in three separate classes on flights of up to 683 mi.

1933 September 27   In Germany four contracts were placed for a dive bomber that was intended to equip Germany's new military air unit. Of the four companies that submitted proposals, Junkers was to receive a development contract in 1934 for what became the Ju 87 Stuka, which first flew in April 1935. The others (Arado, Blohm und Voss and Heinkel) were rejected. In the Sturzbomber (dive bomber) program, Germany attempted to develop aircraft with a capability inspired when Ernst Udet witnessed U.S. Navy dive bombing tactics at Cleveland, Ohio.

1933 October 2   The old German firm of railway engine and locomotive engineers, Goathaer Waggonfabrik A.G. (GWF), reopened its Aircraft Construction Department. Although it would not emulate its World War I success in building bombers, the first Gotha aircraft of the new organization, the Go 145 trainer, achieved astonishing success. Designed by Dipl. Ing. Albert Kalkert and built of wood, the biplane first flew in February 1934. More than 10,000 were built in Germany, Turkey and Spain, and its service use extended well into the 1950s.

1933 October 15   One of the most important British aero engines of this decade and the next had its origins in the Rolls Royce P.V.12, which made its first test run on this date. Predecessor to the Merlin, the P.V.12 was designed and developed by Rolls Royce as a private venture, and they capitalized on their experience with the 1,600-HP R engine for the Supermarine S.6B that had won the 1931 Schneider Trophy. In July 1934, the P.V.12 would pass its 100-hr. test and demonstrate 625 HP for take-off and 790 HP at altitude. By the end of its development more than 10 years later, the ultimate Merlin version would produce 2,030 HP.

1933 October 18   The Grumman XF2F-1 made its first flight, piloted by James H. Collins, prior to its being delivered to Anacostia Naval Air Station for tests. Developed as a shipboard fighter, the aircraft was ordered into production on May 17. 1934, and entered service with the U.S. Navy beginning February 1935. The aircraft had a slightly higher loaded weight than the prototype that had been ordered November 2, 1932, with a top speed of 231 MPH at 7,000 ft. and a maximum range of 985 mi. The F2F-1 carried two 0.30-in. machine guns, and some F3F-1 types developed from the F2F-1 were still in service when the United States went to war against Japan in December 1941.

1933 October 20   Erhard Milch, the head of the German ministry of aviation (RLM), and Hermann Göring addressed more than 60 aircraft manufacturers and ancillary suppliers to deliver plans for German air expansion and rearmament. There was still debate within the political and military hierarchy as to how ambitious the expansion plan should be. After this meeting, however, plans were put into effect for transforming German industry to munitions support, placing it on a strategic planning schedule more reminiscent of wartime than peaceful defense structures. Whatever the finally agreed numbers, the German aircraft industry knew it had a virtually open checkbook.

1933 October 28   The U.S. Navy ordered the Consolidated Model 28 (XP3Y-1) designed by Isaac M. Laddon for comparative tests with the Douglas XP3D-1 for which engineering studies had been ordered on May 20, 1933, and for which a prototype order would be placed February 11, 1934. Out of these activities would emerge the Consolidated PBY Catalina. Designed to replace the P2Y, it had a parasol wing mounted as a semicantilever with a faired, internally braced, central support supplemented by two struts on each side. With retractable wing-tip floats and power from two 825-HP Pratt & Whitney R-1830-58 radial engines, it would carry a 2,000-lb. bomb load and four machine guns.

1933 October   Responding to discussions between aircraft design chief Sydney Camm and the British Air Ministry in August 1933, the Hawker Co. showed initial design configurations of a monoplane fighter based on the Fury biplane. What emerged was inspired by discussions between Sydney Camm and Maj. John Schaular Buchanan on future fighter needs. Referred to as the Fury Monoplane, the aircraft was to have a 660-HP Rolls Royce Goshawk like the Hawker P.V.3 biplane, which had been prepared unsuccessfully for the F.7/30 specification. The Fury monoplane was in effect, little more than a beefed-up Fury.

1933 October   The first flight of the Polikarpov I-15, the TsKB-3 Chaika, took place with Valerii P. Chkalov at the controls. The aircraft had been designed as a successor to the I-5 and was given a gull configuration on the upper wing, which had a span of 32 ft. The fuselage was 20 ft. in length and carried a single 710-HP Cyclone SGR-1820-F3 engine. The I-15 had a top speed of 229 MPH and a range of 340 mi. It was used in Spain, China, and many Russian theaters, some being retained well into the early 1940s.

1933 November 1   The German state railway (Deutsche Reichsbahngesellschaft) began flying the Dornier Do.F on its night freight and mail service between Berlin and Königsberg via Danzig. Other routes opened soon, including Berlin-Breslau and Münster-Stuttgart via Munich. It is believed that seven Do.Fs were operated by the state railway as the Do.11Da. Services to the rail network were also provided by Junkers Ju 52/3m aircraft.

1933 November 15   In what turned out to be a crucial stage in British air rearmament plans, the Defense Requirements Committee was established with a mandate to examine the armed services and to recommend to the cabinet measures necessary to overcome deficiencies. The report was submitted February 28, 1934, and although it toed the government line, endorsing the wisdom of abandoning the ''10-Year-Rule,'' it positively identified Germany as the ''ultimate potential enemy'' and went so far as to suggest—accurately enough—that she might engage in aggressive policies within ''five years.''

1933 November   The prototype Focke-Wulf Fw 56 Stösser flew for the first time with the registration D-JSOT. Designed as a high-wing monoplane trainer, it was the first aircraft with which designer Kurt Tank (later of Fw 190 fame) became involved from the outset. During 1935 it won out against the He 74 and the Ar 76 as a home defense fighter, about 1,000 being built in all, many going to flying clubs. The Fw 56 had a wingspan of 34 ft. 6 in., a length of 25 ft. 3 in. and a loaded weight of 2,196 lb. Powered by a 240-HP Argus As 10C 8-cylinder in-line engine, it had a maximum sea level speed of 173 MPH and could climb to 3,280 ft. in just over 2 min.

1933 December 22   Built for Air France, the Société Aéronautique Française (originally known as the Constructions Aéronautiques E. Dewoitine) D.332 three-engine transport aircraft left Paris for a flight to Saigon (now Ho Chi Minh City, Vietnam) under the command of Maurice Noguès. The D.332 could carry eight passengers in comfort over a range of 1,242 mi. Powered by three 575-HP Hispano-Suiza 9V 9-cylinder air-cooled engines, the aircraft had a wingspan of 95 ft. 2 in. and a length of 62 ft. 2 in. Registered F-AMMY and named *Émeraude*, the D.332 arrived in Saigon December 28 after a total flying time of 48 hr. The Dewoitine transports remained in service until the late 1940s.

1933 December 31   The Polikarpov I-16, designated the TsKB-12 by the Central Constructor's Bureau, made its first flight with test pilot Valerii P. Chkalov at the controls. In 1934 it would become the first monoplane fighter with enclosed cockpit and retractable undercarriage to enter service with any air force. The I-16 had a wingspan of 29 ft. 1 in., a length of 19 ft. 8 in. and power from a single 710-HP Cyclone SGR-1820-F3 radial engine. Performance included a top speed of 245 MPH, a service ceiling of 31,000 ft. and a range of about 500 mi. The I-16 remained in service throughout World War II although replacement by more modern types had begun by 1943.

1933 December   Built in prolific numbers as a major training aircraft, the Yokosuka K5Y1 made its first flight with a production decision coming in the following month. The K5Y2 floatplane version was developed, and although Yokosuka built only 60, seven other Japanese aircraft manufacturers built the type for the navy. Powered by a 340-HP Hitachi Amakaze 11 9-cylinder radial, the K5Y1 had a wingspan of 36 ft. 1 in., a length of 26 ft. 5 in., a top speed of 132 MPH at sea level and a climb rate of 9,845 ft. in 13 min. 32 sec. The aircraft was given the code name Willow and was used during World War II.

1934 January 1   The Rhineland program of German air force expansion became effective, in which it was planned during 1934 and 1935 to produce a total 3,715 new aircraft for the Luftwaffe. This represented a doubling of the monthly production rate and a four-fold increase over that of January 1933. In July, this plan was expanded to call for a total production of 4,021 military aircraft by September 30, 1935, and an increase in monthly production from 72 in January 1934 to 293 in July 1935. The total plan included 832 new bombers, 51 dive bombers, 245 fighters, 590 reconnaissance aircraft, 149 naval aircraft and 2,154 trainers, liaison and miscellaneous types.

1934 January 14 Designed for the Australian government as a fast 10-seat passenger aircraft, the de Havilland D.H.86 made its first flight. Bearing more than a superficial resemblance to the twin-engine D.H.84 Dragon, it was almost twice the size and was also the first four-engine de Havilland aircraft. Powered by four 200-HP Gipsy Six engines, it had a span of 64 ft. 6 in., a length of 46 ft. 1 in. and an all-up weight of 9,200 lb. (11,000 lb. with the 205-HP Gipsy Six Series II). The D.H.86B had a range of 800 mi., extended from the 450 mi. of the prototype and 760 mi. of the D.H.86A. Several of these aircraft continued in use after World War II.

1934 January 31 In the preceding 12 months, German military aviation had grown expansively by whatever criterion was used to measure the increase. Employment in aircraft manufacturing plants had risen from 2,813 to 11,102, and employment in aircraft engine factories had gone up from 1,175 to 5,769, a more than four-fold increase in employment over a year. Monthly production had increased from 31 a year before to a current 72, and although most planes were of old designs, the prospects for the next two years looked bright as many new aircraft were on the drawing boards.

1934 February 3 The first scheduled trans-Atlantic airmail service between Berlin and Rio de Janeiro, Brazil was inaugurated by Luft Hansa. The journey was made in four stages, beginning with the Berlin-Seville, Spain leg flown by a fast He 70, followed by a stage to Bathurst (now Banjul), Gambia, using a Ju 52/3m. From there, the mail was put aboard a Dornier Wal named the *Taifun,* catapulted into the air from the bow of the tender *Westfalen* anchored in the harbor and flown to Natal, Brazil, where it was transferred to a Junkers W.34 of Syndicato Condor and flown to Rio.

1934 February 9 Pres. Roosevelt canceled the air mail contracts provided for in the Kelly Act of Feb. 2, 1925, effective February 19. The action followed allegations of fraudulent practice on the part of the postmaster general in allocating contracts to private operators. The USAAC began an emergency airmail service February 19, but poor weather over the entire country caused the president to suspend flights between March 11 and March 18, after which it continued to carry out this service until June 1.

1934 February 17 The first airmail flight from Australia to New Zealand was flown by Charles T. P. Ulm in his Avro Ten, a license-built Fokker F.VIIB/3m registered as VH-UXX. Powered by a 330-HP Wright Whirlwind and named *Faith in Australia,* the aircraft made the crossing in 14 hr. 10 min. The same aircraft was used by Stephens Aviation Ltd. in 1941 to evacuate people from New Guinea to Australia.

1934 February 18 At precisely 10:00 P.M. pilot Jack Frye and copilot Eddie Rickenbacker began a transcontinental flight from the Union Air Terminal at Los Angeles to Newark, N.J. in a DC-1, stopping at Kansas City and Columbus. They accomplished the flight in a total duration of only 13 hr. 4 min., 3 hr. ahead of schedule. On the eve of the cancelation of airmail contract flights ordered by Pres. Roosevelt on February 9, it demonstrated the level of progress made in civil aviation fueled by fierce competition from rival mail carriers, a stimulus without which the DC-series would never have emerged.

1934 February 19 Northrop delivered the first of 24 Gamma light bombers to the Chinese government. Based on the Gamma 2C, each aircraft was powered by a 710-HP Wright SR-1820-F3

radial engine and had a retractable tub fitted to the underside of the fuselage behind the wing for a bomb aimer. A 0.30-in. machine gun was fitted to the rear of the cabin enclosure, operated by the bomb aimer. In addition, four similar guns were fixed in the wings. The maximum bomb load was 1,600 lb. All 24 aircraft had been delivered to the Chinese by September 21, 1934, and aircraft of this type were the kind to be used against the Japanese.

1934 February 23 The prototype Lockheed Electra made its first flight with test pilot Marshall Beadle at the controls as it took off from Lockheed's Burbank, California facility. It was the first product of the newly reopened Lockheed Aircraft Corp. The Electra was aimed at the airline market and given two 450-HP Wasp Jr., SB engines, which, when restrictions were introduced in the United States over single-engine passenger-carrying flights, proved prudent and a clear marketing advantage over a single-engine design first favored by the company President Lloyd Carlton Stearman. The Electra had a wingspan of 55 ft. and a length of 38 ft. 7 in. with capacity for 10 passengers.

1934 February The Japanese navy issued a definitive specification for a modern fighter that evolved as a requirement from the April 1932 decision for greater reliance on the domestic Japanese aircraft industry and less dependence on foreign products. Issued as the 9-Shi specification, it called for an aircraft with a maximum speed of 217.5 MPH (350 km/hr.) at 9,845 ft. (3,000 m), a wingspan not to exceed 36 ft. 1 in. (11 m) and a length no greater than 26 ft. 3 in. (8 m) with armament of two 7.7-mm machine guns. This specification led to the Mitsubishi Ka-14, which entered service as the navy's type 96 Carrier Fighter Model 1 (A5M1).

1934 March 8 The British air estimates for 1934–35 were announced and showed a very small increase over preceding years, with four more RAF squadrons and a new aircraft carrier for the navy. Since 1921 annual expenditure on military aviation in Britain had remained under £20 million, staying around £16–18 million since 1926. It was to be the last year of sublime indifference to Germany's ominous war preparations and the total failure of the disarmament talks at Geneva, where Britain had unsuccessfully tried to ban military aircraft altogether and proposed unworkable compromises that had little effect other than to divert the nation's attention while other powers built up their air forces.

1934 March 14 Promising added sophistication over more conventional, continuous wave radio detection methods, the pulse radio detection and ranging technique was authorized as a research project at the radio division of the U.S. Naval Research Laboratory. Headed by Dr. A. Hoyt Taylor, the Radio Division was to experiment with a concept developed by Leo Young. When received back as an echo, microsecond pulses of radio energy transmitted at intervals several tens to several thousands of times longer than a single pulse would provide information on range and bearing of the reflective object. The entire apparatus could be installed on a ship, potentially enhancing aircraft detection.

1934 March 26 Piloted by John Lankester Parker and with three passengers on board, the first landplane derivative of the Short Kent flying boat took to the air for the first time. Named *Scylla* (G-ACJJ), the big biplane was followed by *Syrinx* (G-ACJK) for the busy Imperial Airways routes into continental Europe. Carrying 38 passengers, they were each 78 ft. 5 in. long and had a wingspan of 113 ft., an all-up weight of 33,500 lb. and a top speed of 137 MPH. The last biplanes built by Short Brothers,

One of the last great biplane airliners, the Short Scylla, *made its first flight on March 26, 1934.*

these two splendidly rigged biplanes were the last of their generation; both flew until 1940.

1934 March 29   Ordered by Pan American Airways on November 30, 1932, from a specification issued August 15, 1931, the Sikorsky S-42 flying boat lifted into the air for the first time. It was quickly put into service, and its first scheduled passenger carrying flight between Miami and Rio de Janeiro, Brazil was on August 16. The S-42 had a conventional boat hull with a length of 67 ft. 8 in. and a wingspan of 114 ft. 2 in. incorporating four 700-HP Pratt & Whitney Hornet radial engines installed in the leading edge. With a gross take-off weight of 43,000 lb., the S-42 had a cruising speed of 170 MPH and a range of 1,200 mi. carrying 32 passengers. It proudly perpetuated the name Clipper.

1934 March 30   Pending the outcome of an inquiry into the alleged fraudulent use of public money in subsidizing U.S. airmail contracts, Pres. Roosevelt ordered new bids for temporary contracts. The USAAC had not been able to adequately cope with the emergency operation of an albeit reduced delivery and route schedule. In the first three weeks of army airmail flights, which began February 20, the USAAC lost nine pilots, some of them on route familiarization flights. Some 45 airlines gathered at the Post Office Department April 20 to bid for new contracts at the somewhat reduced rate of 45 cents per mile. The temporary contracts would become permanent.

1934 March   The Nakajima E8N1 biplane made its first flight. It was designed by engineer Kishiro Matsuo as a two-seat reconnaissance seaplane with a wingspan of 36 ft. and a length of 28 ft. 11 in., and it was powered by a 580-HP Nakajima Kotobuki 2 KAI1 9-cylinder radial engine. In October 1935, it was accepted by the Japanese navy as the Type 95 Reconnaissance Seaplane Model 1 and was used widely from warships and aircraft tenders. It remained in production until 1940, and the E8N2 model was active in the Pacific war, later duties including liaison and communications.

1934 April 11   Following the cancelation of the private U.S. airmail contracts, American Airlines Inc. was formed to replace the old American Airways leasing aircraft operated by the former entity. Operations commenced May 5, and new equipment arrived in the form of the DC-2, which started scheduled runs in December. Seeing the possibilities of this aircraft on night flights

and wishing to combine its efficiency with the comfort of the Curtiss Condor, American Airlines' president, C. R. Smith called Donald Douglas and suggested he design a sleeper version of the DC-2. This was the inspiration for the famous DC-3, although Douglas was uninterested in developing this model until an advance order for 20 arrived from American Airlines.

1934 April 11   Comdr. Renato Donati of the Italian Regia Aeronautica set a new world altitude record by flying a much-modified Caproni Ca.113 biplane to a height of 47,352 ft. The wing area of the Ca.113 had been increased from the usual 34 ft. 5 in. to 46 ft. 5 in. for this attempt, and the engine was fitted with a supercharged Bristol Pegasus radial manufactured under license by Alfa Romeo. This same aircraft was also used by the Contessa Carina Negrone in 1935 to set a new altitude record for women of 39,402 ft.

1934 April 17   The D.H.89 Dragon Rapide, a scaled-down version of the four-engine de Havilland D.H.86, reduced almost to the same dimensions as the D.H.84, made its first flight from Hatfield, England with H. S. Broad at the controls. Using construction techniques pioneered by the larger aircraft, the Dragon Rapide became a highly popular transport aircraft, 728 being built over a 10-year production period. A military version, the Dominie, entered service with the RAF and served throughout World War II.

1934 April 17   Designed as a modification of the Fairey T.S.R.I., the T.S.R.II made its first flight. One of the most incongruous aeronautical success stories of World War II, it was eventually accepted by the Royal Navy for its Fleet Air Arm as the Swordfish. First in service during February 1936, it already looked 10 years out of date yet served with distinction in convoy duties and fleet protection roles. With a wingspan of 45.5 ft. (17 ft. 3 in. folded), a length of 36 ft. 4 in. (40 ft. 11 in. with floats) and power provided by a 690-HP Bristol Pegasus IIIM or 750-HP Pegasus XXX, the Swordfish could carry a 1,610-lb. torpedo or 1,500 lb. of bombs.

1934 April 20   The USSR created the award "Hero of the Soviet Union" and immediately bestowed it upon seven civil and military pilots who rescued 111 survivors from the icebreaker *Chelyuskin* stranded on an ice floe off the northeast coast of Siberia. They were M. V. Vodopyanov, I. V. Doronin, N. P. Kamanin, S. A. Levanevskii, A. V. Lyapidevskii, V. S. Molokov and M. T. Slepnev. Automatically bringing with it the Order of Lenin, this award was thrice given to top Soviet fighter ace of World War II, Ivan Nikolai Kozhedub with 62 victories; and single awards were given only to G. A. Rechkalov (58 victories), N. D. Gulaev (57), K. A. Yevstigneev (52), D. B. Glinka (50), A. F. Klubov (50) and eight others with less than 50 victories.

1934 April 23   The last biplane produced by Douglas, the XO2D-1 floatplane ordered for trials by the U.S. Navy, made its first flight at Anacostia. Designed to compete with the Curtiss XO3C-1, a predecessor of the Seagull, the aircraft was powered by a 550-HP Pratt & Whitney R-1340-12 9-cylinder air-cooled radial but failed to beat out Curtiss for a production contract. The XO2D-1 was used later by Douglas as a company trials aircraft.

1934 April   The Mitsubishi Ka-9, an aircraft designed to a far-seeing requirement defined by Adm. Isoroku Yamamoto for a long-range, land-based navy attack bomber, took to the air for the first time, piloted by Yoshitaka Kajima. Designed by Sueo Honjo, the Ka-9 was powered by two 500-HP Hiro Type 91 12-cylinder engines and had the then-phenomenal range of 3,265 mi.

It inspired a rewritten specification known as 9-Shi, which called for a bomber capable of carrying a 1,764-lb. warload. Nakajima Hikoki K. K. company tried to compete with the Mitsubishi Ka-15, an improved version of the Ka-9, with its LB-2, but lost out.

1934 April   The first product of the Bücker Flugzeugbau set up at Johannisthal, Berlin in 1932, the Bü 131 Jungmann made its first flight, piloted by Joachim von Köppen. Powered by an 80-HP Hurth HM 60R 4-cylinder in-line engine, the Bü 131 had been designed by Swede Anders J. Andersson as a sports biplane suitable for aerobatic and display purposes but also useful as a trainer. Used by Czechoslovakia, Finland, Hungary, Spain, Sweden and Switzerland, it achieved considerable success throughout Europe, more than 1,200 being built by Japan as the Kokusai Type 4 (Ki 86) powered by a 110-HP Hatsukaze for the army and as the Watanabe-Kyushu Type 2 Momiji K9WI for the navy.

1934 May 8   New Zealand aviatrix Jean Batten began her third attempt at a new women's solo flight record between England and Australia when she took off from Lympne, Kent in her two-seat D.H.60M Moth light biplane (G-AARB). Batten arrived in Darwin, Northern Territories on May 23, having flown the England-Australia route in 14 days 22 hr. 30 min., beating Amy Johnson's 1930 record by more than four days.

1934 May 11   The first Douglas DC-2, a stretched production version of the DC-1, powered by two Wright Cyclone SGR-1820-F3 engines made its first flight. It was the first of 24 production models ordered by TWA. With a crew of two and a capacity for 14 passengers, the DC-2 had a wingspan of 85 ft., a length of 62 ft., a loaded weight of 18,560 lb. and a cruising speed of 190 MPH at 8,000 ft. Airline operations began May 18, and it began an 18-hr. Newark-Los Angeles service with one stop at Chicago. The DC-2 swept the Boeing 247 trimotors from the prime routes.

1934 May 25   Set up September 25, 1933, to investigate alleged misuse of public funds in selecting airlines for airmail contracts and in the use of U.S. government funds for subsidizing the routes, a Senate committee chaired by Sen. Hugo L. Black of Alabama reported its conclusions. It found that in the period 1931–33 the postmaster general had paid out $56 million in subsidies to airlines and received $18 million in airmail revenue. Operators' costs were only $20 million, which meant they were making a net profit of $34 million. The expansion of passenger-carrying services had clearly been funded by American taxpayers.

1934 May   Developed progressively from single-seat Fury Monoplane first displayed to the British Air Ministry in October 1933, detailed design work at Hawker's began on what was now called the Interceptor Monoplane. Since January, Sydney Camm's design team had been given permission to use the Rolls Royce P.V.12 engine. Armament was to have comprised two Vickers guns mounted on the fuselage and two Browning guns mounted in the wings, but revisions to match specification F.5/34 issued early in 1934 changed the monoplane to an eight-gun fighter, and tests were conducted with this arrangement at the National Physics Laboratory, Teddington.

1934 June 1   The USAAC made the last airmail flight authorized during the emergency period following cancellation of the Kelly Act on February 9. Just 200 officers and 324 men using 148 combat aircraft and some B-10 bombers struggled to maintain airmail deliveries on 16,000 mi. of routes—down from 27,000 miles normally operated by the private airlines—flying 347 tons of mail over 1.6 million mi. during the emergency. Yet there were problems: Many aircraft crashed, and the emergency high-lighted deficiencies in the USAAC, which prompted greater attention to resources.

1934 June 4   A Savoia Marchetti S.M.73 flew for the first time powered by three 600-HP Gnôme-Rhône Mistral 9Kfr radial engines. Designed as a low-wing monoplane transport aircraft carrying a crew of five and 18 passengers, it began operations with the Belgian airline Sabena in 1935 and resulted in a diverse range of variants and derivatives. A military version, the S.M.81 Pipistrello, could carry an internal bomb load of up to 2,205 lb. and had a wingspan of 78 ft. 9 in. and a length of 57 ft. 3 in. Twelve aircraft of this type were the first from Italy sent to Gen. Franco during the Spanish Civil War, and S.M.81s served throughout Italy's involvement in World War II (June 1940–September 1943).

1934 June 15   In an unfortunate choice of name in light of subsequent events, Lufthansa (the name changed from Luft Hansa earlier in the year) introduced its Blitz service between Berlin, Hamburg, Cologne and Frankfurt using the fast Heinkel He 70 low-wing monoplane transport aircraft. The service opened with He 70D-0 D-UDAS named *Habicht* (Hawk) and was followed by a shared service with Rohrbach Rolands on the Berlin-Vienna-Budapest-Belgrade-Sofia-Salonica route. With its elliptical wing, the He 70 was R. J. Mitchell's aerodynamic reference when he designed the Spitfire.

1934 June 17   Piloted by M. M. Gromov, the *Maxim Gorky*, the only Tupolev ANT-20 made its first flight from Moscow Central Aerodrome. A giant aircraft with a wingspan of 206 ft. 8 in., the ANT-20 had a length of 108 ft. and a maximum take-off weight of 92,593 lb. It was powered by eight 90-HP M-34FRN engines, six in the wing leading edge and two in tandem above the fuselage center-section. Capable of carrying up to 80 people, it was destroyed May 18, 1935, with the loss of all 46 people on board when an I-5 attempted an unauthorized loop around the aircraft's wing and crashed into it. An astonishingly advanced aircraft for its day, 100 technical institutions combined to design the ANT-20.

1934 June 22   Designed for the Dutch airline KLM on its Far East routes, the Fokker F.XXXVI made its first flight. Powered by 750-HP Wright Cyclone SGR-1820-F2s, it was the first four-engine aircraft designed and built by Fokker. It had a wingspan of 108 ft. 3 in., a length of 77 ft. 5 in., a loaded weight of 36,376 lb., a cruising speed of 149 MPH and a range of 838 mi. It accommodated four crew and 32 passengers, or 16 sleepers for overnight flights. Good though it was, the challenge of the DC-2 destroyed its potential market, and only one was built. It was eventually sold to the British firm Scottish Aviation and was scrapped in 1940.

1934 July 16   In Britain, the Ministerial Disarmament Committee announced a plan for expansion of military aviation known as Scheme A, which was expected to make the country ready for war within 5 to 8 years. The scope of this plan would be enlarged on July 18 when the cabinet stated that it could not "delay any longer measures (to) . . . bring our air forces to a level (near) . . . that of our nearest neighbour." Under Scheme A, 41 new RAF squadrons and 820 aircraft would be added within four years, raising home defense strength from 42 to 75 squadrons. The RAF had about 800 aircraft on strength already, with about 550 in England. Under Scheme A, the RAF would have 25 fighter and 39 bomber squadrons.

1934 July 19   At an Air Ministry armament conference in Britain, future fighter needs were discussed by RAF and armament experts from which arose specification F.5/34. This called for a six- or eight-gun fighter with a speed greater than 275 MPH at 15,000 ft., a climb rate of 20,000 ft. in 7.5 min. and an operating ceiling of 33,000 ft. Tests at the Aeroplane and Armament Experimental Establishment showed that a fighter flying at these speeds would need a higher rate of fire than could be satisfactorily achieved with the existing Vickers and Lewis guns.

1934 July 19   Lt. Col. H. H. Arnold commanded a flight of 10 USAAC Martin B-10 twin-engine monoplane bombers on a long-distance formation flight from Bolling Field, Washington, D.C. to Fairbanks, Alaska, arriving after flying time of 25 hr. 30 min.; the return flight took 26 hr. Arnold's aviators completed the 8,000-mi. round-trip survey flight in good condition, demonstrating, as they had intended, the durability of their new aircraft. Arnold later became chief of the USAAC. For the formation distance flight, he was awarded the Mackay Trophy.

1934 July 19   As part of trials aimed at qualifying the airship USS *Macon* and her parasitic escort fighters, Curtiss F9C-2 Sparrowhawks were released to scout for the airship USS *Houston,* which was carrying Pres. Roosevelt back from the Pacific. Without any form of landing gear, the Sparrowhawks were entirely dependent on their parent airship for safe recovery and landing, but the lack of wheels and struts improved performance measurably. The aircraft successfully located the president's airship before returning to the *Macon.*

1934 July 23   The British Air Ministry issued specification B.3/34 calling for a long-range heavy bomber to replace the Hendon and Heyford biplanes, even though these were only just then joining the RAF. The specification called for a bomber capable of carrying a 2,500-lb. bomb load a distance of 1,250 mi. at 15,000 ft. and was issued to Armstrong Whitworth Fairey, Handley Page and Vickers. It resulted in selection of the Vickers (Wellington) and the Armstrong Whitworth (Whitley) designs. Vickers developed a design originally prepared for specification B.9/32 issued in 1932 and produced the world's first bomber utilizing geodetic construction, a metal airframe design using a lattice-work stressed skin frame.

1934 August 29   The Challenge de Tourisme Internationale (International Tourist Challenge) began with a promising entry from Germany, the Messerschmitt Bf 108 (designed as the M 37). The aircraft failed to make better than fifth place, when structural weakness resulted in a crash, it had almost been withdrawn from the contest. The aircraft went on to become highly successful, being used by the Luftwaffe for liaison and communications. After the war, the French produced the same plane as the Nord 1001. The Bf 108 had a wingspan of 33 ft. 10 in. and a length of 26 ft. 5 in. and was powered by a 225-HP Hirth HM 8U engine. It had a loaded weight of 2,981 lb., a top speed of 188 MPH and a range of 621 mi.

1934 September 3   Eager to show off the new all-metal B-10 bombers, Col. Henry H. Arnold left March Field under orders from Gen. MacArthur to take the first squadron from California to New York as quickly as possible in a demonstration of rapid deployment. The squadron departed Bolling Field at 2:30 A.M. for Amarillo, Tex. and refueled there, but a combination of poor gasoline and bad weather forced a detour through Louisiana. Further delays at Atlanta prevented Col. Arnold getting to Mitchel Field within 24 hr., as he had hoped, but total flying time was 18 hr. 10 min.

1934 September 4   Responding to a British Air Ministry specification (F.36/34) for a high-speed, single-seat monoplane fighter,

Hawkers submitted a design tender that would emerge later as the Hurricane but was at this time known as the Interceptor Monoplane. Calculations and tests at the National Physics Laboratory, Teddington, indicated the Interceptor Monoplane would have a top speed of 330 MPH at 15,000 ft. At a mock-up review in Kingston, Surrey on Jan. 10, 1935, engineers explained that the Interceptor would carry eight machine guns in the wings.

1934 September 7   The prototype Hawker Hardy (serial no. K3013) two-seat, general-purpose biplane made its first flight. It was two years before production commenced, but the RAF received 47 of this type and used them in the Middle East (No. 6 Squadron flew Hardys in the Palestine rebellion and No. 30 Squadron operated them in Iraq), and as a patrol aircraft on the border between Kenya and Somaliland in 1940. Essentially similar to the Audax, the Hardy had a loaded weight of 5,005 lb., mounting a fixed forward-firing Vickers gun, an aft-facing Lewis and two 112-lb. supply panniers for small bombs. Some were even used for dive-bombing.

1934 September 8   The de Havilland D.H.88 Comet twin-engine monoplane racer made its first flight. One of three ordered initially, G-ACSP had been built for record-breakers Jim and Amy Mollison. Of wooden stressed skin construction, the Comet had a wingspan of 44 ft. and a length of 29 ft.; two 230-HP Gipsy Six R engines provided a top speed of 237 MPH, cruising speed of 220 MPH and a range of 2,925 mi. Only five Comets were ever built, three for racing, one for the French government as mail aircraft and one as a record-breaker used by Tom Campbell Black and J. C. McArthur in their attempt to set a new Hatfield-Cairo record, which they did, covering 2,240 mi. in 11 hr. 8 min. on August 8, 1935.

1934 September 12   An important link between the British single- or twin-gun biplane fighters of the first half of the decade and the eight-gun monoplane fighters that would enter service from the end of 1937 was the Gloster Gladiator, the prototype of which made its first flight. With four Browning guns, two in the wing and two in the fuselage, the rugged Gloster S.S.37 biplane had a wingspan of 32 ft. 3 in., a length of 27 ft. 5 in. and a top speed of 253 MPH. It entered service with the RAF in February 1937. Though replaced by Hurricanes and Spitfires by 1940, a few flew with great distinction in Norway, Malta and Africa.

1934 September 12   The prototype Hawker Hind (serial no. K2915), latest in the wide range of designs from the Hawker drawing boards, made its first flight. Essentially a Hart with a cut-down rear gunner's cockpit and an aft-firing Lewis in addition to the forward-firing Vickers gun, the Hind was a two-seat light bomber similar to its predecessor but with a maximum loaded weight of 5,298 lb. (versus 4,554 lb.) and a tail wheel instead of a skid; it was the only Hart or derivative to have a wheel at that position. The Hind began to replace Harts in the RAF from December 1935 and served for about three years before themselves being superseded by the Battle, Hampden and Blenheim monoplane bombers.

1934 September 22   A novel attempt to fly nonstop from England to India in a small Airspeed A.S.5 Courier single-engine monoplane, refueled en route, ended in a near-disaster when the pilot, Sir Alan Cobham, had to make a forced landing at Halfar, Malta. Cobham took off from Portsmouth Airport at 5:30 A.M., and met up with a Handley Page W.10 over Selsey Bill, southern England before proceeding to a second rendezvous over Malta, which it reached at 4:15 P.M. Unable to take on extra fuel when a broken throttle connection prevented a synchronization of speed

Winner of the 1934 race between Mildenhall, England and Melbourne, Australia: the D.H.86 Comet racer.

with the refueling airplane, Cobham, with Sqdn. Ldr. Helmore on board, headed for Halfar, only just making it down as the engine progressively deteriorated.

1934 September 26 The Boeing board gave formal approval to proceed with the Model 299, a four-engine bomber concept responding to an Army Air Corps requirement for a multi-engine bomber capable of carrying a 2-ton bomb load and possessing a range of 1,000 mi. Although the design team was headed by Boeing president Claire Egtvedt, Edward C. Wells, an assistant project engineer, was largely responsible for what would emerge as the B-17. Of conventional semimonocoque construction, the bomber would have a crew of up to eight, including four gunners manning five enclosed defensive machine gun positions (nose, dorsal, ventral and two waist).

1934 September Two representatives of the British Air Ministry, C. H. Keith and Maj. H. S. V. Thompson, visited the United States to negotiate a licensing agreement by which the Colt Automatic Weapon Corp's Browning machine gun could be manufactured in Britain. Several modifications were necessary, including changing the caliber from U.S. 0.30-in. to the British 0.303-in. It was arranged that the Birmingham Small Arms Co. would manufacture the gun, providing the RAF with a modern replacement for the Vickers and Lewis guns and one that would be suitable for the eight-gun fighter defined by an RAF specification (F.37/34), to emerge on the Hurricane and the Spitfire.

1934 October 1 An amendment to the U.S. Air Commerce Act prohibited the use of single-engine aircraft by airlines operating at night or over terrain where suitable emergency landing sites were not available. This severely limited the market for the single-engine Northrop Delta and helped stimulate orders for aircraft like the Boeing 247, the Lockheed Electra and the DC-2. The Delta was relegated to the executive market, which, although small, was clearly here to stay.

1934 October 7 One of the most important Soviet bombers of World War II, the Tupolev ANT-40 stressed-skin monoplane, made its first flight powered by two water-cooled Hispano-Suiza engines. With a wingspan of 62 ft. 4 in. and a length of 66 ft. 8 in., production ANT-40s known as the SB-2 had a pair of 730-HP Wright Cyclone SGR-1820-FF2 engines providing a top speed of about 250 MPH and a range of between 350 mi. and 780 mi. depending on the variant. More than 6,600 SB bombers had been built when production ended in early 1941, and the type saw service in Spain, Mongolia, Finland and the Far East.

1934 October 11 Vought received a U.S. Navy order for the XSB2U-1 torpedo bomber, the first all-metal low-wing monoplane for the navy of its type. With a Pratt & Whitney radial engine and crew of two housed in a cockpit covered by a single glasshouse canopy, the Vindicator was a rugged design. However, in case the monoplane proved too radical, the navy also ordered the XSB3U-1 biplane from Vought on February 7, 1935. The SB2U-1 had a wingspan of 33 ft. 3 in., a length of 28 ft. 2 in. and power from a single 700/750-HP Pratt & Whitney R-1535-82 with main wheels that retracted backward into the lower wingroot. In tests during 1936, the monoplane proved superior, and it was ordered as the SB2U-1 in October 1936.

1934 October 20 The MacRobertson England-Australia air race began with three D.H.88 Comet racers, flown by Jim and Amy Mollison, Owen Cathcart-Jones and Ken Waller and C. W. A. Scott and Tom Campbell Black, getting off the ground from Mildenhall, Suffolk with 12 other contenders. These included a commercial DC-2 from the Dutch airline KLM carrying passengers and a Boeing 247D. The red-painted Comet with white letters G-ACSS and the name *Grosvenor House* inscribed on the side was first to reach Australia, Scott and Campbell Black landing at Flemington Race Course, Melbourne, 11,333 mi. from Mildenhall after 70 hr. 54 min. 18 sec. The KLM DC-2 came in second shortly thereafter.

1934 October 22   Charles Kingsford Smith and Capt. P. G. Taylor flew their Lockheed Altair 8D from Australia across the Pacific to the United States, the first to make the eastbound crossing. Their Altair (serial no. VH-USB) had been constructed as a Sirius 8A; bought from Victor Fleming, it was refitted with a retractable landing gear. Named *Lady Southern Cross,* it made a nonstop flight from Suva to Honolulu, a distance of 3,197 mi. in 25 hr. 5 min. en route to Oakland, Calif. Registered G-ADUS, the Altair 8D was later lost, along with Sir Charles and Tommy Pethybridge during a flight across the Andaman Sea between India and Burma (now Myanmar).

1934 October 23   The Italian pilot Francesco Agello established an FAI-ratified speed record for piston-engine seaplanes of 440.683 MPH (which still stands today), at that time an absolute world air speed record. Designed and built for the Schneider Trophy race, the Macchi M.C.72 was a mixed wood and metal low-wing monoplane with a wingspan of 31 ft. 1 in., a length of 27 ft. 3 in. and power provided by two coupled 1,500-HP 12-cylinder piston engines (50,000 cc) set one behind the other in the forward fuselage driving two, twin-bladed, metal, contra-rotating propellers on the same shaft.

1934 November 4   The first Junkers Ju 86 made its first flight before entering service with Lufthansa. Designed as a bomber also capable of being used as a freight- and passenger-carrying twin-engine monoplane powered by the 600-HP Jumo 205C, it had a wingspan of 73 ft. 10 in. and a length of 57 ft. 2 in. Though not a great success as a commercial aircraft, at least 25 were operated as military aircraft while occupying the civil register prior to the official acknowledgement of the Luftwaffe. The Ju 86 carried two crew and 10 passengers and had a range of 683 mi. at 224 MPH. From 1936 it was delivered to the Luftwaffe as a bomber capable of carrying a warload of up to 2,000 lb.; about 1,000 were eventually built.

1934 December 1   The British Air Ministry issued Supermarine a contract valued at £10,000 for the construction of a prototype Type 300 four-gun fighter. Designed by R. J. Mitchell's team, it had been refined from the Type 224 flown in February 1934 in response to specification F.7/30 of October 1931. Initially projected to have a 660-HP Rolls Royce Goshawk, the Type 300 was finally designed to have the Rolls Royce P.V.12, later called Merlin, and to carry an elliptical wing of NACA 2200 section, with a thickness ratio of 13% at the chord and 6% at the tip. Designer Beverley Shenstone corresponded with Ernst Heinkel to explore ways of copying the smooth surface of the He 70 onto the Type 300.

1934 December 20   In London, Parliament approved the scheme put forward by Imperial Airways whereby Imperial Airways would carry airmail at a fixed rate for first-class service anywhere in the British Empire with the exception of Canada and the West Indies. To facilitate this service and carry passengers too, Short Brothers were commissioned to build the S.23 Empire flying boat. During 1935 a contract was signed for a composite combination of a modified four-engined Empire flying boat named Maia and a four-engined seaplane named Mercury carried on its upper fuselage. The so-called Short-Mayo Composite would, it was hoped, provide the range for the smaller seaplane to reach America with a full load of mail after being lifted to altitude by the flying boat.

1934 December 25   French aviator Raymond Delmotte became the first man to officially fly faster than 500 km/hr. when he piloted his Caudron C.460 to an FAI record 505.848 km/hr.

(314.32 MPH) at Istres, France. The C.460 had a wingspan of 22 ft. 2 in., a length of 23 ft. 4 in., a wing area of 74.27 sq. ft. and a weight of 1,709 lb. Powered by a 370-HP Renault engine, the Caudron C.460 was a C.450 with retractable landing gear, which was itself a successor to the 360-series racing airplanes. The C.450/460 was developed beginning January 1932 when the Caudron brothers retained the services of technical director Marcel Riffard, joined later by the equally brilliant young engineer Georges Otfinovsky.

1934 December 31   A major step toward the development of the USAAC as an independently administered service was made when the War Department gave authorization for the formation of the general headquarters of the air corps at Langley Field in Hampton, Va. The three tactical wings of the new organization were based at Langley, March Field in Riverside, Calif. and Barksdale Field in Bossier City, La. Brig. Gen. Frank M. Andrews was appointed to command the headquarters and also became a member of the general staff, an appointment that greatly increased the army air corps' influence at U.S. military planning level. The new establishment was to become effective from March 1, 1935.

1935 January 1   Based on success with the Rhineland Program begun January 1, 1934, Erhard Milch announced a revised Luftwaffe expansion plan that envisaged the production of a total 9,853 new military aircraft between January 1, 1934, and September 30, 1936, and an extra 5,832 aircraft for the 12 months beginning October 1, 1935, added to the existing Rhineland Program scheduled to end September 30, 1935. The majority of aircraft were bombers and attack planes, reflecting prevailing defense doctrine that emphasized assault at the expense of conventional defense against an aggressive enemy.

1935 January 7   The Tachikawa Ki-9 biplane trainer made its first flight, powered by a 350-HP Hitachi Ha-13a radial engine. The aircraft was accepted by the Japanese army, and the type remained in service until the defeat of Japanese forces in 1945. After the war, the Ki-9 soldiered on under the flag of the Indonesian People's Security Forces. With a wingspan of 33 ft. 10 in., a fuselage length of 24 ft. 8 in. and a loaded weight of 3,142 lb., the Ki-9 remained in production for 10 yr., more than 2,600 being produced by the end of World War II.

1935 January 11   Amelia Earhart became the first woman pilot to fly solo between Hawaii and the United States. She took off from Wheeler Field, Oahu, Honolulu, in driving rain to fly her Lockheed Vega across the eastern Pacific to Oakland, Calif. The aircraft had 500 gal. of fuel, a two-way radio, a rubber raft in the event of ditching and several items of emergency equipment. Flying through a clear night and into a gathering dawn, Earhart landed after 18 hr. 15 min. to the cheers of 10,000 people who thronged the airfield.

1935 January 17   The large, Latécoère 521, trans-Atlantic flying boat made its first flight from Biscarosse, France. With a wingspan of 161 ft. 9 in. and a length of 103 ft. 9 in., it was powered by six 800/860-HP Hispano-Suiza 12Ybrs engines. With an operating weight of 81,571 lb. when carrying 30 passengers on the Atlantic route, the 521 had an operating weight of 92,595 lb. and capacity for 70 passengers on shorter Mediterranean routes. Capturing several distance, speed and load records in 1937, the 521 made several flights to America, as did a second aircraft, the 522. Three armed versions were ordered by the French Navy. Two were sunk and the third withdrawn in 1942.

1935 January 22   Set up by the U.S. Air Mail Act of 1934, the Federal Aviation Commission, which came into being July 11, 1934, under the chairmanship of Clark Howell, submitted its first report encouraging a sympathetic government oversight to stimulate competition in the aviation industry and to set standards by which it could expand. Pres. Roosevelt disagreed and tried to enact legislation for greater controls and regulations. During the year, the House of Representatives passed legislation giving airlines three-year airmail contracts rather than the existing annual agreements. This helped provide stability without controlling civil operations unduly.

1935 January 28   The Tizard Committee (Committee for Scientific Survey of Air Defense), including physicists A. V. Hill and P. M. S. Blackett in addition to H. E Wimperis, director of scientific research at the Air Ministry, met to discuss Britain's air defenses. They learned from Wimperis that A. F. Wilkins, assistant to the famous scientist Ronald Watson-Watt, had carried out experiments proving the implausibility of using intensive radio transmissions to disable aircraft in the air, citing the extraordinary power levels necessary for such beam weapons.

1935 February 3   The death of the German aircraft designer Prof. Hugo Junkers was announced, 25 years after his first patent was issued for a flying-wing design. Junkers had helped transform aircraft technology, first with the pioneering influence of his all-metal transport aircraft and then by the impact his Ju 52/3m would have on aviation in the 1930s and throughout World War II. From the rugged Ju 87 dive-bomber to the massive six-engine Ju 290 built in 1936, Junkers aircraft remained at the forefront of German aviation from 1915, when the J 1 made its first flight, to 1945.

1935 February 4   Designed to the 9-Shi fighter specification issued by the Japanese navy in February 1934, the Mitsubishi A5M, powered by a 550-HP Nakajima Kotobuki 5 radial engine, made its first flight at Kagamigahara, Japan. The army was also interested and ordered prototypes, which stimulated a competition ultimately won by Nakajima with their Ki-27. The navy achieved great success with their A5M models (nicknamed Claude by the Allies), particularly in the Sino-Japanese conflict that flared again during 1937. The A5M had a wingspan of 36 ft. 1 in., a length of 25 ft. 4 in. and a single radial engine of various types and power between 550 HP and 710 HP.

1935 February 12   The giant American airship *Macon* was destroyed when a violent gust of wind struck her off Point Spur on the way to Sunnyvale, Calif. at the end of an exercise. The airship was driven up to a height of 4,850 ft. and at 5:39 P.M. plunged into the sea, killing 2 out of 83 crewmembers on board. The *Macon* had made 54 flights totaling just over 1,798 hr. With her went all hopes for large U.S. patrol airships and the parasite concept of shepherded aircraft retained in on-board hangars and deployed through a trapeze system. It was an end foreseen when *Macon*'s sister ship, *Akron*, had been lost on April 3, 1933.

1935 February 24   The prototype Heinkel He 111a made its first flight from Marienehe at the hands of Flugkapitän (Flight Captain) Gerhard Nitschke. Powered by two 660-HP BMW VI 6,0Z engines, it derived from a specification for a medium bomber issued through clandestine instructions in 1934. Designed by Siegfried and Walter Günter officially as a transport aircraft, the He 111a (later V1) had an elliptical wing with a precise span of 82 ft. 0.75 in., modified in later aircraft (for instance 74 ft. 1.75 in. on the first production bomber version capable of carrying

2,200 lb). The commercial airliner version was rolled out March 12, the bomb bay becoming a passenger smoking compartment!

1935 February 26   By special decree, effective March 1, 1935, Adolf Hitler separated the German Air Force from the Reichsheer (the army) and the Reichsmarine (the navy), creating an independent force of the Reichsluftwaffe, which soon became known formally as the Luftwaffe. Total strength comprised 20 aircraft squadrons (land- and sea-based) and 20 training stations, the auxiliary bombing units under the aegis of Lufthansa and the emergency units under the Air Ministry (Reichsluftfahrtministerium, or RLM). The 16 front-line squadrons included five bomber, three fighter, five reconnaissance and three naval. By August 1, 1935, the total had grown to 48 front-line squadrons. March 1 was declared Air Day.

1935 February 26   Following the January 28 meeting of the Tizard Committee, RAF Sqdn. Ldr. R. S. Blucke, commander of the Wireless and Electrical Flight, Farnborough, flew a Handley Page Heyford bomber across a special test range at Daventry where short-wave radio transmitters had been set up. Dr. A. P. Rowe, Ronald Watson-Watt and A. F. Wilkins observed a cathode ray tube on the ground and saw an oscillograph of the aircraft as it flew over, with clear rise and fall sine curves as the Heyford approached and then receded. This crucial test had been set up when the Tizard Committee met with Air Marshal Philip Joubert de la Ferté on February 21 at RAF Uxbridge. It proved that radio waves could detect and track aircraft in the air.

1935 February   Under the command of Lt. Col. Ralph Royce, a team of Army Air Corps personnel conducted cold temperature flying tests using 17 different types of aircraft. The trials took place from Michigan to Montana and developed and evaluated new procedures for all aspects of winter operations. The trial aircraft were equipped with a combination of wheel and ski main landing gear to assess their effectiveness on snow. During the test period, operations were interrupted twice to fly emergency mercy missions to save the lives of civilians in danger from the extreme cold.

1935 March 9   Typical of the entrepreneurial spirit very much alive outside the club of ever stronger major airline operators, the tiny British company Crilly Airways Ltd. was formed with capital of only £12,000. Two days later it began flights between Doncaster and Croydon with a D.H.84 Dragon and from April 2 twice-daily Leicester-Bristol and Leicester-Norwich services. From May 18, a Nottingham-Leicester-Northampton service was offered three times daily, and during June and July, flights converged on the seaside holiday resort of Skegness from Nottingham and Leicester twice daily, bringing holidaymakers from the industrial midlands.

1935 March 14   The German Luftwaffe began a series of evocative name dedications for flying squadrons and groups, reinvigorating nationalistic fervor and reviving nostalgia for the air war of 1914–18. The first dedication was to 132 Fighter Squadron at Döberitz-Damm, which became Jagdgeschwader Richthofen Nr. 2 (Richthofen Fighter Group No. 2). During April, Bomber Group I./154 became Geschwader Boelcke and an offshoot of J.G.2 became Geschwader Immelmann. With such assertive messages of German militarism, applicants flooded to the new Luftwaffe to accommodate the anticipated expansion.

1935 March 15   The Dornier Do 18, a replacement for the supremely successful Wal flying boat, made its first flight, carrying the registration D-AHIS and the name *Monsun*. The all-metal structure supported a wing spanning 77 ft. 9 in. on a braced pylon above the 63 ft. 2 in. fuselage. Power was provided by two 540-HP Junkers Jumo 5 diesel engines placed in tandem within a common enclosure on top of the wing center-section, driving pusher and tractor propellers respectively. Just over 100 Do 18s were built, and though production ended in 1939, the type served extensively with the Luftwaffe.

1935 March 18 Resembling the increasingly lauded Douglas DC-2, the Fiat G.18 made its first flight. Designed by Guiseppe Gabrielli, the twin-engine, low-wing monoplane began its service life with Avio Linee Italiane in 1936, and nine aircraft of this type were eventually built. With a wingspan of 82 ft. and a length of 61 ft. 8.5 in., the G.18 accommodated a crew of three and 18 passengers. It was powered by two 700-HP Fiat A.59R 9-cylinder radial engines and had a cruising speed of 211 MPH, a ceiling of 26,902 ft. and a maximum range of 1,025 mi.

1935 March 23 The cargo ship *North Haven* departed San Francisco carrying equipment for five air bases and two villages as well as 74 construction staff, 44 Pan American airline personnel, 250,000 gal. of aviation fuel, power supplies, windmills, motor launches, storage dewars, generators, sheds, tools, and supplies. Over several months, engineers would construct flying boat bases at Midway, Wake Island and Guam ready for the through-route from San Francisco to Manila, the Philippines, island-hopping all the way, before the end of the year. Existing bases at Honolulu and Manila were consolidated for the expanded air traffic.

1935 March 24 The prototype Avro 652A (serial no. K4471) Anson made its first flight at Woodford in England. Designed as a coastal patrol landplane and based on the Avro 652 four-passenger aircraft (which was ordered by Imperial Airways and flown for the first time January 7), the Anson was powered by two 295-HP Armstrong Siddeley Cheetah VI radials. Inspired by success with twin-engine monoplanes in America, the Anson had a wingspan of 56 ft. 6 in., a length of 42 ft. 3 in., a cruising speed of 158 MPH and a range of 660 mi. When it entered service with No. 48 Squadron on March 6, 1936, it was the first RAF monoplane to have retractable landing gear, albeit cranked up and down by hand. Ansons were used by the USAAC and the RCAF. The RAF finally retired its last Anson after a flypast on June 28, 1968.

1935 March 28 Ordered by the U.S. Navy on October 28, 1933, the Consolidated XP3Y-1 flying boat made its first flight, and on June 29, an order for 60 PBY-1s was placed. This shifted the aircraft from a patrol to a patrol-bomber category. The XPBY-1 made its first flight on May 19, 1936, with add-on contracts for 116 PBY-2 and PBY-3 versions that year and for the first 33 PBY-4s in December 1937. The type quickly became established, 14 U.S. Navy squadrons being equipped with the aircraft by 1938. The PBY series capitalized on Consolidated's experience with flying boats to good effect.

1935 April 3 Spin research and stability problems were tackled directly by NACA when it inaugurated operational use of the new 15-foot spin tunnel at Langley Memorial Aeronautical Laboratory, Langley, Va. With a 15-ft. open-throat test section, the facility was driven by 150-HP electric motor, providing a simulated maximum speed of 40 MPH but variable to the rate of the falling airplane model. A clockwork motor would set controls in the model to achieve automatic spin recovery. During World War II, every military aircraft design was tested in the facility.

1935 April 12 The Bristol Type 142 twin-engine, low-wing monoplane made its first flight at Filton, England. Designed as a fast light transport aircraft, newspaper proprietor Lord Rothermere ordered the type built for his personal use to counter, he said, claims about the superiority of the DC-1 and show the Air Ministry that a light transport aircraft could be adapted as a faster bomber than contemporary fighters such as the Gloster Gladiator, thus stimulating British air expansion. Called Britain First, the Type 142 had a wingspan of 56 ft. 4 in., a length of 39 ft. 9 in. and power provided by two 650-HP Bristol Mercury VIS 2 radials. It led directly to the Bristol Blenheim

1935 April 13 The first England-Australia passenger service was inaugurated by Imperial Airways and QANTAS between London and Brisbane. The first flight on the round-trip service from Brisbane took place on April 17. A single fare for the 12,754-mi. route cost £195, but the first through passengers were not carried on the route until April 20 due to heavy booking on the 48 individual stages. The entire journey took the first two through-passengers twelve-and-a-half days to complete.

1935 April 15 Ordered on June 30, 1934, the first of two contenders for a U.S. torpedo-bomber development contract made its first flight when the Douglas XTBD-1 monoplane took to the air powered by a single 800-HP Pratt & Whitney XR-1830-60 radial engine. Its competitor, the Great Lakes XTBG-1 biplane, was delivered to the navy on August 20, 1935, but its performance was inferior to the Douglas, which entered service as the TBD-1 Devastator in October 1937 as the U.S. Navy's first all-metal monoplane aircraft, powered by a 900-HP R-1830-64. With a wingspan of 50 ft. and a length of 35 ft., the TBD-1 carried one fixed and one flexible 0.30-in. machine gun and the option of a 1,000 lb. torpedo. The type was withdrawn during 1942.

1935 April 16 A Pan American Airways Sikorsky S.42 flying boat took off from Alameda, Calif. on the first leg of a route survey flight to Honolulu that took 18 hr. 37 min. Meticulous care was taken to plot each planned passenger route with care and safety. Stripped of seats and modified for a range of almost 3,000 mi., the S.42 had conducted a nonstop survey flight between Miami and the Virgin Islands and back on March 23. It took off for the Honolulu-Midway stage on June 12, and between August 9 and October 5, it surveyed the Midway-Wake-Guam stages.

1935 April 26 Operational requirements (British Air Ministry) chief, Sqdn. Ldr. Ralph Sorley, visited the Supermarine works to revive progress on the Type 300 four-gun fighter defined by specification F.37/34 issued January 3. He recommended that the Type 300 be included among the contenders for an eight-gun day-and-night fighter defined earlier in April by Air Ministry specification F.10/35. From this date forward, the Type 300 would be designed for that role but known as the Supermarine F.37/34 fighter. Sorley also advised Air Marshal Sir Hugh Dowding that both the new Supermarine and Hawker fighters be ordered into production "off the drawing board" and before the first flight.

1935 April Designed from the DC-2 to a military specification calling for a bomber capable of carrying a 2,000-lb. bomb load 1,020 mi. at 200 MPH, the Douglas DB-1, powered by two 850-HP Wright R-1820-G5 radial engines, was completed prior to flight trials at Wright Field beginning August. It competed against the Boeing 299 and the Martin 146 but was selected for production in January 1936 due largely to the unit price of $58,500 compared with $99,620 for each Boeing 299. Designated B-18, 350 were built of this and the B-18A version, each of which had a wingspan of 89 ft. 6 in., a length of 57 ft. 10 in., a maximum weight of 27,673 lb. and a maximum 4,000-lb. bomb capacity. The two models were superseded in 1942 and 1943 by B-17s.

1935 April   The prototype of the purely civil version of the Junkers Ju 86 made its first flight, powered by Junkers Jumo 205C diesel engines. Designated Ju 86b, and later Ju 86B in the production model, it was a contemporary of the Heinkel He 111; but unlike that aircraft, distinct military and civil versions were designed. The Ju 86 was designed with full cooperation between Lufthansa and the German Air Ministry. During 1936, Lufthansa put it into service, and the Swiss operated one, adding a second in 1937. Orders from South Africa followed, and Australia operated one for a brief period.

1935 May 8   The prototype Henschel Hs 123 dive-bomber designed to a specification drawn up by Ernst Udet in 1933 made its first public appearance. Former W.W.I. ace Udet had been drawn into the new Luftwaffe and regarded himself as chief test pilot. In competition with the Fieseler Fi 98a, the Hs 123 proved superior, although rigorous flight testing at Rechlin tore the upper wings from two of the three prototypes. Strengthened, the type entered service with the Luftwaffe later this year. Powered by an 880-HP BMW 132Dc radial, the HS 123A-1—which took part in blitzkrieg attacks on Poland, France and the Low Countries in 1939 and 1940—had a wingspan of 34 ft. 5 in., a length of 27 ft. 4 in., a top speed of 212 MPH and a range of 534 mi.

1935 May 15   Designed by Donovan A. Berlin, the prototype Curtiss P-36, the Model 75, made its first flight just 12 days before the army air corps competition for a successor to the Boeing P-26. With a wingspan of 37 ft. and a length of 28 ft. 3.5 in., it was powered by a 900-HP Wright XR-1670-5 or 700-HP Pratt & Whitney R.1535 and had a top speed of 281 MPH, almost 50 MPH faster than the Boeing. Designed as a metal monoplane with retractable landing gear and enclosed cockpit, it served along with Seversky P-35 as a stopgap until the later generation of high-performance monoplane fighters epitomized by the P-40 came into use five years later.

1935 May 21   Assertions by senior Nazi officials that Germany already possessed equivalent air power to Britain forced a stepping up of expansion schedules. Scheme C, which replaced the Scheme A formulated in July 1934 (an interim scheme had been rejected by the cabinet), anticipated a total 150 RAF squadrons, of which 123 would be based at home, including 35 fighter and 68 bomber squadrons. The expansion, to be completed by the end of March 1939, was to have provided the RAF with 1,804 aircraft by that date.

1935 May 28   The most famous German fighter of all time—the Messerschmitt Bf 109—made its first flight from Augsburg at the hands of Flugkapitän Hans Dietrich Knötsch. Designed as an all-metal, low-wing, stressed-skin monoplane, it flew for the first time with a 640/695-HP Rolls Royce Kestrel 12-cylinder V engine. (Production models were capable of accepting either the Junkers Jumo 210 or the Daimler Benz DB 600 engine.) Inspected by veteran pilot Ernst Udet, who said it would "never make a fighter," the Bf 109a (later redesignated V1) was entered in military trials at Travemünde in October.

1935 June 4   From a small British manufacturer came the Armstrong Whitworth A.W.23 bomber-transport, which made its first flight after assembly at the Coventry works. Designed to specification C.26/31 for an aircraft capable of carrying troops or bombs (the RAF had been looking for a replacement for the Victoria

since 1932 and had settled for its derivative the Valentia), it competed for production orders against the Handley Page H.P.51 and the Bristol Type 130 Bombay. The A.W.23 had a light-alloy main-wing spar for lightness covered with metal sheet back to the rear of the spar, the rest of the wing being fabric. This design was used successfully on the Whitley bomber of 1936.

1935 June 19   The first Vickers Wellesley took to the air as the G.4/31 monoplane flown by test pilot Mut Summers; a parallel biplane design had first flown on August 16, 1934, but was subsequently canceled when a production order for the monoplane was issued September 10, 1935; eventually 176 were built. Barnes Wallis designed geodetic construction for the Wellesley, which had a wingspan of 74 ft. 7 in. and a length of 39 ft. 3 in. Powered by one 925-HP Bristol Pegasus XX, the two-seat general purpose bomber had a bomb load of 2,000 lb., two defensive gun positions, a cruising speed of 188 MPH and a range of 1,160 mi. It joined the RAF in April 1937.

1935 June 23   The Bristol Type 130 bomber-transport, later named Bombay, made its first flight from Filton, near Bristol. Designed to specification C.26/31, it had a wingspan of 96 ft. and a length of 67 ft. 9 in., and power was provided by two 750-HP Bristol Pegasus IIIM3 engines. Production aircraft had two Bristol Pegasus XXIIs that provided a cruising speed of 160 MPH at 10,000 ft. and a range of 2,230 mi. Exceptionally late into service, the first Bombay reached the RAF in 1939. Only 50 were built, but the type saw widespread use as a casualty evacuation aircraft in North Africa and Italy during World War II.

1935 June 26   The French engineer and former army pilot Maurice Claisse flew the Breguet-Dorand gyroplane for the first time and achieved forward speeds of 18 to 30 MPH. Designed by Louis Breguet and René Dorand, the Gyroplane Laboratoire was the first flight-proven product of the Syndicat d'Études du Gyroplane formed by the two men in 1931. It was powered by a Hispano-Suiza engine driving two co-axial, contra-rotating rotors attached to a body adapted from a Breguet 19 fuselage. It introduced cyclic pitch for lateral movement and collective pitch for vertical motion. Ahead of its day, it achieved a sustained flight of 1 hr. 2 min. 45 sec. in 1936.

1935 June   Air headquarters (Koku Hombu) of the Imperial Japanese Army, which was responsible for the design and development of Japanese army aircraft ordered three aircraft manufacturers to design two prototypes each of an advanced fighter. All three prototypes, from Kawasaki, Mitsubishi and Nakajima, emerged as low-wing monoplanes characteristic of designs appearing in Europe and the United States. Mitsubishi entered a derivative of their A5M, then under way for the navy, and Kawasaki produced the Ki-28 and Nakajima the successful Ki-27. These designs represented the creditable levels of aircraft design achieved by Japanese engineers.

1935 July 1   Intrepid US aviators brothers Fred and Algene Key landed their Curtiss Robin high-wing monoplane after remaining airborne continuously for 633 hr. 34 min., having made 107 aerial refuelings in the 26 days beginning June 4. A specially fitted platform around the aircraft facilitated in-flight maintainence, and food, fuel and sundry supplies were transferred to the aircraft from a second Robin via a specially installed upper hatch. The aircraft survived severe turbulence, an on-board fire and several major malfunctions. Al Key performed a minor operation on himself to remove an abscess from his mouth on radio instructions from the ground.

1935 July 7 The enterprising Crilly Airways Ltd. began a Sunday service linking Norwich, Ipswich, Southend and Ramsgate with a twice daily Leicester-Liverpool run from August 1. Beginning October 1, Crilly began Leicester-Norwich-Croydon, Leicester-Bristol and Leicester-Croydon services using one D.H.84 Dragon and three Monospar S.T.25s. On February 1, 1936, Crilly undertook a survey flight from London to Lisbon using a Fokker F.XII, with a night stop at Madrid. A return flight via Madrid and Bordeaux was made February 4, but the Spanish denied overflight rights for scheduled services. A Bristol-Bournemouth service began during July 1936, but the company was liquidated September 9, 1936.

1935 July 9 The USAAC allocated the designation XBLR-2 to a giant Douglas bomber concept, a single example of which (XB-19) was ordered September 29, 1936. (A similar design for Sikorsky's XBLR-3 was rejected.) The XB-19 first flew on June 27, 1941, powered by four 2,000-HP Wright R-3350-5 radials providing a cruising speed of 135 MPH and a range of 7,300 mi. carrying a 6,000-lb. bomb load. Supplemented by external bomb racks, the internal load of 18,700 lb. could be increased to a total bomb load of 37,100 lb. for short flights. With a gross weight of 140,000 lb. and 10,350 gal. of fuel, the XB-19 had a crew of 11 to 18 men and 12 machine guns in 10 positions. Used to evaluate technical problems with large bombers, the XB-19 stimulated consideration of a truly intercontinental bomber resulting in the B-36.

1935 July 10 The Bell Aircraft Corp. was founded by ex-Consolidated personnel Lawrence D. Bell, Raymond P. Whitman and designer Robert (Bob) J. Woods with start-up capital of $500,000. The men set up their own company and took over Consolidated's facilities when their old company relocated from Buffalo, N.Y. to California. The work force was offered the opportunity to stay on with the new owners. Bell had begun working for Glenn Martin in 1925 at the age of 17 and joined Consolidated in 1928 as sales director before rising to vice president. Consolidated contracted with Bell for subassemblies on the PBY.

1935 July 11 The Imperial Japanese Army Air Headquarters (Koku Hombu) authorized design and development of a high-speed reconnaissance aircraft, which would emerge from Mitsubishi as the Ki-15 low-wing monoplane powered by a 550/750-HP Nakajima Ha-8 radial engine. With a top speed of 298 MPH at 13,125 ft., the aircraft first flew in May 1936 and entered service the following year. By June 1938, the Ki-15-II had emerged, powered by a 900-HP Army Type 1 14-cylinder radial providing a top speed of 317 MPH at 14,205 ft. The type was worked to good effect in the Sino-Japanese conflict of 1937 and a further version, the Ki-15-III, had a top speed of 329 MPH.

1935 July 22 Air Marshal Sir Hugh Dowding, air member for research and development on the Air Council, presented a report to the British Air Defence Research Committee about the practical applications of "radio direction finding." Dowding was keen on the idea of using radar for detecting aircraft at long range, thereby providing an interval of warning time in which defensive fighters could be scrambled before bombers reached their targets and dropped their bombs. This was an important step in the development of a chain of radar stations around the eastern and southern coast of Britain, which would be pivotal during the Battle of Britain in 1940.

1935 July 24 Development in Britain of radio direction finding (RDF) took a step nearer fruition when three Hawker Harts from the RAF tested the Orfordness radio range by creating a reflected

Designated as the XLBR-2, the Douglas XB-19 was the last of the U.S. long-range bomber concepts.

image displayed on an oscilloscope at a distance of 20 mi. from the transmitter when they split up to fly in separate directions. The Harts had been flying at 7,000 ft. and were detected with an error of just over 1,000 ft. in height.

1935 July 28 Chief Boeing test pilot Leslie Tower piloted the prototype Model 299 bomber on its first flight, 11 days after the plane was rolled out. Powered by four 750-HP Pratt & Whitney R-1690E Hornet radial engines—a novel concept at the time—it had a length of 68 ft. 9 in. and a wingspan of 103 ft. 9 in. The Model 299 had been built in competition with the Douglas DB-1 and the Martin 146, which was little more than an overgrown B-10. When the Model 299 flew 2,100 mi. from Seattle to Wright Field on August 20 in just 9 hr. 3 min. at an average speed of 233 MPH, it all but clinched a production order for what was, in 1935, a novel concept with its four engines. Unfortunately, a fatal crash on October 30 knocked it out of the running.

1935 July 30 Lt. Frank Akers, U.S. Navy, carried out the first blind landing aboard an aircraft carrier when he flew his OJ-2 equipped only with standard instruments from the San Diego Naval Air Station to the USS *Langley* and landed safely on the flight deck. He was not made aware of the carrier's location but successfully snagged the no. 4 arrester wire as he flew his aircraft in, unable to see the flight deck due to a special hood that had been fixed across the cockpit precluding vision outside. For this remarkable feat, Lt. Akers was later awarded the Distinguished Flying Cross.

1935 July Precursor to the G3M Nell, the Mitsubishi Ka-15 made its first flight as a medium bomber for long-range, land-based naval attack duties. It was powered by two 600/750-HP Hiro Type 91 12-cylinder engines with a wingspan of 82 ft. and a length of 54 ft. and entered service as the Navy Type 96 Attack Bomber Model 11 (G3M1). These saw extensive use against the Chinese and participated in the Pacific war but were being replaced by 1942. The definitive version, the G3M3, had a range of 3,871 mi. In all, just over 1,000 Nells were built.

1935 August 8 Precursor to the M.S.406, the first French monoplane fighter with a retractable landing gear to enter service, the Morane-Saulnier M.S.405-01 low-wing monoplane made its first flight powered by a 860-HP Hispano-Suiza 12Ygrs 12-cylinder V engine. The M.S.405-02 had a modified wing platform and a different engine variant. An initial order for 50 aircraft of this type placed in 1937 was changed to embrace the derivative M.S.406, 1,000 of which were ordered in March 1938 with 572 on strength by September 1939. The M.S.406 had a wingspan of 34 ft. 9 in., a length of 26 ft. 9 in., an 860-HP Hispano-Suiza 12Y-31 engine and a top speed of 302 MPH.

1935 August 19 The winning contender for a requirement issued by the U.S. Navy stipulating a carrier-based dive-bomber, the Northrop XBT-1, made its first flight and was eventually ordered into production as the BT-1, deliveries beginning in 1937. The requirement had been issued June 1, 1934. Bids were also received for a biplane design from three companies (Curtiss XSBC-3, Great Lakes XB2G-1, and Grumman XSBF-1) as well as two monoplanes (Brewster XSBA-1 and Vought XSB2U-1). The BT-1 had a length of 31 ft. 10 in., a wingspan of 41 ft. 6 in. and a single 825-HP Pratt & Whitney R-1535-94 radial engine.

1935 August 23 No. 84 Squadron, RAF, searched for the location of a Handley Page H.P.42 *(Horsa)* that had left Basra for Bahrain the night before. *Horsa* had force-landed in the desert 100 mi. to the south of Bahrain because the Basra take-off signal had not been received at the point of destination and no landing lights illuminated the strip. When the parched passengers were found safe, they had been forced to strip in 140°F heat of the desert. American authoress Jane Smith was found wearing nothing but her knickers, which were autographed and presented later to No. 84 Squadron in appreciation.

1935 August At the behest of the *Daily Express* newspaper, a curious little airplane built by amateur aviator Henri Mignet was brought from France to England where it toured southern coastal towns, demonstrating its capabilities. Called the Pou-de-Ciel (literally, Flying Louse) and popularly known as the Flying Flea, it was the first aircraft designed for construction by amateurs from a series of plans drawn by Mignet. Diminutive in size, it had two wings in tandem and a large tail. Several fatal accidents gave the Pou-de-Ciel a checkered reputation, and it was eventually banned in France.

1935 September 13 Howard Hughes took the world air speed record from the French when he set a new record of 352.388 MPH in the Hughes H-1 racer designed by Richard Palmer and powered by a Pratt & Whitney Twin Wasp engine. With Joseph Nikrent as the timer and record-breaking pilots Amelia Earhart and Paul Mantz observing, Hughes used the Irvine ranch in Santa Ana, Calif., for the attempt. On September 12, Hughes attained average speeds of 302 MPH, 350 MPH and 334 MPH on each of three runs. He ran the fourth leg next day and increased the previous record by 39 MPH.

1935 September 13 The last flight of a USAAC aircraft powered by a World War I Liberty engine took place when a Douglas BT-1 flew from Fort Clark, Tex. to Kelly Field. This aircraft was a dual control trainer version of the O-2K, which had been developed from the DT navy torpedo aircraft to compete in two army competitions for observation aircraft. One competition was for Liberty-engined aircraft, the other for designs using the Packard 1A-1500 engine. The army eventually placed an order for 46 O-2 aircraft equipped with Liberty engines. Curtiss won the Packard competition with its XO-1.

1935 September 15 A Seversky SEV-3 amphibious monoplane established a new world air speed record for amphibious aircraft, which was still standing in 1992. The SEV-3, the first one built by Seversky, was powered by a 710-HP Wright Cyclone and

achieved a record 230.413 MPH. Founded in 1931, the Seversky Aircraft Corp. employed Alexander Kartveli as chief designer, who produced the SEV-3 as a basic design from which it was intended diverse versions and variants would emerge for a variety of roles and purposes. From the SEV-3 emerged the SEV-2XD two-seat experimental demonstration aircraft. The SEV-1XP single-seat fighter contender for the 1936 USAAC fly-off, was developed from the SEV-2XD and eventually ordered into production as the P-35.

1935 October 1 Allied British Airways was formed by merging United Airways, which had begun service in April 1935, and Spartan Airlines, operating since April 1933. The new company was to be controlled by Whitehall Securities and from October 29 was to be known as British Airways Ltd. It acquired Hillman's Airways, operating since April 1932, on December 11, 1935, and British Continental Airways, operating since April 1935, on August 1, 1936. Beginning January 1, 1936, British Airways began operating from Heston Airport and supported a London-Amsterdam-Hamburg-Copenhagen-Malmö, Sweden, service from February 17 using D.H.86 biplanes. British Airways started using Gatwick Airport south of London from May 17, 1936, although it was not officially opened until June 6. On February 7, 1937, the operational base moved to Croydon.

1935 October 1 Lieferplan (production plan) No. 1 began as a further refinement of Luftwaffe aircraft production. Set down by Erhard Milch, it combined the January 1, 1935, Rhineland Program extension and incorporated further advances in production schedules. It adopted a target of 11,158 aircraft for the period January 1, 1934, through April 1, 1936, adding 1,305 to the earlier schedule. It envisaged new 3,820 combat aircraft for the Luftwaffe, 462 combat aircraft for the navy and 6,876 trainers, liaison and miscellaneous aircraft. Of the combat inventory, there were to be 1,849 bombers and 970 fighters in the Luftwaffe.

1935 October 1 The newly formed Luftwaffe set up an experimental dive-bomber unit at Schwerin, Germany, equipped at first with Heinkel He 50, He 51 and Arado Ar 65 aircraft; a year later it got its first Henschel Hs 123A-1 types. The Schwerin unit became known as I./St.G 162, which indicated it was the first group of the Immelmann Geschwader, and operated with II./St.G 162 and another unit, I./St.G 165 at Kitzingen. It was I./St.G 162 that first operated the Junkers Ju 87 Stuka and evaluated the aircraft before working out operational tactics.

1935 October 3 Italian air forces were committed in anger when Benito Mussolini attacked Ethiopia with 320 aircraft supporting a mechanized assault. Most were Caproni Ca.101 transport-bombers, but eight fighter squadrons, including three equipped with Fiat CR. 20 biplanes, were operational. Also involved were two-seat Ro.37 reconnaissance bomber biplanes built by I.M.A.M. (Industrie Meccaniche e Aeronautiche Meridionali). A few Caproni Ca.111 twin-float seaplanes were deployed, as were some Ca.133 high-wing, twin-engine bombers along with the Savoia-Marchetti S.M.79. Fearing disruption to merchant traffic through Suez, the British sent some squadrons to the Middle East, but none saw action.

1935 October 14 U.S. Navy Lt. Comdr. K. McGinnis and Lt. (jg) J. K. Averill, pilot T. P. Wilkinson and a crew of three took off in the prototype Consolidated XP3Y-1 from Cristobal Harbor, Canal Zone, Panama and flew to Alameda, Calif. nonstop. The 3,443.3 mi. were completed in 34 hr. 45 min. and established a FAI-certified Class C straight-line distance record for seaplanes of 3,281.383 mi. (5,540 km). The aircraft was powered by two

825-HP Pratt & Whitney engines. Lt. Comdr. McGinnis had secured the straight-line distance record on January 11, 1934, at 2,399 mi. when he commanded a flight of six P2Y-1 flying boats from San Francisco to Pearl Harbor.

1935 October 30 The Boeing Model 299 crashed and burned out when elevator locks were inadvertently left in place during a routine test take-off at Wright Field. In the resulting pitch-up and stall caused by reverse action on the trim tab, Maj. Ployer Hill was killed, test pilot Leslie Tower was fatally injured, and the rest survived. Although the Model 299 had been favored as a new bomber, it was disqualified from the competition, and an order granted to the Douglas DB-1, which became the B-18 in service. However, the army awarded Boeing an order for 13 test models of the 299 on January 17, 1936.

1935 October A fighter competition was held at Travemünde, Germany to select a new fighter for the Luftwaffe. Entries included the Arado Ar 80, the Focke Wulf Fw 159, the Heinkel He 112 and the Messerschmitt Bf 109. The latter two were both favorites, but the Bf 109, at 290 MPH, was 12 MPH faster than the He 112. With the exception of the Fw 159, which was powered by a 610-HP Junkers Jumo 210, all entrants had a 640/695-HP Rolls Royce Kestrel engine. Both favorites received a production order for 10 prototypes. Some Rumanian He 112s saw action in World War II, and a few were supplied to the Japanese, but the type was generally rejected in favor of the Bf 109.

1935 October Built for Pan American Airways in a parallel procurement to the Sikorsky S.42, the first Martin M-130 (registration no. NC14716) flying boat was test-flown across the Atlantic. Named *China Clipper* (joined later by *Philippine Clipper* and *Hawaiian Clipper*), it had a wingspan of 130 ft., a length of 91 ft., a gross takeoff weight of 52,000 lb. and a speed of 130

MPH. With capacity for 32 passengers, it was almost twice as expensive as the Sikorsky S.42 but featured luxury equipment, a galley and several technical advantages over its competitor. It was powered by four 800-HP Pratt & Whitney R-1830 Twin Wasp engines.

1935 October The first confirmation of the existence of the still-secret Dornier Do 17 medium bomber was obtained when an aircraft of this type appeared publicly at Bückeberg airfield. It had been built and flown during 1934, and because of its long, thin fuselage, it was dubbed the Flying Pencil. Designed to a Lufthansa mailplane specification, it emerged as a fast (222 MPH) bomber with a wingspan of 59 ft., a length of 53 ft. 4 in. and two 660-HP BMW VI 12-cylinder engines. Devoid of passenger space, it was never used as a mailplane but joined the Luftwaffe in early 1937 as the Do 17E-1. With a bomb load of 1,650 lb., later increased to 2,205 lb., it had a maximum range of 310 mi.

1935 November 6 The prototype Hawker Hurricane (serial no. K5083) made its first flight from Brooklands, England with Hawker chief test pilot Flt. Lt. P. W. S. Bulman at the controls. With a wingspan of 40 ft., a length of 31 ft. 6 in and a normal loaded weight of 5,672 lb., the Hurricane prototype had a top speed of 310 MPH at 15,000 ft. and a climb time of 22.5 min. to 30,000 ft., initial climb rate being 2,400 ft./min. Powered by a 1,025-HP Rolls Royce Merlin C, it was clearly the fighter of the future and a bright star indeed in the potential range of replacement aircraft during air expansion plans about to develop.

1935 November 11 The USAAC and the National Geographic Society teamed to support an ascent using the balloon *Explorer II* to reach a record height of 72,395 ft. over Rapid City, S.D. This was a new world altitude record and would stand for 20 yr. The intrepid balloonists were Captains Albert Stevens and Orvil

Ancestor of a family of World War II German bombers, the first prototype Dornier Do 17 took to the air for the first time in 1934.

Anderson. They made their ascent beginning 4:00 A.M. in a 3.7 million cu. ft. balloon with an inflated diameter of 192 ft. Maximum height was reached at 12:19 P.M. with touchdown 125 mi. from the take-off point after a flight time of 8 hr. 13 min. Several scientific instruments were carried aloft and made important measurements of the stratosphere.

1935 November 14 Designed by R. B. Noorduyn of Noorduyn Aviation Ltd., the prototype Norseman I made its first flight. Later to become one of the most popular Canadian utility aircraft ever built, the Norseman was a high-wing monoplane with a wingspan of 51 ft. 8 in., a length of 33 ft. 1 in. and a single 600-HP Pratt & Whitney R-1340-AN1 9-cylinder radial. With a range of 1,150 mi. and a top speed of 155 MPH and capable of operating with wheels, skis or floats, it served with the Royal Canadian Air Force, the Royal Canadian Mounted Police (RCMP) and several other air forces (even after 1945), including the United States, which ordered 749 under the designation C-64A.

1935 November 15 The chief of the Bureau of Aeronautics for the U.S. Navy issued a formal specification calling for a fighter design competition that would lead to contracts for a modern shipboard fighter to replace current biplane designs. One of these, the Grumman XF4F-1, was prepared as a biplane but never built. It was followed quickly by the XF4F-2 monoplane, which would be ordered as the F4F Wildcat in 1939, and more than 7,800 of which would be built. The second design resulting from this requirement was the Brewster F2A Buffalo, which emerged in 1938 as the first Navy monoplane fighter. Both types would form the first echelon of modern carrier fighters after the attack on Pearl Harbor.

1935 November 21 The Russian pilot V. K. Kokkinaki set an unofficial altitude record when he achieved a height of 47,818 ft. flying a Polikarpov I-15 single-engine biplane fighter. This was 433 ft. above the confirmed FAI record, which had been achieved on April 11, 1934, by the Italian pilot Donati flying a Caproni Ca.114A modified single-seat fighter. This aircraft had been designed in 1933 for the Region Aeronautica but failed to receive any orders. The Polikarpov I-15 would form part of the Soviet munitions supply sent to Spain one year later for the Republicans fighting Gen. Franco. Others were used in the Sino-Japanese conflict, and some saw service in World War II.

1935 November 22 American Lincoln Ellsworth and Canadian Herbert Hollick-Kenyan took off in their Northrop Gamma, *Pole Star,* equipped with skis to fly 2,500 mi. from Dundee Island, on Graham Land, Antarctica, south to the U.S. research base Little America across the Ross Sea. Just over half way, they set down on the ice, and after 19 hr. took off; after only 30 min., poor weather forced them to land again. Attempting to fly again on November 27, a blizzard forced them down after 50 min. A week later they dug themselves out, and on January 4 flew south for 3 hr. landing 125 mi. from the Ross Sea with fuel for one hour. Next day they flew to within 4 mi. of Little America but spent 10 more days trying to reach base on foot.

1935 November 22 The first scheduled airmail service across the Pacific Ocean began when a Martin Model 130 flying boat operated by Pan American Airways took off from San Francisco's Alameda Airport for Manila via Hawaii, Midway, Wake Island and Guam under the command of Capt. Ed Musick. The flying boat made its first stop at Honolulu after 21 hr. and reached its destination in a flight time of 59 hr. 48 min. The first scheduled weekly passenger service was inaugurated on October 21, 1936, beginning a permanent commercial service interrupted only

by the war with Japan. Also on November 22, Pan American secured landing rights at Auckland, New Zealand.

1935 December 9 The prototype of the Curtiss SBC Helldiver carrier-based scout bomber, which would join the U.S. Navy in July 1937, made its first flight as the XSBC-2. Designed as a monoplane when ordered on June 30, 1932, the aircraft appeared originally under the designation XF-12C-1 carrier-based fighter, then as the XS4C-1 scout aircraft and finally as the XSBC-1 scout bomber. It crashed in September 1934, and when redesigned as a biplane, it emerged as the XSBC-2. Despite the identity crisis, the Helldiver developed into a worthwhile bomber able to carry a 500-lb. bomb for a range of 590 mi. or a 1,000-lb bomb on shorter flights.

1935 December 17 The first Douglas Sleeper Transport (DST), eventually known as the DC-3, made its first flight from Clover Field in Santa Monica, Calif. piloted by Carl A. Cover with Ed Stineman and Frank Collbohm also on board. The DST had a wing span of 95 ft., a length of 64 ft. 5.5 in. and a loaded weight of 24,000 lb., and power was supplied by two Wright Cyclone SGR-1802-G2 engines. It had a cruising speed of 192 MPH and a ceiling of 20,800 ft. Chief designer Arthur Raymond had redesigned the DC-2 with rounded sides and a new nose, making even more numerous changes than envisaged by American Airlines when they requested the type. As the DC-3, this aircraft would revolutionize air transport in the 1930s and 1940s, becoming a workhorse for at least 30 years. Many were still flying in 1992.

1935 December 27 The Army Air Corps provided a spectacular end-of-year community aid activity when it was called upon to use its aircraft to bomb targets on Hawaii! But it was not to quell an over-festive populace. The rumbling volcano Mauna Loa was pouring forth lava that threatened to engulf communities at Hilo. By bombing out certain pinpoint targets, the lava flow was diverted from its favored, topographic course.

1935 December The British government approved plans to build five radar early warning stations between Bawdsey and the South Foreland, protecting the Thames estuary and the approaches to London. In September it had been agreed to expand the work of the radar experimental establishment at Orfordness and to move it to Bawdsey Manor, not far from Felixstowe on the south coast of England. The ultimate objective was to build a chain of such stations around the south coast of Britain and up as far north as the Tyne River.

1935 Detailed design work began on two potential heavy bombers, the Boeing XBLR-1, later XB-15, on which work had begun as early as January 1934, and the Martin Model 145-a, or XB-16. The latter had four in-line engines recessed into a 140-ft. wing with retractable dorsal and ventral gun turrets on an 84-ft. fuselage supporting horizontal tail and twin fin/rudder assemblies. Although never built, the final XB-16 configuration incorporated four tractor engines buried in the wing leading edge and two pusher engines in the trailing edge on a 173-ft.-span wing. With twin tail booms, the aircraft had a design length of 114 ft. 10 in. Cross weight would have been 104,880 lb., speed 140 MPH and range 3,300 mi. with a 2,500-lb. bomb load.

1936 January 4 The Vought XSB2U-1 made its first flight, more than two years after being ordered by the navy as an all-metal, low-wing, monoplane scout bomber that would be named Vindicator. Powered by a 700-HP Pratt & Whitney R-1535-78 radial engine, the XSB2U-1 had a wingspan of 42 ft., a length of 33 ft. 2 in. and a gross weight of 5,916 lb. With a long glass-house cockpit enclosure for two, the production SB2U Vindicator ordered in October had a 34-ft. fuselage, a gross weight increased to 6,232 lb. (9,421 lb. for the SB2U-3) and power from an 825-HP R-1535-02 radial. The aircraft had one fixed and one flexible 0.50-in. gun, a cruising speed of 152 MPH and a range of 1,120 mi.

1936 January 10   The civil transport version of the Heinkel He 111 bomber was revealed to the public for the first time at the Berlin Tempelhof airport. Named *Dresden,* it was operated by Lufthansa and had evolved from the military model, which made its first flight in February 1935. Registered D-AHAO, the He 111 V4 could carry up to 10 passengers in two separate compartments and was the forerunner to the He 111C model, of which six were built during the summer of 1936 and named *Nürnberg, Leipzig, Köln, Königsberg, Breslau* and *Karlsruhe.*

1936 January 13   American aviator Howard Hughes began a record-breaking sprint across the North American continent from Burbank, Calif. to Newark, N.J., a journey completed January 14 after 9 hr. 26 min. 10 sec. at an average speed of 259 MPH. Flying the most powerful Northrop Gamma fitted, at his instruction, with a 1,000-HP Wright SR-1820-G2 radial engine, this was the latest in a series of record-breaking flights by the enigmatic Hughes. Born in December 1905, Hughes took flying lessons and achieved his license in 1927, by which time he was a multi-millionaire in charge of his father's oil business. Philanthropist, fortune-maker and businessman extraordinaire, he formed Hughes Aircraft in 1934 to design racing aircraft.

1936 January 17   The USAAC ordered 13 Boeing Y1B-17 four-engine bombers (previously identified as the Boeing Model 299), the first of which made its first flight on December 2, 1936. Externally, the Y1B-17 was identical to the Model 299, but the four Pratt & Whitney S1E-G Hornet (R-1690) engines of the earlier model were changed for four 850-HP Wright Cyclone SGR-1820-39 engines and the complement was reduced from eight to a crew of six. The first of 13 production Y1B-17s was delivered to the army on January 11 and the last on August 4, 1937. Gross weight was up from 32,432 lb. on the Model 299 to 34,880 lb., cruising speed was 217 MPH versus 140 MPH, service ceiling was 30,600 ft. versus 24,620 ft., and range was 1,377 mi. with a bomb load of 8,000 lb. versus 3,101 mi. with a bomb load of 4,800 lb.

1936 January 22   The U.S. Navy's newest aircraft carrier, the USS *Ranger,* arrived at Cook Inlet, Alaska, where it had been sent to carry out cold-weather operations tests. The full range of aircraft and ship support equipment was flexed in efforts to flush out weaknesses in operating equipment and procedures. The results of the equipment tests and trials were analyzed, and several important equipment and procedural changes made as a result of this shakedown.

1936 January   Opting for quantity rather than quality, the USAAC ordered 133 Douglas DB-1 bombers, designated B-18, because the quoted quantity production price was only 59% of the price quoted by Boeing for the Model 299 (B-17). Yet the production B-17 would be 38% faster and have a service ceiling 12,100 ft. higher and a range of 2,400 mi. with a bomb load of 4,000 lb. versus only 1,200 mi. with a 4,400-lb. bomb load. The B-18 had one 0.30-in. gun in each of three defensive positions; the production B-17 had six 0.50-in. guns and one 0.30-in. gun. The B-18 had a wingspan of 89 ft. 6 in., a length of 56 ft. 8 in. and two 810/930-HP Wright R-1820-45 engines.

1936 February 10   Ernst Udet, the German fighter ace of World War I, was appointed by Hermann Göring as inspector of fighters and dive-bombers in the German Air Ministry (RLM). Udet had a lot of experience as a pilot, but his knowledge of aeronautics was not technically advanced, and his appointment June 9 as head of the technical supply department (Technisches Amt) at the insistence of Adolf Hitler was unsound. Udet was to become increasingly frustrated with the excess demands on military preparedness made by Hitler and would increasingly displease the Führer.

1936 February 15   The Japanese army issued a specification for a twin-engine heavy bomber to replace the Mitsubishi Ki-20 and the Mitsubishi Ki-1. It called for an aircraft with an operating altitude of between 6,560 ft. and 13,125 ft. with an endurance in excess of 2 hr. at 186 MPH, a maximum speed of 248.5 MPH at 9,845 ft. and a climb time of 9,845 ft. in 8 min. Defensive guns were to be provided in nose, dorsal and ventral locations; it was to hold with a crew of four, a standard bomb load of 1,653 lb. and a maximum bomb load of 2,205 lb. This specification resulted in the Mitsubishi Ki-21, which first flew on December 18, 1936, and its unsuccessful competitor, the Nakajima Ki-19.

1936 February 29   The Sikorsky Aircraft Co. submitted a secret design to the USAAC that became known as Project M5-35 for a giant bomber given the designation XBLR-3. Had the aircraft been built, it would have had a 205-ft. wingspan, a wing area of 4,614 sq. ft., a length of 120 ft. and a height of 35 ft. Powered by four 1,600-HP Allison XV-3420-1 engines, the aircraft would have had a gross weight of 119,977 lb. and a fuel load of almost 8,000 gal.! With a cruising speed of 130 MPH, it would have had a range of 7,650 mi. Canceled in favor of the XBLR-2 (XB-19) from Douglas, it was the last of the long-range bomber concepts.

1936 February   Douglas showed United Air Lines initial design studies of a four-engine airliner theoretically capable of twice the carrying capacity of the DC-3 and with a range of 2,200 mi. Sought by United, the project needed financial backing from other airlines, and a month later American, Eastern, Pan American and TWA joined United in each paying $100,000 for a single prototype to be designated DC-4E. Capable of carrying 42 passengers, or 30 in full sleeper configuration (incorporating a bridal room!), the increasing complexity of the aircraft eventually forced Pan American and TWA to withdraw in favor of the Boeing 307.

1936 February   In the first adaptation of its type, the Polikarpov I-16UTI two-seat fighter-trainer gained its flight acceptance certificate from the Soviet state authorities. Redesigned to accommodate a pupil for conversion familiarization, the I-16UTI had a blind flying student canopy over one of the open cockpits for instrument rating and a black curtain over the pilot's head for total blind flying tests. This aircraft was also known as the UTI-4, but the concept became a familiar trend for several Soviet fighters.

1936 February   The British government approved air expansion Scheme F, which was to replace Scheme C, approved May 21, 1935. Scheme F called for a front-line force at home of 1,736 aircraft in 124 RAF squadrons by March 31, 1939, and an overseas force of 468 aircraft in 26 squadrons with 312 aircraft in 37 squadrons in the Fleet Air Arm, providing a total force strength of 2,516 aircraft in 187 squadrons. With the fighter strength left unchanged at 420 aircraft, the light bomber category (Hawker Hart, Hind and Fairey Gordon) was upgraded to medium bomber with Hampden, Battle and Blenheim and heavy-medium Wellingtons.

1936 March 4　The last great passenger-carrying airship, a veritable behemoth in its day, took to the air for the first time. With a length of 803 ft. 10 in., a diameter of 153 ft. 6 in., a capacity of 7,062,940 cu. ft. and a payload capacity of 41,887 lb., the German dirigible LZ 129, the *Hindenburg*, was powered by four 1,320-HP Daimler-Benz DB 602 diesel engines. Designed to use helium, which is safer, it was instead built for hydrogen because the United States, which had a monopoly on the supply of helium, refused to grant an export license for the gas to Nazi Germany. The *Hindenburg* made its first Atlantic crossing in the record time of 64 hr. 53 min. on May 6.

1936 March 5　Vickers test pilot J. "Mutt" Summers took the prototype Supermarine Type 300 (F.37.34) fighter (serial no. K5054) into the air for the first time (although there is circumstantial evidence that this flight took place on March 6). Later named Spitfire, the aircraft had a wingspan of 37 ft. 8 in., a length of 29 ft. 11 in., an all-up weight of 5,200 lb. and power provided by a 990-HP Rolls Royce Merlin C engine. Tests demonstrated a top speed of 335 MPH (later increased to 348 MPH) at 16,800 ft. with a service ceiling of 35,400 ft. An order for 310 Spitfires was received at Vickers Supermarine on July 28, under Specification F.16/36 back-dated to June 3.

1936 March 7　In support of the military occupation of the Rhineland, the Luftwaffe's III./Jagdgeschwader 134 and I./Sturzkampfgeschwader 165 units were transferred to Köln Butzweilerhof, Cologne and Düsseldorf. Two Staffeln (units) of the 165 Dive-Bomber Group were sent to Frankfurt am Main airport, and a third went to Mannheim. Although equipped with 1,000 rounds of ammunition each, the aircraft were not in a combat-ready condition, and the entire operation was incapable of serious response to a military challenge from the occupying powers.

1936 March 10　The first Fairey Battle (serial no. K4303) made its first flight with Chris Staniland at the controls. An all-metal, low-wing medium bomber, it was designed to specification P.27/32, originally issued in August 1932, as a replacement for the Hawker Hart. More than 2,200 Battles were built, less than half of which served with the RAF, the rest being exported to Australia and Canada as trainers and target-tugs. The aircraft was obsolete when war came and suffered heavily during efforts by the RAF to stem the German invasion of France in May 1940. The Battle had a wingspan of 54 ft., a length of 42 ft. 4 in. and a single 1,030-HP Rolls Royce Merlin.

1936 March 15　Having successfully interested the investment bankers O. T. Falk & Partners to put up money for the design and development of a gas turbine engine, following a favorable report from consulting engineer M. L. Bramson, the firm Power Jets Ltd. was formed, enabling Frank Whittle to begin the detailed design. The investors began discussions with British Thompson Houston (BTH) Ltd. about the manufacture and assembly of Whittle's engine, and an order was signed on June 17. The first engine had a single-stage centrifugal compressor and was designated WU, for Whittle Unit. Whittle completed his tripos at Cambridge University and remained there doing postgraduate work, a means of keeping him at work on the engine.

1936 March 17　Piloted by Alan Campbell-Orde, the prototype Armstrong Whitworth A.W.38 Whitley (serial no. K4586) made its first flight from Whitley airfield near Coventry, England. Ordered into production off the drawing board, the Whitley was a descendent of the A.W.23 bomber-transport and had a light alloy monocoque fuselage. The Whitley had a wingspan of 84 ft., a length of 69 ft. 3 in., a loaded weight of 28,200 lb. and a maximum bomb load of 7,000 lb. with a range of 1,650 mi. with a 3,000-lb. bomb load. It joined the RAF in March 1937, replacing the Heyford, and formed an important stopgap during the early part of World War II, along with the Hampden and the Wellington.

1936 March 28　NACA commenced operational use of the newly constructed 8-ft.-high speed tunnel (8-Foot HST) at the Langley Memorial Aeronautical Laboratory, Langley, Va. Built as a companion to the full scale tunnel, operational since May 1931 and capable of simulated speeds of up to 118 MPH, the new facility could test models and components to 575 MPH (Mach 0.75). The test section comprised an igloo-shaped building with 12-inch thick concrete walls to withstand the inward pressure due to the Bernoulli effect. Technicians and engineers were subjected to an equivalent 10,000 ft. altitude pressure and wore protective suits and oxygen masks. The 8-Foot HST was deactivated in 1956.

1936 March　Nowhere was the impending threat of another war in Europe better seen than in the response to German and Italian military expansion defined by the British air estimates for 1936–37. The amount requested for parliamentary approval was £50.7 million, almost double the figure for the previous year. In two years, expenditure on military air needs had grown almost threefold, from £17.5 million, a sum similar to that spent in 1921.

1936 March　Two people key to the German development of turbojet aircraft were employed by Ernst Heinkel. Dr. Hans Joachim Pabst von Ohain began secret tests with jet propulsion at Heinkel's Marienehe facility, following preparatory work at Göttingen University. Heinkel also employed von Ohain's assistant from Göttingen, Max Hahn. Von Ohain had been an assistant of Prof. Pohl and brought considerable theoretical knowledge to Heinkel to work on the assembly of the first test engine, designated He S-2A and demonstrated in September 1937 to deliver a thrust of 176 lb., followed six months later by a more powerful engine running on petrol rather than hydrogen.

1936 March　Prof. Ronald Watson-Watt, a British scientist working on radar detection of enemy aircraft, secured a major breakthrough in the development of related techniques when he demonstrated the ability of his radar equipment to determine the bearing and hence the position of an airborne object when integrated with the range and the altitude. The radar equipment could detect aircraft up to 75 mi. away, a capability that served as a force multiplier because it did away with the need for standing patrols, conserved aircraft and pilots and allowed controllers to more effectively vector fighters onto targets.

1936 March　In France, flight tests got under way with a revolutionary, variable geometry biplane called the Varivol, designed by Jacques Gérin and built at the Compagnie Francaise d'Aviation with tests conducted in the wind tunnel at Chalais-Meudon. The wing area of the biplane could be increased from 67.81 sq. ft. to 279.86 sq. ft. by rolling outwards from the fuselage additional spruce leading and trailing edge segments along the full 38 ft. 7 in. span of the fixed, duralumin wing section. The extensible sections, controlled by electric motors, were literally rolled up inside the fuselage when retracted. The 25 ft. 5 in. fuselage was of welded steel construction, metal covered forward and fabric covered aft. The Varivol was irreparably damaged November 29.

1936 April 15 The Brewster XSBA-1 scout dive-bomber appeared for flight trials with the U.S. Navy powered by a Wright R-1820-4 engine and showed a top speed of 242 MPH; it was sent back for a 950-HP R-1820-22, and in 1937 it attained 263 MPH. The fastest U.S. dive-bomber thus far, it had a retractable landing gear, an enclosed bomb bay with a 500-lb. capacity, perforated wing flaps doubling as dive brakes and two crewmembers in separate cockpits within a common "glasshouse" enclosure. This was the first aircraft from Brewster Aeronautical Corp. The Naval Aircraft Factory was ordered to build 30 in 1938 as the SBN-1, but production problems delayed delivery of the first until the end of 1940; the last was not finished until March 1942.

1936 April 29 American Airlines officially accepted the Douglas Sleeper Transport (DST), soon to be called the DC-3, at Phoenix, Ariz. to avoid paying sales tax in California where the aircraft had been built. From Phoenix it was sent back to Santa Monica for 50 hr. of flight tests and route-proving trials before American formally took it over on July 11. In February 1942, the USAAC purchased it and leased it to TWA, where it was used as a cargo carrier designated C-49E until October 15, 1942, when it crashed in bad weather and was destroyed.

1936 April The first North American BT-9 two-seat basic trainer ordered for the Army Air Corps made its first flight having been assembled in the new North American facility at Inglewood, Calif. North American Aviation Inc. had changed in 1935 from being a holding company to a design and manufacturing company, divesting its interests in air transport operations. Beginning with a facility at Dundalk, Md., North American opened the Inglewood factory in January 1936. General Aviation (the subsidiary of General Motors Corp. that had originally been Fokker Aircraft Corp.) joined North American Aviation as its manufacturing division. It brought with it the precursor of the BT-9 known as the NA-16. The aircraft was an adaptable trainer with a cruising speed of 147 MPH and twin Browning 0.30-in guns.

1936 April The first flight of one of the most notable German aircraft of World War II, the Fieseler Fi 156 Storch, took place less than four years after Fieseler Flugzeugbau began building airplanes. The Storch was the epitome of short takeoff and landing (STOL) design, with Handley Page slots and trailing edge extended flaps, a length of 32 ft. 6 in., a wingspan of 46 ft. 9 in. and a 240-HP Argus As 10C-3 8-cylinder, inverted V-engine providing a cruising speed of 81 MPH and exceptionally low stalling speed of less than 25 MPH. More than 2,500 were built for liaison, army cooperation, rescue duty and medical work in the Luftwaffe.

1936 May 2 American parachutist Clem Sohn made a jump over Hanworth, England using a novel form of flexible wing attached to his arms, legs and body. By spreading his legs and arms, the bat-like wings enabled Sohn to glide toward the ground from an altitude of 10,000 ft. He made several turns in the air using his wings and deployed a parachute at 1,000 ft. to arrest his rate of descent. Although reminiscent of early would-be aeronauts, Sohn's efforts preceded development in the United States of inflatable wings that would be used in tests in the 1960s to generate lift during descent. This work would lead to hang gliding and, in turn, small powered flying machines in the 1980s known as microlights.

1936 May 4 Amy Mollison (née Johnson) left Gravesend, England at the start of a record-breaking flight to Cape Town, South Africa, only a month after a previous attempt failed when her Percival Mew Gull was damaged at Colomb Béchar (now Bé-

char), Algeria. Flying Mew Gull G-ADZO, Mollison arrived at Cape Town on May 7 having flown the 6,400-mi. West Coast route in 3 days 6 hr. 26 min. (a flying time of 54 hr. 37 min.) taking 11 hr. 9 min. off the record. Leaving Cape Town on May 10, Mollison arrived back in England after 4 days 16 hr. 17 min., having covered 7,863 mi. The two-way cumulative transit distance of 14,263 mi. took a total of 7 days 22 hr. 43 min. of flying time, or 12 days including the stopover.

1936 May 11 Piloted by Cyril F. Uwins, the Bristol Type 138A High Altitude Monoplane made its first flight. Designed to Air Ministry specification 2/34 by a team led by Frank Barnwell, the aircraft was built to achieve an altitude of 54,000 ft. through light wood construction, a fixed landing gear and a supercharged 500-HP Bristol Pegasus P.E.6S rotary engine. With a wingspan of 66 ft., making it the largest single-seater to date, and a length of 44 ft., it had an all-up weight of 5,310 lb. and a speed of 123 MPH. The Type 138A secured an altitude record of 15,230 m (49,967 ft., the first altitude record to exceed 15,000 m) on September 28, 1936, and 16,440 m (53,937 ft.) on June 30, 1937.

1936 May 12 The prototype Messerschmitt Bf 110 V1 made its first flight from Augsberg-Haunstetten airfield, Germany piloted by Rudolf Opitz. Designed as a twin-engine, long-range strategic fighter, it was a cantilever, low-wing monoplane with a duralumin flush riveted skin and powered by two Daimler Benz DB 600 12-cylinder inverted-V engines, although early production models had the Junkers Jumo. The first major production model, the Bf 110C-1, had a wingspan of 53 ft. 4 in., a length of 39 ft. 7 in., a cruising speed of 217 MPH at 13,780 ft. and a range of 1,070 mi. Ineffective as a day fighter, it was to prove a valuable night fighter and served with the Luftwaffe from February 1939.

1936 May 15 In a classic demonstration of how minor design detail changes can significantly enhance the performance (and prospects) of an aircraft, British test pilot Jeffrey Quill flew the prototype Supermarine Spitfire (serial no. K5054) with a new propeller tip subtly redesigned to avoid control problems due to the speed of sound. It immediately gave the Spitfire an extra 13 MPH, increasing top speed from 335 MPH to 348 MPH and making it a creditable challenge to the Hawker Hurricane, with which it was to compete in military trials held at Martlesham Heath. Chief designer R. J. Mitchell was not privileged to see the Spitfire achieve greatness. He died June 11, 1937, at the age of 42.

1936 June 3 Germany lost its most vocal advocate of a strategic bombing force when Lt. Gen. Walther Wever, the first Luftwaffe chief of air staff, died. The chief of the technical supply department, Oberstleutnant Wilhelm Wimmer, had successfully argued the case for a bomber capable of reaching targets as far from central Germany as Scotland or the Urals, and during the summer of 1935 Wever had issued a specification resulting in contracts for the Dornier Do 19 and the Junkers Ju 89, both four-engined bomber prototypes. These were canceled by his successor, Lt. Gen. Albert Kesselring, who favored a tactical role for the Luftwaffe. An improved heavy bomber specification was issued, resulting in the Heinkel He 177.

1936 June 3 The British Air Ministry awarded a contract to Hawker for 600 Hurricane Mk.1 fighters, the first of a new breed of high-speed, eight-gun interceptors for the RAF. This was the biggest peacetime order placed in Britain to date and epitomized the magnitude of the transition from the old to the new era; Hawker still had 500 Hart biplane variants to build for the RAF. The first production Hurricane Mk.1 flew on October 12, 1937, powered

First of the RAF's eight-gun monoplane fighters, the Hawker Hurricane would prove a rugged and adaptable aircraft.

by a 1,030-HP Rolls Royce Merlin II, and the first deliveries reached No. 111 Squadron, RAF, in December 1937. Rapid production and delivery contrasted with the sluggish start to Spitfire production.

1936 June 15 With J. "Mutt" Summers at the controls, the prototype Vickers Wellington (serial no. K4049) made its first flight powered by two 915-HP Bristol Pegasus X radial engines. Benefactor of the geodetic construction pioneered in aircraft by the Wellesley, the Wellington was designed by Barnes Wallis and proved to be a rugged, forgiving aircraft capable of surviving major damage. Affectionately known as the Wimpey, it had a wingspan of 86 ft. 2 in., and a length of 60 ft. 10 in. and could carry a 4,500-lb. bomb load over a range of 1,540 mi. or a 1,500-lb. load over 2,200 mi. Just over 11,400 Wellington bombers were built, becoming the backbone of RAF Bomber Command in the first two years of World War II.

1936 June 15 Designed as an army cooperation monoplane to replace the Hawker Hector biplane, the prototype, high-wing Westland Lysander (serial no. K6127) made its first flight piloted by Harald Penrose. With a wingspan of 50 ft. and a length of 30 ft. 6 in., it had a 890-HP Bristol Mercury XII engine and a loaded weight of 5,920 lb. Just over 1,400 Lysanders were built, the first operational model joining the RAF in June 1938. The type was used for artillery-spotting and reconnaissance. A special version with long-range tanks flew more than 400 spy-dropping operations into occupied Europe. The Lysander was finally retired in 1946.

1936 June 16 The USAAC ordered 77 Seversky P-35 all-metal, cantilever, low-wing monoplane fighters, developed from the SEV-1XP by way of a modified version, the SEV-7. The P-35A had a wingspan of 36 ft., a length of 26 ft. 10 in. and a gross weight of 6,118 lb. With two 0.50-in. and two 0.30-in. machine guns, it was not on the same level as the British or German equivalents, but it provided the army air corps with an interim fighter of relatively modern design. At the April 1936 fly-off in which the P-35 was selected, Curtiss had entered its Model 75; although it placed second, three were ordered under the designation Y1P-36 on August 5.

1936 June 21 Designed to a specification issued in 1932, the Handley Page H.P.52 Hampden prototype (serial no. K4240) made its first flight. It was ordered into production in August, and the first reached the RAF in August 1938. In all, almost 1,500 Hampdens were built in Britain and Canada before the type was withdrawn from Bomber Command in September 1942, although it soldiered on as a torpedo bomber with Coastal Command. Characterized by its unusually thin, boom-like rear fuselage with four defensive gun positions, the Hampden had a wingspan of 69 ft. 2 in., a length of 53 ft. 7 in., a loaded weight of 18,756 lb. and a maximum bomb load of 4,000 lb. over 1,200 mi.

1936 June 22 The U.S. Navy ordered a prototype monoplane fighter, the XF2A-1, from Brewster; designed as Model B-139, it would become the first monoplane fighter to serve with the navy. It had a fat, all-metal fuselage with cantilever mid-wing arrangement and fabric-covered control surfaces. The landing gear was designed to retract fully into the underside of the forward fuselage, and the pilot had an enclosed cockpit. Tailwheel and arrester hook were provided for carrier operations. This aircraft made its first flight in December 1937 and entered service as the F2A Buffalo in June 1940; the improved F2A-3 followed in late 1941.

1936 June 25 Designed to specification 28/35 issued by the Air Ministry, the prototype Bristol Blenheim (serial no. K7033) made its first flight. It had been developed from the Bristol Britain First monoplane built in 1935. The first RAF contract for the three-man light bomber had been placed in August 1935, and the first production aircraft reached No. 114 Squadron in March 1937. With a wingspan of 56 ft. 4 in. and a length of 39 ft. 9 in., the Blenheim I had a loaded weight of 12,500 lb. and could carry a 1,000-lb. bomb load. It had a range of 1,125 mi. and a cruising speed of 200 MPH with two 840-HP Bristol Mercury VIII engines. The redesigned Blenheim IV served with Bomber Command until August 1942.

1936 June 26 Achieving what some have regarded as the first true helicopter flight (because the design set the trend for future designs and was a true progenitor), the first Focke-Wulf Fw 61 lifted into the air for 45 sec. and landed vertically. Building upon experience constructing Cierva autogyros, Prof. Heinrich Karl Johann Focke designed his helicopter from the fuselage and engine of an F4 Stieglitz trainer but with the propeller cut back to the diameter of the engine so that it served only as a cooling fan. The horizontal tail was set on top of the vertical fin, and two sets of three-bladed articulated rotor assemblies were positioned either side of the fuselage on outriggers.

1936 June The U.S. Coast Guard ordered five Hall PH-2 flying boats powered with two Wright R-1820-F51 Cyclone radial engines. They were to help the Coast Guard patrol large areas of the coast and to serve as rescue flying boats for emergencies. The Coast Guard also obtained seven PH-3 biplane flying boats with special modifications adapting them to the needs of the service. Some of these flying boats would see service during World War II and were used for antisubmarine operations.

1936 June The Mitsubishi F1M catapult-launched, short-range observation biplane made its first flight, having been designed to a 10-Shi specification aimed at replacing the Nakajima E8N1. Equipped with a central float and two outrigger floats, the F1M had a wingspan of 36 ft. 1 in., a length of 31 ft. 2 in. and a single 660/820-HP Nakajima Hikari 1, 9-cylinder radial. Mitsubishi alone built over 500 of the F1M2 variant, the most popular, and some were also built by the Twenty-first Naval Air Arsenal.

The F1M2 had two fixed forward-firing 7.7-mm machine guns and a single, flexible, rear-firing 7.7-mm.

1936 July 3 The first C-class Empire flying boat built by Shorts as the S.23 design, made a brief 14-min. first flight piloted by John Lankester Parker. The last word in luxury travel for Imperial Airways passengers flying to Africa or the Far East the S.23 was designed to carry 17 passengers and 2 tons of mail. The first of 42 Empire flying boats (G-ADHL, named *Canopus*), was a high-wing monoplane with a wingspan of 114 ft., a length of 88 ft., an all-up weight of 40,500 lb. (later 52,500 lb.), a maximum speed of 200 MPH and a range of 760 mi.; a few later versions got up to 3,300 mi. Power was provided by four 920-HP Bristol Pegasus XC engines.

1936 July 14 The administrative and operational structure of the RAF's metropolitan force was reorganized into several separate commands: fighter, bomber, coastal and training. Some time later, Training Command was separated into Flying and Technical Training commands, and Army Cooperation, Balloon, Maintenance and Transport commands were added. Hitherto, metropolitan air forces were under the centralized authority of Air Defense Great Britain (ADGB) headquarters, which was now abolished. Fighter Command had three groups, Bomber Command six and Coastal Command three. Although Coastal Command continued for a while to be responsible for the Fleet Air Arm, that force was soon subsumed into the Royal Navy.

The air chief marshal, Sir John M. Steel, was appointed air officer commander in chief (AOCinC) Bomber Command, replaced by Sir Edgar R. Ludlow-Hewitt on September 12, 1937, (who was serving in that position when war broke out in Europe in September 1939). AOCinC, Fighter Command was A.C.M. Sir Hugh C. T. Dowding, who remained in that position until November 1940. AOCinC for Coastal Command was Air Marshal Sir Arthur M. Longmore, replaced on Sept. 1, 1936, by A.M. P. B. Joubert de la Ferté, who is in turn replaced on August 18, 1937, by A.C.M. Sir Frederick W. Bowhill. AOCinC Training Command was A.M. Sir Charles S. Burnett, replaced July 1, 1939, by A.C.M. Sir Arthur M. Longmore.

1936 July 14 Powered by four 840-HP Nakajima Hikari 2, 9-cylinder, air-cooled radial engines, one of the most successful prewar Japanese flying boats made its first flight when the prototype Kawanishi H6K took to the air piloted by Katsuji Kondo. Influenced greatly by Short Brothers in England, the flying boat had a wingspan of 131 ft. 3 in., a length of 84 ft. 1 in. and a maximum weight of 50,760 lb. With a cruising speed of 150 MPH at 3,280 ft. and a range of 2,500 mi., the H6K was used on bombing as well as maritime reconnaissance missions, and several were used as transport aircraft.

1936 July 15 A specification (B.12/36) calling for design of a high-performance heavy bomber was issued by the British Air Ministry. It called for a four-engine bomber with a wingspan not to exceed 100 ft. (so that it could use existing hangars), a speed of at least 230 MPH at 15,000 ft. with a range of 1,500 mi. and a maximum bomb load of 14,000 lb. The resulting aircraft was to be defensible from all quarters by machine guns mounted at several trivets. Shorts entered their S.29, the Short Stirling, which entered service in August 1940 as the first four-engine RAF heavy bomber since the Handley Page V/1500 designed at the end of World War I; Supermarine's Type 316 was not developed.

1936 July 25 Lufthansa pilot Flugkapitän Henke flew Spanish Nationalist Capt. Francisco Arranz to meet with Hitler at Bayreuth and request military assistance in the struggle against so-

cialist factions. Following a consultation with Reichsmarschall Hermann Göring and Werner von Blomberg, Hitler gave his permission for military support. Military plan Sonderstab W was set up the following day under Gen. Wilberg to coordinate preparations. Twenty Junkers Ju 52/3m were to be dispatched for air-lifting troops, and six Heinkel He 51 fighters along with 20 20-mm antiaircraft guns were to be sent by sea. This was the vanguard of a support program that would commit Germany and Italy to the support of Gen. Franco until March 1939.

1936 July 27 The Luftwaffe sent the first of 20 Junkers Ju 52/3m g3e bombers piloted by Flugkapitän Alfred Henke from Berlin-Tempelhof to Tetuan in Spanish Morocco and began ferrying Nationalist troops from Africa to Spain the following day. Carrying 22 Moroccan soldiers, this represented the first air transport activity conducted by the Luftwaffe. By the end of August, 7,350 troops had been ferried across the Mediterranean Sea in 461 flights; 5,455 troops were ferried on 324 flights during September, and the following month 1,157 troops were airlifted on 83 flights before the activity was canceled on October 11. A total of 285 tons of materiel were airlifted in the same period, in an effort that helped Gen. Franco consolidate his forces for an attack on Seville.

1936 August 11 Under the socialist government of Léon Blum, France's private aircraft companies were drawn into state ownership by authorization of the Nationalization of Military Industries Act, approved by the senate on this date. All companies working on aircraft, engines, armament and ancilliary equipment were to be grouped geographically into the National Aeronautical Construction Society (Sociétés Nationales de Construction Aéronautiques), in each of which the state was a two-thirds owner.

1936 August 14 Expansion of the use of German aircraft to support fascist units in the Spanish Civil War began with a bombing raid by a Ju 52/3m commanded by Oblt. Rudolf Freiherr von Moreau und Hoyos in which the battleship *Jaime I* was knocked out from a height of 1,500 ft. In another incident, a Ju 52/3m belonging to Squadron B, based at Tablada and equipped with nine Junkers, bombed a column outside Madrid. Nine days later an attack took place on the Getafe airfield, and on August 25 the Cuatro Vientos airfield close to Madrid was bombed. The capital city itself was hit on August 27 and 28. After November, the Spanish Nationalist Junkers units were backed up with Ju 52/3m bombers operated by Kampfgruppe 88, comprised military of three Staffeln, each equipped with 12 aircraft.

1936 August 22 A Junkers Ju 86 (civil registration D-AXEQ) owned by Junkers and named *Bückeberg* took off from Dessau, German on a nonstop flight to Bathurst (now Banjul), Gambia on the coast of West Africa. With a ground run of 1,476 ft., the 21,605-lb. aircraft took off with 1,174 gal. of fuel. It contained no windows but had otherwise been modified very little. After a flight of 20 hr. the Ju 86 landed on August 23 having flown a total distance of 3,603 mi. There were still 33 gal. of fuel remaining when the aircraft landed, sufficient for a further 100 mi.

1936 September 4 Flying a Percival Mew Gull (serial no. VP-KCC) named *The Messenger,* Beryl Markham from South Africa took off from Abingdon, England to become the first woman to fly the Atlantic Ocean from east to west. She landed on a mud flat at Baleine Cove, Cape Breton Island, Canada when she ran out of fuel, the aircraft tipping over into a layer of mud 6 ft. deep. Powered by a 200-HP Gipsy Six engine, the Mew Gull flew the 2,612 mi. in 21 hr. 35 min. This aircraft had been entered for the Schlesinger Air Race from England to South Africa,

Precursor to a more famous type, the Junkers Ju 86E represented the resurgence of the German aircraft industry in the 1930s.

but the damage sustained on landing prevented it from entering that contest.

1936 September 5 Lufthansa made the first of four round-trip mail proving flights between Lisbon, Portugal, and New York via the southern route. Two Dornier Do 18 flying boats, were flown from Lisbon to Horta in the Azores, where they were loaded aboard the depot ship *Schwabenland*. Still at Horta, the planes were catapulted into the air in an attempt to conserve fuel for the long flight; however the 4.5 g-force exerted on the crew was almost intolerable. Some routes went via Hamilton, Bermuda en route to New York, but on September 11, D-ARUN *(Zephyr)* flew from Horta direct to New York in 22 hr. 12 min. with 10 hr. of fuel remaining on board. The trials ended October 20 when the Do 18s were directed to the South Atlantic route.

1936 September 8 The British Air Ministry issued specification P.13/36, which ultimately resulted in development of the Avro Manchester (and thus the Lancaster) and the Handley Page Halifax. The specification stipulated design of a twin-engine medium bomber capable of carrying a maximum 4,000-lb. bomb load, at a cruising speed of 275 MPH, with a range of 3,000 mi. and a ceiling of 28,000 ft. Avro, Handley Page and Hawker responded with designs, although the Hawker concept drawn up by Sydney Camm was rejected and came to nothing.

1936 September 10 The first Soviet contingent sent to support socialist forces in the Spanish Civil War arrived with 18 Polikarpov I-15 biplane fighters. Another 12 aircraft of this type arrived later on the freighter *Bolshevik*, and by the end of the month, 200 pilots had landed in Spain along with 31 Tupolev SB-2 bombers and full supplies of munitions and stores. About 1,500 Soviet Air Force engineers and ground personnel were in Spain to support the effort, and on October 16 the boat *Yakov Smushkevich* brought 50 more pilots and 100 ground personnel. The first of the Polikarpov I-16 monoplane fighters arrived by the end of October.

1936 September 12 Bearing more than a superficial resemblance to the Douglas DC-2, the prototype Nakajima Ki-34 twin engine transport made its first flight at Ojima in Japan. Nakajima built the DC-2 under license and designed their own smaller version for short routes. It had a wingspan of 65 ft. and a length of 50 ft. 2 in. with power provided by two 580-HP Nakajima Ko-

tobuki 2-I 9-cylinder radial engines or two 710/780-HP Nakajima Ha-1b radial engines in the production model. The Ki-34 served as a transport aircraft with the Japanese navy, more than 300 being built in all.

1936 September 15 The first U.S. Navy aircraft carrier, the largely experimental USS *Langley*, was redesignated to the role of seaplane tender as the ship was no longer capable of operating the current and projected families of carrier-based aircraft. This reduced the U.S. Navy carrier strength to four: *Ranger, Lexington, Saratoga* and *Yorktown*. (The latter was launched April 4, 1936, and was commissioned September 30, 1937.) The forward third of the *Langley*'s flight deck was dismantled, leaving only the aft two-thirds maintained for seaplane stowage. *Langley* was eventually converted to a short-deck tender and aircraft ferry, a role she filled during World War II until sunk by the Japanese in Far East waters with the loss of 16 lives on February 27, 1942.

1936 September 18 A signal event in the progress of American civil transport services was taken when American Airlines introduced the Douglas DST (DC-3 with sleeper equipment added) between Newark, N.J., and Glendale, Calif. With the DST, American could offer a 17.5-hr. service with only three stops and no plane changes. Previously, the service required a plane change—from DC-2 to Curtiss Condor at Fort Worth, Tex.—and nine stops on a 23 hr. 23 min. flight time, only a small improvement on the 1934 service that required two airlines, two changes of aircraft and 15 stops in a 25 hr. 35 min. transit time.

1936 September 29 Held to mark the Empire Exhibition in Johannesburg, South Africa, the Schlesinger Air Race with prizes totaling £10,000 began when nine contestants left Portsmouth, England at one-minute intervals. Indicative of how flight times were tumbling, the winning Percival Vega Gull (G-AEKE) piloted by C. W. A. Scott and Giles Guthrie reached Rand Airport, Johannesburg in an elapsed time 52 hr. 56 min., flying the 6,150 mi. at an average flying speed of 156.3 MPH. They were the only entry to finish the race. Preoccupied with military expansion plans, the aviation industry now had less time for air races, this being one of the last before World War II.

1936 September A series of arrested landings were conducted by the French with the carrier *Béarn* in the world's first tests with a twin-engined monoplane involving flights on and off an aircraft carrier. The twin-engine Potez 56E had been designed by Louis Coroller as an executive transport, the first one flying on June 18, 1934. Potez 56Es were each fitted with an arrester hook for deck trials. Of essentially wood construction, this low-wing cantilever monoplane had single fin and rudder, a wingspan of 56 ft. 6 in., a length of 38 ft. 10 in. and a maximum takeoff weight of 6,570 lb.; it was powered by two 185-HP Potez 9Ab radial engines.

1936 October 1 Production plan no. 4, the fourth German Luftwaffe modernization schedule in a series that began October 1, 1935, envisaged a total 18,000 new military aircraft produced by domestic industry between January 1, 1934, and March 31, 1938. There had been two interim updates since the first production plan. This one was important because it included many new combat types that would play important roles in World War II, including the Bf 109, Ju 87 and Do 17. As a consequence, major industry retooling was necessary, which hampered expanded production. Industrial floor space for aircraft assembly would increase from 323,000 sq. ft. in May 1933 to 10.775 million sq. ft. in May 1938.

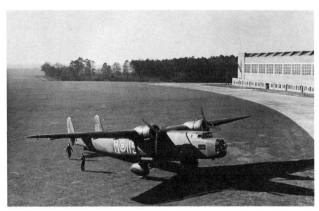

Called upon to play a role early in World War II, the RAF's Harrow II represented an old design retained for duty.

1936 October 5   The first flight from England to New Zealand began when Jean Batten left Lympne, Kent in Percival Mew Gull G-ADPR named *Jean*. She came down at Darwin, Australia after a flight of 5 days 21 hr. 3 min., bettering the previous solo record by 24 hr. 16 min. and setting a record that stood for more than 44 years. Later, Jean Batten flew on to New Zealand, arriving after the fastest crossing of the Tasman Sea by flying the 1,200 mi. in 8.5 hr. Her elapsed time from England to New Zealand was 11 days 1 hr. 25 min. On another flight that began August 18, 1937, Jean Batten took the Australia-England record for a female at 5 days 18 hr. 15 min., which stands unbroken today.

1936 October 10   Derived from the Handley Page H.P.51 troop carrier, the Harrow made its first flight as one of the first British monoplane bombers to enter service with the RAF, which it did from January 1937. Pressed into service as a bomber to fulfill the new modernization scheme then coming into force, the Harrow never saw active service as a bomber. At the outbreak of war, it was deployed instead as a transport aircraft and served in that role until April 1945. The Harrow had a wingspan of 88 ft. 5 in., a length of 82 ft. 2 in. and a loaded weight of 23,000 lb. with a 3,000-lb. bomb load. Power was provided by two 925-HP Bristol Pegasus XX engines providing a cruising speed of 163 MPH and a range of 1,250 mi.

1936 October 15   Representative of a new generation of Japanese army air force aircraft destined to bring it fully up to date as a modern fighting force, the exceptionally maneuverable Nakajima Ki-27 low-wing cantilever monoplane fighter powered by a 650-HP Nakajima Ha-1a radial engine made its first flight. Pitted against competing designs from Mitsubishi and Kawasaki, the Ki-27 went into production fitted with a pair of synchronized 7.7-mm machine guns and became operational from July 1938. The Ki-27 had a wingspan of 37 ft. 1 in., a length of 24 ft. 8 in. and a top speed of 292 MPH at 11,480 ft.

1936 October 21   The first scheduled passenger through service between San Francisco and Manila got under way when a Pan American Martin M-130 flying boat (*China Clipper*, the first built) departed for the Philippines, stopping at Hawaii, Midway, Wake and Guam. Two more Martin flying boats, named *Philippine Clipper* and *Hawaiian Clipper*, had been introduced earlier in the year. The flying boats would fly a weekly service with a round-trip elapsed time of 13 days, including two days at Manila. To accommodate the passengers, the islands of Midway, Wake and Guam had been fitted out with new hotels, solar water heaters,

comfortable furniture, showers, landscaped gardens and electricity.

1936 October 22   Piloted by Herbert G. Brackley, the first Short C-class Empire flying boat (G-ADHL, *Canopus*) left Rochester, near the Thames estuary, England on the first leg of a proving flight to Alexandria, Egypt, from where it would return on the first scheduled Imperial Airways flight using this luxury flying boat. At Lake Bracciano, Rome, Capt. F. J. Bailey took over and flew it to Alexandria. The scheduled return flight was made via Athens and Mirabella to Brindisi in just over 7 hr. on October 30. Capt. Bailey also made the first scheduled outbound flight on November 2, 1936.

1936 October 26   The British Joint Planning Committee (Capt. Tom Phillips, Royal Navy, Col. Sir Ronald Adam, Army, and Gp. Capt. A. T. Harris, RAF) completed a secret report wherein it was assumed that a war with Germany was inevitable. In the event Germany launched an attack from the Low Countries, Britain should bomb Luftwaffe airfields and supply depots. If the attack came through France, Britain must send a modest expeditionary force, and the RAF should attack communication and supply lines. It grossly overestimated the effects from enemy bombing against domestic targets in the first week, claiming 150,000 casualties (one-third this number of British civilians would die throughout World War II).

1936 October 28   Designed to a specification from the technical department of the German Air Ministry for a long-range strategic "Ural Bomber" issued in summer 1935, for an aircraft capable of attacking central Russia, the Dornier Do 19 made its first flight powered by four 600/715-HP Bramo 322H 9-cylinder radial engines providing a cruising speed of 155 MPH at 6,560 ft. and a maximum range of 994 mi. With four defensive gun positions (in nose, tail, dorsal and ventral positions) proposed in production versions, the cancellation of the Ural Bomber concept preceded completion of two other Do 19 prototypes, and the program was abandoned along with the only other contender, the Junkers Ju 89. The Do 19 had a wingspan of 114 ft. 10 in., a length of 83 ft. 6 in. and a maximum loaded weight of 40,785 lb.

1936 November 1   Luftwaffe units operating in Spain came under the command of Maj. Gen. Hugo Sperrle. Known as the Legion Condor, with 4,500 men, it grew to 6,000 by January and eventually to 16,000. The Nationalists under Gen. Franco would have the advantage of 285 front-line German aircraft at peak, and Mussolini would supply almost 800 aircraft and 50,000 soldiers from Italy. The Republicans were supported by Soviet Polikarpov I-15 and I-16 fighters, which outclassed the German He 51. The initial strength of the legion was 48 Ju 52/3ms in the bomber role, 48 Heinkel He 51 fighters, 12 Heinkel He 70 reconnaissance aircraft and small numbers of Hs 123s and He 112s in addition to antiaircraft batteries.

1936 November 4   The first engagement between Soviet and Nationalist air forces took place over Madrid during the Spanish Civil War. Ten Polikarpov I-15 biplane fighters jumped an Italian Ro.37 reconnaissance biplane (built by the Breda-owned Romeo company) escorted by two Fiat Cr.32 fighters, a type that in August had formed the La Cucaracha squadron fighting for the Nationalists. The Fiats were shot down, but the Ro.37 escaped. Soviet aircraft built up to number more than 430 by the end of 1937, but the appearance of the Bf 109 brought an end to an advantage previously held by the Soviet I-16. Soviet aircraft comprised about 90% of Republican air power and the withdrawal of Soviet support in late 1938 was a severe blow. Of 1,409 Soviet aircraft sent to Spain, 1,176 had been destroyed.

1936 November   One of the first mercenaries to travel from America to the civil war in Spain in hope of adventure, fame and fortune, Bert Acosta sailed from New York with race-car driver Edward Schneider, Gordon Berry and Maj. Frederick Lord, who had flown in the British Royal Flying Corps during World War I. With a deal that would give them $375 a week, they were to receive a special bonus for every aircraft flown by the Nationalists shot down. Far from ready fame, they were given unarmed biplanes hastily converted as bombers. For the next two years, many Americans would travel to Europe in search of adventure.

1936 November   Mitsubishi, Nakajima and the Eleventh Naval Air Arsenal were awarded a production contract for the B4Y1 carrier-borne torpedo bomber. Designed by Yokosuka, the biplane had a wingspan of 49 ft. 2 in., a length of 33 ft. 4 in. and a single 600-HP Hiro Type 91 12-cylinder liquid-cooled engine. The biplane was produced as a new attack bomber and made its first flight toward the end of 1935. The type was used in the second Sino-Japanese War, but never saw combat in the Pacific war.

1936 December 2   Ordered by the U.S. Army in January 1936, the first of 13 Boeing Model 299 bombers made its first flight as the Y1B-17 powered by four 930-HP Wright GR-1820-39 radial engines with Maj. John D. Corkille at the controls. All 13 Y1B17s had been delivered by August 1937, trials being conducted with 12 aircraft flown by the Second Bomb Group at Langley Field. Assertions from the navy that they should protect U.S. shores from attack scaled down the first order for production B-17Bs to 39; ultimately 12,731 B-17 bombers were built. The Y1B-17 had a wingspan of 103 ft. 9 in., a length of 68 ft. 4 in., a gross weight of 42,600 lb., five 0.30-in guns and a 10,496-lb. bomb load. Cruising speed was 217 MPH with a range of 1,377 mi.

1936 December 18   Designed to the specification issued February 15 calling for a twin-engine heavy bomber, the Mitsubishi Ki-21 made its first flight as a competitor to the Nakajima Ki-19. Capable of carrying a maximum bomb load of 2,205 lb., the Ki-21 entered service as the Army Type 97 Heavy Bomber Model 1A. Its competitor was not ordered, but Nakajima built the Type 97, and total production exceeded 2,000, less than 700 of which had been built by the design marquee. Named Jane (after Gen. Douglas MacArthur's wife) by the Allies, the Type 97 was a cornerstone of Japanese army bombing operations. It had a wingspan of 73 ft. 10 in., a length of 52 ft. 6 in., and a normal range of 932 mi.

1936 December 21   Bearing the German civil registration D-AQEN, the prototype Junkers Ju 88 V1 made its first flight from Dessau with Flugkapitän Kindermann at the controls. Designed as a high-speed bomber (Schnellbomber), work on the Ju 88 and contenders from three competing manufacturers started January 1936. Powered by two 1,000-HP Daimler Benz DB 600A engines, the prototype crashed after a few test flights, but the type was ordered into production and joined the Luftwaffe in 1939. The most popular variant, the Ju 88A4, had a wingspan of 65 ft. 7 in., a length of 47 ft. 3 in. and a maximum speed of 292 MPH at 17,390 ft.

1936 December 22   Flying the Short Empire flying boat G-ADHM named *Caledonia,* Capt. Cumming of Imperial Airways made a nonstop flight from Marseilles, France to Southampton, England in just over 4 hr., returning from a journey that began

nine days earlier. Leaving London on December 13 with 5.5 tons of mail for India, Capt. Cumming carried out a proving flight for new routes east. On the return journey, he made the 1,700 mi. from Alexandria, Egypt to Marseilles in just over 11 hr.

1936 December 27   Piloted by M. M. Gromov, the Petlyakov Pe-8 prototype made its first flight. Designed initially by A. N. Tupolev and originally designated ANT-42, this aircraft was the only heavy bomber used by the USSR during World War II. With four 930-HP M-34FRN engines, the Pe-8 could carry a maximum 10,000-lb. bomb load. It had a maximum speed of 250 MPH, a service ceiling of 27,560 ft. and a range of 2,920 mi. with a 4,000-lb. bomb load. Compromised in development when its chief proponents were imprisoned by Stalin, only 79 aircraft of this type were built. The Pe-8 had a wingspan of 128 ft. and a length of 77 ft. 5 in.

1936 December   Designed as a four-engine long-range Ural Bomber to a German Air Ministry specification issued during the summer of 1935, the Junkers Ju 89 V1, bearing the civil registration D-AFIT, made its first flight powered by four 1,075-HP Junkers Jumo 211A engines. With a wingspan of 115 ft. 8 in., a length of 86 ft. 11 in. and a maximum loaded weight of 61,290 lb., the Ju 89 carried a 3,520-lb. bomb load, had a cruising speed of 196 MPH and a service ceiling of 22,965 ft. Two aircraft were built before the program was terminated on April 29, 1937, the Ju 89 being, along with the Do 19, one of only two early candidates for the role of strategic bomber in the new Luftwaffe.

1936   During the year, Junkers completed and flew the first of two EF 61 high-altitude bomber prototypes designed to achieve sustained flight at heights considerably in excess of 40,000 ft. With a high-aspect ratio wing of 88 ft. 7 in. span and a fuselage length of 47 ft. 1 in., the EF 61 V1 was powered by two 950-HP Daimler Benz DB 600A 12-cylinder liquid-cooled engines. The aircraft had a cylindrical fuselage forward of the wing and a semispherical nose section containing the pressurized crew cabin. The first prototype crashed in September 1937, as did the second three months later. Although flown as the world's first pressurized bomber, it never saw service.

1937 January 14   Based on reports from the Joint Planning Committee (JPC) about Germany's projected air strength, the British Air Staff formulated an updated expansion plan known as Scheme H and delivered it in a memorandum to the cabinet. It called for an increase in first-line bomber strength of from 1,022 by April 1939, projected Scheme F, to 1,630, raising the total metropolitan force to 2,422 (instead of 1,736). This was based on a JPC prediction that Germany would have 2,500 first-line aircraft. Gen. Erhard Milch assured Air Vice-Marshal Christopher Courtney that Germany would stop at 1,620, and Scheme H was dropped. Newspapers owned by Lord Rothermere continued to warn of German air expansion.

1937 January 16   The French Lioré et Olivier 45.01 four-seat medium bomber made its first flight more than two years after a specification had been issued. With substantial dihedral on the horizontal tail supporting twin fins, the aircraft had a wingspan of 73 ft. 10 in., a length of 56 ft. 4 in. and, in the production version, two 1,140-HP Gnôme-Rhône 14N 48/49 radial engines. Out of 1,783 ordered, only 452 had been delivered when the Vichy government was formed to collaborate with the German occupation forces. Declared void, the old order was replaced by one for 225, which the Nazis allowed the French to build for themselves from late 1941.

1937 January One of the most effective carrier-borne torpedo bombers in the world, the Nakajima B5N made its first flight. Designed as a replacement for the Yokosuka B4Y1 biplane, the B5N had a wingspan of 50 ft. 11 in., each wing hinged to overlap the cockpit, and a length of only 33 ft. 9 in. The aircraft was designed for carrier operations, and 144 B5Ns were sent to attack Pearl Harbor on December 7, 1941. The most powerful variant carried a single 970-HP Nakajima NK1B Sakae 11 14-cylinder radial engine. The B5N had a bomb- or torpedo-carrying capacity of 1,764 lb., a cruising speed of 159 MPH at 6,560 ft. and a normal range of 590 mi.

1937 February 9 Designed to specification 0.27/34, the first Blackburn B-24 prototype (serial no. K5178) of the Skua two-seat dive-bomber made its first flight, to become in November 1938 the first modern cantilever monoplane with flaps, retractable landing gear and variable pitch propeller to enter the Fleet Air Arm service. Production delays forced the navy to introduce the Fairey Fulmar ahead of the Skua, but 190 Skuas were eventually delivered by March 1940. Capable of carrying a single 500-lb. bomb and with four wing-mounted machine guns and a manually operated Lewis in the rear cockpit, the Skua had a wingspan of 46 ft. 2 in. and a length of 35 ft. 7 in. With a 890-HP Bristol Pegasus XII, the Skua had a cruising speed of 144–165 MPH and a range of 760 mi.

1937 February 18 The Short Empire flying boat G-ADHM named *Caledonia* made a nonstop flight from Southampton, England, to Alexandria, Egypt, covering the 2,222 mi. in 13 hr. 5 min. This effectively demonstrated the ability of the Short flying boat to fly across the Atlantic Ocean. From March 5, when the new flying boat base at Hythe opened, no more Imperial Airways landplane flights were scheduled to destinations other than in Europe. The first survey flights in Africa with the Short Empire flying boat named *Cambria* took place after several more long-distance flights, with *Caledonia,* and these ended June 4 after a 20,000-mi. survey of the continent. *Caledonia* and *Cambria* were then prepared for Atlantic proving flights.

1937 February 22 The British government approved reciprocal trans-Atlantic services involving Pan American and Imperial Airways. Having opened up the Pacific route to the Philippines and begun a regular, reciprocal service with Imperial between Bermuda and New York on June 18, Pan American was eager to open a US-European route using new flying boat technology epitomized on the American continent by the Boeing 314, which it had ordered July 21, 1936, and by the Boeing S-307, which it would order March 15. Access to these routes by machines equal, if not superior, to the new Imperial Airways flying boats presaged a new era in air travel, the application of which would, unknowingly at this point, await peace after another world war.

1937 February 26 Powered by an 840-HP Fiat A.74 RC 38 14-cylinder radial engine and piloted by test pilot Giovanni de Briganti, the first Fiat G.50 cantilever low-wing fighter made its first flight at Marina di Pisa, Italy. Likely to spin, the aircraft had a wingspan of 35 ft. 11.5 in., a length of 25 ft. 7 in., a top speed of 293 MPH and climb time of 7.5 min. to 19,685 ft. Armed with two synchronized Breda-SAFAT 0.5-in. machine guns, 778 G.50s were built, and the type served briefly in Spain during 1939, then against France in June 1940 and England in late 1940. With a range of only 416 mi., applications were limited, but some were sent to Finland where they served until 1947.

1937 February 28 One of two aircraft designed to replace the Kawasaki Ki-3 light bomber, the Mitsubishi Ki-30 made its first flight powered by the reliable Mitsubishi Ha-6 14-cylinder, air-cooled radial engine. Possessing a wingspan of 47 ft. 9 in., a length of 33 ft. 11 in. and a cruising speed of 236 MPH with a range of 1,056 mi. the Ki-30 had an undistinguished career, although 686 were built. Built as the second Ki-3 replacement, the Kawasaki Ki-32 made its first flight a few weeks after the Ki-30; it was powered by a 775/850-HP Army type 98 12-cylinder, V, water-cooled engine. It had a wingspan of 49 ft. 2 in., a length of 38 ft. 2 in. and a maximum bomb load of 992 lb. The Ki-32 had two 7.7-mm machine guns, and a total of 854 were built.

1937 February The USAAC ordered the first batch of 238 North American O-47 three-seat observation monoplanes, which brought a refreshingly up-to-date look to this class of military aircraft. Originated by the General Aviation Manufacturing Corp. before it was absorbed into the newly oriented North American Aviation Inc., the aircraft was powered by a 975-HP Wright R-1820-49 radial engine and had a wingspan of 46 ft. 4 in., a length of 33 ft. 7 in. and a gross weight of 7,636 lb. With a cruising speed of 200 MPH, it had an endurance of just over 2 hr. and carried a fixed Browning 0.30-in. gun in the wing and a flexible gun in the rear cockpit. Although a few were destroyed by Japanese attacks on remote islands, most O-47s spent the Pacific war as target tugs.

1937 March 5 Operating Stinson Reliants on mail pick-up flights, a specialized technique using equipment for snatching and/or dropping mail while performing low passes, All American Aviation was founded to serve 58 small communities in Pennsylvania, Delaware, Maryland, West Virginia and Ohio. The company was eventually renamed Allegheny Airlines and in 1959 would introduce a no-book, walk-on service for spare seats at 36% discount. Allegheny became US Air on October 30, 1979, after having merged with Mohawk Airlines on April 12, 1972.

1937 March 17 The first of four Sikorsky S.42B flying boats, modified from the basic model with an additional 2,000 lb. take-off capability, departed from San Francisco on the first leg of the first Pan American survey flight to New Zealand. Piloted by Capt. Ed Musick, the S.42B arrived at Auckland on March 29 and flew back to Honolulu on April 20. The first commercial Pan American service to New Zealand began December 23, 1937, using the S.42B. On the second flight, the aircraft was destroyed and its crew, including Capt. Musick, killed in a refueling fire at Pago Pago, Eastern Samoa, on January 11, 1938. So began a disappointing year for Pan American in which the Pacific routes were clearly shown to be unprofitable.

1937 April 1 Reacting to severe shortages of raw materials, ambitious German rearmament plans were substantially modified to focus on modern combat aircraft. Production plan no. 5 called for a cumulative aircraft production total of 18,620 between January 1, 1934, and October 1, 1938. This was replaced by production plan no. 6 in September, covering the period through March 1939 and concentrating on fewer models but larger numbers of each type. It envisaged a cumulative total of 22,200 aircraft produced by April 1, 1939. Subsequently, production plan no. 7 leveled cumulative production at 22,681 by June 30, 1939. The rate of expansion had peaked, and emphasis was now being placed on streamlining industry.

1937 April 1 Formed in June 1923, the New Zealand Permanent Air Force became the Royal New Zealand Air Force as an independent military body. For the next several years, the RNZAF grew by steady expansion until World War II introduced a pressing need for crew training. More than 13,000 air crew, of which almost 6,000 were pilots, received some or all of their flight training in New Zealand during the war. Supplemented by U.S. combat aircraft, the RNZAF made a creditable contribution to the war in the Pacific. In 1990, the RNZAF had a strength of 4,200 men and women, 43 fixed-wing combat aircraft and seven naval and 12 air force helicopters.

1937 April 6 The Japanese pilot Masaaki Inuma, with Kenji Tsukagosha as mechanic and navigator, took off from Tachikawa, Japan in the second prototype Mitsubishi Ki-15 at the start of a flight to London. Designed as a single-engine reconnaissance aircraft, the Ki-15 had a wingspan of 39 ft. 4 in., a length of 27 ft. 10 in. and a 640/750-HP Army Type 94 9-cylinder, air-cooled radial. Named *Kamikaze* (Divine Wind), the aircraft was given the civilian registration J-BAAI and flown to London at a record attempt to mark the coronation of King George VI. Inuma arrived in London 94 hr. 18 min. after leaving Japan, covering the 9,542 mi. in a flying time of 51 hr. 17 min. 23 sec., averaging 101.2 MPH.

1937 April 10 Trans-Canada Airlines (TCA) was formed as a direct result of the Trans-Canada Air Lines act, 1937. The new airline was created as a publicly owned company and had a starting capital of $5 million with 50,000 shares owned by the Canadian National Railway. The first president of TCA was H. J. Symington. The first survey flight across the continent from Vancouver took place on July 7, and the first scheduled service between Vancouver, British Columbia and Seattle, Wash. began September 1 followed by a Vancouver-Winnipeg freight service on March 1, 1938, the first of a rapidly expanding operation. In 1952 TCA carried a million passengers in one year for the first time, and in 1964 the airline became Air Canada.

1937 April 12 Following combustion tests first held October 2, 1936, the Whittle WU gas turbine engine was bench run for the first time at the BTH factory at Rugby, England. Controlled by Whittle himself, the engine was run up to 1,000 RPM by an electric motor, and then the pilot was ignited. The main fuel valve was opened up at 2,000 RPM, and the engine quickly accelerated through 8,000 RPM before elements of the engine glowed red. It was later discovered that pooled fuel in the bottom of the large combustion chamber ignited to cause the runaway condition. Testing of the WU was stopped on August 23 for modifications.

1937 April 20 Built to allow aeronautical engineers to test the flight, stability and free flight aspects of aircraft models without the expense of testing full-scale designs, the 5-ft. free flight tunnel was declared operational by NACA at the Langley Memorial Aeronautical Laboratory, Langley, Va. It was powered by a 5-HP electric fan at a maximum speed of 25 ft./sec., with controls to permit tracking of the model as it moved on input through control wires linking it to an operator station. Engineers had complained that the full scale tunnel was unacceptable for control tests, the aircraft frequently crashing into the tunnel wall.

1937 April 26 In raids that began March 29 on the "Iron Belt" surrounding Bilbao, Spain, Heinkel He 111B-1 bombers of the Legion Condor bombed the town of Guernica between 4:30 P.M. and 7:30 P.M. The planned target had been a bridge used to carry traffic delivering supplies to Nationalist forces in Balbao, but poor visibility and a general lack of familiarity with the aircraft and its bomb-release gear resulted in 1,600 deaths and almost 900 injured, almost all civilians. After the bombers left, He 51 fighters strafed the streets, which accounted for a high percentage of the total casualty list. Communists cited this as a deliberate attempt by German aircraft to kill civilians, and the Guernica incident fueled their efficient propaganda machine.

1937 April The world's first aircraft powered by a liquid rocket motor made its first flight when Flugkapitän Erich Warsitz flew the Heinkel He 112 into the air but crashed as the motor malfunctioned. Powered by a 2,000-lb. thrust motor provided by Dr. Wernher von Braun, burning liquid oxygen and alcohol, the He 112 was flown at Kummersdorf, a suburb of Berlin. After modifications to the engine design, Warsitz persisted with his trials and eventually made a fully successful flight several months later. Nevertheless, a competing rocket motor built by Walter and operating on a hydrogen peroxide and paste catalyst was preferred and selected for later experiments.

1937 April One of the more famous names in military aviation came into existence with the founding of SAAB (Svenska Aeroplan Aktiebolaget) in Sweden. With a factory at Trollhättan, the company was monopolized with orders from the Kungl Svenska Flygvapnet (Royal Swedish Air Force) and in 1939 merged with airplane builders Svenska Järnsvagsverkstäderna Aeroplanavdelningen, a Swedish manufacturer formed in 1930. Until then, military orders had been shared between the two companies. The first SAAB products were license-built Junkers Ju 86 from Germany. The first domestic design was the L.10, or SAAB-17, an all-metal reconnaissance aircraft with retractable undercarriage, which made its first flight on May 18, 1940.

1937 May 6 At 7:23 P.M., the giant German dirigible *Hindenburg* was destroyed when it burst into flames while trying to moor to a mast at Lakehurst, N.J. It had left Frankfurt on May 4, and its crew of 61 with 36 passengers had flown the Atlantic under the command of Max Pruss, arriving over the Empire State Building, N.Y. at 3:30 P.M. on the sixth. A total of 22 crew and 13 passengers died as the flaming hulk sank to the ground, watched by a distressed radio reporter commenting live on the incident. Various theories were expounded as to the cause of the disaster—lightning, a broken stay wire causing a static spark, even sabotage—but the actual cause was never found.

1937 May 7 A milestone in the evolution of pressurized aircraft, the Lockheed XC-35 made its first flight at Burbank, Calif. before being delivered to Wright Field where Lt. Ben Kelsey would conduct a highly successful series of high-altitude pressure tests. Specially adapted from the Electra (and given special c/n 3501), the aircraft was ordered by the War Department in June 1936. With two 550-HP turbosupercharged Pratt & Whitney XR-1340-43 radial engines, the XC-35 was sealed with a neoprene tape provided by Du Pont. With an interior/exterior pressure differential of 10 lb./sq. in., the XS-35 was the world's first successful pressurized aircraft.

1937 May 8 The German dirigible *Graf Zeppelin* arrived back at Freidrichshafen for the last time, condemned by the loss of the *Hindenburg* to premature retirement. *Graf Zeppelin* had carried 16,000 fare-paying passengers on 590 flights in the eight yr. 10 mon. since it first flew, having covered 1,053,389 mi., equivalent to 44 flights around the earth's equator. The recently completed *Graf Zeppelin II* was also retired at this time. *Graf Zeppelin* was not broken up until May 1940, but by that time, the dream of Count Ferdinand von Zeppelin that the airways of the world would be full of giant passenger-carrying dirigibles had died, almost 37 years after his first rigid airship took to the skies.

1937 May 8 For the first time, a powered aircraft was flown to a height of more than 50,000 ft. when Lt. Col. Mario Pezzi of

The Hindenburg *bursting into flames at Lakehurst, N.J., on May 6, 1937, ending hopes of an airship renaissance.*

the Italian Air Force piloted a specially modified Caproni Ca.113, the Ca.161 bis, to an altitude of 51,384 ft. With a 14-cylinder 700-HP Piaggio XI radial engine, the aircraft broke the existing record of 49,967 ft. Lt. Col. Pezzi was chief of the high altitude school in Italy and wore a special pressure suit. On October 22, 1938, Lt. Col. Pezzi flew the same aircraft to a new record height of 56,050 ft., which had, between his flights, been reset on June 30, 1938, by Flt. Lt. M. J. Adam of the RAF in a Bristol Type 138A at 53,937 ft.

1937 May 10 The Focke Achgelis Fa-61 made the world's first autorotation of a rotary-winged flying machine when it descended from a height of 1,300 ft. with the engine switched off and its rotors spinning freely. It came in for a perfect landing, adding great confidence to autogyro operating safety. The achievements of this remarkable flying machine attracted the attention of the 25-year-old woman test pilot Hanna Reitsch, who demonstrated it to Charles Lindbergh when he visited Germany. Lindergh was greatly impressed with the helicopter, calling it the most striking aeronautical development he had ever seen.

1937 May 19 Japanese plane makers Mitsubishi and Nakajima were authorized to prepare designs for a new experimental navy fighter aimed at a production model capable of replacing the Mitsubishi A5M. The specification was revised in October to facilitate a maximum speed of 311 MPH at 13,125 ft., a climb time of 9,840 ft. in 9.5 min., an endurance of at least 1.5 hr. or 6 to

8 hr. at cruising speed, and a takeoff run of less than 230 ft. Moreover, the fighter had to have two 20-mm cannon and two 7.7-mm machine guns with the option of carrying two 132-lb. bombs. Mitsubishi employed Jiro Horikoshi to head the design team, which eventually produced one of the most famous aircraft of World War II, the Mitsubishi A6M Reisen (Zero).

1937 May 29 One of the most successful Grumman aircraft and Grumman's first twin-engined plane, built in relatively small numbers, the high-wing G-21 Goose amphibian first took to the air piloted by Bud Gillies and Robert L. Hall. The first 12 G-21s were powered by the 450-HP Pratt & Whitney Wasp Jr. SB radial engine. Some 345 G-21s were built and supplied to the military forces of 12 countries. With a wingspan of 49 ft. and a length of 38 ft. 3 in., the Goose had a loaded weight of 3,402 lb., a maximum sea level speed of 195 MPH and a range of 795 mi. The Goose had a wide range of applications, and some were still airborne in the early 1990s.

1937 June 2 Just over one month after the cancellation on April 29 of the German Ural Bomber program and the two contenders, the Dornier Do 19 and the Junkers Ju 89, Heinkel received authorization to proceed with a full-size mockup of Projekt 1041. This had been developed by Heinkel following definition of an improved strategic bomber program about one year before and would ultimately lead to the Heinkel He 177 Greif. The specification driving Projekt 1041 anticipated the aircraft carrying a 2,000-

lb. bomb load 4,160 mi., producing a top speed of more than 335 MPH and stressed to perform shallow-angle dive-bombing.

1937 June 18   The first of two long-distance flights from the USSR to the United States began when Soviet airmen V. P. Chkalov, G. F. Baidukov and A. V. Belyakov flying a Tupolev ANT-25 with red wings and tail took off from Moscow. After 63 hr. 25 min., they landed at Portland, Maine, having flown a distance of 5,674 mi. This followed on an unsuccessful attempt to fly to the United States that began July 20, 1936, and ended after 56 hr. 20 min. when the ANT-25 came down after 5,709 mi. on the island of Ood, subsequently named Chkalov, off Sakhalin in the sea of Okhotsk. The second successful, long-distance flight with the ANT-25 began July 12, 1937, when M. M. Gromov, A. B. Yumashyev and S. Z. Danilin flew from Moscow to San Jacinto, Calif., flying 7,146 mi. in 62 hr. 17 min. and breaking the straight-line distance record.

1937 June 23   The USAAC ordered a prototype Lockheed XP-38 designed to specification X-608 defining a high-altitude interceptor with a top speed of more than 360 MPH at 20,000 ft., 290 MPH at sea level and a climb time of 6 min. to 20,000 ft. Designed by Hall L. Hibbard and Clarence L. ''Kelly'' Johnson, the P-38 Lightning was superlative in many respects. It was the first military project for Lockheed, the first twin-bomb/twin-engine interceptor in the USAAC, the first with a top speed of 400 MPH, the first with a turbosupercharged Allison in-line engine, the first USAAF fighter to shoot down a German aircraft, first to escort Allied bombers to Berlin, first to land in Japan after the surrender, heaviest fighter in service and the only U.S. fighter in production throughout World War II, more than 11,000 being built.

1937 June 25   The first Pan American survey flight over the North Atlantic route began when the Sikorsky S.42B named *Clipper III* left Port Washington, N.Y. for Shediac, New Brunswick. The second flight on June 27 got to Botwood, Newfoundland, and the third flight, on July 3, went to Shediac, Botwood, Foynes (in Ireland) and Southampton, England. The last proving flight, a repeat of the third, was flown beginning August 22, six days after a survey flight of the southern route calling at Bermuda, the Azores, Lisbon, in Spain and Marseilles, France before Southampton. Pan American had received the permission of the British government to perform reciprocal North Atlantic services with Imperial Airways.

1937 June 25   Using two Focke Wulf Fw 61 helicopters, designated V1 and V2, the first of several FAI-certified records for this class of aircraft were accomplished. The German pilot Ewald Rohlfs took the V1, registered D-EBVU, to a height of 2,439 (8,001.95 ft.) and secured an endurance record of 1 hr. 20 min. 49 sec. The second Fw 61, registered D-EKRA, achieved a speed of 122.553 km/hr. (76.151 MPH) over a 12.43-mi. (20 km) closed-circuit course. This same helicopter also took the record for distance in a straight line, achieving 16.4 km (10.19 mi.). On October 25, 1937, the German aviatrix Hanna Reitsch would fly the Fw 61 a straight-line distance of 108.974 km (67.713 mi.) and in June 1938, Karl Bode would achieve a distance of 230.248 km (143.069 mi.) and on January 29, 1939, an altitude of 3,427 m (11,243.44 ft.).

1937 June 30   The U.S. Navy awarded Martin a contract for a full-size prototype Model 162 twin-engine patrol flying boat to challenge the Consolidated PBY and to retain its now established position in flying boat design. As it turned out, the Model 162 was markedly superior to the PBY when it appeared in 1939.

Martin built a 25%-scale model known as the Model 162A, and the prototype was designated XPBM-1. The design featured a gull wing, and the prototype had a flat tail with vertical fins. This was changed later when the tail was given dihedral, canting the fins inward and giving the aircraft its characteristic appearance.

1937 June 30   The U.S. Navy received the four USAAC airships in its inventory when the air corps abandoned its airship program. The four airships (TC-10, -11, -13 and -14) were handed over with army designations, but only the last two were employed by the navy. TC-13 had been built by Goodyear in 1933 and had a length of 233 ft. and a volume of 360,000 cu. ft. TC-14 was built by Air Cruisers Inc. in 1935 with a car produced by Mercury Corp. It had the same dimensions as the TC-13. TC-11 had been the first of its kind to have a metal car and had a length of 195 ft. 9 in., a diameter of 44 ft. 6 in. and a volume of 200,600 cu. ft.

1937 July 1   Varney Air Transport reflected the growing nature of domestic airline operations by changing its name to Continental Air Lines Inc. Formerly known as the Southwest Division of Varney Speed Lines, which had begun operations in 1926, it began operations July 15, 1934, having been set up by Walter T. Varney and Louis H. Mueller. Its name changed on December 17, 1934, to Varney Air Transport Inc., and modest expansion began when Walter Varney withdrew and an investor named Robert Six came in. When Varney became Continental, it moved headquarters to Denver, Colo.

1937 July 1   The Soviet state airline, Aeroflot, opened one of its most important international routes—between Moscow and Stockholm, Sweden via Riga, Latvia. It was serviced by Tupolev ANT-35 twin-engined, low-wing, monoplane transport aircraft, the first of which had flown first on August 20, 1936, and a few Douglas DC-3s. This was the second of two important international air routes opened by Aeroflot, the other being the Moscow-Kiev-Prague route first flown in 1936. The ANT-35 had a wingspan of 68 ft. 3 in., a length of 49 ft. and a cruising speed of 224 MPH with a range of 1,020 mi.

1937 July 2   World-famous record-breaking aviatrix Amelia Earhart disappeared without trace, along with copilot Fred Noonan, while attempting to fly around the world in a Lockheed Model 10-E (serial no. NR16020) powered by two 600-HP Pratt & Whitney Wasp S3H1 radial engines, the most powerful version of the Electra. They departed Oakland, Calif. on May 21 and Miami on June 1. From Natal, Brazil, they flew across the South Atlantic to Africa, up to Arabia, Calcutta, Bangkok and Singapore, interspersed with refueling stops. From Lae, New Guinea, they took off on one of the longest legs of the trip aiming for Howland Island in the Pacific, only 2 sq. mi. in size. Radio messages indicated they were lost and searching for land, but nothing more was heard from them.

1937 July 3   Designed and produced for the Royal Netherlands Naval Air Service, the Dornier Do 24 V3 prototype (serial no. D-ADLR) flying boat made its first flight from the Bodensee powered by three 890-HP Wright R-1820-F52 Cyclone radial engines. (V1 and V2 had flown in 1938.) The Dutch received 11 Do 24s from license-builder Weser-Flugzeugbau and built a further 25 themselves. With a wingspan of 88 ft. 7 in. and a length of 72 ft. 2 in., the Do 24 was similar to its predecessor, the Do 18, and had a loaded weight of 39,249 lb. and a range of 1,800 mi. The Dutch flew Do 24s against the Japanese in the East Indies, and the Germans flew them against the Allies in Europe.

1937 July 5 To coincide with Pan American Sikorsky S.42B (serial no. NC16736, *Clipper III*) flying from Botwood, Newfoundland to Southampton, England via Foynes, a Short Empire flying boat (serial no. G-ADHM, *Caledonia*) piloted by Capt. Wilcockson departed Foynes at 6:00 P.M. just three hours before the Clipper left Botwood. This was the first in a series of dual survey flights involving Pan American and Imperial Airways on the North Atlantic route mutually agreed upon at the beginning of the year for reciprocal schedules from the United States to England. In October, *Caledonia* would begin survey flights of the Southampton-Azores leg.

1937 July 7 The USAAC ordered 210 Curtiss Model 75 all-metal, cantilever wing, monoplane fighters designated P-36, powered by a 1,050-HP Pratt & Whitney R-1830-13 radial engine. Worth just over $4.113 million, this order, the largest single order awarded for a U.S. military aircraft since 1918, resulted from a fly-off involving a lone Y1P-36 during the 1937 Pursuit Aircraft Competition. More than 1,000 P-36s would be built for domestic and export markets. The P-36 had a wingspan of 37 ft. 3 in., a length of 28.5 ft., a gross weight of 5,650 lb., a top speed of 313 MPH and a normal range of 825 mi. Armament comprised single 0.50-in. and 0.30-in. machine guns.

1937 July 15 The first successful aircraft to be designed and produced by the Hamburger Flugzeugbau G.m.b.H. subsidiary of Blohm und Voss, the Bv 138 twin-boom high-wing flying boat, took to the air designated Ha 138 V1. It was developed as a long-range maritime reconnaissance flying boat and had a hull reminiscent of a Dutch clog. The main production model, of which 227 were built, was powered by two 880-HP Junkers Jumo 205D engines providing a cruising speed of 146 MPH and a range of 3,105 mi. This version did not enter service until March 1941. Preceded by 52 earlier prototypes and variants, the Bv 138 had a wingspan of 88 ft. 7 in., a length of 65 ft. 3 in. and a loaded weight of 32,413 lb.

1937 July 23 The International Military Aircraft Competition at Dübendorf near Zürich provided the picturesque venue for the first major demonstration of the Messerschmitt Bf 109. Three Bf 109B versions were there as well as the V13, powered by a 950-HP Daimler Benz DB 600 engine that would be used to raise the world landplane speed record in less than four months time. Although revealed publicly for the first time at the 1936 Olympic Games in Berlin, the Bf 109 created a profound sense of German aeronautical vitality, the significance of which was not lost on other European countries.

1937 July 27 The Short S.21 Maia flying boat (G-ADHK), the lower component of a composite aircraft adapted from the design of the Empire flying boat to carry a four-engine seaplane called Mercury on its upper fuselage, made its first flight from the Medway River, England. It had a wingspan of 114 ft., a length of 84 ft. 11 in., an all-up weight of 38,000 lb. and a maximum speed of 200 MPH. The aircraft had a ceiling of 20,000 ft. and a range of 850 mi. When launching the Mercury seaplane in flight, a maximum weight was limited to 27,000 lb. Initially equipped with pylons to support the seaplane, which were removed in 1940, Maia was destroyed by German bombing while moored at Poole, Dorset on May 1, 1941.

1937 July 27 Officials from the British and Irish governments met in Dublin with representatives of Imperial Airways and Pan American to discuss areas of common interest, such as postal services, weather forecasts and signal codes, and to review experimental and pioneer flights in the expanding global network of civil air operations. This was following in February 1938 by a follow-up conference in Canada, at which they agreed to standardize communications procedures and weather forecasting. A third conference in Dublin in March 1939 resulted in the Transatlantic Air Service Safety Organization (TASSO).

1937 July 27 Designed by Focke-Wulf as a 26-passenger long-range airliner, the Fw 200 V1 (eventually registered D-AERE) made its first flight almost exactly one year after Deutsche Lufthansa ordered the type. With a wingspan of 108 ft. 3 in. and a length of 78 ft. 3 in., the four 750/875-HP Pratt & Whitney S1E-G 9-cylinder radial engines provided a cruising speed of 202 MPH at 9,842 ft. and a range of 776 mi. Some went to Denmark, and Lufthansa had a few when war broke out, but the potential of the aircraft for military transport and long-range reconnaissance was quickly recognized. It was in a military role that the Fw 200 Condor was to achieve fame.

1937 July 29 The British cabinet decided to transfer full administrative and operational control of the Fleet Air Arm from the RAF to the Admiralty, a move fought for long and hard by the Royal Navy. Yet, whereas the RAF was getting modern monoplane fighters and bombers, the FAA would soldier on with outdated, outclassed biplanes, going into World War II with nothing more modern than a navalized version of the Gloster Gladiator, the landplane version having flown first in 1934. The final move came following a review by Sir Thomas Inskip.

1937 July 29 Designed to challenge the Douglas transports and further develop the Electra, Lockheed conducted the first flight of the Model 14 Super Electra powered by 875-HP Pratt & Whitney Hornet S1E-G radial engines. The first production aircraft went to Northwest Airlines, and the type would evolve into the Hudson. The Super Electra had a wingspan of 65.5 ft., a length of 44 ft. 4 in. and a maximum weight of 17,500 lb. With a cruising speed of up to 240 MPH, the Super Electra was competitive with the DC-3 (207 MPH), but the capacity was less, and a series of accidents sapped faith, resulting in its domestic demise in 1939, although foreign airlines continued to operate it with success.

1937 July The German Air Ministry set up a rocket aircraft research program called Projekt X, conducted in great secrecy at the German Research Institute for Gliding (Deutsches Forschungsinstitutt für Segelflug, or DFS) and involving Dr. Alexander M. Lippisch. The institute had expanded in 1933 to embrace several novel and experimental projects. This work would lead directly to the DFS 194, intended to serve as a test vehicle for rocket motors and as an aerodynamic precursor to operational, rocket-propelled, flying-wing concepts.

1937 August 3 Just three days after delivering the last of 13 Y1B-17 preproduction flight evaluation bombers, Boeing received an order for 119 production B-17B, C and D models, the first of which would fly on June 27, 1939, and be delivered on December 20 that year. The B-17B had the same wingspan as the Y1B-17, a length of 67 ft. 11 in. and a maximum weight of 46,650 lb. The four 1,000-HP Wright R-1820-51 radials provided a top speed of 291 MPH and a cruising speed of 231 MPH, increased to 323 MPH and 250 MPH respectively for the B-17C with 1,200-HP Wright R-1820-65 engines with a maximum weight of 49,650 lb. Range was 2,000 mi. with a 4,000-lb. bomb load.

1937 August 11 Designed around the Frazer-Nash hydraulically operated turret with four 0.303-in. Brownings, the prototype two-seat Boulton Paul Defiant (serial no. K8310) made its first flight from Wolverhampton, England. The Defiant had a wingspan of 39 ft. 4 in. and a length of 35 ft. 4 in. with the turret and gunner placed immediately behind the pilot. Developed to a concept more applicable to World War I than modern air combat requirements, the two-seat fighter followed the bristol F2B and Hawker Demon in concept. It was to prove fatally outdated during the war with Germany. Powered by a 1,030-HP Rolls Royce Merlin III, the Defiant had a top speed of 303 MPH and a climb time of 1,900 ft./min.

1937 August 13 Ordered by the U.S. Navy on June 29, 1935, the giant Sikorsky XPBS-1 flying boat made its first flight, powered by four 1,050-HP Pratt & Whitney XR-1830-68 Wasp radials generating a top speed of 227 MPH, a ceiling of 23,100 ft. and a range of 3,170 mi. carrying a 4,000-lb. bomb load. With a wingspan of 124 ft. and a length of 76 ft. 2 in., the XPBS-1 was the first American aircraft to have nose and tail gun turrets, housing 0.50-in. guns, and twin 0.30-in. machine guns in waist locations. The navy eventually ordered the Consolidated PB2Y, and Sikorsky never reached production.

1937 August 14 An early application of air power in the second Sino-Japanese War began when 38 Mitsubishi G3M2 Model 21 bombers hit parts of Hangchow and Kwangteh in China, making the first transoceanic bombing raid ever carried out. Riding the tail of a typhoon, the bombers fought through appalling weather 400 mi. across the Formosa Strait to strike targets on mainland China 1,250 mi. from their base at Taipei on the island of Formosa. The following day, additional raids took place from a base at Kyushu. Japanese bombers were subsequently based in China where raids could be planned into the inner areas of the country.

1937 August 15 Two Blohm und Voss Ha 139 twin-float, twin-fin, four-engined seaplanes began a series of seven round-trip flights between Horta, in the Azores, and New York, operating from the German depot ships *Schwabenland* and *Friesenland* and averaging 143.5 MPH on the westbound run and 154.7 MPH on the eastbound return. With a wingspan of 88 ft. 7 in. and a length of 64 ft., the Ha 139A had a maximum catapult weight of 38,581 lb. and a range of 3,293 mi. at a cruising speed of 161.5 MPH. Built by the Blohm und Voss subsidiary Hamburger Flugzeugbau G.m.b.H, D-AJEY *Nordwind* and D-AMIE *Nordmeer* were characterized by anhedral wing sections inboard of the four 605-HP Junkers Jumo 205C engines.

1937 August 28 Derived from the Junkers Ju 89 long-range bomber project, the Ju 90 four-engine, low-wing transport made its first flight. With twin fins and a rectractable landing gear, the Ju 90 could carry up to 40 passengers and had a range of 1,300 mi. It had a wingspan of 114 ft. 11 in., a length of 86 ft. 3 in., a cruising speed of 199 MPH at 9,842 ft. and a service ceiling of 18,044 ft. Pressed into service with the Luftwaffe during 1940, only 20 of the type were built, and it was used in supply operations into Stalingrad before it was retired late in 1943.

1937 September 1 One of the most unusual fighters of the interwar years, the Bell XFM-1 Airacuda, made its first flight. Designed as a heavily armed attack fighter against the impending generation of heavy, long-range bombers, it had a wingspan of 69 ft. 10 in. supporting two nacelles, each with a 37-mm gun and a gunner in the front and a 1,150-HP Allison V-1710-13 pusher in the rear. The fuselage was 44 ft. 10 in. in length with a two-man crew in tandem, and a gunner with an 0.30-in. gun in each of two rear fuselage blisters. Top speed was 271 MPH and range 800 mi. Unwieldy and highly vulnerable in the air, it would have been no match for fast escort fighters. Although nine YFM-

1 were ordered in 1939, the type never entered operational service.

1937 September 2 The first Grumman monoplane fighter, the XF4F-2, made its first flight. Powered by a 1,050-HP Pratt & Whitney R-1830-66 14-cylinder radial, the aircraft had a wingspan of 34 ft., a length of 26 ft. 5 in. and a loaded weight of 5,535 lb. It crashed in April 1938 and was rebuilt as the XF4F-3, prototype of the F4F-3 Wildcat, first of the Grumman ''cat'' family of navy aircraft, with 7,825 built. The F4F-3 had a wingspan of 38 ft., a length of 28 ft. 9 in., a top speed of 328 MPH at 21,000 ft. and a range of 845 mi. With six 0.50-in guns, it was well armed if not always the equal of its enemies in combat. The plane entered service in November 1940.

1937 September 4 The first victories credited to the Mitsubishi A5M were obtained against three Curtiss Hawk II and IIIs of the Chinese air force. Although the A5M went on to secure stunning victories, European and American air force officials failed completely either to see or appreciate the significance of this new generation of Japanese fighter aircraft. Unliked by their pilots at first, the A5M monoplane was soon to make a great impression upon those tasked with taking it into action. It also helped direct, and confirm, the strategy for Japanese armament plans.

1937 September 5 The Short S.20 Mercury seaplane (G-ADHJ) powered by four 340-HP Napier-Halford Rapier engines, which provided a range of 3,900 mi. with 1,000 lb. of mail when launched from the upper fuselage of the Short S.21 Maia flying boat in flight, made its first flight from the Medway, England. Further independent flights took place before Mercury was mated to the upper fuselage pylons of Maia and carried into the air on January 20, 1938. (Test pilot John Parker had inadvertently become airborne during trials the previous day.) Mercury had a wingspan of 73 ft., a length of 51 ft. and an all-up weight of 20,800 lb. Mercury was handed over to the RAF in 1940 and broken up at the end of 1941.

1937 September 8 The Northrop Corp. was dissolved five months after the Douglas Aircraft Co. purchased the remaining 49% of shares that it did not hitherto own in the company. Douglas had owned 51% since January 1932, and made the April 5 share purchase in an attempt to settle labor problems developing at the El Segundo, Calif. plant. The U.S. War Department threatened to cancel its orders generated at that plant, which forced Douglas to make swift moves to secure their future interest by totally absorbing the former subsidiary and embracing it as the El Segundo Division of Douglas. Labor problems persisted and worsened for a while, but the dispute was eventually settled.

1937 September The first successful bench test of a gas turbine engine in Germany was carried out by Pabst von Ohain working for Ernst Heinkel. Using hydrogen at first, design changes resulted in the use of gasoline by the end of the year. In this latter series of tests, a thrust of 1,100 lb. was recorded for the He S-3 engine, which had been designed with a control capability similar to a throttle arrangement. These tests were parallel to similar work being conducted in England by Flt. Lt. Frank Whittle, on less extravagant resources and with equal success.

1937 September The Japanese navy authorized Mitsubishi to begin development of the G4M, one of the most sucessful bombers of World War II and the Japanese bomber with the largest production run—all told, 2,446 were built. Named Betty by the Allies, the G4M derived from the 12-Shi specification calling for an attack bomber capable of carrying a 1,764-lb. torpedo 2,300 mi. and achieving a top speed of 247 MPH at 9,845 ft. The G4M was to replace the navy Type 96 Attack Bomber, the Mitsubishi G3M, which entered service in 1936 and which was used against the Chinese in late July 1937.

1937 October 1 The German Air Ministry issued development contracts for the Focke-Wulf Fw 189 and the Henschel Hs 129, close-air-support aircraft. Designed to a requirement for a heavily armored ground attack plane, the two competing designs would both see operational service, but not until 1942, after several years of indecision. The aircraft were each to have two relatively low-powered engines, at least two 20-mm cannons in addition to machine guns and armor protection for the engines and the crew. The aircraft also had to be as small as possible.

1937 October 1 For the first time, lapstraps became compulsory on British airlines. The great improvement in airline safety had caused a lapse in the habit, but for general safety reasons, it was made a mandatory requirement. Additional safety regulations for aircraft capable of carrying more than 10 passengers required two fire extinguishers to be carried, and oxygen equipment was mandatory for all flights above 15,000 ft. Moreover, an artificial horizon and directional gyroscope were required to be carried in the cockpit.

1937 October 7 The USAAC ordered a single prototype of the Bell XP-39 Airacobra, the first single-engine fighter with a tricycle landing gear ordered by the U.S. Army. The tricycle landing gear had been suggested by Bob Wood as a way to optimize installation in the nose of the American Armament Corp. 37-mm cannon, around which the aircraft was conceived. A unique feature to make room for the gun was the location of the Allison V-1710 engine in the rear fuselage behind the cockpit. Bell calculated a top speed of 400 MPH at 20,000 ft. for a gross weight of 5,550 lb., and the XP-39 was first flown in April 1938 after which close examination by NACA resulted in some modifications and refinements.

1937 October 11 The American aviator Charles Lindbergh made the second of five formal visits to Germany, more than a year after his first visit (which began July 22, 1936), and inspected aircraft facilities during a two-week stay. Lindbergh sent reports of his impressions to Washington affirming that if the United States did not heed German air expansion, "We shall be doomed to the same position of air inferiority as France . . . and Britain. Germany has outdistanced France . . . Germany is superior to Britain. England is a country composed of a great mass of slow, somewhat stupid and indifferent people. Germany has developed a huge air force while England has slept and France has deluded herself with a Russian alliance."

1937 October 15 The largest American aircraft to date, the Boeing XB-15 (formerly XBLR-1), made its first flight with Eddie Allen at the controls. Designed to the "Project A" requirement of May 1934, the XB-15 had a wingspan of 149 ft., a length of 87 ft. 7 in. and a maximum loaded weight of 70,700 lb.; power was supplied by four 1,000-HP Pratt & Whitney R-1830-11 radial engines. The crew of 10 had rest quarters, a kitchen, lavatory, and, for the first time in an aircraft, a 110-volt electrical supply. The XB-15 had a cruising speed of 171 MPH and a range of 3,400 mi. with a bomb load of 2,511 lb. Maximum bomb load was 12,000 lb. It was converted in 1943 to the XC-105 cargo carrier and gross weight was increased to 92,000 lb.

1937 October 16 Designed to replace a generation of biplane flying boats for the RAF, the Short S.25 Sunderland made its first flight with John Parker, Harold Piper and George Cotton on board. Developed from a design common to the S.23 Empire-class flying boats for Imperial Airways, 749 were built, and the type remained in service with the RAF from mid-1938 through May 1959; five remained with the RNZAF until March 1967, almost 30 years after the first flight. With a wingspan of 112 ft. 9 in. and a length of 85 ft. 4 in., the Sunderland II and III versions were powered by 1,065-HP Bristol Pegasus XVII engines providing a top speed of 213 MPH and a range of 2,980 mi.

1937 October 20 The British air minister, Lord Swinton, submitted RAF expansion Scheme J to the government, which called for a total 2,387 aircraft in the metropolitan force and 644 overseas by March 1941, with the bomber force expanded to match German levels. It was not approved by the cabinet and reflected the disagreement on criteria for assessing the needs of the RAF. Some thought Germany would only succeed if aiming for a knockout blow and that emphasis should be placed on defensive forces, whereas air chiefs believed the strategic bombing offensive would be more important in defeating Germany.

1937 November 2 Gen. Erhard Milch, Luftwaffe, reported back to Adolf Hitler on his recent visit to England at the request of the British government in attempts to placate fears on German air expansion. Milch had reciprocated a visit earlier in the year made by Air Vice Marshal Christopher Courtney to German factories and Luftwaffe units. Of his impressions, Milch advised Hitler that Winston Churchill, who had opposed his visit, was "undoubtedly the submerged iceberg on which Germany might founder."

1937 November 4 The American pilot Frank W. Fuller, winner of the 1937 Bendix Trophy Race, made a record north-south flight from Vancouver, British Columbia to Agua Caliente, N. Mex., covering the distance of 1,225 mi. in 4 hr. 54 min. at an average speed of 150 MPH. Battling strong headwinds, Fuller used only 670 HP of the 1,200 HP available from his Pratt & Whitney Twin Wasp engine.

1937 November 6 Successor to the Savoia-Marchetti S.M.73, the S.M.75 made its first flight powered by three 750-HP Alfa Romeo 126 RC.34 engines. With accommodation for up to 30 passengers, it was the first civil Savoia-Marchetti to feature retractable landing gear, and it had a watertight all-wood wing structure with a welded steel tube fuselage with metal, plywood and fabric exterior covering. The S.M.75 was operated as an airliner by Ala Littoria, and some were pressed into military service during 1941 before a special military version, the 75bis emerged. One civilian version was flown from Rome to Tokyo and back in 1942.

1937 November 11 In an enormous boost to the morale and prestige of the new Luftwaffe, Dr. Ing. Hermann Wurster became the first German pilot flying a German aircraft to break the world air speed record for landplanes. In the specially modified Messerschmitt Bf 109 V13 (D-IPKY), he was awarded a homologated speed of 610.95 km/hr. (379.62 MPH). The aircraft was fitted with a specially boosted Daimler Benz DB 610R.III engine capable of short bursts of 1,650 HP. The 600-series engine was earmarked for the production Bf 109D, which had the 960-HP DB 601Aa and preceded the first long-term production version, the Bf 109E, with a 1,100-HP DB 601A engine with fuel injection and better superchargers.

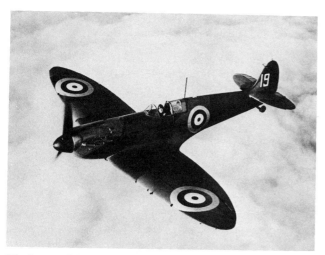

The immortal Spitfire: designed by R. J. Mitchell, built by Supermarine and, under license, other plane makers.

1937 November 17 An Air Inquiry Committee was set up in the House of Commons, England, under Lord Cadman to investigate allegations of inefficiency and waste at the government-subsidized Imperial Airways. Lord Cadman's report, issued early 1938, recommended the expansion of air services into Europe under British Airways, with Imperial Airways concentrating on the intercontinental routes. The lack of medium-size British airlines was also criticized, and the government was encouraged to strengthen links between the civil and military aviation sectors. This led to an upgrading of the Department of Civil Aviation within the government.

1937 November 25 Responding to the new world air speed record seized by Germany on November 11, the Air Ministry decided to continue efforts formulated during the summer to fly a specially modified Mk.1 Spitfire (Supermarine Type 323) (serial no. K9834), designated N.17, on a world speed attempt. Powered by a special Rolls Royce sprint Merlin, which in tests in January 1938 demonstrated 2,100 HP, the N.17 was to have a course pitch four-blade propeller and a reduced wingspan of 33 ft. 8 in. with rounded tips. Guns and unnecessary protuberances were removed, and the skin flush riveted. A special streamlined canopy replaced the conventional type, and a tail skid replaced the wheel.

1937 November Under the command of Gen. Volkmann, the Legion Condor operating in the Spanish Civil War reached its peak level of equipment and force capability. It comprised 40 Heinkel He 111 bombers, five Dornier Do 17 bombers, three Ju 87 dive-bombers, 45 Bf 109 fighters, four He 45s and eight He 59s. Only the Soviet Polikarpov I-16 could outclass the Bf 109. The Legion operated in conjunction with 146 Spanish and 134 Italian aircraft and was proving to be a valuable testing ground for tactics and operational plans. The Junkers Ju 87 in particular was singled out by Germany for trials in the Spanish Civil War and was sent to that country for evaluation.

1937 November The emergence of a new family of modern combat aircraft developed in Germany and Italy was reflected in several new records obtained by these countries. On November 22, a Heinkel He 111 carried a 2,000-lb. (1 ton) load over a distance of 621 mi. (1,000 km) at a speed of 313 MPH. On November 30, an Italian Savoia-Marchetti S.M.79 carried a 4,000-lb. load for 621 mi. at an average speed of 275.96 MPH. These bombers were not particularly outstanding compared to those of other countries but indicated a level of capability, particularly for Germany, for which the country had been traditionally favored by circumstances.

1937 December 12 The Japanese Air Headquarters (Koku Hombu) delivered to Mitsubishi a specification defining a long-range reconnaissance aircraft with an endurance of 6 hr., a cruising speed of 249 MPH, a top speed of 373 MPH at 13,125 ft. and rear defensive armament. Developing what would be known as the Ki-46 (nicknamed Dinah by the Allies), design bureau chief Tomio Kubo adapted theoretical calculations inherent in the Ki-39 twin-engine long-range escort fighter and benefited from studies at the Aeronautical Research Institute of the University of Tokyo. The aircraft was to have a two-man crew, a long, slender fuselage and a thin wing section.

1937 December 17 Designed in competition with the Sikorsky XPBS-1, the Consolidated XPB2Y-1 flying boat took to the air for the first time, powered by four 1,050-HP Pratt & Whitney XR-1830-72 Twin Wasp radials. Capable of carrying an 8,000-lb. bomb load, the PB2Y Coronado joined the U.S. Navy following an initial production order dated Match 31, 1939. The PB2Y-3 had a wingspan of 115 ft., a length of 79 ft. 3 in. and a gross weight of 68,000 lb. with a cruising speed of 141 MPH and a range of 1,490 mi. Although the Coronado was underutilized more than 230 Coronados were eventually built and 10 were used by the British to ferry supplies across the Atlantic during the war.

1937 December 24 Piloted by Macchi test pilot Giuseppe Burei, the first Macchi Castoldi M.C.200 took to the air. First in a line of Italian World War II fighters that never maintained the pace of technology development set by the United States and Britain, the M.C.200 was the first Italian all-metal, monoplane fighter with retractable landing gear and a covered cockpit. With a top speed of 313 MPH and an 870-HP Fiat A.74 14-cylinder air-cooled radial engine, the Saetta (Lighting) entered service in 1939, seeing action in North Africa between 1941 and 1943 before being replaced by the M.C.202.

1937 December 28 Concerned at the lack of military preparedness and aware to a greater extent than most of the gathering war clouds in Europe, Pres. Franklin D. Roosevelt sought from Congress an increase in Army Air Corps strength from an inventory of 1,352 to 2,320 by 1940. On December 12, the American gunboat *Panay* had been accidentally sunk by Japanese aircraft in China; moreover, European countries were arming rapidly with modern fighters and bombers. The air corps itself was doubtful of the long-range bombing role and preferred to allocate funds for tactical, twin-engine bombers and fighters instead of investing, as it soon would have to, in strategic forces.

1937 December 29 In an intrepid endeavor to photograph the remote and mysterious mountains of the Ruwenzori range, 600 mi. northwest of Mount Kilimanjaro between Uganda and Zaire, Richard and Mary Light took off in their Bellanca powered by a supercharged 550-HP Wasp engine with a range of 1,000 mi. and a ceiling of 25,000 ft. As they struggled for altitude up the east and west flanks of the range at 15,000 ft., Mary Light took pictures while her husband piloted the airplane. Climbing around the magnificent slopes of Mount Stanley, Mary Light collapsed from the cold, and her husband returned her to base, where she spent three days recovering.

1937 December No. 111 Squadron, RAF, at Northolt became the first operational Fighter Command unit to receive the Hawker Hurricane, which replaced Gloster Gauntlet biplanes. The new fighters were more than 100 MPH faster and carried eight 0.303-in. machine guns, compared to the twin Vickers of the Gauntlet. It is interesting to note, however, that in the preceding month it was with a Gauntlet of No. 32 Squadron that the RAF first carried out an interception from ground radar when a biplane from that squadron was vectored onto a civilian airliner coming up the Thames River.

1937 December One of the oldest and most established partnerships in aviation came to an end when Henri and Maurice Farman retired from aviation, 30 years after Maurice bought his first Voisin biplane and 37 years after the 17-year-old Maurice had gone up in the air on his first balloon flight. The most notable Farmans of the day were the 200-series four-engine heavy bomber family and the NC.223 mailplane, which had first flown in June 1937 and which was developed into the F.223 bomber that would first fly January 18, 1938.

1937 December Originating as a twin-engined, two-seat fighter, work began on the Kawasaki Ki-45 Toryu (Dragon Killer) through a specification demanding a maximum speed of 335 MPH at 11,480 ft., an endurance of 4 hr. 40 min. at 217 MPH and an operating height of 6,560 ft. to 16,405 ft. In addition, it had to have two forward-firing and one flexible, rear-firing machine gun and be powered by two license versions of the (British) Bristol Mercury engine, the 820-HP Nakajima Ha-20b. The Ki-45 emerged as a development of the Ki-38, which had been proposed in competition with the Nakajima Ki-37 and the Mitsubishi Ki-39.

1937 December The first Achi D3A (named Val by the Allies) was completed with a 710-HP Nakajima Hikari 1 9-cylinder, air-cooled radial engine prior to a first flight that took place in January 1938. With a wingspan of 47 ft. 2 in., a length of 33 ft. 5 in. and a loaded weight of 8,047 lb., its fixed, spatted landing gear was hardly the epitome of modernization. Yet the Val was the first type to drop bombs on American soil when it attacked the Pacific fleet at Pearl Harbor. It could carry a 551-lb. bomb under the fuselage and two 132-lb. bombs under the wings. A total of 1,495 Vals were eventually built, and the type served throughout the war, ending its days in a kamikaze role.

1938 January 11 Two USAAC officers recommended changes in the structure of the air corps during an aviation conference, stressing that air power possessed by the United States was surpassed in many important areas by air forces in other countries. Maj. Gen. Frank M. Andrews, commander of the general headquarters, USAAC, said that personnel strength was lower than that of many foreign air forces and demanded an increase in and acceleration of flying training programs for new recruits. Maj. James H. Doolittle claimed that standards in European aviation were higher than those in the United States and recommended the creation of a secretary of state for air.

1938 January 15 Deutsche Lufthansa flew a Heinkel He 116 airliner, developed during 1937, from Hamburg on the first leg of a journey to Natal, Brazil via Paris, Marseilles, Oran, Las Palmas and Dakar, the first landplane to fly the South Atlantic mail route. Similar in appearance to the He 111, the He 116 had a wingspan of 72 ft. 2 in., a length of 45 ft. and four 240-HP Hirth HM 508B 8-cylinder inverted-V engines. Designed to operate across the South Atlantic and on Far East routes, it was underpowered for the defined mission, and only three were built.

In 1939, a modified version would become the first aircraft to fly more than 10,000 km (6,213 mi.) in less than 50 hr.

1938 January 18 Eighteen Consolidated PBY flying boats left San Diego for a nonstop flight to Hawaii, which they completed in about 20 hr. flying time. As part of a Pacific defense line stretching from the Aleutians more than 5,000 mi. to the Samoan Islands, bisecting Hawaii on the way, the U.S. Navy planned a force of 250 aircraft on Hawaii with provision for 600 during emergencies. In addition, airfield facilities were to be improved with provision of a 5,000-ft. runway, eight double hangars and special bomb-proof installations. Increased aggression in China played a major part in alerting U.S. government concern to Japan's future ambitions.

1938 January 20 The Armstrong Whitworth A.W.23 bomber-transport, first flown in June 1935, was used in the first flight refueling tests with a Short Empire flying boat named *Cambria*. Flying over Southampton water, England, the two aircraft demonstrated how fuel could be transferred from one to the other by a trailing line, thus facilitating trans-Atlantic flights otherwise prohibited by the unrefueled range of the flying boat. The Air Ministry had loaned the A.W.23 to Flight Refueling Ltd. for preparatory trials that had begun during the previous summer.

1938 January 22 Designed by Heinrich Hertel and Siegfried Günter as a late competitor for fighter production orders, despite the expanding production orders for the favored Messerschmitt Bf 109, the Heinkel He 100 (originally He 113) made its first flight with test pilot Gerhard Nitschke. With a wingspan of 30 ft. 10 in., a length of 26 ft. 10 in. and extraordinary emphasis placed on commonality of parts and minimum rivets for ease of assembly, the He 100 was doomed because its design relied on the 1,000-HP Daimler Benz DB 601 12-cylinder inverted-V engine, an engine heavily earmarked for the Bf 109 and therefore not readily available .

1938 January 24 Three Italian Savoia Marchetti S.M.79 bombers began a record long-distance flight to South America from Guidonia Airport near Rome. Commanded by Col. Attileo Bieso, Capt. N. Moscatelli and Lt. Bruno Mussolini, the three aircraft flew the fastest connection between Rome and Rio de Janeiro, Brazil and arrived at their destination in a flight time of 41 hr.

First flown on January 20, 1938, the Short Mayo was an attempt to provide a trans-Atlantic service.

32 min. The flight clearly demonstrated the levels of technical capability achieved by Italian aviation, as it was intended to do.

1938 February 2   The Dutch East Indian Air Force was formed as an autonomous military power for integrated operations with the army and navy of the Netherlands, which ruled the East Indies as a colony. As of 1991, the successor Indonesian Air Force has a complement of 24,000 personnel and approximately 75 combat aircraft, mostly A-4 and F-5 fighters and ground attack planes, and the navy has 18 combat aircraft and 12 armed helicopters, including nine Westland Wasp HAS-1s.

1938 February 6   Unrecorded by camera, still or movie, the Short Mayo composite aircraft, comprising the four-engine Short Mercury floatplane carried on top of the Short Maia flying boat, achieved in-flight separation for the first time when, with Harold Piper at the controls, Mercury lifted away from Maia. Taxi trials had begun January 1; a brief leap into the air took place January 19, the day before the first official takeoff in the mated configuration. Newsreel footage of in-flight separation was taken on the second such event February 23, and both aircraft began extensive trials before Mercury was fitted with supercharged Rapier VI engines in June.

1938 February 10   In a remarkable demonstration of engine performance and reliability, Sqdn. Ldr. J. W. Gillan, commanding officer of No. 111 Squadron, RAF, flew from Turnhouse, outside Edinburgh, to Northolt airport, near London, covering the 327 mi. in 48 min. at an average speed of 408.75 MPH. Encouraged by a very strong tail wind, the flight was made with the Merlin engine held above 2,950 RPM for the entire journey. From Bedford south to Northolt, Gillan maintained a gentle dive at 380 MPH indicated air speed. This dash did much to restore morale to Hurricane pilots who had suffered several crashes and accidents due to unfamiliarity with handling the fast new monoplanes.

1938 February 15   Led by Col. Robert Olds, six Boeing Y1B-17 bombers from the USAAC Second Bombardment Group at Langley Field, Va. began a goodwill tour of South American cities. Over the next 12 days, the planes visited Lima, Peru, Buenos Aires, Argentina, and Santiago, Chile before returning via the Panama Canal Zone. In Buenos Aires, the crew helped celebrate the inauguration ceremonies of Pres. Roberto Ortiz. A valuable objective on the 12,000-mi. flight was the opportunity to test the Y1B-17 in a variety of climatic and geographical operating environments. The aircraft passed with flying colors.

1938 February 16   The British cabinet received a briefing on air expansion Scheme K, the latest in efforts to shape British rearmament in the air to match German plans. Although Scheme K was not accepted (neither was Scheme J nor Scheme L) it began the emphatic shift from offensive bombers to defensive fighters by proposing a first-line force of 1,360 bombers and 532 fighters, as compared with Scheme H of January 1937, which proposed 1,659 bombers and 476 fighters. Approved in November 1938, Scheme M called for a force of 812 bombers and 638 fighters.

1938 February 18   In a supreme test of endurance and reliability, the Sahara Rally began in North Africa. Having been organized by the Royal Italian Aero Club, the event attracted 23 contestants and comprised a grueling race in inhospitable and rugged terrain where men and machines were tested almost to destruction. Despite the appalling conditions, only 10 contestants failed to make it to the finish line.

1938 February 23   The British Empire air mail program was extended to the Far East by the first flight of a Short Empire flying boat (G-ADVE, named *Centurion*) from Southampton, England to Karachi, as the first flight without surcharge on a series of scheduled routes covering Egypt, Palestine, India, Burma, Celyon and Malaya. A QANTAS aircraft (VH-ABB) accompanied the flying boat to Karachi and continued on to Singapore. The route-proving flight to India and Singapore had been conducted beginning February 17 using the Empire flying boat G-AEUG named *Coogee*.

1938 February 24   The Japanese trading organization Mitsui & Co. Ltd. acquired the license to build the DC-3 twin-engine airliner in Japan. Production was to be carried out by Showa Hikoki Kogyo KK following detailed inspection and examination of 20 DC-3A aircraft delivered to Japan, thirteen were fitted with Wright Cyclone engines and seven with Twin Wasp engines. Eventually, Japanese manufacturers would build 414 DC-3s for the Japanese navy, designated Type O transports.

1938 February 25   Designed by Dr. Ing. Richard Vogt of the Blohm und Voss Hamburger Flugzeugbau as an army cooperation aircraft to replace the Henschel Hs 126, the asymmetric Bv 141 made its first flight. Offset to port when referenced to the wing mid-span position (full span 57 ft. 3 in.), the fuselage (length 45 ft. 9 in.) carried a single 865-HP BMW 132N 9-cylinder, air-cooled radial with the crew nacelle offset to starboard. This unconventional layout aimed at maximizing all-round visibility. Although only 13 were built, the aircraft's lack of success did not deter Vogt from designing other asymmetric aircraft, including the P.177 and the P.194.

1938 March 9   A new parachute descent record of 35,450 ft. was achieved by the French parachutist James Williams when he jumped from the rear cockpit of a ANF Les Mureaux 113 high-wing monoplane after taking off from the airfield at Chartres. Dropping to a height above the ground of 650 ft. in 2 min. 50 sec. before opening his parachute, Williams easily achieved a world free-fall record. The Les Mureaux 113 evolved as an early member of a family of reconnaissance aircraft designed by the engineer André Brunet for Les Ateliers de Constructions du Nord de la France et des Mureaux, which had been set up before World War I by M. Pélabon.

1938 March 12   The implementation of Operation Otto took place when German troops crossed the Austrian frontier accompanied by aircraft on reconnaissance and fighter patrol duty to consolidate the annexation of Germany's old ally. Aircraft of K.G. 155 circled Vienna, dropping propaganda leaflets, after which they landed at the airport followed by scores of transport aircraft. There was no resistance because political decisions had been made that to resist was futile and would lead only to bloodshed and full military occupation. The Austrian Air Force was merged with the Luftwaffe by March 16, and a Luftwaffe command was set up under Maj. Gen. Alexander Löhr, headquartered in Vienna.

1938 March 15   De Havilland D.H.88 Comet racer G-ACSS began a record-breaking flight from England to New Zealand and back in what some regard as the most notable success of the Comet's achievements. With Arthur Clouston and Victor Ricketts, the Comet (named *Australian Anniversary* for this attempt) left Gravesend at 8:17 P.M. and arrived at Blenheim, New Zealand at 4:57 A.M. on March 20, having set a record time of 4 days 8 hr. 7 min. The return flight began at 10:02 A.M., March 21, ending 5:40 P.M. March 26, after a record return flight of

26,450 mi. in 5 days 20 hr. 27 min., a return flight time of 10 days 21 hr. 22 min.

1938 March 15   The British air estimates for 1938–39 were presented to the House of Commons, detailing expenditure on aviation of £73.5 million pounds, an increase of almost 50% in two years. Britain was in the midst of a political feud over defense spending that toppled several leading politicians who were blamed for Britain's lack of preparedness and the sense that the nation was on a massive spending spree. German production lines were building an estimated 600 aircraft per month, while British production was around only 300 per month.

1938 March 18   Only seven months after its first flight, the prototype Heinkel He 115 V1 began a series of flights breaking eight seaplane speed records by carrying loads between 1,100 lb. and 4,400 lb. over distances of 1,000 km (621 mi.) and 2,000 km (1,242 mi.) at an average speed of 204 MPH. The He 115 V1 first appeared with a fully glazed nose, a configuration typical for later models, but the record-breaking aircraft had a wooden nose faired in. The He 115 was a twin-float seaplane with a wingspan of 72 ft. 2 in., a length of 45 ft. and a loaded weight of 15,719 lb. With just over 500 built during World War II, the He 115 was the Luftwaffe's most successful seaplane.

1938 March   Douglas and Boeing described two large bomber concepts to the USAAC. Neither received a contract for prototype development because they were considered too expensive. Douglas put up the DB-4, a four-engine long-range bomber version of the DC-4 with a range of 1,000 mi. carrying 20,000 lb. of bombs, or a 4,000 mi. range with a bomb load of 4,500 lb. Boeing's contender, the Model 316, was given the designation Y1B-20. It would have had a gross weight of 87,600 lb., a range of 4,000 mi., a cruising speed of 242 MPH and a service ceiling of 31,200 ft. This design was refined and eventually developed into the Model 345, which was ordered into prototype stage by the army as the B-29.

1938 March   The Air Staff in Britain issued a paper titled "Considerations Affecting the Design of an Ideal Bomber Aircraft for the Royal Air Force," which had been prepared by Gp. Capts. R. D. Oxland, R. H. M. S. Saundby and John Slessor to repel criticism from such eminent former officers as Sir Hugh Trenchard that the RAF was unwisely shifting from offense to defense as the primary policy of deterrence. Unable to explain publicly that secret developments with air defense technologies, such as radar, considerably enhanced the role of the fighter rather than the probable survivability of the bomber, the paper did influence procurement strategies resulting in orders for 200 Avro Manchester, 200 Short Stirling and 100 Handley Page Halifax bombers off the drawing board.

1938 April 6   The Bell XP-36 made its first flight when test pilot Jimmy Taylor took it into the air at Wright Field, Dayton, Ohio. Test data on later flights demonstrated a top speed of 390 MPH, a cruising speed of 325 MPH and a climb time of 5 min. to 20,000 ft. Powered by a 1,150-HP turbosupercharged Allison V-1710-17 in-line engine, the XP-39 originated when Bob Woods designed a fighter interceptor with the engine mounted mid-fuselage to make room for a centrally mounted 37mm cannon firing through the propeller boss and two 0.30-in. machine guns. Without armament, the XP-39 had a gross weight of 5,550 lb. After tests, the USAAC made changes that emphasized the close support role.

1938 April 16   Bench tests with the modified Whittle WU gas turbine engine began again. Since August 1937, Whittle and engineers at British Thompson Houston Ltd. in Rugby, England had changed the U-shaped combustion chamber to a single straight-through design. Using makeshift parts and overworked components, the engine failed on May 6 and was severely damaged. In the interim, the British Air Ministry had become interested in the gas turbine and on the advice of the Aeronautical Research Committee placed contracts for detailed engineering reports. The Air Ministry agreed to fund a second rebuild for continued tests.

1938 April 16   American automobile magnate Henry Ford dedicated the relocated home and bicycle workshop of the Wright brothers in a ceremony attended by leading aviation personalities. Ford had purchased the buildings, dismantled them and created them again at Dearborn, Mich., establishing the historic buildings as a national monument.

1938 April 18   On what proved to be the last Australia-England solo record-breaking flight before the outbreak of World War II, H. F. Broadbent made a dash from Darwin, Australia beginning at 3:00 A.M. and ending at Lympne, England at 10:51 P.M. April 23, after a flight of 5 days 4 hr. 21 min. In Percival Vega Gull G-AFEH, Broadbent had travelled 9,612 mi. at an average speed of 77.4 MPH. Broadbent had flown to Australia from Lympne on March 12, but a forced landing in the Netherlands East Indies damaged the Vega Gull, and he went on to Australia by QANTAS before returning to collect the aircraft and fly it to the mainland.

1938 April 20   Designed as an army cooperation aircraft capable of operating from rough landing strips, with excellent visibility forward and to either side, the Tachikawa Ki-36 made its first flight, only 11 months after the Air Headquarters (Koku Hombu) issued the specification. A bid from Mitsubishi was rejected. The Ki-36 achieved fame in the role for which it was designed and as a trainer. Powered by a 470/510-HP Army Type 98 9-cylinder, air-cooled radial, it had a span of 38 ft. 8 in., a length of 26 ft. 3 in. and a loaded weight of 3,660 lb. First blooded in the Sino-Japanese conflict, it served throughout World War II, and 2,723 were built by Tachikawa and Kawasaki.

1938 April 20   The British Purchasing Commission, including Air Comm. A. T. Harris of Bomber Command, arrived in the United States to review American aircraft designs and discuss possible orders for expansion of the RAF. As a result of this visit, the British placed orders in June for the Lockheed Hudson and the North American BC-1, known as the Harvard 1 in RAF service. The first of 200 Hudsons on the initial order were docked at Southampton, England on February 15, 1939, with assembly carried out at a Lockheed subsidiary near Liverpool. The first Harvards were delivered to No. 3 Flying Training School, Grantham, Lincolnshire. The British Commonwealth air forces would eventually buy 5,000 Harvards.

1938 April 21   The NACA Langley Aeronautical Laboratory took delivery of the Brewster XF2A-1 in efforts to improve its top speed, which had been disappointingly low at 250 MPH. Using the full-scale wind tunnel, Langley suppressed protuberances such as exhaust stacks and gunsights to add 31 MPH. This improvement impressed the U.S. Navy, which placed a production order for 54 on June 11. Langley worked on 19 new aircraft types between this date and November 1940 in a drag clean-up program that dramatically improved performance. The XF2A was the first aircraft to use the NACA-230 series of wing shapes, which would be used on all U.S. combat planes during World War II with the exception of the P-51 Mustang.

1938 April 22 Eastern Air Lines was bought for a total $3.5 million from its owners, North American Aviation, by a group of financiers headed by America's top-scoring World War I air ace, Edward ("Eddie") V. Rickenbacker. The rival operator, Transcontinental and Western Air, were outbid in their attempts to acquire control of Eastern. Rickenbacker would build up the "Great Silver Fleet" comprising the popular DC-3 airliner and nurse the airline through the post-World War II years. Rickenbacker retired from Eastern in 1963.

1938 April 29 The 14th Boeing Y1B-17, originally designed as a high-altitude static test vehicle, was completed as a flyable airframe to test superchargers for the Wright radials and made its first flight as the only Y1B-17A built. It served well as a company test bed for various supercharger designs, which helped give later B-17 variants, and other Boeing models, the added power necessary for increased performance demands in the early 1940s. With flights routinely conducted at heights of up to 38,000 ft., the B-17 program was assured a long and healthy production future.

1938 May 12 Capt. N. H. White assumed command of the U.S. Navy's sixth aircraft carrier, the USS *Enterprise* (CV-6), during her commissioning ceremony at Newport News. During World War II, the "Big E" as she was to be affectionately known, developed a reputation for being the "fightingest ship in the navy" and survived 20 out of the 22 major naval air actions of that conflict. Her aircraft would claim 911 enemy aircraft destroyed and 71 ships sunk; she was claimed to have been sunk several times. Despite many attempts to save her after World War II, the *Enterprise* was finally cut up for scrap in 1959.

1938 May 17 The Naval Expansion Act was authorized, which permitted the United States to build more aircraft carriers and to program the deployment of "not less than" 3,000 naval aircraft. As a result of this act, the USS *Hornet* (CV-8) and USS *Essex* (CV-9) were laid down in 1939 and 1941 respectively. The *Hornet* was to follow the design of the *Yorktown*, but the *Essex* was a completely new design with an overall length of 899 ft., a flight deck beam of 147 ft. 6 in. and a fully loaded displacement of 39,800 tons. Out of an authorized construction program involving 32 ships, 24 would be built, of which 17 would see action during World War II. The *Essex* (later CVA-9, then CVS-9) was not scrapped until 1973.

1938 May 21 The last production Dornier flying boat, the Do.26, made its first flight. With the registration D-AGNT and the name *Seeadler* Sea Eagle, the Do.26 V1 was followed by D-AWDS, second of two originally ordered by Deutsche Lufthansa for nonstop flights between Lisbon, Portugal and New York. With a design range of 5,592 mi., the Do.26 V1 was powered by two 600-HP Junkers Jumo 5C engines, and the V2 had 700-HP Jumo 5Ds. Four Do.26 V3s were delivered to the airline, being completed as the Do.26D, as were three more for the Luftwaffe.

1938 May 23 In the belief that the biplane fighter still had a future in modern air forces, the Italian Fiat company developed the C.R.42 Falco, which made its first flight this day. The C.R.42 had evolved from the earlier, and successful, C.R.32 and was powered by an 840-HP Fiat A.74 R1C 14-cylinder radial that provided a speed of 267 MPH and a service ceiling of 33,465 ft. Paradoxically, the biplane was several months behind production of the new monoplane Fiat G.50, but despite the fact that the

C.R.42 was outdated the Italians bought 1,781, and a few even served as night attack aircraft with the Luftwaffe later in World War II.

1938 May Col. Robert Olds, USAAC, led a demonstration flight of three Y1B-17 bombers 725 mi. out into the North Atlantic to rendezvous with the Italian luxury liner *Rex,* en route to New York, fly low over its decks for photographers and drop leaflets welcoming the passengers to American waters. Supporters of the long-range bomber concept lost ground to Army Air Corps chiefs who preferred buying twin-engine, medium-range bombers to buying fewer but more powerful types. Moreover, the navy objected to what it considered an infringement of its military responsibilities and the informal agreement between the army chief of staff and the chief of naval operations restricting Army Air Corps flights to within 100 mi. of land.

1938 May The first trans-Atlantic delivery made by an aircraft manufacturer to an overseas customer took place when Lockheed dispatched a Model 14-H Super Electra powered by two 875-HP Pratt & Whitney D1E-G Hornet radials to the Polish airline LOT. From the Lockheed factory at Burbank, Calif., the aircraft (SP-LMK) was flown to Central and South America, across the South Atlantic to West Africa and from there up to Europe and on to Poland. LOT had ordered 10 Super Electras; three Model 14-Hs were flown out to England and subsequently operated by BOAC, formed through the amalgamation of Imperial Airways and British Airways.

1938 June 6 In preparation for an attempt at the world absolute air speed record, Ernst Udet flew the Heinkel He 100 V2 to an average 634.473 km/hr. (394.2 MPH), seizing the 100 km (62.1 mile) closed-circuit record from the Italians. Test pilot Flugkapitän Herting was scheduled to make the flight, but Udet, visiting Wüstrow where the attempt was to take place, was asked by Ernst Heinkel to fly the aircraft himself. Publicity implied that the He 112, then on offer to foreign air forces, had made the flight in a version known as the He 112U, and close-up photographs, which would have revealed the aircraft as an He 100, were prohibited.

1938 June 7 The first of six Boeing 314 flying boats ordered by Pan American for the North Atlantic run made its first flight. Powered by four 1,500-HP Wright Double Cyclone 14-cylinder radials, the aircraft was the biggest commercial aircraft of its day. With a wingspan of 152 ft. and a length of 106 ft., the flying boat had a maximum takeoff weight of 82,500 lb. and could carry up to 74 passengers on short trips or 30 between California and Hawaii. Although each cost $550,000, they were luxuriously appointed and were a considerable improvement on the Martin 130, which they had been designed to replace. The first aircraft was built with a single fin and rudder, but this was replaced with triple fins and twins rudders, and the other five planes were given the same tail assembly.

1938 June 7 Piloted by Carl Cover, the first Douglas DC-4E prototype made its first flight from Clover Field, Santa Monica, Calif. With a large horizontal tail surface and three fins, the aircraft had a wingspan of 138 ft. 3 in., a length of 97 ft. 7 in. and four 1,475-HP Pratt & Whitney R-2180-S1A1G 14-cylinder, air-cooled radial engines. The DC-4E had a cruising speed of 200 MPH and a range of 2,200 mi., but performance left a lot to be desired. When measured on engineering and maintenance costs, it was not competitive against the DC-3, and the supporting airlines and Douglas decided to develop the smaller and more efficient DC-4.

1938 June 15 The two-dimensional low-turbulence tunnel was declared operational at the NACA Langley Memorial Aeronautical Laboratory, Langley, Va. Built at a cost of $103,000, it was designed to study ice formation on aircraft and measure the effect of very low-level turbulence on airfoils. Makeshift refrigeration equipment was provided, and the walls of the 3-ft. by 7 ft. 6 in. test section lined with crude insulation. Later modified to test low-drag potential of different airfoil sections, it was dismantled in 1947.

1938 June 30 In response to specifications issued February 1, the U.S. Navy ordered prototype examples of the Grumman XF5F-1 Skyrocket twin-engine fighter and the Vought (model V-166B) XF4U-1 single-engine fighter. The XF5F-1 first flew in April 1940, and although possessing an astonishing 2,630 ft./min. climb time, it was totally unsuitable for carrier work in almost every other way. The Vought XF4U-1 was designed by Rex B. Beisel around the 1,800-HP Pratt & Whitney XF-2800 Double Wasp with supercharger, and as the F4U Corsair, the aircraft would achieve fame throughout World War II and the Korean War, being the last U.S. piston-engine fighter in production; the last was completed in December 1952.

1938 July 7 Operated by the RAF Long Range Development Unit commanded by Wg. Comdr. O. R. Gayford, four Vickers Wellesley bombers (serial nos. L2638, L2639, L2680 and L2681) took off from RAF College Cranwell, England at 4:15 P.M. for the Persian Gulf before looping back and landing at Ismailia, Egypt, a distance of 4,300 mi. flown in 32 hr. Powered by 840-HP Bristol Pegasus XXII engines driving Rotol constant-speed propellers, each aircraft carried three crewmembers under the overall command of Sqdn. Ldr. R. G. Kellett. Other aircraft were commanded by Flt. Lt. H. A. V. Hogan, Flt. Lt. A. N. Combe and Flt. Lt. P. H. Dunn. The flight broke the record for long-distance formation flying and was considered a rehearsal for the absolute distance record attempted in October 1938.

1938 July 7 The de Havilland company wrote to Sir Wilfrid Freeman, the British Air Council Member for research and development, proposing design and development of a wooden bomber equipped with Rolls Royce engines and optimized in configuration and layout for speed and altitude. De Havilland argued that nonessential workers in the furniture- and cabinet-making industry could be directed in wartime to assembly of a bomber streamlined like the D.H.88 or the D.H.91 Albatross airliner. During the fall, a design evolved around a fast, unarmed aircraft with a two-man crew and twin Rolls Royce Merlin engines and carrying a 1,000-lb. bomb load, 1,500 mi. Thus began development of what would emerge as the D.H.98 Mosquito.

1938 July 8 Hermann Göring convened a meeting of top German aircraft manufacturers and informed them that Germany was on a collision course with war and that industry was required to redouble efforts for rearmament and weapons production. The occupation of Austria had temporarily alleviated the financial crisis facing Germany by providing greatly increased manufacturing capacity. This, plus the growing crisis in Czechoslovakia and the imposition of a 10-hour work day in the aircraft industry, helped focus production plans around existing models. The Junkers Ju 88 was favored as the standard bomber, and the Luftwaffe expected to phase out the Do 17 and the He 111 in October 1939.

1938 July 10 Howard Hughes, with crewmembers Harry Connor, Tom Thurlow, Richard Stoddart and Ed Lund, began a record-breaking round-the-world flight at 7:30 P.M. in a specially modified Lockheed Super Electra. They cut in half the time set

by Wiley Post in a flight that began July 15, 1933. Starting and finishing at Floyd Bennett Field, N.Y., with stops at Paris, Moscow, Omsk, Yakutsk, Fairbanks and Minneapolis, they completed the flight in 91 hr. 14 min. 10 sec. with a flying time of 71 hr. 11 min. 10 sec. at an average speed of 206.1 MPH. Hughes made extravagant preparations, including radio communication, navigation and weather forecasting that set new standards for airline travel.

1938 July 17 Setting out from Floyd Bennett Field, N.Y. ostensibly to return to California, whence he came, Douglas Corrigan claimed he set his compass incorrectly when he began a west-to-east crossing of the Atlantic, landing in Ireland July 18, after having completed 3,150 mi. in 28 hr. 13 min. Corrigan had flown nonstop to New York from Long Beach, Calif., but on hearing of his plan to fly the Atlantic, the condition of his Curtiss Robin led the Civil Aviation Authority to forbid the attempt. For his "error" in not setting the compass correctly when he agreed to return to California, he has been known ever since as "Wrong Way Corrigan."

1938 July 21 The first commercial crossing of the North Atlantic by Imperial Airways began when the four-engine seaplane Mercury piloted by Capt. D. C. T. Bennett took off from the upper fuselage pylons of the Short flying boat called Maia while airborne over Foynes on the Shannon. Accompanied by A. J. Coster as wireless operator, Capt. Bennett flew Mercury 2,930 mi. in 20 hr. against stiff headwinds to land in Boucherville, Montreal the following day. This was the first trans-Atlantic crossing for the Short Maia-Mercury composite, accomplished with less fuel than anticipated. After flying on to Port Washington, Long Island, N.Y., the return journey was made via Boucherville, Botwood, Horta and Lisbon.

1938 July 21 The first of 13 experimental test runs between Horta in the Azores and New York began with the Blohm und Voss Ha 139B D-ASTA, named Nordstern (North Star). Launched by catapult from the depot ships Schwabenland and Friesenland, the Ha 139B had a wingspan of 96 ft. 9 in., a length of 64 ft. 5 in. and a maximum catapult weight of 38,691 lb. Cruising speed was 168 MPH and range 3,666 mi. The metal floats were divided into 12 watertight compartments attached to the wings by streamlined mountings. Power was provided by four 605-HP Junkers Jumo 205C heavy-oil engines. This and the two Ha 139A seaplanes were deployed with the Luftwaffe when war broke out in 1939.

1938 July The Women's Auxiliary Territorial Service (WATS) was formed in Britain, providing a women's arm of the RAF for the first time since the Women's Royal Air Force had been disbanded after World War I. Flouting attempts to keep the WATS under control of the War Office so its members could be at the disposal of either the army or the RAF, the Women's Auxiliary Air Force (WAAF) was formed in June 1939, replacing the WATS and firmly aligning the new service with the RAF. By September 3, 1939, it comprised 230 officers and 7,460 airwomen, a number that swelled to 170,000 by 1945.

1938 July Flown by the designer Kurt Tank, the Focke-Wulf Fw 189 Uhu (Owl) tactical reconnaissance aircraft made its first flight, powered by two 430-HP Argus As 410 12-cylinder inverted-engines. With twin tail booms and glazed forward and rear crew enclosures, the Fw 189 had a wingspan of 60 ft. 4 in., a length of 39 ft. 6 in. and a maximum loaded weight of 9,193 lb. The aircraft remained in production until February 1943, after 864 had been built, serving a variety of support roles.

1938 August 1 Piloted by Dr. Ing. J. Hermann Wurster, the Messerschmitt Me 209 V1 made its first flight powered by a 1,800/2,300-HP Daimler Benz DB 601ARJ 12-cylinder, inverted-V, liquid-cooled engine. Designed to seize the world speed record, the aircraft was a dangerous brute to fly and arose from the P.1059 project established in 1937. It had a wingspan of 25 ft. 7 in., a length of 23 ft. 9 in. and a gross weight of 5,545 lb. Only four were built as record breakers, but the type was resurrected in 1943 as a potential successor to the Bf 109. The second Me 209 flew in February 1939 but crashed two months later. The third was used only briefly for test flights, and the fourth became the prototype in 1939 for an unsuccessful fighter derivative.

1938 August 1 The largest mass, long-distance, formation flight began when 41 U.S. Navy Consolidated PBY-1 flying boats took off from Seattle, Wash. en route to San Diego. Flying a total air distance of 1,400 mi., they demonstrated increasing crew confidence in, and satisfaction with, the PBY design. With a wingspan of 104 ft. and a length of 65 ft. 10 in., the PBY-2 was ordered in July 1936, followed by the PBY-3 with two 1,000-HP R-1830-66 engines and the PBY-5 with two 1,050-HP R-1830-72 engines. These later models had blisters over hatch covers either side of the rear fuselage, a familiar recognition feature of the aircraft that would soon be immortalized as the Catalina.

1938 August 4 The first production Spitfire delivered to an operational RAF squadron arrived at Duxford, Cambridgeshire. Spitfire Mk.1 (serial no. K9789) was the first to join No. 19 Squadron, RAF, commanded by Sqdn. Ldr. Henry Cozens. He made his first flight in the type seven days later and was pleasantly surprised by its performance compared with the Gloster Gauntlet the unit operated at the time. When Britain declared war on Germany on September 3, 1939, the RAF had 306 Spitfires in 10 fully equipped squadrons and one squadron converting to the type. In comparison, more than 500 Hurricanes had been delivered, equipping 17 squadrons. Supermarine had problems gearing up production of the Spitfire, while Hawker was more experienced with handling large orders.

1938 August 10 The Focke-Wulf Fw 200 V1 four-engine airliner began a nonstop flight from Berlin to New York, covering the 3,970 mi. in 24 hr. 55 min., and averaging 164 MPH. Named *Brandenberg* and given the designation Fw 200S-1, for Sonder (Special), the aircraft was registered D-ACON, having already made a long-distance flight June 27 between Berlin and Salonika via a short stop at Cairo registered as D-ADHR. Another long-range flight began November 28, when D-ACON flew from Berlin to Tokyo with stops at Basra, Karachi and Hanoi in a journey that lasted 48 hr., of which 42 hr. 18 min. was accumulated flying time.

1938 August 22 The Civil Aeronautics Act signed by Pres. Franklin D. Roosevelt on June 23 came into effect with authority over route certification and a new federal agency, the Civil Aeronautics Authority, to administer the act. The administration released $7 million in funds to help modernize the national airways and provide updated communication equipment. The first chairman of the agency was the industrialist Edward J. Noble, and one of its early acts was to authorize construction of Washington National Airport, which opened June 1941.

1938 August 23 The American racing and record-breaking pilot Frank Hawks was killed along with his mechanic when his Gwinn Aircraft Aircar became entangled in telephone lines shortly after taking off from East Aurora, N.Y. The Aircar had been designed to be as foolproof as possible, docile to fly and safe in every aspect of its handling and performance. The irony was that Frank Hawks had claimed 214 records flying some of the most unstable and difficult high-performance aircraft in a spectacular career of high-speed, high-performance aviation. One of his most notable activities was to tour all (then) 48 states for the Will Rogers Memorial Commission.

1938 August 24 The Sterman Hammond JH-1 radio-controlled target drone was fired upon by the U.S. Navy for the first time during a series of trials with the USS *Ranger* (CV-4). Unusual in layout in that it had a twin-boom pusher configuration, the JH-1 was the first navy aircraft to have a tricycle landing gear since the early Curtiss biplanes. Its single Menasco XL engine gave the drone a maximum speed of 130 MPH. The navy bought two JH-1s and carried out experiments with radio control equipment first before handing them over to operational training activities involving antiaircraft practice. On this occasion, the JH-1 was making a simulated bombing attack.

1938 August The first of 1,730 Dornier Do 217 bombers made its first flight powered by two 1,075-HP Daimler Benz DB 601A engines. Essentially an enlarged Do 215 a redesignated Do 17Z, it differed from earlier variants by having a larger, glazed nose section. With a wingspan of 63 ft. 4 in. and a fuselage length of 59 ft. 8 in., the first major production version (Do 217E) was powered by two 1,580-HP BMW 801ML engines providing a cruising speed of 245 MPH, a maximum range of 1,430 mi. and a maximum bomb load of 8,818 lb. The next major development would add the role of night fighter to the Do 217J, which appeared in 1941.

1938 September 11 During Civil Aviation Week in Sweden, mock attacks by 70 aircraft of the Swedish Air Force demonstrated over Stockholm's Bromma airport. Simulated bombing raids were made on the Houses of Parliament and the railway station, the national bank and other public buildings. In a bid to get Swedes air-minded and to alert them to the dangers of aerial attack, the exercise mirrored increasing concern throughout Europe and Scandinavia that war was imment. The Swedish government was concerned that people should understand the danger and heed civil defense measures.

1938 September 12 The Guggenheim School of Aeronautics at the Massachusetts Institute of Technology inaugurated the use of the recently completed Wright Brothers High Pressure Wind Tunnel. The device was the first of its kind built in the United States and was designed and constructed to simulate atmospheric conditions at various speeds and altitudes. The tunnel allowed engineers to experiment with flight conditions in the substratosphere, as high as 35,000 ft. at speeds of up to 400 MPH. The tunnel could accommodate wingspans as large as 8 ft.

1938 September 15 The first Lockheed Model 14-WF62 Super Electra, delivered to British Airways for the UK-West Africa service, carried Prime Minister Neville Chamberlain from Heston, England to Oberwiesenfeld Airport, Munich, Germany on a historic mission for diplomatic talks with Adolf Hitler about the rising crisis over Czechoslovakia. The flight took just over 3 hr. and in bumpy weather was a poor introduction to flying for the prime minister, although he was to make two more visits within the next two weeks. British Airways eventually bought eight Super Electras.

1938 September 22 Maj. Gen. Henry H. "Hap" Arnold was officially appointed chief of the U.S. Army Air Corps following the death on September 21 of Maj. Gen. Oscar Westover in an aircraft accident at Burbank, Calif. Westover had held that position since 1935 when he replaced Maj. Gen. Benjamin D. Foulois. Maj. Gen. Arnold was to become one of the supreme architects of strategic air power in World War II and would shape the forerunner of Strategic Air Command.

1938 September 23 Responding to the Czechoslovakian crisis induced by cession of the Sudetenland to Germany and only a day before general Czech mobilization, Imperial Airways flew a Handley Page H.P.42W G-AAXC *(Heracles)* to evacuate residents of Prague to London. *Heracles* had first flown on August 13, 1931, gained its certificate of airworthiness on August 31, 1931, and began life by sharing heavy London-Paris traffic with two other H.P.42 airliners. These stalwart old biplanes served Imperial Airways well. Up to the outbreak of war in September 1939, they carried passengers on 2.3 million flight mi. without one passenger being lost.

1938 October 1 Operation Green, the code name for the German occupation of the Sudetenland, began. Approximately 500 German aircraft would participate, while held in reserve were 400 fighters, 600 bombers, 200 dive-bombers and ground attack aircraft with 30 reconnaissance planes. Full occupation was completed 10 days later, and Czechoslovakian resistance had been deterred by the first full-scale Luftwaffe alert for action. Luftwaffe paratroopers at Oberschleissheim, near Munich, had been put on standby. Concerned now that he might have to fight Britain, Hitler ordered an air armament program to bring the Luftwaffe up to an operational state capable of waging war against Britain or France, which at this point it did not have.

1938 October 1 National Air Travel Week began in the United States to mark the 10th anniversary of the start of scheduled commercial air transportation and was intended to encourage tens of thousands of people to take their first flight by offering $2 joyrides. The airlines saw it as an opportunity to advertise the advantages of air travel, and across the nation, educational activities helped stimulate air-mindedness.

1938 October 6 The world seaplane distance record set when a Focke-Wulf Fw 200 flew 3,970 mi. from Berlin to New York in a flight that began August 10, 1938, was broken when the Short Mercury seaplane took off from the top of the Short Maia composite aircraft over Dundee, Scotland and headed south to land on the Orange River in Africa. Piloted by Capt. D. C. T. Bennett with 1st Off. Ian Harvey as radio operator, the seaplane carried extra fuel in the floats. Fighting through icing conditions over southern England, strong winds over the Sahara, tropical thunderstorms over the equator and the reluctance of a fuel pump that broke, necessitating the transfer of float fuel by hand pump, they achieved a record distance of 5,997.43 mi. in 41 hr. 56 min., a seaplane record that stands to this day.

1938 October 9 Officials from the U.S. Civil Aeronautics Authority and the Department of Commerce witnessed the demonstration of two new flying aids aboard a Boeing 247 owned by United Air Lines and specially modified to serve as a flying laboratory. The flight took place over New York and included demonstrations of the use of a radio altimeter and an automatic direction finder. Both instruments were to become vital aids in the development of safe bad-weather and night-flying capability.

1938 October 11 The prototype Westland Whirlwind (serial no. L6844) took to the air for the first time at Yeovil, England. Powered by two 885-HP Rolls Royce Peregrine I engines, it was the first single-seat, twin-engine fighter to enter service with the RAF

when it began to equip No. 263 Squadron in December 1940. Although it had a top speed of 360 MPH at 15,000 ft. and carried four 20-mm guns in the nose, it was not a great success, and some of the total 112 built were operated as fighter-bombers, carrying a bomb load of up to 1,000 lb. Of all-metal, stressed-skin construction, the Whirlwind had a wingspan of 45 ft. and a length of 32 ft. 9 in.

1938 October 11 Developed as a landplane version of the successful Ha 139, Blohm and Voss designed the Ha 142, which made its first flight registered D-AHFB. Powered by four 880-HP BMW 132H-1 9-cylinder radials, it had a cruising speed of 202 MPH and a range of 2,420 mi. Intended as a mailplane for Deutsche Lufthansa, the Bv 142 (redesignated from the second prototype) was given machine guns in five defensive positions and evaluated as a strategic maritime reconnaissance aircraft. The Bv 142 had a wingspan of 96 ft. 11 in., a length of 67 ft. 2 in. and a maximum loaded weight of 36,508 lb. Including prototypes, only four were built and the type never succeeded in Luftwaffe service.

1938 October 14 One of the three great American fighters of World War II, the Curtiss P-40, made its first flight as the Model 75P (XP-40). Essentially a modified P-36 with a promising new Allison in-line engine, the P-40 was dated before it flew but provided a quick and ready solution to USAAC problems of equipment and production needs. Submitted along with seven other Curtiss, Seversky, Lockheed and Bell designs, the USAAC ordered 524 P-40 fighters on April 27, 1939. Powered by a 1,040-HP Allison V-1710-33 supercharged engine, it had a top speed of 357 MPH and armament of two 0.50-in. and two 0.30-in. machine guns. Before production ended, 13,738 had been built.

1938 October 15 The RAF's first twin-engine monoplane torpedo bomber, which would serve with Coastal Command from November 1939 until 1943 when it was phased out, the prototype Bristol Beaufort (serial no. L4441) made its first flight. Basically a development of the Blenheim, the Beaufort had a wingspan of 57 ft. 10 in., a length of 44 ft. 7 in. and crew of four with twin 0.303-in. guns in nose and dorsal positions plus a bomb load of 1,500 lb. or a 1,605 lb. torpedo semirecessed in the fuselage. Power came from two 1,130-HP Bristol Taurus VI engines, giving a cruising speed of 200 MPH and a normal range of 1,035 mi. In all, 1,013 Beauforts were built.

1938 October 18 The American pioneering aviator Charles A. Lindbergh received the Order of the German Eagle, with Star, at the direct order of Adolf Hitler. Lindbergh was in Germany carrying out an inspection of airfields and facilities, and the award was presented personally by the head of the Luftwaffe, Field Marshal Hermann Göring. Lindbergh was the first American citizen to receive this honor and the first American to receive an award at the direct order of Adolf Hitler.

1938 October 22 Flying an Italian Caproni Ca.161bis, the Italian aviator Mario Pezzi achieved a record height of 17,083 m (56,046 ft.). This was ratified by the FAI as an absolute world altitude record and remains so today as the greatest altitude reached by a conventional, piston-engined aircraft on a measured flight monitored by calibrated instruments.

1938 October 25 Three RAF Wellesley bombers from the Long Range Development Unit at Cranwell, England left Upper Heyford for Ismailia, Egypt, from where they were to make an assault on the distance record. The Wellesleys with serial no. L2838, and its three-man crew commanded by Sqdn. Ldr. R. G. Kellett, and serial no. L2680, commanded by Flt. Lt. A. N. Combe, arrived in Darwin, Australia on November 7, having flown non-stop the 7,158 mi. from Ismailia in 48 hr., averaging 150 MPH; serial no. L2639, commanded by Flt. Lt. H. A. V. Hogan, was forced to refuel at Koepang on the island of Timor, 400 mi. from Darwin, and made it to Darwin the next morning. Held until 1946, the world distance record was homologated at 7,157.7 mi.

1938 October 26 The Douglas Model 7B, one of the most important twin-engine light bombers of World War II and precursor to the DB-7 and A-20 Havoc and Boston bombers, made its first flight. Powered by two 1,100-HP Pratt & Whitney R-1830-S3C3-G 14-cylinder, air-cooled radials, it had defensive armament on dorsal and ventral positions and the option of either six 0.30-in guns in an unglazed nose section or a bomb aimer's nose and 2,000-lb. load (or 4,000 lb. on later models). The French were the first to order the DB-7, and the British bought a large number; the Dutch used them in the Far East, 2,901 were sent to Russia, and U.S. air forces used the type throughout World War II. In all, 7,478 were built.

1938 October 26 Following a bench test failure in April of the modified Whittle WU gas turbine engine, the device was rebuilt with 10 separate combustion chambers replacing the single chamber of straight-through design and then put through its first test. This was the definitive conceptual design layout of early gas turbine engines that would power many of the early British and American aircraft using turbojet power. This third WU configuration was successfully employed on numerous engine tests until a turbine disc failure wrecked it on February 22, 1941, by which time a flight test engine, the W.1, was being built.

1938 October In response to concerns about the lack of U.S. preparedness for a defensive war, the USAAC drew up plans for a total force strength of 7,000 aircraft. Believing that a war in Europe was inevitable and that American production capacity would be the only way Britain and France could build up adequate forces to repel Germany, Pres. Roosevelt requested that the War Department draw up schedules for a standing strength of 10,000 U.S. aircraft, of which 3,750 were to be combat planes. Among others, the new USAAC chief Maj. Gen. H. H. Arnold argued that funds could be better divided between aircraft and much needed operational and training facilities, and the president settled for a force of 6,000 planes.

1938 November 7 Released by the German chief of the operations staff, Col. Hans Jeschonnek, the Concentrated Aircraft Procurement Program compiled by the Luftwaffe general staff defined the forces that were to be built up by late 1942 and used against Britain and France in the event of war. It allocated 30 Kampfgeschwaders (bomber squadrons) for a strategic air attack on England, 15 Geschwaders (groups) for medium bombing attack on France with 13 Seekampfgeschawaders (Marine Bombing Group) reserved for naval targets, including attacks on shipping, harbors and minelaying duties. The report called for as many He 177 long-range bombers as the aircraft industry could manufacture to complement the Ju 88 in the 58 bombing squadrons. The report was adamant that Germany would not be ready for war with Britain before late 1942.

1938 November 11 Britain's minister of state for air, Sir Kingsley Wood, announced to Parliament that the government wished to develop international air transport through an amalgamation of Imperial Airways and British Airways. The unified organization would be owned by the government and shareholders bought out. Former chairman of the British Broadcasting Corp., Lord Reith

would head the new nationalized airline, which was to be known as the British Overseas Airways Corp. (BOAC). From new offices close to Victoria Station, London, Lord Reith and his deputy Leslie Runciman drafted the guidelines for the new corporation. The Bill creating BOAC became law on August 4, 1939, and the new airline became effective April 1940.

1938 November 12 After the Dornier Do 19 and Junkers Ju 89 fell short of expectations, the technical office of the German Ministry of Aviation placed an order for six (later 12) experimental prototypes of the Heinkel Projekt 1041 heavy, long-range aircraft defined by the ''Bomber A'' requirement laid down in mid-1936. Designated He 177, the aircraft displayed several innovative features. Each wing housed two coupled Daimler Benz DB 601 engines (known as the DB 606) side-by-side linked by a common gear case, the two crankshafts driving a single propeller. The He 177 also had a remotely controlled gun barbette in the nose.

1938 November 12 Hanna Reitsch flew the powered version of the tailless aircraft designed by the Horten brothers. Powered by an 80-HP Hirth HM 60R driving a pusher propeller, the Ho II was tested at Darmstadt at the request of Ernst Udet, who wanted an evaluation of this remarkable machine. The flying wing had a span of 54 ft. 1 in. and an area of 334.3 sq. ft. It had first been fitted with an engine in 1935, a year after glider tests began with this type. The Horten brothers began work on their tailless designs in 1931 after experimenting with glider models and achieved modest success with the Ho I before they destroyed it in 1934.

1938 November 19 Developed as a civilian transport aircraft from the Savioa-Marchetti S.79 bomber, the first S.M.83 (I-LUCE) made its first flight powered by three 750-HP Alfa Romeo 126 RC.34 9-cylinder, air-cooled radial engines. Designed at first to carry 10 passengers, aircraft used on the South Atlantic between Natal and Rio de Janeiro beginning December 1939 carried 6 people and 2,204 lb. of mail, and a special version operating the Rome-Natal run carried no passengers and 1,102 lb. of mail. Ala Littoria operated four, and Sabena bought three for the Brussels-Congo run.

1938 November 30 A record flight time across the United States for light aircraft—those weighing less than 700 lb.—was established by American pilot Johnny Jones when he flew his 50-HP Aeronca across the continent. Jones took off from Los Angeles on November 29 and landed 30 hr. 37 min. later at Roosevelt Field, N.Y. During the flight, his aircraft used 123 gal. of fuel and eight pints of oil for a total fuel cost of $123.

1938 December 10 The first Lockheed Hudson Mk. 1 (serial no. N7205) began flight trials at Burbank, Calif. under the maker's designation Model B14L. Developed in February 1938 from the Model 14 super Electra as a land-based maritime reconnaissance aircraft, it had been ordered by the British purchasing commission during April and would have a wingspan of 65 ft. 6 in., a length of 44 ft. 4 in., a height of 11 ft. 10 in. and a loaded weight of 17,500 lb. Top speed was 246 MPH at 6,500 ft., and range was a credible 1,960 mi. Thus began Lockheed's long association with land-based maritime reconnaissance aircraft. Deliveries to its RAF customer began Feb. 15, 1939.

1938 December 12 The prototype Nakajima Ki-43 Hayabusa was rolled out in secret at the Ota plant ready for its first flight to be made during early January 1939. Designed to a specific instruction from the army, signaling an end to competitive bidding, it was powered by a 925-HP Nakajima Ha-25 double-row,

14-cylinder radial engine with supercharger, providing a top speed of 308 MPH and a climb rate of 5.5 min. to 16,405 ft. Performance improved with later versions equipped with more powerful engines. The Ki-43-II had a wingspan of 35 ft. 7 in., a length of 29 ft. 3 in. and a maximum weight of 6,450 lb. with two 12.7-mm machine guns. One of the most important Japanese fighters, 5,919 of all types were built by August 1945.

1938 December 16 Powered by a 550-HP Pratt & Whitney R-1340-AN-2 Wasp engine, the first K-2-series airship designed and built for the U.S. Navy was delivered to Lakehurst, N.J. for trials. These were significantly different from the K-1 generation of 1931 and emerged when the U.S. Navy took over responsibility for American military blimps in 1937. More than 70 K-2-series airships were built, varying in capacity between 414,000 cu. ft. and 456,000 cu. ft. Most were operated as patrol airships, but some were used for training.

1938 December 21 Appointed to the cabinet of the British government to handle civil defense preparations, Sir John Anderson described to Parliament an air-raid protection shelter designed for general use. Comprising a U-shaped corrugated iron shield designed to protect four occupants against blast and bomb splinters, inadequate nevertheless against close or direct hits, the shelter would become one of the familar sights of wartime Britain in the gardens of homes everwhere. The production plan envisaged the manufacture of 2.5 million ''Anderson'' shelters, and when Britain declared war on Germany on September 3, 1939, 1.5 million shelters had been constructed.

1938 December 30 Set up in October under Rear Adm. Arthur B. Cook, U.S. Navy, the Committee on Future Research Facilities recommended the addition of a second NACA research center. Following a visit to Europe by NACA's director of aeronautical research, Dr. George Lewis, it was believed necessary to expand the scientific study of flight in the light of new German research centers and in support of expanding military resources in the United States. Authorized by Congress on August 9, 1939, the new facility was to be named the Ames Aeronautical Laboratory, and a committee under Col. Charles A. Lindbergh decided to locate it at Moffett Field, Calif., site of an army air training base.

1938 December 31 Developed as a 33-passenger airliner version of the Boeing Model 299 and ordered by the USAAC as the B-17 bomber, the Boeing Model 307 Stratoliner made its first flight. With wings, engines and tail from the Model 299, the Model 307 had a revolutionary new pressurized fuselage, enabling it to operate at 14,000 ft. With a wingspan of 107 ft., a length of 74 ft. 4 in. and a maximum weight of 42,000 lb., the Stratoliner had a cruising speed of 220 MPH and a range of 2,390 mi. The first crashed, but TWA took five, which were pressed into the USAAC in 1942 as the C-75. Pan American had three, and Howard Hughes had one. All nine planes survived the war.

1938 December The 23,200-ton German aircraft carrier *Graf Zeppelin* was launched but destined never to serve on operational patrols due to a change of priorities and an emphasis on the battleship and the heavy cruiser. Known as Plan Z, Adm. Erich Raeder conceived a German carrier task force able to maul British merchant fleets and naval forces by 1944. The Messerschmitt Bf 109T was developed as a carrier-fighter beginning late in 1939, before the decision to abandon the *Graf Zeppelin*. The Me 155 carrier fighter evolved from the Bf 109G but was abandoned for the same reason, the design eventually becoming the Blohm and Voss Bv 155 high-altitude fighter.

1938 December The first Messerschmitt Bf 109E-O fighters with the powerful new 1,175-HP Daimler Benz DB 601A engine reached JG 132 at Düsseldorf in Germany. The E-3 had a top speed of 348 MPH at 13,120 ft., a climb time of 3.1 min. to 9,840 ft. and a maximum range of 410 mi. With a wingspan of 32 ft. 4 in. and a length of 28 ft. 4 in., the E-3 had a loaded weight of 5,523 lb. With fuel injection, two 20-mm cannon in the wings and two 7.9-mm MG 17 machine guns in the nose, the Bf 109E was a formidable fighter, more than a fitting match for the Spitfire and Hurricane. It was to serve throughout the Battle of Britain until the aerodynamically refined Bf 109F appeared in late 1940.

1939 January 2 Alexander Leppisch and 12 other employees left the D.F.S. factory and joined the Messerschmitt A.G. at Augsburg, Germany and set up Abteilung (Section) L. They took with them the designs for the tailless gliders (DFS 193 and 194), which were intended to research the aerodynamics of delta-winged airplanes but which would provide an airframe within which Walter rocket motors could be tested. Heini Dittmar went with Lippisch, but Paul Opitz stayed at DFS; both would play important roles in the development of a rocket-propelled fighter. The former Projekt X went to the Technischen Amtes (Technical Office) of the Reichsluftfahrtministerium (German Air Ministry) where its name was changed to Messerschmitt 163, using a redundant type number originally allocated to a failed competitor to the Fw 156.

1939 January 12 President Roosevelt presented a strong message to Congress asserting that the USAAC and U.S. naval aviation were ''utterly inadequate'' for America's defense responsibilities. Congress approved authorization of $300 million on a force of a maximum 6,000 aircraft, with $180 million of the total spent on combat planes. The War Department worked out a schedule of production with the USAAC that detailed 5,500 aircraft, 3,251 of which were to be procured by June 30, 1941, when it was planned to 48,203 personnel in the army air corps.

1939 January 17 A U.S. Post Office contract was issued to Eastern Air Lines for the operation of the world's first regularly scheduled, rotary-winged, commercial aircraft service. Using a Kellett KD-1B autogyro, the service carried passengers from the roof of the Philadelphia Post Office to the nearby Camden (N.J.) Airport and was the first regularly scheduled roof-top service for any form of flying machine. Services began July 6 and used the roof of the new post office building, which had been specially constructed for autogyro services. Eastern operated the service for approximately one year.

1939 January 23 A Curtiss Hawk 75A Mohawk, the export version of the P-36 Hawk fighter, precursor to the famous P-40 series, reportedly achieved a terminal speed of 575 MPH during a vertical dive from 22,000 ft. The phenomenal speed was achieved prior to delivery to the French following orders placed with Curtiss for a substantial number of these aircraft with 1,050-HP Pratt & Whitney R-1830-SC3G engines. The rated maximum speed was 313 MPH. The French ordered their first 100 Mohawks on May 13, 1938, and followed it with an order for another 100; deliveries began May 1939.

1939 January 25 The USAAC issued a specification to American aircraft manufacturers calling for a medium high-speed bomber with a crew of five, capable of carrying a 2,000-lb bomb load and four defensive 0.30-in. guns. The imperative to provide the Army Air Corps with large numbers of bombers shortened the procurement cycle, and two of the bidding manufacturers were selected for production contracts before their respective prototypes had flown. On August 10, the USAAC gave North American an $11.77 million contract for 184 of its NA-62 design, to be designated B-25 in service, and Martin got an order worth $15.8 million for 201 of its Model 179, to be designated B-26.

1939 January 25   The USAAC closed entries for the next generation of fighters following release of its "Requirements for the Fighter Competition," which stipulated medium altitude interception and attack against medium bombers. Although the Army Air Corps made it known they favored in-line engines on grounds of performance and reliability, four of the eight contenders for selection had radial engines, including the Curtiss H75-R, the Seversky XP-41 and the XP-43 with turbosupercharged engines and the Curtiss XP-42. The Curtiss XP-40, Bell XP-39 and Lockheed XP-38 had conventional engines. Orders resulting from these contenders would be placed April 27.

1939 January 27   Piloted by Lt. Benjamin S. Kelsey, the XP-38 twin-engine, twin-boom fighter made its first flight from March Field, Calif. At 13,964 lb., the XP-38 had a gross weight greater than some bombers, yet with two 1,150-HP turbosupercharged Allison V-1710-11/15 engines, it had a top speed of 413 MPH, although most early production models had a top speed of about 395 MPH, a climb time of 6.5 min. to 20,000 ft. and a maximum range of 1,390 mi. Designed by Hall L. Hibbard and Clarence L. Johnson, the production P-38 ordered September 20, 1939, had a 37-mm cannon and four 0.50-in. machine guns in the nose. It had a wingspan of 52 ft. and a length of 37 ft. 10 in.

1939 January 29   The Focke-Wulf Fw 61 twin-rotor helicopter made the last prewar German record for an aerial vehicle of this class when Karl Bode flew it to an altitude of 11,240 ft. 6 in. With a rotor diameter of 23 ft., the Fw 61 had a loaded weight of 2,100 lb. and power from its 160-HP Bramo Sh 14A radial engine provided a top speed of 76.4 MPH, a cruising speed of 62 MPH and a range of 143 mi. The Fw 61 was little more than an experimental precursor to successors designed in 1939 for civil transport duties, a function militarized during the war for rescue and support roles epitomized by the Focke Achgelis Fa-266 Hornisse.

1939 January   Designed to a specified Imperial Japanese Army requirement for a heavy, twin-engine fighter, the Kawasaki Ki-45 Toryu (Dragon Slayer) was rolled out prior to first flight. Originally designed in competition with parallel efforts from Nakajima and Mitsubishi, the Ki-45 was the only contender when these two giants dropped out. Nevertheless, it was the end of 1942 before the type reached combat zones. It eventually found its niche as a night fighter, and a version was specially designed for the task. A total of 1,701 of all models eventually came off production lines. The Ki-45 was effective at harassing B-24s and in defense of the Japanese homeland during low-level night raids by B-29s.

1939 February 5   The British racing and record-breaking pilot Alex Henshaw took off from Gravesend Airport, England at 3:25 A.M. on the outward leg of an attempt on the London-Cape Town return flight record, one of the last such efforts before war broke out in Europe. Flying a modified Percival Mew Gull with a 205-HP Gypsy Six Series II engine, he landed at Wingfield Aerodrome, Cape Town at 6:59 P.M. on February 6, having flown 5,997.9 mi. in 39 hr. 25 min. at an average flying speed of 152 MPH. After 27 hr. 19 min. at Cape Town, Henshaw departed for England at 10:18 P.M. on February 7, arriving at Gravesend at 1:51 P.M., February 9, a flying time of 39 hr. 36 min. at an average 151 MPH.

1939 February 14   The single example of the giant Boeing XB-15 four-engine bomber was used to help victims of an earthquake in Chile. Operated from its base at Langley Field in Virginia, the aircraft delivered 3,250 lb. of medical supplies in a flight that took 29 hr. 53 min. Underpowered and expensive to produce, the USAAC had favored quantity over quality and rejected the XB-15 for the role for which it was designed; but experiences such as the relief of Chilean earthquake victims convinced the army to redisignate the XB-15 in 1943 as the XC-105 transport aircraft. Fitted with special cargo doors and hoists, it helped demonstrate the value of large aircraft serving as troop or cargo transports.

1939 February 18   Continuing an established tradition of navy flying boat designs, the Martin Model 162 made its first flight as a serious rival to the Consolidated PBY. Built in lesser numbers, it had superior performance and demonstrated a maximum speed of 198 MPH and a range of 2,137 mi. But it was big, with a wingspan of 118 ft., a length of 80 ft. and a gross weight of 58,000 lb. The production model PBM-1 was powered by two 1,600-HP Wright R-2600-6 engines and entered service with the U.S. Navy in 1941. Eventually named Mariner, the PBM had a successful service record and orders totaled 1,370 (the last 36 of which were amphibians) before production ended in 1949.

1939 February 20   Designed to fly short-haul routes with an economy of performance similar to that of the DC-3 on the longer routes, the Douglas DC-5 made its first flight from El Segundo with Carl Cover at the controls. Powered by two 900-HP Wright Cyclose GR-1820-F62 radials, it had a wingspan of 78 ft., a length of 62 ft. 2 in. and a loaded weight of 20,000 lb. accommodating 16 passengers and a crew of three. The type ran into aerodynamic problems, and although six were ordered, by the time design changes had eradicated the problems, the war was on and orders were cancelled. Nevertheless, seven were supplied as R3D-1 and -2 types for the navy and Marine Corps, respectively.

1939 February   The prototype Bü 181 Bestmann (D-ERBV) made its first flight, the initial model of several thousand built by Bücker that were to become standard Luftwaffe trainers during World War II. With a loaded weight of only 1,650 lb., the Bü 181 was used for towing gliders and for transporting Panzerfaust antitank rocket launchers. Powered by a 105-HP Hirth HM 504 in-line engine, it had a cruising speed of 121 MPH and a ceiling of 16,400 ft. with a range of 497 mi. After World War II, the type was built by Fokker in Holland, by AB Hagglund och Söner in Sweden and by Zlin in Czechoslovakia.

1939 March 3   The founder and owner of the Irving Parachute Co., Leslie L. Irvin, was awarded the Royal Aeronautical Society Gold Medal at Wakefield, England for his "outstanding and meritorious accomplishments in parachute design." Irving parachutes had become world-famous, and in many countries, they were standard equipment for civil and military pilots alike. The company name differed from its owner's because Leslie Irvin was frustrated with sales and advertising responses that continually, and some would say naturally, added a "g" to the end of Irvin, so he formalized the arrangement and called his company Irving.

1939 March 9   The British air estimates for 1939-40 (beginning April 1, 1939) were announced in the House of Commons, revealing unprecedented levels of spending for defense; of £523 million, aviation would get £220.6 million. The manpower strength of the RAF stood at 100,000 personnel, up from an average 34,000 in 1934, and an additional 18,000 were to be recruited by the fall. Responding to threats to peace in Europe, France aimed to build 500 aircraft a month in addition to 635 recently purchased from the United States, bringing to 1,000 the total bought from the United States with the intention of increasing that to 2,500 by early 1940.

1939 March 14   The prototype Martin 167W three-seat reconnaissance bomber was delivered to Wright Field for evaluation, having been adapted for possible export to France and Britain from a failed contender for a USAAC specification calling for an attack bomber. Only a few Martin 167Fs, as they became known, were delivered to France before the German invasion in May 1940, but the British purchased a total 225 and used them mostly in the Middle East. With a wingspan of 61 ft. 4 in. and a length of 46 ft. 8 in., the Maryland, as it was known by the British, had a top speed of 278 MPH, a range of 1,080 mi. with a maximum 2,000-lb. bomb load and armament comprising four Brownings in the wings and in mid-upper and ventral positions.

1939 March 23   Hungary attacked Slovakia (granted autonomy in October 1938 to create a new Czecho-Slovakia out of the former Czechoslovakia), and six aircraft from each of three bomber squadrons operating Junkers Ju 86K-2s were used to bomb targets across the Uh River. Fighter protection from two squadrons operating Fiat C.R.-32 biplanes backed up the Heinkel He 170s of a reconnaissance unit. Slovakia had declared independence on March 14 and had only a handful of aircraft comprising Avia B-534 fighters and Letov S-328 reconnaissance bombers along with some B-71 bombers (a license-built version of the Soviet SB-2), and all were still marked up with the Czech-Slovak insignia. Slovakia was defeated within 48 hours. Former Czecho-Slovak pilots would flee their newly occupied country and join the French and the British.

1939 March 24   American woman air record-breaker Jacqueline Cochran achieved a women's altitude record of 30,052 ft. 5 in. over Palm Springs, Calif. in a Beechcraft Model 17. Cochran went on with her flying achievements to become one of the most famous women aviators of all time. For more than 20 years she remained in the forefront of racing and record-breaking flights, culminating in what many regard as her finest achievement when, on May 1, 1953, she became the first woman to fly faster than the speed of sound.

1939 March 30   Piloted by Flugkapitän Hans Dierterle, the Heinkel He 100 V8/R (serial no. D-IDGH) seized the absolute world air speed record from Hermann Wurster, who had flown his Bf 109 to 379 MPH. The pilot took off at 5:23 A.M. and achieved four legs of a course at Oranienburg to record an average speed of 463.92 MPH, adding 70 MPH to the previous record. When news of this reached Britain, preparations of the Speed Spitfire (N.17) for a similar attempt were abandoned since the aircraft could not have achieved such a high speed in its planned configuration. N.17 was adapted for photographic reconnaissance trials and ended up as the personal mount of Air Commo. J. N. Boothman.

1939 March 30   The U.S. Navy contracted with the Newport News Shipbuilding & Dry Dock Co. for the next U.S. aircraft carrier, the CV-8 *Hornet*, which was the first to be funded after the termination on Dec. 31, 1936, of the Washington Treaty. Laid down in 1934, the 25,500-ton *Yorktown* and the 25,000-ton *Enterprise* had set new performance standards, carrying about the same number of aircraft as the 20,500-ton *Ranger* but with better performance, turn circle and defensive armament. With a loaded displacement of 29,100 tons, the *Hornet* had an overall length of

827 ft. and a flight deck beam of 114 ft. *Hornet* was sunk in October 1942.

1939 March   Russell Conwell Newhouse was awarded the annual Lawrence Sperry award for the greatest advance made in aeronautics during the preceding year. His citation was for "the development and first practical application of the terrain clearance indicator." Newhouse had developed this device, also known as the absolute altimeter, through Bell Telephone Laboratories. The system had been publicly demonstrated in October 1938 when fitted on board a Boeing 247 flying laboratory of United Air Lines.

1939 April 1   Trans-Canada Air Lines began operating the first passenger air service across Canada. The route had been opened March 1 by the first airmail run from Montreal to Vancouver via Ottawa, North Bay, Kapuskasing, Winnipeg, Regina and Lethbridge. The first passenger flights over the route were made by two Lockheed Model 14-H2 Super Electra twin-engine airliners powered by the 875-HP Pratt & Whitney S1E2-G Hornet radial, taking off from Montreal and Vancouver and making simultaneous 2,411-mi. flights on reciprocal headings.

1939 April 1   The Mitsubishi A6M1 made its first flight from Kagamigahara, Japan. Powered by a 780-HP Mitsubishi Zuisei 13 radial engine and piloted by test pilot Katsuzo Shima, the A6M1 achieved its objectives, but the A6M2, which first flew on December 28, was a superior design. Powered by the 950-HP Nakajima NK1C Sakei 12 14-cylinder, air-cooled radial, it had a top speed of 331 MPH, a climb time of 7 min. 27 sec. to 19,685 ft., a normal range of 1,160 mi. and a service ceiling of 32,810 ft. The A6M2 had a wingspan of 39 ft. 4 in., a length of 29 ft. 9 in. and a loaded weight of 5,313 lb.

1939 April 4   A developed version of the Brewster XSBA-1 carrier-based bomber was ordered into production for the U.S. Navy as the SB2A Buccaneer. Designed in 1934, the XSBA-1 had been given a more powerful engine in 1937, and 30 had been ordered as SBN-1s in September 1938; but the first would not be delivered for more than two years. With a wingspan of 47 ft. and a length of 39 ft. 2 in., the SB2A was bigger than the SBN-1 and had a gross weight of 14,289 lb. versus 6,759 lb. to accommodate a 1,000-lb. bomb load. Defensive armament comprised twin 0.50-in guns in the fuselage, two 0.30-in guns in the wings and two in a dorsal turret. The RAF purchased some, which they named Bermuda and used as target tugs.

1939 April 8   The U.S. Navy ordered the first 36 Douglas SBD-1 torpedo bombers derived from the Northrop BT-1, which first flew August 19, 1935. Redesigned to have a fully retractable undercarriage, the first of the type (the XBT-2) was a modified BT-1 from the production line. The navy would eventually order 5,321 of the Dauntlesses, 783 of which were delivered to the army. The SBD played a valuable role in the early years of the Pacific war, serving meritoriously at the Battle of Midway. With a 1,000-HP Wright R-1820-52 radial, the SBD-3 had a top speed of 250 MPH, cruising speed of 152 MPH and a range of 1,345 mi. carrying a 1,000-lb. bomb load.

1939 April 26   Fitted with a specially prepared 2,770-HP Daimler Benz DB 601ARJ engine, Messerschmitt Me 209 VI (D-INJR) claimed the last FAI speed record before World War II when Flugkapitän Fritz Wendel achieved an average 755.138 km/hr. (469.22 MPH), albeit only marginally better than the record set by Hans Dierterle in the Heinkel He 100 V8 less than a month before. Nevertheless, this speed record for piston-engined aircraft would stand for more than 30 years until American Darryl G.

Greenamyer beat it by almost 19 MPH. Fritz Wendel had taken over as chief test pilot and crashed in the Me 209 V2 (D-IWAH) on April 4, 1939.

1939 April 27 As a result of a competition that closed January 25, the USAAC ordered several examples of three aircraft that would, in various ways, play an important role in World War II. It ordered 524 Curtiss P-40s, although this was later reduced to 199 so that 140 Hawk fighters of a similar configuration could be completed for France. Also ordered were 13 Lockheed YP-38 fighters, delivery of the first being achieved in March 1941. Before delivery, however, the army ordered several hundred production-series P-38s and several variants before the British placed an order for 143 aircraft of the same type with the designation Lightning Mk.1. Also ordered were 12 Bell YP-39 Airacobras, first of 9,585 eventually built (of which 4,773 went to Russia).

1939 April Exploiting the absence of Alexander de Seversky during a sales trip to England, the directors of the Seversky Aircraft Corp. voted him off the board, changed the company name to Republic Aviation Corp. and refinanced it with Alexander Kartvelli as vice-president and director of technical operations. Seversky had imprudently invested in development of unlikely contenders for production orders, and the company was in a poor financial state, verging on collapse. Seversky would spend the rest of his life writing, acting as a consultant and speaking at prestigious aeronautical events.

1939 May 11 Air units of the Imperial Japanese Army Air Force went into action against Russian forces when fighting broke out on the Manchukuo border with Outer Mongolia. In the days ahead, Japanese air forces increased to 200 fighters, most of them Nakajima Ki-27 fighters. In what became known as the Nomonhan incident, lasting five months, the Japanese claimed the Russians pitched 3,000 aircraft against them and that they shot down 1,340. In reality, the Russians had only 450 fighters on the front and shot down 215 for 120 of their own lost in action. As with air fighting over Spain, the Polikarpov I-16 proved more than a match for its adversaries.

1939 May 12 The USAAC ordered 13 of the Seversky AP-4 (army designation YP-43), which had been entered for the USAAC competition of January 25, 1939. The initial order was followed in 1940 with one for another 53 given the type name Lancer. Although similar to the P-35 yet heavier, the P-43 was underpowered and lacked performance commensurate with European fighters. A more powerful 1,400-HP Pratt & Whitney powered P-44 named Rocket was proposed, but the USAAC rejected this when the AP-10 (late, P-47) was unveiled. Nevertheless, the P-43 was kept going, the army eventually buying 272, of which 108 went to the Chinese to help them fight the Japanese.

1939 May 12 The Messerschmitt Me 209 V4, registered D-IRND, made its first flight as the prototype of a fighter the company proposed. The plane was doomed from the outset because the basic design (P.1059) had evolved as a high-speed record-breaker unsuited to such a radical role reversal. With wingspan of 30 ft. 6 in. and increased wing area aimed at improving handling, it was fitted with a standard Daimler Benz DB 601 engine that required a large underwing radiator, which needed a larger wing that was unable to accommodate armament. Reduced to two MG 17s and one MK 108 firing through the propeller arc, the aircraft's performance was dramatically compromised, and it showed little improvement over the Bf 109.

1939 May 14 Designed to Specification B.12/36, the prototype Short Stirling four-engine bomber (serial no. L7600) made its first flight with John Lankester Parker at the controls, Sqdn. Ldr. Eric J. Moreton in the right seat and George Cotton as flight engineer. The Stirling owed much to the Empire-class and Sunderland flying boats, using a similar high-wing design necessitating a complicated and stalky landing gear. This gave the aircraft a distinct pitch-up attitude on the ground. After a 20-min. flight, the prototype came in to land, a brake seized, and the gear collapsed, rendering structural damage too great to repair.

1939 May 15 The U.S. Navy ordered a prototype Curtiss SB2C dive-bomber to compete with the Brewster SB2A, designated XSB2C-1 and first flown November 18, 1940. Named Helldiver from the earlier Curtiss SBC biplane of the same name first flown in 1933, 6,650 of this rugged two-seat, all-metal, mid-wing monoplane would be built, the last being retired 1949. With extra armor, self-sealing tanks and, in later versions, wing-mounted rockets and up to 2,000-lb. of bombs and radar, Helldivers were the mainstay of naval dive-bombing operations from 1943. With a gross weight of 16,616 lb., a wingspan of 49 ft. 9 in., a length of 36 ft. 8 in. and a 1,900-HP Wright R-2600-20, the Helldiver had a cruising speed of 158 MPH and a range of 1,165 mi.

1939 May 20 The first regularly scheduled trans-Atlantic airmail service was inaugurated by the Boeing 314 (serial no. NC18603) *Yankee Clipper,* commanded by Capt. A. E. Laporte of Pan American World Airways and carrying 1,804 lb. of mail. The first aircraft of this type had been delivered January 27, 1939, and was immediately operated on the Pacific service, replacing the Martin M-130, *Hawaiian Clipper,* which had crashed in July 1938. The last of six Boeing 314s was delivered June 16, 1939, two being assigned Pacific services and four on North Atlantic routes. *Yankee Clipper* had been delivered to Pan American at Baltimore February 24 and christened by Mrs. Franklin D. Roosevelt on March 3.

1939 June 1 The Focke-Wulf Fw 190 V1 (D-OPZE) made its first flight from Bremen powered by a 1,550-HP BMW 139 18-cylinder, two-row radial engine, piloted by Flight Captain (Flugkapitän) Hans Sander. Tasked with designing a supplementary fighter to the Bf 109, senior engineer R. Blaser produced what many regard as the definitive radial-engined fighter of World War II. Given the choice of either in-line or radial, design engineer Kurt Tank selected the radial engine to the surprise of many. Initially fitted with a ducted spinner, a NACA cowling was eventually installed, and prototypes adopted the 1,660-HP BMW 801C-0. With stressed duralumin skin, the Fw 190 had good all-round visibility and a wide-track main landing gear that offered better handling than the Bf 109.

1939 June 4 The first flight evaluation aircraft of the Consolidated PBY ordered by the British began a survey flight around the Indian Ocean. Known as the Model 28-5, *Guba II* (NC777) was piloted by Capt. P. G. Taylor. The 17-day, 9,022-mi. route took the aircraft to Port Hedland, Batavia, Christmas Island, Cocos, Diego Garcia, the Seychelles and Mombasa. Requested by the British and Australian governments, the flight demonstrated the ability of the flying boat to serve the Indian Ocean ports. The Model 28-5 was subsequently delivered to the Marine Aircraft Experimental Establishment, Felixstowe, England.

1939 June 13 The aircraft carrier USS *Saratoga* completed two days of replenishment at sea from the tanker USS *Kanawha,* demonstrating at-sea refueling activities and capabilities. These trials helped develop techniques for extending the range of carrier patrols as a means of covering greater expanses of ocean, reducing the need to return to port and greatly improving operating efficiency and effective deployment radius. The procedure and capabilities would serve the navy well during extended Pacific campaigns in World War II.

1939 June 27 The first production Boeing B-17B (serial no. 38-211) made its first flight from Seattle, 22 months after an order for B-17B, -C and -D models. Designated Boeing Model 299M, the B-17B nearly crippled the company, Boeing losing $12,000 on each aircraft. Gambling that big production orders for the heavy bomber would soon materialize, the company backed its instincts and produced the 39 aircraft on order by March 1940. The B-17B had a range of 2,400 mi. with a 4,000-lb. bomb load and dispensed with the nose turret seen on the YB-17A, replacing it with a ball and socket joint. This gave the aircraft a cleaner nose arrangement until the introduction of the chin turret on the B-17G model.

1939 June 28 The first regularly scheduled passenger service across the North Atlantic began with the luxurious Pan American Boeing 314 flying boat named *Dixie Clipper* commanded by Capt. R. O. D. Sullivan carrying 22 passengers. It had conducted the first survey flight March 26 flying from Baltimore to Foynes, Ireland via the Azores, Lisbon, Biscarosse, Marseilles and Southampton, England, calling at Southampton, the Azores and Biscarosse on the return leg. The first scheduled flight using the northern route began July 8. The standard fare was $375 one-way or $675 round-trip.

1939 June 30 The diminutive Heinkel He 176 made its first full rocket flight when it was taken into the air by test pilot flight captain (Flugkapitän) Erich Warsitz. Powered by a Walter HWK RI-203 rocket motor operating on hydrogen peroxide and methanol, which could be throttled to deliver between 100 lb. and 1,100 lb. of thrust, the flight lasted a mere 50 sec. It was repeated next day and witnessed by Erhard Milch, Ernst Udet and members of the German Air Ministry. In a display of new aircraft types on July 3, the He 176 was witnessed by Adolf Hitler and Hermann Göring. Despite abortive attempts to get it developed as a fighter—the aircraft was severely underpowered—it was abandoned as a project and ended up in the Berlin Air Museum, where it was destroyed in an air raid.

1939 June The first prototype of the Mitsubishi Ki-51 was delivered by the factory for trials leading to service introduction of this ground attack and reconnaissance aircraft in China. Derived from the equally successful Ki-30 light bomber, it was liked by pilots and ground crew, being easy to fly and simple to maintain. A total 2,385 Ki-51s (known as Sonias) were built and used throughout the war. The derivative Ki-71 (named *Edna* by the Allies) had a retractable landing gear and a more powerful engine than the 950-HP Mitsubishi Ha-26-II. With a wingspan of 39 ft. 8 in. and a length of 30 ft. 3 in., the Ki-51 had a top speed of 263 MPH and a 441-lb. bomb load, two wing-mounted 12.7-mm machine guns and a single 7.7-mm in a flexible rear mount.

1939 July 6 The McDonnell Aircraft Corp. was incorporated in the state of Maryland, offices being rented from American Airlines alongside Lambert Field in St. Louis, Mo. Starting with limited resources and meager prospects, James McDonnell would see his company grow steadily through wartime production needs to become the leading supplier of jet aircraft to the U.S. Navy and build the spacecraft to put the first Americans in space. Almost 28 years after its formation it would take over the Douglas

Aircraft Co. and forge one of the greatest aircraft manufacturing companies of all time.

1939 July 6 The world's first scheduled helicopter service began operations between the roof of the Philadelphia Post Office and nearby Camden (N.J.) Airport. Operated by Eastern Airlines, the Kellett KD-1B used for this service was an open cockpit, tandem two-seat autogyro. The service lasted a year. The next efforts at a regular service resulted in a CAB license to fly five routes between Chicago and 32 suburban communities in 1946, but this failed to get off the ground.

1939 July 17 Developed from the Bristol Beaufort, the Beaufighter prototype (serial no. R2052) made its first flight exactly two weeks after the British Air Ministry agreed to transform Bristol's private venture into an official project and order 300 of the type. Taking the wings and elements of the fuselage and tail and combining them with a new forward nose section and engines, Bristol developed the Type 156 beginning in late 1938 into what would become one of the best radar-equipped night fighters of World War II. With a wingspan of 57 ft. 10 in. and a length of 41 ft. 8 in., the Beaufighter had a top speed of 333 MPH and a range of 1,470 mi. Equipped with up to four 20-mm and six 0.303-in. guns, it could carry a 2,127-lb. torpedo, and 5,500 served with the RAF from August 1940 to May 1960.

1939 July 25 A direct product of British Air Ministry specification P.13/36 issued in September 1936, the first Avro Type 679 (serial no. L7246) made its first flight from Ringway (Manchester), England as the *Manchester I* with Capt. H. A. Brown at the controls. With two 1,750-HP Rolls Royce Vulture in-line engines, it was underpowered and unreliable. Stressed for dive-bombing, the fuselage could carry a 10,350-lb. bomb load, and the first of 209 entered service with the RAF in November 1940, only to be withdrawn 19 months later after persistent engine failures. With a wingspan of 90 ft. 1 in. and a length of 70 ft., the Manchester is remembered best as the progenitor of the famous, and extremely sucessful, Lancaster.

1939 July 26 Australian flying enthusiast and Dufaycolor (color film processing company) director Sidney Cotton left England for Berlin in a Lockheed Model 12A (G-AFTL) on a mission to photograph German military installations for British intelligence. Under cover of his company, Cotton recruited World War I aviator Schöne (an aquintance of Göring) as his German sales representative, providing reason to fly his modified 1,500 mi.-range Lockheed to Berlin. In January Cotton began work with the French Deuxième Bureau photographing new airfields and installations around Mannheim and Italian North Africa airfields during the spring. The last mission was on September 1, after which Cotton set up the RAF Photo Development Unit.

1939 July 27 The first of 38 Douglas B-23 Dragon bombers made its first flight. A streamlined version of the B-18 and powered by two 1,600-HP Wright R-2600-3 Cyclone radial engines, the aircraft was obsolete before it entered army service later in the year. The 38 B-23s procured replaced an equal number of B-18s, canceled in favor of the improved aircraft. Twelve were later converted into UC-67 transport aircraft, and some served as patrol aircraft that eventually were used for training activities.

1939 July Designed as a replacement for the Ki-32, the first Kawasaki Ki-48 prototype twin-engine light bomber was completed a year before the first production aircraft and initial deliveries to the Forty-fifth Sentai. Stimulated by the phenomenal performance of the Soviet SB-2, which persistently evaded interception due to its speed and performance at altitude, the Ki-48 emerged from the drawing board with a wingspan of 57 ft. 4 in., a length of 41 ft. 4 in. and, in a developed production version (Ki-48-IIb), two 1,150-HP Nakajima Ha-115 radials. With a 1,764-lb. bomb load, the aircraft had five machine guns in three defensive positions. A total of 1,977 Ki-48s were eventually built.

1939 August 1 The British Parliament debated civil defense procedures and heard from Sir John Anderson that 1.9 million men and women in Britain had been recruited to civil defense jobs, including fire-fighting, air-raid warning and policing of the general public. Fearful of the consequences of an all-out German bombing attack similar to those carried out by belligerent powers in Spain during the Spanish Civil War, the government had been divided on how best to protect the public. Schemes for deep underground concrete shelters had been rejected on the grounds that they would cost too much and take too long to build.

1939 August 5 The first experimental trans-Atlantic airmail service operated by Imperial Airways began when a Short Empire-class flying boat (G-AFCV) piloted by Capt. J. C. Kelly left Southampton for New York, via Foynes, Botwood and Montreal. A Handley Page Harrow II tanker (G-AFRL) was based at Shannon, with two (G-AFRG and G-AFRH) at Botwood for in-flight refueling. Whereas the Pan American Boeing 314 could make the trip without refueling, the Short flying boats were hard put to equal this capability, and Imperial Airways struggled hard to maintain its side of the reciprocal flight agreement.

1939 August 7 In a most bizarre act of aggression, Japanese pilot Daisuke Kanbara decapitated the pilot of a Chinese aircraft he had forced to the ground on the border between Manchukuo and Mongolia. After getting the Chinese pilot to crash-land his aircraft, Kanbara put down his own aircraft swiftly alongside the Chinaman and drew from the cockpit the Samurai sword he apparently took along in case such an opportunity presented itself. Striding boldly up to the Chinaman, who by this time had left his machine, Kanbara expedited the coup de grace, got back into his aircraft and took off.

1939 August 17 The first military version of the Douglas DC-3 was ordered by the USAAC as a command transport powered by two 1,200-HP Pratt & Whitney R-1830-21 radials and equipped with military equipment such as communication sets. Designated C-41A, it was a derivative of the DC-3A and preceded some 10,000 military versions of the famous aerial workhorse. Just over a year later, on September 16, 1940, the first batch of the C-47 military version was ordered to join a line of DC-2 derivatives known in the USAAC as the C-32, C-33, C-34 and C-39. Converted to have a DC-3 wing center-section, tail and landing gear, the one C-38 (DC-2) held by the Army Air Corps was the forerunner of a fully militarized DC-3.

1939 August 20 Beginning at 6:00 A.M., 100,000 Soviet troops, 1,000 artillery pieces, 800 tanks and almost 300 aircraft attacked the Japanese Kwantung Army in an effort to push them back from the contested border between Manchukuo and Outer Mongolia. The Kwantung Army operated about 500 aircraft and soon began to suffer heavily. Air supremacy was gained by the evening, and SB-2 bombers struck rear echelons, airfields and Japanese supply depots. The Soviets displayed excellent coordination between ground and air units, foreshadowing ground support roles they would exploit against the Germans. An armistice signed September 16 left both sides with 200 aircraft destroyed.

1939 August 20 The first reported example of a successful air-to-air combat using rockets fired from a monoplane fighter took place when five Polikarpov I-16 Type 10 fighters attacked a small formation of Mitsubishi A5M fighters over the Khalkin Gol River in Manchuria during the Russo-Japanese War. The I-16s had been adapted to carry four 82-mm RS rockets on the underside of each wing. Commanded by Capt. Zvonariev, the Russian fighters engaged the Japanese aircraft, and when the Russians returned to base, they claimed to have brought down two aircraft by rocket fire.

1939 August 26 Bearing the civil registration J-BACI, a Japanese Mitsubishi G3M2 bomber converted for use as a transport aircraft and powered by two 1,075-HP Kinsei 45 engines began a flight around the world beginning at Tokyo airport. Sponsored by the Mainichi Shimbun press and publishing company of Osaka and the Tokyo Nichinichi Shimbun newspaper, the flight was completed October 20. War had broken out in Europe, and the aircraft was unable to visit London, Paris or Berlin as planned, bypassing northern and central Europe. Total distance traveled was 32,850 mi. in 194 flying hr. for an average flying speed of 169 MPH. Several earlier goodwill flights had taken the transport derivative to Teheran and Rome.

1939 August 27 The first flight of an aircraft powered by a turbojet engine took place in Germany at the Heinkel airfield, Marienehe, when Flugkapitän Erich Warsitz piloted the Heinkel He 178 V1 on a brief, but successful, trip around the field, aborted when the plane sucked in a bird that stalled the engine. With a wingspan of 23 ft. 3 in. and a length of 24.5 ft., the He 178 had a loaded weight of 4,396 lb. With its HeS 3b engine delivering 1,102 lb. of thrust, the plane had inadvertently become airborne August 24 during taxi trials. Witnessed by Udet and Milch on its second flight November 1, the He 178 achieved 373 MPH, but major airframe redesign would have been needed for better performance. It was destroyed in a 1943 air raid.

1939 August An instructor at the U.S. Army Air Corps Engineering School at Wright Field, Ohio, Ezra Kotcher prepared and completed a paper he had been asked to write on potential problems facing future aeronautical designs. In it he advocated the construction and flight testing of research aircraft propelled by turbojet and rocket engines to explore transonic flight. The paper was circulated through NACA and read by Gen. H. P. Arnold. Kotcher absorbed calculations in a paper by Lt. Col. H. Zornig during the mid-1930s showing the plausibility of supersonic flight, and he was also motivated by advocates such as Theodore von Karman.

1939 August After leaving Douglas a year after it obtained total ownership of the old Northrop Corp., John ("Jack") K. Northrop set up Northrop Aircraft Inc. His friend, test pilot and TWA captain Edward Bellande, introduced Jack Northrop to businessman LaMotte T. Cohu, who saw the role American industry would soon come to play in the procurement needs of European countries. He decided to invest in Northrop and became chairman and general manager, leaving Jack Northrop as president and chief engineer. Dirt was moved on the new plant at Hawthorne, Calif. on September 30, and work started on parts for Consolidated flying boats and the N-3PB seaplane bought later by Norway.

1939 August Designed as a high-speed twin-engine bomber capable of unescorted missions, the Nakajima Ki-49 Donryu (Storm Dragon) made its first flight. With two 1,080-HP Nakajima Ha-5 KAI radials, and 2,420-HP Nakajima Ha-117 radials in the definitive version, the Ki-49-IIa had a 2,205-lb. bomb load, a range of up to 1,833 mi. and a top speed of 306 MPH. Only 819 were built, but it was the first Japanese bomber with a tail turret, carrying 12.7-mm guns in nose, tail and dorsal positions in addition to a 20-mm cannon in the dorsal turret and two 7.7-mm guns in beam positions. The Donryu had an undistinguished career, and some were converted to suicide missions, carrying an explosive load of 3,527 lb.

1939 September 1 Germany invaded Poland. The 54 Wehrmacht divisions of more than 1.2 million men in two army groups, commanded by Col. Gen. Gerd von Rundstedt in the north and Col. Gen. Fedor von Bock in the south, were supported by 2,093 Luftwaffe aircraft. The Poles had only 25% of their 40 divisions mobilized and approximately 460 combat-ready aircraft, of which just over one-half were reconnaissance, one-third fighters and about 10% bombers. Due to a lack of equipment, only 340 Polish pilots, 250 observers and 210 air gunners were able to fight. Ironically, 10% of Polish air losses were due to mistaken identity from friendly forces. Deployed as an adjunct of the Polish Army, air squadrons were under the command of Marshal Rydz-Smigly.

Upon final orders transmitted to all relevant Luftwaffe units on the preceding day, Junkers Ju 87 Stukas were the first German aircraft to take off at the beginning of the blitzkrieg on Poland when three aircraft of 3./St.G.1 led by Oblt. Bruno Dilley took off from Elbing to bomb approaches to the Dirschau bridge. Their bombs were released just 8 min. later at 4:34 A.M., 11 min. before the official declaration of war. Of 348 Stukas, 300 were operational in all nine existing Stukagruppen along with 789 Heinkel He 111s in 21 groups and 319 operational Dornier Do 17s in nine groups. The 36 Henschel Hs 123 dive-bombers would achieve success out of proportion to their vintage, but it was the Stukas that instilled a sense of fear wherever they went, inviting a sense of invulnerability that was to prove misplaced in later conflicts.

The first German aircraft lost in World War II was shot down by an aging and obsolete fighter of the Polish Air Force. At approximately 5:30 A.M., Lt. Wladyslaw Gnỳs of No. 121 Squadron flying a PZL P.11c successfully attacked a Luftwaffe Junkers Ju 87. Fitted initially with a Gnôme-Rhône-built 515-HP Bristol Jupiter radial, the P.11 first flew in August 1931 and was equipped for service use with two light machine guns. The Polish Pursuit Brigade shot down 42 German aircraft for a loss of 37. In the 16 days before the effective neutralization of Polish air resistance, fighter units were officially credited with 126 confirmed victories, 10 probables and 14 badly damaged.

In the initial attacks on Poland, the Luftwaffe sent waves of bombers against Warsaw, while others were sent to ports and harbor installations on the Baltic coast, ground facilities and military bases, including supply depots and airfields. In anticipation of sending surprise paratroop units to the area east of Posen, four groups of Ju52/3m stood ready in Silesia, but the drop was never ordered, and they joined five other groups to shift supplies and logistics for the Wehrmacht and advancing Luftwaffe units.

1939 September 1 Originally held in reserve, fewer than 200 Bf 109E fighters, out of 1,088 in Luftwaffe units, were sent to fight in Poland, and these were withdrawn after a week when fighter opposition all but dissolved. The Bf 110 initially escorted the bombers but Polish PZL P.11 fighters were more maneuverable and in the first engagements evaded the heavier twin-engine fighters. Five Polish aircraft were, however, shot down by the Bf 110Cs escorting He 111 bombers during the afternoon. The Bf 110 was eventually dispatched on ground strafing duties when Polish aircraft were driven from the skies.

1939 September 1 U.S. Army chief of staff Gen. George C. Marshall reviewed a report for the secretary of war on the optimum use of airpower in hemispheric defense and concluded a strategy that legitimized Army Air Corps plans for a long-range bombing force. The Aeronautical Board originated the survey in March 1939 and concluded that long-range bombers were essential to guarding the southern access routes to the United States via the Caribbean and Central America. Whereas bombers had been frowned upon, they were now considered a key asset in air defense through strikes at enemy resource centers, so much so that fighter development lagged behind that of other countries and that of other types of American aircraft.

1939 September 2 The only bombing raid into German territory made by Polish aircraft after the attack by Wehrmacht and Luftwaffe forces began in the early morning hours when 2nd Lt. Malinowski of No. 41 Reconnaissance Squadron took off from Zdunowo, north of Modlin, to determine the position of the German Third Army. About 30 min. after crossing the German border at 9:40 A.M., the pilot of the PZL P.23 Karaś spotted cavalry units. At 10:25 A.M., the aircraft was shot at by antiaircraft batteries on the road between Wielbark and Chorzele. Shortly before 11:00 A.M., the crew dropped eight bombs on the railway station at Nidzica, landing back at Zdunowo at 11:27 A.M.

1939 September 2 Because of imminent war with Germany, the last two scheduled air races planned to take place in Britain on this date (before 5 yr. 8 mon. of continuous conflict brought a halt to all but essential war activities) were canceled. At Birmingham, 12 entrants had signed on for the King's cup air race, which would have been held in four sections of five 20-mi. laps for a total of 400 mi. The Wakefield Challenge Cup, which gathered interest from 14 entrants not taking part in the King's Cup race, would have consisted of three sections of four 20-mile laps.

1939 September 2 The Advanced Air Striking force of the RAF comprising Squadron Nos. 12, 15, 40, 88, 103, 105, 142, 150, 218 and 226 of No. 1 Bomber Group flew from England to France in anticipation of a war with Germany. The 10 squadrons were equipped primarily with the Fairey Battle. Of the 160 Battles that set out, 159 arrived, one having ditched in the English Channel. Ground crews were shipped by sea, but the aircraft were bombed up before departure so they could be operationally ready on ar-

The Fairey Battle prototype took to the air in May 1937 and would be pressed into service early in World War II.

The RAF rearmed for fear of a resurgent Germany—but with many outdated designs, like this Fairey Battle of No. 63 Sqdn.

rival. Long past their heyday and outclassed as a medium bomber in the role for which they were designed, the Battles were used as armed reconnaissance aircraft.

1939 September 3 On the day Britain and France declared war on Nazi Germany, Britain had a first-line strength of 1,660 aircraft (2,200 reserves), France 1,735 (1,600) and Germany 4,320 (4,900). Of these first-line totals, the British had 536 bombers (plus 1,450 in reserve), France 463 (total) and Germany 2,130 (plus 2,400 reserves). Britain had 608 first-line fighters, France 634 and Germany 1,215. The balance was made up of long-range reconnaissance aircraft, of which Britain had none, France had 444 and Germany had a total 560, including army cooperation aircraft, coastal reconnaissance and naval aircraft. By comparison, the USAAC—which would not join the war for more than two years—had 800 front-line aircraft.

British military air personnel strength stood at approximately 186,000 officers and men, comprising 118,000 in the regular RAF, 24,500 in the RAF Regular Reserve, 21,000 in the RAF Volunteer Reserve and 22,500 in the Auxiliary Air Force. The strength of the regular RAF was less than half what it had been in November 1918. Dramatically outnumbered, the RAF braced itself for an onslaught; but confidence was high as Lt. Col. H. M. Trenchard visited RAF units and found that the men were "what I had not thought possible—better than in the last war."

The Luftwaffe had approximately 390,000 officers and men, more than three times the strength of the British RAF, with 1,300 bomber crews, 160 long-range reconnaissance crews and 450 seaplane crews for multi-crewmember aircraft. In all, including those in schools, the Luftwaffe had 3,960 crews. In addition, attributed to Luftwaffe strength, 900,000 men served with Flak units and antiaircraft regiments, an additional 100,000 in signals units, 60,000 on construction projects and 80,000 were employed

on maintenance and supply. By comparison, the USAAC had a strength of 26,000.

At precisely 12:03 P.M., 48 min. after the British prime minister Neville Chamberlain announced that England was at war with Germany, the RAF undertook its first operational sortie. A Bristol Blenheim IV (serial no. N6215) of No. 139 Squadron based at Wyton, piloted by Flt. Off. A. McPherson and carrying Comdr. Thompson, Royal Navy, and Cpl. V. Arrowsmith, took off on a reconnaissance flight. From an altitude of 24,000 ft. over the Schillig Roads, the aircraft took 75 photographs showing three German capital ships, four cruisers and seven destroyers. The Blenheim landed at 4:50 P.M., and at 6:15 P.M., 18 Hampden and nine Wellington bombers took off from Scampton, Waddington and Mildenhall to attack the warships. Failing to find them in storms and darkness, the Wellingtons returned at 10:40 P.M. followed by the Hampdens at 12:02 A.M.

On the night of the first day Britain found itself at war with Germany for the second time in 21 years, No. 4 Group RAF began penetration flights using 10 Whitley III bombers from Nos. 51 and 58 Squadrons to drop bundles of propaganda leaflets on Germany in what was known as Operation Nickel. The Whitleys dropped 26,000 lb. of paper amounting to 6 million sheets on Hamburg, Bremen and the Ruhr. Dubbed "bumph raids" by their frustrated crews, the aircraft were prevented by government policy from bombing German soil. The raids were suspended April 6, 1940, after 65 million leaflets had been dropped in an effort described later by Sir Arthur Harris as having no other purpose than to supply "the Continent's requirements of toilet paper."

1939 September 4 On its first attack of the war, No. 2 Group RAF Bomber Command sustained severe losses when it sent 15 Blenheims from Squadron Nos. 107, 110 and 139 to attack German warships at Wilhelmshaven. The raid was authorized on the basis of an intelligence flight carried out by Flt. Off. A. Mc-Pherson of No. 139 Squadron during the morning. Five Blenheims failed to return—No. 107 Squadron lost four out of five aircraft sent out and No. 110 Squadron lost one out of five; No. 139 Squadron could not find the warships. Two Wellingtons were lost out of 14 sent from Nos. 9 and 149 Squadrons (No. 3 Group) on a raid in which a British warship was very nearly attacked, and one aircraft bombed Esbjerg, 110 mi. off target! Combined losses for the day were 7 out of 29 (24%).

1939 September 5   In the first four days of the attack on Poland, the Luftwaffe flew 4,806 sorties against railways, highways and military facilities with a further 3,746 sorties against enemy gun batteries, emplacements, strong-points and protected positions. The total 8,552 sorties represented an average 2,138 sorties/day. This policy of striking transportation allowed the Poles to marshal only 37 of their 45 infantry divisions, 11 of their 16 cavalry divisions and only seven border guard brigades. By September 8, all movement on the routes Poznan-Kutno-Warsaw, Krakow-Radom-Deblin and Crakov-Tarnov-Lvov had been halted. This prevented the Poznan Army from inflicting heavy damage on the German eighth and tenth armies (Army Group South) on their drive toward Warsaw and is a landmark in the development of air-land warfare.

1939 September 5   Pres. Franklin D. Roosevelt announced the United States was an official neutral in the European war five days after he had appealed to all sides not to bomb unfortified towns or wage war on civilians. He ordered the U.S. Navy to deploy ships and aircraft to conduct protection patrols in the West Indies and along the eastern seaboard. The first navy squadrons deployed to their assignments September 11, and the navy in Washington passed along to the British all information received from aerial patrols about the presence and disposition of German surface and subsurface shipping.

1939 September 6   In an engagement in which Spitfires and Hurricanes first fired their guns in anger, the RAF and antiaircraft batteries on the ground shot down three British aircraft with the loss of one pilot. Alerted by the Chain Home radar station at Canewdon, Spitfires from No. 74 Squadron scrambled to intercept suspected German raiders coming in over the English Channel. A technical fault at the station misrepresented aircraft from the west and showed them on the screen coming from the east. As more aircraft scrambled, the size of the ''raiding'' force grew larger. Two fighters shot down by Spitfires were Hurricanes from No. 56 Squadron, and a Blenheim from No. 64 Squadron was brought down by antiaircraft fire. There were no German aircraft anywhere near the Thames River.

1939 September 9   In what became known as the Battle of Kutno, the Polish Gen. Kutrzeba used a continuous flow of intelligence reports from reconnaissance aircraft to harry the flank of the German Eighth Army across the Bzura River for 48 hr. until massive Luftwaffe air power on September 11 blunted Polish attacks. Far to the east, the Fourth Panzer Division was already at the outskirts of Warsaw, but a fierce fight with armor and artillery pinned down Gen. von Rundstedt, causing him to request air strikes to knock out Polish armor and artillery. The Thirtieth Infantry Division had been badly mauled in a brilliant application of timely air intelligence which, for two brief days, temporarily threatened German progress.

1939 September 14   The Vought-Sikorsky VS-300 helicopter made its first vertical ascent with Igor Sikorsky at the controls of his tethered machine. Powered by a 75-HP 4-cylinder Lycoming

engine, it had a 28-ft. diameter main rotor and a single antitorque tail rotor at the end of an enclosed boom. The first free flight was made on May 13, 1940, when the VS-300 was powered by a 90-HP Franklin engine and the tail had been modified to include two tail outriggers, each supporting a 6 ft. 8 in. diameter propeller for lateral control. On May 6, 1941, the VS-300 remained aloft for 1 hr. 32 min. 26 sec., beating the record set by Germany's Fw 61.

1939 September 17   In conformity with the Nazi-Soviet Pact, the USSR attacked Poland's eastern border north and south of the Pripet Marshes and the Soviet Air Force struck unprepared airfields at Kovel, Dubno and Luck, where most Polish bomber and fighter groups had withdrawn to and where the aircraft of the Carpathian Army were stationed. By this time, only remnants of the Polish Air Force remained, and the Soviet attack removed all hope of regrouping ground forces in the east. During this day and the next, more than 100 Polish aircraft escaped to Romania but were pressed into the service of the Romanian Air Force to be used later along the Eastern Front against the Soviet Union.

1939 September 22   At a meeting of the Supreme War Council, a request from the French for six British fighter squadrons totaling 80 aircraft to be sent to the continent was turned down. This would have supplemented the four squadrons of Hurricanes sent as part of the Air Component of the British Expeditionary Force. Despite renewed requests in October, Air Marshal Hugh Dowding could not accept the resulting attrition of metropolitan defense forces deemed necessary in the event of a sudden attack on Britain by the Luftwaffe. Nevertheless, exercising an option provided by the cabinet, the Chief of the Air Staff Sir Cyril L. N. Newall sent two squadrons of Gladiators in November.

1939 September 25   In approximately 1,500 sorties, the Luftwaffe dropped 536 tons of bombs and almost 80 tons of incendiaries on Warsaw, using 240 Stukas and 30 Ju 52/3ms in a final attempt to subdue the country's government and force it to surrender. It was the culmination of eight days of bombing on Warsaw. Smashed and ineffective water supplies prevented fires from being fought, and considerable damage and loss of life ensued. During the night, 13 Polish aircraft left Mokotow airfield for Hungary, one PZL P.11 carrying Lt. Col. M. Izycki, who would go on to command the Polish Air force in England as an adjunct of the RAF.

1939 September 25   The first German aircraft to be shot down by the British in World War II was put out of action by a Blackburn Skua of No. 803 Squadron Fleet Air Arm piloted by Lt. B. S. McEwen from the aircraft carrier HMS *Ark Royal*. The victim was a Dornier Do 18D flying boat from 2/Kü.Fl.Gr. 106 based at Norderney and on patrol over the Great Fisher Bank in the North Sea. The *Ark Royal* was accompanied by the battleships HMS *Nelson* and HMS *Rodney* and by the battlecruisers HMS *Hood* and *Renown*. After being forced down onto the water, the Do 18D was sunk by the guns of HMS *Somali*, and its crew taken on board. Two other Dorniers escaped.

1939 September 26   On the first operational flight of the Junkers Ju 88a, Aircraftman 1st class (Gefreiter) Carl Frank piloting one of four aircraft returned to his base at Westerland/Sylt to erroneously report the sinking of the British aircraft carrier HMS *Ark Royal*. Having been alerted by reports of the carrier, and four escorting warships, from three Dornier Do 18Ds on patrol, the four Ju 88As located the five ships and attacked with bombs. The pilots reported that Frank's aircraft scored a hit on the *Ark Royal* with one of two 1,102-lb. SC 500 bombs and that bombs from the other aircraft struck the four escorts. In reality, the *Ark Royal* was not hit, and a single bomb bounced off HMS *Hood* without exploding.

1939 September 28 Its air force impotent, Poland surrendered to Germany one day after the collapse of Warsaw and 11 days after 20 Soviet divisions attacked Poland from the east as part of an arranged division of the country agreed to by Hitler and Stalin. Contrary to German propaganda, the Polish armed forces made good account of themselves and inflicted severe injury on the Luftwaffe. Although the Poles lost 333 aircraft, the Germans lost 285 (including 78 twin-engine bombers, 31 Ju 87s, 67 Bf 109s and 12 Bf 110s) with 279 severely damaged and 734 crewmembers dead. In four weeks, Germany had lost three times the aircraft it lost in the three years of the Spanish civil war. About 7,500 Poles escaped through Romania to fight for France in the Armée de l'Air and, after France collapsed, to England where they formed Polish squadrons in the RAF.

1939 September 29 Success with the six Boeing 314 flying boats on the Pacific and Atlantic services led Pan American to order six more of the improved and higher performance model designated 314A. These were to be delivered between April 1941 and January 1942. Pan American had been forced to suspend the full trans-Atlantic service when war broke out between Britain and Germany on September 3, the northern route being terminated at Foynes, Ireland and the southern route at Lisbon, Portugal. Both countries were neutral. All Pan American northern route Atlantic services were stopped October 3 for the winter.

1939 September 29 Three days after RAF Bomber Command began major reconnaissance sweeps in search of warships as targets of opportunity, five out of 11 Hampdens from Nos. 61 and 144 squadrons were shot down by German fighters off the Frisian Islands that skirt the North Sea coast of Germany. The first flight, on September 26, had been uneventful, no targets presenting themselves, but the 45% loss rate was too high to accept. These were, however, relatively isolated losses. In 394 sorties in the last four months of the year, most were carried out without any losses. Yet the inescapable conclusion that unescorted bombers penetrating industrial areas of Germany were going to sustain unacceptable losses had not yet been realized.

1939 September The Bloch M.B.161 Languedoc 33-seat passenger airliner designed and built by the Société National de Constructions Aéronautiques du Sud-Oest (SNCASO) made its first flight in France three years after a specification outlined by Air Afrique resulted in the precursor Bloch 160. After nationalization of the French aviation industry in 1936, Bloch and Blériot merged to form the SNCASO. The Languedoc had a wingspan of 96 ft. 5 in., a length of 79 ft. 7 in. with power from four 1,100-HP Gnôme-Rhône 14N-48/49 radials. Air France ordered some, but the war intervened and Germany ordered 20 in 1942, although delaying tactics prevented their being delivered.

1939 September The Japanese navy drew up a forward-thinking specification for a high-speed interceptor capable of 373 MPH at 19,685 ft. and of reaching that height in not more than 5.5 min. The aircraft was to be an interceptor in the purest sense and have little design consideration for dogfighting. Moreover, it had to have a landing speed of less that 81 MPH and, for the first time, armor protection for the pilot. This specification would result in the powerful—and fast—Mitsubishi J2M Raiden (Thunderbolt).

1939 October 4 The last Polish missions of aerial resistance against Nazi occupation were flown during the Battle of Kock 66 mi. southeast of Warsaw where preparations for Hitler's victory parade were under way. Operating in support of Gen. Kleeburg's unit, two RWD 8 parasol communication and liaison aircraft flew reconnaissance missions along with one P.W.S. The last RWD 8 returned during the morning and could not take off again because the unit had run out of fuel. The RWD had dropped hand grenades on the enemy.

1939 October 6 Designed to replace the SOC seagull biplane scout and observation seaplane for the U.S. Navy, the Curtiss XSO3C-1 made its first flight 17 mon. after the first order. Powered by a 600-HP Ranger V-770-8, the navy bought 794, of which 250 were on behalf of the British navy. With a wingspan of 38 ft. and a length of 35 ft. 8 in., the monoplane was not popular, and its predecessor outlived it in operational use. With a large central float and outriggers, it could carry a bomb load of up to 500 lb. and had an 0.30-in. forward-firing machine gun in addition to an 0.50-in. gun on a flexible mounting in the rear cockpit.

1939 October 6 The prototype Hawker Tornado (serial no. P5219) single-seat interceptor designed to specification F.18/37 made its first flight at Langley, Buckinghamshire with P. G. Lucas at the controls. It had been designed to carry the new 24-cylinder Rolls Royce Vulture. With a maximum speed of almost 400 MPH, the Tornado was the first British aircraft to encounter compressibility problems necessitating removal of the under-wing air intake to a chin position, and it made its first flight in this configuration on December 6, 1939. The aircraft was not a success, and only three other examples were built, one equipped with the 18-cylinder Bristol Centaurus radial engine.

1939 October 8 A Lockheed Hudson of No. 224 Squadron became the first RAF aircraft, and the first American aircraft in combat, to shoot down a German aircraft in World War II. The aircraft was a Dornier Do 18D of 2./Kü.Fl.Gr. 106 and the action took place off Jutland, site of the famous World War I naval battle. Hudsons had first entered service with the RAF during the summer, becoming operational with No. 224 Sqdn., Coastal Command, at Gosport. The Hudson had two fixed forward-firing 0.303-in. machine guns operated by the pilot, and it was with these that the Dornier was shot down. The Hudson also had a dorsal turret housing twin 0.303-in. guns, one in the ventral position and provision for two in the midships position.

1939 October 11 Dr. Alexander Sachs, director and economic adviser to the Lehman Brothers investment concern in New York, delivered a letter from Albert Einstein to Pres. Roosevelt calling upon the government to fund an atomic bomb project. He also carried a memo from Leo Szilard, one of two physicists who demonstrated on March 3 that self-sustaining atomic chain reactions might be possible and outlining progress to date. Concerned by German progress in the field, Einstein and other scientists urged parallel development of an atom bomb. Roosevelt asked Brig. Gen. Edwin M. Watson to organize a working group to define the concept. Thus began official sanction for U.S. nuclear weapons.

1939 October 11 Commercial flights between London and Paris were resumed following suspension on the outbreak of war with Germany. In a special agreement between Air France and Imperial Airways, Dewoitine D.338 and Armstrong Whitworth Ensign airliners provided service twice daily between Heston, England, and Paris. Services were indefinitely suspended June 13, 1940, a month after Hitler attacked France and the Low Countries. Air

France would not resume the Paris-London service until October 22, 1945.

1939 October 16 The first air combat victory scored by the RAF, and the Spitfire, against an enemy aircraft in World War II took place over the Firth of Forth, Scotland. Nine Junkers Ju 88As from I/KG 30 attacked shipping near the Forth Bridge during the first German air raid on a Royal Navy base. The cruiser HMS *Southampton* was hit, and damage was inflicted on the cruiser HMS *Edinburgh* and the destroyer HMS *Mohawk*. Spitfires from Nos. 602 and 603 squadrons, Royal Auxiliary Air Force, intercepted the German bombers and Sqdn. Ldr. Ernest E. Stevens from No. 603 Squadron shot down a Junkers, which crash-landed in the water off Port Seton. Three crewmembers were taken prisoner. Another raider was destroyed by flak.

1939 October 23 Piloted by test pilot Katsuzo Shima, the prototype Mitsubishi G4M made its first flight, just over two years after the 12-Shi specification calling for a new navy attack bomber. Mitsubishi would eventually build 2,446 G4Ms, and the type entered service during 1941, getting a trial run in China beginning with an attack on Chungking. Dubbed Betty by the Allies, the G4M had a wingspan of 82 ft. and a length of 65 ft. 8 in. with two 1,530-HP Mitsubishi MK4A Kasei II radials. A wide variety of defensive armament characterized various derivatives, although most versions could carry a 2,205-lb. bomb load. With a cruising speed of 196 MPH, the G4M had a range of 3,749 mi. a major asset during the early years of the war.

1939 October 25 The prototype Handey Page Halifax (serial no. L7244) made its first flight from RAF Bicester with J. L. B. H. Cordes at the controls. Designed as a twin-engine bomber to be powered by Rolls Royce Vulture engines, an order of September 3, 1937, changed the configuration to four Rolls Royce Merlins. With a wingspan of 98 ft. 10 in. and a length of 70 ft. 1 in., the Halifax Mk.I entered RAF service in November 1940. Armament comprised two 0.303-in. guns in a nose turret and four in a tail turret with provision for guns amidships. Capable of carrying a maximum bomb load of 13,000 lb., the Halifax had a range of 1,860 mi. with a 5,800-lb. bomb load, and 6,176 were built for the RAF.

1939 October 28 The first German aircraft shot down on British soil was claimed by Spitfire pilots of Nos. 602 and 603 squadrons, RAuxAF. A section from each squadron was patrolling the coast at 10,000 ft. when they were alerted by bursts of antiaircraft fire. A lone Heinkel He 111P (unit marking IH + JA) of Stab/KG 26 was attacked and forced to crash-land after a brief fight. Two crewmembers were dead, but the pilot, Lt. Rolf Niehoff, was wounded and taken prisoner together with an uninjured fourth crewmember. The aircraft came down on heath land six miles from Haddington, about 15 miles southeast of Edinburgh, Scotland.

1939 November 19 The Heinkel He 177 V1 prototype took to the air for the first time piloted by design engineer Frank for a 12-min. flight terminated by a rapidly rising engine temperature. With a wingspan of 103 ft. and a length of 67 ft. 6 in. the aircraft had a loaded weight of 52,734 lb. Performance was dissapointing and fell substantially below the specification for the ''Bomber A,'' which led to its design. Weight grew rapidly as modifications were made, the first production model reaching a maximum loaded weight of 66,139 lb. when it joined IV/KG 40 in August 1941 for trials in the antishipping role. Not for another two years would the aircraft be seriously committed to major operational duties.

1939 November 22 A Heinkel He 115 seaplane from 3./Kü.Fl.Gr 106 dropped a mine off Southend, near the Thames estuary. It was defused at low water by a bomb disposal squad from HMS *Vernon* led by Lt. Comdr. J. G. D. Ouvry. After the bomb was removed and disassembled, technical details about the device were gleaned from which countermeasures were developed. The most effective method was the use of low-flying Vickers Wellingtons to destroy mines deployed below the tide level, the aircraft itself carrying a 48-ft. diameter magnetized ring capable of activating the mine while the aircraft passed overhead at a low, but safe, altitude.

1939 November 22 The first amphibious Consolidated PBY made its first flight with a retractable tricycle undercarriage. Converted from the last of the PBY-4 line, the XPBY-5A proved the added landing gear did little to alter the aircraft's performance, and the U.S. Navy received the first amphibious models in late 1941, by which time the British name, Catalina, had been universally adopted for all PBY aircraft. At the outbreak of war in September 1939, the RAF had ordered the first 30 of more than 650 Catalinas as the flying boat/amphibian commenced a distinguished combat career with the British air forces. Several later versions evolved, and the parent company eventually built 2,398 PBYs before production ended in April 1945.

1939 November 30 Operating from an airfield near the Estonian town of Paldiski, Soviet bombers attacked Helsinki in support of a general invasion of Finland that began when armies totaling almost a million men rushed across the border, which was defended by 300,000 Finns. The first wave attacked shortly after 9:00 A.M., and around noon, Viipuri and Petsamo were also attacked. Faced by 900 Soviet aircraft, albeit mostly old I-15 and I-16 fighters, the Finnish Air Force comprised only 145 aircraft purchased from British, German, Italian and French manufacturers, but it put up a spirited and credible resistance and not before March 13, 1940, was the country subdued by the Soviet Union's overwhelming numerical superiority.

1939 November Mitsubishi test pilot Maj. Fujita took the prototype Ki-46 into the air for the first time from Kagamigahara near Nagoya. One of the most aesthetic Japanese aircraft, code-named Dinah by the Allies, the two-seat reconnaissance aircraft entered service for flight trials a year later. It had a top speed of 335 MPH (391 MPH for later models) and a ceiling of 35,530 ft. With a wingspan of 48 ft. 3 in. and a length of 36 ft. 1 in., the Ki-46 had a maximum loaded weight of 14,330 lb. A total 1,742 of several versions was built, each equipped with a single 7.7-mm rear-firing machine gun or one 37-mm cannon mounted at an angle in the fuselage with two 20-mm cannon in the nose.

1939 December 1 Finnish Air Force pilot Capt. Eino Luukkanen took off from Immola at 5:30 A.M. as one of two fighters on patrol over Vuoksenlaakso and spotted a Soviet Tupolev SB-2, which he shot down, the first successful victory over Soviet aircraft of the Winter War. The commander of the Finnish Air Force, Gen. J. F. Lundquist, had formed 31 aircraft into No. 24 Fighter Squadron immediately after the Soviet attack November 30. Stationed at Immola, they were there to protect the vital power station at Imatra, about 30 mi. north of Viipuri.

1939 December 3 Responding to an order from the British government for ''a major operation (to destroy) an enemy battle cruiser or pocket battleship,'' the RAF began daylight raids on German shipping when 24 Wellingtons from Nos. 38, 115, and 149 squadrons attacked targets near Heligoland. Although attacked by German fighters, with the loss of one Messerschmitt,

RAF pilots preparing to meet the Luftwaffe in combat as German forces gathered for an attack on France and the Low Countries.

no British bombers were lost; and one German minesweeper was sunk by a bomb that went through its hull from a height of 7,000 ft. A second daylight raid on December 14 resulted in the loss of six out of 12 Wellingtons to antiaircraft fire and German fighters.

1939 December 3   The second Short Stirling (serial no. L7605) made its first flight and went on to perform extensive flying trials prior to service introduction of the first production machines with No. 7 Squadron, RAF, at Leeming in August 1940. This was the first four-engine RAF bomber squadron since 1919. With a wingspan of 99 ft. 1 in. a length of 87 ft. 3 in. and a cruising speed of 215 MPH at 15,000 ft., the Short Stirling had a range with 5,000-lb. bomb load of 1,930 mi. Power was provided by four 1,590-HP Bristol Hercules XI 14-cylinder, air-cooled radials. The Stirling was the only British bomber of World War II designed from the outset with four engines, and the RAF received a total of 2,221 before production ended. A subsequent Mk.V version was developed as a troop transport.

1939 December 17   An agreement was signed by the Dominion Government of the British Empire whereby Canada, Australia, South Africa, Southern Rhodesia, India, New Zealand, the Middle east and the Bahamas would train British air crews for war duty. Known as the Empire Air Training Scheme, later the British Commonwealth Air Training Plan, it developed to include 175 training schools in addition to the 153 in the British Isles. Between 1940 and 1945 they trained collectively, 205,582 air crew and pilots (137,739 from Canada alone) in addition to 88,022 from Britain. The United States also trained more than 14,000 air crew in five flying schools.

1939 December 18   Twenty-four RAF Wellington bombers from Nos. 9, 37 and 149 squadrons assembed over Kings Lynn, Norfolk for attacks of opportunity on German shipping in the Schillig

Roads and Wilhelmshaven. Two were forced to return with engine trouble. Detected by an experimental Freya early warning radar station, the bombers were incessantly attacked by German fighters, only 10 of the 22 returning safely to England. Two German fighters were shot down, but no results were obtained from the bombing effort. The disastrous operation shattered confidence in the ability of close formation bombers to adequately defend themselves in daylight raids, and Bomber Command switched to night raids, a policy that persisted for almost five years.

1939 December 29   The first Consolidated XB-24 made its first flight from Lindbergh Field, San Diego, piloted by William Wheatley. With 19,256 B-24s and derivatives built between 1939 and 1944, more aircraft of this type were built for U.S. and Allied air forces than any other American aircraft. Designed originally to a U.S. Army specification calling for performance improvements over the B-17, the B-24 had a wingspan of 110 ft. and a length of 63 ft. 9 in. and was powered by four 1,200-HP Pratt & Whitney R-1830 series engines. It had a maximum speed of 292 MPH, a cruising speed of 228 MPH, a ceiling of 30,500 ft. and a range of 2,200 mi. (2,850 mi. for the B-24D), with up to 8,800 lb. of bombs and 10 0.50-in. guns.

1939   In the year that war broke out in Europe and World War II seemed inevitable, the Soviet Union produced more aircraft than any other country, assembling 10,382 versus 7,500 in 1938 and 3,578 in 1937. Next came Germany with 8,295 (compared with 5,235 and 5,606); Britain with 7,940 (2,827 and 2,153); Japan with 4,467 (3,201 and 1,511); France with 3,163 (1,382 and 743); and the United States with 2,195 (1,800 and 949). In the last three years, the USSR had built 21,460 aircraft, Germany 19,136, Britain 12,920, Japan 9,179, France 5,288 and the United States just 4,944. Production totals should not be interpreted as reflecting operational strength; as many older types were withdrawn in these years and raw production figures take no account of the roles for which the planes were obtained.

1939 To study high Reynolds number propeller and wing shapes, NACA declared operational the new $1.1 million, 19-ft. pressure tunnel at the Langley Memorial Aeronautical Laboratory, Langley, Va. This was the first facility in the world to combine large size and high pressure and provided engineers with a 19-ft. closed-throat test section where speeds of up to 330 MPH could be simulated and observed on experimental surfaces. In 1955, NACA began conversion of the facility to a transonic dynamics tunnel, and many aircraft were tested at higher Reynolds numbers than could be accommodated by the propeller research tunnel of 1927.

1940 January 6 At 12:03 P.M. Capt. Jorma Sarvanto of the Finnish Air Force attacked a formation of seven Soviet Ilyushin DB-3 bombers, and within four minutes shot down a record six aircraft, leaving another Finnish pilot to shoot down the seventh. The tenacious resistance of Finnish pilots more than compensated for numerically inferior equipment. Stalin was forced to dispatch another 600 modern Soviet aircraft to the Finnish front, bringing the total to 2,000. Reinforcements to Finland comprised 33 Gladiators, 17 Lysanders and 24 Blenheims from Britain, 76 Morane-Saulniers and Koolhovens from France, 17 Fiats from Italy, 12 Gladiators from Sweden, 44 Brewsters from the United States and 25 Gladiators from South Africa.

1940 January 10 Delayed in Münster, Germany, en route to a staff meeting and carrying top secret plans for the invasion of France and the Low Countries, Luftwaffe Maj. Helmut Reinberger accepted the offer of a ride in a Messerschmitt Bf 108 piloted by Maj. Erich Hönmanns. After taking off from Loddenheide airfield, the pilot got lost in fog and, after accidentally cutting off the fuel to his engine, came down at Mechelen, Belgium, 15 mi. north of Brussels. Maj. Reinberger made several desperate attempts to destroy the papers, but they were captured and examined by the Belgian general staff. Although having been reported as pivotal in getting Hitler to change plans for the invasion of France and Belgium, the incident did in fact have nothing to do with the actual changes made to "Case Yellow."

1940 January 13 The Yakovlev I-26 (Ya-26, then designated Yak-1 in December 1940) made its first flight with test pilot Yu. I. Piontkovskii at the controls. With a mixed-construction fuselage, wooden wing and enclosed cockpit with retractable landing gear, it was the first of more than 30,000 Yak fighters built during World War II. Powered by a 1,050-HP M105P 12-cylinder V piston engine, the Yak-1 had a top speed of 336 MPH and a range of 435 mi. with one 20-mm ShVAK cannon mounted on the engine and one 12.7-mm machine gun in the fuselage plus mountings for two 220-lb. bombs on underwing racks. Subsequent development of the Yak-1 resulted in the Yak-9, which first flew during 1942 with metal wing; while later variants had a 1,650-HP Klimov VK-107A engine and a top speed of 434 MPH. Armament included two cannons, two machine guns and two bomb racks.

1940 January The Japanese newspaper *Asahi Shimbun* asked the University of Tokyo Aeronautical Research Institute to design an aircraft capable of flying more than 9,321 mi. (15,000 km) at a speed of at least 186 MPH (300 km/hr.). The management wanted to stage a nonstop Tokyo-New York flight to outdo their principal competitor, the *Mainichi Shimbun,* who had sponsored a round-the-world flight by a modified Mitsubishi G3M2. Designated A-26 (*A* for *Asahi Shimbun* and 26 for the then Japanese

year 2600), it was formally assigned the project number Ki-77 by designer and manufacturer Tachikawa Hikoki K.K. Detailed engineering drawings began in the fall of 1940, but minor problems delayed completion and the first flight, which took place on November 18, 1942.

1940 February 3 The formal contract for design and construction of the first British jet-propelled aircraft was awarded to the Gloster Aircraft Co. to specification E.28/39, and the project would initially be known by this number. The E.28/39 was to be powered by a W.1 gas turbine engine developed by Power Jets Ltd. to a design originated by Frank Whittle under a contract awarded in March 1938. The design of the E.28/39 was conceived by George Carter who envisaged a small, compact, low-wing, semimonocoque monoplane with a single fin and rudder and a tricycle landing gear. Two aircraft were ordered with serial numbers W4041 and W4046.

1940 February 5 The U.S. Army issued performance and mission requirements for a class of Superbomber, based loosely on work conducted by Boeing since March 1938 on its projected Model 334. At that time, responding to a design study from the USAAC for a pressurized version of the B-17 with tricycle landing gear, Boeing worked in-house in the absence of government funds and modified the concept in July 1939 with Model 334A. This is considered the direct ancestor of the B-29. The new performance requirements issued this month called for a 400 MPH bomber with a range of 5,333 mi. carrying a 2,000-lb. bomb load. This would result in Model 345 submitted May 11, 1940.

1940 February 15 Responding to early reports of air engagements in Europe and initial intelligence about aircraft vulnerability, the commander in chief, U.S. Fleet, recommended the use of leak-proof and selfsealing fuel tanks on U.S. Navy aircraft to minimize fire and explosions to aircraft damaged during attack. He also suggested the use of armor-plating for pilots and observers as minimum mandatory protection against gunfire and shrapnel. The bureaus of Aeronautics and Ordnance had been experimenting since 1937 with various forms of protection for combat aircrew and had conducted several tests with alternative materials and configurations.

1940 February 22 Sqdn. Ldr. Douglas Farquhar of No. 602 (City of Glasgow) squadron, RAuxAF, took the first British gun-camera film of an enemy aircraft under attack while shooting down a Heinkel He 111 over Coldingham, Berwickshire, Scotland. The squadron had been equipped with Spitfire Mk.1 fighters in May 1939 and had been based at Drem, Scotland since October 13, 1939. Gun cameras would become increasingly important for adding information about aircraft attacked in the air, frequently being the impartial arbiter between contested kills.

1940 February 22 The Luftwaffe inadvertently bombed and sunk the German destroyer *Leberecht Maass,* believing it to be an Allied merchant ship. Ordered by X Fliegerkorps to resume bombing attacks on British shipping, 4. Staffel of KG 26 took off at 5:54 P.M. Heinkel He 111P, with unit marking, 1H + JM piloted by Feldwebel Jäger with Unteroffizier Schräpler as observer and bomb aimer flew north for 1 hr. before turning west across the southern tip of Sylt, picking up the Hörnum navigation beacon guiding it at a bearing of 241° across the North Sea. White foam was spotted at 7:20 P.M., and the aircraft attacked, dropping four 110-lb. SC 50 bombs, of which only the third hit. At 7:45 P.M., a second run released four more bombs on the ship *Max Schultz,* which set it on fire. Both ships sank with the loss of 578 lives.

1940 February 24   Piloted by P. G. Lucas, the prototype Hawker Typhoon (serial no. P5212) made its first flight powered by the 2,100-HP, 24-cylinder, Napier Sabre engine, giving production versions a top speed of 412 MPH at 19,000 ft. Equipped with the characteristic chin radiator scoop to avoid compressibility problems encountered by the Tornado (see October 6, 1939), the Typhoon was built as the second of two contenders for specification F.18/37 demanding a single-seat interceptor equipped with 12 Browning machine guns. The Typhoon entered service with No. 56 Squadron, RAF, in September 1941, but it achieved success in the close air support/ground attack role. Total production was 3,330 for the RAF, and the type remained in service until the end of the war in Europe.

1940 February 26   The U.S. Army Air Corps established its Air Defense Command, and on March 15, Brig. Gen. James E. Chaney assumed command at its headquarters at Mitchel Field, Long Island, N.Y. Largely administrative in practice, it was established to control and coordinate the air defenses of the continental United States against hostile attack. It had few resources to put such an edict into operation, especially for the global role of protecting U.S. possessions it had originally been expected to achieve.

1940 February 27   Development of the Vought Model V-173 was initiated with the award of a contract to design a revolutionary fighter aircraft of almost circular planform powered by two powerful engines driving large propellers. A theory proposed by Charles H. Zimmermann suggested that an aircraft of this shape would take off and land at very low speed yet have higher cruising speeds than conventional aircraft and have immunity from stall or spin. Zimmermann joined Vought in 1937 and convinced company president Eugene E. Wilson of the concept by demonstrating with a small radio-controlled model.

1940 March 1   A contract was awarded by the technical office of the German State Ministry of Aviation for three prototype twin-jet Messerschmitt Me 262 aircraft. It had been initiated during the fall of 1938 under the designation Projekt 1065, a design contract that stipulated an airframe capable of accommodating two BMW axial-flow turbojets expected to produce a thrust of 1,320 lb. but an engine that was still in the design stage. When Messerschmitt submitted its design on June 7, 1939, it was presented as an all-metal, low-wing, cantilever monoplane with fully retractable undercarriage and two BMW P3302 turbojets buried in the wing-roots. Maximum speed was calculated at 560 MPH. Messerschmitt had been ordered to build a mock-up prior to the prototype order.

1940 March 1   Overcoming official reluctance, de Havilland received a contract to specification B.1/40 for 50 wooden D.H.98 Mosquito bomber aircraft powered by two Rolls Royce Merlin engines. Designed at Salisbury Hall, London Colney, England by a team headed by R. E. Bishop, the Mosquito had been conceived as a 400 MPH, high-altitude, unarmed bomber. The Mosquito was designed as a private venture beginning October 1938. Pushed forward by the personal enthusiasm of Sir Wilfred Freeman, Air Council member for research, development and production, detailed design work had begun December 29, 1939, for an aircraft capable of carrying 1,000 lb. of bombs for 1,500 mi.

1940 March 12   The Treaty of Moscow, ending the Finno-Russian War, was signed with Finland ceding parts of Karelia to the USSR. During the conflict, which began November 30, 1939, 684 Soviet aircraft had been destroyed, including 240 shot down by Finnish fighters; 31 Fokker D-XX1 fighters alone accounted for 120 Soviet bombers. The Finns lost 67 aircraft, 42 of them in combat. The Soviets were in haste to finish the war because Stalin had been informed by his secret police that Britain and France were planning to bomb the oilfields at Baku on the Caspian Sea. The intelligence information indicated there were to be attacks from nine bomber squadrons on the 122 refineries, achieving complete destruction in 10 to 45 days, the French operating from Cizre, Turkey, the British from Mosul, Iraq. None of this was true.

1940 March 16   During the early hours following a propaganda leaflet raid over Warsaw, the crew of Whitley V (serial no. N1387) lost their way and, believing themselves to be over France, inadvertently landed in Germany. The aircraft from No. 77 Squadron, RAF, was commanded by Flt. Lt. Tomlin and had flown from Villeneuve, France, to Warsaw. Running into bad weather and a strong headwind on the way back, they climbed to 18,000 ft. to fly over dense cloud and, short on fuel, concluded from dead reckoning that they were over friendly territory once more. When they came down to select a suitable field, a short burst from an antiaircraft battery prompted the crew to switch on their lights. After rolling to a halt, they hailed approaching peasants, who promptly informed them that they were in Germany, pointing to the direction of France. Hastily retreating to the Whitley, the crew took off and made it safely back to French territory.

1940 March 16   Jim Ibister, the first British civilian killed by a German air raid in World War II, died on the doorstep of his cottage in the Bridge of Waithe, a hamlet four mi. from Stromness on the Island of Orkney off the coast of Scotland. Aged 27, Ibister ran outside to help a neighbor when her house was hit and was himself struck by the blast of an exploding bomb dropped by a Heinkel He 111 of KG/26. He was buried during a service at St. Magnus Cathedral conducted by his brother-in-law, Rev. T. G. Tait, and was survived by his son Neil, then aged three mon. Ibister was the first of 60,411 British civilians killed during air raids in World War II.

1940 March 19   Mounting a reprisal raid to a German attack on Scapa Flow March 16 in which one man died and seven were injured, the first British civilian casualties of the war, 30 Whitleys and 20 Hampdens of RAF Bomber Command set out on the first RAF night bombing raid. A Whitley of No. 102 Squadron (serial no. N1380) became the first RAF aircraft to drop a bomb on German soil during World War II. The target was the seaplane base at Hörnum on the North Frisian island of Sylt. In all, 43 aircraft reached the target, 191 (250-lb. and 500-lb.) bombs and 1,360 (4-lb.) incendiaries were dropped, and only one Whitley was lost. The British government had ordered Bomber Command to carry out the raid against a target that held no civilian occupants.

1940 March 26   Test pilot Eddie Allen took the Curtiss CW-20 into the air for the first time from St. Louis. Developed as a prototype airliner powered by 1,700-HP Wright R-2600 engines, the aircraft caught the attention of the army due to its unusually spacious fuselage. As a result of this flight, a contract was eventually placed for 46 aircraft to the same design, only smaller, although it was still the largest twin-engined airplane to see service with the USAAC/USAAF. Called Commando and designated as the C-46, more than 3,000 of this transport aircraft were eventually built for the army. Designed originally in 1937 for carrying 36 passengers, the C-46 could lift 40 fully equipped troops and carry cargo along its stressed floor.

1940 March 30 The prototype LaGG-1 single-seat fighter took to the air powered by a 1,100-HP Klimov M-105P engine and a 23-mm cannon located between the cylinder banks and two 12.7-mm UB machine guns in the forward upper decking. Designed by a bureau set up in September 1938 run by Semyon A. Lavochkin, V. P. Gorbunov and M. I. Gudkov and known as LaGG, it was also known as the I-22. Unique in being constructed from plastic impregnated wood covered by stressed Bakelite plywood skinning, the armament of production fighters was sized down to one 20-mm cannon and two 7.62-mm guns in efforts to alleviate bad handling characteristics. The LaGG-1 had a wingspan of 32 ft. 2 in., a length of 28 ft. 11 in., a height of 14 ft. 5 in. and a loaded weight of 7,451 lb. with a top speed of 373 MPH and a range of 410 mi.

1940 April 4 The first of three prototype Curtiss P-40 Warhawk fighters, designated Hawk 81-A, made its first flight powered by a 1,040-HP Allison V-1710-33 engine. Last of a great line of Curtiss fighters that began with the true parent of the first Hawk, the PW-8 of 1923, the first major production model was the P-40B, which was delivered to the USAAC, the designation P-40A applying to the British Tomahawks. The P-40B had armor protection for the pilot and two 0.30-in. wing-mounted guns in addition to two 0.50-in. cowling-mounted guns. The first overseas deployment was with the Thirty-third Pursuit Squadron to Iceland on July 25, 1941, followed by further deployments to the Philippines.

1940 April 5 Designed as a high-altitude interceptor to a TsKB design study (Project X), the MiG-1 took to the air powered by a 1,350-HP Mikulin AM-35A V engine. This was the first production aircraft from the OKB (experimental design bureau) headed by Artem I. Mikoyan and Mikhail Y. Gurevich and was given the official designation I-200. Of mixed construction, the MiG-1 had a wingspan of 35 ft. 5 in., a length of 26 ft. 9 in. and a height of 8 ft. 7 in. with one 12.7-mm and two 7.62-mm machine guns. The fighter had a top speed of 390 MPH at 22,965 ft. and a range of 454 mi. but handled badly and had poor maneuverability. It was soon developed into the MiG-3, which made its first flight in November 1940.

1940 April 8 The USN placed a contract with Grumman for two prototypes of the XTBF-1, later named Avenger, a chunky mid-wing monoplane that would become the U.S. Navy's standard carrier torpedo bomber of World War II. The navy had issued a specification on March 25, 1939, calling for an aircraft capable of 300 MPH, a loaded range of 1,000 mi., a ceiling of at least 30,000 ft. and a stalling speed with torpedo of only 70 MPH. Thirteen design proposals from six manufacturers were submitted. The first XTBF-1 flew on August 7, 1941, and the type saw its first action at Midway on June 4, 1942. In all 9,839 Avengers were built, and the plane flew with nine navies.

1940 April 8 The first operational sortie of a special German antishipping Fernaufklärungstaffel (Long Range Reconnaissance Squadron) with Fw 200C-0 and Fw 200B aircraft was conducted when, accompanied by He 115s from Kü.Fl.Gr 506, they patrolled the North Sea looking for Royal Navy units. Toward the end of this month, the Fw 200 unit was renamed 1./KG 40. It had been set up just before the attack on Poland in September 1939 when Luftwaffe chief of air staff Gen. Hans Jeschonnek ordered Oblt. Edgar Petersen to apply his knowledge as a reconnaissance pilot to maritime patrol missions and adapt the long-range, four-engine aircraft to that role. In June 1940 1./KG 40 was renamed I Gruppe and given the first military version of the Fw 200C-1 with defensive armament and bombs.

1940 April 9 Operation Weserübung (Weser Exercise) got under way at 5:00 A.M. when German troops crossed the Danish border and units of the Kriegsmarine supported seaborne landings on the Danish and Norwegian coast. It was followed 90 min. later by paratroop landings at Aalborg East and West airfields and 20 min. after that by airborne infantry put down aboard some of the 571 Ju 52 transport aircraft made available. Success would have been impossible without what was, then, the largest airborne operation in war mounted by eight Kampfgeschwader zur besonderen Verwendung (bomber groups for special operations), seven of which had been specially formed for Weserübung.

1940 April 9 About 3.5 hr. after German seaborne landings at Norwegian ports, Luftwaffe attacks were directed against Stavanger/Sola and Oslo/Fornebu airfields. A British Airways Junker Ju 52/3m transport (G-AFAP, on strength from January 28, 1938, named *Jason*) was captured by the Germans at Oslo. By early afternoon the Oslo/Kjeller airfield had also been taken, and large numbers of fighters and bombers arrived to use this facility as a forward base from which to mount further attacks. During the day, 180 German aircraft arrived at Stavanger/Sola, and on April 10 the airfields at Trondheim/Vaernes and Kristiansand were captured by the Germans. Ju 52s flew in 29,280 personnel, 259,300 gal. of gasoline and 2,619 tons of supplies.

1940 April 10 United Air Lines began the first economy service in commercial airline rates by charging $13.90 for a flight between San Francisco and Los Angeles via intermediate stops. The Sky Coach service was offered on Boeing 247s, which had been fully depreciated by the airline and were capable of carrying 10 passengers. The service ceased April 23, 1942, when the USAAF integrated United's transport fleet for military operations.

1940 April 10 Sixteen British Fleet Air Arm Blackburn Skua dive-bombers from their base at Hatston, near Kirkwall in the Orkney Islands, crossed 330 mi. of the North Sea to carry out a dawn attack on the German cruiser *Königsberg*. Seven aircraft from No. 800 Squadron, led by Capt. R. T. Partridge, Royal Marines, and nine from No. 803 Squadron led by Lt. W. P. Lucy, sank the cruiser as she lay alongside Skoltegrund Mole, Bergen, Norway. Only one Skua was lost during this operation, but when the two squadrons put to sea on HMS *Ark Royal* to support the Royal Navy and Royal Marines' Narvik operation on April 21, almost all the Skuas were lost as they failed to find the carrier, ditched at sea, were shot down or landed on Norwegian soil.

1940 April 11 The first coordinated torpedo attack from an aircraft carrier took place when Fairey Swordfish biplanes from Nos. 816 and 818 Squadrons, Fleet Air Arm, operating off HMS *Furious*, took off to attack two German cruisers reported to be lying off Trondheim. The cruisers were not found but two destroyers were, and one was sunk. As if to make amends, on April 13, a Swordfish flown by Petty Officer F. C. Rice and Lt. Comdr. W. L. M. Brown as observer so successfully spotted for the Royal Navy that six German destroyers were sunk by HMS *Warspite* and a seventh was bombed by the aircraft, which sank in Ofot Fjord.

1940 April 24 Eighteen Gloster Gladiators of No. 263 Squadron, RAF, took off from the deck of HMS *Glorious* to fly 180 mi. across the sea in a heavy snow storm to land on the frozen Lake Lesjaskog 40 mi. from the north Norwegian town of Andalsnes. The next day, 10 Gladiators were shot up on the ground;

but the pilots of the remaining eight made more than 30 sorties and shot down several German aircraft, roaming and bombing at will before three of their group were lost. On April 26, the remaining five Gladiators operated from an emergency strip at Setnesmoen, but two were shot down, two became unserviceable, and there was no fuel for the remaining aircraft. They had flown 49 sorties, made 37 attacks and secured two confirmed He 111s shot down. The personnel were evacuated on April 28 in a cargo vessel.

1940 April A special delegation from Tokyo returned from Stuttgart, Germany with design blueprints for the liquid-cooled Daimler Benz DB 601A and several engines as manufacturing patterns together with right for license production of the engine in Japan. Production got under way at the Kawasaki Akashi plant, and within three months the first Ha-40 engine appeared with certification of all ground tests and full production clearance for what was identified as the 1,100-HP Army Type 2 engine. Kawasaki meanwhile had designed potential airframes for fighters designed to use the new engine, and in February the Japanese Air Headquarters (Koku Hombu) ordered the multi-role Ki-60 and Ki-61 heavy and light fighters respectively.

1940 May 10 Backed up by waves of bombers and fighters, the German army struck at Belgium, Holland and Luxembourg in a surprise attack that began at 5:30 A.M. Airborne troops dropped into the fortress of Eben Emael, paratroop gliders landed near the three bridges across the Albert Canal in Belgium, and 12 He 59 floatplanes carried infantry on a one-way mission to the center of Rotterdam near the two bridges over the Nieuwe Maas. Fourteen Luftwaffe bomber geschwader, five dive-bomber geschwader and 12 fighter groups (Jagdgeschwader) supported the assault. The Dutch had only 125 military aircraft (of which 65 were destroyed on the first day), the Belgians had only 180, and the French Air Force comprised only 400 operational fighters and 100 bombers in the northeast theater within a total combat force available of about 1,000 aircraft.

1940 May 10 On the day the German armed forces attacked Belgium and Holland, the Luftwaffe began the most concentrated aerial bombardment and application of air power the world had yet seen. It had 3,530 operational aircraft at its disposal for what was code-named *Fall Gelb* (Case Yellow) from a total first-line strength of 4,500. For Case Yellow, there were 1,300 long-range bombers, 380 dive-bombers, 860 Bf 109 fighters, 350 twin-engined Me 110 fighters, 300 long-range reconnaissance planes and 340 army cooperation (support) aircraft operating within Luftflotte 2 (Kesselring) and Luftflotte 3 (Sperrle). In addition, there were 475 transport aircraft, mainly the Ju 52 and 45 gliders. On this day too, the Luftwaffe suffered the heaviest loss of aircraft by any air force in one day when 304 planes were destroyed, 51 damaged and 267 crewmembers killed.

The RAF in France comprised 10 medium bomber squadrons and two fighter squadrons of the Advanced Air Striking Force and 13 squadrons of the British Air Force in France (BAFF, otherwise known as the Air Component), including four fighter squadrons, for a total of approximately 400 aircraft. But most were equipped with medium bombers, and there were only four Hurricane squadrons. The RAF response to the German invasion was slow, the first reaction beginning around midday when 32 Fairey Battles flew to attack German columns advancing through Luxembourg. Only 19 returned, every one damaged. The Hurricanes flew 208 sorties and claimed 42 German aircraft for the loss of four and six damaged. On May 22, the RAF evacuated Merville, its last base in France.

1940 May 10 Capable of carrying a crew of two in a pressurized cabin, the Arado Ar 240 V1 made its first flight powered by two 1,075-HP Daimler Benz DB 601A engines. The aircraft had been designed to have FA-13 remotely operated gun barbettes from Rheinmetall-Borsig, but these were troublesome, and the aircraft project itself was cancelled in December 1942—but not before it had demonstrated its high speed performance, making a dash at close on 400 MPH over Britain. The Ar 240 had been proposed as a fast reconnaissance/night fighter/interceptor much like the British Mosquito. But the inability of the Germans to produce an aircraft of this type with gun barbettes is in marked contrast to a wide range of aircraft with this feature developed by the Allies.

1940 May 11 Boeing submitted its Model 345 design study to the USAAC in response to a requirements draft issued during February. As a result of this submission, Boeing received a $85,652 appropriation for wind-tunnel tests on June 17 with extra funds provided June 27. On August 24, Boeing was awarded a $3,615,095 contract for two prototypes and a static test model with the formal army designation XB-29. In May 1941, the company received a letter contract for 250 production aircraft, increased to 500 seven months later. The XB-29 was to be the first pressurized bomber equipped with remote-control, power-operated gun turrets with a wing loading far in excess of previous aeronautical experience.

1940 May 13 A navalized derivative of the Bell P-39 Airacobra, the XFL-1 Airabonita, made its first flight powered by an Allison XV-1710-6 delivering 1,150 HP. Given a conventional tailwheel landing gear with the main legs moved from the rear toward the forward edge of the wing, an arrester hook at the tail and several vital changes to equipment and systems, flight trials revealed inherent deficiencies and the aircraft was not considered suitable for carrier work. By the time the XFL-1 appeared, the navy already had the fighters it wanted, and it was never ordered into production.

1940 May 14 At 12:00 noon, Lt. Col. von Choltitz commanding the German Sixteenth Infantry Regiment demanded the immediate surrender of Rotterdam from his position alongside the Ninth Panzer Division near the Meuse bridge. The Twenty-second Infantry Division under Lt. Gen. Count Sponeck was being hard-pressed northwest of the city, and the Dutch commander in charge of the city, Col. Scharroo, refused. At 1:25 P.M., aircraft of K.G.54 took off to bomb the city. Surrender negotiations began while they were in the air, and though 43 planes received recall messages, 57 bombers dropped 96 tons of high explosives, destroying 25,000 homes, killing more than 900 people and leaving 78,000 homeless. The Dutch surrendered next day, the royal family having escaped to safety in England.

1940 May 15 The commander in chief of RAF Fighter Command, Air Chief Marshal Sir Hugh C. T. Dowding, successfully argued before the British War Cabinet led by the newly appointed prime minister, Winston S. Churchill, that remaining fighter squadrons should not be sent to France but retained in Britain for what he believed would be an impending Battle of Britain. As of May 12, there were 10 RAF Hurricane squadrons in France, and on May 13 the equivalent of two more flew across the English Channel to France. The RAF had lost 219 aircraft in the five days through May 14, mostly Battles and Blenheims. In response to the German bombing of Rotterdam, the Cabinet also approved a bombing campaign against industrial targets in the Ruhr.

1940 May 15 Messerschmitt submitted to the technical office of the German State Ministry for Aviation changes and redesign features for the twin-jet Projekt 1065 aircraft, the Me 262. Adopting BMW turbojet engines, the company wanted to move installation from the wingroots to separate nacelles situated at approximately quarter-span to accommodate an increase in the engine size without unduly compromising the aerodynamics. Approval for the changes was granted in July, and the following month construction began at the Augsburg factory. However, problems with development of the BMW turbojet caused Messerschmitt to adopt the Junkers Jumo 004, which had also been the recipient of a 1939 development contract.

1940 May 16 Pres. Franklin D. Roosevelt called for a complement of 50,000 military aircraft for the army and the navy and annual production of 50,000 aircraft to meet projected U.S. defense requirements. This was impossible to achieve, even given the resources of the United States, and the War Department requested an Army Air Corps of 18,000 aircraft by April 1, 1942, and annual production of 18,000 aircraft thereafter. The president approved this plan June 18, and on June 26 Gen. Marshall sanctioned the First Army Objective, which called for 12,835 aircraft and 54 combat groups operating 4,000 aircraft with a staff of 220,000 officers and men by April 1942.

1940 May 26 The evacuation of 338,226 British and French troops from Dunkirk began and was completed June 12 with 239,555 having been taken out through the harbor and 98,671 taken off the beaches. Where possible the RAF flew cover for small boats that carried the men back to the southeast coast of England. Fighter Command harried German efforts at preventing this exodus, and during the nine days of the seaborne rescue, the RAF flew 3,561 sorties of which 2,739 were flown by fighters, 651 by bombers and 171 by reconnaissance aircraft. During this period also, the RAF flew cover from the aircraft carriers HMS *Furious* and HMS *Glorious* for the evacuation of the British Expeditionary Force from Narvik, Norway, but the *Glorious* was sunk June 8 by the *Scharnhorst* and the *Gneisenau*.

1940 May 29 The prototype Vought XF4U-1 Corsair made its first flight, powered by a 2,000-HP XR-2800-4 Double Wasp radial engine and carrying one 0.50-in. and one 0.30-in. gun in each wing and special compartments in the wings for 10 bomblets for use against bombers. By the end of the year, the XF4U-1 achieved a top speed of 404 MPH, and the U.S. Navy ordered 584, the first of 12,571 eventually built, with the first deliveries beginning October 3, 1942. The F4U-1 had a wingspan of 41 ft., a length of 33 ft. 4 in. and a gross weight of 14,000 lb. Top speed was 417 MPH at 19,900 ft., and the range was 1,015 mi. Produced in 1946, the F4U-5 had a top speed of 470 MPH and a climb rate of 3,780 ft./min.

1940 June 4 The British Overseas Airways Corp. began a twice weekly service between Heston airport near London and Lisbon, Portugal, using D.H.91 Albatros four-engined airliners. It was scheduled to link up with the Lisbon-New York service operated by Pan American and thus maintain a vital air route with the United States. The service opened with a link via Bordeaux in southwest France, but when France fell to the Germans, this was changed. A Dutch KLM DC-3 flown to Britain when Germany attacked Holland on May 10 was used from August for a direct route from London to Lisbon.

1940 June 10 Exactly one calendar month after Hitler's attack on Belgium, Holland and Luxembourg, and with the fate of France sealed, Italy's Benito Mussolini declared war on these countries

A primary offensive bomber in the 1940 Battle of Britain, the Heinkel He 111 had been developed in the mid-1930s.

and Britain, effective the following day. The Regia Aeronautica had 1,796 combat aircraft in Italy, including 783 bombers, 594 fighters, 268 reconnaissance aircraft and 151 seaplanes. On June 12 the First Wing took off from air bases in northern Italy to bomb targets in southern France using Fiat Cicogna bombers while Fiat CR.42 Falco fighter-bombers attacked shipping off the Mediterranean coast of France.

1940 June 11 The Regia Aeronautica began bombing raids on Malta at 4:45 A.M. with an attack from 14,000 ft. by 10 S.M.79 aircraft on Grand Harbour and the airfield at Hal Far. This tiny 17-mi. by 9-mi. Mediterranean island was in a strategic position to control the Allied shipping lanes, serve as a base to harry Axis shipping and mount raids on Sicily and Italy. Until Hurricanes were delivered by HMS *Argus* on August 2, only six Gladiators were available for air defense, and of these, only three were airworthy at any one time. Kept flying with spares from another six unserviceable Gladiators, the myth arose that only three aircraft (*Faith, Hope,* and *Charity*) kept the Axis air forces at bay.

1940 June 12 The first production helicopter, the German Focke Achgelis Fa 223 Drache, was flown for the first time. Originally designated Fa 226 Hornisse, it had evolved in early 1939 from the Fa 61 as a six-seat civil transport for Deutsche Lufthansa. The 40 ft. 2 in.-long fuselage had an extensively glazed nose

The view that many German airmen saw of England: forward from the bomb-aimer's position in the nose of a Luftwaffe Heinkel He 111.

section with the 1,000-HP BMW-Bramo 323 Q3 Fafnir engine located in the center-section driving two 39 ft. 4.5 in. diameter rotors attached to outriggers. A horizontal tail surface was set atop the vertical fin/rudder assembly. Despite ambitious production plans, air raids prevented all but nine from flying before the end of the war.

1940 June 14 The first British air attack on Italy took place when nine Fairey Swordfish torpedo bombers from No. 767 Squadron, Fleet-Air Arm, led by Lt. Comdr. G. C. Dickens flew from Hyères in southern France to raid Genoa. Four days later the 24 aircraft were flown to Bône in Algeria, and the squadron was split up, the training section returning home to England and the operational components flying to Malta on June 22 to become No. 830 Squadron, FAA, operations beginning June 30 against oil tanks at Augusta, Sicily. From then on, for a period of nine months, the Swordfish contingent, never more than 27 biplanes strong, sank an average 50,000 tons of Axis shipping per month.

1940 June 14 The U.S. Naval Expansion Act permitted an increase in aircraft carrier tonnage, from 40,000 tons set in the Expansion Act of May 17, 1938, to 79,500 tons. Aircraft strength was revised upward from "over 3,000" in the previous act to 4,500 operational aircraft. The funds allowed by this act provided for completion of the *Hornet* (CV-8), which had been laid down in September 1939, and for construction of the *Essex* (CV-9), which would be laid down in 1941.

1940 June 22 The French government surrendered to the German occupational forces, and the Battle of France was over. Since May 10, the Germans had lost 1,279 aircraft, including 522 bombers, 109 dive-bombers, 193 Bf 109s, 107 Me 110s and 184 transport aircraft in their campaign against France and the Low Countries. France lost an estimated 757 aircraft, and the RAF lost 959, including 453 Hurricanes and 67 Spitfires. The majority of Hurricanes were lost either to ground attack or abandoned during the hurried evacuation of airfields overrun by the Germans. Combined, the Allied air forces lost, including Belgium and Holland, just over 2,000 aircraft.

1940 June 26 Equipped with their own home-built Hurricanes, No. 1 Squadron, RCAF, arrived in Britain, the first Canadian Air Force unit to arrive in the British Isles. It became operational at Northolt, near London, on August 17 after working up at Middle Wallop and Croydon learning, as the U.S. airmen who followed them would, the vagaries of the English language and the peculiar use of radio slang spoken by the British. The squadron shot down its first Germans on August 26, the day they lost their first pilot when Flying Off. R. L. Edwards flying Hurricane (serial no. P3874), built at Langley, Buckinghamshire, England, was shot down by a Dornier Do 215 over North Weald at 3:26 P.M.

1940 June 28 The U.S. Congress passed the Vinson-Trammel Act, which reduced the profit companies could make on military contracts from 12% to 8% of the contract price. This was in recognition of the enormous profits that could be made from expanded munitions production and, with an eye to a possible war and the vast government funds that would be expended, it was aimed at limiting criticism that private industry was profiteering from war work. It was also known as the "Most Bangs for the Buck Act," for obvious reasons.

1940 June 30 The five-man Civil Aeronautics Authority (CAA) was transferred to the United States Department of Commerce and its name changed to the Civil Aeronautics Board. The Civil

Aeronautics Board was to be responsible for civil aviation in the United States, and the first administrator for Civil Aeronautics was Lt. Col. Donald H. Connolly.

1940 June 30 Just three days after all formal hostilities ceased in France, Reichsmarschall Hermann Göring issued a Luftwaffe directive for a detailed plan for the destruction of the RAF prior to an invasion of Britain. The plan called for nuisance raids until combined operations could begin in the Battle for Britain. On July 2, Hitler followed with an overall order to assemble air, army and naval attack and invasion plans. On July 4, the Luftwaffe began coordinated attacks on shipping in the English Channel and in ports along the south coast of England, from bomber bases set up in northern France and protective fighter units in the Pas de Calais.

1940 July 3 Unintentionally, test pilot Vance Breese took the Northrop N-1M flying wing into the air for the first time when it bounced off the ground for several hundred yards during high-speed taxi tests at Baker Dry Lake, Muroc Army Air Base, Calif. Designed by Jack Northrop, who wanted to build the optimum "clean" airplane, the N-1M evolved through technical discussions with Theodore von Karman at the California Institute of Technology. It had a wingspan of 38 ft., a wing area of 300 sq. ft., a length of 17 ft. and a takeoff weight of 3,900 lb. Powered by two 120-HP Franklin engines driving pusher propellers, it had a top speed of 200 MPH. Jack Northrop's first tailless design had been built in 1928 as the X-216H, dubbed *Flying Wing*.

1940 July 8 The first commercial airline flight by passengers in a fully pressurized airliner took place when Transcontinental and Western Airline (TWA) flew one of its five SA-307B Stratoliner airliners from Burbank, Calif. to Long Island, N.Y. First flown on December 31, 1938, the Boeing Model 307 was a transport version of the Model 299H/B-17C, which was to make its first flight as a bomber on July 21, 1940. The Stratoliner was more than just a converted bomber. It had a greatly enlarged new fuselage compared to the B-17, a completely different rudder/fin arrangement and leading edge slots on the increased wingspan of 107 ft. 3 in. The Stratoliner had a range of 2,390 mi.

1940 July 10 On the day some historians consider to be the start of the Battle of Britain, Luftwaffe attacks continued to press RAF Fighter Command as they had for two weeks. A major air battle took place over the Dover area where a convoy was trying to get out of the English Channel. More than 100 aircraft were involved in the dogfight that ensued during the afternoon, No. 111 Squadron, RAF, in the thick of displaying its unique head-on attack tactic to disrupt the bombers. Disruption was complete. Only one German bomb scored a direct hit, on a schooner, which sank.

1940 July 10 The fourth Messerschmitt Bf 109F series prototype made its first flight, powered by one of the new 1,350-HP Daimler Benz DB 601E. The Bf 109F had modified underwing radiators, reduced span wing leading edge slots and ailerons, a deeper but more symmetrical cowling and significantly enlarged spinner. The Bf 109F-3 was the first production model to have the DB 601E, and typical performance figures were a top speed of 388 MPH at 21,325 ft., a climb time of 2.6 min. to 9,840 ft. and a maximum range of 442 mi. or 528 mi. with drop tank. Various combinations of 20-mm engine-mounted cannons and two 7.9-mm MG 17 or 15-mm MG 151 machine guns were installed. The first Bf 109F, the F-2 version, reached III/JG 26 under Maj. Gerhard Schöpfel during May 1941.

1940 July 12   Pan American Airways began fortnightly airmail service from San Francisco to Auckland, New Zealand via Hawaii, Canton Island and New Caledonia. From December, the New Caledonia stop-off was deleted in favor of Fiji. Aircraft used for these flights was the Boeing 314. Survey flights had been conducted in August and November 1939, and route certification was granted by the Civil Aeronautics Board on June 7, 1940. Passenger flights began September 13, 1940.

1940 July 15   The first of seven American volunteer pilots who would fight alongside British pilots in the Battle of Britain, Pilot Off. W. M. L. Fiske arrived at No. 601 Squadron, RAF, based at Tangmere near the south coast of Britain. Plt. Off. Fiske died of wounds on August 17. The other pilot officer volunteers were A. G. Donahue, DFC (No. 64 Squadron), J. K. Haviland, DFC (No. 151 Squadron), V. C. Keogh (No. 609 Squadron), P. H. Leckrone (No. 616 Squadron), A. Mamedoff and E. Q. Tobin (both of No. 609 Squadron). All except Plt. Off. Fiske survived the Battle of Britain, but only Plt. Off. Haviland survived the war.

1940 July 16   Signed by Adolf Hitler, War Directive No. 16 was issued to the German army, navy, and air force. Hitler explained that because "England, in spite of her hopeless military situation, shows no signs of being ready to come to an understanding, I have decided to prepare a landing operation . . . preparations must be completed by the middle of August." Hitler went on to direct the Luftwaffe "to prevent interference by the enemy Air Force . . . To destroy coastal fortresses . . . to destroy important transport highways . . . and to attack approaching enemy naval forces." Thus began preparations for what would become the Battle of Britain, first by attacking convoys and ports and then by switching to control of the skies over Britain.

1940 July 19   The U.S. Army awarded a contract to the Platt LePage Aircraft Co. for a helicopter. Designed by Havilland H. Platt and Laurence LePage, late of Pitcairn Autogyro Co. and the Kellett Aircraft Corp., the XR-1 won the army tender with a machine vaguely similar to the German Fw 61. It was powered by a 450-HP Pratt & Whitney R-985 situated in the center of a conventional airframe with a single rotor at the tip of two streamlined pylons. There were two seats, and the machine sat on a conventional undercarriage. It had a rotor diameter of 30 ft. 6 in, and weighed 4,800 lb. It made its first flight in May 1941 and spent less than 92 hr. in the air before being retired.

1940 July 20   In response to the shift from day to night raids by RAF bombers, Luftwaffe chief Hermann Göring ordered Col. (Oberst) Josef Kammhuber to set up a night fighter force (Nachtjagdgeschwader), and by the end of November three had been formed. When war broke out in September 1939, there were only two night fighter squadrons equipped with Arado Ar 68 biplanes, joined soon after by two Bf 109 and one Bf 110 squadrons. By the end of 1940, Kammhuber had 164 night fighters. Most were standard Bf 110s and Junkers Ju 88s equipped with special radio equipment and painted black. Not for a year, however, would Kammhuber get significantly improved air defense radar.

1940 July 21   Ordered in September 1939, Boeing flew the first of 38 B-17C four months after the last B-17B had been rolled off the production line on March 30. It eliminated the side gun blisters, the ventral blister was replaced by a metal "bathtub" housing, and the single nose socket in the transparent section was replaced by two side gun sockets. Additionally, self-sealing fuel tanks and armor protection was provided. Twenty B-17Cs would be delivered to the RAF, which named it Fortress I. The B-17C

could carry a 4,000-lb. bomb load 2,400 mi., and improved engines gave it a speed of 323 MPH at 25,000 ft. Similar, but with an added crew member, the first of 42 B-17Ds flew on February 3, 1941.

1940 July 22   The Luftwaffe circulated to senior officers its detailed staff instructions for air operations in support of the invasion of Britain to be conducted primarily by Luftflotte 2 in northwest France under Kesselring and Luftflotte 3 in southwestern France under Sperrle. Luftflotte 5, in Scandinavia, was too far from Britain to do anything other than carry out diversionary attacks. Luftflotten 2 and 3 had 769 serviceable long-range bombers, 656 single-engine fighters, 248 dive-bombers, 168 twin engine fighters, 48 long-range reconnaissance aircraft and 46 coastal reconnaissance aircraft. By August 1, the RAF had 649 serviceable and 258 unserviceable fighters.

1940 August 8   Traditionally regarded as the first day in the Battle of Britain, the intensive air operations mounted by the Luftwaffe were no real part of that campaign but rather an opportunistic assault on a convoy, code-named PEEWIT, of 20 merchant ships and nine Royal Navy escort vessels passing through the Straits of Dover. Luftflotte 3 organized 57 Ju 87 dive-bombers escorted by 20 Bf 110s and 30 Bf 109s to attack PEEWIT, and RAF fighters only partly disrupted the onslaught. Another attack by 82 Ju 87s and 68 escort fighters in the afternoon left 16 merchant and four naval ships either sunk or badly damaged. Throughout the day in all areas, the Luftwaffe lost 46 aircraft, and the RAF lost 21.

1940 August 10   One of the most successful Italian fighters of World War II, the Macchi M.C.202 Folgore, made its first flight as a reworked and re-engined M.C.200 Saetta. Powered by an important Daimler Benz DB-601A-1 liquid-cooled engine which radically altered the aircraft's appearance and gave it a modern streamlined look, the M.C.202 had a wingspan of 34 ft. 8 in., a length of 29 ft. and a height of 9 ft. 11.5 in. Top speed was a creditable 370 MPH at 16,405 ft. and service ceiling a worthy 37,730 ft. with a range of 475 mi. Production machines were to be powered by a license-built version of the DB-601, the 1,175-HP Alfa Romeo RA.1000 RC 41-I inverted V-12 piston engine.

1940 August 13   Postponed from August 10 because of bad weather, this was *Adler Tag* (Eagle Day), the day set for the start of *Adlerangriff* (Attack of Eagles) prior to *Unternehmen Seelöwe* (Operation Sealion), the German invasion of England. A key flaw in the German plan lay in underestimations of RAF strength in a Luftwaffe intelligence document *(Studie Blau)* dated July 16 concerning British resources and operating bases. It contained outdated information and was also inaccurate about the speed of RAF repair and aircraft replacement, which would frustrate field commanders when they would consistently encounter stronger opposition than German intelligence predicted. Today the Germans flew 1,485 sorties and lost 39 aircraft, the RAF lost 14 planes in the air and 47 (only 1 of which was a fighter) on the ground.

1940 August 15   On a day that produced some of the bitterest fighting in the Battle of Britain, the Luftwaffe mounted 1,786 sorties from Luftflotten 2, 3 and 5, attacking targets along the south coast of England, around the southeastern counties and up along the Thames estuary and on northeast England from the Humber estuary to Sunderland. The RAF mounted a stiff and aggressive defense, accounting for 71 German aircraft destroyed and 19 seriously damaged, and 30 RAF fighters were lost and 12 damaged. However, 16 RAF bombers were destroyed on the ground, so equivalent totals are 90 German aircraft out of action (71 completely destroyed) with 58 British aircraft out of action (46 destroyed).

1940 August 17 The first American volunteer serving with the RAF to die on duty succumbed to terrible burns sustained the day before when his Hurricane (serial no. P3358) was shot up and strafed at 1:05 P.M. while landing back at RAF Tangmere during a Luftwaffe airfield attack. Plt. Off. William Fiske of No. 601 Squadron put his aircraft down as the Luftwaffe was raining bombs down upon the runway and the hangars. Managing to dodge the bombs and the holes, he came to a stop, but before he could leave his aircraft it was hit and quickly became a raging inferno. Only with extreme bravery was the ground crew able to extricate his body and get him to hospital.

1940 August 18 The reputation of the much-feared Junkers Ju 87 Stuka dive bomber was dealt an irrevocable blow by the RAF when Hurricanes of Nos. 43 and 601 squadrons and Spitfires of Nos. 152 and 602 squadrons shot down or badly damaged 22 Stukas of St.G 77 during an afternoon attack on the Chain Home radar installation at Poling on the south coast of England just 3 mi. inland from the seaside town of Littlehampton. The first major Stuka attack on England was on August 8 when 18 were shot down or damaged; by today a total of 76 aircraft out of 220 Stukas were lost.

1940 August 19 Following a particularly heavy day of air fighting over England, Göring ordered his senior officers to Karinhall for a conference that turned into a contemptuous tirade of abuse and bitter complaint that they had failed to smash the RAF. He ordered sweeping reorganization of the fighter groups and replaced older leaders with young officers like Adolf Galland and Johannes Trautloft. In the preceding four days, the Germans had lost 249 aircraft, damaged or destroyed, to the RAF's 134 fighters lost. So far this month, the RAF had lost 106 pilots. German intelligence, once again wide of the mark, calculated only 300 serviceable RAF fighters remained when in reality there were more than twice that number.

1940 August 19 The North American (NA-62) B-25 Mitchell made its first flight powered by two 1,700-HP Wright R-2600-9 radial engines. As a development of the privately developed NA-40, the NA-62 was heavier and had twice the bomb load, and its wider fuselage afforded side-by-side seating for the pilot and copilot. Almost 11,000 Mitchells were built, and the type served widely in the USAAC/USAAF and with Allied air forces. It had a wingspan of 67 ft. 7 in., a length of 54 ft. 1 in. and a crew of up to six, depending on the mission. The B-25 had a top speed of 315 MPH at 15,000 ft. and a range of 1,350 mi. Bomb load was 3,000 lb.

1940 August 24 A shift in Battle of Britain strategy unfolded as the Luftwaffe began to concentrate on trying to destroy RAF Fighter Command by attacking inland cities like London, thus drawing remaining defensive forces to the protection of civilian areas. In this way, it was hoped to break the RAF's control of the skies over south and southeast England. The Luftwaffe moved fighter forces from northwest France to the Pas de Calais area where they could mount better protective cover for the massed bomber formations that would attempt to smash the RAF fighter squadrons south and southeast of London.

1940 August 25 In the late evening, RAF aircraft took off on the first British bombing raid on Berlin. The War Cabinet sanctioned the raid after German bombs fell on London and other

British cities the night before. About 43 of the 103 Whitleys, Wellingtons and Hampdens went to Berlin; six Hampdens and three Blenheims were lost during attacks on this and other cities. Bombing was inaccurate, and only two people in Rosenthal were slightly injured. This raid and others over successive nights had no military value. They were desperate attempts to raise morale at home, but they inflamed German anger.

1940 August 28 Developed as a reaction-powered experimental aircraft by Secondo Campini and Caproni, the Caproni Campini N.1 made its first flight at Taliedo with Maro de Bernadi at the controls. Campini formed his company, S. Campini per Velivoli e Natani a Reazione, in 1931 for research into reaction motors. He designed a device powered by a 900-HP Isotta-Fraschini radial engine driving a ducted-fan compressor in which air passed through a variable nozzle exit pipe into which fuel could be injected and burned. The low-wing monoplane had a length of 43 ft. and a wingspan of 52 ft. with a maximum weight of 9,250 lb. and a top speed of 233 MPH. On November 30, 1941, it flew 168 mi., and today the aircraft is preserved in the Museo della Scienza Tecnica in Milan.

1940 August 29 The Luftwaffe began to increase the severity of their night raids on cities in the south, the midlands and the north of England, consolidating what would become known as the ''Blitz.'' In these raids, increasing use of German radar would permit on-target attacks on dark nights and in poor weather conditions. Fighter Command losses were relatively light tonight, with only nine aircraft shot down for 16 bombers destroyed and 15 badly damaged.

1940 August 31 With the explicit intention of destroying the British will to continue the fight by attacking its cities and wearing down the resources of RAF Fighter Command, several waves of enemy aircraft spread across southeast England from early morning on nuisance raids to harry the Spitfires and the Hurricanes. These free-wheeling raids were characteristic of fighter force (Jagdwaffe) tactics and ran counter to the orderly precision with which the RAF went about its business of defending Britain. All day the country was attacked, and at night 160 German bombers hit major cities. In all, the Luftwaffe lost 60 aircraft including 26 Bf 109s, and the RAF lost 37 fighters.

1940 August In Germany, powered flight trials began with the tailless DFS 194 delta-wing research aircraft carrying an 882-lb. thrust Walter HWK I-203 rocket motor. A ban had been imposed in February 1940 on all research projects not likely to reach operational status within 12 months, and work on Projekt X and the Me 163 rocket-powered research aircraft was stopped. Seeking to find a way to keep work going, Lippisch and his team married the motor to the metal airframe and achieved a top speed of 341.8 MPH with excellent handling qualities. Because of this, work on the Me 163 was resumed, and three prototypes built to use the HWK R-II-203 engine, which the German Air Ministry stipulated should be capable of throttle settings between 331-lb. and 1,653-lb. thrust.

1940 August Designated Nakajima Ki-44 Shoki, the Japanese interceptor destined to bear the brunt of defending the homeland against initial USAAF B-29 raids made its first flight. Speed and climb rate was emphasized at the expense of maneuverability, and the Ki-44 adopted the 1,250-HP 14-cylinder, twin-row, Nakajima Ha-41 engine rather than one of the more conventional Japanese aero engines. The Ki-44 was accepted by the army air force in September 1941, fitted with two 7.7-mm fuselage mounted and two 12.7-mm wing-mounted machine guns. The K-44-IIb had a maximum weight of 6,598 lb. and could reach 16,405 ft. in 4 min. 17 sec.

1940 September 2 An agreement was signed giving the United States 99-year leases for air and naval bases on British territories in the Bahamas, Jamaica, St. Lucia, Trinidad, Antigua and British Guiana and in Bermuda and Newfoundland in return for 50 four-stack destroyers from World War I. In a separate agreement, the United States acquired a base on Dutch Guiana. Thus began the accumulation of lands and territories for the use of Army Air Corps hemispheric defense plans, the stationing of airmen and aircraft beginning in Bermuda on November 15 with Patrol Squadron 54 based on the seaplane tender USS *George E. Badger* (AVD-3).

1940 September 5 The first German fighter-bomber raids on England took place when 4./JG 26 sent its Bf 109s equipped with bomb racks. Dubbed Jabo, an abbreviation of Jagdbomber, the Bf 109 had external stowage locations for a single 250-kg (551-lb.) or four 50-kg (110.25-lb.) bombs. The following day a Bf 109E-7 from 6./LG 2 was brought down by antiaircraft fire and forced to land at Hawkinge, Kent. Examined by the Royal Aircraft Establishment, Farnborough, it was found to have Jabo racks, the first German fighter so equipped to be brought down over England.

1940 September 7 In a mass daylight air raid on London, 965 aircraft comprising 348 Luftwaffe bombers and 617 fighters approached the Thames estuary across a 20 mi. front stacked 2 mi. upward from 14,000 ft. and stretching back 40 mi. toward continental Europe. It was the first of 57 consecutive day and night raids on London and the beginning of a concentrated sequence of heavy air attacks on British cities that would last until the end of May 1941, when the bomber squadrons on Luftflotten 2 and 3 would largely be withdrawn for service on the Eastern Front. Göring personally controlled the daylight attack, and in this and the follow-up raids during the night, 436 Londoners lost their lives, and 1,600 were seriously injured. The Luftwaffe lost 63 aircraft, the RAF 42. Although the Battle of Britain would not be considered to have ended before late October, the switch from airfield to city targets signaled the collapse of German plans for an early invasion of Britain.

1940 September 7 Conceived originally as a trans-Atlantic passenger-carrying flying boat, the Blohm und Voss Bv 222 Wiking made its first flight bearing the civil registration D-ANTE with Flugkapitän Helmut Wasa Roda at the controls. Powered by six 1,000-HP BMW-Bramo Fafnir 232R radials, it had a wingspan of 150 ft. 1 in., a length of 120 ft., a height of 35 ft. 9 in. and a maximum loaded weight of 108,000 lb. Because it now had no civil job, the Bv 222 was tested for its potential as a military transport, and it became the largest flying boat to go into service during World War II. The specially formed Luft-Transportstaffel (See) 222 received its first Bv 222 (the V1 prototype) on May 10, 1942, but in keeping with the changed maritime reconnaissance role, this was changed to Aufklärungsstaffel (See) 222 at the end of 1942 and to 1.(Fern)/See-Aufklärungs-Gruppe 129 in 1943.

1940 September 11 Hurricanes of Nos. 46, 249 and 257 squadrons, RAF, successfully intercepted the first and only serious bombing raid by Italy's Regia Aeronautica on the British mainland. The Italian raid was staged as a reprisal for RAF raids on Italian targets, which had begun on the night of June 11/12 when 36 Whitleys were sent across the Alps (only nine bombed

the assigned area in Turin, 23 failed even to cross the mountains and turned back). The Italians sent 10 Fiat B.R.20 bombers, of which seven were shot down, escorted by 40 Fiat C.R.42 fighters, of which four were shot down.

1940 September 13 Preproduction models of the Mitsubishi A6M2 serving with the Twelfth Rengo Kokutai (Combined Naval Air Corps) of the Japanese Navy saw their first combat action in China. During this and later engagements, the A6M2 Reisen (Zero) shot down 99 Chinese aircraft for the loss of only two and helped Japan's naval fighter pilots learn combat tactics and optimum operational use of the aircraft. In September 1941, they were withdrawn as war clouds gathered in the Pacific, and production aircraft were modified as a result of experiences in China. When Japan attacked the United States on December 7, 1941, of 521 carrier fighters, 328 (63%) were Zeros.

1940 September 15 On what is generally regarded as the day the Luftwaffe lost the Battle of Britain, a second mass daylight air raid on London took place followed by an evening raid on Southampton. During the day, Prime Minister Winston Churchill visited the operations headquarters of Air Chief Marshal Sir Keith Park, commander in chief of No. 11 Group, RAF Fighter Command, at Uxbridge. In the heat of the battle, Churchill asked Park where his reserves were. Park replied cooly, "There are none." Nevertheless, the Luftwaffe lost 80 aircraft, the RAF lost 35, and Adolf Hitler realized his invasion plan was not feasible. Two days later orders were issued to dismantle equipment on German-occupied Dutch airfields that would have been used in Operation Sealion, without which an airborn invasion was impossible.

1940 September 16 Luftwaffe chief Hermann Göring ordered yet another switch in tactics that would, he said again, destroy the RAF "in four or five days." He planned to achieve this by resuming daylight fighter-bomber sweeps of RAF airfields and by attacks on aircraft factories and manufacturing centers, while the night bombers raided London and other English cities. From September 21, main aircraft production centers would be raided both by day and by night.

1940 September 19 No. 71 Squadron, RAF, was re-formed at Church Fenton, Yorkshire, England, having been disbanded on February 28, 1918, as the first of three Eagle squadrons manned by American volunteers. It was equipped in October with Brewster Buffalo fighters ordered in 1939 by the British Purchasing Mission to the United States and in the following month by Hurricanes. No. 121 Squadron re-formed on May 14, 1941, at Kirton-in-Lindsey, Lincolnshire, and No. 133 Squadron re-formed on August 1, 1941, at Coltishall, Lincolnshire, both with Hurricanes. All three squadrons were transferred as the 334th, 335th and 336th Fighter Squadrons to the Fourth Fighter Group, USAAF, on September 29, 1942.

1940 September 22 The first of five prototype turbojet-powered fighter aircraft built by Heinkel, the He 280 V1, made its first unpowered flight when it was towed into the air by a Heinkel He 111 and released for a glide back down to the ground. A general expansion of Heinkel turbojet development had begun when Max A. Meuller left the Junkers Magdeburg factory and joined the Rostock-Marienehe team to produce the HeS 30 while the existing Heinkel team, headed by Dr. Hans Joachim Pabst von Ohain, worked on a centrifugal engine, the HeS 3/6. Both engines would be tested in the He 280, an all-metal, mid-wing, twin-engine monoplane with a tricycle landing gear and high-mounted tail and twin fin/rudder units.

1940 September 27 The final fighter-bomber attack on Britain with Bf 110 twin-engine fighters took place. Flying without fighter cover four out of 19 attacking the Bristol area were shot down. A fighter-bomber unit designated Erprobungsgruppe (Test-Group) 210 had been formed under Hptm. Walter Rubensdörffer in early July, but losses were heavy and the Bf 110, though fast, was vulnerable to the nimble RAF fighters. The Bf 110 was increasingly unable to operate during daylight, and groups could only form a defensive ring if attacked. Hptm. Martin Lütz, the new commander of Epr Gr 210, was one of those killed during the Bristol raid when he fell to the guns of a Hurricane from No. 504 Squadron, which had moved to Filton near Bristol the day before.

1940 October 12 Designed as an armored attack aircraft by Ilyushin, the Il-2 Sturmovik made its first flight and was quickly ordered into mass production, reaching a quoted 300 per month by August 1941. If Soviet figures are correct, the Il-2 was produced in greater numbers than any other aircraft in history, 36,163 being built by November 1944 when production ended. With a 1,665-HP (later 1,720-HP) Mikulin AM-38 (AM-38F) V-12 engine, the Il-2 had a wingspan of 47 ft. 11 in., a length of 38 ft. 2 in. and a maximum loaded weight of 14,021 lb. Typical performance was a maximum speed of 269 MPH, ceiling of 14,845 ft. and a range of 475 mi. Armed with two 23-mm cannons and two 7.62-mm guns in the wings and one 12.7-mm machine gun for the rear gunner, the Il-2 could carry up to six 220-lb. bombs in addition to underwing rockets. This aircraft did as much as any other to win the ground war on the Eastern Front between 1941 and 1945.

1940 October 15 Designed for Alpine crossings from Italy into Central Europe, the Fiat G.12 transport aircraft made its first flight, powered by three 770-HP Fiat A.74 14-cylinder, two-row, air-cooled radial engines. A derivative, the G.12 RTbis, was developed to support nonstop airline operations between Rome and Tokyo. With a loaded weight of 46,737 lb., the aircraft had a range of 5,592 mi. and made its first flight in 1942. Derivatives of the G.12 appeared as late as 1949.

1940 October 26 Designed by North American engineers Raymond Rice and Edgar Schmued to a specification delivered by the British Purchasing Commission for a European fighter, requirements that could not be met by existing U.S. aircraft, the NA-73 made its first flight powered by a 1,100-HP Allison V-1710-F3R engine. Because North American had manufactured for a foreign customer, the USAAC stipulated the first two should be delivered to Wright Field for evaluation. Armed with four 0.30-in. and two 0.50-in. wing-mounted guns and two 0.50-in. guns in the fuselage, it entered service with the RAF as the Mustang 1 in October 1941. With a wingspan of 37 ft. 1 in. and a length of 32 ft. 2 in., the Mustang had a loaded weight of 8,600 lb., a top speed of 390 MPH at 8,000 ft. and a range of 1,050 mi.

1940 October 31 As if to emphatically underline the positive end to the Battle of Britain, only a few Luftwaffe aircraft raided England, and not a single aircraft was lost in combat to either the Germans or the RAF this day. There has never been a definitive accounting of aircraft lost in the Battle of Britain, but the most accurate estimates give the Luftwaffe losses totaling 1,882 aircraft and 2,662 aircrew with the RAF losses at 1,265 aircraft (of which 1,017 were from Fighter Command, 130 from Coastal Command and 118 from Bomber Command) and 1,494 aircrew. Fighter Command lost 537 pilots (36% of the total RAF losses)

out of 3,084 fighter pilots who served during the Battle of Britain, Bomber Command 718 and Coastal Command 280.

1940 November 1 The growing importance of the defense of the Hawaiian islands was marked when all USAAC elements in that region were renamed as units of the Hawaiian Air Force under the direct administrative control of the U.S. government's Hawaiian Department. It had only 117 aircraft, but within a year that force would number 231, making it the largest single contingent for any U.S. possession anywhere in the continental U.S. or overseas.

1940 November 11 The first organized ferry flight of U.S.-built aircraft across the North Atlantic began when Capt. D. C. T. Bennett led a formation of Lockheed Hudsons from Gander, Newfoundland to Northern Ireland in 10 hr. 30 min. The North Atlantic Ferry Service was organized to expedite the delivery of U.S. aircraft to Britain and was set up by the Canadian Pacific Railway (CPR) on the suggestion of the British Ministry of Aircraft Production. The CPR established an Air Ferries Department under the command of Maj. G. E. Woods Humphrey, an ex-director of Imperial Airways.

1940 November 11 In a three-quarter moon, a force of 21 Fleet Air Arm Swordfish from Nos. 813, 815, 819 and 824 squadrons attacked the Italian navy in Taranto harbor and sank three battleships, severely damaged two destroyers and a cruiser, disabled two auxiliary vessels and badly damaged shore installations, oil tanks and sea-plane hangars. For the first time, a major naval force had been knocked out from the air, and the Japanese used this as a model for their attack on Pearl Harbor. The first wave of 12 Swordfish took off from HMS *Illustrious* at 8:30 P.M. 180 mi. from Taranto, followed by the second wave of nine at 9:30 P.M. Eleven aircraft carried torpedoes, six had bombs, and four had flares. The flares were dropped over the target at 11:00 P.M., and only one aircraft was lost in each of two attacks.

1940 November 14 On a relatively clear night with a full moon, 552 German bombers of Luftflotten 2 and 3 set out to attack the English city of Coventry using the X-Geräten navigational radio beam system over England for the first time. Code-named Moonlight Sonata, it was one of the first raids in a new strategic bombing campaign aimed at industrial targets as well as London and aero-engine plants. In all, 449 bombers, primarily Heinkel He 111s, found Coventry and dropped 554 tons of high explosives and 31,716 incendiaries in 881 cans. Bombing went on from 7:20 P.M. through 5:35 A.M. November 15, killing 568 and injuring 863 civilians.

1940 November 25 The first Martin B-26 made its first flight from the plant in Baltimore with chief engineer William K. Ebel at the controls. As the aircraft had been ordered straight from the drawing board, the first few were reserved for trials. Powered by two 1,850-HP Wright R-2800-5 engines, the B-26 had a maximum bomb load of 5,800 lb., a top speed of 315 MPH and a range of 1,000 mi. Deliveries to the USAAF got under way in 1941, and the first units were deployed overseas, to Australia, in February 1942. The aircraft was difficult to introduce due to the high landing speed that necessitated special training for crew conversion.

1940 November 25 Exactly 30 days after ACM Sir Charles F. A. Portal replaced Marshal of the RAF Sir Cyril L. N. Newall as Chief of the Air Staff (a position he would retain for the duration of the war), Air Marshal Sir W. Sholto Douglas took over RAF Fighter Command from ACM Sir Hugh Dowding. It presaged a shift from the defensive protection of the British Isles to offensive attacks on targets in France and the Low Countries with fighter sweeps colloquially known as ''Rhubarbs,'' which began in January. On October 5, 1940, Air Marshal Sir Richard E. C. Peirse took over RAF Bomber Command from Sir Charles Portal, who had replaced ACM Sir Edgar R. Ludlow-Hewitt on April 3, 1940. When the bombers joined these continental raids, they were known as ''Circuses.''

1940 November 25   The prototype D.H.98 Mosquito bomber (serial no. W4050) made its first flight at Hatfield, England. The second prototype D.H.98 (serial no. W4052) served as the progenitor of all fighter versions and first flew on May 15, 1941. The third prototype (serial no. W4051) flew on June 10, 1941, as the first reconnaissance variant (Mk.I). The Mk.I entered service with the RAF in June 1941 with the first sortie being flown on September 20. The bomber version (Mk.IV) entered RAF service in No. 2 Group during November 1941, and the first sortie was flown May 31, 1942. The fighter variant (Mk.II) joined the RAF in January 1942 with the first night sortie on April 27/28. All versions had a wingspan of 54 ft. 2 in., fuselage length varied between 40 ft. 6 in. and 44 ft. 6 in., and maximum loaded weights were up to 23,859 lb. Top speed was 436 MPH for the fastest version, the P.R.Mk.VIII.

1940 December 18   The first successful launch of a rocket-propelled Henschel Hs 293A radio-controlled bomb took place in Germany. Since January, a team lead by ex-Junkers engineer Prof. Dr. Herbert A. Wagner had been working at Henschel on air-to-ground missiles. The first unpowered model was developed under the code FZ 21, but a powered version had a single 1,320-lb. thrust Walter HWK 109-507B bi-propellant rocket motor that provided thrust for 10 sec., boosting speed to 120 MPH above release speed, and a maximum terminal speed of 560 MPH. It was first used in action on August 25, 1943, attacking destroyers in the Bay of Biscay. A television-guided version was built and tested in 1944.

1940 December 21   The first SC 2500 (5,500-lb.) bomb developed for use by the Luftwaffe was dropped on London's Victoria railway station by a specially adapted Heinkel He 111 of III/KG 26, demolishing the Central Signal Box and closing the station completely until December 24, when daylight rail traffic resumed using hand signals. Only He 111H-5 and H-6 aircraft, with a maximum permitted overload bomb weight of 5,550 lb., were cleared to carry the SC 2500, which was suspended beneath the center fuselage. Takeoff and handling characteristics with the new bomb were such that only very experienced pilots were chosen to fly these aircraft.

1940 December 23   The first U.S. all-cargo air service was inaugurated by United Air Lines when at 11:30 P.M. a flight left New York for Chicago, where it arrived at 3:40 A.M. local time the following morning after stopping in Cleveland. The service supplemented the mixed passenger-cargo services and received a boost with the Christmas rush. The service was terminated May 31, 1941.

1940 December 23   Conceived in 1937 as a long-distance record-breaker for Germany's Third Reich, the Messerschmitt Me 261 made its first flight, powered by two 2,700-HP DB 606A/B 24-cylinder engines mounted on an 88 ft. 2 in. span wing and set either side of a pencil fuselage 54 ft. 9 in. long, with twin fins and rudders set on a horizontal tail. The engines were two pairs of coupled DB 601s mounted side by side with each pair driving a two-bladed 15 ft. 1 in. propeller. Work on the Me 261 had stopped just before the war, but was resumed to gain technical information. The Me 261 had a range of 6,831 mi., a cruising speed of 248 MPH and a ceiling of 27,060 ft. Only three were built, the last serving as a reconnaissance aircraft with a special reconnaissance group, Aufklärungsgruppe/Ob.d.L. from 1943.

1940 December 29   In what was described at the time as ''The Second Great Fire of London,'' 136 German bombers of Luftflotten 2 and 3 attacked the capital, dropping 140 tons of bombs

First flown at Baltimore, Md., on November 25, 1940, the Martin B-26 Marauder would become a stalwart of World War II.

The Avro Lancaster made its first flight on January 9, 1941, and quickly became the RAF's most effective heavy bomber.

and 22,068 incendiaries and killing 163 and injuring 509 people in a concentrated raid around the city itself. The raid lasted less than 3 hr. 15 min. (from 6:17 to 9:30 P.M.) and engulfed most of the old and historic part of the city of London "square mile." The Guildhall and eight churches built by Sir Christopher Wren were destroyed, and eight hospitals were damaged. The tidal Thames River was unusually low, hampering firefighters and limiting water supplies for fireboats. Many conflagrations were left to burn. Although ringed by fire, Wren's St. Paul's Cathedral miraculously escaped destruction.

1940 December 31   The Kawanishi H8K1 heavy flying boat designed for maritime reconnaissance made its first flight, powered by four 1,530-HP Mitsubishi MK4A Kasei 11 14-cylinder, air-cooled radial engines. With a wingspan of 124 ft. 8 in. and a length of 92 ft. 4 in., it was bigger than the Short Sunderland, with a maximum loaded weight on some versions of 71,650 lb. The H8K1 made its first combat sortie on the night of March 4/5, 1942. The aircraft had 20-mm and 7.7-mm machine guns in up to eight defensive gun positions and could carry torpedoes, bombs or depth charges to a maximum loading of approximately 4,400 lb. In all, 167 H8K1 were built.

1940 December   One of the most outstanding, yet unrecognized, Japanese aircraft of World War II made its first flight at Yokosuka. The D4Y Suisei was powered by a Daimler Benz DB 600G engine in lieu of the license-built version of the DB 601A known as the Aichi Atsuta. (Later versions were powered by a 1,400-HP AE1P Atsuta.) The Yokosuka D4Y Suisei was Comet by name and comet by nature, with a speed of 360 MPH (comparable to the British Mosquito) and a range of up to 2,417 mi. Like its British counterpart, it was utilized for bomber, reconnaissance and night fighter roles. With a wingspan of 37 ft. 9 in. and a length of 33 ft. 6 in., the D4Y had a maximum loaded weight of 10,463 lb. A total 2,038 of these carrier-based dive-bombers were built.

1940   During the year, the USAAC accepted 5,054 aircraft, comprising 60 heavy bombers, 62 medium bombers, 891 light bombers, 1,422 fighters, 65 reconnaissance aircraft, 233 transports, 2,320 trainers and 1 communications aircraft. As of June 30, 1940, the USAAC had on strength a total 2,966 aircraft, comprising 54 heavy bombers, 478 medium bombers, 166 light

bombers, 477 fighters, 414 reconnaissance aircraft, 127 transports, 1,243 trainers and 7 communications aircraft.

1941 January 9   The Avro Lancaster (serial no. BT308) made its first flight from Woodford, England and was delivered to the Aircraft Experimental Establishment, Boscombe Down, for trials. The first production Lancaster flew on October 31, 1941, and made the first operational sortie of its distinguished career on April 17, 1942. The Lancaster was originally known as the Manchester III, a development of the twin-engine Manchester powered by the unsuccessful Rolls Royce Vulture, before Avro replaced them with four Merlins transforming an already promising aircraft into a spectacular bomber. With a wingspan of 102 ft., a length of 69 ft. 4 in. and an all-up weight of 50,000 lb. (up to 72,000 lb. on one variant), the Lancaster could carry a 14,000-lb. bomb load 1,660 mi. or a single 22,000-lb. bomb 1,040 mi.

1941 January 23   One of the most unusual Japanese aircraft of World War II was authorized when Kawasaki received the formal go-ahead for their Ki-64 steam-cooled fighter. It was powered by two Kawasaki Ha-201 engines mounted forward and aft of the pilot's seat, producing 2,350 HP and driving three-bladed contra-rotating propellers. The unconventional aircraft incorporated 18.5 gal. of water in each wing vented through radiator surfaces contiguous with the wing surfaces and flaps. Only five flights were made beginning December 1943, but Kawasaki estimated a top speed of 435 MPH.

1941 February 6   Disillusioned by unrealized claims that Britain could be defeated by Göring's Luftwaffe alone, Hitler's War Directive No. 23 was issued commanding that the blockade of Britain's imports be the prime objective for the German Air Force. In cooperation with the German navy, Britain was to be starved into submission as the Luftwaffe destroyed the ports, sank supply convoys and smashed the armaments industry. It is significant that Hitler decided in this directive that "no decisive success can be expected from terror attacks on residential areas."

1941 February 7   Gloster Aircraft receive a contract from the British Ministry of Aircraft Production for 12 jet fighters to an F.9/40 specification issued November 1940. It had been written around Gloster's own design for a twin-jet fighter raised by George Carter, submitted in August 1940 and finalized in December. The order was later reduced to eight aircraft, one of which would be set aside in an exchange deal with the United States for a P-80. The F.9/40 would be named Meteor, changed from Thunderbolt to avoid conflict with the American fighter of that name, and the Rover W.2B engine would be called Welland.

1941 February 9   Since August 1, 1940, when I/KG 40 began to seriously harass Allied merchant vessels in the North Atlantic with its Focke-Wulf Fw 200C Condor antishipping sorties, the group had sunk 363,000 tons of shipping and 85 ships. With a nominal strength of 15 aircraft, though rarely with more than six to eight aircraft operational, the unit had accounted for 24% of the 1.5 million tons sunk and 28% of the 292 Allied ships lost in the North Atlantic during the same period. By late summer, when merchant ships equipped with catapult-launched fighters became available and escort carriers appeared, the Condors were ordered not to initiate an engagement.

1941 February 10   From its base at Oakington, England, No. 7 Squadron, RAF, carried out the first bombing raid with the Short Stirling, the first operational RAF four-engine bomber since the Handley Page V/1500 of 1919. Three aircraft dropped 56

500-lb. bombs on oil storage tanks at Rotterdam, Holland in a night raid. The RAF would receive 2,221 Stirlings, of which 769 would be lost, 641 due to enemy action. The Stirling would drop 27,821 tons of bombs and lay 20,000 mines. It had a wing span of 99 ft. 1 in., a length of 87 ft. 3 in. and a loaded weight of 70,000 lb. and could carry a maximum bomb load of 14,000 lb. a distance of 590 mi. With a bomb load of 3,500 lb., range was 2,010 mi. The Stirling had a maximum speed of 210 MPH.

1941 February 10 In the first British airborne parachute operation of World War II, Armstrong Whitworth Whitley Mk.Vs of Nos. 51 and 78 squadrons, RAF, dropped paratroopers near Campagna, Italy with a mission to destroy the viaduct at Tragino. Unfortunately, they were unable to do more than disrupt water supplies for more than two days, and the paratroopers were captured walking to the coast where a British submarine was scheduled to pick them up and return them to England. On the second airborne operation, on the night of February 27/28, paratroopers dropped by 10 Whitleys from No. 51 Squadron, RAF, achieved all of their objectives when they retrieved secret German radar equipment from a coastal Würzburg site at Bruneval, France.

1941 February 14 A new objective for USAAC pilot training goals was established with the aim of passing 30,000 new military pilots from the air training schools each year. The program had expanded from 300 a year to 1,200 a year prior to the start of European hostilities in September 1939 and then to 7,000 with new goals announced in June 1940. The First Aviation Objective of July 1940 had further increased this to 12,000 new pilots each year, and now even that major goal was increased 250%. Nine new training schools has been opened during 1939, and by the end of 1941, there would be 41 primary air training centers for U.S. military pilots.

1941 February 19 Enacting the orders contained within Hitler's War Directive No. 23, the Luftwaffe began a renewed, concentrated bombing campaign against ports and industrial areas in the British Isles that would continue unabated until Luftflotten 2 and 3 were moved east prior to the German invasion of the USSR in June. This night was the first of 81 consecutive nights of air raids on Portsmouth, Plymouth, Bristol, Avonmouth, Swansea, Merseyside, Belfast and Clydeside as well as on the main centers of aircraft production in Nottingham, Coventry and the Birmingham area. By the end of this campaign in June, 40,000 British civilians had been killed and 236,000 had been injured; not until the end of 1942 would casualties suffered by Britain's armed forces equal that of her civilian populations.

1941 February 25 The Messerschmitt Me 321 Gigant heavy glider was first towed into the air, by a Junkers Ju 90. Adolf Hitler had postponed the seaborne invasion of Britain on October 12, 1940, and switched short-term priorities to the invasion of the USSR. To more effectively assist an airborne assault on Britain following a quick defeat of the USSR, a Grossraumlastensegler (large-capacity cargo glider) was ordered. The German Air Ministry's Technical Office (Technische Amt) produced a specification to which Messerschmitt and Junkers responded on November 6, assigned designations Me 263 and Ju 322. The latter was unsuccessful, but the redesignated Me 321, the first of 200 Gigant aircraft, entered service in August 1941. It had a wingspan of 180 ft. 5 in., a length of 92 ft. 4 in. and a maximum overload weight of 86,860 lb.

1941 February 25 The Protivo-Vosdushnaya Oberona Strany (PVO-Strany), or National Air Defense Force, was formed within the Soviet air force. It was later to become an independent force

with its own commander in chief and would assume responsibility for the air defense of the motherland. Later, this would involve not only aircraft but early warning technologies as well as ground-to-air missile air defense systems. In 1954 it became an independent arm of the Soviet armed forces and ranked third in size behind the strategic rocket forces and the ground forces. The PVO-Strany was, however, slow to organize itself to optimum effect and had hardly begun to emerge before the German invasion of the USSR.

1941 February In Japan, the Air Headquarters (Koko Hombu) drafted a specification for the type of bomber it wanted to succeed the Nakajima Ki-49 Donryu and instructed Mitsubishi to build three prototypes of what would emerge as Japan's finest bomber of World War II: the Ki-67 Hiryu (Flying Dragon). Chief engineer Ozawa designed a slim, mid-wing monoplane powered by two fan-cooled Mitsubishi Ha-104 radial engines. The Koku Hombu wanted the aircraft to operate at an altitude of 13,125–22,965 ft., have a maximum speed of 342 MPH, have a range of 435 mi. carrying a 1,102-lb. bomb load, have a maximum bomb load of three 551-lb. or eight 220-lb. bombs and carry a crew of six to ten with four defensive gun positions.

1941 March 9 Responding to increased German attacks on British ports and incoming supply convoys, Prime Minister Churchill wanted to switch bombing raids from strategic targets to the sources of these threats, and the Air Ministry sent the order to RAF Bomber Command this day changing the target objectives for the next four months. The commander in chief of the RAF Bomber Command, Sir Richard Peirse, was frustrated in being taken away from his strategic targets, especially when the spring weather could have improved results. RAF raids on the French U-boat bases forced the Germans to expend resources on bombproof shelters, and capital ships were frequently attacked at Brest.

1941 March 10 The first operational sorties carried out by the four-engine Handley Page Halifax were flown against targets at Le Havre, France this night when six aircraft of No. 35 Squadron, RAF, flew out from Leeming, England, accompanied by eight Blenheims. The aircraft had been accepted at Leeming in November 1940, but the squadron moved to Linton-on-Ouse, Yorkshire a month later. No aircraft were lost to enemy action, but one of the Halifaxes was incorrectly identified and shot down by an RAF fighter on the way back. Two nights later three Halifaxes of No. 35 Squadron were among 85 other aircraft when they became the first four-engine RAF bombers to hit targets in Germany, striking shipyards at Hamburg.

1941 March 17 Reacting to growing awareness of the development of gas turbine engines in Britain, the chief of the U.S. Navy Bureau of Aeronautics authorized a small committee to examine the potential of such powerplants to military aircraft. The committee examined reaction propulsion in general to study the potential of jet propulsion for primary power as well as supplementary, assisted takeoff propulsion. The committee conducted its work under the direction of NACA.

1941 March 26 The USAAC set up its Technical Training Command to direct and administer the new projects and air weapons programs and to provide technical training and schooling for the tens of thousands of technicians and service crews needed for the dramatic expansion of the air corps. This was a much welcomed additional link in the chain of command for noncombat activities and would help control the support facilities and spares infrastructure. Also in March, the Materiel Division was split, leaving the old organization to handle procurement with a new Maintenance Command handling supply and maintenance.

1941 March 27 Under the title of ABC-1, the first of two U.S. reports was issued on an Anglo-American alliance should the United States be drawn into the European war. It stated that should the United States become embroiled in the war, "the High Command of the United States and the United Kingdom will collaborate continuously in the formulation and execution of strategic policies and plans." The second report, ABC-2, was issued March 29. A British delegation had visited Washington, D.C. in late 1940 to probe the possibility of such cooperation. This followed upon an American visit to London on August 6, 1940, by three military observers.

1941 March 31 Two Vickers Wellington bombers, one each from Nos. 9 and 149 squadrons, RAF, dropped the first 4,000-lb. bombs on Emden during a raid on the German city this night involving six Wellingtons; five others went to Rotterdam and a further 28 attacked Bremen. Each bomb carried a parachute for retarded descent, a concept known as "land-mine" when dropped by the Germans and "cookie" or "blockbuster" when dropped by the RAF. The 4,000-lb. bomb required modifications to the bomb bay of the Wellington and was the biggest bomb in service to date.

1941 March The Second Aviation Objective for the USAAC was approved by the U.S. War Department, calling for further increases in U.S. military air power in anticipation of involvements in Europe. Under the new plan, the USAAC would have 84 combat groups by June 30, 1942, equipped with 7,800 operational combat aircraft and 400,000 officers and men, almost double the combat resources of the First Aviation Objective announced in June 1940. Within three months, Congress had authorized the purchase of 50,000 aircraft for the army and the navy.

1941 April 2 After more than 40 towed gliding flights, the Heinkel He 280 V1 made its first flight from Marienehe powered by two 1,102-lb. thrust HeS 8 engines and with Fritz Schäfer at the controls. Following a demonstration for senior Luftwaffe and RLM officials on April 5, the aircraft was given strong support, and development of more powerful engines was approved. The engine's inventor, Max Meuller, left Heinkel at the end of the year, and his engines were abandoned. The aircraft was re-engined with Junkers Jumo 109 engines and soon ran into competition from the Me 262.

1941 April 6 To secure Greece and the Balkans, German forces attacked the Serbian border in Operation Marita. Yugoslav airfields and fortifications were hit by Luftwaffe attacks, and 32 German aircraft were shot down. In several engagements, Yugoslav Bf 109s fought Luftwaffe Bf 109s. Beyond this first day, little air opposition faced the Germans, but with an assault on Greece beginning April 14, the Luftwaffe faced defending Greek and RAF aircraft until the 30 RAF planes withdrew to Malta April 22 and Greece capitulated a day later. Yugoslavia had capitulated on April 17.

1941 April 6 Tasked with the job of destroying threats to convoys and merchant shipping, RAF Coastal Command sent a Bristol Beaufort of No. 22 Squadron to attack the German battleship *Gneisenau* in harbor at Brest, France. Piloting the only one of four Beauforts sent to find the battleship, Flying Officer Kenneth Campbell released his torpedo during a low-level attack only 30 ft. above the water, severely damaging the ship. Campbell's aircraft was shot by flak, and the pilot was posthumously awarded

the Victoria Cross. Kept in harbor for repairs from this attack and a bombing raid on the night of April 9/10, the *Gneisenau* was finally recalled to Germany and took part in the daring channel dash of February 12, 1942.

1941 April 10 The first four-engined land-based aircraft built in Japan, also the first Japanese aircraft to have a retractable tricycle undercarriage, made its first flight. Developed and built out of the Douglas DC-4E prototype clandestinely procured via Mitsui Trading Company for Greater Japan Air Lines, the Nakajima G5N Shinzan (Mountain Recess) was powered by four NK7A Mamoru 11 14-cylinder radial engines. The Japanese believed the DC-4E represented all they needed to know about large aircraft but had never developed the experience to design indigenously. However, the Japanese had chosen a flawed design, and changes made by Nakajima only exacerbated the defects.

1941 April 11 The USAAC issued a specification to industry for what would emerge as the world's first hemispheric strategic bomber, that is, an aircraft capable of hitting an enemy's vital resources on the other side of the world to the continental United States. The aircraft was expected to carry a 10,000-lb. bomb load 5,000 mi. and to have a maximum bomb load of 72,000 lb., a top speed of 240–300 MPH. The primary mission was the bombing of European targets from bases in the United States. Of four designs submitted, the USAAF selected the Consolidated Model 37 and awarded a contract on November 15, 1941, for two XB-36 (model 37) prototypes. The selected design had a slightly swept wing of 230-ft. span, six pusher engines along the trailing edge, a circular-section fuselage, twin fins and rudders and a gross weight of 278,000 lb.

1941 April 15 Pres. Roosevelt sanctioned the formation of the American Volunteer Group (AVG), under Gen. Claire Lee Chenault, a force of U.S. airmen who volunteered to fight for Gen. Chiang Kai-shek's forces in China against the Japanese. The first group of 110 pilots and 150 mechanics sailed from San Francisco July 7, 1941, under the guise of actors, bankers, clerks and entertainers bound for Toungoo airstrip 150 mi. north of Rangoon, Burma. They had 100 P-40 Tomahawks with which to train, the first combat taking place on December 20, 10 days after a reconnaissance of Japanese-occupied Thailand.

1941 April 18 Powered by a single Junker Jumo 210G 12-cylinder, liquid-cooled engine in the forward section of the fuselage in lieu of the turbojets for which it had been designed, the Me 262 was taken into the air for the first time by Fritz Wendel. Problems with development of the BMW 003 turbojet designs led Messerschmitt to examine the alternative Junkers Jumo 004. Airframe testing was necessary in advance of engine installation, and a plan to use two rocket motors instead of turbojets was examined and rejected on grounds of safety. The first 1,015-lb. thrust BMW 003 turbojets arrived at Messerschmitt during November 1941 and were subjected to static tests prior to a first flight attempt.

1941 April Tests were carried out on a hydraulic wing-folding mechanism fitted to the last Grumman F4F-3, designated XF4F-4. The device had been conceived by Roy Grumman as a means of increasing the number of aircraft that could be parked on a carrier deck by 150%. The "sto-wing" reduced span from 38 ft. to 14 ft. 4 in. with outboard wing panels rotating almost vertically as they swung aft to rest alongside the rear fuselage. The production version, designated F4F-4, had manually folding wings, and service deliveries began May 1941. Previously, on February 9, 1937, the British Blackburn Skua had demonstrated a folding wing mechanism in which the wing leading edge was folded upward as it pivoted back.

1941 May 3   The U.S. Naval Aircraft Factory initiated Project Roger to install airborne radar equipment in U.S. Navy aircraft. This project gave a much-needed boost to the development of U.S. Navy radar equipment, and research was conducted in close cooperation with the Massachusetts Institute of Technology and with the Naval Research Laboratory. In a separate part of the program, the navy asked the Radio Corporation of America (RCA) to design and develop a radio altimeter, a device that would quickly become an important piece of blind-flying equipment.

1941 May 4   Capt. D. C. T. Bennett made the first proving flight in the North Atlantic return ferry service when he took off in a Consolidated Liberator AM258 from St. Hubert airport, Montreal, Canada to fly to Squires Gate, Blackpool, England. The following day the first westbound service was flown by Capt. A. B. H. Youell. Later, the terminals were changed to Dorval, Montreal, and Prestwick, Scotland. Operational flights began July 1 when Lt. Caleb V. Haynes took off from Bolling Field, Washington, D.C. for Prestwick via Montreal and Gander, Newfoundland. On June 26, 1941 the USAAC made a permanent arrangement with Pan American to fly ferry and supply routes to North Africa.

1941 May 6   The XP-47B, the first of 15,683 Republic Thunderbolts, was piloted by L. L. Brabham. The XP-47 of 1939 and XP-47A of 1940 had been an attempt at a lightweight fighter with a 1,150-HP liquid-cooled Allison V-1710-39 engine. It was under-armed, and a revised design called the XP-47B was presented June 12, 1940, for a barrel-shaped heavyweight powered by a 2,000-HP Pratt & Whitney R-2800 18-cylinder twin-row radial. With a length of 35 ft. and a wingspan of 40 ft. 9 in., the P-47B had a gross weight of 13,360 lb. It was armed with eight 0.50-in. machine guns, had a top speed of 429 MPH at 27,800 ft., a climb rate of 6.7 min. to 15,000 ft. and a range of 550 mi. The Fifty-sixth Fighter Group accepted its first P-47s in November 1942.

1941 May 10   The third of three major Luftwaffe night raids on London started 2,154 separately reported fires, killed 1,436 people, seriously injured 1,792, left 35% of all streets in the Greater London area impassable and all but one main-line train station inoperable for several weeks. Some fires, even some streets, were left to burn themselves out, and one raged for 11 days. In each of the two earlier attacks on April 16, and 19, more than 1,000 people had been killed, and in total more than 148,000 homes had been destroyed. On all three nights, the Luftwaffe flew 1,904 sorties and dropped 2,627 tons of high explosives and 10,845 incendiary cans. This was the worst night for London in a continuing series of air raids on Britain that would peter out toward the end of May.

1941 May 10   Shortly after 5:45 P.M., Adolf Hitler's deputy Rudolf Hess took off from Augsburg, Germany in a Messerschmitt Bf 110D with additional fuel tanks bound for Scotland on a one-way mission, reputedly to sue for peace with pro-Nazi elements in Britain. He descended by parachute to Floors Farm near Busby, and his Bf 110D crashed 11 mi. northwest of Dungavel House, home of the Duke of Hamilton, near Bonnyton Moor not far from Glasgow. He claimed he wanted to discuss terms with the duke, whom he saw alone while in custody on May 11. Hess was detained for the remainder of his life, spending his last 40 years at Spandau Prison, Berlin, where he died on August 17, 1987, and was buried in a family plot on August 26.

1941 May 24   The first of two torpedo-bomber attacks on the German battleship *Bismarck* in the North Atlantic began with the launch at 10:00 P.M. of six Fairey Fulmars and nine Swordfish from the carrier HMS *Victorious*. Their inexperienced crews almost attacked HMS *Norfolk* 23 mi. astern of the *Bismarck*, and under intense fire and bad weather hit the *Bismarck* with only one torpedo. For 31 hr., the *Bismarck* was lost, but a Catalina piloted by Ens. Leonard Smith, U.S. Navy, sighted her again at 10:30 A.M. May 26. A torpedo attack from HMS *Ark Royal* that afternoon mistakenly identified HMS *Hood* for the *Bismarck*, but the cruiser expertly avoided the 11 torpedoes launched at her. *Bismarck* was finally struck by three torpedoes launched by the bombers from 8:47 P.M. that night. British warships finished her off next day.

1941 May 20   The occupation of Crete began when 493 Luftwaffe Junkers Ju 52/3m transports air-lifted 10,000 paratroopers and supplies to the airfield at Maleme. He 111H bombers pounded the opposition, leaving 80 towed DFS 230 gliders to set down 750 troops and consolidate the position. Attacked by the British, troop transports used the coastal strip as a landing area, but losses to artillery fire mounted fearfully, 150 transport planes and 5,600 men being lost. Facing 50,000 British troops, Operation Merkur (Mercury) was the biggest, and the last, German airborne assault of World War II. By June 1, it had secured its objective, giving the Luftwaffe the airfields of Iraklion and Kastelli.

1941 May 24   The first of two torpedo-bomber attacks on the German battleship *Bismarck* in the North Atlantic began with the launch at 10:00 P.M. of six Fairey Fulmars and nine Swordfish from the carrier HMS *Victorious*. Their inexperienced crews almost attacked HMS *Norfolk* 23 mi. astern of the *Bismarck*, and under intense fire and bad weather hit the *Bismarck* with only one torpedo. For 31 hr., the *Bismarck* was lost, but a Catalina piloted by Ens. Leonard Smith, U.S. Navy, sighted her again at 10:30 A.M. May 26. A torpedo attack from HMS *Ark Royal* that afternoon mistakenly identified HMS *Hood* for the *Bismarck*, but the cruiser expertly avoided the 11 torpedoes launched at her. *Bismarck* was finally struck by three torpedoes launched by the bombers from 8:47 P.M. that night. British warships finished her off next day.

1941 May 26   Developed at the request of the Air Headquarters (Koku Hombu) for the Imperial Japanese Army, the Kayaba Ka-

Affectionately known as the ''Stringbag,'' the Fairey Swordfish would play a vital antishipping role during World War II.

l two-seat observation autogyro made its first flight at Tamagawa powered by a 240-HP Argus As 10c 8-cylinder inverted-V, air-cooled engine. With a takeoff run of only 98 ft., it could be made to hover in still air and turn a full circle, show a top speed of 102.5 MPH and climb to 3,280 ft. in 3 min. 20 sec. Carrying two 132-lb. torpedos, the Ka-1 became the first armed autogyro to enter operational service. Kayaba Industrial Co. built around 240 Ka-1s and a single Ka-2 for antisubmarine duties around coastal waters.

1941 June 2 The first U.S. Navy escort carrier, the AVG-1 *Long Island* was commissioned at Newport News, Va., having been converted from the 9,000-ton, 492-ft. long *Mormacmail*. Conceived and first proposed December 13, 1940, by Adm. William F. (Bull) Halsey, U.S. Navy, as a stopgap, the escort carrier was a converted cargo ship capable of carrying a small number of aircraft for defense of the convoys. First estimates were that the *Mormacmail* could be converted within 18 mon., but Pres. Roosevelt cut that to three months. The United States built 127 escort carriers and the British built five.

1941 June 14 The Martin 187 Baltimore made its first flight, and the prototype (serial no. AG685) arrived in Britain during October, the first of 1,575 that would be delivered exclusively to the RAF as a light bomber. It had been ordered as a development of the Martin 167W Maryland, rejected by the USAAC as a three-seat reconnaissance bomber in 1939 and ordered by the French but diverted to Britain when France fell to the Nazis. The Baltimore had a wingspan of 61 ft. 4 in., a length of 48 ft. 6 in. and a height of 17 ft. 9 in. It had the capacity of carrying a 2,000-lb. bomb load and a top speed of 302 MPH. It had a crew of four and carried four 0.303-in. guns in the wings, two or four in a dorsal turret and two in a ventral position. The aircraft was used exclusively in the Mediterranean theater.

1941 June 17 Prewar aviatrix Jacqueline Cochran became the first woman to ferry a bomber across the Atlantic. Despite opposition from male pilots who believed women were not strong enough to handle the controls of a heavy bomber for long hours on the ocean crossing, Cochran appealed to her friend, the British minister of supply, Lord Beaverbrook, who cleared her for a series of 60 test takeoffs and landings in Montreal, Canada, after which she was licensed for the ferry flights. The male ferry pilots threatened to strike, citing the apparent downgrading of their task by allowing a woman to do the same job! The compromise was that she had to relinquish the controls to her copilot, Capt. Grafton Carlisle, for takeoff and landing.

1941 June 19 Just three days before Hitler's attack on the USSR, with most of the German bombers now ready for the eastern offensive, the tally of damage to Britain during the year-long blitz brought somber reading. Almost 45,000 civilians had been killed, 86,000 seriously injured and 150,000 slightly injured. Two million homes had been destroyed or damaged (1.3 million in London alone)—15% of all homes in the British Isles. About 7% of all British homes had been damaged beyond repair. Aircraft production had never been seriously hampered, output increasing from 2,831 military aircraft in the first three months of 1940 to 4,515 during the same period in 1941; only 0.5% of oil reserves had been depleted.

1941 June 22 At precisely 4:15 A.M. on the morning after the longest day of the year, the German armed forces attacked the Soviet Union in the opening blows of Operation Barbarossa, the biggest land and air assault in history. A German communist defector had warned Stalin the previous day of imminent attack but

was shot for being alarmist. On the Eastern Front, the Luftwaffe had 1,945 combat aircraft and 930 transport, reconnaissance and liaison aircraft, to which could be added 980 aircraft operated by Romanian, Hungarian, Croatian, Finnish and Italian units for a grand total of 3,855, of which 2,770 were front-line combat aircraft. Elsewhere, the Luftwaffe had 780 aircraft with Luftflotten 3 and 5 in western Europe and Norway, 370 with Fliegerkorps X and Fliegerführer Afrika in the Mediterranean and North Africa, and 190 held for the air defense of Germany. For Operation Barbarossa, the Germans deployed 3.2 million soldiers in 153 divisions along a 1,000-mi. front from the Baltic to the Black Sea with the following air fleets: Luftflotte 1 ([Generaloberst] Col. Gen. Alfred Keller) with I Fliegerkorps and eight Finnish squadrons supporting Army Group North under (Generaloberst) Col. Gen. Wilhelm Ritter von Leeb; Luftflotte 2 ([Feldmarschall] Field Marshal Albert Kesselring) with I and II Flakkorps and II and VII Fliegerkorps supporting Army Group Center under (Feldmarschall) Field Marshal Fedor von Bock; Luftflotte 4 ([Generaloberst] Col. Gen. Alexander Lörh) with IV and V Fliegerkorps and Romanian, Italian and Hungarian units supporting Army Group South. Soviet air forces in the west numbered more than 7,500 combat aircraft, with 4,000 aircraft east of the Urals, but Luftwaffe intelligence estimated them at 5,500, poorly equipped and badly trained. In fact, the Red Air Force had begun a re-equipment program and had 2,030 Yak-1, MiG-3 and LaGG-3 fighters and 709 Pe-2 light bombers and Il-2 close support aircraft. Nevertheless, the bulk of its fighter force still comprised biplanes like the I-15 and obsolescent monoplanes such as the I-16. (General Leutnant) Lt. Gen. P. F. Zhigarev commanded the Voenno-Vozduzhoye Sily (V-VS), or Soviet air forces, and reported direct to (Marshal Sovetskogo Soyuja) Marshal Timoshenko and Stalin. In the opening hours of the attack, the Germans caught the Russians by surprise. By noon the Soviet air forces had lost more than 800 aircraft (some sources say 1,000), and at the end of the first day had lost 322 aircraft in air-to-air combat and 1,489 on the ground at 66 airfields for a grand total loss of 1,811, almost 25% of their total force west of the Urals. By the end of the second day, a total 3,000 Soviet aircraft had been destroyed, and 72 hr. after the initial attack, the Red Air Force had been all but eliminated in the air. By June 29, the Red Air Force had lost a total of 4,017 aircraft against the loss of 150 Luftwaffe aircraft, clearing the way for sweeping gains on the ground.

1941 June 30 The first Jagdgeschwader to achieve 1,000 confirmed air combat victories exceeded this figure on a day when JG 51 shot down 96 Soviet aircraft and Germany's premier air ace, Oberst Werner Mölders, increased his score by a phenomenal 11 "kills." Born in Gelsenkirchen on March 18, 1913, Mölders became what many regard as Germany's greatest fighter pilot ever, named on July 27, 1940, to succeed Theodore Osterkamp as Geschwaderkommandeur. With his victory score at 68, Mölders took JG 51 to the Eastern Front, and within days of the invasion of the USSR had exceeded the 80 victories of Manfred von Richthofen, who until then held the greatest number of air victories attributed to a German pilot.

1941 June 30 The U.S. Navy had on hand a total 3,437 aircraft, including 1,774 combat types, 183 for transport and utility, 1,444 for training and 31 for miscellaneous duties. The navy had a total of 15,175 aviation personnel on active duty, of which 4,446 were officers including 3,483 pilots and 11,269 enlisted men including 629 pilots.

The U.S. Navy ordered two prototype F6F Hellcat shipboard fighters from Grumman under the designation XF6F-1 and -2. Developed from the F4F Wildcat, the Grumman's first monoplane fighter, the Hellcat would become one of the most important Navy fighters from early 1943. It evolved from lessons learned during the first 18 mon. of war in Europe and from early operational tours with the Navy's first generation monoplane fighters. The XF6F-1 was powered by a 2,000-HP Wright R-2800-10W engine and the XF6F-2 had the supercharged R-2800-21. Subsequent design changes were made, and these two aircraft were redesignated XF6F-3 and -4.

1941 June   The first Focke-Wulf Fw 190A-1 production fighters began to arrive with the Luftwaffe. A special unit of selected personnel from II/JG 26 had been established at Rechlin-Roggenthin with six Fw 190A-0 in March. In July the first A-1s arrived with 6./JG 26, which began to convert from their Bf 109E-7s, II Gruppe being fully equipped by September. Production increased from 224 by the end of 1941 to 1,878 in 1942, representing 40% of all 1942 single-engine fighter production. The Fw 190A-3 had a span of 34 ft. 5 in., a length of 28 ft. 10 in., a loaded weight of 8,770 lb., a maximum speed of 382 MPH at 19,685 ft. (418 MPH at 21,000 ft. with override boost for 60 sec.) and a climb time of 12 min. to 26,250 ft. and a ceiling of 34,775 ft.

1941 July 2   The first air combat victories claimed by American fighter pilots serving with the British Eagle squadrons were achieved when 12 single-seat Hurricanes of No. 71 Squadron, RAF, and 12 twin-engine Blenheim light bombers on a "Circus" raid across France in the vicinity of Lille were jumped by Luftwaffe Bf 109s with the loss of one Hurricane and two Blenheims. The objective had been the Lille power stations, and the Hurricanes were there to defend the bombers as well as add to the attack.

1941 July 2   Lt. Col. Louis E. Woods, U.S. Marine Corps, commisioned the first U.S. Marine Corps Wing, the first such structure to be set up within the U.S. Marines. Marine Aircraft Wing One was formed at Quantico, Va. and comprised the elements of Marine Air Group One with the addition of a headquarters squadron. The success of the formation as a flexible command structure resulted in four more Marine Aircraft Wings during World War II.

1941 July 8   The first operational raid conducted by the RAF using the newly acquired Boeing Fortress I, the British designation for a batch of B-17Cs purchased from the United States, took place during the day when three aircraft of this type from No. 90 Squadron attacked Wilhelmshaven. The mission was flown from Polebrook near Peterborough, England. The aircraft had

Pioneering airborne radar, the Bristol Blenheim achieved its first success with this equipment on the night of July 2/3, 1941.

joined this squadron in May. In the months ahead, the RAF would fly the Fortress I at 30,000 ft. on individual sorties, but due to poor operating techniques and bad equipment, the aircraft was not used to its best, 26 out of 51 sorties being aborted. The Fortress Is were moved to Coastal Command in October 1942 and used for maritime reconnaissance.

1941 July 9   Four months after having been assigned to maritime threats, RAF Bomber Command was redirected back toward strategic targets in a memorandum from the Air Ministry that required it to turn its attention to attacking and dislocating "the German transportation system and to destroying the morale of the civil population as a whole and of the industrial workers in particular." However, the difficulties and teething troubles with introducing the new four-engine bombers (Lancasters, Stirlings and B-17s) would hamper operations, and the numbers of operational aircraft never seemed to reach projected levels; meanwhile, the ageing Hampdens, Whitleys and Wellingtons soldiered on doing night raids.

1941 July 10   The prototype Blohm und Voss Bv 222 six-engined flying boat began a series of long-distance flights to qualify the aircraft for a productive use of its prodigious lift capacity. In seven flights between Hamburg, Germany, and Kirkenes, Norway, the aircraft lifted 143,300 lb. of cargo and 221 casualties back to Hamburg. Between October 16 and November 6, the Bv 222 transported 66,140 lb. of cargo and evacuated 515 casualties between Athens and Derna, Libya. During these flights, a maximum range of 4,350 mi. was established, and the aircraft achieved a maximum speed of 239 MPH at 7,765 ft.

1941 July 20   Army Regulation 95-5 was issued creating the United States Army Air Forces (USAAF), retaining the air corps and the GHQ Air Force until they were dissolved on March 9, 1942. Earlier, the War Department had directed the establishment of our air forces: Northeast, Northwest, Southeast and Southwest, later renamed First, Second, Third and Fourth Air Forces, respectively. This was predicated by a decision by Gen. George C. Marshall on February 28, 1941, that the air defense of the United States should be the responsibility of the air forces and, on April 12, the War Department directed that each air force should have a bomber command and an interceptor command.

1941 July 31   Having been ordered for the RAF by the British Purchasing Commission, the Lockheed Ventura made its first flight, powered by two 2,000-HP Pratt & Whitney GR-2800 S1A4-G radial engines. Lockheed had already developed the Hudson from its Super Electra, and the Ventura was a development from the unsuccessful Model 18 Lodestar, which was an attempt to improve the commercially uncompetitive Model 14 Super Electra. The Ventura had a wingspan of 65 ft. 6 in., a length of 51 ft. 2 in., a height of 11 ft. 1 in. and a loaded weight of 26,000 lb. The RAF received 394 Venturas beginning mid-1942, and 380 operated with Commonwealth Air Forces.

1941 August 1   The U.S. Navy began airborne tests at Boston airport of a microwave radar developed by the Naval Radiation Laboratory. The aircraft used was the XJO-3 (Navy designation for the Lockheed Model 12 Electra Junior fitted with tricycle landing gear it purchased in October 1938 for deck-landing trials with twin-engine aircraft). Tests conducted through October 16 proved detection of surface vessels up to 40 mi. away and radar-guided vectored approaches on enemy aircraft up to 3.5 mi. distant. On August 7 a plan was issued for installing search radar in naval patrol aircraft with British air interception radar tested in a Douglas SBD Dauntless.

1941 August 3   A Hawker Sea Hurricane Mk.1 piloted by Lt. R. W. H. Everett, Royal Navy, was launched from a catapult mounted on the deck of the British merchant ship HMS *Maplin* to successfully attack and destroy a Focke-Wulf Fw 200C Condor, the first time such an operation had resulted in the destruction of an enemy aircraft. The concept had been developed from an October 1940 directive from the Directorate of Research and Development (Air) for one catapult-launched defensive fighter to be carried by suitable merchant ships for convoy defense, the Hurricane thus launched having to be ditched after the offensive flight. The first CAM (catapult aircraft merchantman) equipped ship, the SS *Michael E,* sailed May 27, 1941, but was torpedoed before the Hurricane could be launched.

1941 August 7   A flight of Red Air Force Ilyushin Il-4 bombers (designated TB-3) made the first Soviet bombing attack on Berlin during the night. The aircraft operated from two islands in the Baltic off the coast of Estonia. Four nights later another attack took place when 11 Petlyakov Pe-8 four-engine bombers flew from Pushkino airfield, the nearest to Berlin that could be used, with a round-trip distance of 1,680 mi. Fourteen Pe-8s had flown to Pushkino for the raid, one nearly getting shot up by Soviet antiaircraft fire (a sad reflection on their view that anything flying must be German!). One crashed on takeoff for the raid, 11 got through, one was shot down by a Soviet fighter, and 6 got back to Pushkino. The rest made forced landings or got lost.

1941 August 12   In the deepest penetration of German air space from the west to date, 54 RAF Blenheim bombers raided Knapsack and Quadrath power stations near Cologne in a daylight operation devised to draw Luftwaffe fighters back away from the Eastern Front. Each Blenheim carried two 500-lb. bombs, and 10 were shot down. Two forces of six Hampdens each also carried out escort raids on St.-Omer and Grosnay in France, and another six Blenheims hit the shipyards at Le Trait, while four Fortresses carried out (their usual) high-level raids on Cologne. In all, 175 fighter sorties were flown with 10 German aircraft claimed for the loss of six Spitfires. Two Blenheims operating as navigation leads were also lost for a total loss of 18 planes.

1941 August 13   Test pilot Heini Dittmar made the first powered flight of the rocket-propelled Messerschmitt Me 163A V1, carrying out a simple takeoff at Pennemünde-West for a brief airfield circuit and landing with limited propellant supply. A wooden mock-up of the aircraft had been delivered to the Walter factory for fit-checks and tests with the 1,653-lb. thrust R II-203b motor, live firings from which began July 18. Rudolf Opitz was drafted into the test program at the instigation of Gen. Ernst Udet, director general of Luftwaffe equipment, who would order eight A-series test aircraft and, on December 1, 1941, series production of the operational B-series configuration.

1941 August 18   Compiled and submitted this day by D. M. Butt, a civil servant in the War Cabinet secretariat, a detailed analysis of RAF Bomber Command operations showed very poor accuracy and bad results of the RAF's bombing operations. From 4,065 individual photographs, it revealed that on average only 25% of crews bombed within 5 mi. of their targets and that on moonless nights only 5% hit within 5 mi. of their targets. In the pollution-shrouded Ruhr region, results were considerably worse. These pictures were submitted only by those crews who claimed to have reached the target, which was only two-thirds of all RAF bomber crews; 33% admitted they never found their objective.

1941 August 25   In the first known instance of parasitic dive-bombers being taken into combat (and for the Soviets, the last),

the Soviet air force operated a Tupoleve TB-3 with two I-16 fighters, each fitted with racks for two 550-lb. bombs. The I-16s (designated SPB for this mission) were carried on struts beneath each wing of the TB-3. The combination carried out a successful raid from an airfield near the Black Sea against the Chernavoda Bridge, Romania, across the Danube River and all three planes returned safely to base.

1941 August 27   RAF Coastal Command captured the German submarine U-570 on her maiden voyage when, at 62° 15 min. N by 18° 35 min. W, her captain, Korvettenkapitän Hans Rahmlow, surfaced and surrendered to an attacking Hudson from No. 269 Squadron piloted by Sqdn. Ldr. J. H. Thompson. Damaged by four depth charges and with water in the batteries producing deadly chlorine gas, U-570 was the first submarine to surrender to an aircraft. Her crew, mostly on their first voyage, were seasick, and the captain was unable to resist their pressures to surrender; he used his dress shirt as a white flag. U-570 was eventually towed to Iceland and commissioned in the Royal Navy as HMS *Graph* until wrecked in 1944.

1941 August   Developed at the request of Oberst Josef Kammhuber, who was responsible for the air defense of Germany, Telefunken A.G. began tests in a Bf 110G of a night radar capable of locking onto enemy aircraft at a distance of 2.5 mi. Known as the FuG 202 Lichtenstein C-0, it led to the simplified mass production version called FuG 212 Lichtenstein C-1; it was sometimes complemented with the addition of the FuG 221a Rosendaal-Halbe, which could lock on to the tail warning radar carried by RAF bombers. With a variety of radar arrays being developed, the Bf 110 was believed by the Luftwaffe to be an ideal night fighter, but its shortcomings would soon become all too apparent.

1941 September 5   The USAAF requested Bell Aircraft Corp. to produce the airframe for a jet-propelled fighter under the designation XP-59A; the XP-59 was in fact a twin-boom pusher fighter already in development at Bell, and the "A" suffix to an existing project number was a ploy to keep the jet secret. Bell submitted plans for its Model 27 by the end of the month, and construction of this mid-wing jet, designed to use the British W.1 engine, got under way during spring 1942. Gen. Henry H. Arnold had been in England during March 1941 when he heard of the imminent flight of the Gloster E.28/39 and made arrangements to have the W.1 engine flown to the United States for General Electric to copy.

1941 September 5   The first of 512 Boeing B-17E (Boeing Model 299-O) bombers made its first flight, displaying the completely redesigned and enlarged tail assembly with span increased from 33 ft. 9 in. to 43 ft. and with a twin-gun dorsal turret just behind the pilot's cabin, a power turret below the fuselage behind the wing and twin-gun manually operated tail armament. The B-17E had a gross weight of 53,000 lb. and had a maximum speed of 317 MPH at 25,000 ft. and a maximum 4,000-lb. bomb load. First deliveries were to the Seventh Bombardment Group, which joined the Nineteenth in Hawaii during December 1941. The first B-17E to Britain arrived July 1, 1942.

1941 September 10   The Soviet rocket-propelled BI-1, designed by a team led by A. Ya Berezniak and A. M. Isayev, supervised by V. F. Bolkhovitinov, made its first unpowered flight when it was towed into the air behind a Petlyakov Pe-2. The first successful ground test of a Soviet liquid-powered rocket motor designed for an aircraft took place in summer 1939 when L. S. Dushkin demonstrated the 310-lb. thrust of his motor in the tail of a glider that, after being towed into the air and cut loose,

With increased wingspan and heavier defensive armament, the first Boeing B-17E took to the air on September 5, 1941.

achieved a speed of 124 MPH. After this, the Soviet Defense Committee commissioned three design teams to build rocket-powered interceptors: Polikarpov and its Malyutka, M. K. Tikhonravov and the Type 302 and the BI-1.

1941 September 11 A detailed plan showing how a military offensive could be mounted simultaneously in Europe and against Japan was presented to Pres. Franklin D. Roosevelt, who had requested the study on July 9, 1941. Formulated by four highly talented officers (Lt. Cols. Harold L. George and Kenneth N. Walker and Majs. Laurence S. Kuter and Haywood S. Hansell), it predicted the defeat of Germany on the destruction of 154 key targets in power, energy and production industries, in which the USAAF would play a major role. To achieve this destruction, the United States would need 6,834 heavy bombers in 98 groups, of which 24 would be equipped with the B-29. In all, said the plan, the USAAF would need 239 combat groups, 108 separate squadrons, 63,467 aircraft and almost 2.2 million men for wars against Germany and Japan.

1941 September 23 For the first time in World War II, an aircraft sank a capital ship when a Luftwaffe Ju 87 Stuka virtually split in two the Soviet battleship *Marat* at Kronstadt. Units from I and III/St.G.2 attacked the Soviet Baltic Fleet in efforts to disable the *Marat* and the *October Revolution.* A previous attempt with 30 Stuka dive-bombers failed as bombs bounced off the Krupp-steel decking of the *Marat,* but diving almost vertically below the level-out altitude of 3,000 ft., Ju 87 Stuka pilot Hans Ulrich Rudel released his specially armored bomb that tore into the magazine and blew up the battleship.

1941 September 30 The battle to capture Moscow began with forward movement of two German army groups: Ninth Army and Panzer Group 3 in the north was to advance forward and meet Fourth Army and Panzer Group 2 at Vyazma about 80 mi. to the Soviet rear and join up with Second Army and components of Panzer Army 2 in the south, joining their pincers at Bryansk for the advance upon Moscow. To help achieve this, Luftflotte 2 absorbed a large part of Luftflotte 1 and Fliegerkorps VIII as well as some units from Luftflotte 4, and Feldmarschall Kesselring was ordered to flank-attack in close support operations. He had

at his disposal 1,320 aircraft, only two-thirds of which were serviceable.

1941 September Jack Northrop met with representatives of the USAAF Material Division to discuss a new strategic bomber based on his flying-wing designs, epitomized by the N-1M, which had been flight-tested for more than a year. Northrop proposed a bomber capable of carrying a 10,000-lb. warload with a 10,000 mi. range at a cruising speed of 300 MPH and a service ceiling of 40,000 ft. Projecting delivery within 24 mon., he received a contract for one prototype XB-35 on November 22, a second aircraft in January 1942 and a further order for 13 YB-35s later that year. To test aerodynamic characteristics, the Air Force ordered four one-third scale N-9Ms.

1941 October 2 Test pilot Heini Dittmar encountered compressibility approaching the speed of sound when he flew the rocket-propelled Me 163A V1 to a speed of 623.85 MPH, 154.63 MPH faster than the existing official world air speed record and the first time an aircraft had exceeded a speed of 1,000 km/hr. (621.37 MPH). Towed into the air by Rudolf Opitz, he cast off at 13,000 ft. and fired the rocket motor to achieve a top speed of Mach 0.84, at which point the nose pitched down violently and the motor stopped from propellant starvation due to negative g force. The Walter R II-203b motor used T-Stoff (80% hydrogen peroxide) and Z-Stoff (sodium/calcium permanganate) propellant with a maximum 116.5 Imp. gal. capacity for 4 min. 30 sec. of powered flight.

1941 October 20 Capt. Ikeda of the Imperial Japanese Army commanded a detachment of Mitsubishi Ki-46-II reconnaissance aircraft on the first of two reconnoiters around areas selected for the planned invasion of the Malaysian Peninsula. The unit had moved to French Indochina from China. The second reconnoiter was carried out two days later, and when hostilities began, the Ki-46-II was deployed to cover reconnaissance duties throughout the theater. With a top speed of 375 MPH and a ceiling of 35,170 ft., the Ki-46-II was able to outrun the inferior Allied fighters, built for European or North American climates and lacking radar from either the air or the ground.

1941 October Developed to tow giant gliders like the Me 321, the five-engined Heinkel He 111Z prototype began flight trials. Essentially two twin-engined He 111H-series bombers with a special wing structure supporting a fifth engine in the middle, the He 111Z (Zwilling) had a wingspan of 116 ft. 1 in., a length of 53 ft. 9 in. and a gap between fuselage center-lines of 42 ft. Empty equipped weight was 47,000 lb. with maximum loaded weight 63,052 lb. Usual towing speed was 137 MPH. Operational use began in early summer 1942 with preparations for the invasion of Malta and continued with emergency supplies to Stalingrad in January 1943.

1941 November 7 A record 392 RAF bombers were sent to raid German targets during the night including 169 dispatched to Berlin and 55 to Mannheim. Seventy-five bombers from No. 5 Group under Air Vice Marshall J. C. Slessor went to Cologne. Thirty-seven aircraft (9.4%) were lost, the majority of which succumbed to icing and the poor weather. This was probably the largest raid the RAF could mount at the time and was an almost desperate—but tragically mismanaged—effort by AVM Richard Peirse to achieve good bombing results.

1941 November 10 The Luftwaffe formally established its fighter-bomber units when 10 (Jabo.)/JG 2 was set up under the command of Hptm. Frank Liesendahl, followed several weeks later by 10 (Jabo.)/JG 26 under Hptm. Karl Plunser with Bf 109E-1/B and E-3/B aircraft. This move helped legitimize the Jabo (fighter-bomber) role, which had first been applied on September 5, 1940, and was followed by an official order from Gen. Hugo Sperrle on March 10, 1942, authorizing the establishment of two fighter bomber squadrons (Jabostaffeln) within JG 2 and JG 26, equipped from August with the more devastating Fw 190.

1941 November 13 Reacting to the Butt Report on RAF bombing operations (August 18) and more immediately to the heavy loss of life on the night of November 7, the Air Ministry informed the commander in chief of the RAF Bomber Command that his strategic offensive against German targets in continental Europe should be reduced in scope pending a complete review of bombing tactics, practice and operational technique as well as leadership and direction. There would not be another major raid on the German capital before January 1943.

1941 November 22 Oberst Werner Mölders died of a broken neck when the Heinkel 111 in which he was flying from Kherson Airport to Lemberg crashed during an attempted landing at Schmiederfeld near Breslau after both engines stopped in bad weather. The first ace ever to score 100 victories (having reached that number on July 15), Mölders had a total victory score of 115, 14 of which were obtained in Spain. He had been appointed Inspekteur de Jagdflieger in September. Commissioned on September 20, 1969, the German guided-missile destroyer D-186 bears his name in commemoration.

1941 November 25 An attempt was made to fly the Me 262 V1 fitted with two BMW 109-003 turbojets with a rated thrust of 1,015 lb. but that actually produced only 992 lb. The aircraft still carried the Junkers Jumo 210G piston engine in the forward fuselage, which had been installed for the first flight on April 18. The attempts were unsuccessful because of repeated turbine failures at takeoff power, and the Me 262 would have to wait for the more powerful Junkers Jumo 004 series engine before it could make its first flight on turbojet power alone on July 18, 1942.

1941 November 30 The first destruction of a German submarine by an aircraft of RAF Coastal Command was achieved when a Whitley Mk.VII of No. 502 Squadron was sent to a location in the Bay of Biscay where intelligence indicated a German submarine was heading for the Mediterranean. In cloudy weather, the ASV (air-to-surface-vessel) radar picked up U-206 at a range of 5 mi., and the aircraft was able to do its job with depth charges it dropped on the target. After 28 mon. of war, it was the first time the RAF had been able to sink one of the most feared and lethal threats to British food and munitions supplies.

1941 December 4 Operation Taifun (Typhoon) launched by the German armies on September 30 as a prelude to taking Moscow ground to a halt a few miles short of its objective. With only around 500 serviceable aircraft, the reinforced Luftflotte 2 had to operate in temperatures below 18° F while now facing superior numbers of Soviet aircraft. In just over four months, the German armies aided by the Luftwaffe had destroyed more than 15,000 Soviet aircraft, 3,200 tanks, 58,000 vehicles, 2,450 artillery pieces, 650 trains and 1,200 locomotives, causing serious damage to 6,300 trains, 1,200 more locomotives and 7,000 rail lines. Although Luftwaffe losses were 2,093 aircraft, only 900 were due to combat, almost 1,200 being due to bad landings and weather; a further 1,361 were damaged.

1941 December 6 As part of its preparations for the attack on Allied shipping, the Japanese Navy moved 27 Mitsubishi G4M1s of the Kanoya Kokutai to Indochina, halting its successful bombing campaign against Chongqing (Chungking) in China in readiness for an attack on the battleships HMS *Repulse* and HMS *Prince of Wales*. The navy retained 93 other aircraft of this type on the island of Formosa, ready for hitting U.S. bases in the Philippines. These aircraft were able to play an important role in assisting ground operations where there was little fighter opposition. In 1942, when they were drawn into attacks on Darwin, Australia, they would suffer from a lack of armor and sealed fuel tanks.

1941 December 7 The Imperial Japanese Navy Air Force attacked U.S. military bases at Hickham Field and Wheeler Field, naval air bases at Ford Island and Kaneohe and ships at anchor in Pearl Harbor, Honolulu without declaration of war in a flagrant violation of international law governing the use of force. The attacking force had at its disposal 23 warships and 376 aircraft, including 108 Mitsubishi A6M2 fighters, 126 Aichi D3A1 dive-bombers and 142 Nakajima B5N2 torpedo bombers from the carriers *Kaga* and *Akagi* in the First Kokusentai (led by Vice Adm. Chuichi Nagumo), *Hiryu* and *Soryu* in the Second-Kokusentai (led by Rear Adm. Tamon Yamaguchi) and *Zuikaku* and *Shokaku* of the Fifth Kokusentai (led by Rear Adm. Yoshimi Hara).

In the Japanese attack on the U.S. Pacific Fleet, the first wave of 183 Japanese aircraft struck at 7:55 A.M., 53 min. after a private manning a radar outpost on Kahuku Point telephoned a report to say he had detected aircraft approaching from the north about 130 mi. distant. In fact, these were 12 B-17s flying in from California, which found themselves caught up in the attack. Largely ignored by the Japanese, only one was destroyed and three damaged. The first attack wave comprised 91 dive-bombers, 49 torpedo bombers and 43 fighters. The second wave at 8:40 A.M. comprised 80 dive-bombers, 54 torpedo bombers and 36 fighters. In all, the 274 attack aircraft dropped 152.7 tons of bombs and torpedoes.

The loss of men and materiel from the Japanese attack on the U.S. Pacific Fleet was devastating. In less than two hours, 2,403 men were killed and 1,178 injured (including civilians, about 4,500 casualties). The U.S. battleships *Arizona, California, Nevada, Oklahoma,* and *West Virginia* were sunk as were the minelayer *Oglala* and the target ship *Utah*. The battleships *Maryland,*

Pennsylvania, and *Tennessee* were badly damaged, and the light cruisers *Helena, Honolulu* and *Raleigh* along with three destroyers, an aircraft carrier and a workshop vessel were lightly damaged. In all, 60% of the entire fleet of U.S. battleships was destroyed. Of 231 aircraft assigned to the Hawaiian Air Force, only 79 were usable, and of 169 naval aircraft, only 82 survived. The U.S. Marine Corps lost 47 out of 48 aircraft. Out of 353 aircraft (sorties), the Japanese lost 9 A6M2, 15 D3A1 and 5 B5N2 aircraft (8.2% of the total) and 55 airmen. U.S. losses would have been greater had the carriers *Saratoga, Lexington,* and *Enterprise* of the Pacific Fleet not been away from Pearl Harbor.

1941 December 8   It was 2:25 A.M. this date across the international date line in the Philippines when Pearl Harbor was attacked by Japan. At the headquarters of the Far East Air Force (FEAF) (named thus on October 28), its commander, Gen. Douglas MacArthur, appointed July 26 by Gen. Marshall, was notified by 3:00 A.M. Total defensive inventory in the Philippines included 162 aircraft, but of these, four P-26s were unusable and 40 of 107 P-40s were still crated. The 17 B-17s at Clark Field north of Manila were ordered airborne but returned at 11:30 A.M. to refuel, 50 min. before 54 Japanese G4M1-3 bombers and 34 A6M2 fighters attacked the base. At 12:40 P.M., 54 G3M1-3 bombers and 50 A6M2s hit the base at Iba 40 mi. from Clark on the west coast of Luzon. The FEAF lost 66 aircraft, including 17 out of 35 B-17s. The Japanese had 112 land-based bombers and 101 fighters on Formosa 520 mi. north of the Philippines.

1941 December 10   Two days after Congress approved a declaration of war against Japan, one day before Germany and Italy declared war on the United States, the first enemy ship sunk by an American aircraft in World War II was sent to the bottom of the Pacific Ocean by a Douglas SBD Dauntless from the carrier USS *Enterprise.* The Dauntless was launched to attack the Japanese submarine I-70, which it sank after a single attack. The *Enterprise* had been at sea 200 mi. west of Pearl Harbor when the Japanese attacked December 7 and was one of three carriers that escaped destruction. The USS *Saratoga* was in San Diego just out of overhaul, and the USS *Lexington* was 425 mi. southwest of Midway.

1941 December 10   Shortly after coming under attack from 52 land-based Japanese torpedo bombers and 34 conventional bombers accompanied by 11 reconnaissance aircraft, the British capital ships HMS *Repulse* and HMS *Prince of Wales* were sunk off Kuantan close to the eastern coast of Malaya at 12:33 and 1:20 P.M. respectively. Of 2,921 officers and men aboard both ships, 2,081 were rescued by fearless action from the escorting destroyers, but 840 died. Only three out of 57 conventional bombs landed on target, but the torpedo bombers gripped the battleships in a crossfire of torpedos impossible to evade.

1941 December 12   The War Department and Gen. H. Arnold called on U.S. airlines to transport men and materiel by working with Ferrying Command, the first agreement being made with Pan American, which extended its Africa service to Teheran, Iran. American Airlines began military operations December 14, and on December 24, TWA agreed to sell five Boeing 307 Stratoliners to the U.S. government.

1941 December 16   USAAC pilot 1st Lt. Boyd D. Wagner, commanding the Seventeenth Pursuit Squadron in the Philippines, became the first American ace of World War II when he shot down his fifth aircraft in three days—he had destroyed four on December 13 during a reconnaissance mission over northern Luzon. Flying P-40E Warhawks, U.S. air units in the Philippines

fought a vicious rearguard action in efforts to stem the pace of Japanese advances, but air power was quickly overwhelmed. Wagner went on to score a total eight victories before he was wounded December 22; he died a year later in an air accident in the United States.

1941 December 20   With sharks' mouths painted on their Tomahawks, the American Volunteer Group known as the Flying Tigers under Gen. Claire Lee Chennault notched up its first victories in an attack on 10 Mitsubishi Ki-21s heading for Kunming from their base in Indochina. Six Ki-21s were shot down, and the rest fled. After Singapore fell on February 15, 1942, the American Volunteer Group moved from Mingalodon, Burma to Magwe on the Chindwin River, and later they battled on against the Japanese from their bases in China. With the United States in the war, the group became the Twenty-third Fighter Group of the China Air Task Force, Tenth U.S. Army Air Force. In seven months as a volunteer force, the Flying Tigers had destroyed 286 aircraft, a further 200 probables, 40 destroyed on the ground and had produced 39 aces; its total losses were 24 aircraft.

1941 December 23   The first C-47-DL, one of 10,196 military transports and derivatives of the Douglas DC-3, was delivered to the USAAF after completion at Long Beach, Calif. Powered by two 1,200-HP Pratt & Whitney R-1830-92 engines, it had a large, two-panel cargo door on the port side of the rear fuselage, reinforced fuselage with appropriate tie-down points for cargo, a 6-in. greater wingspan than the commercial DC-3 and a capacity for up to nine 100-gal. fuselage tanks in addition to the integral 804-gal. capacity tanks (822 gal. on the civilian version). Some derivatives could carry up to 28 airborne or parachute troops or 14 stretchers and 3 attendants.

1941 December 27   The Luftwaffe had 1,332 bombers, 1,472 fighters and 326 dive-bombers in its inventory for the three theaters of war in which it was now engaged: the Western Front, the Mediterranean/North Africa region and the Eastern Front. This represented just 144 more aircraft than it could muster at the commencement of Operation Barbarossa, yet it now had more than twice the area to support and there were major military offensives yet to come. In the six months of fighting on the Eastern Front, the Luftwaffe had mounted 180,000 sorties, but only 730 out of 1,700 combat aircraft in the east were still serviceable, and 85,000 out of 100,000 Luftwaffe vehicles in the USSR were unusable.

1941 December   The state of U.S. aviation had improved favorably for civilian and commercial applications, but U.S. air defenses were still only just beginning to pick up to international standard. Passenger-miles had increased five fold from 267 million in 1935 to 1.369 million in 1941 as a portent of what it would become after the war. U.S. military aircraft production for December totaled 2,464 aircraft, and the country had a grand total of 2,846 first-line aircraft; of these, only 1,157 were considered comparable to front-line aircraft in Europe and Japan. On the day Japan attacked Pearl Harbor (December 7), the USAAF had 23,000 officers, 275,000 enlisted men and 16,000 cadets with a total inventory of 12,000 aircraft of all types.

1941 December   Developed for the Imperial Japanese Army Air Force as the only fighter with long, tapered nose and high aspect-ratio wings, the sleek Kawasaki Ki-61 Hien (Swallow) began flight trials powered by a Japanese-built Daimler Benz DB 601A engine designated Ha-40. Late in 1942, the aircraft entered service use as the Army Type 3 Fighter Model 1A armed with two fuselage-mounted 12.7-mm guns and two wing-mounted 7.7-mm guns. The fighter had a top speed of 368 MPH at 15,945 ft. and a climb time of 5 min. 31 sec. to 16,405 ft. Some 3,078 were built, and although it never did overcome engine troubles, it was the only match for some of the faster U.S. fighters.

1941 During the year, the USAAF had accepted 15,861 aircraft comprising 1 very heavy bomber, 313 heavy bombers, 460 medium bombers, 2,396 light bombers, 3,784 fighters, 203 reconnaissance aircraft, 398 transports, 8,036 trainers and 270 communications aircraft. As of June 30, 1941, the USAAF had 6,777 aircraft on strength, comprising 120 heavy bombers, 611 medium bombers, 292 light bombers, 1,018 fighters, 415 reconnaissance aircraft, 144 transports, 4,124 trainers and 53 communications aircraft.

1942 January 4 Japanese Kawanishi H6K4 flying boats of the Yokohama air unit (Kokutai) under Vice Adm. Eijii Goto's Twenty-fourth Air Flotilla began raids on Simpson Harbor and Vunakanau airfield at Rabaul, New Guinea. A major naval air assault began January 20 when 120 A6M2s, D3A-1s and Nakajima B5N2s from the carriers *Zuikaku, Shokaku, Kaga* and *Akagi* of Adm. Nagumo's First Koku-Kantai struck the airfield and supply depots. In a general thrust south and east to cut air and sea links between the United States and Australia, a main seaborne landing force of 5,300 men took Rabaul early in the morning of January 23.

1942 January 10 The Allied command structure known as ABDA (American, British, Dutch, Australian) was established at various locations under Field Marshal Sir Archibald Wavell to administer the war in Southeast Asia. The air component was under the control of A.C.M. Richard E. C. Peirse, who was moved to this new position from RAF Bomber Command following a disastrous tenure there. In all, about 310 combat aircraft were available, including the Seventh and Forty-third Bombardment Groups with elements of the Nineteenth Bomber Group, USAAF, all under Maj. Gen. L. H. Brereton. P-40E fighters arrived in Australia to form the U.S. Seventeenth Pursuit Group, and the Australians put six squadrons of Hudsons into the fray.

1942 January 11 The first Japanese airborne assault of the Pacific war took place when 324 marine troops of the First Yokubetsu-Rikusentai were dropped on Manado on the northern tip of Sulawesi by L3Y1s, Navy Type 96 transport aircraft, which were actually converted Mitsubishi G3M1 bombers. Next day the airfield was operational with A6M2 fighters of the Twenty-third Air Flotilla. On January 24, further landings took place at Balikpapan, Borneo and Kendara, Sulawesi, and Ambon Island, Ceram, in the Indonesian archipelago.

1942 January 14 Pres. Roosevelt approved a program for the production of 45,000 combat aircraft and transports in 1942 and 100,000 in the following year. These procurement plans were generated by a parallel plan to build up the USAAF to 115 combat groups. By August and September, the Air Staff were calculating that only with production of 131,000 aircraft in 1943 would the United States gain air supremacy over Germany and Japan. The War Production Board moderated these goals and retargeted 1943 production for 107,000 aircraft, of which 85,000 were actually produced.

1942 January 14 The Vought-Sikorsky XR-4 helicopter made its first flight powered by a 165-HP Warner R-500-3 engine. A development of the VS-300 of 1939, it constituted the first operational military helicopter for the U.S. armed services when it was ordered in quantity. In all, 130 R-4s were built and used by

the USAAF, the U.S. Coast Guard and the RAF. The R-4 had a single, 38-ft. diameter rotor layout with a fuselage length of 48 ft. 2 in. and a height of 12 ft. 5 in. The helicopter had a top speed of 75 MPH, a climb time of 45 min. to its service ceiling of 8,000 ft. and a range of 130 mi.

1942 January 28 The U.S. Army Eighth Air Force came into being at Savannah, Ga. under the command of Col. Asa N. Duncan. It was initially a headquarters organization, but it grew rapidly into the primary U.S. strategic air force for the European theater of operations. Maj. Gen. Carl Spaatz decided that the "Eight" would form the nucleus for the build-up in Britain of an air force that would bomb occupied Europe and German territory by day, leaving the RAF to continue night bombing. Initially designated Fifth Air Force on January 2, it was changed January 6 to Eighth Air Force when Fifth, Sixth and Seventh Air Force designations were applied to air units for U.S. possessions and protectorates.

1942 January 31 Northeast Airlines signed an agreement with the U.S. government to begin scheduled operations in the North Atlantic region, beginning February 13 with a flight from Presque Isle, Maine to Gander, Newfoundland, via Moncton, New Brunswick; Goose Bay and Stephenville. On April 5, it was extended up through Argentia, and on April 24 to Narsarsuak. The service extended to Stornoway, in the Outer Hebrides off Scotland, on the night of July 3/4. In this way, the U.S. government subsidized a network of civilian leased/chartered services that would underpin development of routes and services for postwar commercial operation.

1942 January Lt. I. M. Chisov of the Red Air Force had a miraculous escape when, without a parachute, he fell from his badly damaged Ilyushin Il-4 twin-engined medium bomber at a height of 22,000 ft. and survived. Achieving a terminal velocity of about 150 MPH, his fall was broken as his body struck the edge of a snow-covered ravine, which he slid down with decreasing speed until he came to a stop. He suffered a broken pelvis and severe spinal injuries.

1942 January Department F of the German Research Institute for Glider Flying (Deutsches Forschungsinstitut für Segelflug, or DFS) adopted for development a proposal for a composite aircraft project known as Mistel (Mistletoe). In this, a Junkers Ju 88 converted into an unmanned flying bomb would be guided to its target by a Bf 109 mounted on struts above the twin-engined aircraft. When the Ju 88 was aligned with its target, the Bf 109 would separate and return. The entire nose section of the Ju 88 was to be replaced by a 7,715-lb. hollow-charge warhead containing 3,800 lb. of high explosive with a 2,205-lb. steel core capable of penetrating 60 ft. of concrete.

1942 February 12 Under concentrated air cover from occupied France and Holland, the German battleships *Scharnhorst* and *Gneisenau* and the cruiser *Prinz Eugen* escaped from Brest, Brittany through the English Channel to Wilhelmshaven and Brunsbüttel, arriving in the early morning February 13. The three ships moved out of Brest at 11:00 P.M. February 11. With Luftwaffe officers aboard each ship and on average 40 fighters often flying in thick fog at mast height to protect the ships, the flotilla was approached by six Swordfish at 1:34 P.M. the next day just after passing the White Cliffs of Dover, England. All were shot down, and five RAF Westland Whirlwind fighters were driven off at 2:45. In all, 242 British aircraft were sent out to attack the convoy, but only 39 found it, and none did serious damage.

1942 February 14 Another large Japanese airborne invasion with 305 troops dropped by 34 Lockheed WG-14s and 21 Ki-21s from the Japanese Army Air Force secured Palembang, Sumatra within two days. The occupation of Timor island 350 mi. northwest of the Australian continent followed on February 20. Next day, Maj. Gen. Brereton, commander-in-chief, Fifth Air Force, decided to evacuate Java. From February 21 until March 1, B-17s from Australia flew fruitless missions against Japanese forces on the island of Bali. On February 22, the ABDA air command structure was disbanded, thoroughly routed by Japanese progress in the theater.

1942 February 14 In a memorandum from the Air Ministry in London to RAF Bomber Command, A. V. M. Bottomley advised, ''It has been decided that the primary objective of your operations should now be focused on the morale of the enemy civil population and in particular the industrial workers.'' This area-bombing directive followed an argument between the chief of the air staff, A. C. M. Sir Charles Portal, and Prime Minister Winston Churchill about the value of strategic air bombardment. A. C. M. Portal formulated a plan in late summer of 1941 calling for 4,000 bombers to devastate 43 important German cities. Churchill refused to accept claims that this would materially affect the outcome of the war but consented to area bombardment.

1942 February 19 Japanese carrier- and shore-based bombers, including the Mitsubishi G4M1, attacked Port Darwin, Australia for the first time, sinking all 17 Allied ships in the harbor. In the air combats that ensued, 22 British and American aircraft were shot down for the loss of five Japanese aircraft, in a stark confirmation of Japan's superiority in the East Indies. In all, 240 people were killed. In retaliation, U.S. Navy attack aircraft struck at Wake and Marcus Islands; American A-24s, B-17s and P-40s also attacked Japanese landing vessels supporting the assault on Bali, which was successful despite Allied air efforts.

1942 February 20 Lt. Edward Henry O'Hare became the first U.S. Navy air ace when he shot down five Japanese aircraft and damaged a sixth on one mission. A force of 17 Japanese bombers was attempting to strike the carrier USS *Lexington,* and the flattop's Wildcat squadron was launched in defense. Only two of the bombers escaped, 12 being shot down by other pilots. The USS *Lexington* was one of only four carriers available to the U.S. Pacific Fleet, now commanded by Adm. Chester W. Nimitz; others were the USS *Saratoga,* USS *Enterprise* and USS *Yorktown.*

1942 February 20 As advance party for the USAAF in Britain, Brig. Gen. Ira C. Eaker arrived in England in a C-47 accompanied by Lt. Col. Frank A. Armstrong Jr., Maj. Peter Beasley, Capts. Fred Castle and Beirne Lay Jr. and Lts. Harris Hull and William Cowart Jr. All wore civilian clothes and went straight to RAF Bomber Command headquarters near High Wycombe, Buckinghamshire. Planned strength for the Eighth Air Force that Brig. Gen. Eaker would command was 60 combat groups with 17 heavy, 10 medium and six light bomber groups with seven observation, 12 fighter and eight transport groups—a total of 3,500 aircraft by April 1943. The Americans moved to their headquarters at Dawes Hill Lodge, High Wycombe on April 15.

1942 February 22 In one of the most significant moves affecting the strategic air offensive against Germany, A. C. M. Arthur T. (later ''Bomber'') Harris took over from A. M. Richard Peirse as commander-in-chief, RAF Bomber Command, a position he would retain throughout the war. From a total 14,369 tons of bombs dropped on the enemy during 1940 and 34,954 tons dropped in 1941, Bomber Command under Harris would expand to a mighty

force that in 1944 would drop 579,384 tons of bombs, devastating many German towns and cities. When Harris took over, Bomber Command had 378 serviceable aircraft and crews out of 547 aircraft on the inventory, of which only 88 were heavy bombers.

1942 February 25 RAF Hurricanes backed up by American Volunteer Group (AVG) P-40s gained temporary dominance in the skies over Rangoon, Burma (now Yangon, Myanmar) when 37 out of 170 Japanese Army Air Force aircraft were shot down on the second of two days of intensive air combat. Rangoon had been subjected to 31 air raids since December 23, and although minor compared to the German air raids on Britain, the panic that resulted drove 400,000 Burmese to flee north more than 1,000 mi. to safety in India, many thousands dying on the way. The Japanese air campaign against Rangoon was in three phases: Dec. 23–25, 1941, January 23–29, 1942 and February 24–25. Rangoon was taken by the Japanese army on March 9, the conquest of Burma being complete on May 15.

1942 February 27 In the Battle of the Java Sea, air and naval units mounted a determined effort to stop 80 Japanese ships approaching Java from the northeast. Despite a large USAAF force of B-17s, A-24s, P-40s and LB-30s, together with five Dutch navy cruisers and 11 destroyers, five ships were sunk by the Japanese near Surabaya. Included was the first U.S. aircraft carrier, USS *Langley,* converted into a seaplane tender, ferrying 32 P-40s to Tjilatjap. Other ships attempted to pick up the P-40 pilots from the *Langley* but were sunk by the Japanese. All the pilots were drowned with the exception of two who got to Australia.

1942 March 3 The largest number of aircraft dispatched on a single raid to one target was conducted by RAF Bomber Command this night when it sent 235 aircraft in three waves to bomb the Renault factory at Billancourt, which was known to be making war materiel for the Germans. More than 400 tons of bombs were dropped in just under 2 hr. Forty percent of the buildings were destroyed and production was halted for a month with the loss of almost 2,300 lorries being built there. And 9,250 people made homeless; 367 French workers who had ignored air raid sirens were killed.

1942 March 10 Last and most successful in a series of air attacks by the U.S. Navy in the southern Pacific area began from the carriers USS *Lexington* and USS *Yorktown* between 7:49 and 8:40 A.M. when 61 SBD Dauntlesses, 25 TBF Avengers and 18 F4F Wildcats were launched in a strike that sank four Japanese transport ships and a number of smaller vessels. The aircraft had flown over the 13,000 ft. mountains of the Owen Stanley Range from the carriers in the Gulf of Papua. Action organized by Adm. Nimitz had begun February 1 with air strikes in the vicinity of the Marshall Islands, and on February 20, the *Lexington* went to hit Rabaul. On February 24 and March 4, Wake and Marcus were hit by aircraft from the *Enterprise.*

1942 March 13 The first successful use of the Gee navigational aid took place this night when 135 RAF aircraft bombed Cologne, Germany using this system. The raid was judged five times more effective per tonnage dropped than earlier raids to Cologne, with rubber factories and engineering works badly hit, 237 fires started and 62 people killed. Two children were finally dug out alive after three days. Gee improved night navigation to a range of about 400 mi. by computing an aircraft's position using signals received from three beams transmitted from widely separate locations in England; it had first been carried by lead bombers on the night of March 8/9.

1942 March 20 In a desperate effort to dislodge Allied resistance on the Mediterranean island of Malta, a large formation of Ju 88 bombers escorted by Bf 110s from III/ZG 26 attacked Takali airfield. Some aircraft carried 2,200-lb. rocket bombs aimed at suspected underground hangars. This followed a three-month build-up of Axis forces under Generalfeldmarschall Kesselring's Luftflotte 2, and five bomber groups had been moved down to Sicily with the task of pulverizing any military operations from Malta. Raids were maintained for three days before the Luftwaffe turned its attentions to convoys once again.

1942 March 20 A "Plan for Initiation of U.S. Army Bombardment Operations in the British Isles" was refined in the United Kingdom, outlining strategic bombing campaigns against Germany from bases in England. Submitted by Gen. Ira C. Eaker, it marked completion of studies between the USAAF and the RAF about combined operations and identified much the Americans had to rely on the British for, acknowledging it would be some time before U.S. activity could achieve full operational status. By June 4, a plan for 3,649 USAAF combat aircraft in Britain had been compiled, and on June 20, Gen. Marshall instructed Gen. Eisenhower that all U.S. air combat units in Britain were to be integrated into the Eighth Air Force.

1942 March 20 Mitsubishi test pilot Katsuzo Shima piloted the J2M Raiden on its first fight. Designed to a 14-Shi specification of September 1939, the J2M2 had a maximum speed of 371 MPH at 17,880 ft. and a climb time of 5 min. 38 sec. to 19,685 ft. Although only 476 were built, the aircraft was powered by a variety of powerplant derivatives of the 1,800-HP Mitsubishi MK4R 14-cylinder, air-cooled radial. As a bomber interceptor it was supreme, having been built for top speed and firepower rather than maneuverability or dogfighting. Because of technical problems, however, it was late 1943 before it began to appear in substantial numbers.

1942 March 26 The Douglas DC-4 airliner made its first flight from Clover Field, Santa Monica, Calif., powered by four 1,450-HP Pratt & Whitney Twin Wasp (R-2000) 2SD1-G radials. Designed as a 25% lighter version of the DC-4E and capable of carrying up to 40 passengers, the DC-4 production line was commandeered by the army and the prototype appeared in military transport configuration as the C-54 Skymaster. By the end of the war, 1,163 aircraft had been produced, of which 839 were still in service with Air Transport Command. Capable of carrying up to 50 troops, the C-54 had a wingspan of 117 ft. 6 in., a length of 93 ft. 10 in., a height of 27 ft. 6 in. and a gross weight of 62,000 lb. In 79,642 trans-oceanic flights, the C-54 made only two ditchings.

1942 March 27 As a typical example of the civil flying maintained by neutral countries, the Swedish airline A. B. Aerotransport began a courier service between Stockholm and Aberdeen, Scotland with connections to London. The airlines used DC-3s, but the service was suspended after two were shot down by the Germans on the night of June 21/22. The service was resumed on August 15. The A.B.A. service to Moscow had been withdrawn when Germany attacked the USSR in June 1941; but A.B.A. maintained a service to Berlin until shortly before the capitulation of Germany in May 1945.

1942 March 28 The first major bombing success by the RAF against a German city took place this night when 234 aircraft hit the old north German town of Lübeck with more than 40 tons of bombs, destroying or seriously damaging 3,401 buildings and lightly damaging 8,411, a total of 11,812, which represented 62% of all buildings in Lübeck, among which were many of great historic interest. The death toll is variously recorded as 312 or 320, in any event the greatest number of Germans killed in a single raid on a German target to date. The Red Cross negotiated with the RAF that Lübeck would never again be bombed because they were using its port for supplies.

1942 April 5 A long-anticipated Japanese air strike on Ceylon (Sri Lanka) began at 8:00 A.M. when Comdr. Fuchida led 53 B5N2s, 38 D3A1s and 36 A6M Reisens in an attack on Colombo and Ratmalana. Forewarned by sightings at 4:00 and 11:59 P.M. April 4 by patroling Catalinas, 36 Hurricanes from the RAF and six Fulmars from the Fleet Air Arm went to intercept the raiders. Fifteen Hurricanes and four Fulmars were shot down for the loss of 18 Japanese aircraft. No. 11 Squadron Blenheims went out to bomb Adm. Nagumo's naval force (comprising the carriers *Akagi, Soryu, Hiryu, Zuikaku* and *Shokaku* with a combined strength of 377 aircraft), but they failed to find it and returned with their bombs.

1942 April 9 A force of 17 RAF Hurricanes of No. 261 Squadron and six Fulmars of No. 873 Squadron, Fleet Air Arm attacked a force of 60 Japanese bombers and 60 escort fighters during a raid on Trincomolee, Ceylon (Sri Lanka). The Allies shot down 15 planes and damaged 17 that failed to reach their carriers; in addition, nine were brought down by antiaircraft fire for a total loss to the Japanese of 41 aircraft. Eight Hurricanes and three Fulmars were shot down. In two raids (April 5 and 9), the Japanese had lost 59 aircraft. As a result, Adm. Nagumo was denied the use of three of his carriers for the Battle of the Coral Sea while they went back for new aircraft, and their pilots were inexperienced when they went to the Battle of Midway.

1942 April 14 To inject commercial airline expertise into military airlift operations, Gen. H. Arnold appointed American Airlines president C. R. Smith to be become executive officer of USAAF Ferrying Command with the rank of colonel. On June 20, Gen. Arnold unified all the separate transport services (including the US Naval Air Transport Service created December 12, 1941) into the Air Transport Command, responsible for ferrying of men and materiel, control and operations of air routes and running of airfields. By the end of the war, it had 26,600 staff and 429 aircraft.

1942 April 18 In a daring propaganda raid designed to boost morale at home, 16 B-25 Mitchell bombers led by Lt. Col. James H. Doolittle took off from the USS *Hornet* for a raid on Japan. Fifteen bombed targets in Tokyo, Kobe, Yokohama and Nagoye 800 mi. away. Each B-25 carried 1,141 gal. of fuel versus the usual 694 gal.; ventral turret, Norden bombsights and tail guns were removed. Unable to reach planned bases in China, the B-25s were ditched or abandoned, one making it to the USSR. Drawn from the Seventeenth Group and the Eighty-ninth Reconnaissance Squadron, most of the crews survived, and Lt. Col. Doolittle received the Medal of Honor.

1942 April 18 A military VIP service with a Boeing 307 Stratoliner began between the United States and Britain, a service that continued for the next three years of war in Europe. In that period, 5,000 trans-Atlantic flights would be made carrying 112,000 passengers and more than 10,000 tons of cargo. Three Boeing 307s were involved. Two others flew a U.S.-Cairo, Egypt service and, from June 1942, a shuttle run between Natal, Brazil and Accra, Gold Coast (Ghana).

The accepted design entry for a U.S. Army medium attack bomber was approved September 10, 1939, and later emerged as the B-25 Mitchell.

1942 April 19 The U.S. Navy carried out two tests to evaluate the practicality of remotely piloted "drone" aircraft. In the first, a BG-1 was launched and visually controlled to impact the water just beyond its target, the wreck of the *San Marcos* in Chesapeake Bay. In the second test, a BG-2 equipped with a TV camera was successfully guided by Lt. M. B. Taylor in an aircraft to a raft 11 mi. away being towed at 8 knots.

1942 April 19 The Macchi M.C.205 Veltro made its first flight. Powered by a 1,475-HP Daimler Benz DB 605 engine (production aircraft had the Fiat RA.1050 RC 58 Tifone, essentially a license-built version of the DB 605), the sleek fighter had a wingspan of 36 ft. 11 in., a length of 29 ft. and a wing area of 205.51 sq. ft. With a maximum speed of 399 MPH at 23,620 ft., the M.C.205 had a service ceiling of 37,090 ft., a climb time of 5 min. 3 sec. to 19,686 ft. and a range of 646 mi. This aircraft was the last in a line of Macchi-Castoldi fighters starting with the M.C.200, first flown on December 24, 1937. Probably the best Italian fighter ever built, the M.C.205 became operational in mid-1943 and served with the Aviazione Nazionale Repubblicana after the Italian armistice of September 8, 1943.

1942 April 23 In reprisal for increased RAF bombing of German towns and cities, the Luftwaffe began a series of raids aimed at destroying British cities of historical or tourist value. Dubbed "Baedeker raids" by the German press in reference to the guide-books of the same name, Hitler spoke openly of a terror attack (*terrorangriffe*) against England. The first raid hit Exeter; this was followed by raids on Bath, Norwich, York, Cowes, Hull, Ipswich, Birmingham, Canterbury, Poole and other famous towns. By August the raids had dwindled and although considerable damage had been inflicted, 14 major attacks having been carried out with the loss of 40 German bombers the Luftwaffe was coming under increasing pressure from RAF night fighters.

1942 April 23 The first de Havilland H.1 turbojet engine called Supercharger, later named Goblin, made its first test run at Hatfield, England. Designed to the centrifugal concept, the H.1 was named after designer Maj. Frank Halford following a go-ahead to produce the engine early in 1941. The H.1 was the first British

production turbojet engine, assembly being compressed between drawing release on August 8, 1941, and this date. De Havilland was also asked to build a suitable fighter, permission for which was given in May 1942 to emerge as the D.H. 100 Vampire.

1942 April 26 Converted from a Mk.V, the first Spitfire Mk.IX (serial no. AB505) was delivered from the Rolls Royce test station at Hucknall, England to the Air Fighting Development unit at Duxford. Powered by a Rolls Royce Merlin 61 series engine, the Mk.IX had a maximum speed of 409 MPH at 28,000 ft., a climb time of 5.7 min. to 20,000 ft. and a ceiling of 43,000 ft. In all, 5,665 Mk.IXs were built, more than any other mark of Spitfire except the Mk.V. The Mk.IX represented the peak performance of the Spitfire design, although the tail was taller and pointed. Service use began with No. 64 Squadron, RAF, in June, and it soon proved itself a good match for the German Fw 190.

1942 April 30 The Fiat G.55 Centauro made its first flight. Powered by a 1,475-HP Fiat RA 1050 RC 58 Tifone engine, the aircraft was a dramatic improvement on the G.50 and had a top speed of 391 MPH and a climb time of 19,685 ft. in 7 min. 12 sec. Only 289 aircraft were built, serving with the Aviazione Nazionale Repubblicana after the Italian armistice. G.50s that survived World War II went to Argentina and were eventually returned and resold to Egypt in 1948.

1942 April Essentially a powered version of the Me 321 glider, the Me 323 Gigant (Giant) began flight trials. It was seriously underpowered, with four 1,140-HP Gnôme-Rhône 14N supercharged air-cooled radial engines. The Me 323 V2 had six smaller engines, and the first major production type, the D-1, appeared in September armed with five 7.9-mm guns in the nose and upper fuselage and up to 10 guns of like calibre in the fuselage. The aircraft had a span of 180 ft. 5 in., a length of 92 ft. 4 in. and a normal loaded weight of 94,815 lb. Cruising speed was 136 MPH, and range was 683 mi. In all, 198 were built, the type becoming operational late in 1942.

1942 May 4 The first of 3,405 B-17F versions was completed by Lockheed Vega at Burbank, Calif. Although outwardly almost

North American B-25 Mitchell medium bombers played an important role throughout World War II.

identical to the B-17E, distinguished only by a new Plexiglass nose, internal changes were numerous, including self-sealing fuel tanks, an extra 1,100 gal. of fuel, a crew of 10, ten 0.50-in. machine guns in defensive positions, a 50% increase in bomb load to 6,000 lb. and revisions to the propellers allowing feathering in flight. Gross weight increased to 56,500 lb., and the B-17F had a range of 1,300 mi. carrying maximum bomb load.

1942 May 4 The world's first major carrier battle and the first naval engagement fought without opposing surface vessels making contact, the Battle of the Coral Sea, began when Rear Adm. Frank J. Fletcher, in charge of Task Force 17, comprising the carriers USS *Yorktown* and USS *Lexington,* launched an air group at 6:30 A.M. from the *Lexington* and struck Japanese forces on Tulagi, which Adm. Shima had taken the previous day. The Japanese light carrier *Shoho* was dispatched to join the Port Moresby invasion group, and the *Yorktown* sailed to join up with the *Lexington* by early hours May 5, stationing an attack group in the path of the Japanese transports.

1942 May 7 The final round in the Battle of the Coral Sea began when aircraft from the Japanese carriers *Zuikaku* and *Shokaku* unsuccessfully tried to attack the carriers USS *Yorktown* and USS *Lexington,* sinking an oiler instead. B-17s from Noumeá, New Caledonia shadowed the carrier *Shoho,* which was hit with 1,000-lb. bombs from the *Yorktown's* Douglas SBD Dauntlesses and sank at 11:35 A.M. Next day at 11:20 A.M., Japanese aircraft struck the *Lexington,* which sank, but the *Yorktown* hit the *Shokaku,* which was forced to withdraw. The Japanese occupation of Port Moresby was deferred, the Japanese having lost a light car-

rier and 80 aircraft, the United States a large carrier and 66 aircraft.

1942 May 15 United Air Lines began military support operations with a flight from Patterson Field, Fairfield, Ohio, to Anchorage, Alaska via seven stops across a distance of 3,489 mi. A trans-Pacific service for USAAF Air Transport Command was opened September 23, covering the 7,350 mi. between San Francisco and Brisbane, Australia in 50 hr. with the new C-54 Skymaster. When military operations ceased March 31, 1945, United had flown 20,000 tons of men and materiel 21 million mi. in 1,700 Pacific and 1,800 Alaskan flights.

1942 May 15 Piloted by Capt. G. Ya Bakhchivandzhi, the first Soviet rocket-propelled fighter made its first flight powered by a 2,425-lb. thrust Dushkin-Shtokolov motor. Five prototypes had been ordered on July 9, 1941, and test pilot B. M. Kudrin made the first flight after being towed into the air and released from a Pe-2 on September 10. Flown at first with retractable skis, the BI-1 had a wingspan of 21 ft. 3 in., a length of 21 ft. and a maximum loaded weight of 3,710 lb. On March 21, 1943, it reached a height of 9,843 ft. in 30 sec. Only seven test aircraft were ever built.

1942 May 18 German troops at Demyansk about 170 mi. southeast of Leningrad were relieved after 91 days of siege by Soviet troops during which period Luftflotte 1 had carried 26,794 tons of supplies, 692,106 gal. of fuel and 15,466 soldiers into the area, bringing out 22,093 wounded. The Luftwaffe lost 262 aircraft and 385 officers and men on these transport missions. The partial supply of Demyansk went on into 1943 with a total 71,442 tons flown in. This was made particularly difficult because one airstrip was only 100 ft. wide and during the winter months there was a cargo weight limit of 1.65 tons to prevent the aircraft from falling through the surface of snow.

1942 May 26 The first of two Northrop XP-61 twin-engine, twin tail-boom aircraft made its first flight powered by two Pratt & Whitney R-2800-10 radial engines. Designed to a general army specification for a night fighter issued late in 1940, the P-61 Black Widow would enter service at the end of 1943 and record its first kill on July 7, 1944, in the Pacific theater. A giant among fighters, the P-61 had a wingspan of 66 ft., a length of 49 ft. 7 in. and a gross weight of 29,700 lb. With a top speed of 366 MPH, it had a service ceiling of 33,000 ft. and a range of 1,470 mi.

1942 May 26 Representatives of the USAAF, the U.S. Navy, the RAF and the Fleet-Air Arm met with British prime minister Winston Churchill in London at the beginning of the Anglo-American Air Conference. The leaders of the various air arms discussed the allocation of airfields and aircraft in Britain to establish the U.S. forces in Britain. Among those taking part were A.C.M. Sir Charles Portal, chief of the Air Staff, Gen. H. H. Arnold and the chief of the U.S. Navy Bureau of Aeronautics, Adm. John H. Towers, the U.S. Navy's third aviator. On June 18, Maj. Gen. Carl Spaatz was appointed to head Eighth Air Force in place of Brig. Gen. H. H. Arnold.

1942 May 29 The first North American P-51 (NA-91) for USAAF orders made its first flight. The P-51 differed from the British Mustang 1A primarily in having the four 0.30-in. and two 0.50-in. wing guns and two 0.50-in. fuselage guns replaced by four 20-mm wing-mounted cannons. The P-51A (first flown on February 3, 1943) and the P-51C (first flown August 5, 1943) had four 0.50-in. guns in the wings, increased to six later. Range with internal fuel was 1,300 mi. or 2,080 mi. with drop tanks, a

Only 117 days after the initial contract, the prototype North American P-51 Mustang took to the air for the first time.

range considerably greater than any other fighter in European operations and one that, when the P-51 flew its first operational mission on December 13, 1943, was of very great significance for bomber escort duty.

1942 May 29   The only Australian-designed fighter to fire its guns in anger during World War II, the Commonwealth CA-12 Boomerang, made its first flight at Fishermans' Bend, Victoria just three months after an order for 105 had been placed by the RAAF. Redesigned by Lawrence Wackett from the 40 North American NA-16 general-purpose monoplanes license-built in Australia as the Wirraway, the CA-12 eventually served with five RAAF squadrons. Being used mainly for ground attacks, no CA-12 ever shot down an enemy aircraft.

1942 May 30   The first RAF "thousand-bomber" raid was conducted this night when 1,047 aircraft were dispatched to Cologne. The force included 602 Wellingtons, 131 Halifaxes, 88 Stirlings, 79 Hampdens, 73 Lancasters, 46 Manchesters and 28 Whitleys, which together dropped 1,603 tons of bombs. The RAF lost 41 aircraft (3.9%). About 2,500 fires were started, 5,420 buildings destroyed or seriously damaged, 7,420 buildings lightly damaged—a total of 12,840 among which were nine hospitals, 17 churches, six schools, four university buildings, four hotels and six department stores. Some 13,010 homes were completely destroyed, and 28,630 domestic buildings were left in various

states of damage; 45,132 people were left homeless, 486 were killed, and 150,000 people fled the city in panic.

1942 June 2   A massive German blitz on the Soviet city of Sevastopol in the Crimea began with 723 sorties by Junkers Ju 88s, Ju 87s and Heinkel 111s flying in support of Army Group South. The intensive effort to smash resistance to German occupation culminated July 4 in the collapse of Soviet forces when the city fell to Gen. Oberst Erich von Manstein's Eleventh Army. In the interim, 23,751 sorties had been flown by the Luftwaffe during which 26,184 tons of bombs were dropped and 123 Soviet aircraft were shot down for the loss of only 31 planes. The Germans had captured 400,000 prisoners, 1,250 tanks and 2,000 guns, including men and materiel captured in the Izyum-Barvenkovo offensive May 17–22, which effectively opened the summer offensive.

1942 June 3   The major naval engagement that many historians regard as the turning point for the Japanese in World War II, the Battle of Midway began. Comprising the First Koku-Kantai (First Carrier Strike Force) under Adm. Chuichi Nagumo, the Japanese heavy carriers *Kaga, Akagi, Hiryu* and *Soryu* and the light carrier *Hosho,* with almost 300 aircraft, formed the spearhead for the invasion of Midway Island. Under Rear Adm. Frank J. Fletcher's Task Force 17 was the carrier USS *Yorktown* (VT-5) and under Rear Adm. Raymond A. Spruance's Task Force 16 were the carriers USS *Enterprise* (VT-6) and USS *Hornet* (VT-7), carrying a total of 223 aircraft, with another 119 located at shore facilities.

1942 June 4   The first phase of the Battle of Midway began at 6:33 A.M. when 108 Japanese attack planes under Lt. Comdr. Joichi Tomonaga hit the islands of Sand and Midway. The force had been detected more than 30 min. earlier by a patrolling U.S. Navy PBY-5. A6M2 Zeros flying top cover for B5N2s and D3A1s were more than a match for U.S. Navy VMF-221s F2As and F4Fs, which found the Japanese fighters too nimble and agile, and 16 B-17Es were unsuccessful in attacking the Japanese carriers. Advised by Lt. Comdr. Tomonaga that a second strike against the islands would be needed, Adm. Nagumo ordered the carrier attack planes rearmed with fragmentation and incendiary bombs, a task that would take 2 hr.

The second phase of the Battle of Midway began at 9:25 A.M. when 41 TBD-1 Devastators and three escorting F4F-4s attacked

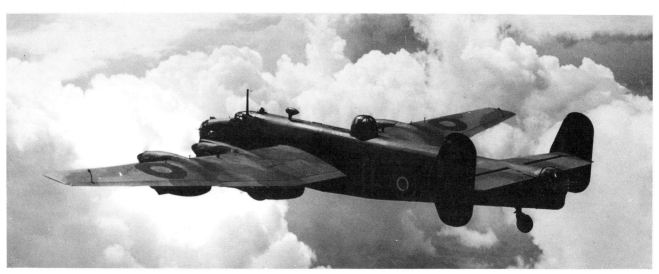

On May 30, 1942, 131 Handley Page Halifax bombers participated in the first "1,000 bomber" raid on Germany.

the Japanese carrier task force under Adm. Nagumo. The presence of the U.S. carriers *Yorktown, Enterprise* and *Hornet* was unknown until discovered very shortly before the attack began, and Adm. Nagumo ordered a rapid rearming of his attack planes with torpedoes and antiship bombs instead of fragmentation and incendiary bombs. Totally outclassed, 36 of the 41 TBD-1s of *Yorktown, Enterprise,* and *Hornet* and their commanders were destroyed by A6M2 Zeros. No Japanese ships had been hit.

The third phase of the Battle of Midway began at 10:25 A.M. when SBD-3s from the *Enterprise* and *Hornet* attacked the Japanese First Koku-Kantai (Carrier Strike Force) and, within 3 min. of beginning dive-bomb attacks from 18,000 ft., had set fire to the carriers *Kaga, Akagi* and the *Soryu,* all of which sank unprotected by air cover. The A6M2s were on the decks refueling and rearming from their earlier decimation of the TBD-1s and were unable to take off and defend the carrier. The Japanese carrier *Hiryu* steamed northeast, found the *Yorktown* and attacked her at 11:58 A.M. and, with torpedoes, at 2:42 P.M. Listing heavily, the *Yorktown* was taken in tow for Pearl Harbor; the *Hiryu* was located and sunk by SBD-3s from *Hornet* and *Enterprise* at 5:05 P.M.

1942 June 5   The fourth phase of the Battle of Midway began with the withdrawal of the remnants of Adm. Nagumo's First Koku-Kantai, which was continually hounded by Seventh Air Force B-17s from Midway Island. USAAF bombers attacked surface ships to a distance of 425 mi. from Midway. After the U.S. carrier *Yorktown* had been hit June 4, Adm. Fletcher relinquished command to Adm. Spruance, who declined to turn west and face Adm. Yamamoto's combined fleet of more than 150 first-class warships, thus ensuring his two carriers remained intact. The already severely damaged *Yorktown* was found by a Japanese submarine and sunk along with a U.S. destroyer, the only U.S. Navy ships lost in the battle, along with 132 aircraft and 307 men. The Japanese lost four carriers, a heavy cruiser, 275 aircraft and 3,500 men.

1942 June 11   The U.S. Eleventh Air Force attacked the Japanese-occupied island of Kiska in the Aleutians for the first time, sending five B-24s and five B-17s from Cold Bay, Alaska. One B-24 was shot down by antiaircraft fire, but all the rest returned safely to base. A US Navy patrol aircraft also discovered the Japanese on Attu Island, signaling the start of a long campaign lasting well into 1943.

1942 June 13   The U.S. Navy made its first operational test with Loran (long-range navigation) equipment with a receiver mounted in a K-2 airship on a flight from the Lakehurst, N.J. Naval Air Station. The system operator, Dr. J. A. Pierce, was able to direct the airship commander on a direct course back to the airship sheds from a distance of 75 mi. offshore. The success of this system led to immediate applications for service use.

1942 June 13   A German reconnaissance aircraft spotted a British convoy of six transport ships, two aircraft carriers, three cruisers and 17 destroyers bringing supplies to the beleaguered Mediterranean island of Malta, and the following day a continuous series of air attacks began. By the time the convoy reached Malta, only two transport ships remained. Throughout the summer, the Luftwaffe kept up an intense attack on the Malta convoys, the last to be so harassed, in August, losing nine out of 14 transports.

1942 June 21   The Soviet airline Aeroflot began relief operations in the Crimea to assist the beleaguered city of Sevastopol. By July 1, 229 night landings had been made, providing 218 tons of supplies and airlifting out 2,162 people, including 1,542

wounded. Earlier, between October 10 and December 25, 1941, Aeroflot had flown 6,235 tons of supplies into the besieged city of Leningrad, evacuating 50,000 people, including 13,208 wounded soldiers. In August 1942, Aeroflot began to supply Stalingrad, flying 46,000 missions by February 1943 and bringing in 2,587 tons of supplies and ferrying out 30,000 men.

1942 June 26   Test pilot Seldon A. Converse made the first flight of a XF6F-3 Hellcat. The first production model flew on July 30 following placement of an order on January 7 for the first 1,080 of 12,275 aircraft eventually built. The F6F-3 was to enter service aboard the USS *Essex* (CV-9) following training at VF-9, Oceana Naval Air Station, Va. With a wingspan of 42 ft. 10 in. and a length of 33 ft. 7 in., the F6F-3 had a maximum weight of 15,487 lb. and a top speed of 375 MPH at 17,300 ft., reached 3,500 ft. in 60 sec., had a ceiling of 38,400 ft. and a range of 1,590 mi. and usually carried six 0.50-in. guns.

1942 June 29   Capt. Charles C. Kegelman, commanding the Fifteenth Bomb Squadron, flew the first official Eighth Air Force mission and became the first personnel member to drop bombs on Germany when his all-American crew of a Douglas Boston accompanied 11 other Bostons from No. 226 Squadron, RAF, from Swanton Morley on a day raid of the marshaling yards at Hazebrouck. In a more somber event, 1st Lt. Alfred W. Giacomini of the Thirty-first Fighter Group was the first Eighth Air Force casualty in Britain when he crashed his Spitfire while landing at Atcham, Shropshire.

1942 June 30   The USAAF had 21,173 aircraft on strength: 846 heavy bombers, 1,047 medium bombers, 696 light bombers, 2,950 fighters, 468 reconnaissance aircraft, 824 transports, 12,610 trainers and 1,732 communications aircraft.

1942 July 1   The first U.S. Eighth Air Force B-17Es destined for the Ninety-Seventh Bombardment Group based at Polebrook near Peterbrough, England flew into Prestwick, Scotland (led by serial no. 41-9085). By July 27, the 180 aircraft of the First, Sixtieth and Ninety-seventh Bomber Groups had arrived in the British Isles, having lost five B-17s and two P-38s en route, two to German disinformation broadcasts on route directions. Their trip had involved a 2,965-mi. flight from Presque Island via Goose Bay, Newfoundland, Bluie West, Greenland, and Reykjavík, Iceland.

1942 July 1   The U.S. Navy had on hand a total 7,058 aircraft (compared to 3,437 on July 1, 1941), including 3,191 (1,774) combat types, 461 (183) for transport and utility, 3,378 (1,444) for training and 28 (31) for miscellaneous duties. The navy had a total of 42,793 aviation personnel on active duty (compared with 15,175 the year before), of which 14,775 (4,446) were officers (9,059 [3,483] pilots) and 28,018 (11,269) enlisted men (732 [629]) pilots.

1942 July 3   The first of seven Martin PB2M/JRM Mars flying boats, the largest the U.S. Navy would operate, made its first flight powered by four 2,300-HP Wright R-3350-8 engines. With a wingspan of 200 ft. and a length of 120 ft. 3 in., it had a gross weight of 145,000 lb., a top speed of 221 MPH and a range of 4,945 mi. With two mess rooms (one for officers) and a shower on board, the aircraft had been rolled out with much ceremony on November 5, 1941, but the maiden flight was delayed because of fire. The first transport mission was flown on November 30, 1943, when Lt. Comdr. W. E. Coney and his crew of 16 carried 13,000 lb. of cargo from the Patuxent River, Md. to Natal, Brazil, a distance of 4,375 mi., in 28 hr. 25 min. nonstop.

1942 July 3 The first firing of a rocket carried by a U.S. Navy aircraft took place when Lt. Comdr. J. H. Hean, gunnery officer of Transition Training Squadron dropped a retro-rocket from a PBY-5A in flight. Designed and developed at the California Institute of Technology, the rocket was expected to provide forward thrust equal to the speed of the launching aircraft, thus allowing the device to fall vertically. Initial service installations were made with PS-63s in February 1943. In other rocket tests, British solid propellant-assisted takeoff rockets were tried out on a Brewster F2A-3 on May 26, reducing takeoff distance by 49%.

1942 July 5 The Luftwaffe played a major role in the destruction of an Allied Arctic supply convoy, PQ 17, when attack aircraft hit the 34 merchant ships in force. In Luftflotte 3, the Luftwaffe had at its disposal 103 Ju 88s, 30 Ju 87s, 15 He 115s, 42 He 111s and 74 assorted reconnaissance aircraft for seeking out and attacking the Arctic supply convoys carrying munitions to the Soviet Union. PQ 17 sailed June 27 from Iceland in fog and was constantly shadowed by Fw 200s of I/KG 40. The last air attack on PQ 17 was made on July 10. In all, 23 merchant ships were sunk, and it would be two months before another convoy set sail.

1942 July 5 Conceived and designed as a pure transport version of the Lancaster bomber, the first Avro 685 York made its first flight at Ringway, England. Largely because of an agreement that the United States would produce all transport aircraft for the Alliance, production did not get under way in strength until 1945–48. With a completely new square section fuselage 78 ft. 6 in. length, married to a Lancaster wing and tail assembly and powered by four 1,620-HP Rolls Royce Merlin T.24s, the York had been designed by Roy Chadwick. Production models incorporated a third, central fin to compensate for fuselage side loads.

1942 July 10 The first of three prototype XA-26 multi-purpose fast attack aircraft made its first flight. Pressed into service for European operations before the end of 1944, it was to be the last attack category aircraft for the USAAF. It was built as a high-wing, tricycle-undercarriage bomber, but the second aircraft was finished as a night fighter with four 20-mm cannons in the belly and four 0.50-in. machine guns in a top turret fired remotely from a gunner's position amidships. The B-26 bomber version was first used in Korea on June 27, 1950, and then as a counter-insurgency aircraft in Vietnam from 1962.

1942 July 12 The Stalingrad Front was formed under Soviet Marshal S. K. Timoshenko. The 600 available air units were split to form two fronts, one facing the Don, the other Stalingrad itself. On August 20, the new Lavochkin La-5 fighters arrived, and in 299 sorties between August 21 and September 16, they shot down 97 German aircraft. The Soviet offensive, known as Plan Uranis, began November 23 with the aim of smashing up the Romanian and Italian forces on the Stalingrad flank.

1942 July 18 Piloted by Fritz Wendel, the first jet-propelled Me 262 V3 to fly independent of supplementary propulsion took to the air from Leipheim near the Messerschmitt plant at Augsburg. The Me 262 was powered by two Junkers Jumo 109-004A-0 engines, each with 1,848-lb. of thrust. On the first attempt, the pilot could not raise the tail of the plane, and he was forced to brake hard to stop at the end of the 3,600-ft. runway, despite a speed of 112 MPH. The cause was ground-deflected jet efflux impinging on the tail and keeping it pinned down. Technicians advised that Wendel jab the brakes at speed to kick the tail up, which he did, becoming airborne for a 12-min. flight.

1942 August 1 The first U.S. Coast Guard antisubmarine operation took place when a Grumman J4F Widgeon piloted by Ens. H. C. White of Squadron 212 based at Houma, La. located and attacked with bombs the German submarine U-166 while patrolling off the Mississippi delta. The presence of the submarine marked the beginning of a new patrol area for German U-boats and an increase in activity along the eastern seaboard and in the Gulf of Mexico. The response was an increase in coastal patrol forces from the U.S. Navy and the U.S. Coast Guard.

1942 August 7 The first U.S. combined forces offensive of World War II in the Pacific began with the carriers USS *Enterprise*, USS *Saratoga* and USS *Wasp* providing air support for a force of U.S. Marines assaulting Guadalcanal and Tulagi in the Soloman Islands. The Japanese sent air support from Rabaul, New Guinea for defending forces, but 16 of the Japanese raiders were shot down for the loss of 10 U.S. carrier aircraft. This was the beginning of a six-month campaign to take Guadalcanal.

1942 August 13 The first guided bomb was tried out operationally by the Italians when a Savoia-Marchetti S.M.79 bomber packed with high explosives was piloted to British warships off the Algerian coast. Equipped with radio guidance equipment, the aircraft maintained its course to an assigned impact point, and the pilot bailed out by parachute.

1942 August 17 The first U.S. Eighth Air Force heavy bomber raid into German-occupied Europe began when the six B-17Es of the 340th and 341st Bomb Squadrons, Ninety-seventh Bomb Group, took off from Polebrook, England to rendezvous with escorting Spitfires over The Naze for a diversion flight. The main attack, comprising 11 B-17s from the 342nd and 414th Bomb Squadrons and one from the 340th Bomb Squadron, departed from Grafton Underwood, near Kettering, for marshaling yards at Rouen/Sotterville in France. The lead aircraft, named *Butcher Shop* (serial no. 12578) was piloted by Maj. Paul W. Tibbets who three years later would pilot the B-29 *Enola Gay*, which dropped the first atom bomb. Sgt. Kent R. West obtained the first air combat kill for an Eighth Air Force gunner.

1942 August 18 The first operational RAF bombing raid to use the new Pathfinder concept was conducted this night when 118 aircraft departed to raid Flensburg, an inlet of the Baltic. Originated by Gp. Capt. S. O. Bufton when he was with No. 10 Squadron, the Pathfinders would illuminate the target by flares and Verey lights to mark the target for the following waves of aircraft. A.C.M. Harris was not convinced at first, but he relented and a Pathfinder Force comprising No. 156 Squadron (1 Group), No. 7 Squadron (3 Group), No. 35 Squadron (4 Group) and No. 83 Squadron (5 Group) was formed, led by the Australian wing Comdr. D. C. T. Bennett.

1942 August 19 In a combined Anglo-Canadian operation in rehearsal for a landing on continental Europe, a force of 6,000 British and Canadian troops conducted an air-supported landing on Dieppe, France, and the first aerial victory was notched up by the Eighth Air Force. The RAF flew 2,339 sorties and the Eighth Air Force flew 123 sorties during the day, including a strike by 22 B-17s on Abbeville/Drucat airfield that caused great damage. In all, 48 German aircraft were destroyed and 24 damaged in return for 114 Allied aircraft lost (eight of which were American-flown Spitfires), and 71 Allied pilots were killed or missing. Second Lt. Samuel F. Junkin Jr. of the 309th Fighter Squadron, 31st Fighter Group, shot down the first Eighth Air Force air combat victory over Europe.

1942 August 20 The U.S. Army Twelfth Air Force was formed at Bolling Field, Washington, D.C. in preparation for the invasion of North Africa in Operation Torch. Initially, administrative elements were put in place followed by establishment strength of combat units. The Twelveth Air Force was to be commanded by Brig. Gen. James H. Doolittle. Operation Torch would take place November 8, 1942, after Lt. Gen. Dwight D. Eisenhower had been named commander, Allied force headquarters (AFHG) on August 7, 1942. Buttressing himself for losing a lot of resources to the Twelveth Air Force and Operation Torch, Maj. Gen. Carl Spaatz subordinated all Eighth Air Force operations to that task.

1942 August 20 The USS *Long Island* made the first U.S. Navy ferry carrier operation in the Pacific when it transported U.S. Marine Corps Dauntlesses and Wildcats to Henderson Field on Guadalcanal, in the eastern Solomons. The aircraft were used to back up U.S. Marine Corps operations on the island and to fly cover against Japanese fighters that came across from Rabaul, New Guinea. USAAF aircraft Bell Airacobras intended for overseas use were requisitioned to help alleviate critical support operations.

1942 August 24 A specially stripped-down, but unpressurized, RAF Spitfire Mk.V pursued and shot down a high-altitude Junkers Ju 86P-2 pressurized reconnaissance aircraft over Egypt. The Ju 86P had been developed in 1940 especially for very high altitude work and given a pressurized crew compartment allowing it to operate at just over 36,000 ft. Pursued to an altitude of 42,000 ft., the Ju 86P-2 was set on fire and crashed in the Mediterranean. As a result of this action, the Germans hastily installed rear-firing machine guns on the hitherto unarmed aircraft, but two more were lost to the Spitfires from Aboukir.

1942 September 1 Eastern Air Lines formed its Military Transport Division (MTD) and in October introduced the Curtiss C-46. With twice the capacity of the DC-3, the C-46 was a valuable addition and, after early teething troubles, took over long-haul routes in the United States and overseas. A Miami-Natal service was introduced in February 1943, and on June 1, 1944, this was extended 1,448 mi. across the South Atlantic to Ascension and from there 1,356 mi. to Accra, Gold Coast (Ghana) using aircraft with extra 250 gal. fuel tanks. Eastern's MTD was disbanded on October 15, 1945.

1942 September 1 No doubt to the extreme satisfaction of the board, which had seen its airline give way to so many national carriers now working for the U.S. government on routes it had once pioneered, Pan American secured a U.S. Navy contract for freight carrying services to Alaska. The contract ended July 31, 1944, but throughout the war, Pan American made 15,000 ocean crossings on other contracts for the government.

1942 September 1 German air ace Hans-Joachim Marseille shot down 17 British aircraft in three sorties while commander of 3./JG 27 in North Africa, the day after scoring 10 kills. Born in 1919, Marseille joined I/JG 27 and went to Africa where he was assigned to 3.Staffel; he shot down his first victim April 22, the day after 3.Staffel arrived in Africa. On November 22, he scored five victories and on June 3, 1942, shot down 10 Kittyhawks, six of them in seven minutes. Victor over 158 enemy aircraft (all his claims have been meticulously researched and confirmed), the "Star of Africa," as he became known, was killed September 30, 1942, trying to escape his aircraft when the engine accidentally caught fire during a routine patrol.

1942 September 2 Incorporating a thin-section laminar flow wing and with a greater length to accommodate fuel tanks shifted from

the wings to the fuselage, the Hawker Tempest made its first flight. Converted from a Typhoon, to which design it owed its origin, the first flying prototype was an Mk.V. Production aircraft were powered by the 2,180-HP Napier Sabre II engine and had a maximum speed of 427 MPH at 18,500 ft. with a climb time of 5 min. to 15,000 ft. The Tempest entered RAF service in April 1944 and distinguished itself as a V-1 and jet killer, shooting down 638 out of 1,771 German flying bombs destroyed in flight by the RAF and accounting for 20 Me 262s.

1942 September 12 The USAAF Eighty-ninth Attack Squadron became the first unit to drop one of the new parachute-fragmentation (para-frag) bombs on the Japanese-held island of Buna, New Guinea. Essentially a parachute-retarded free-fall bomb, the device enabled the attacking aircraft to strike from a much lower altitude than had hitherto been possible using free-fall bombs. The parachute increased accuracy because it reduced the random factors such as wind and descent angle of the ballistic trajectory while harnessing the drop dynamics to precisely known factors related to the parachute.

1942 September 21 The XB-29 prototype made its first flight from Boeing Field, Seattle with Eddie Allen at the controls. The production B-29s had a wingspan of 141 ft. 3 in., a length of 99 ft. and a gross weight of up to 141,000 lb. and could carry a maximum bomb load of 20,000 lb. with armament stripped. The aircraft had a maximum speed of 358 MPH at 25,000 ft., a service ceiling of 31,850 ft. and a maximum range of 5,830 mi. Defensive armament comprised up to 12 0.50-in. guns and one 20-mm cannon in five positions. The first B-29 Superfortress unit, the Fifty-eighth Very Heavy Bombardment Wing, was activated June 1, 1943, with its first mission on June 5, 1944, against Japanese-occupied Bangkok.

1942 September 23 A trans-Pacific air transport service was begun by United Air Lines on behalf of the USAAF Air Transport Command. The route began in San Francisco, Calif. and covered 7,350 mi. to Brisbane, Australia via Honolulu, Canton Island, Fiji and New Caledonia, maintaining a flight path as far away as possible from Japanese air operations. Aircraft used were C-54 Skymasters, military transport versions of the Douglas DC-4A.

1942 September Jack Northrop participated in feasibility studies of a rocket-powered flying-wing interceptor and received a contract for development of three MX-324 gliders that were to aerodynamically qualify the concept. The MX-324 was to have a

The first 400-MPH fighter for the RAF, the Hawker Typhoon proved an equal match for the German Focke-Wulf 190.

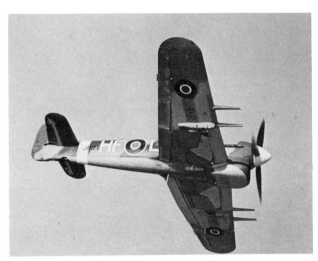

The Hawker Typhoon first flew on February 24, 1940, but not until 1942 did the RAF receive this robust fighter-bomber in quantity.

wingspan of 32 ft. and a length of 12 ft. with the pilot lying prone in the forward center section of the all-wing airplane to enable him to survive higher g-force loads. The rocket interceptor was designated XP-79, and three prototypes were ordered in January 1943. Secret at the time, the aircraft was designed to slice the tails off enemy bombers by ramming them with its armor-plated structure.

1942 September   In the only air raid carried out by a Japanese aircraft on the continental United States, a Yokosuka E14Y1 carried close to the west coast of America by the submarine I-25 dropped four 167.5-lb. phosphor bombs on woods adjacent to the coastal town of Brookings, Ore. Flown by Warrant Officer Nobuo Fujita, the floatplane had a wingspan of 36 ft. 1 in., a length of 28 ft. and a loaded weight of 3,527 lb. The E14Y1 had a range of 548 mi. and a cruising speed of 104 MPH. Intended to start forest fires and create panic, nobody at Brookings even noticed the raid. In 1962 Fujita presented his Samurai sword to the town and in 1985 sponsored three Brookings high school juniors on a trip to Japan.

1942 October 1   Piloted by Bell's chief test pilot Robert M. Stanley, the XP-59A made its first flight, powered by two General Electric Type I-A turbojets mounted to the lower surface of the wing/fuselage joint, marking the first flight of a U.S. turbojet-powered aircraft. The XP-59A had a wingspan of 45 ft. 6 in., a length of 38 ft. and a wing area of 385 sq. ft. with a gross weight of 13,700 lb. It had a maximum speed of 413 MPH at 30,000 ft. and a ceiling of 46,200 ft., roughly comparable to the Spitfire Mk.IX or the Fw 190. Production models of the P-59 Airacomet carried one 37-mm and three 0.50-in. guns in the nose. Only three XP-59As, 13 YP-59As, 20 P-59As and 30 P-59Bs were built before remaining orders were canceled on October 30, 1944, in favor of the superior P-80.

1942 October 9   The first U.S. bombing raid involving more than 100 aircraft took place when 108 aircraft—84 B-17s and 24 B-24s—took off from England to hit industrial targets in German-occupied France. It was also the first operational Eighth Air Force mission for the B-24 Liberator. Although only 79 aircraft were effective over the target area (two collided with each other en route but returned safely), only four aircraft were lost, and

two had to ditch on the way back. During the war, the Eighth Air Force suffered 450 such ditchings involving 4,370 crewmembers, of which 1,547 were rescued.

1942 October 19   A major air offensive began four days ahead of the planned Second Battle of Alamein in North Africa. For more than a year, Allied air power had been built up to a dominant position. There were now 96 operational Allied squadrons in the Middle East, with 1,500 front-line aircraft, 1,200 of which were in Egypt and Palestine. Facing them were 3,000 Luftwaffe and Regia Aeronautica aircraft throughout the Mediterranean, only 689 of which were in Africa. The main battle began at 9:40 P.M. October 23 when 456 British guns opened up simultaneously backed by another 500 guns to support a sustained artillery bombardment. By then the Allied air forces had dominant control of the skies.

1942 October 21   British Overseas Airways Corporation (BOAC) flew its first experimental passenger flight to the Soviet Union between Prestwick, Scotland and Ramenskoye, outside Moscow. The aircraft was a Liberator Mk.1 piloted by Capt. J. R. Percy and made the overnight flight in a nonstop time of 13 hr. 9 min. carrying two other crew members and eight passengers.

1942 November 3   The busiest day for the Allied air forces supporting ground armies fighting the Second Battle of Alamein saw the RAF fly 1,208 sorties to drop 396 tons of bombs on German and Italian positions. The Americans flew 125 sorties, of which 53 were bombing missions. The British lost 16 fighters with 11 damaged. In the period of October 23 to November 4 when the main battle was won by the Allies, the RAF flew 10,405 sorties and lost 77 aircraft, and the Americans flew 1,181 sorties and lost 20 aircraft. The Germans flew 1,550 sorties and lost 64 aircraft, and the Italians flew 1,570 sorties, losing approximately 20 aircraft.

1942 November 4   The first of eight French Latécoère 631s powered by six 1,650-HP Gnôme-Rhône P.18 engines made its first flight, six years after the French Air Ministry issued a specification for a trans-Atlantic flying boat capable of carrying 40 passengers a distance of 3,728 mi. With a wingspan of 188 ft. 5 in. and a length of 142 ft. 7 in., the 631 had a wing area of 3,760 sq. ft. and a loaded weight of 157,300 lb. Air France used the type briefly after the war before a crash on August 1, 1948, led to its withdrawal.

1942 November 7   Operation Torch began as Allied troops landed in North Africa. The command of air forces was divided between Eastern Air Command, controlled from eastern Algeria by the RAF's A.M. Sir William Welsh, and Western Air Command in Morocco, controlled by U.S. Maj. Gen. James H. Doolittle. This separation of command resulted in poor communication and was indicative of a general lack of dialogue between the Operation Torch command and the indigenous North African command structure. The Germans began massive consolidation in Tunisia, bringing in the relatively new Fw 190s and greater numbers of strike aircraft from Sicily.

1942 November 8   For the first time, U.S. pilots in U.S. aircraft found themselves fighting U.S. aircraft flown by pilots of the Vichy French air forces in Morocco and French North Africa. Douglas DB-7s of GB II/23 and Curtiss Hawk 75s of GC I/5 attacked U.S. landing positions on the coast, and by the end of the day the French had lost 30 aircraft. The Vichy government had been able to recover 84 Hawks when it took over control of German-occupied France in July and August 1940.

1942 November 12 The U.S. Ninth Air Force was formed out of the U.S. Army Middle East Air Force (USAMEAF), commanded by Gen. Lewis H. Brereton, in a plan to consolidate North African forces in preparation for the drive across the Mediterranean and on through Sicily, Crete and Italy. The first air raid on Italy by the Ninth Air Force took place December 4 when B-24s hit ships and naval installations at Naples.

1942 November 15 Designed as a night fighter and developed into the best of its kind in the Luftwaffe, the Heinkel He 219 Uhu (Owl) made its first flight more than two years after its conception as a private venture. With a top speed of 416 MPH, it was the only aircraft capable of combating the fast RAF Mosquito. The Owl was introduced in April 1943 for development of tactics, shortly after which during a 10-day period it shot down 20 RAF bombers. With a wingspan of 60 ft. 8 in. and a length of 51 ft., it had a ceiling of 41,668 ft. and a normal range of 960 mi.

1942 November 23 Dubbed "Flying Flapjack," the most radical conventionally engined aircraft ever built made its first flight when Chance Vought test pilot Boone T. Guyton took the V-173 into the air for the first time. In an effort to apply the ultimate in low aspect-ratio wing design propounded by Charles H. Zimmerman in 1933, the U.S. Navy V-173 had a blended wing-body of circular plan section, 26 ft. 8 in. long with a "span" of 23 ft. 4 in. and two 8-HP Continental engines driving 15 ft. 6 in. diameter propellers. Designated XF5U-1, the proposed fighter development was canceled in 1947.

1942 November 25 To relieve Field Marshal Friedrich von Paulus and the encircled Sixth Army at Stalingrad, the Luftwaffe began a massive airlift using the 11 groups of Ju 52/3m transports of Luftflotte 4 and, from November 30, Heinkel He 111s of VIII Fliegerkorps. By January 11, 1943, two days before the first of two airfields at Stalingrad was overrun by the Soviets, the aircraft of VIII Fliegerkorps flew 3,196 sorties carrying 1,817 tons of fuel, 1,347 tons of ammunition and 2,227 tons of food while Kampfgeschwader 55 (bomber group 55) contributed a further 3,594 tons. By January 31, 1943, when von Paulus surrendered the Sixth Army, no fewer than 490 transports of the transport unit (Transportverbände) were lost, of which 266 were Ju 52/3m transports.

1942 November The Bristol Aeroplane Co. completed refinements to the design of its "100-ton Bomber" project designed initially to meet Air Ministry Specification B.8/41 for a heavy bomber capable of carrying a load of 10,000 lb. at 300 MPH over a range of 4,000 mi. With eight Bristol Centaurus engines paired to drive four propeller shafts through the wing trailing edge, the bomber would have weighed 225,000 lb. and had a range of at least 5,000 mi. The needs generated by B.8/41 were, it was decided, adequately met by increasing Lancaster production. The Bristol project matured into the Type 167 Brabazon.

1942 December 6 Operating separately from a diversionary raid by 84 B-17s attacking Lille, France, a day attack by 93 aircraft of RAF Bomber Command struck the Philips radio and valve factory at Eindhoven, Holland; fourteen planes were lost. Flown at low level (no fewer than 23 of the 79 aircraft that returned had been damaged by bird strikes) in clear weather, the Venturas, Bostons and Mosquitos so damaged the factory that production was not back to normal for six months. The raid killed 148 Dutch and seven Germans.

1942 December 20 Six Mosquitos of No. 109 Squadron, RAF, were sent this night to bomb the power station at Lutterode, a small Dutch town near the German frontier, using "Oboe" for the first time. The first Oboe-dropped bombs were released by Sqdn. Ldr. H. E. Bufton and his navigator, Flt. Lt. E. L. Ifould. Oboe was a navigation system by which aircraft were guided by signals transmitted to and from two stations in England. A pulse was transmitted to the aircraft when the plane was over the target where bombs were to be dropped.

1942 December 23 The British government set up a committee under Lord Brabazon of Tara to examine the needs of a revitalized postwar civil aircraft program. The Brabazon Committee reported on February 9, 1943, recommending development of five types of aircraft: (1) a long-haul (trans-Atlantic) airliner capable of accepting turbo-prop engines, eventually developed as the Bristol Type 167 Brabazon; (2) short-haul piston-engined airliners, eventually developed as the Airspeed A.S.57 Ambassador and the Vickers-Armstrong V.S.630 Viscount; (3) medium-haul aircraft, represented by the Avro 689 Tudor; (4) a turbojet mail-carrying airliner, developed as the de Havilland 106 Comet; and (5) small feeder liners becoming the Miles Marathon and the de Havilland 104 Dove.

1942 December 26 The Kawasaki Ki-78 made its first flight at Gifu, powered by a 1,175-HP Daimler Benz DB 601A with the modification of a water-methanol injection boosting power momentarily to 1,550 HP. Originated in 1938 as the KEN III project to break the world speed record, the Ki-78 proved capable of only 434.9 MPH at 11,539 ft., far short of the 528 MPH it was designed to achieve. After the 32d flight, trials were suspended on January 11, 1944.

1942 December 27 Test pilot John Myers piloted the first Northrop N-9M flying wing, powered by two 275-HP Menasco air-cooled engines driving pusher propellers. With a wingspan of 60 ft. and a length of 17 ft. 10 in., it had a wing area of 490 sq. ft., a takeoff weight of 7,100 lb., a top speed of 257 MPH and a service ceiling of 21,500 ft. The fourth aircraft, dubbed N-9MB was later fitted with two horizontally opposed 300-HP Franklin engines. The first N-1M crashed in early 1943, but the others, performing spectacular turns and stunning acceleration climbs, flew for three years in a test program that paved the way for the XB-35.

1942 December The Messerschmitt 264 Amerika Bomber made its first flight powered by four 1,700-HP BMW 801 engines. Designed in 1940 to attack the United States should America enter the war and approved to the prototype stage in 1941, the aircraft had a wingspan of 141 ft. 1 in., a length of 63 ft. 7 in. and a maximum loaded weight of 123,460 lb. carrying a maximum bomb load of 4,460 lb. With a top speed of 339 MPH at 20,015 ft. and a service ceiling of 26,250 ft., the Me 264 had a range of 9,320 mi. at 207 MPH. Three prototypes were built, but subsequent events eliminated the bomber's role.

1942 During the year, the USAAF accepted 41,092 aircraft, including three very heavy bombers, 2,576 heavy bombers, 3,271 medium bombers, 4,055 light bombers, 9,102 fighters, 223 reconnaissance aircraft, 1,738 transports, 16,978 trainers and 3,146 communications aircraft.

1943 January 1 Luftwaffe strength reflected increased production quotas under Erhard Milch to gird the German air force for major campaigns to come. First-line strength was recorded as 1,135 long-range bombers, 270 ground attack aircraft, 1,245 single engine fighters, 495 twin engine fighters, 400 long-range re-connaissance, 275 tactical reconnaissance and 135 coastal aircraft for a total 3,955. There were 1,445 aircraft on the western front, 1,530 on the eastern front, and 855 in the Mediterranean and the Balkans; 125 aircraft were non-operational.

1943 January 3   The First and Second Bomb Wings, U.S. Eighth Air Force, sent 72 B-17s and 13 B-24s from England to bomb the St. Nazaire submarine pens in the first formation bombing conducted by the USAAF. Only 68 aircraft found the target, and of these seven were lost and 47 damaged. This was the heaviest attack yet on the submarine pens, and the formation faced fierce fighter opposition while causing major damage, although intelligence estimates exceeded the actual damage incurred. In all air operations, reconnaissance would consistently overestimate damage done to hardened concrete structures.

1943 January 9   The first Lockheed Model 049-46-10, later named Constellation, made its first flight from Lockheed Air Terminal with Boeing test pilot Eddie Allen (on loan) at the controls. In June 1939, TWA had requested a trans-continental airliner capable of cruising above 250 MPH, and Lockheed came up with the Model 49 capable of carrying 44 passengers and powered by either four Pratt & Whitney Double Wasps or four Wright Double Cyclones. When war broke out, the USAAF requisitioned the prototypes as transports, and production aircraft were designated C-69 before they were accepted for service in July.

1943 January 9   In a change of role from maritime patrol to transport aircraft, 18 Fw 200s of 1. and 3./KG 40 flew to Stalino in south Russia and were redesignated KGrzbV 200 under the command of Maj. Hans-Jürgen Williers to fly supplies into the besieged garrison at Stalingrad where Gen. von Paulus's Sixth Army was under attack. Quite soon Soviet troops overran the airfield, and the aircraft had to drop supplies by parachute, but during February, the Fw 200s were withdrawn to Berlin-Stakken and redesignated 8./KG 40.

1943 January 27   The U.S. Eighth Air Force carried out the first USAAF air raid on Germany when the First BW dispatched 91 B-17s and B-24s from England just after 11:00 A.M. to bomb the Wilhelmshaven naval base. Due to bad weather and poor navigation, only 55 aircraft reached the target, none of them B-24s. Overall, three were shot down (only one B-17), and 43 were damaged. Two B-17s attacked Emden as a target of opportunity.

1943 January 30   De Havilland Mosquito bombers of No. 105 Squadron, RAF, penetrated German airspace to bomb Berlin for the first time in daylight at precisely the time Reichsmarschall Hermann Göring was scheduled to address a Nazi rally. The three aircraft dispatched returned safely and were followed in the afternoon by three more Mosquitoes from No. 139 Squadron that bombed precisely at the time propaganda minister Dr. Josef Goebbels was due to speak. The aircraft flown by Sqdn. Ldr. D. F. Darling and Flt. Off. W. Wright was shot down, and the crew killed.

1943 January 30   A force of 148 RAF bombers carried out a night raid on Hamburg using the H2S navigation system for the first time. This involved a primitive form of on-board radar constructing a crude image of the ground below. It did not rely on transmitted signals and therefore freed the bomber from range limitations inherent with the Gee navigational aid. It was named H2S after the chemical formula for hydrogen sulphide, a colorless gas with the odor of rotten eggs, when Lord Cherwell remarked that it "was a stinking shame that it had not been developed

Fast, built primarily of wood, and adaptable to fighter, bomber and reconnaissance roles: the de Havilland Mosquito B.IV.

earlier." Although unsuccessful on this night, H2S would become a valuable target alignment aid.

1943 February 9   A major turning point in the Pacific war occurred when all Japanese resistance on Guadalcanal ended with the surrender of the last ground forces. In the long, hard battles for this island, the Japanese had lost 18 surface ships, six submarines, about 800 aircraft and approximately 2,000 crack airmen. On Guadalcanal, 2,400 Japanese had been killed for the loss of 1,600 Americans. With Guadalcanal as a staging point, the reoccupation of the Solomon Islands was next on the Allied agenda.

1943 February 11   The Ryan Aeronautical Corp. received a U.S. Navy contract for the XFR-1 powered by a hybrid combination of reciprocating engine for normal flight and a turbojet for takeoff and boosted power requirements. Nine manufacturers had responded to the request for a carrier escort aircraft, and the Ryan Model 28 was selected. The reasoning behind the hybrid was a need to combine the high performance of the turbojet with the limitation of short takeoff runs (off carrier decks) and the need for the long-mission duration of piston-engined planes.

1943 February   No. 41 Squadron, received the first Spitfire Mk.XII powered by the 1,735-HP Rolls Royce Griffon engine. The modified design incorporated a large spinner in place of a four-blade propeller and a larger tail; length increased to 31 ft. 10 in. with a wingspan of 32 ft. 7 in., a height of 11 ft. and a loaded weight of 7,280 lb. Substantially changing the outline of the Spitfire from its original shape, a Griffon-engined Mk.IV had

Developed during the first half of 1942, the Spitfire Mk.IX was built in greater numbers than any other variant except the Mk.V.

first flown on November 27, 1941. The Mk.XII, of which only 100 were built, had a maximum speed of 393 MPH at sea level, a climb time of 6.7 min. to 20,000 ft. and a range of 329 mi. No. 91 Squadron received its Mk.XIIs in April.

1943 March 3   A modified Piaggio P.108 bomber (serial no. MM 24318) took to the air at Albenga, Italy for the first time, fitted with a massive 102-mm 90/53 naval gun weighting 3,307 lb. with a muzzle velocity of 2,296 ft./sec. The proposal to fit such a massive weapon was made by Ettore Muti who had considerable influence in the Fascist Party and was able to get Ansaldo San Giogio to adapt the gun for installation. With 50 shells weighing 44 lb. each, gun and ammunition would gross 5,500 lb. The first in-flight firing trials took place on March 30, but the armistice was signed before the plane flew in combat.

1943 March 5   The fifth prototype Gloster F.9/40 (Meteor) (serial no. DG206) became the first of its type to fly when test pilot Michael Daunt took it into the air at RAF College Cranwell, England. Powered by two 2,000-HP de Havilland H.1 turbojet engines, the F.9/40 had a wingspan of 44 ft. 3 in., a length of 41 ft. 3 in. and a loaded weight of 13,300 lb. Designed for a W.2B engine built by Rover, powerplant troubles had kept the aircraft grounded since taxi trials using this engine began July 22, 1942. Maximum speed was 420 MPH at 30,000 ft. with a climb time of 17 min. to that altitude.

1943 March 5   In the first raid of what A.C.M. Sir Arthur Harris called his ''Battle of the Ruhr,'' 442 RAF bombers (of which 303 were four-engined heavies) set out for Essen in the Ruhr to hit at the industrial heartland of Germany. The campaign would be waged until spring 1944 and make optimum use of Oboe, Gee and H2S navigational systems and the greater number of heavy bombers becoming increasingly available. All these factors, coupled to effective use of the Pathfinder force, gave the RAF a modern strategic bombing arm for the first time in World War II.

1943 March 22   In one of the most novel methods for destroying enemy bombers, Luftwaffe fighter pilot Lt. Heinz Knocke of 5./JG 1 achieved the first success with an antibomber bomb system dropped from his Bf 109G. Equipped with an SC 250 (550-lb.) bomb specially fitted with a time fuse, the idea was to fly above U.S. bomber formations and drop the bomb into the box formation of aircraft below. It was unusual at best and unlikely as a long-term solution to solve the problem of increasingly heavy Allied air raids, and little operational use was made of the idea.

1943 March 24   In a plan conceived by A.V.M. Sir Harry Broadhurst, which proved one of the most effective uses of tactical battlefield air support in this war, the RAF Desert Air Force carried out major strikes against enemy rear positions defending the Tebaga Gap on the flank of the German line in Tunisia. Waves of ground attack aircraft struck artillery and antitank positions opening a path for the advancing British Eighth Army under Gen. Montgomery, which had been held down by fire.

1943 March 25   RAF Transport Command was formed under A.M. Sir Frederick W. Bowhill for the specific purpose of ferrying aircraft overseas, operating cargo movements along trunk routes and within operational theaters, supporting military operations by dropping supplies or paratroops and carrying politicians or senior military officers around the world. It started with just 70 aircraft and by the end of the war had grown into the largest RAF command with 12 groups and 58 squadrons with more than 500 operational aircraft.

1943 March   Consolidated Aircraft Corp. and Vultee Aircraft Inc. merged, forming the Consolidated Vultee Aircraft Corp., the latest in a series of take-overs that gathered up Thomas-Morse Aircraft Corp. in 1929, Hall-Aluminium Aircraft Corp. and the Stinson Aircraft Corp. in 1940. The first merger step had been taken in December 1941 when Vultee acquired 34% of Consolidated's common stock, and the two had close management links from January 1942.

1943 April 7   Masterminded by Adm. Yamamoto and known as Operation I-Go, the Japanese launched an all-out campaign to destroy air power in the Solomon Islands with 110 A6M Zero fighters and 67 D3A carrier bombers attacking a convoy off the east coast of Guadalcanal, shipping at Koli Point and a task force at Tulagi. In the ensuing air battles, P-38s, P-39s and Wildcat fighters claimed 39 Japanese aircraft shot down for the loss of seven Allied fighters. On April 11, the Japanese again attacked, this time with 150 aircraft; I-Go concluded with an attack on Port Moresby by 200 aircraft the following day and achieved modest success.

1943 April 8   The first P-47B Thunderbolts to carry out an offensive sweep went to war with 23 aircraft of the Fourth, Fifty-sixth and Seventy-eighth Fighter Groups, US Eighth Air Force, carried out a patrol of northeast occupied Europe along the Pas de Calais. Earlier, on March 10, 14 P-47s and 12 Spitfires had been sent on an offensive patrol off Walcheren Island, but radio interference at high engine power levels prevented intership communication. The first P-47 bomber escort mission was flown on May 4. The P-47 was well liked, but range limitations were a serious flaw to bomber escort requirements. During the war, 5,222 P-47s would be lost in action, of which 1,723 were due to non-combat causes.

1943 April 17   In the heaviest opposition experienced to date, the First Bomber Wing, U.S. Eighth Air Force, lost 16 B-17s out of 115 that were sent to bomb aviation plants at Bremen, Germany during the early afternoon. Only 107 had been effective at the target, and 39 aircraft were damaged, 161 crewmembers being either killed or missing in action. These losses halted optimism that fighter protection was not an essential prerequisite for large bomber formations, and the commanding general, Ira C. Eaker, requested 20 fighter groups to neutralize German fighter opposition.

1943 April 18   Reacting to intelligence information that the commander of the Imperial Japanese Navy, Adm. Isoroku Yamamoto, would arrive at Ballale, 16 U.S. Thirteenth Air Force P-38 Lightnings intercepted his formation of two bombers and six escorting Zero fighters at 9:40 A.M., 2 hr. 15 min. after take-off. The P-38s had flown a circuitous path from Guadalcanal up the Bougainville coast to intercept Adm. Yamamoto off Kahili. A four-plane attack section went in to down the Mitsubishi G4M bombers, and Capt. Thomas G. Lanphier and 1st Lt. Rex T. Barber shot down the aircraft carrying the Japanese commander.

1943 April 18   The Ninth Air Force was credited with shooting down 52 out of a formation of more than 100 German Ju-52 transport aircraft caught with escorts over the Cape Bon, Tunisia area ferrying supplies between Italy and Tunisia. Under Operation Flax, Allied air units were hounding the air route in attempts to starve out remaining Axis resistance in North Africa. In 18 days beginning April 5, 432 German transport aircraft were destroyed for the loss of 35 Allied fighters. All fighting in North Africa ceased when the Axis powers there surrendered May 13, and 250,000 men were taken prisoner.

1943 April   One of the best fighters to enter service with the Imperial Japanese Army Air Force toward the end of World War II, the Nakajima Ki-84 Hayate made its first flight. It entered service in March 1944 and revealed superiority in handling and performance over many other Japanese and Allied fighters. With a top speed of 392 MPH at 20,080 ft., 427 MPH under "War Emergency Power," it had a climb time of 5 min. to 16,405 ft. and an action radius of 497 mi. incorporating 1.5 hr. combat at maximum range. In just 17 mon., 3,382 Ki-84s were built, but most suffered from inferior workmanship.

1943 May 7   The Sikorsky XR-4 helicopter conducted landing trials aboard the merchant tanker *Bunker Hill* in a demonstration conducted by the Maritime Commission on Long Island Sound. The pilot, Col. R. F. Gregory, USAAF, made 15 flights. As a result of these successful trials, a joint venture was begun with representatives of the British air forces, the British Admiralty and U.S. naval services as well as NACA to expedite evaluation of the helicopter in an antisubmarine role, the first formal military function declared for the helicopter.

1943 May 16   In an attempt to paralyze essential industrial work in the German Ruhr, 19 Lancasters of the specially formed No. 617 Squadron, RAF, took off for a night raid on the Möhne, the Eder and the Sorpe dams vital for electricity. Formed on March 21, 1943, the "Dam Busters" were led by Wg. Comdr. Guy Gibson. Only 11 aircraft reached the targets, five breached the Möhne Dam, three breached the Eder, and the Sorpe and Schwelme dams were hit but not breached. All Lancasters carried special bouncing bombs designed by Barnes Wallis. Approximately 1,294 people were drowned on the ground, including 493 Ukrainian slave workers, and 53 crewmembers were killed. German war munition production was hardly affected by the dam raid.

1943 May 17   During a conference chaired by Brig. Gen. Franklin O. Carroll, chief of the USAAF Engineering Division, Lockheed was invited to design and build a prototype turbojet fighter des-

ignated XP-80 for which a formal letter contract was issued June 24 for Project MX-409. It had been preceded by the late 1942 L-133 design, which so impressed the USAAF that it transferred to Lockheed Bell's XP-59B design studies and specifications and drawings for the Halford H.1B turbojet. The XP-80 mock-up was inspected July 20–22, and the prototype (serial no. 44-83020) was officially accepted November 16.

1943 May 21   The Boeing B-17G, the last production model of the type, made its first flight; the first production aircraft was completed September 7. The aircraft had a new chin turret housing twin 0.50-in. guns, staggered waist gun positions giving each gunner more room and numerous minor changes. Maximum bomb load was increased to 9,600 lb., and gross weight was increased to 65,500 lb. Cruising speed was 150 MPH at 5,000 ft. with a climb time of 37 min. to 20,000 ft. It was built in greater numbers than any other version, 8,670 being assembled, of which 4,750 were lost in combat, a higher percentage than for any other B-17 model.

1943 May 23   Increasingly preoccupied with mounting reprisal bombing raids on Britain and Allied shipping in the Atlantic, rather than attacking the increasingly large armadas of aircraft threatening Germany, Adolf Hitler demanded development of a new long-range bomber at an aircraft manufacturers conference at Obersalzburg. Heinkel received a contract to develop the He 277, a version of the He 177 with four engines, each mounted separately. Only two were built, the first flying late in 1943 and the second in February 1944. All long-range bomber projects were finally canceled on July 3, 1944, in favor of increased fighter production.

1943 May 27   The last daylight raid carried out over Germany by RAF Bomber Command was mounted when 14 Mosquitoes were sent from No. 105 and 139 squadrons to attack glassworks and a Zeiss optical instruments factory at Jena, Germany. Two aircraft were lost on the way out, 11 bombed the targets with

The first of 8,670 B-17G bombers took to the air for the first time on May 21, 1943.

An Italian bomber in North Africa, brought down by the RAF Desert Air Force during the demise of Axis power in the region in 1943.

great accuracy, and two more were lost when they crashed in England. The round-trip had been across 500 mi. of enemy-occupied Europe.

1943 June 10   BOAC began a regularly scheduled service between RAF Lyneham, Wiltshire, and Moscow. Six proving flights had been conducted between January 4 and March 4, and the service used Consolidated Liberator transport variants of the four-engined bomber. The route went via North Africa, Cairo, Habbaniyeh, Pahlevr (Iran) and Astrakhan. The first aircraft to make the scheduled flight was G-AGHG (military serial no. AM262), which was returned to the RAF in September 1944.

1943 June 11   The Italian-held island of Pantelleria, situated in the Mediterranean between Sicily and Tunisia, surrendered after a month of intensive bombing. Since May 8, the Northwest African Tactical Air Force under A.M. Sir Arthur Conningham, combining the RAF's No. 205 Group, the B-17s of the U.S. Twelveth Air Force and the B-24s of the U.S. Ninth Air Force, dropped 6,800 tons of bombs in 5,285 sorties, of which 1,650 tons was dropped June 10. Thoroughly demoralized, the Italian forces surrendered as the seaborne invasion took place.

1943 June 11   During the night, Maj. Werner Streib of I/NJG 1, operating from Venlo in the Netherlands, encountered and shot down five RAF Lancaster bombers while flying one of the newly operational Heinkel He 219 Uhu night fighters. Surprisingly, the type was ordered out of production in favor of the Ju 388J and the Focke-Wulf Ta 154, neither of which appeared during the war. An exceptional aircraft, the He 219 was the first operational German aircraft to have a tricycle landing gear, the first to incorporate an ejection seat and the first to place the armament behind the pilot, thus preventing him from being temporarily blinded when the guns fired at night.

1943 June 15   Developed since late fall 1940 to make use of the impending availability of BMW and Junkers gas-turbine engines, the Arado 234 Blitz reconnaissance bomber made its first flight at Rheine, north of Münster, with Flugkapitän Selle at the controls. The Ar 234 became the first operational turbojet bomber when it joined (special air attack unit) Sonderkommando Götz in September 1944. Powered by two 1,980-lb. thrust Jumo 004B turbojets, it had a maximum speed of 461 MPH at 19,685 ft., a maximum range of 967 mi. with a 1,100-lb. bomb load and a maximum bomb load of 3,300 lb. The Ar 234 had a wingspan of

46 ft. 3 in., a length of 41 ft. 5 in. and a maximum weight of 21,715 lb.

1943 June 16   The last major Japanese air raid on Guadalcanal took place when a force of 120 aircraft converged on Allied shipping. They were met by more than 100 Allied fighters in what turned out to be the largest single Allied air victory of the Solomon Islands campaign. The Japanese lost 79 aircraft shot down in combat and 17 more to antiaircraft fire. Only six Allied fighters were lost, but the Japanese damaged three ships and did considerable damage on Guadalcanal.

1943 June 20   The first RAF shuttle raid took place during the night when 60 Lancasters were sent from England to bomb the Zeppelin works at Friedrichshafen before flying on to land in North Africa. German night fighters waiting for the bombers were confused when they failed to return, and no Lancasters were lost. This was also the first use of the technique where a single lead aircraft controlled the raid by marking the target for following aircraft. It had been pioneered by No. 5 Group, and Gp. Capt. L. C. Slee was master bomber this night, although he had to hand over to his deputy aircraft, commanded by Wg. Comdr. G. L. Gomm, when his Lancaster developed engine trouble.

1943 June 22   The first large daylight bombing raid conducted by the U.S. Eighth Air Force took place when 235 B-17s were sent to a synthetic rubber plant at Hüls in the Ruhr and 42 B-17s with 136 escorting P-47s were sent to Antwerp. Only 183 B-17s got to Hüls, but 39 B-17s bombed Antwerp. Eleven B-17s sent to Hüls were YP-40 gunship conversions of the B-17F. These carried the B-17G chin turret, an extra dorsal turret and twin waist guns each side. Some YB-40s had up to 30 machine guns and cannon. The first YB-40 bomber escort mission had been flown May 29 as a stop-gap measure until long-range escort fighters arrived. Only 20 B-17Fs were converted as gunships.

1943 June 24   The Messerschmitt 163B V1 prototype rocket fighter made its first flight with the definitive 3,750-lb. thrust Walter R II-211 (HWK 109-509) engine. The Me 163B carried 3,717 lb. of "T-stoff" (80% concentrated hydrogen peroxide) and 1,032 lb. of "C-Stoff" (57% methyl alcohol, 30% hydrazine hydrate, 13% water), a total hypergolic propellant load of 4,749 lb. within a maximum loaded weight of 9,500 lb. The Me 163B had a wingspan of 30 ft. 7 in., a length of 19 ft. 2 in. and a wing area of 199.132 sq. ft. It had a top speed of 596 MPH between 10,000 ft. and 30,000 ft.

1943 June 25   To soften up targets for Operation Husky, the invasion of Sicily, planned for 2:45 A.M. July 10, the heaviest air assault of the campaign began when 130 B-17s of the Northwest African Air Force dropped 300 tons of bombs on Messina. The Luftwaffe had about 290 aircraft in Sicily, of which 143 were ready for combat, together with 63 serviceable Italian aircraft, a low number due to several weeks of intensive aerial bombardment by the Allies.

1943 June 25   Luftwaffe bomber pilot Oberstlt. Hajo Herrmann set up JG 300 under Oberstlt. Kurt Kettner to introduce a new form of night air defense using searchlights and flares to illuminate raiders for attack from free-ranging night fighters operating without radar and so outside the increasingly effective jamming techniques employed by the Allied air forces. Known as "Wilde Sau" (Wild Boar), the technique worked well, and two other Jagdgeschwader were formed: JG 301 under Maj. Helmut Weinreich and JG 302 under Maj. Manfred Massinger, all three formed into Jagddivisionen 30.

1943 June 25 Two prototypes of one of the most remarkable aircraft of its day, the privately proposed Douglas XB-42 Mixmaster, were ordered. Powered by two 1,325-HP Allison V-1710-125 engines mounted in tandem behind the cockpit and driving two contra-rotating pusher propellers in the tail, it first flew on May 6, 1944, and had a top speed of 488 MPH at 14,000 ft., a range of 2,100 mi. and capacity to carry an 8,000-lb. bomb load. Designed by E. F. Burton and Carlos C. Wood to have an exceptionally streamlined surface, the XB-42 was never put into production but was used as the basis for the first U.S. jet bomber, the XB-43, ordered on March 31, 1944.

1943 June 30 The USAAF had on strength a total of 49,018 aircraft comprising two very heavy bombers, 4,421 heavy bombers, 4,242 medium bombers, 1,689 light bombers, 8,010 fighters, 486 reconnaissance aircraft, 4,268 transports, 22,849 trainers and 3,051 communications aircraft.

1943 July 1 The U.S. Navy had 16,691 aircraft on hand, of which 8,696 were for combat, 878 for transport and utility, 7,021 for training and 96 for miscellaneous duty. There were a total of 148,024 U.S. Navy aviation personnel on active duty, including 41,805 officers (20,847 pilots) and 106,219 enlisted men (774 pilots). The Marine Corps had a total 57,934 aviation personnel on active duty comprising 7,317 officers (4,898 pilots) and 50,617 enlisted men (132 pilots).

1943 July 5 In the last major aerial battle between Luftwaffe and Soviet air forces, 800 German bombers, ground attack and antitank aircraft backed up a massive German attack at Kursk in Operation Zitadels. The Germans had 2,100 operational aircraft against more than 5,000 available to the Russians. The Soviets sent 132 ground attack aircraft protected by 285 fighters of the Red Seventeenth Air Army under Gen. Sudetz to raid VIII Fliegerkorps airfields. During the day, the Soviets lost 176 aircraft, the Germans 260. By July 8, the Germans had lost 854 aircraft, the Russians 566, and in August the Luftwaffe had only 1,775 aircraft in the east, having lost 2,183 in three months. They faced 8,000 Soviet aircraft.

1943 July 5 Hptm. Hans Ulrich Rudel demonstrated the effectiveness of the new Junkers Ju 87G-0 when single-handedly he destroyed 12 Russian T-34 tanks. Rudel had been conducting trials with the new tank-buster version of the infamous Stuka dive-bomber, equipped with a single 37-mm Flak 18 cannon under each wing. Tungsten ammunition was used, which exploded only after penetrating the tank's armor. Rudel was asked to form a special Panzerstaffel for antitank duties and designated 10.(Pz)/St.G 2. Operationally, II Gruppe with its Fw 190s was tasked with flying shotgun for the Ju-87Gs.

1943 July 9 The British First Airlanding Brigade comprising 2,075 men in 137 Airspeed Horsa and Waco Hadrian gliders towed by Albemarles and Halifaxes was flown during the night to an assault on the Sicilian Ponte Grande Bridge near Syracuse along with 100 C-47s carrying U.S. troops at the start of Operation Husky. With a dark night and poor navigation, 69 gliders went down in the sea with loss of life, and 59 missed their planned target, some crashing up to 25 mi. away. Similar navigation errors by 226 C-47s of the U.S. Fifty-second Troop Carrier Wing caused paratroops to be dropped all over the countryside. To their credit, the troops achieved almost all of the planned objectives.

1943 July 18 While on patrol off the coast of Florida, the U.S. Navy airship K-74 attacked a surfaced German U-Boat, the U-134, and the airship was shot down during the exchange of fire.

On the day that Italy's capital was bombed from Tunisia for the first time, B-26s attacked Ciampino airfield, Rome.

This was the one and only time during World War II an airship was brought down by a submarine. U-134 had been damaged by the exchange and limped across the Atlantic to the Bay of Biscay, surviving two attacks in the process only to be sunk by bombers when she reached her destination.

1943 July 19 The Allies bombed Rome for the first time from Tunisia and the newly acquired base on the Mediterranean island of Pantelleria. During the morning, 158 B-17s of the Northwest African Air Force and 112 B-24s of the U.S. Ninth Air Force in Libya bombed the city and its environs, attacking rail yards, killing 166 people and injuring 1,659. In the afternoon, Ciampino airfield was attacked, and five groups of B-25s and B-26s bombed airfields at Littorio and Centocelle. Farther south, operations in Sicily had almost decimated the Luftwaffe and units of the Regia Aeronautica. Only 25 Axis aircraft remained in flying condition; 1,100 had been either shot down or destroyed on the ground.

1943 July 24 Drawing upon the combined resources of a by-now much larger RAF Bomber Command than when he became commander-in-chief in February 1942, A.C.M. Sir Arthur Harris sent 791 bombers to raid Hamburg in the first of a series of four devastating attacks in 10 days on this north German port. The series of raids on Hamburg were called Operation Gomorrah, and a similar plan for raids centered on Essen were known as Operation Sodom. Some 2,284 tons of bombs were dropped in a 50-min. period by the 728 aircraft that reached the target, killing 1,500 people. Next day, during early evening, 100 B-17s of the First Bomber Wing, U.S. Eighth Air Force, dropped 196 tons of bombs on the city, followed by a further 126 tons by 54 B-17s July 26.

1943 July 27 The most devastating raid in the annals of strategic bombing thus far was prosecuted by 729 RAF bombers dropping 2,326 tons of bombs in the second of six raids on Hamburg between July 24 and the night of August 3. During this night, in very unusual weather conditions, a violent firestorm erupted, killing an estimated 40,000 people, destroying 16,000 multi-story apartment blocks and causing 1.2 million people to flee the city after the 3-hr. firestorm. The RAF returned again two nights later with 707 bombers dropping 2,318 tons and again on the night of August 2 during a violent thunderstorm. In the six raids, the RAF dropped more than 9,000 tons of bombs and the U.S. Eighth Air Force 250 tons, killing an estimated 60,000 people, equal to the number of British civilians killed in the 5 yr. 8 mon. of war.

1943 July 28   The first U.S. Eighth Air Force aircraft lost to air-to-air rockets fired from a German fighter was shot down when a B-17 of the 385th Bomb Group received a direct hit from a 21-lb. Wfr.Gr.42 spr projectile. Carried in special launch tubes under the wings of certain Fw 190 and Me 110 fighters, the rockets could be fired outside the range of a bomber's defensive armament, time-fused to detonate at 3,600 ft. Although difficult to line up on a bomber, a direct hit was invariably fatal.

1943 July 29   Although it made short flights three days earlier, the first formal flight of the first Bell helicopter, the Model 30, took place at Gardenville, near Buffalo, New York. Designed and developed by Arthur M. Young, it had a 32-ft. rotor powered by a 160-HP Franklin air-cooled engine. Young had been working on helicopter designs for 15 yr. and joined Larry Bell on November 21, 1941. In June 1942, a small team set up shop at Gardenville from which the Model 30 emerged on a cold winter morning 6 mon. later.

1943 August 1   Drawn from the U.S. Ninth Air Force and elements of the Eighth Air Force in Britain, 177 B-24s set out from Benghazi, Libya to bomb the vital oil refineries at Ploesti, Romania on a 1,550-mi. round-trip mission; all but 13 bombed the target. Two newly formed Messerschmitt units, I/JG 3 and IV/JG 27 with Bf 109Gs, lay unsuspectingly in the path of the approaching bombers, which were severely mauled by these and flak around the target. Flying most of the way at rooftop height, sometimes as low as 40 ft., 54 B-24s (30.5%) failed to return, and 532 crewmembers were lost. Very little damage was done to the refineries, despite wartime propaganda to the contrary.

1943 August 5   The Women Air Force Service Pilot (WASP) organization was formed out of several separate organizations previously responsible for ferrying aircraft over the North Atlantic. Many of these women pilots were only 18 years old with less than 200 hr. of flying time. Before the WASPS were disbanded on December 20, 1944, they had flown 60 million mi., delivered 12,650 aircraft of 77 different types and flown 50% of all fighters delivered to England. Of the 1,830 WASPs, 38 lost their lives. Whereas male ferry pilots were offered flying careers after the war, the women were dismissed.

1943 August 17   The U.S. Eighth Air Force sent 146 B-17s to raid the Messerschmitt factory at Regensburg, 230 B-17s to bomb the ball-bearing complex at Schweinfurt and 240 P-47s on bomber penetration escort, a total of 616 aircraft. Only 127 aircraft got through to Regensburg and 188 to Schweinfurt, but 724 tons of bombs were dropped in all, the Fourth Bomber Wing Regensburg bombers flying on to North Africa but losing 24 (16.4%) with 51 damaged. The First Bomber Wing B-17s were also badly mauled, with 36 (15.6%) lost and 121 damaged. Only three fighters were lost. These raids demonstrated the heavy losses the USAAF was prepared to take while building up toward major strategic offensives.

1943 August 17   Responding to intelligence reports that the Germans were developing rocket-powered aircraft and ballistic missiles on the Baltic island of Peenemünde, 560 RAF bombers dropped 2,000 tons of bombs on the secret research facility. About 180 Germans and 500 to 600 foreign workers were killed. As a result, the V-2 ballistic rocket program moved to Blizna, Poland for flight tests; but damage was not as severe as estimated by the RAF. Drawings offices and engineering development continued

In July 1943, the Bell Model 30—first in a long line of Bell helicopters—made its first flight at Gardenville, New York.

at Peenemünde, separate sections of which were run by the Luftwaffe for the Fi-103 flying bomb (V-1) and antiaircraft rocket programs and by the German army for the A-4 (V-2) ballistic missile.

1943 August 18   Designed to a USAAF specification arising from successful trials with the Vought-Sikorsky R-4 helicopter, the Model 327 (R-5) made its first flight at Bridgeport, Conn. Powered by a 450-HP Pratt & Whitney R-985-AN-5 engine driving a 48-ft. rotor, it had tandem seating for two, a maximum speed of 106 MPH, a service ceiling of 14,400 ft. and a range of 360 mi. Helicopters of this type were adopted by the USAAF as the H-5 and by the U.S. Navy as the HO2S. They were used extensively by rescue services and in Korea during the mid-1950s. From this design, the company developed the successful commercial S-51 derivative.

1943 August 25   The first operational use of stand-off glide bombs took place when 12 Dornier Do 217E-5s of II/KG 100 based at Cognac attacked Allied destroyers in the Bay of Biscay with Henschel Hs 293A-1 missiles. The winged missile had a span of 10 ft. 3 in., a length of 11 ft. 9 in. and a weight of 2,304 lb. containing a 649-lb. explosive charge. Powered by a rocket motor slung beneath the main body of the missile, the Hs 293 was tracked visually to the target and controlled by radio signals sent from the Dornier, continuous corrections being applied by an operator using a small control stick in the launch aircraft. No hits were scored in this attack, but two days later, the corvette HMS *Egret* was sunk with a missile.

1943 August 30   McDonnell was issued a contract for the first jet ordered for shipboard operations. It was the first in a long line of jet fighters for this relatively new company. Designed for offensive patrols at 15,000 ft., the FH-1 Phantom originated as two XFD-1 prototypes, each powered by two 1,600-lb. Westinghouse WE-19XB-2B turbojets. The company had been given a letter of intent on January 7, and mock-ups had been completed and inspected by June 3, although construction did not begin before January 25, 1944.

1943 August 31   The U.S. Ninth Air Force based in Cyrenaica, North Africa, was ordered to prepare for the invasion of the continent. Headquarters were at Sunninghill Park near Ascot, Berkshire. The Ninth was redesignated Tactical Air Force and would perform that role, softening up beaches, cutting communications links and following through with support of the ground forces. It was the beginning of a gradual converging of forces toward the common goal of liberating occupied Europe.

The Do 217, the definitive Dornier Do 17 development, first came into operation with Hitler's Luftwaffe in 1940.

1943 August 31 The U.S. Navy's Grumman F6F Hellcat went to war for the first time when the F6F-3s of navy squadrons VF-9 (USS *Essex*), VF-5 (USS *Yorktown*), and VF-22 (USS *Independence*), Task Force 15, hit Japanese-occupied Marcus Island. Later this day Lt. Richard Loesch scored the Hellcat's first aerial combat victory. Grumman built a total 12,275 Hellcats between June 1942 and November 1945. Operated in combat for just under 2 yr., primarily in the Pacific, it is credited with having destroyed 5,156 enemy planes (4,947 by carrier-based units and 209 by land-based units), which is 55% of all enemy aircraft shot down by U.S. Navy and U.S. Marine Corps units. Moreover, only 270 Hellcats were lost in combat during World War II, an outstanding kill ratio of 19.1:1.

1943 August Reacting to the significant increase in frequency and intensity of Allied bombing raids into Germany, the Luftwaffe took steps to increase its fighter defense forces and transferred during the month 12 fighter Gruppen (groups) to the defense of the Reich. These included I and II/ZG 1 and III/ZG 26, all from southern Italy. On July 24, Allied bombers began using strips of aluminum foil dropped in flight to confuse German early-warning radar equipment. Visual attack procedures known as Tame Boar (Zahme Sau) were introduced on August 17 whereby two-seat Bf 110s got in among the bomber streams and selected targets at will from relatively close range. The concept was pioneered by Col. von Lossberg.

1943 August The prototype six-engine Junkers Ju 390 long-range bomber, developed to a requirement for bombing the United States, made its first flight. Powered by the 1,700-HP BMW 801D engine, it had a wingspan of 165 ft. 1 in., a length of 112 ft. 2 in. and a loaded weight of 146,477 lb., calculated to have a maximum speed of 314 MPH at 19,686 ft. and a maximum range of 6,027 mi. It was designed to have a 3,960-lb. bomb load and defensive armament in nose and tail positions. Delivered for trials in January 1944, it once crossed the Atlantic and got to within 12 mi. of New York City before returning safely to Germany, its capacity to cross the Atlantic having been demonstrated.

1943 September 9 The Ruhrstahl/Kramer X-1 (Fritz X) radio-controlled free-fall bomb was successfully used to sink the 50,952-ton Italian flagship *Roma*, which came under attack from 12 Dornier 217K-2s of III/KG 100. The attack came a day after Gen. Eisenhower accepted the complete surrender of all Italian forces. The X-1 was 4 ft. 5 in. across its tail fins, with a length of 10 ft. 8 in. and a body diameter of 1 ft. 10 in. It was used September 13 to hit and sink the clearly marked Red Cross hospital ship *Newfoundland* and on September 16 to badly damage the British warship HMS *Respite*.

1943 September 12 In one of the most spectacular commando operations of the Mediterranean war, nine DFS 230C-1 gliders fitted with special nose-mounted braking rockets accompanied by a Fieseler Fi 156 Storch high-wing monoplane landed on a plateau alongside the Campo Imperatore Hotel at the peak of the Gran Sasso Massif. The mission of Sturm Abteilung Skorzeny (attack unit Skorzeny) led by SS-Hauptsturmführer Otto Skorzeny was to rescue the imprisoned Italian dictator, Benito Mussolini, who had been held captive since July 25. He was flown out in the Fi 156 piloted by Maj. Gerlach and delivered to Hitler via Rome.

1943 September 12 The first operational use of the British 12,000-lb. "Tallboy" bomb took place when eight RAF Lancasters of No. 617 Squadron carried out a postponed raid on the Dortmund-Ems canal. Two aircraft put their bombs on the target without the desired result, and five Lancasters were lost. After the heavy losses in the dam-busting raid on the night of May 16/17, RAF Bomber Command had ceased low-level attacks, and No. 617 Squadron was tasked for high-altitude precision bombing.

1943 September 14 The Imperial Japanese Navy issued a specification for a four-engine bomber to replace the twin-engine Mitsubishi G4M. Failure to come up with a twin-engine replacement sooner had pushed the navy to ask manufacturers to incorporate four engines. It was expected to have a maximum speed of 368

MPH, reach 26,245 ft. in 20 min., carry a bomb load of 8,816 lb. for 2,300 mi. and have all-round defensive armament. Lessons of 1942 proved the worth of a long-range land-based attack bomber, and the design evolved into the Nakajima G8N Renzan.

1943 September 20   Geoffrey de Havilland, son of the company's founder and now chief test pilot, flew the first D.H.100 Vampire into the air at Hatfield, England. Powered by a 2,700-lb.-thrust de Havilland H.1 turbojet engine, the prototype (serial no. LZ548/G) was succeeded by production models with a twin-tail boom arrangement, a wingspan of 40 ft., a length of 30 ft. 9 in. and an all-up weight of 10,480 lb. The Vampire entered service with No. 247 Squadron, RAF, in April 1946, and its design was the ancestral configuration for derivatives and developments culminating in the Sea Vixen that remained in service with the Fleet Air Arm until 1974.

1943 October 1   The Junkers Ju 352 Herkules of mixed wood and steel construction made its first flight. The aircraft evolved from the Ju 252 transport and was designed to restrict demand on essential raw materials, especially light metal alloys. There were also changes in tail surface design, and the Ju 352 incorporated a Trapoklappe ramp, which hydraulically raised the rear fuselage for loading. Powered by three 1,000-HP Bramo 323R-2 air-cooled radials, the Ju 352 looked like an enlarged Ju 52. Its only real application was in dropping agents behind enemy lines.

1943 October 5   U.S. Navy Task Force 14 commanded by Rear Adm. A. E. Montgomery began a two-day strike on Wake Island during which many new operational tactics and procedures were carried out. The task force had six new aircraft carriers, seven cruisers and 24 destroyers and employed techniques that executed battle operations with one group of six carriers, two groups of three carriers or three groups of two carriers. Handling tactics for multi-carrier task forces had been devised by Rear Adm. F. C. Sherman and his staff in the South Pacific war zone.

1943 October 5   The Luftwaffe formed new ground attack wings consolidating dive-bomber, ground support and fast attack bomber units under a new General der Schlachtflieger (slaughter fliers), Oberst. Hubertus Hitschold. The Junkers Ju 87D was to be replaced by the Fw 190F and G variants, but new aircraft were to be sought for ground attack. Much had been learned on the Eastern Front about air-land battles, and the Luftwaffe reacted to needs generated by demands made on ground forces in Russia. On October 7, night ground attack units were formed, some using the aging Arado Ar 66 biplane.

1943 October 8   In what amounted to the most far-sighted project of its day, the British controller of research and development at the Ministry of Aircraft Production, A.M. Sir Ralph Sorley, authorized Miles Aircraft to proceed with development of a 1,000-MPH research aircraft under specification E.24/43. Classified top secret, Miles was to work with the Royal Aircraft Establishment, Farnborough, and the National Physical Laboratory on what would eventually be designated the M.52.

1943 October 13   A plan put forward by Brig. Gen. Kenneth B. Wolfe to use B-29s in raids against Japan from permanent bases near Calcutta, India using forward staging bases in China was approved by Gen. H. H. Arnold. A decision had also been recently made to use the B-29 in the war against Japan exclusively and not to deploy it into the European theater. Assigned to introduce the new bomber, the Fifty-eighth Very Heavy Bombardment Wing had been working up to receive the aircraft and

four Bomb Groups (40, 444, 462 and 468) would move to India in the spring of 1944.

1943 October 14   In a second major bombing raid on the German ball-bearing works at Schweinfurt, the U.S. Eighth Air Force suffered heavy losses but caused considerable damage that dispersed production. Of 351 B-17s and B-24s that took off from bases in England, only 320 could form up in the prevailing bad weather, 31 of the 60 B-24s that took off being forced to land again. Of the 320 dispatched, only 229 made it to the target and dropped almost 500 tons of bombs. Twenty-eight bombers were shot down on the way; 32 failed to make it back, for a total 60 (18.75%) aircraft lost. A further 7 were written off, and 13 were in various states of damage. In all, 599 airmen were killed or missing with 40 wounded.

1943 October 15   Developed as a transport but introduced into the Luftwaffe as a replacement for the Focke-Wulf Fw 200 anti-shipping aircraft, the Junkers Ju 290 became operational with 1./Fern-Aufklärungsgruppe 5 at Mont de Marsen. Formed on July 1 and consolidated during November by 2. Staffel, this unit worked its Ju 290s far into the North Atlantic acting as the eyes for German U-boats and the Fw 200 Kondor maritime reconnaissance bombers of KG 40. The Ju 290 had a range of 3,820 mi. and was powered by four 1,700-HP BMW 801D engines.

1943 October 16   The U.S. Navy accepted its first helicopter, the Sikorsky YR-4B (HNS), at Bridgeport, Conn. following a 60-min. flight by Lt. Comdr. F. A. Erickson of the U.S. Coast Guard. The YR-4B could carry a crew of two and one stretcher case suspended beneath the main body of the helicopter. The first emergency use was on January 3, 1944, when 40 units of blood plasma were flown from New York City, N.Y. to Sandy Hook for the relief of survivors from an explosion aboard the destroyer USS *Turner*. The flight took place amid snow and sleet that had grounded fixed-wing aircraft.

1943 October 26   The Dornier Do 335 Pfeil made its first flight a year after the requirement for a single-seat unarmed intruder carrying a 1,100-lb. bomb load at 495 MPH had been issued.

Orville Wright (center) and Col. Frank Gregory with the Sikorsky XR-4 prototype tested throughout 1943.

Truly unique and radical in its design, the Do 335 incorporated two 1,900-HP Daimler Benz DB 603 12-cylinder, inverted-V engines mounted fore and aft of the cockpit and driving separate tail- (pusher) and nose- (tractor) mounted propellers. With a wingspan of 45 ft. 3 in. and a length of 45 ft. 5 in., the Do 335 had a top speed of 474 MPH at 21,325 ft. and a cruising speed of 426 MPH at 23,610 ft.

1943 October 31 The first U.S. Navy air combat kill achieved with the aid of on-board air-interception (AI) radar was recorded when Lt. H. D. O'Neil of Squadron VF(N)-75 out of Munda, New Georgia successfully located and shot down a Japanese Mitsubishi G4M Betty attack bomber. Flying a Vought F4U-2 Corsair, O'Neil was vectored to the area of the target by Maj. T. E. Hicks and Tech. Sgt. Gleason from Marine Squadron VMF(N)-531. The action took place over the ocean off Vella Lavella. Twelve Corsairs had been modified to carry AI radar.

1943 November 2 Encouraged by favorable reports from General der Jagdflieger Adolf Galland and at the invitation of Willy Messerschmitt, Reichsmarschall Hermann Göring paid a visit to the Messerschmitt works at Augsburg to investigate optimistic claims about the Me 262 turbojet-powered fighter. When asked by Göring if the Me 262 could carry bombs, Messerschmitt casually concurred, opening the door on the aircraft's misapplication, and when Hitler saw the aircraft November 26, he ordered that it be developed as a fighter-bomber.

1943 November 15 RAF Fighter Command was renamed Air Defense of Great Britain (ADGB), effective this date, with Air Marshal R. M. Hill taking over as commander-in-chief from A.M. Sir Trafford Leigh-Mallory. On October 15, 1944, ADGB reverted to RAF Fighter Command, and A.M. Hill was replaced by A.M. Sir James M. Robb on May 14, 1945.

1943 November 18 Under Rear Adm. C. A. Pownall, Task Force 50 comprising six heavy carriers and five light carriers began the campaign that would ultimately lead to the capture of the Marshall Islands in the central Pacific with the first phase of the occupation of the Gilbert Island group. In two days, air power attacked airfields and defensive installations followed by Marine Corps landing support at Tarawa and Makin atolls November 21. During November 10–18, aircraft from eight escort carriers had protected assault shipping and then flown combat air patrols and close support missions as they landed. Squadron VF-1 flew off the escort carriers USS *Barnes* and USS *Nassau* November 25 to land on Tarawa airstrip.

1943 November 18 One of the greatest tests of RAF Bomber Command began when 440 Lancasters and four Mosquitoes started a new campaign of night raids on Berlin that would severely test the morale of British bomber crews flying across 500 mi. of occupied Europe to reach one of the RAF's most distant objectives. The main campaign was relaxed after February 1944, by which time 7,403 sorties had been flown on 14 major raids with the loss of 384 aircraft (5.2%), although a few raids took place through the end of March. By then, the RAF had other priorities associated with the impending invasion of Europe. They did, however, force the Germans into consolidating their air defenses.

1943 November 27 The U.S. Navy issued a letter of intent to Grumman for two prototype XF8F-1 carrier-fighters proposed by the manufacturer as replacement for the F6F Hellcat. The F8F Bearcat first flew on August 31, 1944, and production aircraft powered by a 2,100-HP Pratt & Whitney R-2800-34W engine had a top speed of 447 MPH at 28,000 ft. and a climb rate of up

to 4,800 ft./min. On November 20, 1946, a Bearcat flown by Lt. Comdr. M. W. Davenport claimed an unofficial time-to-height record of 10,000 ft. in 1 min. 35 sec. A total 1,265 F8Fs were built, and more than 40 years later, the civilianized Bearcat would be a prominent attendee in national air races and speed record attempts.

1943 November The only aircraft designed from the outset to be carried aboard a submarine for an offensive military role was completed when Aichi finished its M6A Seiran floatplane, with a wingspan of 40 ft. 2 in., a length of 38 ft. 2 in. and a maximum weight of 9,800 lb. Powered by a 1,400-HP Aichi AE1P Atsuta 30 engine, it had a maximum speed of 295 MPH at 17,060 ft. and a range of 739 mi. The M6A was designed for use with the new 4,500-ton I-400 class submarine, which had a watertight deck hangar. A total of 28 M6As were built, and in July 1945, submarines put to sea carrying three floatplanes apiece. Their mission was to bomb the Panama locks, but the war ended before they carrried out the attack.

1943 November Oberst Siegfried Kneymeyer was appointed chief of technical air armament services in the Reichsluftfahrtministerium (German Air Ministry), bringing radical ideas for the future of German military aircraft production. He advocated halting production of all conventionally powered bombers in favor of turbojet-powered bombers and of swiftly moving across to jet fighters. Kneymeyer was responsible for priority being given to research and development of new jet aircraft such as the Junkers Ju 287 and to technologies such as swept wings for supersonic flight.

1943 December 13 The U.S. Eighth and Ninth Air Forces dispatched 1,462 aircraft to bomb targets in Bremen, Kiel, Hamburg and Schipol airport, Amsterdam; this was the greatest number of aircraft so far put together for a single day's operations. A total 430 escort fighters including P-47s, P-38s and P-51s flew sorties, the latter using drop tanks giving them a round-trip range of almost 1,000 mi. This marked the beginning of daylight raids routinely escorted by long-range fighters, one of the most welcome improvements to USAAF bombing operations.

1943 December 17 At a commemorative dinner in Washington, D.C. celebrating the 40th anniversary of the first flights of Orville and Wilbur Wright in 1903, Pres. Roosevelt announced that, at Orville's request, the original Wright Flyer was to be brought back from England and displayed at the Smithsonian. It had been restored in 1916 using many original materials and loaned for exhibition in England, but a label on Dr. Samuel Pierpont Langley's Aerodrome A in the Smithsonian claiming it to be the "first heavier than air machine capable of flight" so incensed Orville that he sent the Flyer to the Science Museum in London. It was returned November 22, 1948, and officially accepted at a dinner December 17, 1948.

1943 During the year, the USAAF accepted 68,600 aircraft comprising 92 very heavy bombers, 9,393 heavy bombers, 5,413 medium bombers, 5,175 light bombers, 17,628 fighters, 284 reconnaissance aircraft, 6,817 transports, 19,491 trainers and 4,307 communications aircraft. By now the USAAF had about 2.3 million officers and men.

1944 January 1 Luftwaffe strength had improved significantly since January 1, 1943, despite severe losses in the Mediterranean campaigns and on the Eastern Front. First-line strength was recorded at 1,580 long-range bombers, 610 ground attack, 1,535 single-engine fighters, 905 twin-engine fighters, 425 long-range reconnaissance, 330 tactical reconnaissance and 200 coastal aircraft for a total 5,585. As to distribution, there were 1,410 on the Western Front, 1,225 in the defense of the Reich, 1,710 on the Eastern Front, 505 in the Mediteranean and the Balkans and 735 nonoperational.

1944 January 8 Designed by Clarence Johnson, the Lockheed XP-80 prototype (serial no. 44-83020) made its first flight from Muroc Dry Lake, Calif. at 9:10 A.M. with Milo Burcham at the controls. It was powered by a de Havilland H.1 turbojet. Production aircraft were powered by the 3,850-lb. thrust General Electric J33. The P-80A had a wingspan of 39 ft. 11 in., a length of 34 ft. 6 in. and a gross weight of 14,500 lb. It had a maximum speed of 558 MPH at sea level and a climb rate of 4,580 ft./min. Armament comprised six 0.50-in. guns in the nose. Two YP-80As were sent to Italy where they saw combat in April 1945.

1944 January 11 In one of the largest day operations mounted by the U.S. Eighth Air Force to date, 663 B-17s and B-24s and 592 escort fighters were dispatched to raid Oschersleben, Halberstadt, Brunswick, Osnabrück and minor targets in Germany. Only 551 were effective at the targets, and a total 60 aircraft were lost with 184 aircraft damaged or written off. For the first time in Eighth Air Force operations, B-24s operated as pathfinders with H2S equipment. It is estimated that more than 200 Luftwaffe fighters tangled with the bombers, 39 being shot down.

1944 January 11 In air combat over German-occupied Europe, Lt. Col. James H. Howard, commander of a squadron flying P-51s with the 354th Fighter Group, U.S. Eighth Air Force, received confirmation on three enemy fighters claimed to have been shot down, and possibly three more, for which he became the only Eighth or Ninth Air Force fighter pilot to be awarded the USAAF Medal of Honor out of 38 recipients during World War II. Born in Canton, China, Lt. Col. Howard (who retired as a brigadier general) shared with Sgt. Archibald Mathies, born in Scotland, the honor of being the only USAAF Medal of Honor holders not born in the United States.

1944 January 12 The prototype Gloster Meteor F.1 jet fighter (serial no. EE210/G) made its first flight with Michael Daunt at the controls. This was the full militarized version of the F.9/40 and carried four 20-mm cannons and a special clear-view canopy. The first operational RAF unit to get the Meteor, No. 616 Squadron, received its first aircraft (serial no. EE219) at Culmhead on July 12. It had a wingspan of 43 ft., a length of 41 ft. 3 in. and a gross weight of 13,795 lb. Powered by two 1,700-lb. thrust Rolls Royce W.2B/23C Welland engines, the Mk.1 had a maximum speed of 415 MPH. (The Mk.8, which would enter service in 1950, would have a top speed of 598 MPH.)

1944 January 18 To prevent German submarines from entering the Mediterranean, the U.S. Navy began patrolling the Straits of Gibraltar with PBY Catalinas fitted with magnetic anomaly detectors (MADs). This equipment measured the changes in the magnetic field made by a large metal object passing through the water. The first successful detection came on February 24 when Catalinas of VP-63 detected, attacked and sank the U-761 with retro-rocket bombs.

1944 January 21 Air Marshal Sir Arthur Conningham was appointed commander of the RAF's Second Tactical Air Force, which was to be responsible for ground attack and support operations for the amphibious forces of the Normandy landings beginning on June 6, 1944. Second Tactical Air Force would comprise 91 squadrons, including RAF, Fleet Air Arm, RCAF, RNZAF and RAAF units. The second air grouping, which would be used for invasion duties, was the Air Defense of Great Britain force with 43 squadrons while the third was the U.S. Ninth Air Force with 165 (U.S.) squadrons.

1944 January 21 During this night, the Luftwaffe returned to bomb Britain in force when Generalmajor Dietrich Peltz, as the Angriffsführer (attack leader) England, sent his bombers to attack towns and cities across southeast England. Under the code name Operation Steinbock ordered by Göring the previous November in retaliation for Allied raids on Germany, a special effort had been made to get every bomber operational and out of 481 aircraft, 431 (89.6%) were ready for flight. By May 1944, these raids had dwindled, giving Britain the vain hope of respite. This was dashed when the V-1 and V-2 raids started.

1944 January 21 Displaying the effectiveness of new radar devices introduced to German night fighter units, 57 RAF bombers out of a force of 648 aircraft raiding Magdeburg this night were shot down, three-quarters of them by the night fighter groups (Nachtjagdgruppen). On the night of January 27/28, 33 Lancasters out of a force of 515 raiding Berlin were lost, and on February 19/20, 78 aircraft out of 823 were shot down. Introduced late in 1943, the FuG 220 Lichtenstein SN-2 avoided frequencies jammed by "windows" (strips of metallic foil dropped by advancing bombers), while FuG 350 Naxos homed in on H2S transmissions and FuG homed in on the RAF's Monica tail-warning radar.

1944 January 22 With resistance from the Luftwaffe in central Italy almost under control and facing only 335 operational aircraft, the Allied air forces supported more than 50,000 Anglo-American troops as they went ashore at Anzio on the western seaboard at the start of a sharp run up to Rome. Tactical support from B-17s and medium bombers helped ground forces move quickly, but progress soon slackened as commanders opted to consolidate rather than dash for victory. On February 10, the Villa Propaganda at Castel Gondolfo, a major center of German war administration, was destroyed.

1944 January 29 Intensive air attacks on Maloelap, Kwajalein and Wotje from aircraft dispatched off six heavy and six light carriers of Task Force 58 opened the battle for the recapture of the Marshall Islands. Japanese air opposition was neutralized on this first day, and U.S. Navy aircraft thereafter hunted enemy submarines and shipping, flying cover for the landings on Kwajalein and Majuro atolls January 31 and Roi and Namur February 1.

1944 January 31 For the first time anywhere, an operational rocket-propelled fighter appeared on the charge roster of an operational combat unit. The unit was 20./JG 1 based at Zwischenahn, and 12 operational Me 163Bs were on hand assigned to Luftflotte Reich. The first combat-ready fighter, the Me 163B V14 had arrived at Zwischenahn earlier in the month, and the unit had been evolving attack strategies on simulated bomber formations. Next month the unit was redesignated 1./JG 400 under the command of Oblt. Robert Olejnik, but not before the end of February did the first MK 108 cannon arrive for installation.

1944 February 15 The U.S. twelfth and fifteenth air forces bombed the sixth-century monastery at Monte Cassino, a powerful bastion of German resistance on the Gustav Line in central Italy. Some 135 B-17s dropped 313 tons of 500-lb. GP bombs and 73 tons of 100-lb. incendiaries on the main buildings and courtyard, while 47 B-25 and 40 B-26 medium bombers dropped

154 tons of 1,000-lb. bombs on the monastry as Fifth Army fired 314 heavy-caliber shells on the gun emplacements. About 400 women and children who had taken refuge in the monastry were among the soldiers killed.

1944 February 16   The prototype Curtiss XSC-1 Seahawk made its first flight, the last in a long line of U.S. Navy scouting aircraft. A stubby, low-wing monoplane, the Seahawk had a wingspan of 41 ft., a length of 36 ft. 4 in. and a gross weight of 9,000 lb. Powered by a 1,350-HP Wright R-1820-62 radial, the SC had a cruising speed of 125 MPH and a range of 625 mi. It entered service as a scout and antisubmarine aircraft with the USS *Guam* in October 1944, but only 10 had been built when contracts for 950 were cancelled on V-J Day.

1944 February 17   In the first major strike on Truk, Vice Adm. Spruance's three fast-carrier groups began a two-day aerial assault, during which 1,250 combat sorties were flown against Japanese installations at the naval base. Dropping 40 tons of bombs, they destroyed 265 out of 370 Japanese aircraft and sank 37 warships and merchant ships totaling 200,581 tons. During this engagement, the first U.S. Navy carrier night attack was carried out by twelve TBF-1Cs of VT-10 (USS *Enterprise*) specially equipped with radar. Success in the initial occupation of the Marshalls beginning January 29 and the two fast-carrier groups to the west had hastened the occupation of Truk from its original target date of May 10.

1944 February 18   A precise, pinpoint attack from very low altitude on the jail at Amiens, France was conducted by three formations of six Mosquitoes from No. 487 (New Zealand), No. 464 (Australian) and No. 21 squadrons, RAF, in attempts to breach the walls and liberate imprisoned French resistance workers. Releasing their bombs from as low as 10 ft., the Mosquitoes breached the walls, killing 50 Germans but enabling 258 prisoners, 12 of whom were to have been shot the next day, to escape.

1944 February 20   The first in a series of raids that would last through February 25 began, a period known as "Big Week" when the U.S. Eighth Air Force attained the true proportion of a strategic bombing force. It began with the first of the Eighth Air Force's "1,000 bomber" raids as 1,003 B-17s and B-24s left for targets in Germany with 835 escort fighters. Only 880 bombers were effective at the targets, but only 21 were lost with 240 damaged for the loss of 229 crewmembers missing or dead. At the end of "Big Week," the Eighth had flown 3,300 sorties and dropped 6,615 tons of bombs for a total loss of 219 aircraft and 1,675 crewmen dead or missing.

1944 March 6   The U.S. Eighth Air Force suffered the heaviest losses of any daylight raid when 75 B-17s and B-24s on a raid over Germany were shot down or destroyed out of a total dispatched force of 730 aircraft, 672 of which reached their targets. To the aircraft lost (11.2%) must be added 353 bombers damaged and 703 crewmen killed or missing. Of 801 fighters dispatched, 11 were shot down.

1944 March 6   The RAF began this night its raids on occupied Europe aimed at supporting Operation Overlord, the Normandy landing, to which RAF Bomber Command had been assigned. Halifaxes and Mosquitoes of Nos. 4, 6 and 8 groups, 267 aircraft in all, hit railway marshaling yards in France. This was followed the next night by a raid with 304 aircraft on the railway yards at Le Mans. Losses were very light during attacks on occupied Europe, in contrast to the losses from raids on German towns and cities beyond the "Kammhuber line," a defensive screen of fighter bases and radar.

1944 March 15   The U.S. Army Air Technical Service Command, the Navy Bureau of Aeronautics and the National Advisory Committee for Aeronautics met at NACA's Langley Laboratory to discuss areas of research necessary for high-speed, transonic aircraft. NACA wanted a conservative, turbojet-propelled design that would eventually mature into a NACA-Navy project. This gave rise to the Douglas D-558 program, while the air force, in less comfortable association, teamed with NACA to produce the rocket propelled Bell X-1 program.

1944 March 25   In trials to develop a maritime role for the de Havilland Mosquito, an aircraft of this type (FB.MkVI, serial no. LR359) carried out the first British carrier-deck landing with a twin engine aircraft. With special, large-diameter propellers and an improvised arrester gear, and piloted by Lt. Comdr. E. M. Brown, the aircraft put down on the deck of HMS *Indefatigable*. The first production Sea Mosquito flew for the first time on November 10, 1945, and the first of 50 entered service with the Royal Navy shortly thereafter.

1944 March 25   The U.S. Fifteenth Air Force made the first operational use of the radio-controlled VB-1 Azon glide bomb, the first U.S. remotely controlled weapon used in action. The VB-1 was a standard 1,000-lb. bomb fitted with a special tail unit that incorporated a receiver operating two rudder control motors, which made it possible to vary the azimuth of descent by up to 200 ft. either side of the downrange path. Because the tail device weighed 164 lb., the VB-1 could only be carried on the 2,000-lb. bomb shackles of a B-24.

1944 March 30   RAF Bomber Command suffered its heaviest losses of the war during a night raid directed at Nuremberg. No sooner had the 795 bombers crossed the English Channel than the Luftwaffe night fighter units were vectored onto two radio beacons astride the path to Nuremberg. For more than an hour, 294 fighters severely mauled the bombers, shooting down 82 on the way to the target. The RAF lost 95 aircraft (11.9%) and 545 crewmembers with 200 wounded. Ironically, the majority of the aircraft bombed Schweinfurt by mistake, killing 70 German civilians in all. By this time, the Germans had 25 operational Nachtjagdgruppen (night fighter units) with 550 aircraft.

1944 March 31   Douglas received a contract from the USAAF changing the XB-42 tandem-engine pusher-bomber prototype into a twin-engine turbojet aircraft and redesignating it the XB-43. Two 3,750-lb. thrust General Electric TG-180 turbojet engines were to be installed in the fuselage previously occupied by the Allison engines of the XB-42. The XB-42 had yet to fly, but Douglas built the first XB-43 from the static airframe of the XB-42, which had been ordered along with two flying prototypes on June 25, 1943.

1944 March   U.S. aircraft manufacturing output this month reached the highest achieved in any country before or since: U.S. industry delivered 9,113 aircraft, compared to 2,464 in December 1941, grossing 44,454 tons compared with 6,121 tons. These figures exceeded the combined aircraft manufacturing output of the rest of the world. This was equal to an annual production output of 109,356 aircraft.

1944 April 3   Forty-two Fleet Air Arm Fairey Barracudas protected by 80 escort fighters attacked the German battleship *Tirpitz* in Kaafjord on the northern tip of Norway. Achieving complete

Allied air operations relied heavily on preflight preparation; here is a model of the Kiel harbor complex.

surprise, the Barracudas scored 15 direct hits, killing 300 of the *Tirpitz*'s crew and starting a massive fire amidships. Fighter cover had been flown in part by Corsairs from No. 1834 Squadron aboard HMS *Victorious,* Hellcats from No. 800 Squadron aboard HMS *Emperor* and Wildcats from No. 898 Squadron on HMS *Searcher*. This was the first time Corsairs had operated from carriers. Early teething troubles were overcome this month by the U.S. Navy, and they soon began operations from U.S. carriers.

1944 April 4   The U.S. Navy issued a contract for design and production of two prototype and 15 production Lockheed P2V Neptune maritime patrol and antisubmarine aircraft. Work on this postwar stalwart of maritime defense began in 1941 as a private venture run by Lockheed's Jack Wassall, but operational priorities delayed work. Unlike its predecessor, the PV-1 and PV-2 that evolved from the Lockheed Model 18, the P2V was purpose-built from the drawing board.

1944 April 14   RAF Bomber Command officially transferred its operations to targets in support of the invasion plans under Operation Overlord, joining the U.S. eighth and ninth air forces in the combined offensive run by Gen. Dwight D. Eisenhower until it was released September 25. The gradual shift to the destruction of communications and transport facilities had begun during March, however, and much of the bombing work over the next seven weeks would combine the destruction of German resources with deception and diversionary attacks in the weeks preceding D-day.

1944 April 17   The prototype Lockheed C-69-LO (Constellation) was delivered to the USAAF testing site at Wright Field, Ohio. Piloted by Howard Hughes and Jack Frye, with three other crewmembers and 12 important passengers, an impressive unofficial record-breaking flight was made from Burbank, Calif., a distance of 2,300 mi., in 6 hr. 57 min. 51 sec.

1944 May 15   At a meeting with NACA requested by the USAAF, represented by Ezra Kotcher, the aims and objectives of a high-speed transonic research program were discussed. NACA wanted a turbojet design, but the air force preferred the use of rocket propulsion. NACA came back July 10 with its proposed configuration for a "Mach 0.999" aircraft; the air force opted for a rocket-powered aircraft shortly thereafter. In important ways, rocket propulsion for manned aircraft helped gather experience and confidence for much later projects like the hypersonic X-15, which went far beyond the capabilities of jet propulsion and prepared the way for manned space projects.

1944 May 27   The first recorded suicide attack by aircraft of the Imperial Japanese Army Air Force took place when four Kawasaki Ki-45 Toryu (Dragon Killer) twin-engine long-range fighters attacked shipping off the coast of New Guinea, with minimal success. Long in gestation, the aircraft entered service during April 1942, more than 3 yr. after the first prototype had been completed. A total of 1,698 Ki-45 were built, and the type was employed in home defense during the closing months of the war.

1944 May 31   Six days before the Allied Normandy landings, the Luftwaffe had a front-line strength of 7,075 aircraft, of which 934 were transports and 761 were nonoperational, leaving 6,314 combat-ready warplanes. They were dispersed as follows: 2,360 on the Eastern Front, 1,519 in defense of the Reich, 827 on the Western Front, 266 in Italy, 262 in the Balkans and 146 in Norway. On the Western Front, II Jagdkorps had just 173 fighters comprising 119 operational Fw 190s and Bf 109s, 92 Bf 110 night fighters and 55 Junkers 88 destroyer-interceptors.

1944 June 1   The first Atlantic crossing carried out by nonrigid airships was successfully completed when a formation of U.S. Navy ZP-14s arrived at Port Lyautey, French Morocco, having covered a distance of 3,145 mi. since setting off from South Weymouth, Mass. on May 29. With stopovers at Argentia, Newfoundland, and the Azores, the blimps made it across in a flying time of 80 hr. They were assigned to antisubmarine patrols around the Straits of Gibraltar at the western neck of the Mediterranean.

1944 June 5   In one of the most intensive periods of aerial attack ever mounted, Allied air support for the run up to Operation Overlord, the invasion of Normandy, had logged within a period of two months 195,200 sorties, of which 71,800 had been conducted by the RAF and 123,400 by the U.S. eighth and ninth air forces. The objective had been to soften up German defenses and attack a large number of targets across wide areas of the continent, confusing the Germans about the exact location of the planned landings. A total 215,430 tons of bombs had been dropped, of which 111,600 had been dropped by the USAAF and 103,830 tons by the RAF. In the nine-week period, a total 1,953 Allied aircraft had been lost, 1,251 by the USAAF (763 by the Eighth Air Force alone) and 702 by the RAF. In all, 12,000 officers and men had been lost.

1944 June 6   Supporting the largest single seaborne invasion ever mounted (D-day), involving 2 million men and 7,000 ships, Allied air units flew a total 14,674 sorties from bases in England between midnight June 5 and midnight June 6. Of this total, 9,018 were flown by the U.S. eighth and ninth air forces and 5,656 were flown by the RAF. Allied air forces had at their disposal 5,212 medium and heavy bombers, 5,409 fighters and 2,316 transport aircraft. During the day, the RAF lost 113 aircraft, and the USAAF lost 59. The first Allied airstrip in France was established June 7 at Asnelles, northeast of Bayeaux.

On the day the Allies landed on the Normandy beaches, the Luftwaffe was able to mount only 319 sorties. There were only the Jagdwaffe units JG 2 and JG 26 in that sector under Luftflotte 3, equipped in the main with Fw 190A-2s and A-3s with the exception of III/JG 26, which had Bf 109G fighters. The fourth fighter-bomber Staffel of each Jagdgeschwader was equipped with Bf 109F-4/Bs, which they had been operating with for more than two years.

1944 June 8   The first operational RAF airfield in liberated Europe was occupied by No. 144 (Canadian) Wing and their Spitfires, led by Gp. Capt. Johnnie Johnson. With a score of 38, Johnson was the top-scoring Allied air ace of the European theater, second overall in the Allied forces only to Maj. Richard Bong who scored his 40 victories in the Far East. After initial training, Johnson had joined No. 616 Squadron, RAF, in August 1940 and from March 1941 flew wing for the legless British pilot Douglas Bader, eventually getting command of No. 610 Squadron before promotion to Wing Commander.

1944 June 8 In a night raid on a railway tunnel near Saumur, the RAF dropped the first 12,000-lb. "Tallboy" bomb from a Lancaster of No. 617 Squadron in quick response to intelligence that a German panzer unit was scheduled to move through. Designed by Barnes Wallis, the bomb was designed to penetrate hardened structures. Bomber Command had been using 12,000-lb. bombs since 1943, but "Tallboy" was built as a scaled-down version of "Grand Slam," a 22,000-lb. bomb then on the drawing board, to split open particularly difficult structures. It was used again several times against U-boat and E-boat pens and, in September and November, in attacks on the German battleship *Tirpitz*.

1944 June 9 The prototype Avro Lincoln (serial no. PW925), designed to a specification calling for a long-range strategic bomber for the Far East, made its first flight at Ringway, England, powered by four 1,680-HP Rolls Royce Merlin 85 engines. The aircraft evolved from the Lancaster, had longer span wings extending to 120 ft., a length of 78 ft. 3 in. and a loaded weight of 75,000 lb. Range was 1,660 mi. with a 14,000-lb. bomb load or 1,040 mi. with a 22,000-lb. bomb. Although it joined No. 57 Squadron, RAF, in August 1945, too late to hit Japan before the war ended, it was used against the Mau Mau in Kenya before it was withdrawn from service in 1953.

1944 June 11 Capt. David S. McCampbell, U.S. Navy, serving as commander of squadron VF-15 aboard the carrier USS *Enterprise,* scored the first of 34 air combat victories that would leave him the highest-scoring U.S. Navy fighter pilot of all time. In one blistering assault on 40 Japanese bombers and 20 fighters June 19, he shot down five aircraft and on October 24 shot down nine Japanese aircraft when he and just six fellow fighter pilots attacked 40 fighters and 20 bombers. McCampbell also logged 20 aircraft destroyed on the ground and remained in the U.S. Navy after the war.

1944 June 15 The first B-29s to bomb Japan took off at 4:24 P.M. from a forward base in China, having flown over the "Hump" (as airmen called the Himalayas) from Calcutta, India beginning June 13. This was the first raid on Japan since Doolittle's raid on April 18, 1942, and involved 68 B-29s, of which 47 reached and bombed the target—the vitally important steel mills at Yawata; seven aircraft and 55 crewmembers were lost. Raids from forward bases in China would continue until the Marianas islands were captured, the first B-29s to Japan flying from there November 24. The first B-29 raid had taken place on June 5 against Bangkok.

1944 June 16 Responding to the first attack on England from German V-1 (Vergeltungswaffe, or Revenge Weapon) flying bombs during the night of June 12/13, RAF Bomber Command began the systematic destruction of launch sites in occupied Europe. Raids on four sites in the Pas de Calais area involved 405 aircraft, including 236 Lancasters. The last in a series of attacks (code-named Rumpelkammer) by ground-launched V-1s was sent off on September 1. Also known as pilotless aircraft, the V-1 was officially known as the Fieseler Fl 103, in reality the first fully operational cruise missile. During the 1950s, cruise missiles would challenge the preeminence of the strategic bomber.

1944 June 19 In the campaign to seize the Marianas, which began June 11, and rapidly build up Saipan for B-29 operations against Japan, Task Force 58 under Vice Adm. M. A. Mitscher successfully launched the Battle of the Philippine Sea. In a continuous day-long attack, the carrier-based aircraft repelled Japanese air attacks, destroying 402 enemy aircraft for the loss of only 20 U.S. pilots in 20 aircraft. Next day, the task force chased and sank the Japanese carrier *Hiryu*. The Japanese were finally ousted from Saipan on July 9, clearing the way for troops to land on Guam July 21 and on Tinian, another air base for bombers, on July 24.

1944 June 20 Returning to the strategic air offensive against Germany after their support of the Allied landings on the Normandy beaches, the U.S. Eighth Air Force dispatched 1,965 B-17s and B-24s with 1,111 fighters on escort and strafing missions into occupied Europe. Of the total 1,607 bombers that hit their targets, 1,257 concentrated on strategic targets in northern Germany, hitting oil refineries, synthetic oil plants, tank ordnance depots and a vehicle assembly plant. In the next three months, the U.S. eighth and ninth air forces would destroy much of Germany's refining capacity to deny the Luftwaffe important fuel for their aircraft, countering increased aircraft and munitions production.

1944 June 21 The U.S. Eighth Air Force began the first of its shuttle missions, landing in Russia after bombing long-range targets in Germany. Under the code name Frantic, 145 B-17s of the Third Bomb Division bombed an oil plant just south of Berlin and continued on to airfields in the USSR, escorted by P-51s that had flown from England using long-range tanks for the outward flight. After dropping their tanks and escorting the B-17s for 580 mi., they crossed the Russian border and diverted to Soviet fighter airfields, leaving the bombers to land at Mirgorod and Poltava.

1944 June 22 The great Soviet summer offensive began along a 435-mi. front extending from the Gulf of Finland down to the Romanian border. In all, 1.7 million Soviet troops, 31,000 guns and mortars and 5,200 tanks and self-propelled guns in 166 divisions pushed against 225,000 German troops in 28 under-manned, and under-equipped divisions. The combined strength of the Soviet air forces amounted to 13,400 aircraft; 6,000 of these were front-line aircraft, including 2,000 fighters, available for this offensive. The Luftwaffe had just 1,780 serviceable aircraft in this sector, under Luftflotten 1, 4 and 6.

1944 June 25 The prototype Ryan XFR-1 Fireball composite aircraft, powered by both turbojet and piston engine, made its first flight. Simple in layout, it had a 1,600-lb. thrust General Electric J31 turbojet and a Wright R-1820-72W radial in the nose and incorporated a tricycle landing gear. The aircraft was delivered to U.S. Navy Squadron VF-66 in March 1945, but the aircraft was withdrawn from service just over two years later when superseded by all-jet aircraft.

1944 June 30 After 25 continuous days of air support for the invasion of Normandy, 163,403 sorties had been flown by the Allied air forces, an average of 6,536 per day, of which 131,263 had been in direct support of those operations. Of these, 85,311 were flown by the USAAF, and 45,952 were flown by the RAF. During the same period, the Luftwaffe was able to mount only 13,829 sorties on the Western Front, so complete was the suppression of German air operations. The Allies lost a total 1,508 aircraft to the Luftwaffe's 808 (1.14% to 5.84%); 6,253 Allied aircrew were lost, of which 5,006 were from RAF Bomber Command and the U.S. Eighth Air Force.

1944 June 30 The Supermarine Spiteful, a converted Spitfire XIV with a new laminar flow wing, made its first flight piloted by Jeffrey Quill. Married to a Spitfire airframe powered by a 2,375-HP Rolls Royce Griffon 69, the new wing gave the plane a top speed of 483 MPH and a maximum climb rate of 4,890 ft./min. at 2,000 ft. Only 17 Spitefuls and two navalized Seafang versions were completed, but the Spiteful is important because it bridged two generations of fighter. Having attached a laminar wing to a Spitfire airframe, Supermarine then used that wing to develop a new fuselage tail and engine for the Attacker, first of a jet breed from Supermarine.

1944 June 30 The USAAF had on hand a total 78,757 aircraft, the highest annual reporting total it would ever achieve in peace or war. It had 445 very heavy bombers, 11,720 heavy bombers, 5,427 medium bombers, 2,914 light bombers, 15,644 fighters, 1,056 reconnaissance aircraft, 9,433 transports, 27,907 trainers and 4,211 communications aircraft.

1944 July 1 The U.S. Navy had a total 34,071 aircraft on hand, including 22,116 for combat duty, 1,939 for transport and utility services, 9,652 for training and 364 for miscellaneous duties. In addition, there were six helicopters for the first time and a record 146 balloons. There was a total 248,324 aviation personnel on active duty comprising 63,963 officers (37,367 pilots) and 184,361 enlisted men (475 pilots). The U.S. Marine Corps had a total 116,525 aviation personnel comprising 14,822 officers (10,416 pilots) and 91,287 enlisted men (41 pilots).

1944 July 2 The first prototype Tachikawa Ki-77 was used by Japan to begin an unofficial attempt to break the world distance record by flying it around a 537.5-mi. circuit between Sinking, Peichengtu and Harbin, Manchuria. The aircraft remained in the air for 57 hr. 12 min., flying 19 circuits to log a distance of 10,212 mi. On April 20, 1943, the second prototype had flown nonstop from Fussa, Tokyo Prefecture to Singapore in 19 hr. 13 min., covering a distance of 3,312 mi., but on July 7 it was lost over the Indian Ocean attempting to fly nonstop between Singapore and Berlin, a distance of more than 8,000 mi.

1944 July 3 Reacting to increased Allied bombing that pounded German transport, armaments and munitions industries by day and night, all Luftwaffe bomber development was finally halted in favor of emergency fighter production. Nevertheless, only four days later a Führer-Befehl (Führer order) ordered jet Me 262 production to concentrate solely on the bomber version. Not until November 4 did Hitler approve the aircraft as a fighter with the proviso that it be capable of carrying a 550-lb. bomb, an order that was ignored.

1944 July 5 The top-scoring U.S. air ace in the European theater during World War II, Lt. Col. Francis S. Gabreski, scored his 28th and last victory. On July 20, he crash-landed in occupied Europe and was taken to Stalag Luft 1 after five days of evading the Germans. Gabreski shot down his first victim August 24, 1943, while commanding the Sixty-first Fighter Squadron and had a total 153 combat missions in P-47 and P-51 fighters. He obtained an additional 6.5 victories in Korea, and retired in 1967 with the rank of colonel.

1944 July 5 The first U.S. rocket-powered aircraft flew under its own propulsion when test pilot Harry Crosby piloted the Northrop MX-334 flying wing to a landing at Muroc Dry Lake, Calif. Converted from the third MX-324 flying-wing glider, the MX-334 was powered by a 200-lb. thrust Aerojet XCAL-200 rocket motor. It had a wingspan of 32 ft., a length of 12 ft. and a wing area of 244 sq. ft. with a takeoff weight of 2,500 lb. Towed into the air by a P-38 piloted by Capt. Martin Smith, the MX-334 was released at 8,000 ft. for the first of several test flights during which air-to-ground data transmissions were conducted for the first time. The MX-334 was never put into production, nor was the XP-79, which was being developed as a rocket fighter.

1944 July 6 The rocket-propelled Me 163 V18 achieved a speed of 702 MPH at low altitude using a new rocket motor. Known as the HWK 109-509C, it had a thrust of 4,400 lb. achieved in incremental thrust steps and supplemented by an auxiliary motor delivering an extra 400-lb. fixed thrust. The V18 landed safely

Epitomizing the new generation of warplanes: a North American P-51 (below) in formation with a Boeing B-17.

Originating from a United Kingdom specification and powered by a Rolls Royce Merlin, the P-51 saw duty in every major theater of war.

but only after its rudder had been torn away in flight. The Me 163B was now operational, and 364 would be built before the end of the war. But while technical developments continued, there was little opportunity to apply them operationally due to the lack of facilities and fuel.

1944 July 6 The Messerschmitt Me 262 V12, a preproduction prototype aircraft, achieved a speed of 624 MPH, the highest ever recorded for an aircraft of this type, during high-speed trials at Leipheim. During the course of these trials, a variety of minor aerodynamic improvements were made, including the use of a streamlined, low drag, cockpit canopy.

1944 July 7 The first air-launched V-1 flying bomb was set on course for London from the underwing carriage of a Heinkel He 111H-22, a designation specifically applicable to the He 111 modified to carry the 4,800-lb. missile. The V-1 was usually launched from a catapult or ''ski-ramp'' on the ground, but the air-launched method increased range from 130 mi. to 320 mi. III/KG 3 was responsible for introducing the new launch method and firing against London 1,176 V-1s between this date and November 10/11.

1944 July 7 During a raid by 1,129 U.S. Eighth Air Force B-17s and B-24s, the special Luftwaffe unit IV(Sturm)/JG 3 shot down 32 bombers for the loss of only two Fw 190A-8/R7s. The unit was an outgrowth of Sturmstaffel (Attack Squadron) 1 formed under the direct control of Hermann Göring in late 1943, its mission being to bring down bombers even by ramming if necessary.

Pilots guilty of infringing rules were sent to the unit and required to sign a declaration that they would bring down at least one bomber on each sortie—by whatever means.

1944 July 17 In support of the U.S. First Army, Lockheed P-38s attacked the defenses and fuel depot at Coutances, southwest of St. Lô, France, using for the first time a jellied explosive called napalm carried in wing tanks. This was the first time napalm was used, and it became a standard fuel explosive, effective for creating fires over wide areas due to the splash effect of the highly combustible fuel.

1944 July 20 During one of the last operations involving the Heinkel He 177, Obstlt. Horst von Riesen commanding KG 1 was leading a force of 80 aircraft when two caught fire while circling the Masury lakes near Rastenburg. Wisely, he ordered them to jettison their bombs. Upon landing, he was promptly arrested and told he would be court-martialed. By coincidence, the bombs had been jettisoned just at the crucial moment the Hitler bomb plot failed. He was suspected of having been careless with his jettison procedures, only being released several hours later, just as the bomb plot was confirmed.

1944 July 26 The first interception of an Allied aircraft by a jet-propelled Me 262 occurred when Flt. Lt. A. E. Wall, RAF, flying in a Mosquito, reported the extraordinary phenomenon of another aircraft rapidly approaching him from the rear. It was an Me 262 flown by Lt. Alfred Schreiber from Erprobungskommando (Test Detachment) 262, Lechfeld, which overtook the

Mosquito and turned to attack, the latter escaping by out-turning the jet and diving for cloud cover. The Mosquito landed at Fermo Airfield, Italy when the pilot suspected structural damage from the violent evasive maneuvers. Luftwaffe claimed this as the first aerial combat victory scored by a jet fighter.

1944 July 29 A USAAF B-29 returning to its forward base at Kiuglai, China from a bombing raid on the Showa steel works at Anshan, Japan was hit by antiaircraft fire and forced to land at Tavrichanka on the shore of Vladivostok Bay in the USSR. Other B-29s put down in Soviet territory on the night of November 10/11 and on November 21, 1944. Impounding the bombers and interning the crews, the Soviets used the B-29 to develop first the Tupolev Tu-4, then the Tu-70 transport aircraft and finally the Tu-20 and Tu-114. The crews were eventually released after repeated protests from the U.S. government.

1944 July Messerschmitt began work on the swept-wing P.1101, which was to have been powered by a Heinkel-Hirth turbojet and had a length of 30 ft. 4 in. and a wingspan of 27 ft. at 40°. Characterized by the placement of its engine in the lower forward fuselage with a circular nose air intake, the P.1101 was secreted away to the Tyrol mountains toward the end of the war, discovered by the Americans and given to Bell in the U.S. where it formed the basis for the X-5.

1944 August 1 American Airlines, the first U.S. airline to post fixed freight charges with the Civil Aeronautics Board, began an all-cargo service between Los Angeles and New York. The airline used DC-3s at first, then introduced Liberators later on. In March 1942, Pennsylvania-Central Airlines had been the first to operate a domestic military cargo service on a scheduled basis.

1944 August 4 Under the code name Aphrodite, the U.S. Eighth Air Force began operations with old bombers stripped of unnecessary equipment and fitted with radio-controlled equipment for glide bomb attacks on special targets. Packed with 10 tons of high explosive, the bomber would be piloted by a crew of two before control was taken over by a "mother" plane flying nearby. The crew would bail out, leaving the "mother" to remotely pilot the "baby" to its target. Several missions were flown against V-1 flying bomb sites, especially the hardened launch stands at Watten, with mixed success.

1944 August 4 The first "kill" attributed to an Allied jet fighter in World War II was secured by Flt. Off. T. D. Dean of No. 616 Squadron, RAF, when he flipped a V-1 flying bomb off course as it flew at 1,000 ft. over Kent, England by deflecting its wings with the wing tip of his Gloster Meteor Mk.1 (serial no. EE216). The flying bomb fell to earth 4 mi. south of Tonbridge. The technique of flipping V-1s by the wing tips was pioneered by Dean after his guns jammed. Of 9,251 V-1s launched against England between June 13, 1944, and March 29, 1945, 4,261 were destroyed, of which 1,979 were credited to the RAF.

1944 August 10 Japanese resistance on Guam came to an end, and the island was secured by elements of U.S. Navy Task Force 58 in a campaign to capture the Marianas that had begun June 11. In that period, the U.S. Navy and Marine Corps had destroyed 1,223 Japanese aircraft and sunk 110,000 tons of enemy shipping.

1944 August 12 Lt. Joseph P. Kennedy Jr. and Lt. Wilfred J. Willy were killed during flight trials of a modified B-24 to be used in an Aphrodite flying bomb mission when an electrical malfunction sent an incorrect electrical signal in the fusing sys-

tem and inadvertently triggered the 25,000 lb. of high explosive packed into the aircraft. The aircraft was to have been flown under radio control to a target after the crew bailed out, relinquishing control to a "mother" plane flying nearby. Lt. Joseph Kennedy was the older brother of John F. Kennedy, president of the United States, 1961–63.

1944 August 14 During this night, under Operation Anvil, troops of the U.S. Seventh Army under Lt. Gen. Alexander M. Patch landed in the south of France largely unopposed and with only 183 U.S. casualties. Within 24 hr., 94,000 men and 11,000 vehicles were put ashore between Toulon and Cannes and drove north toward Lyons, which they reached September 3. In support of Anvil, Allied air units flew transport and glider missions to land 9,000 paratroops, and a total of 4,000 sorties were flown during the first night. The escort carriers USS *Tulagi* and USS *Kasaan Bay* combined with a Royal Navy task force to support air operations.

1944 August 16 The first combat between rocket-powered and conventionally powered aircraft took place after five Me 163Bs climbed almost vertically from their base at Brandis to attack a formation of B-17s and B-24s en route to inland targets. The first two sliced through the bombers without result, but a third badly cut up a B-17, which limped home. The Me 163 (Werke No. 163100) flown by Lt. Hartmut Ryll was suddenly attacked by a P-51 flown by Lt. Col. John B. Murphy of the 370th Fighter Squadron, 359th Fighter Group, the pilot reporting head and chest injuries before his aircraft hit the ground and exploded. This is the first reaction-powered aircraft to be shot down.

1944 August 16 The forward-swept wing Junkers Ju 287 V1 experimental aircraft made its first flight powered by four 1,980-lb. thrust Junkers Jumo 109-004B-1 turbojets, two mounted in nacelles either side of the forward fuselage and two in similar nacelles slung beneath the wing trailing edge. Assembled from the fuselage of an He 177, the tail unit of a Ju 388 and with main landing wheels from a Ju 352 and nose gear from a captured B-24, it made only 17 flights before work on potential bomber projects was dropped in favor of fighters. The sole prototype was captured by the Russians.

1944 August 20 A Kawasaki Ki-45 two-seat, twin-engine fighter piloted by Sgt. Shigeo Nobe of the Fourth Sentai Squadron deliberately rammed the B-29 *Gertrude C.* of the 468th Group over Yawata, Japan in the first recorded instance of a successful in-flight suicide attack. The right wing of the Ki-45 stuck in the wing of the B-29 outboard of the port outer engine, and the rest of the Japanese aircraft cartwheeled across the bomber, causing it to disintegrate. Pieces smashed into B-29 *Calamity Sue,* which also went down out of control.

1944 August 28 In the first recorded defeat of a jet fighter in combat, two fighter pilots of the U.S. Eighty-second Fighter Squadron, Seventy-eighth Fighter Group, shared credit for bringing down a Messerschmitt Me 262 near Termonde, Belgium. Leading a flight of four P-47s at 11,000 ft., Maj. J. Myers spotted a fast-flying aircraft close to the ground. Diving down, the four aircraft identified it as a jet, and Maj. Myers shared the claim with Lt. M. D. Croy after they strafed the fighter and chased it to a forced landing. The pilot, Oberfeldwebel Hieronymous Lauer, escaped to fly again.

1944 August 31 Since June 1, the Luftwaffe lost a staggering 11,074 aircraft on all fronts, with Jagdkorps II in the west covering western France and Belgium losing an average 600 fighters

On August 4, 1944, a Republic P-47J reached a speed of 504 MPH, the first airplane to exceed 500 MPH in level flight.

per month. However, in spite of remorseless heavy bombing of aircraft production and supply plants, the German aircraft industry began to compensate for these losses, by this date delivering more fighters than had been destroyed. By the end of July, the Jagdwaffe had 1,900 single-seat fighters (23% more than on January 1), and they would have 3,200 by mid-November.

1944 September 2 The last aircraft to be brought down by a biplane fighter came to earth in a small meadow near the village of Radvan in central Slovakia. The Junkers Ju 52/3m of the Hungarian air arm piloted by Lt. Gacko had been the victim of an Avia B.534 biplane equipped with four fuselage-mounted 7.7-mm machine guns and flown by Warrant Officer Frantisek Cyprich. The Avia B.534 and its pilot were flying for the forces of the Slovak National Uprising, which on August 29 had begun a civil war just before the Germans took over.

1944 September 8 The RLM Technical Office met to draw up the specification for a Volksjager (People's Fighter) to be powered by a BMW 003 Sturm turbojet engine. Seven days later the submitted proposals from contenders were examined, and a Blohm und Voss design was judged the best. Heinkel complained after the company's design had been rejected, but their protest was overturned, and the RLM confirmed its choice of the Blohm und Voss projekt 211 design. However, the RLM decision was reversed by direct order from Göring's headquarters near Rastenburg, East Prussia on September 23, and the He 162 was reinstated.

1944 September 10 First of the postwar USAAF transport aircraft, the Fairchild C-82A Packet made its first flight. Powered by two 2,100-HP Pratt & Whitney R-2800-85 radial engines, it had twin tail booms for rear fuselage loading and a gross weight of 54,000 lb. Only 220 Packets were built before production ended in September 1948, but a successor, the C-119 Flying Boxcar, with a larger fuselage and a gross weight of 72,700 lb., went into service during late 1949. A wide range of derivatives was built before the type was superseded by the C-130 and retired in 1975.

1944 September 14 Col. Frank B. Wood, Maj. Harry Wexler and Lt. Frank Reckford of the USAAF flew into the eye of a hurricane for the first time, starting a series of scientific investigations that goes on today. A Douglas A-20 equipped with special meteorological instruments but otherwise unmodified flew through the violent winds to the eye in a successful effort to record data that would prove invaluable in understanding both the dynamics of such weather systems and the ability of aircraft to survive their ferocity.

1944 September 15 Under a plan to sink the German battleship *Tirpitz*, code-named Operation Paravane, 26 RAF Lancasters flew from Yagodnik 20 mi. south of Archangel'sk in the USSR to where the *Tirpitz* lay in Alten Fjord, Norway. Aircraft from Nos. 9 and 617 squadrons had flown out four days earlier. The raid involved 20 aircraft loaded with 12,000-lb. Tallboy bombs and six with 499–500-lb. "bobbing" bombs that sank before rising underneath the ship. *Tirpitz* was badly damaged and moved so she could be used as a fixed artillery platform, but the RAF finally capsized her in a Tallboy raid November 12.

1944 September 17 More than 20,000 paratroops, including the British First Airborne Division and the U.S. Eighty-second and 101st Airborne divisions, were airlifted to Arnhem, Eindhoven and Nijmegen by 3,887 aircraft, including 500 glider-tug combinations, at the start of Operation Market. Conceived as a means of maintaining the pace of the Allied advance upon German-occupied territory, the airborne force included 1,113 bombers and 1,240 fighters. It was linked with Operation Garden, an attempt by the Second Army under Gen. Montgomery to outflank the Germans and march on Arnhem. The operations were a failure, the last troops being pulled out on September 25.

1944 September 25 The oil and gas industry of the Third Reich were made the priority for the combined Allied bombing offensive of Germany. Secondary priorities were jointly the disruption of road, rail, waterway and other transport systems and the destruction of tank and motor vehicle production facilities. RAF Bomber Command commander-in-chief, A.D.M. Sir Arthur Harris, disagreed with the concensus, and sought to target areas of large industrial production as well as urban areas to wear down civilian morale.

1944 September 30 The occupation of Palau and Morotai, supported by widely spaced operations from four carrier groups of Task Force 38, ended with major air strikes at airfields and enemy shipping around Manila and in the central Philippines. In action that began August 31 with attacks on Bonin and Volcano islands, fighter sweeps were conducted against Mindanao and to support Marine Corps landings on Morotai while the entire Fast Carrier Force struck Palau between September 6 and 8. Since August 31, 893 enemy aircraft had been destroyed along with 67 warships and merchant ships, totaling 224,000 tons.

1944 September The last production version of the Messerschmitt Bf 109 appeared with the K-series, essentially the G-10 with production refinements and standardization. Powered by a 2,030-HP Daimler Benz DB 605DCM engine, the Bf 109K-4 had a top speed of 452 MPH at 19,685 ft. and a climb time of 3 min. to 16,400 ft. and 6.7 min. to 39,370 ft. Deliveries began January 1945 and quickly replaced earlier G-series variants.

1944 October 1 The world's first scheduled helicopter mail service began, comprising four routes radiating from Los Angeles International Airport to the downtown post office, the San Fernando Valley, San Bernardino and the Newport Beach areas. A three-year certificate was awarded by the Civil Aeronautics Board (CAB) to Los Angeles Airways, which had been incorporated May 11. Sikorsky S-51s were used, and in July 1951, the CAB extended the license and authorized the carrying of passengers.

1944 October 7 The first air combat victories formally credited to a fully operational jet fighter unit were achieved by the Luftwaffe's Kommando Nowotny named for and headed by Maj. Walter Nowotny. Intercepting 25 B-24s from the Second Bomb Division attacking the Magdeburg/Rothensee oil refineries, Fw Lennartz and Oberfähnrich Russel flying Me 262s each claimed an aircraft shot down, but four Me 262s were claimed by USAAF fighters before the day was out.

1944 October 10 In the opening phase of the occupation of Leyte, 17 U.S. aircraft carriers of Task Force 38 under Vice Adm. M. A. Mitscher struck airfields on Okinawa and other islands of the Ryukyu group, with attacks on Luzon the following day. In these opening two days, the Japanese lost 804 aircraft, 438 of which were to aerial combat. The U.S. Navy secured control of the skies by the time the landing on Leyte took place October 20. During continuing operations in November, the Japanese lost a further 770 aircraft.

1944 October 14 Under Operation Hurricane, the most concentrated attack of the war, the RAF sent 1,013 heavy bombers accompanied by escort fighters to Duisburg while the U.S. Eighth Air Force sent 1,251 B-17s and B-24s to the Cologne area escorted by 749 fighters. Bomber losses totaled only 19 aircraft out of 2,264 (0.84%), and 1 fighter was lost. No German aircraft were seen, testimony to the attrition of the Luftwaffe fighter forces. During the night, the RAF sent 1,005 aircraft to bomb Duisberg and 240 to finally destroy Brunswick. In this 18-hr. period, the Allies dispatched 3,509 bomber sorties and dropped 14,400 tons of bombs on three targets, of which 9,850 tons had been dropped by the RAF on Duisberg. These were the largest totals of the war.

1944 October 15 The first Japanese kamikaze attack on a U.S. Navy carrier took place when Rear Adm. Arima, commander of the Twenty-sixth Air Flotilla, crashed his Yokosuka D4Y and its 500-lb. bomb onto the deck of the USS *Franklin,* killing three and wounding 12. The ship was a component of Task Group 38.4 off Luzon attacking Japanese airfields in preparation for the Leyte landings.

1944 October 19 Japanese Vice Adm. Takijiro Onishi arrived at Clark Air Base in the Philippines and ordered Executive Officer Tamai of the 201st Kokutai to form a special kamikaze attack force. During the evening, 24 volunteers were selected under the command of Lt. Yukio Seki, and the next day they were deployed to bases at Mabalacat and Cebu with A6M Zeros, each carrying a single 500-lb. bomb fitted to the ventral drop tank rack. The first successful attack resulted on October 25 when Lt. Seki and four other pilots from Mabalacat sank the escort carrier USS *Saint Lô* and a U.S. cruiser and damaged another escort carrier, the USS *Kitkun Bay.*

1944 October 23 The prototype Nakajima G8N Renzan made its first flight, powered by four 2,000-HP Nakajima NK9K-L Homare 24 radials. With a wingspan of 106 ft. 9 in., a length of 75 ft. 3 in. and a gross weight of 70,879 lb., it was bigger than the Avro Lancaster. The largest aircraft of its type built in Japan, the navy G8N had a maximum range of 4,639 mi. and a cruising speed of 230 MPH. Only four were built, and the type was scrapped due to shortage of materials and the collapse of any strategic function for the bomber.

1944 October 26 Japan's top scoring air ace, Lt. Hiroyoshi Nishizawa, was killed when a transport aircraft in which he was flying was jumped by two Grumman F6Fs over Calapan, Mindoro and shot down. Born January 27, 1920, Nishizawa of the Imperial Japanese Navy scored his first kill on February 3, 1942, and at the time of his death, he was officially credited with 87 victories. (His score is uncertain because in June 1944 units ceased recording victories by individual; some authorities quote up to 150 kills, and official accounts log between 60 and 70. Subsequent research would support a figure of 87 victories.) During the Battle of the Solomons on August 7, 1942, he shot down seven aircraft.

1944 October Tests began with an Me 262A-series jet fighter as a night interceptor fitted with SN-2 Lichtenstein radar flown by Oberst. Hajo Herrmann of Jagddivision 30. The pilot reported good results from these tests, and the two-seat Me 263B-1a/U1 was converted for this role. Performance was hampered by the radio and radar antennae, slowing the aircraft's top speed by 37 MPH. Despite production plans for the Me 262B-2a, only one prototype was flying when the war ended.

1944 October The first Focke-Wulf Fw 190D-9 single-seat fighters powered by the 2,240-HP 12-cylinder Junkers Jumo 213A-1 joined III/JG 54 at its base in Oldenburg. Developed from the Fw 190A-8 with a new wing and a change from radial to in-line engine, the D-9 had a wingspan of 34 ft. 5.5 in., a length of 33 ft. 5 in. and a maximum loaded weight of 10,670 lb. With a top speed of 426 MPH at 21,650 ft., it had a climb time of 2 min. 6 sec. to 6,560 ft. and 7 min. 6 sec. to 19,685 ft. The Fw 190D-9 was an attempt to produce an interim high-altitude fighter pending availability of the Ta-152.

1944 October The first production versions of the ultimate Focke-Wulf 190 derivative, the Ta 152H-0, were delivered to Test Unit (Erprobungskommando) 152 at Rechlin under Hptmn. Bruno Stolle. Designed as a high-altitude fighter, it was powered by a 2,050-HP Junkers Jumo 213E-1 and had a wingspan of 47 ft. 4.5 in., a length of 35 ft. 2 in. and a maximum loaded weight of 11,502 lb. It had a maximum speed of 472 MPH at 41,010 ft., an initial climb rate of 3,445 ft./min. and a ceiling of 48,550 ft.

1944 November 1   The first flight over Tokyo during World War II by a U.S. land-based aircraft was carried out by Capt. Ralph D. Steakley flying from the Marianas in an F-13, a photo-reconnaissance version of the B-29. In addition to standard bombing equipment, the F-13 was equipped with three K-17B, two K-22 and one K-18 aerial cameras. In 1948, aircraft of this configuration were redesignated RB-29 and RB-29A under the revised nomenclature for USAF aircraft. Only 118 B-29s were converted to F-13 specification.

1944 November 1   With an eye on more peaceful skies, the Chicago Conference convened a meeting on civil aviation that would last through December 7 and result in the formation of the International Civil Aviation Organization (ICAO). The United States had wanted an ''open-skies'' policy and naïvely bunched all European countries into a single entity without considering the individual needs of each, causing hostility from the British, represented by Lord Swinton. Under Adolf Berle, the U.S. delegation helped form a Freedom of the Air policy, agreed to by all participants, allowing limited concessions on freedom to land in foreign countries.

1944 November 3   Japanese general Sueyoshi Kusaba presided over the launch of the first of 9,300 bomb-carrying balloons released from Japan into the prevailing jet stream across the Pacific. The idea of long-range balloon bombs evolved from studies begun as early as 1933. According to reports, about 1,000 balloons made the 6,200-mi. crossing to the continental United States, but only 285 are recorded as having come to earth, each carrying a 33-lb. antipersonnel bomb and two incendiaries intended to start fires. The first sighting was made November 4 by a navy patrol plane 66 mi. southwest of San Pedro, Calif.

1944 November 5   Demonstrating the remarkable capabilities of the B-29, the U.S. Twentieth Air Force flew a round-trip bombing mission from Calcutta, India to Singapore, a round-trip distance of almost 4,000 mi. Their target was the King George VI docks, and the 53 B-29s hit them with remarkable accuracy, one 1,000-lb. bomb being positioned to within 50 ft. of the aim point. The raid put the docks out of action for three months and severely hampered Japanese Navy operations.

1944 November 9   The Boeing 367-1-1, a prototype XC-97 transport aircraft ordered by the USAAF in January 1942, made its first flight. Derived from the B-29, it had the bomber's wings, tail, undercarriage and engines but with a double-lobe fuselage of two intersecting circular cross-sections. Known as the C-97 Stratofreighter, it began its service life in October 1947; 888 of the type were built before production ended in 1956. Capable of carrying 134 fully equipped combat troops, 83 stretcher patients or up to 12 tons of cargo, many were converted into aerial tankers designated KC-97.

1944 November 13   Railway Air Services began a scheduled civil air service from Croydon, near London, to Liverpool and Belfast, Northern Ireland, the first civil air service into or out of London since September 1939. The aircraft was a D.H.86B Rapide (G-ACZP) flown by Capt. C. W. S. Clark outbound and Capt. D. C. Harrison inbound.

1944 November 18   One of the most spectacular Japanese aircraft of World War II, the Mitsubishi Ki-83 made its first flight powered by two 2,200-HP Mitsubishi Ha-211 Ru turbosupercharged, 18-cylinder radials. Designed as an exceptionally clean long-range escort fighter, it had a top speed of 438 MPH at 29,530 ft., a climb time of 10 min. to 32,810 ft. and a service ceiling of 41,535 ft. Equipped with four nose cannons, it was equal to the D.H.103 Hornet in performance; but it came too late and only four prototypes were built.

1944 November 24   The U.S. XXI Bomber Command flew its first mission from Saipan in the Marianas to bomb targets in Japan at the commmencement of a campaign that would last until the final mission to Japan was flown on the night of August 14/15, 1945. Led by Seventy-third Bomber Wing commander Gen. Emmett O'Donnel Jr. in *Dauntless Dotty,* 111 B-29s set out to bomb Tokyo, but 17 aborted on the way and nine were unable to release their bombs due to mechanical problems. The first B-29 had arrived on Saipan October 12, less than 4 mon. after the marine invasion began.

1944 November 29   The Japanese supercarrier *Shinano* was sunk by four torpedoes from the American submarine USS *Archerfish* just 10 days after it had been completed. Built up from the third hull of the *Yamato* family of battleships, the *Shinano* had a displacement of 71,890 metric tons and a waterline length of 840 ft., making it the biggest warship of all time except for the American supercarriers of today in the *Enterprise, Nimitz* and *Forrestal* classes. In contrast, the biggest American carrier of World War II, the USS *Saratoga* (CV-3), had a displacement of 48,550 tons. *Shinano* was one of 25 Japanese carriers of World War II.

1944 November 30   Bell Aircraft Corporation design engineer Robert Woods visited with Ezra Kotcher at his Wright Field office and was concerned at the latter's fruitless attempt to gather support from U.S. aircraft companies for the proposed MX-524 transonic rocket-propelled research aircraft. Bell's Robert Wolf had been a keen supporter of transonic flight research and in December 1943 proposed at a conference that industry build a turbojet-powered aircraft funded by the military and tested by NACA. Woods committed his company to build this aircraft, eventually known as the Bell X-1.

1944 November   In the United States, a unique propulsion company was formed when Roy E. Marquardt and George P. Tidmarsh set up the Marquardt Aircraft Co. in Van Nuys, Calif. Marquardt specialized in ramjet research and engine development, contemporarily one of the most advanced concepts in aircraft propulsion, and received a contract to develop a 20-in. diameter subsonic ramjet. The company went on to produce some of the most advanced propulsion concepts in the world, including the hydrogen-fueled, air-breathing engine for the USAF in the 1960s.

1944 November   The Reichsluftfahrtministerium (German Air Ministry) issued a specification for a simple fighter to achieve quicker production potential than the Heinkel He 162 Salamander in a desperate last effort to build up the number of defensive fighters available for the Third Reich. Only three manufacturers responded (Blohm und Voss, Heinkel and Junkers) to a specification calling for the use of a pulse-jet engine similar to that employed in the V-1 flying bomb.

1944 November   The Siebel Flugzeugwerke at Halle, Germany received plans for the DFS 346, a supersonic fighter of all-metal, semi-monocoque, duralumin construction. The plane was so configured that the pilot lay in a prone position, occupying a pres-

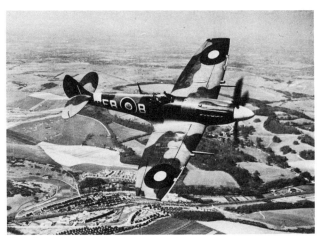

The clipped-wing Supermarine Spitfire Mk. XII equipped with cannon and machine gun was the first Spitfire with the Griffon engine.

surized nose section. Preoccupied with Junkers subcontracted work, Siebel did little on the project before war's end, but the Soviets took the plans and built the DFS 346. The first flight took place when the DFS was dropped from a captured B-29 forced down near Vladivostok.

1944 December 5 Under Operation Grubworm, the USAAF began the movement of the Chinese Fourteenth and Twenty-second divisions from Burma back to Cnahyi, Kunming, Luliang and Yunnani in China. The USAAF airlifted 25,000 Chinese troops, 396 U.S. soldiers as "advisers," 1,596 animals, 42 jeeps, 48 howitzers, 48 heavy mortars and 48 antitank guns. Under the command of Col. S. D. Grubbs, the Tenth Air Force flew 1,328 missions, losing only three aircraft before the airlift was completed on January 5, 1945.

1944 December 6 Designed as the Volksjager (People's Fighter) to a specification issued September 8, the Heinkel He 162 Sala-mander made its first flight just 67 days after Heinkel had been awarded the contract on September 30. Powered by a 1,764-lb. thrust BMW 003 E-1 turbojet mounted on top of the fuselage behind the cockpit, the aircraft had a wingspan of 23 ft. 8 in., a length of 29 ft. 8 in. and a loaded weight of 5,490 lb. The Volks-jager concept was developed by Karl Otto Sauer, chief of the technical department under Albert Speer's Ministry for Arma-ment and Ammunition, as a mass production home defense fighter. Troublesome to handle, the He 162 was too late to see combat, although some American pilots reported tangling with it.

1944 December 8 A direct copy of the Messerschmitt Me 163, the Mitsubishi J8M1 Shusui rocket fighter made its first flight when it was towed into the air by a Kyushu K10W1. Manufac-turing rights on the German Walter HWK 109-509 engine had been obtained earlier by Japanese military attachés in Berlin, but a submarine carrying technical data on the Me 163 and its engine was sunk in late 1943. On its first powered flight on July 7, 1945, the aircraft crashed, and no other prototypes flew.

1944 December 14 U.S. naval air support for the landings on Mindoro involved six escort carriers of Task Unit 77.12.1 and Marine Corps shore-based units in a two-day operation at the end of which the Japanese had lost 341 aircraft. Fighter sweeps over Luzon heralded the impending invasion of the main Philippine islands, which would begin in January 1945.

1944 December 16 In a last desperate effort to push the Allies back to the North Sea coast, 24 German divisions start a massive counterattack in the Ardennes known as the Battle of the Bulge. With a theoretical first-line strength of 1,500 aircraft in the area and a total of 2,360 aircraft, the Luftwaffe was never able to mount much more than 800 sorties a day. On December 24, the Allied air forces flew 3,823 sorties, of which 1,243 were flown by the British, dropping 1,521 tons of bombs. After this, the Luftwaffe was driven back to airspace over Germany, unable to mount more than 60–80 aircraft over the battle each day, most of those flying at night.

1944 December 17 The top-scoring U.S. air ace of all time, Maj. Richard I. Bong of the U.S. Fifth Air Force shot down his 40th and last victim, a Nakajima Ki-43, over the Philippines. Born September 24, 1920, the first of nine children, Bong opened his score December 27, 1942, with an Aichi D3A. Throughout the war, Bong flew P-38s in three tours: December 1942–No-vember 1943, February–April 1944 and October–December 1944. He was killed in a flying accident August 6, 1945, when the P-80 he was piloting crashed on takeoff at the Lockheed plant in Burbank, Calif.

1944 December 17 The 509th Composite Group, U.S. Twen-tieth Air Force, was established at Wendover airfield, Utah under the command of Col. Paul W. Tibbets with Lt. Col. Thomas J. Classen as his deputy. The group's only combat unit was the 393rd Bomb Squadron commanded by Maj. Charles W. Sweeney and was equipped with specially modified B-29s, each with fit-tings to carry and drop one of two types of atomic bomb. A top-secret unit, the 509th had its own administrative and technical units to maintain its complete independence from other USAAF operations.

1944 December 28 The first U.S. Marine Corps squadrons as-signed to a fleet carrier, and the first units to operate the Vought F4U Corsair, became operational with the USS *Essex* when squadrons VMF-124 and VMF-213 joined Air Group 4 aboard the carrier at Ulithi Atoll. The 36 Corsairs were dispatched to consolidate air-strike power against possible threats from increas-ingly active kamikaze action.

1944 During the year, the USAAF accepted from manufactur-ing factories a total 69,956 aircraft, the highest annual total U.S. armed forces would ever achieve. It comprised 1,161 very heavy bombers, 14,887 heavy bombers, 5,228 medium bombers, 3,861 light bombers, 24,174 fighters, 95 reconnaissance aircraft, 9,276 transports, 7,578 trainers and 3,696 communications aircraft.

1945 January 1 The U.S. Navy issued a contract to North American Aviation for the company's first jet fighter, the NA-134, which entered operational service in 1948 as the FJ-1 Fury. The aircraft was to lead directly to the most famous North Amer-ican aircraft of the post-World War II era, the F-86 Sabre. The XFJ-1 flew for the first time on November 27, 1946, and service models were powered by the 4,000-lb. thrust Allison J35-A-2 turbojet. The FJ-1 had a top speed of 547 MPH at 9,000 ft. and an initial climb rate of 3,300 ft./min. By mid-1949, the aircraft was retired, only 30 having been built.

1945 January 1 Under Operation Bodenplatte, the Luftwaffe launched an all-out effort to destroy the Allied airfields in liber-ated areas of Europe and as many aircraft as possible on the ground. The Luftwaffe had concentrated 2,360 aircraft for the Battle of the Bulge December 16, 1944, but could deploy just 800 fighters and fighter-bombers for Bodenplatte. In the event,

150 Allied aircraft were destroyed for the loss of 270 German aircraft. This was the last major Luftwaffe offensive. By February 1, the Luftwaffe had only 1,000 aircraft in the west, of which 600 were single-engined fighters.

1945 January 3 U.S. Navy Task Force 38 of the Third Fleet and Central Pacific Forces launched an air offensive against Formosa and the Ryukyus with a combined force of nine heavy and 12 escort carriers followed by a two-day attack on Luzon beginning January 6 and on the Formosa-Pescadores-Ryukyus area again on January 9. In this period, over 100 Japanese aircraft were destroyed and 40,000 tons of shipping sunk. Seventh Fleet carriers covered the Luzon Attack Force as it moved up for a landing in Lingayen Gulf, but kamikaze pilots sank the escort carrier *Ommaney Bay* (CVE-79) on January 4.

1945 January 3 In the first of a series of test raids on Japanese cities with incendiary bombs, 57 B-29s operating from the Marianas bombed the docks and urban areas of Nagoya with less-than-anticipated results. Washington had requested incendiary raids, and Gen. H. Arnold was convinced that Japanese cities were ripe for this sort of attack, but there was opposition to any attempt to deflect Twentieth Air Force bombers from precision bombing with high explosives. The next test raid was on February 4 when 69 B-29s raided Kobe followed February 25 when 172 aircraft burned out a square quarter-mile of downtown Tokyo.

1945 January 9 With Seventh Fleet carrier-based air cover, the invasion of Luzon began. Operations in the South China Sea involved 14 fast carriers and 926 aircraft in air strikes along 420 mi. of the coast of Indochina. On January 12, 32 ships and a large number of smaller boats totaling in all 149,000 tons were sunk. Moving north to avoid a typhoon, the strike force hit Hong Kong, the coast of China and Formosa on January 15, sinking a further 62,000 tons of shipping. On the run-out through the Balintang Channel January 20, the task force hit Formosa, the Pescadores and Okinawa again. In three weeks, 600 Japanese aircraft and 325,000 tons of shipping had been destroyed.

1945 January 13 Close air support backing up the British Fourteenth Army in Burma reached a new peak when 54 RAF bombers hit the Japanese military quarter in Mandalay, killing 1,000 people and destroying 70 major buildings. It was just two days short of three years since the Japanese invasion of Burma. Since early 1943, the British had been pushing hard, without much success, to retake the country and building in the process a major air lift to supply the troops pressing down toward Mandalay from India.

1945 January 20 The Imperial Japanese Army ordered Nakajima to design a simple, easy to build, suicide aircraft for the impending defense of the homeland. The prototype Ki-115 was completed in March, a conventional low-wing monoplane powered by a 1,500-HP Nakajima 23 14-cylinder radial with provision for two solid propellant rockets under each wing to increase speed in a dive. None were ready in time for operational use, but the design is testimony enough to the desperate final days of Japan's warring adventures.

1945 January 26 The prototype McDonnell FH-1 Phantom made its first flight, powered by two 1,165-lb.-thrust Westinghouse 19 XB-2B engines. Originally designated XFD-1, the prototype was redesignated XFH-1, removing the *D* to avoid confusion with Douglas aircraft. The Phantom entered service in late 1947, only 60 being built. The FH-1 had a wingspan of 40 ft. 9 in., a length of 37 ft. 3 in. and a maximum weight of 12,035 lb. With a top

speed of 479 MPH, it was not much faster than conventional fighters, but it had a climb rate of 4,230 ft./min. and a service ceiling of 41,100 ft.

1945 January In a single month, the USAAF Air Transport Command flew 5,000 flights over the "Hump" (the Himalayas) between India and China. In one month, 44,000 tons of materiel was air-lifted at an average of about 1,500 tons per day, an apt climax to flights along this route, which began in 1942 and burgeoned into the most consistently intensive airlift operation of World War II. It was with the experience and organization of operations such as these that postwar U.S. airlines would dominate civil air operations.

1945 February 1 One of the most effective Japanese army single-seat interceptors of World War II made its first flight when the Kawasaki Ki-100 took to the air, powered by a 1,500-HP Mitsubishi Ha-112-II 14-cylinder double-row radial. In a sense, it was Japan's equivalent to the German Focke-Wulf Fw 190, for that aircraft had demonstrated how a bulky radial engine could be married to a slim fuselage. Essentially a reengined, redesigned Ki-61 Hien, the Ki-100 had a top speed of 360 MPH at 19,685 ft. and proved a worthy mount for ambitious fighter pilots. Only 384 were built, and though it served only five months, it earned the healthy respect of those who flew it and those who flew against it.

1945 February 13 Allied plans to mount massive air raids on German cities causing confusion and panic in order to stimulate the final collapse of Germany were realized this night in Operation Thunderclap when 805 RAF bombers hit Dresden in two waves. They dropped 2,660 tons of bombs in a mix of high explosives and incendiaries, creating a firestorm and an unknown number of dead. Evidence indicates a probable toll of around 55,000, roughly equal to all the British civilian dead due to World War II. In all, 80,000 buildings were destroyed and 95,000 damaged, leaving 45,000 unaffected. More than 250,000 people were made homeless and driven out of the city.

1945 February 14 In a continuation of Operation Thunderclap and the RAF raid on Dresden the previous night, 311 U.S. Eighth Air Force B-17s dropped 850 tons of bombs on marshaling yards in the city, while escort P-51 fighters strafed roads in the surrounding countryside. Refugees had doubled Dresden's residential population of 1 million, and many fled along these roads. During the night, a further raid by 211 B-17s dropped 512 tons of bombs, and exactly three weeks later another raid by 406 B-17s dropped 1,190 tons. In four raids, the city had received 4,700 tons of high explosives and incendiaries.

1945 February 16 U.S. Navy Task Force 52.2 under Rear Adm. C. T. Durgin commenced air strikes from nine escort carriers (supplemented later by two more escort carriers and a strike carrier) in support of the impending landings on Iwo Jima. Task Force 52.2 was joined for the February 19 Iwo Jima landings by Task Force 58 under Vice Adm. Mark A. Mitscher, who had been attacking Japan with nine heavy and five escort carriers since February 16. He returned to attacks on Tokyo Bay beginning February 24 and struck Okinawa and the Ryukyus March 1. By March 16, the day Iwo Jima was secured, his ships and planes had destroyed 648 Japanese aircraft and 30,000 tons of merchant shipping.

1945 February 21 Germany's top-scoring night fighter pilot, the 23-year-old Maj. Heinz-Wolfgang Schnaufer of NJG 4 shot down two Lancasters in the predawn hours and during the evening, before midnight, seven more Lancasters, bringing his one-day total to nine. Five days earlier a British military radio station broadcast birthday greetings to this "Night Ghost of St. Trond." After the war, Maj. Schnaufer and his Bf 110 were brought to England, his aircraft displayed in Hyde Park, London. He died July 15, 1950, from injuries sustained in a car accident two days earlier.

1945 February 22 Begun at 1:00 P.M. Operation Clarion was an all-out attempt by the Allied air forces in Europe to destroy as far as possible, within 24 hr., all means of transportation and communication still open to the Germans. It involved 9,000 aircraft operating from bases in England, France, Belgium, Holland and Italy, and attacks covered an area of 250,000 sq. mi. The U.S. eighth and ninth air forces flew 1,709 heavy bomber sorties against targets in north, central and southwestern Germany. By now there was very little air resistance from the Luftwaffe.

1945 February 27 A Messerschmitt Me 262C-1a flown by Flugkapitän Karl Bauer performed the first flight of this aircraft with an auxiliary propulsion system in addition to the two Junkers Jumo turbojets. Fitted with a Walter 109-509A-2 rocket motor delivering a thrust of up to 3,740 lb., the Me 262 reached a height of 38,400 ft. in 4.5 min. These tests led to development of a turbojet/rocket motor designated 109-003R providing 2,205-lb. of thrust for 3 min. Calculated to give the Me 262 a climb time of 42,640 ft. in 2 min. 20 sec., it was not fully developed, and only five flights took place before the war ended.

1945 February 28 Oblt. Lothar Siebert was killed while carrying out the first manned flight of the vertically-launched rocket interceptor, the Bachem Ba 349 Natter. Launched by four solid-propellant Schmidding 109-533s giving a combined thrust of 10,560 lb. for 10 sec., the interceptor carried a liquid-propellant Walter 109-509A-2 sustainer delivering a maximum thrust of 3,750 lb. for 70 sec. The Natter rose for 1,650 ft. before the canopy came away. The interceptor rolled on its back and climbed at a shallow angle through 4,800 ft. before nosing into the ground.

1945 March 4 At precisely 1:51 A.M., Junkers Ju 88G-6 D5+AX (Werke No. 620028), piloted by Hptm. J. Dreher and carrying a crew of three from night fighter unit 13./Nachtjagdgeschwader 3, became the last aircraft to crash on British soil during World War II. Confused by a car's headlights, the aircraft hit a tree while attacking the airfield at Elvington and crashed at Sutton upon Derwent, Yorkshire, killing all four crewmembers. Two other Ju 88s had crashed in separate incidents at 1:37 and 1:45. The last German aircraft to reach Britain during hostilities was a Ju 188A-3, which landed in Fraserburgh, Scotland, on May 2 with five members of 9./KG26 escaping from Trondheim, Norway.

1945 March 10 In a devastating demonstration of the effectiveness of incendiary raids on Japanses cities, 279 B-29s hit urban areas of Tokyo in the early hours killing 83,000 people, a death toll from a single raid never exceeded in the the annals of aerial warfare. The bombers dropped 1,675 tons of bombs, and in the firestorm that developed, 15.8 sq. mi. of Tokyo were completely burned out with the destruction of 267,000 buildings (25% of the total). One B-29 bombing late was caught in a thermal draught and thrown 5,000 ft. higher. As the aircraft retreated, the sky-glow could be seen from a distance of 125 mi.

1945 March 14 A Lancaster (serial no. PD112) piloted by Sqdn. Ldr. C. C. Calder of No. 617 Squadron, RAF, dropped the first 22,000-lb. bomb close to the Bielefeld viaduct, shattering its

structure and destroying a 300-ft. section. Known as the "Grand Slam," the bomb was an earthquake type designed to shatter structures through tremors created by the explosion; fourteen 12,000-lb. Tallboy bombs were also carried by Lancasters on this raid. Carrying the main train line from Hamm to Hanover, the viaduct had resisted seven attacks beginning February 22. No. 617 Squadron would drop another 40 Grand Slams before the end of the war.

1945 March 18 One of the most enduring U.S. Navy carrier-based attack bombers of the postwar era, the Douglas XBT2D-1 made its first flight 8 mon. after the initial order. A total of 3,180 would be built before production ceased in 1957. Designed around the chunky 2,500-HP Wright R-3350, it could carry a warload of up to 8,000 lb. under its wings and would enter service in late 1946 as the AD-1 Skyraider, better known as "Spad" to its devotees. Used extensively throughout the Vietnam War, the Skyraider had a span of 50 ft., a length of 38 ft. 2 in. and a gross weight of 18,263 lb. with a cruising speed of 198 MPH and a range of 95 mi.

1945 March 18 At the start of the Okinawa campaign, Vice Adm. Mitscher's 10 heavy and six light fast carriers of Task Force 58 began an intensive five-day softening up process, destroying 528 Japanese aircraft, followed by preinvasion strikes on the island March 23. Increasingly, kamikaze attacks were hitting hard at U.S. Navy carriers and support ships, and from March 26 Rear Adm. C. T. Durgin's Task Group 52.1 and its 18 escort carriers joined Vice Adm. Mitscher's force for preassault strikes on Okinawa.

1945 March 18 In a major air action where Luftwaffe Me 262 units claimed 14 USAAF aircraft shot down during a major air raid by the Eighth Air Force, the jet fighters used R4M air-to-air rockets for the first time. Attached to wooden racks, each Me 262 carried 12 rockets under each wing. Fired within 0.003 sec., the battery of 24 missiles were made to converge on a bomber at 1,800 ft. Designed by Kurt Heber and built by DWM at Lübeck, each 8-lb. rocket contained 17.6 oz. of the explosive Hexagon, and because the ballistics were similar to the MK 108 cannon, a standard Revi 16B gunsight was fitted in the cockpit.

1945 March 19 In the last of five night incendiary raids on Japanese cities conducted by Gen. Curtis LeMay beginning March 10, 290 B-29s dropped a mixture of high explosives, napalm and incendiary bombs on Nagoya during the early hours. The first fire raid on Nagoya since the January test raids had taken place in the early hours of March 11 involving 285 B-29s. The third fire raid hit Osaka with 274 B-29s in the early evening of March 13 followed with a raid by 307 B-29s on Kobe in the early hours of March 16. The March fire raids burned out a total 32 sq. mi. in the four cities, and the conflagrations were so intense that on occasion thunderheads formed from the fire thermals and lightning struck the aircraft.

1945 March 20 The last Luftwaffe air raid on the British Isles took place, during which the last German aircraft shot down by the RAF over Britain fell into the sea after being attacked by a Mosquito Mk.XXX from No. 125 Squadron, RAF. It was a Ju 188 that crashed 10 mi. northeast of Cromer in the final hour before midnight. Since the first British civilian death in a Luftwaffe air raid on March 16, 1940, 51,509 civilians had been killed and 61,423 seriously injured by German aircraft. An additional 6,148 had been killed and 17,981 seriously injured by V-1 flying bombs, and a further 2,754 killed and 6,523 injured by V-2 ballistic missiles.

1945 March 23 The Allied ground assault across the lower reaches of the Rhine River began with Allied air forces flying more than 8,200 sorties, of which 4,900 were flown by fighters and fighter-bombers. Considered by both sides to be the symbolic frontier to the German heartland, the Rhine had first been crossed on March 7 at Remagen and then on March 22 at Nierstein. For two days, massive aerial bombardment had prepared for this major offensive in the south, with U.S. eighth and ninth air forces flying 2,800 sorties on March 21 and 2,700 on March 22.

1945 March 24 The U.S. eighth and ninth air forces flew more than 5,000 sorties, 2,000 of which were transport-glider combinations of IX Troop Carrier Command air-lifting the British Sixth Airborne and the U.S. Seventeenth Airborne divisions plus their equipment, supplies and ammunition. They were put down on the eastern side of the Rhine and north and northwest of Wesel as the British Second and the U.S. Ninth armies were crossing the river to the northwest and the southeast. Fighter-bombers laid an intensive carpet of fragmentation bombs prior to the landings. In all, more than 3,000 Allied fighters supported Operation Varsity.

1945 March 25 In a USAAF air raid on industrial facilities near Letov, outside of Prague, the Heinkel He 177 V38 prototype, specially adapted to carry the German atom bomb, was damaged beyond repair. It had been at Letov since 1942 with its wings removed and modifications made to the bomb bay enabling the aircraft to carry an air-drop weapon, should it ever fly again. The atom bomb project was far from producing a practical weapon although the Luftwaffe had earmarked other He 177s that would be adapted for such a mission. Work was stopped in August 1944.

1945 March 27 The U.S. Twentieth Air Force began B-29 operations in support of the Okinawa campaign, with more than 150 aircraft from the Marianas hitting Tachiarai and Oita airfields and the Omura aircraft factory. Mines were laid in the Shimonoseki Strait by 97 B-29s in the first of many such operations. A second mine-laying operation three days later blocked the approach to Sasebo and southern approaches to Kure and Hiroshima.

1945 March 31 With the war in Europe almost over and the Pacific war coming to a climax, the British Commonwealth Air Training Program was officially terminated. During the war, it had produced 137,739 aircrew, of which 54,098 had been pilots. Training took place in Commonwealth countries and the Dominions to relieve pressure on British operational units and to permit training to take place without fear of attack.

1945 March Construction of three prototype Henschel Hs 132 turbojet-powered dive-bombers began at the Schönefeld factory. The end of hostilities prevented the only prototype of the V1, anywhere near completely built from making a flight before it was finished and taken to the Soviet Union. Designed as a dive-bomber so as to avoid problems with conventional bomb sights on high speed jets releasing their loads in straight and level flight, the pilot lay prone in the nose to withstand the 12 g incurred in a dive.

1945 April 1 The first successful Japanese rocket-propelled suicide attack took place when a Yokosuka MXY7 Ohka of the 721st Kokutai damaged the battleship USS *West Virginia* and others damaged three transport vessels. It had first been taken into attack on March 21. The Ohka was a small, manned projectile carried to the vicinity of a target by a parent aircraft and released, following which the "pilot" ignited either a rocket motor or a turbojet depending on the variant. With a terminal velocity of 576 MPH, it had a range of up to 73 mi. and carried variable-sized warheads of up to 2,646 lb.

1945 April 6 The first in a series of mass suicide attacks by Japanese kamikaze pilots involved 400 human bombs flown this day against the U.S. Navy's Task Force 58 supporting the battle for Okinawa. By May 28, 1,500 Japanese kamikaze aircraft and pilots had flown against U.S. naval forces with eight heavy and one light carrier from Task Force 58 hit as well as three escort carriers of Task Force 52, the last on June 6.

1945 April 7 Moving south toward Okinawa from its base at Tokuyama on the southern coast of Honshu, a Japanese task force of one light cruiser, eight destroyers and the world's biggest battleship, *Yamato,* was spotted by U.S. submarines off the Bungo Strait. A force of 380 dive-bombers and torpedo bombers was launched from Task Force 58 at 10:00 A.M. with the Japanese warships 250 mi. away. For defense, the 71,000 ton *Yamato* had 146 25-mm antiaircraft guns, but by 2:25 P.M., it had been sunk with the loss of 3,063 lives. Out of 10 Japanese warships, only four destroyers survived.

1945 April 7 The last major Luftwaffe fighter operation took place when 120 Bf 109Gs of Ram Commando (Rammkommando) Elbe attacked 1,300 USAAF bombers escorted by 850 fighters. Only 15 German aircraft returned from a melee in which 50 bombers and six escorting fighters had been brought down. The unit had been formed by Oberst. Hajo Herrmann as a last-ditch method of stopping Allied bombers. Herrmann commanded IX Fliegerdivision with its 150 Bf 109s. Most of the volunteer pilots were inexperienced, with only one or two flights to their credit.

1945 April 25 The last offensive bombing mission conducted by the U.S. Eighth Air Force took 554 B-17s and B-24s to targets in southeast Germany. No aircraft were lost, and there was only one loss out of 539 fighter escort and patrol missions. It had been 967 days since the first operational mission from England, and in that time the "Mighty Eighth" had flown 332,904 heavy bomber sorties, of which 274,921 were effective, and dropped 714,719 tons of bombs for an average bomb drop per sortie of 2.147 tons. The Eighth Air Force was to continue flying leaflet and food supply dropping missions through May 8, by which time a total of 5,548 aircraft had been lost, 2,452 to enemy fighters and the rest to flak and accidents. On average, planes flew 60 sorties before being lost.

1945 May 2 During the night, RAF Bomber Command carried out its last raid of World War II when 126 Mosquitoes attacked Kiel in two raids one hour apart. The last Bomber Command fatalities of the war occurred when two Halifaxes, supporting the Mosquitoes, collided with the loss of 13 airmen. RAF Bomber Command had flown operational missions on 1,481 (71%) of all calendar nights since the war began and on 1,089 days. In all, 389,809 sorties had been flown, on which 1,052,936 tons of bombs had been dropped for an average bomb drop per sortie of 2.7 tons. In all, Bomber Command lost 8,953 aircraft and 47,268 crewmembers, 67% of all RAF personnel killed or missing on operations during the war. Average sorties per lost aircraft was 43.5.

1945 May 5 The only U.S. citizens known to have been killed in the continental United States from enemy bombs died when they pulled at a Japanese bomb that had been carried across the Pacific on a balloon—one of 9,300 launched beginning November 3, 1944. A woman and five children in Lakeview, Oreg. died after finding the strange-looking object caught in thick bushes and tugging at it, causing it to explode. Hitherto silent on the potential threat, the U.S. government then issued a general warning.

1945 May 7   At precisely 2:41 A.M. General Jodl signed surrender terms on behalf of the German High Command simultaneously to both Western and Eastern commanders, a ceasefire to take effect at midnight on May 8/9. So ended just over 5 yr. 8 mon. of war in Europe during which German aggression resulted in almost 40 million dead, of whom more than 20 million were civilians, with countless more millions permanently injured in body and mind. In that period, 4 million Germans passed through the ranks of the Luftwaffe; 320,000 were killed and 230,000 seriously injured. Of the dead, 70,000 were air crew killed on operations, with 25,000 air crew wounded.

1945 May 8   On this last day of war in Europe, figures showed that of 99,406 aircraft received by the Luftwaffe, 79,405 (79.8%) had been destroyed. Only 40,738 (51.3% of total losses) were attributable to enemy action, 38,667 (48.7% of total losses and 38.9% of all aircraft delivered) being due to accidents. Between late 1939 and early 1945, German fighter production had increased from 24% to 77.8% of all aircraft delivered, and four fighter models had accounted for 55% of all aircraft delivered: the Bf 109 (28,103 received), Fw 190 (20,001), Bf 110 (5,762) and Me 262 (1,294). Peak delivery had been achieved in 1944, when 36,953 aircraft were received by the Luftwaffe.

Luftwaffe operations with the rocket-propelled Me 163 fighter came to an end when II/JG 400 surrendered at Husum to elements of an RAF regiment. In all, 364 Me 163s had been built, 279 being production aircraft, but fewer than one-quarter saw operation service. Me 163 pilots were credited with having shot down at least 16 aircraft for the loss of six rocket planes. Production had been stopped in February to conserve diminishing resources for more conventional aircraft. So ended the operational career of the world's only rocket fighter deployed and used in combat.

In the period from September 1, 1939, to the cessation of air combat, Luftwaffe fighter pilots logged 70,000 victories, out of 120,000 Allied aircraft destroyed, of which 45,000 were Soviet and 25,000 mostly British and American aircraft. Of 28,000 men who served as Luftwaffe fighter pilots, only 1,400 survived the war. Under the most stringent rules of confirmation, the Jagdwaffe produced over 3,000 aces (5 or more victories), while the RAF (including Canada, Australia and New Zealand) produced 868, the USAAF in Europe 262, the USSR 162 and France 130. Five other countries produced a total 118 aces. In all, 10 Allied groups or countries generated 1,540 aces, about half the total for the Luftwaffe.

In the period since September 1, 1939, the Jagdwaffe produced 107 fighter pilots with confirmed victory scores of 100 or more; the highest-scoring ace, Erich Hartmann, had 352. The leading aces among the Allies were, by nationality, a USSR pilot, with 62 confirmed kills; RAF (including Canada, Australia and New Zealand), 38; France 33; USAAF (Europe), 28; Czechoslovakia, 28; ''Eagle Squadron,'' 25; Poland, 18; Norway 16; and South Africa 15. The combined total of all nine Allied leading aces (263 victories) came to only three-quarters the score credited to Germany's highest scoring ace, and 467 Jagdwaffe aces scored more than the top RAF ace.

1945 May 8   Top-scoring Luftwaffe fighter of all time, Maj. Erich Hartmann secured his last, and 352nd, air combat victory when he shot down a Soviet fighter over Czechoslovakia. Since his first victory on November 5, 1942, he averaged a ''kill'' every

2.5 days for 30 months of air combat action on the Eastern Front. ''Bubi'' Hartmann flew 1,425 missions, survived more than 800 combats and 13 accidents, rode his fighter through 12 crash landings and only jumped by parachute once. Born April 19, 1922, he joined the reconstituted Luftwaffe in 1959, after having spent 10 years as a Soviet prisoner. He commanded JG 71 ''Richthofen'' before retiring.

1945 May 17   The Lockheed P2V Neptune made its first flight, powered by two 2,300-HP Wright R-3350-8 engines. This land-based patrol aircraft saw service with the U.S. Navy for two decades from its introduction in March 1947 and operated with the Argentinian Commando de Aviacion Naval into the 1980s. The P2V also operated with the naval air arms of Australia, Brazil, Canada, Chile, France, Japan, the Netherlands, Portugal and the United Kingdom.

1945 May 18   North American Aviation received a contract from the USAAF for three prototype jet fighters adapted for land use from the XFJ-1 Fury being built for the U.S. Navy. Called XP-86, it incorporated a straight-through inlet/exhaust arrangement with the engine set in the mid-fuselage position just behind the pilot. The overall design was approved June 20, but in August, NAA incorporated captured German research to develop a swept wing based on the study of an Me 262 wing, which resulted in a year's production delay.

1945 May 29   For the first time on a fire-bombing raid, 454 Twentieth Air Force B-29s on a daylight bombing raid to Yokohama were escorted by 101 P-51s from VII Fighter Command. Anticipating enemy fighters, Gen. Curtis LeMay had ordered the escorts, which in the ensuing air battles shot down 26 aircraft for the loss of three P-51s, the B-29s claiming six Japanese fighters for the loss of seven bombers. Fighter escorts became routine, but on one raid June 1, 27 fighters out of 148 on their way to rendezvous with 458 B-29s for an attack on Osaka were lost, due to collisions caused by extreme turbulence.

1945 June 7   In the last of Gen. Curtis Lemay's great city raids on Japan with massed formations of B-29s, 409 bombers dropped incendiaries and high explosives on industrial, transport and army arsenal areas of Osaka, destroying 55,000 buildings and 2 sq. mi. of the city. In the period between the fire raid on Nagoya March 19 and this date, the U.S. Twentieth Air Force flew 5,538 strategic sorties against Japanese cities and industrial areas in addition to tactical support for the Okinawa campaign, to which it was exclusively committed between April 17 and May 11.

1945 June 9   Switching from massed air raids on major cities, Gen. Curtis LeMay sent 110 Twentieth Air Force B-29s to three separate industrial targets in Narao, Atsuta and Akashi. Beginning on the night of June 16/17, LeMay attacked medium-size cities with populations of 60,000–300,000 on a list of 25 urban zones believed crucial to achieving an air victory before an invasion of the Japanese mainland. By the end of hostilities on August 15, the Twentieth Air Force had razed 58 such cities to the ground in raids that put up to 784 aircraft out on a single night.

1945 June 21   Naval air units of Task Force 38 (renamed from Task Force 58 when it was transferred May 28 to Third Fleet under Adm. W. F. Halsey) ended an intensive 96-day campaign to capture Okinawa during which period 3,022 Japanese aircraft had been destroyed by U.S. Navy and Marine Corps units. Japanese resistance on Okinawa had all but ended in a campaign that had been waged since March 18 for the loss of 12,500 U.S.

Army and Navy lives and about 125,000 Japanese. Carriers had flown more than 40,000 combat sorties, dropping 8,500 tons of bombs and expending 50,000 air-to-ground rockets. Shore-based U.S. Marine Corps units dropped 1,800 tons of bombs and fired 15,865 rockets.

1945 June 22 Piloted by Vickers test pilot J. "Mutt" Summers, the prototype VC1 Viking made its first flight. Sponsored by the British government and developed as an interim short-haul airliner before the Brabazon projects matured in the 1950s, it was based on the Wellington bomber. It accommodated a crew of three and 21 passengers with a range of 1,500 mi. at 190 MPH and was powered by two 1,675-HP Bristol Hercules 130 engines. The Viking began work with British European Airways (BEA) in September 1946, and 163 were built, as well as 263 Valetta RAF transport aircraft and 163 Varsitys for RAF conversion training.

1945 June 25 The National Skyway Freight Corp. was founded by Robert Prescott, one of Gen. Chennault's "Flying Tigers" who operated C-46 transport aircraft over the "Hump" between India and China. At first the company flew the strange-looking Budd RB-1 Conestogas before acquiring C-47s and C-54s. In February 1947, it changed its name to the Flying Tiger Line Inc. and was known as the Flying Tigers until bought by Federal Express in 1990.

1945 July 1 The U.S. Navy had on hand a total 40,912 aircraft, the highest U.S. Navy figure ever achieved at an end-of-fiscal-year inventory, of which 29,125 were for combat, 2,897 for transport and utility, 8,370 for training and 520 for miscellaneous duties. There were also 27 helicopters. The navy had a total 319,147 aviation personnel on active duty, the highest end-of-fiscal-year figure, comprising 77,344 officers (49,380 pilots) and 241,803 enlisted men (439 pilots). With another all-time peak return, the U.S. Marine Corps had a total 111,710 aviation personnel on active duty comprising 15,309 officers (10,229 pilots) and 96,401 enlisted men (47 pilots).

1945 July 10 As a component of U.S. Navy Third Fleet under Adm. W. F. Halsey, Vice Adm. J. S. McCain's Task Force 38 (of 14 carriers) began intensive air strikes against the Tokyo plains area of Japan at the start of a softening up process prior to the invasion of the southern Japanese islands under Operation Olympic, scheduled to begin November 1. Strikes shifted to northern Honshu and Hokkaido on July 14–15 and back again to Tokyo July 17 and Yokosuka July 18. Between July 24 and 30, attacks moved up past Osaka to Nagoya and back again before departing the Tokyo area for the atomic bomb drop.

1945 July 29 Japanese opposition in Burma finally came to an end following an intensive nine days of British air attacks where the RAF had flown 3,045 sorties and dropped 750 tons of bombs. In the air and ground actions during this period, 10,000 Japanese were killed. In the Burma campaign, 96% of 615,000 tons airlifted to the British Fourteenth Army went by air, of which 75% was carried by the USAAF, and 315,000 troops flown in and 110,000 casualties flown out. In March alone, 94,300 tons of supplies had been carried in by air.

1945 August 1 In the largest night attack mounted by the U.S. Twentieth Air Force, 627 B-29s carried out a fire raid on the Japanese cities of Hachioji, Toyama, Nagaoka and Mito, 120 other aircraft bombed the Kawasaki petroleum facilities, and 37 laid mines around the coast. The total of 784 aircraft out of 836 dispatched represented the peak of strategic operations mounted by Twentieth Air Force in a single day during World War II.

This was the penultimate strategic air raid before the first atomic bomb was dropped on August 6, a raid on the night of August 5/6 sending more than 600 B-29s to four cities and mine-laying duties.

1945 August 6 At 9:15 A.M., the first atomic bomb to be used in war was dropped from the B-29 named *Enola Gay* and piloted by Col. Paul W. Tibbets, accompanied by a B-29 camera aircraft (No. 91) and an instrumented B-29 *Great Artiste* and preceded by B-29 *Straight Flush* on a visibility run. Dubbed *Little Boy*, the bomb had a length of 10 ft. 6 in., a diameter of 2 ft. 4 in. and weighed 8,900 lb. Released at 31,600 ft., it exploded 50 sec. later, 2,000 ft. over Hiroshima, with a yield of 15,000 tons of TNT (30 million lb., or 1,364 times the biggest conventional bomb). It destroyed more than 80% of the buildings, killing more than 70,000 people out of 245,000 residents. *Enola Gay* landed back at Tinian at 2:58 P.M. after a flight time of 12 hr. 13 min.

1945 August 6 After the atom bomb had been dropped on Hiroshima, U.S. president Harry S Truman said of the Japanese that "If they do not now accept our terms they may expect a rain of ruin from the air, the like of which has never been seen on this earth." This belied the fact that the United States had only two bombs in 1945. Not for 2 yr. would it have more than 10 and not before May 1949 would the United States have its first production-line bomb. Notwithstanding, 8 yr. after the first production bomb appeared, the United States stockpile would exceed 5,000 atomic bombs.

1945 August 7 The only Japanese turbojet-powered aircraft of World War II, the Nakajima J8N1 Kikka made its first flight at the Kisarazu Naval Air Base, piloted by Lt. Comdr. Susumu Takaoka and powered by two 1,047-lb.-thrust Ne 20 engines, a copy of the BMW 003. The prototype made only one more flight before the project was terminated August 15. The J8N1 was stimulated by the Me 262 and bore considerable likeness to it. It had a wingspan of 32 ft. 10 in. and a length of 26 ft. 7 in. with a top speed of 433 MPH at 32,810 ft., an altitude it could reach in 26 min.

1945 August 9 The second of only two atomic bombs dropped in war fell from B-29 *Bock's Car* piloted by Maj. Charles W. Sweeney, at 11:58 A.M. and from a height of 28,900 ft. About a minute later, it exploded over Nagasaki with an explosive yield of 21,000 tons of TNT, killing about 35,000 people and destroying just under 1.5 sq. mi., creating much less damage than at

In the aftermath of the Nagasaki atomic bomb, dropped August 9, 1945, air power took on new and awesome proportions.

Hiroshima three days before. Dubbed *Fat Man,* the plutonium bomb had a length of 10 ft. 6 in., a diameter of 5 ft. and a weight of 10,000 lb. Kokura, the primary target, had to be abandoned for Nagasaki due to bad weather.

1945 August 9   Vice Adm. J. S. McCain's Task Force 38 resumed air strikes on the Japanese mainland until Adm. W. F. Halsey sent a message at 6:35 A.M. August 15 ordering the cessation of all hostilities. A carrier strike against Tokyo had already taken place, and another had to be recalled. Since July 10 when intensive U.S. Navy air strikes against Japan started, 1,223 Japanese aircraft had been destroyed along with 23 warships and 48 merchant ships grossing 285,000 tons.

1945 August 10   In a not unrepresentative example of the weather faced by Allied pilots in Burma, 16 Spitfires from No. 615 Squadron, RAF, attempted to fly from Palel on the Imphal plain to Calcutta, India. Running into a very large cumulonimbus cloud only 30 mi. out, one aircraft was thrown from 5,000 ft. to 11,000 ft., four were destroyed and their pilots killed, four pilots had to bail out by parachutes and all of the remaining eight arrived at their destination with hands cut up in attempts to fight the controls. These were new operating conditions for airmen schooled in the less violent weather of Europe and North America.

1945 August 14   The last air raids by the U.S. Twentieth Air Force were carried out against Japan. They begin with 302 B-29s hitting the naval arsenal at Hikari and the army arsenal at Osaka and with 108 B-29s striking the marshaling yards at Marifu. During the night, more than 160 aircraft bombed Kumagaya and Isezaki, and 132 flew nonstop from the Marianas on a 3,650-mi. round trip to bomb the Nippon Oil Co. at Tsuchizakiminato, the longest round trip bombing raid from the Marianas. The unconditional surrender of Japan was announced by U.S. Pres. Harry S Truman before the B-29s returned. Ironically, the last B-29 lost in the war was mistakenly shot down by Soviet fighters on August 29.

1945 August 15   The last B-29 returned to the Marinas from a raid on Tsuchizakiminato shortly after the formal announcement of Japan's acceptance of peace terms. This was the last of 29,155 effective sorties completed by aircraft of its type. In just 14 months, B-29s had dropped 171,060 tons of bombs, burned out 175 sq. mi. of 66 Japanese cities, virtually destroyed the Japanese munitions industry and laid 12,000 mines. The average bomb drop per sortie was about 5 tons. In all, 350,000 Japanese civilians had been killed, 480,000 injured, 9.2 million made homeless and 2.21 million homes demolished in the fire raids and the two atomic bomb drops, for the loss of 414 aircraft and 3,015 B-29 crewmembers and 80 fighters. It is estimated the strategic raids killed an additional 550,000 and injured 820,000 Japanese on military duty or war work.

1945 August 15   At the end of the U.S. Twentieth Air Force strategic bombing of Japan, the effects of the B-29 raids had drastically reduced aircraft production. Between mid-1941 and the end of the third quarter 1944, Japanese aircraft production increased six-fold but was to be halved from that in nine months as industry was hit by air raids. Overall, war production had been reduced by 53% between September 1944 and this date. Production of merchant ships and motor vehicles had been reduced by 82% and 96% respectively since the beginning of the war.

1945 August 15   At precisely 5:40 A.M., a Nakajima C6N Saiun was shot down by fighter pilot Lt. Comdr. Reidy, U.S. Navy, the last Japanese aircraft to be shot down in World War II. Five

minutes later the war was officially over. The aircraft type had been developed in 1942 as a long-range, carrier-borne reconnaissance aircraft. Powered by a 1,820-HP Nakajima NK9B Homare 11, it was eventually adapted to a home defense night fighting role, and it was in that role that it enters this history.

1945 August 31   To this date during 1945, the USAAF took acceptance at the factory of 29,725 aircraft comprising 2,507 very heavy bombers, 3,771 heavy bombers, 1,636 medium bombers, 1,732 light bombers, 12,149 fighters, 247 reconnaissance aircraft, 4,236 transport aircraft, 1,309 trainers and 2,138 communications aircraft. As of this date, the USAAF had 63,715 aircraft on hand, including 2,865 very heavy bombers, 11,065 heavy bombers, 5,384 medium bombers, 3,079 light bombers, 16,799 fighters, 1,971 reconnaissance aircraft, 9,561 transport aircraft, 9,558 trainers and 3,433 communications aircraft.

Since January 1, 1940, the USAAC/AAF had received 230,288 aircraft: 3,764 very heavy bombers (1.63% of total), 31,000 heavy bombers (13.46%), 16,070 medium bombers (6.99%), 18,110 light bombers (7.86%), 68,259 fighters (29.64%), 1,117 reconnaissance aircraft (0.48%), 22,698 transport aircraft (9.86%), 55,712 trainers (24.19%) and 13,558 communications aircraft (5.89%). In all, the United States spent $45 billion on aircraft during World War II, about 25% of the near $200 billion spent on munitions. As an example of U.S. production capacity, in 1944 one Ford plant turned out 46,000 tons of airframes, almost the total output of Japanese aircraft for that year and 50% of the German output.

1945 September 2   The formal surrender of Japan was signed on the USS *Missouri* in Tokyo Bay by Mamoru Shigemitsu on behalf of the Emperor of Japan and the Japanese government and by Yoshijiro Umezu for the Japanese Imperial General Headquarters. Within hours, a C-54 left Tokyo airport for Washington, D.C., carrying film of the historic event, making a new record of 31 hr. 25 min. between the two cities. So ended World War II, the bloodiest conflict the world has ever known with 55 million dead of whom 31 million were civilians, including almost 6 million murdered Jews. Of that total, more than 1 million civilians in Britain, Germany and Japan had been killed in air raids.

On V-J Day, the USAAF had 33,235 first-line aircraft on hand, having lost 22,948 aircraft in combat operations since December 1941. Production output league tables per manufacturer since July 1, 1940, were headed by North American Aviation (having produced 41,188 aircraft); Consolidated Vultee (30,903); Douglas (30,696); Curtiss (26,154); Lockheed (18,926); Boeing (18,383); Grumman (17,428); Republic (15,603); Bell (13,575); Martin (8,810); and Chance Vought (7,890): Douglas put out the highest gross tonnage of aircraft, followed by Consolidated, Boeing and North American, which produced fighters.

1945 September 5   The prototype Douglas C-74 Globemaster I transoceanic cargo transport made its first flight. At the time the largest cargo aircraft in production, only 14 were built as orders were canceled on V-J Day. Powered by four 3,000-HP Pratt & Whitney R-4360-27, 28-cylinder radials, the C-74 had a normal range of 3,400 mi. and capacity for 125 troops, 115 stretcher cases or 48,150 lb. of cargo. Pan American placed an order for 26 as the DC-7—not to be confused with the later airliner given that designation—but canceled the order in 1947.

1945 September 11   Project MX-743 was born when Bell engineers Stanley Smith, Jack Strickler, Paul Emmons, Jack Woolams, Harold Hawkins, Charles Fray and Robert Stanley met to discuss a successor to the straight-wing transonic X-1 then being built. Swept-wing research at Bell and data from captured German test results gave confidence that such a configuration was vital for truly supersonic flight between Mach 1 and 2. Designated Bell Model 52, it was submitted to the USAAF at Wright Field on October 1.

1945 September 12 In the previous 15 days, 185 Douglas C-54 Skymasters with 15 in reserve at Manila, Guam and Saipan flew the first elements of the U.S. occupation force from Kadena airfield, Okinawa, to Japan. In this period, the C-54s made 3,646 flights carrying 23,456 troops and military personnel with more than 2,200 tons of cargo. The build-up of U.S. transport aircraft during the war put the United States in the forefront of commercial aviation in the immediate postwar years, and no opportunity was lost to press home this advantage as European industries, sapped of their resources, struggled to compete.

1945 September 19 No. 273 Squadron, RAF, flew into Tan Son Nhut airfield, Saigon with Spitfire IXs 17 days after the communist rebel leader Ho Chi Minh declared the independence of republican Vietnam. After the Japanese surrender September 2, the British administered the Japanese disarming process, but the Chinese armed the Communist Viet Minh. After an attack on Tan Son Nhut on October 13, the Japanese were rearmed to fight them since they were still in the country. The Japanese pilots flew 2,000 sorties by the time their Gremlin Task Force was disbanded in January 1946.

1945 September 20 Test pilot Eric Greenwood flew a Gloster Meteor F.1 (serial no. EE227) specially converted to accommodate two Rolls Royce R.B.50 Trent turboprop engines, the first time engines of this type had powered an aircraft in flight. The flight took place at Church Boughton, England with the 18th production Meteor having previously completed 80 flying hr. with No. 616 Squadron, RAF. It went to Rolls Royce at Hucknall to receive the Trents and 7 ft. 11 in.-diameter five-bladed Rotol propellers.

1945 September 25 Designed by R. E. Bishop to a stated Brabazon Committee requirement (concerning postwar civil aviation needs), the de Havilland D.H.104 Dove made its first flight, piloted by G. H. Pike. With two 330-HP Gypsy Queen 70-3 engines, early production aircraft carried between 8 and 11 passengers 1,000 mi. at 165 MPH (179 MPH for later models). It replaced the D.H.89 Dragon Rapide but was expensive to buy and costly to operate. Nevertheless, more than 500 were built and operated by airlines around the world.

1945 September 28 With four officers and four press correspondents, six C-54 Skymasters from the USAAF Air Transport Command began a 23,279-mi. round-the-world flight, which was completed in a record time of 149 hr. 4 min., a flying time of 116 hr. 23 min. at an average 200 MPH. Completed October 4, the event was instituted as a weekly event by C-54 Skymasters thereafter as rehearsal for possible long-range deployments due to unforseen emergencies.

1945 October 1 The first annual general meeting of the International Air Transport Association (IATA) took place at its new headquarters in Montreal, Canada. The articles of association had been accepted at the International Airline Operators Conference in Havana, Cuba April 16–19 when 41 airlines from 25 countries signed, and many more followed over the following months. A successor to the International Air Traffic Association formed in 1919, IATA was to be a self-governing watchdog and ethical policing service for airlines large and small.

1945 October 8 The Short Empire flying boat *Coriolanus* became the first QANTAS airliner into Singapore after the war with Japan, less than a month after the Japanese surrender in Southeast Asia. It departed Sydney, New South Wales October 4, and the return flight was made October 12–17 with 34 Australian POWs. *Coriolanus* opened the route between Sydney and Fiji via Noumea and Brisbane beginning November 19 and would log 2,523,641 mi. in 8,500 flying hr. when on December 20, 1947, it became the last Empire flying boat to retire.

1945 October 9 BOAC began a survey flight from Hurn, England to Lima, Peru via West Africa, Argentina and Chile when Capt. O. P. Jones departed at the controls of an Avro Lancastrian (G-AGMG). The Lancastrian was a converted Lancaster, the first (serial no. R5725) being a Mk.III converted by Victor Aircraft Ltd. Avro completed the first of 74 Lancastrians in early 1945. As early as May 12, BOAC had opened a United Kingdom-West Africa-Cairo passenger service using DC-3s; these were supplemented by Halifaxes for freight transport beginning October.

1945 October 17 In response to attacks on British military units in the Netherlands East Indies covering the Recovery of Allied Prisoners-of-War & Internees (RAPWI) program instituted August 16, 904 Wing, RAF, including two RAF regiment squadrons, landed at Batavia. They began a year-long campaign to suppress aggression from Sukarno and to stabilize the country for the evacuation of ex-POWs. The British recognized the new Republic of Indonesia, which Sukarno declared September 16, but Sukarno refused to accept that Britain, itself a colonial power, would permit independence from the Dutch.

1945 October 29 The first post-World War II Farnborough air show began with a display of captured German aircraft as well as British types the public had not hitherto had the chance to inspect. A flying display included fly-bys of the Short Shetland flying boat, and several engines were displayed on stands, setting the scene for future air displays in this small Hampshire town that for so long had been home to the Royal Aircraft Establishment.

1945 November 6 U.S. Navy Ensign Jake C. West landed the hybrid Ryan FR-1 Fireball on the deck of the USS *Wake Island* using the jet engine alone, thus becoming the first pilot to land a turbojet aircraft on the deck of an aircraft carrier. The first deck landing by an all-jet aircraft was performed by Lt. E. N. Brown (RNVR) on December 3 when he put his Sea Vampire down on the British carrier HMS *Ocean*. Brown's aircraft (serial no. LZ551) was the converted Mk.1 third prototype Vampire and preceded production of the Sea Vampire, which joined the Royal Navy in March 1948.

1945 November 7 Piloted by Gp. Capt. H. J. Wilson, RAF, the camouflaged Gloster Meteor EE454 named *Britannia* raised the absolute world air speed record to 606.25 MPH in a high-speed dash across Herne Bay, England. It was also the first time a turbojet-powered aircraft established a world air speed record. The previous record had been set by Fritz Wendel in a Messerschmitt Bf 109R on April 26, 1939, and the new British speed raised that by 137 MPH.

1945 November 10 BOAC and South African Airways began a joint service between Hurn Airport, Hampshire, England and Johannesburg, South Africa, using a fleet of 13 Avro York transports. Each aircraft was equipped with 12 sleeper berths, the route taking passengers via Tripoli, Cairo, Khartoum and Nairobi. The RAF operated Yorks as transport aircraft until March 1957, and

256 were eventually built and operated by several foreign and domestic British airlines.

1945 November 20 A Boeing B-29 flew a record distance of 8,198 mi. in 35 hr. 5 min. at an average 234 MPH. The aircraft had a double crew, and 11,110 gal. of fuel with a takeoff weight of 141,000 lb. The flight began along a 10,280-ft. runway at Guam with the overloaded aircraft flying at 50 ft. for the first few hours and ended at Washington, D.C. Planning to run all four engines at 30% for fuel conservation, severe vibration resulted in one being shut down with three engines run at 40% for an astonishing specific fuel consumption of 1.35 gal./mi. compared to a usual consumption of 2.0–2.5 gal./mi. depending on winds.

1945 November 25 Transcontinental and Western Airways conducted a proving flight between Washington, D.C. and Paris, France with the first of a civil production batch of Lockheed 049 Constellation airliners. A special invitation flight on December 3 preceded a scheduled service beginning February 6, 1946, three days after Pan American became the first commercial user of the Constellation. Previously, Constellations had been completed to military specifications. With a crew of three and capacity for two attendants and five passengers, its range of 2,290 mi. with maximum payload of 18,400 lb. was an outstanding performance for the day.

1945 December 3 The first USAAF jet fighter unit, the Thirty-first Fighter Squadron of the 412th Fighter Group at March Field, Calif., received its first P-80A Shooting Star at the start of a long and successful career. It would serve in time with 76 different USAF squadrons, and from it would evolve the F-94 Starfire and the T-33 trainer. The T-33 would remain in service with the USAF through 1988 and, long into the 1990s, would form the personal air-transport for NASA astronauts, 50 years after its progenitor first entered service.

1945 December 8 The most successful of early postwar helicopters, Bell's Model 47, made its first flight and went on to gain the first helicopter license and certificate issued by the CAA. Powered by a 178-HP Franklin 6V4-178-B32 engine, the Bell 47B had a 35-ft. 1.5-in. rotor, a loaded weight of 2,100 lb., a cruising speed of 80 MPH and a range of 212 mi. Numerous variants followed, the last being the 47J-2A two-seat executive transport and the TH-13T two-seat trainer of 1964, each with 260-HP engines.

1945 December 14 Bell Aircraft Corp. received a contract from the USAAF for two XS-2 supersonic, swept-wing research aircraft designed to extend the flight test corridor beyond the transonic performance projected for the straight-wing X-1. The new wing for the Bell X-2 was developed after trials with the L-39 (built by Bell for the U.S. Navy as the first U.S. swept-wing aircraft) had tested full-scale the theoretical estimates that had been written up about low-speed handling of swept-wing designs.

1945 December 21 The Consolidated-Vultee XP-81 became the first American turboprop aircraft to fly when it took to the air powered by a 1,650-SHP General Electric XT31-GE-1 engine in addition to a 3,750-lb. thrust Allison J33-GE-5 turbojet. The aircraft had been flying since February on the power of its jet engine alone. The turbojet concept evolved when in late 1943 the USAAF asked the company to build a long-range escort fighter powered by a combination of a turboprop for endurance at cruising speed and a jet engine for high speed. The aircraft was a disappointment and was abandoned.

1945 December 22 One of the most outstanding post-World War II general aviation aircraft, the Beech Model 35 Bonanza, made its first flight. Characterized by a butterfly tail unit, it had a wingspan of 32 ft. 10 in. and a length of 25 ft. 2 in. Powered by a 285-HP Continental E185-1 air-cooled engine and capable of 184 MPH, or 172 MPH in cruise, the standard Model 35 had a range of 750 mi. at 8,000 ft. On March 7, 1949, William P. Odom began a nonstop flight of 4,957 mi. between Hawaii and Teterboro, N.J., in a modified Bonanza. By July 1962, 7,000 Bonanzas had been delivered, and the type was still in production 45 years after the first flight.

1946 January 1 The Société National Air France was reestablished as France's premier airline at the start of a postwar build-up that would set it among the great airlines of the world. A cross-channel service between London and Paris had opened October 11, 1945, and during 1946 a full European network would be consolidated and trans-Atlantic services reestablished.

1946 January 1 The United Kingdom Air Ministry transferred the management and operation of London's Heathrow airport to the Ministry of Civil Aviation and removed all wartime restrictions on civil aviation. Heathrow was to grow into London's principal airport. Located west-southwest of London in the county of Middlesex, it expanded into one of the world's busiest airports. BOAC began using Heathrow instead of Hurn on May 28 for its U.K.-Australia service, and the airport was officially opened three days later with the first arrival of Constellations of Pan American Airways and American Overseas Airways on route-proving flights prior to commercial operations.

1946 January 7 The U.K. aircraft firm English Electric received a British government contract for detailed design of a high-altitude bomber powered by two Rolls Royce AJ65 turbojet engines, later named Avon. The aircraft was known as the English Electric A1 and would mature into the Canberra, Britain's first jet bomber. Studies began in early 1944 when the Ministry of Aircraft Production asked W. E. W. Petter of Westland Aircraft to design a jet fighter-bomber. Petter moved to English Electric and developed the A1 as an unarmed bomber to replace the Mosquito.

1946 January 9 The first post-war Soviet airliner, the Ilyushin I1-12, made its first flight piloted by V. K. Kokkinaki and his brother Konstantin. Designed in 1943 as a replacement for the I1-2, a license-built Douglas DC-3, the I1-12 entered service on August 2, 1947. It was the first commercial aircraft with a tricycle undercarriage and feathered propellers, but although 1,500 were built, it had marginal performance and was uneconomical to fly. It led to a complete redesign designated I1-14, of which 2,500 were built for worldwide export, the first flying on September 20, 1950.

1946 January 18 Western Airlines became the first commercial operator to fly the civilianized C-54 on scheduled airline service. This aircraft was surplus to military requirements. There had been 839 aircraft of this type with the USAAF when the war ended, and many were sold at $90,000 each or leased to U.S. airlines. National began using C-54s in February followed by United on March 1. In airline use, these aircraft reverted to their original designation as DC-4 Skymasters.

1946 January 21 The U.S. War Department announced that the personnel strength of the USAAF had already been reduced from its peak of 2.372 million in 1944 (and 2.282 million in 1945) to 900,000 and that it would stabilize at around 400,000.

In fact, it reached a post-World War II low of 305,827 in 1947 before increasing to a post-World War II peak of 919,835 in 1957. In 1992, personnel strength stood at 486,819. As of the beginning of fiscal year 1991 (October 1, 1990), the USAF had 6,724 aircraft, of which 3,855 (57%) were more than 15 yr. old.

1946 January 25   Test pilot Jack Woolams flew the first Bell XS-1 rocket research aircraft (serial no. 46-062) for the first time during an unpowered descent after being dropped from the belly-mount of a converted B-29 operating out of Pinecastle AFB, Florida. The XS-1 had a wingspan of 28 ft. and a length of 30 ft. 11 in. It had been rolled out at the Bell plant at Wheatfield, N.Y. on December 27 and was flown to Pinecastle January 19 by B-29 45-21800 piloted by Harold Dow.

1946 January 26   The McDonnell XFD-1 Phantom made its first flight powered by two 1,165-lb. static thrust (s.t.) Westinghouse 19 XB-2Bs. On March 7, the U.S. Navy ordered 100 (only 60 were built), and in service, it was designated FH-1 to avoid confusion with the *D* designation used for Douglas aircraft. VF-17A became the first unit to operate the FH-1, and it also served as the first USMC jet fighter. With a maximum speed of 479 MPH and a range of 980 mi., it was quickly replaced by more promising types such as the Grumman F9F-2 Panther and McDonnell F3H Demon.

1946 January 26   Col. William H. Councill, USAAF, flew a Lockheed P-80A Shooting Star from Long Beach, Calif. to New York City, in a record-breaking time of 4 hr. 13 min. 26 sec., a distance of 2,470 mi. at an average speed of 584.82 MPH. With wing-tip fuel tanks increasing on-board fuel capacity from 285 to 485 gal., maximum range for the production P-80A was now a highly creditable 1,440 mi. On this day, extraordinary meteorological conditions gave the P-80A a tail wind of 120–165 MPH all the way.

1946 January   Having transferred control of Saigon and the surrounding airfields, including Tan Son Nhut to the Vietnamese and the French, British army units and RAF squadrons withdrew or were disbanded, some returning to Burma. Since September 11, 1945, when the British moved in, more than 2,700 Viet Minh and 40 Allied troops had been killed. During March 1946, the French Armée de l'Air had 30 Spitfires and 23 C-47s, the Spitfires flying 600 sorties, dropping 28 tons of bombs and firing 150,000 rounds of ammunition during the month. Even the C-47s were pressed into use as bombers, dropping 15 tons of explosives.

1946 February 3   The first commercial use of the Lockheed Model 049 Constellation was inaugurated by Pan American with the aircraft's first scheduled service between New York and Bermuda. On February 5, TWA inaugurated a Washington-New York-Paris flight with their Constellations—permission had been granted July 5, 1945—opening the first trans-Atlantic service to compete directly with Pan American.

1946 February 4   Against a scheduled trans-Atlantic crossing time of 17 hr. for a Douglas DC-4, a Pan American Lockheed Constellation flew from New York's La Guardia airport to Hurn airport, near London, in a flying time of 12 hr. 9 min. The flight was carried out in three stages: New York to Gander, Newfoundland (a distance of 1,020 mi. in 4 hr. 33 min.); Gander to Shannon, Ireland (1,775 mi. in 6 hr. 36 min.); and Shannon to Hurn (1 hr.). It carried 29 passengers and generally flew at 17,000 ft. to make use of winds.

1946 February 11   The United States and the United Kingdom signed an agreement in Bermuda setting out the principles by which air rates and frequency of international air services should be set. It was agreed that routes should be established by common consent, that the IATA should set the fares and that the frequency of flights by respective countries should be subject to controls by their respective governments to insure equitable market share. France signed a charter of this type on March 27, and the Bermuda Agreement became a standard upon which bilateral air agreements would be based in the future.

1946 February 15   Developed from the Douglas DC-4/C-54, the prototype DC-6 made its first flight. This was the beginning of a lengthy commercial career that would last more than 40 yr., 704 DC-6s being built for airlines around the world. With a pressurized cabin, a cruising speed of 315–330 MPH and a maximum payload range of 3,340 mi., the DC-6 was powered by four 2,100-HP Double Wasp radials and could accommodate 48–52 passengers. First deliveries began to American Airlines on November 20. A stretched DC-6A cargo version appeared in 1949, followed by a passenger derivative, the DC-6B, capable of carrying up to 102 in high-density seating in 1951.

1946 February 28   One of the most enduring operational post-World War II jets made its first flight when the prototype Republic XP-84 took to the air from Muroc AFB, Calif. Developed as a straight-wing, jet-propelled successor to the P-47 Thunderbolt, this aircraft was designated P-84 Thunderjet in service and began operational trials with the Fourteenth Fighter Group, USAAF. Redesignated F-84 in 1948, 4,455 aircraft of this type were built, of which 1,936 were a special fighter-bomber version known as the F-84G. Operational for the first time in 1951, the F-84G was the first single-seat fighter-bomber capable of dropping tactical nuclear weapons. It had a top speed of 622 MPH, a range of 2,000 mi. and a bomb load of up to 2,000 lb.

1946 February   On hearing reports of German research into transonic aircraft and Germany's work on swept-wing configurations and believing that their own aerodynamicists had been working up a technological blind alley, the British Ministry of Supply stopped all work on the supersonic Miles M.52. Air Comdr. Frank Whittle resigned from Power Jets February 9 in protest over this decision of Prime Minister Clement Attlee's Labour government. "We have not the heart to ask pilots to fly" at supersonic speed, said Sir Ben Lockspeiser, U.K. Director of Scientific Air Research, when explaining the action of the government, effectively condemning British manufacturers to await U.S. results—when offered.

1946 March 21   The USAAF Strategic Air Command was formed under the command of Gen. George C. Kenney and was to be responsible for strategic bombing. In time, it would carry the air-launched strategic nuclear deterrent role, one leg of a "triad" of strategic nuclear deterrence. The U.S. Navy would assume responsibility for the third leg of the strategic triad, submarine-launched ballistic missiles, when they were developed during the late 1950s. Between May 1, 1946, and July 1, 1957, Strategic Air Command was also responsible for defending escort fighters, flying F-84s, in up to six wings. Tactical Air Command was formed under Lt. Gen. E. R. Quesada and would be responsible for tactical air operations, including control of the air over a battlefield, tactical nuclear weapons delivery and ground support for the land forces. Air Defense Command was formed under George E. Stratemeyer and would be responsible for the defense of the North American continent and Hawaii.

1946 April 3 In the third of four contracts for carrier-based jet fighters it would award in the three years beginning spring 1943, the U.S. Navy contracted with Douglas for three prototype XF3D-1s, ultimately known as the Skyknight. As a rugged all-weather fighter, it was not to fly for almost two years. The fourth navy jet fighter contract was awarded April 22.

1946 April 22 Continuing the ''cat'' name tradition set by Wildcat, Hellcat, Tigercat and Bearcat, plus a nonstarter called Kitten, Grumman received a U.S. Navy order for its first jet fighter design, the F9F Panther. Not for 19 mon. would the XF9F-2 make its first flight, but it became the best of the first generation U.S. Navy fighters.

1946 April 24 The I-300 (MiG-9) twin-jet fighter prototype made its first flight at the hands of A. N. ''Lesha'' Grinchik, the first flight by a Soviet pilot in a Soviet-built jet aircraft. The aircraft had been put together by the Mikoyan-Gurevich bureau as a mid/straight-wing, low-risk design accommodating two 1,760-lb. static-thrust (s.t.) RD20 engines. The I-300 had a maximum speed of 656 MPH at 16,405 ft., a range of 684 mi. and a ceiling of 42,653 ft. It is believed that more than 1,000 were eventually built.

Taken into the air by test pilot Nikhail I. Ivanov immediately after the I-300 (MiG-9), the Yakovlev Yak-15, the second Soviet jet aircraft, made its inaugural flight. This was the lightest fighter ever built, with a loaded weight of 5,809 lb. including two NS-23 machine guns and ammunition. Work had started February 1945 at the behest of Stalin, and the aircraft began taxi trials in October, during which several ''hops'' had been made. Probably for political purposes to favor aircraft designed by the Mikoyan-Gurevich bureau, the first formal flight was held back until the MiG I-300 was ready.

1946 April 24 In the United States, Winged Cargo Inc., a private commercial cargo-glider company, made its first test with a DC-3 pulling a freight version of the Waco Hadrian glider. Developed as a troop glider in 1941, the Hadrian could accommodate 15 fully equipped troops or up to 3,710 lb. of military cargo— small vehicles, howitzers or supplies. Winged Cargo's bizarre scheme to use low-cost government surplus equipment never caught on.

1946 April 27 The world's first twin-engine helicopter made its first flight when the McDonnell XHJD-1 Whirlaway took to the air. It was powered by two 450-HP Pratt & Whitney R-985-AN-14B 7-cylinder radial engines driving 46-ft. diameter rotors on pylons either side of the fuselage. With a fully loaded weight of 11,000 lb., the XHJD-1 had a cruising speed of 90 MPH with 10 people on board, a ceiling of 12,900 ft. and a range of 300 mi. It was used until June 1951 for research.

1946 April Boeing received a contract for two prototype XB-47 jet bombers. All-jet bomber studies began at Boeing during late 1943 and resulted in design proposals for the Model 424 in March 1944 (a jet version of the B-29) and the Model 432 design in December, which had engines in the fuselage rather than underwing pods like the B-47. In September 1945, acting on information garnered during a tour of German research facilities, the Model 448 appeared carrying four engines in the forward fuselage and two engines aft with a swept-back wing. In October, the engines were reconfigured in underwing pods and later still in twin inner and a single outer pod beneath each wing with a bicycle landing gear and wing-tip outriggers.

1946 May 5 The first of three D.H.108 tailless research aircraft made its first flight piloted by Geoffrey de Havilland at Woodbridge, Suffolk, England. It had been designed for research into the behavior of swept wings and played a valuable role influencing the design of the D.H.106 Comet airliner and the D.H.110 twinboom fighter. Attached to a standard Vampire fuselage, the 43° swept wing had 15% greater area than the Vampire and spanned 39 ft. The three aircraft varied in length between 24 ft. 6 in. and 26 ft. 9 in.

1946 May 17 The first all-jet U.S. bomber made its first flight when the Douglas XB-43 became airborne at the hands of Bob Brush and Russell Thaw. With a maximum bomb load of 6,000 lb., it had a range of 1,100 mi., a maximum speed of 515 MPH and a service ceiling of 38,500 ft. Powered by two 3,750-lb. s.t. General Electric J35-GE-3 turbojets, the XB-43 had a wingspan of 71 ft. 2 in., a length of 51 ft. 2 in. and a maximum loaded weight of 39,533 lb. Only two were built, the USAAF selecting the B-45 instead.

1946 May 22 In the first of a rapid succession of helicopter records, a Sikorsky R-5 piloted by USAAF Maj. F. T. Cashman raised the straight-line distance flight record for helicopters from 230.48 km (143.22 mi.)—achieved by Karl Bode in a Focke-Wulf Fw 61 on June 20, 1938—to 1,132 km (703 mi.). On November 14, an R-5 piloted by Maj. D. H. Jensen established the first 1,000 km (621.4 mi.) unloaded closed-circuit speed record at 107.25 km/hr. (66.65 MPH); and on February 10, 1947, Maj. E. M. Cassell raised the altitude record from 3,427 m (11,244 ft.)—set by Karl Bode in an Fw 61 on January 29, 1939—to 5,842 m (19,168 ft.).

1946 May 22 De Havilland Aircraft of Canada conducted the first flight of their prototype two-seat DHC-1 Chipmunk with Patrick W. P. Fillingham at the controls. Conceived in 1945 when DHC was advised by its U.K.-based parent company to design a trainer as well as the bush aircraft it wanted to produce, the Chipmunk was adopted by the RAF as their ''ab initio'' trainer with 735 being built as Tiger Moth replacements and serving well into the 1970s. The DHC-1 had a wingspan of 34 ft. 4 in., a length of 25 ft. 8 in., a loaded weight of 2,000 lb. and a maximum speed of 138 MPH.

1946 June 24 In plans to give carriers a nuclear strike capability, the U.S. Navy ordered prototypes of the North American AJ Savage, which, with a gross weight of more than 52,000 lb., was by far the heaviest aircraft ordered for shipboard use. The aircraft was to have two 2,400-HP Allison 2800-4W piston engines for cruise and a 4,600-lb. s.t. Allison J33-A-19 in the rear fuselage for overtarget speed to escape the effects of an atomic blast. The aircraft first flew on July 3, 1948, and equipped navy units between September 1949 and 1959.

1946 June 25 Northrop test pilot Max Stanley, copilot Charles Fred Bretcher and flight engineer Orva Douglas flew the first XB-35 ''flying-wing'' bomber prototype on its maiden flight. It had a wingspan of 172 ft., a wing area of 4,000 sq. ft., a length of 59 ft. 1 in. and a takeoff weight of 209,000 lb. Powered by four 3,000-HP Pratt & Whitney R-4360 Wasp Major engines driving eight 8-ft. diameter contra-rotating pusher propellers, the XB-35 had a maximum speed of 391 MPH, a range of 7,500 mi. and a bomb load of 10,000 lb. Two XB-35s and one YB-35 were flown.

1946 July 1 In a weapons effects test, B-29 *Dave's Dream* (serial no. 44-27354) piloted by Maj. Woodrow P. Swancutt of the 509th Bomb Group dropped a 21 kiloton Nagasaki-type atomic

First flown in June 1946, the revolutionary Northrop XB-35 was ahead of its time and fell victim to lobbying from builders of more conventional airplanes.

bomb on 83 ships grouped around the USS *Nevada* lying off Bikini in the Pacific. The bomb missed the *Nevada* by 2,130 ft. in what was dubbed the "Able" shot, one in a series of atomic tests known as Operation Crossroads involving 42,000 people, including 2,200 from Strategic Air Command under Brig. Gen. Roger M. Ramey. A second bomb was detonated underwater July 25, and several aircraft provided photographic coverage, data collection and vital monitoring.

1946 July 11   A Lockheed Constellation owned by TWA crashed during a training flight near Reading, Pa., and the type was grounded from July 12 through August 23. The Model 049 had been introduced on TWA's transcontinental service between New York and Los Angeles March 1, and it had a commanding 50 MPH cruise-speed advantage over the more spartan, unpressurized DC-4. Nevertheless, American and United pressed ahead with plans to introduce their competitor, the DC-6.

1946 July 21   Piloted by Lt. Comdr. James Davidson, U.S. Navy, the prototype McDonnell XFD-1 (later XFH-1) Phantom became the first U.S. all-jet aircraft to operate off a U.S. aircraft carrier when it landed aboard the USS *Franklin D. Roosevelt*. Production would begin in the following year with deliveries from July 23, 1947. VF-17A was the first navy unit to operate the FH-1 (as

it was known in service), with the last of 60 delivered May 27, 1948.

1946 July 24   A fitter with the Martin-Baker company in the United Kingdom, Bernard Lynch became the first person to eject from an aircraft in flight when he was propelled from the rear cockpit of a specially modified Meteor F.3 at 320 MPH and a height of 8,000 ft. Formed by Sir James Martin in 1929, the Martin-Baker Aircraft Co. made the first ground test of a seat carrying a 200-lb. "dummy" weight on January 20, 1945, followed by the first live ride up the 16-ft. near-vertical test rig January 24. Dummy ejections from a Boulton Paul Defiant in flight began May 11, 1945.

1946 July 27   The prototype Supermarine Attacker (serial no. TS409) made its first flight from Boscombe Down, England, piloted by Jeffrey Quill. The first prototype was powered by a 4,300-lb. s.t. Rolls Royce Nene 3 turbojet engine; subsequent aircraft had the 5,000-lb. s.t. version that became standard. The Attacker had a top speed of 590 MPH at sea level, a range of up to 1,090 mi. with ventral tank and a ceiling of 45,000 ft. Adopting the laminar flow wing of the Spiteful, it was the first Supermarine jet and the first Fleet Air Arm jet fighter when first deployed in 1951.

1946 July 31 Agreement was reached for the formation of one of the world's foremost airlines, the Scandinavian Airline System (SAS), by bringing together the principal airlines of Sweden (Svensk Interkontinental Luftrafik), Denmark (Det Danske Luftfartselskab) and Norway (Det Norske Luftfartselskap). In the emerging rush for postwar commercial services, the U.K. airline BEA was about to form, and Air France was rising strongly to take second place behind it. This move by the Scandinavian countries was a successful bid to seriously challenge their competitors.

1946 August 1 A new U.K. airline, the British European Airways Corp., was formed under the Civil Aviation Act of 1946 with a board chaired by Sir Harold Hartley. The initial fleet comprised 21 DC-3s that had been taken over from the BEA division of BOAC. The first service was an 8:40 A.M. flight from Northolt (London) to Marseilles, Rome and Athens. The British South American Airways Corp. was also founded on this date with six Avro Lancastrians and four Avro Yorks.

1946 August 8 The prototype Convair XB-36 (serial no. 42-13570) powered by six 3,500-HP Pratt & Whitney R-4360-25 engines made its first flight from Fort Worth, Tex. This was the biggest USAAF/USAF bomber of all time and the aircraft with the biggest wingspan of any U.S. air forces would operate. With a wingspan of 230 ft., a wing area of 4,772 sq. ft., a length of 162 ft. 1 in. and a gross weight of 328,000 lb., it could carry a standard bomb load of 72,000 lb., or 84,000 lb. on later variants, and 12 20-mm cannons in six defensive positions. The aircraft had a crew of 15, a maximum range of 8,175 mi. and a cruising speed of 202 MPH.

1946 August 9 In the first of two incidents, communist fighters forced down an unarmed USAAF C-47 transport aircraft over Yugoslavia, and detained its 10 occupants. On August 19, another C-47 was fired upon and four of its occupants killed. Responding to a strong note of protest by the U.S. government, President Tito of Yugoslavia gave an assurance that foreign registered aircraft would not be fired upon in the future.

1946 August 17 The first American to jettison himself from an aircraft in flight using an ejection seat was a Sgt. Lambert, USAAF, flying in the second seat of a specially modified twin-engined Northrop P-61 flying at 302 MPH, 7,800 ft. above the ground. Lambert was serving at Wright Field, Ohio when he volunteered for the tests with the first U.S. ejection seats.

1946 August 19 On orders from the Kremlin following a display at Tushino, Mikoyan and Gurevich was told to have 15 I-300s ready for the October Revolution Day parade. Commissar Pavel Yu Dementeyev was sent to the factory where 60,000 drawings were prepared. Bribed to work night and day to build them by hand without tooling or jigs due to a post-war lack of resources, the work forced delivered all 15, only to have the parade canceled due to fog. In May 1947, the aircraft was officially accepted as the MiG-9 with more than 1,000 built.

1946 August 30 The British Minister of Civil Aviation, Lord Winster, announced that BOAC would acquire six Boeing Stratocruisers, the commercial version of the C-97 developed from the B-29, for its trans-Atlantic service. Britain would, said the ministry, purchase up to 200 civil "aircraft of the future" from the United States, an admission of how far development of competitive British civil aircraft had fallen behind America during the war when priorities in the United Kingdom were on military programs.

1946 September 3 Established March 15 on plans announced at the March 12 declaration of major USAAF changes, the USAAF Air University was inaugurated by Gen. Carl Spaatz. Established at Maxwell Field near Montgomery, Ala., it was intended to act as a center of excellence to provide "professional military education" for USAAF officers, NCOs and civilian employees. Maj. Gen. Muir S. Fairchild was the first commander. As of 1992, it had 2,800 military and 1,800 civilian permanent staff with more than 20,000 military personnel completing courses each year.

1946 September 4 In Britain, the Ministry of Supply ordered two prototype D.H.106 Comet four-jet airliners. Design work had begun in 1944 to fill the requirement set by the Brabazon Committee, and based on plans and performance projections put up by de Havilland, BOAC placed an order for 10 in December 1945. A design team led by R. E. Bishop evaluated a wide variety of configurations, finally settling on a relatively conventional aircraft powered by four 4,450-lb. s.t. de Havilland Ghost 50 engines.

1946 September 7 Grp. Capt. E. M. Donaldson, RAF High Speed Flight based at Tangmere, England, established a new world air speed record of 615.78 MPH in a Gloster Meteor F.4 (serial no. EE549) just off the south coast between Worthing and Littlehampton. The High Speed Flight had been reformed July 12 and was equipped with three Gloster Meteor F.4s (including serial nos. EE550 and EE548) for the record attempt before being disbanded again September 26.

1946 September 12 The seventh display held by the Society of British Aircraft Constructors opened at Radlett, England, the first since World War II. In four days, representatives from 50 countries attended the exhibits from 194 U.K. aircraft manufacturing and ancillary companies with 55 aircraft on display in the park. Many of these aircraft took part in the flying displays. On the last day, the Royal Aeronautical Society held its garden party at Radlett.

1946 September 16 The first and only U.S. air freight carrier (as opposed to mixed passenger/freight) to operate successfully on a transoceanic route came into existence as Seaboard & Western Airlines, with its first flight to Europe made on May 10, 1947, with a C-54 to Luxembourg. Gaining business in the late 1940s through the International Relief Organization, it opened a scheduled freight service to Europe on April 10, 1956. Saved from financial collapse in 1961, it began operating Canadair CL-44s and changed its name to Seaboard World Airlines on April 26, 1961.

1946 September 19 After a year of struggling against the new Indonesian nationalists under Sukarno, the RAF handed over responsibility for air operations in the Dutch East Indies to the Dutch, who proceeded to build up their air force in the region. During the month, No. 31 Squadron, RAF, completed its relief duties and was disbanded. In a year, it had air-lifted 127,800 Allied POWs and internees and 26,000 tons of freight in 11,000 sorties.

1946 September 20 The prototype Martin XP4M-1 Mercator made its first flight. The latest in a series of U.S. Navy hybrid propulsion designs, it had two Pratt & Whitney R-4360 radial engines for sustained flight and two Allison J-33 jet engines for high speed and acceleration. The patrol bomber had been ordered July 6, 1944, and deliveries of the nine production aircraft began June 28, 1950.

1946 September 27 Geoffrey de Havilland, son of the founder of one of Britain's most famous aircraft manufacturers, lost his life when the D.H.108 tailless research aircraft he was flying broke up and crashed. The second of three prototypes, serial no TG306 suffered structural failure at Mach 0.875 as the pilot was diving down low over the Thames estuary near Gravesend, Kent from a height of 10,000 ft. The first D.H.108 had crashed May 1, 1950, during stall trials, and the third crashed February 15, 1950, reportedly due to oxygen starvation to the pilot.

1946 September 29 An RATO-assisted Lockheed P2V Neptune took off from Perth, Western Australia at the start of a long-distance, nonstop, record flight covering 11,235.6 mi. in 55 hr. 17 min. Named *Truculent Turtle,* the P2V weighed 85,240 lb. and carried 8,592 gal. of fuel and a crew of four. Originally scheduled to land at Washington, D.C., the P2V was forced to put down at Port Columbus, Ohio; however this distance was sufficient to establish a new FAI distance record for piston-engine aircraft.

1946 September 30 NACA engineer Walter C. Williams took four other engineers to the USAAF test facility at Muroc, Calif. to set up test and instrumentation equipment for the scheduled, but highly secret, powered flights with the Bell X-1. NACA had been asked by the USAAF in December 1945 to supervise the transonic flights, and the first team, under "Walt" Williams, went to Pinecastle for the January 19 glide test. On October 9, six more NACA engineers for Williams's team arrived at Muroc.

1946 October 6 A USAAF B-29 named *Dreamboat* landed in Cairo, Egypt after a 10,865 mi. flight from Honolulu in 39 hr. 35 min. The route took the aircraft over the North Pole via Alaska and on over Paris, Berne and Venice. The crew was commanded by Col. C. S. Irvine.

1946 October 30 The Soviet MiG OKB prepared the first manufacturing and production drawings of the 5,000-lb. s.t. Rolls Royce Nene 2 turbojet engine for its I-310 swept-wing fighter, the MiG-15. The British exported 10 engines to MiG during September followed by 15 more in March 1947 and 30 more later that year. The Soviets stripped down the engines and, from detailed examination of the components, prepared the first drawings. It is estimated that this cut by two years the development time of the revolutionary Soviet fighter.

1946 November 3 The U.S. Navy nonrigid airship XM-1 commanded by Lt. H. R. Walton landed at Naval Air Facility, Glynco, Ga., after a record flight of just over 170 hr. The flight began at Lakehurst, N.J. October 27 and went to Savannah, Ga., the Bahamas, Florida, Cuba and back up to Glynco. This remained the absolute unrefueled flight duration record for any form of airborne craft for 40 yr. until Dick Rutan and Jeana Yeager completed a nine-day round-the-world flight on December 23, 1986.

1946 November 15 The 17th Paris Air Show opened at the Grand Palais des Champs-Elysées and closed December 1, the first such show since 1938. Britain dominated the exhibit due to the uncertain state of France's own aircraft industry and the absence of any U.S. participation. The next show was in 1949, and in 1951 the biennial event moved to June at Le Bourget, where it has remained ever since.

1946 November 18 The U.K. airline BEA introduced ex-Luftwaffe Junkers Ju 52/3m.g8e aircraft on its London (Croydon)-Liverpool-Belfast route. Operated for BEA by Railway Air Services, 11 aircraft (G-AHBP and G-AHOC to G-AHOL) had been

converted by Short & Harland Ltd. of Belfast and were given the name Jupiter. G-AHOK had an accident at Renfrew, Scotland on January 26, 1947, and was written off, and most of the others were scrapped in February 1948.

1946 November In the first known instance in which atomic-bomb-carrying B-29s were used as instruments of international diplomacy, Col. James C. Selser toured west European capitals and flew along the border with communist eastern Europe following the incidents of August 9 and 19 in which two USAAF C-47s had been forced down over Yugoslavia. Selser was commander of the Forty-third Bombardment Group and brought six B-29s to Rhein-Main, Germany for two weeks, returning to the U.S. in early December.

1946 December 9 Test pilot Chalmers H. "Slick" Goodlin piloted the No. 2 Bell XS-1 on the first rocket-powered flight test of the type. Dropped from a B-29 over Muroc Dry Lake, Calif. at 11:54 A.M., the XS-1 weighed 12,012 lb. and fell 10 sec. from 27,000 ft. before the first and second of four chambers on the single 6,000-lb. thrust Reaction Motor Inc. XLR11-RM-3 rocket engine were ignited, each chamber delivering 1,500-lb. thrust. The second chamber was shut down at a speed of 330 MPH and re-ignited at 35,000 ft. until the XS-1 had reached a speed of Mach 0.79, when both chambers were shut for a dive to 15,000 ft.; all four chambers were again ignited for a few seconds before the engine was shut down.

1947 January 1 The British Air Ministry issued a specification calling for a jet bomber capable of flying at 45,000 ft. carrying a 10,000-lb. atomic bomb at 500 MPH with a range of 3,500 mi. Under specification B.35/46, Avro, Armstrong-Whitworth, Bristol, English Electric, Handley Page and Short Brothers were invited to tender offers on January 9, and the design conference to consider proposals was held July 28. From these studies would come designs ordered as prototypes of the first U.K. "V-Bombers," the Avro Vulcan, the Handley Page Victor and, an outsider, the Vickers Valiant.

1947 January 3 The RAF King's Flight was reestablished under Air Commodore E. H. Fielden, the captain of the flight, at RAF Benson in England. Four Vickers Viking C.Mk.II aircraft were assigned to the flight, two (V.L.246 and V.L.247) for royal transportation, one (V.L.245) for carrying staff members and one (V.L.248) for carrying maintenance crew and parts. The passenger seats designated for the Royals carried special parachutes incorporated in the plush design and a compartment in the extreme rear of the two personnel aircraft carried secret service men.

1947 January 8 In the first successful demonstration of the slotted-throat wind tunnel, NACA engineers Ray H. Wright and Vernon G. Ward from the Langley Laboratory attached to the Langley 16-ft. High-Speed Tunnel a parasitic tunnel that produced transonic flow from longitudinal slots in the throat of the primary tunnel. The first major installation of a slotted-throat tunnel would be at Langley Laboratory in December 1949.

1947 January 11 The XF2D-1, the prototype McDonnell F2H Banshee carrier-borne fighter, made its first flight powered by two 3,250-lb. s.t. Westinghouse J34-WE-34 turbojets. Essentially a slightly larger but 85% heavier development of its predecessor and with twice the engine power, the F2H was, at 532 MPH, more than 50 MPH faster than the FH-1 Phantom. The Banshee entered U.S. Navy service in March 1949, and by September 1952 364 had been built. The type remained operational until 1962.

1947 January 29   Under Operation HIGHJUMP a U.S. Navy Douglas R4D Skytrain transport piloted by Comdr. William N. Hawkes took off from the USS *Philippine Sea* 660 mi. off the Antarctic continent carrying the famous polar aviator Rear Adm. Richard E. Byrd. This was the first of six R4D aircraft ferried from Norfolk, Va., to take off for the hop to the U.S. Antarctic base Little America, and it was also the first time the R4D had operated off a carrier.

1947 March 10   The first Swedish jet fighter, the SAAB-21R, made its first flight, powered by a 3,000-lb. s.t. de Havilland Goblin 2 turbojet. Unusually, it was a successful adaptation of a piston-engine aircraft. Formed in 1937, the Svenska Aeroplan A.B. produced the SAAB-21, which first flew on July 30, 1943, as a low-wing cantilever monoplane with a rear-mounted engine driving a pusher propeller and twin booms supporting the horizontal tail. To this design, the only successful pusher-fighter of World War II, was fitted the turbojet engine of the SAAB-21R with 60 built for service from 1950.

1947 March 12   At precisely 1:00 P.M., President Harry S Truman addressed a joint session of U.S. Congress and a radio audience across the nation with a message that was to have far reaching consequences for the growth and expansion of U.S. military air power. Laying out what became known as the Truman Doctrine, the president sought to assure free people everywhere that the United States would come to their aid in the fight for democracy wherever that struggle was challenged by oppression. This would provide the nascent USAF (officially formed September 18) with the blueprint for building a global force capable of waging total atomic war.

1947 March 16   In attempts to counter an offensive by Viet Minh forces in Indochina, Dauntlesses brought to the area by the French carrier *Dixmunde* went into action from Tan Son Nhut airfield northwest of Saigon. In cooperation with the Armée de l'Air, the Aéronavale prepared a reciprocal offensive to free Hoa Binh, and in April 500 French paratroops were dropped from C-47s and Ju 52/3m transports. In a major operation in October, Dauntlesses dropped 65 tons of bombs in 200 sorties; 15,000 French troops were involved, 6,000 Viet Minh were killed.

1947 March 16   As a development of the Convair Model 110, designed in 1945 as a DC-3 replacement and first flown on July 8, 1946, the Convair Model 240 medium-range airliner made its first flight powered by two 2,100-HP Pratt & Whitney R-2800-S1C3-G radial engines. Having placed an order for 75, American Airlines put the Convair 240 into service during June 1948 as a supplement to their new fleet of Douglas DC-6 four-engine airliners.

1947 March 17   Powered by four 4,000-lb. thrust General Electric J35-A-4 turbojets built by Allison, the prototype XB-45 made its first flight from Muroc, Calif., piloted by George Krebs. Ordered during 1945, it was an interim step between piston-generation bombers and the advanced Boeing XB-47 class that took advantage of swept-wing research and high subsonic cruise capability. The B-45 Tornado entered service in November 1945 with the Forty-seventh Brigade at Barksdale AFB, near Bossier City, La. and was the first U.S. all-jet bomber to become operational. It had a bomb capacity of 20,000 lb., a cruising speed of 456 MPH and a range of 1,910 mi.

1947 April 15   The NACA/U.S. Navy Douglas D-558-1 Skystreak research aircraft made its first flight, piloted by Eugene F. May. Powered by a 5,000-lb. s.t. Allison J35-A-11 turbojet, it

had a length of 35 ft. 8 in., a wingspan of 25 ft. and a maximum speed at sea level of 651 MPH. The second D-558-1 flew 27 test flights before it was handed over to NACA in November, the month the third Skystreak was delivered. The second aircraft crashed in May 1948, halting the program for 11 months; the first aircraft was only used by NACA for spares; the third D-558-1 continued test flights until June 10, 1953.

1947 April 24   The U.S. Navy Bureau of Aeronautics awarded the Ryan Aeronautical Co. a $50,000 contract to explore vertical takeoff and landing (VTOL) concepts applicable to carrier-borne combat aircraft. The advantages for minimizing deck space were apparent and thought sufficiently viable to warrant further analysis. Under the guidance of project design engineer Ben Salmon, Ryan defined the Model 38 fighter as weighing 7,700 lb. and using rocket-assisted takeoff and a J33 turbojet for sustained flight. This work resulted in the X-13 Vertijet.

1947 April 27   United Air Lines began a transcontinental route between New York and Los Angeles using the DC-6 on a 10-hr. service with only one stop, at Lincoln, Nebr. The first DC-6 had been delivered by Douglas in November 1946, and certification procedures delayed this important competitor from challenging TWA and its luxurious Constellation, which it began using on transcontinental services March 1, 1946. But just as TWA lost its edge when the Constellation was grounded between July 12 and September 20, 1946, so too did United when the DC-6 was grounded November 12, 1947.

1947 May 16   The USAAF Strategic Air Command conducted a mock air attack on New York when 101 B-29s theoretically dropped bombs on targets across the city. This followed the first "Maximum Effort" exercise beginning April 11 with a raid on Los Angeles and was to be followed by a raid on Chicago August 1. The most telling feature of the spectacular mock attack on New York was that contrary to expectations, only 77% of the force could get off the ground, 30 B-29s being unfit for flight on this day.

1947 May 28   At the behest of the British Ministry of Civil Aviation, Flight Refuelling Ltd. conducted an experiment using converted Avro Lancasters to determine the feasibility of in-flight refueling for commercial airliners on long-distance routes. In the first of 22 such flights, Sir Alan Cobham, chairman of Flight Refuelling, accompanied A.V.M. D. C. T. Bennett on the 3,355-nm (4,091-mi.) flight from London to Bermuda in Lancaster G-AHJV (formerly LM639). A Lancaster tanker from Santa Maria, the *Azores,* rendezvoused with G-AHJV to deliver 1,700 gal. of fuel.

1947 May   The Soviets claimed to have exceeded Mach 1 during a test flight of the DFS 346, designed and built by the Deutsches Forschungsinstitüt für Segelflug and captured by the Russians as they overran Nazi Germany at the end of the war. Begun by DFS as a supersonic fighter powered by two Walter 109-509B rocket engines delivering a total thrust of 4,410 lb, the DSF 346 was projected to be capable of reaching 1,320 MPH (Mach 2). Siebel took it over just before the war ended, and the Russians kept the project alive at Podberezhye, using a USAAF B-29 they had captured, to carry it to an altitude of 33,000 ft.

1947 June 17   Pan American began the world's first round-the-world commercial service when it started flying Lockheed Constellations and fully utilizing routes on which it held licenses to operate. The eastbound flights starting from New York were not global circumnavigations because they terminated at San Francisco; Pan American would not get transcontinental routes for 20 yr. The fare for the 21,642-mi. flight was $1,700 and included stops at Gander, Shannon, London, Istanbul, Karachi, Calcutta, Bangkok, Shanghai, Tokyo, Manila, Guam, Wake, Midway and Honolulu before reaching San Francisco. In the inaugural flight, passengers were delivered back to New York July 1.

1947 June 19 Piloted by the chief USAAF test pilot, Capt. Albert Boyd, a Lockheed P.80R Shooting Star powered by a boosted 4,500-lb. s.t. General Electric J-33 turbojet engine raised the world air speed record to 1,003.6 km/hr. (623.738 MPH), which was the first homologated FAI speed record to exceed 1,000 km/hr. The record was achieved over four runs across a 1.86-mi. course at Muroc Dry Lake, Calif.

1947 June 25 The first Boeing B-50 made its first flight, powered by four 3,500-HP Pratt & Whitney R-4360 engines giving an almost 60% power increase over the B-49 from which it was adapted. In all, 371 B-50s were built, of which 136 were converted to an air-refueling role that kept the type in USAAF service until 1965. Although an improvement on the B-29, it was only a marginal improvement at a time when piston-engine bombers were about to be withdrawn in favor of jet bombers. Nevertheless, the B-50 entered service in January 1948 and remained with Strategic Air Command until 1955.

1947 June 27 The Tupolev Tu-12 made its first flight as the first Soviet jet-engined bomber designed from the outset for turbojet power. Initiated in mid-1946, it was designed to use a Soviet copy of the Rolls Royce Nene engine married to an airframe that evolved from the Tu-2. With a wingspan of 61 ft. 10 in. and a length of 53 ft. 11 in., the Tu-12 had a loaded weight of 34,656 lb. The two engines were carried in the mid-wing position and provided a maximum speed of 487 MPH at 16,400 ft. The Tu-12 was only a precursor to more advanced designs, and only a few were built.

1947 July 16 The world's first jet-powered flying boat, the first of three Saunders Roe SR.A/1s (serial no. TG263), made its first flight, piloted by Geoffrey Tyson at Cowes, England. Designed in 1943 as an island-hopping flying boat, the SR.A/1 emerged with a wingspan of 46 ft., a length of 50 ft. and a maximum weight of 16,000 lb. It was powered by two 3,230-lb. s.t. Metropolitan-Vickers F.2/4 Beryl axial-flow turbojets and had a top speed of 512 MPH.

1947 July 28 The principal director of technical development at the British Air Ministry telephoned the heads of Avro and Handley Page to tell them that their respective designs for the jet "V-Bombers" had been provisionally accepted and that pending confirmation of wind tunnel tests prototypes would be ordered. The H.P.80 would be developed into the Victor, and the Avro 698 would emerge as the Vulcan. Technically advanced, it would be 10 yr. before they became operational.

1947 August 9 Three Sikorsky Hoverfly helicopters, the British version of the Sikorsky VS-316 (designated R-4 in USAAF service) were assigned to the King's Flight to carry the king's mail daily between Dyce Airport, Aberdeen, Scotland and his home at Balmoral. The service was scheduled to run until September 28, but flights could only be made on 25 days because of bad weather or turbulence. The RAF had received its first helicopters in 1945 at the new Helicopter Training Flight, Andover, England.

1947 August 20 In the first of two FAI world air-speed records achieved this month by the first Douglas D-558-1 turbojet re-

search aircraft, Comdr. Turner F. Caldwell, U.S. Navy, flew the first Skystreak to a ratified speed of 1,030.826 km/hr. (640.663 MPH). On August 25, Maj. Marion Carl, USMC, raised this to 1,047.131 km/hr. (650.796 MPH) in a second D-558-1. The record would stand for more than a year.

1947 September 1 Following the partitioning of India, four U.K. airlines, including BOAC, executed Operation Pakistan and, in the space of 15 days, carried 7,000 people from Delhi to Karachi, the new capital of the new state of Pakistan, returning with about 1,500 people to Delhi. In addition, food, medicines and supplies were flown to Delhi and Lahore in an operation under the overall control of Air Commodore H. G. Brackley.

1947 September 2 The first of a new generation of elegant jet-propelled Hawker aircraft, the P.1040 (serial no. VP401), took to the air at Boscombe Down powered by a 4,500-lb. s.t. Rolls Royce Nene I. The P.1040 originated during late 1944 and accommodated its engine in midfuselage with dual intakes and a bifurcated exhaust either side of the fuselage just aft of the wing. The design had stimulated interest at the Admiralty in a naval fighter and specification N.7/46 was met with authorization to proceed with the prototype Hawker Sea Hawk as a development of the P.1040.

1947 September 18 The United States Air Force was established under Gen. Carl A. Spaatz, who officially took up his appointment September 26 in a "paper" change; he had been the commanding general of the USAAF since February 9, 1946. The first secretary of the air force was Stuart Symington, effective this date. Also on this date, the new secretary of defense, James V. Forrestal, approved transfer of military and civilian personnel from the U.S. Army Air Force to the Department of the Air Force and the USAF in Order No. 1. Armed with the Truman Doctrine of March 12, this was the most significant action for the expansion and development of strong military air power.

1947 September 22 The USAF completed the first automatic trans-Atlantic flight when a C-54D-1-DC (serial no. 42-72461) of the All Weather Flying Center flew from Stephensville, Newfoundland to Brize Norton, England, a distance of 2,400 mi. From takeoff to landing, the aircraft was on auto-pilot, although it did carry a crew to take over in the event of a malfunction.

1947 October 1 The first North American XP-86 (serial no. 45-59597) flew for the first time, powered by a 3,750-lb. s.t. Allison J35-C-3 engine and piloted by George Welch. The world's first swept-wing fighter in the air, it had a span of 37 ft. 1 in., a length of 37 ft. 6 in. and a gross weight of 16,357 lb. Flight tests with production P-86A revealed a top speed of 675 MPH at 2,500 ft., a maximum climb rate of 7,470 ft./min. and a ceiling of 48,300 ft. with a range of 783 mi. carrying six 0.50-in. guns in the nose. The P-86A had a 4,850-lb. s.t. J47-GE-1 engine and entered service in mid-1949.

1947 October 14 The No. 1 Bell XS-1 (serial no. 46-062) piloted by USAF Maj. Charles E. "Chuck" Yeager became the first aircraft to pass through the speed of sound after being dropped from the belly of a B-29 (serial no. 45-21800) at 10:26 A.M. from a height of 20,000 ft. Yeager test-fired all four XLR11-RM-3 rocket-motor chambers in pairs, then began a climb under the combined power of the first and third chambers before igniting the second and fourth chambers for a climb to 35,000 ft. and Mach 0.95. With chambers two and four shut down again, he began to level off at 40,000 ft., then ignited a third chamber and slowly accelerated to Mach 1.06, about 700 MPH, at 43,000 ft.

Yeager shut off the motor with 30% propellant remaining, coasted through 45,000 ft. and returned to earth at the end of a 14-min flight after separation.

1947 October 21   The first of three Northrop YB-49 types made its first flight from Hawthorne, Calif. carrying pilot Max Stanley, copilot Charles F. Bretcher and flight engineer Orva Douglas. The YB-49 was a jet-engined version of the XB-35 with eight 4,000-lb. s.t. Allison J-35-A-15 turbojets providing a maximum speed of 493 MPH and a range of 3,155 mi. The USAF had approved in June 1945 a Northrop suggestion that jet engines be fitted to two converted YB-35 piston-engined flying-wing bombers.

1947 October 24   The first of 466 Grumman Albatross amphibians built between 1947 and 1961, the XJR2F-1, made its first flight just two years after the 345th and last Grumman Goose left the production line. Designed to replace the Goose for the U.S. Navy, the Albatross had a wingspan of 80 ft., a length of 60 ft. 8 in. and a maximum loaded weight of 33,000 lb. With two 1,425-HP Wright R-1820 engines, it had a cuising speed of 150 MPH and a maximum range of 2,680 mi. The Goose and Albatross would both serve the U.S. Navy for more than 35 yr.

1947 October 31   The first British pressurized airliner, the Avro Tudor, began scheduled airline service with British South American Airways. Originating in 1943 as a long-range airliner developed from the Lancaster bomber, it first flew on June 14, 1945, but BOAC stipulated no fewer than 343 modifications and finally canceled its options. A crash on August 23, 1947, took the life of Avro's chief designer Roy Chadwick, and more crashes in January 1948 and January 1949 sapped confidence in what should have been Britain's premier postwar long-range airliner. Only 46 were built.

1947 November 2   Piloted by Howard Hughes, the H-4 Hercules, named simply *Flying Boat* because that was what it was, made its one and only flight for 60 sec., traveling just over 1 mi. at 80 MPH across Long Beach Harbor near Los Angeles, Calif. The H-4 had a wingspan of 319 ft. 11 in. (still the greatest span of any aircraft), a length of 218 ft. 8 in., a height of 79 ft. 4 in. and eight 3,000-HP Pratt & Whitney R-4360 engines. Designed and built by a team led by Hughes as a military transport flying boat, it weighed 400,000 lb. and was made almost entirely from wood, hence its nickname *Spruce Goose*. It is presently on display at Long Beach Harbor.

1947 November 12   All Douglas DC-6 airliners were grounded through March 21, 1948, after an aircraft crashed at Bryce Canyon National Park, Utah, killing all 52 passengers and crew. The day before, another DC-6 had burst into flames but managed to land at Gallup, N. Mex. The aircraft were returned to flight status after an intensive investigation revealed that the fires had been caused by fuel venting into cabin heaters. The DC-6 remained successful, 704 being built between 1946 and 1958; and more than 200 were still in service by the mid-1970s.

1947 November 23   The Convair XC-99 (serial no. 43-52436) made its first flight piloted by Russell R. Rogers. Built as a transport version of the B-36 six-engine bomber, it had a new two-deck fuselage but retained the wings and tail unit of its parent. The XC-99 could carry 400 fully equipped troops or up to 101,000 lb. of freight, and after delivery to the USAF in May 1949, it served on several special missions until retired in 1957.

1947 December 10   The first of three Douglas D-558-II Sky-rocket swept-wing research aircraft was trucked to the NACA test center at Muroc Dry Lake, Calif. On January 29, 1946, Douglas received permission to change the last three of six D-558-1 Sky-streak turbojet research aircraft into swept-wing aircraft powered by both turbojet and rocket engines in an airframe adapted to accept new design concepts stimulated by German wartime research.

1947 December 17   Piloted by Bob Robbins and Scott Osler, the first of 2,032 Boeing B-47 Stratojet strategic bombers made its first flight from Boeing Field, Seattle to Moses Lake AFB in central Washington. Powered by six 6,000-lb. s.t. General Electric J47-GE-25 engines, the B-47B had a gross weight of 180,000 lb., a maximum speed of 617 MPH and a range of 4,000 mi. and could carry a 20,000-lb. bomb load. It carried only two 0.50-in. defensive tail guns and a crew of three. Strategic Air Command operated the B-47 from 1951 through 1967, with a maximum 1,543 B-47s on strength in 1958.

1947 December 30   The first MiG I-310 prototype made its first flight, piloted by Viktor Nikolayevich Yuganov. Powered by a 5,000-lb. s.t. Rolls Royce Nene 2 turbojet engine, the production MiG-15 had a wingspan of 33 ft. 1 in., a length of 32 ft. 11 in. and a maximum weight of 10,692 lb. The MiG-15 had a maximum speed of 652 MPH at sea level, a climb time of 2.3 min. to 16,400 ft. and a ceiling of 49,869 ft. with a range of 882 mi. More than 5,000 single-seat fighters and several thousand two-seat trainers would be built before production ceased in 1951, the type entering service in 1948.

1947   Resulting from the worst U.S. civil aviation accident record to that date, Pres. Truman set up a special board of inquiry on air safety chaired by CAB chairman James M. Landis. During the year, there had been 36 incidents within the airspace of the continental United States, and in a two-week period during mid-year, 143 people had been killed. The findings were ambiguous, and no single cause had been identified. All, however, appeared to indicate that air safety had not matured as rapidly as air transport.

1948 January 13   Two ex-RAF officers, Sqdn. Ldr. Jack Hemmings and Flt. Lt. Stuart King, took off from London's Croydon Airport in a Miles Gemini at the start of a survey of Africa to determine the suitability of aircraft for missionary work in undeveloped countries. Established as the Mission Aviation Fellowship, this unsung application of air transport blossomed into a world-wide network of almost 150 aircraft operating in 25 countries logging 125,000 flights annually. An established charity and still in operation, MAF is nondenominational and uses a wide range of fixed- and rotary-winged aircraft.

1948 January 17   The three Boeing 314A flying boats operated by BOAC on the Bermuda-Baltimore route were retired, to be replaced by Lockheed Constellations. The three Boeings (G-AGBZ *Bristol*, G-AGGA *Berwick* and G-AGCB *Bangor*) began operations with BOAC in mid-1941. Since then they had flown 29,100 hr., carried 42,000 passengers, logged 4,238,867 mi. and made 596 trans-Atlantic flights. The last Boeing 314A (G-AGBZ) flown by Capt. J. W. Burgess flew the Bermuda-Baltimore route this day while Constellation G-AHEN, *Baltimore*, flew the Baltimore-Bermuda route.

1948 January 30   At approximately 10:30 P.M., the 76-year-old pioneering aviator Orville Wright, the man acclaimed as the first pilot of the first powered flying machine, died in a hospital at Dayton, Ohio of a heart attack he had suffered three days before.

The Boeing B-47 took to the air for the first time in December 1947, displaying all the design features of post-World War II aircraft: jet engines, swept-back wings and low thickness-ratio airfoils.

It was his second, the first heart attack had been on October 10, 1947. Orville Wright was buried February 2.

1948 February 4   The first swept-wing NACA/U.S. Navy Douglas D-558-II research aircraft made its first flight, piloted by John F. Martin. The aircraft was powered by a 3,000-lb. thrust Westinghouse J34-WE-40 turbojet, but not until mid-1949 was the four-chamber 6,000-lb. thrust Reaction Motors XLR-8-RM-5 motor fitted to the #1 aircraft for combined turbojet/rocket trials. In addition to the jet fuel, tankage included a 195-gal. alcohol tank in the rear fuselage, a 180-gal. liquid oxygen tank forward, an 11-gal. hydrogen peroxide tank and 7 helium vessels for tank pressurization.

1948 February 14   Forty-five Turkish air force officers arrived in the United States for technical and staff training with the USAF as one in a succession of one-shot arrangements made by informal agreement with the joint chiefs of staff to foster foreign self-defense capabilities in line with the Truman Doctrine. These informal arrangements were the precursor to Pres. Truman's proposals for the Mutual Defense Assistance Program of 1949.

1948 February 16   During a combined training exercise involving the USAF and the RAF, six B-29 Superfortresses were inter-cepted over Brighton, on the south coast of England, during a flight from Germany. The B-29s had deployed from the United States as part of an exercise in long-distance operations and as a display of Strategic Air Command's capabilities to operate on a global basis. Despite the effort, serious shortcomings gave cause for concern about efficiency, morale, discipline and overall war-fighting capabilities.

1948 March 10   NACA test pilot Herbert H. Hoover became the first civilian to exceed the speed of sound when he flew the No. 2 Bell XS-1 to a speed of 703 MPH (Mach 1.065). It was the 74th flight of an XS-1 and the 31st flight of the No. 2 aircraft, which had made its first powered flight October 11, 1946. Over-all, NACA test pilots made 55 of the 158 X-1 program glide and powered drops, Bell test pilots (all civilians) made 37 drops, and Air Force pilots made 66 flights. The fastest X-1 flight was flown by Maj. Chuck Yeager on May 2, 1949, when he achieved 927 MPH (Mach 1.45)—Yeager also made 35 X-1 flights, more than any other pilot. The last X-1 flight was on October 23, 1951.

1948 March 22   The first Lockheed TF-80C two-seat trainer prototype of the F-80 Shooting Star made its first flight. (The designation was changed to T-33 on May 5, 1949.) Powered by a 4,600-lb. s.t. General Electric J33-A-35, the aircraft had a wingspan of 38 ft. 10 in. and a length of 37 ft. 9 in. It was one of the most successful trainers, with 5,691 being built for the USAF and the U.S. Navy and for countries receiving it under the Mutual Defense Assistance Program. The type was also license-built in Japan.

1948 March 23   The prototype Douglas F3D Skyknight (the XF3D-1) made its first flight powered by two 3,000-lb. s.t. Westinghouse J34-WE-22 engines, later replaced by 3,400-lb. s.t. J34-WE-36s. (The plane was originally designed around the 4,600-lb. s.t. J46-WE-3 engine, but that engine was abandoned.) In all, 268 Skyknight night fighters were built with initial service use in U.S. Navy unit VC-3 beginning in February 1951. The type became a mainstay in the Korean conflict—credited with shooting down more enemy aircraft than any other Navy type—as well as in Vietnam, before finally being retired in 1970.

1948 March 23   Test pilot Gp. Capt. John Cunningham set a new FAI-ratified world altitude record of 18,118 m (59,446 ft.) during tests with the third production D.H.100 Vampire (serial no. TG278) with 4-ft. wing-tip extensions and a special hood for the de Havilland Ghost turbojet that was to be fitted to aircraft of this type. The previous altitude record—17,083 m (56,046 ft.)—had been set by Mario Pozzi on October 22, 1938.

1948 March 28   The USAF Strategic Air Command completed a series of tanker plane trials with specially converted B-29s with the designation KB-29M. Carrying a jettisonable 2,300-gal. fuel tank in the bomb bay, and hose and reel and modifications drawing on the aircraft's main fuel supply for refueling operations if needed, Boeing converted 92 B-29s at the Wichita Plant 2, which was specially reopened for this purpose. Boeing designed a special "flying boom," and this was installed on each of 116 modified B-29s given the designation KB-29P in 1950–51.

1948 April 5   BEA Vickers Viking G-AIVP named *Vimy,* with a crew of three commanded by Capt. John Ralph and 10 passengers, crashed when a Soviet Yak fighter collided with the airliner. The Viking was at 1,500 ft. beneath a 3,000-ft. cloud base and right down the middle of the approach path as it prepared to land at Gatow airport, Berlin at the end of a routine London-Hamburg-Berlin flight. The Yak dived below the airliner and pulled up sharply, slicing off its starboard wing. The Yak crashed in the Soviet sector of Berlin, the Viking in the British sector.

1948 April 6   The world's first airliner to fly with turbojet power, the Vickers Type 618 Viking (G-AJPH, formerly VX856) made its first flight from Wisley, England, piloted by J. "Mutt" Summers. Later converted to test the 5,000-lb. s.t. Rolls Royce Nene and provide data on high-altitude civil flying requirements, on July 25—the 39th anniversary of Blériot's historic first channel crossing by air—the aircraft flew from London to Villacoublay, Paris in 34 min. 7 sec. at an average speed of 384 MPH. The Nene-Viking's top speed was 457 MPH, but it had a range of only 312 mi., compared to 1,700 mi. for a Viking 1B.

1948 April 14   Lord Nathan, Britain's minister of aviation, opened the new flying boat terminal at Berth 50, Southampton on the south coast of England. BOAC had been operating Short Hythe flying boats from there since the beginning of the month, when the facility at Poole, Dorset was closed. The Hythes were converted ex-RAF Sunderlands. The mayoress of Southampton christened the first BOAC Short Solent, *Southampton*—a slightly fatter version of the Sunderland—capable of carrying 30 passengers up to 3,000 mi. at 250 MPH.

1948 April 26   North American Aviation test pilot George Welch became the first man to exceed the speed of sound in a turbojet-powered aircraft—and a standard fighter at that—when he nosed the XP-86 into a shallow dive and reached a speed just in excess of Mach 1. This was only the 14th time an aircraft had broken the sound barrier, and George Welch was only the fifth man to do so. All previous flights had been made with the two Bell XS-1 rocket aircraft.

1948 April 30   The prototype Martin P5 Marlin (XP5M-1) made its first flight, powered by two 3,450-HP Wright R-3350 radial engines. The Marlin would enter service with the U.S. Navy almost exactly 2 yr. later, incorporating a Martin PBM Mariner wing and upper hull combined with an improved lower hull of higher length/beam ratio. A major redesign in 1953 produced the P5M-2 version with a T-tail, a cruising speed of 150 MPH and a range of 2,050 mi. It could carry up to four 2,000-lb. bombs, mines or torpedoes. In all, Martin built 239 Marlins, the last leaving the U.S. Navy in 1967.

1948 May 3   Howard C. Lilly, the first NACA pilot to lose his life on duty and the first pilot who had flown at supersonic speed to die, was killed when the Douglas D-558-I he was flying caught fire after takeoff and crashed. To date, the Skystreaks had completed 127 flights without a major incident, and this was the 18th flight of the #2 plane. Pending findings of a board of inquiry, all Skystreak operations with the two remaining aircraft were stopped. Research flights with #3, D-558-I, resumed April 22, 1949.

1948 May 14   The state of Israel formally achieved independence and prepared for immediate attack from its Arab neighbors. Altogether, the nascent Israeli Air Force had only 54 aircraft comprising a motley collection, mostly Taylorcraft J-2 Cubs, ex-RAF Austers, C-47s and various east European and redundant U.S. light aircraft. Facing Israel, Jordan and Lebanon had no aircraft, Iraq had 10 Harvards based in Jordan, and Syria also had 10 Harvards. Egypt had 15 Spitfire Mk.IXs, five C-47s and four Lysanders. Only the preceding day, Egyptian fighters had attacked Israel at several places, supporting ground assaults from Lebanon and Syria.

1948 June 1   A new U.S. Department of Defense Military Air Transport Service (MATS) was consolidated under the command of USAF Lt. Gen. Laurence S. Kuter. MATS had been established at the direction of Defense Secretary James V. Forrestall to transport by air people, materiel, military mail and general cargo for the army and the navy as well as the USAF. Starting out with a motley collection of 824 transport aircraft (766 from the army and 58 from the navy), it grew by 1956 to a fleet of 1,435 planes serving 115,000 global air route mi. On January 1, 1966, its name changed to Military Airlift Command.

1948 June 1   American Airlines introduced its new Convair 240, soon known as the Convair-Liner, the first pressurized twin-engined aircraft to enter commercial service. It could carry 40 passengers at 235 MPH and soon became a favorite. Western Airlines began their first Convair-Liner flights September 1, and three more domestic U.S. airlines and Pan American bought the aircraft. United Air Lines was instrumental in sponsoring development of the stretched version, the Convair 340.

1948 June 1   The first U.K. public mail service operated by helicopters began when a Sikorsky S-51 (G-AKCU) opened the service with a flight between Peterborough and several locations in East Anglia. Dispatched in a ceremony attended by the mayor of Peterborough, Capt. J. Theilmann piloted the helicopter on its first run with 140 lb. of mail. A second S-51 (G-AJOV) piloted by Capt. G. A. Ford accompanied the first as far as Norwich, the fifth of 13 stops. The service operated six days a week but was discontinued September 25 after 30,046 lb. of mail had been delivered.

1948 June 3　The first air victory by an Israeli Air Force pilot was achieved when Modi Alon flying an Avia C-210 attacked and shot down a C-47 belonging to the Egyptian Air Force. The Egyptian aircraft had been on a bombing raid to Tel Aviv; a second aircraft of the same type was damaged. Despite this success, throughout the continuing support given by Israeli aircraft to ground forces countering Arab attacks, several were lost to ground fire. Bigger and better aircraft began to arrive to be a part of Israel's air force, including Beaufighters, P-51s and even B-17s on July 15.

1948 June 11　The USAF designation for fighters and reconnaissance aircraft underwent a change. Whereas fighters had been given the prefix *P* since 1925, they would henceforth be assigned the letter *F,* and whereas reconnaissance aircraft had been assigned the letter *F* since 1930, they would now be assigned numbers in the *P* series. Type numbers would continue unchanged so that, for instance, the North American P-86 retained its type number and became the F-86.

1948 June 18　Adding a hemispheric capability to the intercontinental bomber force of B-29s and B-50s, Strategic Air Command activated the first two air-refueling units, the Forty-third Refuelling Squadron at Davis-Monthan AFB in Arizona and the 509th Air Refuelling Squadron at Roswell AFB in New Mexico. The first KB-29Ms began arriving at the end of the year with their trailing hoses and grappel hooks developed by the British. It would be two years before the KB-29Ps with their flying-boom arrangement would join Strategic Air Command.

1948 June 20　At the suggestion of Lt. Gen. Kenney, the first Strategic Air Command Bombing Competition was held at Castle AFB in Calif. to stimulate improvements in bombing accuracy, which in the previous two years had become abysmal. Three crews from each of 10 B-29 bombardment groups participated in the competition, which lasted a week, and each crew made three visual releases and three radar releases from 25,000 ft. The Eighth Air Force swept the board, with top honors going to the Forty-third and 509th Bombardment Groups.

1948 June 26　On the first day of what would be known as the Berlin airlift, U.S. Air Forces Europe (USAFE) under Gen. Curtis E. LeMay impressed C-47s as available to lift 80 tons of milk, flour and medicine into the beleaguered city of Berlin. The Soviet Union had blocked all surface routes through East Germany, leaving only the air routes as a politically viable means of getting supplies through to the 2 million people. On June 29, USAF Brig. Gen. Joseph Smith took over the Berlin Airlift Task Force and by July 20 had 54 C-54s and 103 C-47s capable of air-lifting 1,500 tons daily.

1948 July 5　Britain's Ministry of Supply ordered three prototype Bristol Type 175 turboprop airliners, which three years later would emerge as the Britannia. The project had evolved in October 1947 during a meeting at Filton, Bristol in response to a BOAC specification calling upon industry to develop an economic long-range airliner. On February 2, the Ministry of Supply called upon BOAC to order 25 Type 175s so they would be in commercial service by the required date of 1954, but the airline

vacillated and the British government stepped in and guaranteed the work.

1948 July 6　The U.S. Navy introduced early-warning functions to airborne units on aircraft carriers when VAW-1 and VAW-2 were commissioned with the Pacific and Atlantic Fleets, respectively. The first navy land-based airborne early-warning (AEW) squadron (VPW-1) had been commissioned April 1, but this was the first application of that role to carriers at sea. The VAWs would train AEW crewmembers and organize early-warning operations throughout the fleet.

1948 July 8　The first RAF operations against communist insurgents in Malaya took place when Spitfires of No. 60 Squadron, RAF, hit a camp near Ayer Karah. This was followed on July 15 by another strike and one on the 16th when 10 communists at a camp in swamps near Telok Anson were killed. These were the opening shots in a lengthy campaign that would drag on through 1951 until military forces went on the offensive to purge the jungle of terrorists, which was effectively accomplished by 1954.

1948 July 8　The first Consolidated-Vultee B-36B, the first fully operational military version of the type, made its first flight. (A B-36A that had joined the Seventh Bombardment Group, Strategic Air Command, at Carswell AFB in Texas on June 26 was unarmed and used for training only.) With a gross weight of 328,000 lb., the B-36B had a maximum speed of 381 MPH at 34,500 ft., a cruising speed of 202 MPH, a ceiling of 42,500 ft. and a range of 8,175 mi. with a 72,000-lb. bomb load. With the introduction of the B-36, Strategic Air Command changed designated "very heavy bomber" B-29s and B-50s to "medium bombers," designating the B-36 a "heavy bomber."

1948 July 8　The Soviet's first successful turbojet-powered bomber, the Ilyushin Il-28, made its first flight, piloted by V. K. Kokkinaki. Developed as a tactical, medium-range rival to earlier Tupolev types, it was pitted against the Tu-73. Although inferior to the Tu-73 in some respects, the Il-28 was cheaper and more maneuverable. Powered by two 5,950-lb. s.t. VK1-A turbojets, the Il-28 had a maximum speed of 560 MPH at 14,760 ft. and a range of 1,550 mi. with a 4,400-lb. bomb load. Eventually, more than 3,000 were produced for 16 countries.

1948 July 14　Six de Havilland Vampires of No. 54 Squadron, RAF, landed at Goose Bay, Labrador after having made the first North Atlantic crossing by turbojet aircraft. The planes took off from Stornoway, Scotland at 10:15 A.M. on July 12 and made the 2,202-mi. crossing in three stages for a total flying time of 8 hrs. 18 min.; 662 mi. to Meek's Field, Iceland in 2 hr. 42 min.; 757 mi. to Bluie West 1, Greenland in 2 hr. 41 min.; and 783 mi. to Goose Bay in 2 hr. 55 min. Cruising altitude was 25,000–32,000 ft. against head winds peaking at 207 MPH.

1948 July 14　A car air-ferry service was opened across the English Channel between Lympne, England and Le Touquet, France by Silver City Airways. The aircraft employed was one of the new Bristol Type 170 Freighters, the first of which had flown on December 2, 1945. The Type 170 was a general-purpose transport with a large, bulbous nose and clam-shell doors for straight-through entry to a deep fuselage. A total of 214 Type 170s were built by 1958. The aircraft used for this service was G-AGVC, and it carried two cars on the inaugural flight.

1948 July 16　A combined announcement by the U.S. Defense Department and the British Air Ministry detailed plans to move USAF fighter and bomber groups to England and Germany by

Bridging the eras of piston- and jet-engined bombers, the Convair B-36 was the world's first hemispheric bomber. Here it supports a trapeze for escorting fighters, an idea never used operationally.

the end of the month. The 301st Bombardment Group with its B-29s was to move to Furstenfeldbruck, Germany, the Twenty-eighth Bombardment Group to RAF Scampton, England and the 307th Bombardment Group to RAF Waddington and RAF Marham, where the newly established U.S. Third Air Division was to be headquartered. The Thirty-sixth Fighter Wing was to move from the Panama Canal Zone to Germany during August. Under the guise of a long-term training program, an informal agreement between the British and American governments reinforced strategic air power in Europe.

1948 July 16   The prototype Vickers VC2 Viscount (G-AHRF) made its first flight at Wisley, England, piloted by J. ''Mutt'' Summers and G. R. ''Jock'' Bryce. Originating in 1944, the Viscount had a protracted gestation but emerged to gain its certificate of airworthiness on July 27, 1950, and was the world's first revenue-earning turboprop airliner. Powered by four Rolls Royce Dart engines and carrying up to 70 passengers at a cruising speed of 352 MPH at 18,000 ft., the definitive 810 series, which appeared in 1958, had a range of 1,760 mi. Vickers made 459 aircraft for U.K. airlines and 43 export customers. Many were still in use more than 40 yr. after the plane's inaugural flight.

1948 July 20   Sixteen USAF Lockheed F-80s of the Fifty-sixth FG landed at Stornoway, Scotland on a reciprocal flight using exactly the same staging routes to that conducted by six RAF Vampires on July 12–14. The 2,202-mi. flight was completed in a flying time of 4 hr. 40 min., with the first leg from Goose Bay, Newfoundland taking 1 hr. 15 min., the second leg taking 1 hr. 45 min. and the final stage to Stornoway achieved in 1 hr. 40 min. Accomplished in a little over half of the time taken by the Vampires, indicated air speed had been about the same (300 knots) with the tail wind accounting for the time difference.

1948 July 23   The first east-west crossing of the Atlantic by a bomber squadron was accomplished by No. 617 ''Dam Busters'' Squadron, RAF, when their 16 Avro Lincolns arrived at Gander, Newfoundland after a flight of 11 hr. 20 min. from RAF Binbrook, England. Led by squadron commander, Wg. Comdr. C. D. Milne, the aircraft eventually flew down to Andrews Field near Washington, D.C., then went on to fly in formation for six hr. over 12 U.S. cities in three states on the eastern seaboard in a contribution to American Army Air Forces Day.

1948 July 23   In an attempt to accommodate the 4,500 tons per day of vital supplies needed by the people of Berlin, Gen. Hoyt S. Vandenburg, USAF chief of staff, ordered Military Air Transport Service to send 72 C-54s (eight squadrons) and 2,500 crew members to USAFE. By the end of the month, the daily airlift total reached 2,000 tons. On July 29, a new Airlift Task Force (later redesignated First Airlift Task Force) under Maj. Gen. William H. Tunner was formed with headquarters at Wiesbaden.

1948 August 1   An Air France Latécoère 631 six-engined flying boat was lost over the Atlantic with all passengers. A second aircraft of this type had been lost during delivery, and following this second accident, the type was withdrawn. The airline had taken delivery of three Laté 631s and began commercial operations with them July 26, 1947. The aircraft originated with a specification in 1936 for a flying boat capable of carrying 40 passengers across the Atlantic and had made its first flight on November 4, 1942.

1948 August 6   Two B-29s of the Forty-third Bombardment Group completed a 20,000-mi. round-the-world flight. With eight stops, the flight was completed in a flight time of 103 hr. 50 min. Scheduled to take 14 days, an extra day was needed when a third

B-29 in the group crashed in the Arabian Sea. The two B-29s that completed the trip were commanded by Lt. Col. R. W. Kline in *Gas Gobbler,* and 1st Lt. A. M. Neal, in *Lucky Lady.*

1948 August 16 Piloted by Fred Bretcher, the Northrop XF-89 Scorpion made its first flight, powered by two 5,440-lb. s.t. Allison J35-A-35 turbojets mounted side-by-side in the fuselage beneath the cockpit. Designed as a two-seat, all-weather interceptor, the Scorpion had a gross weight of 42,241 lb., a maximum speed of 636 MPH and an initial climb rate of 8,360 ft./min. Delivered for service use in 1951, the type went through a succession of variants, and a total of 1,050 were built before it was superseded by the F-102 in 1957.

1948 August 23 Developed as a radical solution to the problem of escort fighters for intercontinental-range bombers, the parasitic McDonnell XF-85 Goblin made its first flight with a 3,000-lb. thrust Westinghouse J34-WE-7 axial-flow turbojet. It had been carried to a height of 20,000 ft. suspended on a trapeze attached to the belly of an EB-29B (serial no. 46-524). After release, the XF-85 was caught in turbulence and smashed into the bomber's belly which shattered its canopy. The pilot, Edwin Schoch, landed safely.

1948 August Bell Aircraft Corp. took possession of the Messerschmitt P.1101 variable geometry research aircraft that had been captured by the U.S. Army at Oberammergau in April 1945 and evaluated by the USAF at Wright Field. Bell suggested modifications that included the ability to change the sweep of the wing in flight from between 20° and 50°. An accident to the P.1101 airframe resulted in construction of two completely new aircraft designated X-5 based on the Messerschmitt design.

1948 September 1 The prototype SAAB-29 made its first flight incorporating design changes resulting from examination of German swept-wing research. It had a remarkable performance for its day, which greatly enhanced the reputation of its Swedish manufacturer. It had a top speed of 658 MPH at 5,085 ft. and a ceiling of 50,855 ft. with a range of 1,678 mi. The first operational swept-wing fighter outside the United States and the USSR, the SAAB-29 entered service with the Swedish Air Force in 1951, and a total of 661 were built.

1948 September 3 Operation Dagger, a major air defense exercise involving the RAF and 90 USAF B-29s, began on the ninth anniversayy of Britain's declaration of war on Germany, the first major British air exercise for 10 years. It involved a simulated mass air attack by B-29s coming over the Dutch coast at 33,000 ft. toward London. This "attack" was met by RAF Meteors and by Lincolns and Lancasters on the first night. A simulated "truce" brought brief respite before massive air "attacks" on London and "mine-laying operations" against major coastal towns.

1948 September 3 The prototype Fleet Air Arm Hawker Sea Hawk (serial no. VP413) made its first flight, fitted with folding wings, four 20-mm Hispano nose cannons and catapult spools. Developed from the P.1040, production models had a 5,000-lb. thrust Rolls Royce Nene RN.4 turbojet engine providing a top speed of 560 MPH at 36,000 ft. and a 288-mi. radius of action from the carrier. As a ground attack fighter-bomber, it would carry two 500-lb. bombs and two fuel tanks. Four foreign navies bought the Sea Hawk, the Fleet Air Arm using the type from March 1953 to December 1960.

1948 September 5 A record 62,282 lb. was air-lifted by a flying boat, constituting the heaviest load flown by air to this date and an all-time record for flying boats. The aircraft, the one U.S. Navy Martin JRM-2, *Caroline Mars* of VR-2 flew the load 390 mi. from the Patuxent River, Maryland to Cleveland, Ohio. The JRM-2 had an upgraded gross weight of 165,000 lb. weight. On May 19, 1949, the JRM-1 *Marshall Mars* carried a record 301 passengers and crew from San Diego to Alameda. On August 22, 1956, Lt. Comdr. Virgil Solomon landed the last Mars flying boat to carry scheduled military passengers.

1948 September 9 Piloted by John Derry, the third D.H.108 flying-wing research aircraft became the first British aircraft to exceed the speed of sound. The event took place at about 10:00 A.M. near Windsor on a routine flight from Farnborough to Hatfield, England during a dive from 40,000 ft. to 30,000 ft. where Derry achieved a speed of almost Mach 1.1, about 700 MPH.

1948 September 15 USAF pilot Maj. Richard L. Johnson set a new world air speed record when he flew a North American F-86A Sabre (serial no. 47-661) at an average speed of 1,079.61 km/hr. (670.981 MPH). This was a standard F-86A with guns and ammunition, and the record was achieved at Muroc Dry Lake, Calif. North American was quick to point out that every Sabre leaving the factory was faster than the official FAI record, and they were right; a regular F-86A was easily good for 677 MPH over the USAF test range.

1948 September 18 The daily delivery of food, fuel and medical supplies into Berlin reached 5,583 tons, exceeding the original estimate of 4,500 tons for daily needs. In a revision of estimated requirements, a new target of 5,620 tons was set, including 1,435 tons of food, 3,084 tons of coal and 255 tons of industrial equipment. Because coal for the coming winter was a prime requirement, 38 C-54Es from Military Air Transport Service were converted to C-54Ms for this special purpose.

1948 September 18 The delta-wing Consolidated Vultee XF-92A research aircraft made its first flight. Originally designated XP-92 as a hybrid jet/rocket fighter, the Model 7002 was kept going to produce a research aircraft with the help of Alexander Lippisch, who had been brought to the United States from Germany after the war. Powered by a 5,000-lb. s.t. Allison J33-A-23, the XF-92A had a wingspan of 31 ft. 3 in., a length of 42 ft. 5 in. and a loaded weight of 15,000 lb. It was retained for USAF/NACA research until a nose gear collapse wrote it off on October 14, 1953.

1948 September 29 Utilizing German research work conducted by the Arado aircraft company, the Chance Vought Co. flew its radical XF7U-1 Cutlass carrier fighter, possibly the worst aircraft ever bought by the U.S. Navy. With twin vertical fin-rudder assemblies set behind the 38° swept wings at approximately mid-span position, the aircraft had elevons on the outer section of its 38 ft. 8 in. wingspan. Powered by two 4,600-lb. s.t. Westinghouse J46-WE-8A turbojets, the F7U had a top speed of 680 MPH at 10,000 ft., a climb rate of 13,000 ft./min. and a range of 660 mi. The Navy bought around 300, a quarter of which were lost in accidents. The type operated from 1951 to November 30, 1957.

1948 October 10 On evaluating the performance and the program plan for the Northrop XF-89 all-weather interceptor, the USAF canceled the 88 Curtiss XP-87 aircraft ordered June 10. First flown on March 5, 1948, the XP-87 had been designed to have four 5,200-lb. s.t. Westinghouse J47-GE-15 engines, but flight trials were carried out with the 3,000 lb. s.t. J34-WE-7, which, although providing a speed of 600 MPH and a climb time of 13.8 min. to 35,000 ft., left the aircraft seriously underpowered. This was the last Curtiss aircraft, and in March 1951 the Curtiss Airplane Division of the Curtiss-Wright Corp. closed and was taken over by North American while the main company diversified into general engineering activities.

1948 October 14   In two days beginning this date, the diminutive parasitic McDonnell XF-85 Goblin No. 2 made three successful separations and hook-ups to a parent EB-29 mother-plane from which it had been designed to operate. The XF-85 had a length of 14 ft. 10 in., a wingspan of 21 ft. 1 in. and a loaded weight of 4,550 lb. It had a calculated top speed of 664 MPH at sea level and an endurance of 30 min. The fourth flight on October 15 ended with an emergency landing as did the fifth flight, and when the No. 1 Goblin made its first flight on April 8, 1949, and suffered a similar fate, the project was canceled.

1948 October 19   Replacing Lt. Gen. George C. Kenney as commander of USAF Strategic Air Command, Lt. Gen. Curtis E. LeMay took over the U.S. strategic bomber force as of this date. An experienced and able leader of World War II, LeMay was a strict disciplinarian, and in his almost nine-year tenure, he was responsible for shaping Strategic Air Command into one of the most efficient and effective instruments of air power anywhere. He adopted a nascent force with relaxed constraints and created a mighty armada with high morale and tight discipline.

1948 October 23   A development of the Focke Achgelis Fa-223, the French SNCASE company's SE 3000 made its first flight. Construction had been assisted by Prof. Focke himself, and this four-passenger helicopter was also adaptable as a heli-crane, with fittings for lifting gear. It also incorporated a welded steel fuselage with fin and rudder and lifting rotors on two outriggers with centers 41 ft. apart. Two other Fa-223s were put together in Czechoslovakia.

1948 November 4   In response to non-scheduled operators offering cut-price deals, Capital Airlines began the first scheduled "coach" service. The inaugural route was between New York and Chicago with a one-third reduction on the standard fare. Capital justified its position by scheduling the service in off-peak periods and by reducing inflight services with a high-density seating arrangement, their DC-4s carrying 60 passengers. Prior to this, air travel had been largely a "first class" service but the age of high density seating would bring an end to luxury travel for all.

1948 November 19   A research precursor to Britain's first swept-wing fighter and ground attack aircraft, the Hawker Hunter, made its first flight when Sqdn. Ldr. T. S. Wade flew the Hawker P.1052 (serial no. VX272) for the first time from Boscombe Down. This plane was on the same design layout as the P.1040 but with swept wings. The second P.1052 (serial no. VX279) was fitted with a swept tail rather than the straight tail of VX272 and was redesignated P.1081 for its first flight June 19, 1950. With a 130-MPH speed advantage over the Gloster Meteor at sea level, some wanted the P.1052 in production as a fighter, but it was retained as a research aircraft pending even better designs.

1948 November 30   A newly installed fog dispersal system (called Fido) was activated at Blackbushe airport, England for the first time. It comprised a series of gas pipes feeding burners that, when ignited, literally burned away the damp air. Lit at 4:12 P.M., it enabled Vickers Viking G-AJFS piloted by Capt. Harding of Airwork, on charter to the Crown Agents for the Colonies, to depart for Gibraltar en route to Accra with urgently needed bank notes for the West African Currency Control Board. Fido improved visibility from 30 yd. to 600–800 yd.

1948 December 7   Built from rubble by the men and women of Berlin in record time, a new airfield opened at Tegel to relieve congestion at Tempelhof, Berlin's prime airport, as the Berlin airlift to relieve the beleaguered city increased. There were now four landing fields in West Germany (Rhein-Main, Wiesbaden, Fassberg and Celle) and three unloading fields (Tempelhof, Gatow and Tegel). At the insistence of the British, a joint traffic control center was set up this month.

1948 December 9   A B-50A and a B-36 completed a nonstop round-trip flight from Carswell AFB in Tex. to Hawaii. Commanded by Maj. J. D. Bartlett from the Seventh Bombardment Group, the B-36 flew more than 8,000 unrefueled mi. in 35 hr. 30 min. The B-50A commanded by Lt. Col. Michael N. W. McCoy from the Forty-third Bombardment Group flew a distance of 9,870 mi. in 41 hr. 40 min. and performed three in-flight refueling operations from KB-29M tankers of the 43rd and 509th Air Refuelling Squadrons.

1948 December 29   The Supermarine Type 510 (serial no. VV106) was flown for the first time by Mike Lithgow. This was the first British jet-engined fighter with sweep on both wing and tail surfaces. Designed to specification E.41/46, it was a swept-wing, jet-engined version of the Supermarine Attacker powered by a 5,000-lb. s.t. Rolls Royce Nene 2, and it was intended to replace the Gloster Meteor. In tests against an F-86A, it proved its equal at altitude, although a poor finish degraded its performance at sea level. This Type 510 was to evolve into the Supermarine Swift.

1949 January 6   An armistice was agreed upon between Israel and her warring Arab neighbors. For the past year, an increasingly powerful, nascent Israeli Air Force, equipped with Czech aircraft bought in April 1948, had supported ground operations against Egypt, Syria, Jordon, Lebanon and Iraq. None of these Arab nations had the air power they would acquire during the 1950s and 1960s, but hostile action by both sides in the air war honed skills that were already being put to use building fighter forces for defense and offense. On separate dates between February 24 and July 20, 1949, an armistice was signed between Israel and Egypt, Lebanon, Jordan and Syria. An uneasy peace prevailed for seven years.

1949 January 17   In rearmament plans for her air force, France planned the license production of several western aircraft, including the de Havilland Vampire, of which it eventually built 500 under the name SE-535 Mistral. France's air force in 1949 had few modern aircraft and impending membership in the NATO defense infrastructure prompted in-depth planning for an expanded military force. In October 1949, an assistance pact signed in Washington, D.C. helped France rapidly improve its air force.

1949 February 4   In the United States, the CAA gave authorization for the full use of ground control approach (GCA) landing aids. These would be used only in conditions of poor visibility caused by fog or bad weather and comprise a ground radar system that would locate the aircraft and a ground controller to talk the aircraft down, providing height, vector and distance-to-go information. Pilots found this system superior to other radar identification aids.

1949 February 8   As if to emphatically stamp its arrival as precursor of a new generation of jet bombers, the Boeing XB-47 completed a nonstop flight from Moses Lake airfield in Washington to Andrews AFB, Maryland in 3 hr. 46 min. Covering the 2,289-mi. distance at an average speed of 607.2 MPH, the six-engined bomber prototype more than halved the existing transcontinental record. Placed in service four years ahead of the longer lived B-52, the B-47 would equip Strategic Air Command in greater numbers than any other jet bomber, 1,367 being in service during the peak year (1958).

1949 February 25   The #3 Douglas D-558-II research aircraft made the first Skyrocket flight incorporating both turbojet engine and rocket motor. (During its first flight January 8, only the turbojet had been operating.) The second D-558-II had only a turbojet engine and made two flights November 2 and 7, 1948, before delivery to NACA; it was returned to Douglas January 1950 for the turbojet to be changed for the rocket motor prior to airdrop research flights.

1949 February 28   The first home-built French post-World War II fighter made its first flight when the swept-wing Dassault MD 450 Ouragan took to the air one year after design completion. Liberated from Buchenwald concentration camp, the French aircraft builder Marcel Bloch set up the Avions Marcel Dassault and immediately forged strong links with the Armée de l'Air. His MD 450 was powered by a 5,070-lb. s.t. Hispano-Suiza Nene 104B and had a maximum speed of 584 MPH at sea level. In all, 350 were built for the French Air Force and in January 1955 it became the first aircraft ordered new by the Israeli Air Force.

1949 March 2   Commanded by Capt. James G. Gallagher, the crew of 14 aboard the Strategic Air Command B-50A *Lucky Lady II* of the Forty-third Bombardment Group, USAF, completed the first nonstop round-the-world flight in 94 hr. 1 min. Flying a distance of 23,452 mi. the B-50A was refueled four times by KB-29 tankers of the Forty-third Air Refuelling Squadron before landing back at Carswell AFB, Tex., its point of departure almost four days before. For this achievement, the crew was awarded the 1949 McKay Trophy given annually since 1912 to the U.S. Air Force person or persons making "the most meritorious flight of the year."

1949 March 9   The prototype Avro Shackleton (serial no. VW126) made its first flight, piloted by J. H. Orrell. The latest development of the Avro Lancaster, the production Shackleton evolved from the Lincoln Mk.III and was powered by four 2,450-HP Rolls Royce Griffon engines, each driving twin, three-bladed, contra-rotating propellers. In service with the RAF as a maritime reconnaissance replacement for U.S.-built Liberators and Fortresses beginning February 1951, it was still on duty, as an airborne early warning (AEW) aircraft, 40 yr. later.

1949 March 12   A B-36 of the Seventh Bombardment Group, USAF, completed a 9,600-mi. unrefueled flight in 43 hr. 37 min. Carrying a crew of 12 commanded by Capt. Roy Showalter, the flight began and ended at Fort Worth, Tex. Capable of carrying four times the bomb load of a B-50A, the B-36 displayed truly awesome, hemispheric range and was a clear sign that the dismemberment of America's air power that followed World War I would not be repeated in the post-World War II era.

1949 March 26   The Consolidated-Vultee B-36D made its first flight powered by four 5,200-lb. s.t. J47-GE-19 turbojet engines mounted in pairs under the outer wing sections in addition to the six pusher engines. In this "six-turning, four-burning" configuration, the B-36D *Peacemaker* truly bridged the piston and the jet bomber eras, boosting top speed to 439 MPH at 35,120 ft.

and raising bomb capacity to 84,000 lb. First flown December 18, the strategic reconnaissance RB-36D carried up to 14 cameras in two of the four bomb bays and had a crew complement of 22.

1949 March 31   The U.S. Navy Bureau of Aeronautics ordered two Douglas XA3D-1 carrier-based attack bombers in the 60,000-lb. class and with nuclear delivery capability. The aircraft was expected to operate from a new class of "super carriers" carrying 54 nuclear attack planes and epitomized by the CVB-58 named *United States*, authorized in the FY 1949 budget but suspended on April 23. Amidst flagging confidence in the survivability of carriers in an atomic age, funds went to the USAF for B-36 production. When the Korean War restored support for carriers, the CVA-59 *Forrestal* became the "super carrier" in reality. *Forrestal* was laid down on July 14, 1952, launched December 12, 1954, and commissioned October 1, 1955.

1949 April 1   Pan American introduced the first of 20 Boeing Model 377 Stratocruiser airliners on its scheduled service between San Francisco and Honolulu. On April 15, they began flying between New York and Bermuda, followed by the New York-London route from June 2. American Overseas Airlines introduced the Stratocruiser on its trans-Atlantic route starting August 17 followed by BOAC on December 6. With up to 100 passengers, 50% more than the Lockheed Model 749 Constellation, at 340 MPH the Stratocruiser was 13 MPH faster at cruising speed and, at 4,200 mi. had about the same range.

1949 April 16   The first flight of the radar-equipped, two-seat, all-weather YF-94 Starfire fighter took place. Powered by a 6,350-lb. s.t. Pratt & Whitney J48-P-5 or P-5A turbojet, the F-94 entered service in May 1950. Developed from the F-80, it had a top speed of 585 MPH at 30,000 ft. and an initial climb rate of 7,890 ft./min. Armament comprised 24 folding-fin 2.75-in. rockets in the nose and 12 in each of two underwing pods.

1949 April 16   U.S. and British transport aircraft supplying blockaded Berlin with vital life-sustaining cargo delivered a record day's total of 12,940.9 tons. To accomplish this, 1,398 aircraft were involved delivering supplies at three Berlin landing fields. In January, the daily food allowance for the rationed Berliner's diet had been raised from 1,600 to 1,880 calories. Beginning July 1948, unofficially dubbed Little Vittles, USAF air crews (encouraged by Lt. Gail S. Halvorsen) dropped from open cargo doors clusters of candy and gum on handkerchief "parachutes" to crowds of waiting children on the approach path to Tempelhof.

1949 April 20   Released from a Sud-Est SE.161 Languedoc "mother-plane," the Leduc 0.10 ramjet-propelled research aircraft made its first powered flight and accelerated to a speed of 423 MPH on half power after being released at 200 MPH. The ramjet engine was capable of 13,228-lb. thrust, but the airframe was limited to Mach 0.85. It had modest sweep, a wingspan of 38 ft. and a length of 41 ft. The pilot sat in a conical forward section behind which was the annular intake for the ramjet mounted in the center fuselage. Lack of funds led to termination of the follow-on fighter project, the Leduc 0.22.

1949 April 21   Displaying the advantages of a flying boat service, a Short Sunderland flew in medical supplies to the besieged frigate HMS *Amethyst* on the Yangtze River and on May 15/16 evacuated 121 British civilians from Shanghai. Proving their worth in the Far East, on April 4, 1948, six Sunderlands of specially formed No. 88 Squadron, RAF, had completed mail ferry flights from Hong Kong to occupation forces in Japan. In 19 months, they had air-lifted 2,368 passengers and 100 tons of mail.

1949 April 26 American pilots Dick Riedel and Bill Harris returned to earth after having remained in the air for exactly 6 wk. 1 min. when they landed their Aeronca Chief back at Fullerton airfield, Los Angeles. Campaigning to get a better airfield, the flight had been sponsored by the 18,000 inhabitants of Fullerton. For the first 4 wk., they flew east and circled around towns in Florida, then returned to Fullerton. Limited to a flight duration of just over 12 hr., fuel tanks in the aircraft were topped up from hand-delivered cans passed up twice daily from a speeding jeep. Fullerton got a better airfield, and the two pilots set a record that stands today.

1949 May 13 The prototype English Electric Canberra piloted by R. P. Beamont made its first flight from Warton, England. Designed to specification B3./45, the Canberra entered service as the first RAF jet bomber in May 1951, replacing Avro Lincolns. Powered by two 6,500-lb. s.t. Rolls Royce Avon 101 engines, it had a maximum speed of 570 MPH at 40,000 ft., a range of 2,660 mi. and a bomb load of 6,000 lb. The Canberra evolved into intruder, reconnaissance aircraft, target tug and training aircraft, with more than 40 still in service 40 yr. after it joined the RAF.

1949 May 15 BOAC introduced the Short Solent flying boat to airline service and operated it on the Southampton, England-Lake Naivasha, Nairobi run three times a week. Capable of carrying 30 passengers by day or 20 by night, the Short Solent was a developed version of the Sandringham, which had been based on the Sunderland. It had, at 236 MPH, a 70 MPH (42%) faster cruising speed than the old Empire flying boats and a range of 3,000 mi., cutting existing schedules almost in half. Solents began serving the Southampton-Karachi service May 26 but were replaced by Avro Yorks November 19.

1949 June 24 Piloted by Douglas's Eugene F. May, the #3 Douglas D-558-II exceeded Mach 1 for the first time, the first Skyrocket to do so. The addition of the rocket motor had increased the speed of the Skyrocket by more than 100 knots, reaching Mach 0.99 at 20,000 ft. or Mach 1.08 at 40,000 ft. with both turbojet and rocket motor on. However, with jet fuel and rocket propellant on board plus JATO takeoff assist bottles, the D-558-II needed 15,000 ft. of runway to take off, and in November the U.S. Navy ordered Douglas to modify it for air-drop research flights.

1949 July 27 Destined to become the first revenue-earning jet airliner, the prototype de Havilland D.H.106 Comet (G-ALVG) made its first flight piloted by John Cunningham. Designed as an all-metal, 36-seat plane, it completed a round-trip from Hatfield, England to Castel Benito, Libya, on October 25 at an average speed of 448 MPH. Powered by four 4,450-lb. s.t. de Havilland Ghost turbojet engines, it had a cruising speed of 490 MPH and a range of 1,750 mi. The second prototype flew exactly one year later.

1949 August 9 Lt. J. L. Fruin of VF-101 became the first American pilot to eject from a U.S. aircraft in emergency escape when his McDonnell F2H-1 Banshee went out of control at 500 MPH and a height of 30,000 ft. Fruin was over Walterboro, S.C., when the incident happened. VF-101 had been the first U.S. Navy unit to receive the twin-jet fighter.

1949 August 23 BOAC inaugurated its first all-landplane service to the Far East with Canadair C-4 *Arcturus* (registration no.

G-ALHJ) beginning a weekly flight from London to Rome, Cairo, Basra, Karachi, Calcutta, Rangoon, Bangkok and Hong Kong. Developed from the Douglas DC-4, only 42 C-4s were built, but BOAC was operating this aircraft until the late 1960s. *Arcturus* was sold in August 1957, but BOAC acquired it back again in 1964, and it was operated at the Heathrow Training School until scrapped in 1970.

1949 September 2 Giving added life to the de Havilland production line, the prototype D.H.112 Venom fighter bomber (serial no. VV612) made its first flight from Hatfield, England. Designed as a more powerfully engined development of the Vampire, the Venom had a 4,850-lb. s.t. Ghost 103 engine that gave it a top speed of 640 MPH and, at 9,000 ft./min., exactly twice the climb rate of its predecessor. In all, 3,268 Vampires were built for 26 air forces, and 1,143 Venoms for seven countries.

1949 September 4 The prototype Bristol Brabazon (G-AGPW) made its first flight at Filton, Bristol piloted by the new company test pilot A. J. Pegg. Powered by eight 2,500-HP coupled Bristol Centauris XX engines, the aircraft had a wingspan of 230 ft., a wing area of 5,317 sq. ft., a length of 177 ft. and a height of 50 ft. Equipped to carry 100 passengers at 250 MPH, it would have had a range of 5,450 mi. Easily the largest aircraft built in Britain, the Brabazon was unable to attract airline orders, and the single flying prototype was broken up in October 1953 with the unfinished second prototype similarly destined for the breakers.

1949 September 4 The first of five Avro 707 delta wing research aircraft (serial no. VX784) made its first flight piloted by S. E. "Red" Esler. Powered by a 3,500-lb. s.t. Rolls Royce Derwent, the aircraft had a wingspan of 33 ft. and a length of 30 ft. 6 in. VX784 crashed on September 30, killing the pilot, but the other aircraft went on to provide much valuable data about the handling characteristics of delta aircraft, contributing to the Vulcan and Concorde programs.

1949 September 19 Last in a long line of Royal Naval Air Service/Fleet Air Arm types built by Fairey, the Gannet prototype (serial no. VR546) was flown for the first time at Aldermaston, England by Grp. Capt. Slade. Powered by a 2,950-HP Armstrong Siddeley Double Mamba 100, it was the world's first aircraft powered by a double-propeller turbine engine, each half of which could be shut down and feathered in flight for economy. With an endurance of almost 5 hr., Gannets served as both anti-submarine search and strike and airborne early warning aircraft before retiring in the late 1970s.

1949 September 30 On the last day of the Berlin airlift, the last USAF C-54 departed Rhein-Main for Berlin, ending Operation Vittles. Since June 26, 1948, American and British transport aicraft had airlifted 2,325,808 tons of cargo. The USAF had flown 1,783,826 tons. The RAF flew 541,982 tons of supplies but had used its aircraft mainly to airlift people, including 50,000 children, invalids and elderly, to warmer places in Western Europe for the 1948 winter. Of the total cargo, 1,586,029 tons had been coal and 536,705 tons had been food.

1949 November 7 Setting a trend that would influence helicopter design for decades ahead, the single-rotor Sikorsky S-55 made its first flight. It was the first helicopter to have a cabin unrestricted by the engine, which was mounted in the nose, and this design evolved into the S-58, S-61, S-64 and S-65. The latter flew with the U.S. air forces under the H-53 designation.

First flown on November 27, 1949, as a modified C-74, the Douglas C-124 Globemaster II was the ultimate development of the DC-4.

1949 November 18   In what was the first flight to carry more than 100 people across the Atlantic, a Douglas C-74 Globemaster I flew from Mobile, Ala. to Marham, England with 103 passengers and crew. The nonstop flight took approximately 23 hr. The aircraft had been utilized to relieve C-54s to fly short hops during the Berlin airlift.

1949 November 27   The prototype Douglas C-124 Globemaster II made its first flight at Long Beach, Calif. Modified from the fifth production C-74, the Globemaster II had a double-deck fuselage and used the wings and tail of its predecessor. With capacity for 200 troops, 123 stretcher cases and 15 medical attendants or 74,000 lb. in cargo, the C-124 had a maximum range of 6,280 mi. Entering service in mid-1950, C-124s served until 1980 as heavyweight Military Air Transport Service work horses, 386 being built.

1949 December 21   The Strategic Air Command Commander-in-Chief, Gen. Curtiss LeMay, received approval from USAF headquarters to dispense "on-the-spot" promotions to outstanding aircraft commanders in the grade of First Lieutenant. LeMay already had 237 promotions to captain awaiting aurthorization to proceed with this policy, instituted by him after the second Strategic Air Command bombing competition. LeMay believed this would help shake up Strategic Air Command and inject a sense of pride in personal performance and stability among the junior officers.

1949 December 22   The first North American F-86D Sabre made its initial flight, piloted by George Welch. Incorporating a recontoured nose with a bulbous upper lip to accommodate a radar unit, this all-weather interceptor variant was powered by a 5,700-lb. s.t. (7,630-lb. s.t. with afterburner) General Electric J47-GE-17 engine and had a top speed of 707 MPH, an initial climb rate of 17,000 ft./min. and a ceiling of 54,000 ft. Armament included 24 2.75-in. rockets. In all, 2,504 "Sabre Dogs" were produced.

1950 January 17   The prototype MiG-17, piloted by I. T. Ivashchyenko, made its first flight. Essentially a refined and improved MiG-15, production aircraft had a completely new wing

and were powered by a 5,732/7,451-lb. s.t. VK-1F afterburning turbojet, giving the aircraft a maximum speed of 711 MPH at 9,840 ft. and a climb time of 1.8 min. to 16,405 ft. About 6,000 MiG-17s were built before production ceased at the end of the decade, with many going to Soviet client countries. The MiG-17 had a wingspan of 31 ft. 7 in., a length of 36 ft. 11 in. and a maximum loaded weight of 13,955 lb.

1950 January 19   Canadian test pilot William ("Bill") A. Waterton took the Avro Canada CF-100 into the air for the first time at Malton, Canada. Powered by two 5,700-lb. s.t. Rolls Royce Avon RA 2 turbojet engines, this all-weather, two-seat fighter was well suited to northern climates, and its initial climb rate of 9,800 ft./min. stood well against contemporary fighters. It was the first operational jet fighter from Canada and 53 were supplied to Belgium. Several variants of the 689 CF-100s appeared, the most powerful carrying two 7,300-lb. s.t. Avro Canada Orenda 11 engines.

1950 January 27   An Anglo-American agreement was signed providing for the eventual supply of 88 Boeing B-29s, known in RAF service as the Washington. The agreement was part of the Mutual Defense Assistance Program under which the United States would supply its allies with equipment important for their self-defense and contribution toward the North Atlantic Treaty Organization, which had come into being on April 4, 1949. The first Washington landed in England March 22 and helped fill the gap between the aging Avro Lincolns and the new generation of jet V-bombers planned for the mid-1950s.

1950 January 30   U.S. Pres. Harry S Truman announced his decision to proceed with development of a thermonuclear, or hydrogen, bomb as the first step in acquiring weapons many thousands of times more powerful than the atomic bomb. In September 1949, Truman had announced that the Soviet Union had detonated its first atomic bomb, and worsening relations with the USSR urged on this new development. The USAF also announced this day strict new regulations prohibiting civil overflights of U.S. atomic research facilities.

1950 February 8   A U.S. Navy Lockheed P2V-3C Neptune set a new long-distance record for carrier-launched aircraft by completing a flight from the carrier USS *Franklin D. Roosevelt* in the Atlantic to San Francisco, covering the 5,823 mi. in 25 hr. 59 min. Commanded by Comdr. Thomas Robinson, the aircraft flew over Charleston, N.C., Jacksonville, Fla. and the Panama Canal, along the coast of Central America and over Mexico.

1950 February 24   The prototype propeller-driven Hunting Percival Provost (serial no. WE522) made its first flight powered by an Armstrong Siddeley Cheetah, replaced by a 550-HP Alvis-Leonides 126 in the production version. It joined the RAF as a basic trainer, providing students with essential flying skills before they graduated to the jet-powered Vampire, and replaced the Percival Prentice in that function. The Provost had a wingspan of 35 ft. 2 in., a length of 28 ft. 8 in. and a loaded weight of 4,400 lb. and was used as a trainer until the 1960s.

1950 March 20   No. 97 Squadron, RAF, arrived at Tengah, Singapore with its Avro Lincoln bombers to hit communist insurgents in Malaya. A development of the World War II Lancaster, the Lincoln had the capacity for carrying 14,000-lb. bomb loads and, with a range of 1,470 mi. at maximum load, was a credible instrument of air power. The RAF did not phase the Lincoln out until March 1963, the last serving at No. 151 Signals Squadron, Watton, England.

1950 March 27 The second prototype Supermarine built to specification E.41/46 (serial no. VV119), and the first true prototype of the Swift swept-wing fighter, made its first flight as the Type 528 piloted by Mike Lithgow. Extensive modifications included lengthening the fuselage by 4 ft., giving the rear fuselage a greater diameter and providing a nose wheel and increased internal fuel capacity. These modifications transformed it into the Type 535 when it resumed flight trials August 23. Reheat was applied for the first time on September 1. Two pre-production Swifts and 100 production aircraft were ordered in November.

1950 April 1 The first British military helicopters in the Malayan theater became operational at Seletar, Singapore. Comprising three S-51 Dragonflys, they evacuated the first casualty retrieved by helicopter on June 6 when a policeman was flown to Johore hospital. By the end of the year, a total of 26 casualties had been evacuated, with 55 in 1951 and 144 in 1952. In January 1953, the Sikorsky S-55s of the carrier HMS *Perseus* arrived to replace the problem-plagued Dragonflys.

1950 April 1 English Electric received a contract for three prototype P.1 supersonic fighter development aircraft. Designed to specification F23./49, the aircraft had to be capable of flying at supersonic speed in level flight with interceptions controlled by ground radar. Following the cancellation of the Miles M.52, a new requirement for a supersonic fighter had emerged, designated Experimental Requirement 103, and it was to this that W. E. W. Petter had designed the P.1 in the summer of 1948.

1950 April 8 An unarmed U.S. Navy Consolidated PB4Y Privateer of VP-26 was shot down with the loss of all 10 crewmembers after being attacked by Soviet fighters during a routine flight over international waters in the Baltic Sea. The plane was flying between Wiesbaden, Germany and Copenhagen, Denmark on a training flight and was last reported by Danish authorities. The PB4Y was the navy version of the B-24 Liberator and was being used by the navy as a patrol and antisubmarine aircraft.

1950 April 18 The only U.S. Navy flying boat to use turboprop engines made its first flight when the prototype Convair R3Y Tradewind took to the air powered by four 5,500-EHP Allison XT40-A-4 engines. Operating as long-range transports, only 11 were built, the first flying in February 1954. With a gross weight of 160,000 lb., the R3Y had a wingspan of 145 ft. 9 in. and a length of 139 ft. 8 in.

1950 April 21 The heaviest aircraft to take off from the deck of an aircraft carrier to date lifted into the air from the USS *Coral Sea*. Piloted by Lt. Comdr. R. C. Starkey of VC-6, the Lockheed P2V-3C had a weight of 74,668 lb. The P2V-3C had been specially modified for carrier work, 11 being so fitted, and on March 7, 1949, a P2V-3C flew off the USS *Coral Sea* with a 10,000-lb. dummy bomb load from a position near the Virginia Capes, across the United States to "bomb" the west coast before returning to land at the Patuxent River NAS in Maryland.

1950 April 28 The first U.S. Navy order for Sikorsky S-55 helicopters was placed for general-purpose and antisubmarine aircraft with delivery commencing in August. A second order included S-55s for troop work with the marines, and it was marine applications of the helicopter that resulted in Sikorsky developing a family of very large helicopters typified by the S-56 and, later, the S-58, S-64 and S-65.

1950 May 3 Britain's first post-World War II aircraft carrier, HMS *Ark Royal*, was launched at Birkenhead on the River Mer-

sey by Queen Mary, the wife of King George VI. Laid down originally as HMS *Illustrious*, *Ark Royal* had a length of 720 ft. and a loaded displacement of 53,340 tons, a ship's crew of 2,345 and provision for fast jets with a 5.5° angled flight deck. Laid down in May 1943, the *Ark Royal* would be completed in February 1955.

1950 May 9 In cooperation with Rotor Stations Ltd., Westland Aircraft Ltd. began operating the United Kingdom's first temporary helicopter service. Flying 90 mi. between Barnes, near London, and Castle Bromwich, Birmingham, it was organized to coincide with the British Industries Fair in Birmingham and made two round-trips Monday through Friday. The pilot, Kenneth Reed, flew one of the 23 Westland-Sikorsky S-51 Mk.1As (G-ALIK) that would appear on the British register. Westland acquired S-51 license manufacturing rights in 1947 and would acquire the S-55 rights in 1951.

1950 May 10 The first de Havilland D.H.114 Heron (registration no. G-ALZL), a stretched version of the Dove, took to the air powered by four 250-HP Gipsy Queen 30 engines; production aircraft would carry a variety of powerplants, including a 340-HP Lycoming engine. Designed as a short- or medium-haul economy air taxi, the Heron was taken on a high-pressure sales tour beginning May 1951, with New Zealand National Airways Ltd. becoming the first customer. The Heron had a cruising speed of 165 MPH and a range of just over 800 mi. Saunders Aircraft of Canada remanufactured the aircraft as the ST-27 powered by two 715-esHP United Aircraft PT-6A-27 engines.

1950 May 17 Transcontinental and Western Air changed its name to more properly reflect its increasingly international operation, becoming Trans World Airlines and thus retaining the familiar abbreviation TWA. Right after World War II, TWA had aggressively attacked Pan American domination over trans-oceanic routes, sending a Lockheed Constellation on a proving flight to Paris on November 25, 1945. In August 1946, TWA linked with Northwest Airlines to provide a round-the-world service extending on from its route to Shanghai, TWA flying east from the United States to Shanghai and Northwest flying across the Pacific from Shanghai to the United States.

1950 June 1 Arizona Airways and Challenger Airlines merged to form Frontier Airlines, creating one of the most successful domestic operators in the United States. Arizona had formerly merged with Monarch, and Challenger had absorbed Summit. From the early 1960s, Frontier would serve the west-central United States from New Mexico to Canada and a spur service east from Denver to Kansas City and up to Omaha.

1950 June 1 The world's first sustained, routinely scheduled helicopter passenger service began when British European Airways started its operation between Speke, Liverpool and Pengham Moor, Cardiff. Using Sikorsky S-51s, the inaugural flight included among its passengers Lord Pakenham, the minister for civil aviation, and Lady Douglas, who were flown from Liverpool to Cardiff in G-AJOV piloted by Capt. J. Theilmann. When the service ceased on March 31, 1951, the S-51s had transported 819 passengers in 1,086 flying hours and 96.5% of scheduled services.

1950 June 2 The U.S. Navy selected the Grumman Model 89 for long-range, low-altitude, antisubmarine patrols operating off comparatively small escort carriers. From an invitation to bid issued January 20, 24 manufacturers responded with proposals on April 27 with only Douglas and Vought getting into the short list from which they were eliminated in favor of Grumman. An important part of the requirement was that the aircraft should operate without direction from the aircraft carrier. The S2F Tracker became one of Grumman's longest-serving aircraft, 1,269 being built between December 1952 and December 1967.

1950 June 3 Piloted by O. P. Hass and powered by a 5,200-lb. s.t. Allison XJ35-A-25 engine, the first Republic swept-wing F-84F Thunderstreak made its first flight as the YF-96A. The designation was changed to YF-84F on September 8, 1950. A second machine flew February 14, 1951, with an imported version of the British Armstrong Siddeley Sapphire engine. The first of 2,713 F-84F production aircraft flew on November 22, 1952, and joined the USAF in January 1954 powered by a 7,220-lb. s.t. Wright J65-W-3. A further 715 reconnaissance RF-84Fs were produced featuring wingroot intakes.

1950 June 25 Communist forces of North Korea invaded the Republic of Korea (ROK) south of the 38th parallel at 4:00 A.M. The ROK Air Force comprised 187 officers, 1,672 enlisted men and 16 aircraft, all small liaison and army cooperation planes. The military force comprised 65,000 men in addition to a police force of 35,000, equipped with light guns and mortars but no tanks or artillery. The North Korean Air Force consisted of 162 aircraft, of which 132 were combat planes, all Soviet.

Only the 500-strong U.S. Korean Military Advisory Group remained of 45,000 American troops that had been in the country during 1947. U.S. Far East Air Force (FEAF) elements based at Japan, Okinawa and the Philippine Islands comprised a total force of 1,172 aircraft, of which 553 were in operational units, 365 being F-80 fighters, in 30 U.S. squadrons equivalent to nine of the USAF's 48 combat wings. Based around a limited defensive capability, the FEAF was ill-equipped or -prepared to wage an aggressive war. In total, the USAF had 411,277 officers and men (18% of peak strength during World War II) and a total inventory of less than 2,500 jet aircraft of all types.

1950 June 26 Reacting to an invasion of the Republic of Korea by communist forces the day before, U.S. air units began to cover evacuation ships in the harbor at Inchon. At 1:33 P.M., a radial-engined communist fighter appeared through clouds and attacked two patrolling North American F-82 Twin Mustang escort fighters. Not knowing whether they should respond, the U.S. pilots evaded an encounter, and the communist pilot broke off in the first air-to-air engagement of the Korean War.

1950 June 27 The first aerial "kill" of the Korean War was credited to the pilot of a USAF F-82 Twin Mustang, Lt. William Hudson, and his radar operator, Lt. Carl Frasee, from the 68th (All-weather) Fighter Squadron, USAF, during a protection patrol on U.S. transport aircraft over Kimpo airfield. The crew of the F-82 came upon two Yak-9s attacking a U.S. fighter and got on the tail of one of them, shooting it down.

1950 June 28 U.S. Fifth Air Force units carried out the first bombing operations against North Korean forces south of the 38th parallel under authorization of a United Nations resolution calling for a military response to the aggression. On the preceding evening B-26s had attacked ground units, and during the afternoon, the Nineteenth Bombardment Group B-29s roamed South Korea seeking targets of opportunity. Communist fighters successfully struck at F-82, B-26 and C-54 aircraft in the air and on the ground. At 5:00 P.M. Washington time June 29, a National Security Council directive authorized search and destroy missions north of the 38th parallel.

1950 June 29 The Gloster Meteor F.8 single-seat day interceptor entered service with the RAF when it joined No. 245 Squadron at Horsham St. Faith. More than 1,000 F.8s would be produced, and the type was to serve as the primary British air defense fighter for 5 yr. until gradually replaced by the Hawker Hunter. First flown on October 12, 1948, the F.8 was powered by two 3,600-lb. s.t. Rolls Royce Derwent 8 engines and had a maximum speed of 590 MPH at sea level with an initial climb rate of 6,950 ft./min. and a range of 980 mi. Armament comprised four 20-mm nose cannon.

1950 July 3 The first naval air operations against North Korean forces began when carrier aircraft from the USS *Valley Forge*, with Air Group 5, and HMS *Triumph* hit targets around Pyongyang. The first U.S. Navy "kills" were achieved when Lt. L. H. Plog and Ens. E. W. Brown of VF-51 flying Grumman F9Fs shot down two Yak-9s. The British employed Carrier Air Group 13 with two squadrons, one flying the Seafire 47, the other the Firefly FR.2. On station these ships formed part of Task Force 77, which would sustain air operations through the end of the war.

1950 July 20 United Nations forces defending South Korea achieved virtual air supremacy and U.S. FEAF intelligence officers estimated that North Korea, as a result of major air attacks and air-to-air combat, had only 65 of its original aircraft left of which only 30 were in serviceable condition. By August 10, North Korean forces were known to have only 35 front-line aircraft, and by the end of the month that figure was down to 18. The North Koreans were known to be pursuing Soviet and Chinese sources for more aircraft.

1950 July 29 The world's first scheduled airline service using turboprop airliners began when BEA started using their Vickers Viscount between Northolt, London and Le Bourget, Paris. The first aircraft to go, registration G-AHRF, was piloted by Capt. R. Rymer carrying 14 paying passengers and 12 specially invited guests. The Viscount was used on this route for two weeks. On August 3, BEA signed an order for 20 Viscounts and on August 15 started the world's first domestic service to use turboprop airliners when it introduced the Viscount on the London-Edinburgh route.

1950 August 3 The first U.S. Marine Corps air units in action against North Korean forces supported the First Provisional Marine Brigade around Changwon when HO3S helicopters and OY observation aircraft from USMC Marine Observation Squadron VMO-6 delivered rations and water and evacuated casualties. This was the first time U.S. helicopters had operated in a war zone; before the conflict was over, rotary-winged aircraft would acquire a reputation and a range of roles hardly envisaged when it began.

1950 August 4 The first medical evacuation by helicopter from a Mobile Army Surgical Hospital (MASH) team took place when an S-51 flew out a casualty from a fire fight along the Pusan Perimeter. Next day, five more casualties were evacuated, some of them from hillsides too steep for jeeps to climb. The first MASH unit had arrived in Korea July 6. The S-51 was designed to carry two pilots and three people on a cramped bench to the rear. In-field modifications enabled a stretcher to be carried across this area, with the patient's legs protruding through the side.

1950 September 4 The first emergency rescue of a pilot from behind enemy lines by helicopter took place when Lt. Paul W. van Boven of the Third Air Rescue Squadron, USAF, flying a Sikorsky H-5, successfully picked up Capt. Robert E. Wayne who had been shot down behind communist lines in Korea. The H-5, formerly designated R-5, was the military version of the S-51.

1950 September 9 In support of the impending Inchon landings to push communist North Korean forces from South Korea, U.S. FEAF Bomber Command started intensive B-29 operations against railheads and marshaling yards in an attempt to disrupt the movement of supplies and materiel. Within four days, the B-29s had severed 46 rail routes, and on September 13 four groups with 60 aircraft attacked rail targets south from Anjou and Hungnam. Also on September 13, two days of intense napalm attacks neutralized communist units on the island of Wolmo-do, which dominated Inchon harbor.

1950 September 17 Two days after the successful Inchon landings, two Yak-3s made the North Koreans' only attack on shipping of the war when they struck the 17,500-ton cruiser USS *Rochester*. One of the two Yaks was shot down by the cruiser HMS *Jamaica*. Such was the intensity of the flying that by the end of the month only two Fireflys and one Seafire were in operational condition with Carrier Air Group 13. On October 10, HMS *Theseus* and CAG-17 relieved HMS *Triumph* with separate squadrons of Fireflys and Sea Furies.

1950 September 18 In support of the breakout from Inchon, 42 B-29s of the Ninety-second and Ninety-eighth Bombardment Groups dropped 1,600 (500-lb.) bombs on two targets, each measuring 1,500 ft. by 15,000 ft. on either side of the Naktong River at Waegan. The precise targeting of 400 tons of bombs into a total area of 1.6 sq. mi. was spectacular and effective. As previously poor weather cleared, tactical air operations increased with 286 close-support sorties being flown. The next day, 361 missions were flown.

1950 September 22 In the first nonstop crossing of the North Atlantic by turbojet aircraft, Col. David C. Schilling flew an F-84 from RAF Manston, England to Limestone, Maine in 10 hr. 1 min. Two aircraft began the flight, which included three in-flight refuelings, but Lt. Col. W. D. Ritchie, flying the other F-84, had to bail out of his aircraft over Labrador when it ran out of fuel against strong headwinds.

1950 September 22 In the only known instance of a large ground force surrendering to an aircraft in the air, 200 communist Korean troops moved to a hill as they had been so ordered by a hurriedly scribbled note, signed "McArthur" (sic), dropped by Lt. George W. Nelson flying a North American T-6 Mosquito carrying a forward air controller. Nelson located some UN patrols and directed them by radio to the hill where the troops surrendered their weapons.

1950 September 24 UN fighter sweeps had achieved surprising levels of success against communist Korean forces. To date, since operations got under way early in July, Fifth Air Force fighter pilots had killed 7,900 troops in strafing and ground attacks using bombs, guns and rockets. Nearly 800 had been killed on September 22, and on this date a total of 1,400 were killed. Communist forces were forced to move into the open as UN forces pushed north. No longer able to choose when they moved along the roads and trackways, the communists were forced to travel during daylight.

1950 September 25 Pres. Truman overruled the CAB and allowed Pan American to buy the assets of American Overseas Airlines for $17,450,000, making it an equal competitor with

TWA on international routes. The two airlines had been trying to merge since their respective boards reached agreement on terms December 13, 1948, but the CAB prevented such a move. Pres. Truman held Pan American in high esteem for its services during World War II and had awarded the Harmon Aviation Trophy to Pan American founder Juan Trippe in 1946 for that contribution.

1950 September 27 All strategic air operations against targets in the far north of Korea were halted by the U.S. Joint Chiefs of Staff following the return of the government of South Korea to its capital, Seoul. The defeated North Korean People's Army had been bombed and strafed into submission and outmaneuvered on the ground. On September 29, U.S. general Douglas MacArthur and South Korean president Syngman Rhee attended a victory parade in the capital. On October 1, Gen. MacArthur prohibited attacks on rail facilities south of the 38th parallel and, from October 4, on enemy airfields south of the 40th parallel.

1950 October 9 Approved by Pres. Truman, the Joint Chiefs of Staff sent Gen. MacArthur a message authorizing that ''in the event of the open or covert employment anywhere in Korea of major Chinese Communist units . . . you should continue the action.'' This allowed air operations to be directed against communist infiltration from China and directly resulted in air-to-air combat with Chinese pilots. The first Chinese incursion came at 4:00 A.M. on October 14 when two Chinese aircraft attacked Kimpo airfield.

1950 October 13 The first Lockheed Model 1049 Super Constellation made its first flight powered by four 2,500-HP Wright 749C-18BD-1s but later with 2,700-HP Wright Double Cyclones for production models. The Model 1049 was stretched in length from 95 ft. 2 in. to 113 ft. 7 in. increasing to 102 the number of passengers carried in a high density arrangement. Developed as a response to the Douglas DC-6, the Super Constellation had a cruising speed of 255 MPH, increased to 305 MPH in the Model 1049G first flown December 7, 1954.

1950 October 20 In support of the Wonsan invasion on the northeast coast of Korea, 71 C-119s and 40 C-47s delivered 2,860 paratroopers and 301.2 tons of equipment beginning at 2:00 P.M. over Sukchon and Sunchon. The entire drop was accomplished within the hour, and although many dropped perilously close to high-tension power lines not spotted in reconnaissance photographs, only one man was killed and 36 injured. The paratroopers belonged to the elite 187th Airborne Regimental Combat Team of the Eleventh Airborne Division.

1950 October 21 Beginning at 10:00 A.M., 40 C-119s dropped 1,093 paratroopers and 106.8 tons of supplies to reinforce the assault forces dropped on the preceding day in the Wonsan invasion. By October 22, the 187th Airborne Regimental Combat Team had engaged 6,000 communist Korean troops, killed 2,764 and taken 3,000 prisoners. The air drops had gone like clockwork, and the almost total lack of any air threat emphasized the importance of air superiority in operations of this sort.

1950 October 31 Since July 13, the strategic bombing offensive against North Korean targets had built to a peak of activity, 30,136 tons of bombs having been dropped to achieve a monthly average of 8,610 tons. This exceeded the 5,500 tons per month average during peak deployment of B-29s from the Marianas Islands in World War II.

1950 November 1 At 1:45 P.M., six Chinese MiG-15 jet fighters appeared over North Korea for the first time and attacked a

North American T-6 and an F-51 Mustang in the first appearance of this Soviet-built fighter in the Korean War. The American aircraft escaped. The day had seen the first indication that communist Chinese air units were intervening in the war. An F-80 was shot down by ground fire from across the Yalu River, dividing opposing forces.

1950 November 8 The first all-jet air battle took place when F-80s from the Fifty-first Fighter Interceptor Wing clashed with Chinese MiG-15s from Antung across the Yalu River opposite Sinuiju, North Korea. The F-80s were escorting 70 B-29s raiding Sinuiju shortly before mid-day with 584.5 tons of 500-lb. incendiary clusters. Lt. Russell J. Brown got on the tail of a MiG-15 and shot it down with his six 0.50-in. guns. This was the first air "kill" of one jet fighter by another.

1950 November 8 The Supermarine Swift prototype (serial no. VV106) became the first swept-wing aircraft to land on and take off from a carrier, HMS *Illustrious*. Three pilots made 12 landings and rocket-assisted takeoffs this day with the carrier proceeding at 22–25 knots and a 50-knot wind down the deck. With two rockets, the aircraft got airborne in 500 ft. with approaches taken at an indicated air speed of 124–134 knots. On the last takeoff, asymmetric rocket assist thrust slewed the aircraft, and on getting airborne, a wing struck a gun turret.

1950 November 9 In the first air combat victory achieved by a U.S. Navy jet, Lt. Comdr. W. T. Amen, commanding officer of VF-111, shot down a MiG-15 while attacking bridges across the Yalu River near Sinuiju in his Grumman F9F-2 Panther. Other MiGs involved in the resulting dogfight fled north of the river.

1950 November 10 BOAC withdrew all flying boats from service, the last of which were Short Solents flown on the Southampton-Johannesburg service. On November 7, these had been replaced by Handley Page Hermes airliners flying via Tripoli, Kano, Brazzaville and Livingstone. Thus ended 26 yr. of passenger flying boat services by Imperial Airways and BOAC. Tasman Empire Airways Ltd. continued to operate Solents until 1960, mostly between Australia and New Zealand, but British use of the flying boat expired in 1958 when Aquila closed its service to the Madeira islands.

1950 November 20 The first British hybrid turbojet/rocket aircraft, the Hawker P.1072, made its first flight combining propulsion from both motors. This aircraft was originally the P.1040 (serial no. VP401) used for Sea Hawk development and reengineered at the Kingston, Surrey works to carry a 2,000-lb. thrust Armstrong Siddeley Snarler ASSn.1 liquid propellant rocket and a 5,000-lb. s.t. Rolls Royce Nene R.N.2 turbojet. The first flight on turbojet power only had been made November 16. After six hybrid-power flights, the project was canceled in early 1951, attention turning to afterburners.

1950 November 23 The U.S. FEAF in Korea began a major air offensive to support a push by the U.S. Eighth Army against communist forces in North Korea. The assault north toward the Yalu River began at 10:00 A.M. November 24, and for two days, the Fifth Air Force flew 345 close support missions as Gen. MacArthur set up a pincer movement, hoping to encircle communist troops. Running into stiff resistance, the Eighth Army was brought to a halt and driven back. Massive reinforcements from China swelled communist ground forces from 200,000 in late November to 500,000 by early December.

1950 November USAF Tactical Air Command began development of a nuclear role for fighter-bombers in Europe, resulting in the development of the Republic F-84G Thunderjet. Advances in nuclear weapons engineering permitted small, low-yield bombs to be deployed on fast, low-flying jets, and the F-84G was the first aircraft to fill this role. Although the aircraft was delivered in 1951, the nuclear delivery role was not operationally available until 1952.

1950 December 6 Republic F-84 Thunderjets of the Twenty-seventh Fighter Escort Wing, USAF, flew their first combat mission from Itazuke, Japan on armed reconnaissance and close-support duties. The ground war in Korea was worsening, and USAF Gen. Hoyt S. Vandenberg had offered an F-84 wing and an F-86 wing on November 8. The two wings departed San Diego at the end of November aboard aircraft carriers. Col. George F. Smith took elements of the Fourth Fighter Interceptor Wing with its F-86s to the crowded air base at Kimpo, South Korea, leaving a rear echelon at Johnson AB, Japan.

1950 December 14 Combat Command flew 393 sorties between this date and December 17, airlifting from Yonpo airfield, Korea 228 patients, 3,891 passengers and 2,088.6 tons of cargo of X Corps. Unable to hold out against communist infiltrators, the airlift began at 9:00 A.M. for round-the-clock operations with aircraft taking off at 5-minute intervals for four days. All the while, during the retreat of the Eighth Army and X Corps, air operations were stepped up to cover the ground forces from increasing Chinese air hostility.

1950 December 17 Lt. Col. Bruce H. Hinton, commander of the 336th Fighter Interceptor Squadron, Fourth Fighter Interceptor Wing, USAF, became the first pilot to attack and destroy a Chinese MiG-15 with an F-86A Sabre. The kill came on the second mission of the day, which departed Kimpo airfield at 2:05 P.M. At 2:45, patrolling at 32,000 ft. and 472 MPH, four MiGs were spotted at 25,000 ft. Jettisoning auxiliary fuel tanks, the Sabres went in to attack the MiGs, which only spotted the USAF jets at the last moment. Col. Hinton fastened on the leader's wing man and fired 1,500 rounds, causing a rear fuselage fire. The MiG crashed 10 mi. southeast of the Yalu River.

1950 December 19 A change in F-86 patrol tactics in Korea required pilots to enter the combat area at high speed, thus having momentum to press home a fast attack and minimize the probability of being out-paced. Previously, since their first operational deployment two days before, Sabre pilots cruised in at relatively low speed to conserve fuel. Patrols were standardized at 16 aircraft, or four flights of four. Vindication of the new tactics came December 22 when two Sabre flights fought more than 15 MiGs and shot down six in a 20-min. dogfight from 30,000 ft. to the treetops.

1950 December 20 Dubbed Operation Christmas Kidlift, 989 small children orphaned by the war in Korea were airlifted out of Inchon in a driving snowstorm by 12 C-54s of the Sixty-first Troop Carrier Group. During the preceding month, the Fifth Air Force chaplains, Col. Wallace I. Wolverton, and Lt. Col. Russell L. Blaisdell had gathered together the orphans and, fearing a communist occupation of Seoul, had taken their young charges to Inchon where they waited for a cargo ship that never came. Gen. William H. Tunner organized the transport aircraft.

1950 December 20 In the first of two tragic records seven months apart, 86 out of 116 men on board a USAF Douglas C-124A Globemaster II were killed when it crashed on takeoff from Lake Moses, Wash. On June 18, 1951, a second C-124A crash near Tokyo resulted in the deaths of 129 people. Despite these two accidents, the Globemaster II would provide safe and reliable service for many years.

1951 January 1 Following a period of respite due to poor weather, the UN air forces began a major campaign to halt the southward progression of communist North Korean forces. The U.S. FEAF flew 564 sorties followed by 531 the next day, 556 on January 3, 498 on January 4 and 447 on January 5. Communist forces had launched an offensive in the area of the Imjin River and along the Chuchon-Hongchon-Wonju axis. During January intelligence estimates indicated air operations caused 19,000 communist casualties.

1951 January 13 A successful attack by a single B-29 on an important railway bridge at Kanggye, North Korea destroyed two spans and prevented its use. The B-29 had used the new 12,000-lb. Tarzon bomb similar to the GB-1 Azon bomb of World War II. With radio-controlled tail fins, the bombs were much more accurate but required experienced handling. In the first drops during December 1950, miss distances were frequently in excess of 500 ft., but accuracy came down to around 100 ft. or less within 3 mon.

1951 January 16 Six Strategic Air Command B-36Ds of the Seventh Bombardment Wing arrived at RAF Lakenheath, after crossing the Atlantic from Carswell AFB, Tex. via Limestone AFB, Maine, accompanied by three C-124A transports and a C-97A Stratofreighter. The first touched down at 5:00 A.M. and the last by 11:15 A.M. On the way, they had flown at altitudes between 700 ft. to 35,000 ft., checking radar and mock target alignment. Before reducing height for the approach to Lakenheath, the giant bombers were ''intercepted'' by RAF and USAF fighters to accompany them in. They returned to Carswell on January 20.

1951 January 19 Consolidated-Vultee was awarded a contract for two XF2Y-1 Sea Dart jet-powered seaplane fighters. In October 1948, the U.S. Navy had launched a competition for a seaplane interceptor. Consolidated's proposal was for a delta-wing design incorporating retractable skis for takeoff and landing. Two air inlets were provided above the wings on top of the fuselage behind the cockpit for the two J34-WE-32 turbojets.

1951 January 23 In a furious air battle around the Yalu River on the border between North Korea and China, 30 MiG-15s stormed into 33 F-84F Thunderjets of the Twenty-seventh Fighter Escort Wing, U.S. FEAF, on a strafing run on Antung airfield. Two flights hit the airfield, and six flights flew top cover, the F-84s claiming four MiGs destroyed, three probably destroyed and four damaged. During the afternoon, the Forty-ninth Fighter Bomber Wing sent 48 F-84s to hit Pyongyang prior to a bombing raid by 21 B-29s of the 19th and 307th Bombardment groups in which 90% of the bombs hit the airfield. From this date on, the FEAF gradually lost its edge over enemy aircraft as increasing numbers of Soviet jet fighters were employed by the Chinese.

1951 January 23 The first of two Douglas XF4D-1 prototypes made its first flight powered by a 5,000-lb. s.t. Allison J35-A-17 turbojet engine. Production F4D Skyray had the 10,500-lb. s.t. Westinghouse J57-P-8B providing a top speed of 695 MPH and an initial climb rate of 18,000 ft./min. Designed by Ed Heinemann as a carrier-based interceptor, the Skyray was a tailless aircraft with a slightly swept wing of extremely low-aspect ratio, having a span of 33 ft. 6 in. and a fuselage length of 45 ft. 8 in. Delayed by test problems, the first of 450 did not enter service until April 1956.

1951 January 31 With 17,000 hr. in his log book and 400 trans-Atlantic crossings to his credit, Pan American Capt. Charles Blair flew his P-51C Mustang *Excalibur III* nonstop from New York to London, covering the 3,500-mi. distance in 7 hr. 48 min. at an average speed of 450 MPH assisted by 130 MPH tail winds. The aircraft had been modified to carry 865 gal. of fuel, giving it a range of 5,000 mi. Unfortunately, the record was not observed by the FAI, and the very outdated record of 20 hr. 29 min. set in 1937 by a Lockheed Electra remained.

1951 February 5 Canadian authorities announced plans to increase defense spending and to inject an extra $5 billion into the defense budget. The RCAF would be expanded to include 40 active and reserve squadrons, an increase of 29, with 11 of the new squadrons going to Europe as part of Canada's NATO commitment. In addition, the U.S. and Canada would set up a defense early warning (DEW) line across North America comprising radar and interceptor squadrons capable of defending the continent from a trans-Arctic Soviet attack.

1951 February 14 At the defense debate in Britain's House of Commons, U.K. Defense Minister Emmanuel Shinwell announced plans to nearly double the strength of the RAF, increasing funds from £222.7 million in 1950/51 to £328.75 million for 1951/52. Already, there were twice as many day fighter squadrons as there had been in 1949, and with Canberras coming into service, the strength of the tactical bombing force was to be considerably increased. Manpower was to increase by 55,000 to 270,000.

1951 February 21 Sqdn. Ldr. A. E. Callard and his crew of Flt. Lt. A. J. R. Robinson and Flt. Lt. A. E. J. Haskett, RAF, departed RAF Aldergrove, Northern Ireland in Canberra, serial no. WD932, at 12:43 P.M. on the first nonstop, unrefueled, trans-Atlantic crossing by a turbojet-powered aircraft. The 2,072-mi. crossing was made in a record time of 4 hr. 37 min. at an average speed of 450 MPH. From Gander, Newfoundland, the Canberra was flown down to Andrews AFB, Washington, D.C. on February 24, a distance of 1,317 mi. covered in 2 hr. 59 min.

1951 February 23 Incorporating the latest swept-wing design technology, the Dassault M.D.452 Mystère single-seat fighter bomber made its first flight in France. Powered by a 7,716-lb. s.t. Hispano-Suiza Verdon 350 turbojet, production aircraft had a maximum speed of 696 MPH and an initial climb rate of 8,860 ft./min. with a range of 569 mi. Later, a two-seat night fighter emerged as well as the Super Mystère, of which almost 500 were produced for the French air force.

1951 March 2 Grumman was awarded a U.S. Navy contract for the modification of three F9F-5 Panthers into a swing-wing configuration with horizontal tail surfaces. Under the original F9F work order, Grumman was to research the possibility of a swept-wing version, and this came to fruition with the order for the prototypes of 1,988 F9F Cougar carrier-based fighters. The sudden appearance of the swept-wing MiG-15 and the inferiority of the straight-wing F-80 and, to a lesser extent, the McDonnell F2H Banshee prompted sudden action to improve the F9F series.

1951 March 6 Production of the English Electric Canberra jet bomber in the United States as the Martin B-57 was implemented by the Air Materiel Command. In seeking a night intruder and fast tactical attack bomber, the USAF evaluated several contenders from U.S. manufacturers including the North American B-45, the Martin B-51 and the North American AJ-1 Savage as well as the Avro Canada CF-100 from Canada. But in a demonstration fly-off at Andrews Air Force Base, Washington, D.C., February 26, Canberra WD932 demonstrated in a stunning flying display why the decision had already been made in favor of the British aircraft.

1951 March 8   The U.S. Navy awarded North American a contract to build three prototype navalized F-86 Sabres as the XFJ-2 in response to increasing numbers of swept-wing Soviet-built MiG-15s appearing in Korea. The FJ-1 Fury with straight wings had been the basis for the swept-wing F-86, and now the navy wanted the benefits of that aerodynamic refinement also. The first prototype flew on December 27, and the first navy order for 300 FJ-2 Furys was placed February 10, 1952. The type entered service in January 1954, and 1,112 were built for the navy and the marines.

1951 March 13   The Australian airline QANTAS began a survey flight from Rose Bay, Sydney to Valparaiso, Chile with a Catalina (VH-ASA). Post-World War II development had begun with flights to London in 1946 followed by services to Japan the following year. Improved equipment, especially the pressurized DC-6s, helped the airline's image and increased the number of passenger-miles flown.

1951 March 15   One of three Boeing C-97A cargo aircraft modified into a tanker configuration and designated KB-97C, refueled a Boeing B-47. The KB-29s had not been compatible even with the B-50, so the conversion of the C-97 was ideal for use with the new fleet of jet bombers. The first operational model, the KC-97E, was delivered July 14, incorporating provision for 7,200 gal. in four additional fuel tanks. In all, Boeing built 811 KC-97's, which served with Strategic Air Command until 1964 and with the Air National Guard until 1977. The KB-29s were retired in 1956.

1951 March 21   General Electric was awarded a USAF contract to build a nuclear-powered turbojet engine designated P-1. Later this year, a direct-air cycle design with metallic fuel elements would be selected for development, with the 17,000-lb. s.t. J53 turbojet as the selected baseline design around which the nuclear source was to be built. In 1953 the project was canceled, as was work on two Convair X-6 aircraft that were to have been derivatives of the B-36 as purpose-built test beds for the powerplants. However, Convair did fly the NB-36, which was to have been used to test the reactor alone, for two years beginning in 1955.

1951 March 23   An airborne assault with the 187th Airborne Regimental Combat Team in Operation Tomahawk dropped 2,011 paratroops from 72 C-119s in support of a U.S. I Corps attack toward the Imjin River in North Korea. In addition, the C-119s dropped 204 tons of supplies as 48 C-46s dropped 1,436 paratroops and 15.5 tons of munitions and supplies. There were only 84 jump casualties and 18 wounded by ground fire with one man killed. During daylight, the U.S. Fifth Air Force flew 168 sorties in support of the operation.

1951 March 23   Benefiting from the increased protection afforded by the F-86s in Korea, B-29s of the Nineteenth and 307th Bombardment Groups attacked rail bridges at Kogunyong and Chongju in northwestern Korea near the Manchurian border in an area known as a ''MiG Alley.'' Screening the bombers, 45 F-86s fought off MiG-15s, and the B-29s reported no hostile contact. The gradual build-up of F-86s took the strain away from the F-80s, and they also proved a fair match for the MiGs, which at first were reluctant to engage the Sabres.

1951 March 31   Contracts were awarded to Lockheed and Consolidated-Vultee for development of experimental vertical takeoff aircraft under the respective designations of XFO-1 and XFY-1. Since 1947 the USAF and the U.S. Navy had been jointly studying vertical flight for jet fighters in an effort to reduce runway lengths and carrier flight decks. These navy contracts were a culmination of studies carried out by several U.S. manufacturers into potential designs for a vertical takeoff escort fighter capable of operating from small ships.

1951 April 2   The USAF Air Research and Development Command (ARDC) became operational, embracing control over the Air Development Force at Wright Field, the USAF Cambridge Research Division, the USAF Flight Test Center at Edwards AFB, Calif. and the Holloman AFB Research & Development Center, N.M. Added later were the Arnold Engineering Development Center at Tullahoma, Tenn., the USAF Armament Center at Eglin AFB, Florida and the USAF Special Weapons Center at Kirtland AFB, New Mexico.

1951 April 11   United Air Lines introduced the new Douglas DC-6B on its New York-San Francisco service, beating Pan American by 18 days. The DC-6B differed from its contemporary, the all-cargo DC-6A, in not having a stressed floor and was essentially a 102-seat passenger version. Introduced on April 16, the DC-6A was 5 ft. longer than the DC-6 and powered by either four 2,400-HP Double Wasp CB16s or four 2,500-HP Double Wasp CB17s, features that the DC-6B retained. In total, 704 DC-6 series aircraft were built, of which 74 were the all-cargo DC-6A and 288 were the all-passenger DC-6B.

1951 April 16   Photographic reconnaissance interpreters with the UN forces in Korea reported ominous signs that the Chinese were building airfields in North Korea in preparation for air support of a major ground offensive from China. Accordingly, an ''airfield neutralization'' program was devised, and the fighter wings moved up to suppress communist air opposition by putting pressure on MiG Alley. Between April 16 and 23, an average 12 B-29 aircraft made daily raids on these airfields.

1951 April 16   Just five days after the inaugural service of the all-passenger DC-6B, the all-cargo DC-6A was introduced by Slick Airways. Awarded an experimental five-year, all-freight operating certificate on August 12, 1949, Earl F. Slick had been hauling freight since March 4, 1946, as a contract carrier, and with a fleet of ex-Army C-46Es, he quickly developed a viable business. But American Airlines also ordered a fleet of 10 DC-6As with the declared intention of competing in the freight market, and Slick merged with Flying Tiger in 1954.

1951 May 1   Eight Douglas Skyraiders and 12 Vought Corsairs from the USS *Princeton* carried out an attack on the Hwachon Dam in communist North Korea. Using aerial torpedoes, they destroyed the dam and released waters held back in the reservoir into the Pukhan River, causing it to flood and delay communist troops from making an easy crossing. This was the first and only use of aerial torpedoes in the Korean War.

1951 May 9   A massive U.S. Fifth Air Force/First Marine Air Wing attack on the communist held airfield garrison of Sinuiju, North Korea was carried out by 312 pilots. F-84s flew top cover, and although 50 MiG-15s took off from Antung across the Yalu River, none would come over and fight. At the end of the day, the garrison had been badly mauled, with 106 buildings destroyed, an exceptionally large fuel dump fired, 26 ammunition dumps blown up and many aircraft destroyed on the ground. It was believed Sinuiju would support the new communist offensive that was to begin May 15.

1951 May 18   The #2 Douglas D-558-II piloted by William "Bill" Bridgeman became the fastest aircraft when it achieved a speed of Mach 1.72 at 62,000 ft., approximately 1,130 MPH. This was also the first time a human being had traveled faster than 1,000 MPH. The previous unofficial record had been set by Charles Yeager in the #1 Bell X-1 when he reached a speed of Mach 1.45 (972 MPH) at 50,000 ft. on May 2, 1949. Bill Bridgeman raised the record again on June 11 when he flew the same aircraft to Mach 1.79 (1,180 MPH) at 64,000 ft.

1951 May 18   The prototype Vickers Valiant (serial no. WB210) made its first flight piloted by J. "Mutt" Summers from the grass airfield at Wisley, England. First of the "V-Bombers" to fly, the production Valiant B.1 had a wingspan of 114 ft. 4 in., a length of 108 ft. 3 in. and a gross weight of 140,000 lb. carrying a maximum bomb load of 21,000 lb. With a maximum speed of 657 MPH at 30,000 ft., the Valiant had a range of 4,500 mi. and was powered by four 10,000-lb. s.t. Rolls Royce Avon 201 turbojets. It became operational with No. 138 Squadron, RAF, in July 1955.

1951 May 20   USAF Capt. James A. Jabara of the Fourth Fighter Interceptor Wing flying F-86s in Korea shot down his fifth and sixth enemy aircraft and thus became the first jet air ace. The kills took place on a day when the Chinese MiG pilots finally broke their reluctance to engage the F-86s and came across the Yalu River to fight, 50 MiG-15s battling 36 Sabres. Jabara completed two tours of duty in Korea and eventually achieved a total 15 air combat "kills," the second-highest-scoring air ace of the Korean War.

1951 May 29   Gen. Hoyt S. Vandenberg, USAF chief of staff since April 30, 1948, described his vision of American air power when giving evidence before the Senate Foreign Relations and Armed Services Committee: "The British Navy, which was superior at one time to all the combined navies of the world, kept the peace for a long period. It kept the United States safe, as a matter of fact, for a long time. My hope is that the United States Air Force can be built to a point where it can do a similar job for the free nations of the world."

1951 June 1   A massive build-up in the size of the Chinese Air Force increased the Chinese inventory from 650 at the beginning of the year to 1,050 combat aircraft. Of no greater importance in the total build-up was the flow of MiG-15 swept-wing jet fighters, which now numbered 450. The failure to exploit a ground offensive that promised to push UN forces far down to the south at the beginning of the year was attributed to the lack of Chinese air power.

1951 June 14   A new series of inexpensive coach-class air fares to East Africa was instituted this day by two British airlines. An Airwork Vickers Viking left Blackbushe and a similar aircraft of Hunting Air Transport left Bovingdon for Nairobi, Kenya. The flights took two days and went via Nice, Malta, El Adem, Halfa, Khartoum, Juba and Entebbe.

1951 June 20   For the first time, communist air units in North Korea used eight Ilyushin Il-10 second-generation Sturmovik ground attack aircraft in a raid on the island of Sinmi-do held by the South Koreans. F-51 Mustangs of the U.S. FEAF intercepted them, shooting down two and damaging three. An additional flight of Mustangs came up and hit six Yak-9 fighters, and a third flight met MiG-15s arriving on the scene. Four MiGs were claimed as damaged, but one P-51 was shot down.

1951 June 20   Piloted by Bell Company test pilot Jean "Skip" Ziegler, the X-5 variable-sweep research aircraft made its first flight powered by a nonafterburning 4,900-lb. s.t. Allison J35-A-17A, modified by Bell to have a lighter tail pipe and changed plumbing. Partial sweep was successfully attempted for the first time on July 27 followed by a full sweep from from 20° to 60° four flights later. The X-5 was handed over to NACA for research programs after which, in 1955, it was returned to the air force.

1951 June 25   On the first anniversary of the communist assault on South Korea, the Red Chinese and the North Koreans were sent a message by Lt. Gen. Matthew B. Ridgway encouraging them to sue for peace. Two days later the Chinese declared they were ready to suspend military operations and discuss peace terms. Meanwhile, in the absence of a formal agreement, the air war continued. Gen. Ridgway replaced Gen. MacArthur as commander of the UN Command and the Far East Command on April 11.

In the first year of the Korean War, the U.S. FEAF had lost 857 men, including 187 killed, 255 wounded, 412 MIA and 3 POW. FEAF had lost 188 fighters, 33 fighter-bombers, nine transports and 17 other aircraft for a total of 247. It dropped 97,000 tons of bombs and 7.8 million gal. of napalm and transported 176,000 tons of cargo and 427,000 people. To air action, the communists had suffered 120,000 casualties, lost 391 aircraft, 125,000 buildings, 24,500 vehicles, 14,200 rail cars, 893 locomotives, 1,695 tanks and 2,700 guns.

1951 July 3   On bomber escort and diversion duties against targets in North Korea, 32 F-84s hit flak batteries in Pyongyang while six B-29s escorted by 33 F-86s dropped 8,500 100-lb. bombs on the airfield runway. In a concentrated attempt to destroy Red China's air arm in North Korea, the airfield neutralization program worked, and on July 12, the Chinese abandoned their efforts at keeping the airfields in North Korea open for use, citing large numbers of people so far being required to repair 69 airfields to help only 30 aircraft maintain operational status.

1951 July 20   The first flight of the Hawker P.1067, serial number WB188, later named Hunter, began when Neville Duke took it into the air at Boscombe Down. Designed as a replacement for the Gloster Meteor, the P.1067 had sweep on all surfaces, capacity for four powerful 30-mm Aden cannons in the nose and power provided by a Rolls Royce Avon turbojet. A wide variety of marks and variants appeared. The Hunter began a 17-year period of service with the RAF in July 1954, and all told 2,241 were built for many air forces around the world.

1951 July 31   In a concentrated series of air attacks since the beginning of June against communist logistics in North Korea, U.S. FEAF units achieved high levels of success with B-26 night intruder operations mounted by the Third and the 452nd Bombardment Wings. In two months, they destroyed 1,245 vehicles and damaged 2,845. Prior to this, in the three months ending June 30, U.S. Marine Squadron VMF(N)-513 using C-47 Firefly gunships, F4Us and F7Fs attacked 11,980 vehicles and destroyed 1,420. In a special "truck-hunting" operation, U.S. Fifth Air Force fighter-bombers accounted for 7,807 vehicles destroyed during January–May with a further 5,941 damaged.

1951 July   The world's first operational night fighter unit, No. 25 Squadron, RAF, received its D.H.113 Vampire NF (night-fighter) 10s replacing Mosquito NF 36s. Developed as a private venture, the prototype of this night fighter variant made its first flight on February 10 and was one of 12 Vampires ordered by

Egypt. When arms were embargoed to Egypt, the aircraft were diverted to adaptation as night fighters. With a gross weight of 13,100 lb., the NF 10 had a maximum speed of 538 MPH and a range of 1,220 mi.

1951 August 5 The first preproduction Supermarine Swift (serial no. WJ960) made its first flight powered by a 7,500-lb. s.t. Rolls Royce Avon RA7 engine. The Swift F.1 had a wingspan of 32 ft. 4 in., a length of 41 ft. 5 in. and a loaded weight of 19,330 lb. With a maximum speed of 680 MPH, it had an initial climb rate of 7,700 ft./min. and a ceiling of 48,000 ft. Several variants were produced, the most successful being the F.R.5 fighter reconnaissance version. The Swift F.1 joined the RAF in 1952 and was retired about 10 years later. Thus, for eight years from 1954, did a Supermarine and a Hawker fighter once again share the front-line defense of Britain.

1951 August 7 The ill-fated McDonnell XF3H-1 Demon made its first flight powered by a 7,200-lb. s.t. Westinghouse J40-WE-6. The 33,900-lb. gross weight of the F3H required the more powerful J40-WE-24, which failed to appear due to design difficulties, and the first 58 production models had the 7,200-lb. s.t. J40-WE-22. After delivery, numerous flying accidents due to engine failure brought a halt to production. In June 1955, the F3H-2 appeared with the 9,700-lb. s.t. Allison J71-A-2. First into service in March 1956, the F3H-2 proved a good aircraft and remained with the U.S. Navy until August 1964.

1951 August 10 Piloted by Tom Brooke-Smith, the first prototype Short S.A.4 (serial no. VX158) jet bomber made its first flight from Aldergrove, England. Powered by four Rolls Royce Avon jet engines in vertical pairs enclosed by nacelles that appeared to clasp the wing from above and below, the aircraft was designed to specification B.14/46 for a 10,000-lb. bomb load. It lost out to the Vickers Valiant, but two prototypes were completed for research purposes.

1951 August 15 Test pilot Bill Bridgeman reached a record altitude of 79,494 ft. in the #2 Douglas D-558-II rocket research aircraft, although this did not qualify for FAI recognition. The previous highest altitude attained by a human being was 72,395 ft. reached by Capts. O. A. Anderson and A. W. Stevens of the U.S. Army in a balloon over South Dakota on November 11, 1935. The FAI altitude record stood at 59,446 ft., achieved by John Cunningham on March 23, 1948, in a D.H.100 Vampire (serial no. TG278).

1951 August 15 Powered by a Rolls Royce Dart, a DC-3 of British European Airways became the first turboprop aircraft operated on a freight run. Named *Sir Henry Royce*, the aircraft flew between Northolt, Middlesex, England and the military airfield at Hanover, West Germany. The Dart engines had been fitted to two DC-3s to speed engine development.

1951 August 17 Developed to answer a need made clear through operations in Korea, the latest and most important variant of the Douglas Skyraider, the AD-5, made its first flight. Incorporating many changes, including a wider fuselage for side-by-side seating, a longer fuselage and increased vertical fin area and a conversion kit enabling it to be adapted as a transport, the AD-5 gave the Skyraider an extended operational career. The last of 3,180 Skyraiders was delivered in 1957.

1951 August 17 Col. Fred J. Ascani, USAF, broke the 100-km closed-circuit record with a speed of 635.686 MPH in his F-86E Sabre jet fighter. The event took place at the U.S. National Air

Races held at Wayne Major Airport, Detroit, Mich. This beat the previous record of 605.23 MPH achieved by John Derry in a D.H.108 in April 1948.

1951 September 1 Having failed to agree to terms during Korean War peace talks that had broken down on August 23, the communist air forces launched an all-out air offensive with as many as 90 MiG-15s appearing over the Chinese border simultaneously. China's MiG-15 strength had now grown to 525. During the month, Fourth Fighter Interceptor Wing pilots reported 1,177 MiG sorties over North Korea with 911 combat engagements. Pressure from the communist air forces now seriously threatened UN ground forces.

1951 September 5 Following five years of intensive study, the USAF awarded Consolidated-Vultee a contract to modify a B-36 to carry a nuclear reactor for tests on airframe, instruments and electronics. The nuclear reactor would be built by General Electric and provide vital research necessary to determine whether an atomic-powered bomber was feasible. A nuclear aircraft would provide virtually unlimited range since the fuel source would have many years of continuous operation.

1951 September 20 The Grumman F9F-6 Cougar swept-wing version of the F9F Panther made its first flight powered by a 7,000-lb. s.t. Pratt & Whitney J48-P-6 turbojet. With a wingspan of 36 ft. 5 in., a length of 41 ft. 7 in. and a gross weight of 20,000 lb., the Cougar had a top speed of 705 MPH at sea level, a climb time of 8.5 min. to 40,000 ft. and a range of 600 mi. The U.S. Navy and Marine Corps bought 1,985 Cougars, bringing to 3,373 the total U.S. Panther/Cougar buy.

1951 September 26 Piloted by John Cunningham, the de Havilland D.H.110 swept-wing twin-tail boom prototype advanced RAF night fighter made its first flight at Hatfield, England. On April 9, 1952, it exceeded the speed of sound in a dive, and on September 6, John Derry was killed when the second prototype broke up during demonstrations at the Society of British Aircraft Companies Show, Farnborough. Modifications kept the first prototype grounded through June 1954. The RAF changed its mind and bought the Javelin, but the Royal Navy remained interested in the D.H.110, which later emerged as the Sea Vixen.

1951 October 3 The U.S. Navy's first Helicopter Antisubmarine Squadron was commissioned at Key West Naval Air Station, Fla. Designated HS-1, the unit was commanded by Comdr. J. T. Watson and would develop operating procedures for search and destroy missions, working with surface ships, shore installations and fixed-wing aircraft.

1951 October 11 The first battalion-strength helicopter lift took place during the Korean War when 12 HRS-1s from the U.S. Marine Air Transport Squadron moved almost 1,000 troops of the First Marine Division a distance of 15 mi. over 3,000-ft. mountains in 156 flights. Operation Bumblebee took approximately 6 hr.

1951 October 16 Experiencing the most intensive pressure of the war from communist jet fighter pilots, F-86 pilots of the U.S. Fourth Fighter Interceptor Wing were credited with nine MiG-15s. In the preceding two months, Chinese MiGs had been brought in to new airfields constructed in North Korea previously destroyed by the U.S. FEAF. Mounting numbers of jet fighters began to tip the balance in favor of the communist air units.

1951 October 23   In one of the fiercest air battles of the Korean War, approximately 100 MiG-15s boxed in 34 F-86s of a screening force deployed to fend off intruders from a major bombing operation against Namsi airfield south of the Yalu River. Eight B-29s escorted by 55 F-84s of the Forty-ninth and 136th Fighter Interceptor wings were circled by 50 MiG-15s, which went in to attack the formations when the USAF pilots refused to be drawn away from their primary role of protecting the bombers. Three B-29s were shot down, five were badly damaged, and one F-84 was lost. B-29 gunners got three MiG-15s, and an F-84 pilot was credited with one.

1951 October 31   In the first month of renewed aerial combat following the breakdown of peace talks in the Korean War, the U.S. FEAF claimed 32 MiG-15s destroyed, 24 by F-86s, for the loss of 15 (including 7 Sabres). UN pilots had reported 2,573 MiG-15 sorties with 2,166 engaged in combat, an increase of 184% in sorties and 237% in contacts over the previous month. Calls had been made for increased UN fighter strength, but these had been refused.

1951 November 26   The prototype Gloster Javelin (serial no. WD804) made its first flight. Developed over several years as a potential replacement for the Meteor, the Javelin had a delta wing with a span of 52 ft. and a length of 56 ft. 3 in. With a gross weight of 42,000 lb. and powered by two 8,000-lb. s.t. Armstrong Siddeley Saphire turbojets, the Javelin had a top speed of 622 MPH, a climb time of 9.8 min. to 45,000 ft. and an operational ceiling of 52,500 ft. It began a 12-yr. tenure with the RAF in December 1955.

1951 December 12   Designed to operate from a 1,000-ft. landing strip and carry a load of 3,153 lb. a distance of 882 mi., the first DHC-3 Otter took to the air at Downsview, Canada with George Neal at the controls. The RCAF bought early models in the series, and the type became a popular and rugged overland light passenger or transport aircraft. With capacity for nine people in addition to the crew of two, the Otter could easily convert to a cargo carrier.

1951 December 31   In the preceding two months, communist air operations over North Korea had continued to increase, with 2,326 sorties in November and 3,997 sorties in December. In three months, the communist forces had increased almost four-fold the number of missions flown by their MiG-15 intruders. A new Chinese air regiment had been moved down to Ta-ku-shan, raising to 290 the complement of MiG-15s at the Antung air base. In addition, the Russians were now supplying the MiG-15 bis with its more powerful engine.

1952 January 3   The prototype Bristol Type 173, the first twin-rotor helicopter designed and built in the United Kingdom, made its first flight piloted by C. T. D. Hosegood. Incorporating two sets of engines and rotors from the Bristol Type 171 Sycamore, it had room for 13 passengers. After a long gestation, its derivative, the Type 192, was evaluated by the RAF and ordered as a short-range tactical transport helicopter. Known as the Belvedere, it entered service in September 1961.

1952 January 4   Pan American World Airways inaugurated the first all-cargo service across the North Atlantic with its recently acquired Douglas DC-6A cargo carrier. On May 1, Pan American introduced its new DC-6B airliner version of the DC-6A on the inaugural flight of the trans-Atlantic "Rainbow" service at tourist fare. Pan American had become Pan American World Air-

ways Inc. on January 3, 1950, a change that reflected the full international nature of its business.

1952 January 8   Bell Aircraft Corp. designer Robert J. Woods urged in a letter to NACA that effort be given to the problems associated with hypersonic flight and the possibility of travel into space involving winged vehicles. Attached was a report from Germany's ex-V2 chief (Maj.) Walter Dornberger proposing a winged vehicle capable of "skipping" across the upper atmosphere. In June the NACA Aerodynamics Committee recommended that Ames and Langley laboratories increase their work on hypersonics.

1952 January 13   The first of 52 Lockheed P2V-5 Neptune aircraft arrived at St. Eval, Cornwall, England to operate under the Mutual Defense Assistance Program with the RAF as maritime reconnaissance aircraft. All 52 were in the United Kingdom by January 27, and the type served with Nos. 36, 203, 210 and 217 Squadrons. They were eventually replaced by the Avro Shackleton beginning March 1957 but helped plug a gap in Coastal Command needs in the face of an expansion in Soviet submarine fleets.

1952 January 22   The de Havilland Comet 1 became the world's first jet airliner to receive a certificate of airworthiness when the U.K. minister of civil aviation, J. S. Maclay, handed over the appropriate documentation to the de Havilland aircraft company at Hatfield, England. The first cabin pressurization flight had been performed on February 21, 1950, and the second prototype was delivered to the Ministry of Supply in April 1951 for a 500-hr. route proving and crew operations program.

1952 February 2   The British Ministry of Supply issued specification F.124T, which had been derived from an RAF operational requirement for a target defense interceptor. It envisaged a single-seat rocket-propelled vehicle launched from a ramp. Although not invited to tender, Saunders Roe developed a design capable of intercepting aircraft at up to 100,000 ft. and submitted it in April. On October 30, Saunders Roe was authorized to proceed with what became the SR.53.

1952 February 10   Maj. George A. Davis Jr., USAF, was awarded a posthumous Medal of Honor for giving up his life this day to protect a formation of fighter bombers over North Korea. Flying an F-86 Sabre, Maj. Davis led his wingman in an attack on 12 MiG-15s about to jump a formation of F-84s. Fighting furiously and shooting down two of the communist fighters, Davis lost his life when the F-86 he was flying was finally overwhelmed. His bravery broke up the MiG attack, enabling the F-84s to escape. Only four Medals of Honor were awarded to members of the USAF during the Korean War.

1952 February 19   The first Bristol Sycamore H.R.12 five-seat helicopter delivered to the RAF arrived at St. Mawgan, England for trials with Coastal Command. The British army received its first Sycamore H.C.1 on September 29, 1951, more than four years after the first Bristol Type 171 took to the air. With a 550-HP Alvis Leonides 73 engine, the H.R.12 had a maximum speed of 127 MPH and endurance of 3 hr.

1952 March 3   In the Korean War, the U.S. FEAF began Operation Saturate during which an around-the-clock interdiction effort would be maintained against North Korean railways. Replacing Operation Strangle, which had been directed between May 31, 1951, and the end of the year as a highway interdiction campaign, Saturate lasted less than three months. But in that period,

243 aircraft were destroyed and a further 290 damaged for the replacement of only 131.

1952 March 13　The Airspeed A.S.57 Ambassador began flight trials on the BEA London-Paris service and became available two weeks later to fare-paying passengers. The Ambassador was designed as a DC-3 replacement to a type requirement issued by the Brabazon Committee and first flew on July 10, 1947. BEA ordered 20 in September 1948 and from June 16, 1952, operated a 90-min. first-class Elizabethan service for a maximum 40 passengers with champagne and a hot lunch. Some A.S.57s were still in service in the early 1970s.

1952 March 14　Responding to the national emergency announced December 15, 1950, as a result of the Korean War, plans had been made to expand the production of nuclear and thermonuclear weapons, and USAF chief of staff, Gen. Hoyt S. Vandenberg, sent a letter to Secretary of the Air Force Thomas K. Finletter urging greater pace for development. On April 29 the air force responded by affirming, ''The objective is to achieve a capability for delivery of thermonuclear weapons at the earliest practicable date.''

1952 March 19　The first North American F-86F took to the air for the first time only nine days before the USAF took delivery of the first operational model. With significant improvements brought on by the Korean War emergency, the F-86F had a new wing leading edge extended 6 in. at the root and 3 in. at the tip to eliminate the need for slats and a slightly more powerful, 5,970-lb. s.t. J47-GE-27 engine. War requirements necessitated a new production facility at Columbus, Ohio, and this was the first product from that assembly line. Of 6,754 F-86s built, 2,539 (38%) were the *F* variant.

1952 April 1　During a speech in Chicago, Secretary of the Air Force Thomas K. Finletter announced that plans were well under way to adapt all U.S. combat aircraft to carry atomic weapons if necessary. Recent developments in miniaturizing atomic devices had brought atomic weapons within the bombload of almost all strategic and tactical aircraft. In 1952 nuclear weapons engineers worked out a thermonuclear device (or hydrogen bomb) that would weigh less than 4,000 lb. and deliver an explosive yield of 250 kilotons. The first 15-kiloton atomic artillery shell joined the U.S. nuclear weapons stockpile this month.

1952 April 1　Top World War II air ace USAF Col. Francis S. Gabreski became an air ace of the Korean War in a period of increasingly hostile Chinese MiG-15 activity. In March and April, 83 communist jets were shot down for the loss of only six FEAF pilots and their fighters. Gabreski would achieve a total 6.5 victories during the Korean War, bringing to 34.5 the total number of victories credited to this airman.

1952 April 1　Nicknamed unflatteringly the ''flying banana,'' the first Piasecki H-21 Workhorse helicopter made its first flight. Based on the U.S. Navy HRP, an earlier design, it was the first tandem-rotor helicopter for the USAF. Powered by a 1,425-HP Wright R-1820-103 piston engine, it had a rotor diameter of 44.5 ft., an overall length of 86 ft. 4 in. and a height of 15 ft. 5 in. The HRP had been ordered by the navy in 1944, but only one was ever accepted. The USAF ordered 195 H-21s with an additional 334 bought by the army.

1952 April 15　The first prototype B-52 Stratofortress, the YB-52 (serial no. 49-231) rolled out March 15, made its first flight piloted by A. M. ''Tex'' Johnson and Lt. Col. Guy M. Town-send from Boeing Field to Moses Lake, Wash. First rolled out on November 29, the XB-52 first flew on October 2, 1952. With a wingspan of 185 ft. and a length of 152 ft., the YB-52 was powered by eight 8,700-lb. s.t. Pratt & Whitney YJ57-8-3 turbojets. Maximum speed was 556 MPH at 40,000 ft., and range was 5,200 mi. at a gross weight of 390,000 lb.

1952 April 17　A concept study undertaken by Bell Aero-systems division of Bell Aircraft Corporation was presented to the USAF Wright Air Development Center. Known as ''Bomi'' (BOMBER-MISSILE), the study had carried forward ideas first propounded by Dr. Eugene Sänger in the late 1930s for a rocket-launched ''antipodal bomber'' capable of skipping across the top of the upper atmosphere. ''Bomi'' was proposed as a Mach 4 vehicle to be boosted to altitudes in excess of 100,000 ft. with a range of 4,000 mi.

1952 April 23　A modified B-36 designated GRB-36F made a successful retrieval and launch sequence in the FICON (fighter conveyor) program whereby a B-36 carried its own defensive F-84E in a modified bomb bay. On May 14, the first flight with an F-84E stowed aboard for takeoff was flown, and by February 20, 1953, 170 airborne launch and retrieval flights had been completed. By that time, emphasis had shifted toward using the FICON concept to carry a fast reconnaissance aircraft to the vicinity of a high-value target, and a contract was awarded to convert B-36s and F-84s for this.

1952 April 26　The Japanese Maritime Self-defense Force was formed as an antisubmarine and maritime patrol force for home defense purposes only. It was to be part of a Security Agency that would eventually control a Japanese Air Self-defense and a Ground Self-defense Force, all three under the command of the Defense Agency, or Boeicho. Combat equipment was to be supplied at first by the United States.

1952 May 2　The world's first regularly scheduled, fare-paying, jet passenger service opened with a BOAC Comet 1 flight from London to Johannesburg. It began at 3:12 P.M. when Capt. A. M. Majendie took off with Comet 1 G-ALYP and 36 passengers for a 2 hr. 34 min. flight to Rome, Italy, where it arrived 9 min. later than scheduled. From there Capt. J. T. A. Marsden took the Comet on to Beirut, Khartoum, Entebbe, Livingstone and Johannesburg, arriving 23 hr. 38 min. after taking off from London.

1952 May 17　New U.S. FEAF tactics were introduced into the Korean War when it was observed that communist MiG-15 jets were coming over the border from Manchuria at heights of between 15,000 ft. and 35,000 ft. instead of the 40,000–50,000 ft. previously experienced. Barrier patrols were consequently lowered to intercept the low flyers while still maintaining the high-altitude cover. U.S. Fifth Air Force flew the highest monthly total of sorties achieved during the Korean War when they notched up 5,190 patrols in May, during which 32 communist aircraft (27 MiGs) were destroyed for the loss of nine.

1952 May 19　The world's first variable geometry fighter made its first flight when the Grumman XF10F-1 Jaguar took to the air. The aircraft appeared to have an assured future when it was proposed, but it was seriously underpowered with its 6,800-lb. s.t. Westinghouse XJ40-WE-6 turbojet engine and was plagued by stability problems on all 32 flights that ended April 25, 1953. It never entered service. The aircraft had in-flight sweep capability of 13.5° to 42.5°.

1952 May 20 Boeing's board approved a plan to invest $16 million and develop the Model 367-80, the 80th design iteration of the basic replacement for the C-97 it had been planning since the end of World War II. It would eventually appear as the Boeing 707 commercial jet airliner in a range of equally long-lived military variants. Boeing had been unable to get the air force interested in a jet cargo-tanker replacement and opted for private investment. The single Model 367-80 was not originally intended as either an airliner or a military transport type, just an experimental demonstrator.

1952 May 23 A prestigious list of VIPs, including Queen Elizabeth, the Queen Mother, Princess Margaret, Sir Geoffrey and Lady de Havilland and other dignitaries, made a special 4-hr. flight around Europe in the new Comet airliner G-ALYR. The flight began from the de Havilland works, Hatfield, England at 12:25 P.M. and lasted 4 hr., covering 1,850 mi. at an average speed of 462 MPH and a maximum speed of 520 MPH.

1952 May 29 In the first use of the air refueling technique in support of an operational combat mission, 12 F-84E Thunderjet fighter-bombers of the 159th Fighter Bomber Group rendezvoused with KB-29 tankers over Taegu using refueling probes on their wing tips to take on extra fuel. The F-84Es had taken off from Itazuke, Japan to attack targets at Sariwon, North Korea before returning to their base in Japan.

1952 May The smallest piloted aircraft ever built and flown was completed and given a test flight by its designer, Ray Stits, at Riverside, Calif. With a tiny enclosed cabin for its single occupant, the Stits Skybaby biplane had a cantilevered wingspan of 7 ft. 2 in., a length of 9 ft. 10 in. and a horizontally opposed Continental C-85 engine delivering 85 HP. The tiny flying machine had a top speed of 185 MPH and an empty weight of 185 lb.

1952 June 16 Soviet MiG-15 jet fighters patrolling the waters of the Baltic Sea intercepted and shot down a Swedish Catalina searching for survivors from a U.S. Douglas DC-3 believed to have been shot down by Soviet MiGs the previous day. Although Soviet air force interceptors had been aggressive since the end of World War II, recent events in Asia had raised tension between the USSR and NATO countries. Soviet pilots were flying MiG-15s in Chinese Air Force colors over Korea, and many top USAF generals wanted to extend the Korean conflict to mainland China and the eastern USSR.

1952 June 17 The U.S. Navy dedicated its Aviation Medical Acceleration Laboratory at the Naval Air Development Center. The facility boasted a human centrifuge with a 110-ft. arm capable of exerting 40 g's on occupants of the gondola. It was set up to conduct research into pilot reactions to extremes of physical stress brought about by high-altitude/high-speed flight and later proved useful in the U.S. astronaut program.

1952 June 21 The U.S. Navy issued a contract to Douglas for prototypes and preproduction A4D Skyhawks designed by Ed Heinemann. Conceived as a lightweight fighter, the Skyhawk was adapted to the role of fighter-bomber prior to presentation to fill a void created by the aging AD Skyraider. With a (then) phenomenal thrust-to-weight ratio of better than 1:1, the A4D was to remain in continuous production for 27 years; 2,960 were built for U.S. Navy and foreign customers, and some were still operational 40 yr. after the type's first flight on June 22, 1954.

1952 June 27 A combined services attack on communist North Korean hydroelectric power supply facilities ended after four days of intensive air operations from USAF and U.S. Navy units in the single most concentrated attack since World War II. In four days, the U.S. Fifth Air Force flew 730 fighter-bomber and 238 counter-air sorties, and the navy flew 546 attack missions, a total 1,514 sorties. More than 1,200 had been flown in the most intensive period June 23–24.

1952 July 10 Lt. Gen. Otto P. Weyland, commanding U.S. FEAF in the Korean War, issued a directive allocating priority to stepping up air pressure on the communist forces in an effort to press peace terms at the negotiating table. Air superiority was considered an essential aspect of that policy, although the Chinese Air Force had reached in June a strength of 22 air divisions with 1,830 aircraft, of which more than 1,000 were fighters. Moreover, there were now 5,360 Soviet air units in the region compared to the North Koreans' 270.

1952 July 11 Operation Pressure Pump mobilized every available UN air unit in the Korean War for a mass assault on 30 targets in Pyongyang. Aircraft from the Royal Navy carrier HMS *Ocean* were involved as well as the U.S. Seventh Fleet, the First Marine Air Wing, the U.S. Fifth Air Force and the Korean Air Force in 1,254 sorties culminating in a night attack by 54 B-29s. Intelligence agents reported 1,500 buildings destroyed and 7,000 casualties, including more than 400 in a direct hit on an air raid shelter housing communist officials.

1952 July 17 A major airlift of 58 F-84G Thunderjets of the Thirty-first Fighter Escort Wing from Turner AFB, Ga. to Misawa and Chitose AFBs, Japan was completed just 13 days after it began July 4. Named Fox Peter One, the transoceanic air movement was supported by KB-29 tankers of the Second and Ninety-first Air Refueling squadrons in the first large-scale deployment of escort fighters utilizing in-flight refueling. The first refueling took place between Turner AFB and Travis AFB, Calif. with a second refueling between Travis and Hawaii. From there the F-84Gs island-hopped via Midway, Wake, Eniwetok, Guam and Iwo Jima.

1952 July 23 Designed to the first specification issued for a jet trainer, the Fouga CM.170 Magister made its first flight. Within two years, the French Air Force had placed an order for 95, although more than 400 were to be produced for the Armée de l'Air with many more built for foreign air forces. Characterized by a "V" tail, the CM.170 had a wingspan of 39 ft. 10 in., a length of 33 ft. and power provided by two 882-lb. s.t. Turboméca Marboré IIA turbojets. Forty years after the plane's first flight, Israel still operated more than 70 CM.170s.

1952 July 29 The first nonstop flight across the Pacific Ocean was conducted by an RB-45C (serial no. 48-042) commanded by Maj. Louis H. Carrington. The flight began at Elmendorf AFB, Alaska and ended at Yokota Air Base, Japan after two in-flight refuelings from KB-29 tankers. The flight earned Carrington and his two fellow crewmembers the 1952 Mackay Trophy.

1952 July 31 The first helicopter crossing of the North Atlantic was accomplished when two USAF Sikorsky H-19s landed at Prestwick, Scotland just after 4:00 P.M. First down was *Hopalong* flown by Capt. Vincent H. McGovern, followed by *Whirlaway* piloted by 1st Lt. Harold R. W. Moore. The first 380-mi. leg of the flight between Westover AFB, Mass. and Presque Isle, Maine had been flown July 15 with the 570-mi. flight to Goose Bay, Labrador completed on July 17. On July 28 they arrived at

Contracted from Douglas on June 21, 1952, the A-4 Skyhawk was the brilliant brainchild of Ed Heinemann.

Bluie West One, Greenland, reaching Keflavik, Iceland on July 29 prior to the last leg, via the Hebrides. Total flying time was 42 hr. 25 min.

1952 August 11   BOAC inaugurated its new weekly service between London and Colombo, the capital of Ceylon (now Sri Lanka), via Rome, Beirut, Bahrein, Karachi and Bombay using the new jet Comet 1 airliner. The 5,925-mi. flight took 21 hr. 35 min., 12 hr. 10 min. less than the time taken with the Argonaut. The Comet (G-ALYU) arrived at Columbo August 12, and the return flight began August 13 but was 3 hr. 42 min. late because of fog and had to be diverted to Prestwick, Scotland.

1952 August 16   The prototype Bristol Type 175 Britannia (G-ALBO) made its first flight from Filton, Bristol, England piloted by chief test pilot A. J. "Bill" Pegg. Powered by four 3,870-EHP Bristol Proteus 705 turboprop engines, initial production models had a wingspan of 142 ft. 3 in., a length of 114 ft., a cruising speed of 335 MPH and capacity for up to 83 passengers. The second prototype was lost in a crash landing, but the first production aircraft flew in 1954.

1952 August 22   The prototype Saunders Roe SR.45 Princess flying boat made its first flight from the Solent off Cowes, Isle of Wight along the south coast of England. With a length of 148 ft. and wingspan of 219 ft. 6 in. the SR.45 had an empty weight of 190,000 lb. and a normal maximum weight of 330,000 lb. Capable of carrying up to 200 passengers, the Princess was powered by ten 2,500-SHP Bristol Proteus 2 powerplants in four coupled pairs driving contra-rotating propellers and two outboard single units. Only one of three prototypes flew, G-ALUN, making 47 flights totaling 96 hr. 50 min. by June 1954.

1952 August 30   Powered by four 6,500-lb. s.t. Rolls Royce Avon R.A.III jet engines, the prototype Avro 698 Vulcan made

its first flight piloted by chief test pilot Wg. Comdr. R. Falk. Designed to carry Bristol Olympus turbojets, which were unavailable for the first flight, the world's first large delta-wing aircraft had a span of 99 ft. and a length of 97 ft. 1 in. with a wing area of 3,554 sq. ft. Later, the four 6,500-lb. s.t. Rolls Royce Avon R.A.3s first fitted to the prototype were replaced by four 8,000-lb. s.t. Armstrong Siddeley Sapphire engines.

1952 September 4   In air battles that raged all day, 73 MiG-15s from north of the Yalu River fought it out with 39 F-86s of the U.S. FEAF over the Chongchon. The FEAF lost four Sabres but destroyed 13 MiGs. At the end of the month, the communist fighter pilots changed tactics and reverted to high-level, high-speed dashes south over the Yalu River, similar to tactics employed in 1951.

1952 September 6   At the Society of British Aircraft Companies Show at Farnborough, England, the first prototype D.H.110 (serial no. WG236) piloted by John Derry, with flight test observer Tony Richards in the second seat, broke up in midair at about 3:45 P.M. on the second public day, killing the crew and 29 spectators on the ground. A further 60 spectators were injured by pieces of the aircraft hurled into the crowd. The flying display continued to its scheduled conclusion.

1952 September 20   Piloted by Douglas test pilot William E. ("Bill") Bridgeman, the one and only X-3 transonic research aircraft made its first flight more than seven years after conception. Designed as a Mach 2 research aircraft, it was powered by two 3,370/4,900-lb. thrust Westinghouse XJ34-WE-17 turbojets and had an unusually long pointed nose, a fuselage length of 66 ft. 9 in. and a wingspan of 22 ft. 8 in. It made only 26 flights, achieved its highest speed of Mach 1.21 on July 28, 1953, and was retired in May 1956.

1952 September NACA published Research memorandum L52H08 *A Study of the Zero Lift Drag Characteristics of Wing-Body Combinations Near the Speed of Sound* and made it available secretly to the U.S. aviation industry. Written by Richard T. Whitcomb, it said that the ideal shape for a streamlined body at transonic speed was not, as had previously been thought, a function of the fuselage diameter but of the total cross-sectional area of the fuselage, wings and tail. This proved to be so and was immediately applied to the design of the Convair F-102, giving it the familiar "wasp waist" shape.

1952 October 15 On "D-Day" for the hoax amphibious landing and paratroop drop in support of a "landing" on the village of Kojo near Wonsan, UN air units in Korea flew paratroops right up to the border before wheeling around before the drop. For several days, intensive air operations had put pressure on the communists in the belief that a major operation was about to take place. During October the U.S. Navy flew 11,004 sorties, their peak monthly total of the war.

1952 October 15 New York Airways began the first helicopter mail service between the metropolitan airports of Idelwild (now Kennedy) and LaGuardia in New York City and Newark, in N.J. Granted a CAB certificate in December 1951, New York Airways used three Sikorsky S-55s. New York Airways was the third helicopter mail carrier in the United States, preceded by Los Angeles Airways (May 11, 1944) and Helicopter Air Services of Chicago (August 20, 1949).

1952 October 16 Developed from a line of Süd-Ouest experimental high-performance aircraft, the first of three prototype S.O. 4050 Vautours made its first flight. The S.O. 4050-01 was a two-seat all-weather fighter, the S.O. 4050-2 a single-seat ground attack aircraft and the S.O. 4050-3, a two-seat bomber that made its first flight in December 1954. Precursor half-scale models had been built with glide-drops from a Languedoc 161 beginning September 26, 1949. Six preproduction models were ordered.

1952 October 20 For the first time, a U.S. airline ordered a foreign make of aircraft when Pan American World Airways placed an order for three Comet 3 airliners, a proposed stretched version of the Comet with a length of 111 ft. 6 in. and capable of carrying up to 78 passengers 2,500 mi. across the Atlantic. Delays caused by BOAC not ordering the Comet 3 until the following year and two accidents in the first half of 1954 caused the reservations to lapse, and Pan American never operated the Comet.

1952 October 23 The first flight took place of the Hughes XH-17 experimental USAF heavy cargo helicopter after two years of extensive testing. Incorporating four long stilt-like legs capable of straddling a cargo container secured to the underside of the fuselage, the XH-17 had a 130-ft. rotor driven by two General Electric J35 turbojets discharging propulsive jets through the blade tips. It had a fully loaded weight of 52,000 lb. and a cruising speed of 60 MPH. Capable of lifting 27,000 lb., it performed many test flights, but the project was canceled in 1953.

1952 October 28 The Douglas XA3D-1 prototype A3D Skywarrior made its first flight, the heaviest aircraft to operate from an aircraft carrier. With a length of 76 ft. 4 in. and a wingspan of 72 ft. 6 in., the Skywarrior had a maximum weight of 82,000 lb. with power provided by two 12,400-lb. s.t. Pratt & Whitney J57-P-10 turbojets. This nuclear-capable bomber with a warload of up to 12,000 lb. had a range of 1,050 mi., a top speed of 610 MPH at 10,000 ft. and entered U.S. Navy service in 1956. In all, 156 flew with eight heavy attack squadrons.

1952 October The prototype precursor to the MiG-19 flew for the first time only 15 mon. after the design for the plane had been accepted. The refined true prototype flew on September 18, 1953. Powered by two 4,079/6,702 lb. s.t. Tumanskii turbojets, the MiG-19 was the first truly supersonic fighter outside the United States, with sweep on all surfaces and rugged adaptability for ground attack work. With a wingspan of 30 ft. 2 in. and a length of 41 ft. 4 in., the MiG-19 had a top speed of 902 MPH (Mach 1.36) and an initial climb rate of 22,635 ft./min.

1952 November 1 The world's first thermonuclear explosion took place under the code name Ivy Mike (for "megatons") at precisely 7:15 P.M. on Elujelab in the Eniwetok atoll. With a yield of 10.4 megatons, it created a fireball 3.5 mi. in diameter, digging a crater 164 ft. deep and almost 1.2 mi. across. The stem of the boiling mushroom reached a height of 130,000 ft. and developed a head 10 mi. high and 100 mi. across. It was 700 times more powerful than the bomb dropped on Hiroshima and created two completely new elements: einsteinium and fermium.

1952 November 2 The first jet versus jet night combat took place just before midnight when a Douglas F3D Skyknight from VMF(N)-513 piloted by Maj. William T. Sutton with Master Sgt. H. C. Hoglind in the second seat intercepted what was subsequently identified as a Yak-15 in the night sky over Korea. Within minutes the Soviet-built aircraft had been shot down in flames. VMF(N)-513 went on to score a further five nighttime victories during the Korean War.

1952 November 3 The prototype SAAB-32 Lansen all-weather fighter, one of the finest aircraft in its class, made its first flight. In 1953 it entered production as the A32A. Approximately 450 all-weather fighters, night-fighters and reconnaissance aircraft were built before production ended in May 1960, the last version being the J32, which was still in service 30 yr. later. The latest versions were equipped as electronic surveillance aircraft.

1952 November 3 The first USAF aircraft fully adapted to carry a thermonuclear bomb flew to Kirtland AFB, N. Mex. when the first B-36 so modified arrived back from the manufacturers (Consolidated-Vultee). An order dated November 28 authorized modification of 36 aircraft. Eventually all B-36s were adapted to carry thermonuclear weapons, except 12 assigned to carry the Rascal air-to-ground atomic device, which was canceled in 1956.

1952 November 19 Flying a F-86D Sabre, Capt. J. Slade Nash, USAF, broke the official FAI-ratified absolute air speed record when he achieved an average 698.505 MPH. The previous record, also achieved by an F-86, had held for more than four years; but the new record would stand for less than eight months. On July 16, 1953, Lt. Col. William F. Barnes, also flying an F-86D, raised the record to 715.75 MPH.

1952 December 3 A C-47 forced down over Hungary by Soviet fighters and impounded along with its crew until a "fine" was paid by the U.S. government began an international incident. The Hungarian consulates in New York and Cleveland, Ohio were closed, and a ban was imposed on U.S. citizens wanting to visit Hungary. The crew of four was released December 28.

1952 December 4 Developed to combat increasing threats from submarine forces, the Grumman XS2F-1 made its first flight. The first of 1,252 production aircraft joined the U.S. Navy in February 1954 powered by two 1,525-HP Wright R-1820-82WA engines providing a cruising speed of 149 MPH and a range of 1,150 mi. With a maximum weapons load of 4,810 lb., the (redesignated) S-2 Tracker evolved into an early warning aircraft, was sold to 13 foreign countries and is still operational outside the United States 40 years after the first flight.

1952 December 24   The prototype Handley Page H.P.80 Victor (serial no. WB771), last to fly of the celebrated V-Bombers, made its first flight piloted by Hedley G. Hazelden with test observer Ian Bennett. The Victor had a wingspan of 110 ft., a length of 114 ft. 11 in. and four 11,000-lb. s.t. Armstrong Siddeley Sapphire 200 turbojet engines. The second prototype (serial no. WB775) made its first flight on September 1, 1954, and the first production aircraft lifted into the air on February 1, 1956.

1953 January 3   The Cessna 310 "executive" aircraft made its first flight powered by two 225-HP horizontally opposed Continental engines. This was the first private aircraft to carry wingtip fuel tanks that enabled the main landing gear to fold up into the wings. Each tip tank held 51 gal. of fuel, but later versions had provision for two supplementary fuel tanks in the wings. The aircraft proved popular, 2,000 being sold in the first 10 yr.

1953 January 5   Reporting on the known strength of communist air units facing UN forces in Korea, Gen. Glen O. Barcus, commander of U.S. Fifth Air Force, indicated increasing concern over the growing number of jet aircraft from the Soviet Union. The Chinese were known to have 1,485 aircraft in Manchuria, including 950 MiG-15s, 165 conventional fighters, 100 Il-28 medium jet bombers, 115 ground attack aircraft, 90 transport planes and 65 of various other types.

1953 January 6   A new post-World War II German national airline came into existence under the name Luftag. Deutsche Lufthansa had made its last flight on April 21, 1945, and the airline was formally liquidated on January 1, 1951. The German state railway and the state of Nordrhein-Westfalen provided provisional stock for the new company, which had nothing whatsoever to do with the old one. Nevertheless, on August 6, 1954, it was officially renamed Deutsche Lufthansa. Today it is known simply as Lufthansa.

1953 January 12   Operational tests began with an angled flight deck on the aircraft carrier USS *Antietam*. The British had invented the angled flight deck and tested it on HMS *Triumph* in 1951 as a means of allowing an aircraft to make a second attempt at landing without plowing into aircraft parked forward. Other British inventions, the steam catapult and the mirror landing system, were incorporated in the USS *Forrestal, Saratoga, Ranger* and *Independence*.

1953 January 23   The last combat sortie flown by the venerable F-51D (former P-51) of World War II was carried out by the Sixty-seventh Fighter Bomber Squadron, Eighteenth Fighter Bomber Group, toward the close of the Korean War. Aircraft of this type had fired 183,034 air-to-ground rockets in 62,607 sorties for the loss of 194 aircraft to communist air attack and antiaircraft fire. Increasingly, the F-86F was coming into its own as a ground attack and strafing aircraft, and the Sixty-seventh was to successfully operate the jet before the war ended.

1953 January 30   The first Boeing B-47E prototype incorporating numerous improvements and changes over preceding models made its first flight. Powered by six 7,200-lb. s.t. General Electric J47-GE-25 engines, it was equipped with a JATO system. Later models had a jettisonable rocket pack providing 33,000-lb. of thrust for takeoff. With a gross weight of 206,700 lb., the B-47E had a top speed of 606 MPH, a service ceiling of 40,500 ft.

and a range 4,643 mi. A total 931 B-47Es and 240 RB-47Es were built, by far the largest number of any B-47 variant.

1953 January 31   Operation Canute, the largest helicopter rescue to date, came into effect this night within hours of a major flood's inundating large areas of Holland and areas of Lincolnshire and East Anglia in Britain. In the coming week, the RAF flew photographic reconnaissance of the flooded areas, and a total 250 U.S., British and Dutch aircraft were involved. Thirty-eight helicopters were used to rescue several thousand people from isolated farms, villages and towns cut off by flood waters. In six days, the helicopters delivered 500,000 sandbags, 50,000 bread loaves and tons of medical supplies.

1953 February 12   Convair received a formal USAF contract for detailed design and assembly of prototype supersonic strategic bomber and reconnaissance aircraft under the respective designations XB-58 and XRB-58. The general configuration was selected March 24, the aircraft having a 60° sweep on a delta wing with four engines mounted separately beneath port and starboard wings, the inner engines mounted on pylons. The fuselage was to have the area-rule design pioneered by Richard T. Whitcomb. According to the schedule, the first production aircraft was to fly in 1956, but technical problems would delay this for 3 yr.

1953 February 16   Capt. Joseph McConnell Jr., a flight leader with the Sixteenth Fighter Interceptor Squadron, Fifty-first Fighter Interceptor Wing, shot down his fifth enemy aircraft and became the Korean War's 27th U.S. fighter ace. McConnell would end the war with 16 kills, exceeding by 1 victory the 15 scored by Maj. James Jabaara, thus becoming the top Korean War air ace. McConnell had to bail out of his F-86 on April 12 but three days later downed his 10th victim. On May 18 he scored 3 kills, his last of the war.

1953 February 21   The first powered flight with the Bell X-1A took place over Rogers Dry Lake, Calif. with Jean Ziegler at the controls. Ordered in December 1947 as more advanced versions of the X-1, four follow-on rocket research aircraft were built. First to be completed, the X-1D had been lost August 22, 1951, when an explosion started a fire and the rocket plane had to be jettisoned from the EB-50A carrier-plane.

1953 March 3   A D.H.106 Comet 1 crashed on takeoff at Karachi, Pakistan, killing all 11 people on board. Bearing the registration CF-CUN and named *Empress of Hawaii*, it was the second Comet delivered to Canadian Pacific. This accident, similar to a nonfatal accident to a BOAC Comet (G-ALYZ) at Rome on October 26, 1952, was caused by the nose being held too high at takeoff, which resulted in a loss of lift. Modifications included drooped wing leading edges.

1953 March 10   The first attack by communist fighters on aircraft flying in the skies of Western European countries took place when two USAF F-84 Thunderjets were attacked by two MiG-15s of the Czech Air Force. Lt. Warren G. Brown, USAF, was shot down and had to eject without sustaining injury. The two F-84s had been flying over Bavaria in West Germany. Two days later an RAF Lincoln on a training flight was shot down by MiG-15s with the loss of all seven crew members. The plane had inadvertently flown over Boizenburg, East Germany because of a navigation error.

1953 March 27   A classified design study requirement was issued by the USAF calling for a "special reconnaissance aircraft" capable of "optimum subsonic cruise at altitudes of 70,000 ft. or

First flown in March 1953, the Bell Model 61 was the first helicopter designed for antisubmarine warfare.

higher'' and a radius of 1,500 mi. carrying up to 700 lb. of reconnaissance equipment. It had been put together between October and December 1952 by Maj. John Seaberg, assistant chief, new developments office, Bombardment Branch, Wright Field, who believed new and efficient turbojet engines fitted to an airframe capable of sustained high-altitude flight would achieve new surveillance objectives. Thus was born the U-2 spy plane.

1953 March   The last F-80C first-generation jet fighter-bomber was retired from the Korean War. F-80 fighter-bombers had flown 98,515 sorties, dropped 33,266 tons of bombs and 8,327 tons of napalm and shot down 37 enemy aircraft for the loss of 143. The last unit to operate the F-80C was the Eighth Fighter Bomber Group (FBG) at Suwon, receiving F-86Fs in return.

1953 April 3   Just over 2 mon. after the world's first jet airliner completed its first 10,000 hrs. of flying, a twice-weekly Comet 1 service from London to Tokyo opened. With a total route distance of 10,379 mi. the journey took 36 hrs. 20 min. and cost £260 one way or £468 return. This was the longest route operated by BOAC and was added to existing routes between London and Johannesburg, London and Colombo, London and Singapore and Paris and Dakar.

1953 April 9   The prototype Convair XF2Y-1 jet-propelled seaplane fighter took to the air for the first time, piloted by E. D. Shannon. It was underpowered with two 3,400-lb. s.t. Westinghouse J34-WE-32 engines. A second prototype (YF2Y-1) had two 6,000-lb. s.t. Westinghouse J46-WE-2 turbojets and managed to exceed the speed of sound in a shallow dive on August 3, 1954.

The YF2Y-1 had a wingspan of 33 ft. 8 in., a length of 52 ft. 7 in. and a gross weight of 16,527 lb. The project was canceled in 1954.

1953 April 10   Initial project evaluation of the Project Bomi studies was completed, with Bell Aircraft Corp. proposing a manned reconnaissance version. The USAF liked the idea, and a one-year contract for detailed study under MX-2145 was awarded to several aircraft companies, including Boeing, in April 1954. As MX-2276, Bell's 400-ton Bomi reconnaissance vehicle would be launched vertically to 259,000 ft. and 15,000 MPH with a range of 12,200 mi.

1953 April 18   The world's first regularly scheduled, sustained passenger service with a turboprop airliner began when a BEA Vickers Viscount named *Sir Ernest Shackleton* (G-AMNY) left London airport for Nicosia, Cyprus via Rome and Athens. The final leg was conducted as a charter flight to Cyprus Airways.

1953 April 24   Two EF-84Bs adapted to attach their wing tips to special wing-tip capture latches on an ETB-29A crashed with their mother-plane during tests aimed at evaluating the feasibility of escort fighters ferried to the war zone by the bombers they were to protect, thus conserving fuel and significantly extending the range of the fighters. The project had some limited success, but turbulence and the difficulty in safely latching on and off the wing-tip pick-up points were never satisfactorily solved.

1953 April 26   Two USAF B-29s dropped leaflets on communist positions near the Yalu River in North Korea offering a

$50,000 reward and political asylum to any pilot defecting with his MiG-15 intact to U.S. forces. After the war, on September 21, Lt. Ro-kum-suk brought over his MiG-15bis although he was surprised to hear of the reward and said he had not seen the leaflets. He was, nevertheless, given the reward and a further $50,000 bonus. His aircraft formed the basis of a detailed technical examination of one of the top Soviet fighters of the day.

1953 April 27 The U.S. Navy ordered prototypes of a second derivative of the F9F Panther designated G-98 by Grumman and F9F-8 by the navy before the new designation F11F-1 from April 1955. Incorporating the new area-rule fuselage and powered by a 9,600/15,000-lb. s.t. General Electric YJ79-GE-3 turbojet, it would become the first navy fighter capable of supersonic speed in level flight, and in a developed version, it was the first to exceed Mach 2.

1953 May 2 On the first anniversary of its first fare-paying jet airline service, a BOAC Comet 1 (G-ALYV) broke up in the air at 11:05 GMT while climbing toward 10,000 ft. 6 min. after taking off from Dum Dum Airport, Calcutta on a scheduled flight to Delhi. All 43 people on board were killed, including 36 adult passengers, an infant and 6 flight and cabin personnel. The aircraft had been commanded by Capt. M. W. Haddon. Wreckage was strewn over an area of eight sq. mi.

1953 May 12 The first Bell X-2 designed for Project MX-743 was destroyed and its pilot, Jean Ziegler, killed while preparing for a drop from the belly of the EB-50A mother-plane at 30,000 ft. and 200 MPH over Rogers Dry Lake, California. The test pilot was in the bomb bay of the EB-50A watching X-2 instrument readings when a massive explosion destroyed the rocket plane and pushed the EB-50A 650 ft. higher. A mass of flaming X-2 wreckage fell to the desert floor.

1953 May 13 Four waves of 59 U.S. FEAF F-84G Thunderjets of the Fifty-eighth Fighter Bomber Wing attacked the Toksan dam 20 mi. north of Pyongyang, North Korea with 1,000-lb. bombs. By nightfall, the 2,300-ft. dam appeared to have withstood the attack, but during the night it gave way. The ensuing flood destroyed 700 buildings, inundated Sunan airfield and washed away five railway bridges. A second raid by 90 Thunderjets breached the Chasan dam three days later.

1953 May 18 Jacqueline Cochrane became the first woman in the world to officially fly faster than the speed of sound when she reached Mach 1.01. The same day she also established a new FAI-ratified 100 km. (62.14 mi.) closed-circuit record when she flew a Canadair F-86E Sabre to an average 652.337 MPH, breaking the existing record by 18 MPH. Her husband, Floyd Odlum, was head of the Atlas Corp. which had just sold shares in Consolidated-Vultee (owner of Canadair) to General Dynamics Corp.

1953 May 18 The Douglas DC-7, powered by four 3,250-HP Wright R-3350 Turbo-Compound engines, made its first flight. Developed in response to Lockheed's L.1049 Super Constellation and ordered by American Airlines, the DC-7 had a wingspan of 117 ft. 6 in., a length of 108 ft. 11 in. and a maximum payload range of 2,850 mi. Essentially a reengined DC-6B with a 40-in. longer fuselage, it was further developed as the DC-7C. This was the first truly long-range commercial transport and had a maximum payload range of 4,605 mi. and a 127-ft. 6 in. wingspan and was capable of carrying up to 94 passengers.

1953 May 25 The prototype North American YF-100A, first of the Century fighters, took to the air from Edwards AFB, Calif.

for the first time, piloted by George Welch. When it entered service with the USAF in November, it was the world's first fighter capable of supersonic speed in level flight, achieving 892 MPH at 35,000 ft. Powered by a 10,000/16,000-lb. s.t. Pratt & Whitney J57-P-21A turbojet, the F-100D had a wingspan of 38 ft. 9 in., a length of 47 ft. 5 in. and a gross weight of 38,048 lb. The F-100 Super Sabre served the USAF and the Air National Guard for more than 25 yr.

1953 May Following tests with a modified F-84E carried on a retracted trapeze beneath a B-36, the USAF ordered Convair to convert 10 B-36 bombers into GRB-36D configurations and Republic to convert 25 F-84Es into RF-84Ks. The GRB-36D would carry the RF-84K to within 1,800 mi. of the objective, releasing it for a fast reconnaissance at up to 629 MPH before returning for retrieval and a return to base with film. The GRB-36D/RF-84K combination were operational for less than 1 yr. beginning late 1955.

1953 June 3 The first B-47s deployed to the United Kingdom from their home base at MacDill AFB, Fla. arrived at Fairford, Gloucestershire as the vanguard of the full 306th Bombardment Wing. The last aircraft touched down June 6, the last one to land setting a new trans-Atlantic record time of 5 hrs. 22 min. over the 3,120 mi. from Linestone AFB, Maine. The 90-day rotational training program continued with the arrival of the 305th Bombardment Wing at Brize Norton, Oxfordshire and Mildenhall, Suffolk as the 306th Bombardment Wing returned home.

1953 June 10 The final experimental test flight for the turbojet powered #3 Douglas D-558-I Skystreak was flown by A. Scott Crossfield. It had flown 82 times since early 1948, 78 of them since April 22, 1949, for NACA. The three Skystreaks had made a total 225 flights exploring aspects of the transonic flight regime, an area of aeronautical research almost exclusively the preserve of the D-558-I, the D-588-II Skyrocket and the Bell X-1 series.

1953 June 14 The prototype Bristol Beverley (serial no. WZ889), the first aircraft designed specifically to air-drop heavy loads, made its first flight from Brough, England with H. Wood at the controls. Flown in precursor form as the Blackburn Universal Freighter on June 20, 1950, it was redesigned for new and expanded supply-dropping roles and joined the RAF in March 1956. With a wingspan of 162 ft. and a length of 99 ft. 5 in., the C.Mk.1 could carry 13 tons in its capacious body and 42 passengers in the tail boom. The plane had a range of 760 mi. at 173 MPH and continued in service until 1967.

1953 June 15 Communist Forces in Korea came under attack in the largest one-day air assault mounted by UN forces as 2,143 missions were flown by the U.S. FEAF, 532 by the U.S. Navy's Task Force 77 and 478 sorties by the U.S. Marine Corps for a total 3,153 missions. The effort was a crushing response to a communist offensive that began June 10.

1953 June 23 In less than two days, the U.S. 315th Air Division moved 3,252 paratroops and 1,770.6 tons of cargo in 53 C-46 and 249 C-119 transport planes of the 187th Airborne Regimental Combat Team from southern Japan to central Korea. Orders to move came on the day the operation began (June 21), and the move was completed by dawn this morning. The move added strength to the U.S. Eighth Army facing threat from communist ground forces.

1953 June In a record month of "MiG kills" in the Korean War, U.S. FEAF F-86 Sabre pilots sighted 1,268 communist jets, attacked 501 and shot down 77. The WAF estimated that FEAF destroyed a further 11 and probably damaged 41, thus disabling up to 129 aircraft for no losses. On June 30, a Korean War record of 16 kills was achieved during a month in which MiG pilots were resuming attacks below 40,000-ft. altitude. During the month five F-86 pilots became aces.

1953 July 20 The first American-built version of the English Electric Canberra twin-jet bomber, the Martin B-57A, made its first flight from Baltimore, the first of 67 RB-57As being delivered to Shaw AFB, S.C. in April 1954. A special high-altitude RB-57D version with extended wings of 107 ft. 6 in. versus 64 ft. on the standard production model was introduced in April 1956. In July 1964 the RB-57F appeared with a span 122 ft. 5 in. and power provided by two 18,000-lb. s.t. Pratt & Whitney TF33-P-11 turbofans in the wings with two 3,300-lb. s.t. J60-P-9 turbojets under the wings.

1953 July 27 The armistice bringing an end to hostilities between communist forces of North Korea and the allied forces of the United Nations came into effect at 10:01 P.M. Since the war began, the U.S. FEAF had flown 720,980 sorties, the U.S. Navy had flown 167,552 sorties, the U.S. Marine Corps 107,303 sorties and friendly UN allied air forces a total 44,873 sorties. In total, UN air forces flew 1,040,708 sorties in 37 mon., an average of 28,127 per month. The FEAF 315th Air Division, responsible for transport, flew 210,343 sorties during the Korean War, moved 2,065,591 passengers, 307,804 wounded and injured patients and 39,763 tons of freight using an average 210 aircraft per day.

Since the Korean conflict began June 26, 1950, UN forces claimed to have destroyed 1,327 tanks, 82,920 vehicles, 963 locomotives, 10,407 railcars, 1,153 bridges, 118,231 buildings, 65 tunnels, 8,663 gun positions, 8,839 bunkers, 16 oil storage tanks and 593 boats and barges. It was estimated that the allied air forces killed 184,808 communist troops. In addition, fighter-bombers or medium bombers (B-29s) were estimated to have cut 28,621 railroad links. FEAF delivered 476,000 tons of ordnance against communist targets, the U.S. Navy 120,000 tons, the U.S. Marines 82,000 tons and friendly UN forces about 20,000 tons.

During the 37 months of the Korean War, UN air forces destroyed 976 enemy aircraft for the loss of 1,041 due to enemy action, of which only 147 were shot down by enemy fighters. An additional 945 were lost due to nonenemy action. Of the total 1,986 aircraft lost, FEAF lost 1,466 (73.8%), the U.S. Marines lost 368 (18.5%) and friendly forces lost 152 (7.6%). FEAF fighter pilots claimed 810 enemy aircraft shot down in combat, of which 792 were MiG-15s. The FEAF lost 139 aircraft to MiG attacks, of which 78 were F-86s.

1953 August 20 The first mass flight by jet fighters over the Atlantic began under Operation Longstride when Col. David C. Schilling, commander of the Thirty-first Strategic Fighter Wing led nine F-84 Thunderjets off the runway at Turner AFB, Ga. The flight included a spare F-84 that accompanied the other eight as far as Savannah, Ga. The eight F-84s reached Nouasseur Air Base, French Morocco after a flight of 10 hrs. 20 min., incorporating three in-flight refuelings from KB-29 tankers. A second flight of 17 F-84s under Col. Thayer S. Olds, commander of the Fortieth Air Division, arrived in England after a flight lasting 11 hrs. 20 min. and including three refuelings.

1953 September 1 The first jet-to-jet aircraft in-flight refueling took place when a YB-47F was refueled by a KB-47G, a standard B-47B converted to evaluate midair refueling using a hose and drogue system first worked out by the British just after World War II. The YB-47F was a standard B-47B modified for the tests. Such refueling proved impractical for the B-47 but future KB-135 jet tankers would have the flying boom system.

1953 September 1 The Belgian airline Sabena inaugurated the world's first regularly scheduled international helicopter service when it started carrying passengers on its Brussels-Lille (France) service and its Brussels-Antwerp-Rotterdam (the Netherlands) service. The Sikorsky S-55 was also employed running a Brussels-Liège-Maastricht (the Netherlands)-Brussels service. In the first year of operations, these services carried 13,000 passengers on 3,500 flights but with an average on-time performance of 83%, still some way short of the 99% usually achieved by fixed-wing airlines.

1953 September 7 Flying an all-red Hawker Hunter (serial no. WB188), test pilot Neville Duke set a new world air speed record, ratified by the FAI, of 1,107.76 km/hr. (727.63 MPH) over a 3-km (1,86-mi.) course off Littlehampton on England's south coast. On September 19, he used the same aircraft to raise the 100 km (62.14 mi.) speed record to 790.6 MPH. On September 25, Mike Lithgow in a silver Supermarine Swift (serial number WK198) retained for Britain the overall speed record and raised it to 1,183.74 km/hr. (735.7 MPH).

1953 September 11 The U.S. Navy Grumman F9F-8 Cougar participated in the first air test of the newly developed XAAM.N7 Sidewinder air-to-air heat-seeking missile when it fired two at a QF-80 Firebee target at 10,000 ft. over the Mojave Desert in California. Development of the missile began in 1948 at the U.S. Naval Ordnance Test Center, China Lake, Calif. and on Nov. 27, 1950, it was given the name Sidewinder. Soviet military spies obtained the design and made a direct copy, which emerged as the AA-2 Atoll.

1953 September 19 BOAC completed the first South Atlantic proving flight for jet air transport when Comet 2 G-ALYT, which had been commanded in turn by Capts. A. P. W. Pain and A. M. A. Majendie, returned to London. Beginning September 13, the Comet 2 had flown first to Lisbon, then Dakar, Recife and on to Rio de Janeiro. The return route had been flown via Natal, Dakar, Casablanca and Madrid. Total flying time had been 31 hrs. 40 min. The Comet 2 had a length of 96 ft., increased all-up weight, power provided by four 7,300-lb. s.t. Rolls Royce Avon engines and a range of 2,100 mi.

1953 October 1 First set up as a private concern on August 1, 1951, Japanese Air Lines was completely reorganized as Japan Air Lines Nihon Koku Kabashiki Kaisha, a restoration of the company as it existed before World War II. The government now held 50% of the $5.5 million capital, and a weekly service opened to the United States for the first time in February 1954, using DC-6B aircraft.

1953 October 3 Flown by Lt. Comdr. James B. Verdin, U.S. Navy, a Douglas F4D-1 Skyray seized the absolute world air speed record with an FAI-ratified average of 1,211.48 km/hr. (752.94 MPH), the only occasion when a U.S. Navy pilot achieved that distinction flying a U.S. Navy aircraft. This was the second of only two absolute speed records broken by U.S. Navy pilots, the previous occasion having been when Comdr. F. Turner took the record on August 20, 1947.

1953 October 9 An RAF Canberra (serial no. WE139) flown by Flt. Lts. R. L. E. Burton and D. H. Gannon won the London-New Zealand air race by covering the 11,796-mi. distance in 23 hrs. 51 min. 10 sec. Flying from London Airport to Harewood International Airport, Christchurch, New Zealand, Capts. W. Ballie, A. S. Johnson and S. E. Jones in the prototype Vickers Viscount (G-AMAV) set the new London-Melbourne, Australia time of 35 hrs. 47 min. at an average speed of 293.7 MPH.

1953 October 24 Designed essentially as a scaled-up version of the delta-wing Convair XF-92A, the prototype YF-102 made its first flight powered by a 16,000-lb. s.t. Pratt & Whitney J57-P-23A turbojet. A second prototype flew on January 11, 1954, but performance for both was poor and below predictions. During early 1954, Convair carried out a detailed study and incorporated area-rule in a redesign of the aircraft, changes that were incorporated in the YF-102A, which made its first flight on December 20, 1954.

1953 October 29 The North American YF-100A Super Sabre broke the existing absolute world air speed record when Lt. Col. Frank K. Everest, USAF, flew the aircraft to an average 1,215.04 km/hr. (755.149 MPH) at Edwards AFB, Calif. This was the last low-level world speed record run. Everest had made 10 Bell X-1 flights and two Bell X-1A flights and would make 13 flights in the Bell X-2, achieving an unofficial speed record of 1,900 MPH (Mach 2.87) on July 23, 1956.

1953 November 20 NACA test pilot A. Scott Crossfield became the first man through Mach 2 when he piloted the #2 Douglas D-558-II Skyrocket to a speed of Mach 2.005 in a slight dive at 62,000 ft. The Skyrocket never again appoached such speeds. For this attempt, the aircraft had been cold-soaked with liquid oxygen loaded several hours before the attempt, ensuring the maximum quantity of propellant could be pumped into the tanks. The #2 Skyrocket made its last flight on December 20, 1956, having completed 103 flights, 82 of which were air-launched.

1953 December 12 On its eighth powered flight, the third flown by Maj. Charles (''Chuck'') Yeager, the Bell X-1A established a new, unratified speed record of 1,650 MPH, Mach 2.435, at 75,000 ft. before it plunged temporarily out of control. This was the highest speed achieved by any first or second generation Bell X-1 series aircraft. The X-1A make the last of its 12 flights July 20, 1955, and the X-1B, first flown September 24, 1954, kept flying through January 23, 1958, when Neil Armstrong, the man who would first walk on the moon, made its last flight.

1953 December 18 Designed to a U.S. Marine Corps requirement for a very large transport helicopter, the Sikorsky XHR2S-1 made its first flight powered by two 1,900-HP Pratt & Whitney R-2800-54 engines driving a 72 ft. diameter rotor. With a length of 64 ft. 11 in. and a fully loaded weight of 31,000 lb., the S-56 was the biggest helicopter flying outside the USSR until the mid-1960s. It could carry 10,000 lb. slung underneath, and inboard cargo loading was eased by a traversing electric hoist with a 2,000-lb. lift capacity. The type entered service in July 1956.

1954 January 10 BOAC Comet 1 G-ALYP commanded by Capt. A. Gibson broke up at an altitude of more than 26,000 ft., killing six crew members and 29 passengers, including six children, 25 min. after taking off from Rome's Ciampino Airport bound for London on the last leg of a flight from Singapore. Fishermen in the Mediterranean saw flaming wreckage fall into the sea between the islands of Elba and Monte Cristo. The BOAC Comet fleet was grounded between January 11 and resumption of Comet services on March 23.

1954 January 12 In a speech in New York City, U.S. Secretary of State John Foster Dulles declared that a U.S. policy of ''massive retaliation'' would be adopted in the future to deter aggression and asserted that ''local defenses must be reinforced by the further deterrent of massive retaliatory power'' in areas of the world where UN forces might be called upon to defend oppressed peoples, similar to the recently ended Korean War. This policy would sustain development of a conventional and nuclear, tactical and strategic, U.S. Air Force.

1954 February 5 NACA concluded a two-day meeting of the Research Airplane Panel that drew representatives from all the NACA field laboratories at which the question of a hypersonic research aircraft to replace the second generation X-1 and the X-2 had been discussed. Chaired by Hartley Soulé, the panel concluded that a completely new aircraft was necessary and directed Ames, Langley, Lewis, the High Speed Flight Station at Edwards AFB, Calif. and headquarters in Washington, D.C. to generate goals requirements.

1954 February 13 The RAF received its first swept-wing fighters when No. 56 Squadron took delivery of the first Supermarine Swift Mk.1. The F.Mk.2 joined the RAF on August 30 but, like its predecessor, suffered a number of fatal accidents caused by design problems. The aircraft found a temporary niche as a low-altitude, high-speed tactical reconnaissance aircraft, defined under the FR.5 designation. The FR.5 was replaced by the Hunter in 1961.

1954 February 24 Flown for the first time on December 16, 1953, the Dassault Mystère IVB became the first French aircraft to exceed the speed of sound in level flight. Powered by a 7,500/9,500-lb. s.t. Rolls Royce Avon R.A.7R, the aircraft had a completely redesigned fuselage compared to the IVb, incorporating a dielectric lip over the nose intake. Production aircraft had the afterburning Atar 101G-21 turbojet.

1954 February 28 Flown by Tony LeVier, the XF-104 (serial no. 53-7786) made its first flight 15 mon. after design began as the Lockheed Model 83. A tactical day fighter, it would become the only aircraft to hold both speed and altitude records simultaneously, and it was the first interceptor to be capable of sustained speeds in excess of Mach 2. Dubbed a ''missile with a man inside,'' the F-104 Starfighter had an anhedral wing with a span of 21 ft. 11 in., a length of 54 ft. 9 in. and a gross weight of 27,853 lb. With a top speed of 1,150 MPH at 40,000 ft., it had the then phenomenal initial climb rate of 54,000 ft./min. and joined the USAF in 1955.

1954 March 1 The first in a series of Pacific tests aimed at producing a hydrogen bomb capable of being delivered by aircraft began under Operation Castle. In a fixture at Bikini, the first device was detonated at 6:45 A.M. local time. Because of a miscalculation in the theory of lithium-7, the 15-megaton explosive yield was 2.5 times the predicted yield, 1,000 times the explosive yield of the bomb dropped on Hiroshima. Because of a sudden change in wind, the mushroom cloud, 70 mi. across, blew radioactive particles on Japanese fishermen almost 100 mi. away.

1954 March 1 A ban on the production of military aircraft in Japan, imposed as part of the terms ratifying the surrender of Japan in 1945, was lifted. An agreement was signed in Tokyo between Kawasaki Aircraft Co. and Lockheed Aircraft Corp. for rights to license-manufacture the T-33A twin-seat jet trainer and the F-94C Starfire all-weather jet fighter. An agreement of January 10 cleared the way for an indigenous Japanese aircraft industry to fill the requirements of the newly forming Japanese Air Self-Defense Force.

1954 March 8   The first flight of the Sikorsky S-58 took place, designated XHSS-1 in a U.S. Navy order issued June 30, 1952. Stimulated to request a bigger version of the successful HO4S (S-55), the navy wanted a large general-utility helicopter. The HSS Seabat had a length of 46 ft. 9 in., a 56-ft. diameter rotor powered by an obliquely mounted 1,525-HP Wright R-1820 radial engine and a gross weight of 14,000 lb. The navy got its first Seabats in August 1955, and the Marines took delivery of the HUS Seahorse in February 1957.

1954 March 13   The siege of the French base at Dien Bien Phu, Vietnam began despite assistance from U.S. air units to buttress flagging French success in holding back the Viet Minh. The airstrip came under concentrated fire from the following week, and on April 1, a French paratroop battalion was dropped in; another followed on April 10. Under the code name Vulture, a U.S. plan was drawn up to use carpet-bombing on communist positions around the perimeter or even use three strategically placed atomic weapons, but the idea was dropped for fear of massive Chinese intervention.

1954 March   In the United States a top secret Strategic Missiles Evaluation Committee set up by the USAF and chaired by Dr. John von Neumann declared that intercontinental ballistic missiles (ICBMs) were feasible. Strategic Air Command, under the command of Gen. Curtis LeMay, appreciated that this might threaten the survivability of the bomber force, and in seeking to stiffen support for the manned penetrating aircraft sought new technologies to gain better aircraft efficiency and performance.

1954 April 1   The first military version of the Convair 340 airliner, the C-131A was delivered to the USAF Military Air Transport Service. With greater wing area than the 240, more powerful engines and capacity to seat 44 passengers, the first Convair 340 had first flown on October 5, 1951. The C-131A could carry 27 stretcher cases or 37 passengers and had a special loading floor. Later, after the first Convair 440 took to the air on October 6, 1955, the USAF purchased six 440s as the C-131D.

1954 April 1   The last operational combat sortie flown by an RAF Spitfire was conducted against terrorists in Malaya by a P.R.Mk.19 of No. 81 Squadron. The squadron had been flying P.R.Mk.19s since 1949 when it was based at Tengah, Singapore. It moved to Seletar in March 1950 and from there regularly flew in support of British antiterrorist operations. Since December 1953, the squadron had been converting to the Meteor P.R.Mk.10. The P.R.Mk.19 had been the last of the photographic reconnaissance Spitfires, the only PR variant to adopt the Rolls Royce Griffon engine.

1954 April 7   BOAC Comet 1 G-ALYY with a South African Airways crew of seven and 14 passengers on board broke up in midair near Naples shortly after taking off from Rome during the early evening. On April 9, following the crashes of May 2, 1953, and January 10, 1954, the Comet's certificate of airworthiness was withdrawn, and all Comet 1 aircraft operated by British, Canadian and French airlines were permanently removed from service.

1954 April 29   The Consolidated-Vultee Aircraft Corp. became the Convair Division of the General Dynamics Corp. when the latter became majority shareholder. Consolidated Aircraft Corp.

and Vultee Aircraft Inc. had merged on March 17, 1943, under the control of Avco Manufacturing Corp. This passed to the Atlas Corp. on November 20, 1947. Henceforth, Consolidated aircraft would simply be known as Convair products.

1954 May 1   On the traditional May Day parade, the Myasishchyev M-4 Bison bomber made its dramatic appearance over Red Square in Moscow. Flown in late 1953, the M-4 was a major accomplishment for the Soviet aviation industry. It had a swept-wing span of 165 ft., a length of 154 ft. 10 in. and power provided by four 19,180-lb. s.t. Mikulin AM-3 turbojets. Maximum speed was 621 MPH at altitude, and range was 6,650 mi. In service in 1956, about 200 were built with tanker versions still operational in the early 1990s.

1954 May 1   The USAF formed an airborne early warning and control division equipped initially with 10 specially modified RC-121C aircraft, military versions of the Lockheed 049 Super Constellation. These aircraft had initially been ordered by the U.S. Navy but were diverted to the USAF. They were replaced later by the RC-121D, 72 of which were built for the the USAF through diverted navy contracts. They had a range of 4,600 mi. and were redesignated EC-12D in 1962.

1954 May 7   The French base at Dien Bien Phu in Vietnam collapsed after several months under siege during which massive air support had been organized flying in relief supplies and strafing the communist Viet Minh. The French lost 2,293 dead with 5,134 wounded, 885 of whom were flown out by helicopter over the next several days. Transport aircraft flew 6,700 sorties, and combat aircraft flew an additional 3,700 missions for the loss of 48 French aircraft.

1954 May 25   A new endurance record for nonrigid airships was set when a dirigible in the ZPG-2 Class commanded by U.S. Navy Comdr. M. H. Eppes flew from the Lakehurst NAS, N.J. to Key West, Fla. in just over 200 hrs. remaining aloft for more than eight days. Developed as antisubmarine patrol airships, the ZPG-2 class led to the ZPG-2W and ZPG-3W operating as early warning airships.

1954 June 3   The Washington-based Capital Airlines announced it had ordered three Vickers Viscount turboprop airliners from Britain and followed this with an order for 37 more in August and another 20 in November. This was the first major order for British aircraft to operate on U.S. domestic services since the D.H.4s of World War I vintage. Capital ordered another 15 Viscounts and 14 Comet jet airliners, but the airline had overextended itself, and these orders were subsequently canceled.

1954 June 21   Maj. Gen. Walter C. Sweeney, USAF, commander of the Fifteenth Air Force, led a flight of three Twenty-second Bombardment Wing B-47s on a nonstop flight from March AFB, Calif. to Yokota Air Base in Japan. With two in-flight refuelings from KC-97 tanker aircraft, the B-47s flew the 6,700 mi. in just under 15 hrs. taking the new six-engine jet bomber to the Far East for the first time. During 1954 increased activity with Strategic Air Command tankers would result in 142,000 aerial refueling operations and more than 3,400 trans-Atlantic and trans-Pacific flights.

1954 June 22   The prototype Douglas A4D Skyhawk (XA4D-1) made its first flight powered by a 7,000-lb. s.t. Wright J65-W-2 engine. Production A4D-1 had the 7,700-lb. s.t. J65-W-4, a wingspan of 27 ft. 6 in., a length of 39 ft. 5 in., an empty weight of 8,400 lb. and a maximum gross weight of 20,000 lb.

Beginning with the A-4E, power was provided by an 8,500-lb. s.t. Pratt & Whitney J52-P-6A. The A-4M had an 11,200-lb. s.t. J52-P-408A allowing 9,155-lb. warload, a top speed of 670 MPH and a tactical radius of 340 mi. with 4,000 lb. of ordnance. The navy took delivery of its first operational Skyhawk in November 1956.

1954 June 24 The USAF announced that the new U.S. Air Force Academy approved in a bill signed by Pres. Dwight D. Eisenhower April 1 would be located at Colorado Springs, Colo. By the end of 1990, 24,000 cadets had graduated from the academy after completing a core curriculum of 91.5 semester hr. Cadets can major in any one of 25 specialized subjects. The goals of the academy include development of the physical and intellectual abilities of its cadets and production of first-class USAF officers.

1954 June 26 The prototype Hunting Jet Provost (serial no. XD674) made its first flight from Luton, England, piloted by R. G. "Dick" Wheldon. Just as the de Havilland Vampire had provided a jet advanced trainer for the RAF, so would the Jet Provost provide a jet basic trainer to replace the piston-engined types. Power was provided by a 1,750-lb. s.t. Armstrong Siddeley Viper ASV.5 engine, and the aircraft had a wingspan of 35 ft. 2 in., a length of 31 ft. 11 in. and a top speed of 330 MPH at 20,000 ft.

1954 June 28 The first Martin B-57B bomber version of the B-57A Canberra copy made its first flight, and the first of 202 was delivered to the 461st Bombardment Group (Tactical) of Tactical Air Command on January 5, 1955. Two other Bombardment Groups (Tactical) in Europe were equipped with this aircraft although the type was retired from Tactical Air Command by mid-1959. Some units still held on to their B-57Bs until transfer to the Air National Guard in 1964. As a tactical night intruder, it had a rotary weapons bay, wing pylons for rockets or bombs and armament of eight 0.50-in. or four 20-mm guns.

1954 June 28 The first USAF Douglas RB-66A Destroyer was flown from the Long Beach, Calif. facility to Edwards AFB by George R. Jansen. Evolved from the U.S. Navy A3D Skywarrior, it was equipped for all-weather night reconnaissance. From this was developed the B-66B light tactical bomber first flown January 4, 1955. Other versions included the electronic reconnaissance RB-66C and the WB-66D weather reconnaissance variant.

1954 June 30 As of this date, the last day of fiscal year 1954, the USAF had accepted 5,662 aircraft in the preceding 12 mo. This constituted a record for post-World War II procurement. Annual acceptance figures for fiscal years showed that the USAF had received 876 aircraft in 1948, 1,278 in 1949, 1,652 in 1950, 1,756 in 1951, 2,814 in 1952 and 4,723 in 1953. From the 1954 peak of 5,662 aircraft, procurement would fall to 4,830 aircraft in 1955 and 3,086 in 1956.

1954 July 9 Representatives of NACA, the U.S. Navy Bureau of Aeronautics and the USAF Scientific Advisory Board met at NACA headquarters in Washington, D.C. to hear from Hartley Soulé, chairman of the Research Airplane Panel, Walter C. Williams of the High Speed Flight Station and John V. Becker and John E. Duberg from the Langley Aeronautical Laboratory. The Langley presentation outlined the requirements for a Mach 7 research aircraft, and it was agreed that this should be circulated among industry and the military.

1954 July 14 The first free flight of the McDonnell XV-1 convertiplane was carried out at the St. Louis, Mo. plant. Designed by the Austrian helicopter pioneer Friedrich Doblhoff, the convertiplane combined the features of a twin boom, twin-tail fixed-wing aircraft with those of a single-rotor helicopter. It was powered by a 525-HP Continental R-975-19 radial engine driving a pusher propeller and a compressor feeding air through rotor tip jets. Used for tests until the end of the decade, on October 10, 1956, the XV-1 became the first helicopter to exceed 200 MPH.

1954 July 15 The Boeing 367-80 made its first flight, with Boeing chief test pilot A. M. "Tex" Johnson at the controls. The four-jet aircraft incorporated much that had been learned in the design and development of the B-47 six-jet bomber. The USAF evaluated it as a potential tanker-transport and in September placed an initial order for a military KC-135A to carry out this role. Boeing then began a major marketing campaign among the airlines to sell the 367-80 as a trans-Atlantic airliner.

1954 July 26 Two U.S. Navy Douglas AD Skyraiders operating off the aircraft carrier USS *Philippine Sea* shot down two Soviet Lavochkin La-7s from the Chinese Air Force that attacked them during a search for survivors from a Cathay Pacific Airways DC-4 airliner that had been shot down off Hainan Island July 23. The Chinese admitted liability for the loss of the airliner and passengers, paying £367,000 compensation.

1954 July 29 Setting a new design configuration that would remain a distinct feature of business jet aircraft, the Morane-Saulnier M.S.760 Paris made its first flight powered by two 882-lb. s.t. Turboméca Marboré II turbojet engines mounted on pods attached to the rear fuselage. With a wingspan of 3 ft. 3 in., a length of 33 ft. and a gross weight of 7,650 lb., it could carry four people with six in a later version.

1954 July 30 The Grumman F9F-9 prototype made its first flight piloted by Corky Meyer from the new Peconic River Facility at Calverton, N.Y. powered by a 7,500-lb. s.t. Wright J65-W-7 turbojet, the F9F derivative soon proved its worth, and orders followed for the more powerfully engined, and redesignated, F11F-1F Tiger. With a wingspan of 31 ft. 7 in., a length of 40 ft. 10 in. and a maximum weight of 23,459 lb., it had a 6,300 ft./min. climb rate and a maximum sea level speed of 754 MPH. On May 2, 1957, it was flown to Mach 2.04 and a height of 80,250 ft.

1954 August 1 The U.S. Navy VTOL fighter contender from Convair designated XFY-1 made its first free vertical takeoff and landing powered by a 5,850/7,100-EHP Allison YT40-A-6. This unusual aircraft stood in a vertical position on its tail and had a short, fat fuselage 35 ft. in length with a near delta wing of 27 ft. 8 in. span, one ventral and one dorsal fin with a total height of 22 ft. 11 in. and two three-blade contra-rotating propellers. The XRY-1 had a gross weight of 16,250 lb. Full transition from vertical to horizontal flight took place in early November.

1954 August 3 The only flying machine built by Rolls Royce and the first British VTOL machine, the "Flying Bedstead" took to the air for the first time. Comprising an open rectangular frame with near-vertical legs at each corner, the device contained two Rolls Royce Nene engines with exhaust ducted downwards 90° thrusting through the center of mass. A pilot sat on a platform on top of the machine with projecting nozzle support trusses fore and aft for pitch control.

1954 August 3 The French Nord 1402 Gerfaut 1A became the first aircraft in Europe to exceed the speed of sound in level flight without thrust augmentation when it was propelled to a speed of just over Mach 1 by its 6,173-lb. s.t. SNECMA Atar 101C turbojet. First flown January 15, the Gerfaut 1A was a delta-wing research aircraft and was followed by the Gerfaut 1B, which flew on February 9, 1955, and by the Gerfaut II, which flew on April 17, 1956.

1954 August 4   The prototype English Electric (serial no. WG760) made its first flight from Boscombe Down, England with Roland Beamont at the controls. Powered by two 8,100/10,300-lb. s.t. Armstrong Siddeley Sapphire Sa.5 engines, the aircraft had a wingspan of 34 ft. 10 in. and a length of 56 ft. 8 in. with a maximum loaded weight of 28,000 lb. By this time, English Electric had received an order for 23 more advanced P.1B fighter prototypes since the P.1A was now considered little more than a development aircraft.

1954 August 5   The first production Boeing B-52A made its first flight and, like the two that followed, was immediately returned to Boeing for flight test programs. The remaining 10 of 13 ordered were completed as B-52Bs. The initial production version differed from the prototypes mainly in having a redesigned cockpit placing the pilots side by side. The first model in service use was the B-52B, flown from the Boeing factory at Seattle to Castle AFB, Calif. by Brig. Gen. William E. Eubank Jr., commander of the Ninety-third Bombardment Wing on June 29, 1955.

1954 August 6   Two B-47s of the 308th Bombardment Wing started out on a 10,000-mi. round-trip from Hunter AFB, Ga. to French Morocco, one aircraft making the flight in 24 hrs. 4 min., the other in 25 hrs. 23 min. Tied into this was a new concept in intercontinental bombing operations whereby B-47s would fly a bombing mission and go on to land at a friendly airfield further along instead of forward-basing and returning to the point of departure. The flights were part of Operation Leap Frog.

1954 August 23   The prototype Lockheed YC-130 made its first flight with Stanley Betz and Roy Wimmer on the flight deck. Designed as a tactical troop drop and cargo transport to requirements generated by the Korean War, the C-130 Hercules would become on of the most efficient and practical aircraft of its type ever built. The initial production version was powered by four 3,750-HP Allison T56-A-1A engines, had a wingspan of 132 ft. 7 in., a length of 97 ft. 10 in. and a maximum weight of 124,200 lb. Lockheed built more than 2,000 for customers in 57 countries.

1954 September 4   The U.S. Navy lost a Lockheed P2V-5 Neptune shot down by two Soviet MiG-15 fighters off the Siberian coast but outside Soviet airspace. The aircraft came from Navy Squadron VP-19, and of the 10 men on board, nine were rescued from the sea but one went down with the plane as it sank after ditching. The Soviets said later they suspected the aircraft of spying.

1954 September 27   The North American F-100A Super Sabre became fully operational with Tactical Air Command's 479th Fighter Day Wing at George AFB, Calif. This unit had received its first F-100A the previous November, but it was only declared in operational readiness today. The aircraft had an effective ground attack role and could carry 5,000 lb. of bombs externally. The aircraft had a poor service and operations record, with more than 500 lost between mid-1956 and mid-1970, but was used extensively in Vietnam and filled a wide range of roles.

1954 September 29   Accomplishing the unprecedented feat of going supersonic on its first flight, the first F-101 took to the air at Edwards AFB, Calif., piloted by Bob Little. Preceded by two prototype XF-88 long-range escort and penetration fighters, the F-101 evolved as an interceptor and tactical bomber with a length of 67 ft. 4 in., a wingspan of 39 ft. 8 in. and a gross weight of 52,400 lb. Powered by two 10,100/14,880-lb. s.t. Pratt & Whitney J57-P-13 turbojets, the F-101 had a maximum speed of 1,094 MPH and an initial climb rate of 39,250 ft./min. The USAF took delivery in May 1957.

1954 October 5   At an executive session of the NACA Aerodynamics Committee at the High Speed Flight Station on Edwards AFB, Calif. comments were proffered from industry representatives on the desirability or otherwise of development of a hypersonic manned research vehicle. Opposition was most vociferous from Lockheed's Clarence L. ("Kelly") Johnson, who believed rocket-powered research planes provided nothing that could be applied to the design of tactical military aircraft. However, the committee passed a resolution formally backing a Mach 7 research aircraft for flight "at several hundred thousand feet."

1954 October 6   The Fairey Delta Two (sometimes F.D.2, serial no. WG774) made its first flight with test pilot Peter Twiss piloting the 13,884-lb. delta-wing research aircraft. Powered by a 10,000-lb. s.t. Rolls Royce Avon series 200 turbojet, it had been designed to explore the supersonic flight regime with two ordered in October 1950. The F.D.2 had a wingspan of 26 ft. 10 in., a length of 51 ft. 7 in. and a height of 11 ft. The aircraft incorporated a hinged nose for increased visibility on landing and would eventually be used to test Concorde SST wing configurations.

1954 October 12   The first USAF jet basic trainer made its first flight when the Cessna XT-37 took to the air piloted by Bob Hogan. Cessna's Model 318 was successful in getting a contract to satisfy the specification issued April 1952. The first production T-37A flew on September 27, 1955, and the type was eventually developed into an armed reconnaissance aircraft, the A-37, a close support aircraft sold especially to the South Vietnamese.

1954 October 18   The U.S. Navy placed a letter of intent with McDonnell for development of a twin-engine attack fighter under the designation AH-1. Work had begun on the fighter at McDonnell in 1953, and the aircraft should have had cannon armament, but the requirement changed, and the aircraft was additionally called upon to perform as a high-altitude interceptor. For that, the guns gave way to missiles, for which a second crew member was added and the designation was changed to F4H-1. Because production of the McDonnell FH-1 Phantom had ceased, the new fighter was to be called the Phantom II.

1954 October   During the month, the USAF formulated a requirement for its B-70 supersonic bomber program, stipulating an aircraft to strike targets at a distance of 3,600 mi. and fly unrefueled in both directions at Mach 3 carrying a wide range of nuclear weapons. Under Weapon System 110A in 1955, initial studies were carried out by North American and Boeing indicating the need for an aircraft of 750,000 lb. gross weight with enormous jettisonable fuel pods on the wings. These were refined during 1956–57, but the project was eventually canceled.

1954 November 4   The last operational Boeing Superfortress, a B-29A serial no. 42-94032, made its last flight from the 307th Bombardment Wing, Kadena AB, Okinawa to the storage facility at Davis-Monthan AFB, Ariz. The last B-50, a D model serial

Developed as the first Bell helicopter with a turbine engine, the XH-13F, a Bell 47G, made its first flight on October 20, 1954.

no. 49-330, was withdrawn from Strategic Air Command service on October 20, 1955, when the aircraft retired from the 97th Bombardment Wing, Biggs AFB, Tex. By this latter date, there were already more than 1,000 B-47s with Strategic Air Command.

1954 November 7   The USAF announced plans for construction of a special laboratory for the detailed design and manufacture of atomic engines for large aircraft. The facility was to be built at Middletown, Conn. at a cost of $15.5 million and was to be finished by 1957. It was to be operated by Pratt & Whitney.

1954 November 15   The Scandinavian Airlines System (SAS) inaugurated the first passenger service following the Great Circle route from Copenhagen, Denmark to Los Angeles via Sondrestromfjord, Greenland and Winnipeg, Canada. This saved 10 hrs. compared to the flight via New York. Due to navigational problems experienced while flying at high latitude close to the magnetic pole, special compensation techniques had to be adopted.

1954 November 19   Col. David A. Burchinal, USAF, commander of the Forty-third Bombardment Wing, landed at Fairford, England after having remained in the air for 47 hrs. 35 min. since taking off from Sidi Slimane, French Morocco on November 17 in a B-47. Intending to fly straight to Fairford, he encountered bad weather and turned back to Sidi Slimane only find bad weather there also. Kept aloft with nine in-flight refuelings, Burchinal waited until the weather cleared at Fairford and landed at his original destination.

1954 December 11   Ushering in new age of super-carrier naval aviation, the USS *Forrestal* (CVB-59), the first new aircraft carrier since World War II, was launched from the Newport News, Va. ship yards. The CVB-59 had a loaded displacement of 78,200 tons, a length of 1,039 ft., a width over the flight deck of 252 ft. and provision for up to 95 aircraft. The *Forrestal* was commissioned on October 1, 1955, seven days after the launch of her sister ship, USS *Saratoga* (CVB-60).

1954 December 14   At a presentation by NACA, the U.S. Department of Defense accepted recommendations to build a Mach 7 research aircraft and directed NACA to control the project. Later in the month the USAF, the U.S. Navy and the NACA formed the Research Airplane Committee, and on December 30, the Air Materiel Command announced a bidders' briefing to be held at Wright-Patterson AFB, Ohio.

1954 December 20   The Convair YF-102A, the definitive pre-production configuration of the Delta Dagger, made its first flight displaying the waisted fuselage of the area-rule concept pioneered by Richard T. Whitcomb. Powered by a 16,000-lb. s.t. Pratt & Whitney J57-P-23 turbojet, the aircraft had a wingspan of 38 ft. 1 in., a length of 68 ft. 3 in., a gross weight of 28,150 lb. Performance included a top speed of 780 MPH at 36,000 ft., an initial climb rate of 17,400 ft./min. and a combat radius of 651 mi. The USAF took delivery of the first of 875 F-102As in mid-1956.

1954 December 23   The first formation ejection took place over Iraq. Eight Venom F.B.1s of No. 73 Squadron, RAF, had taken off from their base at Habbaniyah on a routine exercise, but six were unable to get back in due to sudden ground fog. Low on fuel, two made emergency belly landings. The other four ascended to 10,000 ft. in a box formation, the lead pair jettisoning their canopies and ejecting at 207 MPH in their Martin-Baker Mk.2F seats. Reporting their position by radio, the rear pair then ejected and spent the night on the ground guarded by local tribesmen.

1955 January 1   The U.S. government issued a general warning about the possible discovery of Japanese balloon-carried bombs that might be found by people and inadvertently detonated causing death and injury. One such live bomb had recently been found in Alaska, and the Defense Department thought several hundred might be found in isolated and remote areas of the United States. About 9,300 such balloons had been released in Japan beginning November 3, 1944.

1955 January 4   The USAF Air Research and Development Command issued System Requirement 12 calling for an unmanned reconnaissance aircraft with a range of 3,450 mi. capable of operating at an altitude of 100,000 ft. On May 12, this was expanded through General Requirement 12 to include a manned aircraft capable of operational readiness by 1959.

1955 January 18   At an airframe bidders' conference organized by USAF Air Materiel Command, industry heard goals and requirements of the proposed hypersonic, Mach 7 research aircraft recently approved as Project 1226. In attendance were representatives from Bell, Boeing, Chance Vought, Convair, Douglas, McDonnell, North American, Northrop and Republic. A separate propulsion bidders' meeting on February 4 drew Aerojet, General Electric, North American and Reaction Motors. Bids on Project 1226 were to be in by May 9, and on May 17 the NACA Research Airplane Committee was to hear briefings.

1955 January 20   The government of South Vietnam reached agreement with United States, Britain and France whereby those countries would supply equipment for the modernization of its land and air forces. Since 1950 the United States had assisted the French against the communist Viet Minh through the Mutual Assistance Advisory Group. After the French defeat at the battle of Dien Bien Phu in May 1954, it was agreed the country would be partitioned at the 17th parallel, with the French out by 1956. On June 1, 1956, the South Vietnamese Air Force was formed with a squadron of F8F-1 Bearcats.

1955 February 4   The first production Avro Vulcan B.Mk.1 (serial no. XA889) made its first flight powered by four 9,750-lb. s.t. Bristol Olympus turbojets. In October it was discovered that wing fatigue could result from g-loads at altitude, so the sweep was reduced from 52° to 42° at half span and increased

Shown here in formation with two English Electric Canberras (in service from 1951), the Vickers Valiant joined the RAF during 1954.

again further outboard. Starting with Vulcan XA890, the aircraft had extended engine nozzles also.

1955 February 9 The Vickers Valiant B.Mk.1 became the first V-bomber to reach operational status when No. 138 (Bomber) Squadron, RAF, declared itself clear for service. Based at Gaydon, England, the squadron was commanded by Wg. Comdr. R. G. W. Oakley. On September 5, two Valiants under the command of Sqdn. Ldr. R. G. Wilson flew from Wittering, England to Singapore, Australia and New Zealand under Operation Too Right, essentially a flag-waving exercise integrated with operational shakedown trials.

1955 February 26 The first supersonic ejection took place when North American test pilot George F. Smith ejected from his diving F-100 off Laguna Beach, Calif. Asked to take up a F-100 for a routine test, George Smith grabbed only his helmet and flew the aircraft in sports shirt and denims. After the controls failed, he escaped at an estimated speed of Mach 1.05. He suffered multiple fractures, a detached retina, damaged lower intestines and hemorrhaged eyeballs. He was unconscious for five days but recovered.

1955 March 1 The first modernized early warning unit covering the east coast of the continental United States, the 551st Early Warning and Control Wing based at Otis AFB, Falmouth, Mass. began operating the Lockheed RC-121D airborne early warning aircraft. They would eventually receive 30 aircraft of this type, a similar-sized unit having already become operational (on May 1, 1954) on the west coast at McClellan AFB, Sacramento, Calif.

1955 March 2 Continuing the progressive evolution of the Dassault single-seat fighter line, the prototype Super Mystère B1 single-seat interceptor made its first flight powered by a 7,500/ 9,500-lb. s.t. Rolls Royce Avon R.A.7R turbojet. Known formerly as the Mystère XX, or Super Mystère IVB1, production aircraft had the 7,275/9,260-lb. SNECMA Atar 101G-21 engine, a speed of Mach 1.2 and an endurance of 70 min.

1955 March 12 The French Süd-Est SE-3130 Alouette II helicopter made its first flight and would become the first turboshaft

helicopter to enter production. Powered by a 400-HP Turboméca Artouste II engine, it had a 33 ft. 5 in. rotor, a length of 31 ft. 9 in. and a fully loaded weight of 3,307 lb. Seating five and with a cruising speed of 106 MPH, it had a range of 329 mi. On June 3, it achieved an FAI-ratified height record for helicopters of 26,934 ft. More than 1,000 Alouette IIs were built for 35 countries.

1955 March 25 The first of two XF-8A prototype single-seat carrier-based fighters made its first flight. Designed to a U.S. Navy specification of 1952 for a supersonic fighter, production F-8 Crusaders were each powered by a 10,700-lb. s.t. Pratt & Whitney J57-P-20A and went into service in March 1957. Unusual in having a high-mounted wing with a variable incidence mechanism for reduced landing speed, the F-8 had a top speed of 1,120 MPH and a range of 1,100 mi. This XF-8A was the last aircraft built by the Chance-Vought company before it became Ling-Temco-Vought.

1955 March A fuels and propulsion panel at NACA met in Washington, D.C. to discuss ideas concerning the possible use of hydrogen as an aircraft fuel in high-flying reconnaissance aircraft. Hydrogen-fueled engines would be capable of stable combustion for sustained flight at and just above 100,000 ft., compared to approximately 45,000 ft. for conventional jet fuel of the day. Taking work done by Edmund R. Jonash, Arthur Smith and Vincent Hlavin, which had been written up on December 23, 1954, NACA's Abe Silverstein applied this to the potential application for military reconnaissance aircraft.

1955 April 3 A new integrated air traffic control center for the south of England became operational at Heathrow Airport west of London, by this time the main airport for England's capital city. The operational control and jurisdiction over the airspace of such a large area under one central control was considered an effective way of maintaining safety in increasingly busy skies. It was also the most effective way of serving the needs of busy airlines and minimizing congestion and landing delays.

1955 April 15 The first landing in England by a German-registered civil aircraft since 1939 occurred. A Convair CV-340 registered D-ACAD, belonging to Deutsche Lufthansa, landed at London Airport at the end of a proving flight from Hamburg, Germany to England. Full services began May 16 with flights linking London, Hamburg, Frankfurt, Dusseldorf and Munich with CV-340 aircraft, D-ACOH and D-ACIG.

1955 April 17 The new control tower at London's Heathrow Airport came into full operation during the evening. Working in conjunction with the new Southern Air Traffic Control Center nearby, the airport control building miniaturized what the larger air traffic control was achieving, controlling movements on the ground and in the air directly within the general flying area of Heathrow. Dubbed by the press the "Tower of London" after the medieval fortress of that name, it was an emphatic declaration of the impending age of turbine- and jet-powered air transport.

1955 May 10 The Federal Republic of Germany was formally admitted to NATO under a protocol issued in Paris on October 23, 1954. On May 12, the USSR renounced its treaties with Britain and France and on May 14 formally established the Warsaw Pact with its client states in Eastern Europe. The accession of West Germany opened the way for establishment of a reconstituted Luftwaffe, whose role within the NATO Central European Command would be, in time of war, to achieve and maintain air supremacy over its territory.

1955 May 15 The United States and Canada reached agreement on the final details of the construction of the Defense Early Warning (DEW) line protecting the North American continent from hostile air attack. It was to comprise a chain of radar stations covering the northern latitudes, from which an airborne attack from the Soviet Union would presumably come.

1955 May 27 The prototype Süd-Est Caravelle (F-WHHH) made its first flight from Toulouse, France, piloted by Pierre Nadot. Although design studies on the first French jet airliner had been under way since 1946, it had not been given direction until 1951. Powered by two 10,000-lb. s.t. Rolls Royce Avon R.A.26 engines, it was handed to an Air France crew for proving trials in May 1956, 3 mon. after the airline had placed an initial order for 12 aircraft.

1955 May The British Ministry of Supply selected the Avro 730 design concept to accommodate O.R.330 calling for a Mach 2.5 reconnaissance aircraft with a range of 5,500 mi. flying at 60,000 ft. Submissions from Handley Page and Vickers were rejected. The air staff believed that performance at this level would render it immune to fighters or antiaircraft missiles. With four turbojets in stacked pairs at each wing tip, the Avro 730 would have a crew of two and a 52-ft. long Red Drover sideways-looking X-band radar incorporated within the 163.5 ft. fuselage. It was to have a wingspan of almost 60 ft.

1955 June 2 An agreement was signed whereby the United States would provide financial assistance to the Italian aircraft division of Fiat for the manufacture and production of a NATO fighter. Called the G.91, the aircraft would be produced at the Turin factory, and three prototypes were ordered for evaluation with the idea that they would result in a fighter sold to European NATO countries. The concept had risen in December 1953 when a NATO requirement for a light fighter/attack aircraft was defined.

1955 June 3 A Canadian Pacific Airlines DC-6B (CF-CUR) *Empress of Amsterdam* under the command of Capt. R. B. Leslie inaugurated a polar route linking Amsterdam, the Netherlands with Sydney, Australia, via Sondrestromfjord, Edmonton and Vancouver.

1955 June 4 Responding to the imminent availability of the Boeing 367-80 jet-powered airliner, Donald Douglas approved the Douglas Aircraft Co.'s DC-8 jet, successor to the DC-7. Concerned with retaining its lead in U.S. civil transport against a bid from Boeing, the company envisaged a four-engined airliner with a triple-spar wing of modest 30° sweep for efficient low-speed handling and a specification filling trans-Atlantic and European route needs. A Douglas team led by Art Raymond and Ed Burton began work on the detailed design.

1955 June 9 Lockheed Aircraft Corp. at Burbank, Calif. announced its new turboprop Model 188 Electra airliner in response to success with the British Viscount and sales of that aircraft to Capital Airlines. On June 8 American ordered 35, and on September 27 Eastern ordered 40. By the time the Electra made its first flight in December 1957, 129 Electras had been ordered by six U.S. and three foreign airlines, and there were provisional orders for a further 48 aircraft.

1955 June 17 The prototype Tupolev Tu-104, powered by two 14,881-lb. s.t. Mikulin RD-3 jet engines and bearing the registration number SSSR-L5400, made its first flight. Developed hurriedly from the Tu-16 bomber, which had flown first in early 1952, the Tu-104 had a wingspan of 121 ft. 2 in. and a length

of 131 ft. 5 in. with a gross weight of 174,000 lb. The wing had a 35° sweep, and the cabin could accommodate 50 passengers. This was increased to 70 with the production Tu-104A version powered by two 19,180-lb. s.t. Mikulin AM-3M engines, which was developed later this year.

1955 June 25 The prototype Dassault M.D.550 Mirage, first in a famous line of top French fighters, made its first flight a year after seeking to fill an Armée de l'Air requirement for a small all-weather interceptor. Powered by two 2,160-lb. s.t. M.D.30R turbojets and one 3,307-lb. thrust SEPR rocket motor, the aircraft had a 23 ft. span delta wing set low on a 37 ft. 9 in. fuselage with a large vertical tail. Neither this nor a proposed Mirage II was powerful enough, and Dassault upgraded the design into the Mirage III.

1955 June 28 RAF Canberra B.Mk.2 (serial no. WH699) *Aries IV* made a record flight between Ottawa and London in 6 hrs. 42 min. at an average speed of 496.825 MPH. The Canberra had previously been in the Arctic region in February 1954 when it flew to Canada for trials and courtesy calls, and during that October, it made the first flight over the North Pole by a British jet aircraft. *Aries IV* was crewed by Sqdn. Ldrs. I. G. Brown, D. Bower and R. A. Seymour.

1955 July 14 The Martin Model 275, U.S. Navy XP6M-1 SeaMaster, multi-role jet flying boat made its first flight. With an all-metal hull and high-set swept wings with a span of 100 ft., the aircraft had a length of 134 ft. and power from four 9,700/13,000-lb. s.t. Allison J71-A-4 turbojets. The SeaMaster was to have entered service with more powerful engines, but an order for 24 was canceled after only three had been built in addition to a total of eight prototypes. With a speed of 633 MPH, they were the fastest flying boats ever built.

1955 July 18 The diminutive Folland Gnat made its first flight as a private venture single-seat fighter that the RAF eventually bought as a trainer designated Gnat T.1 With a 4,230-lb. s.t. Bristal Siddeley Orpheus 100 engine, it had a wingspan of 24 ft., a length of 31 ft. 9 in. and a loaded weight of 7,400 lb. The trainer had two seats in tandem and joined the RAF Central Flying School in February 1962 as the standard advanced trainer. The Red Arrows flew the Gnats in their air displays until 1978 when they changed them for Hawks.

1955 July 27 A Lockheed Constellation belonging to the Israeli airline El Al was shot down by Bulgarian antiaircraft batteries as it flew along the border with Greece in the latter country's airspace. The aircraft, registration 4X-AKC, was flying from Vienna, Austria to Lod when it was attacked by ground fire and by Bulgarian fighters that put several rounds through its fuselage. All 58 people on board were killed.

1955 August 1 The USAF began research into zero-gravity by simulating the effects using T-33 jet trainers and F-80 Shooting Stars. The aircraft were flown on a parabolic curve culminating in a rapid rate of descent equal to the free-fall speed of a body of equal mass above the earth at that altitude. This created the effect of zero-gravity for up to 1 min. in a technique that would be used many times by the USAF, the U.S. Navy, NACA and NASA in the years ahead.

1955 August 2 From the flat surface of Groom Dry Lake in south-central Nevada, the first Lockheed U-2 spyplane took to the air piloted by Tony LeVier and powered by a 10,500-lb. s.t. Pratt & Whitney J57-P-37 engine. With a high-aspect ratio wingspan of 80 ft. 2 in., a length of 49 ft. 8 in. and a gross takeoff weight of 22,100 lb., the U-2 could carry more than 750 lb. of reconnaissance, surveillance or intelligence-gathering equipment. It could reach an altitude in excess of 65,000 ft. and had a normal range of 3,455 mi. It proved to be one of the most valuable intelligence-gathering assets of all time.

1955 August 3   The first RAF pilot to eject at supersonic speed left his diving Hawker Hunter at Mach 1.1 and 25,000 ft. when it failed to respond to the controls during a high-speed dive. Flying Officer H. Molland survived very high g forces until the barostat automatically opened the parachute at 10,000 ft. and put him down in the sea off Felixstowe on the east coast of England. He suffered two black eyes from blast at ejection.

1955 August 20   Col. H. A. Haines, USAF, flying a F-100C Super Sabre broke the world absolute air speed record when he recorded an average 1,323.03 km/hr. (822.135 MPH). The F-100C had been developed as a fighter-bomber version of the Super Sabre fighter. It was the first time an officially ratified speed record had been claimed above Mach 1 and was almost 70 MPH faster than the previous record set by the YF-100 almost 2 yr. before.

1955 August 23   The first one-day return flight across the Atlantic was completed when an RAF Canberra returned across the Croydon, England marker, having crossed from Floyd Bennett U.S. Navy field, N.Y. in 6 hr. 16 min. 19.5 sec. at an average speed of 550.35 MPH. The outbound leg began at 7:18 A.M. when the Canberra crossed the marker and flew the 3,457.96 mi. to Floyd Bennett field in 7 hr. 29 min. 56.7 sec. at an average speed of 461.12 MPH, a summed average of 481.52 MPH for the 14 hr. 21 min. 45.4 sec. flying time.

1955 August 23   The first Westland Widgeon single-rotor helicopter made its first flight at Yeovil, England as a development of the Dragonfly, which was essentially a license-built Sikorsky S-51. The Widgeon had a length of 41 ft. 3 in. and a rotor of 49 ft. 2 in. and was powered by a 520-HP Alvis Leonides 521/1 engine; it had capacity for five people. Although only 15 Widgeons were built, the design set Westland on the road of becoming an independent helicopter design marque.

1955 September 3   Sqdn. Ldr. J. S. Fifield ejected from the rear sear of a modified Gloster Meteor Mk.7 piloted by Capt. J. E. D. Scott while the aircraft was still traveling along the ground at 120 MPH. This ground-level ejection, the first ever, proved that a modified Martin-Baker Mk.3 ejection seat could save the lives of pilots in difficulty during takeoff or landing. With only a 1.5 sec. delay between firing the ejection gun, imparting a vertical velocity of 80 ft./sec., and parachute deployment, Sqdn. Ldr. Fifield was safely back on the ground six sec. after leaving the Meteor.

1955 September 20   Seeking solutions to high-speed flight problems, the Nord 1500 Griffon I made its first flight powered by a 6,300/8,370-lb. s.t. SNECMA Atar 101G21 turbojet engine. With a wingspan of 26 ft. and a length of 46 ft., the needle-nosed aircraft had a large air intake beneath the forward fuselage directly under the cockpit and forward canard surfaces for pitch trim. In this configuration, the aircraft could achieve a speed of 940 MPH at 10,000 ft.

1955 September 21   In a special inaugural run, the British airline Skyways Limited introduced a special air-coach service with passengers taken by coach from London to Lympne, Kent, by

DC-3 to Beauvais-Tille and from there to Paris by coach again. Capts. J. S. Morgan and E. R. Skemp flew DC-3s G-AMWV and G-ANAE, and regularly scheduled services began on September 30.

1955 September 30   North American Aviation Inc. was formally notified that it had been selected to pursue detailed design and manufacture of three Project 1226 (X-15) hypersonic research aircraft, and on December 6, the company received a formal USAF contract. NAA had earlier notified the NACA/USAF team that it now had too much work on and wanted to pull out. An arrangement was found to allow them to continue when it was agreed that the work schedule could be extended.

1955 October 10   Helicopter Training Unit 1 (HTU-1) departed Tampico, Mexico on the carrier USS *Saipan* (CVL-48) after a week of disaster relief aid work following flooding that stranded local communities. The helicopters rescued 5,439 people from treetops, roofs and areas cut off by the waters and airlifted 183,017 lb. of supplies and medicines.

1955 October 13   Pan American World Airways announced orders worth $96 million for 25 Douglas DC-8s and 20 Boeing 707-100 four-jet airliners. These were the first bookings for the Boeing jet and got the commercial airliner project started. Calculated annual production rates on the new generation of U.S. jet airliners were four or five times that of the DC-7 or the Super Constellation, and fears of a monopoly position loomed again as they had just after World War II.

1955 October 16   The Boeing Model 367-80 made a round-trip flight from Seattle to Washington, D.C. in a total flying time of 8 hrs. 8 min. at an average speed of 579 MPH. Aided by winds, the east-west leg was flown in 3 hrs. 58 min. at an average speed of 592 MPH and west-east leg was flown in 4 hrs. 8 min. at an average speed of 567 MPH. This was a valuable contribution to the intensive sales campaign under way to sell the Model 367-80 as a commercial airliner.

1955 October 22   A massive 52,550-lb. long-range tactical fighter-bomber with a warload of up to 14,000 lb., the Republic YF-105A Thunderchief took to the air for the first time. The definitive F-105D was powered by a 16,100/24,500-lb. s.t. Pratt & Whitney J75-P-19W turbojet giving it a top speed of 1,390 MPH at 38,000 ft., a cruising speed of 584 MPH and a combat radius of 780 mi. Affectionately known as the ''Thud,'' the F-105 entered service in May 1958 and would serve the USAF for almost 26 yr.

1955 October 25   Designed to intercept transonic bombers, the double-delta SAAB-35 Draken made its first flight in a design configuration first tested by its precursor, the SAAB-210, on February 21, 1952. Two other prototypes of the SAAB-35 followed, and the type was ordered into production in 1956. The novel design also incorporated a tricycle landing gear with two small tailwheels, which permitted a tail-down landing position for maximum wing braking effect, which cut rollout to 2,000 ft.

1955 October   The British Ministry of Supply modified the O.R.330 specification being met by the Avro 730 to include a bomber role to satisfy Air Staff needs for a Mach 2+ V-bomber replacement. This was subsequently revised to accommodate a 50 ft. long stand-off missile housing a 1 MT nuclear warhead in a large weapons bay. The powerplants were also changed to comprise eight turbojets in packs of four at each wing tip, the span being increased to 65 ft. 7 in. and length reduced to 159 ft. The first flight was expected in November 1959.

1955 November 1 A United Airlines DC-6B with four people on board broke up in the air and was destroyed when a bomb planted by John G. Graham went off shortly after takeoff from Denver, Colo. Graham had placed the bomb on board shortly after taking out insurance on the life of his mother, who was a passenger on the airliner. Graham, who had intended to make a claim for $13,400, was sentenced to die in the electric chair.

1955 November 11 Two competitive Phase I design contracts for Weapon System 110A, the supersonic nuclear intercontinental bomber, were awarded to North American and Boeing following a USAF presentation to six companies on July 13. The bids were to be returned by October 1956. (Lockheed and Convair were already working on WS-125, a nuclear-powered bomber concept.) The WS-110A companies came up with such outlandish concepts that they were rejected. WS-110A was restructured into six-month feasibility studies conducted in the first half of 1957.

1955 November 18 The first Bell X-2 made its first powered flight when an EB-50A released the aircraft for flight. Piloted by Lt. Col. Frank Everest, USAF, it achieved a speed of 627 MPH (Mach 0.95). The X-2 had a wingspan of 32 ft. 3 in. and a length of 45 ft. 5 in. with a gross weight of 24,910 lb. Power was provided by a two-chamber Curtiss XLR-25-CW-3 rocket motor that could be throttled between 2,500-lb. and 15,000-lb. of thrust; the upper chamber produced a maximum 5,000 lb., the lower chamber 10,000 lb. of thrust.

1955 November 24 The Fokker F.27 Friendship made its first flight, powered by two Rolls Royce Dart 507 series turboprop engines. The first production aircraft entered service with Aer Lingus in late 1958. Powered by two 2,320-ESHP Rolls Royce Dart Mk 536-7R turboprop engines, it had a wingspan of 95 ft. 1 in., a length of 77 ft. 3 in. and a maximum weight of 44,996 lb. With a cruising speed of 298 MPH and a range of 1,197 mi. with 44 passengers, the type soon became popular, and almost 800 were eventually built.

1955 November Designated Ye-50, the first of more than 11,000 MiG-21 supersonic single-seat fighters made its first flight piloted by V. P. Vasin but with a relatively low-thrust engine and a small rocket motor in the tail for added thrust. With a span of 23 ft. 5 in., a length of 51 ft. 8 in. and a gross weight of up to 22,723 lb., the MiG-21 was powered by a variety of powerplants with thrusts generally between 12,000 and 14,000 lb. A wide range of variants was produced, and the type is likely to be in service with some air forces 50 yr. after its first flight.

1955 December 2 A succession of jet airliner records and "firsts," including the first trans-Pacific flight by a jet airliner, was to be set during a round-the-world flight by Comet 3 G-ANLO, which began its journey at Hatfield, England with takeoff at 10:54 A.M. Via Cairo, Bombay, Singapore and Darwin, the Comet reached Sydney 44 hrs. 18 min. after takeoff in a flying time of 24 hr. 53 min. From there it flew to Melbourne and, on December 9, to Perth for a 2-hr. stop before a high-speed dash back to Sydney, covering the 2,047 mi. in a record 4 hrs. 22 min. The Comet 3 was considered the development precursor to the stretched Comet 4.

1955 December 10 The Ryan X-13 Vertijet made its first flight powered by a 10,000-lb. s.t. Rolls Royce Avon RA.28-49 engine. Designed as a nonvectoring vertical takeoff and landing

research aircraft, it had a delta-wing span of 21 ft., a length of 23 ft. 5 in. and a large vertical tail giving a height of 15 ft. 3 in. Designed to be launched vertically, then transition to horizontal flight, it gave some impressive demonstrations.

1955 December 12 De Havilland Comet 3 G-ANLO left Sydney, Australia on the second part of its round-the-world flight that began December 2. Crossing the Tasman Sea to Auckland in 2 hrs. 40 min. it flew to Fiji in 2 hr. 54 min. and from there to Honolulu, covering the 3,178 mi. in 6 hr. 56 min. and arriving December 14. Two days later it made the 2,707-mi. flight to Vancouver in 5 hr. 48 min., becoming the first jet airliner to cross the Pacific Ocean.

1955 December 15 The Bell X-1E, the re-built #2 X-1, made its first powered flight with NACA test pilot Joseph A. Walker. It had been modified to carry a very thin, 4% thickness/chord ratio wing. Powered by an advanced XLR-11 engine, the X-1E reached a speed of Mach 2.24 (1,478 MPH) on October 8, 1957, the second highest speed achieved in the X-1 program. The last X-1E flight, its 26th and the last of all X-1 flights, was flown November 6, 1958. All but the last four, flown by John McKay, were made by Joseph Walker.

1955 December 18 The Beech 73 Jet Mentor, the first U.S. lightweight, single-engined turbojet trainer, made its first flight as a private venture in the vain hope of persuading the USAF to adopt it. Powered by a 920-lb. s.t. Continental YT69-T-9, it had a wingspan of 32 ft. 9 in., a length of 30 ft. and a maximum weight of 4,450 lb. At one point, it appeared the Royal Canadian Air Force might buy the type, but nothing came of negotiations.

1955 December 20 The round-the-world publicity flight of Comet 3 G-ANLO, the first carried out by a jet airliner completed its journey at 10:51 A.M. when it landed at Hatfield, England, having traveled a cumulative distance of 29,934 mi. in a total flying time of 66 hr. 43 min. The Comet 3 had left Vancouver on December 18, flying to Toronto and Montreal before making the 3,240 mi. crossing of the Atlantic in 6 hr. 18 min., becoming the first jet aircraft to circumnavigate the globe.

1955 December 28 May Hymans, president of Air France, announced reservations for 24 French-built Süd-Est Caravelle jet airliners and 10 Boeing four-jet airliners based on the Model 367-80 and known as the 707. The Belgian airline Sabena also announced it would reserve options on 3 Boeing 707s. On December 21, SAS had ordered seven DC-8s at a cost of $14.3 million including spare parts.

1956 January 8 Pan American announced that it had carried a record number of passengers across the North Atlantic in 1955, an announcement that did little to quell fears that the airline was about to become a monopoly. In 1955, Pan American flew 20,851 people from the United States to Europe, representing a 36% increase over the total for 1954. With a spate of new orders for turboprop and jet airliners, the U.S. aviation industry as a whole reported a boom for manufacturing and servicing sectors.

1956 January 18 Lt. Gen. Donald L. Putt, USAF deputy chief of staff for development, called a meeting with senior officers at the Pentagon to discuss a proposed high-altitude, hydrogen-fueled reconnaissance aircraft presented to him on a recent visit from the chief of Lockheed's design department (known as the "skunk works"), Clarence L. ("Kelly") Johnson. Putt wanted a 6-mon. period for study and experiment and appointed Norman C. Appold to study hydrogen-fueled engine work and report back to him.

1956 January 20   The first prototype Supermarine N.113 (Type 544) bearing the serial WT854 made its first flight from Boscome Down, England, with Mike Lithgow at the controls. The swept-wing N.113 had an area-ruled fuselage and a powerful Rolls Royce Avon 200 series engine. It had evolved from the straight-wing Type 508 jet, which carried a butterfly tail. The Type 508 was redesignated the Type 525 when it acquired swept-back wings. When the design configuration of the Type 525 was given a conventional swept-back tail, it became the Type 544 (N.113). The Type 544 was precursor to the Scimitar, which was to appear in 1957 as the first Royal Navy fighter capable of supersonic flight and the first for the Fleet Air Arm designed to carry atomic weapons.

1956 January 25   The British Ministry of Supply announced that it had set up a research project involving BOAC, BEA, Avro, de Havilland, Bristol, Handley Page, Rolls Royce, Short Brothers and Vickers-Armstrong to examine the prospect for a British supersonic transport (SST). For more then a year each company had employed small teams to work on theoretical concepts for such an aircraft.

1956 February 1   Plans were announced for the creation of a pilot training scheme for the new Luftwaffe, a scheme put together by the Air Planning Group at the West German Ministry of Aviation. Projected equipment levels envisaged a force of 1,320 jet-powered combat aircraft and propeller-driven transports, with 324 Hawker Hunters purchased from the United Kingdom. Other aircraft would include F-84s, F-86s and F-100s in a total of four fighter wings, eight fighter-bomber wings, three reconnaissance wings and five transport wings.

1956 February 10   One of the great pioneers of military aviation in Britain, a staunch advocate of strategic air power and the first chief of the Air Staff (1918), the Right Hon. Sir Hugh Montague Trenchard, GCB, OM, GCVO, DSO, first Viscount and Baron of Wolfreton, died at his home in Sloane Avenue, London at the age of 83. Known affectionately as the "Father of the Royal Air Force," Trenchard was born February 3, 1873. He failed examinations for military service but joined the militia, and in 1895 went to India where he met Winston Churchill. Trenchard served in South Africa during the Boer War (1899–1902) and joined the Royal Flying Corps in 1912. During World War I (1914–18), Trenchard became commandant of the RFC and established offensive strategies adopted by the RAF when it was formed in 1918.

1956 February 20   Reporting back to Lt. Gen. Donald L. Putt, USAF, at the Pentagon on prospects for building a hydrogen-fueled test engine, Norman C. Appold recommended that Pratt & Whitney be given a contract to build one. The recommendation was approved and given the project name Suntan. Lockheed was contracted for six CL-400 hydrogen-burning reconnaissance aircraft designed to fly at Mach 2.5, 100,000 ft. above the earth. Contracts for competing designs were eventually let, and a design from Boeing received favor for a while, but the whole idea was dropped.

1956 February 20   A new helicopter charter service began in Norway under the name of Helikopter Service A/S with the objective of flying passengers and freight to the more remote areas of the country. The helicopter was ideally suited for these duties, and technical developments and improved performance helped encourage new services to exploit rotary-winged aircraft. Helikopter Service A/S eventually moved into oil-rig supply services for North Sea platforms.

1956 February 24   No. 46 (Fighter) Sqdn, RAF, took delivery of the first operational Gloster Javelin delta-wing, two-seat, all-weather fighter following interminable delays due to accidents and development problems. Over the next decade, a total 406 Javelins in improved variants would enter service, the last finally being released from RAF service in April 1968. The type incorporated U.S. radar, and later versions were equipped with Firestreak anti-aircraft missiles.

1956 March 8   Lockheed Aircraft Corp. announced that the Royal Dutch airline KLM had placed an order for 12 of the new 66–85 seat Lockheed Electra airliners. This was the first European order for a U.S. turboprop airliner and raised confidence that the company had been right to aim for the medium-haul market and not compete with Boeing and Douglas in the long-haul jet market.

1956 March 10   The world air speed record was claimed by a British pilot flying a British aircraft. In the last hour of morning, Peter Twiss flew the Fairey F.D.2 (serial no. WG774) at 38,000 ft. on two timed runs between the south coast town of Chichester and Royal Naval Air Station Ford. The first run was clocked at 1,117 MPH and the return (westerly) run was at 1,147 MPH giving a mean of 1,132 MPH (1,821.39 km/hr.) or Mach 1.731. It beat the old record of August 20, 1955, by 310 MPH (38%) and was the first FAI speed claim to exceed 1,000 MPH. This was the last time a British pilot flying a British aircraft would break the absolute air speed record.

1956 March 20   The USAF Air Research and Development Command issued a contract to Bell Aero-systems for Reconnaissance System 459L (named Brass Bell). On September 21, 1955, Bell had received a Special Reconnaissance System 118P contract emphasizing altitude in a Mach 15 rocket-launched vehicle, but Brass Bell emphasized range. In June, System Requirement 126 Project ROBO (ROcket-BOmber) contracts were awarded to numerous aircraft manufacturers in the United States.

1956 March 22   The prototype Tu-104 (Registration no. SSSR-L5400) flew into London's Heathrow Airport, causing intense interest. Just after midday, an RAF PR Canberra (serial no. WT512) flew slowly over the top of the Tu-104. Unknown officially in the west until its arrival, the aircraft carried Gen. Ivan Serov, head of Soviet security services on a mission to prepare for the visit of Nikita Khrushchev and Marshal Bulganin to England in April.

1956 March   NACA became aware of USAF Air Research and Development Command studies initiated this month on two projects: a manned ballistic rocket system and a manned glide rocket system. Envisaged as a successor to the X-15 and capable of Mach 12, the manned glide rocket was of interest to NACA, and a study group was set up by Floyd Thompson to investigate the concept. It would focus on research objectives and goals, setting Mach 15 as the target for a boost-glide concept incorporating interference lift integrating the aerodynamic effects of wings and fuselage instead of treating them separately.

1956 April 5   The first fully arrested deck landing of the de Havilland Sea Vixen took place aboard HMS *Ark Royal* with the semi-navalized prototype XT828, which had been built at Christchurch, England. It would be March 20, 1957 before the first fully navalized Sea Vixen (XJ474) took to the air. It had a hydraulically steerable nose wheel, folding wings which reduced the span from 51 ft. to 22 ft. 3 in. and incorporated a pointed nose radome.

1956 April 23   The first Douglas C-33 Cargomaster flew with a crew commanded by J. C. Armstrong. Conceived by USAF in 1951, the requirement stemmed from lessons in the Korean War. The C-133 was a high-wing transport capable of lifting 110,000 lb. of cargo comprising anything from ballistic missiles to jeeps. With a wingspan of 179 ft. 8 in. and a length of 157 ft. 6 in. it had a gross weight of 286,000 lb. and was powered by four 6,500-SHP Pratt & Whitney T34-P-7WA turboprops. The C-133A could carry 52,000 lb. a distance of 4,000 mi. Military Air Transport Service took delivery of the first of 35 in late 1957.

1956 April 25   Th increasingly dominant position U.S. aircraft manufacturers were gaining in the airliner market was strengthened by several different orders. Orders totaling 128 Lockheed Electra turboprop airliners were reached when Western Air Lines announced it would buy nine aircraft for $7 million. On April 24, Deutsche Lufthansa had announced orders for four Boeing 707 jet airliners, and on May 9, Trans-Canada Air Lines announced orders for four DC-8s.

1956 May 1   The German firm of Bölkow-Entwicklungen K.G. was founded from a civil engineering company that had been formed 3 yr. earlier in Stuttgart by Ludwig Bölkow. The company was to play an important role in the future development of an indigenous German aerospace industry when its design team merged in 1959 with those of Messerschmitt and Heinkel. It quickly became the most diversified company in the German aerospace industry, developing sporting, touring and sailplane aircraft as well as helicopters, electronics and rockets.

1956 May 17   The Douglas DC-7C ''Seven Seas'' received its certificate of airworthiness. Powered by four 3,400-HP Wright R-3350-18EA-1 radials, the aircraft had a cruising speed of 355 MPH, a maximum range of 5,640 mi. and a maximum gross takeoff weight of 143,000 lb. The DC-7C represented the peak of piston-engine airliner development and a total of 121 would enter service, Pan American becoming the first operator on June 1.

1956 May 20   The first hydrogen bomb dropped from an aircraft was released from a B-52 of the Ninety-third Bombardment Wing piloted by Maj. David Critchlow during a series of intensive tests under Operation Redwing carried out in the vicinity of Bikini Atoll. The test event was named Cherokee, and the device was a B-36 bomb developed jointly by the USAF, U.S. Navy and Los Alamos Scientific Laboratory. It was detonated at a height of 4,350 ft. with a probable explosive yield of 2 megatons.

1956 June 20   The U.S. Navy commissioned the first in a new class of ships, the amphibious assault ship USS *Thetis Bay*, a former escort carrier modified from the *Anzio* class to carry 15 to 20 helicopters. The Korean War had revealed a specific need for helicopter assault capabilities, and conversion of an existing hull was the quickest and cheapest method of achieving support for that.

1956 June 21   Convair announced orders for 40 of its planned CV-880 four-jet airliners, 30 going to Trans World Airlines and 10 to Delta Airlines. Convair had announced in April plans to build a smaller, faster competitor to the Boeing 707 and Douglas DC-8. The aircraft was first called simply *Convair Skylark*, then

Golden Arrow and finally *Convair 660* before its definitive designation CV-880.

1956 June 24   During the Tushino Air Display in Moscow, two new Sukhoi fighters, a swept-wing Su-7 and a delta-wing Su-9, appeared in public for the first time. Permitted after Stalin's death to reopen his design bureau, Pavel Sukhoi produced in 1955–56 the first in a line of top-class combat aircraft. The Su-7 was powered by a 19,842-lb. s.t. turbojet and went into service during 1958. About 2,000 Su-9 and Su-11 derivatives, each powered by a 22,046-lb. s.t. engine, were built for operational use beginning in 1959.

1956 June 29   North American was awarded a U.S. Navy letter contract for design and development of the A3J nuclear attack aircraft. With high performance and all-weather capability among carrier-based aircraft it was second in size and weight only to the Douglas Skywarrior. The aircraft was to incorporate a wide range of highly advanced concepts and be capable of Mach 2 performance at a great range. In 1962 the designation was changed to AJ-5 and the aircraft became known as the *Vigilante*.

1956 June 30   The worst civil air disaster to date resulted in 128 people losing their lives when a Lockheed L-1049 Super Constellation of Trans World Airlines and a United Airlines DC-7 collided over the Grand Canyon in Arizona. The two aircraft had departed Los Angeles Airport three minutes apart, the Super Constellation bound for Kansas City, Kans., the DC-7 for Washington, D.C. Heavy thunderstorms were in the area and both aircraft were flying on similar patterns when the Constellation requested to fly at 1,000 ft. above the cloud ceiling of 20,000 ft. while the DC-7 was at a fixed height of 21,000 ft.

1956 July 4   The first operational U-2 spyplane flight took place when a single aircraft known as Article 347—(no U-2 had serial numbers or block plates on any part)—took off from Wiesbaden, West Germany. Operated for the CIA, two aircraft had been moved in April from Groom Lake, Calif. to a clandestine unit named First Weather Reconnaissance Squadron Provisional located at Lakenheath, England. The flight carried the U-2 over Moscow, Leningrad and the Baltic. The CIA aircraft could be detected by Soviet air defense radar and on the second flight they protested, but the U.S. did not respond or acknowledge the protest.

1956 July 7   The D.H.106 Comet C.Mk.2 entered service with No. 216 Squadron, RAF, at RAF Transport Command, Lyneham, England when the first of 10 arrived for duty with the world's first military jet air transport unit. It had a capacity for only 44 people, and the RAF received in February 1962 the first of five Comet C.4s with capacity for 94 and an increased cruising speed of 542 MPH. The type was retired in June 1975.

1956 July 23   The Dassault Etendard II made its first flight powered by two 2,425-lb. s.t. Turboméca Gabizo turbojets. Derived from the Mystère family, the aircraft was smaller, with swept surfaces and a tricycle landing gear. Developed in response to NATO interest, it was abandoned in favor of the Etendard VI, which had a single 4,859-lb. s.t. Bristol Siddeley Orpheus BOr.12 and first flew on March 16, 1957. When Fiat got the contract to build the G.91 to the NATO Basic Military Requirement No.1 (NBMR-1), it too was dropped.

1956 July 24   Developed as a private venture to free the design from the rigid specification of Nato requirement (NBMR.1), Dassault carried out the first flight of the Etendard IV, which was ordered by the Aéronavale. With power provided by a 9,700-lb.

s.t. SNECMA Atar 08B turbojet, the Etendard IVM interceptor entered service in January 1962 aboard the French carriers *Clemenceau* and *Foch*. It had a wingspan of 31 ft. 6 in., a length of 47 ft. 3 in., a top speed of Mach 1.08 and a combat radius of up to 1,000 mi.

1956 August 9 The prototype Fiat G.91 single-seat tactical strike and light reconnaissance aircraft made its first flight powered by a Fiat-built 5,000-lb. s.t. Bristol Siddeley Orpheus 803 turbojet. With a wingspan of 28 ft., the aircraft had a gross weight of 12,125 lb., a top speed of 668 MPH at sea level and a combat radius of 200 mi. As a ground attack fighter, the G.91 became operational with the Italian Air Force in February 1959 and with the German air force under a license-built agreement.

1956 August 21 A new U.S. national FAI-ratified air speed record and a speed record for U.S. combat aircraft was set when Comdr. R. W. Winslow, U.S. Navy, flew a Chance-Vought F-8U1 Crusader at a measured speed of 1,015.428 MPH over the Mojave Desert, Calif.

1956 August 23 The first nonstop helicopter flight across the continental United States was completed when a Piasecki H-21 covered the 2,160 mi. between San Diego and Washington, D.C. in 31 hrs. 40 min. The USAF bought 201 H-21s, and the U.S. Army purchased 334 and used them for cargo transport and the movement of personnel, each helicopter capable of lifting 14 troops or 12 stretchers. In U.S. Army service, it was given the name Shawnee.

1956 August 31 The first Boeing KC-135A (serial no. 55-3118) made its first flight and was taken over by the USAF on January 31, 1957. Named Stratotanker, it became operational with the Ninety-third Air Refueling Squadron on June 18, 1957, with a flying boom assembly providing fuel at a maximum transfer rate of 1,000 gal./min. The entire internal load of 31,200 gal. could be used either by the KC-135A or its recipient charges.

1956 September 2 A Vickers Valiant piloted by Wg. Comdr. L. H. Trent landed at RAF Marham, England after having been the first V-bomber to cross the Atlantic nonstop. It had taken off from Loring AFB, Maine and made the journey in 6 hr. 25 min. The outward flight had been made 2 wk. earlier by way of Prestwick, Scotland and Goose Bay, Newfoundland.

1956 September 10 Originating as a developed version of the F-100 Super Sabre, the North American YF-107A made its first flight powered by a 17,220/24,500-lb. s.t. Pratt & Whitney YJ75-P-9 turbojet. With a split intake above the fuselage directly behind the cockpit, the aircraft had area ruling, a swept-wing span of 36 ft. 7 in., a length of 61 ft. 10 in. and a gross weight of 39,750 lb. Although the YF-107A displayed a top speed of 1,295 MPH at 36,000 ft., Tactical Air Command chose the Republic F-105, and the F-100 became the last fighter ever built by North American.

1956 September 15 The Indian Air Force ordered 25 Folland Gnat single-seat lightweight fighters and negotiated for the license manufacture of the type by Hindustin Aircraft Ltd., Bangalore, India. The Gnat proved a modest seller, being purchased by Finland and Yugoslavia in addition to serving with the RAF as an advanced trainer. In the fighter role, it had a top speed of Mach 0.98, a climb time of 5 min. 15 sec. to 45,000 ft. and a 500-mi. radius of action.

1956 September 15 The Tupolev Tu-104 went into regularly scheduled service with Aeroflot on its Moscow-Omsk-Irkutsk route. At this time, it was the only turbojet airliner in service (since the withdrawal of the Comet 1 series in April 1954). BOAC would not fly the Comet 4 series on scheduled services for another two years. During this month, the Tu-104A set many records with payload/altitude and load-carrying capabilities.

1956 September 24 The reconstituted German air force formally came into existence as the Luftwaffe der Deutschen Bundesrepublik. On October 7, RAF chief of the Air Staff, Sir Dermot Boyle, who had succeeded Marshal of the Royal Air Force Sir Bertram Dickson on January 1, hosted a delegation led by Lt. Gen. Josef Kammhuber, who had commanded Luftflotte 5 during World War II. The visitors remained in Britain through October 13 and were given tours of industrial facilities, RAF bases and research establishments.

1956 September 27 Just 20 days after setting an unofficial altitude record for manned aircraft of 126,200 ft., the sole remaining Bell X-2 was lost along with its pilot Capt. Melburn Apt. The X-2 was released from its EB-50D at 31,800 ft. and 230 MPH and, on full thrust, accelerated to Mach 1 at 43,000 ft. and a gradual nose-over at 72,000 ft. Descending on a shallow flight line to 62,000 ft., the X-2 reached Mach 3.196 (2,094 MPH) and lost control to inertia coupling. Apt jettisoned the escape capsule but was unable to release his parachute.

1956 October 1 During final approach into London Airport, Avro Vulcan serial no. XA897 carrying A. M. Sir Harry Broadhurst, commander-in-chief, RAF Bomber Command, and six crewmembers crashed when the aircraft touched down short of the concrete runway, tore off its landing gear and went out of control. Broadhurst and the pilot, Sqdn. Ldr. D. R. Howard, ejected safely, but the other four, in downward firing seats, were killed. The Vulcan had just completed a 26,000-mi. goodwill tour of the Far East.

1956 October 10 To meet the challenge of the Douglas DC-7C, the first airliner capable of flying nonstop in either direction across the North Atlantic, the Lockheed L-1649 Starliner made its first flight. Supported by an order for 25 aircraft from TWA, it was a complete redesign of the L-1049 Super Constellation. With a wingspan of 150 ft. and a length of 116 ft. 2 in., it had a gross weight of 160,000 lb., capacity for 99 passengers and four 3,400-HP Wright 988TC-18EA-2 Turbo-Compound engines moved further outboard for quieter travel.

1956 October 11 The first British air-dropped atomic bomb was released from a Vickers Valiant of No. 49 Squadron, RAF, commanded by Sqdn. Ldr. E. J. G. Flavell over Maralinga, Southern Australia. The device exploded with a yield of 10 kilotons. In all, two Valiants, 10 Canberras, four Hastings, two Whirlwind helicopters and four Varsities supported the test. Britain's first atomic test had been conducted on October 3, 1952, in the Monte Bello islands off the northern coast of Australia aboard the frigate HMS *Plym*.

1956 October 20 Flt. Lt. A. W. ("Bill") Bedford, RAF, flew a Hunter T.Mk.7 from London to Rome, a distance of 891.7 mi. in a time of 1 hr. 34 min. 28.5 sec. at an average speed of 566.1 MPH. Five days later he returned with the same aircraft in a time of 1 hr. 40 min. 9.7 sec. at an average speed of 533.93 MPH. Both flights represented record flights for point-to-point times and no doubt were used by the company in the strenuous efforts already under way to sell the Hunter overseas.

1956 October 22 Just 16 mon. after starting design work on a contender for Weapon System SS443-L, the Bell Model 204 helicopter made its first flight as the XH-40. In June 1955, Bell won the U.S. Army competition for a helicopter to carry out general utility work, evacuate casualties and train pilots. The production model designated HU-1A Iroquois had a length of 42 ft. 8 in., a rotor diameter of 44 ft., a width of 8 ft. 3 in. and 700-SHP Lycoming T53-L-1A turboshaft engine, making it the first turbine-powered aircraft in U.S. Army service.

1956 October 30 At 3:00 P.M. an order was given to the RAF to prepare for the bombing of Egyptian airfields and at 4:15 Egypt was given an ultimatum to the effect that unless it withdrew its forces from the Suez Canal region force would be used to eject them. Egyptian Pres. Gamal Abdel Nasser had nationalized the canal on July 26 and moved troops in to control the flow of international shipping contravening an agreement signed by Egypt. A combined French/British force was mobilized and neutralization of Egypt's air potential was considered prerequisite for early success.

1956 October 30 A U.S. Navy Douglas R4D under the command of Rear Adm. G. L. Dufek landed on the ice at the South Pole using skis attached to the landing gear legs. Not since Robert Falcon Scott stood on the same spot in January 1912 had men vested that precise location. The R4D was a variant of the DC-3, 568 transports of which had been procured by the navy.

1956 October 31 The first British air attack on Egypt began at 7:30 P.M. when aircraft from Malta took off, joined two hours later by aircraft from Cyprus. The RAF had five squadrons of Canberra B.6s and four squadrons of Valiant B.1s at Malta and seven squadrons of the Canberra B.2 on Cyprus, a total of 285 aircraft. The first bombs were dropped at 10:30 P.M. by a Canberra (serial no. WH853) of No. 12 Squadron, RAF. The Royal Navy flew Sea Hawks against targets bringing to 500 the total number of sorties flown by the allies this day. On the following day, some Egyptian aircraft escaped south.

1956 November 2 Continuing the air attacks on Egyptian targets, French carrier aircraft joined in with strikes on Port Said. From November 3, tactical targets were attacked, and Royal Navy carriers supported air operations with HMS *Eagle* and HMS *Albion* in the eastern Mediterranean. HMS *Eagle* withdrew on November 4, a day the Royal Navy carriers flew 355 sorties.

1956 November 5 The final phase of the air operation against Egyptian forces began when 27 Hastings and Valettas from six squadrons dropped 600 paratroopers of the Third Battalion, Parachute Regiment, and part of No. 16 Parachute Brigade on locations around the Suez Canal. Air support was provided by aircraft from HMS *Albion* and HMS *Eagle* while HMS *Bulwark* withdrew to rearm and take on fresh supplies. The French dropped 500 men from Noratlas and C-47 aircraft, and these were reinforced by 100 British troops the same day. The drops were a complete success.

1956 November 5 Set up by the British Ministry of Aviation, the Supersonic Transport (SST) Aircraft Committee met for the first time chaired by Morien B. Morgan. In 1954 he had reported findings of a small committee from the Advance Fighter Project Group set up to look at the possibility of building an SST. In attendance were representatives for nine British aircraft manufacturers and four engine builders. The committee ordered detailed studies from Handley Page of their Mach 2.2 H.P.109 design and from Bristol of their Mach 2.2 Type 198. The latter would even-

tually be rescoped into the Type 221 and then the Type 223 with four Olympus engines.

1956 November 6 The USAF Air Research and Development Command formally grouped its work on a manned glide rocket system begun during March into Project HYWARDS, an acronym for hypersonic weapons research and development system, defined as System Requirement 131. This was a support research program combining Brass Bell and ROBO.

1956 November 7 A ceasefire in the Suez Canal area was ordered, taking effect from 2:00 A.M. On the previous day, a Canberra had been shot down by an Egyptian MiG-17. In all, the allied forces destroyed 260 Egyptian aircraft on the ground, the RAF dropped 1,439 (1,000-lb.) bombs, Canberras flew 278 sorties, Valiants flew 49 sorties, and the RAF flew 44 photo-reconnaissance missions. HMS *Eagle* carried out 621 sorties, dropped 72 (1,000-lb.) bombs, 157 (500-lb.) bombs and launched 1,448 air-to-ground rockets.

1956 November 8 The world altitude record for balloons was raised to 76,000 ft. by Lt. Comdr. M. L. Lewis, U.S. Navy, and Malcolm D. Ross in the gondola of a plastic balloon named *Stratolab*. They ascended from Rapid City, S.D. and descended to a point near Kennedy, Nebr., 175 mi. away from their starting point. The previous record had been set in 1935.

1956 November 11 Test pilot B. A. Erickson piloted the prototype Convair XB-58 (serial no. 55-0660) from Fort Worth, Tex. With an area-ruled fuselage, four 15,600-lb. s.t. General Electric J79-GE-5A engines and a delta wing, the production B-58A had a wingspan of 56 ft. 10 in., a length of 96 ft. 9 in., a gross weight of 163,000 lb. and a maximum refueled weight of 176,890 lb. Not for nearly 3 yr. would the first production aircraft fly, but this Mach 2+ nuclear bomber was more than 200 MPH faster than any fighter in the sky.

1956 November 11 A 2-wk. mass exercise involving more than 1,000 B-47s and KC-97s of the USAF Strategic Air Command ended successfully. The exercise had been two closely coordinated operations called Power House and Road Block and represented the peak of Strategic Air Command efficiency with its new and growing fleet of jet bombers. Ten years after its formation, Strategic Air Command's operational bomber fleet had grown tenfold and included 148 B-36s, 1,306 B-47s and 97 B-52s.

1956 November 18 The enduring family of French delta-wing fighters of the Dassault Mirage line began with the first flight of the Mirage III-001. In just a month it had exceeded Mach 1.5 and with a 9,900-lb. s.t. Atar 101G2 and with a supplementary rocket boost motor reached Mach 1.8. With superior performance and adaptability, the French ordered the type into production as their primary single-seat, multi-mission combat aircraft.

1956 November 24 In a 2-day exercise named Quick Kick that began today, four B-52s of the Ninety-third Bombardment Wing joined four B-52s from the Forty-second Bombardment Wing for a nonstop flight around the perimeter of the United States. The most notable achievement was that of Lt. Col. Marcus L. Hill Jr., who flew his B-52 from Castle AFB, Md. around the 15,535-mi. perimeter in 31 hrs. 30 min. via four in-flight refuelings from KC-97 tankers. Had the KC-135 been available, it was estimated the flight would have taken only 28.5 hrs.

1956 November 28 The world's first jet vertical takeoff and landing (VTOL) transition from the vertical to horizontal flight took place 6,000 ft. over Edwards AFB, Calif. when the Ryan X-13 Vertijet was put through its paces. Designed to operate from a transport trailer, it did just that for the first time publicly on April 11, 1957, and on July 30, 1957, gave a stunning impression of what the future held for VTOL technology before 3,000 people outside the Pentagon in Washington. Unfortunately, the future held nothing for the X-13 itself, which was canceled a year later.

1956 December 3 Northeast Airlines of Boston, Mass. announced a deal with the Bristol Aeroplane Co. for a fleet of five Britannia-series 305 airliners, the first deliveries to take place in October 1957. These negotiations fell through, however, and the aircraft were sold off to charter companies in the United States and Latin America.

1956 December 13 In the USAF Air Research and Development Command altitude simulation chamber at Dayton, Ohio, Maj. Arnold I. Beck was given a simulated altitude of 198,770 ft. wearing a protective suit and helmet. This was only 65,230 ft. short of the actual altitude at which the atmosphere ends and the vacuum of space begins.

1956 December 17 The first taxi trials of the Short SC.1 (serial no. XG905) VTOL aircraft took place at the Belfast, Northern Ireland factory. With a wingspan of 23 ft. 6 in. and a length of 29 ft. 10 in., the SC.1 was powered by a group of four lightweight 2,000-lb. s.t. Rolls Royce RB.108 engines, developed as VTOL engines following tests with the "Flying Bedstead" and installed thrusting directly down. A fifth engine of the same type was to provide horizontal propulsion.

1956 December 23 The first of five flights with a specially modified Martin B-57 equipped with a hydrogen fuel system for one of its two engines and a conventional JP-4 fuel system for the other took place. The first test was not a great sucess, but the third through fifth tests beginning February 13, 1957, went well. The tests were part of the Bee Project, formulated and organized by Col. Norman C. Appold of the power plant laboratory at the Wright Air Development Center in the fall of 1955.

1956 December 26 The prototype Convair F-106A made its first flight from Edwards AFB, Calif. Designed to Weapon System WS201B as an improved F-102, it soon became a completely new aircraft powered by a 17,200/24,500-lb. s.t. Pratt & Whitney J75-P-17 turbojet providing a top speed of 1,327 MPH and an initial climb rate of 42,800 ft./min. With a delta-wing span of 38 ft. 3 in. and an area-ruled fuselage length of 70 ft. 9 in., the F-106A Delta Dart was, like its predecessor, armed exclusively with rockets and missiles.

1957 January 11 The first production Supermarine N.113 Scimitar (serial no. XD212) made its first flight powered by two 11,250-lb. s.t. Rolls Royce Avon Mk.202 turbojets. It had a wingspan of 37 ft. 2 in. and a length of 20 ft. 6 in. with a gross weight of about 40,000 lb. Armament comprised four 30-mm Aden cannons and provision for up to four 1,000-lb. bombs, rockets or missiles. The Royal Navy took delivery of the first Scimitar and formed up No. 803 Squadron during mid-1958 for service about HMS *Victorious*. The last of 76 Scimitars was delivered in 1960.

1957 January 16 Five B-52Bs of the Ninety-third Bombardment Wing, commanded by Maj. Gen. Archie J. Old, Jr., commander of the U.S. Fifteenth Air Force, began Operation Power Flite, the first nonstop round-the-world flight by turbojet aircraft.

The lead aircraft *Lucky Lady III* (serial no. 53-0394) was commanded by Lt. Col. James H. Morris. Supported by KC-97 tankers, one B-52B had been unable to take on fuel at the first rendezvous point and a second, spare aircraft landed at Brize Norton, England. The other three went on to complete their flight, landing at March AFB, Calif., having flown 24,325 mi. in 45 hr. 19 min.

1957 January A NACA study group set up by Floyd Thompson to work on the USAF Project HYWARDS concept issued its first report suggesting Mach 18 as the design goal, carrying aerothermodynamics far beyond the level that would be achieved with the Mach 7 X-15. During the year, the proposed configuration was tested in wind tunnels at Langley Laboratory. This work would lead to an aerodynamic configuration eventually selected for the NASA Space Shuttle. Ames Aeronautical Laboratory meanwhile came up with configurations from which would emerge the "lifting body" concepts.

1957 February 1 BOAC began using the first of their 91-seat Bristol Britannia 102-series turboprop airliners, known affectionately as the "whispering giant," and introduced it on to the London-Johannesburg service via Rome, Khartoum and Nairobi on a scheduled time of 22 hr. 50 min. Cruising speed was 362 MPH for the new airliner. Later, BOAC introduced the Britannia on its services to Australia, Tokyo, Colombo, Singapore and Hong Kong.

1957 February 13 BEA began operations with their new, improved Vickers Viscount 802 turboprop airliner, the first of which, *Sebastian Cabot* (G-AOJD), was put on the London-Glasgow route. The first international flight, London to Amsterdam, was on February 15. With four 1,900-SHP Rolls Royce Dart R.Da.7/1 MK 525 engines providing a cruising speed of 357 MPH, the 800 series evolved into a "stretched" Viscount with a fuselage length of 85 ft. 8 in. (versus 88 ft. 11 in. on the first series), a range of 1,610 mi. and capacity for up to 65 passengers.

1957 February 19 The first ascent and hover by a "flat-riser" VTOL aircraft took place when the experimental Bell X-14 sucessfully lifted into the air. Powered by two 1,750-lb. s.t. Armstrong Siddeley Viper A.S.V.8 turbojets with exhaust deflected directly down through the center of gravity or toward the rear, the X-14 had a length of 25 ft. and a wingspan of 34 ft. with a gross weight of 4,269 lb. It differed from the "tail sitters" by ascending with the longitudinal axis parallel to the ground rather than perpendicular to it.

1957 March 5 Grumman won a U.S. Navy competition for a new airborne early warning and air intercept control (AEW/AIC) aircraft with its Design 123 concept and began work on mockups, which were inspected October 14–18. The navy wanted aircraft in this category with a higher cruising altitude so that greater areas of the sea and the sky could be covered. The navy placed an initial order in December for the design that would mature into the E2 Hawkeye.

1957 March 7 In a brilliant adaptation of the Antonov An-8 twin-piston engine transport aircraft, the An-10 Ukraina made its first flight piloted by Ya. I. Vernikov and V. P. Vazin. Utilizing four 4,000-EHP Ivchyenko turboprops, the An-10 had a length of 105 ft., a wingspan of 124 ft. 8 in. and provision for up to 90 passengers. It entered service with Aeroflot in July 1959 and was hailed by the Soviets as the "most economical airliner in the world," a valid statement only when operating costs incorporated subsidized fuel.

1957 March 11   A Lockheed L-1049H Super Constellation convertible cargo/passenger aircraft carried a record nonmilitary load of 41,746 lb. between Newark, N.J., and Burbank, Calif., a distance of 2,451 mi. The L-1049H was the last civil version of the Super Constellation and had first flown on September 20, 1956. In all, 53 were built for 14 customers. As with the L-1049G, wingtip tanks could be carried, increasing fuel capacity to 7,750 gal.

1957 March 15   A U.S. Navy ZPG-2 nonrigid airship set a new unrefueled endurance record when it landed, having remained aloft for 264 hr. (11 days) 12 min., beating the record set by the *Graf Zeppelin* in 1929. Commanded by Comdr. J. R. Hunt, the 1,011,000 cu. ft. airship took off from its base at Weymouth, Mass. on March 4 and flew to Africa, then returned to Key West, Fl. The airship was 343 ft. in length and powered by two Wright R-1300-2 Cyclone radial engines.

1957 March 20   The first production de Havilland D.H.110 Sea Vixen F.A.W.1 (serial no. XJ474) made its first flight at Christchurch, England. It took part in sea trials aboard HMS *Ark Royal* and together with the second aircraft (serial no. XJ475) made 166 deck landings on HMS *Centaur*. The first Sea Vixen unit, No. 892 Squadron, RNAS, became operational on the type July 2, 1959, almost eight years after the first flight of the D.H.110. Powered by two 10,000-lb. s.t. Rolls Royce Avon 208 turbojets, it had a wingspan of 50 ft., a length of 55 ft. 7 in. and a gross weight of 37,000 lb.

1957 March 25   The Vought F-8A Crusader became operational with U.S. Navy Squadron VF-32 based at Cecil Field, Fl. The Crusader had a wingspan of 35 ft. 2 in., a length of 54 ft. 6 in. and a gross weight of 34,000 lb. Although employed as a carrier-based fighter, it could carry up 5,000 lb. of ordnance and four fixed forward-firing 20-mm Colt cannons. An RF-8A version had flown on December 17, 1956, and 14 were supplied to the navy. The first of 187 F-8Es with a 16,900-lb. s.t. Pratt & Whitney J57-P-20A was delivered in January 1959.

1957 March 27   Developed for use by USAF Air Defense Command as a long-range interceptor to specifications for Weapon System WS-217A, the two-seat McDonnell F-101B made its first flight. It now had the capacity to carry two Douglas MB-1 (Genie) nuclear air-to-air rockets as well as three Falcon missiles in its weapons bay. Its mission would be to fire nuclear missiles into massed formations of enemy bombers. The F-101B had a length of 71 ft. 1 in., a gross weight of 52,400 lb. and a combat radius of 694 mi.

1957 March 28   The prototype Canadair CL-28 Argus made its first flight from Cartierville, Canada, piloted by W. S. Longhurst and crew. Adapted to the RCAF need for a maritime patrol replacement for Avro Lancasters by using the wing, tail and landing gear of the Bristol Britannia, it had a wingspan of 142 ft. 3 in. and a length of 128 ft. 3 in. Powered from four 3,700-HP Wright R-3370 TC981 EA-1 engines, it had a cruising speed of 207 MPH and a range of 5,086 mi.

1957 March   Project engineer Ralph Hooper at Hawker Aircraft Ltd. prepared an initial layout drawing of a VTOL proposal given the company project designation P.1127. It evolved from an idea put forward by French engineer Michel Wibault whereby a conventional aircraft engine could be made to direct its exhaust through two or four involutes directed backwards or downwards by swivel action thus permitting vertical or horizontal flight according to

the vector of the exhaust flow. Bristol devised such an engine known as the BE.53.

1957 April 1   The first of the USAF Strategic Air Command's seven tactical fighter wings (operating F-84s) to be phased out of Strategic Air Command was transferred to Tactical Air Command; three more were later transferred to Tactical Air Command and three were inactiviated on July 1. With the slow phaseout of the B-36, there was diminishing need for the F-84s because the B-47 and B-52 jet bombers did not need escorts. From a peak of 209 aircraft in 1954, Strategic Air Command now had only 76 B-36s, reducing to 22 in 1958, the last operational year for B-36s with Strategic Air Command.

1957 April 4   A Defense White Paper of unusual significance was released by Britain's defense minister, Duncan Sandys. There was to be no supersonic successor to the V-bombers as had been planned and no manned fighters after the operational version of the English Electric P.1B since, it asserted, air defense would in future rest upon surface-to-air missiles. The British strategic nuclear deterrent was also to be shifted from bombers to the Blue Streak land-based intercontinental missile.

1957 April 4   The first English Electric P.1B (serial no. XA847) single-seat interceptor made its first flight with Roland Beamont at the controls. Ordered on February 26, 1954, it was the precursor to 20 development aircraft, all of which were flying by the end of September 1959, and in May 1960 two of these aircraft took part in the annual air defense exercise. The P.1B was powered by two 11,250/14,500-lb. s.t. Rolls Royce Avon R.A.24R turbojets. Maximum speed was around Mach 2.

1957 May 15   Under Operation Grapple, Britain detonated its first hydrogen bomb in an air-drop from a Vickers Valiant (serial no. XD818) of No. 49 Squadron, RAF, 45,000 ft. above Malden Island, one of the Line Islands in what is now Kiribati. The bomb detonated 8,000 ft. above the surface with an explosive yield of about 1.4 megatons. The aircraft was commanded by Wg. Comdr. K. G. Hubbard and six more drops of more powerful weapons were carried out by September 11, 1958, A.C.M. Sir Harry Broadhurst, commander-in-chief of RAF Bomber Command, having arrived the previous day in a Vulcan to witness the last test under Operation Grapple.

1957 May 16   Newly appointed as a test pilot for Saunders Roe, Sqdn. Ldr. John Booth piloted the first hybrid-propulsion SR.53 fighter contender. Powered by a throttleable 8,000-lb. thrust de Havilland Spectre rocket motor and a 1,640-lb. s.t. Armstrong Siddeley ASV.8 Viper turbojet, it had a maximum level speed of Mach 2 and a climb time of 2 min. 12 sec. from brakes off to 50,000 ft. The SR.53 had a wingspan of 25 ft. 1 in., a length of 45 ft. and a maximum weight of 18,000 lb.

1957 May 17   An imported Sikorsky S-58 was used by Westlands in Britain to install a Napier Gazelle gas turbine engine in place of the original Wright R-1820 piston engine. The modification required a slightly longer nose but worked well and suited a requirement from the Royal Navy for a single helicopter to carry out both hunter-strike and general purpose duties. From this experimental installation, Westland evolved the Wessex.

1957 May 21   The second of the three V-bombers to join the RAF entered service when two Avro Vulcan B.Mk.1s arrived with No. 83 Squadron on loan from No. 230 Operational Conversion Unit. Both units were based at RAF Waddington, Lincolnshire. The B.Mk.1 was powered by four 11,000-lb. thrust

The Avro Vulcan joined the RAF in 1957 and proved the most enduring of the three V-bombers.

Bristol Olympus 101 turbojets, later by 12,000 lb. and then 13,000 lb. s.t. versions. The production Vulcans featured the new wing with a compound taper on the leading edge.

1957 June 1   Trans World Airlines launched its nonstop trans-Atlantic service with the first of the Lockheed L-1649 Starliners on the New York-Paris run. On September 30, TWA inaugurated a nonstop Los Angeles-London service. Eastbound flights took 19 hr. 10 min.; westbound flights took an average 21 hr. 5 min. The Starliner had a cruising speed of 290 MPH and a maximum payload range of 4,940 mi., 6,180 mi. with an 8,000-lb. payload. Too late to seriously compete with the coming jet age, it stands alongside the DC-7C as the epitome of piston-engine air transport at the end of an era.

1957 June 11   The first USAF U-2 (serial no. 56-6696) was delivered to the 4080th Strategic Reconnaissance Wing at Laughlin AFB, Tex. by Col. Jack Nole. The Air Force U-2's were finished in all-aluminum rather than the all-black of the CIA aircraft. Five more aircraft designated WU-2As had a sampling orifice in the nose to scoop in air. For many years, they conducted the most intensive sampling of air for radioactive contamination analysis ever conducted.

1957 June 28   The first Boeing KC-135A turbojet tanker was delivered to the USAF 93rd Air Refueling Squadron at Castle AFB, Calif. On November 11–12, the vice-chief of the Air Staff, Gen. Curtis LeMay, piloted KC-135A (serial no. 55-3126) nonstop 6,322.85 mi. from Westover, AFB, Mass., to Buenos Aires, Argentina in 13 hr. 2 min. 51 sec. and on the return flight November 13 flew a direct, 5,204-mi. route back in 11 hr. 3 min. 57 sec. On November 25, the last two KB-29P tankers were transferred out of the Twenty-seventh Air Refueling Squadron.

1957 June 29   The first nonstop flight by an airliner between London and Vancouver, Canada took place when a Bristol Britannia series 311 (G-AOVA) flew the 5,100-mi. in 14 hr. 40 min. The series 311 was powered by four 4,120/4,450-EHP Bristol Proteus turboprop engines and had a range of 5,310 mi. at a cruising speed of 357 MPH carrying 139 passengers.

1957 June   The first British helicopter to be developed for antisubmarine duties in an offensive role, the Westland Whirlwind H.A.S.7 entered service with the Royal Navy's Helicopter Flight

of No. 700 Squadron. Previous versions of the Whirlwind had not had an offensive role, equipped only for noncombat duty. Over time, the Whirlwinds so-adapted gradually replaced the Fairey Gannets, and the Whirlwind was in turn replaced by the Westland Wessex H.A.S.1 during the early 1960s.

1957 July 4   The prototype Ilyushin Il-18 turboprop medium-haul airliner made its first flight piloted by V. K. Kokkinaki. Designed to an Aeroflot requirement, it had capacity for 75 passengers and was initially powered by four 4,000-EHP NK4 engines providing a cruising speed of 388 MPH. The Il-18 was designed to operate from sparsely serviced airfields and on primitive routes. Production continued throughout the 1960s, and approximately 800 were built.

1957 July 19   The first live-firing of a nuclear-tipped Douglas Genie air-to-air missile was successfully conducted under the direction of the Las Alamos Scientific Laboratory. It was released from a Northrop F-89J Scorpion over Yucca Flat, Nev. at a height of 15,000 ft. The 1.5 kiloton nuclear warhead was detonated by ground command at a range of 6.2 mi. with USAF observers directly underneath to demonstrate the apparent absence of ill effects.

1957 July 27   The USAF Tactical Air Command completed a week-long series of exercises in which aircraft practiced long-range missions to drop tactical nuclear weapons. A unit of B-57s flew on simulated raids to South America, F-100s flew missions to North Africa with in-flight refueling simulating long-distance strikes, and B-66s flew from the U.S.-Canadian border to "targets" in Puerto Rico.

1957 July 31   The North American DEW line was declared fully operational protecting the continent from surprise attack and providing target location and tracking information for air defense networks. The USAF Air Defense Command and the Royal Canadian Air Force had a joint program of cooperation to deploy their forces to counter hostile intruders, and their forces included an increasingly large force of interceptors equipped with nuclear air-to-air missiles.

1957 August 12   Lt. Comdr. Don Walker flew his F3D Skyknight onto the deck of the USS *Antietam* off Pensacola, Fl. using an experimental automatic landing system for the first time. This was the first in a long series of tests that would culminate in the first operational landing using standard production equipment on June 13, 1963. By August 20, more than 50 successful automatic landings had been performed to prove the concept should it ever be needed in the event the pilot was disabled or unconscious.

1957 August 19   Maj. David G. Simmons, USAF, established a new world altitude record for ascent in a balloon when he reached a height of 101,516 ft. Most of the day was spent at approximately this altitude before slowly descending to the ground. On June 28, an unmanned 200-ft. diameter balloon with a capacity of 3.75 million cu. ft. lifted 2 tons of equipment to a height of 104,000 ft.

1957 August 28   A record altitude for manned aircraft was achieved by the RAF Canberra serial no. WK163 piloted by chief test pilot for Napier, M. Randrup, who flew the aircraft to 70,310 ft. with the aid of a Double Scorpion rocket motor. There were aircraft, like the U-2, that theoretically had the ability to exceed this altitude. The Canberra bomber force in the United Kingdom was being gradually phased out as the V-bombers began to enter service, although the RAF would continue to operate the type in the Far East, and No. 45 Squadron, RAF, received its B.Mk2s in November.

1957 August 31 The substantially modified second prototype Avro Vulcan (serial no. VX777) made its first flight with a new wing design that would characterize the B.Mk.2. With the delta-wing span increased by exactly 12 ft., the leading edge had a further increase in compound taper giving increased chord in the outer section and providing an area of 3,964 sq. ft. and improving aerodynamic performance. The first production B.Mk.2 flew in August 1958 and began to equip RAF squadrons in 1960. The Mk.2 eventually had four 20,000-lb. s.t. Bristol Olympus 301 turbojets.

1957 August At the end of a USAF feasibility study worked on by North American and Boeing in attempts to find a practical supersonic intercontinental Mach 3 bomber, both companies incorporated boron fuels in propulsion systems. But North American also adopted the compression-lift principle in which the massive bomber would ride on its own shock wave. Tests in wind tunnels over the next few months proved the concept would work, at least in theory.

1957 August The first complete drawings of the Hawker P.1127 VTOL project were made, incorporating a Bristol BE.53/2 engine that had been modified in concept by project engineer John Fozard to have a bifurcated exhaust flow feeding four rotatable involutes creating a four-post flat-rising vertical takeoff aircraft. The engine now had a theoretical thrust of 9,000 lb., and work progressed at Bristol to build a prototype for tests.

1957 September 1 The first Luftwaffe operational fighting unit came into existence with the formation of Jagdbombergeschwader 31, which was renamed Jagdbombergeschwader Boelcke on April 21, 1961. Equipped with F-84F Thunderstreaks, in June 1962 it was to become the first Luftwaffe unit to take part in a NATO exercise. Prior to the formation of Jagdbombergeschwader 31, Luftwaffe activity had concentrated on training and organizational build-up.

1957 September 1 The British Army Air Corps formally came into existence again, having been first operated between 1942 and 1950, when it was divided into the Glider Pilot Regiment and the Parachute Corps. The army air corps would have responsibility for air observation duties and light liaison with aircraft up to a maximum weight of 4,000 lb., helicopters becoming the prime equipment.

1957 September 4 The Lockheed CL-329 JetStar made its first flight at the Lockheed Air Terminal as the first flying contender for the USAF's UCX (utility transport experimental) requirement, for which North American was also building a contender known as the NA-246 Sabreliner. Both manufacturers followed the example of Morane-Saulnier with its M.S. 760 and put the engines in pods attached to the rear fuselage. When the military requirement evaporated, Lockheed went for the business market and finally got the USAF to buy the type in 1960.

1957 September 9 The British Ministry of Supply issued a letter for industry clarifying General Operational Requirement No. 339 (GOR.339), which called for an advanced Canberra replacement capable of supersonic dash, low-level strike and operations from bombed runways and soft fields. At a meeting on September 16, Sir Cyril Musgrave addressed representatives from every major U.K. planemaker, informing them that only a team of two

or three firms would receive the contract and that GOR.339 was to form the basis for an amalgamation of separate companies into industrial blocks.

1957 September 11 Pan American inaugurated its "Polar Route" service between London and San Francisco across Frobisher Bay and Baffin Island, using four-engined DC-7C airliners. On September 30, Trans World Airlines started a similar service using the Lockheed L-1649 Starliner. This was an optimum flight path for long-range aircraft that could fly nonstop across the United States and the North Atlantic in one hop.

1957 September 19 Funds for the USAF Project Suntan hydrogen-fueled aircraft program were cut by two-thirds when opposition to the concept gathered ranks in the Pentagon, a surprising opponent being the originator of the idea, Lockheed's Clarence K. ("Kelly") Johnson. Different approaches to high altitude, Mach 2+ reconnaissance flights and the inherent risk of large quantities of hydrogen in a single aircraft were arguments against the project.

1957 September One of the greatest leaps in helicopter design took to the air when the Mil Mi-6 made its first flight piloted by R. I. Kaprelyan. Designed as a heavy transport helicopter, it had a length of 108 ft. 10 in., a single five-blade rotor of 114 ft. 10 in. driven by two 5,500-SHP TV2-BM turbine engines and a wing of 50 ft. 2 in. With a gross weight of 93,695 lb., the Mi-6 accommodated up to 120 people and could lift up to 44,000 lb.

1957 October 1 Gen. Thomas S. Power, commander-in-chief of USAF Strategic Air Command since July 1 when he replaced Gen. Curtis LeMay, ordered a One-Third Ground Alert condition at several bases in the United States and abroad. Preparing for the time when Strategic Air Command bases could be threatened with attack from intercontinental ballistic missiles, Operation Try Out conducted earlier this year proved that with changes Strategic Air Command bases could maintain one-third base force levels at constant armed readiness capable of getting airborne in less than 15 min.

1957 October 3 Powered by four 12,000-SHP Kuznetsov NK-12 turboprop engines driving contra-rotating propellers, the Tu-20-derived Tupolev 114 Rossiya made its first flight. It was the largest commercial airliner ever built until surpassed by the Boeing 747 20 yr. later. It had capacity for up to 220 passengers, a length of 177 ft. 6 in., a wingspan of 167 ft. and a gross weight of 385,000 lb. A cruising speed of 478 MPH coupled with a range of 5,561 mi. made this the ultimate turboprop airliner.

1957 October 10 Integrating results from three earlier study programs under the code names ROBO, HYWARDS, and Brass Bell, the USAF Air Research Development Command issued a development plan for System 464L, named Dyna-Soar for "dynamic soaring." It was to be a follow-on research progam to the X-15 and use rocket boost to propel a winged vehicle to hypersonic speed in the outer atmosphere. The first release of funds for 464L was approved on December 21, and a request for bidders was put out to industry at that time.

1957 November 6 The first untethered flight of the Fairey Rotodyne (serial no. XE521) took place at White Waltham, England with W. R. Gellatly and J. G. P. Morton at the controls. The Rotodyne had a fuselage length of 58 ft. 8 in. with a centrally mounted 104-ft. rotor driven by blade-tip compressed air jets from two 3,000-EHP Napier Eland N.E1.3 turboprops. These engines were attached to the high-mounted wing, which had a span of 46 ft. 6 in. Using the rotors for vertical flight and the Elands for forward flight, the wing contributed 85% lift, the remainder coming from the auto-rotating rotor.

1957 November 29 The Kaman Aircraft Corp. was awarded a U.S. Navy contract to develop a high-performance, all-weather helicopter for a wide variety of missions, including guard duties at naval stations and on aircraft carriers, gunfire observation, reconnaissance, personnel transfer, casualty evacuation and tactical air controller duties as well as its primary mission of serving as a search and rescue helicopter. Kaman had been building helicopters for the U.S. Navy since 1951.

1957 December 6 The prototype Lockheed 188 Electra made its first flight powered by four 3,750-EHP Allison 501-D13 turboprop engines. With a wingspan of 99 ft. and a length of 104 ft. 6 in. it could carry 66 to 80 passengers a distance of 2,770 mi., or 3,500 mi. for the Model 188C with increased tankage. Patronized by the airlines to begin with, only 170 were built as it was quickly superseded by jet airliners, but Lockheed successfully turned it into a U.S. Navy maritime patrol aircraft with the designation P3V Orion.

1957 December 12 Maj. Adrian Drew, USAF, piloted a McDonnell F-101A Voodoo to an FAI-ratified absolute world speed record of 1,207.34 MPH (1,943.03 km/hr.), homologated from two passes over a course near Los Angeles. This surpassed the record previously set by Britain on March 10, 1956, by 75 MPH, but it would stand for only five months.

1957 December 14 The West German defense minister announced that the United States would provide F-84F Thunderstreak fighter-bombers for nine Luftwaffe fighter-bomber wings. These would not be equipped to carry nuclear weapons, conforming to an agreement that nuclear weapons could be held on German soil by non-German NATO forces but that they could not be operated or used by any of the German armed forces.

1957 December 19 Two important events with the Bristol Britannia turboprop airliner occurred. BOAC introduced the series 312 on its London-New York service, and El Al carried out a proving flight for its New York-Tel Aviv service, flying the 6,200 mi. in just over 15 hr. at an average speed of 401 MPH with a series 313 Britannia. The first scheduled service on this route began December 22. The BOAC flight was commanded by Capt. A. Meagher in G-AVOC and was the first trans-Atlantic service to use turboprop airliners.

1957 December 20 The first Boeing 707-100 made its first flight powered by four 12,500-lb. s.t Pratt & Whitney JT3C-6 turbojet engines. With a wingspan of 130 ft. 10 in., a length of 144 ft. 6 in., a gross weight of 257,000 lb. and a cruising speed of 571 MPH, it was almost 200 MPH faster than the smaller turboprops and could carry 124 to 179 passengers (more than twice as many as the Britannia) a distance of 3,075 mi. The first six 707s, designated Model 707-121, went to Pan American.

1957 December 23 North American Aviation was awarded a USAF contract from WS-110A to develop an intercontinental Mach 3 bomber based on its July submission to a 6-mon. feasibility study. A special 45-day Phase I extension had been granted to work through alternate configurations and concepts. The bomber would be designated B-70, and in response to development of a Soviet ICBM and a Soviet earth satellite launched in October, the schedule envisaged a mock-up review in March 1959, first

flight in December 1961 and the first combat-ready wing in August 1964.

1957 December 24 The U.S. Navy awarded a contract to Sikorsky for development of the S-61 into an antisubmarine/hunter-killer helicopter. The design had to be capable of accommodating a weapons load of 840 lb. and all-weather operation and have a water-tight hull. The S-61s were to weigh about 50% more than the HSS-1 Seabat and would bear the name Sea King and the designation HSS-2, later H-3. From this design would stem a wide range of civil and military versions.

1957 December 24 Orders from the British Ministry of Supply for five Saunders Roe SR.177 supersonic fighters incorporating hybrid propulsion were canceled. Proposed in 1954, the SR.177 was a development of the SR.53 concept that would have had a 10,000-lb. thrust de Havilland Spectre 5A rocket motor and a 14,000.-lb. s.t. de Havilland Gyron Junior DGJ.10-1 turbojet with afterburner. It would have had a top speed of Mach 2.35 and a climb time of 3 min. 6 sec. from brake release to 60,000 ft. The Germans had shown interest, and the Heinkel Co. paid a visit, but requirements changed.

1957 December A painter was commissioned to paint a sign alongside the Christmas tree at the entrance to the new USAF Strategic Air Command headquarters at Offutt AFB, Neb. with the words "Maintaining Peace Is Our Profession" but was unable to find space for the word "Maintaining." Tree officers Lt. Col. Edward Martin and CWO Ben Kohot elected to omit that word. Visiting headquarters, Col. Charles T. Van Vliet of the Eighth Air Force saw the sign and took the idea back to Westover AFB, Mass. Other Eighth Air Force units copied it, and "Peace Is Our Profession" was adopted as the new Strategic Air Command slogan.

1958 January 14 The Australian carrier QANTAS inaugurated its round-the-world service by dispatching two Lockheed L-1049G Super Constellations in opposite directions. *Southern Aurora* (VH-EAO) flew east across the Pacific and the United States to London where, on January 17, it met *Southern Zephyr* (VH-EAP), which had flown west across the Indian Ocean and the Middle East. Both aircraft continued on their prescribed headings and arrived back at Melbourne, Australia on January 20. QANTAS was the first non-U.S. airline to carry passengers across the United States.

1958 January 26 The USAF Eighty-third Fighter Interceptor Squadron of Continental Air Defense Command became the first unit to become operational with the Lockheed F-104 Starfighter. When production ended in 1978, 2,578 Starfighters had been built, 1,789 under license in Canada, Italy, Holland, Germany and Japan under military aid programs and 48 in co-production. Only 741 were built in the United States, and of these only 296 served with the USAF.

1958 January 31 The prototype North American T-2 Buckeye took to the air for the first time. Powered by two 2,950-lb. s.t. General Electric 085-GE-4 turbofans, it had a wingspan of 38 ft. 2 in., a length of 38 ft. 8 in. and a gross weight of 13,180 lb. Top speed was 521 MPH at 25,000 ft. The Buckeye entered service as a U.S. Navy trainer in the second half of 1959, and the last T-2s left the service in mid-1973.

1958 February 4 The world's first nuclear-powered aircraft carrier, the CVAN-65 USS *Enterprise* was laid down at the Newport News shipyard. When carrying 80 to 95 aircraft, it would form the core of a formidable strike force equipped with some of the most powerful aircraft in the U.S. Navy's inventory and represented a political statement about power projection that was well noted by America's potential adversaries.

1958 February 12   The British government announced plans for BEA to purchase 24 de Havilland D.H.121 Trident airliners. Designed to a specification issued by the airline in August 1956, the Trident would have three jet engines in the tail—two mounted on external pods faired into the rear fuselage with the bulbous enclosure for the third engine's air intake situated forward of the vertical tail. BEA wanted a short/medium-haul airliner capable of operating from 6,000-ft. runways.

1958 February 13   In a British defense white paper, it was announced that production of nuclear bombs for the RAF had started and that "stand-off" weapons were being developed for the V-bombers. This referred to the Blue Steel rocket-propelled, air-launched strategic missile with a range of 200 mi. It had already been tested by air-drop under full control and during 1958 would be fired live with a dummy warhead.

1958 February 15   The first production SAAB-J35A Draken made its first flight, powered by a 17,262-lb. s.t. afterburning Flygmotor RM6B, a license-built Rolls Royce Avon. The double-delta single-seat interceptor had a wingspan of 30 ft. 10 in., a length of 50 ft. 4 in. and a gross weight of 27,998 lb. With a top speed of Mach 2 (1,320 MPH) and a combat radius of 348 mi., it was well received when it joined the Swedish Air Force in February 1960. In all, 525 Drakens were built, with some still in service in 1991.

1958 February 21   It was announced by the RAF that its Canberras in Germany had been given a nuclear capability and that they had been equipped to carry U.S. tactical weapons. Britain was developing its own range of tactical nuclear weapons, but for the interim, the RAF would depend on U.S. technology.

1958 March 8   Although not directly associated with aviation, the decommissioning of the last of America's four *Iowa*-class battleships, the USS *Wisconsin,* signaled the dominance now achieved by naval air power over conventional surface fleets. The *Missouri* had been decommissioned on February 26, 1955, the *New Jersey* on August 21, 1957, and the *Iowa* on February 28, 1958. The *New Jersey* was recommissioned briefly during the Vietnam War, and all would be recommissioned briefly, beginning in 1982 when even carrier power was deemed not to fill every U.S. Navy requirement.

1958 March 25   The Avro Canada CF-105 Arrow made its first flight powered by two 23,500-lb. s.t. Pratt & Whitney J75-P-3 turbojets. It had been developed as a replacement for the CF-100 Canuck and incorporated some advanced technical innovations, one of which was the 4,000-psi hydraulic system. (Hydraulic systems of this pressure did not appear on an operational aircraft before the North American B-1.) With a delta-wing span of 50 ft. and a length of 77 ft. 10 in., the CF-105 was canceled on February 20, 1959.

1958 March 26   An F-100D was flown for the first time from a zero-length launcher similar to atom-proof shelters being designed for protecting USAF Tactical Air Command aircraft from destruction on exposed airfields. Propelled by a 150,000-lb. thrust Astrodyne rocket motor, the F-100D was accelerated to flying speed along a short rail. The F-100D was capable of carrying a load of 7,040 lb. on underwing pylons, and North American built a total of 1,274.

1958 April 1   Airline operators introduced economy-class fares on trans-Atlantic services to and from the United States; the new fares were about 20% below first-class rates. The post–World War II boom in civil air transport rang the death-knell for prestigious first-class services. The need to optimize seat-mile costs and the higher density seating capacity of turboprop and turbojet airliners, plus the greater number of people now willing and able to pay for air travel, eroded prewar attention to personalized service.

1958 April 9   The Handley Page Victor B.Mk.1 entered operational service with the RAF, the last of the V-bombers to do so. The first production Victor had made its first flight on February 1, 1956, incorporating a 40-in. nose extension to improve the center of gravity and a reduction in the height of the vertical fin. The last of 50 Victor B.Mk.1s was delivered to the RAF in February 1961. As a tanker, the Victor would still be in service during the early 1990s.

1958 April 9   An English Electric Canberra B.6 (serial no. WT207), which had been used by No. 76 Squadron, RAF, for high-altitude air sampling over Australia, exploded 56,000 ft. above Monyash, England, causing the two-man crew to execute the highest emergency ejection to date. Flt. Lt. John de Salis and Flg. Off. Patrick Lowe were in free-fall for 4 min. at 130 MPH and a temperature as low as −57°C before their parachutes opened at 10,000 ft. They landed safely.

1958 April 10   The Fairey Rotodyne made a full transition from vertical to horizontal flight for the first time at an altitude of 4,000 ft. In 70 previous test flights, the Rotodyne had built up to speeds of 125 MPH and an altitude of 6,800 ft. By the end of October, transitions were being effected within 30 sec. and at heights as low as 300 ft. During these successful trials, a serious marketing campaign began to sell the Rotodyne as a passenger aircraft, and Kaman negotiated a licensing agreement for U.S. sales and service, but the aircraft failed to get the orders necessary to sustain development.

1958 April 18   A U.S. Navy Grumman F11F-1 Tiger piloted by Lt. Comdr. George C. Watkins raised the FAI-ratified absolute world altitude record for manned aircraft when he flew to a measured altitude of 23,448 m (76,932 ft.). The record would stand only two weeks before a French pilot broke it on May 2.

1958 April 21   New York Airways introduced the Vertol Model 44B twin-rotor helicopter on its commercial services and became the first airline to operate a helicopter with internal seating for passengers laid out like a conventional, fixed-wing airliner. The Model 44B had capacity for 15 passengers arranged in pairs along the right side of the fuselage with an aisle down the left side.

1958 April 21   The first of a succession of Lockheed A-series studies carried out for the CIA began, from which a high-altitude, Mach 3+ reconnaissance aircraft evolved. In competition with General Dynamics and a balloon-launched ramjet concept from the U.S. Navy, designs A-1 through A-12 culminated in a delta-wing aircraft fabricated from titanium and powered by two turbo-ramjet engines. More conservative than the Mach 6 General Dynamics proposal, Lockheed was selected to build Article 12 in a project managed by the USAF.

Following its first untethered flight on November 6, 1957, the Fairey Rotodyne promised a commercial success that never came.

1958 April 24 Lockheed won a U.S. Navy contract to adapt the unsuccessful 188 Electra turboprop airliner as the P3V Orion maritime patrol and antisubmarine aircraft. Revised to match U.S. Navy specification No. 146, the Orion was born from the third Electra prototype. It flew for the first time as a YP3V-1 aerodynamic precursor on August 19. It carried a dummy electromagnetic anomaly detection boom out the tail and a simulated weapons bay in an under-fuselage bulge.

1958 April 27 The first production de Havilland Comet 4 flew from Hatfield. The aircraft now capable of crossing the North Atlantic, BOAC had ordered 19 for its London-New York service. Powered by four 10,500-lb. s.t. Rolls Royce Avon 524 engines, the Comet 4 had a range of 3,225 mi. and a cruising speed of 503 MPH. It was put through a rigorous proving season, and on September 17, the first Comet 4 flew from London to Gander, Newfoundland in 5 hr. 47 min. at the start of a tour of North and South America.

1958 April 30 Probably the most advanced ground attack aircraft of the time, the prototype Blackburn N.A.39 (serial no. XK486) made its first flight from the Royal Aircraft Establishment at Thurleigh, England. It had been designed and developed in under three years to a specification calling for a low-level intruder able to fly at high subsonic speed with impunity under enemy radar coverage. Powered by two 7,100-lb s.t. de Havilland Gyron Junior DGJ.1 turbojets, the aircraft was rugged and versatile, with a weapons load of 8,000 lb. split between internal bays and underwing stores points.

1958 May 2 A Süd-Ouest S.O. 9050 Trident II piloted by M. R. Carpentier set a new world altitude record for manned

aircraft by reaching a height of 79,452 ft. with the aid of two 1,760-lb. thrust G.A.M.D.30 engines and a 6,614-lb thrust SEPR.631 rocket motor. The aircraft had first flown on July 17, 1955, and on April 4, 1958, claimed a new time-to-height record of 15,000 m (49,200 ft.) in 2 min. 37 sec. One of the first hybrid-propulsion projects, it was preceded by the S.O.Espadon, a derivative of which carried rocket motors on the wing tips.

1958 May 7 The third FAI world altitude record within 3 wk. was set by Maj. H. C. Johnson, USAF, in a Lockheed F-104A when he reached a height of 91,243 ft. The aircraft was powered by a 9,600/14,800-lb. s.t. General Electric J79-GE-3B turbojet engine. These had been retrofitted to all F-104As, replacing the original J79-GE-3A engines.

1958 May 12 The first preproduction Dassault Mirage IIIA powered by the new 13,228-lb. s.t. Atar 9B turbojet and carrying a modified delta wing made its first flight. With a length of 51 ft. and a wingspan of 26 ft. 1 in., it had a gross weight of 30,203 lb. and maximum speed of Mach 2.2 with a ceiling of 59,055 ft. and a combat radius of 391 mi. with a 1,765-lb. warload. Trainer, all-weather interceptor and fighter-bomber variants appeared also.

1958 May 16 Piloted by Capt. Walter W. Irvin of the USAF, a Lockheed F-104A Starfighter raised the FAI-ratified absolute world air speed record for manned aircraft to 2,259.18 km/hr. (1,403.79 MPH). This was the first world speed record to exceed 2,000 km/hr., less than 11 yr. after Col. Albert Boyd had been the first through the 1,000-km/hr. barrier.

1958 May 17 In Operation Pipeline, four U.S. Navy F3H Demons and four F8U Crusaders were flown nonstop across the

A Comet 4, first flown April 27, 1958, with long-range, leading edge, supplementary wing tanks.

North Atlantic as part of a rapid-deployment concept to test the ability of pilots, support crew and aircraft to quickly move aircraft from the U.S. East Coast to the Sixth Fleet in the Mediterranean Sea.

1958 May 21   The prototype Dassault Etendard IVM made its first flight adapted from the basic Etendard IV to meet stringent specifications from the Aéronavale. It soon proved a formidable addition to the French carrier force, which in addition to the ex-British *Colossus* class (renamed *Arromanches*) was to comprise the *Clemenceau* (launched December 21, 1957) and the *Foch* (to be launched July 23, 1960).

1958 May 24   The Bell X-14 made its first full transition from hovering flight to horizontal flight, moving from vertical lift-off to forward motion in less than 30 sec. The X-14 was handed over to NACA in October 1959, and two General Electric J85-5 turbojets were installed for a flight research program beginning in 1961. When replaced by two J85-19s in 1971, it was redesignated X-14B until a hard landing on may 29, 1981, ended its 24-yr. flying program.

1958 May 26   The 335th Tactical Fighter Squadron of the Fourth Tactical Fighter Wing, USAF, based at Eglin AFB, Fla, became the first unit operational with the F-105B Thunderchief, the first aircraft of its type to be deployed. It had first flown on May 24, 1957, and only 75 were built before the first of 610 F-105D variants replaced it. These, in turn, were superseded by 143 F-105Fs, a large number of which were converted to Wild Weasel duties in Vietnam as the earlier variant took the brunt of the Rolling Thunder campaign (1965–68).

1958 May 27   Arguably the most outstanding combat aircraft of the turbojet era, the McDonnell XF4H-1, prototype of the F-4 Phantom II, made its first flight from Lambert Field, St. Louis. It was powered by two 9,300-lb. s.t. General Electric J79-GE-3A engines instead of the planned GE-8 version. As yet, it had no anhedral on the outer wing panels or dihedral on the tail. Ugly to some, the epitome of rugged air combat survivability to many, the Phantom became legendary through Vietnam and will undoubtedly endure through 50 yr. of service, which it will celebrate in the year 2010.

1958 May 30   Less than three years since the company had approved development, the Douglas DC-8 made its first flight, from

Long Beach, Calif. to Edwards AFB, captained by A. G. Heimerdinger, and remained airborne for 2 hrs. 7 min. First certified on August 31, 1959, the basic domestic version was powered by four 13,000-lb. s.t Pratt & Whitney JT3C-6 turbojets. It had a wingspan of 142 ft. 5 in., a length of 150 ft. 6 in. and a maximum cruising speed of 559 MPH with up to 176 passengers.

1958 June 2   Test pilot Tom Brooke-Smith, flying the Short SC.1 VTOL research aircraft conducted a full transition from vertical to forward flight, hover, side-movement and reversing under full control. The first hover flight had been made on May 23, and in development of VTOL techniques, the aircraft was used to test an autostabilization system. Tests went on until October 2, 1963, when a failure caused the SC.1 to turn turtle and crash, killing test pilot J. R. Green.

1958 June 9   A second airport for London, England, called Gatwick and located 25 mi. due south of the city center, was opened by Queen Elizabeth, who arrived at 10:45 A.M. in a de Havilland Heron of the Queen's Flight. Traffic at Heathrow was building above expected levels, and this second airport was a vital part of plans to expand air services into and out of the London area. The first commercial use of the airport was by a Transair Viscount, which had departed May 30, but a BEA DC-3 Pionair charter flight to the Channel Islands was the first official departure, a few minutes after the opening ceremony.

1958 June 15   The first of two Westland Westminster aerodynamic test helicopters for a 40-seat transport design made its first flight, powered by two 2,400-SHP Napier Eland 229 turboshaft engines. With a length of 86 ft. 9 in. and a rotor diameter of 72 ft. it had an all-up weight of 33,000 lb. and a range of 210 mi. at 115 MPH. The second flew on September 4, 1959. Nothing came of the type, but the development experience proved valuable in later helicopters.

1958 June 16   The USAF awarded parallel contracts to Boeing and Martin Aircraft for 12- to 18-mon. studies of a hypersonic boost-glide vehicle under the System 464L Dyna-Soar program. Nine aircraft companies had responded to the call for bids issued December 21, 1957, including Republic, Lockheed, North American Aviation, Douglas, McDonnell, Convair, a Martin-Bell team, Boeing and Northrop. (Bell was eventually eliminated as partner of Martin.) It was left to the winners to decide whether to include a capability for the aircraft to achieve orbital flight.

1958 June 20 The first Westland-built Wessex (serial no. XL727) derivative of the Sikorsky S-58 made its first flight. It had the capacity for carrying 16 fully equipped troops or 12 commercial passengers at a cruising speed of 115–127 MPH. The Wessex HAS Mk.1 joined the Royal Navy in 1961 and was still doing yeoman duty 30 yr. later. In the interim, the type had been developed for the civil aviation market, and it was also sold as a military helicopter to four foreign countries.

1958 June 29 Two Strategic Air Command KC-135As made a record run between London and New York in 5 hr. 53 min. 12.77 sec., having made a New York-London crossing in 5 hr. 29 min. 14.64 sec. two days earlier. The aircraft were from the Ninety-ninth Air Refueling Squadron and were to have been accompanied by a third, which crashed on takeoff at Westover AFB, Mass., killing 15 people. On September 17, a KC-135 established a straight-line unrefueled distance record of 10,229.3 mi. in 13 hr. 45 min. 46.5 sec. and on September 24, another aircraft lifted a record 78,089.5 lb. to 6,562 ft.

1958 July 3 USAF Strategic Air Command selected the name Valkyrie for the B-70 strategic bomber program from a competition that drew more than 20,000 entries. The aircraft was named after the mythical Norse maidens who roamed across the skies mounted on horses, deciding the fate of battle victims. B-70 prime airframe contractor North American had begun selecting subcontractors in May while engine contractor General Electric developed its boron-fueled YJ93-GE-5.

1958 July 5 The Bristol Type 192 derivative of the Type 173, the first twin-rotor helicopter to fly in Britain, made its first flight. Powered by two 1,300-SHP Napier Gazelle N.Ga.2 engines, it had a length of 54 ft. 4 in., a rotor diameter of 48 ft. 8 in. and capacity for up to 18 fully equipped troops. In service as the Belvedere, it was finally withdrawn in 1969.

1958 July 8 Sqdn. Ldr. Christopher Walker, RAF, was killed when the U-2 spyplane he was flying crashed during a flight from McLaughlin AFB, Tex. Walker was found dead in his ejection seat 1,000 ft. from the wreckage of the aircraft. Walker, along with RAF pilots John MacArthur, David Dowling and Michael Bradley, had been sent to train at McLaughlin AFB in May following a visit by a U-2 to the Royal Aircraft Establishment, Farnborough, England in November 1956.

1958 July 30 The prototype de Havilland (Canada) DHC-4 Caribou made its first flight. With outstanding STOL characteristics, it could clear a 50-ft. obstacle with a full load in only 1,185 ft. from a ground run of 725 ft. and land over a 50 ft. obstacle in 1,235 ft with a 670 ft. run-off. The DHC-4 had a wingspan of 95 ft. 7 in., a length of 72 ft. 7 in. and two 1,450-HP Pratt & Whitney R-2000 D5 Twin Wasp engines.

1958 August 23 The U.S. Federal Aviation Act came into existence, creating the Federal Aviation Agency (FAA) as of this date, which absorbed the Civil Aviation Authority, and simultaneously abolishing the Airways Modernization Act of August 1957. The first FAA chariman was Gen. E. R. (''Pete'') Quesada who had formerly been the chairman of the Airways Modernization Board. Among the FAA's first objectives were to improve aircraft safety and increase pilot training requirements for military and civil aviation.

1958 August 31 The prototype North American A-5 Vigilante carrier-based attack bomber made its first flight, followed quickly by a move to production. With a gross weight of 79,588 lb., it

was the heaviest aircraft operated by the U.S. Navy and had a wingspan of 53 ft., a length of 76 ft. 6 in. and a top speed of Mach 2.1 with a combat radius of 1,500 mi. Powered by two 10,800-lb. s.t. General Electric J79-GE-8 engines. it entered service in August 1962.

1958 September 14 Test pilot John Cunningham flew the first Comet 4 (serial no. G-APDAS) a distance of 7,925 mi. between dawn and sunset, leaving Hong Kong in the morning and arriving at London with the sun 2 hr. from setting. Total flying time had been 16 hr. 16 min., and only two stops had been necessary, the first at Bombay for 1 hr. and the second at Cairo for 1 hr. 6 min. The same aircraft left London September 17 for a second tour of the Americas, including Canada, Mexico, Peru, Paraguay, Brazil, and the United States.

1958 September 16 Designed to match a USAF UTX (utility trainer experimental) requirement, the first North American NA-246 made its first flight. Powered by two 3,000-lb. s.t. Pratt & Whitney J60 engines mounted in pods attached to either side of the rear fuselage, the first of 213 military T-39As entered service with the air force in 1962. Developed as a business jet powered by two 3,700-lb. s.t. Garrett TFE731-3-1D engines, it had a wingspan of 50 ft. 5 in., a length of 46 ft. 11 in., a maximum weight of 24,000 lb. and a range of 2,763 mi., more than 600 being built by 1992.

1958 September 19 The Kaman H-43 Huskie made its first flight as the first helicopter ordered into production for firefighting and crash rescue activities. Powered by a Pratt & Whitney R-1340-48 piston engine, it had twin two-blade rotors on separate posts above the squat body, giving a length of 25 ft. and a span across the rotors of 51 ft. 6 in. The basic design evolved into the H-43B with an 860-EHP Lycoming T53-L-1B turbojet and entered service with the USAF in June 1959, following the first of 18 H-43As that saw service from November 1958.

1958 September 24 For the first time, an aircraft was shot down by another aircraft using a heat-seeking infrared missile. It happened over the Formosa Straits when 14 F-86Fs of the Chinese Nationalist Air Force Third Fighter Wing armed with Sidewinder missiles attacked 20 Red Chinese MiG-15s. The F-86Fs claimed 10 MiGs destroyed, of which four were said to have been shot down by the Sidewinder. Over the following six weeks, a total 31 MiG-15 and MiG-17 fighters were claimed against a loss of only two F-86Fs.

1958 October 1 The National Aeronautics and Space Administration (NASA) formally replaced the National Advisory Committee for Aeronautics (NACA), having been so enacted through the National Aeronautics and Space Act signed by Pres. Eisenhower on July 29. The bill to create NASA had been proposed April 14 following lengthy congressional debate. Senate Armed Services Committee hearings between November 25, 1957, and January 23, 1958, had sought ways of elevating U.S. air and space research to meet perceived threats from the Soviet Union after the first test flights of their ICBM and the launch on October 4, 1957, of Sputnik 1.

1958 October 4 The first two-way jet airliner service over the North Atlantic began when BOAC Capt. R. E. Millichap captained Comet 4 G-APDC from London to New York in 10 hr. 22 min., carrying the chairman Sir Gerard d'Erlanger and stopping only at Gander. Simultaneously, Capt. T. B. Stoney commanded G-APDB from New York to London in 6 hr. 11 min., carrying managing director Basil Smallpiece. At 13:35 GMT, the two aircraft passed each other 300 mi. apart at 47° W. The weekly service became daily from November 13.

1958 October 15 The first of three North American X-15 hypersonic research aircraft was rolled out just over 2 yr. 4 mon. after the production go-ahead. It was shipped to Edwards AFB, Calif. from the Los Angeles plant on October 17 to begin a 5-mon. static test program. The X-15 had a length of 49 ft. 10 in. without pitot probe and 50 ft. 3 in. with the probe, a wingspan of 22 ft. 4 in. and a height of 11 ft. 7 in. It had a within-wheel nose leg and two rear fuselage skids.

1958 October 26 Pan American made the first trans-Atlantic flight between New York and Paris-Le Bourget with the first of its Boeing 707-121 jet airliners (serial no. N711PA) carrying 111 passengers, the largest number that had ever boarded a scheduled flight. Pan American was the busiest trans-Atlantic airline. Because BOAC had introduced its longer-range Comet 4, the British airline replaced TWA for a while as the second-ranking Atlantic carrier. TWA had only the out-paced Lockheed Super Constellation. Eventually, with only half the seating capacity of the new Boeing jets. BOAC's Comets lost out to the U.S. airline.

1958 October 26 The first major production variant of Strategic Air Command's new eight-engine bomber, the B-52G made its first flight incorporating many modifications that would keep this aircraft in serivce well into the 1990s. The most visible difference between the B-52G and the earlier variants was the reduced height of the tail, lowering overall height to 40 ft. 8 in. versus 48 ft. Increased internal tankage and two fixed outer-wing tanks allowed an unrefueled range of 7,500 mi. Provision was made for carrying two AGM-28 Hound Dog supersonic stand-off bombs.

1958 November 25 The English Electric P.1B prototype (serial no. XA847) became the first British aircraft to exceed Mach 2 in level flight. The aircraft was presently involved in an intensive development program prior to full production. On October 23, at a ceremony at Farnborough, the chief of the Air Staff, Marshal of the Royal Air Force Sir Dermot Boyle, broke a bottle of champagne over the nose of XA847 and named the type Lightning before test pilot Roland P. Beamont gave a spectacular flying display.

1958 December 4 The VEB-152-II jet airliner powered by four 6,950-lb. s.t. Pirna jet engines made its first flight in the German Democratic Republic. Developed by the Flugzeugwerke Dresden, it had been ordered by the East German Deutsche Lufthansa and by the Polish airline L.O.T., engine thrust on production aircraft being raised to 7,270-lb. s.t. The aircraft had a conventional fuselage 107 ft. in length and a high swept-wing spanning 86 ft. 7 in. carrying paired engines in pods at mid-span. It had capacity for 72 passengers with a range of 1,242 mi.

1958 December 5 The first production Lockheed Electra was delivered to American Airlines, the first of 35 ordered by the airline. The Electra would not realize its proper commercial potential in the waning need for turboprop airliners. Also, a series of highly publicized accidents early in its service life would deter operators. Yet the Electra probably came closest of any turboprop airliner to meeting the operating economics of the jets.

1958 December 6 The first in a series of U-2 spyplane missions over China was conducted. The aircraft would carry out detailed overflights of the Zhejiang (Chekiang) and Jiangxi (Kiangsi) regions around Shanghai. U-2 activity had been expanding this year. In September the CIA had flown missions over Egypt to identify

British and French movements and monitor the build-up in the Suez Canal region. During this year also, a U-2 unit was sent to Bodo, Norway to monitor atmospheric pollution from nuclear weapons testing, which in 1958 increased to 77 explosions, compared to 32 in 1957 and 18 in 1956.

1958 December 10 The first regularly scheduled U.S. domestic jet airline service was inaugurated. Leasing a Boeing 707-121 from Pan American, National Airlines flew the first such service between New York and Miami. The trip was completed in a record time of 2 hr. 15 min.

1958 December 29 The first of 20 Bristol Britannia C.1 transport aircraft for the RAF (serial no. XL635) made its first flight powered by four 4,445-HP Bristol Siddeley Proteus 255 turboprop engines. It had a maximum loaded weight of 185,000 lb. and could carry 113 troops, 53 stretcher cases or 37,400 lb. of freight. The C.1 entered service in 1959, and one aircraft made a 4,160-mi. flight nonstop from Palisadoes Airport, British Honduras to St. Mawgan, England. The Britannia was retired from military service in January 1976, and some were sold to freight charter services.

1958 At least six attempts to launch small earth-orbiting satellites were made during the year by the U.S. Navy using an existing redesigned missile named Caleb and the Douglas F4D Skyray as the launch aircraft. The Caleb cost approximately $50,000 and weighed 3,000 lb. It had a length of 16 ft. 8 in. and a diameter of 24 in. and would have been capable of placing a mass of 50 lb. in low-earth orbit.

1959 January 1 Vickers-Armstrong and English Electric were awarded a contract for a new light bomber known as the T.S.R.2, conforming to Operational Requirement 343 (which had evolved from a specification known as GOR.339 outlined on September 9, 1957) performing tactical, strike and reconnaissance duties. It was said to be the most demanding specification ever put together for the British aircraft industry. Vickers would lead the design effort, which evolved from an English Electric P.17 proposal, and Bristol Siddeley would provide a developed 22R version of the 593 Olympus engine.

1959 January 8 Designed originally to fill the needs of the 1955 British O.R.323 for a medium-range freighter, the Armstrong Whitworth A.W.650 Argosy (G-AOZZ) made its first flight with Eric Franklin at the controls. More than 2 yr. earlier, the military role had vanished, and what was designated the A.W.66 became the A.W.650 civil transport as a private venture. The first customer to receive the type was Riddle Airlines Inc. of Miami in August 1961. The Argosy had a wingspan of 115 ft., a length of 86 ft. 9 in. and four 2,020-EHP Rolls Royce Dart 536 turboprop engines.

1959 January 20 Designed to a requirement issued by BEA on April 15, 1953, the Vickers type 950 Vanguard, successor to the Viscount, made its first flight. The aircraft for BEA were powered by four 4,985-ESHP Rolls Royce Tyne Mk.506 turboprop engines and could carry 132 pasengers. It had a wingspan of 118 ft., a length of 122 ft. 10 in. and a maximum range of 2,070 mi. at 412 MPH. Only 43 were built, BEA putting the first to work in December 1960.

1959 January 27 The first Convair CV-880 (Model 22) jet airliner flew, powered by four 11,200-lb. s.t. General Electric CJ-805-3 turbojets providing a cruising speed of 557–615 MPH and a maximum payload range of 3,450 mi. With provision for up to

The first of only two North American XB-70As ever built took to the air for the first time on February 4, 1959.

110 passengers, the Model 22 had been developed for domestic use and was to form the basis for an intercontinental version, the Model 30, otherwise known as the CV-990, which would be faster and carry more people.

1959 January 29 At the 27th annual meeting of the Institute of Aeronautical Sciences in New York, U.S. manufacturers discussed the prospects for supersonic transport (SST) aircraft. Presentations by Convair, Douglas and Boeing agreed that such a venture was possible but that the market was not yet ready. General Electric and Pratt & Whitney said there were no barriers to building engines for an SST, but all thought that sonic boom effects would restrict use and limit revenue.

1959 February 1 The Royal Canadian Air Force took over management of the defense early warning line across the continent of North America. The DEW line had been set up and operated by the USAF. The RCAF would still report to the North American Air Defense (NORAD) center at Colorado Springs, Colo., from where the system coordinated radar coverage toward the Arctic Circle and communicated with fighter units.

1959 February 11 A U.S. meteorological balloon achieved a record height of 146,000 ft. carrying a special package of detectors sending information by radio signal to the ground. In the never-ending quest for information about the atmosphere, the significantly increased altitude being flown by military aircraft stimulated a series of research projects designed to improve scientific understanding of the upper atmosphere.

1959 February 12 The last Convair B-36 Peacemaker was retired from the USAF Strategic Air Command. The B-36J (serial

no. 52-2827) had been assigned to the Ninety-fifth Bombardment Wing at Biggs AFB, Tex. and was flown to Amon Carter Field, Fort Worth, where it was placed on display as a permanent memorial. The peak year for the B-36 inventory had been 1954, when 209 aircraft of this type were in service. For the first time, Strategic Air Command now had an all-jet bomber force. Technically, Britain had had an all-jet bomber force from early 1958, when the last B-50 Washingtons were retired.

1959 February 20 The first Handley Page Victor B.Mk.2 (serial no. XH668) made its first flight, powered by four 19,750-lb. s.t. Rolls Royce Conway R.Co.17 Mk.201 turbojet engines and a modified wing with a span of 120 ft. and a loaded weight of 175,000 lb. The Mk.2 had a combat radius of 1,725 mi. and a service ceiling in excess of 60,000 ft. Warload comprised 35 high-explosive 1,000-lb. bombs, or a variety of nuclear weapons, including the Blue Steel stand-off bomb. The B.Mk.2 entered service with the RAF in 1965.

1959 March 10 With North American test pilot A. Scott Crossfield in the cockpit, the #1 X-15 rocket-powered research aircraft made its first captive-inactive flight suspended by a pylon beneath the starboard wing of modified B-52 carrier-plane. The size of the X-15 prohibited it from being carried in a B-50 under-fuselage configuration as had been the case with previous air-launched research aircraft. One B-52A and one B-52B had been modified for this project after delivery on February 4, 1958, and January 6, 1959, respectively.

1959 March 11 Designed to a U.S. Navy specification issued on September 23, 1957, the prototype Sikorsky S-61 (designated YHSS-2) Sea King made its first flight. It was ordered into production as the SH-3A, entering service with the U.S. Navy in September 1961. This amphibious helicopter had alternative General Electric T58 or Bristol Siddeley-Gnôme engines driving a five-blade rotor with a diameter of 62 ft. The S-61 had a length of 54 ft. 9 in. and a maximum takeoff weight of 21,500 lb. A civilian S-61L derivative could carry 30 passengers in a lengthened fuselage.

1959 March 18 The West German Luftwaffe contracted with Lockheed for the license manufacture of the F-104G Starfighter; Messerschmitt would eventually build a total of 260. At first the contract anticipated production of the F-104G in Germany for all European NATO countries participating in the re-equipment purchase, but this was amended when agreements with individual countries allowed production by indigenous manufacturers. Fokker built 350 F-104 variants in the Netherlands, Fiat built 444 in Italy and Canadair built 340 in Canada.

1959 March 26 The first production Breguet 1050 Alizé three-seat, carrier-based antisubmarine aircraft was delivered to the Aéronavale. The aircraft had flown first on October 6, 1956, and, powered by a 1,950-SHP Rolls Royce Dart R.Da21 turboprop engine, had a wingspan of 51 ft. 2 in. and a length of 45 ft. 6 in. The Alizé had a patrol speed of 138–207 MPH and an endurance of 5 hr. 10 min. and could carry a single torpedo, three 353-lb. depth charges, four homing rockets or six air-to-ground rockets.

1959 March 31 A BOAC round-the-world service began when Bristol Britannia 312 G-AOVT departed London-Heathrow bound for Hong Kong via New York, San Francisco, Honolulu and Tokyo, arriving at its destination in time to meet a Comet 4 (G-APDH) that had flown from London April 1 and arrived in Tokyo April 3. It picked up the Britannia passengers next day and returned to London. Because of a trans-Pacific rights dispute, regularly scheduled service did not start before August 22.

1959 March With an eye to developing it into a high subsonic VTOL ground-attack aircraft, approval was granted at Hawker Aircraft, Kingston, England for construction of a prototype P.1127. The aircraft was to be powered by a BE.53/3 engine that would incorporate bleed-air fed to wingtip jets for reaction control and stability in the nonaerodynamic lift phases of V/STOL flight. Still lacking British government support, the project attracted the interest of NASA in the United States.

1959 April 10 The first USAF Northrop T-38A Talon trainer derivative of the N-156 lightweight fighter made its first flight. Production aircraft were powered by two 2,680-lb. s.t. General Electric J85-GE-5A turbojets and had a wingspan of 25 ft. 3 in. and length of 46 ft. 4 in. With a maximum speed of 805 MPH at 36,089 ft. and an initial climb rate of 28,500 ft./min., the T-38A entered service in March 1961. The type has gained fame as the first supersonic trainer for the USAF and as the personal transport for the U.S. astronauts.

1959 April 14 The Grumman YAO-1 made its first flight from Bethpage, N.Y. The only fixed-wing aircraft ever to be specially designed for the U.S. Army was developed after the Korean War by a joint Army-Marine Corps requirement to replace the Cessna L-19 and Bird Dog observation aircraft. The resulting OV-1 Mohawk entered service with the Seventh Army in Germany during 1961. With a wingspan of 47 ft. 10 in. and a length of 41 ft., it was powered by two 1,150-SHP Lycoming T53 series engines, had a cruising speed of 207 MPH and had a range of 1,230 mi.

1959 April 15 The first scheduled service with the Tupolev Tu-104B airliner, powered by two 21,384-lb. s.t. Mikulin RD-3M-500 engines, began on Aeroflot's Moscow-Leningrad route. Increased in length to 131 ft. 5 in., the aircraft could carry 100 people over a maximum range of 1,303 mi. at a cruising speed of 466–497 MPH. The design incorporated the fuselage and flaps of the Tu-110 with the wings, tail and landing gear of the Tu-104A. Added advantages included moving the under-fuselage cargo bay loading door from the centerline to the starboard position.

1959 April 23 The USAF conducted the first successful live firing of the GAM-77 Hound Dog strategic air-to-surface missile from a B-52D. With a length of 42 ft. 6 in. and a wingspan of 12 ft., the Hound Dog carried a 7,500-lb. s.t. Pratt & Whitney J52-6 turbojet in an underslung rear pod giving it a range of 710 mi. It carried a 1 megaton warhead and was to be carried by the B-52G and B-52H or earlier variants when suitably modified. First delivered to the 4135th Strategic Wing, Eglin AFB, Florida, it would remain in the Strategic Air Command inventory through 1976. A peak inventory of 593 was reached in 1963.

1959 April 23 The British Ministry of Aviation asked the Hawker Aircraft Co. to prepare cost and manufacturing estimates for two prototype V/STOL design concepts around the P.1127 research vehicle. Eager to find a replacement for the Hunter ground-attack aircraft and mindful of the increasing vulnerability of fixed airfields to missile attack, the RAF was intrigued by the possibility of a high-performance combat aircraft operating from unprepared fields.

1959 April 26 The Süd-Est Caravelle jet airliner entered service with SAS. The second prototype was leased to the airline for it to make a flight from Copenhagen, Denmark to destinations in the Middle East. The first inaugural flight by Air France took place on May 6 when a production aircraft was flown from Paris, France to Istanbul, Turkey. Powered by two 10,500-lb. s.t. Rolls Royce Avon R.A.29 turbojets, the Caravelle had a wingspan of 112 ft. 6 in. and a length of 105 ft. with a range of 1,150 mi.

1959 May 15 The RAF gave up its last flying boat when the last two Short Sunderlands of No. 205 Squadron, were flown from Seletar airfield, Singapore for the last time. They had been in service 21 yr. and contributed their unique role in war and peace. During the British North Greenland Expedition of 1951–54, they had operated during the summer when the lakes were ice-free. Five Sunderlands moved 250 tons of equipment from Young Sound on the northeast coast to base camp at Britannia Lake only 800 mi. from the North Pole.

1959 May 19 The first passenger service between South America and the United Kingdom was inaugurated when Aerolineas Argentinas introduced the Comet 4 to replace the DC-6. BOAC was to follow with its Comet 4 service beginning January 25, 1960, but in the interim, Aerolineas Argentinas became the first airline to operate jet airliners between South and North America when the Comet was introduced for that service on June 7, 1959.

1959 June 1 BOAC inaugurated the first regularly scheduled jet airliner service between Europe and the Far East. Comet 4 G-APDE flew outbound from London to Singapore and arrived June 3. The return flight was made by Comet 4 G-APDM, which arrived in London June 5. The competition between the jets and the turboprops heated up when TWA began its nonstop Chicago-London service June 5 with the Lockheed L-1649A doing the journey in 13 hr. 10 min. and making the return trip in a scheduled time of 15 hr. 50 min.

1959 June 4 A new lightplane record was set when American aviator Max Conrad landed his Piper Commanche at New York after having flown 7,683 mi. nonstop from Casablanca, Morocco. The Commanche, which first flew on May 24, 1956, was powered by a 180-HP Lycoming, had a wingspan of 36 ft., a length of 24 ft. 9 in. and capacity for four people. When production ended in 1973, a total 4,708 had been built.

1959 June 8 Piloted by A. Scott Crossfield, the #1 X-15 rocket research aircraft made its first glide drop from a B-52 carrier-plane at 37,550 ft. and reached a speed of Mach 0.79 during the descent. Four captive-inactive flights with the B-52 had been conducted to date, each with some technical difficulty. Two more captive flights were completed, the first with full rocket propellant tanks, prior to the first powered flight on September 17.

1959 June 12 The first Lockheed C-130B transport aircraft was delivered to the USAF 463d Troop Carrier Wing. Powered by four 4,050-eHP Allison T56-A-7A engines and Hamilton Standard propellers, 128 out of 230 of this type went to the USAF. Some were modified as WC-130B weather reconnaissance aircraft and others as electronic intelligence-gathering aircraft.

1959 June 16 A U.S. Navy Martin P4M-1Q Mercator of Navy Squadron VQ-1 was on a routine patrol over international waters off the coast of Japan when two Soviet MiG-15s attacked it without provocation. The aircraft was hit several times, and the controls became difficult to handle, some being inoperable. One of the crewmembers had been wounded by gunfire, and the aircraft was only just able to make it to an emergency landing at Miho, Japan.

1959 June 17 The prototype Dassault Mirage IVA delta-wing strategic bomber made its first flight. Designed to a requirement for an indigenous nuclear bomber issued in 1954, the two-seat aircraft was essentially a scaled-up Mirage III. It had a wingspan of 38 ft. 10 in., a length of 77 ft. 1 in. and two 15,432-lb. s.t. SNECMA Atar 9K turbojet engines providing a maximum speed of 1,454 MPH or Mach 2.2 at 40,060 ft. carrying a 60 kiloton nuclear weapon or up to 16,005 lb. of stores. The first of 62 joined France's L'Armée l'Air in 1964.

1959 June 30 The first of nine preproduction Bell HU-1A Iroquois helicopters, powered by 700-HP Lycoming T53-L-1A engines, joined the USAF. The aircraft was soon dubbed the ''Huey,'' a reference to the ''helicopter-utility'' category under which it was ordered. Deliveries of the HU-1A were completed in 1961, when some were sent to South Korea, a year after the first overseas deployment had taken two from the Eighty-second Airborne Division on exercise to the Panama Canal Zone.

1959 July 2 The first of four prototype Kaman HU2K-1 Seasprites made its first flight. This was followed by an initial production batch of 12 and orders for a further 102. With a 1,250-SHP General Electric T58-GE-8B turboshaft engine driving a 44-ft. diameter rotor, it had a length of 52 ft. 2 in., a cruising speed of 124 MPH and a range of 620 mi. Filling a wide range of duties, it was the object of a conversion program into the SH-2 during the early 1970s.

1959 July 3 The first ground attack version of the Hawker Hunter, the F.G.A.9 (serial no. XE617) made its first flight. Designed to succeed the now-aging de Havilland Venom, the Hunter F.G.A.9 contender was in competition with the Folland Gnat as a possible replacement when the RAF reviewed both types in 1958. The initial order was for conversion of some Mk.6s into

the ground attack role, giving the aircraft capacity for carrying 1,000 lb. of external stores.

1959 July 9 A Vickers Valiant B.Mk.1 (serial no. XD861) of No. 214 Squadron, RAF, was flown from a flying start over London-Heathrow to a landing at Cape Town, South Africa, constituting the first nonstop flight between those two capital cities. The aircraft, captained by Wg. Comdr. M. J. Beetham, was flown 6,060 mi. in 11 hr. 28 min., with two in-flight refueling operations.

1959 July 13 To celebrate the 50th anniversary of the first crossing of the English Channel by air, a Paris-London air-land race was held. Sqdn. Ldr. Charles Maughan, RAF, made the quickest time of 40 min. 44 sec. It began with a 4-min. motorcycle dash from the Arc de Triomphe to Issy-les-Moulineaux followed by a 3 min. 44 sec. Bristol Sycamore flight to Villacoublay. A Hunter T.7 was used for the cross-channel leg to Biggin Hill airfield in southern England in 18 min. 28 sec. It took 7 min. 30 sec. by Sycamore helicopter to Chelsea Embankment, London, with 6 min. 30 sec. by motorcycle to Marble Arch, the difference in time taken up with changeovers and customs.

1959 July 14 Maj. V. Ilyushin, son of the famous aircraft designer, broke the existing world altitude record for manned aircraft with a flight to 94,659 ft. in the new Sukhoi Su-9. The aircraft bore a very close resemblance to the MiG-21, but the prototype had a bulbous lip carrying a fire control radar. This was changed to a central cone within the circular nose air intake on later production aircraft.

1959 July 26 The longest possible descent on record was achieved when Lt. Col. William H. Rankin of the U.S. Marine Corps ejected from his Nought F8U Crusader at a height of 47,000 ft. As he fell into violent thunderstorms, he was continually thrown up by vertical air currents, only coming safely back to earth in North Carolina 40 min. after he left his ailing aircraft.

1959 July 29 The first jet airliner service between Sidney, Australia and San Francisco, Calif. was completed by QANTAS's Boeing 707-138B *City of Canberra*. This was also the airline's first scheduled jet flight over the Pacific Ocean. QANTAS had taken delivery of its first of six aircraft of this type in June, all powered by four Pratt & Whitney JT3D-1 engines.

1959 July 30 The prototype private venture Northrop N-156F made its first flight, piloted by Lew Nelson. Designed for the lightweight fighter market and to be compatible with the Military Assistance Program for foreign purchase, it was powered by two 3,500-lb. s.t. General Electric J85-GE-5 turbojets, and had a wingspan of 25 ft. 3 in. and a length of 45 ft. 1 in. Maximum speed with two wingtip Sidewinder air-to-air missiles was Mach 1.3, and ferry range 2,230 mi. After three years of hard selling, Northrop would eventually receive an order for F-5 lightweight fighter versions.

1959 August 10 In the supersonic B-70 bomber program, it was decided to abandon the boron-fuel concept for General Electric YJ93-GE-5 afterburning engines. Another version of that engine, the GE-3, would be used, burning a refined jet petroleum fuel called JP-6. This had the effect of cutting 10% off the B-70's range, calling for a single KC-135 refueling rendezvous to accomplish the stipulated range of at least 8,055 mi.

1959 August 25 During an acceptance trial with the Douglas A3D Skywarrior, VAH-1 pilot Lt. Comdr. Ed Decker took off

Chosen by 30 countries around the world as a low-cost fighter, the Northrop F-5 was adapted for many roles, including reconnaissance and training.

from the flight deck of the carrier USS *Independence* with a deck weight of 84,000 lb., making it the heaviest aircraft ever to fly from a carrier. VAH-1 had been operating aboard the *Enterprise* since 1956.

1959 August 29 Known as Project Oxcart and managed by the USAF, the contract for a CIA high-altitude, high-speed reconnaissance aircraft designated A-12 was awarded to Lockheed. Unlike earlier proposals that envisaged a hydrogen-burning aircraft, the A-12 would use the relatively conventional propulsion of a Pratt & Whitney JT11D. Some consideration was soon given to a penetrating, unmanned, remotely controlled drone, which was to be launched from the A-12.

1959 September 13 At the 20th Society of British Aircraft Companies display at Farnborough, England, Hawker chief test pilot A. W. ("Bill") Bedford stunned the crowds when he performed 13 inverted spins (for the 13th of the month) from a height of 15,000 ft. in his two-seat Hawker Hunter T.7 trainer G-APUX. Colored smoke marked the trail of his aircraft, which was performing the first public dislay of inverted spins.

1959 September 17 Piloted by A. Scott Crossfield, the #2 X-15 research aircraft made the first powered drop from a B-52. Propelled by a Reaction Motors XLR-11, because the XLR-99 for which the aircraft was designed had not yet reached operational readiness, the X-15 attained a speed of 1,393 MPH (Mach 2.11) and a height of 52,341 ft. Some 23 flights with the XLR-11 would be made by the X-15 before the XLR-99 was first used in flight on November 15, 1960.

1959 September 18 United Air Lines and Delta Air Lines inaugurated services with the Douglas DC-8 series 10, with a mixed-class capacity for 124 people and a maximum payload range of 4,330 mi. Full certification had been granted on August 31, only 15 months after the plane's first flight, which compared very well with the 4 yr. 3 mon. for the Boeing 707. Nevertheless, the DC-8 was almost a year behind the Boeing in getting into service.

1959 September 23 The ambitious North American F-108 Rapier supersonic interceptor that had been evolving for 2 yr. was canceled. Designed to be a miniature version of the B-70, it was to have been powered by two 30,000-lb. s.t. General Electric J93-GE-3 turbojet engines and achieve a dash speed of Mach 3

as an escort for the giant bomber. Design gross weight was 102,000 lb. with a projected length of 84 ft. 10 in. and a wingspan of 52 ft. 10 in.

1959 September 30 Croydon airport outside London, once known as London's airport and the center of British civil air transport for almost 40 yr., was officially closed, formally superseded by Heathrow (which opened on May 31, 1946) as London Airport. Croydon's traffic was taken up by nearby Gatwick, which had recently been opened.

1959 October 13 The Nord 1500-02 Griffon II achieved a speed of Mach 2.19 on the combined operation of its 7,716-lb. s.t. SNECMA Atar 101E3 turbojet engine and a ramjet engine. The ramjet engine was installed within the ducting of the turbojet engine, which was used to accelerate the aircraft to sufficient speed for the ramjet to take over. The Griffon II had first flown on January 23, 1957, and could have achieved higher speeds than it did but for limitations placed on the kinetic heating of the aircraft's skin.

1959 October 15 Just a month after its first flight, the first production B-58A Hustler made a 1,680-mi. flight in 1 hr. 10 min. with one in-flight refueling and maintaining a cruising speed of more than Mach 2 for over 1 hr. The first prototype had flown without its ventral weapons pod, an integral part of the aircraft's aerodynamic profile. The second prototype had flown for the first time on February 16, 1957, followed by 30 trials of aircraft operating with a special unit drawn from the 6592d Test Squadron and the 3958th Operational, Test and Evaluation Squadron.

1959 October 31 A developed version of the basic USAF Military Air Transport Service Cargomaster, the first Douglas C-133B, took to the air, powered by four 7,500-SHP Pratt & Whitney T34-P-9W turboprop engines. Two primary operating advantages were that the new model had rear-loading clam-shell doors and a near-25% increase in payload/range, carrying 52,000 lb. a distance of 4,000 mi. Military Air Transport Service ordered 15, the first being delivered to the 1,501st Air Transport Wing in March 1960.

1959 October 31 The first de Havilland Comet 4C made its first flight, powered by four 10,500-lb. s.t. Rolls Royce Avon 525B engines and with wingspan increased to 114 ft. 10 in. At an increased maximum takeoff weight of 160,000 lb. the Comet 4C had a maximum low payload range of 4,285 mi. and a maximum payload range of 3,350 mi., almost double that of the Comet 1. The Comet 4C combined the wings and fuel tankage of the Comet 4 with the longer fuselage of the Comet 4B.

1959 November 1 BOAC started its first Comet 4 service between London and Sydney when G-APDL flew out of Heathrow to Australia via Beirut, Karachi and Singapore. The aircraft arrived in Sydney November 3 and the first westbound service left November 4 and arrived in London the following day, a round trip of 23,384 mi. flown in 60 hr. 57 min. at an average speed of 383.66 MPH.

1959 November 2 The world's first rigid-rotor helicopter took to the air when the Lockheed CL-475 made its first flight powered by a 140-HP Lycoming VO-360-A1A engine. (Rigid rotors are movable in pitch for feathering purposes only.) Seeking improvements to handling characteristics as well as operating cost and efficiency, Irven Culver and a small team developed a small model to test the concept, and from that the CL-474 was built with a rotor diameter of 32 ft. and a loaded weight of 2,000 lb.

First flown on November 11, 1954, the Convair B-58 Hustler was the first U.S. supersonic bomber.

At the end of its trial, it was handed over to the Smithsonian Institution.

1959 November 9 The USAF selected Boeing for a contract to build the Dyna-Soar hypersonic boost-glide vehicle, now designated Weapon System 620A. On December 15, project control was moved to the Wright Air Development Division at Wright-Patterson AFB, Ohio, which was formed the same day and also assumed control of the glider, responsibility for the booster segment moving to the U.S. Army Ballistic Missile Division. Funds for Boeing were released after a Phase Alpha review had been completed on April 1, 1960.

1959 November 16 Capt. Joseph W. Kittinger Jr., USAF, set a new record for free-fall parachute jumps when he ascended to a height of 76,400 ft. in the open gondola of a balloon before stepping out for a free-fall of 12,400 ft. Kittinger had taken off from White Sands AFB, N. Mex. and survived on bottled oxygen when his altitude exceeded the safe limit for open breathing. Kittinger became a specialist in high-altitude balloon ascents and record parachute jumps.

1959 November 17 At a meeting of the Dayton-Cincinnati section of the U.S. Institute of Aeronautical Sciences, Douglas Aircraft Co. representative Dr. V. V. Holmes said it was technically possible to build a supersonic transport in 1963–65 but that operating conditions would make it preferable in 1968–70 and that it was unlikely airlines would operate them before 1970–75. Talk of an SST among manufacturers was more positive, and moves on the West Coast had been made by Douglas, Convair and Lockheed to form a consortium to share development costs and work on an SST.

1959 November 25 The Lockheed YP3V-1 made its first flight just under 4 mon. after winning a competition for the next U.S.

Navy high-performance antisubmarine aircraft. The name Orion was given to the aircraft toward the end of 1960, and two years later the designation of this aircraft was changed from P3V to P-3. The first preproduction aircraft would not fly for another 17 mon. but development of a special bomb bay and the equipment to fill it would continue for several years.

1959 December 2 The first BOAC Comet 4 service between London and South Africa began when G-APDK left Heathrow for Johannesburg, arriving December 3. The first return flight left that day, but weather diverted the aircraft from Rome to Naples. The total round-trip distance of 11,169 mi. was flown in 32 hr. 29 min.

1959 December 3 Seeking ways to balance the budget and rely in the future more on ballistic missiles than manned penetrating bombers, U.S. Budget Bureau director Maurice Stans canceled the USAF B-70 program, which was working toward a Mach 3 bomber for Strategic Air Command. Only one XB-70 prototype was to be allowed to continue, and related work was reduced to a minimum. The first flight was put back by 1 yr. to December 1962 followed by a limited 5-yr. flight test program.

1959 December 5 The Avro Canada Model 1 Avrocar made its first flight at Malton, Canada. Designed in cooperation with the U.S. Army to the WS-606A requirement calling for a land mobile vehicle capable of operating over swamps and estuaries, it was circular with a central fan for vertical air-cushion lift and three Continental J69 turbojets for power. The Avrocar was taken to the United States where NASA began tests on May 17, 1961.

1959 December 13 Six years after its first flight, Moulton B. Taylor's Aerocar was granted FAA certification. Designed as a road car with detachable wings and tailplane, the developed Aerocar III had a span of 34 ft., a length of 23 ft. as an aircraft and a length of 11 ft. as a car, a gross weight of 2,100 lb. and a 143-HP Avco Lycoming O-320-A1A flat-four-piston engine. Only six Aerocars were built, but between them they notched up 200,000 mi. on the road and 5,000 flying hr.

1959 December 14 Joe B. Jordan in a USAF Lockheed F-104C reached a new record altitude of 31,502 m (103,389 ft.), the first pilot, and the first aircraft, to exceed a height of 100,000 ft. A U.S. Navy McDonnell F4H Phantom II piloted by Comdr. Lawrence E. Flint had reached a new FAI-ratified record altitude of 98,556 ft. on December 6.

1959 December 15 Maj. J. W. Rogers, USAF, achieved a new absolute world air speed record with an average speed of 2,455.74 km/hr. (1,525.95 MPH) in a Convair F-106A Delta Dart at Edwards AFB, Calif. This was the last world speed record achieved by an operational combat fighter, the rest being taken by special aircraft prepared either for a record attempt or developed for a unique role such as high-speed reconnaissance.

1960 January 18 Test engineer Marion McKinney installed a one-sixth aerodynamic model of the Hawker P.1127 V/STOL prototype in a wind tunnel at the NASA Langley Research Center and found it stable and capable of controlled ascent, translation and forward flight. On February 4, it was made to perform the first transition to simulated forward flight. From the United Kingdom, Hawker chief test pilot A. W. ("Bill") Bedford and Hugh Merewether flew the X-14 to familiarize themselves with VTOL operating techniques.

1960 January 28 During sessions at the 2d Supersonic Transport Symposium held at the annual meeting of the Institute of Aeronautical Sciences in New York's Astor Hotel, proponents of the SST submitted a wide range of design specifications, and manufacturers spoke confidently of producing an SST by the mid-1960s. It was also noted that a government subsidy to develop an SST was being considered by the Aviation Subcommittee of the Senate Interstate and Foreign Commerce Committee to block any possible Soviet lead in this field.

1960 January 29 The Japanese government concluded an agreement with Lockheed whereby the Mitsubishi company would be allowed to build under license the F-104J Starfighter. The F-104J was similar to the F-104G being built under license in Europe but would be equipped as an all-weather interceptor and would have a Japanese-built J79-1H1-11A turbojet engine. The first F-104J was flown on June 30, 1961, and a total 207 were built for the Japanese.

1960 February 13 France detonated its first atomic weapon and thus became the fourth nation to develop an indigenous nuclear capability. The device was exploded in the Sahara Desert and would lead to development of nuclear weapons for the newly evolving French nuclear deterrent. France already had U.S.-supplied atomic weapons deployed with two squadrons of F-100 fighter-bombers under NATO rules, but these would no longer be present after France withdrew from NATO in 1966.

1960 February 20 The first of only 37 Boeing 707-400 airliners built began the first nonstop flight from London to Bombay on its way to join Air India, the first of an initial order of six for that airline. BOAC had been first to order the new type, 18 of which were delivered beginning in April. Powered by 17,500-lb. s.t. Rolls Royce Conway 50B bypass engines and with reduced payload, the 400-series had a range of 6,955 mi. and a maximum

payload range of 4,720 mi. This was the only version of the Boeing 707 to be powered by British engines.

1960 February British Aircraft Corp. Ltd. was formed combining the Bristol Aeroplane Co., the English Electric Co. Ltd. and Vickers Ltd. This was the second major block grouping of Britain's aircraft manufacturers to emerge. Hawker Siddeley absorbed Folland in 1959 and put in bids for de Havilland, which it acquired in 1960. The third block grouping was Westland Aircraft, which took over Saunders Roe in 1959 and acquired Bristol Helicopters and Fairey in 1960.

1960 March 3 The longest nonstop flight ever made by an RAF aircraft was completed when a Vickers Valiant B.Mk.1 (serial no. XD858) piloted by Sqdn. Ldr. J. H. Garstin flew around the British Isles for a total distance of 8,500 mi. aided by two inflight refuelings. The aircraft belonged to No. 214 Squadron, and the pilot was practicing for a nonstop flight from England to Singapore, which he completed on May 26 after flying a Valiant B.Mk.1 (serial no. WZ390) 8,100 mi. in 15 hr. 35 min.

1960 March 15 The USAF Forty-third Bombardment Wing of the Strategic Air Command was formed at Carswell AFB, Tex. following a move from Davis-Monthan AFB, Ariz. as the first unit to operate the B-58A Hustler supersonic bomber. Introduction of this Mach 2 + aircraft called for special training and work-up procedures. The first B-58A arrived August 1 when Gen. Thomas S. Power, commander-in-chief of Strategic Air Command, accepted it. A second wing, the 305th Bombardment Wing, would also operate this aircraft. Strategic Air Command would eventually receive 116 aircraft of this type.

1960 March 25 The first NASA flight in the X-15 hypersonic research program got under way when test pilot Joseph A. Walker made the first of his 25 flights in this aircraft. The #1 X-15 was air-dropped from its B-52 carrier-plane for a Mach 2 (1,320 MPH) flight to 48,630 ft. using the interim Reaction Motors XLR-11 engine.

1960 March 31 Tests designed to demonstrate the continued viability of U.S. Navy non-rigid airships in anti-submarine operations ended when one of two fleet squadrons completed an exercise that had begun September 15, 1959, off the eastern seaboard of the United States. In that period, airships of the ZPG class maintained active patrols in some of the worst weather recorded in the North Atlantic. The first phase of the operation ended January 31 and the second phase began February 1. During the second phase one ZPG-2 airship remained aloft for 95.5 hr. Airships of this type had been designed to remain airborne for no more than 55 hr.

1960 April 1 BEA started operating de Havilland Comet 4Bs when Capt. A. N. Werner flew *RMA Walter Gale* (G-APBM) from Tel Aviv to London by way of Athens and Rome. Simultaneously, Capt. W. Baillie flew *RMA William Denning* (G-APMD) between London and Moscow, the first such service to be operated by BEA under reciprocal arrangements with Aeroflot. Ordered by BEA in April 1958, the short-haul Comet 4B was stretched 3 ft. 2 in. to accommodate a total 102 passengers with cruising speed increased to 532 MPH and range reduced to 2,570 mi.

1960 April 9 A CIA overflight of the USSR by a U-2 spyplane provided evidence that the Soviets were quickening the pace of their intercontinental ballistic missile (ICBM) capability. Major construction and expansion at the two ICBM testing sites in Khazakhstan and at Plesetsk, near Archangel, were observed, and a second flight was considered necessary to confirm this and provide additional information. It was not until May that the weather was good enough to mount that flight, flown by Francis Gary Powers.

1960 April 13   The British government announced in London that the de Havilland Blue Streak intercontinental ballistic missile was to be abandoned and replaced by Skybolt stand-off missiles purchased from the United States and carried by the Avro Vulcan B.Mk.2. The decision to cancel Blue Streak after five years of development work in association with Rocketdyne of California was based on cost and the fact that existing V-bombers could be made the basis for sustaining a nuclear strike capability without full development and operations costs of a completely new delivery system.

1960 April 19   The Grumman A-6 Intruder made its first flight when the A2F-1 took to the air powered by two 8,500-lb. s.t. Pratt & Whitney J52 turbojets. Later production A-6A models would have the 9,300-lb s.t. J52-P-8. With a wingspan of 53 ft., 25 ft. 4 in. folded, and a length of 54 ft. 9 in., the A-6 could carry 18,000 lb. of ordnance on centerline and wing stations with a cruising speed of 481 MPH and a normal range of 1,350 mi. Designed to a U.S. Navy requirement for a close-air support and interdiction aircraft, Grumman won the contract on December 20, 1957.

1960 April   The results of the Phase Alpha review of the USAF Dyna-Soar program were released confirming Boeing as the prime contractor. The review had examined alternate configurations, program schedules and flight objectives. It confirmed a three-step approach. Step one was to start in July 1963 with 20 air-drops, followed by unmanned suborbital flights beginning November 1963 and manned suborbital flight beginning November 1964. Parallel studies were to define a military reconnaissance system.

1960 May 1   A veteran of 27 U-2 spyplane flights for the CIA, Francis Gary Powers was brought down over Sverdlovsk (now Yekaterinburg) in the U-2 identified as Article 360 from an altitude of just over 67,000 ft. Apparently subject to structural breakup from the concussive effects of a salvo of up to 14 Soviet SA-2 missiles, one of which shot down a MiG-19, Powers ejected after activating a ''melt-down'' system to destroy sensitive equipment. Powers' overflight began at Peshawar, Pakistan and was to have ended 3,788 mi. away at Bodo, Norway. A second flight penetrated elsewhere as an unsuccessful diversion. Powers went on trial in Moscow and spent five years in prison before being returned to the United States in 1962.

1960 May 4   The USAF issued Specific Operational Requirement 182 defining the tasks to be assigned a new strategic military air transport aircraft for the Military Air Transport Service. The new aircraft was to be jet-powered, and a design competition was set up. Lockheed, Boeing, Convair and Douglas put up competing designs, and Lockheed was selected on March 13, 1961, to build the prototype of the C-141 StarLifter, a name indicating it as the ''star'' of the new transport capability. The C-141 was to be developed under the designation SS476L.

1960 May 12   A record test parachute drop of a 35,000-lb. mass was made from Lockheed C-130 in flight. The aircraft had been built for tail-drops, and the design made it practical for zero-height drops where parachute-retarded loads were rolled out the back only a few feet above the ground.

1960 May 15   Delta Air Lines introduced the Convair CV-880 into service just 14 days after the plane received FAA certification. Although faster than the Boeing 707 and the DC-8, it was not as efficient, and it ran third in a race in which only two contenders had a realistic chance of receiving strong order books. Only 48 were built, of which 26 went to TWA and 17 to Delta.

1960 May 17   Royal Dutch Airlines, KLM, celebrated the 40th anniversary of the London-Amsterdam service by naming their Douglas DC-8 airliner PH-DCC, *Sir Frank Whittle*. This was done in honor of the work Whittle had done in developing the jet engine. Whittle was among the passengers carried between London and Amsterdam as was H. (''Jerry'') Shaw who had been on the inaugural flight 40 yr. earlier.

1960 May 27   BOAC began using Boeing 707-436-series aircraft on its London-New York route when Capt. T. B. Stoney commanded G-APFD as it left Heathrow during the morning. The first eastbound flight was commanded out of New York by Capt. Nisbett in the same aircraft during the evening, arriving London-Heathrow the following morning. Stoney had flown into London with G-APFD on April 29 from the Boeing factory at Seattle, Wash. and made the 4,900-mi. journey in 9 hr. 44 min.

1960 June 3   A U.S. Marine Corps UH-34D completed a successful test-firing of the Martin Bullpup ASM-N-7A air-to-surface guided missile. This comparatively old missile, ordered into development in 1954, had been redeveloped into the N-7A version with significant improvements. Its application to helicopter operations emphasized the diversifying roles of rotary-winged aircraft. The U.S. Marine Corps ordered its first UH-34D, S-58 derivative, in October 1954, and deliveries began in February 1957.

1960 June 14   The USAF issued Specific Operational Requirement 183 calling for a Tactical Fighter Experimental (TFX) F-105 replacement. It evolved from a meeting between NASA's John Stack and acting commander-in-chief of Tactical Air Command, Brig. Gen. Frank Everest, in which the advantages of variable geometry were extolled and a working solution to previous problems was found by placing pivot points outboard of the fuselage. TFX was to be capable of Mach 2.5 at altitude and Mach 1.2 at low level.

1960 June 24   The first Avro 748 (G-APZV) made its first flight at Woodford, England with chief test pilot J. G. Harrison. Powered by two 1,740-HP Rolls Royce Dart 514 turboprop engines, it was designed as a replacement for the DC-3 (and 381 were built), but it fell far short of that objective. The 748 had a wingspan of 103 ft. 5 in., a length of 67 ft. and a cruising speed of 281 MPH with a maximum payload range of 812 mi.

1960 July 1   A Soviet MiG fighter piloted by Capt. Vasily A. Polyakov shot down a USAF RB-47 of the Fifty-fifth Strategic Reconnaissance Wing while operating in international airspace over the Barents Sea. Of the six-man crew, four were killed, but copilot Bruce Olmstead and navigator Capt. John R. McKone were held by the Russians for 7 mon. and accused of spying. They were returned to the United States on January 24, 1961, just four days after the inauguration of President John F. Kennedy.

1960 July 1   In a shakedown trial of the Gyrodyne QH-50A helicopter drone, the first landing at sea aboard the USS *Mischer* took place. The unmanned, remotely controlled helicopter drone was developed from a contract in April 1958. The device was only 8 ft. 10 in. in length with a 72-HP Porsche YO-95-6 flat-four engine driving a 20-ft. rotor. With an all-up weight of 578 lb., it could carry two homing torpedoes up to 33 mi. away from the ship before returning to be recovered. The U.S. Navy received 758 QH-50 drones.

1960 July 1   At Offutt AFB, Nebr., Strategic Air Command began operational testing with an airborne command post comprising one of five specially converted KC-135s of the Thirty-fourth Air Refueling Squadron. Tanker aircraft were placed on 15-min. alert. (Strategic Air Command bombers had been on 15-min. alert for 2 yr.) When airborne, the command posts could take over command of Strategic Air Command activities in the unhappy event that the primary command centers on the ground were destroyed.

1960 July 1   British United Airways came into being, combining the activities of Airwork, Hunting-Clan, Air Charter, Morton Air Services, Olley Air Service, Transair, Airwork Helicopters and Bristow Helicopters. Through the merger of these separate, independent companies, the new holding group became the largest U.K. commercial air operator next to BOAC and BEA. Forty percent of the shares were divided equally between Blue Star Line and Furness Withy and 32% divided equally between Clan Line and British & Commonwealth Shipping.

1960 July 5   The first Boeing 720 service began with an inaugural run on United Air Lines's Chicago-Denver-Los Angeles route. Developed from the Boeing 707 as a short/medium range version for a maximum 165 passengers, the Model 720 was 8 ft. 4 in. shorter than the standard 707-100 and was powered by four 12,000-lb. s.t. Pratt & Whitney JT3C-7 engines attached to pylons on a substantially modified wing incorporating double taper inboard of the inner engines. The first of 154 had flown on November 23, 1959.

1960 July 31   After 12 yr. of operations against communist terrorists in Malaya, the RAF declared an end to Operation Firedog, although there were still groups operating in Thailand. A Malayan Auxiliary Air Force had been formed in 1950, which grew into the Royal Malayan Air Force in 1958 when the country achieved independence. Helicopters had played a particularly important part in the operations, evacuating 4,673 people since 1950.

1960 August 2   As a result of major decisions made in 1957, changes in British defense policy caused a reduction in the planned number of Victor B.Mk.2 bombers. Handley Page had proposed modifications enabling the B.Mk.2 to carry two Skybolt missiles, but the original plan to have the aircraft carry the Blue Steel stand-off bomb was retained, notwithstanding arguments that with Skybolt the bomber could attack two targets instead of one.

1960 August 4   The #1 North American X-15 rocket-powered research aircraft achieved its highest speed yet when NASA pilot Joseph A. Walker reached a speed of Mach 3.31 (2,196 MPH) and a height of 78,112 ft. The aircraft was still fitted with its XLR-11 motors and would be returned to North American on February 8, 1961, for installation of the XLR-99. It was returned to Edwards AFB, Calif. on June 10, 1961, and made its first flight with the more powerful engine on August 10, 1961.

1960 August 11   The first man-made object returned intact to earth from space was retrieved by a U.S. Navy HRS-3 helicopter operating from the ship *Haiti Victory*. The object was an oblate sphere from the USAF Discoverer 13 reconnaissance satellite that had been launched the day before. A retro-rocket brought the

capsule back down through the atmosphere on its 17th orbit of the earth, and it was picked up less than 3 hr. after hitting the water, 330 mi. northeast of Honolulu.

1960 August 12   The #1 North American X-15 reached a new unofficial record height of 136,500 ft. when it was flown to that altitude and a speed of Mach 2.52 (1,772 MPH) by USAF test pilot Capt. Robert M. White. White was one of five USAF test pilots that would fly the X-15, including Maj. Michael J. Adams, Capt. Joseph M. Engle, Capt. William J. Knight and Maj. Robert A. Rushworth. Together they would account for 89 of the 199 X-15 drops flown by USAF pilots, with Rushworth flying 34, the most of any USAF pilot. North American Aviation test pilot Scott Crossfield flew 14 missions, five NASA pilots flew a total of 91 missions, and U.S. Navy pilot Forrest S. Peterson flew 5 missions.

1960 September 4   The wide acceptance, sales potential and superior performance of the Boeing jet airliner was demonstrated in no better way than when Capts. J. M. B. Botes and S. Pienaar took the first Boeing Model 707-344 to enter service with South African Airways from Seattle, Wash. to Jan Smuts Airport, Johannesburg. They flew the 11,445-mi. distance in 21 hr. 35 min. The inaugural flight of the Boeing 707 Springbok service between Johannesburg and London began October 1.

1960 September 17   The first commercial Comet 4 service with East African Airways began when Capt. P. Henn commanded VP-KPJ from London to Nairobi, Kenya via Rome, Khartoum and Entebbe. The return flight took place on September 19, and a weekly series of flights to Dar-es-Salaam began on September 22. These flights were operated in a BOAC pool involving other aircraft. East African Airways took delivery of three Comet 4s in all.

1960 September 18   In an effort to demonstrate the low-altitude mission capabilities of the high-flying supersonic B-58A, an aircraft of this type (serial no. 58-1015) was flown from Fort Worth, Tex. to Bakersfield, Calif. via El Paso and Phoenix at a height of between 100 ft. and 500 ft. At no time did the flying speed drop below 690 MPH, and the pilots reported a good ride, excellent handling characteristics and good visibility from the cockpit.

1960 September 21   North American Aviation was contracted to build one YB-70 in addition to the single XB-70 it had been contracted to build, which was scheduled for a first flight in December 1962. Despite cancellation of production and operational plans for this Mach 3 Strategic Air Command bomber at the end of 1959, Congress had voted additional funds on July 31 to complete the XB-70 to full weapons status and for the USAF to build two XB-70s in addition to the YB-70 from North American.

1960 October 5   The first production Macchi M.B.326 single-seat advanced trainer and light attack aircraft made its first flight. The prototype had flown on December 10, 1957, and production aircraft powered by a 2,500-lb. s.t. Rolls Royce Viper turbojet had a wingspan of 34 ft. 8 in. over tip tanks, a length of 34 ft. 11 in. and a gross weight of 8,300 lb. The M.B.326 entered service with the Aeronautica Militare Italiano (Italian Air Force) in February 1962. A wide range of variants from two-seat trainer to ground attack evolved from the M.B.326.

1960 October 6   The British minister of aviation, Harold Watkinson, awarded a full development contract to British Aircraft Corp. for two ground test and nine flying T.S.R.2 aircraft. In association with this advanced aircraft program, an Avro Vulcan (serial no. XA494) was to be used to test the 13,300/30,600-lb. s.t. Bristol Siddeley Olympus B.01.22R engines, two of which the T.S.R.2 would carry. At this time, the aircraft had a projected performance of Mach 1 at sea level and Mach 2+ at altitude and a 1,150-mi. tactical radius.

1960 October 16   The last BOAC Comet 4 service between London and New York was flown, ending just over 2 yr. of trans-Atlantic jet passenger service. In that period, Comet 4s had made 2,304 Atlantic crossings with two aircraft initially operating a weekly service extended later to two services a day. On-time arrival had been achieved on 73% of westbound flights, 89% arrived within one hour of the scheduled time. There were no in-flight engine failures and on only one flight was an engine prudently shut down when a fuel control unit malfunctioned.

1960 October 21   The prototype Grumman E-2A Hawkeye maritime airborne early warning aircraft, designated W2F-1, made its first flight with the unusual configuration of dihedral on the horizontal tail surface and four vertical fins. The E-2A Hawkeye entered U.S. Navy service in January 1964. Distinguished by a large circular radome, the aircraft had a wingspan of 80 ft. 7 in., 29 ft. 4 in. folded, a length of 56 ft. 4 in., a gross weight of 54,830 lb. and a crew of five. The E-2A had a cruising speed of 297 MPH, a service ceiling of 28,800 ft. and a range of 1,650 mi.

1960 October 21   The prototype Hawker P.1127 V/STOL aircraft (serial no. XP831) made its first tentative hop into the air with chief test pilot Bill Bedford at the controls, broken leg in plaster following a minor accident. The P.1127 had a wingspan of 24 ft. 4 in., a length of 49 ft. and a loaded weight of 11,800 lb., although stripped to the essentials it was under 10,000 lb. for the first flight. Power was provided by the 10,500/13,500-lb. s.t. Bristol Pegasus engine. The first free hovering flight was achieved on November 19.

1960 October   The USAF announced it had been conducting studies on an aerospace-plane capable of operating between the outer atmosphere and space by ingesting large quantities of air at hypersonic speed. This reflected increasing optimism for the air-breathing ramjet engine concept studied and tested in working models by the Marquardt Corp. The company would go on to develop the idea of an air-breathing, hydrogen-fueled aerospace vehicle, although government support would stop short of development.

1960 November 15   The Reaction Motors XLR-99 single-chamber rocket motor of 50,000-lb. thrust at sea level, 57,850 lb. at 100,000 ft., was used for the first time on an X-15 flight. Flown by North American test pilot A. Scott Crossfield, the #2 aircraft reached a speed of Mach 2.97 (1,960 MPH) at 81,200 ft. on 50% power. Seven days later the first in-flight restart was conducted when the #2 X-15 reached Mach 2.51 (1,656 MPH), and on Scott Crossfield's last X-15 flight, December 6, he reached Mach 2.85 (1,881 MPH) and 53,374 ft.

1960 November 16   The first Canadair CL-44 made its first flight from Cartierville in Canada with W. S. Longhurst and G. T. McLean on the flight deck. Adopting the wings, tail and landing gear from the Bristol Britannia, the CL-44 had a fuselage 136 ft. 10 in. in length and a wingspan of 142 ft. 4 in. with four 5,730-ESHP Rolls Royce Tyne RTy.12 turboprop engines. Developed as an enlarged transport version of the CL-28, a cargo-carrying

variant had a rear-loading swing-tail, and a stretched version could accommodate 189 passengers.

1960 December 1   Boeing Co. president William Allen decided to authorize development of the Boeing 727 three-jet airliner for short- and medium-haul services. Boeing had been studying the concept for four years, and with competitors entering the market, a decision was made to proceed despite the low prospective order book for the type. The concept was to adopt the tri-engine configuration now becoming popular for smaller jet transports, leaving a clean 32° swept wing. The Boeing 727 would eventually appear in greater numbers than any other jet transport except the Boeing 737, with 1,832 built when production ended.

1960 December 8   The first British round-the-world jet service began operations when BOAC started operating its Boeing 707-436 twice-weekly service from London to Hong Kong by way of New York, San Francisco, Honolulu and Tokyo. This route had previously been flown using turboprop Bristol Britannias. The Boeing link connected with the BOAC Comet 4 westbound service between Hong Kong and London, the first of which departed December 11. Since shutting down its trans-Atlantic Comet service, BOAC had concentrated its jet airliners on eastern and southern routes.

1960 December 14   A B-52G of the USAF Fifth Bombardment Wing at Travis AFB, Calif. completed a record flight of 10,078.84 mi. without refueling in a time of 19 hr. 44 min. The aircraft had been commanded on this flight by Lt. Col. T. R. Grissom on a closed-loop circuit from Edwards AFB, Calif. to El Paso, Tex., Andrews AFB, Md., Ernest Holloman AFB, Newfoundland, Eielson AFB, Alaska, Philip, S. Dak. and back.

1960 December 20   The first Douglas DC-8 Series 50 made its first flight powered by four 17,000-lb. s.t. Pratt & Whitney JT3D-1 turbofan engines. Engine power had been steadily increased from the 13,500-lb. s.t. Pratt & Whitney JT3C-6 used in the domestic Series 10 version, and now enhanced efficiency made further improvements in the aircraft's sales potential. Douglas converted some early DC-8s into Series 50 standard at the request of owner airlines.

1960 December 29   The first production McDonnell F4H-1 Phantom IIs were delivered to U.S. Navy Squadron VF-101 for trials and transition training. With the emphasis on missile armament, these aircraft represented a new era for naval aviators, achieving full performance commensurate with their traditionally more powerful land-based contemporaries. The F-4 would be the first naval aircraft to achieve high prominence as a land-based fighter and attack aircraft.

1961 January 12   The first in a series of 14 world speed and altitude/payload records set by the Convair B-58 Hustler was achieved when Maj. Henry J. Deutschendorf and his crew averaged 1,708.82 km/hr. (1,061.81 MPH) around a 2,000-km (1,248-mi.) circuit carrying a 2,000 kg (4,409 lb.) payload. On January 14, Maj. Harold E. Confer and his crew set records in categories for aircraft carrying 2,000 kg, 1,000 kg and no loads over a distance of 1,000 km averaging 1,284.73 MPH (2,067.58 km/hr.).

1961 January 18   USAF Strategic Air Command announced it had been carrying out trial operations with an airborne alert concept for 2 yr., during which 6,000 sorties had proven the feasibility of keeping a number of nuclear-armed B-52s in the air at all times. This move was made in response to continued build-

Authorized on October 18, 1954, the McDonnell F-4 emerged as the free world's most versatile jet fighter.

up of Soviet land- and sea-based ballistic and cruise missiles. A 50% ground alert posture, whereby half the operational B-52 force was ready for flight within 15 min. at one time was achieved in July 1961.

1961 January 24   The Convair CV-990 jet airliner made its first flight. It was powered by four 16,100-lb. s.t. General Electric CJ-805-23 turbojet engines and had a wingspan of 120 ft., a length of 139 ft. 5 in., a maximum loaded weight of 244,200 lb. and provision for up to 121 passengers. Incorporating antishock cones on the wing trailing edge, it had a projected cruising speed of 621 MPH and a maximum payload range of 4,997 mi., but flight trials showed a top cruising speed of only 584 MPH and the need for many modifications. Only 37 aircraft were built.

1961 February 1   USAF Strategic Air Command announced that the first elements of the Ballistic Missile Early Warning Systems (BMEWS) were operational at Thule AB, Greenland. Other BMEWS sites at Clear, Alaska and Fylingdales, England would be brought to operational status at later dates. The BMEWS system comprised a network of radars capable of detecting and tracking ballistic missiles or nuclear warheads appearing over the horizon and of warning defense networks in the United States and overseas.

1961 February 1   The only other airline apart from BEA to operate the Vickers Vanguard turboprop airliner began regularly scheduled operations when Trans-Canada Airlines started a Montreal-Vancouver service with one of their 23 aircraft. The route went via Toronto, Winnipeg, Regina and Calgary. Fully scheduled services with BEA began March 1 following interim services begun in late 1960. Had jet airliners not arrived when they did, aircraft like the Vickers Vanguard would have been in the forefront of commercial operator lists.

1961 February 3   A limited number of KC-135As modified to operate as part of a continuously manned airborne command post began round-the-clock operations under Operation Looking Glass. Each aircraft carried a team of Strategic Air Command general officers in constant touch with Strategic Air Command headquarters and linked to Strategic Air Command bases throughout the country. Each aircraft was airborne for approximately 8 hr. before being replaced by another. In this way, a preemptive missile

strike against Strategic Air Command command posts on the ground would not eliminate the chain of command and control over retaliatory forces.

1961 February 14   Defense Secretary Robert McNamara of the United States informed the U.S. Navy that its recently declared Fleet Air Defense Fighter (FADF) requirement would be merged with the USAF TFX requirement for a supersonic tactical fighter-bomber. The U.S. Navy had wanted to relieve the F-4H in the air defense role by the early 1970s. In attempting to make their requirement compatible with TFX, the navy removed the ground attack role, which resulted in the navy Attack Experimental (VAX) program that led to the Vought A-7.

1961 February 20   The U.S. Marine Corps placed an order for 14 Boeing-Vertol assault helicopters. Developed from the civilian Vertol Model 107-II, which had first flown in April 1958 and designated Model 107M, the H-46 Sea Knight (as it became known) had a mission requirement to lift 4,000 lb. of cargo or 17 fully equipped troops a distance of 115 mi. at 150 MPH. Folding rotor blades were essential for stowage on aircraft carriers and rapid loading or unloading was mandatory.

1961 March 6   The first of 152 Boeing B-52H strategic bombers made its first flight. Developed specifically to carry the Douglas Skybolt air-to-surface missile, it was powered by eight 17,000-lb. s.t. Pratt & Whitney TF33-P-3 turbofan engines that provided a maximum speed of 630 MPH at 40,000 ft. and a maximum unrefueled range of 12,000 mi. The first B-52H arrived with Strategic Air Command on May 9. Because of the subsequent cancellation of the Skybolt missile, the B-52H carried two Hound Dog missiles plus 20,000-lb. of nuclear or conventional weapons.

1961 March 7   The #2 North American X-15 became the first manned aircraft to exceed Mach 4 when pilot Capt. Robert M. White reached a speed of 2,905 MPH, which, at the altitude of 77,450 ft., was Mach 4.43. This was the first NASA mission flown with the XLR-99 single-chamber rocket motor installed. The #2 aircraft would be used during the year for a number of record altitude and speed runs. On this flight, it carried a special patch of temperature-sensitive paint on the nose to measure the amount of heat at that point.

1961 March 7   The USAF declared the McDonnell GAM-72A Quail decoy operational with Strategic Air Command. The first Strategic Air Command test-drop from a B-52G of the 4135th Strategic Wing had been conducted on June 8, 1960. The Quail was a small, cropped delta-wing vehicle with a span of 5 ft. 4 in. and a length of 12 ft. 10 in. powered by a 2,450-lb. General Electric J85-GE-7 jet engine. When released from a B-52, it resembled closely the radar signature of that aircraft and operated as a decoy target for antiaircraft artillery radar or radar-guided missiles.

1961 March 13   The Hawker P.1127 V/STOL aircraft made the first conventional flight with Bill Bedford at the controls during a test at the Routal Aircraft Establishment, Bedford and remained airborne for approximately 22 min. Further flights gradually increased the flying envelope through 400 knots and a height of 30,000 ft. before the aircraft was delivered to Dunsfold on March 25. The flight test program was sharply divided into vertical flights and horizontal flights, gradually bringing the two together for the first full transition on September 12.

1961 March 28   Pres. John F. Kennedy addressed a special session of Congress on the revised FY 1962 defense budget and announced a request for increased funds to place one-eighth of Strategic Air Command's B-47 and B-52 inventory, about 180 aircraft, on airborne alert and to commit 50%, about 730 aircraft, to 15-min. ground alert.

1961 April 5   The first Dassault Mirage IIIE long-range intruder version of the basic Mirage III made its first flight. The length was increased by 2 ft. 6 in. and a British Marconi blind low-level navigation and ground-attack radar was provided. It had a 14,110-lb. s.t. SNECMA Atar 9C turbojet engine. Evolving into the Mirage 5 and Mirage 50, 1,410 aircraft of this series were built for 20 countries; 532 Mirage IIIEs were built for 13 air forces. A force of 30 French aircraft each carried a 30 kiloton AN-52 nuclear weapon.

1961 April 7   A Strategic Air Command B-52 from the USAF Ninety-fifth Bombardment Wing was shot down by an F-100 of the 188th Fighter Interceptor Squadron of the New Mexico Air National Guard over Mount Taylor, N. Mex. Piloted by Capt. Donald Blodgett and Capt. Ray Nobel, the B-52 came under a simulated attack from two F-100s flown by 1st Lt. James Van Scyoc and Capt. Dale Dodd. During a final pass, the outer missile of two Sidewinders under the port wing of Lt. Van Scyoc's aircraft fired due to moisture short-circuiting the firing mechanism. The pilots and electronics warfare officer Capt. George Jackson survived, but 2nd Lt. Glen Blair and Capts. Steve Carter and Peter Gineris were killed.

1961 April 10   In the United States, production of B-70 Mach 3 bomber prototypes was to be limited to just three aircraft—two XB-70s and one YB-70. These aircraft were to be completed as high-speed aerodynamic test vehicles. The new defense secretary, Robert McNamara, had wanted to cancel the program, but a compromise was achieved that preserved investment to date but eliminated government obligations to find major funds in the future.

1961 April 10   For the first time during the severe weather of an Antarctic winter, a Lockheed C-130 BL Hercules of the U.S. Navy, VX-6 piloted by Comdr. Lloyd E. Newcomer with a double crew of 16 men and a special crew of five, landed back at Christchurch, New Zealand, having evacuated a Soviet exchange scientist from the U.S. Byrd Station. The scientist, Leonid Ku-

perov, had been suffering from an acute abdominal condition, and this was the only way to get him to hospital.

1961 April 21   The #2 North American X-15 piloted by Capt. Robert M. White, USAF, became the first aircraft to travel faster than 3,000 MPH when it achieved a speed of 3,074 MPH, or Mach 4.62, at a height of 105,000 ft. To achieve this, the engine was shut down and then started again in flight for a double-phase burn. This was the 15th free flight for the #2 X-15.

1961 April 24   The Tupolev Tu-114 turboprop airliner began a scheduled service nonstop on the Moscow-Khabarovsk route, a distance of 4,337 mi. The first route-proving flight had been flown on March 10, 1960, and this was followed by a second on March 17, 1961, carrying 170 passengers. The scheduled block time for the journey was 8 hr. 15 min. This was the first regularly scheduled service for the Tu-114.

1961 April 28   An experimental derivative of the MiG-21 was used by the Soviets to set a new world altitude record for manned aircraft. A Ye-166A flown by Col. G. Mossolov of the Soviet Air Force reached a height of 113,898 ft. (34,713 m). The aircraft was fitted with an augmented 13,228-lb. s.t. TDR Mk.R-37F turbojet supplemented by a GRD Mk.U2 rocket motor.

1961 May 4   Comdr. M. D. Ross and Lt. Comdr. V. A. Prother, both U.S. Navy, ascended in the gondola of their *Stratolab* balloon to a new FAI-ratified record altitude of 113,740 ft. They had been launched from the deck of the USS *Antietam* in the Gulf of Mexico and took 2 hr. 36 min. to reach maximum height over Mobile, Ala. The event ended tragically when Prother slipped from the helicopter recovery sling after splashdown and died about 1 hr. later. The previous record had been that achieved by Capt. J. Kittinger, USAF, when he reached a height of 102,800 ft. in August 1960. The new U.S. Navy record would stand unbroken for at least the next 30 yr.

1961 May 9   The British Aircraft Corp. announced the development of the BAC 111 short- and medium-haul airliner, which had begun life as the Hunting H.107 32-seat airliner of 1956. In the intervening period, the design was upgraded to incorporate turbofan engines and provide seating for 59, but it failed to stimulate interest until the corporation bowed to market wishes and redesigned it to take up to 90 passengers.

1961 May 10   A Convair B-58A Hustler from the Forty-third Bombardment Wing flown by Maj. Elmer E. Murphy, USAF, and his crew received the Aero Club de France Blériot Trophy for flying for more than 30 min. at a speed in excess of 2,000 km/hr. (1,242.8 MPH). The actual average speed was 1,302 MPH (2,094.9 km/hr.) over a 669.4-mi. distance that was flown in 30 min. 45 sec.

1961 May 19   The U.S. Army selected submissions from Bell and Hiller as winning contenders for the light observation helicopter competition for which designs had been submitted by Vertol, Cessna, Gyrodyne, Hughes, Kaiser, Kaman, Lockheed, McDonnell, Republic and Sikorsky as well. The army ordered five prototypes of the Bell HO-4 and the Hiller HO-5 and would order five HO-6s from Hughes at a later date.

1961 May 19   An Avro Vulcan B.Mk.2 flew for the first time with two Bristol Siddeley Olympus 301 turbojets rated at 20,000-lb. s.t. and two Olympus 201s rated at 17,000-lb. s.t. in the first of a series of flights to qualify the more powerful engine for retrofitting to operational RAF aircraft. When fitted with four

Olympus 301s, the Vulcan B.Mk.2 had a maximum speed of 645 MPH at 40,000 ft., a sea level speed of 530 MPH, a high altitude tactical radius of 2,300 mi. and a service ceiling of 65,000 ft.

1961 May 19 The first of 18 C-135A Stratolifter cargo versions of the KC-135A made its first flight. The first three were converted tankers, the rest purpose-built by Boeing; 30 more were completed as C-135Bs with Pratt & Whitney TF33-P-5 turbofans. The aircraft could carry up to 126 combat ready troops. Deliveries to Military Air Transport Service began on June 9 as part of the service's modernization program.

1961 May 24 Three U.S. Navy McDonnell F4H-1 Phantom II aircraft competing for the Bendix Trophy improved on the existing coast-to-coast record for nonstop flights by averaging 870 MPH across the 2,421.4-mi. run between Los Angeles and New York. The aircraft flown by Lt. R. F. Gordon and Lt. (j.g.) B. R. Young made the fastest Mach 1+ dash, completing the distance in 2 hr. 47 min.

1961 May 26 A Convair B-58A Hustler piloted by Maj. W. R. Payne and crew flew nonstop from Carswell AFB, Tex. to Paris, a distance of 5,183 mi., in commemoration of the 34th anniversary of the Lindbergh Atlantic crossing. It was refueled three times by a KC-135A Stratotanker. During a portion of this flight, the aircraft set a new point-to-point record by flying from New York to Paris, a distance of 3,669 mi. in 3 hr. 19 min. 41 sec. These flights did more than break records, they contributed valuable performance and high speed systems qualification trials.

1961 June 1 United Air Lines absorbed Capital Airlines to become the biggest airline in the world, with services to 116 cities and a fleet of 267 aircraft. Capital had begun as a small airline formed in 1926 to operate one of the first airmail charters. It was taken over by Pennsylvania Air Lines in November 1930. In November 1936, it merged with newcomer Central Airlines to become Pennsylvania-Central Airlines and on April 21, 1948, was renamed Capital Airlines. Bad financial problems forced the buyout from United.

1961 June 1 The prototype Breguet 941 STOL aircraft made its first flight. Powered by four 1,200-SHP Turboméca Turmo IIID turboprop engines, the high-wing aircraft was designed to the deflected-slipstream technique whereby propeller slipstream blows over the surface of the entire wing and across full trailing edge flaps and ailerons. The aircraft had a wingspan of 76 ft. 1 in. and a length of 76 ft. 8 in. It could clear a 50-ft. obstacle just 935 ft. after takeoff, which at maximum payload required a run of 902 ft. Only four transports were purchased for the Armée de l'Air.

1961 June 17 Four years after its inception, the first supersonic fighter designed and built in Asia, the Hindustin HF-24 Marut, made its first flight in India, powered by two 4,850-lb. s.t. Rolls Royce Orpheus 703 turbojets and with a wingspan of 29 ft. 6 in. and a length of 52 ft. Incorporating swept wings and tail, it was designed by a team run by the ex-Focke-Wulf design chief Kurt Tank. In addition to 129 built as fighters, there were 18 Marut Mk.1T trainers. The fighter had a maximum speed of Mach 1.02 and a combat radius of 246 mi.

1961 June 21 An Avro Vulcan (serial no. XH481) of No. 617 Squadron, RAF, began the first nonstop flight from England to Australia. Commanded by Sqdn. Ldr. M. G. Beavis, the crew took 20 hr. 30 min. to fly the aircraft 11,500 mi. En route it rendezvoused with Vickers Valiant air-refueling tankers operating

out of Cyprus, Pakistan and Singapore. Experiments giving the Valiant an air-refueling role had been conducted during 1959 by No. 214 Squadron, RAF, at Marham.

1961 June 23 The #2 North American X-15 became the first manned aircraft to exceed Mach 5 when Capt. Robert M. White flew it to a height of 107,700 ft. and a speed of Mach 5.27, or 3,603 MPH. The type of reentry flown by the X-15 induced visible heat effects on the wing surfaces. A minor malfunction resulted in a partial loss of cabin pressure during the flight.

1961 June 28 Following a review of the tragic loss of one of their four ZPG-3W airships in June 1960, the U.S. Navy formally abandoned airship operations. Designed specifically for antisubmarine work, the ZPG-3W had a crew of 12, a capacity of 1,516,300 cu. ft., a length of 403 ft. and a diameter of 85 ft. with a height of 118 ft. and two 1,500-HP Curtiss Wright engines, the largest nonrigid airships ever built.

1961 June 30 Following a declaration from Iraq's ruler, Abdul Karim Kassem, that Kuwait was part of his country and the movement of armed forces south from Baghdad, Nos. 8 and 208 Squadrons, RAF, were moved with their Hawker Hunters to Bahrein from Khormaksar, Aden Protectorate, and Eastleigh, Nairobi. Two Avro Shackletons from No. 37 Squadron and No. 88 Squadron with its Canberras were moved to Sharjah. The Hunters flew into Kuwait on July 1 following a formal request for assistance followed by Britannias and Canberras. HMS *Victorious* arrived in the Persian Gulf with Gannets and Sea Vixens on July 9. The show of force suppressed territorial ambitions.

1961 July 9 At the Tushino Airport, Moscow, flyby, the Myasishchyev M-50 bomber (later code-named *Bounder*) made its first appearance. With a length of 187 ft. 10 in. and a wingspan of 121 ft. 4 in. over two tip-mounted engines, it was powered by four 28,660/40,000-lb. s.t. Koliesov ND-7F turbojets, the inner pair of which were mounted on pylons beneath the wings just outboard of mid-span. The M-50 had a top speed of Mach 1.83 (1,212 MPH) and a ceiling of 66,000 ft.

1961 August 7 The Soviet Beriev Be-10 jet-powered flying boat set a new speed record for its class of 912 km/hr. (566.69 MPH) over a 25-km course. The aircraft had been flown by N. Andryevskii and two crew. Payload records were set during September when the Be-10 flew a 1,000-km circuit carrying 5 tons and reached a height of 12,753 m (41,775 ft.) carrying 10 tons (22,050 lb.). The Be-10 had a swept-wing span of about 82 ft., a length of about 108 ft. and two 14,330-lb. s.t. Lyul'ka AL-7RV turbojets nestled between the high-set wingroots and the fuselage. Only four preproduction aircraft were built.

1961 August 16 The first development aircraft of the Bell UH-1D helicopter made its first flight, featuring a larger (48-ft. diameter) rotor, a longer (40 ft. 4 in.) fuselage and a 1,100-SHP Lycoming T53-L-11 turboshaft engine. The cabin volume was increased from 140 cu. ft. to 220 cu. ft. and capacity was upgraded for a pilot and 12 troops. Purchased by the U.S. Army as an infantry transport helicopter, it began operational duty on August 9, 1963, with the Eleventh Air Assault Division at Fort Benning, Ga.

1961 August 21 The Douglas DC-8 Series 40 prototype became the first commercial airliner to exceed the speed of sound (Mach 1) in a shallow dive, during flight tests with Rolls Royce Conway engines at a height of 40,350 ft. Observed and calculated speeds showed an actual Mach number of 1.005–1.01, calculated to be 667 MPH at that altitude. Tracking cameras on the ground and on-board instruments were used to record the event, which took place during a flight from Long Beach to Edwards AFB, Calif.

1961 August 24 Beginning this date through October 12, U.S. aviatrix Jacqueline Cochrane flying a Northrop T-38A Talon set a wide range of records for women, achieving an altitude record of 56,071 ft., a distance record of 1,492 mi., a 100-km (62.14 mi.) closed circuit speed record of 784.337 MPH and a 15-km (9.32 mi.) course speed of 844.2 MPH.

1961 September 10 The conclusions and recommendations of Project Horizon, a detailed review of U.S. civil aviation for the decade ahead, came out favorably on the side of a U.S. supersonic transport aircraft. The review had been commissioned by Pres. John F. Kennedy and was put together by a presidential task force headed by FAA administrator Najeeb Halaby.

1961 September 12 The first in-flight transition from vertical to horizontal flight and back with the Hawker P.1127 were made in separate flights by test pilots Bill Bedford and Hugh Merewether in the prototype (serial no. XP831). Thus was the aircraft of first V/STOL to achieve vertical takeoff, hover, translate to forward flight and accelerate to near-sonic speed. Before the end of the year, it had marginally exceeded Mach 1 and in late December achieved Mach 1.2 during a dive.

1961 September 21 The first Boeing-Vertol YHC-1 (CH-47 Chinook) made its first flight following more than two years of development for what would emerge as one of the most versatile military transport helicopters ever flown. With a length of 51 ft. and two 57-ft. diameter rotors driven by two 2,200-SHP Lycoming T55-L-5 turbines, it could lift 33 troops, 27 paratroops or 24 litters at a cruising speed of 150 MPH for a radius of 200 mi. Thirty years later, it was still in production, more than 1,000 having been built and engine power having almost doubled.

1961 September 29 The U.S. Defense Department issued requests for proposals on the USAF/U.S. Navy requirement for a tactical fighter-bomber/fleet defense fighter. The requirement was heavily biased toward the USAF need for Mach 1.2 at sea level, which necessitated a heavier aircraft than the navy would have liked. By December 6, bids were in from Boeing, Lockheed, McDonnell, North American, Republic and a General Dynamics/Grumman team.

1961 September 30 The French cruiser helicopter carrier *La Resolue* was launched in affirmation of the importance now being placed on helicopters in defense applications. The ship would subsequently to renamed *Jeanne d'Arc,* replacing a training cruiser of that name when it was retired from service. *La Resolue* had a displacement of 13,000 tons fully loaded and a length of 590 ft. with a beam of 78 ft. With provision for eight helicopters, it was designed to carry a battalion of 700 men and a complement of 1,050.

1961 October 2 The British minister of aviation Peter Thorneycroft and French transport minister Robert Buron met to discuss possible collaboration on a supersonic transport (SST). As a result, the British Aircraft Corp. and Süd Aviation were asked to embark upon a collaborative effort. The two companies held their first meeting in London on October 13 to discuss how they would integrate work, supposing the plan were to be given a formal go-ahead.

1961 October 7 The Soviet MiG Ye-166 high-speed experimental aircraft captured the FAI-ratified 100-km (62.14-mi.) speed record with a measured average of 1,492 MPH (2,401 km/hr.), more than 100 MPH faster than the previous record set by an F4H-1 Phantom II in September 1960. The Ye-166 had a delta-wing span of 29 ft. 5 in., a length of 59 ft. and a 22,050-lb. s.t.-augmented AL-7F providing a top speed of Mach 2.82 and a ceiling of 82,000 ft.

1961 October 7 The Soviet Kamov Ka-22 compound helicopter, piloted by D. K. Yefremov and V. V. Gromov, set a new world record for the 15/25 km class by averaging 356.3 km/hr. (221.4 MPH). Publicly displayed for the first time at Tushino on July 9, it had a length of 73 ft. 10 in. and a wingspan of 67 ft. between the center-lines of two 65 ft. 7 in. tip-rotors driven by two 5,500-SHP Soloviev D-25V engines. These also powered two forward-facing propeller assemblies through a clutch progressively transferring power as required.

1961 October 11 Flown by Capt. Robert M. White, USAF, the #2 North American X-15 became the first aircraft to carry a pilot more than 200,000 ft. above the surface of the earth during a flight that reached a speed of 3,647 MPH, Mach 5.21, and reached an altitude of 217,000 ft. During this flight, the outer panel of the left windshield cracked. The flight tested a new reaction control concept whereby gas jets stabilized the aircraft in an environment in which atmospheric pressure was only 0.1% that at the earth's surface.

1961 October 21 The Breguet 1150 Atlantique made its first flight just under two years after receiving an order for a Lockheed P2V replacement for NATO forces. The original requirement had been written up in 1958. Powered by two 6,105-EHP Hispano-built Rolls Royce Tyne RTy.20 Mk.21 turboprop engines, the Atlantique had a wingspan of 119 ft. and a double-bubble fuselage with a length of 104 ft. 2 in. After 87 had been produced for France, Germany, Italy, the Netherlands and Pakistan, a developed version, the Atlantique 2, was flown for the first time in 1981.

1961 October 28 The first rolling vertical takeoff was accomplished at Dunsfold, England with the Hawker P.1127 as part of its continuing flight development program. Accomplished by first directing the engine exhaust gases to the rear and then gradually rotating to a down-thrusting vector when the wings began to generate lift, the V/STOL aircraft could carry much greater loads when this operating technique was used.

1961 November 9 The first man-powered aircraft to get off the ground was pedaled into the air at Lasham, England by Derek Piggott, who managed to remain airborne for a distance of 150–200 ft. at a height of about 5 ft. The vehicle was designed and built by a group of graduates from Southampton University led by Anne Marsden, Alan Lasserie and David Williams, supported by Prof. E. J. Richards of the University's aeronautical engineering department. It had a span of 80 ft., a length of 25 ft. and weighed 124 lb. empty.

1961 November 9 The #2 North American X-15 became the first manned aircraft to exceed Mach 6 and the first to exceed 4,000 MPH. Piloted by Capt. Robert M. White, USAF, it reached a height of 101,600 ft. and a speed of Mach 6.04 (4,093 MPH). Thus was the design flight speed achieved just over 2 yr. after the first powered drop from its B-52 carrier-plane. During the flight, the 21st for the #2 aircraft and the 45th of the program, the outer right windshield shattered but the pilot was not injured.

1961 November 22 Lt. Col. Robert B. Robinson flying a McDonnell F4H-1F Phantom II set a new FAI absolute world air speed record when he piloted the aircraft to an average speed of 1,606.51 MPH (2,585.43 km/hr.), more than 75 MPH faster than the previous record set by a Convair F-106 Delta Dart on December 15, 1959. Although the rocket-powered X-15 had by this date achieved a speed of more than 4,000 MPH, it was placed by the FAI into a special category of "aerospacecraft," which also included manned orbiting spacecraft.

1961 December 9 An RAF Avro Vulcan B.Mk.2 (serial no. XH537) carried out the first drop tests with dummy Douglas Skybolt missiles at the West Freugh range in Scotland. In the next year, a detachment of 200 RAF personnel under the command of Wg. Comdr. Charles Ness would operate at Eglin AFB, Fla. as the British Joint Trials Force scheduled to test Skybolt missiles on the Vulcan.

1961 December 11 In the first direct U.S. involvement in Vietnam, the 15,700-ton aircraft ferry USS *Card* arrived at Saigon with two U.S. Army companies operating Piasecki H-21 Shawnee helicopters. On December 23, the first helicopter assault was staged by 30 Shawnees from the Fifty-seventh Transportation Company (Light Helicopter), which put troops down near a village believed to be a communist stronghold 12 mi. west of Saigon.

1961 December The USAF announced it had selected a powerful derivative of the Titan ICBM to fire the Dyna-Soar winged space vehicle into orbit following initial air-launched drops from a B-52 carrier-plane. The Titan III was being developed by the USAF as a satellite launch vehicle and was to be sufficiently powerful to carry the winged vehicle directly into orbit.

1962 January 9 The first production de Havilland D.H.121 Trident made its first flight powered by three 10,400-lb. s.t. Rolls Royce RB.163/1 Spey turbofans. With a wingspan of 89 ft. 10 in. and a length of 114 ft. 9. in., the D.H.121 could carry 88 to 95 passengers at 586 MPH a distance of 1,530 mi. It was ordered by BEA but failed to interest other airlines until the Trident 1E version was first flown in November 1964. With seating for 115 to 139, China's CAAC bought 33 Trident 2Es powered by three 11,960-lb. s.t. Speys.

1962 January 11 A USAF B-52H (serial no. 60-0040) of the 4136th Strategic Wing, Strategic Air Command, based at Minot AFB, N. Dak., completed a record 12,532.28-mi. (20,168.78-km) unrefueled flight when it landed at Torrejon AB, Spain, having flown from Kadena AB, Okinawa. The aircraft weighed exactly 488,000 lb. at takeoff and flew at 40,000–50,000 ft. with a top speed of 662 MPH. This record would stand for almost 25 yr. until the unrefueled round-the-world flight of Dick Rutan and Jeana Yeager ended on December 23, 1986.

1962 January 24 The first two U.S. Navy McDonnell F4H Phantom II fighters of a batch of 29 were delivered to the USAF Tactical Air Command at Langley AFB, Va. for test and evaluation. U.S. Navy trials, and the array of records claimed by this aircraft, demonstrated its superiority over existing land-based fighters, and interest had developed in buying it for the USAF.

1962 January 31 The U.S. Defense Department decided to award parallel follow-on study contracts for the USAF/USN TFX requirement to Boeing and a General Dynamics/Grumman team. The Boeing contender was preferred, but a second contract extension in April 1962 failed to fill requirements and a third contract was given to the two contenders in June 1962. At this submission, both competing bids were declared satisfactory with Boeing clearly in the lead.

1962 February 5 A U.S. Navy helicopter piloted by Lt. R. W. Craffton, U.S. Navy, and Capt. L. K. Keck, USMC, became the first to exceed 200 MPH in an officially sanctioned trial flight. The helicopter, a Sikorsky HSS-2 Sea King, was flown along a special course along the Connecticut shoreline from Milford to New Haven, qualifying for the 15/25 km record at an average 210.65 MPH.

1962 February 16 The Aviation Traders ATL.98 Carvair made its first overseas flight by flying from Southend, England to Ostende, Belgium across the English Channel. A modified DC-4 with a longer, bulbous, forward fuselage with a side-swinging nose surmounted by the flight deck permitted front-loading access for five cars forward and 22 passengers in the rear. It derived its name from "car-via-air" and was operated by Channel Air Bridge to replace its old Bristol Superfreighters. In all, 21 were built.

1962 February 23 A Douglas DC-8 Series 50 established a new long-distance record for commercial transport aircraft when it flew nonstop between Tokyo and Miami, a distance of 8,705 mi. flown in 13 hr. 52 min. This record greatly exceeded the previous long-distance record, increasing it by 1,700 mi. The estimated maximum range advertised for the DC-8-50 was 6,900 mi. in still air and with no reserves.

1962 February 23 An Avro Vulcan (serial no. XA894) made its first flight after modifications to fit it with a fifth 20,000-lb. s.t. Bristol Olympus 301 engine for special tests associated with the T.S.R.2 and Concorde supersonic airliner projects. The engine was recessed into the area usually occupied by the bomb bay with bifurcated intakes on the underside of the main air inlets. Just 100 flying test hours were completed with this configuration before the aircraft was burned out on the ground on December 3.

1962 February 26 The Fairey Rotodyne was canceled by the British minister of aviation Peter Thorneycroft, despite interest from New York Airways, BEA and the military in Britain. Fairey Aviation and Westland Aircraft had merged on February 8, 1960, and that plus pressure of work from taking over Bristol helicopter work allowed the project to wither away.

1962 February 28 The first live Convair B-58A escape-pod ejection with a man inside was performed while the aircraft was flying at 565 MPH, 20,000 ft. over Edwards AFB, Calif. After 26 sec., a parachute was deployed, and the subject landed on the ground 8 min. later. The B-58A incorporated three separate escape pods to protect each occupant from supersonic blast if used above Mach 1. In March a small bear was successfully used for a supersonic ejection test at Mach 1.3 and 35,000 ft.

1962 March 1 Los Angeles Airways set up the world's first commercial service using turbine-powered, multi-engine helicopters. The helicopter selected was the Sikorsky S-61L, which could accommodate up to 28 passengers. This commercial derivative of the S-61A had a cruising speed of 136 MPH and a maximum range of 350 mi. Chicago Helicopter Airways had hoped to be the inaugurating airline with the S-61L but had to defer its order on January 2, 1962.

1962 March 3 The U.S. Navy claimed F-4H-1 Phantom II climb-tree records with flights on February 21 and March 1 and 3.

These were 34.523 sec. to 3,000 m (9,843 ft.), 48.787 sec. to 6,000 m (19,686 ft.), 61.629 sec. to 9,000 m (29,529 ft.), 77.156 sec. to 12,000 m (39,372 ft.) and 1 min. 54.548 sec. to 15,000 m (49,215 ft.).

1962 March 5 Crewed by pilot Capt. Robert G. Sowers, navigator Capt. Robert MacDonald and defense systems operator Capt. John Walton, a Convair B-58 (serial no. 59-2458) of the Forty-third Bombardment Wing broke three records during a round-trip between New York and Los Angeles in 4 hr. 41 min. 14.98 sec. The fastest trans-continental crossing between Los Angeles and New York was accomplished in 2 hr. 58.71 sec. at an average speed of 1,214.65 MPH. The third record notched the fastest time between New York and Los Angeles. This flight brought the award of the Bendix Trophy, Distinguished Flying Crosses and a personal congratulation from Pres. John F. Kennedy.

1962 March 18 The first Convair CV-990 to enter service in the United States inaugurated the type on the American Airlines route between New York and Chicago. Swissair introduced the CV-990 when it began using this aircraft, which it named *Coronado,* on its service to Rio de Janeiro and São Paulo on February 25. Several technical difficulties were experienced, and the type was retrofitted with improvements under which it then became the CV-990A. This was to be the last commercial airliner built by Convair.

1962 March 30 The USAF ordered a unique version of the U.S. Navy McDonnell F-4H Phantom II, designating it F-110A Spectre. Aimed at filling the Specific Operations Requirement 200 calling for a close-air support, interdiction and counter-air aircraft, the USAF ordered one F-110A and two YRF-110A photo-reconnaissance variants. Under the reclassification of USAF/U.S. Navy designations to remove conflicting numbers, the name Spectre was removed and these aircraft became the F-4C and the RF-4C respectively.

1962 March 31 F-4H-1 reached 20,000 m (65,620 ft.) in 2 min. 58.5 sec. and, on April 3, 25,000 m (82,025 ft.) in 3 min. 50.44 sec. The 25,000-m record and the 3,000-m record claimed March 3 were taken by Lt. Comdr. John W. Young, who in September would be chosen as a NASA astronaut and would go on to make six space flights, including the first Gemini mission, the fifth moon landing and the first space shuttle flight. Young was maintenance officer of VF-143 at Miramar NAS, California.

1962 April 12 Lt. Comdr. Del W. Nordberg, U.S. Navy, claimed a new climb time for powered aircraft of 6 min. 11.43 sec. to 30,000 m (98,430 ft.). The flight took place at Point Mugu, Calif. and, with records for intermediate climb-time altitude from 3,000 m claimed on March 3 and for climbs to 20,000 m and 25,000 m flown on March 31 and April 3, completed a clean sweep of all the FAI climb-time categories by the F-4H-1.

1962 April 14 U.S. Army pilot Capt. Leland F. Wilhelm took the 3,000-m (9,843-ft.) helicopter climb-time record when he piloted a Bell YHU-1D Iroquois to that altitude in 2 min. 14.6 sec. Only the day before, Capt. Boyce B. Buckner had flown his Iroquois to a height of 6,000 m (19,686 ft.) in 5 min. 51 sec., both records ratified by the FAI for helicopter classes.

1962 April 14 The first of two Bristol Type 188 research aircraft (serial no. XF923) made its first flight piloted by chief test pilot G. L. Auty and powered by two 14,000-lb. s.t. de Havilland Gyron Junior DGJ 10 turbojet engines. Designed to explore kinetic heating effects through sustained supersonic cruise, excessive fuel consumption reduced its true value. With a length of 71 ft. and a wingspan of 35 ft. 1 in., the Type 188 had a maximum speed of 1,200 MPH. The second machine (serial no. XF926) entered service on April 29, 1963.

1962 April 19 The first live firing of the Douglas XGAM-87 Skybolt air-launched ballistic missile was successfully completed when a test round was dropped from a B-52G out of Eglin AFB, Fla. After a full first-stage firing, the second stage failed to ignite. It failed to perform as required in four other test launches on June 29, September 13, September 25 and November 28. The stand-off weapon had a range of 1,150 mi.

1962 April 22 Jacqueline Cochrane became the first woman pilot to fly a jet aircraft across the Atlantic, from New Orleans to Hanover, Germany with stops at Gander and Shannon. The aircraft she used was a Lockheed JetStar. In flying the 5,120 mi., she claimed a total 49 FAI world records for the flight.

1962 April 26 Lockheed test pilot Lou Schalk flew the first of 15 top-secret single-seat A-12 spy-planes (serial no. 60-6924) from the USAF Groom Lake research facility in Nevada. Powered by two 32,000-lb. s.t. Pratt & Whitney JT11D-20B turbo-ramjets, the A-12 had a length of 98 ft. 9 in. (102 ft. with pitot tube), a wingspan of 55 ft. 7 in., a wing area of 1,605 sq. ft. and a gross weight of 120,000 lb. Top speed was Mach 3.6 (2,400 MPH) with an operational ceiling of 92,500 ft. and a range of 2,500 mi.

1962 May 1 During a visit to London, the U.S. defense secretary, Robert McNamara, commented that the Kennedy administration would commit $30 million to the operational development of the Hawker P.1127 as a V/STOL strike aircraft and its Bristol Pegasus engine. By this time, the U.K. government had held discussions with their German counterparts and received tepid interest in a joint Anglo-German project to move the P.1127 from its "official" research status to operational precursor for a combat aircraft.

1962 May 9 The Sikorsky S-64 Skycrane made its first flight after a development program instigated by a specification from the German Defense Ministry for a cargo-lifting helicopter. With provision for five crewmembers and capable of carrying 60 troops or a maximum load of 20,760 lb., the S-64 had a length of 70 ft. 3 in. and a 72-ft. diameter rotor powered by two 4,620-SHP Pratt & Whitney JFTD12A-1 turboshaft engines. With a cruising speed of 110 MPH and a range of 191 mi., five CH-54As were acquired by the U.S. Army followed by an order for 37.

1962 May 21 Hawker Aircraft Ltd. received a British government contract for 9 P.1127 V/STOL development aircraft to be used for service evaluation trials in a multinational unit involving personnel from Britain, the United States and Germany. Formally signed January 16, 1963, each country would pay for three aircraft and contribute one-third of the operational and support costs of the unit. Designed to provide a considerably improved 18,000-lb. thrust, the Pegasus 5 engine would be de-rated to a thrust of 15,500-lb. for the evaluations.

1962 June 3 In the worst single-aircraft disaster to date, an Air France Boeing 707 (F-BHSM) *Château de Sully* was destroyed while attempting to take off from Orly Airport, Paris. Of the 123 passengers and 10 crew on board, only two stewardesses survived. They were seated in the rear of the jet airliner. One of the stewardesses reported severe vibration before the pilot seemingly aborted the takeoff. This was the fifth Air France jet accident in less than 2 yr., the others being minor incidents.

1962 June 7 A B-52H of the Nineteenth Bombardment Wing from Homestead AFB, Fla. set a new record for nonstop unrefueled distance flown on a closed circuit with an FAI-ratified distance of 18,245.05 km (11,336.92 mi.). The flight began and ended at Seymour Johnson AFB, N.C. and routed the aircraft via Bermuda, Sondestrom, Greenland and Key West, Fla. The record had not been beaten as of January 1992.

1962 June 13 Capt. Richard H. Coan, USAF, set a new closed-circuit distance record for helicopters when he flew a Kaman H-43B Huskie 656.258 mi. This beat the previous record of 625.464 mi. set by a Soviet Mil Mi-1. During mid-year, the Huskie designation was changed to HH-43B.

1962 June 26 The USAF announced that it had changed the designation of its winged reentry vehicle and that it would no longer be known as Dyna-Soar but rather by the experimental classification X-20. The USAF said this more properly reflected the nature of the project. On August 7, a memorandum of understanding with NASA was released defining areas of research that would be conducted by the air force in support of the manned space programs of Mercury, Gemini and Apollo, thus hoping to buttress the X-20 against cancellation by appearing to make it an important part of aerospace research.

1962 July 7 Soviet air force pilot Georgiy Mossolov established a new world air speed record when he flew a MiG Ye-166 at an average speed of 2,681 km/hr. (1,665.89 MPH). On September 11, P. Ostapyenko piloted a Ye-166 to a record sustained altitude of 22,670 m (74,380 ft.) in level flight.

1962 July 7 The Lockheed VZ-10 Hummingbird VTOL research aircraft made its first flight. Powered by two 3,000-lb. s.t. Pratt & Whitney JT12A-3LH turbojet engines, one on either side of the fuselage above the wing position, vertical lift was obtained by opening diverters that deflected the exhaust down through under-fuselage apertures. With a length of 32 ft. 8 in. and a mid-wing span of 25 ft. 8 in., the Hummingbird continued to carry out flight research until it was destroyed in an accident in March 1969.

1962 July 17 For the first time, a manned aircraft reached a height in excess of 300,000 ft. Piloted by Capt. Robert M. White, USAF, the #3 X-15 was flown to a height of 314,750 ft. and a speed of Mach 5.45 (3,832 MPH) with an ascent inclination of 41° and a reentry angle of 23° that induced severe vibration and yawing during the descent phase. Because the nominal division between atmosphere and the vacuum of space is regarded as 50 mi. (264,000 ft.), this was the first flight of a winged vehicle for which the pilot received astronauts' wings.

1962 July 20 A joint USAF-NASA ad hoc committee comprising about 30 people began work on an aero-space plane (ASP) that would provide earth-to-orbit and return capability and a conventional aircraft capable of hypersonic speed and an unrefueled range of 5,000 mi. There had been several proposals already to develop the X-15 into such a vehicle by replacing the B-52 carrier-plane with a modified ballistic missile.

1962 July 25 Lt. A. Newman, U.S. Navy, of the Naval Ordnance Test Station, China Lake, Calif., piloted a McDonnell F4H-1 Phantom II to a height of 36,000 ft. and released a Caleb two-stage, solid-propellant rocket, which ignited and accelerated

to a height of 725 mi. Under Project Hi-Hoe, the test proved the validity of air-launched, antisatellite weapons and, potentially, the use of standard aircraft to launch small satellites.

1962 July 29 The USAF contracted with Curtiss-Wright for two Model 200 VTOL transport aircraft designated X-19. Developed as a private venture, the configuration included four tilting propeller assemblies, one each at the tips of two sets of wings set one behind the other. Powered by two 2,200-SHP Lycoming T55-L-5 turboshaft engines, the X-19 had a forward wingspan of 19 ft. 6 in. and a rear wingspan of 21 ft. 6 in. with a fuselage length of 42 ft. 1 in. and a gross weight of 13,660 lb.

1962 July 29 The first Vickers Type 1100 VC-10 airliner (G-ARTA) made its first flight, powered by four 21,000-lb. s.t. Rolls Royce Conway RCo42 turbofan engines in pairs either side of the rear fuselage. Developed to a 1957 BOAC requirement for a long-range airliner for commonwealth routes, it had a wingspan of 146 ft. 2 in., a length of 171 ft. 8 in. and capacity for 115 to 135 passengers. The VC-10 had a cruising speed of 552 MPH and a maximum payload range of 5,400 mi.

1962 August 8 During a special high-temperature research flight, Maj. Robert A. Rushworth, USAF, piloted the #2 X-15 rocket-propelled research aircraft to a speed of Mach 4.4 (2,943 MPH) and a height of 90,877 ft. At this relatively low altitude for the speed engaged, external surfaces reached a maximum temperature of about 900°F. During the 8-min. flight, Rushworth piloted the aircraft through a series of maneuvers to test various aerothermal profiles.

1962 August 29 A CIA U-2 spyplane overflight of Cuba discovered a Soviet military build-up on the island, and the previously scheduled bimonthly survey of the country was increased to weekly surveillance. Since the program's inception in 1953, the CIA had held tenacious control over the U-2 activities. The USAF wanted to take over the CIA spyplane flights and finally managed to get permission for the Cuba missions on October 9.

1962 August 31 A USAF U-2E "strayed" over the Soviet-occupied island of Sakhalin in the northwest Pacific, provoking sharp complaints from the Soviet authorities. The United States assured the Soviet government that overflights of the USSR had been prohibited since the flight of Francis Gary Powers resulted in Soviet SAMs bringing down the CIA-operated aircraft on May 1, 1960.

1962 September 9 A Nationalist Chinese U-2 spyplane was shot down over communist China and, concerned about the safety of U-2 overflights of Cuba, Pres. Kennedy ordered a halt to these flights until October 5. During the interval, Soviet missile-carrying cargo ships off-loaded their cargoes at Havana and accelerated deployment. The Nationalist Chinese had been used by the CIA to obtain information on the communist military build-up and on China's emerging atomic weapons program.

1962 September 18 The U.S. Defense Department changed the system of aircraft designation to avoid conflicting number systems between the U.S. Air Force and the U.S. Navy. From this date all military aircraft would carry a fixed number-letter combination irrespective of the operating service. Thus, the Navy F-4H-1 Phantom II became the F-4B while the USAF version, instead of becoming the F-110A as it would have under the old system, became the F-4C. Bomber designations reverted to B-1 after the North American B-70.

1962 September 19 Named "Pregnant Guppy" because of its appearance, a radical modification of a Boeing 377 Stratocruiser converted it into a heavy-lift cargo carrier for oversize objects, which flew for the first time on this day. Converted by On Mark Engineering, it had a 16 ft. 8 in. plug inserted in the fuselage and a completely new roof structure that allowed loads up to 19 ft. 9 in. to be inserted. To facilitate loading, the complete rear fuselage could be unbolted and moved to one side. It began operations during 1963 when it was leased to NASA for transporting spacecraft sections.

1962 October 2 The Tupolev Tu-124 short-haul airliner began operations on the Aeroflot service between Moscow and Tallin. Powered by two 11,900-lb. s.t. D-20P turbofan engines, the first Soviet airliner to use turbofans, it was similar to the Tu-104 in appearance but smaller, with a wingspan of 83 ft. 10 in., a length of 100 ft. 4 in. and capacity for up to 60 passengers. Only around 100 standard Tu-124s were built, and a special luxury version for VIPs was also built.

1962 October 14 A USAF U-2E piloted by Maj. Steve Hayser of the 4080th Strategic Reconnaissance Wing returned to the United States with photographic evidence that Soviet ballistic missiles were being set up in Cuba. From the pictures, they appeared to be intermediate or intercontinental missiles that would threaten U.S. towns and cities practically to the Canadian border. A U.S. Navy Lockheed P2V also returned reconnaissance pictures of the Soviet freighter *Omsk* with oblong crates on deck suggesting missiles.

1962 October 16 The first Boeing-Vertol CH-46A Sea Knight twin-rotor helicopter made its first flight. Officially accepted in 1964, 624 were to be built by 1970 for the U.S. Navy and the U.S. Marine Corps. Powered by two 1,400-SHP General Electric T58-GE-10 shaft turbine engines driving two 51-ft. diameter rotors, the helicopter had a length of 44 ft. 10 in. and a gross weight of 23,000 lb. It had a cruising speed of 154 MPH and a range of 230 mi.

1962 October 18 The first free flight of the Dassault Balzac V-001 VTOL research aircraft took place following the first tethered flight tests on October 12. Built to carry out research for the projected Dassault Mirage III-V V/STOL fighter, it had one 4,850-lb. s.t. Bristol Siddeley Orpheus turbojet and eight vertically mounted 2,200-lb. s.t. Rolls Royce RB.108 lift-jet engines in pairs fore and aft of each main wheel bay.

1962 October 22 Pres. Kennedy publicly announced the build-up of Soviet intermediate-range ballistic missiles on Cuba. Since October 17, there had been an average six or seven U-2 overflights each day, and since October 14, the USAF 4080th Strategic Reconnaissance Wing had flown 20 missions over Cuba. Low-altitude overflights by McDonnell RF-101Cs had also taken place. By December 6, the 4080th Strategic Reconnaissance Wing would have flown 102 Cuba missions since October 14.

1962 October 26 USAF Strategic Air Command received its last B-52, an H model (serial no. 61-040) and the last three B-58A Hustler supersonic bombers (serial nos. 61-2078 to 61-2080). It was in this year that Strategic Air Command reached peak strength with the B-52, 639 aircraft being in the inventory. The USAF now had no strategic or long-range bomber in development or production except the research-oriented XB-70. On October 30, Defense Secretary McNamara asked the USAF to begin drawing up plans for a B-52 replacement.

1962 October 27 Maj. Rudolph Anderson, USAF, of the 4080th Strategic Reconnaissance Wing flying a U-2 spyplane mission over Cuba was shot down by a Soviet SA-2 Guideline SAM, one of a large number deployed to Cuba in protection of the Soviet intermediate-range SS-4 missiles. Ironically, the Soviets had already decided to withdraw their missiles from Cuba, U.S. Navy patrol aircraft having observed them stopped at sea on the 26th. On October 28, the Soviets announced they would comply with the U.S. request to withdraw the missiles from Cuba. One unprecedented, secret protocol to the agreement granted the United States the right to make U-2 spyplane flights over Cuba.

1962 October 29 The Douglas DC-8F Jet Trader cargo/passenger aircraft made its first flight, powered by four 18,000-lb. s.t. Pratt & Whitney JT3D-3 turbofans. With a maximum cargo-lifting capacity of 95,282 lb. and a gross weight of 318,000 lb., a typical load mix would carry 54 passengers and 54,500 lb. of cargo over a maximum stage of 4,000 mi. Up to 189 economy-class seats could be fitted with cargo bulkheads removed.

1962 October 31 Aeroflot introduced the Antonov An-24 on its Kiev-Kherson route, less than 3 yr. after the aircraft's first flight on December 20, 1959. Designed as a short-haul, 32-seat airliner powered by two 2,515-EHP Ivchyenko AI-24 turboprop engines, it had a wingspan of 95 ft. 9 in. and a length of 77 ft. 2 in. More than 1,000 had been built when production ceased in 1978. Cargo versions and 44-seat variants were developed resulting in a An-24V capable of accommodating 50 people.

1962 November 7 U.S. defense secretary Robert McNamara recommended to Pres. Kennedy that the Skybolt ALBM be canceled and the following day the British ambassador was informed that it had been. The reason given was that the launch aircraft would be vulnerable to antiaircraft defenses and that it was technically flawed, but the real reason was the Skybolt's cost. This decision sealed the fate of Britain's nuclear deterrent. Having already been shifted from Blue Streak missile to Skybolt-armed Vulcans, it was now destined to be put aboard British-built submarines armed with Polaris missiles from the United States.

1962 November 9 During a routine research flight in which it was to have reached a height of 120,000 ft., NASA test pilot John B. McKay piloted the #2 X-15 back down to the ground when the throttle failed at 35% thrust and the engine was shut down. Landing with excess fuel on board, the left rear landing leg collapsed, flipping the aircraft over on its back and substantially damaging the airframe. It was decided to rebuild the aircraft at North American's Los Angeles plant.

1962 November 24 The U.S. Defense Department awarded General Dynamics/Grumman the contract to build the USAF/U.S. Navy TFX fighter bomber/fleet defense fighter. Defense Secretary Robert McNamara had overturned the decision of the selection committee when it chose Boeing, and the ensuing lengthy congressional hearings vindicated his objectivity. A contract was signed December 21 for the TFX, designated F-111A for the USAF and F-111B for the navy. At an estimated $5.445 billion, it was the biggest aircraft program awarded to date.

1962 November 29 The French ambassador in Britain, Geoffroy de Courcel, and the British minister of aviation, Julian Amery, signed an agreement for the development and production of a supersonic airliner designed to cruise at Mach 2.2 powered by Olympus 593 engines developed by Bristol Siddeley, with SNECMA providing about one-third the effort. France would contribute about 60% of airframe work which would be developed by Süd-Aviation and the British Aircraft Corp. The first flight was scheduled for 1966 and cost to the United Kingdom was predicted at a maximum 85 million pounds.

1962 December 7 The Süd-Aviation SA 3210-01 Super Frelon helicopter made its first flight. This was a development of the SA 3200 Frelon first flown on June 10, 1959. Powered by three 1,320-EHP Turbom/eca Turmo IIIC2 shaft-turbine engines driving a 62-ft. diameter main rotor, it had a length of 75 ft. 11 in. and a gross weight of 26,455 lb. Developed with technical assistance from Sikorsky and built with help from Fiat in Italy, the Super Frelon would have a long and successful life. The aircraft was still in widespread service in the early 1990s, employed by several air forces as a heavy-duty helicopter for transport, airborne assault, and ambulance duties.

1962 December 8 The Bell HO-4 U.S. Army light observation helicopter contender made its first flight, the first of the three designs ordered in May 1961. Developed as Bell Model D-205, it was powered by one 250-SHP Allison T63 shaft turbine engine driving a single rotor. In the initial contracting, the Model 205 would not be successful. Developed by Bell as the Model 206 Jet Ranger, however, it would be resubmitted to the army in 1968 and receive an initial order for 2,200.

1962 December 21 Pres. John F. Kennedy and Prime Minister Harold Macmillan concluded four days of meetings at Nassau in the Bahamas with a joint statement declaring agreement had been reached for the United States to supply Britain with the Polaris submarine-launched ballistic missile instead of the now-canceled Skybolt air-launched missile. Britain would supply the submarines and the warheads. This effectively transferred the British nuclear deterrent from air to sea-based forces.

1962 December 27 The first production batch of six top-secret Lockheed SR-71 Blackbird spy planes developed from the A-12 precursor test-bed that was ordered. They were to be heavier, two-seat versions of the A-12 designed for CIA-controlled spying and surveillance missions. In addition to the pilot, there was a second crew member to be called the reconnaissance systems officer who would control the electronic sensors and electronic warfare equipment.

1963 January 7 Aeroflot began a regularly scheduled service between Moscow and Havana, Cuba, using their long-range turboprop Tupolev Tu-114 airliner. Although the aircraft had a range of more than 5,500 mi., an intermediate stop was necessary and the airline set up stop-over facilities at Murmansk. Nevertheless, a reduction in carrying capacity was necessary, 120 passengers being the maximum number carried on this service. Later in the year, Aeroflot began using the Tu-114 on a nonstop flight between Moscow and Delhi, India.

1963 January 13 U.S. helicopters from the Port Lyautey NAS at Rota, Spain and from the USS *Springfield* completed a 7-day maximum-effort relief operation ferrying survivors from flooded areas of Beth and Sebou in Morocco. About 26 tons of supplies, including food and medical aid, were flown in, and 320 people were evacuated to safety.

1963 January 15 FAA administrator Najeeb E. Halaby asked the agency's SST advisory group to provide a detailed cost and operating report of a Mach 3 airliner by May 1. Meanwhile, competing design outlines from Boeing/North American and Douglas/McDonnell/Republic groups were submitted to the USAF Technical Systems Division for analysis under the separation of

roles whereby the Defense Department examined technical aspects, the FAA operating and management decisions and NASA the aerodynamics.

1963 January 17 The first Short Skyvan (G-ASCN) light transport aircraft made its first flight at Sydenham, Northern Ireland with Denis Taylor at the controls. Powered initially with Continental piston engines, a Turbo-Skyvan was quickly developed powered by two 520-ESHP Astazou turboprops. Featuring a high-aspect ratio wing of 64 ft. 1 in. developed by Hurel Dubois in France and a box-shaped fuselage 39 ft. 9 in. in length, it had a stall speed of 73 MPH, a cruising speed of 173 MPH and a maximum range of 465 mi.

1963 January 28 The Hiller Model 1100, designated OH-5A, was the second of three selected finalists in the U.S. Army light observation helicopter competition to fly. Powered by a 250-SHP Allison T63-A-5 turboshaft engine driving a 35 ft. 5 in.-diameter rotor, it had a length of 29 ft. 9 in. Armament was to comprise a variety of optional rocket pods. The OH-5A was not selected by the army.

1963 January The Ilyushin Il-62 made its first flight, fitted with temporary engines. Designed as the Soviet Union's first intercontinental jet transport aircraft, it had a wingspan of 141 ft. 9 in. and a length of 160 ft. 9 in. with four 23,150-lb. s.t. NK-8-4 turbofan engines. Accommodating up to 186 people, the Il-62 became one of the more familiar Soviet aircraft at international airports during the 1970s. First into service with Aeroflot on March 10, 1967, it was developed into a stretched version seating 195 and a total of approximately 250 Il-62s were built for eight countries.

1963 February 1 The Dassault Mirage III-R reconnaissance version of the delta-wing fighter made its first flight. The Armée de l'Air ordered 50 of the type equipped with seven ONERA cameras in the nose and similar air-to-air armament as that carried by the Mirage III-C. On June 14, Jacqueline Auriol set a new women's speed record when she achieved an average 2,030 km/hr. (1,275 MPH) in an aircraft of this type.

1963 February 8 The first Hawker P.1127 prototype (serial no. XP831) carried out the first V/STOL operation from an aircraft carrier when test pilot Bill Bedford flew vertical takeoffs and landings on the flight deck of HMS *Ark Royal* off Portland in the English Channel. Assisted by Hugh Merewether, the trials demonstrated tactical advantages in operating V/STOL aircraft without having to turn the carrier into wind and were to presage a unique application for its successor, the Harrier.

1963 February 9 The first of 1,832 Boeing 727 tri-jet airliners made its first flight. Powered by three 14,000-lb. s.t. Pratt & Whitney JT8D-1 turbofans, production aircraft had a wingspan of 108 ft., a length of 133 ft. 2 in. and a gross weight of 152,000 lb. The 727 could carry up to 129 passengers in a high-density configuration or 94 in a combination of first-class and economy at 532 MPH for 1,150 mi. The Boeing 727 became the first jet aircraft allowed to operate from New York's LaGuardia airport.

1963 February 12 The first production Hawker Siddeley HS 125 made its first flight just one day less than six months after the prototype first took to the air. Designed as a business jet and a utility aircraft for the armed forces, it had a wingspan of 47 ft. and a length of 47 ft. 5 in. with power provided by two 3,100-lb. s.t. Bristol Siddeley Viper 521 turbojet engines. It did well for itself, continuing in production for more than 25 yr., after which more than 600 had been sold.

1963 February 14 The RAF announced that No. 617 Squadron had gone operational with the first Avro Blue Steel stand-off bombs. Other units followed in turn—Squadron Nos. 27 and 83 with Vulcan B.Mk.2 and Squadron Nos. 100 and 139 with Victor B.Mk.2. With a range of 200 mi., each bomber carried a single missile. The strategic nuclear deterrent would progressively shift to the Royal Navy's four Polaris submarines from 1968, and the last Blue Steel was withdrawn from service in 1975.

1963 February 22 In Antarctica, U.S. Navy Lockheed LC-130F Hercules piloted by Comdr. William H. Everett with Rear Adm. James R. Reedy and passengers of VX-6 carried on a 3,470-mi. flight from McMurdo Station to the Shackleton Mountain across unknown and uncharted territory. The flight across the South Pole and back established a record for distance flown in the Antarctic. The first trans-Antarctic flight would take place on October 1, 1963.

1963 February 25 The prototype Transall (Transporter Allianz Group) C.160 made its first flight. Developed by a Franco-German consortium, the high-wing transport was sold to both countries as well as to Turkey and South Africa. Powered by two 6,100-ESHP Rolls Royce Tyne RTy.20 Mk.22 turboprops, it had a wingspan of 131 ft. 2 in. and a length of 106 ft. 3 in. and was capable of carrying either 93 troops, 88 paratroops or 35,274 lb. of cargo. Some 179 C.160s were produced up to 1972, but production opened a second time in 1977 when the French ordered 29 more aircraft all of which were delivered by 1985.

1963 February 27 Built as one of three contenders for the light observation helicopter category, the Hughes OH-6A Cayuse made its first flight powered by a 317-SHP Allison T63-A-5A turboshaft engine. On May 26, 1965, this helicopter was declared the winner, 1,417 being built for the U.S. Army. The OH-6 had a 26 ft. 4 in.-diameter rotor, a length of 30 ft. 4 in. and a gross weight of 2,700 lb. From this design, essentially a military version of the Hughes 386, successors such as the Model 500 Defender and the Model 530 would emerge from the same manufacturer.

1963 April 1 FAA administrator Najeeb Halaby announced selection of Lockheed and a Boeing/North American (NAA) team to conduct detailed airframe studies of a possible commercial supersonic transport aircraft. Lockheed would be awarded a $950,000 contract to carry out research in three areas, and Boeing/NAA would carry out work on six areas at a cost of $850,000. It was agreed that the U.S. government would provide $1.8 million toward development costs, with industry funding up to $1.6 million.

1963 April 8 Without a single order to back it, Douglas announced it would produce a short- to medium-haul airliner to compete with the Caravelle, the BAC 111 and the projected Boeing 727, while getting ahead of the Boeing 737 with which it would compete. As it happened, the Douglas DC-9 would rank third behind the Boeing 727 and the Boeing 737 for numbers built, with around 1,000 sold before the MD-80 derivatives gave it a new lease on life.

1963 April 10 The Entwicklungsring-Süd VJ 101C single-seat experimental VTOL aircraft made its first free hover powered by six Rolls Royce RB.145 engines, two in the under-fuselage mounted vertically and two in each wingtip pod capable of piv-

oting from forward to vertical thrust. Consolidated in 1959, the pooled design bureau of Bölkow, Messerschmitt and Heinkel formed the EWR (Entwicklungsring) to design a Mach 2 VTOL fighter. Research into hover and stability had been conducted by a test rig, which made its first free flight on March 13, 1962.

1963 April 11 Maj. Robert A. Rushworth, USAF, piloted the #1 X-15 rocket research aircraft to a speed of Mach 4.25 (2,864 MPH) and a height of 74,400 ft. in the first of a new series of science and research flights. The aircraft carried a U.S. Army KC-1 camera in the underside of the nose to measure optical distortion caused by shock-wave interaction, air flow and aerodynamic turbulence. This research was important for studies into operational, hypersonic reconnaissance aircraft.

1963 April 12 Flying a Lockheed F-104G Starfighter, Jacqueline Cochran of the United States set a new FAI-ratified world air speed record for women with an averaged 1,273.2 MPH over the 15/25-km course. The aircraft was flown at an altitude of 30,000 ft. for this record. Cochrane took the 100-km (62.14 mi.) closed-circuit women's speed record May 1 at 1,203.686 MPH.

1963 April 13 Americans Don Piccard and Ed Yost from South Falls, S. Dak. became the first people to fly across the English Channel in a hot-air balloon. They took off from Rye, England and reached Gravelines, France in just under 4 hr., flying mostly at an altitude of 13,000 ft.

1963 April 18 The first Northrop X-21A made its first flight at the start of a research program aimed at evaluating boundary layer control techniques. Essentially a converted Douglas WB-66D, the aircraft incorporated laminar flow control and was the first serious attempt to tackle the enduring problem of boundary layer drag caused by turbulence across the wing. Inspired by John Northrop, the company employed the Swiss Dr. Werner Pfenninger who had worked for the Germans following his pioneering tests in this field during 1936.

1963 May 3 Lockheed engineers W. H. Statler, R. R. Heppe and E. S. Cruz summarized their remarkable work on the Lockheed Model 186 (XH-51A) rigid-rotor helicopter in a paper to the American Helicopter Society in Washington, D.C. Funded by the U.S. Army and the U.S. Navy, the XH-51A was powered by a 550-SHP Pratt & Whitney PT6B-9 turboshaft engine driving a three-blade 35-ft. rotor. The second machine was modified to have a compound engine and eventually went to NASA. Despite a top speed of 206 MPH, it failed to attract customers.

1963 May 13 North American Aviation received a contract to rebuild the severely damaged #2 X-15 as the X-15A-2 to exploit the full potential of the airframe by extending the burn duration of the XLR-99 rocket engine. To do this, two external drop tanks carrying a total 13,500 lb. propellant would be fitted and provision made for in-flight test of an externally mounted scramjet engine. The X-15-A2 was returned to Edwards AFB on February 19, 1964, and given a captive test on June 15, 1964.

1963 May 14 In a high-speed run to test dynamic and kinetic heating effects, Maj. Robert A. Rushworth, USAF, piloted the #3 X-15 rocket research aircraft to a speed of Mach 5.2 (3,600 MPH) and a height of 95,600 ft. Wired with 600 surface sensors, the aircraft was flown to a 90° bank angle. Temperatures up to 900°F on its Inconel-X skin provided valuable data on aero-thermal forces and their effects on a hypersonic vehicle.

1963 May 27 The first USAF F-4C made its first flight, powered by two 10,900/17,000-lb. s.t. General Electric J79-GE-15 engines. The aircraft retained the folding wings and arrester gear of the navy fighter, but dual controls were fitted into the two-place cockpit. Armed like its navy counterpart with four Sparrow missiles, the aircraft had no gun armament but ample provision for 16,000 lb. of weapons and stores including up to 1,340 gal. external fuel load. The USAF received a total of 583 F-4Cs and 503 of the RF-4C reconnaissance variant.

1963 June 4 Pan American announced a provisional order for six Anglo-French Concorde supersonic airliners. Air France and BOAC would receive the first two aircraft followed by the first Pan Am aircraft, and the delivery sequence would alternate until the sixth had been delivered. Panair do Brasil had also placed provisional orders for three Concordes.

1963 June 5 Pres. Kennedy announced that his administration would seek funds for the sponsored development of a supersonic transport aircraft and in presentations to Congress later in the month indicated that he expected industry to pay for 25% of the development and return to the government a royalty on each aircraft sold. Moreover, the U.S. government, he said, would pay no more than $750 million for the research and development phase.

1963 June 11 The first two-seat Republic F-105F mission trainer made its first flight. First of the F-105 two-seaters, it joined the USAF beginning in December and proved its worth in Vietnam on Wild Weasel missions, when 86 of the 143 delivered were converted for that job and given the designation F-105G. With an extended fuselage, taller tail and second cockpit, the F-105F/ G was retired to the Air National Guard and made its last flight in 1983.

1963 June 13 Lt. Comdr. R. K. Billings in an F-4A Phantom and Lt. Comdr. R. S. Chew Jr., flying an F-8D Crusader, became the first pilots to carry out fully automatic carrier deck landings with production support equipment. The qualification took place aboard the USS *Midway* (CVA-41) off the coast of California. It was the culmination of 20 yr. of research and almost 6 yr. of technical development with experimental automatic ''hands-off'' carrier landing systems.

1963 June 17 The first Sikorsky S-61R heavy transport helicopter made its first flight. Developed from the standard S-61 into the USAF-designated CH-3C, it had a hydraulically operated rear ramp, an internal winch for 2,000-lb. loads and capacity for 25 troops, 15 stretchers or 5,000-lb. internal cargo or 10,000 lb. on an external sling. The USAF acquired 120 and employed them extensively in Vietnam, where they earned the nickname ''Jolly Green Giant.''

1963 July 4 The first landing of a single-engine aircraft at the North Pole was successfully accomplished when Bob Fisher and Cliff Alkefer of the University of Alaska Arctic Research Center flew their Cessna Model 180 from Point Barrow, Alaska. This aircraft had a normal maximum range of 925 mi. but flew with overload fuel on board.

1963 July 6 The first Vickers Viscount bought by the People's Republic of China left Britain with a British crew en route to its new owners. The national airline CAAC had ordered six Viscounts. These were the first aircraft to break the Soviet monopoly on China's aircraft procurement.

1963 July 19 NASA test pilot Joseph A. Walker piloted the #3 X-15 research aircraft to a new record height of 347,800 ft. and a speed of Mach 5.5 (3,710 MPH) on a flight devised to measure

air density at extreme altitude. To do that, the pilot released a 30-in. diameter nitrogen-filled balloon on a 100-ft. line trailed behind the aircraft. This information supported trajectory design for lifting reentry vehicles.

1963 July 25 A Partial Test Ban Treaty banning the testing of nuclear weapons in the atmosphere, outer space or under water came into force. The last U.S. atmospheric test had been conducted on November 4, 1962, when a Nike Hercules rocket was launched. The last time an aircraft dropped a nuclear weapon was on October 30, 1962, when a B-52 dropped a parachute-retarded device over the Johnston Island area in the Pacific, under the test name Housatonic, for the Lawrence Livermore Laboratory. U.S. aircraft dropped a total of 52 nuclear weapons on test since June 30, 1946. The preferred delivery vehicles were, in order, the B-50, the B-45, the B-36 and the B-52.

1963 July 31 The YF-5A made its first flight powered by two 2,720/4,090-lb. s.t. General Electric J85-GE-13 turbojet engines. Selected in May 1962 as the U.S. Defense Department's ''Freedom Fighter'' for participating countries in the Military Assistance Program, the F-5 remained in production until 1987, and a total of 2,610 had been built. The F-5A light tactical fighter and the F-5B two-seat trainer were developed into more potent versions during the early 1970s.

1963 August 2 In the opening minutes of the day, just after midnight, a McDonnell F3B Demon piloted by Lt. Roger Bellnap launched a two-stage Sparroair missile while nearly vertical at a height of 30,000 ft. The missile reached a height of 66 mi. carrying scientific instruments in the nose. There were to be five such launches in all in a U.S. Navy program designed to qualify the performance of air-launched space probes shot to ballistic trajectories.

1963 August 7 The first Lockheed YF-12A (serial no. 60-6934) made its first flight. A precursor Mach 3.35 interceptor powered by two 32,500-lb. s.t. Pratt & Whitney JT11D-20B turbo-ramjets, it was derived from the A-12. The YF-12A was a two-seat aircraft designed to carry Hughes GAR-9 (AIM-47A) air-to-air missiles in three fuselage bays. Only three aircraft were built, used extensively for flight research and sensor testing until the last flight on November 7, 1979.

1963 August 15 The FAA requested design bids for a supersonic airliner capable of carrying 125 to 160 passengers and for engines to power it. For Phase 1, submissions were presented in January 1964 by Boeing, Lockheed and North American while engine-makers General Electric and Pratt & Whitney submitted designs for augmented turbojets in the 35,000–40,000-lb. class. North American was eliminated, and only Lockheed with the CL-823 design and Boeing with the Model 733 went through to Phase 2.

1963 August 16 NASA test pilot Milton O. Thompson piloted the M2-F1 lifting body research vehicle when it was towed into the air for the first time by a C-47 released at 10,000 ft. and 120 MPH for a free glide lasting 2 min. before landing on Rogers Dry Lake, Calif. at about 90 MPH. Authorized in September 1962, the M2 evolved as the brainchild of NASA engineer Robert D. Reed for testing optimum reentry vehicle shapes for high lift/drag shapes. It took the form of a flat-topped half cone with a width of 13 ft., a length of 20 ft., a height of 10 ft. and a weight of 1,140 lb. with pilot.

1963 August 20   The British Aircraft Corp. BAC 111 Series 200 made its first flight powered by two 10,600-lb. s.t. Rolls Royce Spey RB.163-2 (Mk.506-14) bypass engines. With a wingspan of 88 ft. 6 in. and a length of 93 ft. 6 in. the aircraft had capacity for 65 to 79 passengers, but development problems resulted in slow success. On October 22, the prototype was lost in an accident that caused the death of test pilot Mike Lithgow, but 230 had been built when production ended in 1985. As the Rombac 1-11, it was built in Romania, the first flying in 1987.

1963 August 22   In what would be the greatest height achieved by an X-15 and by a manned aircraft without going into orbit, NASA test pilot Joseph A. Walker piloted the #3 X-15 to an altitude of 354,200 ft. (67.083 mi.). Considering that some manned spacecraft have dipped in their orbits around the earth to as low as 87 mi., this was indeed a landmark in the history of aviation, less than 60 yr. after the first powered flight. The purpose of the flight was to measure reentry stability and control techniques.

1963 October 1   A Lockheed C-130 Hercules of the U.S. Navy under the command of Rear Adm. James R. Reedy, made the first transpolar flight across Antarctica. Equipped with skis, the aircraft departed Capetown, South Africa and flew to McMurdo Sound, Antarctica, covering the 4,700 mi. in a flight time of 14 hr. 31 min. This flight inaugurated the U.S. Navy's Operation Deep Freeze '64, a logistics support operation.

1963 October 7   The first flight of the Lear Jet Corp.'s Learjet 23 took place, 3 yr. after the formation of the parent company, then known as the Swiss American Aviation Corp. A classic name in twin-engined executive jets, the first model in this successful family of aircraft was powered by the 2,850-lb. s.t. General Electric CJ6190I turbojet mounted in pods on either side of the rear fuselage. With a wingspan of 35 ft. 7 in., a length of 42 ft. and a maximum takeoff weight of 12,500 lb., the Learjet 23 had a cruising speed of 570 MPH and a maximum range of 2,300 mi.

1963 October 16   In Operation Greased Lightning, a B-58A (serial no. 61-2059) of the USAF 305th Bombardment Wing, Bunker Hill AFB, Ind. set a new world record time of 8 hr. 35 min. 20.4 sec. flying 8,028 mi. from Tokyo to London nonstop. Piloted by Maj. Sidney J. Kubesch, the aircraft took off from Kadena AB, Okinawa and flew across Japan, Alaska, northern Canada, Greenland, Iceland and London prior to landing at RAF Greenham Common. It also set new record times of 3 hr. 9 min. 41.8 sec. from Tokyo to Anchorage, Alaska at an average speed of 1,093.44 MPH, and 5 hr. 24 min. 54 sec. for the flight from Anchorage to London at an average 826.91 MPH.

1963 October 22   The USAF and the U.S. Army completed Exercise Big Lift during which the 13,336 men of the Second Armored Division from Bergstrom AFB, Tex. were lifted to three airfields in Germany and five in eastern France within 63 hr. 40 min. Military Air Transport Service used 23 C-135s, 18 C-133s, 98 C-124s, 30 C-130s and 35 C-118s in the exercise. In support, a strike force of 18 F-105s, 36 F-100s, eight RF-101s and six RB-66s flew nonstop from Dow and Loring AFBs, Maine to three airfields in Germany, refueled en route by KC-135s.

1963 October 24   It was announced at the Pentagon, Arlington, Va. (just outside Washington, D.C.) that Australia had decided to buy 24 TFX aircraft from the United States instead of T.S.R.2 aircraft from Britain. The RAAF was to procure the F-111A variant as a replacement for its Canberra force. The purchase price was quoted at $224 million, including spares and crew training in the United States. Australia would be given 24 B-47s on loan

Last of the Stratofortress derivatives, the final Boeing B-52H came off the production line on October 26, 1963.

until the F-111As could be delivered, which was estimated to be in 1967. Events would delay actual delivery until 1973.

1963 October 30   The longest nonstop flight to date by a commercial jet airliner was completed when a Douglas DC-8 belonging to Swissair completed a flight from Long Beach, Calif. to Beirut, Lebanon. Under the command of Capt. Siegfried Hale, the aircraft flew the 7,460 mi. in a time of 13 hr. 58 min.

1963 October 31   FAA deputy administrator Gordon Bain responded to a suggestion from Continental Air Lines president Robert F. Six that the United States join forces with Britain and France in development of a supersonic airliner. He categorically denied validity to the idea, saying that there was little except money the United States could contribute at this relatively advanced stage of the project and that neither Britain nor France had ever suggested cooperating with America. In fact, Britain had been rebuffed by the Eisenhower administration when it sought cooperation.

1963 November 11   The Fleet Air Arm of the Royal Navy formed its first Small Ship Flight using Westland Wasp light antisubmarine helicopters aboard Leander-class frigates. Small ship flights equipped with Wasps would operate from an increasing number of navy frigates. The Wasp began life as the Saunders Roe P.531, first flown in July 1958. The Wasp had a 710-SHP Rolls Royce Nimbus 103 turboshaft engine driving a 32 ft. 3 in.-diameter rotor. The Wasp had a length of 40 ft. 4 in. and could carry two homing torpedoes.

1963 November 19   The FAA announced its program of delivery allocation for U.S. supersonic transport aircraft as they came off the production line. U.S. airlines would receive the first four of the initial seventy built, with priority going to trans-Atlantic carriers. After that, foreign airlines would get the remaining 66 with preference there, too, going to trans-Atlantic operators.

1963 November 20   The first of two Curtiss-Wright X-19 VTOL research aircraft made the first hover flight but was damaged in a crash-landing. The second flight took place June 25, 1964, followed by the first controlled hover on August 7, 1964. A crash on August 25, 1965, brought cancellation of the entire program 4 mon. later. The aircraft had achieved 50 flights totaling just under 4 hr.

1963 December 10   Impressed by the pace of NASA's manned space program and balking at the costs involved plus the apparently minimal advantage in the X-20, U.S. Defense Secretary Robert McNamara announced the outright cancellation of the X-

A Lockheed C-141 taking to the air. It was first flown on December 17, 1963, with the last one delivered February 28, 1968.

20 winged aerodynamic space vehicle and the transfer of all research into unmanned experimental reentry body and lifting-body programs.

1963 December 10   During a routine flight of the Lockheed NF-104A, test pilot Charles ("Chuck") Yeager narrowly escaped death when his aircraft got into an uncontrollable flat spin at 90,000 ft. Yeager managed to eject when the aircraft had fallen to 10,000 ft. The NF-104A was modified to carry one 6,000-lb. thrust Rocketdyne AR-2 rocket engine above the tailpipe and below the tail to give astronauts experience with handling aircraft in rarefied air at altitudes of up to 130,000 ft.

1963 December 16   Under Operation Halo at El Centro, Calif. 13 parachutists from the U.S. Army and the USAF carried out a record mass jump when they free-fell from a height of 45,000 ft. after jumping from a Lockheed C-130. They opened their parachutes at 2,500 ft. This exceeded the previous record set in 1961 when nine Soviet parachutists jumped from 36,650 ft. The Halo (high altitude, low opening) tests were an exercise in putting men on the ground quickly.

1963 December 17   The Lockheed C-141 StarLifter made its first flight, powered by four 21,000-lb. Pratt & Whitney TF33-P-7 engines, and was the first strategic jet transport aircraft for Military Air Transport Service. It had a wingspan of 160 ft. 1 in., a length of 145 ft., a gross weight of 316,600 lb. and provision for 154 troops, 123 paratroops, 80 litters or 90,000 lb. of cargo. The first C-141A base became operational at Travis AFB, Calif. on April 23, 1965. The aircraft would quickly become a familiar sight in Vietnam with an almost daily service across the Pacific.

1963 December 25   Returned from discussions with Soviet aviation officials in Moscow where he exchanged technical details for a New York-Moscow service, FAA administrator Najeeb Halaby declared that the USSR was building a supersonic transport aircraft "very similar" to the U.S. plan. An arch advocate of supersonic transport to keep the United States ahead of rivals in the aviation world, Najeeb Halaby was only the latest in a line of people reporting Soviet SST plans during 1963.

1964 January 5   The Short Belfast, the first military transport aircraft with a fully automated landing system, made its first flight powered by four 5,730-EHP Rolls Royce Tyne R.Ty.12 Mk.101 turboprop engines. Ordered by RAF Transport Command, the aircraft had a wingspan of 158 ft. 9 in. and a length of 136 ft. 5

in. It had capacity for up to 150 troops, and the first of 10 aircraft for No. 53 Squadron, RAF, arrived at the unit in January 1966. The squadron was disbanded in September 1976, leaving only the C-130 as the RAF's strategic freighter.

1964 January 6   In a tactical training exercise to test long-range overseas deployment, 18 USAF Lockheed F-104 Starfighters were moved from the west coast of the United States to Europe. The aircraft departed George AFB, Calif. and put down at Moron AB, Spain after a flight of 10 hr. 20 min. The aircraft had flown a total distance of 6,150 mi. and were refueled six times in the air.

1964 January 6   A U.S. Supersonic Transport Evaluation Group was formed under the overall jurisdiction of the FAA. It was to have 210 members, with representatives from the FAA, NASA, CAB, USAF, U.S. Navy and the Department of Commerce. The group was to complete evaluation of the initial industry proposals due January 15 from Boeing and Lockheed. Airlines meanwhile would examine the proposals by the end of March, and FAA administrator Najeeb Halaby was to announce the future direction of the SST on May 1.

1964 January 15   The FAA received submissions for a supersonic transport airframe from Boeing, Lockheed and North American and propulsion submissions from Pratt & Whitney, General Electric and Curtiss-Wright. The Lockheed configuration was a double-delta designed to carry 218 passengers at Mach 2.65. Boeing envisaged an arrow-shaped wing in a configuration carrying 150 passengers at Mach 2.7. Propulsion designs would be capable of speeds up to Mach 3.

1964 February 1   The first Boeing 727-100 to enter airline service started operations with Eastern Air Lines on its Philadelphia-Washington-Miami service. United Air Lines introduced the type on its San Francisco-Denver service February 6, followed by American Airlines on its New York-Chicago run April 12 and TWA on the Indianapolis-New York service June 1.

1964 February 7   The FAA announced that Air France and BOAC had each reserved six delivery positions for the U.S. supersonic commercial transport aircraft. This increased to 10 the number of airlines holding reservations, raising to 63 the total number of aircraft ordered to date.

1964 February 11   Ling-Temco-Vought (LTV) won a U.S. Navy design competition for a light attack aircraft. Announced May

17, it called for an in-service target of 1967. LTV received bonus points for basing its submission on the F-8 Crusader, a product of the old Chance-Vought company before it was absorbed on August 31, 1961. Designated A-7, the new aircraft had less sweepback than the F-8 but with no variable wing incidence. With a shortened and strengthened fuselage it was to be capable of carrying up to 15,000 lb. of ordnance.

1964 February 21 U.S. Marine Air Group 26 at New River, N.C. became the first USMC unit to receive the Bell UH-1E, a derivative of the UH-1 Iroquois helicopter first flown on October 22, 1956. Powered by a 1,100-SHP Lycoming T53-L-11, 250 UH-1Es were purchased for the Marines with a further 20 bought as crew trainers. The navy would procure new versions of the Iroquois from 1970, which led to armed versions similar to those evolved for the U.S. Army.

1964 February 29 Pres. Lyndon Johnson publicly acknowledged the existence of the Lockheed A-12 Mach 3 + spy-plane program and showed a picture that was actually a YF-12A. This top-secret program embracing A-12s, YF-12s and SR-71s was thus cleared to set several FAI world class records the following year and for A-12 designer Clarence (''Kelly'') Johnson to receive a well-earned Collier trophy for 1964.

1964 March 2 The White House released a report compiled by Eugene R. Black and Stanley J. Osborne recommending increased U.S. government subsidy for the supersonic commercial transport. Whereas the original plan announced by Pres. Kennedy envisaged the U.S. government paying 75% of the then estimated $1 billion development cost, the new review proposed a U.S. government subsidy of up to 90%, citing the inability of manufacturers to meet the balance under the original scheme.

1964 March 3 Using a duplex flight control system, the world's first fully automated landings made by a commercial airliner specifically designed for that purpose took place at the Royal Aircraft Establishment, Bedford, England. Piloted by Hawker Siddeley test pilot Jimmy Phillips, Trident G-ARPG made six successful landings as well as four more at the company's Hatfield airfield. Many passengers were to applaud the forward thinking of the old de Havilland company when their Trident carried them into fog-bound airports while other aircraft were diverted.

1964 March 5 The USAF B-70 program was cut back, and only two XB-70 prototypes were to be completed. With the first of these nearing rollout, North American Aviation was forced to scrap the YB-70, which it had been building since 1962. A decision had been made to allow the aircraft a flight research program that would support the U.S. supersonic airliner program. An unsuccessful attempt had been made by the USAF in July 1963 to get funds for an operational fleet of 60 RS-70 reconnaissance-strike versions.

1964 March 6 At a technical meeting of IATA in Beirut, Concorde builders BAC and Süd-Aviation provided details of an increase in the size of the aircraft. It was to have delta-wing span of 184 ft. 2 in. versus 170 ft., and have a length of 83 ft. 10 in. versus 77 ft. Maximum takeoff weight was projected to be 326,000 lb. with a 26,000 lb. payload. To date, 43 Concordes had been ordered by eight airlines on the proviso that the aircraft would not cost more than $10 million.

1964 March 7 The first of 9 Hawker Siddeley Kestrel F(GA).1 service evaluation aircraft made its first flight, powered by a 15,500-lb. s.t. Bristol Siddeley Pegasus 5 engine. With a wing-

span of 22 ft. 11 in. and a length of 42 ft. 6 in., it had a maximum loaded VTOL weight of 14,500 lb. or 17,000 lb. overload for STO. The Kestrel had a top speed of Mach 0.92 (710 MPH at sea level or 635 MPH at 36,000 ft.) and a service ceiling of 55,000 ft.

1964 March 7 The prototype of Egypt's first home-built fighter made its first flight as the Helwan HA-300. Powered by a 4,850-lb. s.t. Bristol Siddeley Orpheus Mk 703-S-10 turbojet, it had been designed by Prof. Willy Messerschmitt for the Spanish Hispano works but transferred to the United Arab Republic (Egypt) where it was assembled at the Helwan Aircraft Works outside Cairo. With a 19 ft. 4 in.-span delta wing, it had a length of 40 ft. 8 in. Only three prototypes were built, and the type was canceled in 1969.

1964 March 26 Rep. Roman C. Pucinski (D.—Ill.) spoke in support of his bill (H.R.8104) to restrict overflight of inhabited areas by supersonic transport aircraft producing an overpressure in excess of 1.5 lb./sq. ft. The FAA had conducted tests over Oklahoma City to measure the strength of public concern over the ''sonic boom'' and received only 2,000 complaints and a lot of pro-SST support. The number of complaints were very low compared to a level of routine complaints in general regarding overflights from military aircraft. Rep. Pucinski said that the FAA overpressure standards were too low and that a more realistic simulation of the level of sonic booms from supersonic transport aircraft should be 3 lb./sq. ft. If applied at that level, he asserted, the public would protest in large numbers.

1964 April 1 Pres. Lyndon B. Johnson signed an executive order establishing the President's Advisory Committee on Supersonic Transport, a powerful interagency body chaired by Defense Secretary Robert S. McNamara. The committee diluted power from the FAA, which under administrator Najeeb Halaby had repeatedly sought to act as a rallying point for pro-SST activists. With the death of Pres. Kennedy in November 1963, the SST had lost one of its most important advocates.

1964 April 9 The prototype de Havilland Canada DHC-5 Buffalo made its first flight. Essentially a larger version of the DHC-4 Caribou, the Buffalo was powered by two 2,850-ESHP General Electric T64-GE-10 turboprop engines, with a wingspan of 96 ft. and a length of 77 ft. 3 in. The DHC-5 could lift 41 fully equipped troops or 24 litters 530 mi. at 212 MPH. Intended for the U.S. Army, they were never ordered as such because of a policy shift moving all fixed-wing transport to the USAF.

1964 April 17 Geraldine Mock of the United States became the first woman pilot to fly around the world. She took off from Columbus, Ohio on March 19 and arrived back after 29 days 11 hr. 59 min. 38 sec. In that period, she had flown a total distance of 23,103 mi. The aircraft she used was a Cessna Model 180 named *Spirit of Columbus,* subsequently presented to the Smithsonian Air and Space Museum in Washington, D.C.

1964 April 21 In a historic shift, the USAF Strategic Air Command had as many ballistic missiles on ground alert as there were manned bombers on ground alert, and for the first time in the history of the U.S. air forces, the primary deterrent was the missile and not the aircraft. The balance would continue to shift increasingly in favor of the missile. By 1970 two-thirds of Strategic Air Command nuclear delivery systems would comprise missiles rather than bombers, and by 1980 three-quarters of the strike force would be in underground silos.

1964 April 27 In the largest operation of its type to date, U.S. Marine Corps Sikorsky UH-34 helicopters air-lifted 420 South Vietnamese troops to the border with Laos to mount an attack on communist positions. These were the redesignated HSS-1 helicopters, military derivatives of the S-61. On March 16, the Pathet Lao had attacked across the Plain of Jars, and on March 19, the United States began armed reconnaissance with USAF RF-101Cs and U.S. Navy RF-8As. This action stimulated the delivery of 50 North American T-28 Texan COIN aircraft to the Royal Laotian Air Force.

1964 May 1 The BAC 221 delta-wing research aircraft WG774 made its first flight powered by a 14,000-lb. s.t. Rolls Royce Avon RA.28R turbojet engine. Taken over by BAC and fitted with an ogive wing to test aerodynamic flight characteristics with a prototype Concorde-shape wing, the Type 221 was the reworked Fairey F.D.2 prototype, which had first flown on October 6, 1954. It had a wingspan of 25 ft., a length of 57 ft. 7 in. and a maximum speed of 1,050 MPH.

1964 May 7 Powered by four 22,500-lb. s.t. Rolls Royce Conway RCo.43 engines and featuring an extended fuselage 171 ft. 8 in. in length accommodating up to 163 passengers, the first Vickers Super VC-10 made its first flight. Gross weight had been increased to 335,000 lb. BOAC had ordered 17 of the type, which had a range of 5,300 mi., and put the first to work on the London-New York route on April 1, 1965.

1964 May 20 The White House authorized full development of the U.S. supersonic commercial transport following evaluation of three airframe and three propulsion contenders. Boeing and Lockheed were to compete for a definitive airframe contract, excluding North American, and General Electric and Pratt & Whitney were to compete for the engine contract, eliminating Curtiss-Wright. The Department of Commerce was to study the economics of the SST, the National Academy of Sciences would advise on sonic boom studies, and the airframe contenders would integrate these studies into design criteria.

1964 May 25 The Ryan XV-5A ''fan-in-wing'' Vertijet VTOL research aircraft made its first flight. Two 2,658-lb. s.t. General Electric J85-GE-5 turbojets could be used to power either two large down-flow fans in the wings or provide conventional thrust for forward flight. A small GE-X376 fan engine in the nose controlled pitch in the hover. Only two aircraft were built, each with a wingspan of 29 ft. 10 in., a length of 44 ft. 6 in. and a loaded weight of 12,236 lb.

1964 June 1 The first Convair 580 turboprop upgrade of the CV-340/440 series made its first fare-paying flight with Frontier Airlines, powered by two 3,750-EHP Allison 501D13D turboprops proving the aircraft with a maximum cruise speed of 355 MPH at 18,000 ft. and a maximum payload range of 645 mi., or 1,570 mi. with an 8,000-lb. load. It could accommodate 52 passengers and gave the old line a new lease. Other improvements would keep the airliner in service for another 20 yr.

1964 June 2 NASA's Flight Research Center at Edwards AFB, Calif. awarded a development and production contract to Northrop for two powered lifting-body vehicles: a powered version of the M2-F1, to be known as the M2-F2, and the HL-10. They were to be delivered 6 mo. apart with the first in late spring 1965. Capitalizing on Northrop's reputation for building cost-effective aircraft, each vehicle cost only $1.2 million. These lifting-bodies were to conduct flight research on the aerodynamics and handling of unpowered reentry vehicles.

1964 June 9 For the first time, Strategic Air Command air refueling tankers were used to support combat operations in Southeast Asia. Four KC-135s from Clark AB, Philippines refueled eight F-100 fighter bombers en route to strike Pathet Lao forces in northern Laos. The tankers remained in southern Laos to refuel two of the fighter-bombers on their way back. The tankers were withdrawn back to Andersen AFB, Guam but reestablished at Clark AFB on August 5 before resuming support operations September 28.

1964 August 5 In Operation Pierce Arrow, 64 aircraft from the carriers USS *Ticonderoga* (CVA-14) and USS *Constellation* (CVA-64) attacked patrol boats in waters off North Vietnam, retaliating for a Viet Cong attack on the destroyers USS *Maddox* and USS *C. Turner Joy*. This was the first U.S. Navy operation against North Vietnam. Other warships were moved up in the following days and on August 7, the United States government put the country on a war footing with the so-called Gulf of Tonkin Resolution. The carrier USS *Ranger* (CV-4) moved in with RA-5C Vigilantes to join the other two and the USS *Bonne Homme Richard* (CVA-31).

1964 August 14 During a flight by the #2 X-15 rocket research aircraft with Maj. Robert A. Rushworth, USAF, piloting, the nose wheel landing gear accidently extended at 3,068 MPH. Peak speed and altitude during the flight was Mach 5.23 (3,590 MPH). After a 9-min. flight, the aircraft landed normally and the nose gear remained intact, but both wheel tires blew on contact with the ground. The first flight of the modified #2 X-15 had been conducted on June 25.

1964 August 14 The last Avro Lancaster to be used anywhere for military duty arrived in Sydney, Australia, piloted by Lt. Pierre Boulier of the Aéronavale. It was flown in from Noumea, New Caledonia, where it had been employed on policing duties within the French Pacific territory. It was scheduled for 3 mon. of display in Australia, after which it was flown to Britain for delivery to the Historic Aircraft Preservation Society.

1964 September 2 An Indonesian C-130B Hercules dropped 96 paratroops at Labis, West Malaysia in support of Indonesian claims to that territory, but the aircraft crashed on the way back to its base. Pres. Sukarno wanted to unite Malaysia, the Philippines and Indonesia and had used air power since the end of 1962 to press toward that objective. The Royal Malay Air Force and elements of the RAAF were on continual patrol to defend the area.

1964 September 21 The first of two prototype North American XB-70A supersonic research aircraft made its first flight, which lasted about 1 hr., and experienced minor technical problems with landing gear retraction, blowing two tires on landing. With a wingspan of 103 ft. and a length of 185 ft., the XB-70A had a loaded weight of 525,000 lb. Powered by six 19,500/31,000-lb. s.t. General Electric YJ93-GE-3 turbojets, it had a design speed of 1,980 MPH at 80,000 ft. and an un-refueled range of 7,500 mi.

1964 September 27 The first T.S.R.2 prototype (serial no. XR219) made its first flight from Boscombe Down, England with Roland P. Beamont and Donald Bowen at the controls. The aircraft had been delivered to Boscombe Down on March 6, and taxi tests began September 2. The T.S.R.2 had a delta-wing span of 37 ft. 1 in., a length of 89 ft. and a normal takeoff weight of 102,200 lb. XR219 was flown to Warton, England on February 22, 1965, for the remainder of its test program.

1964 September 29 The LTV XC-142A V/STOL tactical transport prototype made its first flight in the conventional mode. With a wingspan of 67 ft. 6 in. and a length of 58 ft. 1 in., it had a design loaded weight of 37,474 lb. As a tilt-wing development aircraft powered by four 2,850-SHP General Electric T64-GE-1 turboprop engines, it could lift 8,000 lb. of freight or 32 equipped troops at 288 MPH for 345 mi. STOL radius or 230 mi. VTOL radius.

1964 October 14 The first U.S. Marine Corps Sikorsky (S-65) CH-53E Sea Stallion assault transport helicopter made its first flight just over two years after it had been ordered. The largest to date in the evolving family of Sikorsky helicopters, it was powered by two 2,850-SHP General Electric T64-GE-6 turboshaft engines providing a cruising speed of 173 MPH and a range of 257 mi. It used main and tail rotors from the S-64 Skycrane.

1964 October 15 The Tripartite Evaluation Squadron was established at West Raynham, England with 10 pilots to evaluate the operational capabilities of the Hawker Siddeley Kestrel VTOL fighter. Commanded by Wg. Comdr. D. McL. Scrimgeour, RAF, with Col. Gerhard F. Barkhorn (ex-Luftwaffe fighter ace, with 301 victories to his credit) as his deputy, it had in total four pilots from the RAF, two from the Luftwaffe, two from the U.S. Army and one each from the USAF and the U.S. Navy. In 11 months of evaluation, the squadron performed 938 takeoffs. Six Kestrels were handed over to the United States for a further 3 yr. of evaluation.

1964 November 1 Prime airframe contenders for the U.S. supersonic commercial transport contract revised their submissions. Boeing proposed two variable-geometry aircraft, one for domestic and one for international traffic, that would carry 215 passengers a maximum distance of 4,000 mi. at a gross weight of 500,000 lb. The Lockheed concept incorporated three alternative fixed-wing options with estimated gross weight of 468,000 lb. Operating costs were 1.96 cents/seat-mile for the Boeing and 2.22 cents/seat-mile for the Lockheed design.

1964 November 1 The first USAF losses in South Vietnam were five Martin B-57s destroyed by a Viet Cong mortar attack on the airfield at Bien Hoa where they were stationed. Total USAF resources in the theater were two squadrons of B-57Bs and nine ground attack squadrons with F-100s and F-105s. Air defense was in the hands of F-102s of the 509th Fighter Interceptor Squadron at Da Nang. Given the paucity of the North Vietnamese Air Force (NVAF) aircraft, this was a reasonable disposition of forces.

1964 November 18 The first of two prototype Grumman C-2 Greyhound transport derivatives of the E-2 Hawkeye made its first flight. Similar to the E-2 but with a fuselage 1 ft. shorter than its predecessor, the aircraft had a maximum loaded weight of 54,353 lb. The U.S. Navy ordered 29, canceled 12, then ordered 39 again in 1982. It had a wider fuselage accommodating 26 passengers or up to 15,000 lb. of cargo for land use or 10,000 lb. for carrier-on-deck operations.

1964 November 30 A joint NASA-Pan American statement revealed that a scheduled Pan American flight between San Francisco and Honolulu had successfully picked up error-free teletype messages from the continental United States for approximately 1 hr. via the experimental communications satellite Syncom III in geostationary orbit over the Pacific. The use of satellites for a wide variety of air-related services would be pursued as communications satellites increased in coverage and capability.

1964 December 2 Four USAF Tactical Air Command McDonnell F-4 Phantoms completed an 18-hr. flight of almost 10,000 mi. in an endurance test of long-range deployment capabilities. To keep the aircraft in the air, the F-4s were refueled several times from Strategic Air Command KC-135 tankers. The aircraft landed at MacDill AFB, Fla. Part of the tests were on the pilots themselves, examining physiological and psychological reactions to the long flight.

1964 December 21 The General Dynamics F-111A made its first flight with Dick Johnson and Val Prahl at the controls, the wings fixed at the 26° sweep position. Designed to sweep its wings fully forward (16°) for slow speeds and back (72.5°) for fast speeds, the aircraft had a swept-wing span of 31 ft. 11 in., an extended wingspan of 63 ft. and a length of 73 ft. 6 in. With a gross weight of 92,500 lb. and power from two 11,500/19,000-lb. s.t. Pratt & Whitney TF30-P-1 turbojet engines, it had a design top speed of 1,650 MPH (Mach 2.5) at 40,000 ft. and 865 MPH (Mach 1.2) at sea level.

1964 December 22 The first prototype Lockheed SR-71A (serial no. 64-17950) took to the air following assembly at Palmdale, Calif. It had a length of 103 ft. 10 in., 107 ft. 5 in. with pitot tube, a wingspan of 55 ft. 7 in. and two 32,500-lb. s.t. Pratt & Whitney JT11D-20B turbo-ramjets. The SR-71 was first acknowledged by Pres. Johnson on July 24, when he erroneously gave it the *SR* designation rather than its "official" designation of RS-71. It had a top speed of Mach 3.35 and an operating ceiling of 80,000 ft. Only 32 were built.

1964 December 22 Presidential approval was granted for full-scale development of the USAF CX-HLS program. An acronym for cargo experimental-heavy logistics system, this requirement had grown out of a CX-4 specification refined from that originally written up for the C-141 StarLifter program. The C-141 failed to meet all the needs of that specification due to a fuselage of insufficient cross section. The CX-HLS led to 3-mon. studies during 1964 at Boeing, Douglas and Lockheed, resulting ultimately in the C-5.

1965 January 13 The first transition to horizontal flight from a hover was made by the LTV XC-142A flown by test pilots John Konrad and Stuart Madison. After taking off, the aircraft transitioned to horizontal flight and circled the airfield before converting back to vertical flight and landing. As an operational transport, it was the first U.S. V/STOL aircraft to be designed for service use rather than purely experimental work. The first hover trials had taken place December 29, 1964.

1965 January 26 In Britain the Ministry of Defense announced that the Vickers Valiant was being withdrawn from service due to metal fatigue in the wings. Along with the Victor and the Vulcan, the Valiant had been assigned a low-level role for survivability due to a major expansion of Soviet SAM defenses. During the year, excessive metal fatigue had been discovered in the Valiant. It had never been designed for low-level flight and was unsuited to the role. Vickers Valiant serial no. XD818, the aircraft that dropped Britain's first hydrogen bomb on May 15, 1957, is preserved at the RAF Museum, Hendon, England.

1965 February 2 British prime minister Harold Wilson announced in the House of Commons that the Labour government was canceling the P.1154 supersonic VTOL project and the HS.681 STOL military transport aircraft. The McDonnell F-4 Phantom and the Lockheed C-130 Hercules were to be purchased from the United States instead. The P.1154 had been developed by Hawker as an advanced supersonic derivative of the P.1127/Kestrel VTOL project. The HS.681 had been formally approved by the Ministry of Aviation on March 5, 1963, as a jet replacement for the Hastings and the Beverly with the RAF.

1965 February 2   A Viet Cong mortar attack on Pleiku, South Vietnam put 18 helicopters and seven aircraft out of action and brought authorization to begin Operation Flaming Dart, the first joint Vietnamese Air Force (VNAF)/USAF/U.S. Navy action against the Viet Cong. Army barracks at Chap Le and Vinh in North Vietnam were attacked, and when mortar attacks were again mounted, Vinh was hit February 11. Concern about growing strength among the Viet Cong and the movement of supplies down the Ho Chi Minh Trail instigated armed reconnaissance sorties over eastern Laos from December 14, 1964.

1965 February 13   The U.S. Joint Chiefs of Staff received political authorization to begin Operation Rolling Thunder against targets in North Vietnam associated with Viet Cong support of armed attacks on South Vietnam. The rules of engagement were left loose and open to interpretation, but there were inhibiting restrictions on military action: Ports were not to be attacked for fear of hitting neutral shipping, and the two main cities in the north, Hanoi and Haiphong, were to be avoided. North Vietnamese Air Force fighters were only to be engaged if they initiated a fight.

1965 February 19   Lufthansa became the first foreign airline to place the first firm order for a major new U.S. civil airliner when it ordered 22 of Boeing's recently unveiled Model 737-100s. It was followed by United Air Lines with an order for 40. A small, twin-engined, short-range airliner, it was a lesson in compactness. Although 39 ft. 5 in. shorter in fuselage length than the 727-100, its passenger cabin was only 10 ft. shorter. Whereas Douglas put a two-man crew on its DC-9, Boeing fueled debate by designing a three-man cabin for its 737.

1965 February 25   The first Douglas DC-9 short- and medium-haul twin-jet airliner powered by the 12,250-lb. s.t. Pratt & Whitney JT8D-5 turbofan made its first flight. With a wingspan of 87 ft. 6 in. and a length of 104 ft. 5 in., it could carry 56 to 90 passengers at 544 MPH for 1,013 mi. Delta Airlines began operations with the DC-9 on December 8. With the Boeing 737, the DC-9 and its derivatives would form the backbone of U.S. domestic short- and medium-airline traffic for more than 30 yr.

1965 February 27   Powered by four 15,000-EHP Kuznetsov NK-12 turboprop engines, the Antonov An-22 Antei made its first flight. The world's largest aircraft at the time, it had a wingspan of 211 ft. 3 in. and a length of 189 ft. 11 in. with a gross weight of 551,146 lb. It could carry massive cargo loads, lifting 221,440 lb. to a height of 25,748 ft. in 1967. Less than 200 were built, and the type served with Aeroflot on strategic cargo routes and with the air force as a heavy transport aircraft.

1965 March 2   The first USAF Rolling Thunder air strikes were carried out against an ammunition base at Xom Bang and the naval base at Quang Khe where Viet Cong received munitions and supplies. In all, 110 aircraft carried out the attacks against North Vietnam, including 50 F-105s, 40 F-100s and 20 B-57s. Rolling Thunder went on until a Christmas truce, by which time the North Vietnamese had built up 2,000 radar-guided antiaircraft artillery pieces. The USAF employed RB-66Cs to jam fire-control radars. Rolling Thunder would continue in phases through October 1968.

1965 March 6   The first nonstop transcontinental helicopter flight across the United States was completed successfully. Flown off the deck of the carrier USS *Hornet* at San Diego, Calif., a U.S. Navy Sikorsky SH-3A Sea King flew 2,116 mi. to the deck of the carrier USS *Franklin D. Roosevelt* off Jacksonville, Fla. This flight also set a new straight-line record for helicopters.

1965 March 17   The FAA granted an air worthiness certificate to a Bendix/Boeing automatic landing system designed for use where downward visibility was reduced to 100 ft. and forward visibility to 1,300 ft. Standard VFR (visual flight rules) clearances required 200 ft. downward and 2,640 ft. forward visibility. This was the first such system to be given FAA clearance for use in the United States and was intended for installation on the Boeing 707 and 720.

1965 March 18   The first U.S. Navy Rolling Thunder operations were carried out when attack aircraft from the carriers USS *Coral Sea* and USS *Hancock* hit munitions and supply dumps at Phu Van and Vinh Son. For 15 days, navy reconnaissance missions had been flown from carriers, and by early April, the first Soviet-built SA-2 Guideline batteries had been spotted.

1965 March 31   At a cabinet meeting of the British Labour government during which agreement could not be reached on the future of the T.S.R.2 supersonic strike aircraft, Prime Minister Wilson summed up and decided to cancel the project. The government decided to buy the General Dynamics F-111 instead, citing £750 million costs on development of T.S.R.2 and production of 150 aircraft versus £450 million for purchase of the same number of the F-111. The T.S.R.2 prototype eventually made it to the Imperial War Museum at Duxford.

1965 April 1   The Nihon Aeroplane Manufacturing Co. (NAMC) YS-11 short- to medium-haul airliner entered service with Japan Domestic Airlines on its Tokyo-Tokushima-Kochi service. Powered by two 2,660-EHP Rolls Royce Dart 542-10 turboshaft engines, it had a wingspan of 105 ft., a length of 86 ft. 3 in. and capacity for up to 60 passengers cruising at 245 MPH for up to 380 mi. The aircraft had been designed through a consortium of six companies, made its first flight on August 30, 1962, and gained certification on August 25, 1964.

1965 April 4   Two USAF F-105s attacking the Ham Rung bridge at Thanh Hoa were attacked by North Vietnamese aircraft and shot down, despite F-100s in the area as fighter cover. But these aircraft were old, and so the Forty-fifth Tactical Fighter Squadron, USAF, with its F-4Cs was moved up to Ubon in efforts to counter attacking fighters mauling the F-105s. The first F-4C brought down by a Soviet SAM site fell on July 24.

1965 April 15   The Süd-Aviation SA-330 tactical assault and logistic transport helicopter made its first flight. Developed for the French Army, it could accommodate 12 troops and would subsequently become one of three projects shared with Westlands in the United Kingdom. Powered by two 1,300-SHP Turnoméca Turbo IIIC.4 turboshaft engines driving a 49 ft. 2 in.-diameter rotor, the Puma had a length of 45 ft. 6 in. and a maximum loaded weight of 14,110 lb. It could cruise at 155 MPH across a normal range of 357 mi.

1965 April 18   The Soviet Union announced that on March 16, 1965, A. V. Fedotov had significantly improved upon the 1,000-km (621.4-mi.) closed-circuit air speed record with 2,000 kg (4,410 lb.) cargo. Flying the Mikoyan Ye-266, he had achieved an FAI-ratified speed of 2,320 km/hr. (1,441.2 MPH), beating by 158 MPH the previous record set by a B-58A Hustler.

1965 April 25 The penetration of the U.S. airline market by the British Aircraft Corp.'s BAC-111 Series 200 began when Braniff Airways introduced that aircraft on its Corpus Christi-Minneapolis/St. Paul route. The aircraft replaced Convair 340/440 aircraft. Mohawk Airlines introduced the BAC-111 on its internal services beginning July 15.

1965 April 28 The first of six Handley Page Victor B.1s converted into tanker aircraft made its first flight. Retaining their bomb-carrying capability, the B(K)1.As had two-point trailing drogue hoses and went straight to No. 55 Squadron, RAF, at Marham for operational duty from May. The first Victor K.1 tanker with sealed bomb bay and a three-point hose arrangement flew on November 2, and aircraft of this type went to No. 57 Squadron, also at Marham. These became operational on June 1, 1966.

1965 May 1 Col. Robert Stephens and Lt. Col. Daniel Andre, both USAF, flew a Lockheed YF-12A to set new world records, achieving a height of 24,462 m (80,258 ft.) in level flight and a 15/25-km closed-circuit absolute speed record of 3,351.5128 km/hr. (2,070.102 MPH). Maj. Walter Daniel and Maj. Noel Warner, both USAF, took the 500-km closed-circuit speed record at 2,644.225 km/hr. (1,643.042 MPH), and Maj. Walter Daniel and Capt. James Cooney took the 1,000 km without payload and with 1,000-kg payload and took the 1,000 km with 2,000-kg payload at 2,718.012 km/hr. (1,688.891 MPH).

1965 May 7 The first flight of the Canadair CL-84 Dynavert V/STOL took place when W. Longhurst carried out a hover. Powered by two 1,500-SHP Lycoming T53 turboprop engines, it had a variable tilt wing that could convert the aircraft from vertical to horizontal flight and two contra-rotating tail rotors for fore-and-aft control in the hover or translation. The CL-84 had a wingspan of 34 ft. 8 in. and a length of 53 ft. 7 in. Technically sound, the concept worked well in practice but the idea never found a market.

1965 May 17 The British and French governments signed a memorandum of understanding for the collaborative development of two major aircraft projects: a tactical strike/reconnaissance aircraft to be known as the Jaguar, and an Anglo-French variable geometry (AFVG) fighter. A Dassault-Breguet team would lead the design effort with British Aircraft Corp. In February the French Turboméca Co. had agreed to work with Rolls Royce on development of its RB.172. The AFVG would eventually be canceled and metamorphose into the multi-role combat aircraft (MRCA), from which the Tornado would emerge.

1965 May 18 The Grumman F-111B naval fleet defense fighter made its first flight from Calverton, New York with Ralph Donnell and Ernie von der Heyden at the controls. Based on the original USAF TFX design met by General Dynamics with the F-111A, it had a swept-wing span of 33 ft. 11 in., an extended span of 70 ft. and a length of 66 ft. 9 in. At a loaded weight of almost 78,000 lb., however, it was nearly 23,000 lb. above the limit stipulated by the U.S. Navy.

1965 May 20 The de Havilland Canada DHC-6 Twin Otter made its first flight with R. Fowler, A. Saunders and B. Hubbard in the cockpit. Developed as a follow-up to the single-engine Otter, the DHC-6 was powered by two 578-ESHP Pratt & Whitney PT6A-20 turboshaft engines. It could carry 14 passengers or 18 in high-density seating and had a wingspan of 65 ft., a length of 49 ft. 6 in. and a cruising speed of 156 MPH with a maximum payload range of 300 mi.

1965 June 13 The Britten-Norman BN-2 Islander light utility transport made its first flight, powered by two 260-HP Lycoming 0-540 6-cylinder engines providing a cruising speed of 153 MPH and a range of 950 mi. for nine passengers. With a wingspan of 49 ft. and a length of 35 ft. 3 in., the aircraft was a great success with more than 1,000 being built for customers in 120 countries. Military versions were developed, and 300 were built under license in Romania.

1965 June 17 The first North Vietnamese aircraft shot down by U.S. aircraft during the Vietnam War were destroyed by two F-4B Phantoms of VF-21 operating off the carrier USS *Midway*. Piloted by Comdr. L. C. Page and Lt. J. E. D. Batson, each F-4B shot down one MiG-17 during a strike escort mission against the Viet Cong barracks at Gen Phu in North Vietnam.

1965 June 18 The first B-52 Operation Arc Light bombing mission against targets in North Vietnam was carried out when 27 B-52Fs from the Seventh and 320th Bombardment Wings, USAF, flew from Guam to attack the Binh Duong area with 750-lb. and 1,000-lb. bombs. Two other B-52s were lost in a mid-air collision before reaching the target area. By December 7, the 320th and 454th Bombardment Wings rotated tours through the Pacific area, carrying out more than 100 missions against the Viet Cong.

1965 July 10 The first USAF air combat victories in Vietnam were scored by two F-4C Phantoms of the Forty-fifth Tactical Fighter Squadron, Twelfth Tactical Fighter Wing, based at Ubon. During a routine escort mission covering for F-105s hitting the Bac Giang bridge outside Hanoi, two F-4Cs flown by Capts. Kenneth E. Holcombe, Thomas C. Roberts, Arthur C. Clark and Ronald C. Anderson tangled with MiG-17s of the North Vietnamese Air Force. Two MiGs were shot down by AIM-9 Sidewinder missiles without loss to the USAF aircraft.

1965 July 16 The North American YOV-10A prototype counterinsurgency aircraft for U.S. Marine Corps battlefield support took to the air for the first time. Successful against several competing bids judged in August 1964, the OV-10 Bronco had a tricycle landing gear and two 715-SHP Garrett-AiResearch T76-G-10/12 turboprop engines with extended nacelles faired into twin tail booms supporting a high-mounted horizontal tail. It had a wingspan of 40 ft., a length of 39 ft. 10 in. and a cruising speed of 223 MPH with a 450-mi. range. The USAF and the U.S. Navy also bought the OV-10.

1965 July 17 The #2 North American XB-70A joined the #1 aircraft in flight tests by taking to the air for the first time between Palmdale, Calif. and Edwards AFB, piloted by NASA chief test pilot Al White and USAF XB-70A test director Col. Joseph Cotton. It reached a speed of Mach 1.4 and an altitude of 40,000 ft. The outer wing sections of the aircraft were designed to pivot downward to improve the compression-lift effect in high cruise speed. They were ''folded'' to the maximum 65° droop position for this flight.

1965 July 24 The first U.S. combat aircraft brought down by guided-missile fire was lost when a Soviet-installed SA-2 Guideline destroyed it south of Hanoi. The aircraft, a USAF F-4C Phantom of the Forty-seventh Tactical Fighter Squadron, Fifteenth Tactical Fighter Wing, was on a sortie during strikes on the Lang Chi munitions factory in North Vietnam when it was hit. The North Vietnamese would rely increasingly on Soviet air defense equipment, following the philosophy in Moscow adopted for Soviet air defenses.

1965 July 24 Flying a USAF RF-101C on a reconnaissance mission over North Vietnam, Majs. Daniel J. Doughty and Marvin R. Reed inadvertently developed a survival tactic that would become enshrined in tactical reconnaissance operations. Approaching their objective, a bridge, at tree-top height to avoid SAM or antiaircraft artillery radar detection, they ''popped up'' to 15,000 ft. for a 2–3 min. photographic run on afterburner and dove down to ground level again before they were locked on by enemy detectors.

1965 August 31 The first Aero Space Lines B-377-SG Super Guppy Stratocruiser conversion made its first flight. The aircraft would be used by manufacturers of hardware for the space program to lift heavy or large loads around the United States. An even bigger conversion job than that conducted for the first Guppy, the Super Guppy had a wingspan of 156 ft. 3 in., a length of 143 ft. 10 in. and a cargo compartment 108 ft. 10 in. in length, 25 ft. wide and 25 ft. 6 in. high. Power was provided by four 4,680-EHP Allison 501-D22C engines.

1965 September 7 Developed from the Model 204 (the UH-1A Iroquois), the Bell Model 209 made its first flight as an interim fire-support helicopter pending availability of the Lockheed AH-56A Cheyenne. Powered by a 1,100-SHP Lycoming T53-L-13 turboshaft engine driving a 44-ft. rotor, it had a length of 44 ft. 3 in. and a loaded weight of 9,500 lb. Armed with a nose-mounted General Electric XM-134 Minigun, it was purchased by the U.S. Army as the AH-1 Cobra, and 1,118 were eventually built, many seeing combat service in Vietnam.

1965 September 7 In a conflict over Kashmir, Sqdn. Ldr. Mohammed Mahmood Alam of the Pakistan Air Force achieved, as far as is known, an all-time record by shooting down four aircraft in the space of 30 sec. The encounter came after Alam and Flg. Off. Masood were scrambled to counter incoming Indian Air Force Hawker Hunters. Flying an F-86F, Alam shot down his first Hunter with the second of two Sidewinder missiles. Minutes later, he attacked four Hunters in tight formation and shot them down with cannon-fire as each maintained its place in an evasive turn.

1965 September 15 Elements of the U.S. First Cavalry Division (Airmobile) began operations at Qui Nhon in South Vietnam. Transported from the United States by the USS *Boxer,* they brought to Southeast Asia a new form of air warfare. Equipped with converted and armed UH-1B Iroquois and, later, specially developed helicopter gunships, it would build to a force of 400 rotary-winged aircraft to forge a new air weapon for close air support operations with the U.S. Army and the U.S. Marine Corps.

1965 September 27 The LTV A-7A Corsair II made its first flight powered by an 11,350-lb. s.t. Pratt & Whitney TF30-P-6 turbofan engine and with a wingspan of 38 ft. 9 in. and a length of 46 ft. 1 in. By this time, the order book held contracts for 182 for the U.S. Navy, and two training units received their first aircraft within a year. With a top speed of 685 MPH at 10,000 ft. and a warload of more than 15,000 lb. (35% of maximum weight), it was a rugged attack bomber, and 1,491 were ultimately built.

1965 September 30 U.S. defense secretary Robert McNamara authorized the USAF to proceed with full development of the C-5 Galaxy. In October Lockheed was notified that its design had

The Vought A-7 first flown in September 1965 would remain in service with the U.S. Navy and Marine Corps for more than 30 years.

won out over submissions from Douglas and Boeing. General Electric had been notified in August that they had been selected to produce the 40,000-lb. s.t.-class engine for the C-5, a strategic military transport aircraft specified by the USAF to be capable of lifting around 200,000 lb. over short distances or 100,000 lb. over 8,000 mi.

1965 September 30 An FAA rule requiring one pilot of commercial jet airliners flying above 35,000 ft. to wear an oxygen mask at all times was modified and from this date raised the altitude to 41,000 ft. At this altitude, the reaction time from anoxia would be much more critical than would a sudden decompression at the lower altitude. The increasing safety levels achieved by production jet airliners rendered this only an extreme precautionary rule, however, and there was lobbying to relax the conservative approach.

1965 September 30 Continental Air Services took delivery of the L-100 civilian derivative of the C-130 military transport aircraft. A demonstrator had first flown on April 20, 1964, remaining aloft for 25 hr. 1 min. Powered by four 4,050-ESHP Allison 501-D22 engines, the L-100 received its certificate of airworthiness on February 16, 1965, and 21 production aircraft were delivered. Continental used its L-100s in Laos, and eight other airlines bought the type before a cargo version, the L-100-20, appeared with a stretched fuselage in 1968.

1965 October 6 USAF Tactical Air Command issued Qualitative Operational Requirement 65-14-F defining the need for an air superiority fighter to replace the F-4. Prior to this, fighters had been viewed as interceptors providing a missile-launching platform for penetration strikes against enemy aircraft. Challenges to that view stipulated the increasing need for a highly maneuverable, dogfighting combat plane, and evidence from Vietnam supported that. QOR-65-14-F was an initial step toward development of the F-X, eventually becoming the F-15 Eagle.

1965 October 25 In a prophetic prediction regarding the preferences among fare-paying passengers, Sir William Hildred, director general of IATA, addressed the assocation's 21st annual meeting and claimed that commercial supersonic aircraft like the Concorde and its U.S. counterpart would have to work hard to regain customers in the mid-1970s that had been wooed on to stretched subsonic airliners by lower fares. He was referring to stretched versions of the DC-8 that would each carry more than 200 passengers by the end of the 1960s.

1965 November 15 Technical assessment of the Boeing and Lockheed supersonic transport designs began under a special 82-member U.S. government technical team including representatives from the FAA, USAF, U.S. Navy and NASA. The 5-wk. analysis would integrate separate studies from the different groups represented and apply test results from wind tunnel research on the various proposed configurations. It was hoped that construction of the first prototype could begin by the end of 1966.

1965 November 15 A modified Boeing 707-300 series intercontinental airliner carrying 40 scientists departed Honolulu on a 26,263-mi. round-the-world flight over both North and South Poles. Sponsored by Rockwell Standard Corp. with participation from the U.S. Weather Bureau and NASA, the flight took just over 2 days. During this time, scientists studied fatigue among the interchanging flight crew and behavioral reactions from the "passengers" in the relatively confined pressurized area and conducted scientific studies of the atmosphere.

1965 November 26 The first RAF Vickers VC-10 C.Mk.1 (serial no. XR806) made its first flight from Weybridge, England. Seven months later the first production aircraft reached No. 10 Squadron at Fairford. With a typical cruising speed of 518 MPH, the VC-10 cut 4.5 hr. off the 25 hr. United Kingdom-Singapore Comet 4C service and 12 hr. off the 31.5 hr. taken by Britannia. Powered by four 22,500-lb. s.t. Rolls Royce Conway 301 turbofans, it had capacity for 150 passengers or 76 litters and six medical attendants.

1965 November 26 The first four USAF F-100F Wild Weasel electronic countermeasures aircraft deployed in Vietnam began operations with the 388th Tactical Fighter Wing at Korat. The F-100Fs were equipped with radar homing and warning radar, signal analyzer and missile launch warning receivers. The Wild Weasel terminology had been created when the original code word, Ferret, was dropped because of its association with an operation from World War II. One F-100F was shot down on December 20, but two days later the unit destroyed its first SA-2 battery.

1965 December 8 U.S. defense secretary Robert S. McNamara announced plans to phase out all Convair B-58A Hustler supersonic bombers and about 350 of the 600 B-52s (including all the C, D, E and F models) by June 30, 1971. Two days later McNamara announced plans to buy 210 supersonic strategic bombers developed from the General Dynamics F-111. Designated FB-111A, it would combine features of the USAAF F-111A and the U.S. Navy F-111B to provide a Mach 2 aircraft capable of carrying over 35,000 lb. of bombs as an interim measure, pending development of an advanced manned strategic bomber.

1965 December 8 The USAF issued a request for proposals on the F-X tactical air superiority fighter to 13 manufacturers, and study contracts were awarded to Boeing, Lockheed and North American on March 18, 1966. Aimed at replacing the F-4 and focusing design emphasis on maneuverability and dog-fighting capabilities, the F-X was required to have a maximum speed of Mach 2.5, infrared and radar-guided missiles and similar radar to the Phantom. Grumman also participated on a nonfunded basis.

1965 December 15 The first daylight USAF gunship mission over Vietnam was conducted by the Fourth Special Operations Squadron at Bien Hoa using C-47s converted to carry three Gen-

eral Electric SUU-11A/A 7.62-mm Miniguns. Thus equipped, and designated FC-47, they were employed on ground strafing missions until the designation was changed to AC-47. The first night sortie took place on December 23. The call sign for the AC-47 was "Spooky."

1965 December 21 Following demonstration flights from the roof of the Pan Am Building in Manhattan, New York City, N.Y., Pam Am began a VIP courtesy service to John F. Kennedy International Airport for Pan Am passengers. This air-lift allowed travelers to check in at the Pan Am building just 45 min. before their flight and then be whisked above the congested road traffic to a landing pad at JFK airport.

1965 December 28 The spot-promotion program at USAF Strategic Air Command set up by Gen. Curtis LeMay in December 1949 was terminated by USAF chief of staff, Gen. John P. McConnell. From this date, all crewmen who had received promotions through the program were notified that they would revert to their original grades on June 30, 1966 and only move up again via the usual channels.

1965 December The USAF conducted "Big Belly" modifications to the B-52D, adapting it to the role of iron-bomb carrier rather than strategic nuclear delivery vehicle as designed. B-52Fs used this year in Vietnam carried up to 51 (750-lb.) bombs, 27 internally and 24 on external inboard wing pylons. The modification would allow B-52Ds to carry 84 (500-lb.) bombs internally and up to 24 (750-lb.) bombs externally for a maximum load of up to 62,000 lb.

1966 January 7 The Lockheed SR-71A entered operational service with the USAF when (serial no.) 64-17956 joined the 4200th Strategic Reconnaissance Wing at Beale AFB, Calif. In mid-year, the wing was reorganized as the Ninth Strategic Reconnaissance Wing and was officially changed to that designation on June 22, 1966. The 349th Air Rescue Squadron, 100th Strategic Reconnaissance Wing, was formed from the 349th (Strategic Reconnaissance Squadron) to operate the dedicated Boeing KC-135Q (SR-71) tanker fleet. These aircraft, of which 56 were built, incorporated an additional TACAN rendezvous antenna and special JP-7 fuel systems.

1966 January 10 Adapted from the OH-4A contender for the U.S. Army light observation helicopter competition, the Bell Model 206A JetRanger five-seat utility helicopter made its first flight powered by a 317-SHP Allison 250-C18 turboshaft engine. With a lightened and refined fuselage 28 ft. 2 in. in length, the Model 206A had a cruising speed of 134 MPH and a range of 359 mi. Just over 2 yr. later this would form the basis for a winning entry in the reopened U.S. Army competition.

1966 January 17 A USAF Strategic Air Command B-52 from Seymour Johnson AFB, N.C., returning from a 10-hr. patrol of the southwestern corner of the USSR with four 1.5-megaton nuclear weapons on board, collided with a KC-135A it was taking fuel from causing both aircraft to crash near Palomares, Spain. Four of the seven B-52 crewmembers ejected safely and survived, but three other crewmembers and all four aboard the KC-135 were killed. One nuclear bomb was found in a river bed, one in the hills and one near some houses. Two bombs had detonated their TNT triggers resulting in 1,400 tons of contaminated soil, which was removed into 4,875 drums.

1966 February 8 The former managing director of British United Airways, Freddie Laker, announced the formation of Laker Airways Ltd., which would offer cut-price air tickets and inclusive tours as well as charter flights. Ten years later, Laker Airways employed 500 people and operated three DC-10s, two Boeing 707-138s and five BAC 111-300/400s. Laker's company, however, failed to survive another decade, although the impact he had on upsetting fixed fares had a dramatic impact on trans-Atlantic travel among the national carriers.

1966 February 11 The last two USAF B-47 bombers were withdrawn from service with Strategic Air Command, leaving only the B-52 and the B-58 in service. The last two B-47s retired were E models (serial nos. 53-2286 and 53-6235) from the 100th Bombardment Wing at Pease AFB, N.H. and the Ninth Strategic Aerospace Wing, Mountain Home AFB, Idaho, respectively. They were transferred to the storage facility at Davis-Monthan AFB, Ariz. The B-58 would be retired by January 1970.

1966 March 2 The USAF received permission to proceed with a rocket-powered research vehicle designed to evaluate lifting-body designs for controlled reentry from space. Designated SV-5P, it was an outgrowth of the SV-5D program involving lifting-body shapes fired into space by an Atlas launch vehicle, also designated X-23A. On July 11, 1967, the SV-5P became the X-24A. It was to be built by Martin Marietta, who had been working on lifting-bodies since 1962.

1966 March 7 French president Charles De Gaulle announced that France would withdraw its personnel from the NATO Military headquarters, end assignment of French forces to international command and request the withdrawal from French territory of all non-French military personnel. As a consequence, the NATO headquarters moved to Brussels and units of the Armée de l'Air in the Fourth Allied Tactical Air Force were returned to France. The United States insisted on the return of former USAF aircraft it had loaned to France.

1966 March 11 The U.S. Army selected the Bell Model 209 as an interim helicopter pending availability of the Lockheed CL-480 (AH-56 Cheyenne) as its advanced aerial fire support system (AAFSS) helicopter. Known as the AH-1 Cobra, the 209 was to become more popularly known as the Hueycobra, signifying the relationship with the originally designated UH-1 Huey, redesignated HU-1.

1966 March 14 The first Douglas DC-8 Series 61 made its first flight. Trading fuel weight for extra payload, the aircraft had a fuselage stretch of 36 ft. 8 in., increasing length to 187 ft. 4 in. and raising high-density seating capacity to 259 but reducing range from 5,750 mi. to just under 4,000 mi. Most seating configurations would support around 180 passengers. In all, 78 aircraft of this type were supplied to Air Canada, Delta, Eastern, JAL, National and United. Maximum payload capability was 71,900 lb.

1966 March 15 One 1.5-megaton nuclear bomb that had fallen from the wreckage of a B-52 and a KC-135 that collided over Palomares, Spain, January 17 was finally located in 2,500 ft. of water 5 mi. off the coast. To find the 5,000-lb., 10-ft.-long bomb, 3,000 sailors, 120 frogmen and four submersibles searched for 2 mon. before locating it. After several unsuccessful attempts to retrieve it, during which it slipped into deeper water, the bomb was finally raised to the surface from 2,850 ft. using a cable-controlled underwater research vehicle.

1966 March 17 The Bell Aerospace Textron X-22A dual-tandem, ducted-propeller VTOL research aircraft made its first flight at Niagara Falls, N.Y. Developed to a NASA/U.S. Navy require-

ment, the aircraft was powered by four 1,250-SHP General Electric YT58-GE-8D turboshaft engines located in pairs at the root of each rear wing driving four ducted propellers attached one each side fore-and-aft pivoted to rotate for vertical or horizontal flight. The X-22A had a width across the rear ducts of 39 ft. 3 in. and a width across the forward ducts of 23 ft., with a length of 39 ft. 6 in.

1966 March 23 The U.S. Army awarded Lockheed a development contract for its CL-840, winner of the competition for the AAFSS, which had attracted 12 company bids. The CL-840 emerged as the AH-56A Cheyenne, but that failed to match needs and it was eventually canceled. In November 1972, a new advanced attack helicopter specification would produce the Hughes AH-64 Apache.

1966 March 25 In the longest flight by an aircraft of this type conducted to date, an F-111A flew from Edwards AFB, Calif. to the General Dynamics plant at Fort Worth, Tex., using a newly developed terrain-following radar designed to keep the aircraft at a constant height above undulating terrain. For this flight, the F-111A maintained an average height of 1,000 ft. for 1,202 mi. across land that varied between 500 ft. and 10,000 ft. above sea level. Low-level penetration was one of the primary requirements placed upon the aircraft.

1966 April 1 The modified "Big Belly" B-52Ds of the Twenty-eight and 454th Bombardment Wings assumed responsibility for Arc Light operations over North Vietnam. At the beginning of the year, Gen. William Westmoreland had requested an increase in sorties from 350 per month to 450 per month, and later in the year, Defense Secretary Robert McNamara authorized first 600 per month and then 800 per month. This was not possible with the aircraft and support infrastructure available, and by November, sortie rates were still only 600 per month.

1966 April 7 A Hughes OH-6A completed the longest nonstop helicopter flight on record, beating the 2,105-mi. nonstop record set by a U.S. Navy Sikorsky SH-3A on March 5, 1965. The OH-6A completed an overland flight from Culver City, Calif. to Ormond Beach, Fla. to raise the record by 125 mi. The total distance of 2,230 mi. was flown in 5 hr. 13 min.

1966 April 13 Boeing announced that Pan American had ordered 25 Model 747 large-capacity wide-body intercontinental airliners, launching what is still the world's biggest production airliner. To minimize airport handling problems, the 37.5° swept wing would be kept as short as possible with triple-slotted trailing edge flaps and Kreuger lift devices so that the wingspan was only 53 ft. greater than the Boeing 707 while the fuselage was 78 ft. longer (50%) than the 707 and had a capacity for more than twice as many passengers. Dubbed the "Jumbo Jet," the Boeing 747 would revolutionize mass air transport.

1966 April 24 The U.S. Seventh Fleet carried out its first air strikes on bases in North Vietnam when A-6 Intruders from the USS *Kittyhawk* hit Kep AB near Hanoi. The A-6 had been introduced to Vietnam on July 1, 1965, when the Sunday Punchers of VA-75 aboard the USS *Independence* flew their first missions from the Gulf of Tonkin. VA-75 successfully pioneered the use of electronics on the A-6A to guide Douglas A-4E Skyhawks on enemy defense acquisition radars.

1966 May 1 U.S. parachutist Nick Piantanida suffered irreversible brain damage during a rapid descent from 57,000 ft. Intending to make a free-fall jump from 124,000 ft. using a pressure suit supplied with oxygen, he called for help when the suit failed during the balloon's ascent, and a signal from the ground electrically severed the gondola of his balloon. The parachute failed to slow him appreciably until he had descended to 20,000 ft. Rapid descent and sudden decompression plus oxygen starvation was responsible for his brain damage.

1966 May 3 The first air-snatch of a man off the ground by an aircraft in flight took place when a Lockheed HC-130H fitted with the Fulton Recovery System picked up Capt. Gerald Ly-Vere, USAF. Having donned a harness attached to a balloon previously dropped by parachute, LyVere was snatched off the ground as the aircraft flew across at 400 ft. and snagged a line attached to the balloon at one end and the man's harness at the other. In a later demonstration with the HC-130H of double recovery, Col. Allison Brooks, USAF, and A-3C (Airman 3rd class) Ronald Doll were retrieved in a double harness.

1966 May 18 At 2:55 P.M., Sheila Scott departed London Airport for Rome on the first leg of a round-the-world flight that would secure for her a record solo time and make her the first British pilot to circumnavigate the globe by air. Scott arrived back at London on June 20, 33 days 3 min. after taking off. She had flown a total distance of just over 31,000 mi. in a flying time of 189 hr. averaging 166 MPH in her Piper Commanche 260B *Myth Too*.

1966 May 27 The McDonnell F-4J Phantom II, the second of only two mass-produced aircraft of this type for the U.S. Navy and the U.S. Marine Corps made its first flight. Powered by two 17,900-lb. s.t. General Electric J79-GE-10 engines, it had drooping ailerons and a slotted tailplane to reduce the takeoff distance, as well as improved radar and ground attack equipment. To the 649 F-4Bs were added 522 F-4Js.

1966 May The Société Aeropéene de Production de l'Avion École de Combat et Appui Tactique (SEPECAT) was formed as an Anglo-French company for the development and production of the Jaguar tactical strike and reconnaissance aircraft. Set up as a complementary organization for integrating work between BAC in the United Kingdom and Breguet in France, SEPECAT was to be responsible for engineering development of the multi-variant aircraft.

1966 June 8 The #2 North American XB-70A was destroyed along with an F-104N piloted by NASA test pilot Joseph A. Walker at the end of a formation photographic assignment also involving an F-5, a T-38 and an F-4B. Flying formation on the starboard wing tip of the XB-70A, the F-104N was caught in its vortex and, flipped on its back, was sucked across the trailing edge from starboard to port, ripping off the bomber's vertical tail fins. Joseph Walker was killed as was XB-70A copilot Maj. Carl Cross, USAF, but the pilot, Al White, survived an ejection from 25,000 ft. as the bomber went down over the Mojave Desert in California.

1966 June 15 Boeing unveiled its refined design for the U.S. supersonic transport aircraft. The Model 2707 replaced the 733, which had featured four podded engines under the center-section with a variable-sweep (20°/74°) wing. The Model 2707 retained the variable sweep wing but moved the engines to the underside of a greatly enlarged horizontal tail, which, when the wing was at full sweep, completed a closed delta shape for these lifting surfaces. With a larger fuselage, the cabin could now accommodate 300 people.

1966 June 27 Lockheed revealed details of its refined Model L-2000 for the U.S. SST competition. It was submitted, along with the Boeing design, to the FAA on September 6. It had a conventional fuselage 273 ft. 2 in. in length for up to 258 passengers and a fixed delta wing with a span of 116 ft. carrying four separately mounted General Electric GE4/J5M or Pratt & Whitney JTF17A-21L engines. With a maximum takeoff weight of 590,000 lb., the L-2000 had a cruising speed of Mach 2.7 at 70,000 ft. and a range of 4,000 mi.

1966 June 27 Ordered by the Royal Navy in 1964, the McDonnell F-4K Phantom made its first flight powered by two 12,250/20,515-lb. s.t. Rolls Royce RB.168-25R Spey 201 turbofans with a 20% larger air intake area. The aircraft also featured a lengthened nose leg and reduced tail anhedral and British ejection seats. The navy ordered 50 F-4Ks, the first of which entered service in April 1968 as the navy's first supersonic fighter. In 1965 the RAF had selected the Phantom as a ground attack fighter, and the first of 118 F-4Ms flew on February 17, 1967, followed by service introduction in July 1968.

1966 June 29 For the first time, strategic targets in Hanoi and Haiphong, North Vietnam, were hit by USAF and U.S. Navy aircraft. F-105Ds from the USAF 355th and 388th Tactical Fighter Wing led by Maj. James Kasler and Lt. Col. James R. Hopkins, destroyed oil tanks and left large fires burning in Hanoi. Simultaneously, 28 Douglas A-4 Skyhawks struck targets in the port of Haiphong.

1966 July 1 A blind bombing system using triangulation to improve accuracy, code-named Project Combat Proof, was introduced, enabling the USAF Third Air Division to put six B-52s on quick reaction alert for rapid response to field commander's requests for strikes on communist targets. It had previously required 24-hr. lead time to prepare target details for the bomber crews. Arc Light operations were restricted to targets no closer than 3,300-yd. from friendly troops. Project Combat Proof was later named Project Combat Skyspot.

1966 July 12 NASA test pilot Milton O. Thompson flight tested the Northrop M2-F2 lifting-body for the first time when he was released from a B-52 carrier-plane at 45,000 ft. over Rogers Dry Lake, Calif. The M2-F2 was a developed, powered version of the M2-F1 and had a length of 22 ft. 2 in., a body width of 9 ft. 7 in. and a weight of 6,000 lb. carrying a 8,000-lb. thrust Thiokol XLR-11 rocket motor. The motor was not installed until the 15th flight on May 2, 1967, but four hydrogen peroxide rockets provided 400 lb. of flare thrust.

1966 August 1 The first stretched version of the Douglas DC-9, Series 30, made its first flight, powered by two 14,500-lb. s.t. Pratt & Whitney JT8D-9 engines with the 15,000-lb. s.t. JT8D-11 as an alternative. The fuselage was stretched by 15 ft., raising capacity to 115 passengers and gross weight went up to 114,000 lb. with freight versions also made available. The inherent stretchability of this adaptable airliner helped stimulate several new and increasingly more efficient versions.

1966 August 8 A unique method of stopping aircraft crashes on takeoff or landing was demonstrated at the Royal Aircraft Establishment (RAE), Farnborough, England when a demonstration aircraft traveling at 80 MPH was stopped in 3 sec. as it ran onto a 400-ft. long gravel bed 7 ft. deep. The RAE suggested that airliners could be stopped in 10 sec. by this technique.

1966 September 1   The 25th Farnborough Air Show put on by the Society of British Aircraft companies introduced foreign aircraft for the first time, the only qualifying criteria being that they contain a minimum amount of British equipment. Reflections of a declining independent British aircraft industry, the annual event had become biennial at the close of the 23rd SBAC show in September 1962. From then on, it alternated with the Paris Air Show.

1966 September 9   In Britain, the House of Commons Public Accounts Committee announced that the development cost of the Concorde supersonic airliner had risen dramatically. It was now expected to cost $1.4 billion, versus the previous projection of $476 million, before completion in 1973. It was said that the increased costs were the result of a recent increase in the size of the aircraft and a shift in the specification.

1966 September 24   An experimental version of the MiG-21 interceptor, designated Ye-76, raised the women's absolute world speed record when the Soviet pilot Marina Solovyeva flew a 500-km circuit at an FAI-ratified average of 2,062 km/hr. (1,281.3 MPH).

1966 September 26   A new record for business jets was claimed by Pan American World Airways when it flew its Dassault Fan Jet Falcon, powered by two 4,200-lb. s.t. General Electric CF700-2C turbofan engines, a distance of 2,388 mi. in 4 hr. 38 min. 28 sec. The flight took place between St. John's, Newfoundland and Lisbon, Portugal and exceeded the previous record set by a North American Sabreliner flown by George Eremea of Petit Jean Air Service in 4 hr. 45 min. 59.4 sec. on October 26, 1953. Pan American had ordered 160 Falcons for its Business Jets Division.

1966 October 3   The sheer scale of the rapidly escalating war in Vietnam was brought home to the American public by a claim in the *World Journal Tribune* that during 1966 the USAF would drop 638,000 tons of bombs on communist targets, more than had been dropped during the Pacific war of 1941–45 or during the Korean War. In reality, this was a reflection of the much greater warload of each B-52, which now had a capacity equal to three B-29s.

1966 October 9   The U.S. Navy claimed its first MiG-21 "kill" in the Vietnam War. An F-8E from VF-162 off the carrier USS *Oriskany* shot down an aircraft of this type, which had been seen with increasing frequency over the previous several months. The *Oriskany* was the second ship from the U.S. Navy's Atlantic Fleet to be transferred to the Vietnam War theater.

1966 October 19   The first of 66 Lockheed C-130Ks destined for the RAF made its first flight, powered by four 4,910-ESHP Allison T56-A-15 turboprop engines. Marshall of Cambridge (Engineering) Ltd. fitted British electronics and avionics equipment, and the type entered RAF service with No. 242 Operational Conversion Unit at Thorney Island in April 1967. It could carry either 92 troops or 74 litters and two medical orderlies.

1966 October 21   The first of five prototype Yakovlev Yak-40 short-haul, tri-jet airliners made its first flight, powered by three 3,307-lb. s.t. AI-25 engines. With capacity for carrying 27 to 32 passengers at 342 MPH for 1,118 mi., it had a wingspan of 82 ft. and a length of 66 ft. 9 in. About 800 aircraft had been completed when production ended in 1976, and the Yak-40 was first put to use with Aeroflot on September 30, 1968. In 1972 Yakovlev began development of a successor, the Yak-42 with capacity increased to 100 seats.

1966 November 1   Air Canada, renamed from Trans-Canada Air Lines on January 1, 1965, became the first airline from the North American continent to operate a routine service from Montreal to Moscow. The service had one stop at Copenhagen, Denmark. As a reciprocal arrangement, Aeroflot began a Moscow-Montreal service using Tupolev Tu-114s on November 4.

1966 December 6   The Luftwaffe grounded its entire fleet of more than 700 F-104G Starfighters following the most recent loss of an aircraft of this type on October 28. Since 1962 the Luftwaffe had lost 65 F-104Gs in accidents from various causes. Several technical reasons were identified as having been responsible for the crashes, resulting in the death of 37 pilots, and following selected technical modifications, the aircraft was returned to flight status on January 4, 1967.

1966 December 22   Pilot Bruce Peterson flew the Northrop HL-10 lifting-body for the first time from Rogers Dry Lake, Calif. when he was dropped from a B-52 carrier-plane at 45,000 ft. and 457 MPH. With a length of 22 ft. 2 in. and a width of 15 ft. 1 in., the HL-10 was a thick delta-body with a flat bottom, round top, three vertical tail fins and an 8,000-lb. thrust Thiokol XLR-11 rocket motor. It had two throttleable hydrogen peroxide rockets providing 500 lb. of thrust for flare-assist. The first flight was nearly a disaster due to minimal lateral control.

1966 December 23   The Dassault Mirage F.1 single-seat fighter made its first flight at the start of a long and successful production line evolved from the Mirage III/5 series. Powered by a single 11,067/15,784-lb. s.t. SNECMA Atar 9K-50 turbojet engine, it had a maximum speed of Mach 2.2 (1,450 MPH) at 40,000 ft. and Mach 1.1 (835 MPH) at sea level. With a wingspan of 27 ft. 9 in. and a length of 45 ft. 11 in., it had a gross weight of 24,470 lb. and could carry 3,500 lb. of ordnance on external racks. Nearly 1,000 had been produced by 1992.

1966 December 29   Selected as a military variant of the Cessna 337 Skymaster, the USAF ordered an initial batch of 145 Cessna O-2As to operate in the forward air controller role in Vietnam. Powered by two 210-HP Continental IO-360-C/D piston engines, the high-wing monoplane had twin booms supporting a horizontal tail with a wingspan of 38 ft. 2 in. and a length of 29 ft. 9 in. Capable of cruising at 144 MPH over a range of 1,060 mi. it had seating for a crew of two and two optional passengers. Deliveries began in March 1967.

1966 December 31   In the United States, the FAA announced Boeing the winner of the competition to build the supersonic transport aircraft. The Model 2707-200 would have a length of 318 ft., a variable geometry wingspan (swept) of 105 ft. 9 in. or (extended) 174 ft. 2 in., and a gross weight of 675,000 lb. carrying up to 350 passengers. Cruising speed was Mach 2.7 at 64,000 ft. and range over 4,000 mi. The General Electric GE4/J5 engines had won the propulsion contract, and a first flight was scheduled for early 1973. Certification was expected in 1978.

1966   Flight tests with the MiG-23 began in the Soviet Union. This air combat fighter was to become the mainstay of Soviet and Warsaw Pact countries as well as many client states. Powered by a 27,550-lb. s.t. Tumansky R-29, it had a wingspan of 46 ft. 9 in./26 ft. 9 in. and a length of 55 ft. 1 in. Performance varied with the many variants produced, but maximum speed was generally around 1,550 MPH with a maximum combat radius of 808 mi. The ground attack version was sufficiently different to warrant the designation MiG-27, which appeared in service around the mid-1970s about two years after the MiG-23 in 1973.

1967 January 2   Operation Bolo, a plan to draw up MiG fighters of the North Vietnamese Air Force, was put into action when Col. Robin Olds of the Eighth Tactical Fighter Wing, USAF, based at Ubon led F-4Cs into action. The Eighth Tactical Fighter Wing Phantoms simulated F-105s in flight profiles, refueling activities and radio channels, thus attracting the communist MiGs to what they thought were easy targets. In all, 366 aircraft including F-4Cs from the 366th Tactical Fighter Wing, six flights of F-105Fs and EB-66 jammers escorted by F-104Cs from the 479th Tactical Fighter Wing were involved. Seven MiGs were shot down.

1967 January 8   Four U.S. Marine Corps CH-53A Sea Stallions from Squadron HMM-463 moved to Marble Mountain near the South Vietnamese base at Da Nang on a shakedown trial lifting weapons and extending the work previously conducted by the CH-46. Under the direction of Marine Air Group 16, 22 more CH-53As were operating from HMM-463 by the end of May. In one spectacular demonstration of its capabilities on January 25, a CH-53A retrieved a damaged UH-34D from the landing platform of a U.S. Navy ship.

1967 February 8   The Swedish SAAB-37 Viggen all-weather, multi-role combat aircraft made its first flight. Powered by a 16,000/26,450-lb. s.t. Svenska Flygmotor RM 8, it incorporated a large rear-mounted delta wing with a span of 34 ft. 9 in. with a large forward canard set high on a fuselage 53 ft. 6 in. in length. Designed as the airborne component of an integrated air-ground defense network, it had a maximum speed of Mach 1 at 165 ft. and 1,360 MPH at 39,370 ft. with a service ceiling of 60,000 ft.

1967 February 10   The Dornier Do 31E V/STOL experimental aircraft made its first flight as a development project funded by the German Defense Ministry. Powered by two 15,500-lb. s.t. Rolls Royce Bristol Pegasus 5 vectored-thrust engines in pods under the wings and four 4,400-lb. Rolls Royce RB.162-4D turbojets in a removable lift-jet pod on each wingtip, the DO 31E had a wingspan of 59 ft. 3 in. and a length of 68 ft. 6 in. with a gross weight of 60,500 lb. First transition from vertical to horizontal flight took place on December 16.

1967 February 22   In Operation Junction City, one of the very few paratroop drops of the Vietnam War took place. Carried by 14 Lockheed C-130 Hercules transport aircraft, 845 paratroopers of the 173d Airborne Brigade were dropped in the only combat air assault carried out during the Vietnam War. In September 1966, in Operation Thayer, five battalions of the 101st Airborne Division had been dropped by C-123s in the Cay Giep mountains. Drops like these were rare and were not continued after this date.

1967 February 24   United Air Lines introduced the stretched DC-8-61 series to operational service, inaugurating the era of the large-capacity airliner. Capable of carrying 180 to 220 people in mixed class, or 259 in a high-density configuration, seat-mile costs were greatly reduced as operating costs for the stretched model increased only marginally compared to the major increase in the number of passengers per flight. The cost benefits helped sell the idea of wide-body, large-capacity airliners to international operators.

1967 February 26   The first U.S. Navy mine-laying operation of the Vietnam War was carried out by seven Grumman A-6A Intruders from Navy Squadron VA-35 operating off the carrier USS *Enterprise*. Led by Comdr. A. H. Barris, the aircraft put

their mines down at the mouth of the Song Ca and Song Giang rivers to deny access to small boats carrying supplies and munitions to the communist forces. The rules of engagement had been relaxed, and from December 1966 it was permissible for waterways to be mined.

1967 February   USAF Arc Light B-52 bombing missions finally reached the authorized level of 800 sorties per month, but this brought Andersen AFB, Guam perilously close to maximum operating capacity, necessitating the use of bases elsewhere. The government of Thailand was approached for permission to carry out strikes from one of their airfields, and on March 22 a B-52 base at U-Tapao was set up from where targets in North Vietnam were easier to reach and the congestion on Guam was relieved.

1967 March 3   Reflecting a world-wide shift away from flying boats, the Soviet flying boat and seaplane manufacturer Beriev produced its first landplane, which flew for the first time, powered by two 740-HP ASh-21 engines. These were replaced by the 960-HP Glushenkov TVD-10B turboprops. With capacity for 15 passengers, one of whom sat alongside the pilot, it had a wingspan of 55 ft. 9 in. and a length of 51 ft. 6 in. It was the last type Beriev was to produce, and its design bureau went into decline after the death of its founder in 1979.

1967 March 6   The USAF issued a request for proposals to 21 aircraft companies for design studies of a low-cost attack aircraft designated A-X. In April preliminary contracts were awarded to Grumman, Northrop, McDonnell Douglas and General Dynamics-Convair. The studies were to define aircraft vulnerability to ground fire and examined the advantages of mounting large cannons in ground attack planes as well as trading between turbofans, turbojets and turboprops, with most favoring the latter as a mode of propulsion.

1967 March 9   The first all-metal sailplane manufactured in the United Kingdom made its first flight. Built by Slingsby Aircraft Co., the T.53 was a two-seater designed for air cadets and fabricated from light alloy with a wingspan of 55 ft. 6 in. and a length of 25 ft. 7 in. The first production aircraft flew in March 1968, but a major fire at the company's office in Kirkbymoorside, Yorkshire, interrupted production. Slingsby went into liquidation in July 1969 and was absorbed by Vickers.

1967 March 12   The first of a new family of air-to-ground weapons was used against the North Vietnamese bridge across the Song Ma waterway when U.S. Navy A-4D Skyhawks released optically-guided AGM-62 Walleye missiles, all hitting within 5 ft. of each other as planned. The Walleye had a length of 11 ft. 3 in. and a diameter of 1 ft. 9 in. with a conventional high-explosive warhead. It was manufactured first by Martin and then also by Hughes.

1967 March 15   The first Sikorsky HH-53B USAF heavy-lift helicopter, which would very soon acquire the nickname "Super Jolly," made its first flight just 6 mon. before entering service with the Thirty-seventh Air Rescue and Retrieval Squadron in Southeast Asia. Developed from the S-65 and adapted from the U.S. Navy CH-53, it carried 1,200 lb. of armor plate and three 7.62-mm Minigun mountings for protection from enemy fire. Operating close to enemy forces, it was employed on crew rescue and had a maximum weight of 42,000 lb. and a range of 540 mi.

1967 March 29   A Pan American World Airways aircraft approaching Wake Island in the Pacific made the first public demonstration of a satellite data link from a civil aircraft. Information from the aircraft's navigation equipment was sent via a specially installed antenna to the NASA communications technology satellite ATS-1 and sent from there to a ground station in the Mojave Desert, Calif., from where it was routed to Kennedy International Airport, N.Y., providing detailed position information.

1967 March 30 Signed by Pres. Johnson, Executive Order No. 11340 established the Department of Transportation effective April 1. It was to be headed by Alan Boyd and united 100,000 employees in several government departments. One of the most challenging programs it would have to master from an early date was the U.S. supersonic transport aircraft, for which it was given responsibility by Pres. Richard Nixon in 1969.

1967 April 7 The Süd-Aviation SA-340.001 made its first flight, powered by a 630-HP Turboméca Astazou IIN turboshaft engine driving a 32-ft. 9-in. rotor. During development, the French entered a joint agreement with the British signed February 22 and subsequently known as the SA-341 Gazelle. Assembled in the United Kingdom by Westlands, it equipped elements of the British Army, the Fleet Air Arm and the RAF. With capacity for five, it had a length of 39 ft. and a maximum loaded weight of 7,495 lb.

1967 April 9 The first Boeing 737-100 made its first flight powered by two 14,000-lb. s.t. Pratt & Whitney JT8D-7 turbofan engines. With a length of 93 ft. 9 in. and a wingspan of 87 ft., it could accommodate 99 to 107 passengers at a cruising speed of 575 MPH across a range of 1,150 mi. Only four airlines bought the series 100, and on August 8 the first 737-200 flew, lengthened by 6 ft. to accommodate 130 passengers in tourist class and with 16,000-lb. s.t. JT8D-9s, -15s or -17s with noise suppression nacelles. Range on the series 200 was increased to 2,136 mi.

1967 April 18 In the first flight of a reciprocal arrangement for two-way airline services between the USSR and Japan, an Aeroflot Tupolev Tu-114 flew from Moscow to Haneda Airport, Tokyo, landing after a flight time of 10 hr. 35 min. Japan Air Lines would begin flights between Tokyo and Moscow for this regularly scheduled service.

1967 April 21 The Süd-Est Caravelle got a new lease on life with the first flight of the Caravelle IIR medium-range, passenger-freight aircraft powered by two 14,000-lb. s.t. Pratt & Whitney JT8D-7 turbofan engines. With a length of 107 ft. 4 in. and a wingspan of 112 ft. 6 in., it could accommodate 89 tourist passengers or 50 passengers in the rear and cargo in a 656.7 cu. ft. forward compartment. The first delivery was to Air-Afrique during the summer.

1967 April 28 The McDonnell Aircraft Corp. and the Douglas Aircraft Co. merged to form the McDonnell Douglas Corp. McDonnell had a boom market with expanding sales of its military and commercial aircraft, spacecraft, rockets and electronics. Douglas had serious cash problems and a shrinking production line, which had fallen from 840 aircraft in 1954 to 190 in 1966. In 1966 McDonnell had net income of $43.21 million on sales of $1.06 billion, and Douglas had income of $27.5 million on sales of $1.05 billion. In 1968, McDonnell Douglas would have income of $98.47 million on sales of $3.6 billion.

1967 May 6 A USAF B-52 flew the 10,000th sortie to North Vietnam since the Arc Light operation began June 18, 1965. In the intervening period, Strategic Air Command aircraft had dropped almost 200,000 tons of bombs on enemy positions, supply lines, fortifications and munitions dumps, effectively converting the giant bomber into a tactical strike aircraft for which it was never designed. During 1967, Arc Light sortie rates almost doubled.

1967 May 9 The product of a joint development agreement between Fokker and the German VFW company, the F.28 Fellowship made its first flight. Powered by two 9,850-lb. s.t. Rolls Royce RB.183-2 Mk.555-15 Spey Junior turbofans, it had a wingspan of 77 ft. 4 in. and a length of 89 ft. 11 in., providing 60 passengers with a cruising speed of 519 MPH over a distance of 627 mi. A later version had a stretched fuselage that increased capacity to 79 passengers.

1967 May 10 Test pilot Bruce Peterson flying the M2-F2 lifting body over Edwards AFB, Calif. suffered near fatal injuries when the M2-F2 disintegrated in a crash. Released from the B-52 carrier-plane at 45,000 ft., the pilot experienced severe "dutch-roll" at 200°/sec and drifted away from the planned runway. Confused by a helicopter in his path, he hit the ground hard sustaining severe injuries but recovered and stayed on at the NASA Flight Research Center as safety officer. Motion picture footage of the crash was later used for opening shots of the TV series "Six Million Dollar Man."

1967 May 19 Developed as an export version of the Mirage III-E, the Mirage 5 made its first flight, powered by a 9,436/13,670-lb. s.t. SNECMA Atar 9C turbojet engine. Refined as a ground-attack fighter capable of carrying a warload of 9,260 lb. on external locations, more than 500 were built for several air forces. The Mirage 5 had a top speed of Mach 2.1 at 39,370 ft. or Mach 1.1 at sea level. Peru was the first country to take delivery of the Mirage 5.

1967 May 23 The first Hawker Siddeley Nimrod M.R.Mk.1 (serial no. XV148) Comet 4 conversion made its first flight, followed by a second prototype on July 31 and the first production maritime patrol aircraft for the RAF on June 28, 1968. It was the first four-engine maritime patrol aircraft in service with any air force. Production aircraft were powered by four 12,160-lb. s.t. Rolls Royce RB.168-20 Spey 250 turbofans, with a wingspan of 114 ft. 10 in., length of 126 ft. 9 in. and a maximum overload weight of 192,000 lb. Range was 5,775 mi.

1967 May 31 In a remarkable example of "real-time" planning, six U.S. Navy attack aircraft on their way back across the Gulf of Tonkin from a strike on North Vietnam got caught short and had to rendezvous with a Strategic Air Command KC-135 commanded by Maj. John H. Casteel, already busy refueling two USAF F-104s. Dangerously short of fuel, an F-8 Crusader was being refueled by an A-3 tanker, which was itself taking on fuel from the KC-135. The A-3 then dispensed fuel to the other five. As a result of this operation, Maj. Casteel and his crew received the Mackay Trophy for 1967.

1967 June 1 The first nonstop helicopter flight across the North Atlantic was completed when two USAF HH-53E Jolly Green Giants commanded by USAF Majors Herbert B. Zehnder and Donald B. Maurras arrived at Le Bourget airfield, Paris for the 27th International Air and Space Show. Traveling 4,160 mi. from New York in 30 hr. 48 min., the helicopters traced the route taken by Charles Lindbergh in 1927 and made nine aerial refuelings on the way. Maximum range with external as well as internal fuel for helicopters of this class was 760 mi.

1967 June 4 The FAA stipulated an increase in the nonrefundable airline reservation charge for Boeing SSTs from $200,000 to $750,000, payable directly to Boeing for development subsidy in lieu of extra government support. To date, 113 aircraft had been ordered under an arangement formalized in November 1963 when $100,000 was required as a down payment followed by a second payment of $100,000 within 6 mon. of the first. Pres. Johnson had approved construction of two prototypes April 29.

1967 June 5 In a preemptive strike planned with meticulous care and executed with disciplined precision, the Israeli Air Force attacked 10 Egyptian airfields in the Sinai Peninsula at 7:45 A.M. with Dassault Ouragan and Mystère fighter-bombers carrying 500-lb., 1,000-lb. and 1,200-lb. armor-piercing bombs and rockets. Beginning at 8:15 A.M., the Israeli Army swept across the Sinai with 700 tanks. By midday, airfields in Egypt itself were attacked, and at 5:15 P.M. the airport at Cairo came under air attack. At the end of the day, the Israelis had destroyed 308 aircraft, including 240 Egyptian, 45 Syrian, 16 Jordanian and seven Iraqi, for the loss of 20, of which only one was lost in aerial combat.

1967 June 8 On the fourth day of what became the "Six-Day War," Israeli aircraft supported the full occupation of the Sinai up to the Suez Canal, while the last faltering resistance from Egyptian MiG-21s was suppressed. On the preceding evening, a UN ceasefire over Jordan had been agreed after Israel captured all three bridges across the Jordan River, releasing forces to push south into Egypt and northeast into Syria. By the end of the day, Israel had destroyed a total of 338 Egyptian and 29 Jordanian aircraft, with 30,000 Egyptian casualties, 5,500 captured and 10,000 vehicles, 500 tanks and 450 artillery pieces destroyed, for the loss of 275 Israeli dead.

1967 June 10 Having obtained an Egyptian ceasefire at 4:35 A.M. June 9, after eliminating 80% of their army, Israeli aircraft struck Syria, smashing armor and destroying lines of communication in an air-ground assault beginning 11:30 A.M. that day. By 4:30 P.M. this day, the Syrians had accepted a ceasefire after suffering 7,500 casualties and losing 300 tanks and artillery pieces in just 29 hr. In the "Six-Day War," the Arabs had lost 452 aircraft for the loss of 46 Israeli aircraft.

1967 June 30 The first McDonnell Douglas F-4E Phantom II, equipped for the first time with a built-in 20-mm M-61A1 cannon, made its first flight, powered by two 17,900-lb. s.t. General Electric J79-GE-17s. Most prolific of all F-4 variants, with 949 eventually built for Tactical Air Command, it retained the semi-recessed Sparrow III AAMs characteristic of earlier models and was eventually retrofitted with leading edge slats. As with the F-4B and F-4C, a reconnaissance version appeared as the RF-4E.

1967 July 7 Two USAF B-52Ds crashed into the South China Sea after colliding in midair. Six crewmembers were killed out of 12, including Maj. Gen. William J. Crumm, commander of the Third Air Division, Strategic Air Command. The following day a third B-52D was lost along with five of the six crewmembers on board when it crashed while attempting an emergency landing at Da Nang AB, South Vietnam.

1967 July 24 At a press conference in London, Technology Minister John Stonehouse announced an agreement whereby a short/medium-haul airliner project would be defined by a European consortium involving Süd Aviation in France and Hawker Siddeley in the United Kingdom with Arbeitsgemeinschaft Airbus (Deutsche Airbus GmbH from September 4) in West Germany. Called the European Airbus Project, it would result in the design and development of a twin-engined A-300 series given government approval on May 28, 1969.

1967 July 29 The U.S. Navy suffered its worst noncombat accident of the Vietnam War, arguably its worst ever, when a Zuni rocket was inadvertently fired horizontally from an F-4 parked on deck into a packed flight deck on the carrier USS *Forrestal*. In the ensuing carnage of exploding ammunition and blazing aviation fuel, 143 men were killed, 21 aircraft were completely destroyed and 43 severely damaged. The carrier, a part of Task Force 77, withdrew and was returned to the United States for repairs, which cost $72 million.

1967 August 1 Further increases in the expected development cost of the Concorde supersonic airliner were declared by the House of Commons Public Accounts Committee. Compared to an estimated $476 million when the program started in November 1962, current estimates were $1.470 billion with an additional $75.4 million probably being needed for research at the Ministry of Technology.

1967 August 1 In the United States, the NASA Office of Science and Technology released a report on sonic-boom tests conducted at Edwards AFB, Calif., where 393 people and 220,570 animals had been subjected to the noise from 261 subsonic and 367 supersonic flights. The finding suggested that people were annoyed more by progressively louder sonic booms than by louder conventional jet engine noise and that the walls of houses were more effective at blocking engine noise than supersonic bangs.

1967 August 4 Built by M. Ward of North Scarle, Lincolnshire, England, the tiny Ward Gnome made its first flight powered by a 14-HP Douglas 2-cylinder, horizontally opposed piston engine. Made of unapproved wood materials, it was not possible to register the aircraft, and because of that, it was limited to a maximum altitude of 10 ft. above level ground, probably the only aircraft to be so restricted. It had a wingspan of 15 ft. 9 in., a length of 11 ft. 6 in. and a range of 50 mi. at 50 MPH.

1967 August 28 Developed from the U-2 spy plane, the Lockheed U-2R made its first flight at North Base, Edwards AFB, Calif., piloted by Bill Park. Bearing strong superficial resemblance to its progenitor, the U-2R had a wingspan of 103 ft., wing area increased from 565 sq. ft. to 1,000 sq. ft., a fuselage length of 63 ft. and maximum takeoff weight raised to over 40,000 lb. A greatly improved handling, performance and payload capability gave the U-2 program a completely new lease on life.

1967 August 30 Following the preparation during July of an extended target list for communist sites in North Vietnam, 24 Douglas A-4Cs from the USS *Oriskany* led by Comdr. Burton H. Shepheard penetrated intensive antiaircraft artillery fire to drop their bomb loads within a 12-sec. period on the main supply bridge southeast of the port of Haiphong; three of the four spans were knocked out. In converting Rolling Thunder to an interdiction of southward-moving supply routes, air attacks aimed at communication routes. Air forces were denied permission to attack massed stocks in the harbor itself, however.

1967 September 1 The U.S. Army New Equipment Training Team (NETT) began converting pilots from the 334th Assault Helicopter Company at Bien Hoa, South Vietnam, to the Bell AH-1G Cobra. The unit was fully equipped and ready by the time the Tet Offensive began in February 1968. The application of the helicopter gunship to support operations was a prelude to more effective and autonomous operations in which gunships were used as independent strike elements.

1967 September 6 In further moves to utilize earth-orbiting satellites for improved commercial aircraft operations, the com-

Epitomizing the era of the helicopter gunship, a Bell AH-1G with chin turret and stub-wings for munitions.

munications satellite *Early Bird* was used to relay information about 120 passengers and cargo loaded onto an airliner prior to the plane's departure from Frankfurt, West Germany to Washington, D.C.'s Dulles International Airport. Facsimiles of the cargo manifest, health certificates and customs declaration forms were forwarded in a test to determine whether airport clearance could be speeded up.

1967 September 11 Operation Neutralize began in which coordinated and sustained strikes were carried out against communist targets in North Vietnam and on concentrations of Viet Cong in the south. A combined attack with artillery, naval gunfire and tactical air power was integrated with B-52 strikes in Phase V of Rolling Thunder, which had begun on March 2, 1965. In this round-the-clock assault on communist units, the bases at Con Thien were relieved of enemy bombardment, although by the end of the year, intelligence indicated a potential build-up around Khe Sanh.

1967 September 11 Lockheed announced the first details of its proposed large-capacity, wide-body commercial transport designed to carry 227 to 300 passengers across a range of 2,127 mi. Powered by three high bypass turbofan engines in the 33,000-lb. s.t. class, it was to have a high-lift wing with double-slotted trailing edge Fowler flaps, inboard Kreuger flaps, outboard leading edge slats and upper surface spoilers with roll control, airbrake and lift dump functions. Lockheed estimated a market for 800 transports of this type.

1967 September 21 The Lockheed AH-56A Cheyenne two-seat attack and escort helicopter began flight trials powered by a 3,435-SHP General Electric T64-GE-16 turboshaft engine driving a 50-ft. 5 in., four-blade rigid rotor, a four-blade antitorque rotor and a three-blade pusher propeller. It had a length of 54 ft. 8 in., could carry 2,000 lb. of weapons on six external pylons attached to small stub wings spanning 26 ft. 7 in. and had a 7.62-mm Minigun in the nose. With a top speed of 253 MPH and a range of 875 mi., it had promise, but serious technical problems caused it to be abandoned in August 1972.

1967 October 3 Flown by USAF test pilot Capt. William J. Knight, the #2 rocket-powered North American X-15 research aircraft achieved the fastest speed it would attain, setting the absolute world speed record for nonorbiting manned aircraft. Launched from a B-52 carrier-plane, the X-15 reached a speed of Mach 6.7 (4,520 MPH) and a height of 102,100 ft. The X-15 was fitted with full ablative covering giving the aircraft an uncharacteristic white color, external propellant tanks and a simulated ramjet engine on the ventral tail.

1967 October 5 The first Shin Meiwa PX-3 long-range maritime patrol flying boat made its first flight in Japan. Developed for the Japanese Maritime Self-Defense Force by a company formed from the old Kawanishi Aircraft Co., the aircraft had a wingspan of 107 ft. 7 in. and a length of 109 ft. 11 in. with power from four 2,850-ESHP General Electric T64-IHI-10 turboprops. In service from 1973 as the PS-1, it had a cruising speed of 196 MPH and a range of up to 2,948 mi.

1967 October 12 The all-weather landing system (AWLS) was certified by the FAA for use on the Lockheed C-141 StarLifter under minimum visibility of 1,200 ft. and a 100 ft. decision altitude, at which point the crew had to decide whether to land or climb away. The system had been developed by Air Force Systems Command and could bring the giant transport aircraft down to within 12 ft. of the runway centerline or within 30 ft. of the selected touchdown spot. It could generate information for either manual or automatic control.

1967 October 14 The first of a much improved and more capable version of the Chinook transport helicopter designated CH-47C made its first flight. Powered by two 3,750-SHP Lycoming T55-L-11 engines, it had a 25% increase in lifting capacity and could now take up to 23,400 lb. of cargo while maximum gross weight increased to 44,800 lb. Speed was increased by 11 MPH, and U.S. Army units began receiving the CH-47C in the spring of 1968.

1967 October 23 The first flight, in landplane configuration, of the amphibious Canadair CL-215 water-bomber to be used for fire-fighting took place less than 2 yr. after the design had been approved. Powered by two 2,100-HP Pratt & Whitney R-2800 engines, it had a wingspan of 93 ft. 10 in. and a length of 65 ft. The fuselage was designed to scoop up 1,200 Imp. gal. of water in less than 20 sec. while planing at 70 MPH. Several aircraft of this type were sold abroad, and the type filled a unique need for Canada's forest-fire-fighting service.

Selected in 1959 and first flown September 21, 1961, the Boeing-Vertol Chinook proved a versatile workhorse.

1967 October 26 Designated the BAC 167, the adapted Jet Provost T.5 made its first flight as a two-seat light strike aircraft powered by a 3,410-lb. s.t. Bristol Siddeley Viper 535 turbojet. With a wingspan of 35 ft. 4 in. and a length of 35 ft. 7 in., it had a maximum loaded weight of 11,500 lb. and provision for two machine guns with up to 3,000 lb. on underwing stores. Named Strikemaster, it has been sold to several small air forces in South America, Africa, the Middle East, the Far East and Africa.

1967 November 4 Soviet test pilot Pyotr Otsapenko achieved a new FAI world speed record of 2,910 km/hr. (1,808 MPH) for a 1,000-km (621.4-mi.) closed circuit carrying a 2,000-kg (4,409 lb.) payload flying the Ye-266, soon to be known in the west as the MiG-25 Foxbat. Designed in 1962–64 as a Mach 3, high-altitude, straight-line interceptor to counter the B-70 and powered by two 20,500/27,120-lb. s.t. Tumanski R-31 turbojets, the MiG-25 had a wingspan of 45 ft. 9 in. and a length of 78 ft. 2 in. with a gross weight of 82,500 lb., a service ceiling of 78,740 ft. and a mission radius of 249 mi. It would enter service in 1970.

1967 November 15 The #3 North American X-15 crashed, killing its pilot Maj. Michael J. Adams, USAF, following a flight to Mach 5.2 (3,570 MPH) and a height of 266,000 ft. During wing-rocking activity for instrumented observation of the exhaust plume, bank angles became excessive and the aircraft rolled to 90° before entering a spin-stall at Mach 5 from 230,000 ft. down to 125,000 ft. when it plunged into a dive inducing high-frequency pitch oscillations and stresses up to 15 g, far more than the design tolerance of 7.33 g, which caused the aircraft to break up.

1967 November 18 The variable geometry Dassault Mirage G made its first flight powered by an 11,684/20,503-lb. s.t. SNECMA TF-306C turbofan. Swept fully forward 22°, it had a span of 42 ft. 8 in. and a length of 55 ft. 1 in. with the trailing edge matching the sweep of the forward edge of the low-mounted tail surfaces when fully swept at 72°. Capable of 840 MPH (Mach 1.1) at sea level and 1,585 MPH (Mach 2.4) at 40,000 ft., it never appeared operationally.

1967 November 28 The first of a second generation "stretch," the DC-9 Series 40, made its first flight with an additional 6 ft. 2 in. increase in fuselage length to 125 ft. 7 in. accommodating up to 125 passengers. Developed for SAS and bought additionally by Thai Airways, the Series 40 had either two 14,500-lb. s.t. Pratt & Whitney JT8D-9s, two 15,000-lb. s.t. JT8D-11s or two 15,500-lb. s.t. JT8D-15s. Range with maximum payload was reduced to 670 mi.

1967 November U.S. defense secretary Robert S. McNamara authorized a further increase in Arc Light B-52 bombing operations against targets in North Vietnam, increasing the monthly level from 800 sorties to 1,200 sorties. This required additional B-52D deployments, utilizing Kadena AB, Okinawa. It also increased KC-135 tanker activity, over 22,000 sorties being flown by these aircraft during 1967 in support of B-52 and fighter operations, during which more than 1.1 million tons of aviation fuel were dispensed.

1967 December 1 The USAF awarded F-X study contracts to General Dynamics and McDonnell Douglas with Fairchild-Republic, Grumman, Lockheed and North American carrying out unfunded studies. On August 11, bids had been solicited from seven manufacturers for a second F-X definition round following the first, which began March 18, 1966. In this second phase,

completed by June 1968, it was agreed that the program would move ahead without prototypes being ordered prior to contract selection. Defense Department officials were concerned about escalating Soviet air power.

1967 December 4 U.S. Navy Squadron VA-147 aboard the carrier USS *Ranger* became the first unit to take the LTV A-7A Corsair II into action over Vietnam. The aircraft had made its first carrier landings aboard the USS *Ranger* in June following activation of the unit as the first A-7A tactical squadron on February 1. With provision for more than 15,000 lb. of external stores, it was a welcome addition to the inventory of navy attack aircraft.

1967 December 11 The first prototype Concorde 001 supersonic transport aircraft (F-WTSS) was rolled out at Toulouse, France. With a wingspan of 84 ft. and a length of 193 ft., it was powered by four 32,825/37,400-lb. s.t. Olympus 593s developed jointly by Rolls Royce in England and SNECMA in France. The aircraft had capacity for up to 128 passengers in high-density seating, but prototypes were never fully furnished for commercial duty, being packed throughout their length with data recorders and instrumentation.

1967 December 28 The first Hawker Siddeley Harrier G.R.Mk.1 (serial no. XB738) made its first flight as the definitive operational RAF V/STOL ground attack fighter developed from the Hawker P.1127, the first such aircraft to enter operational service with any air force. Powered by a 19,000-lb. s.t. Bristol Siddeley Pegasus 101, it had a wingspan of 25 ft. 3 in., a length of 46 ft. 4 in. and a maximum VTOL weight of 16,000 lb. and STOL weight of 22,000 lb. Capable of carrying 4,000 lb. of ordnance, it had a maximum speed of 680 MPH and a 600-mi. combat radius.

1967 December 29 The last RB-47H (serial no. 53-4296) was retired from duty with the Fifty-fifth Strategic Reconnaissance Wing, Offutt AFB, Nebr. when it flew to Davis-Monthan AFB, Ariz. The last B-47 bomber variant had been retired February 11, 1966, but this retirement was the final operational flight for aircraft of the type. Introduced in 1951 as the first all-jet Strategic Air Command bomber, with 1,367 on charge in 1958, the plane had been deployed in greater numbers than any other USAF bomber since World War II, a record that will probably stand for all time.

1968 January 16 Prime Minister Harold Wilson announced to the House of Commons in London that his Labour cabinet had decided to cancel the order for 50 General Dynamics F-111Ks as the RAF's deep strike aircraft following cancellation of the T.S.R.2 in March 1965. To this date, the British government had spent £240 million in real-year costs on both projects. Also announced was Britain's withdrawal from east of the Suez Canal and the retirement of the carrier force by the end of 1971. The Phantoms and Buccaneers would be transferred to the RAF.

In a signal to all Royal Navy stations following the debate in the British Parliament over defense cuts that would eliminate the fixed-wing carriers by the end of 1971, Vice Adm. Gibson, flag officer, Naval Air Command, sent the following message: "If the Fleet Air Arm fussed unduly about political decisions affecting its future, we should all have gone stark raving mad some years ago . . . but as usual we have our duty to do. We have a challenge and we will, with God's help, and our own professional pride, keep our standards."

1968 January 22 A B-52G carrying four free-fall nuclear bombs crashed and burned on sea ice at North Star Bay while attempting an emergency landing at Thule AB, Greenland. Radioactive material leaked into the area, and a major clean-up operation was conducted. Not before September 13 was the area cleared of all detectable radioactive debris.

1968 January 22   One day after the North Vietnamese began an all-out offensive against the U.S. Marine Corps base at Khe Sanh, close to the demilitarized zone, Gen. William Westmoreland ordered full activation of Operation Niagara, which combined air elements of the U.S. Army, Navy, Air Force and Marine Corps in an air offensive. An additional 26 B-52s were flown from the United States to Kadena AB, Okinawa to support the 1,200 sorties per month authorized by Defense Secretary Robert McNamara and to help pound communist positions, at times within 1,000 yd. of the Khe Sanh perimeter.

1968 January 30   North Vietnam launched the Tet Offensive involving upwards of 50,000 North Vietnamese troops and Viet Cong drawn from the countryside into the towns of South Vietnam. The offensive's combination of open offensive and clandestine terrorism made air strikes and air support operations difficult and did much to change the nature of the war by seeming to inject a sense of despair among Western analysts, in a year when the U.S. government would change from Democrat to Republican hands.

1968 February 19   American Air Lines ordered 50 McDonnell Douglas DC-10 wide-body airliners, effectively giving the go-ahead on this ambitious program, so recently made possible by the merger of Douglas with McDonnell. Having lost the CX heavy-lift military transport contract, Douglas had wanted to exploit its design for commercial use but lacked the necessary funds. In late April, United Air Lines ordered 60 DC-10s, and by the fall, McDonnell Douglas had decided upon a 250 to 340 seat, twin-aisle configuration utilizing three engines and a wing with 35° of sweep.

1968 February 22   Boeing president William M. Allen announced that the first flight of the Boeing 2707 supersonic airliner would be delayed by 1 yr. to 1972 to allow the company more time to make refinements in the design. This decision had been reached with the full approval of the FAA and the Department of Transportation. Boeing was in the process of transforming the series 200 into the series 300, which would adopt a fixed delta with conventional tail surfaces instead of a variable-sweep wing configuration, and sandwich skins instead of machined skins.

1968 February 27   Developed from the C-130 Hercules transport aircraft under Project Gunship II, the AC-130A went into action over the Ho Chi Minh Trail in Vietnam for the first time. Equipped with flare dispensers, two 40-mm cannons, two 20-mm cannons and two 7.62-mm Miniguns, 11 aircraft were modified as gunships, some getting a 105-mm howitzer in place of a 40-mm cannon. Only one was shot down during the war.

1968 March 8   The U.S. Army reopened its light observation helicopter competition, originally won by Hughes with the OH-6, and named Bell the winner with its Model 206, which had been developed from the Model 205. Designated H-58 Kiowa, it had a 420-SHP Allison T63-A-720 turboshaft engine driving a 35-ft. 4-in. rotor. With a length of 32 ft. 7 in. and a gross weight of 3,200 lb., it had a maximum speed of 138 MPH and a range of 300 mi. The first of more than 2,000 was delivered to the U.S. Army on May 23, 1969.

1968 March 25   Six USAF F-111As of the 428th Tactical Fighter Squadron deployed to Takhli, Thailand in the Combat Lancer

evaluation program flew their first combat missions over Vietnam. They had arrived in Thailand March 15 after flying the 7,000 mi. from Nellis AFB, Nev. via Guam, with five in-flight refuelings. One aircraft was lost in Thailand on March 28 in dense jungle, and a second was brought down 375 mi. north of Bangkok two days later because of a failure in the tailplane control unit, after which the four remaining aircraft were temporarily grounded.

1968 March 28   As a result of numerous development problems and a dramatic overweight condition, the Grumman F-111B U.S. Navy fleet defense fighter was canceled when the U.S. Congress refused to permit continued funding of the project. It did, however, allow continued development of the Hughes AWG-9/AIM-54 Phoenix missile, which it said could be applied to future programs. The Phoenix was an advanced, long-range, air-to-air missile that would form the primary air defense weapon system of the Grumman F-14 Tomcat.

1968 March 29   Lockheed formally launched the L-1011 Tri-Star large-capacity, medium-haul, wide-body airliner, announcing orders for 25 from Eastern (with 25 on option), 33 from TWA (with 11 on option) and 50 from Air Holdings. The latter was a holding company through which aircraft would be supplied to British Airways, Air Canada and Cathay Pacific, a political move to offset objections to the selection of the British Rolls Royce RB.211 turbofan engines for an American aircraft. The TriStar was a large-capacity, twin-aisle airliner aimed at the domestic market. It had begun life as a concept drawn up in 1966 to meet an American Airlines specification.

1968 April 5   Replacement F-111As for the two lost in March over Thailand arrived at Takhli, Thailand from Nellis AFB, Nev. Shortly after the aircraft was restored to flight status, evaluation missions began, but another F-111A was lost on April 27, and the five remaining aircraft were again grounded for several days. When another F-111A was lost in Nevada, an engineering examination revealed structural failure due to an improper weld.

1968 April 6   The first of two LTV YA-7D prototypes made its first flight. Selected by the USAF in 1966 as an attack fighter adapted from the U.S. Navy Corsair II, production aircraft had the more powerful 14,500-lb. s.t. Allison TF41-A-1 turbofan, a gross weight of 42,000 lb. and total combined external load capacity of 20,000 lb. The A-7D entered service in 1970, and 479 were eventually procured, with many going to the Air National Guard where they serve today.

1968 April 8   The siege of the U.S. Marine Corps base at Khe Sanh and its 6,000 occupants in the northern part of South Vietnam ended after the most concentrated period of bombing to this date. In 77 days, the USAF had dropped 96,000 tons of bombs, of which the B-52s dropped 54,000 tons in 2,548 sorties. On some days, 45 B-52 and 300 tactical fighter-bomber sorties were flown against communists pressing upon the base perimeter. USAF transport aircraft had dropped 8,120 tons of medical supplies and rations, and an aditional 4,136 tons and 2,676 personnel had also been flown into the base.

1968 April 30   In the most radical restructuring of the RAF since its formation April 1, 1918, Fighter Command and Bomber Command ceased to exist and were amalgamated into a single Strike Command with headquarters at High Wycombe, the former headquarters for Bomber Command. The changes had begun in August 1967 with the renaming of Transport Command as Air Support Command. In June 1968, flying and Technical commands would merge into Training Command, and in January 1969, Signals Command would join Strike Command. Coastal Command, a misnomer for long-range maritime surveillance, would merge into Strike Command in 1970.

1968 May 5   The Grumman Gulfstream II became the first executive jet to complete a nonstop flight across the Atlantic, flying 3,500 mi. between Teterboro, N.J. and Gatwick Airport, London. The Gulfstream II had made its first flight on October 2, 1966, and was an attempt to follow the Lockheed JetStar and the North American Sabreliner in the executive market. Powered by two 11,450-lb. s.t. Rolls Royce RB.163-25 Spey Mk.511-8 turbofans in the by-now familiar rear fuselage pods, it had a wingspan of 68 ft. 10 in. and a length of 79 ft. 11 in. with a cruising speed of 496 MPH and a range of 3,680 mi.

1968 May 25   Developed for the U.S. Navy as a purpose-built, four-seat, electronic counter-measures (ECM) aircraft, the Grumman EA-6B Prowler made its first flight. The EA-6B was powered by two 9,300-lb. s.t. Pratt & Whitney J52-P-8A turbojet engines, and it bristled with electronic warfare systems. It had a wingspan of 53 ft., a length of 59 ft. 5 in. and a maximum overload weight of 63,177 lb. The Prowler had a cruising speed of 466 MPH and a range of 1,628 mi.

1968 June 30   The first of five development Lockheed C-5A Galaxy military transport aircraft, the heaviest and biggest in the world to this date, made its first flight. The C-5A had a wingspan of 222 ft. 8 in., a length of 247 ft. 10 in. and a gross weight of 769,000 lb. Capable of carrying a maximum payload of 265,000 lb. over short distances and with a maximum range of 3,500 mi. with a 220,000-lb. payload, it had a cruising speed of 537 MPH at 30,000 ft. It was precisely the sort of aircraft the USAF had wanted ever since the Berlin Airlift, but costs prevented procurement in the desired number, only 81 being built for the Military Airlift Command.

1968 July 1   Boeing submitted a progress report on the Model 2707 supersonic transport aircraft to the FAA and indicated each aircraft would cost $41.2 million and that total development and certification costs would be about $2.96 billion. Advance payments from airlines could account for $905 million, Boeing and General Electric could provide $595 million, requiring $1.5 billion in government-guaranteed loans. First flight trials were scheduled to begin in September 1972.

1968 July 12   The last U.S. Navy flying boat, a Martin SP-5B Marlin, was retired from active service and presented to the Smithsonian Institution at a special ceremony at the Patuxent NAS, Md. The Marlin's retirement marked the end of an era that began July 1, 1911, with the flight of the U.S. Navy's first aircraft from Lake Keuka in Hammondsport, N.Y. The SP-5B was the designation applied, since reassignment of designations in 1962, to the P5M-2S, which was the last of several Marlin variants.

1968 July 13   The first production General Dynamics FB-111A strategic bomber made its first flight, initially powered by two TF30-P-12 engines used in the canceled F-111B. Production aircraft were to have 20,350-lb. s.t. Pratt & Whitney TF30-P-7 turbofan engines providing a maximum speed of Mach 2.2 (1,450 MPH) at 40,000 ft. and a range of 4,100 mi. with external fuel. Capable of carrying up to 37,500 lb. of bombs, it was intended as an interim replacement for the retired B-58A and the canceled B-70A, but planned procurement of 210 was cut to 76.

1968 July 16   The first commercial airline service between the United States and the USSR was inaugurated when an Aeroflot

Ilyushin Il-62 landed at New York's Kennedy International Airport with 97 Soviet officials and other passengers on board, and, having flown via Copenhagen, a Pan American World Airways Boeing 707 touched down at Moscow's Sheremtyevo airport. The Boeing 707 carried dignataries and press representatives, followed by a second Boeing 707 carrying revenue-paying passengers.

1968 July 17   Representatives from Britain, Germany, Italy, Canada, the Netherlands and Belgium signed a memorandum of agreement to carry out joint studies on a multi-role aircraft for 1975, known as MRA-75. Since France withdrew from the Anglo-French variable geometry (AFVG) project in June 1967, talks about a common combat aircraft had been held between the United Kingdom, Germany and Italy beginning July 13, 1967. The U.K. variable geometry (UKVG) project was renamed advanced combat aircraft, and the other MRA-75 signatories had joined the venture by May 1968.

1968 July 19   Following the cancellation of the F-111B variable geometry fleet defense fighter, the U.S. Navy issued five $1 million contracts to Grumman, LTV, General Dynamics, North American and McDonnell Douglas for proposals matching a VFX specification calling for an advanced Mach 2+ interceptor and carrier defense aircraft. From this the F-14 would evolve as one of the U.S. Navy's most sophisticated aircraft.

1968 August 5   The world's first commercial airstrip for STOL operations came into operation at New York's La Guardia Airport. Given the name STOLport, it featured a 1,095-ft. runway for visual takeoff and landing only, almost 3,000 ft. shorter than the next shortest runway at the airport. On September 1, other STOLports opened at Washington National Airport, Dulles International Airport and at Friendship Airport, Baltimore.

1968 August 20   The French test pilot Andre Turcat began a series of runway taxi tests with the prototype Concorde at France's Toulouse-Blagnac airport. The first taxi run went for a distance of 1.2 mi., and the runway was used several times for further tests of undercarriage, brakes, engines and control systems. The powerful and noisy engines, the only engines with reheat to power a commercial airliner, drew curious crowds long before the first flight.

1968 August 23   The first McDonnell Douglas F-4M Phantom II arrived at No. 226 Operational Conversion Unit, RAF Conningsby, England, the first of 138 RAF Phantoms. No. 6 Squadron became the first operational RAF fighter squadron to convert to the Phantom, which also assumed the ground attack role until replaced by Jaguars beginning 1974, at which point it reverted to duty as an interceptor. The Phantom began to replace some Lightnings in that role during 1974 until replaced in turn by the Tornado F.Mk.2 from 1986. Coincidentally, McDonnell Douglas delivered its 3,000th Phantom on September 5, 1968, the 4,000th on February 1, 1971 and the 5,000th on May 24, 1978. When production ended in 1979, a total 5,197 F-4s had been built serving 12 air forces.

1968 September 4   The Australian minister of defense formally "accepted" the first of 24 General Dynamics F-111C fighter-bombers ordered from the U.S. government on October 24, 1963, with delivery July–November 1968. The plane was promptly returned to General Dynamics, and the RAAF would not get its first operational F-111Cs for a further 5 yr., making do wth 24 F-4s on loan while the manufacturer sorted out serious structural

On missions over South Vietnam during the late 1960s, the USAF Douglas AC-47 Gunship extracted new jobs for the DC-3 derivative.

problems. Meanwhile, the total price for the 24 aircraft increased from $90.75 million to $320 million.

1968 September 8   Developed as a joint venture between BAC in the United Kingdom and Breguet in France, the E-01 two-seat trainer prototype of the Jaguar single-seat tactical strike fighter made its first flight. With a wingspan of 27 ft. 10 in. and a length of 50 ft. 11 in., the strike fighter had two 4,600/6,900-lb. s.t. Rolls Royce-Turboméca RB.172/T-260 Adour turbofans, a maximum speed of Mach 1.1 (820 MPH) at 1,000 ft. and a warload of up to 10,000 lb. in addition to two 30-mm cannons.

1968 September 11   Developed at the USAF Cambridge Research Laboratories, the largest research balloon ever put together was launched from California with instruments designed to measure the upper atmosphere and the interaction of the sun with the stratosphere. With a volume capacity of 28.7 million cu. ft., the polyurethane envelope was more than twice the volume of the previous biggest balloon. It flew for 18 hr. to a height of 158,000 ft. before descending at Needles, Calif.

1968 September 30   The world's biggest commercial airliner, the Boeing 747-100, was ceremoniously rolled out at the new factory at Everett, Wash. on its 18 wheels arranged in a unique configuration designed to spread the enormous 735,000 lb. gross load of the Jumbo Jet. The aircraft had a wingspan of 195 ft. 8 in., a wing area of 5,500 sq. ft., a length of 231 ft. 4 in. and a height of 63 ft. 5 in. The initial version was powered by four 43,000-lb. s.t. Pratt & Whitney JT9D-2 engines.

1968 September 30   The USAF requested bids from eight manufacturers for the F-X single-seat tactical air-superiority fighter designed to replace the F-4 and put dogfighting back on the agenda for combat pilots. Only Fairchild-Hiller, General Dynamics, McDonnell Douglas and North American responded, and on December 30, three $15.4 million project definition studies were awarded to Fairchild-Hiller, McDonnell Douglas and North

American. Technical proposals were to be in by June 1969 followed by costs and development schedules in August.

1968 October 23   During a flight test evaluation of the rotor system dynamics on the Sikorsky CH-53, the helicopter was put through an impressive range of maneuvers that included loops and rolls. Given the size and mass of this large rotary-winged aircraft, the characteristics exhibited by the type were a dramatic display of refined technologies that had evolved since the helicopters were first seriously developed at the end of World War II.

1968 October 24   NASA test pilot William H. Dana piloted the #1 X-15 on its last flight, achieving a speed of Mach 5.04 (3,682 MPH) and a height of 250,000 ft. In 199 flights since June 8, 1959, the X-15 had achieved a total flight time of 30 hr. 13 min. 49.4 sec., reaching a maximum height of 354,200 ft., a maximum speed of 4,520 MPH (Mach 6.7) with 5 hr. 58 min. 52 sec. above Mach 4, 1 hr. 25 min. 33 sec. above Mach 5 and 1 min. 18 sec. above Mach 6. The #1 aircraft was delivered to the Smithsonian Institution, Washington, D.C., in May 1969, and the #2 aircraft went to Wright-Patterson AFB, Ohio.

1968 October   The third operational fixed-wing gunship employed in Vietnam began operations when the Lockheed AC-119, a converted Fairchild C-119, took to the air on its first combat mission. Adapted in the Project Gunship III program, they were expected to replace the AC-47s operating since December 23, 1965. Four fuselage-mounted gun pods each containing one six-barrel 7.62-mm GAU-2 Minigun were installed with additional avionics, night-illumination equipment and flares. The USAF procured 52 AC-119s.

1968 November 1   Pres. Johnson halted Rolling Thunder bombing operations against North Vietnam as part of a planned drawback of U.S. military units to transfer the defense of South Vietnam to its own people (Vietnamization). B-52s would be heavily engaged in Commando Hunt operations aimed at cutting transshipment routes from the north, a combined operation involving all U.S. air units against fuel dumps and supply lines. During this effort, antiinfiltration sensors dropped in jungle areas were tested for effectiveness, monitoring movement as communist units moved south. Developed under the "Igloo White" program, these sensors included seismic detectors attached to spikes dropped from aircraft that, when impaled in the jungle, transmitted signals monitoring the movement of communist supply trucks along the Ho Chi Minh Trail.

1968 November 13 NASA test pilot John A. Manke completed the first powered flight by the HL-10 lifting-body research aircraft after igniting two of the four XLR-11 rocket chambers and climbing from 39,700 ft. to 43,250 ft. and achieving a speed of Mach 0.84 (524 MPH). The first powered flight attempt had to be abandoned October 23 when only one of the XLR-11's rocket chambers fired. The first four-chamber flight took place on August 6, 1969, when the HL-10 reached a speed of 1,020 MPH (Mach 1.54) and 76,100 ft.

1968 December 11 Süd-Aviation and Hawker Siddeley simultaneously announced a change in the projected A-300 Airbus project, with a resizing designated A-300B. Extensive market surveys and engineering design considerations had reduced the overall size of the projected airliner, making it less costly for airlines and more economic for operators. This resizing gave the U.K. government the excuse it sought to withdraw from the project.

1968 December 30 In a new role for the McDonnell F-4 Phantom, the USAF began to use this adaptable aircraft as night escort and flak suppression aircraft for the Lockheed AC-130 gunships. Using high intensity illumination, the converted transport aircraft harried supply columns along the Ho Chi Minh Trail, but without

fighter escorts to deter the Soviet-built interceptors, they were sitting targets for communist North Vietnamese MiGs.

1968 December 31 As a measure of how civil and commercial flying had expanded, there were a registered total of 10,740 airports, heliports and seaplane bases in the United States, an increase of 344, or 3.3% over 1967. The total comprised 555 heliports, 411 seaplane bases and 28 landing sites in offshore locations. Of the total, 64% were privately owned.

1968 December 31 The world's first supersonic transport aircraft to fly, the Tupolev Tu-144, took to the air, powered by four 28,660/38,580-lb. s.t. Kuznetsov NK-144 turbofans. Conceived in 1963 and ordered the following year, it was presented in model form at the 1965 Paris Air Show. The Tu-144 had a double-delta-wing span of 75 ft. 5 in., a length of 196 ft. 10 in. and a maximum takeoff weight of 330,000 lb. It had a design speed of Mach 2.35 (1,550 MPH) at up to 65,600 ft. and a maximum range of 4,040 mi. Under this designation, a series of changes and modifications would be made to the basic design before the project was abandoned.

1969 January 10 The prototype Mitsubishi MU-2G light business executive and utility transport made its first flight as a successful variant of the MU-2 first flown on September 14, 1963. This successful company had developed the twin-engined, high-wing aircraft beginning 1956, 5 yr. after the peace treaty had been signed with Japan, and more than 800 were eventually built in all variants. Powered by two 705-ESHP Garrett AiResearch TPE331-1-151A turboprops, the MU-2G had a wingspan of 39 ft. 2 in. and a length of 39 ft. 6 in.

1969 January 14 Grumman was awarded a definitive contract to develop the F-14 as the winning contender for the U.S. Navy VFX requirement. Responding to a request for bids issued June

In full-scale production by 1968, the Hughes (McDonnell Douglas) MD-500 proved a versatile attack and surveillance helicopter.

18, 1968, five manufacturers submitted proposals for this tandem two-man, long-range fighter by June 21, and Grumman and McDonnell Douglas were selected for final designs on December 15. Grumman's Mike Pelehach had been working on Design 303 since the fall of 1967, when it was clear the F-111B was unable to meet U.S. Navy requirements.

1969 January 14 The second major accident aboard the aircraft carrier USS *Enterprise* occurred off Hawaii and resulted in the death of 28 personnel and injuries to 344 with 15 aircraft destroyed. It began when a Zuni rocket attached to an F-4 Phantom accidentally launched horizontally, causing explosions and fire. It put the carrier out of action for about three months and cost $56 million to repair.

1969 January 28 Eastern Airlines vice president A. Scott Crossfield summarized the results of 8 wk. of test at the new STOLports in Washington, Boston and New York. He said that the airline was drafting a specification for a purpose-built STOL airliner able to carry 125 passengers at 250 MPH with takeoff and landing speeds as low as 70 MPH. Douglas had been looking at a version of the French Breguet 941 STOL transport aircraft with which Eastern had carried out experiments at the STOL-ports.

1969 February 4 Following the end of its flight research program, announced January 13, the sole surviving XB-70A was flown from Edwards AFB, Calif. to Wright-Patterson AFB, Ohio, a 3 hr. 15 min. flight that delivered the Mach 3 bomber-cum-research aircraft to the USAF museum. It had made 83 flights and its sister-plane, destroyed as a result of a midair collision on June 8, 1966, had made 46, generating a total flying time of 252 hr. 37 min. during which 106 hr. 48 min. were spent at supersonic speed, 51 hr. 34 min. at Mach 2 or over, 22 hr. 43 min. at Mach 2.5 or over and 1 hr. 48 min. at Mach 3 or over.

1969 February 9 The first Boeing 747-100 made its first flight at Everett, Wash. By the end of the year, more than 188 were on order for 29 operators, and in just over 20 yr., the order book would grow to more than 1,000. The Boeing 747 had a cruising speed of 590–625 MPH at 35,000–37,000 ft., a range with maximum payload of 4,600 mi. and a range with minimum payload of 7,080 mi. With capacity for up to 490 passengers, it had a wide range of optional possibilities for utilizing a shortened upper deck immediately behind the flight deck as cocktail bar, sleep area or extra seats.

1969 March 2 After a lengthy succession of taxi and runway tests, the first prototype Concorde 001 (F-WTSS) made its first flight, with Andre Turcat at the controls. The aircraft was powered by four 32,835/37,420-lb. s.t. Rolls Royce Bristol/SNECMA Olympus 593 Stage O turbojets providing an estimated cruising speed of Mach 2.05–2.1 (1,350–1,385 MPH) at 55,000–62,000 ft. and a maximum payload range of 4,020 mi. The first flight lasted 29 min.

1969 March 19 The U.S. defense secretary announced an initial order for 12 Hawker-Siddeley Harrier V/STOL ground attack fighters, designated AV-8A, for the U.S. Marine Corps. Opposition in the USAF and the U.S. Navy was unable to quell enthusiasm among the Marines for the versatile little combat plane. The first order was funded through the FY1970 budget (beginning July 1, 1969), and subsequent orders would be placed for 30 each year for 3 yr. beginning FY1971. Later, 20 two-seat AV-8A trainer versions were built.

1969 March 26 The Panavia Aircraft G.m.b.H. was formed for the design and development of the multi-role combat aircraft (MRCA), which evolved from the MRA-75 study of 1968. With headquarters in Munich, West Germany, this European industrial consortium included participation by BAC in the United Kingdom, Fiat in Italy, Fokker in the Netherlands and Messerschmitt-Bölkow in West Germany. On March 14, agreement had been reached on the basic configuration of the strike aircraft that would emerge as the Tornado.

1969 March The U.S. Navy set up the "Top Gun" school at Miramar NAS, Calif. where fighter pilots would attend special courses for 4 wk. Included were 75 hr. of classroom instruction and 25 hr. of flight training in which combat maneuvers and simulated dogfighting would qualify students for grades that ultimately carried the accolade of "Top Gun" pupil. The idea arose from experience of air combat in Vietnam and the clear need to give fighter pilots realistic training.

1969 April 9 The second prototype Concorde 002 (G-BSST) made its first flight from Filton, England, piloted by Brian Trubshaw. Two prototype and two preproduction Concordes were built, followed by 16 production aircraft, of which 14 were available for sale. British Airways and Air France procured 7 aircraft each, making them the most exclusive airliners ever built for routine commercial use. The two preproduction Concordes flew for the first time on December 19, 1971 (from Filton) and on January 10, 1973 (from Toulouse).

1969 April 14 An unarmed U.S. Navy Lockheed EC-121M Warning Star electronic airborne early warning aircraft on a patrol over international waters across the Sea of Japan was attacked by aircraft from North Korea and shot down with the loss of all 31 on board. This incident was one of several that had taken place since the end of the Korean War in 1953 but was worst in the number of lives lost.

1969 April 17 The Martin X-24A lifting-body research vehicle made its first glide descent from the underwing carry position of a B-52. With a bulbous, wedge-shaped, rounded top and bottom but with a flat underside to the rear of the mid-fuselage, the X-24A had a width of 13 ft. 8 in. (defined by canted fins with rudders either side of the rear fuselage, which also supported a central fin) and a length of 24 ft. 6 in. It had a loaded weight of 11,000 lb., an 8,480 lb. thrust XLR11 rocket motor plus two 500-lb. thrust hydrogen peroxide engines for flare and landing control.

1969 April 24 The first two-seat Hawker Siddeley Harrier T.Mk.2 (serial no. XW174) made its first flight from Dunsfold, England. With a length of 56 ft., the T.Mk.2 had the same wingspan as the G.R.Mk.1 and identical lifting capacity. But the T.Mk.2 featured a longer nose, accommodated a two-place tandem cockpit, an extended tail cone and an enlarged ventral fin. The first aircraft crashed on June 4, but the second flew on July 14, and the first to equip No. 223 OCU (Operational Conversion Unit), RAF, at their permanent base at Wittering arrived during July 1970.

1969 May 9 NASA test pilot John A. Manke piloted the HL-10 lifting-body research vehicle to supersonic speed for the first time, the first time any of the three lifting-bodies had exceeded the speed of sound. After being carried aloft by a B-52, the HL-10 was boosted on three chambers of its four-chamber rocket motor to a speed of Mach 1.12 (743 MPH) and a height of 53,300 ft. in a flight across Four Corners, Calif. that lasted 6 min. 50

sec. The first four-chamber flight boosted the HL-10 to Mach 1.54 (1,018 MPH) and a height of 75,800 ft. on August 6.

1969 May 11 "The Great Transatlantic Air Race of 1969," a commemorative challenge sponsored by the British newspaper *The Daily Mail* in honor of the 50th anniversary of the first crossing of the Atlantic, ended at midnight. It had opened May 4 and attracted almost 400 entrants competing for 21 prizes worth a total of $150,000 in separate categories. The fastest times were New York-London, Lt. Comdr. Peter Goddard, Royal Navy, in an F-4, 5 hr. 11 min. and Sqdn. Ldr. Graham Williams in a Harrier, 5 hr. 49 min.; London-New York, Sqdn. Ldr. Lecky-Thompson in a Harrier, 6 hr. 11 min. and Sheila Scott in a Commanche light aircraft, 24 hr. 48 min.

1969 May 21 A Lockheed C-5A Galaxy military transport aircraft took off at a weight of 728,100 lb.—100 lb. heavier than the designated gross takeoff weight—setting a new world record. The previous best from the C-5A had been 703,826 lb. On October 11, 1970, the Boeing 727-200 made its first flight with a design maximum takeoff weight of 775,000–800,000 lb., depending on engines, and on December 26, 1982, the Antonov 124 had its first flight with a design maximum takeoff weight of 892,872 lb. On December 21, 1988, the Antonov 225 made its first flight with the phenomenal design maximum takeoff weight of 1,322,750 lb.

1969 May 28 A consortium of French and German manufacturing teams, which had come together with formal government approval to form the European Airbus project, decided to go ahead with the twin-jet A-300B short- to medium-haul airliner, formalized by an agreement signed by French and German ministers. The British government decided not to participate, but Hawker Siddeley put private money in to maintain an interest and would eventually build the wings. Süd Aviation in France and Deutsche Airbus in Germany were soon joined by a Fokker-VFW team from the Netherlands and CASA from Spain. The multinational company eventually formed was called Airbus Industry.

1969 June 3 Boeing test pilot Don Knutson flew the 747 Jumbo Jet across the Atlantic for the first time in 9 hr. 8 min. to put in a spectacular appearance at the 28th Paris Air Show. The aircraft was flown from Seattle-Tacoma Airport in Washington state to LeBourget Airport, Paris. Fourth off the assembly line, the aircraft averaged 570 MPH but at times reached a top speed of 656 MPH.

1969 June 5 The Tupolev Tu-144 supersonic airliner became the first aircraft of its class to fly through the sound barrier when it exceeded Mach 1 at a height of 36,000 ft. It achieved supersonic speed about 30 min. after takeoff following a full systems check. The Soviet news agency Izvestia incorrectly claimed this was the first supersonic flight by a commercial airliner, seemingly unaware that a DC-8 had gone through Mach 1 on August 2, 1961.

1969 June 30 An improved version of Sikorsky's big Skycrane cargo lifter made its first flight. Designated CH-54B, it had two 4,800-SHP Pratt & Whitney JFTD12A-5A turboshaft engines, increased maximum loaded weight of 64,700 lb., increased fuselage length of 80 ft. 7 in. and a 4,000-lb. increase in payload lifting capacity. It also featured twin main wheels either side of the space usually occupied by the cargo pallet and new gearbox. A civil version was designated the CH-54E, and Rowan Air Cranes used it for oil operations.

1969 July 2 In renewed air fighting, Israeli Air Force fighters shot down four Egyptian MiG-21 fighters penetrating Israeli air space. Since the ceasefire following Israel's preemptive strike during the 1967 Six-Day War, sustained harrassment from Egypt and Syria kept a constant tension in the Middle East. On July 8, seven Syrian MiG-21s were claimed by Israel, and on September 9 the Israeli Army received air support in a major attack on the Egyptian training camp at Ras Abu-Daraj.

1969 July 14 U.S. Navy Squadron VA-122 became the first unit to operate the LTV A-7E Corsair II incorporating a head-up display (HUD) in the cockpit. Projecting essential flight and navigation information on the forward windshield, it helped pilots maintain visual contact with the view forward. Head-up displays would become an essential component of cockpit aids for all modern combat aircraft.

1969 July 15 U.S. defense secretary Melvin R. Laird ordered a reduction in Arc Light bombing raids against targets in North Vietnam. Sortie rates would be cut from a monthly peak of 1,800 to 1,600. During early October, this would be reduced again to 1,400 per month as the United States continued to reduce the level of its forces participating in the Vietnam War. By June 1, 1971, monthly sortie rates would be down to 1,000 when there were just 42 B-52s operating from the base at U-Tapao in Thailand.

1969 August 1 The first Lockheed S-3A Viking carrier-based search and strike antisubmarine aircraft made its first flight. Having won the U.S. Navy VSX competition issued in 1967, Lockheed built the high-wing S-3A to fly with two 9,275-lb. s.t. General Electric TF34-GE02 turbofan engines. It had a wingspan of 68 ft. 8 in., a length of 53 ft. 4 in. and a gross weight of 52,539 lb. With internal provision for four MK-46 torpedoes or mines or depth charges, it had a cruising speed of 426 MPH and a search radius of 530 mi.

1969 August 6 The biggest helicopter ever built, the Soviet Mil V-12 secured an unbeaten world lifting record for rotary-winged aircraft by carrying 40,205.5 kg (88,636 lb.) to a height of 2,255 m (7,400 ft.) with V. P. Koloshchyenko at the controls. First flown July 10, 1968, the V-12 was powerered by two pairs of 6,500-SHP D-25VF engines driving two five-bladed rotors on outriggers. With a span over the rotors of 219 ft. 10 in. and a length of 121 ft. 4 in., it could carry up to 120 people or a normal payload of 55,115 lb.

1969 August 8 Just over 60 yr. after the formation of one of the world's oldest and most venerable aircraft manufacturing companies, Handley Page Ltd. went into voluntary liquidation, and Barclays Bank appointed a receiver. The company had been penalized by the British government when it declined to merge with either BAC or Hawker Siddeley after the death of Sir Frederick Handley Page in 1962, and it was unable to rely on government money. Despite efforts to save it, the company was finally closed on June 1, 1970.

1969 August 16 Flying an ex-U.S. Navy Grumman F8F-2 Bearcat (registration no. G-58B), U.S. record-breaker Darryl Greenamyer set a new world air speed record for piston-engined aircraft when he averaged 776.449 km/hr. (482.485 MPH) over a 3-km (1.86-mi.) course. Set on April 26, 1939, the previous record had remained unbroken for more than 30 yr. It would be another 10 yr. before Greenamyer's record was broken. Records were now getting close to the theoretical maximum achievable with a piston engine driving a propeller.

1969 August 20 Developed as a counter-insurgency aircraft powered by two 1,022-ESHP Turboméca Astazou XVIG turbo-props, the Argentinian FMA IA 58 Pucara made its first flight with interim engines. With a wingspan of 47 ft. 7 in., a length of 45 ft. 7 in. and a maximum weight of 13,668 lb., it had a horizontal tailplane mounted high on the fin above the rudder and could carry a variety of weapons as well as two 20-mm Hispano cannons and four 7.62-mm FN machine guns.

1969 September 5 The Rolls Royce RB.199 engine was selected for the European multi-role combat aircraft project against competition from Pratt & Whitney and General Electric in the United States. A Rolls Royce-led European engine group was selected to carry out detailed design and development. The Avro Vulcan would be used as a flying test bed for the new engine. Set up in October, Turbo-Union was 40% owned by Rolls Royce, 40% by the German engine-makers Motoren-und-Turbinen-Union München G.m.b.H. and 20% by Fiat in Italy.

1969 September 15 First of a new Cessna family of turbofan-powered executive jets, the Model 500 Citation, powered by two 2,500-lb. s.t. Pratt & Whitney (Canada) JT15D-4 engines, made its first flight. With a wingspan of 51 ft. 8 in. and a length of 47 ft. 2 in., it would carry 6 to 10 passengers at 443 MPH for almost 2,000 mi. During the prototype assembly period and shortly after, the company carried out several design changes, and not for two years was the aircraft available to customers.

1969 September 25 The first operational General Dynamics FB-111A was delivered to the 340th Bombardment Group, USAF, at Carswell AFB, Tex. This was the first new bomber for Strategic Air Command since the B-58A had been delivered on August 1, 1960. On October 8, the Strategic Air Command commander-in-chief, Gen. Bruce K. Holloway, officially received the aircraft (serial no. 67-7193) from Maj. Gen. Lee V. Gossick, commander of the USAF Systems Command's Aeronautical Systems Division. After two more had been delivered, all F/FB-111s were grounded, following the December 22 crash of an F-111A at Nellis AFB, Nev.

1969 September In an attempt to interest the Argentinian Navy in the V/STOL Hawker Siddeley Harrier, a demonstration aircraft was used in deck trials aboard the carrier *Veinticinco de Mayo*, a 19,896-ton vessel in the Colossus class bought from the British in 1948. The Argentinians declined but had they accepted there would most probably have been the first air-to-air combat between V/STOL aircraft when Britain went to retake the Falkland Islands in 1982.

1969 October 1 The first Hawker Siddeley Buccaneer multi-role, two-seat, strike and reconnaissance aircraft for the RAF was delivered to No. 12 Squadron at RAF Honington. Powered by two 11,100-lb. s.t. Rolls Royce RB.168 Spey Mk.101 turbofans, it had a maximum speed of Mach 0.85 (645 MPH) at 250 ft. and a tactical radius of more than 500 mi. on a "hi-lo-hi" mission. It had been selected for the RAF following cancellation of the F-111K and the Anglo-French variable geometry fighter project to serve until the Tornado became available.

1969 October 1 Süd Aviation test pilot Andre Turcat piloted the Anglo-French Concorde prototype 001 through the sound barrier for the first time. He achieved a speed of Mach 1.05 (693 MPH) after taking off from the Toulouse-Blagnac airport. The aircraft was flown to a height of 36,000 ft. for the first supersonic run with only the two outer engines at full power. The inner engines were at less than maximum thrust. The Concorde 001 exceeded 1,000 MPH for the first time on December 13 on a 2 hr. 10 min. flight, during which it was supersonic for 57 min.

1969 October 31 In the world's longest airliner hijacking flight, U.S. Marine Lance Cpl. Raphael Minichiello of Seattle, Wash. ordered the pilot, Capt. Donald Cook, to fly to Denver and then on to Kennedy International Airport, N.Y. From there he demanded to be flown overseas, and the aircraft took off for Rome, completing a 6,900-mi. diversion from its original flight plan. The Marine was captured and indicted for piracy and hijacking; he spent his jail sentence in Rome's Queen of Heaven jail.

1969 November 3 The USAF issued a call for proposals to meet the requirements of its advanced manned strategic aircraft (AMSA), which it wanted as a high-subsonic, low-altitude penetration aircraft and a supersonic, high-altitude stand-off bomber. A large internal weapons bay was an important feature of the specification, as were defensive and offensive avionics. Competing bidders included airframe manufacturers North American, General Dynamics and Boeing and engine-makers General Electric and Pratt & Whitney.

1969 November 24 NASA's supercritical wing was flight-tested on a North American Rockwell T-2 Buckeye for the first time from the manufacturer's plant at Columbus, Ohio. So named because they were carefully designed so that the air flow across the wing would have a (''supercritical'') Mach number as close as possible to the speed of sound, the concept came from Richard T. Whitcomb of the Langley Research Center. He had earlier devised the ''area-rule'' concept for supersonic aircraft and would conceive wingtip ''winglets.''

1969 December 11 The Hawker Siddeley Trident 3B prototype (G-AWYZ) flew for the first time with three 11,930-lb. s.t. Rolls Royce RB.163-25 Mk.512-5W Spey turbofans. Designed to accommodate a fourth powerplant in the tail, the 5,250-lb. s.t. Rolls Royce RB.162-86 turbojet, it made the first flight with all four engines installed on March 22, 1970. Designed as a high-capacity, short-range version of the earlier Trident model, it could carry up to 152 passengers at 533 MPH for 1,094 mi. It had a wingspan of 98 ft. and a length of 131 ft. 2 in. When production ended in 1975, 117 had been sold.

1969 December 23 U.S. defense secretary Melvin R. Laird announced McDonnell Douglas the winner of the F-X air superiority fighter competition for a single-seat combat plane to be designated F-15. The USAF wanted 749 aircraft for three Tactical Air Command wings, two USAF Europe (USAFE) wings and one Pacific Air Force (U.S.) (PACAF) wing. The initial contract was for 20 aircraft, 18 single-seat F-15As and two TF-15As later redesignated F15B. The USAF selected the Pratt & Whitney F100-PW-100 engine for the F-15.

1969 Intelligence sources became aware of the imminent flight trials of a new Soviet swing-wing medium bomber later known as the Tupolev Tu-26 Backfire. Backfire-A was also designated Tu-22M and appeared in limited numbers. It was followed by the Backfire-B and the advanced production version Backfire-C, in service from 1985. This had a wingspan of 112 ft. 6 in./76 ft. 9 in., a length of 130 ft. and power provided by two 35,000/50,000-lb. s.t. Kuznetsov turbofans. With a maximum takeoff weight of 285,000 lb. and a maximum bomb load of 26,460 lb., the Tu-26 had a maximum dash speed of Mach 2 (1,320 MPH) at 39,370 ft. and a combat radius of up to 2,160 mi.

1969 All registered U.S. airlines moved a total 159 million passengers during the year, compared to less than 17 million exactly 20 yr. earlier. In 1969 airlines accounted for 75% of the common carrier passenger-miles between U.S. cities. In 1969, 18.3 million passengers traveled by air between the United States and other countries (compared with 2.2 million in 1949), and U.S. scheduled airlines carried 3.2 billion ton-miles of freight.

1970 January 1 The French government formed the Société Nationale Industrielle Aérospatiale (SNIA) following the merger of Sud-Aviation, Nord-Aviation and a group of companies in the SEREB group. The SNIA was currently the largest aerospace company in Europe, with 105.38 million sq. ft. of facilities and 37,000 employees. Products included satellites, spacecraft and missiles as well as the traditional areas of fixed-wing and rotary-winged aircraft.

1970 January 4 A Britten-Norman Islander (G-AXUD) flown by Capts. W. J. Bright and F. I. Buxton won the British Petroleum England-Australia air race, held in commemoration of the flight 50 yr. earlier by Keith and Ross Smith. The time, handicapped by 88 hr. 10 min., was 80 hr. 20 min. There were 77 entries in three classes, restricted to piston-engined or turboprop-powered aircraft up to a maximum all-up weight of 12,500 lb. Second came a Cessna 310 flown by J. A. Masling and G. Williams in 68 hr. 2 min. but handicapped by 20 hr. 8 min. to generate a "race" time of 88 hr. 10 min.

1970 January 13 A Pan American World Airways Boeing 747 landed at Heathrow Airport, London from John F. Kennedy International Airport, N.Y. on a proving flight prior to the inaugural revenue service scheduled to begin later in the month. The aircraft carried 361 passengers, mostly Pan American staff, and became the first aircraft to cross the Atlantic with more than 300 people on board. The flight time was 6 hr. 30 min.

1970 January 16 The last two B-58A Hustlers were withdrawn from USAF Strategic Air Command and flown to Davis-Monthan AFB, Ariz. They had been serving with the 305th Bombardment Wing, Grissom AFB, Ind., and at Davis-Monthan, they joined 82 other B-58As that had been located there since retirements began on Nov. 3, 1969. At peak in 1964, Strategic Air Command had 94 B-58s in service. By the end of this year, Strategic Air Command had accepted 46 out of a maximum 72 FB-111As it would have on strength by 1974, numbers declining gradually thereafter.

1970 January 22 The first revenue-earning Boeing 747 flight between New York and London touched down at Heathrow when a trouble-plagued Jumbo Jet arrived from John F. Kennedy International Airport. Originally scheduled to depart late evening the previous day, an overheated engine kept it grounded until 1:52 A.M. TWA began operations with the Boeing 747 on its New York-Los Angeles route February 25, with a Pan American aircraft leased to American beginning their continental service March 2. Continental started Chicago-Los Angeles-Honolulu service June 26, and Northwest began using the Jumbo Jet on the Chicago-Seattle-Tokyo service starting July 1.

1970 February 15 The USAF issued a request for proposals on a lightweight, inexpensive fighter that could fill needs in small air forces facing a threat from Soviet-built MiG-21s. The initial contenders were a stripped F-4 Phantom concept, a modified F-104 Starfighter known as the CL-2000 and a supersonic derivative of the Northrop F-5. LTV was also proposing a lightweight version of the F-8 Crusader.

1970 February 16 No. 1 Squadron, RAF, became the first unit to operate the Hawker Siddeley Harrier G.R.Mk.1 on overseas deployment when the squadron moved to Akrotiri, Cyprus. No. 1 Squadron had been at Wittering since July 18, 1969, when it had become the first operational squadron to be fully equipped with V/STOL aircraft. Oldest of the RFC/RAF squadrons, No. 1 had been disbanded in June 1958 but re-formed a month later by renumbering the former No. 263 Squadron, RAF.

1970 February 19 The first of two Canadair CL-84 tilt-wing V/STOL aircraft (serial no. CX8401) developed for a military evaluation program for the Canadian armed forces made its first flight. Designated CL-84-1, it had Lycoming T53 turboprop engines leading to proposals for a CL-84-1C production version and a 16-passenger CL-84-1D powered by 1,900-SHP T53-19A engines. Proposed growth versions could have carried up to 70 passengers, but the market never materialized for this highly promising aircraft.

1970 February 24 Britain's only fixed-wing aircraft carrier, HMS *Ark Royal*, was given a new lease of life and recommissioned for service on this day. Incorporating an 8.5° angled flight deck and powerful steam catapults, the £30-million, three-year re-fit equipped her for service with the Buccaneer and the Phantom; she also continued to operate the Gannet airborne-early-warning aircraft. Despite this effort, the *Ark Royal* had only 10 yr. to live before it was replaced by "commando" carriers equipped with Harrier V/STOL.

1970 March 19 The first powered flight of the Martin X-24A lifting-body research vehicle was made with test pilot Jerauld Gentry in the tiny cockpit. The aircraft was carried aloft by a B-52 carrier-plane and released for a rocket-boosted flight to Mach 0.865 (571 MPH) and a height of 44,384 ft. The X-24A went supersonic for the first time on October 14, achieving its fastest speed (Mach 1.6/1,036 MPH) on March 29, 1971. The X-24A made its last of 28 free flights on June 4, 1971.

1970 March 22 The first Hawker Siddeley Trident 3B made its first flight powered by three 11,960-lb. s.t. Rolls Royce Spey RB.163-25 Mk 512-5W turbofans and a 5,250-lb. s.t. Rolls Royce RB.162 turbojet mounted at the top of the rear fuselage below the rudder. The first Trident 3B had flown with just the three Speys on December 11, 1969. The aircraft had capacity for 128 to 171 passengers, a cruising speed of up to 601 MPH for a maximum range of 1,658 mi. Unlike earlier Tridents, it enjoyed modest success, 117 being built by the time production ended in 1975.

1970 March 28 The first North Vietnamese MiG-21 shot down since the cessation of Rolling Thunder bombing activity on North Vietnam on October 31, 1968, was claimed by Lt. Jerome E. Beaulier and Lt. (jg) Stephen J. Barkley flying an F-4 from VF-142 off the aircraft carrier USS *Constellation* (CVA-64). The Phantom had been on routine escort duty accompanying an unarmed U.S. Navy reconnaissance aircraft near Thanh Hoa, North Vietnam, when it was attacked by the communist fighter.

1970 April 10 Adding to the sales potential of one of McDonnell Douglas's most successful aircraft, the latest A-4M Skyhawk made its first flight. With a loaded weight of 24,000 lb. and a warload of 8,200 lb., the A-4M had a ribbon drag-chute allowing the aircraft to operate out of 4,000 ft. runways, enlarged and improved cockpit canopy, additional ammunition for the 20-mm cannon and self-contained engine starter. To date, 2,400 Skyhawks had been delivered.

1970 April 13 Following substantive negotiations between the respective governments of the United Kingdom and the USSR, dignitaries representing their respective foreign services signed an agreement permitting BOAC to make commercial overflights of Siberia on its scheduled London-Tokyo service. The USSR had a substantial number of intercontinental ballistic missile fields along the trans-Siberian railway, but use of this route cut a major portion of the flight and reduced travel times.

1970 April 16 In a Notice of Proposed Rulemaking, the U.S. Department of Transportation announced its intent to press forward with a ban on all supersonic flights by civil aircraft over the United States, except for those manufacturers who could demonstrate that a particular Mach number would not induce a sonic boom that reached the ground. There would, however, be flight test areas reserved for experimental work on research aircraft. It had been generally believed that a ban would only be imposed on flights across dense urban areas. Opponents had until June 15 to reply.

1970 April In Bersatu Padu, a major military airlift operation in Malaysia, RAF Air Support Command carried out the largest operation conducted by it or its predecessor, RAF Transport Command. In 4,358 flying hr., RAF aircraft lifted 2,265 passengers, 1,503,920 lb. of freight, 350 vehicles and 20 helicopters. The exercise involved air forces from five countries.

1970 May 7 The USAF issued requests for proposals on the A-X attack aircraft and asked 12 companies to bid. Only six responded to a specification defining an antiarmor support aircraft for ground forces with survival a priority in a high-threat air-defense environment. Boeing, Fairchild Hiller Republic, Cessna, General Dynamics, Lockheed and Northrop put in bids by the deadline of August 10. Only Boeing departed from twin turbofans by proposing a turboprop-powered design.

1970 May 13 The British Aircraft Corp. announced a multi-million-pound order for the supply of refurbished Canberra bombers recently retired from the RAF to Argentina. They were to be used in the Argentinian Air Force as bombers and low-altitude strike aircraft. They would still be in service 20 yr. later.

1970 May 15 The FAA ordered an increase in separation between a Boeing 747 and smaller aircraft on landing and takeoff from 4.8 km (2.98 mi.) to 8 km (4.97 mi.) in trailing distance and 300 m (984 ft.) in height following wake turbulence tests involving a C-5A and an F-104. Considerable disturbance in the air around and behind the Jumbo Jet increased the danger of an accident to following aircraft. An interim order requiring separation distances of 16 km (9.94 mi.) and 600 metres (1,969 ft.) was revoked.

1970 May 21 The 18,340-ton amphibious assault ship USS *Guam* withdrew from the coastal region of Peru following an extended mercy mission during which it had flown in more than 200 tons of relief supplies and transported 1,000 evacuees and medical patients on 800 flights. The *Guam* had been supporting a wide-scale rescue operation following a massive earthquake that killed 50,000 people and made almost 1 million homeless. Prior to leaving, the Peruvian government hosted the crew in Lima.

1970 June 1 The first production Lockheed C-5A Galaxy heavy-lift transport aircraft was delivered to Military Airlift Command at Scott AFB, Charleston, W. Va. Only the previous year an earlier plan to equip six squadrons had been changed, reducing the procurement level by one-third to four squadrons. By the end

of 1970, the USAF had placed orders for a total 81 C-5As, less than one-third the number originally projected when the USAF issued the CX-HLS specification.

1970 June 5 Following a request to bid on the USAF advanced manned strategic aircraft (AMSA) program, North American Rockwell was awarded a contract to design and build the supersonic B-1A bomber as the B-52 replacement for Strategic Air Command. Embracing five prototypes and two static-test airframes, the initial swing-wing B-1A contract was worth $1.35 billion. It was the first major Defense Department program since introduction in 1969 of a ''flybeforebuy'' process in which prototypes would be flown first before production contracts would be issued. On February 11, 1971, two prototypes were dropped from the work package.

1970 June 9 A U.S. Marine Corps Sikorsky CH-53A helicopter set a new record for inter-city travel when it flew between the Wall St., New York City heliport and Washington Hospital Center, Washington, D.C. in 1 hr. 17 min. 11 sec. from wheels-off to wheels-on. This powerful helicoper had a maximum speed of 196 MPH at sea level on the power of its two 3,925-ESHP General Electric turboshaft engines. The flight had been arranged between Sikorsky and Pan American World Airways to demonstrate the efficient use of helicopter inter-city flights.

1970 June 17 In the wake of continuing problems with the JT9D-3 engines for the Boeing 747, a spokesman for Pratt & Whitney said that problems with the blade-retaining mechanism in the big turbofans had caused technical difficulties. A large number of postponements and delays had angered passengers, causing concern among the operators that the new generation of large-capacity, wide-body jets would be spurned by passengers.

1970 June 23 The Australian Minister of Defense announced a decision by his government to lease 24 McDonnell Douglas F-4E Phantoms pending resolution of technical difficulties that delayed acceptance of 24 General Dynamics F-111Cs by the Royal Australian Air Force. The variable-geometry strike fighters had been built, but continuing engineering difficulties with USAF aircraft of this type prevented the Australians from accepting their variant.

1970 July 2 The tandem two-seat SAAB Sk 37 trainer version of the SAAB-37 Viggen made its first flight. A rear cockpit took the place of the forward fuel tank and some electronics equipment with bulged canopy, twin periscopes and a taller fin with increased surface area. The first poduction aircraft was delivered to the Swedish Air Force conversion unit F15 at Söderhamn.

1970 July 17 The HL-10 lifting-body research vehicle made its last flight, the second of two performed since installation of three 500-lb. thrust Bell Aerosystems hydrogen peroxide engines in place of the XLR-11 four-chamber rocket motor. Configured to evaluate handling characteristics of a lifting-body assisted by terminal propulsion in the landing phase, the two flights demonstrated increased pilot work load and control problems due to the higher approach speed.

1970 July 18 The first of two prototype Aeritalia G.222 general purpose military transport aircraft made its first flight. Originally designed to a NATO requirement dating to 1962, it was first proposed in four separate configurations, but only one was actually developed. Powered by two 2,970-SHP General Electric CT64-820 turboprops, it had a wingspan of 94 ft. 6 in., a length of 74 ft. 5 in. and a maximum takeoff weight of 57,320 lb. The Italian Air Force ordered 44.

1970 July 22   The German, British and Italian governments announced their satisfaction with the definition stage of the Panavia Tornado program and initiated full-scale development by signing a memorandum of understanding. Another review in March 1973 passed the aircraft for the production investment phase. Definitive allocation of participation levels were: Britain 42.5%, West Germany 42.5% and Italy 15%.

1970 July 23   Boeing was awarded a definitive contract to develop and integrate the airborne warning and control system (AWACS) based on the Boeing 707-320B airframe. Two prototypes designated EC-137D were to be built for comparative tests using separate look-down radars designed by Hughes Aircraft and Westinghouse Electric. Following these tests, the Westinghouse radar was selected on October 5, 1972, and on January 26, 1973, the USAF gave its approval for full scale development of the E-3A, later named Sentry.

1970 August 10   In further extension of agreements previously reached between the United States and the USSR, respective government agencies agreed to permit Pan American and Aeroflot to operate reciprocal service to Leningrad and Washington, D.C. Agreement was also reached to increase the number of flights between the two countries from two per week to six per week. The United States had refused a Soviet request for commercial overflights of respective continental land masses.

1970 August 20   The prototype of a private venture two-seat attack helicopter from Sikorsky made its first flight, designated S-67 Blackhawk. Developed from the S-66 originally submitted unsuccessfully to the U.S. Army for its advanced aerial fire support system (AAFSS) requirement, the S-67 was powered by two 1,530-SHP General Electric T58/T51A1A turboshaft engines driving a 62-ft. diameter rotor. It had a length of 64 ft. 9 in. and a maximum weight of 28,000 lb. With a top speed of 218 MPH and a 12,997-lb. warload, it carried a powerful 30-mm multibarrel cannon.

1970 August 22   The prototype Aermacchi M.B.326K single-seat operational trainer and light ground attack aircraft made its first flight, powered by a 4,000-lb. s.t. Rolls Royce Viper Mk.632-43 turbojet. With a wingspan over tip tanks of 35 ft. 7 in. and a length of 35 ft., it had a maximum permitted speed of 576 MPH and a combat radius of 167 mi. carrying 2,822 lb. of external weapons. This was the latest development in a progressive series of M.B.326s from Aermacchi, a company stimulated by Lockheed investment since 1959.

1970 August 24   Two USAF Sikorsky HH-53C helicopters completed a nonstop trans-Pacific crossing from Eglin AFB, Fla. to Da Nang, South Vietnam, aided by refueling encounters with Lockheed C-130 tankers. The crossing logged 9,000 mi. but was delayed when the helicopters were grounded for 48 hr. in Alaska due to bad weather. The longest nonstop leg was the 1,677-mi. flight from Shemya Island in the Aleutians to Misawa AB in Japan.

1970 August 29   The prototype Douglas DC-10 made its first flight, the first new large-capacity, wide-body turbofan airliner to fly after the Boeing 747. The domestic market for the DC-10 had been diluted by the impending arrival of the Lockheed L-1011 TriStar. The first production series had a typical capacity for 225 to 270 passengers, a length of 181 ft. 5 in., a wingspan of 155

ft. 4 in. (increased later to 165 ft. 4 in.) and a maximum takeoff weight of 430,000 lb. It was usually powered by three 40,000-lb. s.t. General Electric CF6-6D turbofans, but other engines were available.

1970 September 11   The first Britten-Norman BN-2A Trislander made its first flight as a derivative of the Islander but with three 260-HP Lycoming O-540-E4C5 6-cylinder piston engines, the third engine being mounted high in the vertical tail driving a tractor propeller. With a wingspan of 53 ft. and a length of 43 ft. 9 in., the Trislander had a cruising speed of 180 MPH and a maximum payload (4,300 lb.) range of 160 mi. or 700 mi. with a 2,400-lb. load. Capable of accommodating up to 17 passengers, it proved a popular transport and feeder-line aircraft.

1970 September 12   The first two of 72 USAF Tactical Air Command General Dynamics F-111E fighter-bombers arrived at RAF Upper Heyford, England. The aircraft had advanced engine inlet systems and new penetration aids as well as sophisticated weapons management systems for a variety of nuclear and nonnuclear stores. The forward basing of Tactical Air Command F-111Es was considered an important part of combat readiness for missions that would carry these aircraft deep into hostile territory across mainland Europe.

1970 October 2   The USAF took delivery of its first Bell Model 212 helicopter. Designated UH-1N, it was powered by two 1,290-SHP Pratt & Whitney Canada PT6T-3 Turbo Twin Pac engines driving a 48-ft. 2-in. rotor. Developed to accommodate a Canadian armed forces order for 50, the U.S. military ordered 141. With capacity for up to 14 passengers, the UH-1N had a length of 42 ft. 5 in. and a range of 261 mi. It was eventually sold to China also, the first U.S. helicopter exported to that country.

1970 October 18   The first Lockheed C-5A Galaxy transport aircraft was destroyed in a catastrophic fire that caused the death of one maintenance man and injuries to another. Suspecting a fuel leak, the mechanics were preparing to drain fuel from the tanks when a series of explosions occurred, causing a succession of fires throughout the aircraft. The accident happened at the Lockheed plant at Marietta, Ga.

1970 October 20   A hypersonic ramjet engine being developed by NASA was tested in the 8-ft. high temperature structures tunnel at the Langley Research Center, Va. A simulated speed of Mach 7.4 was reached at a temperature of 2,000°F in trials aimed at determining optimum use of different materials in such an engine. NASA was carrying out research on propulsion systems for hypersonic vehicles.

1970 October 28   The U.K. minister of supply, Frederick V. Corfield, announced in the House of Commons that the development cost of the Anglo-French Concorde supersonic airliner had risen once again to an estimated $1.98 billion. This was an increase over the most recent estimate of $1.7 billion, attributable, it was said, to minor technical changes and production needs. The government had made a commitment to the project in the wake of a succession of cancellations applied to British aircraft projects over the last several years.

1970 October 29   The "Early Birds of Aviation" held an annual convention in Washington, D.C., comprising U.S. pilots who had flown solo before December 17, 1916. Among the attendees was "Tiny" Broadwick, who had parachuted from an airplane in 1913, Walter Waterman, who built his own glider in 1909 from plans published in *Popular Mechanics*, and Roy Waite,

Aircraft have long been used for advertising, a role epitomized here by the Pitts S2S aerobatic plane operated by the Rothmans tobacco company.

who in 1912 dropped 20 flour bombs on two battleships in Boston harbor.

1970 November 4 The French Concorde test pilot Andre Turcat flew the prototype 001 through Mach 2 for the first time. The event took place during a 90-min. flight, the 102d test flight from Toulouse-Blagnac, France. The Soviet supersonic transport, the Tupolev Tu-144, had reportedly reached a top speed of 2,150 km/hr. (1,336 MPH) during a test flight on May 26. When the Concorde made its first flight on March 2, 1969, it had a projected operational cruising speed of Mach 2.2 (1,450 MPH), but subsequent flight trials established an optimum cruising speed of Mach 2.04 (1,354 MPH) at 51,300 ft.

1970 November 16 The first Lockheed L-1011-1 TriStar made its first flight less than 3 mo. after its rival on the U.S. domestic market, the DC-10. Production aircraft were powered by the 42,000-lb. s.t. Rolls Royce RB.211, which provided a cruising speed of 540 MPH for a typical mix of 256 passengers a distance of up to 2,878 mi., about 1,200 mi. less than the DC-10. The TriStar had a wingspan of 155 ft. 4 in., a length of 178 ft. 8 in. and a maximum takeoff weight of 430,000 lb.

1970 November 16 The first Hawker Siddeley AV-8A Harrier destined for the U.S. Marine Corps was formally handed over in the United Kingdom to its new customer. The designation implied it to be an attack aircraft in the V/STOL category. Early models for the USMC had the 20,000-lb. s.t. Rolls Royce Pegasus 102, but later models had the 21,500-lb. s.t. Pegasus F402-RR-401. The AV-8A had a warload of 5,300 lb., and the first of three Harrier squadrons started working up in April 1971.

1970 December 3 Serious antisupersonic transport lobbying dealt a serious blow to the future of the Boeing 2707 when the U.S. Senate voted 52-41 in favor of canceling all government funds for the project. For the first time, pro-SST activists were forced to defend their program, and Pres. Richard M. Nixon came out strongly in favor of the supersonic transport on December 5. Vigorous lobbying and support from the House of Representatives deferred a final decision and retained funding through March 31, 1971.

1970 December 18 The USAF ordered four prototypes of two competing designs for its A-X ground attack aircraft program. Northrop received a $28.9 million contract for two YA-9 aircraft, and Fairchild Republic was awarded $41.2 million for two YA-10s. Dissatisfaction with the "buy from the drawing board" approach used by then-Defense Secretary Robert McNamara in procuring the USAF/USN F-111 resulted in an A-X fly-off decision to compare contenders in the air.

1970 December 21 The first Grumman F-14A Tomcat variable geometry U.S. fleet defense fighter was flown for the first time at Calverton, N.Y. by Robert Smyth and William Miller. The aircraft had a swept span of 38 ft. 2 in., an extended span of 64 ft. 1 in., a maximum takeoff weight of 74,349 lb. and power provided by two 20,600-lb. s.t. Pratt & Whitney TF30-P-412 turbofans. The F-14A had a maximum speed of Mach 2.34 at 40,000 ft. or Mach 1.2 at sea level.

1970 December 30 The first Grumman F-14A crashed at Calverton on its second flight, and the crew, William Miller and Robert Smyth, ejected safely but only just; Miller got out only 0.4 sec. before impact. Examination of the wreckage revealed total hydraulic failure due to a comparatively simple problem that did nothing to challenge the aircraft's basically sound design.

1971 January 14 The first McDonnell Douglas F-4EJ Phantom II destined for Japan made its first flight from the manufacturer's plant at St. Louis, Mo. Selected by Japan on November 1, 1968, as the replacement aircraft for its aging fighter force, Japan was to receive two aircraft built in the United States, assemble 11 in Japan and license-build 126. Fourteen RF-4EJ reconnaissance versions were also ordered to replace the North American RF-86Fs.

1971 January 20 The first development aircraft for an improved U.S. Navy early warning capability made its flight as the Grumman YE-2C, ordered in April 1968 to provide needed improvements essential to effective use of new fleet defense fighters like the F-14A Tomcat. Essentially identical in aerodynamic configuration to the E-2A but with improved engines, the E-2Cs joined the navy on operations in November 1973. Capable of tracking large aircraft at 290 mi., small aircraft at 230 mi. and cruise missiles at 115 mi., the E-2C has exhibited an impressive performance.

1971 January 22 A U.S. Navy Lockheed P-3C Orion set a new world record for heavy turboprop-powered aircraft on long-distance flights by flying 6,857 mi. over the great circle route from Atsugi NAS, Japan to Patuxent River NAS, Md. Piloted by Comdr. Donald H. Lilienthal and an eight-man crew, the aircraft actually flew 7,010 mi. to avoid the Soviet-occupied island of Sakhalin, but the lower figure was the FAI-accepted distance, which took 15 hr. 21 min.

1971 January 28 The last defoliation mission carried out by U.S. Special Air Services in Vietnam was flown by UC-123B sprayers operating with the 310th Tactical Air Squadron. In all, 50,000 tons of Agent Orange, a mixture of chemical poisons capable of clearing wide areas of vegetation, had been sprayed across 6.2 million acres of land under the code Ranch Hand. USAF operators fell victim to dioxin poisoning as did many Vietnamese on the ground. Defoliated areas are estimated to remain barren for approximately 100 yr.

1971 January U.S. Navy attack aircraft operating off the USS *Hancock*, the USS *Ranger* and the USS *Kitty Hawk* flew 3,214 sorties against supply and logistics targets in Vietnam in attempts to halt the consolidation of munitions in the south. Almost 1,000 trucks per day were observed moving in daylight and Grumman A-6 and LTV A-7 attack aircraft proved particularly effective against these targets.

1971 February Operating from two U.S. Navy aircraft carriers stationed close to Vietnam, attack planes increased their sortie rate to an average of 122 per day. Whereas Grumman A-6 aircraft had been used exclusively for strikes against Viet Cong and North Vietnamese supply routes, this work was extended to night strikes with LTV A-7 attack planes. A 40% increase since January in truck movements south necessitated the additional sorties.

1971 March 9 The NASA supercritical wing devised by Langley Research Center's Richard T. Whitcomb was flown for the first time on a modified F-8A Crusader. Previously a T-2 Buckeye had been used to test-fly a portion of a supercritical wing. Because the variable wing incidence on the standard F-8A was not acceptable with the supercritical wing, the much higher landing speed required use of the dry lakebed at Edwards AFB, Calif.

1971 March 16 Adapted from the Kaman H-2 Seasprite rescue and utility helicopter, the SH-2D made its first flight. Developed to meet the interim needs of a U.S. Navy light airborne multipurpose system (LAMPS) requirement, the new version of the H-2 had a high-power search radar under the nose and appropriate antisubmarine warfare equipment. Production helicopters were powered by two 1,350-SHP General Electric T58-GE-8F engines driving a 44-ft. rotor. With a maximum overload weight of 13,300 lb., the SH-2F had a cruising speed of 150 MPH and a range of 445 mi.

1971 March 21 The prototype Westland Lynx made its first flight after 3 yr. of development as one of three cooperative ventures between the British helicopter company and Süd Aviation. Powered by two 900-SHP Rolls Royce BS.360-07-26 engines driving a 42-ft. diameter rotor, the Lynx had a length of 38 ft. 3 in. and a maximum takeoff weight of 8,000 lb. Ordered by the British and the French armed services, this multi-purpose transport helicopter sold well at home and abroad.

1971 March 24 As a result of votes in the U.S. Senate and House of Representatives to cancel the Boeing supersonic transport, Boeing's vice president for industrial relations said that cancellation of the project would require the company to lay off about 7,000 workers. Of that total, 4,500 people working directly on production would be dismissed within 7 wk. The elaborate, full-size mock-up was eventually sold to a promotion specialist who put it in a Florida amusement park.

1971 March 25 Developed to meet a military requirement for an Antonov An-12 replacement, the Ilyushin IL-76 made its first flight prior to appearing at the 29th Paris Air Show at the end of May. Powered by four 26,455.lb. s.t. Soloviev D-30KP turbofan engines, the IL-76 had a wingspan of 165 ft. 8 in., a length of 152 ft. 10 in. and a maximum takeoff weight of 374,785 lb. carrying a maximum payload of 88,185 lb. With a maximum payload range of 3,107 mi., it bore a remarkable resemblance to the Lockheed C-141 but was larger.

1971 March During the month, U.S. Navy strike sorties against logistical supply routes from North Vietnam and Laos down into the south increased significantly as the communists sought to use a lull during peace talks to resupply their forces. The navy flew a total 4,535 sorties during the month compared with 3,461 in

February. In April, the sortie rate would fall back to 3,648, but 15 of these were bombing missions into North Vietnam.

1971 April 1 The U.S. Navy's first helicopter squadron dedicated exclusively to mine countermeasures work, HM-12, was commissioned at Norfolk NAS, Va. Employing 15 Sikorsky CH-53A Sea Stallions on loan from the U.S. Marines towing magnetic and acoustic mine activators, the unit eventually received the Sikorsky RH-53D specially built to carry out these duties. With a fuel tank in each sponson and a flight refueling probe, maximum weight was increased to 50,000 lb. and two 0.50-in. machine guns provided for detonating stubborn mines.

1971 April 16 The U.S. Navy became the second military force to operate the world's sole V/STOL strike fighter when VMA-513 received the first of three Hawker Siddeley AV-8A Harrier aircraft at its base at Beaufort Marine Corps Air Station, S.C. The marines had received the first aircraft in England the previous year following which a special ceremony had been held at the U.S. Naval Air Test Center, Patuxent River, Md. Combat evaluation tests continued with earlier tests on ex-RAF Kestrels, designated AV-6A.

1971 April 26 An SR-71 of the Ninth Strategic Reconnaissance Wing, Beale AFB, Calif., made a record-breaking 15,000-mi. flight from its base and back on a trial-simulated mission. During the flight, Lt. Col. Thomas B. Estes and Maj. Dewain C. Vick flew the aircraft at speeds in excess of Mach 3 and at altitudes above 80,000 ft. for certain portions of the mission. There were also several in-flight refuelings with KC-135 tankers. The crew received the Mackay Trophy and the Harmon International Trophy for 1971.

1971 May 8 A further development of the Mirage G variable-geometry experimental fighter, the swing-wing, two-seat Mirage G8, made its first flight, powered by two 15,873-lb. s.t. SNECMA Atar 9K-50 turbojets. Wing sweep could be varied between 23° and 73° and with a maximum takeoff weight of 51,367 lb., the G8 had a top speed of Mach 2.5 at 41,000 ft. or Mach 1.3 (990 MPH) at sea level. The Mirage G was one of an evolving family of experimental swing-wing fighters, which also included a proposed naval version, none of which were deployed operationally.

1971 May 20 Despite last-ditch efforts to save it from cancellation, the U.S. House of Representatives decided to go along with a Senate vote removing all funds from the U.S. supersonic transport. This signaled an end to work on the two Boeing 2707 prototypes that had been on hold since March votes canceling all funds had been challenged by rescue bids in which the House temporarily reversed its judgment. Orchestrated largely by Sen. William Proxmire, the anti-SST lobby proved too strong for proponents of commercial supersonic transport.

1971 May 27 At the opening of the 29th Paris Air Show at Le Bourget, Paris, a gathering together of some of the most remarkable aircraft ever built emphasized the enormous progress made in less than 68 yr. of powered flight. Present were the world's first supersonic airliner to fly (Tupolev Tu-144), the two Anglo-French Concorde prototypes (001 and 002), the world's biggest helicopter (Mil Mi-12), the world's largest aircraft (Lockheed C-5A Galaxy), one of the latest large-capacity wide-body airliners (Lockheed L-1011) and more than 200 private aircraft. In addition, there was a piece of rock from the moon.

1971 May 28 Speaking at the 29th Paris Air Show, Soviet aviation minister Pavel Yu Dementeyev told a press conference that the supersonic Tupolev Tu-144 airliner had already flown at a speed of 1,527 MPH at 20,000 ft. and that it had completed several hundred flying hours. Tu-144 designer, Alexei N. Tupolev, also said that Pan American World Airways president Najeeb E. Halaby, former head of the FAA, had expressed interest in the airline acquiring some for its international services. The Tu-144 was also said to be scheduled to enter service with Aeroflot in late 1973, but it was not until November 1, 1977, that the aircraft began commercial passenger service.

1971 May 28 The first of two prototype Dassault-Breguet Mercure 100 series large-capacity, wide-body transport aircraft made its first flight. Designed to carry 132 passengers and maximum payload 466 mi. at 533 MPH, the Mercure had a wingspan of 100 ft. 3 in., a length of 114 ft. 4 in. and a maximum takeoff weight of 119,227 lb. It bore a remarkable resemblance to the Airbus Industrie A300, although it was only two-thirds the size of its more illustrious successor. Unfortunately, only one customer ordered 10 aircraft of what turned out to be an expensive, heavily government-subsidized project.

1971 June 1 British aviator Sheila Scott left London-Heathrow in a twin-engined Piper Aztec on a round-the-world flight covering a total distance of 34,000 mi. during which she claimed seven world records. Scott arrived back at London on August 5. During her flight, she participated in a unique experiment whereby selected physiological reactions had been measured and sent to a ground station in Fairbanks, Alaska, via the earth-orbiting Nimbus 4 weather satellite, and then to the NASA Goddard Space Flight Center in Greenbelt, Md.

1971 July 23 The prototype Project N2 made its first flight in Australia from the Government Aircraft Factory airfield at Avalon. Designed as a STOL transport, it had a military payload of 3,300 lb. and was to have been developed into several civil versions serving Australia's outback territory. The aircraft had ejection seats for the two-man crew, self-sealing fuel tanks and ordnance points externally. The interest by the Australian Army in buying this 14-seat transport caused serious friction with the air force, which resented intrusion by the army into aviation.

1971 July 29 The NASA Flight Research Center at Edwards AFB, Calif. announced that the Martin X-24A was to be rebuilt into a new configuration designated X-24B and returned to research activities for a new program of flights. The aircraft was to use the same XLR11 rocket motor but with increased thrust due to higher combustion chamber pressures. The shell of the X-24A was delivered to Martin Marietta on December 15, and the transformed aircraft arrived back at Edwards AFB on October 24, 1972.

1971 August 5 The inaugural revenue-paying service with the McDonnell Douglas DC-10 wide-body airliner was flown by American Airlines between Los Angeles and Chicago. This came just one week after American got its first DC-10 from the manufacturer. United Airlines had also received its first DC-10 on the same day and carried out its first revenue flight on August 16. American had planned to make its inaugural flight August 17 but moved it up 12 days to beat its rival into the air. Full FAA certification had been granted July 29.

1971 August 9 The U.S. government Emergency Loan Guarantee Board approved a $250 million guarantee to Lockheed—the entire amount under its jurisdiction—in an effort to save the company from bankruptcy. Lockheed had loans of $400 million and advance payments of $100 million on TriStar orders and needed

further loans that required government guarantees. This was part of an international rescue package involving the British and U.S. governments, the airlines, Lockheed and Rolls Royce, the latter having gone into voluntary liquidation earlier in the year.

1971 September 4 The Concorde supersonic airliner made its first crossing of the Atlantic when prototype 001 took off from Toulouse, France on a flight to Rio de Janeiro, where it arrived September 6 on the eve of Brazil's independence day. It made intermediate stops at Isla do Sal and Cayenne, French Guiana. The prototype flew on to São Paulo for the opening of the French 1971 exhibition in Brazil and for demonstration flights for airlines and government officials before returning to France.

1971 September 9 The governments participating in the multirole combat aircraft (Tornado) program announced their satisfaction with the program to date. Six prototypes were to be built as planned, with the first expected to fly at Manching, West Germany late in 1973. The Luftwaffe expected the first of a planned 420 in service by March 1977, the RAF expected to buy 380, and Italy's Aeronautica Militare would take 100 of the planned production run of 900 aircraft.

1971 September 10 The first of three VFW-Fokker VAK 191B V/STOL research aircraft made its first flight from Bremen, West Germany. Of comparatively conventional swept-wing layout, this aircraft had one Rolls Royce RB.162-81 lift engine at front and back with a vectored thrust RB.192-12 in center-section for transition and forward flight. The project was technically the most ambitious from Germany since World War II and a bold start for the partnership that formed Zentralgesellschaft VFW-Fokker in 1969.

1971 September 16 Two Pakistan Air Force F-86 Sabres were intercepted by the Indian Air Force over the Khasi-Jaintia hills of Assam and turned back into Pakistani air space. This followed increased tension between the newly declared state of Bangladesh (formerly East Pakistan) and India, preceded by intrusions of Indian air space by Pakistani Mirage fighters during July when two aircraft flew low over Srinagar airfield and again in September when three aircraft buzzed Nowshera, Jammu. Outnumbered by the Indian Air Force, Pakistan bought MiG-19s from China and Mirage fighters from France.

1971 September 29 An engine fell off a USAF Lockheed C-5A during preparations for a training flight at Altus AFB, Okla. After an investigation, the USAF announced that the problem was a structural failure of critical elements of the engine pylon. This particular aircraft had accumulated 1,300 hr. of flying time and had made 3,000 landings. Other aircraft of this type were immediately examined, and seven C-5As were grounded temporarily pending superficial strengthening.

1971 October 27 The French Aéronavale completed seven days of trials with the shipboard Jaguar M-05 prototype aboard the carrier *Clémenceau* off Lorient where 12 takeoffs and landings were made. The maximum takeoff weight achieved was 27,170 lb., but additional tests at higher landing weights achieved were canceled when cracks were discovered in the engine mountings. Despite strenuous efforts to sell the navalized version, the Aéronavale eventually bought the Super Etendard instead.

1971 October U.S. Navy strike sorties against communist Vietnam reached a low for the year when aircraft from the aircraft carriers USS *Midway* (through October 10), *Enterprise* (from October 11) and *Oriskany* launched 1,024 ordnance missions, only

30 of which were in South Vietnam. Sortie rates had descended from 2,645 in May to 2,431 in June, 2,001 in July, 1,915 in August and 1,243 in September. They would increase again to 1,766 in November and 2,462 in December before collapsing to 113 by March 1972 before a massive increase during "Linebacker I" raids, which began in May 1972.

1971 November 2 The first production Jaguar E two-seat version was flown for the first time at Toulouse-Blagnac by test pilot Bernard Witt. The flight lasted about 1 hr., and the aircraft was cleared for delivery to the Armée de l'Air early in 1972. French orders were for 32 of the two-seat version and for 43 of the single-seat aircraft with options on a further 24 for a total order-book of 99.

1971 November 3 A U.S. Army Sikorsky CH-54B laid claim to several records, including a sustained level altitude with zero payload of 11,189.5 m (36,711 ft.), an altitude of 9,545.4 m (31,317 ft.) with a 1,000-kg (2,205-lb.) load, an altitude of 9,321.1 m (30,581 ft.) with a payload of 2,000 kg (4,410 lb.), an altitude of 7,817.2 m (25,647 ft.) with a payload of 5,000 kg (11,025 lb.) and an altitude of 5,120 m (16,789 ft.) with a payload of 10,000 kg (22,050 lb.). It also claimed three climb time rates with a best performance of 6 min. 15.2 sec. to 9,000 m (29,529 ft.).

1971 November 4 The U.S. National Capital Planning Commission approved plans for the greatest museum of air and space achievement anywhere in the world. The Smithsonian Institution, for long the nation's depository for U.S. achievement in exploration and discovery, wanted to spend $40 million on a new air and space museum that would bring together all the aircraft and space vehicles that represented important stages in the development of aviation and rocketry. Museum director Michael Collins, an Apollo 11 astronaut, spoke for 90 min. on the project, which was approved by the Fine Arts Commission November 17.

1971 December 3 At 5:54 P.M., the Pakistan Air Force launched a preemptive strike against airfields in northwest India with F-86s and B-57s. The attacks were sparsely supported and spread too thin for optimum effect, failing to do much damage except at Amritsar where the runway was seriously damaged and a radar installation was destroyed. Next day the Indian Air Force hit back in a successful attempt to clear the skies of enemy aircraft, giving its ground forces freedom to move across the border with Pakistan.

1971 December 6 In an air-combat lesson that appeared to endorse the new realization in USAF thinking, that dogfighting was still a necessary part of a fighter pilot's life, a delta-wing MiG-21 air-superiority fighter easily out-maneuvered a Lockheed F-104 interceptor in the Indo-Pakistani war and shot it down. Concerned about adherence to a philosophy that said all fighters were missle-launching platforms (like the F-104) and nothing more, Tactical Air Command had begun the shift back toward a true combat fighter with the FX competition and this incident supported that view.

1971 December 7 At a meeting between the British Minister for aerospace, Frederick Corfield, and the French transport minister, Jean Chamant, in Paris, a sales price on the Anglo-French Concorde supersonic airliner was agreed. The approximately $33.8 million (£13 million) price was higher than the airlines had anticipated but too low to recoup government development costs on sales of the estimated market of 200 to 250. In fact, only 14 were

sold, seven to the British and seven to the French national airline Air France.

1971 December 15 After 56 yr. 8 mon. overseas, a world record for military air units, No. 8 Squadron, RAF, was disbanded when it returned to England from Sharjah near Dubai on the Persian Gulf. The squadron had been formed on January 1, 1915, at Brooklands, England and was posted to Gosport five days later before leaving for St. Omer, France on April 15, 1915. Apart from periods when it was briefly disbanded, it had remained overseas ever since.

1971 December 16 A ceasefire in the war with Pakistan brought peace once more between India and her nearest neighbor after almost 2 wk. of ground and air attack. Bangladesh (East Pakistan) had flown 30 sorties, while the India Air Force had flown 1,978; West Pakistan flew 2,840 sorties while the Indians flew approximately 4,000. Wild claims led to the Pakistani's announcing the destruction of 106 Indian aircraft, probably around 65 in reality; the Indians claimed 94 but actually destroyed about 40. The war cost total casualties of about 11,000 dead and 37,000 wounded.

1971 December 19 In a graphic demonstration of how the possession of air power could embolden politicians, Egypt's president Anwar Sadat publicly announced his decision to resume attacks against Israeli targets at every opportunity, shortly after he had concluded negotiations with the Soviet Union for 12 more Tupolev Tu-16 maritime patrol and strike bombers. As with the existing inventory of Egyptians Tu-16s, Soviet naval air crew were to man the new aircraft.

1971 December 31 An ICAO report acknowledged the remarkable fact that, 36 yr. after its first flight, there were 1,470 Douglas DC-3s in U.S. airline service, more than any other single type of aircraft. Next most widely used aircraft was the Boeing 727, of which 832 were in service.

1971 December The U.S. Navy made the first operational use of laser-guided bombs (LGBs) with aircraft based on the USS *Constellation* against targets in North Vietnam, hitherto considered impregnable. In 16 test drops against roads and antiaircraft batteries, the weapon proved remarkably effective, and during the coming year, it was to be used with great effect against steel bridge structures and emplacements built into solid rock.

1971 December The number of registered U.S. aircraft landing facilities during the year exceeded 12,000 for the first time. There were now 12,070 airports, heliports and seaplane bases, an increase of 261 over the figure for 1970, despite 354 of the 1970 list having been abandoned and deregistered in 1971. Texas had the most landing facilities with 1,128, followed by Alaska with 762 and California with 746. Of the national total, 7,652 were privately owned, and 4,418 were publicly owned.

1971 December The Soviet supersonic transport aircraft, the Tupolev Tu-144, reached a maximum speed of 1,566 MPH, equivalent to Mach 2.37, at 60,700 ft. This represented a slight increase above the target design speed of Mach 2.3. The Soviets planned to present the aircraft at the upcoming Hanover (West Germany) Air Show with a fuselage configured with seating for up to 180 passengers compared to a projected capacity for 120 in pictures of the prototype.

1972 January 3 NASA issued a request for proposals for 6-mon. studies on new propulsion systems for quiet STOL aircraft and clean operation on takeoff and landing. Evaluations and measurement of noise, emission levels, thrust performance, size and weight would enable the agency to define current capabilities and to advise on future directions for this market. Two companies were to be selected, and production of an experimental quiet, clean engine was expected to get under way later in the year.

1972 January 6 The USAF issued a request for proposals for a lightweight fighter (LWF) that was required to have a takeoff weight of under 20,000 lb., a top speed of up to Mach 1.6 and an operational ceiling of between 30,000 ft. and 40,000 ft. with a fast climb rate, high maneuverability, good dogfighting capability and range and rapid turnaround combined with ease of maintenance. Nine companies were asked to bid, and Boeing LTV, Lockheed, General Dynamics and Northrop responded.

1972 January 10 The Kaman KA-100 SAVER (stowable aircrew vehicle escape rotoseat) made its first free flight powered by a 420-lb. s.t. Williams WR-19 turbofan engine. The device had been developed for the U.S. Naval Air Development Center as a means of providing a pilot with propulsion after ejecting from a disabled aircraft. It consisted of a small gyroplane fitted integrally within the ejection seat. After ejecting from the aircraft in the normal way, the device would unfold within 7 sec., deploying a powered auto-rotating two-blade rotor.

1972 January 21 The first four-seat Lockheed S-3A Viking antisubmarine aircraft took to the air from Palmdale, Calif. piloted by John Christiansen and Lyle Schaefer. Powered by two 9,275-lb. s.t. General Electric TF34-GE-2 turbofan engines, the S-3A had provision for four MK-46 torpedoes, bombs, rockets or mines and could patrol for 7.5 hr. at 184 MPH or operate over a high altitude search radius of 530 mi. at 426 MPH or a combat range of 2,900 mi. The S-3A had a wingspan of 68 ft. 8 in. and a length of 53 ft. 4 in.

1972 January 24 The USAF issued a request for proposals on an advanced medium STOL (AMST), which could be developed eventually into a larger successor to the C-130 tactical transport. By March 31, Bell, Boeing, Fairchild Republic, Lockheed and McDonnell Douglas had submitted bids, and on November 10, the USAF awarded preliminary design contracts leading to orders for two prototype Boeing YC-14 and two prototype McDonnell Douglas YC-15 contenders. The only stipulation in the design was that the aircraft carry 27,000 lb. of cargo 450 mi. from a 2,000-ft. takeoff and 38,000 lb. for 3,000 mi.

1972 February 8 The U.S. Joint Chiefs of Staff authorized a B-52 sortie level of 1,200 per month following a suspected build-up in the movement of communist forces into South Vietnam. This necessitated 29 more B-52s being deployed to Guam on standby for a further increase in sortie levels at the request of Gen. Creighton W. Abrams, Jr., commander, U.S. Military Assistance Command Vietnam, and Adm. John S. McCain Jr., commander-in-chief, Pacific. Five B-52 units were deployed to Andersen AFB, Guam.

1972 February 9 The first of two specially modified Boeing 707-320B civil airliners serving as AWACS prototypes, designated EC-137D, made its first flight and was delivered to the USAF. Equipped with a Westinghouse AN/APY-1 radar system complete with large external radome and filled-in window apertures, the aircraft were reconfigured to production E-3A standard in 1977 and 1978 and returned to the USAF. The first of 34 production E-3A Sentry AWACS aircraft was delivered in March 1977.

1972 February 16 Defense Minister Helmut Schmidt of Germany and Defense Minister Michel Debré of France signed an agreement in Paris authorizing development of the Franco-German Alpha Jet, 2 yr. after the proposal was first considered by the two countries. It was an attempt to combine two separate requirements, the Armée de l'Air wanting a trainer and the Luftwaffe wanting a light attack aircraft. Assembled by Dassault-Breguet, the first Alpha Jet was to be ready in 1973 with the second assembled by Dornier in 1974.

1972 February 17 The NASA Langley Research Center, Va. announced that it had developed a fully automated helicopter landing system and demonstrated its effectiveness and safety with engineers and pilots operating from Wallops Station. Automated approaches had been demonstrated from 2–3 mi. out, with the auto-guide system activated at an approach speed of 60 MPH and a height of 800 ft. As the helicopter intercepted the landing guidance path, it locked on to the guidance beam, enabling it to hover above the landing spot and slowly lower itself to the ground from 50 ft.

1972 February 20 A USAF Lockheed HC-130H Hercules piloted by a crew commanded by Lt. Comdr. Ed Allison set a new world record for unrefueled flight by turboprop aircraft. It flew a distance of 14,052.94 km (8,732.5 mi.) between the Taiwanese base of Ching Chuan Kang AB and Scott AFB, Ill. The previous record for unrefueled flight by turboprop aircraft had been set by a U.S. Navy P-3C Orion on January 22, 1971, when it flew a distance of 6,857 mi.

1972 February 29 NASA hosted a major conference at Edwards AFB, Calif. on the results of its supercritical wing research. Despite having ailerons to break the theoretical maximum smoothness over the airfoil, the F-8A used to test the concept demonstrated an increase of 15% in transonic efficiency. Engineers predicted a 2.5% increase in profits for airliners using supercritical wing design concepts, and TC-15, YC-14 and Sabreliner 65 aircraft employed a supercritical wing as well as several foreign designs.

1972 March 1 NASA announced a cooperative joint endeavor between the USAF and the U.S. aerospace industry to develop a quiet experimental STOL transport, dubbed QUESTOL, and an advanced medium STOL transport, dubbed AMST. The joint effort was signed by Dr. James C. Fletcher on behalf of NASA and Dr. Robert C. Seamans Jr. on behalf of the USAF. A special USAF/NASA STOL Coordinating Council was co-chaired by the assistant secretary of the Air Force and the NASA associate administrator for Aeronautics and Space Technology.

1972 March 30 Accompanied by an invasion force of 40,000 communist North Vietnamese moving south across the demilitarized zone, a rocket and artillery barrage signaled the onslaught that had been expected for several weeks. Almost immediately, the U.S. Joint Chiefs of Staff ordered an increase in B-52 bombing sorties to 1,800 per month. In addition, 28 B-52Gs were sent to Guam. Although they could not carry the load of a modified B-52D, they were able to fly round-trip missions without refueling. With these aircraft, the Arc Light force had 133 B-52s at its disposal capable of mounting 2,250 sorties per month.

1972 April 1 A ban on night flying into and out of London-Heathrow, the world's busiest international airport for regularly scheduled traffic, came into effect as a means of reducing the noise impact on local residents. No flying was to be permitted between 11:30 P.M. and 6:00 A.M. each night between April 1 and October 31. This ban followed 7 yr. of restricted night movements in which only 3,500 night flights were allowed in and out per year. Opponents of this restriction said that in reality only an average of 17 flights were flown each night during the summer months when traffic was at peak.

1972 April 13   The USAF ordered four prototypes of two contenders for its LWF program in the first competitive flight evaluation contest for two decades. Two General Dynamics Model 401 designs were to be built as YF-16s under a $37.9 million contract as well as two Northrop P-530 Cobra prototypes as the YF-17 for a contracted cost of $39 million. The first flights of each aircraft were set for early 1974 and Wright-Patterson AFB, Ohio was to be in charge of the fly-off whereby each prototype would accumulate 300 hr. flying time demonstrating their respective capabilities.

1972 April 20   The U.S. Department of Transportation issued a $1.3 million contract to the Atomic Energy Commission's Lawrence Livermore Laboratory for research into the environmental effects of a high-flying fleet of airliners projected for 1985–90. This was to be part of the DOT's climatic impact assessment and provide a detailed assessment of the effect of subsonic and supersonic aircraft on temperature, cloud formation and stratospheric shielding of ultraviolet radiation by the ozone layer and on changes that may result from the emission of propellants at high altitude.

1972 April 26   The inaugural revenue-paying service of the Lockheed L-1011 TriStar was flown by Eastern Air Lines just 12 days after the aircraft received its FAA approval for full commercial use. The aircraft had been saved by a U.S. government loan guarantee agreed to on August 9, 1971, a deal that also helped the U.K. government save TriStar engine-builders Rolls Royce in an international backing for commercial aviation that was based on politics rather than sentiment but which nevertheless reflected the large financial risk in launching new airliners.

1972 April 28   A Grumman F-14A Tomcat fired an AIM-54 Phoenix missile for the first time from the U.S. Navy Missile Center at Point Mugu, Calif. Developed by Hughes Aircraft, it was intended to equip the F-111B. Designed to intercept targets from sea level to 60,000 ft. simultaneously, the fire control system could handle separate target equations, and on one test on November 21, 1973, a full F-14A load of six Phoenix missiles was fired at six separate targets for simultaneous guidance. On April 28, 1972, a Phoenix intercepted its target at a distance of 126 mi.

1972 April   As a result of increased activity due to the communist offensive that began March 30, the U.S. Navy flew a total of 6,083 sorties during the month, of which 4,833 were against targets in South Vietnam, the rest against targets in North Vietnam. The carriers USS *Coral Sea* and USS *Hancock* were on station when the offensive began and the USS *Kitty Hawk* was ordered to join them on April 1 with the USS *Constellation* ordered in on April 2. By the end of the month, the navy was flying an average 300 sorties per day.

1972 May 1   A DHC-5 Buffalo modified by Boeing to have a powered wing utilizing boundary layer control, an augmentor-flap system, drooped ailerons, redesigned spoilers and full span-leading edge slots made its first flight from Seattle, Wash. Designated C-8A, it also had Rolls Royce Spey engines with vectored thrust mounted to a reduced-span wing of 78 ft. 9 in. It was found that the C-8A could clear 35 ft. after a takeoff run of

965 ft. at 45,000 lb. Much work over many years contributed valuable data to the NASA quiet-STOL research effort.

1972 May 9   In Operation Pocket Money, three Grumman A-6A and six LTV A-7E attack aircraft laid a total of 36 mines in Haiphong Harbor with 72-hr. timers to allow clearance of shipping. Nine ships departed, 27 remained, and Soviet supply ships en route diverted. Thus began an extensive campaign during which 11,000 MK 36 and 108 special MK 52-2 mines were planted in Haiphong, Hon-Gai, Cam Pha, Quang Khe, Dong Hoi and Thanh Hoa.

1972 May 10   The USAF and the U.S. Navy began Operation Linebacker I, a concentrated bombing campaign against North Vietnam and supply routes to the south that was maintained through October 22 when Pres. Nixon halted bombing north of the 20th parallel.

This was the most concentrated air combat day of the Vietnam War, U.S. Navy fighter pilots from the USS *Constellation* and the USS *Coral Sea* shooting down eight MiG fighters. Lt. Randy Cunningham and Lt. (jg) William Driscoll flying their F-4 Phantom gained the first triple-kill victory of the war in Vietnam. With their victories over two MiGs on January 19 and May 8, they were the first MiG aces of the war.

1972 May 10   The first of two prototype Fairchild Republic YA-10A ground attack contenders for the USAF A-X ground attack role made its first flight. Powered by two 9,065-lb. s.t. General Electric TF34-GE-100 turbofan engines in barrel-pods either side of the upper rear fuselage, it had a wingspan of 57 ft. 6 in., a length of 54 ft. 4 in. and a maximum takeoff weight of 47,200 lb. including 16,000 lb. of ordnance on up to 11 external locations and a 30-mm Gatling gun with 1,350 rounds.

1972 May 11   A stubborn and resilient target in North Vietnam succumbed to modern technology when a single 3,000-lb. M18 laser-guided bomb demolished for good the Paul Doumer Bridge over the Red River near Hanoi. It had been virtually destroyed the previous day when F-4Es hit it with 2,000-lb. laser-guided and eletro-optical-guided bombs. In strikes that began August 11, 1967, 3,000-lb. bombs and 94 tons of ordnance had failed to destroy it.

1972 May 12   Despite last efforts to extend the production line with improved versions, McDonnell Douglas delivered the last DC-8, a Series 63, to SAS. It was the 556th aircraft of its type. The DC-8-63 incorporated the wing and fuselage of the Series 61 with the engines of the Series 62, 18,000- or 19,000-lb. s.t. Pratt & Whitney JT3D turbofan engines and had been intended for use on trans-Atlantic stages but was limited to the New York-Amsterdam route at best, being unable to stretch as far as Rome.

1972 May 25   NASA test pilot Gary Krier piloted a modified LTV F-8C Crusader on its first flight in the digital fly-by-wire (DFBW) program at the Flight Research Center, Edwards AFB, Calif. Fitted with an electronic control system developed by NASA engineer Melvin Burke, the test program successfully demonstrated how flight control could be improved with fly-by-wire and how much smoother air travel could be with sensors responding rapidly to slight movement in the aircraft's attitude.

1972 May   Responding to a massively increased effort by the communist North Vietnamese to attack targets in South Vietnam, the U.S. Navy flew 7,239 ordnance sorties, of which 3,949 were against targets in the north. The U.S. Marine Corps flew 1,502 air attack support sorties into South Vietnam compared to 543 in

April. The four U.S. Navy carriers that converged on the area during early April were joined by the USS *Okinawa* and the USS *Coral Sea* to give the strongest naval air presence in the region since the war began.

1972 June   The bombing of North Vietnam with B-52s reached an all-time peak with 3,150 sorties being flown during the month in extended Arc Light operations calling upon B-52Ds at U-Tapao AB, Thailand and Andersen AFB, Guam and B-52Gs also at Guam. The strength of the U.S. Eighth Air Force had been increased from 50 B-52s at the beginning of the year to a peak of 200. By the end of the month, 55,803 sorties had been flown in the three months since the start of the communist offensive March 30.

1972 July 27   The McDonnell Douglas F-15A made its first flight, at the hands of test pilot Irving Burrows. Powered by a 19,000/25,000-lb. s.t. Pratt & Whitney F100-PW-101 turbofan, it had a wingspan of 42 ft. 9 in., a length of 63 ft. 9 in. and a maximum takeoff weight of 56,000 lb. With a top dash speed in excess of Mach 2.5, a sustained top speed of Mach 2.3 at 36,000 ft. and supersonic cruise close to the ground, the F-15A had a 20-mm cannon and could also carry 16,000 lb. of external ordnance.

1972 August 2   The first Lockheed U-2 operating from NASA's Ames Research Center on remote sensing calibration work with high resolution cameras using black and white and infrared film, took photographs of a forest fire in Big Sur country around California's Monterey County. Photographs from 25,000 ft., 45,000 ft. and 60,000 ft. were used by the forestry officials to plan ways of fighting the fire that enabled firefighters to contain 50% of the fire within 24 hr.

1972 August 4   The first operational AGM-69A SRAM (short-range attack missile) was delivered to the Forty-second Bombardment Wing, Loring AFB, Maine. With a length of 14 ft. and a diameter of 18 in., the SRAM weighed 2,230 lb. and contained a 170 kiloton W-69 nuclear warhead. Powered by a rocket motor giving the missile a range of up to 100 mi., 20 could be carried by each B-52G and B-52H, and the FB-111A could carry six, two internally. Strategic Air Command modified 281 B-52G and Hs to carry the missile.

1972 September 4   At the biennial Society of British Aircraft Companies Show, Farnborough, England, the event became a display of European aircraft and ancillary products when it opened with access for all European aircraft whether or not they incorporated U.K. products. Previously, only aircraft from the United Kingdom, or foreign aircraft equipped with British components, were permitted to exhibit. As before, non-European aircraft could display only if they had British engines.

1972 September 16   The USAF successfully tested a powered balloon it believed could be used to carry surveillance equipment to assigned locations and left to float in areas difficult to access. Flown at the White Sands Missile Range, the POBAL (powered balloon) had a 9-kW electric motor driving a 39-ft. propeller and a 9 ft. by 2 ft. 6 in. steering rudder on an extended tail boom. The helium-filled balloon could be slowly moved from place to place and left to float at an appropriate place and altitude for up to 12 hr. before it was returned on electronic commands signaled from an operator.

1972 September 16   A two-day celebration of the USAF's 25th anniversary began at Andrews AFB, Md. with flying displays from air force units displaying front-line equipment. Demonstra-

tions included a C-130 demonstrating the low-altitude parachute extraction system (LAPES), an HC-130 refueling an HH-53 helicopter, a KC-135 refueling a B-52 and a fire-fighting drill displayed by an H-42 helicopter team. In the static display were an F-111A fighter, an FB-111A bomber, an SR-71 reconnaissance aircraft, a C-5A Galaxy and a T-38 trainer.

1972 September 20   The supersonic Tupolev Tu-144 made a 1,700-mi. flight from Moscow to Tashkent in 1 hr. 50 min. It incorporated several changes from the first prototype. The nose had been lengthened, and additional windows had been fitted in the drooping visor that could be lowered for landing. The design of the air intakes had been revised, and the nose and main landing gear legs had been repositioned. Inside, the flight engineer's position had been moved forward to the flight deck, and the cabin was fitted for 140 passengers.

1972 October 3   On its first deployment to Vietnam since 1968, a General Dynamics F-111A was lost on its first combat mission; a second aircraft was lost on October 17. There had been pressure to return the aircraft to combat evaluation, and two squadrons of 24 aircraft each were deployed with the 474th Tactical Fighter Wing at Takhli, Thailand, about 575 mi. from Hanoi. It was believed that technical problems that caused the 1968 losses had been overcome and that the aircraft should be given a chance to prove itself.

1972 October 5   The USAF selected the Westinghouse AN/APY-1 radar for its new generation of E-3A Sentry AWACS aircraft. The radar had a span of 24 ft. and a depth of 5 ft. housed within a rotating radome 30 ft. in diameter and 6 ft. deep supported above the fuselage by two stiff streamlined legs. From a normal operating altitude of 30,000 ft., the E-3A would "see" a maximum distance of up to 300 mi., or 237 mi. to the curvature of the earth, and up to 80,000 ft.

1972 October 8   A McDonnell Douglas DC-10 Series 40 began a 7-day demonstration tour of Asia, the United States and South America. It set three new point-to-point records on the 30,411-mi. tour. The 7,677-mi. Los Angeles-Hong Kong route was flown in 14 hr. 44 min., the 7,800-mi. Honolulu-Buenos Aires flight was completed in 14 hr. 18 min., and the 6,300-mi. Rio de Janeiro-Los Angeles leg was completed in 11 hr. 52 min.

1972 October 10   The two prototype Northrop YA-9A and the two prototype Fairchild Republic YA-10A contenders for the USAF A-X ground attack requirement began 250 hr. of testing during which Maj. George P. Lynch's Joint Test Force evaluated each design. The Northrop YA-9A had a wingspan of 58 ft., a length of 53 ft. 6 in. and a maximum takeoff weight of 42,000 lb. Powered by two 7,500-lb. s.t. Lycoming YF102-LD-100 turbofans buried in the underwing-fuselage junction, it had a 20-mm Gatling gun and up to 16,000-lb. of ordnance.

1972 October 18   The first European Airbus A300B-1 made its first flight from Toulouse, with Max Fischl and Bernard Ziegler at the controls. Powered by two 51,000-lb. s.t. General Electric CF6-50C engines, it remained airborne for 85 min. The B-1 had a length of 167 ft. 2 in. with a wingspan of 147 ft. 1 in., and the B-2 had a length of 175 ft. 11 in. The first B-2, the third A300B completed, made its first flight on June 28, 1973, powered by two 49,000-lb. s.t. CF6-50A engines. The A300B could carry 281 passengers at 526 MPH for 1,615 mi.

1972 October 23   Operation Linebacker I was stopped, and all tactical bombing operations north of the 20th parallel were brought to a halt as the North Vietnamese once again returned to the peace talks. The U.S. Navy had flown 23,652 sorties against the communists since operations escalated on May 10. U.S. aircraft carriers involved in Linebacker I included the USS *Enterprise*, the USS *Constellation*, the USS *Coral Sea*, the USS *Hancock*, the USS *Kitty Hawk*, the USS *Midway*, the USS *Saratoga*, the USS *Oriskany* and the USS *America*.

1972 October 27   The world's largest balloon, with an internal volume of 47.8 million cu. ft., was successfuly launched by the USAF Systems Command from Chico, Calif. Carrying a 250 lb. load of scientific instruments that had been developed for the air force by Cambridge Research Laboratories, it reached a record altitude of 170,000 ft., beating the previous record of 162,000 ft. achieved in 1969. The primary purpose of the exercise was to evaluate the technology of thin-film balloons and the characteristics of high-altitude parachutes.

1972 November 10   The directors of North American Rockwell Corp. voted in favor of changing the company's name to Rockwell International Corp. during a meeting at El Segundo, Calif. North American had merged with Rockwell on September 22, 1967. This decision removed the famous manufacturing name that had itself been an amalgam of several smaller companies since December 6, 1928, when Clement Keys formed North American Aviation Inc. The change was aproved by the shareholders on February 15, 1973.

1972 December 18   On the day that U.S. bombing of North Vietnam was resumed following the breakdown of peace talks in Paris, 129 B-52s flew operations in three waves against the Kinh No storage depot 9 mi. north of Hanoi as well as three airfields and 11 SAM sites on the first day of Operation Linebacker II. The first wave struck between 8:01 and 8:12 P.M. followed by the second between midnight and 12:15 A.M., December 19 and the third between 4:43 and 4:58 A.M. Preceded by F-111A strikes on MiG airfields and F-4s dropping chaff, the attacks also involved EB-66s, EA-3s, EA-6s, A-7s, F-105s, EC-121s and H-53s. Three B-52s were lost in the raid.

1972 December 19   On the second day of Linebacker II, during the early hours of the first three attack waves, a MiG became the first combat claim of a B-52. Targets in Hanoi were hit along with a thermal power plant for the first time. Transshipment routes were bombed, and targets struck on the previous day were revisited. No B-52s were lost on this second day of what would become known as the "eleven-day war."

1972 December 20   On the third day of Linebacker II, the first of three B-52 attack formations on the Gia Lam rail yards in North Vietnam dropped its bombs at 8:00 P.M., but the ground defenses were waiting—two aircraft were shot down over Hanoi, and several more severely damaged. From the second wave, six B-52s were diverted away from the intense SAM and AAA fire without crossing the target, and from the third wave, only 90 out of 99 sorties were effective. Six B-52s were destroyed on a night when more than 220 SAMs were fired.

1972 December 21   Operation Linebacker II had been planned to last three days, and the three B-52s lost on day one and the six lost on day three caused grave concern. Nevertheless, it was decided to keep up the pressure and continue the bombing. Major changes in approach patterns to the target were made to confuse ground defenses, and all B-52 sorties this night flew from U-Tapao. Two were shot down. Next day, day five of Linebacker

II, the B-52Ds flew strikes against Haiphong's rail network and marshaling yards as well as gasoline dumps.

1972 December 26   Following a 24-hr. respite Christmas Day, Linebacker II raids against North Vietnam resumed with a carefully planned series of seven raids by 120 B-52s against 10 targets. More than 100 support aircraft were also involved in what was the most concentrated bombing raid ever conducted in war. In a 15-min. period, 113 B-52s dropped their entire load of more than 3,000 tons of bombs for the loss of only two aircraft, one of which crashed just short of the runway at U-Tapao, killing four crewmembers.

1972 December 29   At midnight on day 11 of Linebacker II, all bombing operations against North Vietnam were brought to a halt as the Paris peace talks showed signs of picking up again. In what had been the most concentrated attack of the war, 729 B-52 sorties had dropped 49,000 bombs with a collective yield of more than 15,000 tons on 24 targets in North Vietnam. Other aircraft dropped an additional 5,000 tons. Only 15 B-52s had been lost despite 1,242 reported SAM firings in the most heavily defended areas on earth. This loss rate of 2% was only acceptable in the short term, but tactics worked out by day four had dramatically reduced the losses.

1972   The war in Vietnam proved the heaviest this year for U.S. Navy operations where a total 51,895 sorties were flown out of a total of more than 117,000 sorties launched by U.S. air forces against targets in the north and the south. The U.S. Navy and the U.S. Marine Corps lost a total of 59 aircraft during the year, but ordnance missions dropped 160,763 general-purpose bombs on South Vietnamese tactical support missions in addition to the 111,859 general-purpose bombs dropped by the U.S. Marine Corps.

1973 January 3   The Aviation Advisory Commission submitted its completed report on the status of U.S. civil aviation to Pres. Nixon. It forecast a decline in U.S. leadership in aviation, which it concluded had been achieved during the late 1940s. It recommended setting up the post of undersecretary for civil aviation in the Department of Transportation and the formulation of a 10-yr. plan for services and programs that would restore the United States to a position of world leadership.

1973 January 7   Cameron Balloons Ltd. of Bristol, England flew for the first time the world's only hot-air airship (G-BAMK) from Wantage, Berkshire. Eventually developed to have a length of 112 ft., a diameter of 45 ft. and a volume of 103,000 cu. ft., the D96 was powered by a propane-burning, 1,600 cc Volkswagen engine driving a large diameter propeller providing the airship with a speed of up to 15 MPH and an endurance of 2 hr. Built originally for a customer in the United States, others were built for customers in six other countries.

1973 January 12   The last air combat victory scored by a U.S. Navy air crew over Vietnam was credited to Lt. Victor Kovaleski and Lt. James Wise in an F-4 from VF-121 operating off the USS *Midway*. The North Vietnamese MiG-21 they shot down was the 57th air combat kill by U.S. Navy and U.S. Marine Corps pilots since the air war began.

1973 January 17   The Japanese Air Self-Defense Force flew 28 intercept missions with its F-104J and F-86F Sabres during an unprecedented incursion by Soviet aircraft. Four Tu-20s and two Tu-16s approached Japanese air space from the northeast and 10 Tu-16s in five pairs approached from the northwest in a simulated strike against Japanese targets. There were four such mass intrusion attempts in the first 3 wk. of the year, compared to nine probing flights for the preceding 12 mon.

1973 January 18   The USAF awarded a contract to Fairchild Republic for 10 preproduction A-10A close support aircraft, the first in this class ordered by the air force. The order would later be amended to six preproduction aircraft, the first of which was to fly in February 1975. Made necessary by experience in Vietnam, the Thunderbolt II—known as "Warthog" by less respectful wags—would emerge as a tough antiarmor attack plane, with survivability amid heavy ground defense fire a priority.

1973 January 27   Four days after an agreement had been reached on a ceasefire in Vietnam following successful negotiations in Paris, U.S. military operations were brought to a halt, ending 8 yr. of war. U.S. bombing operations against targets in Laos continued until April and in Cambodia until all bombing ceased on August 15. In 8 yr. 2 mon., 124,532 B-52 sorties had been flown, dropping 2.949 million tons of bombs for the loss of 31 aircraft, 15 to enemy action.

During the course of the war in Vietnam, the USAF had lost a total 2,257 aircraft to operational or combat causes, 2,118 USAF personnel had been killed on active duty, 3,460 had been wounded, and 586 were missing or had been captured. The estimated cost on operations alone was $3.123 billion. The U.S. Army had operated a total of approximately 10,000 helicopters during the war, of which 2,249 had been destroyed with the loss of 90 pilots killed and 400 injured. The U.S. Navy lost 529 fixed-wing aircraft and 13 helicopters, and the U.S. Marines lost 193 fixed wing and 270 helicopters in action. U.S. air forces had lost a total 5,511 fixed-wing and rotary-winged aircraft.

1973 January 31   Exercising their option to withdraw, Pan American and TransWorld Airlines decided not to buy 13 Anglo-French Concorde supersonic airliners, a decision followed shortly by American Airlines. Production was reduced as a result of this decision, brought about by the cancellation of the U.S. SST, by the higher than expected cost of the Concorde and by moves being made to ban the Concorde from landing at U.S. airports. Firm orders now stood at five for BOAC and four for Air France with options on six for Eastern, four for QANTAS, three each for Continental, Lufthansa, Braniff, JAL and China, and two each for Air India, Mexico and Iran Air.

1973 February 9   The first Embraer EMB-110 Bandeirante was delivered to the Brazilian Air Force. The company had been established on August 19, 1969, to promote Brazilian aeronautical products, and the first EMB-110 took to the air on October 26, 1968. With a wingspan of 50 ft. 2 in. and a length of 46 ft. 8 in., the EMB-110 was powered by two 680-HP Pratt & Whitney PT6A-27 turboprops and could accommodate 12 passengers. With a cruising speed of 260 MPH, it had a range of up to 1,150 mi. Remarkably successful, more than 500 were sold within 15 yr.

1973 February 15   The first production model of the highly successful and capable Dassault-Breguet Mirage F.1 made its first flight. Just as the Mirage III had proven to be an export winner, the F.1 would sustain that tradition. Air forces throughout the Middle East as well as South America, Spain and Greece bought this Mach 2.2 multi-mission aircraft. Capable of carrying a warload of 8,818 lb., it also had two 30-mm cannons as standard armament.

1973 February 21   A Boeing 727 belonging to Libyan Airlines and registered SA-DAH was intercepted by an Israeli Air Force F-4E Phantom II over the northern tip of Great Bitter Lake, Egypt, near the Suez Canal. The F-4E fired upon the airliner, forcing it to crash land. Of the 13 people on board, 10 died in the aircraft as it broke up and burst into flames.

1973 February 28   The first McDonnell Douglas DC-10-30CF made its first flight at Long Beach, Calif. Essentially a freight version of the DC-10 Series 30, it was capable of being adapted from a passenger-carrying aircraft into a cargo carrier overnight and derived from a long-range version of the airliner, carrying additional fuel and with the wingspan increased by 10 ft. The DC-10-30 had a maximum payload range of 6,850 mi. carrying 49,000 lb. of cargo.

1973 March 15   NASA announced it had selected Lockheed and Boeing to carry out structural technology work on an arrow-wing supersonic aircraft configuration for the Langley Research Center. In funding approved by Pres. Nixon, NASA was to evaluate the various supersonic airliner shapes that could reduce sonic booms, improve payload capability, increase performance and prepare a technology base for the time the United States decided to develop an SST. Begun under the original Advanced Supersonic Technology program, NASA would change the name in 1974 to Supersonic Cruise Aircraft Research Program and in 1979 to Supersonic Cruise Research.

1973 March 16   The last of 282 Aérospatiale (originally Sud-Est) Caravelle 12 twin-turbofan airliners was delivered to its customer, Air Inter, ending one of the most successful French commercial aircraft projects that had kept the type in production through a range of variants for 18 yr. The Caravelle 12 had an extended fuselage with a length of 118 ft. 10 in. and capacity for 140 passengers. The Caravelle continued to serve well into the next decade, and military transport versions were to be found in various parts of the world more than 15 yr. after the Caravelle was delivered to Air Inter.

1973 March 23   French defense minister Debré settled a contentious furor between senior officers in the Aéronavale and the French engine-makers SNECMA when the wishes of the naval air arm to have its Super Etendard shipboard strike fighter equipped with Pratt & Whitney engines was overturned. The J52-P-408 had been shown to have a better specific fuel consumption at certain corners of the power envelope than the SNECMA Atar 8K-50. Diminishing SNECMA order books countered a technical decision.

1973 April 6   Delivered 4 mon. ahead of schedule, the first Northrop F-5E Tiger II for the USAF was delivered to the 425th TF (Tactical Fighter) Training Squadron at Williams AFB, Ariz. Successful winner of the International Fighter Aircraft competition in November 1970, the Northrop F-5A-21 was redesignated F-5E and was a single-seat replacement for the F-5A trainers employed to tutor foreign pilots serving on these aircraft in their native air forces. A two-seat F-5F followed, and when production ended in 1986, 1,200 had been built.

1973 April 10   The first Boeing T-43A navigation trainer ordered by the USAF on May 27, 1971, made its first flight. Essentially a converted Boeing 737-253, it was equipped with 19 navigator stations down the length of the fuselage, with 12 for basic students, four for advanced students and three for instructors. All 19 aircraft were assigned to the 323d Flying Training Wing at Mather AFB, Calif. and four were later transferred to the Colorado Air National Guard.

1973 April 12   John H. Warner, secretary of the U.S. Navy, announced that the navy in cooperation with the United Kingdom would conduct an 8-mon. study of an advanced Harrier concept using a more powerful Pegasus 15 series engine with a design thrust of 24,900 lb. The studies would involve Hawker Siddeley and McDonnell Douglas in examining an advanced technology wing and Rolls Royce and Pratt & Whitney in engine development with a view to possible U.S. involvement in a manufacturing program for an improved and more powerful V/STOL aircraft.

1973 April 13   The Scottish Aviation Jetstream 201 made its first flight at Prestwick. Last product of the dissolved Handley Page company, the aircraft had been rescued by Jetstream Aircraft Ltd. and then bought over by Scottish Aviation. It was powered by two 940-ESHP Turboméca Astazou XVI turboprop engines, with a wingspan of 52 ft. and a length of 47 ft. 1 in. It was ordered by the RAF as a multi-engined pilot trainer to replace the Vickers Varsity, which had served in that role since October 1951.

1973 April 19   Avro Vulcan B.Mk.1 XA903 began flight tests with a Turbo-Union RB.199-01 powerplant attached to a specially adapted housing beneath the center fuselage. Destined for the Panavia Tornado, the engine had made a successful bench run on September 27, 1971, and the Vulcan would gradually explore the flight regime up to an altitude of 50,000 ft. and a speed of Mach 0.92. Supersonic testing to Mach 2 would be carried out in the National Gas Turbine Establishment at Pyestock, England.

1973 April 27   In the United States, the FAA brought into effect a ruling that prohibited civil aircraft from traveling at supersonic speed over any part of the land mass or the territorial waters of the United States. Exempt were those areas where tests had shown that supersonic flight would not cause a "measurable sonic boom overpressure to reach the surface." This was a major blow to the Concorde sales force and a further erosion of optimism in the commercial propects for supersonic transport.

1973 May 21   Further roles for the Swedish SAAB-37 Viggen multi-mission combat aircraft matured it into the SF 37 all-weather armed reconnaissance derivative, which made its first flight. Equipped with a modified nose containing cameras and related equipment, the aircraft could conduct reconnaissance missions any hour of the day or night in all kinds of weather. Deliveries to Squadron F13 began in April 1977. On December 10, the SF 37 maritime reconnaissance version of the Viggen began to replace the S 32C Lansen with deliveries to Squadrons F17 and F21 in 1978.

1973 June 1   The Royal Australian Air Force finally received the first of its 24 General Dynamics F-111C fighter-ground attack aircraft at Amberley AFB, Brisbane. For 5 yr., the aircraft awaited changes and modifications, and all the time the price kept increasing. Against an original price of $146 million in U.S. dollars, the actual costs worked out to be $398 million, an inflation of 173% in the 10 yr. since the aircraft had first been ordered. Twenty years later, the RAAF still had 22 of the aircraft in service.

1973 June 3   The Tupolev Tu-144 appearing at the Paris Air Show at Le Bourget airport, Paris crashed on a village, killing all six crewmembers, including the pilot, Mikhail Kozlov, and seven people on the ground. A further 28 were injured. The supersonic commercial transport came down on the French village of Goussainville after attempting critical flight maneuvers. The aircraft was reported to have displayed seemingly uncontrol-

lable pitch just before it fell to the ground. The official report into the crash was never publicly released in the West.

1973 June 13   Developed from a basic Boeing 747-200B airframe, the first of three E-4A advanced airborne national command post (AABNCP) aircraft made its first flight. Replacements for the now aging KC/EC-135 series, the E-4A was powered by four 54,750-lb. s.t. Pratt & Whitney JT9D engines. The 747-200B had flown on November 12, 1970, with a new record all-up weight of 820,700 lb. Used as flying command posts, the E-4A could carry increased battle staff and more equipment, and it possessed greater range and endurance.

1973 June 20   During a test flight for weapons trials from the U.S. Navy Missile Center, Point Mugu, Calif., a Grumman F-14A shot itself down when an AIM-7 Sparrow missile failed to clear the aircraft and recontacted. The crew ejected to safety with the F-14A traveling at about 700 MPH at 5,000 ft. and were picked up from the water by helicopter. The F-14A had been assigned its initial carrier trials aboard the USS *Forrestal* in June 1972.

1973 June 22   The U.S. Army issued two contracts for competing concepts submitted by Bell and Hughes Aircraft in response to a request for bids on an advanced attack helicopter issued November 1972. Bell would build two prototypes of its proposed Model 409, designated YAH-63, and Hughes would build two prototype Model 77s, designated YAH-64. The resulting fly-off would result in a single contractor to be selected in December 1976. The Bell Model 409 would be powered by two 1,500-SHP General Electric YT700-GE-700 turboshaft engines and have a gross weight of 13,500 lb.

1973 July 25   The Soviet pilot Alexander Fedotov achieved a new world altitude record of 36,240 m (118,898 ft.). He was flying a Mikoyan YE-266, a specially adapted version of the MiG-25. The previous record achieved by a Soviet E-66A more than 12 yr. earlier had been exceeded by just over 5,000 ft. This record would stand for more than 4 yr. before being raised again by a Soviet pilot.

1973 July 26   The first flight of the Sikorsky research aircraft designated S-69 (XH-59A) took place. Designed to evaluate the advancing blade concept rotor system under a contract issued by the U.S. Army Air Mobility Research and Development Laboratory, it was powered by a 1,825-SHP Pratt & Whitney Canada PT6T-3 Turbo Twin Pac driving co-axially mounted twin, contrarotating 36-ft. rotors and two 3,000-lb. s.t. Pratt & Whitney J60-P-3A turbojets mounted in pods on either side of the fuselage, which had a length of 40 ft. 9 in.

1973 August 1   The NASA/USAF Martin Marietta X-24B lifting-body made its first unpowered glide flight from a B-52 carrier plane. Rebuilt from the redundant X-24A, it featured an extended nose, flat bottom and rounded top with a highly swept delta wing and three vertical fins, the outer pair canted outward. It had essentially the same propulsion as the X-24A, a length of 37 ft. 6 in. and a span of 19 ft. 2 in. with a height of 10 ft. 4 in. and a gross weight of 13,000 lb.

1973 August 15   The U.S. bombing of Cambodia by B-52s ended after more than 8 yr. of almost constant operations in Southeast Asia and 9 yr. of air strikes by fighter-bombers. In that period, Strategic Air Command tankers had flown 194,687 sorties and carried out 813,878 in-flight refueling operations in the course of which they had transferred in the air a total 1.4 billion gal. of aviation fuel.

1973 August 17 The U.K. Ministry of Defense released details of an order from Spain for six single-seat and two two-seat Hawker Siddeley Harrier Mk.55 V/STOL aircraft. Because of political considerations due to Franco's hold on power, the order was routed through the United States where the aircraft were designated AV-8S and TAV-8S respectively. Deliveries began in November 1976, and the aircraft, named Matador, served with the 8a Escuadrilla with the Spanish Navy at Rota, Cadiz.

1973 August 29 In the United Kingdom, Hawker Siddeley announced government pledges of 46 million pounds in support for a new short-range transport having quiet engines, economic performance and grass-strip landing capability. Designated HS 146-100, the initial series would be configured for up to 88 passengers and be equipped with four engines with the first flight scheduled for the end of 1975. In the irony that stems from missed opportunities, the oil crisis of 1973–74 brought temporary shelving of development plans for the very aircraft that eventually would do much to improve short-haul operating economics.

1973 September 12 Grumman carried out the first flight of the F-14B, so-designated because it was powered by two 28,000-lb. s.t. Pratt & Whitney YP401-P-400s instead of the 20,900-lb. s.t. TF30-P-412A in the F-14A. In an attempt to upgrade the Tomcat, Grumman planned on the more powerful model, which was to pattern an F-14C variant, incorporating the more powerful engine and advanced avionics. The end of the war in Southeast Asia and a decline in the U.S. Navy budget inhibited such plans, and the aircraft was put into storage after only 33 hr. of flying.

1973 September 20 During the first visit to the United States by the Anglo-French Concorde supersonic airliner, Pres. Nixon awarded test pilots Andre Turcat and Brian Trubshaw the Harmon International Aviation Trophy at a special White House ceremony. The Concorde had flown to Dallas-Fort Worth regional airport at Grapevine, Tex. from Caracas, Venezuela in time to celebrate the September 21 dedication of what was the world's largest airport. Concorde carried 32 officials and journalists and a 10-man crew.

1973 September 26 Japan Air Lines received the first of seven Boeing 747-SR46s, a short-range high-density version of the Jumbo Jet. With a maximum takeoff weight of up to 735,000 lb., the airliner had capacity for a maximum of 550 passengers due to reduced numbers of galley and toilet positions for the short-range flights. Structural modifications were made for increased takeoff/landing cycles, and the undercarriage was also modified for a larger number of operations.

1973 October 6 At 2:00 P.M. on the day of Yom Kippur, the Jewish Day of Atonement, 900 tanks of the Syrian Army supported by Sukhoi Su-7s and MiG-17s, struck at Israel across the Golan Heights and invaded 12 mi. beyond the 1967 ceasefire line. Five minutes after the attack began, Egypt swarmed across the Suez Canal at 11 points under a 2,000-piece artillery barrage and 250 sorties by Egyptian aircraft hitting Israeli positions in the Sinai. Pressed hard, the Israeli Air Force fought a defensive operation but lost 30 aircraft.

1973 October 7 Responding to an Arab attack on Israeli forces, an Israeli counter-strike against the Egyptian Army on the east bank of the Suez Canal and hardened airfields west of the canal brought little result, Israel losing 20 fighters against 12 Egyptian aircraft shot down. Against Syria, Israel lost about 30 aircraft. The next day Israel make some progress in halting the armored assault over the Golan Heights with repeated close support missions, but against Egyptian forces, the Israelis were hard-pressed to stem the eastward push.

1973 October 8 Driven by an Wankel-type rotary engine, the two-seat RFB/Grumman Fanliner made its first flight. Developed jointly by the West German firm of Rhein-Flugzeugbau GmbH (RFB) and Grumman, the aircraft utilized the wings and tailplane and the AA-5A Cheetah and a new fuselage incorporating a ducted-fan engine. The RFB had been set up in 1956 to develop fiber-glass aircraft wing and fuselage structures and had built an amphibious design in 1970.

1973 October 9 With the Arab-Israeli conflict rapidly evolving into a war of attrition, El Al airliners were requisitioned to fly in supplies to Israel, and 80 Soviet air force transports (An-12 and An-22) plus 20 Aeroflot aircraft flew from bases in the Ukraine to Cairo with munitions and missiles for Egypt. The USAF began air-lifting what would amount to 22,345 toms of supplies in C-5As and C-141s to Israel. An additional 5,500 tons were flown in by El Al and 68 F-4s and A-4s were delivered to Israel by sea and from European USAF bases.

1973 October 15 In the Arab-Israeli war, Israel turned the tables on Egypt and Syria, with strong counter-attacks across the Suez Canal and back across the Golan toward Damascus. Most of the Egyptian SAM sites were rendered impotent as new U.S. F-4s strafed ground targets and attacked Egyptian aircraft in the air. The Egyptians were flying 500 sorties daily to compensate for SAM sites, destroyed by Israeli fighter-bombers. Jordan had entered the war following the invasion of Syria by Israel on October 11.

1973 October 21 The world's first electrically powered aircraft made its first flight in Austria. Named the Militky Brditschka MB-E1 (Electric 1), the powered sailplane was run by a Bosch electric motor powered by rechargeable batteries driving a propeller. The airframe was modified from a HB-3 sailplane. The concept would not catch on, and later powered sailplanes from the designer, Heinz W. Brditschka, reverted to the more conventional piston engine.

1973 October 24 A final ceasefire in the Arab-Israeli conflict brought an end to hostilities in a war that brought Israel closer to defeat than at any other time in its history. Losses had been great. In 11,233 sorties in 19 days, Israel lost 115 aircraft although 48 McDonnell Douglas F-4s and 80 McDonnell Douglas A-4s were supplied as replacements. The Egyptians lost about 242 aircraft, the Syrians 179 and the Iraqis 21. Against the total Arab air losses of 442, the Israelis had scored a 3.8:1 advantage. But the West, too, paid a price, as the Arabs quadrupled the price of oil in revenge for its support of Israel.

1973 October 26 The first Dassault-Breguet/Dornier Alpha Jet 1 made its first flight at Istres, France. Powered by two 2,976-lb. s.t. SNECMA/Turboméca Larzac 04-C5 turbofan engines, it had a wingspan of 29 ft. 11 in. and a length of 40 ft. 4 in. for the trainer and 43 ft. 5 in. for the close support version. Several hundred examples were produced for the Armée de l'Air and the Luftwaffe as well as foreign orders for several countries. The trainer/strike fighter had a maximum speed of 622 MPH and a combat radius of 217–323 mi.

1973 October 31   The last Comet 4 retired from service by a U.K. air operator stood down when Comet 4B G-ARJL completed a service from London to Paris-Le Bourget more than 21 yr. after the first Comet 1 began revenue-earning operations on May 2, 1952. This particular aircraft had made its first flight on May 19, 1961, and began operations at Heathrow under BEA ownership on May 31, 1961. In April 1970, it began flying with BEA Airtours Ltd.

1973 November 1   NASA test pilot Einar Enevoldson and USAF test pilot Maj. Stu Boyd carried out the first flight of an F-111A with a supercritical wing for tests to evaluate the benefit of this concept for military aircraft design. Known as TACT (transonic aircraft technology), the program amply demonstrated considerable performance improvements, generating twice the lift of a conventional F-111A wing at transonic speed. Quickly fed to the industry, it became an important consideration for future manned combat aircraft.

1973 November 15   The NASA/USAF X-24B lifting-body made its first powered flight from Edwards AFB, Calif. after being carried to 45,000 ft. by its B-52 carrier plane. The aircraft achieved a maximum speed of 597 MPH, or Mach 0.917, and a height of 52,764 ft. In a flight research program that ended November 26, 1975, the X-24B made 36 drops, including 24 powered flights, six glide flights and six test flights. Maximum altitude of 74,130 ft. was reached on May 22, 1975, top speed of 1,163 MPH (Mach 1.76) on October 25, 1974.

1973 December 13   The first of two General Dynamics YF-16 single-seat air superiority fighters was rolled out from its assembly plant at Fort Worth, Tex. Designed to meet the USAF lightweight fighter requirement, it had a 25,000-lb. s.t. Pratt & Whitney F100-PW-100 turbofan engine in a fuselage with characteristic underside chin air intake set behind the inclined ejection seat. The YF-16 had a length of 46 ft. 11 in. and wingspan of 30 ft. Armed with a 20-mm M-61A rotary cannon and 500 rounds, it also came with two AIM-9 Sidewinder AAMs. The second prototype was rolled out May 9, 1974.

1974 January 7   The Iranian government signed a formal letter of intent to purchase 30 Grumman F-14A Tomcats from the U.S. government for deployment with the Imperial Iranian Air Force. Deliveries were to begin in January 1976 at the rate of two per month. The origin of this order rested on the visit to the shah of Iran by Pres. Nixon in May 1972. The shah wanted either F-14 or F-15 interceptors to counter increasingly frequent Soviet overflights of Iranian airspace.

1974 January 9   The first full prototype of a highly unusual three-seat agricultural, twin-boom aircraft made its first flight as the WSK-Mielec M-15, the world's first turbofan-powered biplane. Designed and built in Poland, it had a 3,307-lb. thrust Ivchenko AI-25 turbofan engine, with an upper wingspan of 72 ft. and a length of 41 ft. 9 in. With a maximum takeoff weight of 12,456 lb., it could cruise at 92–99 mph and operate over a maximum range of 372 mi. Twin chemical containers between the wings carried 766 gal. of liquid or 4,850 lb. of dry chemicals.

1974 January 24   NASA announced a contract awarded to United Air Lines where by the airline would design, develop and test-fly a package of instruments for a Boeing 747 to measure dust particles in the air, the effect of jet efflux on the upper atmosphere, weather and human health, and changes in the ozone layer shielding against ultraviolet rays. The aircraft's flight would be made over

From flight tests that began during 1972, the McDonnell Douglas F-15 proved an indomitable air-superiority fighter.

the continental U.S. and Hawaii, and another Boeing 747 operated by Pan American would fly similar missions over international air routes.

1974 January 24   The USAF announced plans to place in production a mobile air traffic control system designated AN/TPN-19 and produced by the Raytheon Co. Developed with the help of USAF Systems Command, it comprised an operational shelter, a surveillance radar and precision approach radar to spot planes at 60 mi. and vector them onto an approach path along a 20-mi. path to landing. It was claimed the system could be set up within 2 hr. at any location.

1974 February 2   The first General Dynamics YF-16 prototype made its first flight from Edwards AFB, Calif. after having been ferried from Fort Worth, Tex. in a C-5A. The prototype had made an unexpected hop during high-speed runway tests on January 20. Although designed as a lightweight air combat fighter, the F-16 was capable of carrying up to 15,200 lb. of ordnance on external locations. With a top speed of Mach 2.2 at 40,000 ft. and Mach 1.1 at 1,000 ft. it had a combat radius of 550 mi. and a ferry range of 2,990 mi.

1974 February 18   Flying a highly unconventional balloon configuration, U.S. Army reservist Col. Thomas Gatch ascended from Pennsylvania in an attempt to cross the Atlantic. The assembly comprised 10 small balloons supporting a sealed and pressurized gondola containing Gatch. Three days later the balloon cluster and its gondola were sighted by a merchant ship at sea. The last reported position was 1,000 mi. west of the Canary Islands, but neither the balloons nor Gatch were ever seen again.

1974 February 20   The first U.S. Navy S-3A Viking squadron became operational when VAS-41 at North Island NAS, Calif. declared readiness. The S-3A carried 60 acoustic listening devices, all of which could be dropped into the sea within 10 sec. and activated to send signals to the patroling aircraft. It represented a major asset for antisubmarine operations and would become the backbone of U.S. Navy maritime patrols.

1974 March 1   Developed for the U.S. Navy and Marine Corps as a heavy-lift multi-purpose helicopter, an adapted variant of the Sikorsky S-65 made its first flight as the CH-53E. Powered by three 4,380-SHP General Electric T64-GE-415 turboshaft engines driving a 79-ft. rotor, it had a length 99 ft. 1 in. and could accommodate 55 troops with a maximum takeoff weight of 73,500 lb. The navy procured 70 of what constituted the heaviest and largest helicopter in the fleet.

1974 March 3 In the world's worst air disaster, a DC-10-10 of Turkish Airlines lost an aft cargo door after taking off from Paris en route to London, resulting in a complete loss of control. The aircraft crashed, killing 346 passengers and crew. This was the second time a cargo bay door had been lost from aircraft of this type. On June 12, 1972, a DC-10-10 of American Air Lines also lost a cargo door during a climb over Windsor, Mich. On that occasion, the aircraft was brought under control and landed safely. Latch modifications became mandatory.

1974 March 18 The first operational U.S. Navy F-14A Tomcat squadron went on duty when aircraft of squadrons VF-1 and VF-2 aboard the carrier USS *Enterprise* flew their first sorties. The carrier was off San Diego, Calif. at the time, and the flights were out over the Pacific Ocean. Each squadron had 12 F-14As in the fleet air defense role for outer-perimeter patrols equipped with Phoenix, Sparrow or Sidewinder missiles which added a new dimension to in-depth battle task force defense.

1974 March 20 The USAF awarded Fairchild Republic, McDonnell Douglas and Rockwell contracts of $1.955 million each for definition studies of the first advanced fighter technology integration (AFTI-1) demonstrator aircraft. The purpose of the program was to bring together all the feasible technology advancements of recent years into a single concept for an experimental trials aircraft. The second phase of AFTI-1 would be to procure two prototype demonstrators for flight tests.

1974 March 22 Grumman performed the first flight of the A-6E Intruder equipped with the TRAM (target recognition attack multi-sensor) for laser-guided weapons. Comprising both infrared and laser equipment in a precisely stabilized turret under the nose, the bombardier/navigator would acquire the target on the radar screen, then switch to the FLIR (forward-looking infrared system) for laser designation, a beam down which laser weapons would ride. The first A-6E/TRAM became operational on the USS *Constellation* in 1977.

1974 April 1 Following a merger in September 1972 between a number of United Kingdom state-owned airlines, British Airways formally began operations. Embracing BOAC, BEA, BEA Helicopters, BEA Airtours, Northeast Airlines and Cambrian Air Ways, British Airways was organized into seven operating divisions and took on strength the collective inventory of aircraft previously operated by the separate merged companies. The most notable demise was that of BOAC, which had been in existence since the merger of Imperial Airways and the original British Airways on November 29, 1939.

1974 April 24 At NASA's Plum Brook Station research facility, engineers tested an experimental hypersonic ramjet engine in a hypersonic wind tunnel that was capable of simulating flight conditions through Mach 7. The water-cooled ramjet engine had been developed by the Garrett Corp. with NASA's Lewis Research Center. It was capable of smooth operation between Mach 4 and Mach 8 using a moving spike inlet and burning a mixture of hydrogen and air.

1974 April James Schlesinger, U.S. defense secretary, announced a redirection of the USAF lightweight fighter require-

ment, formalized by the YF-16 and YF-17 competitive fly-off, into the air combat fighter, which would allow the aircraft to retain a mission-adaptable option for foreign purchase. This effectively opened the way for the aircraft to form the backbone of NATO air defense procurement over the next decade and opened a massive export potential measured in billions of dollars.

1974 May 8 Six years after it ceased to operate as a bomber, the last operational variant of the Handley Page Victor emerged as the K.2 refueling tanker, the first of which (serial no. XL233) arrived this day with No. 232 Operational Conversion Unit, RAF. There were to be 27 K.2s in all, ironically converted by a facility at Woodford that had once belonged to Avro, the parent company of the Victor's main competitor, the Vulcan. Thirty-five years after the first Victor bomber joined the RAF in late 1957, the type was still in service as an in-flight tanker.

1974 May 23 Air France introduced the Airbus Industrie A300B2 wide-body, medium-haul airliner into revenue-earning service with the first of six aircraft that had been delivered May 11. The inaugural flight was made between Paris and London on the power of two 51,000-lb. s.t. General Electric CF6-50C turbofan engines. Certification had been gained on March 15 after a 1,600-hr. flight-test program in which both French and German examiners had granted it a certificate of airworthiness.

1974 June 9 The Northrop YF-17 made its first flight at Edwards AFB, Calif. and became the first U.S. aircraft to exceed Mach 1 in level flight without re-heat. Test pilot Hank Chouteau kept the YF-17 in the air for 61 min. Powered by two 15,000-lb. s.t. General Electric YJ101-GE-100 turbojets, the aircraft had a wingspan of 35 ft. and a length of 56 ft. with a maximum takeoff weight of around 30,000 lb., a maximum speed of Mach 2.2 at 40,000 ft. and Mach 1.1 at 1,000 ft.

1974 June 9 The Iranian government ordered an additional 50 Grumman F-14A Tomcat air defense fighters to add to the 30 already ordered earlier in the year. In doing so, it rejected the offer of 53 McDonnell Douglas F-15A Eagles. As part of the deal, 350 Grumman employees would be based at Esfahan, 200 mi. south of Teheran, where the aircraft were to be deployed. When the shah fell in 1978, Iran had received 77 F-14As, but no more than 10 to 15 were serviceable by the time the Americans withdrew.

1974 June 10 The initial development phase for an advanced Harrier known as the AV-16 was completed, but the British government decided that further participation by British industry was unwarranted and that there would be only marginal participation for the rest of the year. Possible U.K. requirements in a U.S. Marine Corps version, to emerge as the AV-8B, were ignored, and participating U.S. companies (McDonnell Douglas and Pratt & Whitney) would employ Hawker Siddeley and Rolls Royce merely as subcontractors to the U.S. program.

1974 June 17 As a marketing exercise aimed at showing how much time could be saved by supersonic air travel an Anglo-French Concorde left Boston's Logan Airport at 8:22 A.M. At the same time, an Air France Boeing 747 left Paris for Boston. The Concorde flew the Atlantic, landed at Paris, spent 1 hr. 8 min. on the ground refueling and made it back across the Atlantic to land at Boston-Logan 11 min. ahead of the Boeing 747.

1974 July 1 No. 111 Squadron became the first RAF interceptor unit to equip with the McDonnell Douglas F-4M, replacing Lightnings the unit had been equipped with since April 1961. It was followed by No. 29 Squadron at Conningsby, England on December 31, a unit that had been operating Lightnings since May 1967. This represented the first time that front-line RAF interceptor squadrons were equipped with U.S. aircraft.

1974 July 19 At a Paris summit meeting, Pres. Valerie Giscard d'Estaing of France and P.M. Harold Wilson of Britain decided to limit production of the Concorde supersonic airliner to 16 aircraft. The French had wanted to expand production to 119 aircraft, but the British Labour government had wanted to cancel it outright. The cost of each aircraft had risen to $40 million, and almost all non-national airlines had withdrawn their reservations. In due course, only 14 aircraft would be available for purchase with seven going to Britain and seven to France.

1974 July 24 A combined U.S. Navy and Marine Corps air-lift evacuated 466 people in just 5 hr. from the Mediterranean island of Cyprus. A conflict between Greek Cypriots and Turkish forces on the island resulted in an uprising when Pres. Mikhail Makarios was replaced by elements of the National Guard and Nicos Sampson was placed in power. CH-46s and CH-53s of Marine unit HMM-162 operating off the helicopter carrier USS *Inchon* carried out the evacuation under protective cover of U.S. Navy fighters from the *Forrestal*. The British evacuated a further 1,164, including holidaymakers.

1974 July 27 A McDonnell Douglas F-15 Eagle made its first flight with the new FAST (fuel and sensor) pack attached to the side of the fuselage air intake and the underside of the wing. The pack could carry an additional 1,538 gal. of fuel, adding 71% to the conventional range with any given payload. This would increase combat radius to 1,323 mi. or ferry range to 3,912 mi. A FAST-equipped F-15 made a trans-Atlantic dash August 26 to appear at the Farnborough Air Show.

1974 August 5 With a volume of 49.5 million cu. ft. and a diameter of 820 ft., the world's largest unmanned balloon was launched by NASA and the U.S. Office of Naval Research from Fort Churchill, Canada. Carrying an 800-lb. package of instruments suspended beneath the giant envelope, which was fabricated from polyethylene 0.0197-in. thick and weighing 3,000 lb., the balloon ascended to a height of 154,200 ft., 500 mi. from its launch point over Hudson Bay before descending to a height of 98,500 ft., at which point a radio command separated the instruments for a parachute descent and recovery.

1974 August 14 The first prototype variable geometry, multimission Panavia Tornado made its first flight from Manching, Germany, with British test pilot Paul Millett at the controls and Nils Meister in the second seat. It had been assembled by Messerschmitt-Bölkow-Blohms, but the first aircraft built in Britain would fly on July 15, 1976, and the first in Italy on February 5, 1977. Powered by two 9,000/16,000-lb. s.t. Turbo-Union RB.199-34R-04 turbofan engines, it had a wingspan of 45 ft. 7 in. or 28 ft. 2 in. swept, with a length of 54 ft. 9 in. and a maximum takeoff weight of 58,400 lb. In service, it would carry a 2.27-mm Mauser cannon and up to 19,840 lb. of ordnance.

1974 August 21 Designed to an RAF requirement issued in October 1971 for a replacement for the Folland Gnat and Hawker Hunter training aircraft, the Hawker Siddeley Hawk made its first flight. Designated as the HS.1182, it was powered by a 5,340-lb. s.t. Rolls Royce Turboméca RT.172-06-11 Adour engine. It had a wingspan of 30 ft. 10 in., a length of 39 ft. 2 in. and a maximum takeoff weight of 16,500 lb. As a light tactical strike

aircraft, it could carry 5,000 lb. of ordnance and had a top speed of 617 MPH.

1974 August 22 The Short SD3-30 third-level airliner made its first flight. Powered by two 1,120-ESHP UACL PT6A-45 turboprop engines, the SD3-30 had a wingspan of 74 ft. 9 in., a length of 58 ft. and capacity for up to 30 passengers and 1,000 lb. of baggage. It had a cruising speed of 180 MPH and a range of 276 mi., or 870 mi. with 20 passengers. Highly popular, the high-wing feeder liner was adopted by many commuter airlines in several countries.

1974 September 1 A Lockheed SR-71 of the Ninth Strategic Reconnaissance Wing, Beale AFB, Calif. crewed by Majs. James B. Sullivan and Noel F. Widdifield, made a record nonstop flight from New York to London in 1 hr. 54 min. 56 sec. at an average speed of 1,806.96 MPH. This substantially beat the previous record that had been set at 4 hr. 46 min. 57.6 sec. by an RAF F-4K in 1969. On September 13, an SR-71 crewed by Capt. Harold B. Williams and Maj. William C. Machorek Jr. set a new world record from London to Los Angeles in a time of 3 hr. 47 min. 39 sec. at an average speed of 1,435.59 MPH.

1974 October 7 General Dynamics and LTV announced joint design of a YF-16 derivative to meet the needs of the U.S. Navy (VFAX) requirement for an attack fighter, and Northrop and McDonnell Douglas announced similar intent for the YF-17. Each would carry approximately 50% more fuel and would have to carry bigger radar dishes compared to the air-combat fighter derivatives of the lightweight fighter contenders. The U.S. Navy indicated a need for about 800 fighter/attack aircraft.

1974 October 17 The first of three Sikorsky S-70 (YUH-60A) tactical transport helicopters designed for the U.S. Army UTTAS (utility tactical transport aircraft system) competition made its first flight. Put out to industry as a specified replacement for the UH-1, the UTTAS resulted in parallel fly-off prototypes from Sikorsky and Boeing-Vertol. With two 1,536-SHP General Electric YT700-GE-700 turboshaft engines driving a 53-ft. rotor, it had a length of 50 ft. 11 in. and a maximum weight of 17,520 lb. A cruising speed of 168 MPH allowed a range of 460 mi.

1974 October 23 The first of two Lockheed C-130s, which would be used in experiments with boron-epoxy-reinforced wing midsections, was delivered to the USAF. It was to participate in 3 yr. of tests involving NASA research facilities for a program of flight evaluation and fatigue checks with the composite, which promised greater strength, lighter weight and more effective aircraft structures. Periodic inspection by Lockheed engineers would determine the probable life of these boron filaments embedded in epoxy resin.

1974 October 28 The prototype Dassault-Breguet Super Etendard made its first flight. Powered by an 11,205-lb. s.t. SNECMA Atar 8K-50 nonafterburning turbojet, it had been developed as an improved version of the Etendard IV-M carrier-based fighter. With a wingspan of 31 ft. 6 in. and a length of 46 ft. 11 in., it had a maximum takeoff weight of 26,455 lb. carrying a warload of 4,630 lb. Transonic in level flight, the Super Etendard had a 450-mi. combat radius and entered service with the Aeronavale in 1978.

1974 November 14 Pres. Gerald R. Ford of the United States accepted on behalf of the USAF the first operational production McDonnell Douglas Eagle, a TF-15A two-seat trainer. The aircraft was assigned to the 555th Tactical Fighter Training Squadron at the Fifty-eighth Tactical Fighter Wing, Luke AFB, Ariz. The purpose of the first TF-15As was to give instructors an opportunity to work up on the new aircraft and devise training and conversion courses from which a syllabus would be written.

1974 November 29 The first of three Boeing-Vertol Model 179 (YUH-61A) tactical transport helicopters built for a fly-off with three Sikorsky S-70s made its first flight in support of the U.S. Army UTTAS requirement. The Model 179 was powered by two 1,536-SHP General Electric YTE700-GE-700 turboshaft engines driving a 49-ft. rotor, and it had a length of 51 ft. 9 in. with a maximum weight of 18,700 lb. It had a normal cruising speed of 170 MPH and a range of up to 700 mi.

1974 December 17 The first McDonnell Douglas DC-9 Series 50 took to the air, the first version to be certificated for new FAA noise standards. Using sound-absorbing materials that had been designed for the engine and nacelles of the DC-10, the Series 50 had smokeless engines and a stretched fuselage accommodating up to 139 passengers. It had been ordered by Swissair, in whose hands it was first used in revenue service in August 1975.

1974 December 23 The first prototype variable-geometry, Rockwell B-1A, supersonic strategic bomber made its first flight from Palmdale, Calif., close to Edwards AFB. In the air only 2 mon. after rollout on October 26, the B-1A was powered by four 30,000-lb. s.t. General Electric F101-GE-100 turbofans, had a wingspan of 136 ft. 8 in., or 78 ft. 2 in. swept, and a length of 146 ft. 8 in. With a maximum takeoff weight of 389,800 lb., it had a potential bomb load of around 80,000 lb. with a top speed of Mach 2.2 at 40,000 ft. or Mach 1.2 at 1,500 ft. A typical mission radius was 3,600 mi.

1974 December 26 Airbus Industrie carried out the first flight of the A300B4. As a long-range version of the basic A300B2, it had the same external dimensions and internal capacity but more powerful engines and a maximum takeoff weight of 30,700 lb. made necessary with the extra fuel. The A300B4 had a range of 3,680 mi. versus 2,648 mi. for the A300B2. French and German certification was obtained on March 26, 1975, followed by FAA approval on June 30, 1976. The Germanair company became the first operator, starting revenue-earning flights on June 1, 1975.

1975 January 12 British Airways introduced a service between London and Glasgow offering guaranteed walk-on seat availability without reservation. The idea had been used by Eastern Air Lines on its shuttle links between Washington, New York and Boston along the eastern seaboard, but this was the first time the idea had been utilized outside the United States.

1975 January 13 The USAF selected the General Dynamics F-16 as its air combat fighter, rejecting the Northrop F-17 following a competitive fly-off. Initial production expectations were for 650 aircraft, but this would grow to more than 1,600 over the years, with more than 1,000 sold to foreign air forces. What began as a lightweight fighter contender ended up filling the advanced combat fighter (ACF) requirement. Prior to initial delivery, more powerful radar and extra wing stations were added to give the aircraft a more versatile role.

1975 January 16 In Operation Streak Eagle, the USAF set new climb-time records with the penultimate research and development McDonnell Douglas F-15A aircraft operating from Grand Forks AFB, N.Dak. The Streak Eagle reached a height of 3,000 m (9,843 ft.) in 27.57 sec., 6,000 m (19,685 ft.) in 39.33 sec., 9,000 m (29,528 ft.) in 48.86 sec., 12,000 m (39,370 ft.) in 59.38 sec. and 15,000 m (49,212 ft.) in 1 min. 17.02 sec. On January 26, Streak Eagle set a record time of 2 min. 41.02 sec. to 25,000 m (82,021 ft.), and three days later it set a time of 2 min. 2.94 sec. to 20,000 m (65,017 ft.). On February 1, it set a time of 3 min. 27.8 sec. to 30,000 m (98,425 ft.).

1975 February 22 The prototype Sukhoi Su-24 Frogfoot close air support aircraft made its first flight. Powered by two 9,921-lb. s.t. Tumanski R-195 turbojets, it had provision for 9,700 lb. in stores plus a standard 30-mm twin barrel cannon. With a wingspan of 46 ft. 11 in. and a length of 50 ft. 7 in. the Frogfoot had a maximum payload range of 466 mi. Frogfoot would be used extensively in Afghanistan in the 1980s and several derivatives evolved, including the two-seat Su-25UB and the export version designated Su-28. About 300 were in service at the end of 1991.

1975 March 7 The Yakovlev Yak-42 medium-range tri-jet transport made its first flight. Powered by three 14,330-lb. thrust

Designed for high-g dogfights, the General Dynamics F-16 entered the flight-test phase in 1974.

Lotarev D-36 turbofan engines, it was a straightforward development of the earlier Yak-40, with capacity for 100 to 120 passengers. It had a wingspan of 112 ft. 2 in. and a length of 119 ft. 4 in. with a cruising speed of 503 MPH and a maximum payload range of 559 mi. or 1,740 mi. with reduced payload. The aircraft entered service with Aeroflot on internal routes late in 1980, and several aircraft were sold overseas.

1975 March 27 The prototype de Havilland Canada DHC-7, known hereafter as the "Dash 7," made its first flight. Designed as a quiet, city-center, short-haul, 50-seat, commercial STOL transport, it had been struggling to emerge for a decade despite efforts by the design company's parent owners Hawker Siddeley to stifle it at birth and prevent competition with the HS.748. Powered by four 1,120-SHP Pratt & Whitney PT6A-50 turboprops, it had a wingspan of 93 ft., a length of 80 ft. 8 in. and a range of up to 1,313 mi. The Dash 7 became one of the most successful short-haul STOL transport aircraft, 111 having been built by 1990.

1975 March 31 A specially modified Royal Canadian Air Force de Havilland CC-115 (DHC-5 Buffalo) made its first flight carrying an inflatable air-cushion landing system beneath the fuselage. Designed and fitted by Bell Aerosystems, it comprised an inflatable rubber bag supplied with air from two turbofans mounted in the fuselage. Perforated underneath to expel a flow of air forming a cushion on which the aircraft could decelerate after landing, the system was tested experimentally but never deployed for operational use.

1975 April 4 A USAF Lockheed C-5A Galaxy heavy transport aircraft crashed with the loss of 178 lives 1.5 mi. short of Ton Son Nhut airfield near Saigon. Most passengers were Vietnamese orphans on their way to Clark AB in the Philippines. The aircraft lost both hydraulic systems after the failure of a rear pressure door at 23,000 ft. about 5 mi. off-shore. This caused the loss of flaps, rudder and elevators, and the crew used ailerons and differential power to turn around in an effort to get back to Saigon.

1975 April 10 The #1 Rockwell B-1 strategic bomber was refueled in the air for the first time by a USAF Systems Command KC-135. Later, on April 21, a Strategic Air Command crew under the command of Lt. Col. Fred C. Hartstein, First Combat Evaluation Group, Barksdale AFB, La., refueled from a KC-135 of the Twenty-second Air Refueling Squadron, March AFB, California. Early tanker tests were important because they allowed handling and maneuverability tests with full fuel loads and varying center-of-gravity positions.

1975 April 15 NASA's Flight Research Center announced the selection of Rockwell International to design and build two sub-scale model aircraft in support of the highly maneuverable aircraft technology (HiMAT) program. After two months of study, NASA was to decide to proceed with the prototypes. Piloted remotely after being dropped by a B-52 carrier plane, the HiMAT vehicle was to demonstrate features that it was thought would form an integral part of future fighters: composite materials, fiberglass structures, electronic controls and so on. The aircraft configuration selected would be a sharply swept canard.

1975 April 19 Responding to a massive invasion of South Vietnam by communist North Vietnamese forces, the carriers USS *Midway, Coral Sea, Hancock, Enterprise* and *Okinawa* deployed to adjacent waters in readiness for an evacuation. With VF-1 and VF-2 on the *Enterprise,* this was the first operational deployment of the F-14A Tomcat. The 1973 ceasefire had been based upon a

U.S. withdrawal in the hope that South Vietnam would be in a position to defend itself. It was not able to do so.

1975 April 29 Amid concentrated shelling by North Vietnamese of the air base at Tan Son Nhut in South Vietnam, Operation "Frequent Wind" reached an intensive phase in desperate efforts to evacuate U.S. government personnel and South Vietnamese granted asylum in the United States. U.S. helicopters took a total 7,014 people out of Saigon, including almost 900 Americans, during the overnight hours, and by April 30, most had been safely delivered to the veritable armada of ships standing by in what some have dubbed "America's Dunkirk."

1975 April 30 Operation Frequent Wind ended after four weeks of growing activity. Since April 1, 51,000 people had been evacuated by air in 19,000 sorties flown by helicopters of the USAF, U.S. Navy and U.S. Marine Corps. In the last two days, these forces had flown 662 helicopter sorties covered by 127 USAF and 173 U.S. Navy fighter sorties with a further 85 sorties flown by the USAF in support operations.

1975 May 2 The U.S. Navy decided to opt for a Northrop YF-17-derived navy air combat fighter (NACF). Teamed with McDonnell Douglas, Northrop had been working up the design for navy application and leaned heavily on its precursor concept, known as the Cobra, from which the USAF lightweight fighter contender had evolved as the YF-17. The high cost of the Grumman F-14A resulted in the navy deciding it wanted a lower cost combat aircraft for general use. The new fighter would be designated F-18.

1975 May 6 In further adaptation of the U.S. Navy LTV A-7 Corsair II, the first of 60 A-7H models for the Royal Hellenic Air Force in Greece made its first flight. Powered by a 14,250-lb. s.t. Allison TF41-A-1, a U.S. built Rolls Royce RB.168-62 Spey, the A-7H was the export version of the A-7D, which had been developed for the USAF. With a warload of up to 15,000 lb. and a tactical radius of 512 mi., the A-7H was a highly versatile tactical strike fighter and would still be in front-line service during the early 1990s.

1975 May 19 Soviet pilots Alexander Fedotov and Pyotr Ostapenko, flying a Mikoyan Ye-266M on separate occasions, set new climb-time records in the USSR. A height of 25,000 m (82,021 ft.) was achieved in 2 min. 34.2 sec., and 35,000 m (114,829 ft.) in 4 min. 11.3 sec. A new grading of altitude, 30,000 m (98,425 ft.) was also set at 3 min. 9.7 sec. These records were later homologated by the FAI.

1975 May 28 A series of Concorde endurance trials for Air France began with the third production aircraft. The flights would end August 2, in which period the aircraft flew 369 hrs., taking in 124 flights and carrying 2,500 passengers. Working toward an operational revenue-earning debut on January 21, 1976, the production aircraft were combining the traditional route-proving function with that of operational endurance evaluation. A similar activity for British Airways began July 7.

1975 June 3 Converted from an early production Mitsubishi T-2 trainer, the first Mitsubishi F-1 single-seat, close air support fighter made its first flight. First flown on July 20, 1971, the T-2 was the first supersonic aircraft designed by the Japanese aircraft industry and made its first supersonic flight on November 19, 1971. Powered by a 5,115/7,305-lb. s.t. Rolls Royce Turboméca Adour turbofan engine, the F-1 had a wingspan of 25 ft.

10 in. and a length of 56 ft. 9 in., exactly as the T-2 but without the rear seat.

1975 June 7 Four European NATO countries, Belgium, Denmark, the Netherlands and Norway, confirmed their decision to adopt the General Dynamics F-16 as the aircraft to replace the F-104 Starfighter. The initial order totaled 348 aircraft, with 116 going to Belgium, 58 to Denmark, 102 to the Netherlands and 72 to Norway. In coproduction agreements, production lines would be set up in Belgium and the Netherlands with about 30 European manufacturers supplying components. Initial orders would be extended, and the F-16 was eventually supplied to many other air forces around the world.

1975 July 4 The first Boeing 747SP, a reduced weight, long-range version of the basic 747, made its first flight. Capable of carrying either four 46,000-lb. s.t. General Electric CF6 series engines or four 50,100–53,110-lb. s.t. Rolls Royce RB.211 series engines, the 747SP had a length of 184 ft. 9 in., compared to 231 ft. 10 in. for the 747-200, and a range of up to 9,212 mi. The 747SP also had a taller tail, raising the overall height by 2 ft. to 65 ft. 5 in. The first aircraft was delivered on March 5, 1976.

1975 July 7 The British-built fourth production Concorde supersonic transport aircraft began an endurance and route-proving program for British Airways that would include 128 flights and 325,000 mi. in 380 flying hr. carrying 2,500 passengers by September 13. Most of the routes were between the United Kingdom and Australia, including seven trips to Melbourne, with other flights to Bahrain, Bombay, Kuala Lumpur and Singapore. The tests ended with six flights out of seven consecutive days between the United Kingdom and Gander, Newfoundland. Full passenger loads were carried on all flights.

1975 July 21 The Cessna Pawnee Division reported that it had delivered its 100,000th single-engined aircraft—a Skyhawk II for the McGhee Implement Co.—since manufacturing of light and business aircraft began in 1929 from five buildings that still held manufacturing and production facilities. Cessna had also built 30,143 multi-engined aircraft and gliders; 3,674 Cessna light aircraft built by Reims Aviation under license in France were not included in the total.

1975 July 23 The first Beech C-12A utility transport aircraft for the USAF and the U.S. Army were delivered to respective services on the same day. Latest in the line of Beech utility aircraft that had served with the U.S. military since 1937, when the navy got its first Model 17 (JB-1), the C-12A was powered by two 850-SHP Pratt & Whitney Canada PT6A-42 turboprop engines and had a wingspan of 54 ft. 6 in. and a length of 43 ft. 9 in. Developed as a military version of the Auper King Air 200, the C-12A could accommodate six passengers.

1975 July 25 The first McDonnell Douglas long-range intercontinental DC-10 Series 40 made its first flight, equipped with three 53,000-lb. s.t. Pratt & Whitney JT9D-59A turbofans, generating a total 20,000 lb. of additional thrust over preceding versions. The Series 40 was supplied initially to Japan Air Lines, which stipulated these particular engines. Other operators accepted the JT9D-20 turbofans at 50,000-lb. s.t.

1975 July 31 The Lockheed F-104 Starfighter was retired from the USAF after almost 18 years in service. Epitomizing the 1950s concept for a fighter armed exclusively with missiles instead of guns or a combination of the two, the USAF had come to reject this philosophy as a result of air combat experience in the 1960s, particularly that gained in Vietnam. Nevertheless, the F-104 served with distinction in many NATO countries and with air forces in the Far East as well as with the U.S. Air National Guard.

1975 August 1 A Douglas KA-3B Skywarrior completed the longest nonstop flight ever made by a carrier-based tactical jet aircraft when it landed at the Alameda NAS, Calif., having flown from the Naval Station at Rota, Spain, a distance of 6,100 mi., in 13 hr. The aircraft was attached to VAQ-208. McDonnell Douglas had modified the Skywarrior during the Vietnam War to serve as ECM/tanker aircraft with the designation EKA-3B. Subsequently, A-3Bs were modified into standard tanker aircraft with a 5,026-gal. fuel capacity and designated KA-3B.

1975 August 4 As part of a series of "shadow" flights, proving runs on projected revenue routes, the fourth production Concorde SST made its first 3,852-mi. flight from Singapore to Melbourne in 3 hr. 37 min. Back in Bahrain on August 11, it carried out several flights to Bombay, India and Kuala Lumpur, Malaysia to evaluate operations in monsoon conditions. A series of North Atlantic runs between London and Gander, Newfoundland commenced August 24.

1975 August 26 The prototype McDonnell Douglas YC-15, contender for the USAF advanced medium STOL transport program, made its first flight, powered by four 16,000-lb. s.t. Pratt & Whitney JT8D-17 turbofans carried in separate nacelles on the high-placed wing, which had a span of 132 ft., reduced later to 110 ft. 4 in. With a fuselage length of 124 ft. 3 in. and a maximum weight of 219,180 lb., the YC-15 had a STOL payload range of 460 mi. with 27,000 lb. and a conventional takeoff/payload range of 2,992 mi. with 38,000 lb.

1975 September 19 The first USAF Strategic Air Command pilot to fly the Rockwell B-1 swing-wing supersonic bomber took the controls of the aircraft for about 2 hrs. in a 6 hr. 30 min. flight from Edwards AFB, Calif. Rockwell test pilots Charles C. Bock and Richard Abrams accompanied Maj. George W. Larson, 4200th Test and Evaluation Squadron. In a gradual expansion of the flight test program, the #3 aircraft flew for the first time on April 1, 1976, followed by the #2 aircraft on June 14, 1976, after doubling as a static loads vehicle for measurement tests.

1975 September 29 The first of two Grumman Gulfstream II shuttle training aircraft made its first flight. Modified to simulate as closely as feasible the descent profile and handling characteristics of the NASA space shuttle, the two aircraft were modified in Bethpage, N.Y. and assigned to NASA's Lyndon B. Johnson Space Center in Houston, from where they would be deployed to the Kennedy Space Center, Fla. or the Flight Research Center, Edwards AFB, Calif. for astronaut familiarization.

1975 September 30 The first Hughes YAH-64 two-seat attack helicopter competing for the U.S. Army advanced attack helicopter requirement made its first flight. Powered by two 1,536-SHP General Electric T700-GE-700 turboshaft engines driving a 48-ft. rotor, it had a length of 48 ft. 2 in. and a maximum takeoff weight of 17,400 lb. A 30-mm gun suspended beneath the copilot/gunner position gave it devastating firepower, and its stub-wings could carry rocket and missile pods, operation of which was integrated with an all-weather, day-night capability.

1975 September The prototype MiG-31 Foxhound made its first flight as a derivative of MiG-25 design technology. Production aircraft were powered by two 33,070-lb. s.t. MKB D-30F-6 turbofan engines, and the aircraft had a wingspan of 45 ft. 9 in., a length of 68 ft. 10 in. and a maximum takeoff weight of about 99,205 lb. With a single cannon in the starboard lower fuselage and up to eight AAMs, the MiG-31 had a maximum speed of Mach 2.3 (1,520 MPH) above 36,000 ft. and a combat radius of up to 870 mi. with two drop tanks. The Soviet air defense forces received the first of this type in 1983, but only 200 were in service by the end of 1991.

1975 September   The Royal Canadian Air Force (RCAF) was absorbed into a single body known as the Canadian Armed Forces with distinct commands for land, sea and air operations. Today, it has a personnel strength of 23,100 and comprises Fighter Group, Maritime Air Group, Tactical Air Group and Training Group.

1975 October 1   The first production Fairchild Republic A-10A Thunderbolt II made its first flight. The aircraft became operational with the 354th Tactical Fighter Wing, Myrtle Beach, S.C. in March 1977 after having worked out through the 355th Tactical Training Wing beginning March 1976. Of a total 739 aircraft that had been planned, the USAF had received 713 by the time production ended in March 1984. The type was deployed in Europe, Alaska and Korea as well as in the Middle East during the 1991 Gulf War, where it proved its worth as a tough and durable ground attack aircraft.

1975 October 25   The fifth production Concorde became the first to exceed twice the speed of sound on its maiden flight. The aircraft took off from Toulouse and reached a speed of Mach 2.11. The sixth production Concorde achieved Mach 2.06 on its first flight from Filton, England on November 5. In anticipation of the first revenue-earning service January 21, 1976, the IATA agreed to a Concorde surcharge of 20% on first-class fares on the Air France service between Paris and Rio de Janeiro and a similar surcharge for the British Airways London to Bahrain service.

1975 November 1   The three Boeing E-4 advanced airborne command post aircraft were placed under the command of the First Airborne Command and Control Squadron (ACCS) at Andrews AFB, Md. The E-4 was fitted with equipment developed for use in the earlier EC-135 aircraft to form the new National Emergency Airborne Command Post. The fourth E-4 was still in the Boeing plant at Seattle being fitted with advanced communications equipment.

1975 November 6   The first of six Harrier GR.Mk.1 V/STOL strike fighters from No. 1 Squadron, RAF, arrived in Belize, formerly British Honduras, in Central America. Believing its former colony to be threatened by Guatemala, the Royal Navy sent ships, and the RAF dispatched Harriers via Goose Bay and Nassau, along with Puma helicopters and Short Belfast freighters. The threat dissipated, and the Harriers were returned to the United Kingdom during April 1976 in crates aboard the transport aircraft.

1975 November 11   The Boeing 747SP began a 29-day world tour beginning and ending at Seattle. During the tour, it made the first nonstop flight from Mexico City to Europe. Visiting 18 cities in a trip covering 72,152 mi. flown in 140 hr. 15 min., the 7,205-mi. direct flight from Mexico to Belgrade was the longest stage on the trip. The most significant stage was the 7,015-mi. nonstop flight between New York and Tokyo, Japan, with 200 passengers on board.

1975 November 22   The Bell YAH-63 two-seat attack helicopter made its first flight, one of two designs selected for a fly-off

in the U.S. Army advanced attack helicopter program. It had a maximum speed of 200 MPH, a maximum cruise of 178 MPH and a range of 300 mi. on internal fuel. Unlike its competitor, the Hughes YAH-64, the Bell concept had the gunner in the rear tandem seat operating a 30-mm gun suspended in a turret beneath the forward seat. The U.S. Army indicated a need for almost 500 attack helicopters.

1975 November   The U.S. Defense Advanced Research Projects Agency and the USAF initiated a program aimed at studying in depth the possibility of building aircraft with a very low radar-cross-section (RCS) so as to make them almost impossible to detect by radar. Such aircraft would achieve this by utilizing radar-absorbent-materials (RAMs) and special faceted design shapes to inhibit reflections back to the source of the beam. Such an aircraft was built and first flown in December 1977 as an experimental survivable testbed. It has come to be know as "stealth" technology.

1975 December 4   The Concorde supersonic airliner received its British certificate of airworthiness, British Aerospace Corp. chairman Sir George Edwards receiving the historic document on behalf of the Anglo-French project. Ten Concordes had accumulated 5,539 hr. 44 min. flying time on 2,480 flights of which 1,511 had gone supersonic for a total time above Mach 1 of 2,006 hr. 52 min. The greatest number of flying hours had been recorded by the second prototype (002) G-BSST, which had flown 812 hr. 7 min. on 437 flights. The greatest accumulated supersonic time had been achieved by the third production aircraft (203), 307 hr. 51 min. on 154 flights.

1975 December 23   The USAF issued a contract to Lockheed for the first of four work packages authorizing modifications to strengthen the C-5A wing-box assemblies. The first contract valued at $28.4 million was to cover engineering analysis and design of modification kits. The second contract would cover production of kits to modify one wing for flight testing and another fatigue testing. The third contract would cover production of the kits; the fourth contract would fund installation on line aircraft.

1975 December 26   The Soviet airline Aeroflot announced the inaugural revenue service of the Tupolev Tu-144, thus becoming the first supersonic airliner to enter commercial service. The aircraft made the first of two weekly return flights from Moscow to Alma Ata, the capital of Kazakhstan, a distance of 2,190 mi., in 1 hr. 59 min. However, the aircraft carried mail and freight only and was not expected to carry fare-paying passengers for several months.

1976 January 5   Transportation Secretary William T. Coleman of the United States called a hearing to investigate the case for allowing the Anglo-French Concorde supersonic airliner to land at U.S. airports. Against claims that the SST was too noisy, polluted the atmosphere and depleted the stratospheric ozone shield, proponents cited increased business opportunities that would arise from reduced travel times between the United States and Europe. They also claimed support from the U.S. aerospace industry through the American Institute of Aeronautics & Astronautics and the Aerospace Industries Association.

1976 January 8   The NASA Flight Research Center at Edwards AFB, Calif. was renamed the Hugh L. Dryden Flight Research Center in memory of the man who had been deputy administrator of NASA from its inception on October 1, 1958, until his death from cancer at the age of 67 on December 2, 1965. For 45 yr.

an ordained Methodist minister, Dr. Dryden had been director of the former NACA from 1947, when he replaced George Lewis, and he was the most senior executive of the advisory committee to see it through to the space age.

1976 January 9 The McDonnell Douglas F-15 Eagle entered service with the USAF when the First Tactical Fighter Wing, Langley AFB, Va. became active with this aircraft. For more than a year, the F-15 had been operated by the Fifty-fifth Tactical Fighter Training Squadron at Luke AFB, Ariz., during which more than 2,000 sorties had been flown. To date, 40 F-15s had been delivered to the USAF, and production was scheduled to rise to nine aircraft per month from April. The First Tactical Fighter Wing received its full complement by the end of the year, when deliveries were made to USAFE.

1976 January 21 At 11:30 GMT, British Airways Concorde G-BOAA commanded by Capt. Norman Todd took off from London-Heathrow for Bahrain at the same instant Air France Concorde F-BVFA took off from Paris-Le Bourget for Rio de Janeiro. These were the first scheduled flights for the world's first operational passenger-carrying supersonic transport. The Air France flight took 7 hr. 25 min. including a 1 hr. scheduled refueling stop at Dakar but the British Airways flight lasted 3 hrs. 37 min. and landing first, thus becoming the first to complete a commercial service between planned destinations.

1976 January 24 The U.S. National Transportation Safety Board published results of airline safety statistics for 1975 showing only 42 accidents and 124 deaths for the year compared with 467 deaths in 1974. The death toll for 1975 was inflated by the crash of an Eastern Air Lines aircraft short of the runway at Kennedy International Airport, N.Y. on June 24 with the loss of 112 lives. Overall, the 1975 figure was the best for 18 yr. with a statistical probability of 0.001 fatalities per million air miles flown.

1976 February 4 U.S. transportation secretary William T. Coleman announced his decision regarding a request from Britain and France that the Anglo-French Concorde be allowed to land at U.S. airports. Hotly contested by environmentalists, the request was granted for a trial period of 16 mon. during which the supersonic airliner would be allowed to land at New York's John F. Kennedy Airport four times a day and at Washington's Dulles Airport twice a day. Not least among the reasons given by William Coleman for granting limited access was the willingness shown by Europeans to accept the Boeing 707 jet airliner.

1976 February 6 Announcing results for 1975, U.S. airlines suffered the second worst deficit on record when they posted notice of $87 million losses, compared to a profit of $250.8 million for 1974. Reasons given were 30% increases in fuel prices, runaway fare discounting in efforts to snatch customers on domestic routes and reduced passenger traffic due to the general recession in world business and trade. The worst annual loss experienced by U.S. airlines was in 1970 when the industry suffered a $100.8 million deficit.

1976 February 10 The first production Westland Lynx HAS.Mk.2 (Helicopter Air Service) helicopter for the Royal Navy (serial no. XZ227) made its first flight at Yeovil, Somerset. The first operational unit to receive the type was No. 702 Squadron in December 1977, which formed up on completion of intensive flight trials. The first production version of the AH.Mk.1 (Army Helicopter) for the British Army (serial no. XZ170) made its first flight on February 11, 1977, and completed operational flying trials in December of that year.

On January 21, 1976, the first commercial Concorde flights began on the London-Bahrain and Paris-Rio de Janeiro routes.

1976 February 20 NASA selected Boeing to build an experimental, quiet, short-haul research aircraft (QRSA) using a de Havilland Canada C-8 Buffalo as the aerodynamic basis for a new design. The program would be coordinated by the Ames Research Center toward an acceptable commercial aircraft for reducing airport noise, environmental impact and congestion at large airports. STOL capability was to be an important part of the research effort with propulsive lift technologies reducing runway length and moving local traffic from big airports.

1976 March 5 The Boeing AGM-86A air-launched cruise missile (ALCM) made its first powered flight after being dropped from a B-52 carrier plane over the White Sands Missile Range, N. Mex. Flying at a height of 35,000 ft., the aircraft dropped the missile, which flew under the power of its turbofan engine for about 11 min. Developed by the USAF as a long-range, stand-off weapon capable of ground-hugging, inertially guided flight for up to 750 mi., the AGM-86 evolved from the ALCM program established on December 19, 1973. The USAF wanted more than 2,000 ALCMs for its B-52 and B-1 force.

1976 March 24 The General Dynamics YF-16 prototype, reengineered as a control-configured vehicle (CCV) for full computerized fly-by-wire tests, made its first flight. Utilizing forward canard surfaces canted downward below the under-fuselage air intake, a flight program began that would fully explore the potential of this inherently unstable, high-g aircraft. Capable of making turns with the wings level and of controlled side-slips or stalls during combat evasion or target alignment, the aircraft restored solid traditions among fighter pilots by providing a highly maneuverable, hands-on dogfighter.

1976 April 7 In a special ceremony at Lock Haven, Pa., Piper displayed its 100,000th aircraft, a Cheyenne turboprop business twin named "Heritage of 76." The celebration ceremony included a Piper Cub, the first airplane manufactured by the company—the 99,999th aircraft delivered was in fact the latest version of that aircraft, the PA-18 Super Cub. Piper claimed that of the approximate 1 million aircraft produced to date, Piper had built 10% and that of all aircraft flying, 25% had been built by Piper.

1976 May 19   U.S. aviator and champion golfer Arnold Palmer completed a FAI light aircraft record-breaking flight around the world in 57 hr. 25 min. 42 sec., accompanied by Robert J. Serling from the National Aeronautic Association and copilots James E. Bir and L. L. Purkey. His flight in the Gates Learjet *200 Yankee* was 28 hr. 43 min. 19 sec. faster than the previous record set by Arthur Godfrey and Dick Merrill in 1966. Covering approximately 23,000 mi., the four men averaged almost 599 MPH and made nine stops in seven countries, presenting bicentennial flags and bronze replicas of the Declaration of Independence.

1976 May 24   British Airways Concorde G-BOAC commanded by Capt. Brian Calvert and Air France Concorde F-BVFA commanded by Capt. Duval arrived together at Washington's Dulles International Airport, having flown the Atlantic from London and Paris respectively at the start of the Europe-U.S. scheduled service. Special presentations and speeches were made as the two gleaming white aircraft stood nose to nose, dignitaries referring, in this U.S. bicentennial year, to the 66 days taken by the *Mayflower* to cross the Atlantic Ocean.

1976 May 25   The first flight of the Boeing E-3A Sentry AWACS fitted with full mission avionics took place just over 3 yr. after authorization of full-scale development. The first aircraft was delivered to the 552d AWAC Wing at Tinker AFB, Okla. on March 24, 1977. The first 24 aircraft ordered were delivered to this standard, but 10 more ordered in 1981 would incorporate improved avionics and the initial aircraft upgraded to an E-3B standard for U.S./NATO operational use.

1976 May 28   Responding to an emergency call for aid, helicopters from HS-4 aboard the USS *Ranger*, with detachments from HC-3 on the USS *Camden*, USS *Mars* and USS *White Plains*, air-lifted flood victims to safety from Central Luzon in the Philippines. Along with helicopters from Cubi Point NAS, U.S. military personnel evacuated 1,900 people and provided 185 tons of relief supplies and 9,340 gal. of fuel.

1976 June 5   A U.S. Navy Grumman A-6 Intruder launched the first fully guided Tomahawk cruise missile over the White Sands Missile Range in New Mexico. Flying at a height of 11,500 ft., the aircraft released the missile for a free flight lasting approximately 61 min. using a turbofan engine for the first time. The flight came only 4 mon. after the first TERCOM (terrain contour matching) test had been carried out using a U.S. Navy Firebee drone.

1976 June 24   Extending the life of the Beech T-34 Mentor primary training aircraft, the U.S. Navy received the first of its T-34C versions ordered in 1973. Beech had built 423 earlier models of the same aircraft. Powered by a 715-SHP Pratt & Whitney PT6A-25 turboprop, the aircraft had a span of 33 ft. 6 in. and a length of 28 ft. 8 in. First selected on June 17, 1954, the Beech T-34 Mentor was powered by a 225-HP Continental O-470-4 engine, had a gross weight of 3,000 lb. and a maximum speed of 188 MPH, compared to 4,000 lb. and 257 MPH respectively for the T-34C.

1976 June 27   An Air France Airbus A300B2 on its way from Tel Aviv, Israel to Paris, France with 256 passengers and 12 crew was hijacked shortly after taking off from Athens, Greece

and ordered to Benghazi to refuel. From there it was flown to Entebbe, Uganda, where the hostages were taken from the aircraft and detained at gunpoint in the terminal building while the terrorists, by this time numbering 16, made demands over Ugandan radio for the release of 53 convicted terrorists from Israeli jails. The Israeli defense forces devised a dramatic air-launched rescue plan to release the hostages, carried out July 3.

1976 June 30   Marking the 50th anniversary of scheduled airline services in the United States, the Air Transport Association noted that in 1926 only 6,000 people were carried between a few cities whereas in 1975 U.S. airlines had carried 205 million passengers on domestic flights and that statistically air travel was 10 times safer than travel by automobile. Freight services in 1975 grossed 4.7 billion ton-miles, although oil price increases and an industry recession had reduced this by 2.5% over 1974.

1976 July 1   Clive Canning arrived in England having flown from Australia in his home-built Thorpe T18 (VH-CMC), the first flight of such distance by an aircraft put together by an amateur from a kit. Canning began his journey June 16 and made it to the United Kingdom in 98 flying hr., flying via West Irian, Celebes, Southern Borneo, Sumatra, Singapore, Thailand, Burma, India, Pakistan, Iran, Bahrain, Saudi Arabia, Cyprus, Greece and France, crossing the English Channel to land at Shoreham.

1976 July 2   The first carried-on-deck (COD) version of the Lockheed S-3 Viking, designated US-3A, made its first flight demonstrating the applicability of that aircraft as a replacement for the Grumman C-1 Greyhound presently used by the U.S. Navy. Adapted for logistical support of carriers at sea, the US-3A had gross weight reduced to 47,601 lb. and provision for carrying a maximum cargo load of 5,750 lb. in the modified bomb bay and two pods on external wing pylons. A projected production version would have had a stretched fuselage and capacity for 11 passengers.

1976 July 3   Israeli special forces troops landed by Israeli Air Force C-130s at Entebbe airport, Uganda, where passengers and crew of an Air France Airbus A300B2 hijacked June 27 were held hostage, fought their way into the terminal building. In an operation that lasted 53 min., the terrorists were overwhelmed and shot, and the hostages flown out to safety via Nairobi, Kenya. About seven MiG fighters were destroyed on the ground at Entebbe to prevent the Ugandans following them. The Israelis claimed later they had received no outside help and had forced the Kenyans to give them fuel and assistance.

1976 July 12   The U.S. Navy phased out the last Douglas C-117D, ending a 35-year-long association with derivatives of the DC-3. The last aircraft of this type was flown to the Davis-Monthan AFB, Ariz. from Pensacola, Fla. The C-117D was originally designated R4D-8, 98 of which had been built from converted R4D models under a Super DC-3 program instigated by Douglas. With new outer wing panels of modest sweep spanning 90 ft. and with two 1,475-HP Wright R-1820-80 radials, the aircraft served as a personnel transport.

1976 July 27   The U.S. Defense Department granted approval to a limited development program of the McDonnell Douglas AV-8B advanced Harrier 4 mon. after the Defense Acquisition Review Council had authorized a flight test program using two YAV-8B aircraft converted from two AV-8As. The British had withdrawn from the program March 15, 1975, but the U.S. Marine Corps wanted about 336 Advanced Harriers with more powerful engines, a supercritical wing and other refinements.

1976 July 27   A Lockheed SR-71A flown by Maj. Adolphus H. Bledsoe and Maj. John T. Fuller, USAF, from the Ninth Strategic Reconnaissance Wing, Beale AFB, Calif. set a 1,000 km (621.4 mi.) closed-circuit speed record of 3,367.221 km/hr. (2,092.29 MPH) on the first of two record-setting days that would establish speed and altitude records still unbroken as of June 1993. It is unlikely that the official record will be broken during this century, although several experimental, classified aircraft have flown considerably faster.

1976 July 28   Capt. Eldon W. Joersz and Maj. George T. Morgan Jr., USAF, flying a Lockheed SR-71A from the Ninth Strategic Reconnaissance Wing, Beale AFB, Calif. set a new absolute world speed record over a 25 km course of 3,529.56 km/hr. (2,193.17 MPH). Also this day, Capt. Robert C. Helt and Maj. Lang A. Elliott, USAF, of the Ninth Strategic Reconnaissance Wing, achieved a sustained altitude record in horizontal flight of 25,929.031 m (85,069 ft.). Neither record is likely to be broken this century unless classified military research aircraft capable of greater speed and altitude are publicly unveiled.

1976 July 29   A memorandum of understanding signed by the governments of the United Kingdom, Germany and Italy formally approved full production for the multi-role combat aircraft Tornado project, authorizing series production of 809 aircraft and placing firm orders for the first 40 aircraft. There were nine Tornado prototypes and one static test airframe as well as one pre-production aircraft to be followed by 385 for the United Kingdom, 324 for West Germany and 100 for Italy.

1976 August 9   The prototype Boeing YC-14 contender for the USAF advanced medium STOL transport aircraft program made its first flight on the power of two 51,000-lb. s.t. General Electric CF6-50D turbofan engines. With a wingspan of 129 ft. and a length of 131 ft. 8 in., it had a gross weight of 251,000 lb. (maximum STOL weight of 170,000 lb.), a cruising speed of 449 MPH and a radius of 460 mi. or 3,190 mi. in the ferry configuration. With the engines positioned so as to blow their efflux over the inboard portion of the wing and trailing edge flaps in an upper surface blowing (USB) concept, the aircraft had remarkable STOL performance.

1976 August 10   The U.S. Senate voted a FY 1977 Defense Appropriations Bill that restricted expenditure of the Rockwell B-1 to just $87 million per month until February 1, 1977. This effectively deferred a full production decision until after the next U.S. president would assume office following the impending election. Deep controversy over the need, capabilities and operational USAF procurement plan for this penetration and stand-off bomber had held votes close to a tie in both the Senate and House of Representatives, with opponents, including Democratic presidential nominee Jimmy Carter, wanting to cancel it.

1976 August 12   The Aermacchi M.B.339X prototype two-seat trainer/ground attack aircraft made its first flight. Developed from the excellent M.B.326 first flown on December 10, 1957, this equally successful aircraft had a wingspan of 35 ft. 7 in. over tip tanks, a length of 36 ft. and a maximum takeoff weight of 13,000 lb. Powered by a 4,000-lb. s.t. Rolls Royce Viper Mk 632-43 turbojet engine, it had a maximum speed of 558 MPH at sea level or 508 MPH at 30,000 ft. The operational M.B.339A would itself form the basis for the single-seat M.B.339K Veltro II.

1976 August 13   The Bell Model 222, the first twin-engined light commercial helicopter developed in the United States, made its first flight, powered by the 650-SHP Avco Lycoming LTS

101-650C. Capable of carrying up to nine passengers, it had a rotor diameter of 30 ft. and a fuselage length of 39 ft. 9 in., with a maximum takeoff weight of 6,700 lb. FAA certification was granted August 16, 1979, with production getting under way 2 mon. later, at which point orders totaling almost 200 had been received.

1976 August 13   The U.S. retired the Grumman HU-16 Albatross almost 29 yr. after the first flight of this amphibian, the last operational navy seaplane. The final water landing was made at Pensacola Bay, Fla., after which it was flown to Sherman Field and from there turned over to the Naval Aviation Museum at Pensacola. So ended 65 yr. of naval aviation tradition during which seaplanes and flying boats had been an established part of the inventory. From this date, the U.S. Navy had an all-wheels air force.

1976 August 18   The first Lockheed Model 1329-25 JetStar II made its first flight, powered by four 3,700-lb. s.t. Garrett-AiResearch TFE 731-3 turbofan engines. A reengined JetStar 731 set up to evaluate the JetStar II configuration had first flown on July 10, 1974, but the production aircraft received its FAA certification on December 14, 1976. Lockheed had built 16 JetStars when production of the initial version ended in 1973, and AiResearch offered reengining services for these earlier models as well as installing the new turbofans on the JetStar II.

1976 August 18   British Airways announced selection of the Lockheed L-1011-500 TriStar, with an initial order for six, to replace the VC-10 and early model Boeing 707 airliners. Powered by the 50,000-lb. class Rolls Royce RB.211-524B, the aircraft was the launch order for this new long-range version that had a fuselage reduced in length by 13 ft. 6 in., capacity for 246 to 300 passengers and maximum gross weight increased to 496,000 lb. This engine was also selected by British Airways for its Boeing 747s, which flew for the first time on September 3.

1976 September 6   Soviet air force pilot Lt. Viktor Balenko landed at Japan's Hakodate commercial airfield on the island of Hokkaido, delivering to the West a MiG-25 Foxbat interceptor in pristine condition. He asked for political asylum and was flown to the United States on September 8. Detailed technical examination of his aircraft revealed it to be a crude engineering compromise with rough welds of cracked surface, valve avionics devoid of any solid-state circuitry, a paucity of instruments, and an ineffective ejection seat.

Typical of the new generation of wide-body airliners, the Lockheed L-1011 TriStar was powered by Rolls Royce engines.

Rolled out on October 22, 1976, the Bell XV-15 was the first NASA/U.S. Army tilt-rotor research aircraft.

1976 September 9 The first Boeing AGM-86A fully guided air-launched cruise missile (ALCM) flight took place over White Sands Missile Range, N. Mex. when a B-52 dropped a test missile. The free flight lasted 31 min., and the ALCM flew between 30 ft. and 180 ft. above the ground to demonstrate terrain avoidance capabilities. By negotiating four TERCOM (terrain contour matching) grid positions detected by its radar, the missile demonstrated guidance capabilities based on preset coordinates. The missile ran out of fuel and crashed short of its test objective.

1976 September 30 The first production Hindustin Aeronautics Limited Ajeet single-seat, lightweight interceptor developed from the Hawker Siddeley Gnat made its first flight, powered by a 4,500-lb. s.t. nonafterburning Rolls Royce Orpheus 701-01 turbojet. Designed as an improved and upgraded Gnat, the aircraft had a maximum speed of 716 MPH and a climb time of 6 min. 2 sec. to 39,375 ft. Four underwing pylon points permitted a variety of external stores in addition to two 30-mm Aden cannons in the bulbous intake fairings.

1976 October 10 The Embraer EMB-121 Xingu made its first flight as Brazil's first pressurized, twin-turboprop, general-purpose aircraft. Powered by the 680-SHP Pratt & Whitney Canada PT6A-28 turboprop, the Xingu had a wingspan of 47 ft. 5 in. and a length of 40 ft. 2 in. With a maximum takeoff weight of 12,500 lb., it had an economical cruising speed of 234 MPH at 20,000 ft. and a maximum payload range of 1,035 mi. With a cabin configured for nine passengers and two pilots, the EMB-121 represented the maturing state of Brazil's active aircraft industry.

1976 October 10 The 57-year-old U.S. balloon-maker Ed Yost, who set out to cross the Atlantic in his helium balloon, was picked up in the water by the German tanker *Elisabeth Bolton* after coming down prematurely 3 hr. earlier about 750 mi. west of the Azores. Ed Yost had broken all previous records by remaining aloft for 107 hr. and traveling 2,500 mi.

1976 October 12 The NASA/U.S. Army rotor systems research aircraft produced by Sikorsky as the S-72, made its first

flight, powered by two 1,500-SHP General Electric T58-GE-5 turboshaft engines driving a 62-ft. rotor in a helicopter configuration. The S-72 also had provision for two 9,275-lb. s.t. General Electric TF34-GE-2 turbofans in compound form attached to two pylons on fixed wings. It had a length of 70 ft. 7 in. with a T-tail spanning 13 ft. 3 in., but in convertiplane configuration, it would have a lower tailplane of 25 ft. span and an upper tailplane reduced to 8 ft. 7 in. The S-72 was scheduled for research on rotor technology at the Ames Research Center.

1976 November 2 A joint announcement by Britain and France confirmed that no more Concorde supersonic airliners would be built beyond the 16 production aircraft already constructed or funded. To date, British Airways had five, Air France had four, and of those in assembly, British Airways would get two and Air France three. Iran had options on two but would not take those up. The cost of the Concorde and essential support equipment was $49.6 million. The decision was announced after a meeting in London between the French transport minister Marcel Cavaille and his British counterpart Gerald Kaufman of the Labour government.

1976 November 5 The U.S. Marine Corps began flight-testing the latest version of the Bell SeaCobra, the AH-1T. Powered by a 2,050-SHP Pratt & Whitney Canada T400-WV-402 twin-turboshaft engine, it could lift 5,392 lb. compared to 2,739 lb. and had a fuselage 48 ft. 2 in. in length compared to 44 ft. 7 in. Later modifications included an ability to carry TOW missiles, and following an initial order for 10 aircraft placed in June 1975, the Marine Corps received its first AH-1T on October 15, 1977.

1976 December 2 The shuttle carrier aircraft, a NASA-modified Boeing 747-123, made its first flight, powered by uprated Pratt & Whitney JT9D-7H engines. Bought from American Airlines for $15 million in 1974, the four-year-old airliner had logged 9,000 flying hr. and was converted to carry the NASA orbiter atop the fuselage. It was fitted with two 200-sq. ft., 900-lb. vertical fins to the extremity of each horizontal tail surface for improved directional stability and a 1,000-lb. mass inertia damper in the nose fitted so as to move laterally on rollers mounted to the floor to damp oscillations caused by air flowing across the orbiter.

1976 December 2 U.S. defense secretary of the outgoing Ford administration, Donald H. Rumsfeld, announced contracts to Rockwell International, General Electric and Boeing for limited production of the B-1 bomber. Work was to proceed on three production models plus long-lead procurement for an additional eight. President-elect Jimmy Carter had advised that he was against production but held out hope for additional study.

1976 December 8 The first full-scale development (FSD) F-16 made its first flight incorporating numerous changes and modifications made to the original YF-16 when it more closely represented the lightweight fighter specification than the operational F-16A would. At first designed to carry an external stores load of 8,000 lb., the eight FSD aircraft could carry 11,000 lb. or 15,200 lb. with reduced fuel load. Operational aircraft would have a reduced fuel load carrying capacity of 20,450 lb., more than the original YF-16 weighed.

1976 December 10 The Hughes AH-64A was named winner of the U.S. Army advanced attack helicopter fly-off competition against the Bell Model 409 (YAH-63A). The AH-64A was to be named Apache. Hughes also received contracts for production of the 30-mm XM230 Chain Gun to be attached to a chin turret in the forward fuselage. The army planned to commence production of 472 Apaches in 1980, and a new facility would be built by Hughes at Mesa, Ariz. to accommodate increased orders.

1976 December 22 Ilyushin test pilot A. Kuznetsov took the first Il-86 airliner into the air. Powered by four 28,660-lb. s.t. Kuznetsov NK-86 turbofan engines, it was the Soviet Union's first large-capacity, wide-body commercial transport aircraft, with a wingspan of 157 ft. 8 in., a length of 195 ft. 4 in. and a maximum takeoff weight of up to 454,150 lb. With a capacity for 234 to 350 passengers, it had a crew of three and a maximum payload of 92,600 lb. The aircraft was subjected to rigorous testing before Aeroflot began operations with the type on December 26, 1980, followed by international services from July 3, 1981.

1976 December 23 The Sikorsky S-70 was declared the winner for the U.S. Army utility tactical transport aircraft competitive fly-off, and the type was selected for development as the UH-60 Black Hawk. With a cabin capacity for 11 fully equipped troops in addition to a crew of three, it could be fitted for medical evacuation, reconnaissance, command and control or troop resupply, and had an 8,000-lb. capacity cargo hook for external lift. The U.S. Army planned to procure 1,107 helicopters of this type by the mid-1980s.

1977 January 2 Designed by Prof. Hidemasa Kimura and built by students at the Nihon University, Tokyo, the Stork B man-powered aircraft controlled by Takashi Katoh achieved a record flying distance of 6,870 ft. between 3 ft. and 7 ft. above the ground at the Shimofusa naval base. Built of wood and metal, the Stork B was the 10th man-powered design from the university. It had a wingspan of 68 ft. 9 in., a length of 28 ft. 11 in. and an empty weight of almost 80 lb. It was propelled by a pusher propeller driven by a chain from the pilot's pedals.

1977 January 6 The first HAL HPT-32 basic trainer for the Indian Air Force made its first flight. Powered by a 260-HP Lycoming AEIO-540-D4B5 flat-six engine, it had a wingspan of 31 ft. 2 in. and a length of 25 ft. 4 in. The aircraft had side-by-side seats for pilot and instructor plus a third seat behind; the cabin could be converted for army liaison work when needed. The HPT-32 had a takeoff weight of 2,756 lb., a stall speed of 68 MPH with flaps up or 68 MPH with flaps down, a maximum speed of 135 MPH and a range of 435 mi.

1977 January 7 Despite major protests from U.S. aircraft manufacturers, the U.S. Coast Guard signed a contract for 41 French-built Dassault-Breguet Falcon 20Gs powered by two 5,300-lb s.t. Garrett AiResearch ATF3-6 turbofans for medium-range surveillance. The aircraft were to be assembled and flown from the Falcon Jet Corp. facilities at Little Rock, Ark. It took a decision by Transportation Secretary William T. Coleman to overrule the protests. Designated HU-25A, the aircraft had a wingspan of 53 ft. 6 in. and a length of 56 ft. 3 in. with a cruising speed of 531 MPH and a range of 2,590 mi.

1977 January 21 In its first year, the Anglo-French Concorde supersonic airliner carried 45,000 passengers on 1,000 revenue departures with a reliability of more than 90%. Load factors averaged 64%, with 70% on the Paris-Washington service, 62% on the Paris-Dakar-Rio de Janeiro run and 36% on the Paris-Caracas service. Overall, British Airways showed a net loss on Concorde services, with break-even on fuel, crew and ground-handling costs. Against a projected annual break-even utilization of 2,750 hr. per aircraft and 65% load factors, Concorde had 1,190 hr./aircraft in the first year.

1977 February 11 U.S. Pres. Jimmy Carter made his one and only flight in a Boeing E-4A national emergency airborne command post (NEACP) aircraft of the First Airborne Command and Control Squadron. He flew from Andrews AFB, Md. to Robins AFB, Ga. It was the first occasion on which a U.S. president had flown in an aircraft of this type.

1977 February 17 The 10,000th Beech Model 35 Bonanza was delivered by the manufacturer just 30 yr. 2 days after the first aircraft had been delivered on February 15, 1947. The aircraft began a series of publicity displays and demonstrations across the United States between the end of February and September. Since its first flight on December 22, 1945, it proved one of the most popular and, with its V-tail, one of the most distinctive, U.S. light and general-purpose aircraft since World War II.

1977 February 18 The first of five captive-inactive flights of the Boeing 747/space shuttle combination took place when the piggy-back combination took off from the NASA Dryden Flight Research Center, Edwards AFB, Calif. The Boeing 747 was flown by Fitzhugh L. Fulton Jr. and Thomas C. McMurtry with flight engineers Victor W. Horton and Louis E. Guidry Jr. on board. The combination took off at 8:30 A.M. and remained airborne for 2 hr. 15 min., reaching a height of 16,000 ft. and a maximum speed of 287 MPH. There was no crew aboard the Shuttle Orbiter 101 *Enterprise* mounted atop the Boeing 747.

1977 February 19 Pres. Carter announced action to stop further development work on an advanced tanker cargo aircraft (ATCA), which USAF Strategic Air Command had been developing as a conceptual deployment-support aircraft. In January, Pres. Ford had announced a program plan for 91 ATCAs, which would have been militarized versions of either the Boeing 747 or the McDonnell Douglas DC-10.

1977 March 10 The result of a requirement raised by the USAF to replace the Douglas EB-66, the first Grumman EF-111A electronic warfare aircraft made its first flight. With a fin-tip pod carrying receivers, a 16 ft. ventral canoe-shaped radome, a fully fitted electronic suite in the space usually occupied by the weapons bay and controls and displays for an electronic warfare officer in the right seat, the empty weight was raised to 55,275 lb., but gross weight was down at 88,848 lb. The first fully equipped EF-111A flew on May 17.

1977 March 13   The Sikorsky S-76 Spirit took to the air for the first time, powered by two 650-SHP Allison 250-C30 turboshaft engines driving a 44-ft. rotor. Designed as a 12-passenger commercial transport helicopter aimed at securing for its manufacturer a larger share of the civil market, it had a length of 44 ft. 1 in. and a maximum takeoff weight of 10,000 lb. With a cruising speed of 144 MPH, it had a range of up to 691 mi. Among the wide range of Sikorsky helicopters available, it was unique in being derived solely from a civil specification.

1977 March 16   The U.S. Army accepted the first production Bell AH-1S HueyCobra equipped with Hughes TOW anti-armor missiles and powered by a 1,825-SHP Avco Lycoming T53-L-703 engine. The AH-1S was a modified AH-19, upgraded with the objective of making it the U.S. Army's primary anti-armor helicopter of the 1980s. The army accepted the aircraft, which was the 1,127th HueyCobra built at Bell's Fort Worth facility.

1977 March 24   The Lockheed YC-141B made its first flight following roll out January 8. The one prototype, stretched StarLifter requested by the USAF had 23 ft. 4 in. fuselage "plugs" fore and aft of the wing, increasing length to 168 ft. 4 in. and load-carrying capacity by 35% to 89,152 lb. Maximum takeoff weight was 343,000 lb., and the C-141B had a maximum payload range of 3,200 mi. with the added advantage of a refueling receptacle. Flying a month ahead of schedule and $4 million under budget, the flight-test program was completed July 1977 with conversion of all 270 C-141As to the B configuration by June 1982.

1977 March 24   The first Boeing E-3A was delivered to the USAF Tactical Air Command's 552d Airborne Warning and Control Wing at Tinker AFB, Okla. Six more were scheduled to arrive by the end of the year, ready for operational duty beginning September 23. To date, Congress had approved purchase of 19 of the 34 E-3As the USAF wanted with deliveries at the rate of 6 per year from March 1978.

1977 March 27   The world's worst commercial air disaster took the lives of 579 people when a Pan American Boeing 747 turned onto the runway ahead of a KLM Boeing 747 as it was taking off from Los Rodeos Airport in Tenerife in the Canary Islands. At speed, the KLM 747 climbed across the top of the Pan American 747, tearing out the upper fuselage and carrying the wreckage on down the runway a distance of 1,488 ft. All those aboard the KLM plane were killed while only 65 people aboard the Pan American 747 survived.

1977 March 29   A world altitude record for gliders was claimed following a flight by British Airways computer technical officer Mike Field in his Skylark 4 to an altitude of 51,580 ft. The ascent was reached in a flight across the Cairngorms in Scotland and exceeded by more than 5,500 ft. the 15-yr.-old record held by the United States. However, the British Gliding Assn. refused to ratify Field's claim and also withdrew claims he made over a period of five yr., saying that the barograph records were not genuine.

1977 March 31   The British defense secretary Frederick Mulley, on behalf of the Labour government, announced that the United Kingdom would not be participating in a proposed NATO

procurement of the Boeing E-3A AWACS aircraft and would be starting full-scale development of its own aircraft to fill this role. A version of the Hawker Siddeley Nimrod would be developed into an AWACS aircraft at a cost of around £300 million including £22 million already spent. It was planned that Hawker Siddeley would convert 11 Nimrod airframes into AEW (airborne early warning) Mk.3 configuration for service from 1981–82.

1977 April 27   At 3:53 A.M. three F-15A Eagles of the Thirty-sixth Tactical Fighter Wing, USAF, took off from their base at Langley, Va. as the first in a series of cells making up three squadrons for duty in Bitburg, Germany. By the end of the year, the wing was completely deployed with USAFE. This was the first time the air-superior F-15A had been deployed to Europe, and the First Tactical Fighter Wing had built up six squadrons, three of which formed the Thirty-sixth Tactical Fighter Wing, for that requirement.

1977 April 29   Put through Parliament by the Labour government, British Aerospace (BAe) officially came into being, absorbing and nationalizing the former companies owned by the British Aircraft Corp. (BAC), Hawker Siddeley and Scottish Aviation. For the first time, all major civil and military aircraft manufacturing in the United Kingdom was under one unified corporation. As early as November 21, 1966, the British government had proposed a merger. In January 1981, the conservative government would de-nationalize BAC, and it became a public limited company.

1977 May 3   The Bell Model 301 tilt-rotor research aircraft made its first free hover under a joint NASA/U.S. Army program. Designated XV-15, the aircraft was powered by two 1,550-SHP Avco Lycoming LTC1K-4K turboshaft engines mounted in nacelles at each wingtip and driving 25-ft. rotors. With provision for tilting for vertical flight and gradual transition to horizontal for forward flight, the gearboxes were interchangeable for safety. The XV-15 had a length of 42 ft. 1 in., a wingspan across the nacelles of 35 ft. 2 in. and a VTOL maximum takeoff weight of 13,000 lb. or 15,000 lb. for STOL.

1977 May 20   The Sukhoi Su-27 Flanker took to the air for the first time as a single-seat, all-weather, counter-air fighter. Roughly the equivalent of the McDonnell Douglas F-15 Eagle, this was the first of two new-generation Soviet fighters to fly, the second being the MiG-29 Fulcrum. However, considerable redesign of the Su-27 was necessary to bring it to definitive production standard, and it did not enter service before 1986, after the MiG-29, which became operational in early 1985.

1977 June 3   A USAF Fairchild A-10 crashed at the Paris Air Show, killing the manufacturer's chief test pilot, Howard W. Nelson. He had 10,000 hrs. experience, had flown 105 combat missions during the Korean War and had logged 500 hr. in the A-10. The first squadron of A-10s was scheduled to go into operational service June 10 at Myrtle Beach AFB, S.C. It was the first major accident for an aircraft of this type since its first flight in 1972 but the sixth air crash at the Paris Air Show in 12 yr.

1977 June 10   The first flight took place of the Britten-Norman Islander fitted with ducted propulsors designed and manufactured by Dowty-Rotol and installed by Miles-Dufon. The seven-blade, variable-pitch fans were contained within broad-chord ducts powered by the conventional Avco-Lycoming engines, which had been relocated to pylons beneath each wing. Test pilot Neville Duke was in charge of tests, which aimed to demonstrate the quiet operation of this radical concept.

1977 June 11 Agreement was reached by the United States and the United Kingdom on a new air services treaty to replace the Bermuda Agreement of 1947, which controlled services on the North Atlantic, Pacific, Bermuda and Caribbean routes. Single airlines from each country would be granted operating licenses to single destinations except on the London-New York and London-Los Angeles routes, where two would be allowed. This opened the way for Laker Skytrain to begin and Pan American and TWA to continue operating these routes.

1977 June 18 The first of three captive-active flight tests with the mated NASA Boeing 747/Space Shuttle Orbiter 101 *Enterprise* began at 8:06 A.M. and lasted 55 min. 46 sec. with astronauts Fred Haise and Gordon Fullerton in the shuttle. The purpose of these three mated flights was to evaluate orbiter systems and crew control handling prior to a series of air-launched drop tests. With a combined takeoff weight of 50,800 lb., the combination reached a maximum altitude of 14,970 ft. and a maximum speed of 208 MPH.

1977 June 28 The first Hawker Siddeley Nimrod AEW trial aircraft, Comet 4 (serial no. XV626) made its first flight following ground tests on the avionics and electronic equipment manufactured by Marconi-Elliott. The aircraft had a large radome beneath the nose and a large fin-tip radome, and additional installations would add an extended rear-fuselage radome. These aircraft were scheduled to replace the Avro Shackleton piston-engined aircraft in the role of long-range maritime surveillance.

1977 June 30 Pres. Carter announced that he was canceling the Rockwell B-1 bomber program but that he was authorizing research and development on the three flying prototypes to continue and the fourth prototype to be completed. This aircraft made its first flight on February 14, 1979, and was the first to carry a full suite of defensive and offensive avionics and weapons systems. Pres. Carter wanted B-1 testing to continue as a hedge against difficulties with an expanded cruise missile program he had authorized instead of the manned penetrating bomber.

1977 July 7 NASA announced it had awarded Boeing a contract to manufacture composite structures for ground tests with a Boeing 727. This work resulted from a research program aimed at lowering fuel costs by 50%, and achieving their aircraft weight reduction was one approach thought worthy of development. The selected composites would comprise high-strength filaments in a polymer matrix, creating a structure lighter, but stronger, than metal. NASA's Langley Research Center was to manage the work over a 3 yr. 6 mon. period.

1977 July 11 The unique Ball-Bartoe Jetwing prototype propulsive-lift research aircraft made its first flight at Boulder, Colo. Designed by O. E. Bartoe Jr. to improve STOL performance and patented by the Ball Corp., the Jetwing was devised as an innovative means of combining propulsive force with augmented lift. It had a 2,200-lb. s.t. Pratt & Whitney Canada JT15D-1 turbofan engine exhausting hot efflux and bypass air through spanwise leading-edge nozzles and across the top of the wing. It had a wingspan of 21 ft. 9 in. and a length of 28 ft. 7 in.

1977 July 19 A special dedication ceremony at the NASA/Langley Research Center formalized the start of work on a national transonic facility. Scheduled to be completed by 1980 at a cost of $85 million, it would use cryogenic nitrogen for realistic simulation of Mach numbers and atmospheric-density ratios. The facility would be used by government and industry as well as research establishments and the scientific community. Speakers

at the dedication included Dr. John J. Martin, assistant secretary of the USAF for research and development, and Donald F. Hearth, the director of the Langley Research Center.

1977 July 22 Responding to an attack on its border town of Sollum by Libyan aircraft, Egypt attacked the air base at the town of Gamal Abdel Nasser south of Tobruk. Further strikes were carried out July 24 during which large numbers of Libyan aircraft were claimed to have been destroyed on the ground. The Libyan base was home to two Mirage and two MiG-23 squadrons. The Egyptians also suffered losses, claimed by Libya to be 14 aircraft. On July 28, the U.S. State Department said it would supply aircraft to Egypt for defensive purposes.

1977 August 12 The first of five air-launched drop tests of the NASA Space Shuttle Orbiter 101 *Enterprise* took place 48 min. after the mated Boeing 747/Orbiter combination took off from the NASA Dryden Flight Research Center, Edwards AFB, Calif. at 8:00 A.M. Piloted by Fred Haise and Gordon Fullerton, the Orbiter separated from the Boeing 747 at a height of 24,000 ft. and a speed of 310 MPH for a free-flight time of 5 min. 22 sec. The last free-flight test took place on October 26.

1977 August 23 Designed by Dr. Paul MacCready and made by the MacCready Company of AeroVironment Inc., a man-powered aircraft named *Gossamer Condor* won the £50,000 Kramer Prize offered to the first person to propel such a device on a figure-eight course. The requirement to fly around two poles 0.5 mi. apart was met by bicyclist Bryan Allen, who completed the course at Shafter, Calif. in a time of 7 min. 27.5 sec. MacCready was working on another design, the *Gossamer Albatross,* with which he hoped to make the first man-powered crossing of the English Channel.

1977 August 31 Soviet test pilot Alexander Fedotov claimed a new world height record for manned aircraft when he climbed to a height of 37,650 m (123,523 ft.). He was flying a Mikoyan E-266M, a specially adapted variant of the MiG-25 Foxbat. In a second flight, the same pilot carried a "payload" of 2,000 kg (4,410 lb.) to a record height of 37,080 m (121,656 ft.). Both records stood as of June 1993.

1977 August The National Aeronautic Assn. announced that the U.S. Powder Puff Derby held during this month was to be the last. Started in 1947, the 30th race was a sentimental journey across the continental United States, with 127 women from many other countries, including Australia, West Germany and even the Bahamas. A shortage of fuel brought on by the energy crisis and funding constraints led the Aeronautic Assn. to decide this would be the last race of its kind.

1977 September 23 Pres. Carter approved a decision by the U.S. Department of Transportation to allow the Anglo-French Concorde supersonic airliner to land at any U.S. airport contingent upon agreement by the local authorities. This announcement came at the end of a 16-mon. trial during which limited services had been allowed at Dulles International Airport, Washington, D.C. and John F. Kennedy International Airport, New York. Miami, Honolulu and Philadelphia had also indicated their interest in receiving Concorde.

1977 September 26 Laker Airways started operations with its one-class economy service between London and New York 6 yr. after the first proposals were submitted for approval to the regulatory bodies in the United States and the United Kingdom. Passengers could book seats only on the day of the flight, with ticket

The Tornado air defense variant emerged in the early 1980s and is seen here with Sidewinder missiles and long-range fuel tanks.

offices open at 4:00 A.M. Tickets cost £59 from London to New York and $135 from New York to London. Laker Airways would operate four DC-10s on the service, offering refreshments and in-flight entertainment.

1977 October 6   The first MiG-29 made its first flight in the Soviet Union. Designed and developed as a twin-engined, single-seat, counter-air combat aircraft, production aircraft were powered by two 11,240/18,300-lb. s.t. Klimov RD-33 augmented bypass turbojet engines providing a maximum speed of Mach 2.3 (1,518 MPH) at 36,000 ft. or Mach 1.06 (805 MPH) at sea level. With a maximum takeoff weight of 40,785 lb., the MiG-29 carried a 30-mm GSh-301 cannon and six R-60 Aphid AAMs. It had a wingspan of 37 ft. 4 in. and a length of 56 ft. 10 in.

1977 October 30   A Pan American Boeing 747SP completed a round-the-world flight over the North and South poles, carrying 165 passengers a distance of 26,382.75 mi. in 54 hr. 7 min. 12 sec. at an average speed of 487.35 MPH. Flying from and to San Francisco, the aircraft stopped at London, Capetown, South Africa and Auckland, New Zealand and set a record for circum-navigating the globe via the poles. It also established a record speed of 479 MPH for the 13,141 mi. between the poles and set several point-to-point records en route. The longest sector was the 7,550 mi. between Capetown and Auckland at 532 MPH with a takeoff weight of 677,000 lb. including 331,500 lb. fuel.

1977 November 1   The Tupolev Tu-144 began regularly scheduled passenger services on the Moscow-Alma Ata (now Almaty, Kazakhstan) route, carrying 140 passengers the full distance of 2,190 mi. in 1 hr. 55 min. The aircraft had been operating on this route since December 26, 1975, and between Moscow and Khabarovsk since February 2, 1977, for cargo and mail services,

but this was the first time Aeroflot claimed to have put the air-craft into routine passenger service. Five out of the first six flights were canceled, and the service was withdrawn without announce-ment on June 1, 1978. In all, 13 Tu-144s had flown, four were used for the passenger flights and two had crashed.

1977 November 15   NASA began a series of Orbiter ferry flight tests with its Boeing 747 shuttle carrier aircraft (SCA) prior to commencing duty air-lifting NASA Orbiters between assembly plants, Edwards AFB, Calif., and the Kennedy Space Center in Florida. The SCA would be routinely employed moving Orbiters from place to place when orbital flight tests began with the first shuttle space flight on April 12, 1981.

1977 November 22   The first regularly scheduled commercial Concorde supersonic passenger service from Europe to New York

First flown on October 6, 1977, the MiG-29 represented Soviet state-of-the-art fighter technology.

was completed at around 8:30 A.M. when Air France and British Airways aircraft arrived at John F. Kennedy Airport from France and England respectively. Despite years of opposition and court hearings, anti-Concorde New Yorkers had been defeated. As summed up by business community representative Gilbert A. Robinson, "The monster never existed except in the minds of those who were against progress." A single Paris-New York fare cost $850, and a London-New York fare cost $716.

1977 December 5 The U.S. Department of Transportation began a series of flights over four days aimed at demonstrating an advanced all-weather microwave landing system using a NASA Boeing 737 at New York's John F. Kennedy International Airport. The International Civil Aviation Organization (ICAO) had tested the equipment as possible replacement for existing instrument-landing systems 40 yr. old, and on February 22, 1978, the British government began a similar series of microwave landing-system tests on the same runway at JFK International. In March 1977, the ICAO all-weather panel had endorsed the design, and other countries, including Australia, had backed the United States in recommending it for operational use.

1977 December 13 Eastern Airlines inaugurated U.S. domestic services with the Airbus A300B4, achieving a significant precedent for the European consortium. The A300B4 was the standard long-range version that had made its first flight on December 26, 1974, and first entered service with Germanair on June 1, 1975. The A300B4-200 was in final design stages and would have strengthened wings, fuselage and landing gear enabling full passenger loads to be carried distances of up to 2,250 mi. or reduced passenger load but with additional fuel tanks to extend range to 3,565 mi.

1977 December 19 Having satisfactorily got a reversal of Pres. Carter's earlier decision, the USAF announced it would order 20 advanced tanker/cargo aircraft (ATCA) designated KC-10A as derivatives of the DC-10-30CF at a cost of $680 million plus $28 million for engineering conversion work. As a freighter, the DC-10A would carry up to 148,000 lb. of cargo a distance of up to 4,600 mi., and as a tanker, it could offload 150,000 lb. of fuel at a mission radius of 2,877 mi. Three underwing and tail refueling booms would be installed as standard equipment.

1977 December 22 The Antonov An-72 STOL transport aircraft made its first flight, powered by two 14,330-lb. s.t. Lotarev D-36 high-bypass turbofan engines in large-diameter nacelles mounted close inboard and located so as to blow efflux across the upper wing and very large multi-slotted flaps. Similar in concept to the Boeing YC-14, the aircraft had a wingspan of 84 ft. 9 in., a length of 87 ft. 2 in. and a maximum takeoff weight of 58,420 lb. The An-72 had capacity for up to 32 or 24 litter patients.

1978 January 1 With the nationalization of the major British aircraft manufacturers, announced in April 1977, the final transfer of assets from the British Aircraft Corp., Hawker Siddeley Aviation, Hawker Siddeley Dynamics and Scottish Aviation into the British Aerospace Corp. (BAe), all identity with the traditional names of U.K. planemakers was obliterated. The divisions of the company would no longer take on the names of the old organizations but would assume identity according to the location of the factories.

1978 January 11 The American Industries Jet Hustler 400A made its first flight, powered by a derated 850-SHP Pratt & Whitney PT6A-41 turboprop in the nose and one 78-lb. s.t. Williams WR19-3-1 turbofan in the tail. With a wingspan of 32 ft. 7 in. and a length of 37 ft. 11 in., the 400A had accommodation for two crewmembers and five passengers in the main cabin. It had a maximum takeoff weight of 7,500 lb. and a minimum-range cruising speed of up to 435 MPH, or 395 MPH and a range of 2,030 mi.

1978 January 23 In the first U.S. Defense Department budget submitted by the new Carter administration, all funds for the advanced medium STOL transport (AMST) aircraft were deleted, effectively bringing to an end a program that had brought about two development aircraft, the YC-14 from Boeing and the YC-15 from McDonnell Douglas. Nevertheless, it was the highest defense budget yet presented to Congress and included continued funding for the McDonnell Douglas AB-8B, the KC-10A and the F-18 Hornet, all programs serving critical needs. Also included was production of an improved Lockheed U-2R, known as the TR-1.

1978 January 27 The USAF announced the first overseas deployment for the Fairchild A-10 close support aircraft. The Eighty-first Tactical Fighter Wing was to get the first aircraft of this kind early in 1979 at RAF Bentwaters and RAF Woodbridge in England. Air crew were to commence conversion training at Davis-Monthan AFB, Ariz. later this year. The A-10 would be a familiar sight over the countryside of East Anglia, England, until they were withdrawn back to the United States in October 1991.

1978 January 31 The British government signed a letter of intent to purchase 30 Boeing Vertol CH-47 Chinook helicopters similar to the CH-47D version expected to enter service with the U.S. Army in the early 1980s. The British had ordered 15 CH-47B helicopters in March 1967 but canceled them in November the same year, paying penalty costs of £500,000. The contracts for this latest procurement would involve 25–30% offsets to the total value of about $200 million (£102.6 million). Deliveries were expected to begin in 1980.

1978 February 1 An usually large selection of modern, high-performance combat aircraft was submitted for the Canadian Armed Forces' new fighter aircraft requirement, which closed this day. Contenders included the Panavia Tornado, the McDonnell Douglas F-15A, the Grumman F-14 Tomcat, the Northrop CF-18L (a Canadian version of the F/A-18), the General Dynamics F-16 and the Dassault-Breguet Mirage 2000. The Canadians were shopping for 120 to 150 aircraft, an order worth approximately Can$2 billion. The Panavia organization had been negotiating with the Canadians since 1972.

1978 February 3 Rocky Mountain Airways became the first customer to put the de Havilland Canada DHC-7 into operational service. It took delivery of the fourth aircraft, following certification by the Canadian Department of Transport on May 2, 1977. Wardair Canada Ltd. became the first to operate the all-cargo version designated DHC-7 Series 101, and the company was actively marketing a maritime version known as the DHC-7R Ranger.

1978 February 16 The NASA Dryden Flight Research Center took delivery of a former USAF Boeing KC-135 cargo-tanker aircraft for research into fuel-saving technologies that might be applied to operational civil and military aircraft. Under a $3 million USAF contract, Boeing would add winglets to the wingtips and perform flights with varying angles of incidence and cant. Theoretical studies had shown advantages in having such attachments.

1978 March 4 Flt. Lt. David Cyster, RAF, an instructor at No. 4 Flying Training School in England, landed in Australia in his Tiger Moth at the end of a journey from England that began February 7 in commemoration of the 50th anniversary of Bert Hinkler's first solo flight from England in an Avro Avian. With a capacity of only 95 gal. in his fuel tank, Cyster had to make numerous stops. His trip was also hampered by a leak that developed shortly after leaving England, as well as poor weather en route.

1978 March 10 The first prototype Dassault-Breguet Mirage 2000 make its first flight, powered by an 18,740-lb. s.t. SNECMA M53-2 turbofan engine. Looking more like a development of the Mirage III/5 family, the delta-wing planform had a span of 29 ft. 6 in. and the fuselage had a length of 50 ft. 3 in. With a maximum takeoff weight of 19,840 lb. the Mirage 2000 had a maximum speed of Mach 2.3 and a tactical radius of 435 mi. carrying four air-to-air missiles and drop tanks. The aircraft had been selected as the primary French combat aircraft for the mid-1980s.

1978 March 10 NASA announced it had received the first HiMAT prototype from Rockwell International. Designed as a highly maneuverable technology demonstrator, HiMAT was a 44% scale model built to display performance envisaged for high-performance combat aircraft in the 1990s. It had a wingspan of 15 ft. 7 in. and a length of 22 ft. 6 in. Featuring a low aspect ratio, swept wing with large-area forward canards and twin tail surfaces emanating from the one-third span position, it could endure 12-g loads, including 8-g turns at Mach 0.9 at 30,000 ft.

1978 March 20 The Bell XV-15 tilt-rotor research aircraft arrived at the NASA Ames Research Center with modifications for remote control. Engineers wanted to test it in the 40-ft. x 80 ft. Ames wind tunnel in 6 wk. of research. The second XV-15 would begin flight trials at Bell after the wind tunnel tests produced necessary results to fine-tune objectives and experiments. The second XV-15 was scheduled to join the first at Ames for an extended period of combined testing.

1978 March 23 Capt. Sandra M. Scott, USAF, assigned to the 904th Air Refueling Squadron, Mather AFB, Calif. became the first woman pilot to perform alert duty at Strategic Air Command. The first female navigators to perform alert duty at Strategic Air Command were Capt. Elizabeth A. Koch, Twenty-second Air Refueling Squadron, March AFB, Calif. and 1st. Lt. Ramona L. S. Roybal, 916th Air Refueling Squadron, Travis AFB, Calif. on April 27.

1978 April 4 Having previously concluded an agreement to operate the Airbus A300 between Paris and Moscow twice weekly, Air France inaugurated the service by taking the first non-Soviet wide-body airliner to the USSR. Under the terms of the agreement, the Soviet airline Aeroflot had the option to begin flights between Moscow and Paris with its own wide-body airliner, the Ilyushin Il-86.

1978 April 7 A former USAF officer, Vincent Loomis, announced he was going in search of Amelia Earhart's aircraft, which disappeared without trace near Howland Island in the Pacific on July 2, 1937. Loomis had flown over the Marshall Islands many times making navigational markings in support of U.S. nuclear weapons tests and believed he had seen wreckage that could be the remains of the aircraft in question. Although a long way from the last reported position, Loomis said a simple navigational error could have taken the plane to the spot he saw.

1978 April 18 The Vickers Viscount became the world's first turboprop airliner to complete 25 yr. of regularly scheduled airline service. A total of 444 Viscounts had been built with 438 sold to 60 operators in 38 countries. Around 130 Viscounts were still in service on this date, 19 of which were with British Airways. Similarly, the Rolls Royce Dart became the first turbine engine to achieve 25 yr. of unbroken commercial service.

1978 April 19 The ICAO voted by 39 to 24 to adopt the time reference scanning beam (TRSB) microwave landing system that had been developed in the United States. It had competed against a British-designed system based on Doppler. Much debate surrounded the relative merits of the two systems, and questions were raised about the ability of the delegates to make subtle technical discriminations. The selected system, however, was expected to become the international standard by 1995.

1978 May 9 The first powered hang-glider, a microflight, to cross the English Channel was flown between England and France by David Cook. The powered glider took just over 1 hr. to make the crossing from Walmer Castle near Deal to a field not far from Calais. The glider used was a Revell VJ-23 of rigid construction powered by a 125-cc go-cart engine that delivered an average 9 HP to a two-bladed propeller, close to that used by the Wright brothers for their historic flights more than 70 yr. before.

1978 May 16 NASA awarded an $80.4 million contract to Pratt & Whitney for advanced technology research into fuel-efficient turbofan engines that might be used in aircraft of the future. The program objective was to reduce specific fuel consumption by as much as 15% while also reducing noise levels, toxic emissions and operating costs. It was part of NASA's aircraft energy efficiency program and was in parallel with a similar contract to General Electric. Both contracts would run 5 yr.

1978 May 22 Boeing Vertol started testing fiberglass rotor blades on a CH-47C Chinook with a view to incorporating blades of this design on future production helicopters of this type. Existing Chinooks would be retrofitted with the blades. The new technology blades were planned for the Model 234 civil version of the Chinook, which British Airways Helicopters had shown keen interest in buying, powered by a 4,200-SHP Avco Lycoming AL5512 turboshaft engine.

1978 June The USAF issued requests for proposals on a wide-body, cruise-missile carrier (CMC) that could be used as a stand-off launch platform for large numbers of pilotless cruise missiles to supplement the B-52 manned penetrating bomber force. Boeing, Lockheed and McDonnell Douglas had each been invited to propose variants of their large commercial transport aircraft. The studies also included the YC-14 and the YC-15 STOL prototypes. The CMC concept arose after Pres. Carter canceled the B-1 and added funds for Tomahawk and air-launched cruise-missile development

1978 July 8 The Boeing quiet short-haul research aircraft (QSRA) made its first flight, powered by four 7,500-lb. s.t. Avco Lycoming YF-102 turbofan engines carried on nacelles forward of and above the blown wing. Designed around the de Havilland Canada C-8A Buffalo, it had a wingspan of 73 ft. 6 in., a length of 93 ft. 3 in. and a gross weight of 60,000 lb. With a cruising speed of 184 MPH, it accommodated two pilots. STOL characteristics were exceptionally good, with a low-speed capability down to 58 MPH.

1978 July 10 Airbus Industrie announced a decision to proceed with development of the A300B10, a shortened version of the

A300 with capacity for 225 passengers, compared to 281 on the B2 and B4. The designation was later changed to the A310. Powered by General Electric, Pratt & Whitney or Rolls Royce engines in the 46,500–50,000-lb. s.t. class, it would have a wingspan of 144 ft., a length of 154 ft. 11 in. and a maximum takeoff weight of 291,010 lb. With a cruising speed of 414 MPH, it would have a maximum payload range of 1,730 mi.

1978 July 11 Approval to commence full development of the BAe 146 was given by the British government, and the first flight of the 70 to 90 seat, quiet, four-turbofan transport aircraft was anticipated for delivery to customers in 1982. First launched in 1973, it was canceled in October 1974, but design teams kept it alive with minimal government funding. Development and production was expected to cost £250 million at 1978 prices and put 7,000 people to work at BAe plants in addition to 5,000 in ancillary industries.

1978 July 14 The Boeing 767 was officially launched when United Air Lines placed an order for 30 aircraft. One of a family of projects offered by Boeing over the past year, the 767 was a 200-seat, twin-jet, wide-body airliner available in several versions. United opted for the 767-200, which had a gross weight of 279,500 lb. and power from two 44,300-lb. s.t. Pratt & Whitney JT9D-7R turbofan engines. It had a transcontinental range of 2,200 mi., sufficient to operate between West Coast and East Coast cities with only one stop. Deliveries were scheduled to begin mid-1982.

1978 August 4 The NASA Lewis Research Center, Cleveland, Ohio, announced that it had teamed with the FAA to host a three-day workshop on aircraft icing at NASA headquarters in Washington. The conference examined technical problems with aircraft icing on fixed-wing and rotary-winged types and explored solutions proposed by government research establishments and industry. Extended icing research had been conducted at Lewis in the 1940s and 1950s, and its work in that period was considered the standard for technical groups to consult.

1978 August 17 The first successful crossing of the Atlantic Ocean by balloon was concluded when the *Double Eagle II* landed in France, having flown 3,680 mi. from Presque Island, Maine in 5 days 17 hr. 6 min. On board were Max Anderson, Ben Abruzzo and Lawrence Newman. The helium balloon passed over Newfoundland, southern Ireland, Wales, southwest England and the English Channel. An attempt the previous month by British balloonists Don Cameron and Maj. Christopher Davey almost succeeded, but they came down in the ocean 103 mi. short of their goal.

1978 August 20 The first British Aerospace Sea Harrier made its first flight following 3 yr. of development after public government approval declared May 15, 1975. The initial orders were to provide aircraft for the antisubmarine cruiser HMS *Invincible* and the antisubmarine carrier HMS *Hermes*. Powered by a 21,500-lb. s.t. Rolls Royce Pegasus Mk 104, it had a wingspan of 25 ft. 3 in., a length of 47 ft. 7 in. and a combat radius of up to 460 mi. The FRS.Mk.1 would take advantage of an inclined "ski-jump" extension to the flight deck for assisted takeoff.

1978 August 29 The prototype Mitsubishi Mu-300 Diamond business aircraft made its first flight, powered by two 2,500-lb. s.t. Pratt & Whitney Canada JT15D-4 turbofan engines mounted in nacelles either side of the rear fuselage. The aircraft had a wingspan of 43 ft. 5 in. and a length of 48 ft. 4 in. with a maximum takeoff weight of 13,890 lb. The MU-300 had a max-

imum cruising speed of 497 MPH and a maximum range of 1,802 mi.

1978 August 31 Eastern Air Lines and British Airways jointly provided the launch orders for the Boeing 757 short/medium-haul commercial transport. Based on the 727 fuselage, the 757 would accommodate up to 233 passengers and adopt Rolls Royce or Pratt & Whitney engines in the 37,000–40,000 lb. class, depending upon customer choice. Eastern ordered 21 but increased that to 27 before the first flight, and BA ordered 19 aircraft. Full development of the Boeing 757 was initiated March 23, 1979.

1978 September 13 The prototype Aérospatiale AS 332 Super Puma, an advanced development of the highly successful SA 330 Puma, made its first flight just over 1 yr. after the first flight of its experimental precursor, the AS 331. Powered by two 1,755-SHP Turboméca engines driving a 49 ft. 2 in. rotor, the Super Puma had a fuselage length of 48 ft. 5 in. With a maximum takeoff weight of 17,196 lb., the Super Puma could lift up to 24 troops in normal seating (versus 16 for the Puma) at 161 MPH for up to 652 mi.

1978 September 25 The U.S. Department of Transportation announced that it would extend to 24 the number of domestic airports equipped with the low-level wind shear alert system (LLWSAS) it had been testing at seven selected airports for the past year. Developed and built by EMR Telemetry of Sarasota, Fla., a small computer sampled measurements from up to five wind sensors distributed around the airfield and alerted the control tower if critical boundaries were observed indicating dangerous wind shear conditions.

1978 September 26 Laker Airways was granted permission to open a Skytrain service between London and Los Angeles on the first anniversary of the inauguration of its London-New York service. A 345-seat DC-10 would be used daily for the walk-on service with a single stop at Bangor, Maine. Fares would be £84 from London to Los Angeles and $162 from Los Angeles to London, with modest increases for the peak months of June, July and August. British Caledonian had hotly contested the license but would concentrate instead on other routes to the United States.

1978 October 6 The Indian government announced a decision it had been pondering for 8 yr. regarding the acquisition of deep-penetration strike aircraft it wanted when it declared in favor of the SEPECAT Jaguar. About 190 aircraft would be needed, the first 40 to be supplied by BAe Warton, England in a deal said to worth around £816 million. The Jaguar won out over the Mirage F1 and the SAAB Viggen.

1978 October 24 Years after turning its back on development of a European medium-haul airliner, Britain finally gained French approval for British Aerospace to join as a full member of the Airbus Industrie consortium. There had been strong opposition following a decision by British Airways to buy the Boeing 757 and reject the proposed Airbus A310. Nevertheless, the United Kingdom would become a full member January 1, 1979, with a 20% share in the organization for a contribution of £25 million.

1978 October 28 The Airline Deregulation Act was signed by Pres. Carter. This would allow U.S. airlines to receive approval to operate routes for which no existing airline held a right on a first-come, first-served basis. Thus were the concessionary powers of the Civil Aeronautics Board abolished. On this day, 23 airlines filed requests for 1,300 new routes, though most of those would be withdrawn. Braniff alone requested 440 but rejected 290 by November 1.

1978 November 8   The first Canadair CL-600 Challenger business transport made its first flight, powered by two 7,500-lb. s.t. Avco Lycoming ALF 502L turbofan engines. In 1976 Canadair acquired the rights from William P. Lear Sr. to design, manufacture and market the LearStar 600 incorporating an advanced technology wing and high-bypass engines. With a wingspan of 61 ft. 10 in. and a length of 68 ft. 5 in., it could carry up to 33 passengers, or 11 in executive layout, and had a cruising speed of 554 MPH and a range of 3,680 mi.

1978 November 9   The first McDonnell Douglas YV-8B advanced Harrier made its first flight at the beginning of an extensive test period that would continue through mid-1979. The aim of the program was to achieve the performance improvements originally set out for the AV-16A. Powered by a 21,500-lb. s.t. Rolls Royce Pegasus (F402-RR-404), it had a wingspan of 30 ft. 3 in., a length of 46 ft. 3 in. and a maximum takeoff weight of 18,850 lb. for vertical takeoff or 29,550 lb. for short takeoff. Vertical takeoff warload was 7,000 lb. or 17,000 lb. for short takeoff. Depending on load, the AV-8B had a combat radius of up to 748 mi.

1978 November 18   The McDonnell Douglas F/A-18 Hornet made its first flight 2 mon. 5 days after it had been rolled out at the St. Louis facility. Powered by two 16,000-lb. s.t. General Electric F404-GE-400 low-bypass turbofan engines, it had a wingspan of 37 ft. 6 in., a length of 56 ft. and a maximum takeoff weight of 33,585 lb. in fighter mode or 47,000 lb. in attack mode, the combat radius being 460 mi. and 633 mi. respectively. The U.S. Navy estimated an initial production need for 185 fighters and 345 light attack aircraft, and the U.S. Marine Corps wanted 270 fighters.

1978 December   The U.S. Aerospace Industries Assn. announced record industry sales of $37.3 billion for the year, up 15% on 1977 due in part to inflation. Industry profits on sales reached 4.7%, up more than 10% over 1977. Overall, aerospace exports had reached the all-time high of $9.3 billion, an increase of $1.8 billion (24%) over the figure for 1977, and led all U.S. industries in the trade balance, with an $8.4 billion surplus on overseas sales making it the most lucrative industry ever created by the United States. The order backlog had jumped 16% over 1977 to stand at $51.4 billion.

1979 January 6   The first production General Dynamics F-16A to enter service with the USAF joined the Sixteenth Tactical Fighter Training Squadron, 388th Tactical Fighter Wing, at Hill AFB, Utah. The first production aircraft had been delivered to the USAF on August 7, 1978, 10 days after its first flight. It was with the 388th Tactical Fighter Wing that the aircraft would obtain combat readiness in October 1980 with the Fourth Tactical Fighter Squadron. In October 1979, the first F-16A assigned to the Fifty-sixth Tactical Fighter Wing arrived at MacDill AFB, Fla.

1979 January 12   British Airways and Air France Concorde supersonic airliners arrived within 2 sec. of each other at Dallas-Fort Worth International Airport's two parallel runways to inaugurate a scheduled service between there and Europe. The aircraft would be operated on an interchange basis by Braniff Airways. They arrived from Washington's Dulles Airport in a flying time of 2 hr. 17 min. but cruised subsonically at Mach 0.95 at an altitude of 31,000–37,000 ft. The British Airways aircraft carried 90 passengers, the Air France Concorde 69.

A fine example of international cooperation, the British Harrier VTOL short-range strike fighter was developed by McDonnell Douglas in the United States into the AV-8B.

1979 January 24   Following the collapse of Britten-Norman, the assets of that company were taken over by the Pilatus Aircraft Co. of Stans, Switzerland. In a deal reached with the receivers, Pilatus would take over the facilities on the Isle of Wight and become responsible for all production and servicing on Islander and Trislander aircraft and for all Britten-Norman facilities owned by Fairey SA in Belgium. Fairey had tried to put Britten-Norman back in business but failed.

1979 January 26   The first General Dynamics F-16A destined for Europe arrived with the First Wing of the Belgian Air Force at Beauvechain followed by the Tenth Wing at Kleine Brogel. On June 6, the first two F-16As arrived in Holland for duty with the Royal Netherlands Air Force and on January 25, 1980, Norway got the first of its F-16As, followed by Denmark on January 28, 1980. Developed in parallel with the F-16A, the two-seat F-16B, which had made its first flight on August 8, 1977, was an important training element in NATO forces familiarization and conversion.

1979 February 3   The first AD-500 nonrigid airship designed by Aerospace Developments and marketed by Multimodal Transport Analysis Ltd. England made its first flight from RAF Cardington, Bedfordshire, home of the pre-World War II British airships R.100 and R.101. It had a length of 164 ft., a maximum diameter of 45 ft. 11 in. and a volume of 181,160 cu. ft. powered by two 200-HP Porsche 6-cylinder air-cooled engines. The AD-500 had a payload of 5,600 lb. to 2,000 ft. With a portfolio of five airship designs and an order from Venezuela, Aerospace Developments would evolve into Airship Industries Ltd.

1979 February 5   Following the overthrow of the shah of Iran by Islamic fundamentalists, it was announced in Washington, D.C. that the new Bakhtiar government had canceled orders for large numbers of U.S. military aircraft, including seven E-3A Sentry AWACS aircraft, 160 General Dynamics F-16As and 11 McDonnell Douglas RF-4E Phantom IIs. Support contracts for the F-14A Tomcat and the Bell AH-1J and Model 214 helicopters were also to be drastically reduced.

1979 February 26   The first McDonnell Douglas F-15C made its first flight at St. Louis, Mo. With additional 2,000 lb. of internal fuel capacity and provision for 13,000 lb. of fuel in conformal Fuel And Sensor Tactical (FAST) packs attached to the fuselage sides, it had a tactical combat radius of 1,305 mi. and a top speed in excess of Mach 2.5 (1,650 MPH) above 36,090 ft. or Mach 1.5 at sea level. The F-15C was procured to supplant the F-15A from the mid-1980s, with a two-seat F-15D replacing the F-15B at the same time.

1979 February 27   The U.S. Navy received the last McDonnell Douglas A-4 Skyhawk. It was the 2,960th Skyhawk built by the company in a production run that had been maintained for 26 yr., longest of any U.S. military aircraft program. The last aircraft was an A-4M attack aircraft ordered by the U.S. Marine Corps but delivered to the navy's VMS-331 squadron at Cherry Point, N.C. The Skyhawk served with many air forces around the world and will constitute front-line equipment well into the next century.

1979 March 9   The Dassault-Breguet Super Mirage 4000, a twin-engined, upgraded development of the Mirage 2000, made its first flight at Istres, France. Declared a private development in December 1975, the Mirage 4000 was powered by two 14,460/21,385-lb. s.t. SNECMA M53 turbofan engines, had a delta-wing span of 39 ft. 4 in. and a length of 61 ft. 4 in. Capable of speeds in excess of Mach 2.3, it had a sustained speed of Mach 2.2 (1,452 MPH) above 36,090 ft. It had two 30-mm cannons and nine external stores locations for up to 15,000 lb. of ordnance.

1979 March 10   The USAF flew two Boeing E-3A Sentry AWACS aircraft to Riyadh, Saudi Arabia to monitor hostilities between North and South Yemen. Concerned about the possible spillover effect of the conflict, Saudi Arabia's royal family had requested U.S. assistance. The aircraft remained over Saudi Arabian territory during these monitoring flights, using its ability to "see" 400 mi. with its Westinghouse APY-1 radar.

1979 March 11   In a test of satellite navigation capabilities, a Lockheed P-3B Orion from the Patuxent River Naval Air Test Center, Md. made the first transoceanic crossing navigating exclusively by satellite. The aircraft flew between Barbers Point and Moffett Field, Calif. in about 6 hr., taking position information from a constellation of Navstar satellites in orbit above the earth. (Navstar is the name of the satellite that constitutes the global positioning system [GPS] and has an atomic clock for extreme time accuracy coded for transmission with the beacon so that on-board instruments determine vector by triangulation and time from the caesium clock.)

1979 March 20   The last Lockheed P-2 Neptune was rolled off a production line in Japan, which had been license-building the type for the Japanese defense forces. It represented the longest production run of any aircraft anywhere, ending 34 yr. of continuous manufacture somewhere in the world. The Neptune had been designed in World War II and during the 1950s and early 1960s remained the mainstay of U.S. Navy antisubmarine warfare patrols until it was replaced by the Lockheed P-3 Orion.

1979 March 31   The British government announced development and production costs for the Concorde supersonic airliner since November 29, 1962, when agreement was reached with France to design and build the aircraft. Through December 31, 1978, the French government spent £543 million on development and £377 million on production (a total of £920 million) whereas the British spent £552 million on development and £346 million on production (a total of £898 million). The total cost of £1.818

billion would increase by a further £101 million, £62 million from Britain, before government funding ceased.

1979 April 20   The 16th and last production Anglo-French Concorde made its first flight at Filton, England with a crew led by Brian Trubshaw. Concorde 216 was to join the British Airways fleet, last in a short line of unique aircraft, for which orders were once projected to eventually exceed 300.

1979 April 23   The last surviving Kawanishi H8K2 flying boat was handed over to the Japanese Museum of Maritime Science in a special ceremony at Norfolk Naval Air Station, Va. Code-named Emily, the large flying boat had been brought to the United States late in 1945 for trials at Patuxent River. During July, the Museum of Maritime Science transferred the aircraft to Tokyo, where it remains today as a proud exhibit of Japanese aircraft engineering.

1979 April   A solar-powered hang-glider named *Solar Riser* was claimed to have made several flights using panels carrying 300 solar cells driving a 3-HP electric motor with a current of 40 volts at 10 amps. Designed by Larry Mauro, it had a 41-in. propeller, a weight of 290 lb., a wingspan of 30 ft. and a calm-weather takeoff run of 100 ft. It was claimed that *Solar Riser* had flown a distance of up to 2,500 ft. maintaining a height of about 40 ft. above the ground. An earlier claim had been made by two Englishmen, Freddie To and David Williams, on December 19, 1978.

1979 May 25   An American Airlines DC-10-10 lost an engine and its wing pylon shortly after taking off from Chicago, Ill. but landed safely. In the ensuing legal confusion, a court grounded the aircraft type and then rescinded that order, but on June 6, the FAA withdrew the aircraft's certificate of airworthiness, which effectively put the aircraft out of action. Countries left to make up their own minds generally followed the U.S. grounding, but Yugoslavia kept flying the DC-10. Finally, on July 13, the aircraft's certificate was restored.

1979 June 5   The £100,000 Kremer Prize offered to the first person to cross the English Channel by man-powered aircraft was won by Bryan Allen when he successfully cycled his *Gossamer Albatross* from Folkstone, England to Cap Gris Nez, France. He covered a distance of 22 mi. in 2 hr. 50 min. maintaining a height of about 10 ft. Designed by Dr. Paul MacCready with sponsorship from the Du Pont Co., the man-powered aircraft had a wingspan of 96 ft. and was developed from the *Gossamer Condor*. It had earlier made a 13-mi. flight lasting 1 hr. 9 min. over the Mojave Desert.

1979 June 13   Two flights of approximately 4,000 ft. each were made at Lasham, England, by a solar-powered hang-glider known as *Solar One*. Conceived by Freddie To and designed by David Williams, *Solar One* had four electric motors delivering a total 4 HP driving a pylon-mounted propeller ahead of the pilot. Power was provided by a battery of nickel/cadmium accumulator cells, which produced electrical energy from sunlight. This enabled *Solar One* to climb for about eight min.

1979 June 20   U.S. Navy Lt. Donna Spruill piloted a Grumman C-1A Trader onto the deck of the carrier USS *Independence* to become the first female pilot to become qualified for on-deck carrier landings with a fixed-wing aircraft. The Trader could accommodate nine passengers and had originated as the TF-1 in 1955, a utility and medium transport derivation of the Tracker antisubmarine search and strike aircraft.

1979 June 27   Six Syrian Air Force MiG fighters were shot down by six Israeli Air Force McDonnell Douglas F-15 Eagles and two Kfir fighters flying cover on a decoy mission over southern Lebanon. Vectored to their prey by a Grumman E-2C, also of the Israeli Air Force, the fighters attacked between eight and 12 MiG-21bis fighters and damaged those not shot down. This was the first recorded ''kill'' for the F-15. On September 24, four MiG-21s were shot down by F-15s after being similarly vectored by the E-2C.

1979 July 10   The first production Panavia Tornado, BT 001 (British Trainer No. 1), made its first flight from Warton, England after having been rolled out on June 5. The first production West German Tornado (GT 001) made its first flight on July 27 followed by the first Italian production Tornado (IT 001) on September 25, 1981. All aircraft were powered by two 9,000/16,000-lb. s.t. Turbo-Union RB.199-34R Mk 101 turbofan engines. BT 001 was delivered to the Aircraft and Armament Experimental Establishment at Boscombe Down, England where it underwent rigorous tests.

1979 July 16   USAF Strategic Air Command completed Global Shield 79, the biggest exercise it had ever carried out, stopping just short of all-out nuclear war. For the first time, it flexed every element of the Single Integrated Operational Plan without actually launching missiles or dropping live nuclear weapons. Strategic Air Command's equipment inventory had changed dramatically over the years. With no sign of a replacement for its 343 B-52s and 65 FB-111As, it had a total 408 bombers and 1,228 Atlas and Minuteman intercontinental ballistic missiles comprising two legs of the strategic triad.

1979 July 17   A fly-off between the General Dynamics AGM-109 Tomahawk cruise missile and the Boeing AGM-86B air-launched cruise missile for Strategic Air Command procurement began when a Tomahawk was dropped from the rotary bomb-bay launcher of a B-52G. The first launch of the AGM-86B followed on August 3, but the missile crashed prematurely on the Utah test range. The AGM-86B was being developed as a long-range version of the AGM-86A. It had a length of 20 ft. 9 in. and a wingspan of 12 ft. with a range of approximately 2,260 mi.

1979 July 23   The British secretary of state for industry, Sir Keith Joseph, said in the House of Commons that the newly appointed Conservative government would offer for public ownership about half the shares in British Aerospace. No part of BAe would be sold to foreign buyers, shares being offered across the company to British citizens or companies. This was the first move to effectively denationalize the British aircraft industry, which had been taken from private ownership by the previous Labour government. From the end of the year, the legal classification of the company would be changed from a statutory corporation to a limited liability company.

1979 July 23   The world's smallest twin-jet aircraft made its first flight in France. Built by Leo Chaques and powered by two 220-lb. s.t. Microturbo TRS-18 turbojets mounted one above the other in the fuselage, the Microstar had a delta wing and canard nose with a span and length of 22 ft. 11 in. each. The aircraft had a gross weight of 1,764 lb. and was reported to have a top speed of 217 MPH.

1979 July 27   The first air-dropped free flight of the Rockwell HiMAT aircraft was conducted from a B-52 carrier plane at 45,000 ft. over the Edwards AFB, Calif. test range. Two previous flights had been conducted with the aircraft retained by the B-52. The

first free flight lasted 22 min. while a controller remotely ''piloted'' the unmanned research aircraft. The HiMAT had a landing skid arrangement for soft touch-down, which was described as working perfectly on this inaugural flight. This first flight was limited to conservative approach and landing techniques.

1979 August 15   The first live air firing of a BAe Sky Flash air-to-air missile was carried out by an RAF Phantom FGR.Mk.2 when it fired a missile against a Meteor U Mk.10 drone over a test range at Aberporth, Wales. With an active radar homing head, Sky Flash had been developed as a replacement for the Sparrow on RAF Phantoms. It was also intended to equip the Tornado F Mk.2, which was expected to enter service with the RAF in 1984.

1979 August 23   The first of 32 BAe Nimrod MR.Mk.1 maritime reconnaissance aircraft retrofitted with modifications transforming it into a MR.Mk.2 type (serial no. XV236) was handed over to No. 201 Squadron, RAF, at Kinloss, Scotland. With 60 times the computing power of the Mk.1, the MR.Mk.2 had advanced Searchwater radar, generally considered the best in the world, the AQS-901 acoustic system compatible with the Australian Barra sonobuoy and Stingray torpedoes.

1979 September 19   The first British Aerospace FRS.Mk.1 Sea Harrier unit was commissioned at Royal Naval Air Station Yeovilton when No. 700A Squadron received its first V/STOL aircraft (serial no. XZ451). It would become No. 899 Headquarters Squadron with eight aircraft, and operational units would comprise Nos. 800, 801 and 809 squadrons for operation with antisubmarine cruisers HMS *Invincible, Illustrious* and *Ark Royal* and the assault carrier HMS *Hermes.*

1979 September 28   U.S. Navy Reconnaissance Attack Squadron 7 (RVAH-7) was disbanded, ending 15 yr. of operations with the North American RA-5C Vigilante. Designed as a nuclear strike aircraft, the Vigilante found its enduring role as a long-range naval photographic reconnaissance aircraft and did valuable work in Vietnam and other areas of the world. The last RA-5C departed Key West NAS November 20; the 156 aircraft were either broken up or employed as drones.

1979 October 18   The first McDonnell Douglas DC-9 Series 80 made its first flight, powered by two 18,500-lb. s.t. Pratt & Whitney JT8D-209 turbofan engines with emergency thrust of 19,250 lb. Fuselage length was increased to 147 ft. 10 in., raising seat capacity to 172 in a high density configuration, and wingspan was increased to 107 ft. 11 in. with an attendant increase in maximum takeoff weight to 140,000 lb. The first aircraft went to Swissair on September 12, 1980, and the type became known first as the Super 80 and then was redesignated MD-80.

1979 October 27   The first prototype Panavia Tornado F Mk.2 air defense version (ADV) made its first flight at Warton, England, piloted by David Eagles with Roy Kenward, project navigator, in the rear seat. The flight lasted 1 hr. 32 min. and reached a speed of Mach 1.2 carrying four dummy BAe Sky Flash AAMs under the fuselage. The ADV was expected to account for 165 of the 384 Tornado aircraft ordered by the British government for service in the RAF. On October 23, the government rejected a plan to buy F-15A Eagles as an interim air defense fighter.

1979 November 27   The first flight of a Boeing 707 fitted with four 22,000-lb. s.t. (derated) CFM-562D1 turbofan engines took place from Boeing Field, Seattle, Wash. This newly manufactured aircraft was adapted in a joint program between Boeing and CFM International and followed earlier plans by Boeing to intro-

Developed for the U.S. Navy, the AEW Grumman E-2C Hawkeye served with air forces in Japan, Israel, Egypt and Singapore.

duce a 707–700 version with these powerplants. However, those plans abandoned, the company offered a reengining service offering operators significantly improved specific fuel consumption over the Pratt & Whitney-engined 707s.

1979 December 3 The first of 30 Lockheed C-130K Hercules destined for the RAF as the C.Mk.3 made its first flight at Marietta, Ga. The RAF had sought a stretched version, and Lockheed engineered a 15-ft. plug in the fuselage, raising capacity from 92 fully equipped troops to 128. The remaining 29 aircraft were produced by Marshall Cambridge (Engineering) Ltd. in a conversion program that was completed in 1982.

1979 December 12 The prototype Sikorsky SH-60B Seahawk made its first flight, powered by two 1,690-SHP General Electric T700-GE-401 advanced technology turboshaft engines driving a 54-ft. 8 in. rotor. Winning contender in the U.S. Navy light airborne multi-purpose system (LAMPS) Mk III competition and selected to build in September 1977, the SH-60B was a derivation of the Sikorsky S-70L selected by the U.S. Army as the UH-60 for the UTTAS role. The U.S. Navy specified a requirement for 204 Seahawks to serve aboard its *Spruance*-class antisubmarine warfare destroyers.

1979 December 14 A most unusual aircraft, the Edgley EA7 Optica, made its first flight. Established in 1974, Edgley designed an observation aircraft with an ''insect-eye'' bulbous nose ahead of a ducted propulsor comprising a five-bladed fixed-pitch fan powered by a 200-HP Avco Lycoming IO-360 engine. With a wingspan of 39 ft. 4 in. and a length of 26 ft. 9 in., it had a maximum weight of 2,725 lb., a cruising speed of 108 MPH, a loiter speed of 57 MPH with a 13-hr. endurance and a range of 650 mi. at 65% power.

1979 December 21 The AD-1 oblique-wing aircraft made its first flight from the NASA Dryden Flight Research Center in California. Airborne for 38 min., the aircraft reached a height of about 1,000 ft. and a speed of about 160 MPH. Developed from an idea by R. T. Jones to improve transonic flight, it had been developed as a joint project between Dryden and the NASA Ames Research Center. The rigid wing could be made to slew diago-

nally as much as 60° in flight so that one side faced 60° forward and the other side 60° backward. Wind tunnel tests at Ames proved the validity of the idea.

1979 December 22 A massive airlift of 5,000 men from the Soviet 105th Guards Airborne Assault Division into Bagram and Kabul, Afghanistan began and was completed December 26, one day before a Soviet-inspired coup replaced the government and its leaders. In 350 sorties flown by An-12, An-22 and Il-76 transport aircraft of the Air Transport Command, a major Soviet military presence was secured to take the roads and open vehicular traffic for reinforcements and consolidation.

1980 January 7 Adding extensive domestic commercial routes to an otherwise exclusively international network, Pan American World Airways acquired National Airlines. The airline's name was to be temporarily retained for market stability and customer ease and for all former operations under that name, but the company was to be totally absorbed within the Pan American corporate structure.

1980 January 21 On the 10th anniversary of the inauguration into revenue-earning service of the Boeing 747, 420 Jumbo Jets had been delivered to 57 operators, and the aircraft had carried a total 266 million passengers in that time. In the latest increase in gross takeoff weight, Boeing 747s for QANTAS were cleared to operate at 833,000 lb. using four 53,000-lb. s.t. Rolls Royce RB.211-524D4 engines with a 6% saving in fuel consumption. Using these engines, the aircraft had a maximum range of 6,275 mi. with 436 passengers and 25,350 lb. of cargo.

1980 January 31 The Israeli Air Force became the first non-NATO country to receive the General Dynamics F-16, at a special ceremony in which Brig. Gen. Amos Lapidot accepted a two-seat F-16B at Fort Worth, Tex. The first seven aircraft were being delivered to the 388th Tactical Fighter Wing at Hill AFB, Utah, where Israeli pilots were to be trained on the type. The Israeli Air Force had orders out for a total 67 F-16As and eight F-16Bs, of which 35 were to be delivered before the end of the year.

1980 February 8 The USAF cruise-missile fly-off between the General Dynamics AGM-109 Tomahawk and the Boeing AGM-86B air-launched cruise missile was completed almost two months behind schedule with the flight of an AGM-86B that, like the first, failed to achieve its objectives. In fact, each missile type had experienced four failures in 10 flights. The USAF wanted to have the first cruise missiles operational with its B-52 by the end of 1982, a capability increased in importance since Carter's cancellation of the B-1 bomber and the greater reliance on a stand-off weapon.

1980 February 14 Japan Air Lines began commercial operations with the highest-capacity airliner ever put into scheduled service when it conducted the inaugural flight of the eighth Boeing 747SR, a short-range version of the basic aircraft strengthened for a greater number of landing and takeoff cycles. Unlike earlier 747SR aircraft delivered to this airline, this aircraft had seating for 550 passengers, 45 in the upper deck. The previously delivered aircraft were to be uprated to carry 530 from their existing configuration of seating for 498.

1980 February 15 The USAF issued a draft request for proposals on a cargo aircraft requirement known as CX calling for a new military transport aircraft capable of lifting large and oversize loads directly into a military theater of operations with extreme STOL capability. Events in the Middle East had defined such a need. The CX was required to have a 19-ft. wide floor and operate in rough-field country with good ground handling and maneuverability. The Defense Department hoped to announce a winner by the end of the year.

1980 February 25 The Israeli deputy minister of defense, Mordechai Zippori, announced indigenous development of a light, single-seat air defense and ground attack fighter named Lavi (Young Lion). With 22% of the structure manufactured from composites and using fly-by-wire control systems, the single-engined aircraft was intended to supplement the F-16A and build up an independent combat aircraft design and manufacturing capability in Israel.

1980 February 29 The disassociation of VFW-Fokker was put into effect as a result of a German desire to focus all national aerospace resources into a single force. The Vereinigte Flugtechnische Werke was to be absorbed into the Messerschmitt-Bölkow-Blohm (MBB) structure, thus creating the third largest aerospace organization in Europe next to Aérospatiale in France and British Aerospace in the United Kingdom, with 34,000 employees. Shareholders included the Krupp Group and two members of the Heinkel family. The separation was back-dated to January 1.

1980 March 4 British Aerospace made the first flight of the BAe (Intercity) 148 powered by Rolls Royce Dart engines fitted with hush-kits. These were claimed to give noise reductions during the approach and landing phase as well as during taxiing on the runway. The hush-kit was to be made available for existing aircraft as well as new models and with a total weight of 15 lb. had no impact on the performance of the aircraft. It was fitted between the nose cowl and the engine intake casing, effectively moving the cowl forward about 3 in.

1980 March 14 Two B-52Hs of the 410th Bombardment Wing, USAF, completed the third nonstop global flight conducted by Strategic Air Command, former flights having been conducted in 1949 and 1957. Commanded by Majs. William H. Thurston and John M. Durham, the two seven-man crews were briefed on the mission at Strategic Air Command headquarters, Offutt AFB, Nebr. for a week prior to the flight. The two aircraft departed March 12 and flew 42 hr. 30 min., during which time they flew 22,285 mi. across the North Atlantic, the Mediterranean, the Indian Ocean, the Strait of Malacca, the South China Sea and the North Pacific, being refueled five times.

1980 March 14 The first Panavia Tornado configured in full-strike aircraft condition made its first flight from Warton, England. The fourth production aircraft and the 19th manufactured Tornado, it was designated BS 001. This aircraft was delivered to Boscombe Down as BT 001 had been. BT 002 would go to RAF Cotesmore for trinational training activities. The first German production aircraft and the first Italian production aircraft were completed as trainers.

1980 March 23 The first Boeing Vertol Chinook HC.Mk.1 destined for the RAF made its first flight, powered by two 3,750-SHP Avco Lycoming T55-L-11E turboshaft engines driving two sets of 60-ft. diameter rotors but with provision for retrofitting with carbon blades. With a total external lift capacity of 20,000 lb., or up to 44 equipped troops in the main cabin, the HC.Mk.1 had a mission radius of 115 mi. The RAF had wanted the Chinook to support the British Army of the Rhine, but the helicopter was battle-tested retaking the Falkland Islands in 1982.

1980 March 25 The USAF selected the Boeing AGM-86B ALCM to equip Strategic Air Command B-52s in a stand-off role, which would provide greater penetration capabilities in an operational role and extend the mission life of the aircraft by removing it from the worst air defense threats. The U.S. secretary of the air force, Hans Mark, announced that the complete contract for 3,418 ALCMs at a cost of $4 billion would go to Boeing, citing better terrain-following performance, superior guidance and cheaper maintainability.

1980 March 28 Gates Learjet became the first manufacturer of light executive and business jets to deliver its 1,000th aircraft, on the same day the company unveiled its Longhorn 50 design. The company boasted 26.2% of the world business jet market of almost 4,000 aircraft. It was followed by the Cessna Citation (with 17.3%), the Dassault-Breguet Falcon (13.9%), the BAe HS.125 (11.6%), the Rockwell Sabreliner (9.9%), the IAI Westwind (7%), the Grumman Gulfstream (6.8%), the Lockheed JetStar (5.3%), the Aérospatiale Corvette (1.1%) and the MBB Hansa Jet (0.9%).

1980 March 28 British Aerospace reinvigorated an old program by flying a new version of the Jetstream for the first time. Designated Jetstream 31, it was marketed in commuter (18- to 19-seat), corporate (8- to 10-seat) or executive (12-seat) versions, powered by two 900-SHP Garrett TPE331-10 turboprop engines. With a wingspan of 52 ft. and a length of 47 ft. 1 in., it had a maximum takeoff weight of 14,110 lb., a cruising speed of 291 MPH and a maximum range of up to 1,275 mi.

1980 March 31 Submissions for the Australian Industrial Participation program inviting Australian companies to become involved in the next round of fighter/ground attack aircraft procurement had to be in by this date. The Australian government was to decide by October whether to buy the McDonnell Douglas F-18 or the General Dynamics F-16. The government hoped to recoup 40% of its investment on these aircraft by involving indigenous industries in final assembly and support contracts. Of the 75 McDonnell Douglas F-18s bought by Australia on October 20, 1981, 73 would be assembled by Aerospace Technologies of Australia Pty. Ltd. and designated ATF-18A.

1980 March A small top-secret group at Northrop working under electrical engineer John F. Cashen and aeronautical engineers Irving T. Waaland and John Patierno decided upon a configuration that would form the basis for the advanced technology bomber, the stealth project that would eventually appear in hardware as the B-2A. Taking research results from the USAF stealth program code-named Have Blue, they decided upon a molded flying-wing shape very different from the faceted shape adopted for the Lockheed stealth fighter flown for the first time on June 15, 1981.

1980 April 10 The Canadian government signed a contract to buy 137 McDonnell Douglas CF-18 Hornets to fill its new fighter aircraft requirement. The contract contained a clause allowing purchase of an additional 10 aircraft based on cost performance between anticipated and ceiling totals. The value of the contract in U.S. dollars was placed between $2.211 billion and $2.369 billion. Within the total were 24 two-seat trainers. The single-seat aircraft were to be almost identical to U.S. Navy aircraft but with a different instrument landing system (ILS) and an additional spotlight for night identification.

1980 April 24 During an aborted attempt to rescue 66 American hostages held in Teheran, Iran since November 4, 1979, when Islamic extremists stormed the U.S. Embassy, seven U.S. Navy

RH-53D helicopters and one USAF EC-130H were destroyed with eight dead and many injured. At a location near Posht-e-Badam in Iran, code-named Desert One, a succession of blunders and mistakes turned the bold attempt into a fiasco. One helicopter collided with the EC-130H, starting a fire. This ignited ammunition, damaging five other helicopters, which had almost run out of fuel waiting for another helicopter to arrive.

1980 May 1 Concerted efforts to lower operating costs of commercial airliners took another step forward when Pan American put into service the first of its Lockheed L-1011-500 TriStars fitted with an active control system that used computers with the Rolls Royce RB.211-524B engines to manage the aircraft powerplants and accrue savings of up to 8%. These aircraft were introduced to replace the Boeing 707–320s. The inaugural service was from New York to Caracas.

1980 May 20 De Havilland Canada announced that it had received letters of intent for 55 DHC-8 (Dash 8) commuter aircraft from 17 operators. The proposed 32- to 36-seat airliner was designed to fill a gap between the company's Twin Otter, carrying 19 passengers, and the Dash 7, carrying up to 50 passengers. The first order was secured from NorOntair (an air transport service of the Ontario Northland Transportation Commission), announced April 2. De Havilland planned to have the Dash 8 certificated for airworthiness by fall 1984.

1980 June 1 With effect from this date, Braniff terminated its interchange agreement with British Airways and Air France whereby it operated Concorde supersonic transport aircraft out of Dallas/Fort Worth, Tex. A doubling in fuel costs and reduced load factors forced this decision, said Braniff, who had operated the service since January 13, 1979. British Airways planned to introduce a sixth Concorde during the summer and increase from 12 to 14 the number of weekly flights to New York and raise from 3 to 4 the number of weekly flights to Washington, D.C.

1980 June 3 Designed for close air support duties against ground targets, the AGM-65E laser-guided Maverick was fired from an aircraft for the first time. The missile was a development of the USAF television-guided weapon and was dropped from a U.S. Marine Corps A-4M Skyhawk at Eglin AFB, Fla. Manufactured by Hughes, the missile was in development by the Marine Corps for use on a variety of USMC and U.S. Navy aircraft.

1980 June 4 The first prototype McDonnell Douglas F-15J was flown for the first time from the manufacturer's plant at St. Louis. The F-15J was the version manufactured for the Japanese, and a six-man team was to take delivery of the aircraft at Edwards AFB, Calif. where they would make eight flights with it before 16 flights with the second prototype. These aircraft were then to be ferried to Nagoya in March 1981, while Japanese assembly of eight preproduction aircraft got under way at the Mitsubishi factory in Komaki, Japan.

1980 June 19 The last Sikorsky S-61 helicopter was delivered to its customer, Siller Brothers Inc. of Yuba City, Calif., ending a production run that had lasted 19 yr. In that time, more than 1,100 S-61 versions had been sold, including 136 civil variants and license-built models in Italy, the United Kingdom and Japan. The S-61 was the first medium-size helicopter to make its mark in a wide variety of civil and military applications.

1980 June 29 USAF Strategic Air Command completed Global Shield 80, an exercise that had first been held in 1979 as a test of the Single Integrated Operational Plan (SIOP), under which all military forces are coordinated for all-out nuclear war. Begun June 20, the operation involved 437 aircraft at 44 bases flying 1,035 sorties for a total 5,506 flying hr. There were nearly 100,000 personnel involved in an exercise that was sprung without prior warning to test reaction time to an emergency alert.

1980 July 1 The Swedish parliament voted to approve preliminary funding for a new fighter attack reconnaissance (Jakt-Attack-Spaning), or JAS, aircraft to succeed the Viggen in the 1990s. The funding covered work through the end of 1981 and would result, it was hoped, in a proposal from the Swedish aircraft industry for an aircraft to carry out this role. It was envisaged that the JAS aircraft would be about half the size of the Viggen.

1980 July 8 A specially modified McDonnell Douglas F-15B two-seat training version of the F-15A Eagle made its first flight as the Strike Eagle, a projected ground attack aircraft for deep interdiction and penetration missions carrying a large warload. Proposed for the new version was a redesigned front cockpit, a suitably adapted rear cockpit fitted out for a weapons systems officer, structural reinforcements for the anticipated takeoff weight of 81,000 lb., common engine bays for optional engines and refined avionics.

1980 July 12 The first of 60 McDonnell Douglas KC-10A cargo/tanker aircraft named Extender made its first flight at Long Beach, Calif. The aircraft had a wingspan of 165 ft. 4 in. and a length of 181 ft. 7 in. with a maximum takeoff weight of 590,000 lb. and a maximum cargo load of 169,370 lb. Maximum cargo/range was 4,370 mi. or 11,500 mi. of an unrefueled ferry flight. The primary advantage of the KC-10A is that it is able to buddy-fly a complete squadron of fighters or ground attack aircraft one-sixth of the way around the globe with all necessary equipment for the fighters to commence operations on arrival.

1980 July 16 The first aerodynamic representation of the BAe Nimrod AEW.Mk.3 made its first flight, powered by four 12,160-lb. s.t. Rolls Royce RB.168-20 Spey Mk 250 turbofans. With a length of 137 ft. 8 in. and a wingspan of 115 ft. 1 in., the airborne early-warning version of the Nimrod maritime reconnaissance aircraft had a maximum endurance of more than 10 hr. and a complement of 10, four of whom were flying crew and the rest a tactical team of electronic warfare specialists. The RAF had hoped to accept the first of 11 AEW.Mk.3s at the end of 1982.

1980 July 21 In a special ceremony at Hill AFB, Utah, the USAF formally assigned the name "Fighting Falcon" to the General Dynamics F-16 single-seat multi-role fighter. General Dynamics had proposed to the USAF prototype development of an advanced tactical-fighter variant with improved supersonic performance, which it designated F-16XL scamp (supersonic cruise aircraft modification program). Featuring extended fuselage and a cranked-arrow delta wing, it would have a cruise of Mach 2.2, more than twice that of the F-16A, 25% more combat radius and a 250% increase in low-altitude penetration weapons load.

1980 August 7 The solar-powered *Gossamer Penguin* made a successful flight for a distance of 2 mi. at Edwards AFB, Calif. piloted by glider pilot Janice Brown. It was designed by Dr. Paul MacCready, who was also working on *Solar Challenger,* which would have a wingspan of 42 ft. and a length of 32 ft. The wing and tail surfaces of *Solar Challenger* would carry 30,000 solar cells for electrical power production to give the airplane a speed of 40 MPH and a range of 100 mi.

1980 August 19 The first Boeing Vertol Model 234 Commercial Chinook made its first flight. Powered by two 4,075-SHP Avco Lycoming AL5512 turboshaft engines driving two 60-ft rotors and with a fuselage length of 52 ft. 1 in., it had four-abreast seating for 44 passengers, a cruising speed of up to 167 MPH and a range of 627 mi. in a special configuration carrying oversize fuel tanks in side fairings. British Airways Helicopters had ordered six of the UT model, which had a range of 264 mi. with maximum fuel.

1980 August 22 The U.S. stealth fighter and bomber projects being worked on by Lockheed and Northrop were made public when Defense Secretary Harold Brown openly declared that the USAF had a technology that ''alters the military balance significantly.'' Under an agreement with the Senate and the House of Representatives, Pres. Carter briefed only eight members of Congress on the stealth projects, but the president had agreed to inform a larger number when annual spending exceeded $1 billion, which it was about to do.

1980 September 22 USAF Strategic Air Command began the first test of the Strategic Projection Force in an exercise called Busy Prairie, which ended September 25, during which 14 B-52Hs of the Fifth Bombardment Wing deployed from Grand Forks AFB, N. Dak. to Whiteman AFB, Mo. They were joined there by EC-135, RC-135, U-2R, KC-135 and C-5 aircraft. The B-52s carried out simulated combat raids over a designated area of central Nevada demonstrating the crew's ability to penetrate air defenses.

1980 September 22 In a surprise attack, Iraqi Air Force bombers attacked 10 airfields in Iran including Ahwaz, Bushmeir, Dezful, Khatami, Meharabad, Omdiya, Sharokhi, Shiraz and Tabriz, at the start of a long and bitter war that would last eight years and result in the deaths of several hundred thousand people on each side. Next day, the Iraqi Army swept across the border into Iran as air action escalated with reciprocal attacks on Teheran and Baghdad. At this stage, the Iraqi Air Force had about 350 combat aircraft and 165 helicopters, and Iran had 325 combat planes and 600 helicopters. The Gulf War, in the air at least, was a model of ineptitude as neither side employed air power to minimize casualties and maximize the operational capability.

1980 October 11 The first two-seat trainer version of the Dassault-Breguet Mirage 2000 made its first flight exhibiting close performance similarities to its single-seat progenitor, the basic Mirage 2000. With a fuselage lengthened by only eight in., the 2000B had a reduced fuel capacity, but in all other respects, it was the same as the standard Mirage 2000. On its first flight, the aircraft reached a speed in excess of Mach 1.3. By this date, four Mirage single-seaters were flying with tests having cleared a load of +9 g and a roll rate of 270°/sec.

1980 October 26 British Caledonian inaugurated its London-St. Louis-Dallas/Fort Worth service by naming its seventh DC-10-30 *James S. McDonnell—The Scottish American Aviation Pioneer* in honor of the cofounder of McDonnell-Douglas who died in August. Born Apr. 9, 1899, James Smith McDonnell was the fourth son of a cotton grower in Little Rock, Ark. An early convert to flying, his father advised him to seek a career in aviation, which he did with remarkable success.

1980 October 29 A flight-test program with a General Dynamics F-16B fitted with the 18,000-lb. s.t. General Electric J79-GE-17X (later designated GE-119) began with the first of 50 flights. It was an effort on the part of the airframe and engine manufac-

turers to exploit the aircraft's sales potential to foreign countries. General Dynamics leased back from the USAF the second F-16B, which it would use to display the aircraft's performance. Designated F-16/79, the Pentagon authorized its sale as an air defense fighter for countries not in need of first-line U.S. combat aircraft, filling a niche between the Northrop F-5 class and aircraft such as the F-15.

1980 November 9 More than 28 yr. after it entered service as the world's first jet airliner, the last Comet was retired from commercial revenue-earning operations. The Comet 4C owned by Dan Air since 1975, when it purchased it from the RAF, made its last flight from Gatwick Airport, London, carrying 119 passengers on a celebration trip. The company had been the only Comet operator for several years and currently had five aircraft for disposal. The very last flight of a Comet was on September 30, 1981, when a Series 4C (G-BOIX, originally RAF aircraft serial no. XR399) was flown by a Dan-Air crew from Lasham to East Fortune, Scotland for permanent display at that airport.

1980 November 13 The first operational U.S. Navy squadron to be equipped with the McDonnell Douglas F/A-18 Hornet was commissioned at Lemoore Naval Air Station, Calif. Known as VF/A-125, it would assume responsibility for training all U.S. Navy and U.S. Marine Corps pilots on this aircraft for combined fighter and attack duties. The two roles had merged with this aircraft, and its multi-purpose role was reflected in squadron training. The first combat-ready Hornet squadron was expected to form up during late 1981.

1980 November 20 The first flight of a significantly modified Lockheed F-104 took place when an MBB test pilot in West Germany flew a CCV (control-configured vehicle)-adapted aircraft for the first time. With fixed canard surfaces to reduce longitudinal static stability to neutral, the aircraft was fitted with a quadrupled digital fly-by-wire system incorporated into the avionics and guidance and control suite. MBB had modified the aircraft to evaluate advanced flight dynamic design possibilities for future fighter aircraft.

1980 November 21 The British pilot Judith Chisholm arrived in Australia from England, having established a new record time of 3 days 11 hr. 2 sec. since she left November 18. This was a substantial improvement on the previous record for a solo flight between London and Australia of 5 days 21 hr. 3 min. set by Jean Batten on October 10, 1936, flying a Percival Gull Six. Judith Chisholm flew a Cessna Turbo Centurion between London-Heathrow and Port Headland, Australia.

1980 December 1 Entries for the U.S. stealth advanced technology bomber (ATB) had to be in by this date. This came more than two months after formulating a response to a Defense Department request for proposals issued in September. Lockheed submitted its proposal under the code name Senior Peg, which closely resembled the F-117A fighter they had been building. Northrop submitted its Senior Ice flying wing concept. The USAF wanted 132 stealth bombers with the first squadron operational by 1987 and anticipated a total program cost of $35 billion. By the end of 1981, Northrop was selected to build the B-2.

1980 December 12 An Alpha Jet fitted with a transonic wing, or Transsonischer Tragflügel (TST), made its first flight at Oberpfaffenofen, West Germany. Designed and fitted by Dornier, the TST had an 18% increase in thickness and was extended forward to a position near the cockpit, with new flaps attached to the trailing edge. The wing was expected either to increase the cruising speed, provide greater lift, or increase payload capability. Substantial testing had been conducted at the French ONERA wind tunnel to qualify the design.

1980 December 14 The inaugural flight of a low-cost, high-frequency service between New York-La Guardia and Washington-National was made when New York Air started revenue-earning operations. Set up by Texas Air Corp., which owned Texas International, the new service competed with Eastern Shuttle and was expected to expand to Newark, N.J., Boston and other locations in New York state. New York Air had six DC-9s and planned to add four more by mid-1981.

1981 January 1 The last aircraft designed by William P. Lear Sr. before his death on May 14, 1978, the Lear Fan Model 2100, made its first flight. Unusual in having twin turboshaft engines in the rear fuselage driving a pusher propeller and a Y-tail with canted upper fins and central lower fin, it was powered by two 850-SHP Pratt & Whitney Canada PT6B-35F turboshaft engines. The Model 2100 had a wingspan of 39 ft. 4 in., a length of 40 ft. 7 in. and a maximum takeoff weight of 7,350 lb. It could accommodate eight people in all with a range of 1,783 mi.

1981 January 8 The first McDonnell Douglas DC-9 Super 82, a Series 80-class aircraft variant, made its first flight with two 20,000-lb. s.t. Pratt & Whitney JT8D-217 engines suitable for ''hot and high'' airports. (Aircraft engine performance is reduced by hot air or by thinner atmosphere and a combination of hot climate and high elevation significantly reduces the load-carrying capacity of aircraft operating from airports with these conditions.) From an airport such as Denver's Stapleton International, which has an elevation of 5,000 ft., the DC-9 Super 82 could carry 155 passengers and baggage a distance of 1,497 mi. The Super 82 was a variant of the basic Super 81.

1981 January 11 The first two Boeing AGM-86B air-launched cruise missiles were delivered to the 416th Bombardment Wing, Griffiss AFB, N.Y., for environmental testing and maintenance training prior to full-scale delivery of the production models for Strategic Air Command. Plans envisaged 172 B-52G bombers fully equipped with 20 air-launched cruise missiles each, eight on an internal rotary launcher and six under each wing on pylons inboard of the inner engines.

1981 January 18 Bell Helicopter passed a milestone in its long and distinguished history when the company delivered its 25,000th helicopter, a Model 222 for Omniflight Helicopters. Since 1970 the company had been operating as an unincorporated division of Textron Inc.; but on January 3, 1982, it was to become a wholly owned subsidiary and change its name to Bell Helicopter Textron Inc. On this day also, Bell delivered the first Model 412, an improved and uprated version of the Model 212, to the ERA Helicopters Company.

1981 January 26 Vital in its early success, Pan American World Airways retired the last of its Boeing 707s after almost 23 yr. of unbroken service as the world's first jet airliner with a truly global sales record. In all, Pan American bought 137 aircraft of this type, including 128 Boeing 707s and nine 720s. The last flight in Pan American colors was made this day by *Jet Clipper Reindeer,* registration N881PA, a charter flight from New Orleans to Philadelphia. The last 24 Boeing 707s owned by Pan American were all based at JFK International Airport, New York.

1981 February 13 Fifty percent of British Aerospace was offered for public ownership for a total sum of £150 million in the first stage of privatization. Employees were to be given 33 shares worth a total £50 with an option to buy additional shares at half price. About one-third of the capital raised by the share offer was to go to the government and two-thirds back into British Aerospace to add to its working capital.

1981 February 16 The third annual Strategic Air Command Emergency War Order practice ended when Global Shield 81, in which more than 100,000 Strategic Air Command personnel had participated, came to an end. Begun January 26, more than 120 Strategic Air Command bombers were dispersed in rehearsal for an emergency alert that involved 30 tankers. Low-level airborne alert missions were flown passively over Colorado, New Mexico, Kansas and Texas. Aircraft were dispersed to foreign countries as well as to overseas possessions such as Guam.

1981 March 17 The first operational McDonnell Douglas KC-10A tanker/cargo aircraft was handed over to Strategic Air Command in a special ceremony at the manufacturer's Long Beach, Calif. plant. Receiving officer Lt. Gen. Edgard S. Harris Jr. was commander of Eighth Air Force, who flew the aircraft to Barksdale AFB, Louisiana. The KC-10A was assigned to Detachment 2 of the 4200th Test and Evaluation Squadron, where it would be fully shaken down. On November 1, it was assigned to the Thirty-second Air Refuelling Squadron, which had just been activated with the second Bombardment Wing also at Barksdale.

1981 March 19 The first of 18 Boeing E-3A Sentry AWACS aircraft for NATO duty arrived at the Dornier factory, Oberpfaffenhofen, near Munich, where mission avionics were installed and checked out beginning April 1. The complete mission-ready aircraft was delivered to NATO on January 22, 1982, with initial operating capability in 1983. The United Kingdom had opted not to participate in the AWACS program, preferring to develop its own version of the Nimrod maritime reconnaissance aircraft into an airborne early-warning aircraft.

1981 March 26 Boeing announced development plans for its 737–300 in response to separate orders earlier this month for 10 aircraft each to US Air (formerly Allegheny) and Southwest Airlines. Essentially a stretched 737–200, the new aircraft had 8 ft. 8 in. added to the length of its fuselage, wingspan increased by 1 ft. 10 in., seating capacity up to 149 in an all-tourist configuration and two 20,000-lb. s.t. CFM56-3 high-bypass turbofan engines. The larger diameter engine cowlings were flattened at the bottom to ensure adequate ground clearance and raised on their mountings so as to carry their upper surfaces in line with the wing leading edge.

1981 March 28 The first Dornier Do.228–100 made its first flight at Oberpfaffenhofen near Munich, West Germany. Developed as a utility and commuter aircraft, Dornier offered two versions of this design, which had been based on the Dornier 128. The 228–100 had accommodation for 15 passengers whereas the larger 228–200 could carry 19 people and had a longer fuselage, 54 ft. 4 in. versus 49 ft. 4 in. In each case, power was provided by two 715-SHP Garrett TPE331–5 turboprop engines, and wingspan was 55 ft. 8 in. The 228 could cruise at 206 MPH with full load with a range of 715 mi. or 1,224 mi. for the 228–100.

1981 April 20 The considerably redesigned Sukhoi Su-27 Flanker-B made its first flight. Powered by two 27,575-lb. s.t. Lyulka AL-31F turbofan engines, it had a top speed of Mach 2.35 (1,550 MPH), above 36,100 ft. and a sea level speed of Mach 1.1 (835 MPH). With a maximum takeoff weight of 66,135 lb., it could carry 10 AAMs in addition to the standard 30-mm six-barrel rotary cannon. The Flanker-B had a wingspan of 48 ft. 3 in. and a length of 71 ft. 11 in. Production started in 1982, and a two-seat version appeared designated Su-27UB Flanker-C.

1981 April 30   The extended period of research and development flights carried out by the four Rockwell B-1 prototypes ended with a last flight by the #4 aircraft. Together, the four B-1s had flown a total 1,895 hr. since the #1 aircraft took to the air on December 23, 1974, at Palmdale, Calif. By October 1978, the B-1 had achieved a maximum speed of Mach 2.2 in level flight. The B-1 was known to be a candidate for revival by the Reagan administration as an interim bomber pending operational deployment of the Northrop B-2 stealth bomber.

1981 May 5   Following agreement reached in March between the governments of Australia and the United States, a Boeing B-52H of the 410th Bombardment Wing, USAF, flew in to RAAF Base Darwin and remained there for two days on public display. On June 22, it conducted its first operational mission from the base, which was a sea search in conjunction with the Royal Australian Air Force. Negotiations lasting several years had culminated in permission to operate from Australian airfields in the event of an international crisis.

1981 May 8   The Dassault-Breguet Atlantic Nouvelle Génération made its first flight at Toulouse-Blagnac. Later designated ATL2, it was an improved and upgraded version of the first series under this name, which equipped the French, German and Italian armed services beginning in 1964. The ATL2 had two 5,665-SHP Rolls Royce Tyne RTy.20 Mk 21 turboprop engines, a wingspan of 122 ft. 9 in. over tip pods and a length of 110 ft. 4 in. Accommodating a normal crew of 12, it was equipped for advanced antisubmarine patrol work and a potential total mission duration of 12 hr. 31 min.

1981 May 11   Test pilot Art Peterson flew the Lockheed ER-2 for the first time at Palmdale, Calif. A civilianized development of the U-2R spyplane, it was configured to the same specification as the USAF TR-1A and in that regard was the first of the new production batch. It had been built for NASA as a high-altitude atmospheric research aircraft and would conduct research at the Ames Research Center, Moffett Field, Calif., where it was delivered on June 10, followed two days later by the first NASA mission. It had capacity for 3,000 lb. of instruments and a range of 3,350 mi. and could loiter for 6.5 hr. at 75,000 ft, from where it would also conduct earth resource observation missions.

1981 May 20   Hughes Helicopters decided to build a working example of its NOTAR (no-tail-rotor) helicopter design following 2 yr. of work under a $2.2 million contract from the U.S. Army Applied Technology Laboratory and the Defense Advanced Research Projects Agency. Hughes had been working since 1975 on an antitorque tailboom that dispensed with the need for a conventional tail rotor and in 1977–78 conducted trials with a working model. Work during this year would concentrate on adapting an OH-6 for full-scale trials.

1981 June 1   The first flight of the Short Brothers 360 took place at Queens Island, Belfast, Northern Ireland, about 6 mon. ahead of schedule. A developed and stretched version of the Short 330, production aircraft were powered by two 1,327-SHP Pratt & Whitney Canada PT6A-65R turboprop engines. With a length of 70 ft. 10 in. and a wingspan of 74 ft. 10 in., the Short 360 had capacity for 36 passengers, with a cruising speed of 243 MPH and a maximum distance of 265 mi.

1981 June 7   In the first planned attack of its kind, eight Israeli Air Force F-16As successfully destroyed an Iraqi nuclear reactor at Osirak near Baghdad. The F-16As took off from their base at Etzion in the Sinai, which was scheduled to be returned soon to Egypt under the terms of the Camp David accord between Egypt and Israel negotiated by Pres. Carter. They were protected by six F-15s that flew higher and were observed by radar. Speaking fluent Arabic, they bluffed their way across Jordan and Saudi Arabia. Two F-16s carried TV-guided smart weapons, and the other six carried 2,000-lb iron bombs, demolishing the target in a single pass at 5:30 P.M.

1981 June 12   The British and Italian governments granted permission for a 9-mon. study to define a replacement for the Sea King helicopter. In June 1980, EH Industries Ltd. was formed in London with ownership between Costruzioni Aeronautiche Giovanni Agusta SpA and Westland Helicopters Ltd. to develop such a helicopter under the designation EH 101. Both governments agreed to have the project handled by the U.K. Ministry of Defense. The EH 101 had grown from the Westland WG 34 design concept first generated in 1977–78.

1981 June 15   The preproduction series Lockheed F-117 made its first flight from a special facility in the Nevada desert. Based on the low-observables studies begun in November 1975, the single-seat low-altitude interdictor had a multi-faceted design and was developed from a program put together by the Defense Advanced Research Projects Agency and the USAF. Full-scale development had begun in November 1978 based on a flight program carried out with an Experimental Survivable Testbed first flown in December 1977. The first F-117A entered service with the 4450th Tactical Group, renamed the Thirty-seventh Tactical Fighter Wing, USAF, in October 1983.

1981 July 3   The first international service with the Ilyushin Il-86 began with an Aeroflot flight from Moscow to East Berlin, East Germany. About 20 of these wide-body, large-capacity aircraft had been built to date and had been used primarily between Moscow and Mineralnye Vody and Moscow and Tashkent (now Toshkent, Uzbekistan). Designed to carry up to 350 people, the high fuel consumption of its Kuznetsov NK-86 engines reduced payload/range capabilities and the aircraft was unable to achieve full capacity.

1981 August 1   The first Lockheed TR-1 derivative of the U-2R spyplane made its first flight powered by a 17,000-lb. s.t. Pratt & Whitney J75-P-13 turbojet engine. With a wingspan of 103 ft. and a length of 63 ft., the TR-1A had a maximum takeoff weight of 30,000 lb. and provision to carry the Hughes advanced synthetic aperture radar system (ASARS) and an X-band side-looking radar for use in the European theater. With a cruising speed of 435 MPH and an operational ceiling above 90,000 ft., it had been rolled out July 15 following restoration of the production line on November 16, 1979.

1981 August 3   Boeing achieved a milestone when it delivered the 4,000th jet airliner it had manufactured, a Boeing 727-200 for Ansett Airlines of Australia. It was exactly 23 yr. since the first Boeing 707 had been delivered to Pan American World Airways. The cumulative total manufactured comprised 940 Boeing 707s, 1,761 Boeing 727s, 778 Boeing 737s and 521 Boeing 747s. All these aircraft were still in production, the Boeing 707 airplane being produced as the USAF E-3A Sentry. The company had orders on the books for 295 more aircraft.

During the early 1980s, the first-generation "stealth" aircraft, the Lockheed F-117A, was flying and in production.

1981 August 15   A new variant of the McDonnell Douglas DC-8, the Series 71, made its first flight powered by four 24,000-lb. s.t. General Electric/SNECMA CFM56-2-1C turbofan engines. Deliveries of these reengined Series 61 aircraft began in April 1982 when Delta Air Lines received the first of 13 aircraft ordered. United Air Lines had ordered 30 conversions from its DC-8-61 fleet. Other versions offered by McDonnell Douglas were reengined Series 62 and Series 63 aircraft as Series 72 and Series 73, respectively.

1981 August 15   The first Boeing B-52G configured for air-launched cruise missiles was turned over to USAF Strategic Air Command's 416th Bombardment Wing, Griffiss AFB, N.Y., fitted with the new offensive avionics system, which was installed to provide improved navigation and weapons delivery. Because the cruise missile was an extremely accurate weapon system, it had to deploy from an accurately known location, and guidance updates prior to release would be an important aspect of success with the system.

1981 August 19   On the second day of a two-day exercise in the Gulf of Sidra off the coast of Libya, two Libyan Air Force Sukhoi Su-22 Fitter C fighters were shot down by two F-14A Tomcats from the carrier USS *Nimitz* when one of them fired a Soviet-built AA-2 Atoll air-to-air missile at a Tomcat. Turning sharply to port to avoid being hit, the first F-14A joined the second in shooting down the two Libyan fighters. AIM-9L Sidewinder infrared homing missiles were used. The incident took place 75–100 mi. south of the *Nimitz* and followed 36 Libyan intrusions into the exercise area on the previous day.

1981 August 24   A decision was made in the United States to commit the McDonnell Douglas AV-8B V/STOL single-seat close support and reconnaissance aircraft to full production, 260 being sought by the U.S. Marine Corps and, in a recent decision, 60

for the RAF. The British procurement was subject to approval by Congress because, after having interested the Americans in the idea of an advanced Harrier, they had pulled out of the program in March 1975. In a joint endeavor, British Aerospace would get about 40% of the work on all USMC/RAF aircraft, and Pratt & Whitney would get 25% of work on the Rolls Royce Pegasus engine.

1981 August 24   The USAF announced it had selected McDonnell Douglas as prime contractor to develop the C-17 long-range cargo aircraft as the winner of its C-X competition. The McDonnell Douglas design had made use of new and advanced technology incorporated in its earlier advanced medium STOL (AMST) work that produced the YC-15. The C-X requirement defined a capability to carry outsize loads usually carried by a Lockheed C-5 in to airstrips accessible only to a C-130.

1981 September 3   The first British Aerospace 146, a Series 100 four-engined, short-range transport aircraft made its first flight at Hatfield, site of the old de Havilland works, piloted by Michael Goodfellow accompanied by Peter Sedgwick. Powered by four very quiet 6,700-lb. s.t. Avco Lycoming ALF502R-3 turbofan engines, the BAe 146 had a wingspan of 86 ft. 5 in., a length of 85 ft. 10 in. (93 ft. 8 in. for the Series 200) with capacity for a maximum 93 (109) passengers and baggage at a cruising speed of 440 MPH for 1,093 (1,150) mi. The Series 200 made its first flight on August 1, 1982.

1981 September 15   The first flight-test mission with a B-52G carrying 12 Boeing AGM-86B ALCMs was conducted by a Strategic Air Command crew with the 416th Bombardment Wing, Griffiss AFB, N.Y. On the 9-hr. flight, the crew evaluated the data and exercised the offensive avionics system to determine mission readiness and to familiarize themselves with operational

Part of a new generation of USAF long-range, heavy-lift aircraft, a Lockheed C-5 refuels from a KC-10 Extender.

procedures. The aircraft carried 12 cruise missiles on underwing pylons.

1981 September 26 The Boeing 767 made its first flight. Powered by two 48,000-lb. s.t. Pratt & Whitney JT9D-7R4D high-bypass turbofan engines, it had a wingspan of 156 ft. 1 in., a length of 159 ft. 2 in. and a maximum takeoff weight of 310,000 lb. With a basic accommodation for 211 passengers in mixed-class configuration, the aircraft had a cruising speed of 529–579 MPH and a maximum payload range of 2,554 mi. An alternative engine for the type was the 47,900-lb. s.t. General Electric CF6-80A.

1981 September 28 The first successful test flight of the Airship Industries Skyship 500 took place at RAE Cardington, England. Developed from the AD-500, which first flew in 1979, it was powered by two 204-HP Porsche engines and had dimensions similar to its predecessor. Utilizing ducted thrust, each propulsor could be moved to provide unusual maneuvering capabilities, and the Skyship 500 was used effectively as a marketing aid for more advanced designs applicable to surveillance observation duties.

1981 October 1 The Ninety-fifth Reconnaissance Squadron of the Seventeenth Reconnaissance Wing, USAF, came into being ready to support deployment of 10 out of 18 Lockheed TR-1A spyplanes to RAF Alconbury, England from February 1983. The aircraft would be fitted with the precision emitter location strike system (PLSS) which, by triangulation using several TR-1As, would provide exact locations of transmitted signals deep inside enemy airspace for attack. TR-1As have been known to fly more than 5,600 mi. unrefueled from Beale AFB, Calif. nonstop to RAF Alconbury on the power of its single engine.

1981 October 2 Pres. Ronald Reagan announced restoration of the B-1 program as an interim strategic bomber pending devel-

opment of the B-2 stealth bomber, which was anticipated for the mid-1990s. The Defense Department was to procure 100 bombers for a planned initial operating capability by 1987, these aircraft assuming a more diverse set of roles than originally anticipated for the B-1. The USAF Scientific Advisory Board recommended maritime, conventional strike and nuclear delivery roles, and Rockwell would build a subsonic development of the basic aircraft, the B-1B.

1981 October 6 For the first time, a wide-body jet airliner was flown with a two-man crew when the Airbus Industrie A300 equipped with a forward-facing crew cockpit (FFCC) took to the air. With digital automatic flight control systems and a push-button crew access to optional flight information modes, the FFCC had been developed for the Indonesian airline Garuda. Powered by Pratt & Whitney JT9D-59A engines, this airline would be the first in the world to operate an aircraft commercially with a two-man crew flight deck.

1981 October 20 Australia's minister of defense, Denis J. Killen, announced that the McDonnell Douglas F/A-18A Hornet had been selected by his government as the winning contender for the new tactical fighter requirement. The RAAF expected to receive the first of 75 Hornets by the end of 1984, assembled and tested at the Australian aircraft factory at Avalon. Offsets of 30% were included in the deal, which was said to offer considerable operating economies over the F-16, runner-up in the contest.

1981 November 20 The Dassault-Breguet Mirage F.1-CR photographic reconnaissance version of the F.1 single-seat fighter made its first flight. Ordered in February 1979 as the successor to the Mirage III-R/RD aircraft in the French Arme de l'Air, the F.1-CR carried an OMERA 40 panoramic camera and an OMERA 35 camera internally with an infrared sensor and an OMERA 360 sight recorder. An underfuselage pod could accommodate additional equipment, and an in-flight refueling probe was standard.

Resurrected by Pres. Reagan, the B-1 was developed into an interim long-range bomber pending availability of the B-2 stealth bomber; cutbacks with the stealth project left the B-1 in mainline service alongside the B-52.

1981 November 23   As part of a rapid deployment joint force exercise code-named Bright Star 82, eight B-52Hs of the 319th Bombardment Wing, USAF, based at Grand Forks AFB, N. Dak. flew the longest nonstop simulated bombing mission in the history of Strategic Air Command. The eight bombers carried out a simulated strike on a runway in Egypt (with the full cooperation of the Egyptian government) mid-point in a 31-hr., 15,000-mi. flight maintained by three heavyweight in-flight refueling operations.

1981 November 25   The first U.S. reconnaissance satellite pictures of a new variable-geometry Soviet bomber were taken to reveal what would later be designated the Tupolev Tu-160 Blackjack. With a wingspan of 182 ft. 9 in./110 ft. 9 in. and a length of 177 ft. 2 in., it had a maximum takeoff weight of 606,260 lbs. carrying a maximum weapons load of 35,935 lb. With a maximum dash speed of Mach 2.07 (1,366 MPH) at 36,090 ft., the Blackjack had a maximum unrefueled range of 4,535 mi. The aircraft made its first flight in 1982 and entered service in 1988.

1981 December 1   The Swedish Parliamentary Defense Committee recommended development of the SAAB-2105 to fill the JAS requirement for a multi-role fighter. The project had been presented by the SAAB company on June 3. It was later renumbered the SAAB-2110 before being given the official designation JAS 39 Gripen (Griffin). It had a similar aerodynamic configuration to the Viggen but would adopt composites for 30% of the structure and be supersonic at all altitudes.

1981 December 7   Lockheed announced that it would terminate production of the L-1011 TriStar wide-body airliner. To date, the company had delivered 220 aircraft with firm orders for a further 24 and options on another 40. Since production began in 1972, the peak year output had been 1974 when 41 aircraft had been delivered. Lockheed cited ''market forces'' influencing its decision and declared that it could not produce the aircraft economically after 1986.

1981 December 8   Jerry Mullen completed the world's longest unrefueled flight made by a piston-engined aircraft when he landed his Javelin Phoenix at Oklahoma City, Okla. He had flown five times around a closed-circuit of 2,014 mi. between Oklahoma

City and Jacksonville, Fla., completing the distance of 10,070 mi. in 73 hr. 2 min. This beat the record set August 1947 when a USAF B-29 flew 8,854.3 mi. A development version of this aircraft was being designed for a nonstop unrefueled flight around the world.

1981 December 17   Hughes Helicopters made the first flight of its radical NOTAR (no-tail-rotor) concept using a converted OH-6. Utilizing a bonded-aluminum honeycomb tailboom incorporating a slot 0.33 in. wide running down the starboard side, pressurized air blown through the inside of the boom flowed out through slot and, mixed with the downwash from the main rotor, down around the boom to provide a force equivalent to the anti-torque action of a tail rotor.

1981 December 22   Grumman was selected to build the X-29A forward swept wing (FSW) research aircraft sponsored by the USAF Flight Dynamics Laboratory and the Defense Advanced Research Projects Agency (DARPA). Grumman lost the HiMAT contract to Rockwell because of a suspected design deficiency in their proposal, which, upon examination by DARPA's Col. Norris Krone, could be solved by adopting a forward-swept wing. He encouraged Grumman to redesign their submission and DARPA to fund a research project.

1982 January 10   Named *Spirit of America,* the first production turbojet Grumman Gulfstream III returned to Teterboro, N.J., having flown around the world in a record time of 47 hr. 39 min. Owned by National Distillers and Chemical Corp., the aircraft carried five crew and five passengers and made refueling stops at Geneva, Bahrain, Singapore, Guam, Hawaii and Chicago. It averaged 524 MPH and generally cruised at between 37,000 ft. and 45,000 ft.

1982 January 26   In the first multiyear procurement on the type, the USAF Systems Command ordered 480 General Dynamics F-16s for delivery between 1982 and 1985. The initial advance of $480.6 million was a downpayment on a bill that was expected to total $3 billion. This was the largest multiyear procurement contract to date. Only 303 F-16s of the originally planned total of 1,388 aircraft anticipated when the first order was placed remained to be delivered.

1982 January 26   The U.S. Defense Department announced cancellation of plans to procure the McDonnell Douglas C-17 and orders for 50 Lockheed C-5N heavy cargo aircraft instead. It also announced plans to continue KC-10A Extender production through the purchase of an additional 44 aircraft. The USAF wanted to continue work on the C-17, however, and lobbied extensively for technologies to remain funded. On July 26, McDonnell Douglas received a $31.6 million USAF contract to do just that.

1982 January 27   Growth in the business jet market was represented by the second manufacturer to produce 1,000 aircraft of a single type when Cessna achieved this total with its Citation twin-jet light executive transport. The first Citation had been delivered in 1972, and 349 were sold. Introduced in 1978, 293 Citation Is were sold prior to the inauguration of the Citation II, of which 358 had been sold. Gates Learjet had delivered its 1,000th production model on March 28, 1980.

1982 February 5   Terminating an agreement reached in May 1981 to cooperate on design and development of a 150-seat passenger airliner known as the MDF-100, Fokker and McDonnell Douglas decided to go their separate ways due to the ''present condition of the worldwide commercial aircraft market.'' Fokker was to concentrate on its F.27 and F.28 line, and McDonnell Douglas declared an intent to proceed with its own design for an aircraft in this class.

1982 February 5 Following a period of reduced revenue income, Laker Airways went into receivership after Freddie Laker, who owned 90% of the shares, asked the Clydesdale Bank to take it into liquidation. Fierce competition from this price-cutting trans-Atlantic carrier had depressed profit in the established airlines, and stock in Pan American, TWA, Northwest and Air Florida jumped between 8% and 11% at news of the Laker collapse. In just 6 yr. Laker had gone from a small charter operator to a major player on the trans-Atlantic routes, helping keep fares low and profits down among his competitors.

1982 February 16 The first production Airbus Industrie A310 was rolled out at the factory in Toulouse, destined for Swissair as the launch customer, and made its first flight on April 3. The design incorporated options for a "wet" tail carrying extra fuel for an extended range of just over 4,000 mi. This additional capacity constituted over half the 22,000-lb. weight difference over the standard A300. The A310 was to come in four versions: the A310-200 all-passenger aircraft, the -200C convertible version capable of being operated on freighter or passenger aircraft, the -200F freighter version and the -300 wet-tail, long-range passenger model.

1982 February 19 One month and six days after roll-out at the Renton, Wash. plant, the first Boeing 757 took to the air on its maiden flight. Powered by two 37,400-lb. s.t. Rolls Royce 535C turbofan engines, two 38,200-lb. s.t. Pratt & Whitney PW2037, or two 40,100-lb. s.t. Rolls Royce 535E4 turbofan engines, the 757 had a wingspan of 124 ft. 10 in. and a length of 155 ft. 3 in. With capacity for between 178 and 239 passengers in a wide variety of configurations, it had a cruising speed of 528 MPH and a range of 2,210 mi., or 5,343 mi. at economic cruise.

1982 February 26 The first production Boeing Vertol CH-47D model of the famous Chinook helicopter line made its first flight. This particular aircraft had already logged 2,650 flying hr. as a CH-47A and its original serial number, 66-19025, was redesignated 81-23381. The U.S. Army took over this helicopter, the first of 436 remanufactured CH-47As planned for conversion, on May 20. The CH-47D became operational with the Eleventh Airborne Division of the Rapid Deployment Force on February 28, 1984.

1982 March 18 The first production model of the BAe Jetstream 31 made its first flight. The type was certificated on June 29 and the first customer deliveries in Germany and the United Kingdom began in December 1982. Interest prompted the manufacturer to promote a maritime patrol version known as the 31EZ with a 360° scan search radar, a purpose-built searchlight and provision for five specialists as passengers.

1982 March 25 Beechcraft celebrated the 35th anniversary of the certification of its first Bonanza, a V-tailed aircraft first flown on December 22, 1945. Since then, the company had delivered almost 15,000 aircraft of that type, including 10,400 of the original design. Subsequent versions evolved over time to maintain the basic aircraft in production for 35 yr. The company marketed a special anniversary version of the Bonanza powered by a 285-HP Continental IO-520-BB engine, optional three-bladed propeller with anti-icing and three-axis autopilot, plus a special paint scheme with logo.

1982 April 2 Following several weeks of military provocation by Argentine armed forces, an Argentine invasion force landed on the Falkland/Malvinas islands in the South Atlantic off the coast of South America, precipitating the largest U.K. military action since the 1956 Suez crisis. The following day Prime Minister Margaret Thatcher told a special cabinet meeting that a large Royal Navy task force was to be mobilized in accordance with a resolution of the UN Security Council calling for Argentina to withdraw. Argentina had about 60 FMA IA 58 Pucará close-support aircraft, 80 A-4 Skyhawks, two squadrons of Mirage IIIEAs and two of Israeli IAI Dagger fighters and nine Canberra bombers in addition to five or six Super Etendards armed with the AS.39 Exocet air-to-surface missile.

1982 April 5 Fighting elements of the Falklands Task Force sailed from Portsmouth on the south coast of Britain on their way to mount an assault on Argentine invasion units. The force included the carriers HMS *Hermes* and HMS *Invincible,* each with nine Westland Sea King helicopters and later with 20 BAe Sea Harriers as fleet defense fighters. The carrier HMS *Illustrious* also had a contingent of Harriers.

1982 April 10 Introducing new technology into the light corporate transport market, the Canadair CL-601 Challenger made its first flight displaying winglets for reduced drag. In addition, the aircraft had two 8,650-lb. s.t. General Electric CF34-1A turbofans, more powerful than engines on its predecessor. With a wingspan of 64 ft. 4 in. and a length of 68 ft. 5 in., the CL 601 had a range of 4,030 mi. and capacity for up to 28 passengers at a cruising speed of 497 MPH.

1982 April 30 An RAF Vulcan bomber took off from Wideawake Air Base on Ascension Island at dusk and bombed the runway at Port Stanley on the Falkland Islands 4,400 mi. away at about 4:30 A.M. May 1 in an attempt to prevent Argentinian aircraft operating from that location. The raid took place from a height of 25,000 ft., and fourteen 1,000-lb. bombs were dropped obliquely at an angle of about 35° so as not to threaten the populated area of the town about 3 mi. away. Carried out in the dark, above cloud cover and without accurate wind data, the raid did not disable the runway.

1982 May 1 At dawn, Sea Harriers from HMS *Hermes* carried out an attack with 1,000-lb. bombs on the Argentine-held Port Stanley airfield in the Falkland Islands and on an airstrip at Goose Green from where Pucará close support aircraft could operate. Sea Harriers from HMS *Invincible* on combat air patrol encountered several Argentine Mirage IIIs and one Argentine Canberra was shot down. Altogether, the Argentines lost 15 aircraft, 12 of which had been destroyed on the ground on this first day of the air war over the Falklands.

1982 May 4 An Argentine Air Force Super Etendard sank the destroyer HMS *Sheffield* with an Exocet air-to-surface missile. Alerted to the presence of the British task force south-southeast of the Falkland Islands by a patrolling Argentine P-2H, the Super Etendard fighters took off from their Rio Grande base and were refueled by KC-130 tankers en route to the area. Both pilots fired their missiles, but one missile ran out of fuel and ditched; the other hit the *Sheffield.*

1982 May 7 Eight BAe Sea Harriers arrived on Ascension Island, having flown nonstop from the United Kingdom in a 9-hr. flight interspersed with several refueling operations. These would bolster the Sea Harrier force, which by now had been reduced to 17 aircraft following a midair collision the day before. Consoli-

Used with effect in the Falklands during 1982, the British Aerospace Harrier GR.Mk.3 shows its laser nose.

dation of air force elements was vital prior to the planned invasion to take the Falkland Islands.

1982 May 12   Braniff International ceased operations and filed for bankruptcy following debts of $670 million and a $300 million loss over 3 yr. Founded in 1928 by Tom and Paul Braniff, the airline filed under Chapter 11 of the U.S. bankruptcy code and preserved its assets intact while it negotiated a rescue package. The airline was resurrected during early 1984 with financial help from Hyatt Inc. It would then operate 30 Boeing 727-200s.

1982 May 21   Air operation during the British invasion of the Falkland Islands provided close support for marines as well as combat air patrols and selected strikes on tactical targets. Helicopters ferried vital supplies ashore. British losses for the day included a Harrier GR.Mk.3 shot down by ground fire near Goose Green, a Wessex HAS.Mk.2 helicopter on board HMS *Ardent* struck by a bomb, a Sea King HC.Mk.5 which crashed into the sea after bird strike on the tail rotor, three Gazelle AH.Mk.1s brought down by ground fire, and a Wessex HAS.Mk.3 damaged by cannon fire trained on HMS *Antrim*.

1982 June 1   The rugged adaptability of the BAe Harrier V/STOL ground attack fighter was ably demonstrated when two aircraft, flown by Flt. Lts. Murdo McLeod and Mike Beech, were flown nonstop 3,800 mi. from Ascension Island to the British Task Force near the Falkland Islands. After multiple refuelings from BAe Victor tankers, the Harriers were put down on the deck of an aircraft carrier, the first deck landings their pilots had made.

1982 June 1   At RAF Waddington, England, the first Panavia Tornado unit became operational when No. 9 Squadron re-formed with this swing-wing, multi-role aircraft. This squadron had been

flying Vulcans since 1962 but had been disbanded April 29. In re-forming with Tornadoes, it effectively closed a chapter in post-World War II RAF history during which the heavy strategic bomber had carried Britain's nuclear deterrent. Now, the Royal Navy had Polaris submarines for that role and the RAF's strike aircraft had a tactical role epitomized by this high-performance aircraft.

1982 June 9   At 2:14 P.M., a force of about 90 Israeli Air Force F-4Es and Kfirs, escorted by F-15 and F-16 fighters, swept up the Bekaa Valley, Lebanon in the first electronic air war. With drones flying over Jordanian and Syrian defenses, a Boeing 707 electronically jamming enemy signals and an E-2C airborne early-warning aircraft vectoring Israeli fighters onto enemy aircraft, 10 out of 19 SAM sites were destroyed within 10 min. A second wave of slightly fewer aircraft destroyed the remaining sites. Almost 100 Syrian MiG-21s and MiG-23s came up, blind without ground radar; about 22 were shot down, without a single loss to the Israelis.

1982 June 10   The first all-female air crew to fly with USAF Strategic Air Command conducted its first mission, a 5-hr. training exercise from Castle AFB, Calif. Under the nickname "Fair Force One," the crew was from the 924th Air Refuelling Squadron and included Capt. Kelly S. C. Hamilton, commander and pilot, 1st Lt. Linda Martin, the copilot, Capt. Cathy Bacon, instructor navigator, 1st Lt. Diane Oswald, navigator, and Sgt. Jackie Hale, boom operator. Hamilton was the only female aircraft commander in Strategic Air Command at this date.

1982 June 14   The Argentine forces on the South Atlantic's Falkland Islands surrendered to British forces, ending their 74-day occupation of the British colony. The British forces had flown 1,335 Harrier sorties since May 1, of which 1,135 were combat air patrols. and had shot down 19 aircraft for the loss of eight, only five of which were in combat. Westland Sea King helicopters logged more than 2,253 sorties, and Victor tankers flew over 600 sorties. Hercules transport aircraft logged 13,000 hr. of flying time. The Argentines had mounted 445 combat sorties, of which only 280 reached their targets.

1982 June 18   An RAF C-130 Hercules transport aircraft of No. 70 Squadron made a record 28 hr. 4 min., nonstop return flight from Ascension Island to the Falkland Islands. While the runway at Port Stanley was closed for extension, the Hercules implemented a recently perfected air-snatch technique in which the C-130 trailed a 150-ft. nylon rope and snagged a mail bag hung between two poles 50 ft. above the ground. For these exceptionally long flights, two auxiliary fuel tanks were fitted in the fuselage with refueling probes.

1982 July 2   The USAF selected the Fairchild design as the next-generation fighter (NGF) to replace the Cessna T-37, which had been serving the military for 25 yr. Designated T-46A, the two-seat primary trainer was expected to fly in 1985, and the USAF announced an intention to buy 650, preceded by two prototypes. The T-46A was to be powered by Garrett turbofan engines, and the aircraft was expected to enter service during 1986. Planning changes would prevent that from happening.

1982 July 3   The General Dynamics single-seat F-16XL made its first flight at Fort Worth, Tex. and featured a cranked-arrow delta wing with a span of 34 ft. 3 in. and a fuselage length of 54 ft. 2 in. The design of the wing incorporated research carried out by NASA and General Dynamics incorporating graphite polymide composites and possessing an area more than twice that of a standard F-16. A second, two-seat F-16XL was built and test-flown October 29 in a program that ended its initial flight phase on May 15, 1983.

1982 July 23   The USAF Strategic Air Command exercise Global Shield 82 ended after eight days of intensive rehearsal for offensive and defensive operations. This year's annual exercise included an expanded operation involving Canadian military forces. USAF Air Defense Command worked cooperatively with the Canadian Armed Forces Tactical Air Group, throwing their combined fighter forces against Strategic Air Command bombers and support forces. This simulated defensive exercise helped defenders work up tactics and offensive elements to evolve strategies dictating how best to repel an air attack.

1982 July 28   The first flight of a DC-3 piston-engined aircraft converted to a turboprop transport aircraft powered by two Pratt & Whitney PT6A engines took place. United States Aircraft Corp., which carried out the conversion, claimed that cruising speed increased from 165 MPH to 215 MPH and that payload increased from 9,400 lb. to 13,128 lb. The company also planned to increase seating capacity from 32 to 36 by adding a small fuselage plug to extend the interior cabin length.

1982 August 4   The first Boeing KC-135R, a reengined USAF KC-135A tanker/cargo aircraft, made its first flight at the start of the biggest retrofit program ever mounted by the USAF intended to keep the tanker fleet operational well into the next century. Powered by four 22,000-lb. s.t. General Electric/SNECMA CFM56-2B-1 engines, the Air Force planned to reengine 390 KC-135s. The CFM56 engines improved efficiency and allowed the KC-135As to offload 65% more fuel in midair refuelings at a 1,725 mi. radius and an average takeoff weight, and 150% more fuel at a radius of 2,875 mi. Increased power enabled the KC-

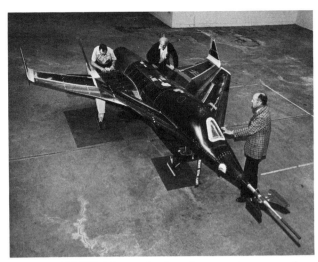

The NASA HiMAT fighter technology demonstrator was used during the 1980s to research new design concepts.

135R to take off and reach an altitude of 2,500 ft. before a standard KC-135A had left the runway. Maximum fuel load with a CFM56-engined KC-135A was 203,288 lb. versus 189,702 lb. with a similar aircraft powered by Pratt & Whitney engines.

1982 August 19   The first airline delivery of the Boeing 767 took place when United Air Lines accepted the ninth aircraft off the production line. An inaugural flight between Chicago and Denver took place September 8 and regular service between Chicago, San Francisco, New York-La Guardia and Boston started September 9. The Boeing 767 replaced the DC-10s used on those routes and accommodated 24 in first class and 173 in coach. As production increased and orders expanded, a significant majority of airlines specified the two-man cockpit offered by Boeing.

1982 August 26   Continuing accidents with the Lockheed F-104 Starfighter brought the total number of Luftwaffe losses to 252 aircraft since 1961 when an aircraft of this type crashed near Munich, West Germany. From a peak loss of 140 per 100,000 flying hours in 1962, the loss rate declined gradually to 10 per 100,000 hrs in 1981–82. The high publicity accorded Luftwaffe F-104 losses frequently failed to recognize the higher loss rates per flying hours in other NATO air forces. However, the German losses were generally attributed to poor training and a lack of adequate conversion training when moving from other, less demanding, aircraft.

1982 August 30   Formerly known as the F-5G, latest in a long line of Northrop lightweight F-5 variants and derivatives, The F-20 Tigershark made its first flight. Developed as an export fighter for countries unwilling to pay for F-16-class aircraft, the F-20 was powered by an 18,000-lb. s.t. General Electric F404-GE-100 turbofan engine. With a wingspan of 28 ft. and a length of 46 ft. 7 in., the F-20 carried two 20-mm cannons, tip-mounted Sidewinders and a weapons load of up to 8,300 lb.

1982 September 28   McDonnell Douglas received a contract to proceed with development of the McDonnell Douglas/BAe U.S. Navy Hawk two-seat trainer under the designation T-45. In a decision announced November 1981, the VTXTS requirement was filled by a planned procurement of 253 Hawk trainers manufactured in the United States and modified for carrier operations as the T-45A with the T-45B designation for the land version. The

T-45B was expected to fly first, and the type would replace T-2C Buckeye and TA-4J Skyhawks.

1982 September 30 The world's first circumnavigation by helicopter was completed when American pilots H. Ross Perot Jr. and Jay Coburn landed their Bell 206L LongRanger *The Spirit of Texas* at Love Field, Dallas, from where they had departed on September 1. In the intervening period, they had covered 26,000 mi. in 29 stages flying over 23 countries. They flew eastward and received permission from the Soviets to land in the Kurile Islands north of Japan. At one point, they were forced to land on the heaving deck of a U.S. container ship pitching through 12-ft. waves in a 50-knot wind.

1982 October 5 The first Boeing 747-300 with a stretched upper deck made its first flight. Announced June 12, 1980, the 747-300 had an upper fuselage extension of 23 ft. 4 in., increasing from 32 to 91 the number of passengers carried behind the flight deck. Operating weight went up to a maximum takeoff weight of 833,000 lb., payload increased to a maximum 150,000 lb., and maximum cruise was improved by Mach 0.01 due to the refined aerodynamics. Swissair and UTA were the first customers to receive their aircraft following certification on March 7, 1983.

1982 October 31 Effective from this date, the long-awaited merger between Continental Airlines and Texas International Airlines took effect with full integration of all airline operations. The combined fleet included 23 DC-10s, 57 Boeing 727s and 39 DC-9s. The Texas Air Corp. established Continental Airlines Corp. to take over both Continental Airlines and Texas International Airlines; it also owned New York Air, which it continued to operate as an independent company.

1982 November 4 The world's longest nonstop, scheduled, revenue-earning service was inaugurated by Pan American World Airways when a Boeing 747SP left Los Angeles, Calif. for a flight to Sydney, Australia. The 7,487 mi. were covered in a flying time of 14 hr. 30 min. and was to become a regular weekly service departing Thursday evenings to arrive in Sydney Saturday on the other side of the international date line. The return flight was to commence in mid-afternoon from Sydney and arrive back in Los Angeles before midnight local time on the same calendar day.

1982 November 29 The first production Dassault-Breguet Mirage 2000C-1 single-seat interceptor made its first flight at Bordeaux-Merignac. Deliveries would begin in 1983 to Escadre de Chasse 1/2 "Cigognes" of the French Armée de l'Air. This unit would receive 10 Mirage 2000C-1 and four Mirage 2000B two-seat trainer versions, the first of which had flown on Oct. 11, 1980.

1982 December 13 A BAe 146 returned to the United Kingdom after a marathon sales and marketing tour that began October 24. The aircraft visited 20 countries, made 98 demonstration flights and made presentations to 31 airlines, receiving serious interest from 12. The BAe 146 (G-SCHH) selected for this tour made its first flight October 19 and was the first of its type to be completed to airline standard. The aircraft flew 130 route sectors in 167 flying hours covering 16,500 mi.

1982 December 15 The first revenue-earning services with the Boeing 767 made inaugural flights with United Air Lines and Delta Air Lines. The United aircraft was powered by two 47,800-lb. s.t. Pratt & Whitney JT9D-7R4D engines, and the Delta aircraft had two 47,900-lb. s.t. General Electric CF6-80A engines.

An optional version marketed by Boeing had a maximum takeoff weight of 335,000 lb., versus 300,000 lb., and two 49,800-lb. CF6-80A2 engines with a maximum payload range of 4,000 mi.

1982 December 16 Four BAe Vulcans of No. 44 Squadron, RAF, scrambled from RAF Waddington, England, to mark the end of more than 25 years of V-bomber service. During the past year, five V-bomber squadrons had been disbanded, an activity slowed by the Falklands campaign. The last squadron, No. 44, was disbanded December 21. The last squadron operating the Vulcan, No. 50, operated the aircraft in a tanker role.

1982 December 26 The world's heaviest aircraft, the Antonov An-124 long-range heavy lift transport aircraft, made its first flight piloted by Vladimir Terski. With a wing span of 240 ft. 5 in. and a length of 226 ft. 8 in., a height of 68 ft. 2 in. and a maximum takeoff weight of 892,872 lb., the An-124 had a cargo capacity of 330,693 lb. With a general configuration similar to the Lockheed C-5, it carried a flight crew of six and space for 88 passengers in the area behind the flight deck above the main cargo hold. Power was provided by four 51,590 lb. thrust Lotarev D-18T turbofan engines.

1983 January 1 Eastern Air Lines flew the inaugural commercial service with the Boeing 757 less than 4 yr. after Boeing announced full production on the aircraft and less than 1 yr. since its first flight. FAA and U.K.-type certification came on December 21, 1982, and January 14, 1983, respectively. Eastern received its first 757 on December 22, 1982, followed by British Airways on January 25. The first British Airways revenue-earning flight was on February 9.

1983 January 3 The newly completed Northrop facility where the stealth bomber code-named Project Senior CJ would be developed was opened for employees to commence work with the advanced systems division. Northrop had purchased an abandoned Ford plant in the Pico Rivera suburb of Los Angeles on April 8, 1982, for $65 million and moved in 4,000 employees who had been working on stealth at Building A-Y across town. It was at Pico Rivera that Northrop would build a 25% scale model of the stealth bomber called Tacit Blue.

1983 January 7 The McDonnell Douglas F/A-18 Hornet became fully operational at U.S. Marine Corps Fighter/Attack Squadron 314 at El Toro Marine Corps Air Station, Calif. It also equipped the Marine unit VMFA-323. Initial work-up had been carried out by the development squadron (VFA-125) at Lemoore NAS, Calif. beginning November 1980 followed by operational and U.S. Navy inspection and survey trials starting early 1982. The U.S. Navy had a requirement for 803 F/A-18s, and the U.S. Marine Corps wanted 316. Deliveries were still in progress in 1993.

1983 January 25 The first SAAB-Fairchild 340 made its first flight 3 yr. after the two companies signed a joint agreement to develop a new regional airliner and corporate transport aircraft. SAAB paid 65% of development costs, built the fuselage and completed final assembly; Fairchild assembled the wings, tail and engine nacelles. Powered by two 1,600-SHP General Electric CT7-7Es, the 340 had a wingspan of 70 ft. 4 in., a length of 64 ft. 9 in. and accommodation for up to 35 passengers in airline configuration or 16 in executive arrangement with a range of 1,048 mi.

1983 January 27 The first BAe FRS.Mk.51 Sea Harrier for the Indian Navy was handed over to the Indian Navy's Sea Harrier Training Squadron established at RNAS Yeovilton, England. The eight aircraft on order were to be deployed with No. 306 Squadron aboard the Indian carrier INS *Vikrant* operating from its base at Goa-Dabolim. Incorporated in the order for eight aircraft were two T.Mk.4N two-seat trainers, which were used at Yeovilton in conjunction with four nonnavalized Harriers for land-based training.

1983 January 31   McDonnell Douglas announced it was launching a new derivative of the DC-9, which would be known as the MD-83. This aircraft was to have 21,000-lb. s.t. Pratt & Whitney JT8D-219 turbofan engines and a maximum payload range of 2,950 mi. carrying 155 passengers and baggage. With a maximum takeoff weight of 160,000 lb. and structural strengthening, the additional range came from two 580-gal. fuel tanks installed under the cabin floor, raising total capacity to 7,000 gal.

1983 February 17   A team from Bell Helicopter and Boeing Vertol presented their design proposal for a tilt-rotor, multi-purpose aircraft to fill the vertical lift aircraft (JVX) USAF/USN program. Bell's experience with the XV-15 program was incorporated in the proposal. Two XV-15 tilt rotor research aircraft had accumulated more than 300 flying hr. by 50 pilots. Boeing applied more than 240 hr. with test models in support of the JVX requirement. The U.S. Army, USAF, U.S. Navy and U.S. Marine Corps expressed a requirement for a total 1,086 aircraft.

1983 February 17   The RAF took delivery of its 100th Panavia Tornado when an RAF crew collected it from Honington, England. The production rate had increased to 110 per year with a planned total procurement cycle of 809 for the air forces of the United Kingdom, Germany and Italy. There had been considerable interest in the aircraft from Greece and Spain, and performance and operating experience from the 25,000 flying hr. now accumulated by this aircraft showed impressive results.

1983 February 24   The youngest pilot known to have made a solo flight in a powered, heavier-than-air, flying machine took to the air for the first time at age 9 yr. 316 days. The flight took place near Mexicali, Mexico, and the aircraft he piloted was a Cessna 150. The previous claimant had been the English boy James A. Stoodley when, in December 1942 at the age of 14 yr. 5 mon., he took his 13-year-old brother John for a joy ride without having received any prior flying instruction.

1983 March 7   In the largest mining exercise of its kind, 10 Strategic Air Command B-52Ds and B-52Gs from the Forty-third Strategic Wing and the Second and Nineteenth Bombardment Wings, were used to lay down mines off the coast of South Korea. This exercise was part of a Team Spirit 83 operation in which U.S. military forces operated in conjunction with friendly forces to rehearse combined activities. The exercise included participation from the USAF, the U.S. Navy, the U.S. Marine Corps and South Korea.

1983 March 23   The first of the Rockwell B-1A swing-wing bombers returned to flight status took to the air when the #2 aircraft conducted a 3.5-hr. flight from Edwards AFB, Calif. It was reintroduced as part of a development program for the B-1B and incorporated several detailed changes. Technically, the #4 aircraft had been returned to flight status when it was brought out of retirement to participate in the Society of British Aircraft Companies Show at Farnborough, England in September 1982. That aircraft was to be modified as an avionics test-bed for the B-1B and was expected to join the #2 aircraft in flight tests in mid-1984.

1983 April 9   Designated PA-48, a modified version of the North American P-51 Mustang made its first flight. Built by Cavalier Aircraft Corp. and taken over by Piper, two prototypes had been ordered as development aircraft for a light tactical strike aircraft aimed at the South American market. Dubbed Enforcer, the aircraft was flight-tested at Eglin AFB, Fla. and at Edwards AFB, Calif., later this year and in 1984. Despite a maximum speed of 403 MPH and a service ceiling of 37,600 ft., the Enforcer failed to attract customers, and the project was abandoned in 1986.

1983 April 23   A Bell and Boeing Helicopter Co. team proposal for the JVX competitive request for bids submitted February 17 resulted in an order from the U.S. Navy for preliminary design of the aircraft over the next 2 yr. To be known as the V-22 Osprey, it was designed for the joint services advanced vertical lift aircraft program that envisaged a tilt-rotor concept for multi-role applications with the USAF and the U.S. Navy, the latter being the administering service. Further contracts in 1985 and 1986 progressed with mock-ups and development of a flight-test program.

1983 April 30   The USAF completed extensive studies of advanced capabilities for the McDonnell Douglas F-15 Eagle using four differently configured aircraft to demonstrate and evaluate varying combinations of mission and load-carrying. Tests were made on advanced radar, and one aircraft operated with a gross weight of 75,000 lb. Other aircraft carried two conformal fuel tanks, three external drop tanks and a 4,000-lb. bomb load. In all, 16 different payload configurations were tested among the nine external stores locations.

1983 May 10   The Westland 30-100, formerly known as the WG 30, entered scheduled commercial service for the first time. It began operations with AirSpur Helicopters in Los Angeles. First flown on April 10, 1979, as a stretched development of the successful Westland Lynx, it was powered by two 1,135-SHP Rolls Royce Gem 41-1 engines driving a 43-ft. 8-in. rotor and had a length of 47 ft. and a height of 15 ft. 6 in. With a maximum takeoff weight of 12,800 lb., the Westland 30-100 had capacity for up to 17 people with a cruising speed of 138 MPH and a range of 219 mi.

1983 May 26   People Express inaugurated low-cost, trans-Atlantic air services with a Boeing 747 flight from London-Gatwick to New York. Fares were $149 or £99 for a one-way ticket and $439 or £299 for a round-trip ticket. During June TWA cut by 25% fares on six London-U.S. routes, reducing from £348 to £258 the cheapest London-New York round-trip ticket and British Airways cut their round-trip London-New York fare to £249 beginning October 1. This fare-cutting war was reminiscent of the situation brought about by Laker Airways.

1983 May 26   British Aerospace signed an agreement with the U.K. government for funding to support detailed design and development of an experimental aircraft program (EAP) prototype to be flying by 1986. For several years, BAe had been conducting privately funded studies with MBB of Germany and Aeritalia of Italy on what had then been designated the agile combat aircraft (ACA). Envisaged as a fixed-wing, high-performance combat aircraft, it was to incorporate advanced structural concepts, including carbon-fiber composites, fly-by-wire controls and an electronic cockpit.

1983 June 20   Flight tests with the Skyfox tactical trainer began at California's Van Nuys airport following an unveiling of the aircraft May 20. Essentially a much-modified Lockheed T-33A,

Anti-armor and airfield denial weapons are the common stores of ground-attack aircraft, as demonstrated by a Panavia Tornado releasing bomblets from a dispenser under its fuselage.

the newly configured aircraft retained all the internal systems and engineering layout within a completely redesigned exterior, power provided by two Garrett TFE731-3 turbofan engines in nacelles attached to the rear fuselage and Martin Baker Mk.10L ejection seats. Skyfox Corp. was seeking orders totaling at least 80 aircraft and had arranged with the Portuguese to set up a production facility in Alverca should the project go ahead.

1983 June 20 The first of four prototype de Havilland Canada DHC-8 Dash 8 fuel-efficient, short-haul transport aircraft made its first flight piloted by Robert Fowler. Powered by two 1,800-SHP Pratt & Whitney Canada PW120 turboprop engines, it had a wingspan of 84 ft. 11 in., a length of 73 ft. and capacity for up to 39 passengers carried for up to 1,025 mi. at 311 MPH. An alternative corporate configuration was available. The cabin was pressurized and air-conditioned.

1983 July 5 The first RAF Lockheed TriStar was put into service when 270 soldiers of the First Battalion, Gloucestershire Regiment, were transported from RAF Brize Norton, England to Edmonton, Alberta. These ex-British Airways L-1011-500 aircraft had been purchased to supplement the existing RAF transport inventory and would eventually total nine K.Mk.1 tanker/passenger, K(C).Mk.1 tanker/cargo and K.Mk.2 aircraft.

1983 July 8 The 1,000th General Dynamics F-16 was rolled out at Fort Worth, Tex. Included in this total were 446 aircraft built in Belgium, Denmark and the Netherlands. Total planned purchase by the USAF now stood at 2,165 aircraft, with a further 255 on order for Israel, Egypt, Pakistan, Venezuela and South Korea.

1983 July 8 The first Airbus Industrie A300-600 made its first flight and was put through its paces for 4.5 hr. The launch order for 11 Series 600 aircraft came from Saudi Arabian Airlines in December 1980. Featuring a major weight reduction program to give it improved performance, the aircraft had a maximum take-off weight of 363,760 lb. and was powered by either two 56,000-lb. s.t. General Electric CF6-80C2-A or two 58,000-lb. s.t. Pratt

& Whitney PW4058. With several refinements, the aircraft had a slightly greater range and could accommodate 16 more people than the A300B4-200.

1983 July 22 Completing the world's first solo circumnavigation of the globe by helicopter, Dick Smith landed his Bell JetRanger at Fort Worth, Tex. from where he had set off on August 5, 1982. From Forth Worth, he had flown 5,620 mi. to the United Kingdom in 61 hr. 11 min., where he arrived August 19, then 12,266 mi. to Sydney in 113 hr. 12 min., which he reached on October 3, and 17,412 mi. from Sydney to Fort Worth in 145 hr. 36 min. beginning May 25. This final leg went via Indonesia, the Philippines, Hong Kong, Taiwan, Japan, the Aleutian Islands, Alaska, Canada, Seattle and Salt Lake City.

1983 July 30 Flying a modified North American P-51D-25 Mustang, Frank Taylor raised the world air speed record for piston-engined aircraft when he reached a speed of 832.12 km/hr. (517.06 MPH) over a 15/25 km course at Mojave, Calif. Named *Dago Red,* his Mustang was powered by a 3,000-HP Rolls Royce/Packard Merlin V-1650-9 engine and bore the serial no. N5410V.

1983 August 19 The last of 250 Lockheed L-1011 TriStars was rolled out at the Lockheed California Palmdale plant. A Series 500, it was one of five that were unsold at the time of completion. In a ceremony at Palmdale, the first TriStar, which had been rolled out on September 1, 1970, and which remained under Lockheed ownership for development work, was present along with the last in the line.

1983 August 29 An 85% scale model of a radical new design concept for a turboprop-powered corporate aircraft designed by Beech Aircraft and built by Scale Composites Inc. made its first flight over the Mojave Desert. The new design featured a swept wing with wing end plates set on a slender tailless fuselage carrying two movable canards and two turboprop engines mounted inboard at the rear. Scaled Composites was owned by Burt Rutan and later became a subsidiary of Beech Aircraft.

1983 September 1 The first preproduction Sikorsky MH-53E airborne mine countermeasures helicopter made its first flight. Developed for the U.S. Navy from the Super Stallion, it had enlarged sponsons for 1,000 gal. of extra fuel over the standard helicopter equipment and specialized equipment for mine detection. The empty weight of the MH-53E was 36,336 lb. Extensive flight trials were held by the U.S. Navy, during which one MH-53E remained in the air on simulated patrol for 20 hr.

1983 September 1 In what would be the final unprovoked attack by Soviet fighters on a civilian airliner, a Sukhoi Su-15 interceptor shot down a Korean Air Lines Boeing 747-200B that strayed inside Soviet airspace west of Sakhalin Island north of Japan. All 269 people on board were killed. Two Soviet air force fighters intercepted the aircraft and closed to within visual distance of the Boeing airliner before flying ahead of it for positive identification. Only then did one of the two fighters fire two heat-seeking missiles. Transcripts of the Soviet air-to-ground communication reveal the pilots spent several minutes identifying the aircraft as a Boeing 747 airliner before conferring with the local Soviet commander, who ordered it shot down. It is possible the pilots believed it to be a military KC-135 but unlikely because of the aircraft's greater size.

1983 September 1 The RAF set up a Tornado Operational Evaluation Unit at the Aircraft and Armament Experimental Establishment in Boscombe Down commanded by Wg. Comdr. J. G. Lumsden. As an RAF Strike Command unit, it was to be responsible for weapons trials and evaluation as well as aspects of electronic warfare, terrain-following and advanced radar operations. The object of this unit, first of its kind for more than 25 yr., was to evaluate the optimum operational techniques and to evaluate a wide variety of tactics and war-fighting activity with full liaison across all RAF units associated with the Tornado.

1983 September 5 A USAF KC-135 of the Forty-second Bombardment Wing, Loring AFB, Maine, commanded by Capt. Robert J. Goodman, saved a Tactical Air Command F-4E that lost power in one engine during an exercise above the Arctic Circle. Directed to land at Gander, Newfoundland 500 mi. away, the F-4E was escorted by the KC-135 but was forced to shut one engine down. Failing power from the second engine caused the F-4E to lose altitude by 20,000 ft. and required the KC-135 to refuel and at times to actually tow the F-4E via the fuel line to the vicinity of Gander where it landed safely.

1983 September 6 In a show of force to suppress violence in Beirut two days after Israeli forces began their withdrawal, the French aircraft carrier *Foch* arrived in Lebanese waters carrying three squadrons of Dassault-Breguet Super Etendards and a reconnaissance unit equipped with Etendard IVPs. A day later the RAF flew in Chinook helicopters and RAF F-4 Phantoms went on quick reaction alert on Cyprus to protect British C-130 Hercules transport aircraft. RAF Buccaneer S.Mak.2Bs were also used with jammers to inhibit newly installed Soviet SAM sites.

1983 September 15 The first official flight of the Agusta A 129 Mangusta light anti-armor helicopter took place in Italy with Commandante Luciano Forzani at the controls. Powered by two 815-SHP Rolls Royce Gem 2 Mk.1004D turboshaft engines driving a 39-ft. rotor, the helicopter had a length of 40 ft. 3 in. and carried four external stores points on two stub wings with a span of 10 ft. 6 in. With pilot and gunner in tandem cockpits, the Mangusta carried a wide variety of weapons and had a maximum speed of 196 MPH and an endurance of 2.3 hr. It had been developed for the Italian Army but with export potential in mind.

1983 September 16 Hawker Hunter F.70s of the Lebanese Air Force attacked antiaircraft batteries and SAM sites operated by Syrian forces and the Druze militia. These aircraft had deployed to a motorway 19 mi. north of Beirut, which they used as a runway since Beirut aiport had been under almost constant threat. One Hunter was shot down and its pilot rescued by a helicopter from the USS *Nimitz,* which had been dispatched to the eastern Mediterranean.

1983 September The USAF Systems Command awarded concept definition study contracts for an advanced tactical fighter (ATF) to replace the McDonnell Douglas F-15 Eagle at the turn of the century. Boeing, General Dynamics, Grumman, Lockheed, McDonnell Douglas, Northrop and Rockwell each received contracts to submit their results by July 28, 1986. The advanced fighter would use an advanced technology engine that would be the subject of separate development contracts. The USAF stimulated a procurement need for 750 aircraft.

1983 October 4 The last B-52D was retired from USAF Strategic Air Command when the last aircraft of this type from the Seventh Bombardment Wing was flown to the storage facility at Davis-Monthan AFB, Arizona. The B-52D was used in permanent displays and at museums, 24 being assigned these duties during 1983 and 1984.

1983 October 6 The first prototype of the Bell OH-58D Kiowa made its first flight following award of a contract to modify up to 578 U.S. Army OH-58As as interim scout helicopters. Under the army helicopter improvement program (AHIP) won by Bell on September 21, 1981, the OH-58D was to be developed from the Bell Model 406 powered by a 650-SHP Allison T703-AD-700 driving a four-blade main rotor. The OH-58D would also feature a McDonnell Douglas/Northrop mast-mounted sight for close combat aerial reconnaissance and a wide range of armament for attack helicopter support missions.

1983 November 6 The Royal Australian Air Force celebrated the 25th anniversary of the inauguration of its fleet of Lockheed C-130 Hercules transport aircraft. During that period, the RAAF had flown a total of 331,000 hr. with the 12 aircraft in its inventory. The first 12 had been C-130As, followed by 12 replacement C-130Es, replaced in turn by 12 C-130Hs. Throughout that time, the RAAF Hercules had flown more than 110 million mi. without a major accident of any kind.

1983 November 16 The first Bell AH-1T + SuperCobra made its first flight powered by two General Electric T700-GE-401 turboshaft engines with a combined power output of 3,250 SHP. Adapted from a U.S. Marine Corps AH-1T, the new variant was evaluated by the military and ordered for the USMC in 1984. Designated AH-1TW, the first of 44 SuperCobras was delivered on March 27, 1986, and incorporated a new rotor based on the bearingless research design originally tested on a Bell Model 680. The U.S. Marine Corps also planned to upgrade an additional 40 AH-1Ts to the 1TW configuration.

1983 November 17 In retaliation for 58 French paratroops and 241 U.S. Marines killed by a suicide bomber in Beirut, 14 Dassault-Breguet Super Etendards from the French carrier *Clemenceau* struck Iranian troops at Baalbek in Lebanon. The Iranians had condoned the bomb attack, which had been carried out on the headquarters of the peace-keeping force. Over the next 2 wk., the United States flew reconnaissance missions across the area.

1983 December 4 Twenty-eight U.S. Navy attack aircraft from the carriers USS *Independence* and USS *John F. Kennedy* deployed in the eastern Mediterranean hit Syrian troop positions and SAM sites in Lebanon along the road from Beirut to Damascus. One A-6E and one A-7E were shot down as the attacking force came under intensive ground fire. The U.S. Navy used laser-guided bombs in this action as the battleship *New Jersey* bombarded targets inshore. On December 3, Syrian SAM sites had fired 10 missiles at two F-14As on reconnaissance.

1983 December 9 The 1,000th Boeing 737 was rolled out at the Renton, Calif. plant, one of 33 aircraft on order for Delta Air Lines. To date, the company had sold 1,114 Boeing 737s and had the biggest customer base in the world. In a footnote to history, Boeing had also delivered the 1,000th 727 to Delta Air Lines in 1972.

1983 December 31 As of this date, Boeing Chinooks operated by British Airways Helicopters on supply flights—begun in 1979—to North Sea oil rigs from locations on the mainland had made 3,971 round-trips, carrying 298,300 people with a load average of 38 people per flight. These helicopters had generated 17,246 total revenue flying hr. and served the Brent, Fulmar, Magnus and Beryl fields.

1983 The largest aviation insurance losses ever were recorded during the year with hull claims totaling $450 million. This compares with $290 million for 1982 and includes 27 total losses, of which four were wide-body jet airliners. Total passenger fatalities world-wide for 1983 had been increased to 988 by the deaths of 269 people when a Korean Airlines Boeing 747 was shot down by the Soviets. In 1983 total fatalities were 553 compared with 355 for 1982.

1984 January 12 The first of 12 preproduction McDonnell Douglas AV-8B Harrier II V/STOL attack aircraft was handed over to the U.S. Marine Corps at a special ceremony at Cherry Point, N.C. At this time, the USMC had a requirement for 336 aircraft incorporating two-seat TAV-8B trainers. Following the first flight of the YAV-8B on November 9, 1978, a series of progressive developments transformed the aircraft into a thoroughly up-to-date weapon system.

1984 January 25 A memorandum of understanding between the governments of Britain and Italy was signed in Rome formally authorizing full development of the EH Industries EH.101 multi-role helicopter. This had been the subject of study and preliminary design work since the binational EH Industries had been formed in June 1980. Overall administration of the project was to be through the U.K. Ministry of Defense. Full-scale development of a naval version of the tri-engined helicopter was approved March 7, and work was to proceed in parallel on a 30-seat civilian version.

1984 January 26 The first production Hughes AH-64A Apache was delivered by McDonnell Douglas to the U.S. Army from its Mesa, Ariz. assembly plant. With plans to equip 34 U.S. Army and National Guard battalions with this twin-engined attack helicopter, the first operational unit, the Sixth Cavalry Brigade (Air Combat), received the Apache in early 1986, and by midyear, its Seventh Squadron, Seventeenth Cavalry, was up to strength. In 1987 the Army National Guard received its first Apache, and the Thirtieth Attack Battalion in North Carolina received 18 of this type.

1984 February 4 The first Sikorsky HH-60A Night Hawk for the USAF was given its first flight, powered by two 1,560-SHP

General Electric T700-GE-700 turboshaft engines. A derivative of the S-70 design, the HH-60A was a combat-rescue version of the military H-60 series with a capability to perform unescorted missions day or night over a radius of 287 mi. at treetop height. Using night-vision goggles and satellite navigation equipment, the crew could home in on a downed crewman. The USAF was unable to get production funding for the HH-60A, and the project was abandoned.

1984 February 24 The first Boeing 737-300 made its first flight following roll-out on January 17 ahead of schedule. As a stretched, reengined derivative of the Boeing 737-200, it was found to handle almost exactly as its predecessor when taken into the air by test pilot James C. McRoberts. It was joined by a second aircraft in March, and certification was granted on November 14, the first delivery taking place on November 28. An executive version of the 737-300, known as the Corporate 77-33, was offered with lavish interior fittings, seating for about 20 and full conference facilities.

1984 February 24 The USAF selected a derivative of the McDonnell Douglas F-15 as the two-seat, dual-role fighter over the General Dynamics F-16XL. The new role would include deep interdiction and high-warload ground-attack missions, day or night and in adverse weather. Under the designation F-15E, the Eagle would acquire a weapons capability of up to 23,500 lb. on external locations. The USAF declared a requirement for 392 F-15Es, the first of which was expected to become operational in 1988.

1984 February 29 Constituting the largest single order in the history of commercial aviation, American Airlines ordered 67 McDonnell Douglas MD-82 short/medium-range airliners and placed options on a further 100, bringing the potential value of the total reserved order to around $3 billion. The initial 67 aircraft had a contract value of about $1.35 billion. American was to receive 25 aircraft per year in 1985 and 1986 and 17 in 1987. If taken up, the other option buys would be delivered through 1991. At this date, American was also negotiating for 15 Boeing 757s.

1984 March 2 Short Brothers of Belfast, Northern Ireland received a £115 million contract from the USAF for the supply of 18 Short 330 light-utility transport aircraft to be designated C-23A. The first of this version was to fly on August 6, and the USAF retained an option of an additional 48 aircraft. Purchased for the European distribution system aircraft (EDSA) program, the C-23A fleet was to be based at Zweibrücken, West Germany for use by the Tenth Military Airlift Squadron of Military Airlift Command ferrying high priority spares between air bases.

1984 March 5 The first production Panavia Tornado F.Mk.2 air defense interceptor made its first flight from Warton, England 3 wk. before a formal roll-out ceremony for this and the second production aircraft. The prototype had first flown on October 27, 1979, and the first operational RAF squadron was expected to form up in 1985 with the first of a total 165 aircraft. The F.Mk.2 carried a 27-mm Mauser cannon, two AIM-9L Sidewinder and four BAe Sky Flash AAMs. The aircraft had a maximum speed of 920 MPH at sea level and Mach 2.2 (1,450 MPH) at 40,000 ft. and a combat radius of 450 mi. with 2 hr. loiter.

1984 March 6 The Airship Industries Skyship 600 made its first flight from Cardington, Bedfordshire, England 13 yr. after its predecessor (Skyship 500) first took to the air. The Airship 600 was a stretched version of the 500 series with accommodation for up to 13 passengers, a volume of 235,400 cu. ft., a length of 193 ft. 7 in. and a maximum diameter of 49 ft. 10 in. Powered by two 225-HP turbocharged Porsche engines, the series 600 had a maximum level speed of 67 MPH and a still air range of 633 mi.

1984 March 12 The governments of Britain, France, Spain and Germany agreed to provide financial aid to launch the Airbus Industrie A320 at an estimated research and development level of $1.7 billion with investment recouped over a production run of 600 aircraft. France and Germany agreed to provide 37.9% each with the United Kingdom providing 20% and Spain 4.2%. The shares of work were 38% to France (Aérospatiale), 30% to Germany (Deutsche Airbus), 26% to the United Kingdom (BAe) and 4.5% to Spain's Construcciones Aeronauticas SA (CASA).

1984 March 13 Gates Learjet rolled out the first of 80 Model 35As for the USAF under a contract received September 19, 1983, for its operational support aircraft (OSA) program. Employed with Military Airlift Command ferrying cargo and medical patients on time-sensitive schedules, the C-21A, as it would be designated, would replace the CT-39 Sabreliner in that role. Under the original agreement, the USAF leased the 80 aircraft from Gates Learjet, but following completion of deliveries in October 1985, a contract to buy was signed September 30, 1986, at a cost of $180 million.

1984 March 20 The last of 713 Fairchild A-10 Thunderbolt IIs was delivered to the USAF. Units equipped with this close support attack aircraft included the Twenty-third and 354th Tactical Fighter Wings in Tactical Air Command, the Eighty-first Tactical Fighter Wings in Europe, the Eighteenth Tactical Fighter Squadron in Alaska and the Twenty-fifth Tactical Fighter Squadron in Korea. In addition, four air force reserve units had the A-10 as well as five air national guard units in the United States. Some work had been done to expand the aircraft's role to a night/adverse weather capability by adding a second seat, but this derivation was not adopted.

1984 March 27 The first nonstop trans-Atlantic flight by a Boeing 767 was made by an El Al (Israeli airlines) aircraft. It had flown from Montreal, Canada to Tel Aviv, Israel, a distance of 5,800 mi., in 10 hr. 52 min. The flight path was required to route the aircraft on a more northerly course because an FAA ruling required twin-engined aircraft to remain within 60 min. flying time of a suitable airport while carrying passengers. On this flight, 90 passengers were carried, although the El Al aircraft had a capacity for up to 224 people at an operational gross weight of 335,000 lb.

1984 March 27 British Airways inaugurated a Concorde service from London to Miami twice weekly. The service operated through Washington-Dulles, necessitating a 50-min. stopover, passengers being removed onto a mobile "people-mover" parked some distance away from the aircraft while it was being refueled. There were insufficient facilities at Dulles to permit passengers access to the terminal building. The overall trip lasted 6 hr. 35 min., a saving of approximately 2.5 hr. over the direct flight by subsonic airliners. The round-trip fare was quoted at £2,509.

1984 March 30 British Aerospace at Filton, Bristol, England delivered the 10th General Dynamics F-111 that had been "re-lifed" for the Twentieth Tactical Fighter Wings, USAF, based in England. Under a program that began in 1978, BAe conducted major maintenance work on all aircraft based in the United Kingdom with a gradual expansion of work until the "re-life" pro-

gram was introduced under contracts worth a total £60 million through 1987.

1984 March 31 The last operational RAF V-bomber squadron was disbanded, ending two decades of service. No. 50 Squadron had been operating Vulcans since August 1961 when it re-formed at RAF Waddington in Lincolnshire. The squadron had been disbanded in October 1959 after a period during which it had been operating English Electric Canberras. The Vulcan had been given an extended life because of the Falkland Islands campaign, but its service career finally came to an end on this date at an RAF base where the first operational Vulcan had taken up duty on July 11, 1957.

1984 April 1 Pan American World Airways expanded its helicopter links in New York by adding a service between Manhattan and the World Trade Center-Battery Park Heliport. Using Bell Model 222s, the existing services between Manhattan and Newark and JFK International airports were to be supplemented by two Westland 30-160s operated by Omniflight Helicopter Services, which operated these flights for Pan American. For non-ticketed Pan American passengers, the single fare on all services was $77, but passengers traveling first or clipper class on Pan American traveled free.

1984 April 8 The RAF Marine Branch was disbanded on this date, having been in existence since the RAF was formed on April 1, 1918. Its principal base at RAF Mount Batten, Plymouth was closed, and its 510 personnel dispersed. In recent years, it had been primarily responsible for training aircrew in sea rescue techniques, search and rescue helicopter winch-training and aircrew survival. It had bases at Alness in Scotland and at Holyhead and Tenby in Wales as well as at Gibraltar in the Mediterranean.

1984 April 12 The first Airbus Industrie A300C4-600 convertible passenger/cargo aircraft made its first flight prior to being delivered to Kuwait Airways, which had ordered three aircraft of this type. The C4-600 had Pratt & Whitney JT9D-7R4H1 engines with enlarged forward cargo-loading doors affording access to the interior main cabin, which could be equipped to carry pallets instead of passenger seats. The maximum freight capacity of 101,400 lb. could be carried over a range of 2,485 mi.

1984 May 12 The Pilatus Britten-Norman CASTOR (corps airborne stand-off radar) Defender made its first flight. With power provided by two 400-HP Allison 250-B17C turboprop engines, the aircraft was fitted with a Ferranti multi-mode acquisition radar housed in a flat, cylindrical housing protruding from the lower portion of the extreme nose. Derived from the Britten-Norman BN-2T Turbine Islander/Defender series, it was adapted to serve the needs of the British army for a surveillance radar to operate in conjunction with a close-look, remotely piloted vehicle.

1984 May 29 The defense ministries of France and Germany signed an agreement authorizing development of a new European antitank helicopter with design and manufacture to be the responsibility of Aérospatiale and MBB. On September 18, 1985, Eurocopter GmbH was formed in Munich to manage the CATH (common attack helicopter) program, which envisaged three versions. Seven development aircraft were to be built, with a first flight expected by 1990.

1984 June 1 What is believed to have been the longest nonstop flight by a twin-engined commercial airliner ended at Addis Ababa airport, Ethiopia, when the first Boeing 767ER for Ethiopian Airlines was flown to its customer base from Seattle, Wash. The total distance of 7,500 mi. was flown in 13 hr. 17 min. carrying 58 people, including the crew. This was the first Boeing 767ER to fly at the optional high gross weight of 345,000 lb.

1984 June 2   Designed and built by Burt Rutan, the Voyager round-the-world contender was rolled out at Mojave Airport, Calif. With a canard layout, the aircraft was built of light composites for extreme strength combined with light weight and had a wing-span of 110 ft. 10 in. with two engines in a tractor-pusher con-figuration set inside a twin-boom tail arrangement. The aircraft had been designed to carry two people around the world on a 25,000-mi. flight expected to be flown at an average altitude of 12,000 ft. in almost 2 wk. of nonstop, unrefueled flight.

1984 June 20   The first reengined KC-135 was transferred to Strategic Air Command after 2 yr. of test and evaluation trials. The KC-135R, newly fitted with four CFM International CFM56 engines, was delivered to the 384th Air Refuelling Wing at McConnell AFB, Kans. from the Boeing plant at Wichita, Kans. and was formally accepted by Gen. Davis from Lt. Gen. Thomas H. McMullen, the commander of the Aeronautical Systems Di-vision, on July 2. The entire fleet of Strategic Air Command KC-135 aircraft was to be reengined over the next several years.

1984 June 21   Operating from Christchurch International Air-port, New Zealand, a KC-10A Extender of the Twenty-second Air Refuelling Wing, USAF, carried out three in-flight refueling operations on a Military Airlift Command McDonnell Douglas C-141B transport aircraft making air-drop deliveries to Antarctic bases at McMurdo Sound and at the South Pole. This was a rou-tine midwinter replenishment but essential for the continuance of base operations and the survival of the occupants. Another flight was conducted June 23.

1984 June 22   Virgin Atlantic Airways began flights between London and Newark with a leased Boeing 747-200B that had been purchased by a British bank from Aerolineas Argentinas. It offered an initial one-way fare of £99 for 2 wk., increasing to £119 hereafter and £110 during the winter of 1984–85. Operating from Gatwick airport outside London, this was the latest fare-cutting service. Run by the Virgin Records Group headed by Richard Branson, the service also offered a sleeperette at £1,013, including limousine service to and from respective airports.

1984 June 22   The Rutan Voyager, built to fly around the world nonstop and rolled out on June 2, made its first flight with Burt Rutan at the controls. A second flight was made two days later, and on July 3 the unconventional aircraft was flown for 90 min. with Jeanna Yeager on board as well. With an empty structural weight of 11,236 lb., the Voyager carried 8,934 lb. of fuel and the interior fuselage, 3 ft. 3 in. wide and 2 ft. 9 in. high, and had room for one person to sleep while the other flew the aircraft.

1984 July 2   The first Dassault-Breguet Mirage 2000s of the French air force were declared operational at a special ceremony at Dijon-Longvic where 2e Escadre de Chasse operated the air-craft. The ceremony marked the inauguration of operational ser-vices with the Mirage 2000. Six single-seat Mirage 2000Cs and four two-seat Mirage 2000Bs were flown over from Mont-de-Marsan by the Escadron de Chasse ½ Cicognes. Capable of nu-clear weapons delivery, the Mirage 2000N was to become oper-ational during 1988.

1984 July 19   The first USAF General Dynamics F-16C was delivered to its customer. Incorporating numerous improvements resulting from the USAF multinational staged improvement pro-

A contemporary of the MiG-29, the Dassault-Breguet Mirage 2000 was adopted as the standard fighter for the French Air Force.

gram, the F-16C incorporated revision for either the Pratt & Whitney F10-PW-220 or the General Electric F110-GE-100 en-gine, which evolved from a USAF alternative fighter engine pro-gram. A comparably modified and refined two-seat F-16D was also introduced, carrying the same changes as the single seat F-16C.

1984 August 6   The first Short C-23A utility transport aircraft ordered by the USAF made its first flight from the Belfast, Northern Ireland plant. Powered by two 1,198-SHP Pratt & Whitney Can-ada PT6A-45R turboprop engines, the C-23A had accommoda-tion for up to nine passengers and two large freight containers or a wide range of payload combinations including two 0.5-ton army trucks. The C-23A had a maximum range of 770 mi. or 225 mi. with full payload.

1984 August 14   At precisely 10:51 A.M., Boeing rolled out from its Renton plant the last 727 it was to produce. Since Feb-ruary 9, 1962, when the first Boeing 727 took to the air, the company had produced 1,832 aircraft of this type. This last air-craft was delivered to Federal Express on September 18, as of which date there were approximately 1,800 727s still flying, in-cluding the first aircraft delivered.

1984 August 16   The ATR.42 twin turboprop regional transport made its first flight. The Franco-Italian Avions de Transport Régional (ATR) consortium had been formed November 4, 1981, to produce a competitive aircraft for this market built by Aéro-spatiale and Aeritalia. Powered by two 1,800-SHP Pratt & Whit-ney PW120 turboprops, it had a wingspan of 80 ft. 7 in. and a length of 74 ft. 4 in. with capacity for a maximum 50 passengers, a cruising speed of 307 MPH and a range of 2,785 mi.

1984 September 12   The biggest military exercise in the United States for 24 yr. ended after eight days of intensive activity when Gallant Eagle 84 came to a close. Coordinated as a U.S. Central Command conventional forces exercise, it involved 44 Strategic Air Command bombers and aviation elements from Strategic Air Command, Tactical Air Command, Military Airlift Command and army operating from a wide range of facilities across the United States. The B-52s alone flew 182 sorties supported by 309 KC-135 and KC-10 missions on refueling operations.

1984 October 3   Boeing sold its 5,000th jet airliner when it announced orders for two 747-300 combination passenger/cargo airliners for Varig, the national airline of Brazil. Boeing had received its order for a jet airliner, a Boeing 707, on October 13, 1955, and the company had averaged 172 orders per year in the ensuing 29 years. In that time, it had sold 982 Boeing 707s, 1,832 Boeing 727s, 1,224 Boeing 737s, 637 Boeing 747s, 139 Boeing 757s and 186 Boeing 767s. This record was unmatched by any other plane maker in the world.

1984 October 18   The first Rockwell B-1B bomber made its first flight. Bearing a strong similarity to the #4 B-1A, its gross weight had increased to 477,000 lb., and major changes to the configuration of the weapons bays and the avionics had also been made. The B-1B was powered by four 30,780-lb. s.t. General Electric F101-GE-102 augmented turbofans and had a wingspan of 136 ft. 8 in. (78 ft. 2 in. fully swept) and a length of 147 ft. With a maximum speed of Mach 1.25 at altitude, it had a low-level penetration speed of 600 MPH and an unrefueled range of 7,455 mi. The B-1B had a maximum bomb load of about 67,000 lb.

1984 November 13   A total of 40 Japanese interceptors were scrambled to intercept nine Soviet bombers approaching Japanese air space. These aircraft included F-15Js, F-4EJs and F-104s. A gradual increase in the number of Soviet intrusions over the past year had brought concern to Japan about that country's intentions. The Soviet Union now had more than 2,000 aircraft deployed within striking distance of Japan, and the recent shooting down of a Korean Airlines Boeing 747 served to highlight the fragile nature of peace in the northern sector of the Pacific rim.

1984 December 1   In a remote-controlled crash of a Boeing 720 derivative of the Boeing 707 to test an Avgard FM-9 fire-retarding additive prepared by ICI, the aircraft suffered severe damage from a conflagration that erupted shortly after the main fireball when the wing severed. As expected, the fireball extinguished itself within 10 sec., but the secondary fire did not extinguish and continued to grow in intensity. The FAA was considering a ruling calling for mandatory use of the fuel additive and had monitored previous tests where the experiments had proved highly encouraging.

1984 December 14   The first of two Grumman X-29A forward-swept-wing (FSW) research aircraft made its first flight piloted by Charles ("Chuck") A. Sewell from Edwards AFB, Calif. Powered by a 16,000-lb. s.t. General Electric F404-GE-400 afterburning turbofan engine and featuring a wing swept forward 33.75° with a span of 27 ft. 2 in., the X-29A had a length of 53 ft. 11 in. and a moving foreplane with a span of 13 ft. 7 in. This FSW research aircraft was to be tested at the Dryden Flight Research Center in California, where it was delivered for NASA flight research beginning April 2, 1985.

1984 December 17   The McDonnell Douglas MD-83 made its first flight powered by two 21,000-lb. s.t. JT8D-219 engines. With a maximum takeoff weight of 160,000 lb., it could carry 155 passengers. FAA certification followed in 1985, and the type entered service with Alaska Airlines and Finnair receiving their aircraft in early 1986. On November 14, 1986, the longest flight ever made by an MD-80 type took place between Montreal and Helsinki, the distance of 3,920 mi. being flown in 7 hr. 26 min.

1985 January 21   Lt. Col. David E. Faught of the Ninety-seventh Bombardment Wing, Strategic Air Command, was engaged in conducting a pilot proficiency exercise aboard a KC-135 when the nose gear failed to extend on a final approach after four touch-and-go landings. With minimum fuel on board, the KC-135 was

kept airborne first by an EC-135, which had to refuel it every 20 min., and then by a KC-10A, which arrived on the scene. When that ran low on fuel, a strip alert tanker refueled the KC-10A, which refueled the KC-135 in turn. After 13 hr. in the air and many unsuccessful efforts at deploying the nose gear, Lt. Col. Faught brought the KC-135 down to an emergency landing with minimal damage.

1985 February 13   An RAF Panavia Tornado GR.Mk.1 carried a BAe defense suppression ALARM (air-launched antiradiation missile) into the air for the first time from Warton, England. The missile was to be carried by the RAF Tornado on deep penetration counter-air and interdiction missions for knocking out SAM and AAA radars ahead of following strike aircraft. Each Tornado could carry a theoretical maximum of nine missiles, but optimum loads would put four missiles on each aircraft, leaving stores points available for the JP233 airfield attack system.

1985 February 19   The first in a series of test flights by a Boeing AGM-86B ALCM over the Beaufort Sea north of Canada began when an ALCM was dropped from a B-52 of the 319th Bombardment Wing, Strategic Air Command. The ALCM flew on across Canada for 4.5 hr. along a corridor 1,500 mi. long and 50 mi. wide from the MacKenzie River Delta along the eastern Rockies to Dawson Creek, British Columbia, east to Primrose Lake near the Canadian Forces Base at Cold Lake, Alberta. At the end of the powered flight phase, a parachute lowered the ALCM to the ground.

1985 February 21   In its first extended deployment at sea, the McDonnell Douglas F/A-18 Hornet began a shakedown tour aboard the carrier USS *Constellation* on a tour that would keep it at sea until August 24. The units involved with proving exercises were the VFA-25 "Fist of the Fleet" and VFA-113 "Stingers" squadrons. At the end of the shakedown, the crews reported that the extended deployment had proven the worth of the aircraft, both as an operational weapon system and as an integrated element of a carrier battle group.

1985 February 26   The first McDonnell Douglas F/A-18 Hornet assembled in Australia made its first flight prior to delivery to the RAAF. This and later two-seaters were to be delivered to the No. 2 Operational Conversion Unit at Williamtown until, by mid-1986, the unit attained full operating status with 14 aircraft. There were to be three operational Hornet squadrons in Australia, two at Williamtown and one at Tindal in the Northern Territory. Each squadron would have 16 aircraft.

1985 March 1   In an attempt to draw customers, Pan American World Airways started an airport-to-door baggage handling service at the New York end of its trans-Atlantic route where passengers' baggage was delivered by the airline to the address of their choice. This prevented passengers waiting for baggage handlers to offload the aircraft, releasing them from the terminal quicker and easing congestion. The fee for this service was $50 per bag up to 70 lb. and 62-in. in size. Purolator Courier was employed to carry out this service on behalf of Pan American.

1985 March 4   A General Dynamics F-16/J79 began eight days of flight tests with a TERPROM (terrain profile-matching) navigation system developed jointly between General Dynamics and British Aerospace. Flight trials were also scheduled for a Panavia Tornado from Warton, England. Utilizing a radar altimeter to establish a match with stored memory of terrain, the system could automatically guide an aircraft at a constant height above the ground over previously surveyed country or supply the pilot with navigational information for manually controlled flight.

1985 March 21 The RAF selected the Brazilian Embraer EMB-312 Tucano for use as its next basic trainer, filling the air staff Target 412 requirement released 2 yr. previously. Replacing the Jet Provost, the Tucano was to be manufactured by Short Brothers of Belfast, Northern Ireland under a special arrangement with Embraer. Several important modifications had been made to the standard Tucano to conform to British requirements. The aircraft was enjoying international success, for in addition to 118 on order for the Brazilian Air Force, Egypt wanted 120, Iraq 80 and Honduras 12.

1985 April 3 Europe's first scheduled international helicopter service was inaugurated with a flight from Dublin, Ireland to Holyhead, Wales. Using a Sikorsky S-61N, Dublin City Helicopters were to operate the service five times daily for a fare of £30 one-way or £53 round-trip. The helicopter was on a 5-yr. lease from British Airways, and British Rail offered combined tickets from U.K. stations to Dublin incorporating the helicopter link.

1985 April 8 The Kingston, England-based Offshore Conferences & Exhibitions Ltd. opened Helitech 86, the first European International Helicopter Technology and Operations Conference, at Aberdeen, Scotland. It was planned as a biennial event concentrating exclusively on rotary-winged technology. The first two-day conference was supported by an exhibition. Aberdeen was chosen as the venue for the conference because of its prominence as an operations base for helicopters used in the North Sea oil industry.

1985 April 12 The slogan that had stood at the gate of USAF Strategic Air Command Headquarters, Offutt AFB, Nebr. and read "Peace Is Our Profession" was removed from its posts after 27 yr. All directional signs reverted to standard USAF plaques. The "Peace Is Our Profession" sign was given to the Strategic Air Command Aerospace Museum located at Offutt AFB in a publicly accessible area where bombers characterizing the history of Strategic Air Command were open to the public.

1985 April 22 McDonnell Douglas delivered the 400th DC-10 and derivative when it handed over the 31st KC-10A Extender to the USAF. Since the first DC-10 Series 10 was delivered on July 29, 1971, the first two operators had become the largest users of the aircraft: American Airlines had 54 DC-10s and United Air Lines operated 50; the USAF was the third largest customer with 31.

1985 June 3 Boeing and United Technologies signed a memorandum of understanding at Le Bourget during the Paris Air Show for joint development of a light agile helicopter to fill the U.S. Army LHX requirement. There had been debate as to whether the army wanted a tilt-rotor design or a conventional rotary-winged aircraft, and the latter was selected in preference to the former.

1985 July 7 The first operational Rockwell B-1B bomber was delivered to USAF Strategic Air Command at the Ninety-sixth Bombardment Wing, Dyess AFB, Tex. The aircraft had been flown from Edwards AFB, Calif. to Offutt AFB, Nebr. on June 27 carrying Verne Orr, air force secretary. It had been planned that Gen. Bennie L. Davis, CinC of SAC, should fly the aircraft to Dyess on June 29, [which was the 30th anniversary of the delivery of the first B-52.] Engine damage prevented that, however, and Gen. Davis collected the fleet prototype from Edwards and delivered that aircraft to Dyess instead.

1985 July 8 The first Airbus Industrie A310-300 made its first flight. This was the world's first commercial airliner to carry a fuel tank in the tailplane incorporating a transfer system for aircraft trim to improve cruising drag and fuel consumption. The aircraft also incorporated a carbon-fiber fin, carbon brakes, wing-tip fences and a modified cockpit for ergonomic efficiency. With a mixed-class configuration of 218 passengers, the A310-300 had a range of 5,280 mi.

1985 July 15 Eastern Air Lines began transatlantic operations for the first time when it flew a DC-10 Series 30 recently acquired from Air Florida from Miami to London-Gatwick. Surprisingly, Eastern had not had one DC-10 among its 284-aircraft inventory until it bought three from the now defunct Air Florida. Eastern operated the Miami-London service daily except Wednesday.

1985 July 26 An Antonov An-124 lifted a payload of 171,219 kg (377,474 lb.) to a height of 10,750 m (35,269 ft.). This exceeded by 53% the maximum weight record for a Lockheed C-5 to a height of 2,000 m (6,562 ft.). Piloted by Vladimir Terski and Alexander Galunenko, the aircraft also took 20 other FAI-ratified records for weight-lifting to specified heights.

1985 July 29 The McDonnell Douglas board of directors decided to market the proposed MD-11, a stretched version of the DC-10, in separate medium-range, long-range and freighter configurations. A derivative of the DC-10 Series 30 with aerodynamic refinements, including outward inclined winglets and cambered aerofoil shapes on the tailplane, the MD-11 would be powered by three engines in the 60,000-lb. class, carry 250 to 405 passengers up to 7,900 mi. and offer extended-range capability for 224 passengers on distances up to 8,870 mi.

1985 August 6 The USAF Aeronautical Systems Division carried out the first full operational flight test of the precision location strike systems (PLSS) using three Lockheed TR-1A reconnaissance aircraft with ground support stations. These aircraft flew a racetrack pattern listening to electronic signals traffic from SAM sites, AAA batteries and radar-directed artillery positions so they could establish their respective positions through

On July 27, 1985, a Lockheed SR-71 seized six major speed and altitude records, recapturing two held by Soviet MiG-25s.

triangulation and coordinate with ground stations the strike aircraft that would have gone to destroy the enemy defense systems.

1985 August 9   Government representatives from the United Kingdom, West Germany and Italy signed an agreement in Turin, Italy for collaboration on the development of a European fighter aircraft (EFA). France and Spain had backed away from an attempt to get a five-nation agreement. The EFA was to be an air-to-air fighter with ground attack as a secondary role. It was expected to be in the 21,500-lb. weight class and operate with a 20,250-lb. s.t. engine. The British wanted about 250, as did the Germans, and the Italians specified 150. Work share was to be 38% each for Britain and Germany with Italy contributing 24%.

1985 August 27   Originally founded by the multimillionaire Howard Hughes, famous for the *Spruce Goose* flying boat, Hughes Helicopters Inc. became the McDonnell Douglas Helicopter Co., a subsidiary of McDonnell Douglas Corp. McDonnell Douglas had taken over Hughes on January 6, 1984, incorporating its plants in California and Arizona. Hughes employed more than 7,000 people and had produced just over 6,400 helicopters, of which more than 4,000 were still flying with civil and military operators in almost 100 countries.

1985 September 10   The first of 50 Lockheed C-5B heavy lift transport aircraft made its first flight from Georgia. It had been rolled out on July 12. The C-5B was dimensionally identical to the C-5A and was powered by four 43,000-lb. s.t. General Electric TF39-GE-1C turbofan engines with a gross takeoff weight of 837,000 lb. and a maximum payload capability of 291,000 lb. These aircraft had been ordered in 1982 after Lockheed submitted a plan for the C-5N (''New'') that incorporated all the modifications and refinements added during the life of the C-5A since it first entered service in 1969.

1985 September 17   A specially adapted but otherwise standard F-15 Eagle launched an ASAT (antisatellite) missile and destroyed a target in space for the first time. Carried beneath the trial aircraft, the missile comprised the first stage of a short-range attack missile (SRAM), an LTV Altair rocket-motor as the second stage and a homing device in the nose. The ASAT missile had a length of 17 ft., a diameter of 1 ft. 6 in. and a weight of 2,700 lb. It was launched at a height of 38,000 ft. with the F-15 climbing at 60°–65° just below Mach 1. The ASAT hit and destroyed the Defense Department P78-1, which had been launched into orbit during 1971.

1985 September 17   The first flight tests of the USAF's common strategic rotary launcher (CSRL) took place when a B-52 carried the weapon carrier into the air for the first time. Installed in a bomb bay, the CSRL was designed to provide suspension for nuclear weapons, conventional bombs and cruise missiles. It had been designed and developed by Boeing, and live tests were to be conducted with cruise missiles dropped at test ranges.

1985 September 26   The Saudi Arabian minister for defense and aviation, Prince Sultan ibn Abdul-Aziz, signed a purchase order for 48 Panavia Tornado IDS interdictor aircraft, 24 Tornado ADV long-range interceptors, 30 BAE Hawk advanced trainers and 30 Pilatus PC-9 basic trainers in a deal worth between £3 billion and £4 billion. Orders for the Tornado would be filled from RAF attrition-replacement production aircraft, and the F.Mk.2 aircraft for the RAF would be similarly delayed as the export orders were filled.

1985 October 8   The USAF issued a request for proposals on its advanced tactical fighter (ATF), which was to replace the F-15 Eagle. An earlier request for design studies generated initial outline concepts from major manufacturers. Boeing, General Dynamics, Grumman, Lockheed, McDonnell Douglas, Northrop and Rockwell were sent copies of the request for response by December 9, to be followed with cost data by December 23. This would then be followed by a 3-yr. demonstration and validation phase leading to a single selection.

1985 October 15   The Fairchild-Republic T-46A trainer ordered by the USAF made its first flight powered by two 1,330-lb. s.t. Garrett F109-GA-100 engines mounted in the fuselage. With a wingspan of 38 ft. 8 in. and a length of 29 ft. 6 in., the T-46A had twin vertical fins and a maximum takeoff weight of 6,817 lb. The USAF became concerned about the Fairchild Republic company when it attempted to sell off the Republic Division that would be responsible for the aircraft, and in March 1986 the contract was terminated after only one had been built.

1985 October 18   The first flight of the AFTI F-111 MAW (mission adaptive wing) aircraft took place from Edwards AFB, Calif. The unique MAW was designed to allow the camber to be altered at will; dispensing with slots, slats, flaps and other lift or dump devices, the smooth composite wing demonstrated the smoothness and lift advantages of a wing of this type. Integrated with the advanced fighter technology integration program, the MAW contract had been awarded by the USAF in 1979.

1985 October 22   Northwest Airlines contracted Boeing for 10 of its newly proposed 747-400s, which, with the same fuselage as the Series 300, would feature 6-ft. wing extensions plus 6-ft.-high winglets, advanced aluminum alloys in the assemblies, lightweight interior components, a digital two-man flight deck, increased fuel capacity and 56,000-lb. s.t. General Electric CF6-80C2 or Pratt & Whitney PW4000 engines. Gross weight would increase to 850,000 lb., and the aircraft would carry 412 passengers a maximum distance of 9,196 mi. Rollout was planned for first quarter 1988.

1985 November 20   The first Panavia Tornado F.Mk.3 made its first flight as the definitive RAF air defense variant of this multirole combat aircraft. It was essentially identical to the F.Mk.2 but with 14-in. engine exhaust nozzle extensions, a Lucas engine control unit, a retractable in-flight refueling probe and several electronic improvements and cockpit updates. It also had provision for four, instead of two, AIM-9L Sidewinder AAMs. The F.Mk.2s were expected to be returned to BAe for upgrade to the F.Mk.3 configuration.

1985 December 13   The Grumman X-29A forward-swept wing research aircraft made its first transonic flight when NASA test pilot Stephen Ishmael reached a speed of Mach 1.05 at 40,000 ft. in the first of two X-29As at the Dryden Flight Research Center, Calif. The ultimate objective was to achieve a speed of Mach 1.72 at 50,000 ft., during which critical flight maneuvers would be conducted for experimental analysis of the aerodynamic characteristics of this unique aircraft.

1985 December 14   The Dassault-Breguet Rafale was rolled out from its factory at St. Cloud, France. Developed originally in the ACX (advanced combat experimental) program as a technology test-bed for a Jaguar replacement, the Rafale was required to attack and destroy a wide range of targets up to 400 mi. from its base with a warload of around 7,700 lb. The Rafale was required to have a high degree of maneuverability and high angle-of-attack

The French Dassault Rafale displays features characteristic of 1990s fighters: delta wing, high maneuverability, fly-by-wire controls and integrated weapon systems.

during combat. The manufacturers wanted the aircraft to make its public debut at the Society of British Aircraft Companies Show, Farnborough, England in September 1986.

1985 December 17 The 50th anniversary of the first flight of the Douglas DC-3 was marked in grand style at several locations around the world where the aircraft still remained in service. None was more lavish than a display that took place at Swatkop, South Africa. A formation of 27 DC-3s swept through the skies in a variety of markings from operators around the world, only three carrying South African markings. At the time of its first flight, the aircraft was known simply as the Douglas Sleeper Transport.

1985 December 31 The USAF awarded McDonnell Douglas a $3.387 billion contract to design and develop the C-17A long-range, heavy-lift cargo transport. The program reversed an earlier decision by the Pentagon announced January 26, 1982, canceling the original C-17, winner of the CX cargo-lifter competition. The USAF expected to buy 210 C-17As at a unit cost of $178 million. This aircraft was to incorporate several technical features providing a capability to lift C-5A-size payloads into rough-field areas reachable only by the C-130.

1986 January 9 Two Lockheed F-104S Starfighters of the Italian Air Force intercepted two Soviet Ilyushin Il-38 maritime patrol aircraft being operated by the Soviets for the Libyan Air

Force and bearing the markings of that country. The Il-38s had threatened to penetrate Italian air space south of Sicily and were escorted away 80 mi. from the southern boundary. The Soviet navy used aircraft of this type to patrol international waters.

1986 January 17 The USAF began operational test and evaluation of the first LANTIRN (low-altitude navigation and targeting infra-red system for night) targeting at McChord AFB, Washington. Developed by Martin Marietta, the two-pod LANTIRN system had separate navigation and targeting elements incorporating subsystems for night operations. The USAF planned to acquire 700, the first in 1987. Development testing had been completed December 20.

1986 January 21 An international organization set up in December 1982 to develop a replacement for the Lockheed C-130 and the Transall C-160 transport aircraft by the end of the century, FIMA (future international civil/military airlifter) representatives met at BAe in Manchester, England and agreed to continue the work indefinitely. FIMA comprised working parties from British Aerospace, Lockheed, Aérospatiale and MBB. It envisaged a high-wing, four-engined aircraft with rough-field capability, a cargo bay 13 ft. 1.5 in. wide and rear loading ramp. The potential sales market of 700–1,000 aircraft would be satisfied by one production line in the United States and one in Europe.

1986 January 23 Delta Air Lines placed an order for 30 of the newly proposed McDonnell Douglas MD-88 medium-range airliners with an option on a further 50 in a launch deal worth around $2 billion. These options were later turned into confirmed orders, making this one of the biggest commercial aircraft buys of all time. The MD-88 would be similar to the MD-82 and use the same derated Pratt & Whitney JT8D-219 engines and accommodate up to 142 passengers in an airframe that used a higher proportion of composites in its construction.

1986 January 23 A joint memorandum of understanding was signed by the U.S. Department of Defense, NASA and the U.K. Ministry of Defense for a 5-yr. study of four competing (Short Take Off Vertical Landing) (STOVL) propulsion systems that would be of value to a future military aircraft. The four concepts included ejector lift, vertical thrust, remote augmented lift and tandem lift. The agreement did not anticipate development of a flying prototype but did form the basis upon which a future agreement could be reached jointly or independently for a successor to the BAe/McDonnell Douglas Harrier.

1986 January 27 Airbus Industrie management decided to proceed with conceptual studies of two new airliners: a twin-engined A330 and a four-engined A340 using a common fuselage and tail assembly and incorporating all-glass cockpits and full fly-by-wire and advanced electronic control systems. Powered by two or four engines in the 60,000+-lb. s.t. category, the A330/340 would extend the Airbus range up into the international class. The A340 was the first major launch into the high density, very-long-range market.

1986 January 30 The first Boeing 767 Series 300 took to the air for the first time, powered by two 48,000-lb. s.t. Pratt & Whitney JT9D-7R4D turbofan engines. Extended by 21 ft. 1 in., the fuselage could accommodate up to 290 passengers and large cargo pallets in the lower hold. Certificated on September 22, the first revenue-earning service of this series began after JAL received its first aircraft on September 25. An optional powerplant was the 50,000-lb. s.t. General Electric CF6-80A2. British Airways placed an order for 11 with options on a further 15 Series 300 types in August 1987.

1986 February 4   In his State of the Union address, Pres. Reagan announced the start of a government/industry program to build an experimental hydrogen-fueled, air-breathing aircraft capable of hypersonic speed within the atmosphere or of being propelled into space by integral propulsion. Dubbed "Orient Express" by the president, it was to be designated X-30 and known formally as the National Aerospace Plane (NASP). It would focus U.S. research and development efforts on an experimental aircraft similar to the X-15 program of the 1950s, stimulating civil and military applications that would be applied to development of a working design.

1986 February 12   At a meeting of shareholders, helicopter-builder Westland PLC received a vote of 67.8% in favor of a rescue plan for the company to prevent its going into liquidation. The proposed plan involved a 21% stake secured between United Technologies in the United States and Fiat in Italy. An alternative plan involved a package from a European consortium comprising BAe, GEC, Aérospatiale, Agusta and MBB, and although this was preferred in some political circles, it was not favored by management or the shareholders. Sikorsky agreed to place five million man-hours of work with Westland over 5 yr.

1986 February 15   The first full-scale Beech Starship 1 made its first flight from Wichita, Kans. Based on design and flight-test results from an 85% model flying since August 29, 1983, and using Burt Rutan's revolutionary application of composites, the Starship 1 had a wingspan of 54 ft. 5 in., a length of 46 ft. 1 in., foreplanes spanning 24 ft. 10 in., a height of 12 ft. 11 in. and a maximum takeoff weight of 14,000 lb. Carrying a crew of two, it was powered by two 1,200-SHP Pratt & Whitney Canada PT6A-67 turboprop engines that provided a maximum speed of 405 MPH and a range with four passengers of 2,506 mi.

1986 February 17   The Saudi Arabian defense minister Prince Sultan ibn Abdul Aziz signed the final order for 134 aircraft from British Aerospace. The deal had been negotiated during the previous year and was finally confirmed with minor changes. In one of the biggest deals ever secured by a British aircraft manufacturer, the Saudis were to receive 72 Panavia Tornadoes, 24 of which were the air-defense version, two Jetstream 31s, 30 Hawk

In the electronic air wars of the 1980s, the Boeing AWACS emerged as a vital component of high-technology air forces.

trainers and 30 Pilatus PC-9s, which were to be fitted out by BAe in England. The Saudis were to return all 18 Lightnings supplied between 1968 and 1972, bringing to 40 the total number of Lightnings returned from that country.

1986 February   The U.K. Ministry of Defense informed GEC Avionics that it had 6 mon. to solve problems with the complex airborne early-warning radar for the Nimrod AEW.Mk.3 and complete development. Long delayed because of technical problems, it had already cost the government £646 million in current dollars, or £882 million at 1986 prices. The MoD was looking at alternative early-warning aircraft, such as the Boeing E-3, Lockheed Orion, the Hercules AEW and the Grumman E-2 Hawkeye. On a 50-50 share basis, the government and GEC were to spend an additional £50 million over the next 6 mon.

1986 March 24   The USAF issued a request for proposals on a new air defense fighter to replace F-4s in 11 air national guard squadrons and required industry to respond by May 9. Possible candidates were the General Dynamics F-16, the Northrop F-20 Tigershark II and the McDonnell Douglas F-4. It was anticipated that the replacement aircraft could be in production by 1987 for operational capability in 1989.

1986 March 24   The first of six former British Airways Lockheed L-1011 TriStar airliners reworked into cargo/tanker aircraft for the RAF was delivered to its customer by Marshalls of Cambridge. The first four aircraft were adapted by Marshalls for the tanker role, and the next two would be fitted as KC.Mk.1 tanker/cargo aircraft. The RAF would also purchase three former Pan American TriStars for conversion by Marshalls to tanker/passenger configurations and designated K.Mk.2 by the RAF.

1986 April 1   The Prince and Princess of Wales opened Terminal 4 at London-Heathrow, simultaneously opening a new metro rail service between London and the outlying airport. Terminal 4 would accommodate anticipated traffic growth from 30 million to 38 million passengers per year, and it was the first terminal to break out of the central area, which had formed the airport's nucleus when it opened. The first air flight began operating through Terminal 4 on April 12. At the same time, plans were confirmed for a major expansion and modernization of Terminals 2 and 3.

1986 April 7   The U.S. Department of Defense and NASA issued contracts for work on the NASP X-30 hypersonic aircraft program. General Electric and United Technologies received about $175 million each for design and development of a large, scramjet, air-breathing engine. Boeing, General Dynamics, Lockheed, McDonnell Douglas and Rockwell each received $32 million for preliminary design of an airframe with fabrication of critical components of the X-30 for tests. It was planned that a final selection of contractors would be made in October 1989 prior to detailed design and assembly and a first flight around 1993.

1986 April 14   Nearly 100 USAF and U.S. Navy aircraft were involved in a coordinated air strike on targets in Libya mounted from air bases in the United Kingdom and from the carriers USS *America* and USS *Coral Sea*. First away were 18 F-111Fs from the Forty-eighth Tactical Fighter Wing at Lakenheath, England and five EF-111As from the 42nd Electronic Combat Squadron (ECS) at Upper Heyford, England, for a 2,900-mi. flight lasting 5 hr. They were refueled by 28 KC-10As and KC-135s, four times outbound and twice inbound. Navy E-2Cs provided command and control and 14 A-6Es, six F/A-18s and six A-7Es hit the Al Jumahiriya barracks and Benina military airfield in Libya. EA-6Bs served as electronic jammers, and F-14As flew cover.

1986 April 16   The British Aerospace experimental aircraft program (EAP) demonstrator finished in pale blue with dark-blue trim, was rolled out with grand ceremony at Warton, England. About half the £160 million originally estimated as development money had been provided by the United Kingdom government, just over 30% by BAe, 12–13% by Italian industry and approximately 7–8% by MBB in Germany. About 50% of £60 million in cost overruns were to be met by the U.K. government because the European fighter aircraft program was considered important for the British aviation industry.

1986 April 23   The first regularly scheduled airship passenger flights began in England after a lapse of almost 49 yr. since the *Graf Zeppelin* LZ 127 landed at Friedrichshafen, Germany for the last time on May 8, 1937. Beginning a regular service of four flights daily from Panshanger Airfield on the outskirts of Welwyn Garden City north of London, Airship Industries' Skyship 500 offered pleasure flights for £100 taking in the sights of London. The service ended in late May.

1986 April 26   The Piasecki Helistat made its first flight at the Lakehurst NAS, N.J. It comprised a redundant U.S. Navy airship and four surplus Sikorsky SH-34J helicopters, with rear fuselages and tail rotors removed, attached to a truss structure with control directed from one of the helicopter cockpits. Capable of lifting 25,000 lb., it was grounded two days later after damage to a front landing gear, but trials resumed a few weeks later. On July 1, it was destroyed when the helicopters broke away, causing the death of an occupant.

1986 April 27   Aeroflot and Pan American World Airways resumed scheduled operations between the United States and the Soviet Union for the first time since Aeroflot suspended this service in 1980; Pan American had stopped in 1978. Using Ilyushin Il-62M aircraft, Aeroflot was to operate weekly round-trip services between Moscow and New York and Moscow and Washington, and Pan American was to operate a weekly Boeing 727 service between Frankfurt and Moscow and a similar weekly service from Frankfurt to Moscow and Leningrad. Connections would be made with the Boeing 747 service from the United States.

1986 May 10   A B-52H carried a full complement of 20 Boeing AGM-86B ALCMs for the first time. It was assigned to the Air Force Test Center at Edwards AFB, Calif. but had been at Carswell AFB, Tex. for modifications enabling it to carry 12 missiles on two underwing pylons and eight internally on a rotary launcher designed by Boeing. The flight was made from Carswell to Edwards, during which the ALCMs were targeted electronically. Simulated launches were made before the aircraft landed.

1986 May 19   The privately developed British Aerospace Hawk 200 single-seat, multi-purpose, lightweight fighter made its first flight at Dunsfold, England, with test pilot Mike Snelling at the controls. With a wingspan of 32 ft. 7 in. over tip-mounted Sidewinder AAMs and a length of 37 ft. 4 in., the Hawk 200 had a 5,845-lb. s.t. Rolls Royce Turbom/eca Adour 871 turbofan engine, a maximum warload of 7,700 lb. on six external pylons and one or two internally mounted 25-mm Aden cannons. With a range of 554 mi., it had a top speed of 644 MPH.

1986 May 20   Construction of a new airport designed to handle quiet STOL aircraft just miles from the center of London began on the Royal Docks on the Thames River. There was to be one 2,500-ft. runway with 7.5° glidepath approaches and capacity to handle 1.2 million passengers per year. British Midland, British

Air Ferries and Bryman Airways all expressed interest in using the airport with de Havilland Canada Dash 7 aircraft.

1986 June 5   The USAF selected the Boeing 747 contender for the project to build the next presidential executive aircraft, designated Air Force One. Under a plan to purchase two 747-200B aircraft and fit four General Electric CF6-80C2-B1 engines, the first aircraft would be delivered to the Eighty-ninth Wing of Military Airlift Command, Andrews AFB, Md. in November 1988 followed by the second 6 mon. later. The president's aircraft was to be certificated for a total complement of 101, including 23 crew.

1986 June 6   Following a memorandum of understanding between Germany and China signed October 3, 1985, a joint bureau was established to coordinate work on a regional airliner powered by two unducted fan engines of 10,000–12,000-lb. s.t. The agreement would enable MBB and the Shanghai Aviation Industrial Corp. to carry out market research and set detailed plans for the development of an aircraft to meet customer needs. In May 1988, a memorandum between MBB and U.S. engine-maker Allison was signed for development of a propfan to power the airliner, which was expected to fly in 1994.

1986 June   Eurofighter/Jagdflugzeug G.m.b.H. was formed to develop the European fighter aircraft (EFA), soon named Eurofighter after the organization formed to manage it. The development of Eurofighter was to be administered by the NATO European Fighter Management Agency (NEFMA) located at the same place as the agency that did a similar job for the Panavia Tornado. Managed by British Aerospace (U.K.), MBB (Germany), Aeritalia (Italy) and CASA (Spain), it would service development and production for a total 800 aircraft.

1986 July 1   The MiG-29 Fulcrum single-seat fighter appeared outside the Soviet and Warsaw Pact territories when six aircraft arrived in Finland. They were visiting the country at the start of a courtesy visit and would return to the USSR July 4 after performing displays at Rissala Air Base. The MiG-29s were based at Kubinka in Russia.

1986 July 4   The prototype Dassault-Breguet Rafale made its first flight at Istres, France, becoming the first of the new generation fighter aircraft using canard surfaces. Powered by two 16,000-lb. s.t. General Electric F404-GE-400 augmented turbofans, the Rafale had a delta-wing span of 36 ft. 9 in. and a length of 51 ft. 10 in. with a maximum takeoff weight of 42,000 lb. On its first flight, the aircraft reached Mach 1.3, 36,000 ft. and pulled 5 g. Maximum design speed was Mach 2. Armament included a 30-mm DEFA 554 gun and provision for 13,000 lb. of ordnance on 12 stores points.

1986 July 7   The U.K. Ministry of Defense closed the submission period for alternative AEW aircraft that it could buy instead of the Nimrod AEW.Mk.3, which had run into technical difficulties. This deadline had been extended and included bids from the traditional suppliers of AEW aircraft as well as one from Airship Industries proposing a specially adapted variant of their Skyship series. Also entering submissions were Pilatus Britten-Norman and a Philips subsidiary MEL.

1986 July 28   Seven competing design teams for the advanced tactical fighter competition had to have their concepts in with the USAF. Two prototypes were to be built, designated YF-22A and YF-23A, from which a winning contender would be selected. Lockheed, General Dynamics and Boeing teamed together to pre-

A Grumman A-6E standing ready as its crew performs a preflight inspection in preparation for an air strike on Libya.

sent a common proposal and McDonnell Douglas and Northrop teamed for an alternative design approach. Rockwell and Grumman submitted individual concepts. Engine contenders were the Pratt & Whitney PW5000, to be designated YF-119 and the General Electric G37, to be designated YF120.

1986 August 6 The British Aerospace advanced turboprop (ATP) regional commercial transport made its first flight, powered by two 2,150-SHP Pratt & Whitney Canada PE124 turboprop engines. Developed as an advanced upgrade on the BAe 748, it had a longer fuselage (length 85 ft. 4 in.) with a redefined nose, improved engines and a swept vertical tail surface. With a wingspan of 10 ft. 6 in., the ATP had a maximum takeoff weight of 49,500 lb. and accommodation for 64 or 72 passengers across a maximum range of 980 mi. British Midland became the first customer, deliveries beginning in late 1987.

1986 August 8 The British Aerospace EAP demonstrator (serial no. ZF534) made its first flight from Warton, England. With a wingspan of 38 ft. 7 in. and a length of 48 ft. 3 in., it was powered by two 9,000/17,000-lb. s.t. Turbo-Union RB199-34R Mk 104D turbofan engines. It had a maximum speed in excess of Mach 2 and extreme maneuverability. It appeared at the Society of British Aircraft Companies Show, Farnborough, where it competed for attention with the French Dassault-Bregnet Rafale, and by November 30 had made 52 flights. After a planned lay-up, it resumed flying in March 1987 and logged its 100th flight on June 14, 1987.

1986 August 11 The Westland Lynx demonstrator (G-LYNX) equipped with special rotor blades and a modified engine raised the world speed record for helicopters from 368.4 km/hr. (228.9 MPH) to 400.1 km/hr. (249.1 MPH). The previous record had been unchallenged since it was claimed by the Soviets with a Mil Mi-24 (A-10) on September 28, 1978. The Lynx carried a special tail unit from the Westland 30, and technology from the British Experimental Rotor Program was applied to the engineering of the rotor. The engine had a water-methanol injection system added.

1986 August 20 The first propfan engine to fly was taken into the air mounted to the starboard side of a Boeing 727-100. The engine was a General Electric GE-36, developed over 4 yr. with help from NASA. The proof-of-concept engine adopted the core of an F404 engine with two rows of scimitar-like external pro-

pulsor blades with a diameter of 11 ft. 8 in. This unducted fan (UDF) generated additional thrust and fuel efficiencies through a pusher fan concept developed in the early 1980s.

1986 August The original Fokker Spin, the first aircraft built by Anthony Fokker in 1911, was returned to the Netherlands from Germany. For more than 40 yr., it had been in the warehouse of the Polish National Aviation Museum at Krakow, after the Germans had confiscated it during World War II. It lacked propeller, wheels and tail unit, but it had a good Renault engine and all the essential elements. Fokker refurbished it and put it on display at the corporate office in Amsterdam.

1986 September 29 The prototype Grumman F-14A Plus Super Tomcat made its first flight powered by two 16,610/27,080-lb. s.t. General Electric F110-GE-400 turbofan engines that characterized the variant. This engine formed the basis for a series of modifications that would appear on an F-14D that Grumman was eager to sell to the U.S. Navy. With revised avionics and upgrades throughout the aircraft, the F-14D was potentially capable of maintaining fleet defense capabilities through the end of the century and beyond.

1986 October 3 A milestone for Canadian aircraft manufacturing was reached when the 7,000th aircraft produced by de Havilland Canada was handed to its customer. A Dash 8 was delivered to Horizon Air, a small operator in the Seattle, Wash. area. Production had begun in 1938 when the nascent company license-built a D.H.82A Tiger Moth aircraft. Of the total manufactured since then, 3,209 had been designed by other manufacturers. The best-selling DHC aircraft was the Beaver, with 1,632 built, followed by the Otter with 466 sold worldwide.

1986 October 7 The USAF took delivery of the 1,715th and last Boeing AGM-86B air launched cruise missile (ALCM) from the Kent, Wash. production facility purpose-built for the ALCM. The last missile was delivered to the Second Bombardment Wing at Barksdale AFB, La., from where the Strategic Air Command B-52s operated. The Boeing ALCM would be carried by the B-1B as well. An upgraded version of the ALCM was in development as well as advanced versions with considerable stealth capabilities.

1986 October 31 The USAF announced it had selected submissions from teams led by Lockheed and Northrop to build competing prototypes for the advanced tactical fighter fly-off. The Northrop/McDonnell Douglas concept would be designated YF-22A and the Lockheed/General Dynamics/Boeing design would be designated YF-23A. The USAF expected to buy around 750 of the F-15 Eagle replacements and to have the aircraft enter operational service sometime in 1995. This date would later slip by several years.

1986 December 11 The first McDonnell Douglas F-15E Eagle two-seat ground attack and air superiority fighter made its first flight. Powered by two 23,830-lb. s.t. Pratt & Whitney F100-PW-220 or two 28,000-lb. s.t. General Electric F110 turbofan engines, the F-15E had a maximum dash speed of Mach 2.35 (1,676 MPH) at altitude or a sustained maximum speed of Mach 2.3, with a ferry range of 3,570 mi. and a maximum warload of 23,500 lb. in addition to one 20-mm M61A1 six-barrel rotary cannon. The aircraft would be operated on long-range deep interdiction missions in bad weather day or night.

1986 December 18 The British defense minister, George Younger, announced cancellation of the BAe Nimrod AEW.Mk.3

program after an expenditure of £930 million. Technical difficulties and escalating cost overruns were the prime reasons given for the halt order. The British government had decided, he said, to buy six Boeing E-3 Sentry AWACS aircraft for the airborne early-warning role at a total cost of £860 million with an option on a further two aircraft. The first aircraft to be powered by CFM56 engines was to be delivered in 1991.

1986 December 23 Richard G. Rutan and Jeanna Yeager completed the first nonstop unrefueled flight around the world made by a heavier-than-air flying machine. In a flight that began December 14 from Edwards AFB, California, the Rutan *Voyager* completed 40,212.139 km (24,986.664 mi.) in 9 days 3 min. 44 sec. at an average speed of 115.8 MPH. During the 14,000 ft. takeoff roll, winglets were damaged and soon broke off. Severe weather several times threatened to end the flight prematurely. Flying west, *Voyager* traveled across the Pacific, the north coast of Australia, the Indian Ocean, the southern tip of Africa, the Atlantic, up the coast of South America and Mexico.

1986 December 30 McDonnell Douglas formally launched a redesigned and improved DC-10 as the MD-11 large-capacity, long-range commercial transport aircraft. Capable of carrying 323 to 405 passengers a distance of up to 5,760 mi., the MD-11 took the DC-10-30 fuselage, extended it by 18 ft. 7 in. and adopted upward and downward outward-inclined winglets and three engines in the 60,000-lb. thrust range. Launch customers had been British Caledonian Airways with an order for nine placed on December 3, Mitsui Co. of Japan for five on December 8 and SAS for 12 aircraft on December 17.

1986 December 31 In Israel, the IAI Lavi single-seat, close support and interdiction fighter made its first flight, powered by a 20,620-lb. s.t. Pratt & Whitney PW1120 turbojet engine. It had a delta-wing span of 28 ft. 10 in., a length of 47 ft. 10 in. and a maximum takeoff weight of 42,500 lb. Equipped with an internally mounted 30-mm cannon, the Lavi had an external stores load of 20,000 lb., a maximum speed of Mach 1.8 (1,188 MPH) and a combat radius of up to 1,324 mi.

1987 January 12 A British Aerospace Harrier GR.Mk.3 made a flight at Boscombe Down Aircraft and Armament Experimental Establishment, England and set new FAI records for Class H, VTOL, aircraft. The Harrier (serial no. XV281) had been stripped prior to delivery at the Rolls Royce Filton plant when, piloted by Sqdn. Ldr. Bernard Scott, it made a record flight to a sustained altitude of 15,500 m (50,850 ft.) and claimed a climb time of 39.48 sec. to 3,000 m (9,843 ft.) and 60.65 sec. to 6,000 m (19,685 ft.).

1987 January 15 Subject to the aircraft being put into full-scale development by Airbus Industrie, Lufthansa decided to order 15 A340 long-range commercial airliners. Within the past month, Airbus had signed an agreement with Internal Aero Engines for the 30,000-lb. s.t. V2500 SuperFan engine, which offered 15% fuel savings, to power the new generation of airliners. The A340-200 would seat 262 people for flights of up to 8,886 mi., and the A340-300 would seat 294 in a longer fuselage on distances up to 8,200 mi.

1987 January 16 The last of 2,610 Northrop F-5s was delivered to the USAF when the final two aircraft off the production line took part in a fly-by at Wright-Patterson AFB, Ohio. In production for 24 yr., the F-5 had been sold to many countries through the U.S. government foreign military sales program. The F-5 had

been built in Canada, Taiwan, South Korea, the Netherlands, Spain and Switzerland, as well as in the United States.

1987 January 23 Glenn Tremmi claimed a world distance record for man-powered aircraft when he flew *Eagle* 60 km (37.3 mi.) in 2 hr. 13 min. The flight exceeded the 22.3 mi. previously set by Bryan Allen in the *Gossamer Albatross,* which in 1977 became the first man-powered aircraft to cross the English Channel. Designed and built by a joint Massachusetts Institute of Technology/NASA team, the aircraft was being prepared for a flight from the Mediterranean island of Crete to mainland Greece in a re-creation of the mythical flight of Daedalus.

1987 February 1 People Express and Texas Air were merged with Continental Airlines, which made Continental the third-biggest airline in the United States. Employing 24,000 people, it was now responsible for 109 domestic and 39 international destinations through 1,500 daily flights. Continental had a fleet of 312 aircraft, including DC-10s, DC-9s, MD-80s, Boeing 747s, Boeing 727s, Boeing 737s and Airbus Industrie A300s.

1987 February 6 The full privatization of British Airways was completed as 7.8 billion shares were applied for a total of 341.4 million offered, a massive over-subscription accommodated by scaling down the number of shares allowed per application. British public applicants received 35.4%, British institutions 36.4%, overseas private markets 0.7%, British Airways employees 8.6%, overseas business markets 16.5% and others 2.7% (totals equal 100.3% due to rounding). About 18–20% of the airline would now be owned by non-British interests.

1987 February 13 The first production Fokker 50 made its first flight from Schipol Airport, the Netherlands. A developed version of the F.27 Friendship, it was powered by two 2,250-SHP Pratt & Whitney Canada PW125B turboprop engines and first flew on December 28, 1985. The Fokker 50 had a wingspan of 95 ft. 2 in. and a length of 82 ft. 10 in. with accommodation for up to 54 passengers and a range of 1,300 mi. at a cruise speed of 282 MPH.

1987 February 19 The first of a planned 15 Boeing E-6A Tacamo survivable, airborne communications aircraft made its first flight. Ordered by the U.S. Defense Department on April 29, 1983, the E-6A was intended to replace the EC-130Q, which had been primarily responsible for communicating with the U.S. Navy Trident submarine fleet. The E-6A would link National Command Authority elements with any submarine anywhere in the world via VHF/UHF links.

1987 February 22 The first commercial aircraft to feature a fly-by-wire control system as standard made its first flight when the 150 to 179 seat Airbus Industrie A320 took to the air. Production aircraft were powered by two 23,500–25,000-lb. CFM56-5-A1 turbofan engines and adopted a single-aisle layout. The A320 had a wingspan of 111 ft. 3 in., a length of 123 ft. 3 in. and a maximum takeoff weight of 145,503 lb. The aircraft had a typical cruising speed of 520 MPH and a range of 2,175 mi.

1987 March 6 A modified Grumman Gulfstream II aircraft began flight tests in the NASA Propfan Test Assessment Program when it made a 90-min. flight at Savannah, Ga. The aircraft carried a modified Allison 570 turboshaft engine on the port wing equipped with a 9-ft. diameter, eight-blade fan developed by Hamilton Standard. The wings had been strengthened, and a special balance boom had been fitted to the starboard wing. Lockheed test personnel were to carry out 150 hr. of flight evaluation in cooperation with NASA's Lewis Research Center.

1987 April 9   The British government announced that the Ministry of Defense was to buy a version of the EH Industries EH 101 utility helicopter to meet the future needs of its armed services for a medium-lift aircraft. There had been an option to buy additional Boeing Vertol Chinooks, but that would not now take place; nor would the United Kingdom participate in the NH-90 program for a joint-European transport helicopter. The government also announced that 50 EH 101s would be purchased to serve the Royal Navy in an antisubmarine role.

1987 April 14   A USAF Rockwell B-1B carried out the longest flight to date with an aircraft of this type. Flying out from Dyess AFB, Tex., the B-1B remained in the air for 21 hr. 40 min. and maintained a high weight throughout five KC-135 refueling exercises. The B-1B flew to within 184 mi. of the Soviet border and covered a total distance of 9,410 mi. The six-man crew was commanded by Lt. Col. Larry M. Jordan and included a total of three pilots, two offensive systems operators and a defensive systems operator.

1987 May 20   Boeing announced the launch of its 737-500 airliner and orders to date of 51 with an option on a further 22. Combining the airframe of a Series 200 aircraft and the engines of a Series 300, the 737-500 was 10 in. longer than the former to maintain center of gravity but shorter than the latter. It was nominally configured for 108 passengers and incorporated technology advances since the earlier generation 737 appeared.

1987 June 5   Airbus Industrie decided formally to launch the A330/340 series of long-range airliners. Orders thus far totaled 89 for the A340 and 41 for the A330 from 10 customers. France was to contribute £590 million, securing its 37.9% share, and Germany would contribute £26.5 million and Britain £450 million. As designed, the A340 would have a wingspan of 197 ft. 10 in., a length of 206 ft. 4 in. and a maximum takeoff weight of 558,900 lb. carrying up to 375 passengers.

1987 June 10   The experimental Boeing Vertol Model 360 Advanced Technology Demonstrator made its first flight powered by two Avco Lycoming AL5512 turboshaft engines delivering a combined output of 4,200 SHP and driving two four-blade rotors. Built as a private venture, the Model 360 had an almost all-composite construction and was about the same size as the CH-46 Sea Knight with a length of 51 ft. and a design takeoff weight of 30,500 lb.

1987 June 19   After having performed 110 research flights in its original configuration, the Grumman X-29 forward-swept-wing demonstrator began a new series of flight trials fitted with a highly calibrated engine for continuous in-flight measurement of performance and instrumentation improvements. Grumman was already working on modifications to the aircraft to permit very high angle-of-attack flights up to 40° and eventually hoped to achieve 70° in a program expected to begin in late 1989.

1987 June 21   A four-man crew headed by Patrick Forticq recreated the circumnavigation of the globe by Howard Hughes in 1938 when they landed back at Paris-Le Bourget after a flight lasting 88 hr. 48 min. Their aircraft was a restored Lockheed 18 Lodestar *Spirit of J&B* sponsored by the J&B Rare Whiskey company. The flight began June 17 and made stops at Svalbard, Fairbanks, Vancouver, Los Angeles, Miami, New York and Gander for a total distance of 14,587 mi. It was completed in a

The European Airbus project gave rise to a wide range of airliners that effectively challenged U.S. leadership in this field and introduced fly-by-controls on airliners for the first time.

time 2 hr. 29 min. less than that taken by Howard Hughes in his Lockheed 14.

1978 July 1   The first of 60 production McDonnell Douglas/ BAe Harrier GR.Mk.5 close support and tactical reconnaissance aircraft was delivered to the RAF at Dunsfold, England. Essentially the U.K. version of the AV-8B developed by McDonnell Douglas and ordered by the U.S. Marine Corps, the GR.Mk.5 replaced the GR.Mk.3 aircraft, which owed its genesis to the first Harrier model. The GR.Mk.5 carried two 25-mm cannons with provision for an external stores load of up to 9,200 lb. within a maximum STO takeoff weight of 29,750 lb.

1987 July 28   General Dynamics made an unsolicited proposal to the USAF that it convert part of future orders for the F-16 to a new variant called Agile Falcon. It would have a 25% greater wing area, better flight control systems and increased use of composites in the airframe. It was a proposed successor to the single-seat/two-seat F-16C/D. In addition, it would utilize the more powerful 32,000-lb. s.t. General Electric F110 turbofan engine. General Dynamics estimated the USAF would want a further 878 F-16s, bringing their total orders to 2,737, of which 500 could be the Agile Falcon.

1987 August 11   The first Israeli Air Force Phantom 2000 made its first flight. Costing $5.6 million per aircraft, it was an upgrade program for the McDonnell Douglas F-4 Phantoms in Israeli service and included structural strengthening to increase fatigue life well into the next century, a new wiring harness, dual redundant avionics buses, new hydraulic line routes, strakes above the engine intake flanks for improved handling and an ergonomically redesigned cockpit layout.

1987 August 15   The first McDonnell Douglas MD-88 made its first flight, powered by two Pratt & Whitney JT8D-219 engines and incorporating built-in windshear detection equipment and many electronic refinements over its predecessors. The company still had orders for more than 400 MD-80-series aircraft, which it had yet to deliver, insuring a long life for this DC-9 derivative.

1987 August 21   The first Boeing 767 test aircraft on loan to the U.S. Army for its airborne optical adjunct (AOA) program made its first flight. Carrying a completely reworked forward upper fuselage, the aircraft had a cupola 86 ft. in length, 9 ft. 7 in. wide and 7 ft. 8 in. high incorporating two infrared sensor modules with 47-in. × 76-in. viewing ports. Apart from two ventral fins added for stabilization, the aircraft remained relatively unchanged from its initial configuration.

1987 August 25   The first Grumman A-6F Intruder II made its first flight, powered by two 10,800-lb. s.t. General Electric F404-GE-400D turbofan engines, and a production aircraft would have a new aluminum/composite wing developed by Boeing. The A-6F also incorporated a new air-to-air radar and greatly improved maintainability. With maximum military warload of 19,000 lb. on underwing stores locations, the A-6F had a range of 1,011 mi. and a maximum speed of 644 MPH.

1987 August 27   The U.S. Department of Defense and NASA announced selection of the Rocketdyne Division of Rockwell International and Pratt & Whitney to develop the hydrogen-fueled scramjet engine for the USAF/NASA X-30 national aerospace plane (NASP). Both companies would pool certain design criteria and work on a cooperative rather than a competitive basis, each company bringing unique strengths in certain critical areas that did not overlap. The technical challenges were judged too great for a single contractor to handle.

1987 September 17   The 70th production Rockwell B-1B broke nine records and set nine new ones during a 5-hr. flight in which it carried a load of 67,300 lb. a distance greater than 5,000 km (3,107 mi.) at an average speed of 655 MPH. Several previous records broken today had been held by the Ilyushin I1-76 since 1975 and by KC-135 and B-52 aircraft from Strategic Air Command. This aircraft also appeared at the 40th USAF birthday celebration at Wright-Patterson AFB, Ohio, September 18. On September 27, a Rockwell B-1B was destroyed when it was damaged following a bird strike, the first of the type to crash.

1987 September 24   The first unrefueled nonstop crossing of the Atlantic by a Panavia Tornado was carried out by a F.Mk.3 aircraft returning to the United Kingdom from tropical trials in Arizona. The aircraft was flown a distance of 2,530 mi. from Goose Bay, Labrador to the British Aerospace airfield at Warton by deputy chief test pilot Peter Gordon-Johnson and project navigator Les Hurst. The aircraft was equipped with four external fuel tanks and armed with four Sky Flash AAMs. Most of the flight was made at a height of 25,000 ft., climbing to 29,000 ft. shortly before descent.

1987 October 7   The U.S. Department of Defense and NASA announced winning contenders for 3-yr. contracts to develop airframe concepts for the USAF/NASA X-30 hypersonic research aircraft. General Dynamics, McDonnell Douglas and Rockwell International were each expected to contribute designs enabling a single contractor to be selected in 1990. In practice, several contractors would handle the work and pool common efforts into an integrated national aerospace research effort unlike anything that had been undertaken heretofore.

1987 October 9   The first EH Industries EH 101 helicopter made its first flight in the United Kingdom. Civil versions of this Anglo-Italian helicopter were to be powered by three 2,000-SHP General Electric CT7-6 turboshaft engines driving a 61-ft. rotor: the navalized version would have three 1,729-SHP CT7-2A engines. With an overall length of 74 ft. 10 in., the EH 101 had a maximum takeoff weight of up to 31,500 lb. with a typical cruising speed of 173 MPH and a range of 402 mi.

1987 November 4   An attempt by British Airways to take over British Caledonian was allowed to proceed by the U.K. Trade and Industry Secretary Lord Young, thus eliminating a major competitor of Britain's premier airline. The U.K. government had been concerned that this might create a monopoly unfair to other, smaller U.K. airlines but the Monopolies and Mergers Commission ruled it an acceptable merger. This gave British Airways an unprecedented hold on British airline operations.

1987 November 13   The defense ministries of France and Germany set up a common antitank helicopter (CATH) program aimed at producing a production helicopter through the Eurocopter consortium signed into being on May 29, 1984. Aérospatiale and MBB would develop jointly two variants for the French and one for the Germans. The French wanted 75 gunships Hélicoptère d'Appui et de Protection (HAP) and 140 anti-tank Panzerabwehr Hubschrauber-2 (PAH-2) variants; the Germans wanted 212 antitank helicopters. The German government was to set up a controlling office in Munich for the CATH program.

1987 December 2   A modified Sikorsky S-72 rotor systems research aircraft made its first flight as the S-72X1 X-Wing-project concept demonstrator. Designed to accommodate a four-blade main rotor 57 ft. 8 in. in diameter, the X-Wing incorporated compressed air blowers along either edge of the aerofoil section, and the rotor was geared to stop turning during forward flight. When stopped, air would be forced to bleed through the rotors aft-facing surface only for roll control. The X-Wing was not attached for this flight, which lasted 40 min., but two blades would be fitted to the rotor shaft for phase two, with all four blades in phase three.

1987 December 9   The long-range version of the Airbus Industrie A300, the Series 600ER, made a first flight prior to delivery to American Airlines. With a fuel tank in the tailplane, the aircraft was powered by two 58,000-lb. s.t. Pratt & Whitney PW4158 engines or the 60,200-lb. s.t. General Electric CF6-80C2A3 and operated at a gross weight of 378,100 lb. It was expected to commence revenue-earning services during April 1988.

1987 December 23   The U.S. Department of Defense issued a contract to a combined General Dynamics/McDonnell Douglas team for detailed design and development of the A-12 advanced tactical aircraft (ATA). As a replacement for the Grumman A-6E in the mid-1990s, the A-12 was to comprise a delta-winged aircraft with extensive stealth capabilities and be powered by two engines. A competing proposal from a Grumman/Northrop/LTV team was rejected.

1987 December 29   The 62%-scale flying precursor of the advanced technology transport aircraft (ATTA) built by Scaled Composites, a subsidiary of Beech, made its first flight at Mojave, Calif., powered by two Pratt & Whitney PT6A-135 turboprop engines. The full-size aircraft would accommodate up to 14 fully equipped troops over a range of 1,150 mi. and operate from 1,000-ft. rough-field runways. The project had been developed to a Defense Advanced Research Projects Agency (DARPA) requirement and would be jointly worked through a Beech/Lockheed team.

1988 January 30   A Boeing 747SP landed back at Boeing Field, Seattle, having circumnavigated the world in a record time of 36 hr. 54 min. at an average speed of 624 MPH. The aircraft made refueling stops at Athens and Taipei and beat the previous record set by Brook Knapp in 1984. Named *Friendship One,* it carried a crew of 18 commanded by Capt. Clay Lucy and 126 passengers, 100 of whom had bought high-priced tickets, proceeds of which would be donated to charity.

1988 February 19   The first Boeing 737-400 made its first flight from Renton, Wash. With a fuselage stretch of 10 ft., optional 22,000-lb. s.t. General Electric CFM56-3B or 23,500-lb. s.t. CFM56-3C turbofan engines and maximum takeoff weight increased to 138,500 lb., the Series 400 had accommodation for up to 168 passengers, a cruising speed of 483 MPH and a maximum payload range of 2,244 mi. Piedmont Airlines was the launch customer and received its first aircraft in September.

1988 February 22   Claimed to be the first aircraft built in Iran since the Islamic revolution, the Fajr made its first flight, powered by a Textron Lycoming TIO-540-SIAD flat-six engine. The aircraft was an adapted version of the Model 300 made by Sequoia Aircraft Corp., Richmond, Va., and designed by David Thurston. It was produced in kit form and had been delivered prior to the events of 1978–79. The aircraft was believed to have been used for training military pilots.

1988 February 23   Contriving to find something to mark the 5,000th flying hour in an RAF McDonnell Douglas F-4 Phantom II, FGR.Mk.2 (serial no. XV582) set a new point-to-point record between John O'Groats and Lands End, the two most famous extremities of the United Kingdom. Flown by Wg. Comdr. John Brady, the officer commanding No. 43 Squadron, and Flt. Lt. Mike Pugh from RAF Leuchars in Scotland, the aircraft covered 594 mi. in 46 min. 44 sec. at an average speed of 770 MPH. The time would have been less had supersonic flight not been banned over land.

1988 February 26   Setting out to beat the round-the-world record set by a Boeing 747SP on January 30, a Grumman Gulfstream IV flew out of Hobby Airport, Houston. With stops at Shannon, Ireland, Dubai, Taipei and Maui, Hawaii, the *Pursuit of Perfection* returned to Hobby in 36 hr. 8 min. 34 sec. The aircraft had flown a total distance of 28,048.589 mi. at an average speed of 637 MPH. This constituted a new FAI world record and a record for aircraft in the 55,000–77,000 lb. weight class.

1988 February 29   The first of two prototype Fokker 100 medium-haul commercial transport aircraft made its first flight, powered by two 13,850-lb. s.t. Rolls Royce Tay 620 engines. Developed from the Fokker F.28 Fellowship, the Fokker 100 had a length of 116 ft. 7 in., a wingspan of 92 ft. 1 in. and capacity for carrying up to 107 passengers a distance of 1,543 mi. Alternative powerplants were available, and one version had a range of 1,836 mi. at a maximum takeoff weight of 98,000 lb.

1988 April 11   At a special ceremony at Oceana NAS, Va., the first Grumman F-14A (Plus) Tomcat shipboard multi-role fighter was officially accepted. It was the first of six aircraft of this type that would be inducted into navy squadron VF-101, an East Coast Fleet Replacement squadron; the first operational squadron was scheduled to receive the aircraft later this year. Grumman was to build 38 new F-14A (Plus) Tomcats and rework 32 existing F-14As into the new standard.

1988 April 15   The Soviet Union announced it had carried out a flight with a modified aircraft equipped to carry a test-bed for an engine capable of running on cryogenic hydrogen and liquified natural gas (LNG). The obvious environmental advantages of aircraft engines running on these fuels promised large sales potential for successful designs, but technical difficulties in handling cryogenic hydrogen and liquified natural gas were thought by many to outweigh the positive aspects of this research.

1988 April 16   The first McDonnell Douglas T-45A Goshawk made its first flight, powered by a 5,450-lb. s.t. Rolls Royce/

Turboméca F405-RR-400 turbofan engine. Derived from the British Aerospace Hawk, the T-45A was built as a U.S. Navy carrier-rated basic and advanced trainer. It had a maximum weight of 12,758 lb., a maximum speed of 620 MPH and a climb time of 7 min. 12 sec. to 30,000 ft. The T-45A had a wingspan of 30 ft. 10 in. and a length of 39 ft. 3 in. with a wing area of 179.64 sq. ft.

1988 April 18   Boeing's first 767ER was delivered to Air Mauritius and in the process set a new world distance record when it flew from Halifax, Nova Scotia to Port Louis, Mauritius, a distance of 8,728 mi., in 16 hr. 27 min. Powered by two General Electric CF6-80C2E4 engines, it had a takeoff weight of 349,206 lb. The manufacturer claimed a distance record for the weight category and a point-to-point record from Halifax to Port Louis.

1988 April 23   The man-powered aircraft Daedalus 88 set a new record for aircraft of this type when it flew 74 mi. in almost 4 hr. from Crete to Santorini in the Mediterranean. The flight had been staged to commemorate the mythical flight of Daedalus and Icarus but ended prematurely when it came down in the sea after losing control as it turned into the wind for a landing. It was piloted by the Greek cyclist Kannellos Kannellopolous, and the distance achieved considerably exceeded that achieved by *Gossamer Albatross* in 1979 during a crossing of the English Channel.

1988 April 25   Defense Secretary George Younger of Britain announced his government's intention to proceed with its participation in the European fighter aircraft program. The United Kingdom would take 33% of the program with Germany also taking 33%, leaving Italy to take 21% and Spain 13%. The four countries had requirements totaling about 800 EFAs, of which Britain needed about 250 to replace the Phantom and the ground attack version of the Jaguar.

1988 April 29   The first Boeing 747-400 made its first flight powered by four 58,000-lb. s.t. General Electric CF6-80C2 engines. Characterized externally by an extended wing with a span of 211 ft. and outward inclined winglets, the 747-400 had the upper fuselage extension of the Series 300, completely redesigned engine nacelle pylons and a modern two-crew digital flight deck. With 412 passengers, it had a range of up to 8,406 mi. but could carry a maximum 660 passengers in high density configuration. Its maximum takeoff weight was 870,000 lbs.

1988 April 30   The USAF Strategic Air Command accepted the last of 100 production Rockwell B-1B bombers in a small ceremony at the North American Aviation plant at Palmdale, Calif. Two months early and within the original cost estimate of $20.5 billion set by Congress, the B-1B program had been an airframe and engine success; but unresolved concerns about defensive and offensive avionics rendered the bomber less capable than projected. The 100th aircraft was flown to 384th Bombardment Wing at McConnell AFB, Kans. by Col. Phillip J. Ford.

1988 May 6   The first McDonnell Douglas F/A-18D Hornet two-seat, night-attack aircraft made its first flight from the St. Louis plant. These aircraft, for use with the U.S. Navy and the U.S. Marine Corps, had the usual stick and throttle controls removed from the rear cockpit and replaced with stationary hand controllers for the use of the weapons systems officer, who would have the added advantage of three color monitors. Upgrade equipment included a Honeywell color, digital, moving map display and a targeting FLIR (forward-looking infrared) display. Crew would use night vision goggles.

1988 May 16 Defense ministers of the United Kingdom, Germany, Italy and Spain signed a memorandum of understanding in Bonn, West Germany, authorizing full-scale development of the European fighter aircraft. Alternative aircraft considered for the role included the McDonnell Douglas Hornet and the Dassault-Breguet Mirage 2000. Contractors involved would be British Aerospace, MDD, Aeritalia and CASA. Engine manufacturers Rolls Royce, MTU, Fiat and Sener would work cooperatively on the powerplant. Eight prototypes were to be funded with an initial operational capability anticipated for the mid-1990s.

1988 May 23 The first of six Bell/Boeing V-22A Osprey tilt-rotor transport aircraft was rolled out at Arlington, Tex. The manufacturers had designed the aircraft for use with all four U.S. armed services, the first time that had been done. It had a wing-span of 84 ft. 8 in. over the rotors, a length of 62 ft. 7 in., height over the tail of 17 ft. 8 in. and two 6,150-SHP Allison T406-AD-400 turboshaft engines. With a maximum STO weight of 60,500 lb., or a normal loaded VTO weight of 47,500 lb., it could accommodate 24 fully equipped troops or 12 litter cases.

1988 June 1 A reengined Boeing 727-200 designed to meet new noise requirements was rolled out by Valsan Partners in the United States. The rear-fuselage side nacelles were fitted with Pratt & Whitney JT8D-200 engines, and the original JT8D was retained in the rear fuselage position but fitted with a hush kit instead of a thrust reverser. Valsan Partners already had 85 orders for reengining work to keep existing Boeing 727s within legal limits.

1988 June 17 The U.S. Customs Service took delivery of the Lockheed P-3 airborne early-warning aircraft under the Blue Sentinel program. The aircraft was to be used to patrol the southern U.S. borders to detect and track drug smugglers. Known as *Blue Canoe,* the aircraft was an ex-RAAF P-3B Orion that had been bought back and modified to carry a General Electric APS-125 radar, the same as that used by the Grumman E-2C in a radome.

1988 June 17 Dassault-Breguet completed its 1,000th Falcon business jet; of these, 949 had already been delivered to customers. The program began in 1962 with the first aircraft of this type under its French name, Mystère, and since then, customers in 66 countries had taken delivery of a Falcon. Both smaller and larger three-engined derivatives had evolved in the two decades since then, and the Mystère was one of the world's most successful business and executive aircraft, claiming particularly successful sales in the United States.

1988 June 27 A Boeing 747-400 weighing 892,450 lb. took off from Moses Lake, Wash. It was the greatest weight ever flown off a runway. This compared with a normal maximum takeoff weight of 870,000 lb. The feat was accomplished during stall and low-speed drag tests, and the aircraft reached a height of 6,562 ft. just 4 min. 49 sec. after rotation. This did not constitute the heaviest load ever flown; a Lockheed C-5A that had taken off at 789,403 lb. had been refueled to a weight of 920,036 lb. in the air on December 17, 1984.

1988 July 3 An Airbus Industrie A300 operated by Iran Air was accidentally shot down over the Strait of Hormuz in the Persian Gulf when the *Ticonderoga*-class cruiser USS *Vincennes* fired a standard missile at what the ship's crew thought was a hostile Iranian Air Force F-14A threatening the U.S. task force. All 290 passengers and crew aboard Iran Air Flight 655, en route from Bandar Abbas to Dubai at 12,000 ft., were killed. The Iranians had a Lockheed P-3 in the area on patrol and two McDonnell

Douglas F-4s. There were no U.S. AWACS in the vicinity at the time.

1988 July 21 In further moves to release all British aircraft companies from public ownership, the U.K. government confirmed its plans to privatize Short Brothers of Belfast, Northern Ireland. The company had borrowed heavily and owed £200 million; it had suffered losses of £37.5 million in 1985–86 and of £20 million in 1986–87. The U.K. government wanted to find a buyer for the entire company but was apparently prepared to sell off any one of the three divisions handling missiles, aircraft and aerostructures.

1988 July 24 Two British Aerospace 146 airliners made the first in a series of noise tests at London-Docklands airport alongside the Thames River. The two aircraft were owned by British Aerospace and by Loganair, and a range of takeoffs and landings were to be made with noise meters and crowds of local residents on site to give their own opinions. Previously, only the de Havilland Canada Dash 7 had been cleared to use the Docklands airport, but the CAA had agreed to tests with the BAe 146 to determine whether it too should be given a license to operate from there.

1988 August 2 NASA commenced flight tests of a specially configured Convair F-106B (serial no. N816NA) at the Langley Research Laboratory, Hampton, Va. The aircraft had been modified to have wing leading-edge vortex flaps, which had been developed at Langley. These flaps could be deflected up to 50° for enhanced maneuverability in transonic flight by improving the lift/drag ratio at this point on the wing by up to 30%.

1988 August 5 A new record for autogyros was set by Wg. Comdr. Kenneth Wallis in a WA-116/F/S autogyro powered by a 60-HP Franklin 2A-120-B engine when he completed a closed circuit course of 623 mi. in a time of 7 hr. 39 min. 59 sec. The speed over the full distance was 81.3 MPH, but 83.3 MPH over a 311-mi. section. The autogyro had a takeoff weight of 728 lb.

1988 August 18 The first electronic combat and reconnaissance (ECR) version of the Panavia Tornado made its first flight at the MBB Flight Test Center, Manching, West Germany. The ECR variant had been ordered by the German government, and 35 of them were to serve with the Luftwaffe. It was essentially a derivative of the Tornado IDS version and was expected to supplant the F-4G Wild Weasel. The aircraft retained an air-to-surface role but did not carry the two 27-mm cannons. Two IDS Tornadoes were used as test beds for the new variant.

1988 September 1 The first of a planned 130 Short (Embraer) Tucano training aircraft was accepted by the RAF when the seventh production aircraft (serial no. ZF141) was handed over to Lord Trefgarne, minister for defense procurement, at a ceremony hosted by Short's managing director Roy McNulty. The aircraft went immediately to the Central Flying School, at which site the ceremony was held. It was to enter service with No. 7 Flying Training School at Church Fenton about 6 mon. later. This was the first peacetime RAF trainer that had originated in a foreign country.

1988 September 7 The McDonnell Douglas STOL and maneuver technology demonstrator (S/MTD) dubbed ''Agile Eagle'' made its first flight at St. Louis. Fitted with provision for two-dimensional thrust vectoring and thrust-reverser nozzles to the two Pratt & Whitney F100 turbofan engines, it was built as a research aircraft for new flight dynamics tests. Adapted from the first two-seat F-15B, it also carried two all-flying foreplanes inter-linked with the vectoring nozzles. The tests would be carried out at Edwards AFB, Calif.

1988 September 19 The first BAe Sea Harrier FRS.Mk.2 aerodynamic test aircraft made its first flight at Dunsfold, England. It featured the new Ferranti Blue Vixen fire-control radar with provision for the new AIM-120 AMRAAM and the BAe Sea Eagle missile. The FRS.Mk.2 represented a mid-life update program incorporating refinements and improved equipment to the Mk.1. The Royal Navy was allowed to order 10 to add to the 36 FRS.Mk.1s it had in the inventory at the end of 1991.

1988 September 28 The Ilyushin Il-96-300 made its first flight in the USSR powered by four 35,275-lb. s.t. Perm (Soloviev) PS-90A turbofans. Developed from the Il-86, the Il-96-300 was a complete redesign with a wingspan of 189 ft. 2 in., excluding upswept, outwardly canted winglets, a length of 189 ft. 2 in. and maximum takeoff weight of 476,200 lb. Up to 300 passengers could be carried at 528 MPH for a maximum range of 4,660 mi. Aeroflot planned to buy 60 Il-96-300s, and the aircraft became the subject of a deal whereby Pratt & Whitney would provide engines for the aircraft to compete in western markets.

1988 October 26 After completing the first circumnavigation of the globe ever conducted by an RAF fighter, four Panavia Tornado F.Mk.3s of No. 29 Squadron returned to RAF Conningsby, England. The 9-wk. tour had taken them eastward through the Far East, Australasia, the Pacific and the United States. Lockheed TriStar tanker aircraft from No. 216 Squadron kept the aircraft fueled in the air, and Lockheed Hercules transport aircraft provided support for ground-handling equipment and spares. The Tornadoes took part in a five-nation air defense exercise in Malaysia, helped celebrate the Australian bicentennial anniversary and participated in the Pennsylvania International Air Show.

1988 October 27 The prototype ATR 72 made its first flight, powered by two 2,160-SHP Pratt & Whitney Canada PW124/2 turboprop engines. Developed as a stretch of the ATR 42, this Franco/Italian regional commercial transport had a wingspan of 88 ft. 9 in. and a length of 89 ft. 1 in. with capacity for up to 50 passengers traveling at 286 MPH for a maximum distance of 742 mi., or 2,727 mi. with no payload. The ATR 72 was the first aircraft with a carbon-fiber wing box. It was manufactured jointly by Aérospatiale and Alenia.

1988 November 1 Boeing/Sikorsky and McDonnell Douglas/Bell each received contracts worth $158 million for the design and assembly of prototype helicopters for the U.S. Army LHX competition. In a period of 23 mon., each team was required to complete detailed designs and build cockpit mock-ups and components for a rotary-winged, light-attack aircraft based on the Allison/Garrett T800 engine. The McDonnell Douglas/Bell proposal was based on their Model 680 with an antitorque (NOTAR) tail. The Boeing/Sikorsky proposal carried a T-tail with a fan-in-the-fin tail rotor, internal weapons bays and a turreted gun.

1988 November 22 At a public ceremony at Palmdale, Calif. the first prototype Northrop B-2A stealth bomber (serial no. 82-1066) was rolled out. Essentially a flying wing, the B-2A had a span of 172 ft., a length of 69 ft. and a height of 17 ft. Powered by four 19,000-lb. s.t. General Electric F-118-GE-110 turbofan engines, it had capacity for a warload of approximately 50,000 lb., including conventional and nuclear free-fall bombs, cruise missiles, SRAMs and sea mines. The design and materials technology employed were optimized around low observables tech-

nology. The USAF expected to order a total 132 aircraft of this type, a figure later reduced to 75.

1988 November 29 The respective governments of the United States and Japan signed a contract for joint development of an aircraft to fill Japan's FS-X fighter requirement. In a program estimated to call for 130 aircraft to replace the F-1 and the F-4EJ of the Air Self-Defense Force by the turn of the century, the Japanese contractor Mitsubishi was to get approximately 45% of the work package. The schedule envisaged assembly of the first aircraft to begin in 1991 followed by flight testing in 1993 and initial deployment in 1997.

1988 December 9 The first SAAB JAS 39 Gripen single-seat, multi-role fighter made its first flight powered by a 12,250/18,100-lb. s.t. General Electric/Volvo Flygmotor RM 12 (F404-40) turbofan engine. With a delta-wing span of 26 ft. 3 in. and a length of 46 ft. 3 in., the Gripen carried two flying foreplanes. Equipped with a 27-mm Mauser BK27 cannon, the SAAB 39 could carry a variety of external stores and was expected to have a maximum speed of Mach 1.2 (914 MPH) at sea level and Mach 2.2 (1,450 MPH) above 36,0000 ft. Combining fighter, attack and reconnaissance roles in a single aircraft, the Swedish Air Force had an initial requirement for 30 Gripen.

1988 December 21 A Pan American World Airways Boeing 747 en route to New York from London's Heathrow Airport exploded at 31,000 ft. over Scotland and came down on the small town of Lockerbie, killing all 259 passengers and crew on board as well as 11 people on the ground. The flight originated at Frankfurt as Pan American Flight 103 when a Boeing 727 carried passengers and baggage to London for the 747 connection. A world-wide investigation was conducted for three years. Late in 1991, U.S. and U.K. officials accused Libyan terrorists of planting the bomb that destroyed the aircraft.

1988 December 21 The world's largest aircraft made its first flight when the Antonov An-225 Mriya took to the air. Powered by six 51,590-lb. s.t. ZMKB (Lotarev) D-18T turbofan engines, it had a wingspan of 290 ft., a length of 275 ft. 7 in., a maximum takeoff weight of 1,322,750 lb. and a potential maximum payload of 551,145 lb. carried in the spacious interior or in a pallet on top of the fuselage. Designed and evolved from the An-124 to carry the Soviet space shuttle, it had a maximum cruising speed of 528 MPH and a typical payload range of 2,796 mi. Only one was built as of 1993.

1989 January 2 The first of two prototype Tupolev Tu-204-100 medium-haul commercial airliners made its first flight, powered by two 35,275-lb. s.t. Perm PS-90A turbofans. With a wingspan of 137 ft. 9 in. and a length of 151 ft. 8 in., the 214-seat airliner had a range of 2,392 mi. and was equivalent to the Boeing 767. Aeroflot had a need for about 350 aircraft of this type, which had a maximum takeoff weight of 219,356 lb. and an economical cruising speed of 503 MPH. Entry into service was scheduled for late 1991.

1989 January 4 In an incident involving two Grumman F-14A Tomcats from the carrier USS *John F. Kennedy*, two Libyan Air Force MiG-23s were shot down over the Mediterranean Sea off the coast of North Africa 70 mi. northwest of Tobruk. The two MiGs had repeatedly ignored evasive tactics by the Tomcats and persisted in threatening the U.S. Navy aircraft. One MiG was brought down by an AIM-7M Sparrow and one by an AIM-9M Sidewinder fired by separate aircraft. Attached to Carrier Air Wing

3, the two F-14As had been on routine patrol when the incident happened.

1989 January 9 The U.S. Defense Department's FY 1990 budget request announced by the outgoing Reagan administration called for cuts involving cancellation of the Bell/Boeing V-22 Osprey. This proposal was later endorsed in the revised defense funding requests issued by Defense Secretary Richard B. Cheney on May 3 when he voiced the conclusions of the new Bush administration. Also deleted was new production of the F-14D and Phoenix missile as well as the AH-64 Apache attack helicopter (after 1990) and a cut by half in funds for the B-2A. Also requested was a transfer of the X-30 national aerospace plane out of the Department of Defense.

1989 January 24 Bell Helicopter Textron started flight tests with its Model 680 equipped with a four-blade bearingless rotor known as the 4BW. The rotor and four-blade assembly had been flight-tested on a Bell AH-1W Super Cobra, which the company had leased from the U.S. Marine Corps, a service that was interested in equipping its AH-1W fleet with this rotor should tests validate theoretical performance improvements. The rotor arms used composite blades with a fiberglass-epoxy yoke attaching the blades to the mast. This same rotor system was adopted by McDonnell Douglas/Bell for their U.S. Army LHX contender.

1989 February 16 The last Northrop F-5E was completed at a small, final-assembly facility at Mojave especially set up for the late order for three aircraft from Singapore. Northrop had produced a grand total of 3,806 F-5/T-38 aircraft over a production period of more than 30 yr. It had ceased full-scale F-5 production in 1987 with delivery of two F-5Es to Bahrain; a total 2,610 F-5 and RF-5 models had been produced altogether. The total also included aircraft built under license in Switzerland, Korea and Taiwan.

1989 March 2 The inaugural revenue-earning flight of the British Aerospace 146 Series 300 took place when Air UK introduced the stretched short-haul airliner on its London-Gatwick to Edinburgh and Glasgow routes. The BAe 146 had a longer fuselage (101 ft. 8 in.) accommodating up to 128 passengers and had four 6,970-lb. s.t. Textron Lycoming ALF502R-5 turbofans. This was the second stretch from the basic BAe 146-100. The Series 200 aircraft had a fuselage length of 93 ft. 10 in. From the end of 1991, all BAe 146s would have four 7,000-lb. s.t. LF507 turbofans increasing the range of the Series 300 to 1,923 mi.

1989 March 16 A mid-life upgrade program for the RAF Panavia Tornado was agreed and covered by a contract issued to British Aerospace. This would cover all operational enhancements identified by the RAF as suitable for keeping the aircraft in pace with technical developments. The work would last several years and give the aircraft a thorough electronics and systems update. A similar program had already begun with Tornadoes operated by the Luftwaffe and the Marineflieger.

1989 March 18 The last Hercules Airbridge mission to the Falklands Islands was flown by the RAF when an aircraft from No. 24 Squadron departed Lyneham, England for Mount Pleasant, which it would reach two days later. With stops at Dakar and Ascension Island, the Hercules was refueled by another Hercules for the long flight to the Falklands. The 14,600-mi. round trip took more than 30 hr., and 650 supply flights had been mounted by the Hercules Airbridge since 1982. These aircraft would now remain at Mount Pleasant on maritime patrol and sup-

port duty, and the TriStar KC.Mk.1 took over the re-supply flights from the United Kingdom.

1989 March 19 The Bell/Boeing V-22 Osprey made its first flight at Bell's Flight Research Center, Arlington, Tex. and remained in helicopter mode throughout. It remained airborne for approximately 15 min. and followed slow taxi runs, the flight culminating in a run-on landing. The flight included out-of-ground-effect hovers and accelerations with a top speed of 23 MPH and an altitude of 30 ft. The Osprey then performed a vertical takeoff followed by another run-on landing.

1989 March 22 The first and only Antonov An-225 built established 106 new FAI world records in several classes, most important of which was a speed of 813.09 km/hr. (505.2 MPH) carrying a payload in the 70–155 metric ton (154,320–341,710 lb.) class around a closed circuit of 2,000 km (1,243 mi.). Also achieved was a record altitude of 12,340 m (40,486 ft.) while carrying a load in the 60–155 metric ton (132,275–341,710 lb.) class. The An-225 took off at a weight of 508.2 tons (1,120,370 lb.) and achieved a height of 2,000 m (6,562 ft.), the heaviest in both instances.

1989 March The world's first supersonic V/STOL fighter made its first flight in the USSR when the Yakovlev Yak-141 took to the air for the first time. Powered by one R-79 34,170-lb. s.t. lift/cruise engine and two 5,180-lb. s.t. Koliesov RD-36-35 lift engines, the Yak-141 had a wingspan of 33 ft. 2 in., a length of 60 ft. 4 in. and a maximum takeoff weight of 30,150 lb. for VTO or 43,100 lb. for STO. With a weapons load of up to 5,700 lb., it had a maximum speed of Mach 1.7 (1,118 MPH) and a STO range of 1,300 mi.

1989 April 3 Developed by Boeing at its Wichita plant, an all-composite wing was flown for the first time on a Grumman A-6E in efforts to circumvent fatigue problems on that aircraft. Plans had been made to fit the new composite wing on the last 21 of the A-6Es still under construction. These aircraft would also have the benefit of new systems integration refinements widening the repertoire of armaments carried by this U.S. Navy attack aircraft. Funds permitting, the navy hoped to modify about half the 342 A-6Es as they came back through the maintenance hangars.

1989 April 13 The McDonnell Douglas MD-80, used for flight trials with the ultra-high bypass (UHB) engine since May 18, 1987, made its first flight carrying the 20,000-lb. s.t. Pratt & Whitney-Allison 578-DX turbofan engine on the port nacelle pylon. Through September 1988, this MD-80 demonstrator had made 137 flights with the General Electric GE-36 propfan engine and had been actively marketing a design proposal known as the MD-91, which would be equipped with propfan engines.

1989 April 17 The fiftieth and last Lockheed C-5B Galaxy heavy-lift transport aircraft was delivered to the USAF. This aircraft was delivered to the Military Airlift Command's 436th Military Airlift Wing stationed at Dover AFB, Del. Having gone through an engineering rework on the wing assemblies, the basic C-5A had given way to technical advancements to produce the upgraded C-5B; at the end of 1991, the USAF had 76 C-5As in addition to 50 C-5Bs.

1989 April 18 An Irish leasing company called GPA Group ordered 308 turbofan airliners valued at a record $16.8 billion in the biggest deal ever struck for commercial aircraft. GPA ordered 30 Airbus Industrie A320s, 24 Airbus Industrie A330/340s, 92 Boeing 737s, 50 Boeing 757s, 40 Boeing 767s, 64 McDonnell

Douglas MD-80s and eight McDonnell Douglas MD-11s. The Boeing order, worth $9.4 billion, is the largest single sale ever made by that company. Airbus Industrie received $4.3 billion worth of orders and McDonnell Douglas $3.1 billion. Revenues for the GPA Group had increased from $155.3 million in 1986 to a projected $1 billion in 1989, with net profit increasing from $25.1 million to $150 million over the same period.

1989 April 27   In West Germany, MBB performed the first flight with the all-composite BK 117 helicopter at Ottobrunn. The engines, hydraulics and gearbox had been utilized from an existing airframe, but the new experimental shell was constructed from 80% carbon-fiber-reinforced plastic and 20% aramid-fiber-reinforced plastic, or Kevlar. There had been 745 separate component parts in the standard BK 117 airframe, but only 105 parts in the new composite airframe. The work had been funded by the German Defense Ministry to demonstrate the practicability of using these materials.

1989 April 28   The governments of the United States and Japan agreed that the General Dynamics F-16 would be the basis for an aircraft to meet Japan's FSX fighter requirement. The arrangement had been made in 1988, but negotiations leading toward a definitive selection had been held up awaiting the incoming Bush administration. The Japanese would produce a special version of the Fighting Falcon at a cost of $42 million, and U.S. companies would receive a 40% share in the development work as well as production of the aircraft.

1989 May 10   The McDonnell Douglas F-15 Agile Eagle, modified to carry thrust-vectoring nozzles and fitted with a flying foreplane, made its first flight with those nozzles attached and operating. Earlier flights had been conducted to evaluate the aerodynamic qualities and handling characteristics of the new configuration, establishing baseline performance before adding the active thrust vectoring element. Also tested had been the new four-channel, digital, fly-by-wire flight control system. Following tests at St. Louis, the aircraft was to be moved to Edwards AFB, Calif.

1989 May 13   In the USSR, the sole Antonov An-225 carried the Soviet space shuttle *Buran* on its back for the first time. Although the record weight of around 1,200,000 lb. was greater than that carried 2 mon. earlier for the FAI record, it was nevertheless well short of the AN-225's maximum potential weightlifting capability of 1,322,750 lb. A second An-225 was in assembly, but this would remain unfinished when funds were withdrawn as problems with the Soviet economy restricted aerospace work.

1989 May 20   Airbus Industrie formally authorized firm contracts to be negotiated with customers of the stretched A320-300. Providing 24% more volume for passengers and 40% more volume for cargo, the Series 300 aircraft would have a fuselage extended in length by 22 ft. 9 in., providing seats for up to 200 people or 186 in a mixed-class configuration. The new aircraft would have optional General Electric CFM56 or IAE V2500 engines and a range of up to 2,085 mi.

1989 May 24   British Aerospace gave the go-ahead for a stretched version of its Jetstream light commuter and executive transport aircraft. Surveys indicated a need for a bigger aircraft capable of carrying up to 29 passengers, and British Aerospace projected a potential sales market for 1,500 such aircraft worldwide. The company hoped to capture 25% of this market with the new aircraft, to be known as the Jetstream 41. Extra baggage space was

to be provided by extending the wing root, and a new wing was to be designed.

1989 May 28   The first of four prototype AIDC Ching-Kuo single-seat, air-defense fighters made its first flight in Taiwan, the country of its indigenous design and assembly. Powered by two 4,820/8,340-lb. s.t. Garrett TFE1042-7 turbofan engines, it carried one 20-mm rotary cannon, six Sky Sword AAMs and a maximum external ordnance load of 9,000 lb. It was built as a replacement for the Northrop F-5 and Lockheed F-104, and design assistance had been provided by General Dynamics. The Garrett turbofans were manufactured in Taiwan by the International Turbo Engine Co.

1989 June 5   The massive Antonov An-225 *Mriya* flew in to Paris-Le Bourget for the 1989 Paris Air Show, carrying the Soviet Shuttle *Buran* on its back. This was the first time either had been seen outside the USSR and the first time the shuttle had been carried for such a distance. When it took off from Kiev to fly to Paris, the combination had a takeoff weight of 1,234,600 lb., the greatest weight ever lifted into the air.

1989 June 13   At a meeting between the U.S. business aircraft-builder Gulfstream and the Soviet aircraft firm Sukhoi, an agreement was reached to investigate the possibility of jointly designing a supersonic executive jet. Designated S-21G, it combined separate studies made by each company during 1987 and 1988. The new aircraft would be a twin-engined tailless design with a wingspan of 65 ft. 3 in., a length of 132 ft. 10 in., a cruising speed of Mach 2 at 60,000 ft. and a range of more than 4,300 mi. Wind tunnel tests were conducted in 1991, after which a final specification was to be agreed upon.

1989 June 30   The first Boeing 737-500 made its first flight from Renton, Wash. The flight lasted 2 hr. 20 min. Capable of carrying up to 132 passengers, the Series 500 had a cruising speed of 494 MPH and a maximum payload range of 1,565 mi., or 3,970 mi. with maximum fuel. Maximum cruising speed was 567 MPH. Power in production aircraft was to be provided by either two 20,000-lb. s.t. or two derated 18,500-lb. s.t. CFM 56-3B-1 turbofans. The first customer to receive the 737-500 was Southwest Airlines, which got the first on order on February 28, 1990.

1989 July 1   Japan's Ministry of International Trade and Industry asked the Japan Aircraft Development Corp. (JADC) to look at the possibility of designing a 75-seat regional transport aircraft. The JADC comprised a consortium of Kawasaki, Fuji, Mitsubishi and NAMC and had been formed to work with Boeing on a proposed airliner designated 757. Boeing withdrew, and the JADC was now to consider joining a joint endeavor between West Germany and China in designing an aircraft known as the MPC-75.

1989 July 17   The prototype Northrop B-2A made its first flight from Edwards AFB, Calif. following a series of runway taxi tests. The crew for the flight, which lasted 1 hr. 51 min., consisted of Bruce Hinds, Northrop chief test pilot, and Col. Richard Couch, USAF director of the B-2 combined test force. The landing gear remained down during the flight, which was maintained below 10,000 ft. The B-2 had a maximum speed of about 600 MPH at 50,000 ft, a maximum payload range of 7,255 mi. on a hi-hi-hi mission, 5,067 mi. on a hi-lo-hi mission or 1,152 mi. on a lo-lo-lo mission.

1989 August 10   The first direct flight between two points in West Germany and East Germany took place when a Lufthansa

The most expensive and hotly contested warplane of all time, the Northrop B-2 stealth bomber first flew on July 17, 1989.

aircraft flew from Frankfurt to Leipzig to inaugurate a new twice-weekly service signaling a thaw in the Cold War. Next day the East German airline Interflug commenced a twice-weekly service between Leipzig and Düsseldorf. The two services were routed through Czechoslovakian air space to avoid flying directly across the border between East and West Germany.

1989 August 17 Setting a new world record for civil aircraft, a Boeing 747-400 of QANTAS Airways flew nonstop from London to Sydney in a record time of 20 hr. 9 min. The 11,156-mi. distance had taken only 3 hr. 6 min. longer than the record time taken by a Concorde supersonic airliner, including refueling stops. It was also a record distance flown by a commercial airliner, the previous best being 10,281 mi. set by a South African Airways 747SP from Seattle to Cape Town. The QANTAS 747-400 carried only 23 passengers and to conserve fuel, it had been towed to the end of the runway for takeoff from London's Heathrow airport.

1989 August 20 At the traditional Aviation Day fly-past at Tushino in the USSR, the Beriev A-40 Albatross was seen publicly for the first time. First flown in 1988, this large multi-role amphibian was powered by two 26,500-lb. s.t. Perm MKB D-30KPV turbofans placed above the rear fuselage and had a normal loaded weight of 150,000 lb. The world's only jet-powered amphibian had a flight crew of four plus space for rescue equipment including power boats and liferafts and up to 60 survivors. The A-40 had a wingspan of 137 ft. 1 in. and a length of 141 ft.

1989 August 29 The USAF issued a request for proposals on its tanker and transport training system (TTTS) program. It wanted to buy 211 aircraft and 14 simulators by 1995 by selecting a design based on an existing executive or business jet. Potential respondents to the request were the Beechjet 400, the Learjet 31 and the Citation SII. Other aircraft that had been previously considered but dropped were the BAe 125, Canadair Challenger, Dassault-Breguet Falcon, Gulfstream Gulfjet, IAI Astra and Rockwell Sabreliner 65.

1989 September 14 The #1 Bell/Boeing V-22 Osprey performed its first full transition from helicopter to wing-borne flight

at the end of the second phase of flight-testing being conducted at the Bell Flight Research Center at Arlington, Va. Earlier, during a series of partial transition to forward flight, the wings were tilted to 45° on September 4. This full transition flight lasted 1 hr. 5 min. while the pilots evaluated a variety of optional engine nacelle angles and flight modes. The V-22 made a conventional run-on landing without attempting a second transition to vertical flight.

1989 September 15 The first production McDonnell Douglas AV-8B Harrier II equipped for night attack was handed over to the U.S. Marine Corps. The aircraft was destined to spend time at the U.S. Naval Weapons Center, China Lake, Calif. before being delivered to the U.S. Marine Corps Air Station at Yuma, Ariz. Of 323 U.S. Marine Corps AV-8Bs ordered, all remaining 156 aircraft yet to be delivered would be completed with night-attack capability.

1989 September 19 The international Helitech exhibition organized by Offshore Conferences & Exhibitions Ltd. of Kingston, England opened with the first appearance in the West of the Kamov Ka-136 Hokum two-seat combat helicopter. Powered by two 2,200-SHP Leningrad Klimov TV3-117 turboshaft engines driving two contra-rotating 45 ft. 10 in. rotors, it had a length of 44 ft. 3 in. and a maximum takeoff weight of about 16,500 lb. Maximum speed was 220 MPH with a wide variety of optional guns, rockets and missiles.

1989 October 3 The last of 37 Lockheed TR-1A spyplanes was delivered to the USAF. All aircraft of this type, which followed the equally successful production run of U-2 spyplanes, were powered by the Pratt & Whitney J75-P-13B turbojet engine. Recent tests by the USAF suggested a possible switch to the General Electric F101-GE-F29 turbofan engine.

1989 October 4 Short Brothers of Belfast, Northern Ireland were acquired by the Canadian corporation Bombardier Inc., ending 46 yr. of U.K. government ownership and eliminating one more aircraft manufacturer from British ownership. The total deal involved £731 million of which £390 million was for writing off debt, £30 million to buy the company and the rest going into restructuring the company and offsetting known losses that would accrue until turnaround.

1989 October 10 McDonnell Douglas announced that it was marketing the MD-90 twin-jet derivative of the original DC-9 family. There were to be three versions of the aircraft, each with different fuselage lengths. Technically based on the MD-80 series, the MD-90 would be powered by two 22,000-lb. s.t. V2500-D2 engines, have a gross weight of 139,000 lb. and carry a maximum 114 passengers 2,762 mi. A larger series aircraft would carry 153 passengers, and the biggest of all would have two 28,000-lb. s.t. V2500D-5 engines.

1989 November 8 In a flight lasting 6 hr. 5 min., the first prototype Northrop B-2A carried out its first in-flight refueling exercise when a KC-10A Extender transferred 40,000 lb. of JP-8 fuel to the stealth bomber. The B-2A had been grounded after the first four flights for tests and checks as well as modifications for the expanded flight-test program following the first five flights. During these Block 1 tests, the aircraft's aerodynamic and handling characteristics were being evaluated prior to the Block 2 low-observables tests to see just how stealthy the aircraft could be.

1989 November 14 An order for 50 McDonnell Douglas MD-90 twin-jet airliners, latest in a long line of DC-9 derivatives, served to officially launch the type. The MD-90 designation had originally been reserved for propfan variants of the DC-9 line, but with the relaxation of fuel prices and the increase in revenue-earning with conventional powerplants, it reverted to a stretched model using turbofan engines. McDonnell Douglas market surveys indicated a potential sales opportunity for up to 800 MD-90s.

1989 November 22 After all funds for continuing operations with the SR-71A Blackbird were deleted from the FY 1990 U.S. Defense Department budget, the aircraft was grounded, pending a final decision on the fate of the inventory. Considerable debate had surrounded this decision. The Defense Department wanted to halt all SR-71A activity a year before, but congressional reluctance to ground this highly valuable aircraft resulted in a stay of execution. The potential appearance of a Blackbird successor plus the availability of space-based intelligence-gathering resulted in cancellation of further funding.

1989 December 8 Boeing's board of directors agreed to market the Boeing 767-X, which would be known as the Boeing 777 if a formal launch was mounted. Based largely on the 767 but with a wider fuselage, the new aircraft would have a twin-aisle cabin and a new wing; capacity would be about 349 people in a mixed-class configuration. The Japanese companies Mitsubishi, Kawasaki and Fuji had been invited to participate in the project. Pratt & Whitney had agreed to develop a growth version of the PW400 at a thrust of up to 80,000 lb., but Rolls Royce offered a 72,000-lb. s.t. Trent 720 and General Electric a new GE90.

1989 December 10 The world's first successful man-powered helicopter took off on its first flight. Designed and put together by students at the California Polytechnic State University, the helicopter was named *Da Vinci* and was the third in a series of previously unsuccessful concepts built at the university. With a rotor diameter of 100 ft., Greg McNeil lifted 7 in. off the ground inside the school's gymnasium.

1989 December 29 The first production McDonnell Douglas MD-530 NOTAR made its first flight at the Mesa, Ariz. plant.

Two similar versions were on offer, and the U.S. Army had drawn up plans for its entire fleet of AH-6 and MH-6 helicopters to be converted to NOTAR configuration. The MD-530N was powered by the Allison 250-C30, but the MD-520N had the 375-HP Allison 250-C20R-2 engine driving a 28-ft. 3-in. rotor. With a length of 25 ft. and a maximum takeoff weight of 3,850 lb., the helicopter had a cruising speed of up to 156 MPH and a maximum range of 285 mi.

1989 Moves were made during the year by the RAF to admit female pilots and navigators following an air force board study that examined the practicality of such a move. Not since the RAF formed on April 1, 1918, had the RAF (or its predecessor, the Royal Flying Corps) allowed women to become pilots or navigators. Women would not be allowed into combat roles and would not be allowed to fly combat aircraft in war. They would, however, be allowed to fly and navigate aircraft on transport duties moving passengers and cargo.

1990 January 5 Operational acceptance of the Boeing E-3 Sentry AWACS for the RAF came a step nearer with the start of airworthiness testing when the first E-3D took to the air for more than 2 hr. at Boeing Field, Seattle. Flight and handling characteristics would be evaluated over a 3-mon. period and varied from the E-3A for the USAF in having wingtip equipment pods and a refueling probe in addition to a receptacle. Part of the evaluation test phase involved refueling with an RAF TriStar and probe-and-drogue refueling with a C-135FR of the French Armée de l'Air.

1990 January 10 The first of five McDonnell Douglas MD-11 long-haul commercial transport test aircraft made its first flight, from Long Beach, Calif. to Yuma, Ariz. Powered by three 61,500-lb. s.t. General Electric CF6-80C2-D1F turbofans, it had a maximum speed of 597 MPH, an economic cruise of 544 MPH and a maximum payload range carrying 405 passengers 5,760 mi. Derived from the DC-10, the MD-11 was 9 mon. late in entering the flight test phase, although the order book stood at 340 aircraft for 30 customers.

1990 January 15 The Atlas Aircraft Corp. of South Africa rolled out its XH-2 Rooivalk two-seat ground support and escort helicopter. Powered by two 1,575-SHP Turboméca Turmo IVC turboshaft engines driving a 49 ft. 6 in. rotor, it had a length of 54 ft. 7 in. and a maximum takeoff weight of more than 17,600 lb. With its two-man crew in tandem, it had a wide array of potential weapons carried on stub-wings, and it boasted a top speed of more than 170 MPH and a maximum range of 460 mi. It made its first flight on February 11.

1990 January 26 The Boeing VC-25A presidential aircraft made its first flight at Wichita, Kans. Built at Everett, the original Boeing 747-200B airframe had been flown to Wichita for extensive rework into the new Air Force One. It was to return to Everett for painting and was scheduled for delivery to the USAF on September 30. A second aircraft of the same type was scheduled for delivery June 30, 1991. Major elements fitted to the VC-25A prior to delivery were the 57 antenna and equipment for mid-air refueling.

1990 January 30 The Royal Navy deployed an antisubmarine Sea King helicopter aboard a frigate for the first time when an HAS.Mk.5 of No. 826 Squadron embarked on a Type 22 frigate HMS *Brave* of the *Broadsword* class. Based at Culdrose, the squadron usually operated two Lynx helicopters to tankers and stores ships of the Royal Fleet Auxiliary, but the Type 22 had the capability of accommodating only one Sea King.

1990 January 31   The first British Aerospace Hawk Mk.66 for the Swiss Air Force was handed over to its new owner at a public demonstration in Switzerland. Twenty aircraft of this type had been ordered by the Swiss with a major contribution from Swiss industry. Each aircraft was assembled in Switzerland at the Federal Aircraft Factory in Emmen. The Hawk Mk.66 was intended to replace the de Havilland Vampire, which had been serving with the Swiss Air Force for 40 yr. Vampires would be retained as target tugs.

1990 February 3   The U.S. Navy accepted the first of 18 Sikorsky HH-60H strike rescue and special warfare helicopters when HCS-4 (helicopter combat support-4) took delivery at Norfolk NAS, Va. HCS-4 and HCS-5 would each operate nine helicopters of this type, with the latter operating from Point Mugu, Calif. This was the first helicopter to be specially developed for the U.S. Naval Air Reserve. The HH-60H could rescue a four-man crew and their equipment in enemy territory during bad weather up to a distance of 289 mi. or covertly set down and pick up eight SEAL members.

1990 February 19   Seven days after the Series 500 gained FAA certification, the Boeing 737 became the most produced commercial airliner when the 1,833d aircraft was rolled from the line at Renton, Wash. Boeing had produced 1,832 727s, and the record-breaker was a Boeing 737-300 destined for delivery to Ansett Worldwide for leasing to British Midland Airways in the United Kingdom. To date, orders to be filled included 1,114 Series 200 aircraft and 49 Series 100 with a further 900 Boeing 737s remaining on order.

1990 February 21   The USAF selected the Beechcraft Model 400A Beechjet light corporate executive transport as its tanker transport training system (TTTS) aircraft. It anticipated inauguration of the Air Training Command's specialized undergraduate pilot training program on this type beginning September 1992. With a wingspan of 43 ft. 6 in. and a length of 48 ft. 5 in., the Model 400A was derived from the Mitsubishi Diamond 2 with two 2,900-lb. s.t. Pratt & Whitney Canada JT15D-5 turbofan engines.

1990 February 21   During tests in France using a General Dynamics F-16 to evaluate the match with a Matra Magic 2 antiaircraft missile, a record performance for the missile was claimed by the test team. In one trial, the Magic 2 was fired from the F-16 at a speed of Mach 1.3 and a height of 20,000 ft. while the fighter was engaging an 8.7 g turn. The Magic missile performed as it was designed to, and these tests served to effectively demonstrate that no firing constraints on the launch aircraft were necessary!

1990 March 6   A Lockheed SR-71A Blackbird set four speed records when it made its last flight. An SR-71A (serial no. 64-17972) raced from the Pacific to the Atlantic, setting a new transcontinental coast-to-coast record of 1 hr. 8 min. 7 sec. across a distance of 2,404 mi. at an average speed of 2,112 MPH. Between Los Angeles and Washington, D.C., it set a new world record of 1 hr. 4 min. 5 sec. and set a record time of 26 min. 36 sec. between Kansas City, Kans. and Washington, D.C. It also logged a new record time of 8 min. 20 sec. between St. Louis, Mo. and Cincinnati, Ohio.

1990 March 10   A Boeing 767-200, the 10,000th jet-powered airliner produced by Boeing, was delivered to Britannia Airways. The delivery was 32 yr. after the first 707-120 had been completed. The total was greater than all the rest of the free-world jet transport output combined. As of March 10, 1990, there were 5,319 Boeing jet airliners operated by 444 companies in 124 countries world wide.

1990 March 14   The first two-seat AMX International AMX-T two-seat operational trainer and maritime attack aircraft made its first flight with Aeritalia's chief test pilot, Comdr. Bragagnolo, at the controls. The single-seat AMX had flown for the first time on May 15, 1984, and was the product of a cooperative venture with Brazil, whereby Alenia built 46.7%, Aermacchi 23.6% and Embraer 29.7%. Powered by a 11,030-lb. s.t. Rolls Royce Spey Mk 807 turbofan engine, the AMX-T had a wingspan of 32 ft. 8 in. and a length of 43 ft. 5 in. with a maximum weight of 28,660 lb. and armament comprising one 20-mm or two 30-mm cannons and a weapons load of up to 8,377 lb.

1990 March 28   Boeing retired the first 747, *City of Everett,* after 21 yr. of work. It was earmarked for the Museum of Flight, an annex of Paine Field, Everett, Wash. where it would join the prototype of the Boeing 707. For 16 yr., it had been stored at Davis-Monthan AFB, Ariz., but its owners, the Smithsonian Institution, decided it was eventually to be moved to the annex to the National Air and Space Museum being set up at Dulles International Airport, Washington, D.C.

1990 March 28   The Soviet Myasishchev M-17 *Mystic* achieved a record altitude of 71,760 ft. for aircraft in the 16–20 metric ton (35,280–44,100 lb.) class. This aircraft was a single-engine prototype of a new high-altitude reconnaissance aircraft powered by a 15,430-lb. s.t. RKBM RD-36-51V turbojet. With a wingspan of 123 ft. and a length of 74 ft. 6 in., it had a height of 15 ft. 9 in. and twin booms supporting a high-mounted horizontal tail surface. It had a maximum takeoff weight of 44,092 lb. and an endurance of 6.5 hr. at 55,775 ft.

1990 April 4   The last of 60 McDonnell Douglas KC-10A Extender tanker/transport aircraft for the USAF was delivered to Seymour Johnson AFB, N.C. The aircraft had been used for extensive tests with the wingtip pod refueling system enabling aircraft thus equipped to refuel three aircraft simultaneously. The tests proved favorable to the concept, and the USAF planned to retrofit this attachment to all Extenders in the inventory.

1990 April 15   Boeing signed a memorandum of understanding with Mitsubishi, Kawasaki and Fuji for each of these Japanese companies to take a 15–20% share in the Boeing 777 with up to 10% of the investment risk borne by the Japanese. Responding to airline reaction, Boeing increased the range and engine thrust for the domestic and international versions on offer. The domestic model would have a range of 5,300 mi. with 353 passengers, and the international model would have a range of 7,600 mi. with 280 passengers in a three-class layout. The General Electric GE90 turbofan was now projected to generate a thrust of 85,000 lb.

1990 April 24   The first civil prototype of the EH Industries EH 101, dubbed Heliliner, made its first flight at Yeovil, England. Powered by three 1,920-SHP General Electric CT7-6 turboshaft engines, the Heliliner would be capable of carrying up to 30 passengers a distance of 580 mi. at a typical speed of 104 MPH. The first civilian prototype was designated PP8, and the second civilian prototype, the PP9, made its first flight on January 16, 1991.

1990 May 4   The second prototype SAAB JAS 39 Gripen single-seat, multi-role fighter made its first flight, albeit for only 14 min., to resume the type's flight test program interrupted February 2, 1989, when the first prototype crashed on landing. There had been some suspicion that the triple-redundant, fly-by-wire flight control system had in some way contributed to the accident, from which the pilot escaped. The third prototype joined the flight test program December 20.

1990 May 24 Orders for the Boeing 747 exceeded 1,000 when Japan Air Lines announced it had ordered 20 more 747-400s. JAL now had a total 104 747s in service or on order with options on 34 more. These aircraft would be powered by the General Electric CF6-80C2 engine and be configured to carry up to 404 passengers in three-class configurations. Deliveries on these aircraft would stretch through 1999.

1990 June 1 Withdrawn from strategic bombing duties with Strategic Air Command, the 59 General Dynamics FB-111As were reassigned to Tactical Air Command when the first two aircraft from the 509th Bombardment Wing at Pease AFB, N.H. were handed over to Tactical Air Command at Cannon AFB, N. Mex. The last FB-111A from this Strategic Air Command wing was expected to have been handed over by the end of the year, at which time the 509th Bombardment Wing would be deactivated. The FB-111As from the 380th Bombardment Wing at Plattsburgh AFB, N.Y. were to hand over their aircraft during 1991. Only a minor internal engineering change was necessary to adapt the aircraft to its new tactical role.

1990 June 22 The first of two advanced tactical fighter contenders to replace the F-15 Eagle was rolled out at Edwards AFB, Calif. when the Northrop/McDonnell Douglas YF-23A was unveiled. This single-seat, air-superiority fighter would be powered by two 32,000–35,000-lb. s.t. Pratt & Whitney YF119-PW-100 or General Electric YF120-GE-100 variable cycle turbofan engines. Featuring a trapezoidal wing with 40° leading edge sweep back and 40° trailing edge sweep forward, it had a span of 43 ft. 7 in. and a length of 67 ft. 5 in. with a loaded weight of 55,000 lb.

1990 July 2 Breathing new life into an aged airframe, a reengined BAC 111 fitted with two Rolls Royce Tay turbofan engines made its first flight at San Antonio, Tex. Converted by Dee Howard Co., the reengined Series 400 and Series 500 aircraft were to be redesignated Series 2400 and 2500 respectively. The company believed that 150 aircraft currently in operation could be reengined and that other refinements, including a glass cockpit, could give this regional airliner a new lease by bringing it fully up to date.

1990 July 12 The last of 59 Lockheed F-117A single-seat, low-altitude stealth interdictor aircraft was delivered to the USAF at Plant 10, Palmdale, Calif. Production had averaged eight annually since the first was delivered in 1982. Initial operational capability had been achieved in October 1983 with the 4450th Tactical Group, which in October 1989 had been redesignated the Thirty-seventh Tactical Fighter Wing. The existence of this unit was not officially recognized until November 1988.

1990 July 20 The U.S. Navy canceled the Lockheed P-7A maritime patrol aircraft program, a $600 million full-scale engineering rework of the P-3C Orion. The manufacturer was under contract to carry out a substantial rework and upgrade of the basic Orion aircraft but maintain 40% commonality with the original P-3C aircraft. The navy found to the contrary that the P-7A had only 5% commonality.

1990 August 2 Iraqi Air Force aircraft supported an unprovoked invasion of Kuwait by 140,000 men in a lightning attack

across the border. Kuwait City had been invaded within a few hours as Iraqi forces moved up to the border with Saudi Arabia posing a serious threat to that kingdom itself. Kuwait had about 50 combat aircraft at two airfields, the northernmost one of which, Ali Al-Salin, was hit by artillery fire that destroyed some aircraft, forcing remaining Mirage F-1Cs to escape to Bahrain and Saudi Arabia. The southern airfield of Ahmad Al-Jabir was evacuated, but F-4UKs operating from adjacent roads kept up attacks on Iraqi forces for two days before they too had to flee.

1990 August 8 The first U.S. combat aircraft ordered to defend Persian Gulf states against aggression from Iraq arrived in Saudi Arabia when F-15Cs of the First Tactical Fighter Wing touched down. In all, six squadrons of F-15C/D fighters were deployed along with five E03A Sentry AWACS aircraft, RC-135 tankers and ground forces of the Eighty-second Airborne Division's ready brigade. The U.S. Navy had the carriers USS *Eisenhower* in the Red Sea and USS *Independence* in the Persian Gulf with the USS *Saratoga* in the process of deploying. The British sent 12 Panavia Tornado F.Mk.3 fighters from Nos. 5 and 29 Squadrons along with tankers and support aircraft.

1990 August 17 The U.S. Civil Reserve Air Fleet (CRAF) Stage 1 was activated in support of the military build-up in the Persian Gulf, which involved more than 20 countries responding to UN resolutions calling on Iraq to withdraw its forces from Kuwait. CRAF Stage 1 gave authority for the U.S. Defense Department to call upon 45 civil aircraft placed under the authority of the commander, USAF Military Airlift Command. In fact, it called up 39 aircraft comprising 18 passenger aircraft and 21 cargo aircraft plus crews. In the biggest mobilization and logistics operation since World War II, a fourth carrier was dispatched to the Persian Gulf August 15 when the USS *John F. Kennedy* was directed from the Caribbean to the Middle East.

1990 August 20 The first 18 of a major deployment of Lockheed F-117A stealth attack aircraft of the 415th Tactical Fighter Squadron, Thirty-seventh Tactical Fighter Wing, USAF, departed Langley AFB, Va. for a 15-hr. nonstop flight to Saudi Arabia. Twenty-two F-117As had flown up from their Tonopah, Nev. base the previous day, two aircraft acting as spares. Refueled en route to the Middle East by KC-10A Extenders, the F-117As were positioned in Saudi Arabia in case they were needed to carry out attack missions against high-value targets in heavily defended areas. The Iraqi military was known to favor Soviet SAM deployment techniques.

1990 August 27 The Northrop/McDonnell Douglas YF-23A took to the air for the first time, the first of two advanced tactical fighter contenders to do so. Piloted by Paul Metz, it remained airborne for 50 min. and reached 25,000 ft. With a maximum speed of Mach 1.2 (915 MPH) at sea level and Mach 1.8 (1,190 MPH) above 36,000 ft., the YF-23A had a combat radius of up to 900 mi. carrying internal fuel and a full load of six air-to-surface missiles in two weapons bays. An important aspect of both this aircraft and the competing YF-22A was the absence of external stores to compromise stealth. The second prototype was flown for the first time on October 26.

1990 August 29 The prototype Lockheed YF-22A advanced tactical fighter contender was rolled out complete with two General Electric YF120-GE-100 variable-cycle turbofan engines uniquely incorporating thrust-vectoring nozzles for enhanced maneuverability. The aircraft had a wingspan of 43 ft., a length of 64 ft. 2 in. and a loaded weight of 55,000 lb. Two prototypes were to be built and flown for evaluation against the two Northrop/McDonnell Douglas YF-23As, and each pair would have one of the two optional powerplants.

1990 September 5 Rolls Royce signed a memorandum of understanding with the Soviet helicopter-maker Kamov for development of the Ka-62R with RTM 322 turboshaft engines. It was to be capable of carrying up to 14 passengers a distance of 372 mi. at 168 MPH. This was the export version of the Soviet civil helicopter, and the Ka-62 intended for domestic use would be used to gain certification. Rolls Royce expected five RTM 322 engines to be supplied during 1993 followed by the first flight of the Ka-62R by 1994.

1990 September 28 A memorandum of understanding between the United States, Spain and Italy was signed, clearing the way for integration of the Hughes APG-65 radar into the McDonnell Douglas AV-8B Harrier II Plus. The last 27 of 280 AV-8Bs would be completed to Harrier II Plus standard with the first flying in 1992. These aircraft would include night attack capability as well as wing refinements to improve performance and the 23,000-lb. s.t. Rolls Royce F402-RR-408 engine. Spain was expected to acquire 18 Harrier II Plus aircraft, and Italy wanted 16.

1990 September 29 The first prototype Lockheed/General Dynamics/Boeing YF-22A made its first flight. Piloted by test pilot Dave Ferguson, the aircraft reached a height of 12,500 ft. and a speed of 288 MPH during its 18-min. flight. Performance figures were similar to those projected for the competing Northrop/McDonnell Douglas YF-23A.

1990 October 10 The first of four Boeing E-3F AWACS aircraft was delivered to the French Air Force when it was flown from Seattle, Wash. to Le Bourget airport outside Paris. It was to receive final outfitting in France where UTA would install radar equipment, computers and general communications equipment. The fourth aircraft was scheduled to be delivered in November 1991, at which time the aircraft would be declared operational. Like the RAF AWACS, the E-3F carried a flight refueling probe as well as a receptacle enabling it to refuel from another tanker.

1990 October 11 The first of two Rockwell/MBB X-31A fighter maneuverability demonstrators made its first flight. Developed jointly between the United States and West Germany, the project was devised to provide a research tool for the enhanced fighter maneuverability program. The X-31A was powered by a 10,600/15,800-lb. s.t. General Electric F404-GE-400 turbofan engine, with a wingspan of 23 ft. 10 in., a length of 43 ft. 2 in. and canard surfaces. Maximum takeoff weight was 15,099 lb., and the X-31A had a maximum speed of 858 MPH with an initial climb rate of 43,000 ft./min.

1990 October 29 Full-scale development of the Boeing 777 was authorized by the board of directors 14 days after United Airlines announced it had placed orders for 34 with an option on a further 34. Designed to compete with the MD-11 and the A330, it would appear initially as a 360-to-390-seat airliner powered by two 70,000-lb. thrust class engines but with growth to 85,000-lb. thrust. Folding wingtips unique to this airliner would reduce parking span from 196 ft. 11 in. to 155 ft. 9 in. With a length of 209 ft. 1 in., the Boeing 777 would have a maximum takeoff weight of 506,000 lb.

1990 October 29 The first production Dassault-Breguet Rafale C single-seat interceptor and multi-role fighter was rolled out from the St. Cloud plant in France. It was dimensionally smaller than the prototype flown for the first time July 4, 1986, and had a wingspan of 35 ft. 9 in. and a length of 50 ft. 2 in. The single 30-mm DEFA gun was now mounted in the starboard forward fuselage, and a twin nose wheel had been adopted. Power was provided by two 10,950/16,400-lb. s.t. SNECMA M88-2 turbofan engines.

1990 November 15 The EH Industries EH 101 development aircraft PP5 carried out its first deck trials when it successfully completed three landing and takeoff cycles on the deck of HMS *Norfolk* as the frigate was engaged on work-up trials. The naval version of this helicopter would be powered by three 11,714-SHP General Electric T700-GE-401A turboshaft engines and serve in the antisubmarine warfare role carrying a wide range of antisubmarine warfare equipment and weapons.

1990 November 21 The NAMC PAC (Nanching Aircraft Manufacturing Co./Pakistan Aeronautical Complex) K-8 two-seat basic trainer and light ground attack aircraft made its first flight, powered by a 3,600-lb. s.t. Garrett TFE-731-2A-2A turbofan engine. Developed jointly by the Chinese and Pakistani air arms, it had a wingspan of 31 ft. 7 in. and a length of 38 ft. With a maximum speed of around 500 MPH and an initial climb rate of 5,905 ft./min., the K-8 had a range of 1,430 mi. Pakistan wanted the initial production models and expected to induct them into the air force during 1993. China was evaluating the type and would decide later on whether it wanted the aircraft in its inventory.

1990 December 31 Martin Baker ejection seats saved their 6,000th life when the four crewmembers of a Grumman EA-6B Prowler from Navy Squadron VAQ-141 were forced to eject during landing on the carrier USS *Theodore Roosevelt*. Immediately after touchdown the arrester wire broke, failing to completely stop the EA-6B, which was about to fall over the bows when the commander, Lt. John Meir, initiated a full crew ejection. As the last man to leave the aircraft, he became the 6,000th person to be saved. The four crewmembers were quickly picked up by an SH-3H Sea King of Navy helicopter squadron HS-9. Martin Baker had made 65,000 ejection seats for 85 air forces.

1991 January 7 U.S. Defense Secretary Richard B. Cheney cancelled the U.S. Navy A-12 stealth attack aircraft citing excess costs, program delays and development problems. A Defense Department cost audit showed that projected development costs of $4.8 billion would be exceeded by at least $2.7 billion and that prime contractors General Dynamics and McDonnell Douglas could give no assurance that this would not increase. The question of how to replace the A-12 in the medium attack role had yet to be decided, Grumman offering adapted variants of the F-14 and McDonnell Douglas the F/A-18.

1991 January 16 The U.S. Defense Department authorized CRAF Stage II activation, theoretically calling up a total of 188 commercial aircraft for USAF logistics supply requirements to the Persian Gulf in Operation Desert Shield. In fact, 59 passenger and 17 cargo aircraft were added to CRAF Stage I, which had been activated August 17, 1990, bringing to 115 the total number of commercial aircraft "drafted" into USAF Military Airlift Command. During the build-up, CRAF aircraft delivered 22% of all air cargo and 69% of air passengers to the theater of operations.

1991 January 17 Following an intensive 5-mon. build-up in Operation Desert Shield, coalition forces in the Middle East began a military offensive with the objective of expelling Iraqi forces

A key element in Operation Desert Storm, the McDonnell Douglas AH-64 Apache attack helicopter possesses stunning firepower and a high level of survivability, a vital mix in air-land warfare.

from Kuwait. Four phases were planned. The first three were to be executed almost simultaneously: strategic air campaign against the Iraqi war machine, communications centers, power supplies and transport networks; an intensive effort to gain complete air superiority over the Kuwait theater of operations (KTO) and concentrated air attacks on the Republican Guard and all ground forces in the KTO as well as reserves in southern Iraq. The fourth phase would be a massive air-land campaign spearheaded by a ground war.

1991 January 17 Operation Desert Storm began at approximately 3:00 A.M. local time with a strike by F-117A stealth attack aircraft on a hardened air defense operations center in southern Iraq and on targets in Baghdad. Army AH-64A Apaches attacked early-warning radar sites in southern Iraq, clearing the way for a wide range of coalition fighters and ground attack planes that began raids on Iraqi forces almost immediately. On the first day, more than 1,300 combat sorties were flown, of which 812 were conducted by fixed-wing aircraft. The U.S. Navy launched 106 Tomahawk cruise missiles. Air threats were light, the Iraqi Air Force choosing to remain on the ground.

1991 January 18 Eastern Air Lines collapsed and all flights were halted, ending almost 2 yr. of operating under bankruptcy court protection to keep its hopes of survival afloat. Eastern had 18,500 employees and a fleet that had declined from 250 aircraft in 1989 to just 170 aircraft that as of this date served 71 cities. Eastern owned only 90 of these 170 aircraft, the remainder being leased. In recent weeks, Eastern had been losing $2.5 million each day and had debts of $3.2 billion despite $600 million received from supporting financial institutions via the bankruptcy court since November 1989.

1991 January 19 The second of two Rockwell/MBB X-31A maneuverability demonstrator aircraft made its first flight after roll-out from Air Force Plant 42, Palmdale, Calif. In the cockpit for this initial flight was Messerschmitt-Bülkow-Blohm's chief test pilot Dietrich Seeck. The first X-31A, which had flown for the first time as recently as October 1990, would rejoin the test program February 14 following the attachment of thrust vectoring paddles.

1991 February 24 At 4:00 A.M. local time, a massive allied ground offensive against Iraqi forces in Kuwait and southern Iraq got under way in Operation Desert Storm. About 2,000 troops of the 101st Airborne Division were airlifted 50 mi. inside Iraq to a desert location code-named Cobra where 300 AH-64A Apache and AH-1G HueyCobras would operate, supported by 118 CH-47s and UH-60As. For four days, ground support from A-10s, F-16s, A-6s, F/A-18s and AV-8Bs was protected by electronic warfare aircraft, while B-52s and FB-111s pounded Iraqi troop concentrations and fire positions.

1991 February 28 After 100 hr. of ground war against the military forces of Saddam Hussein, U.S. Pres. George Bush ordered a complete halt to all allied military operations in southern Iraq. Since the air war began in January, the allied air forces had deployed 2,790 fixed-wing aircraft and flown a total of 109,876 sorties, of which about 60% were combat missions. About 50% of the numerical coalition force was contributed by the USAF, 27% by the other allied air forces, 16% by the U.S. Navy and 7% by the U.S. Marine Corps. Allied air forces dropped a total 88,500 tons of munitions of which 7,400 tons were precision-guided.

Total air losses during Operation Desert Storm included 68 aircraft, of which 56 had been U.S. (only 35 of which were combat related), seven had been RAF (six combat related), three Saudi Arabian, one Kuwaiti and one Italian. The Iraqi Air Force was assessed to have lost 240 aircraft, of which 42 had been lost in combat, 61 had been destroyed on the ground and 137 had fled to Iran. Loss rate for the 46 coalition aircraft destroyed in combat represented a 0.04% attrition rate.

When hostilities ceased over the liberation of Kuwait, the USAF had successfully demonstrated the capabilities of the world's first operational low-observables attack aircraft. Of 42 F-117As deployed to the Middle East in support of Operation Desert Storm, none had been lost. The F-117As flew approximately 2% of all 65,000 attack sorties mounted by coalition air forces. On 1,300 missions, it dropped more than 2,000 tons of bombs, struck 40% of the strategic target list and flew 6,900 hr. The F-117A was the only aircraft to operate over downtown Baghdad.

During the air war against Iraqi forces in occupation of Kuwait, beginning on the first day of the air war January 17, U.S. forces launched a total 288 BGM-109 Tomahawk cruise missiles, of which 264 were successful in reaching their objective. Missiles had been launched from U.S. Navy warships including a submarine in the Red Sea, but the success with this weapon strengthened arguments for its continued deployment with attack aircraft. Never had such a high concentration of cruise missiles been launched over such a short period of time.

At the end of hostilities against Iraqi forces in retreat from their recent occupation of Kuwait, the Royal Air Force completed offensive activities under Operation Granby. In the 6 wk. of the air offensive, the RAF had flown 4,000 combat and 2,500 support sorties and delivered 3,000 tons of ordnance. The total weapons load included 6,000 bombs dropped, of which 1,000 had been laser-guided and 100 had been loads of Hunting JP233 airfield denial weapons. Jaguars fired about 700 high-velocity rockets, but in the absence of any serious response from the Iraqi Air Force, no air-to-air weapons had been fired by the RAF.

When hostilities against Iraq by coalition forces ended, the military action by 22 countries came to a halt. Apart from the United States and the United Kingdom, France had provided a large force of carrier-borne helicopters as well as Mirage F.1CR-200s, Mirage 2000Cs, Jaguar As and a wide range of support aircraft. Argentina supplied transport aircraft and helicopters, Australia sent ship-based helicopters, Belgium provided two transport aircraft, Canada sent CF-18 Hornets and helicopters as well as communications and EW aircraft, Egypt stood by with F-16s and Mirage 2000s, Italy sent Tornado interceptors and Kuwait flew A-4s, Mirage F.1s and Hawks. The Saudi Arabian Air Force possessed five ground attack and three fighter squadrons.

1991 March 20 USAF McDonnell Douglas F-15s on patrol over Iraq attacked and shot down an Iraqi Air Force Su-22 Fitter over Tikrit. It was flying in violation of a ceasefire agreement signed by Iraq on March 3 that prohibited any military air activity by Iraq. The Su-22 was one of two thought to have been sent to attack Kurdish rebels and had been detected by a Boeing E-3 Sentry AWACS aircraft. The second SU-22 evaded the F-15s and quickly landed. The ceasefire agreement failed to prohibit helicopter flying so Iraq could move supplies and medical aid. Exploiting this loophole, Saddam Hussein ordered gunships to attack rebel groups.

1991 March 20 Successfully evading U.S. radar alert networks looking south from Florida, Cuban Air Force pilot Maj. Orestes Lorenzo Perez landed at Key West NAS claiming political asylum. Flying a MiG-23 Flogger, the 38-year-old pilot managed to successfully avoid detection until an air traffic controller spotted the aircraft circling the airfield. He had ostensibly taken off from his air base in Cuba on a training flight and quickly switched to a 90-mi. dash for freedom.

1991 April 1 That solid edifice of British aeronautical research and development—the Royal Aerospace Establishment—ceased to exist when the Defense Research Agency came into being. Absorbing the old (it was founded in 1912) and familiar RAE, Farnborough name into a new organization also embracing other naval and military research establishments, the DRA was set up by the U.K. government in attempts to streamline and integrate British defense-related research and development activity into a single, cost-effective entity.

1991 April 5 After 2 yr. of evaluation, the U.S. Army selected a helicopter design submitted jointly by Boeing Helicopters and Sikorsky, known as First Team, for its light helicopter (LH) requirement. The First Team all-composite design incorporated a tandem two-seat cockpit, five-blade main rotor, and T-tail with shrouded tail rotor. With fly-by-wire fiber-optic controls and internal weapons bays for up to eight Hellfire and four Stinger, four Hellfire and two Stinger, or two Hellfire and eight Stinger missiles, it would also carry a ventral turret-mounted triple-barrel 20-mm Gatling gun. Named RAH-66 Comanche, the army wanted 1,292 LHs, but orders could reach almost 1,700.

1991 April 8 An agreement was reached whereby de Havilland Canada would be sold to Aérospatiale of France and Alenia of Italy. The owners of DHC, Boeing, had been unable to put the company in profit, and the European consortium wanted de Havilland Canada to take more international contracting work. It would continue to manufacure the Dash 8 but would also tool up for work on major subsystems for Boeing and Airbus Industrie as well as several other major aircraft companies.

1991 April 12 The Iraqi foreign minister, Ahmad Hussein Khuddayer Al-Sammaraei, claimed Iraq had 148 aircraft in Iran and wanted them all back. These planes included 115 Iraqi Air Force combat aircraft and 33 airliners. Iran claimed to have only 22 Iraqi aircraft and said they believed the coalition forces must have shot the rest down before they reached Iran. Iran said it would send back the aircraft that defected only if requested formally through the United Nations. However, a systematic process

On April 23, 1991, the USAF selected the YF-22 as the design base from which its F-15 replacement would be built by a team led by Lockheed.

of repainting was underway to give the impounded aircraft Iranian markings.

1991 April 23 The USAF announced selection of the Lockheed/General Dynamics/Boeing YF-22A, powered by the Pratt & Whitney F119 turbofan, as its advanced tactical fighter. After a demonstration and validation fly-off against the YF-23A, the YF-22A had been selected as much for the strength of the management team as for the technical superiority of the design. The engineering development and manufacturing phase would be worth around $11 billion and run from contract award in mid-year through 1999. Nine prototypes, two two-seaters and two ground-test structures would be built, with the first flying in 1995 and the first of 750 production aircraft completed in 2001.

1991 April 27 The prototype Eurocopter Tiger antitank and ground support helicopter flew for the first time at Marignane, France. Formerly known as the CATH, this multi-role helicopter was one of five development prototypes powered by two 1,285-SHP MTU/Rolls Royce/Turboméca MTR 390 turboshaft engines driving a 42 ft. 8 in. rotor. With a length of 45 ft. 11 in. and a maximum weight of 13,227 lb., the Tiger had a maximum cruising speed of 174 MPH and an endurance of almost 3 hr. Orders from France and Germany were now expected to total 427.

1991 April 30 In an unprecedented assault by nature, 50% of the Bangladesh Air Force, about 30 aircraft including almost its entire fighter force, was destroyed by a 20-ft. tidal wave and 140 MPH winds that swept across Chittagong-Patenga Air Base. Despite advance warnings, the aircraft had not been moved from their vulnerable location. Damage was caused not only by the wind and water. A cargo ship had been carried from the sea to the middle of the airfield, wreaking havoc as it was dragged across the runways. Very few aircraft and helicopters were left to help with the relief operation.

1991 May 17 In line with announced cut-backs in U.S. defense spending, the USAF announced closure of its facilities at Bentwaters and Woodbridge in East Anglia, England by September 1993. These bases, officially RAF stations, would revert to U.K. government use. The 72 A-10A attack aircraft would return to the United States, as would A-10As and TR-1As at Alconbury. The Twenty-first and Sixty-seventh Special Operations squadrons currently at Woodbridge would move to Alconbury. In 1990, the USAF had announced the withdrawal of 66 F-111Es and 12 EF-111Es from Upper Heyford, England and 72 F-111Fs from Lakenheath. Thus, by 1994, the numerical strength of USAF aircraft in the United Kingdom would fall by more than 200, leaving only 48 F-15Es at Lakenheath.

1991 May 17   The last piloted Convair F-106B was retired after 32 yr. of continuous flying. Released by the USAF in February 1970, it had operated at the NASA Langley Research Center since 1976 on development work, and then the aircraft moved to the Dryden Flight Research Center before it was transferred back to Langley in January 1979. While at Langley, it carried out scientific meteorological work and research on vortex flap flow.

1991 May 19   The first Dassault-Breguet Rafale C01 made its first flight at Istres, France and exceeded Mach 1 and reached 36,000 ft. on its first flight. For this flight, the aircraft had a takeoff weight of 27,550 lb. and a roll before takeoff of 1,300 ft. accelerating to Mach 1.2 without afterburner. As designed, the agile fighter had a maximum speed of Mach 2 (1,320 MPH) above 36,000 ft. and a tactical radius of 679 mi. with combined underwing tanks and warload of a maximum 17,639 lb.

1991 May 24   For the first time in the history of aviation, more than 1,000 people were lifted into the air at the same time by the same aircraft. In an airlift dubbed Operation Solomon, an El Al Boeing 747-200C Combi, converted to passenger standard with very high-density seating for 760, squeezed 1,200 people on board for a flight from Addis Ababa to Israel. The aircraft had been modified to accommodate as many people as possible and support the evacuation of 14,000 Ethiopian Jews from Addis Ababa. Pressed into service, Boeing 707s carried 500 people, Boeing 747s configured for 454 passengers flew out with 920 on board, Boeing 767s carried 430 and Boeing 757s up to 360.

1991 May 26   The first Boeing 767 to crash came down 150 mi. northwest of Bangkok's Don Muang International Airport, Thailand, killing all 213 passengers and 10 crewmembers on board. The Boeing 767-300ER of Lauda Air was on a flight from Bangkok to Vienna when it went down in hilly country at 11:18 P.M. local time. Rescuers reported they could not find any piece of the aircraft greater than 6 ft. in size. The flight originated in Hong Kong with 125 people on board, 88 joining the flight at Bangkok. A terrorist bomb was suspected of causing an explosion that caused the crash.

1991 May   When the last Boeing E-3D AWACS aircraft rolled out at the assembly plant at Renton, Wash., it was destined to be the last 707 airframe built. Despite efforts to keep the line open with an attempt to get additional E-3 orders, the line closed at the end of August after 1,011 airframes had been assembled. Of this total, 878 were for commercial customers; these included 154 Boeing 720 aircraft, a derivative of the 707. There were still 422 commercial 707s in use around the world.

1991 June 13   The Learjet 60, most powerful of the family to date made its first flight, powered by two 4,400-lb. s.t. Pratt & Whitney Canada PW305 turbofan engines. Accommodating up to nine passengers, the Learjet 60 had a wingspan across upswept winglets of 43 ft. 9 in., a length of 58 ft. 8 in. and a maximum

weight of 22,750 lb. Based on the Model 55C, the Model 60 had a longer fuselage and better appointments together with more efficient engines. It had a 51,000 ft. ceiling and a range of up to 3,100 mi.

1991 June 26   Built by Westinghouse Airships at Weeksville, N.C., the 220-ft.-long Sentinel 1000 airship took to the air in free flight for the first time with Carl Daley and Scott Danneker at the controls. With a volume 354,000 cu. ft. and power provided by two modified Porsche engines in gimballed housings, the airship was being marketed as an early-warning, maritime patrol airship capable of serving drug enforcement agencies in silent, nighttime surveillance. Westinghouse had been teamed with Airship Industries in the United Kingdom but acquired all the British rights when that company went into liquidation.

1991 July 1   The long-serving Avro Shackleton was finally retired from RAF service when the AEW.2 based at Lossiemouth was formally stood down at a ceremony held at RAF Waddington to induct the Boeing E-3D Sentry as Britain's new airborne early-warning shield. The Shackleton had served the RAF for more than 40 yr. As a derivative of the Lancaster and its predecessor the Manchester, its retirement closed a chapter in RAF history during which a common design had served king, queen and country for almost 51 yr.

1991 July 5   Airbus Industrie announced orders for 75 A300-600F freighters for Federal Express with 25 firm orders, 25 confirmed but subject to cancellation and 25 on option. This was one of the largest orders ever placed for a commercial aircraft. All would be powered by the General Electric CF6-80C2 engine for delivery beginning in 1994. Federal Express would use them to replace Boeing 727s on domestic services, but they would also be used on international flights. If taken up, the 75 A300s for Federal Express would make it the biggest operator of the aircraft and raise to 699 the number of firm orders accepted by Airbus Industrie.

1991 July 9   The U.K. defense white paper outlining the government's future defense plans indicated reduction in the RAF's personnel strength from 89,000 to 75,000 by the mid-1990s and a reduction from 18,000 to 16,000 in civilian support staff. Some aircraft procurement decisions made in former years would be rescinded, notably the purchase of 34 Tornados, although Harrier conversions to a GR.Mk.7 configuration would continue. A decision on the strategic nuclear stand-off missile for the RAF was deferred until after the next general election.

1991 July 10   In being since 1925, the Royal Observer Corps was disbanded in a cost-saving move by the British government. Formed to provide an early warning of air attack through the use of volunteers trained to observe and report suspicious air movements, it received "Royal" status in 1941 when it had contributed so much to the detection of incoming enemy aircraft during the Battle of Britain. From 1955 it had been responsible for detecting nuclear fallout patterns in the event of a nuclear war involving the United Kingdom. The Royal Observer Corps had 9,000 volunteers and a paid staff of 170 civil servants.

1991 July 15   A specially modified F/A-18 high-angle of attack research vehicle (HARV) was flown by a NASA test pilot for the first time at the Dryden Flight Research Center. Equipped with thrust-vectoring nozzles and a closed-loop controlled, three-axis command system, the unique aircraft would be flown on takeoff and landing like a normal aircraft, only switching to use of the vectoring guide vanes when at 15,000–35,000 ft. and speeds below Mach 0.7. NASA developed the system as a low-cost approach to research on fast-jet thrust vectoring.

1991 August 3 The USAF awarded contracts for the engineering and manufacturing phase of the F-22 program, awarding $9.6 billion to the Lockheed/General Dynamics/Boeing team for airframe development and $1.4 billion to Pratt & Whitney for development and manufacture of the 33 F119-PW-100 engines. The first prototype was to serve as a full-scale engineering mock-up, leaving the second prototype to continue flight tests at Edwards AFB, Calif.

1991 August 12 Fending off bids from Trans World Airlines, Delta Air Lines successfully shored up nonprofitable Pan American World Airways by agreeing before bankruptcy court judge Cornelius Blackshear to inject $455 million and focus Pan Am's services in Latin America. The 64-year-old airline had been floundering for several years and currently operated under Chapter 11 protection from bankruptcy. TWA chairman Carl C. Icahn had said he wanted to buy Pan American for $1.3 billion and United bid $465 million against Delta's initial offer of $310 million.

1991 August 12 The F-15 STOL and maneuver technology demonstrator program ended after 3 yr. of tests at Edwards AFB, Calif., successfully validating the concept it had been set up to probe. It showed that a modern combat aircraft with modifications could operate into a 1,500-ft. × 50-ft. runway strip at night, without lights, through a 200-ft. cloud deck and a strong crosswind and stop with full thrust reversal. In 140 flights accumulating 179 hr. of tests, the modified F-15 explored two-dimensional thrust-vectoring and thrust-reverser capabilities.

1991 August 28 The U.S. Naval Air Systems Command issued a formal request for concept formulation and definition studies on the AX medium attack A-6 replacement. Strike missions and antisurface warfare were expressly stipulated as priority with air-to-air combat second and stealth capability an essential aspect of the competing designs. The navy expected to finance up to five separate studies at $20 million each and wanted the concept proposals in by October 29. Procurement plans envisaged 575 aircraft, with the first delivered in 2005.

1991 September 15 The first McDonnell Douglas C-17 heavy lift transport aircraft made its first flight, powered by four 41,700-lb. s.t. Pratt & Whitney F117-PW-100 turbofan engines. With a wingspan of 165 ft. and a length of 74 ft., it had a maximum takeoff weight of 580,000 lb., a maximum payload of 110,000 lb. or provision for up to 102 equipped troops. Offering short-field performance and a range of up to 3,225 mi., the C-17A had a cruising speed of 508 MPH. The USAF wanted 120 C-17s with the first in service during 1993.

1991 September 30 On the last day of FY 1991, the USAF concluded its safest year of flying since its formation 44 yr. previously. In 3.69 million flying hr., the USAF averaged an accident rate of 1.11 per 100,000 hr. compared to a next best of 1.49 the previous year and a running average of 1.64 over the preceding decade. Deaths from noncombat flying were 18, compared to 43 the previous year, and an annual average of 64 over the preceding decade. The number of aircraft destroyed in noncombat operations also fell to 38 from a previous low of 48 3 yr. earlier against an annual average of 54 over the last 10 yr.

1991 September 30 The U.K. Ministry of Defense signed a memorandum of understanding with the Italian Defense Ministry

covering production of the EH 101 helicopter, which was to take place at the Agusta facility in Italy and at the Westland plant at Yeovil, England. This came exactly 4 wk. after the Royal Navy signed an order for 44 helicopters of this type. The memorandum also allowed the respective manufacturers to market the helicopter commercially. A potential market for 750 EH 101s existed in naval, utility and civil applications.

1991 September Plans were developed at the Pentagon for substantial restructuring of the USAF. Strategic Air Command and Tactical Air Command were to be abolished and replaced by a single Air Combat Command, which would also assume responsibility for some tankers and transport aircraft previously operated by Military Airlift Command. A new Air Mobility Command would replace Military Airlift Command in the global support role and also operate some tankers previously operated by SAC. The restructuring would take effect from January 1, 1992.

1991 October 14 The U.K. Ministry of Defense announced cuts in low-altitude flying over Britain. The RAF had agreed, it said, to reduce by 30% over 3 yr. the amount of low-altitude flying carried out by fast jets. It pointed out that with the substantial reduction in the number of U.S. aircraft stationed in the United Kingdom that number would drop naturally. However, responding to pressure from public opinion and from a reassessment of what constitutes proper training, the numbers would be further reduced as change of policy.

1991 October 25 The first Airbus Industrie A340 made its first flight from Toulouse just 3 wk. after it had been publicly unveiled at the plant. The aircraft was taken on its 3 hr. 40 min. maiden flight by test pilot Pierre Baud, who reported that it was uneventful and that the aircraft handled as well as an A320. This was the first four-engined airliner built by Airbus Industrie. There were to be six prototype aircraft that would carry out a flight-test program involving 2,000 flying hr. by the end of 1992. The first A340 into service was scheduled for Lufthansa in January 1993.

1991 October 29 The deadline for submissions in the U.S. Navy AX request for proposals on an attack aircraft in lieu of the cancelled A-12 arrived. Only six days earlier, Northrop joined the General Dynamics/McDonnell Douglas team with a proposal heavily biased by earlier work on the A-12. Other submissions involved a completely new design from a McDonnell Douglas/LTV team, a Grumman/Boeing/Lockheed proposal also proposing a new aircraft and Lockheed/General Dynamics/Boeing with a derivative of the F-22. The U.S. Navy wanted 400 to 500 AX aircraft to replace A-6s.

1991 October 31 U.S. Geological Survey geophones and sensors in California picked up unusually loud sonic booms calculated to have been caused by aircraft flying at Mach 3 and a height of between 23,000 ft. and 33,000 ft. Indicative of flight paths trending south to north, two booms 1 min. 40 sec. apart clearly resulted from two separate aircraft and were probably caused by highly classified hypersonic aircraft operating from facilities in the Nevada desert.

1991 November 1 Delta Air Lines took over the Pacific and Silk Route services from an ailing Pan American World Airways, taking on 6,600 former Pan American employees to raise Delta's total personnel strength to 73,000, 8,800 of whom were pilots. Delta absorbed 52 surplus Pan American aircraft and expanded its inventory to 527 aircraft. It added 60 flight listings to provide 2,690 daily operations, trans-Atlantic services expanding from 92 to 195 round-trips each week. Delta expanded overnight from serving cities in 34 countries to cities in 57 countries.

1991 November 8 Aurora Flight Services supported NASA test engineers and technicians for the first flight of the Perseus high-altitude unmanned drone. Aurora had been contracted by NASA to design and build a sailplane-like aircraft capable of operating at 85,000 ft. using liquid oxygen to drive a rotary engine. The prototype made its flight near Edwards AFB, Calif. The full size vehicle would have a wingspan of 59 ft. and weigh 1,300 lb. NASA expected Aurora to have a flight-ready vehicle by mid-1993.

1991 November 14 Test engineers on the Rockwell/MBB X31A program cleared the aircraft for 40° angle-of-attack trials, which were completed a week later. This represented the first post-stall flight achieved in the program and represented an important milestone for the aircraft, which was expected to fly at the full 70° angle of attack imminently. The #2 aircraft had been flown on the 40°-flight by Rockwell test pilot Fred Knox.

1991 November 19 The new Aérospatiale As 365X Dauphin high-speed helicopter prototype broke the world speed record at 230 MPH (371 km/hr.). Flown by Guy Dabadie, chief test pilot, Bernard Fouques, test flight engineer, and Michael Sudre, flight engineer, it captured the FAI weight record by carrying a load between 3 metric tons (6,615 lb.) and 3.5 metric tons (9,922 lb.) over a 3-km (1.86-mi.) course. The AS 365 had first flown on March 31, 1979, powered by two 733-SHP Turboméca Arriel 1C2 turboshaft engines.

1991 November 20 In a tragic sign of the deteriorating political situation in the Soviet Union, a Mil Mi-8 helicopter belonging to the Union of Sovereign States unsuccessfully proposed by Mikhail Gorbachev was shot down by surface-to-air missile in Azerbaijan, causing it to crash with the loss of all 23 people on board.

The helicopter had been carrying senior government officials from Moscow to this troubled hot-spot when it was attacked by local rebel groups.

1991 November 22 In Vienna, a historic conference to clear the way for unrestricted overflight of Soviet airspace ended with a commitment to complete an "open skies" treaty in March 1992. Negotiations had been going on since 1989, and the proposed treaty was to be signed by all NATO countries. It had been monitored by former Warsaw Pact members and agreed to by them as well as by the recently independent former Soviet states. Under the treaty, unrestricted overflights would be carried out for purposes of arms verification.

1991 December 4 Pan American World Airways ceased operating and informed all its crews at 9:00 A.M. to continue scheduled services back to John F. Kennedy International Airport or Miami International Airport. Protected under Chapter 11, Delta Air Lines had extended a $140 million credit line to Pan American, but the airline had already spent $115 million and was losing money at the rate of $3 million per day. When asked by bankruptcy court judge Cornelius Blackshear how long Pan American could survive without money from Delta, experts were unanimous in declaring "35 minutes!"

1991 December 22 The first fixed-wing aircraft carrier built by the Soviet Union arrived at Severomorsk, the home port of the Northern Fleet, where it was to be based. Named *Admiral Nikolay Kuznetsov,* the carrier was required to leave the Black Sea port of Sevastapol so as not to cause contention with claims by the Ukraine that, as it had declared independence from the Union of Sovereign States, it would "own" all military equipment on its territory. The second aircraft carrier in this class was expected to begin sea trials in 1992. A larger, nuclear-powered carrier under construction would go to sea in 1996, provided its original construction schedule was maintained.

GLOSSARY

aerofoil/airfoil a body, such as a wing or a propeller, designed to provide a reactive force when placed in a flow of air

aerofoil shape the shape of a lifting surface, such as a wing, attached to an airplane

aileron the movable part of an airplane wing hinged so that it can be made to move up or down, controlling the airplane's rolling motion

airframe the structure of an airplane, generally without the power plant installed

airspeed the speed of a body moving through air in relation to the speed of the air

all-up weight the weight of a fully loaded airplane

altitude the height of an object above a reference point, e.g., the ground below or the sea; where unqualified, it refers to height above sea level

amphibious an airplane capable of landing or taking off from water or land

angle of attack the angle between the direction of the flow of air and the chord of a wing

anhedral the downward inclination of an airplane wing in relation to the lateral axis

area rule method of design for obtaining minimum drag by maintaining a constant cross-sectional area at the wing-fuselage juncture, obtained by reducing the diameter of the fuselage invariably creating a coke-bottle shape

aspect ratio the ratio of the span of a wing to its mean chord; low-aspect ratio indicates that, relative to its span, the chord is greater than it would be for a high-aspect ratio wing

autogyro a self-propelled aircraft deriving lift from unpowered, rotating blades

balcony a toroidal structure attached to the lower part of a balloon where crew and passengers can walk

ballonet a gas compartment in a balloon or dirigible used to control buoyancy (from the French *ballonnet,* or little balloon).

balloon a large, impermeable bag designed to contain a gas lighter than air, enabling it to rise; may have a basket, gondola or balcony for passengers

barnstorm to fly airplanes in stunt shows held periodically in different locations

barrage balloon a number of balloons tethered to the ground by wires to deter low-flying enemy aircraft

bay a pair of contiguous struts and attendant rigging attached between the wings of a biplane in the axis of the chord

biplane an airplane with two wings placed one above the other

blown wing an airplane wing designed to augment lift with supplementary air blown across the upper surface by compressors attached to the engines

bombsight a mechanical or electrical sighting device for bomb aiming

boundary layer the layer of air closest to the surface of the airplane over which it flows, having a lower rate of flow than the bulk of the air because of its adhesion to the solid surface

buddy-fly the refueling of one airplane by another in such manner so as to directly feed the engines of the airplane being supplied with fuel

camber the curvature of a wing or lifting surface from the leading edge to the trailing edge

canard originally, an airplane designed to carry the tailplane forward of the wing or wings, but more recently used to refer to any aircraft with a separate airfoil surface for lift or control forward of the wing or wings

canopy the partial or complete transparent covering over the pilot or crew positions of an airplane

cant the inclination from true vertical or horizontal

car (airship) the cabin or gondola designed to carry crew or passengers and usually suspended beneath the envelope

chain drive the use of a chain to transfer motion from one wheel to another

chord a straight line connecting two points on a curved surface; when applied to aircraft, the distance between the leading and the trailing edge surfaces of a wing

clockwork motor a purely mechanical motor operating through the released energy of a coiled spring

coal gas a mixture of gases produced by the distillation of bituminous coal and used in some balloons

composite wing a wing fabricated from composite materials, which are produced from artificial materials usually combined in a matrix for added strength with light weight

compressed-air motor a motor operated by the pressure of air raised above sea-level pressure by a compressor

conformal fuel tank an airplane's external fuel tank shaped so as to fit flush with the underside of the airframe and thus achieve minimum aerodynamic drag

contra-rotating propellers two sets of contiguously mounted propellers each revolving in an opposite direction to the adjacent set, thereby canceling out torque

dash speed generally referred to as the speed of a high performance jet when operating its engines at full power for maximum, but not fuel-efficient, speed

de-rate reduce the potential power of an engine to a lower value for some gain, either in reliability or fuel saving

dihedral   the upward inclination of an airplane wing in relation to the lateral axis

dirigible   a rigid airship; that is, an airship with a rigid frame within which are contained rigid or nonrigid gas bags

drag ropes   ropes that are suspended from a balloon or airship so as to trail along the ground and slow its speed

dual monoplane   a monoplane with two sets of wings arranged in approximately the same axis

elevator   the horizontal control surface on an airplane used to control pitch (up and down) motion and usually attached to the tailplane

envelope   the gas bag attached to the interior structure of a dirigible and containing the lighter-than-air gas for lift; the gas bag of a balloon

escadrille   a French squadron of military airplanes

flap   a movable surface attached to the trailing edge of an airplane wing generating additional lift for takeoff and drag for landing

flat-six engine   a 6-cylinder engine arranged with three cylinders in two horizontally opposed banks driving a common crankshaft

flight angle   the angle of an airplane's flight path with respect to a horizontal axis

flight refueling boom   a rigid boom attached to the rear fuselage of a tanker airplane with a connector for locking onto a flight fueling receptacle of another airplane in flight, enabling fuel to be transferred from the tanker

flight refueling drogue   a mechanical device usually attached to a rigid pole or flexible hose trailed from the rear of an airplane in flight to which a second airplane can attach itself and receive fuel via the connection while flying in formation

flight refueling probe   a protruding, sometimes retractable, rigid boom attached to the nose or side fuselage of an airplane for mating to the drogue trailed on a hose by a tanker airplane

flight refueling receptacle   an opening, usually covered by a flap or door, into which a flight refueling boom from a tanker airplane can be inserted for the transfer of fuel

floatplane   an airplane designed for operation from water with a conventional fuselage to which is attached a float shaped like the underside of a boat

fly-by-wire   refers to the control system of an airplane designed to operate by computer or pilot-induced commands via electrical wires rather than mechanical linkages

foreplane   a lifting or control surface attached to the forward fuselage; interchangeable with "canard"

forward elevator   an elevator attached to a foreplane

forward-swept wing   the wing of an airplane designed so that the tip is forward of the root attachment point to the fuselage, a configuration that delays the onset of wingtip stall

gas jet reaction control   gas produced from nonthermal chemical action, released under pressure as a jet through a small orifice to generate reactive forces in rarefied air; used where there is insufficient air for the proper working of aerodynamic flight controls

glider   an airplane capable of gliding or soaring in air currents without the use of an engine, although an engine may be carried

gondola   a car or cabin suspended from a balloon or dirigible

gross takeoff weight   the maximum permitted take-off weight, also referred to as gross weight

ground attack   an airplane carrying out low altitude attack with bombs, rockets or machine guns, usually in support of ground forces

heavier-than-air flying machine   a flying machine that does not depend on buoyancy for support but gains lift from aerodynamic forces

helicopter   an aircraft capable of vertical flight that derives its lift not from wings but from rotating overhead blades

high-bypass ratio engine   also known as a turbofan engine, a type of reaction engine where a low compressor fan driven by a turbine and housed in a short duct forces air rearward where it mixes with exhaust gases to increase thrust

hi-hi-hi   (also hi-lo-hi and lo-lo-lo) where hi indicates high altitude and lo indicates low altitude; the three separate phases of the flight profile of a military airplane en route to its target: approach phase, target, return phase (e.g., hi-lo-hi indicates the airplane flight to and from the target at high altitude but descent to a low altitude for the attack)

hull   when used in connection with Zeppelin dirigibles, the outer rigid structure formed from light-alloy girders

hush-kit   special equipment attached to an airplane and its engines to reduce noise

hydraulics   control surfaces and moving parts on an airplane and/or its engines operated by pressure transmitted through a pipe by a liquid such as oil

hydrogen   a flammable, colorless gas, the lightest and most abundant element with an atomic weight of 1.007 and a density of 0.0899 kg/cubic meter; used in balloons and airships

incidence   the angle between the line of the wing chord and the longitudinal axis of the fuselage

inherent stability   an airplane designed to maintain a normal straight and level position in the air when the flying controls are set at neutral

in-line engine   a multi-cylinder internal combustion engine in which the cylinders are placed in a vertical position one behind the other forming a straight row

interdiction   the act of using a fighter airplane to gain control of the skies over a given territory

interdictor   a fighter airplane used to seek and destroy enemy aircraft from a given area

jet   an airplane powered by a reaction engine obtaining its oxidizer from the ambient atmosphere

jump jet   common parlance for a vertical takeoff airplane

lifting-body   a blended wing-body structure designed so that at least 50% of the lift derives from the design of the fuselage underbody as the wings

loiter   the action of a military airplane remaining airborne in a designated area for some specified purpose such as surveillance or observation

Mach speed   the ratio or the speed of an airplane in air relative to the speed of sound in the same medium at the same pressure and temperature

mainplane   the wing or main lifting surface of an airplane, as against the tailplane or subsidiary lifting surface

mast-mounted sight   an optical device mounted to a mast on top of a helicopter rotor hub

monoplane   an airplane with only one pair of wings

oblique wing   a straight wing pivoted at an angle to an airplane's fuselage

parasol monoplane   a monoplane with its wing attached to a set of struts above the fuselage in the manner of a parasol, or umbrella

payload capacity/capability   the calculated, maximum weight carrying capacity of a fully fueled airplane

pitch   movement of an airplane in the longitudinal axis around the lateral axis

pitot   a small tube attached to the exterior surface of an airplane and connected to a nanometer for measuring the total pressure of incoming air and thereby the velocity of the airplane

plane   an aerofoil or lifting surface of an airplane

planform   the shape of an airplane when viewed from above

probe and drogue refueling   *see* flight refueling entries

propfan engine   a turbofan engine incorporating a set of broad-bladed propellers attached to the rear of the engine casing and driven by a shaft from the turbine

pusher biplane   a biplane powered by an engine and propeller assembly mounted in the rear of the fuselage

pusher propeller   the propeller of a pusher engine moving air in a similar manner to the way the screw mounted in the stern of the ship moves it forward through water

radome   the aerodynamic and weather protection shroud covering radar equipment and the dish antenna

ramjet   a type of jet engine in which fuel is burned in a duct using air compressed by the forward speed of the aircraft

reaction motor   similar to a jet engine in principle but one that carries its own oxidizer and fuel for combustion in a rocket motor

reaction-powered   powered by a reaction, or rocket, motor

reengine   the process of removing the engine of an airplane and replacing it with a more efficient type

Reynolds number   nondimensional parameter representing the ratio of the momentum forces to the viscous forces in the fluid flow

rollout   the distance taken by an aircraft to stop following touchdown

rotary-winged   a classification denoting heavier-than-air craft that obtain their lift from rotors, versus fixed wings

rotation   the act of pulling the nose wheel of an airplane off the ground immediately prior to achieving independent flight

run-on landing   a method of landing a helicopter so that it approaches the landing point at a steep rate of descent inclined somewhat to the vertical and dumps energy by rolling to a stop like a fixed-wing airplane

scout helicopter   generally used to refer to helicopters employed for military scouting duties

scramjet   a supersonic ramjet that obtains thrust from the ingestion of supersonic air through a duct in the nose, enabling the combustion of fuel

seaplane   an airplane designed to operate from water, the lower fuselage shaped like the bottom of a boat and incorporating one or two steps cut into the underside

sesquiplane   a biplane on which the surface area of the lower wing is less than 50% the surface area of the upper wing

side-curtain   fabric covering two contiguous interplane struts, defined as a "bay," between the wings of a biplane

side slip   the action of an airplane dropping one wing (or pair of wings, if a biplane) and slipping sideways due to loss of lift

sortie   usually applied to a preplanned operational mission carried out by a military aircraft

span   the total width of an airplane wing from one tip to the other

sponson   a float attached to the underside of a floatplane, seaplane or flying-boat wing; usually near the tip, to prevent it touching the water

sprung undercarriage   the landing gear of an airplane designed to attenuate the undulations of the ground by incorporating springs in the vertical or horizontal struts

stabilizer   an American term for the horizontal tailplane stores point

static test   the test of an engine strapped to a fixture instrumented to determine its operating performance

stores point   an attachment point on the underside of an airplane wing or fuselage to which external equipment, such as fuel tanks, bombs, rockets or gun pods, can be attached

structural limit   a defined level of imposed stress beyond which an airframe or part of an airplane would structurally fail

supercritical wing   a technique for shaping airfoil (wing) designs to raise the drag-divergence mach number as close as possible to the speed of sound, reducing drag by discouraging the formation of shock-waves and greatly improving the performance of the airfoil in the process

swept wing   a wing attached to a fuselage so that leading and trailing edges incline back toward the tail by a designed amount

tail plane   the horizontal tail assembly of an airplane providing longitudinal stability; referred to as a stabilizer in the United States

tandem wing design   two sets of biplane wings, both sets attached to the fuselage at different locations, one set ahead of the other

thickness ratio   the ratio of the thickness of a wing to the chord, usually referenced to a particular point along the wing but if not stated usually the maximum thickness of the wing

tilt rotor   rotors mounted to the drive shaft in such a way that they can be moved from vertical to horizontal drive by moving them through a maximum 90°

tractor engine   an engine driving a propeller assembly mounted forward of the cylinders and usually attached to the nose of the fuselage or forward section of the wings

tricycle undercarriage   an airplane landing gear arranged with wheels under the wings or fuselage and a third wheel under the nose

triplane   an airplane with three wings stacked vertically one above the other

turbofan   *see* high-bypass ratio engine

turboprop   an engine utilizing hot gases to drive a turbine connected to a shaft and a propeller rather than using the gases for maximum thrust as in a jet engine

turboshaft   *see* turboprop

undercarriage   the landing gear of an airplane designed to operate from land

unducted fan a fan engine that does not incorporate a duct through which air is channeled to compressors

variable geometry an airplane wing pivoted at its attachment point to the fuselage so that the degree of wing sweep-back can be changed in flight, thus varying the geometry of the wing to optimize it for different flying conditions

wallowing successive waves of pitch motion around the lateral axis

wet tail an airplane's tail designed so as to contain fuel as a supplement to main fuel tanks in the wings and fuselage; generally used in airliners as a means of extending range

wing box a structural element in the wing designed to transmit torsional, compression and tension loads

wing end plates vertical plates attached to wingtips and set at approximate right-angles to the mean wing dihedral

wing loading the relative gross weight of an airplane per unit area (square feet or square meter) of the wing

wingroot the structural interface between the wing and the fuselage

wing warping a method of aerodynamic control whereby the wings are twisted around the longitudinal axis to effect roll control, performing the function of ailerons; exclusive to early aircraft

yaw the action of an airplane turning about its vertical axis, said to yaw from side to side

Zeppelin a rigid airship designed and built by Count von Zeppelin or the company he operated

ABBREVIATIONS

AAA   antiaircraft artillery

AABNC   advanced airborne national command post

AAC   Army Air Corps

AAFSS   advanced aerial fire support system

AAM   air-to-air missile

AB   air base

ACA   agile combat aircraft

ACCS   airborne command and control

ACF   air combat fighter

ACM   air chief marshal

ACTA   advanced cargo tanker aircraft

ACX   advanced combat experimental

Adm.   admiral

ADV   air defense version

AEW   airborne early-warning

AFB   air force base

AFTI   advanced fighter technology integration

AFVG   Anglo-French variable-geometry (fighter)

AHIP   army helicopter improvement program

AIC   air intercept control

ALBM   air-launched ballistic missile

ALCM   air-launched cruise missile

AM   air marshal

AMRAAM   advanced medium-range air-to-air missile

AMSA   advanced manned strategic aircraft

AMST   advanced medium STOL

AOA   airborne optical adjunct

ASARS   advanced synthetic aperture radar system

ASAT   antisatellite

ASP   aerospace plane

ASV   air-to-surface vessel

ASW   antisubmarine warfare

ATA   advanced tactical aircraft

ATF   advanced tactical fighter

ATP   advanced turboprop

ATTA   advanced technology transport aircraft

AVM   air vice marshal

AWACS   airborne warning and control system

AWLS   all-weather landing system

BAC   British Aircraft Corporation

BAe   British Aerospace

BEA   British European Airways

BMEWS   ballistic missile early-warning system

CAB   Civil Aeronautics Board

Capt.   captain

CAS   chief of the air staff

CASA   Construcciones Aeronauticas SA

CASTOR   corps airborne stand-off radar

CATH   common attack helicopter

CCV   control-configured vehicle

CIA   Central Intelligence Agency

COD   carried-on-deck

COIN   counter-insurgency

Col.   colonel

Comdr.   commander

Comm.   commodore

CRAF   civil reserve air fleet

CSRL   common strategic rotary launcher

CVAN   attack aircraft carrier, nuclear-powered

CVB   U.S. aircraft carrier designation

CVL   light carrier

CX   heavy-lift (U.S. military air-transport specification)

DARPA   Defense Advanced Research Projects Agency

DEW   defense early-warning

DFBW   digital fly-by-wire

EAP   experimental aircraft program

ECM   electronic countermeasures

493

EDHP   European distribution system aircraft

EFA   European fighter aircraft

EHP   equivalent horsepower

ESHP   estimated static horsepower

EWR   Entwicklungsring GmBH

FAA   Federal Aviation Administration (U.S.)

FADF   fleet air defense fighter

FAI   Federation Aeronautique Internationale

FCS   flight control system

FEAF   Far East Air Force (U.S.)

FFCC   forward-facing crew cockpit

FG   fighter group

FIMA   future international civil/military airlifter

Fl. Abt.   Feldflieger Abteilungen (German: field flying section)

Flg. Off.   flying officer

FLIR   forward-looking infrared system

Flt. Off.   flight officer

FSD   full-scale development

FS   fighter squadron

FSW   forward-swept wing

FY   fiscal year

g   gravity or gravity force

Gen.   general

Gp. Capt.   group captain

HARV   high-angle of attack research vehicle

HCS   helicopter combat support

HiMAT   highly maneuverable aircraft technology program

HP   horsepower

Hptm.   Hauptmann (German: captain)

HUD   head-up display

IATA   International Air Transport Association

ICAO   International Civil Aviation Organization

JACD   Japan Aircraft Development Corp.

JAL   Japan Air Lines

JAS   Jakt-attack-spaning (fighter attack reconnaissance)

JATO   jet assisted takeoff

JG   Jagdgeschwader (Fighter Group)

JVX   vertical lift program

KAL   Korean Air Lines

Kptlt.   Kapitänleutnant (German: lieutenant captain)

LAMPS   light airborne multi-purpose system

LANTIRN   low-altitude navigation and targeting infrared system for night

LAPES   low-altitude parachute extraction system

LHX   light helicopter experimental

LLWAS   low-level wind shear alert system

LPSS   precision emitter lovation system (2144)

Lt.   lieutenant

LWF   lightweight fighter

MATS   military air transport service (USAF)

MBB   Messerschmitt-Bölkow-Blohms

MiG   Mikoyan and Gurevich

MRCA   multi-role combat aircraft

NACA   National Advisory Committee for Aeronautics

NACF   navy air combat fighter

NAMC   Nihon Airplane Manufacturing Co.

NAS   naval air station

NASA   National Aeronautics and Space Administration

NASP   national aerospace plane

NATC   naval air test center

NATO   North Atlantic Treaty Organization

NEACP   national emergency airborne command post

NEFMA   NATO European Fighter Management Agency

NETT   new equipment training team

NGF   next-generation fighter

NORAD   North American Air Defense

NOTAR   no-tail-rotor (helicopter)

Oberst   Colonel

Oblt.   Oberleutnant (German: first lieutenant)

OKB   manufacturing design bureau (Russian)

O.R.   operational requirement

OSA   operational support aircraft

PACAF   Pacific Air Force (U.S.)

PLSS   precision location strike systems

POBAL   powered balloon

QESTOL   quiet experimental STOL

QSRA   quiet, short-haul research aircraft

RAAF   Royal Australian Air Force

RAF   Royal Air Force

RAM   radar-absorbent material

RATO   rocket-assisted take off

RAuxAF   Royal Auxiliary Air Force

RCAF   Royal Canadian Air Force

RDC   radar cross section

RLM   Reichsluftfahrtministerium (German Air Ministry)

RMA   Royal Mail Ship

RN   Royal Navy

RNZAF   Royal New Zealand Air Force

ROBO   rocket-bomber

SAM   surface-to-air missile

SAS   Scandinavian Airline Systems

SAVER   stowable aircrew vehicle escape rotoseat

SBAC   Society of British Aircraft Companies

SCA   shuttle carrier aircraft

scamp   supersonic cruise aircraft modification program

SEPECAT   Societé Européene de Production de l'Avion E.C.A.T.

Sgt.   sergeant

SHP   shaft horsepower

SIOP   Single Integrated Operational Plan

SLCM   submarine-launched cruise missile

S/MTD   STOL and maneuver technology demonstrator

SNECMA   Societe Nationale d'Etude et de Construction de Moteurs d'Aviation

Sqdn. Ldr.   squadron leader

SRAM   short-range attack missile

SST   supersonic transport

s.t.   static thrust

STAC   Supersonic Transport Aircraft Committee (U.K.)

St.G   Stukagruppen

STO   short takeoff

STOL   short takeoff and landing

TACAN   tactical air navigation

TACT   transonic aircraft technology

TERCOM   terrain contour matching

TERPROM   terrain profile matching

TFX   tactical fighter experimental

TOW   tube-launched, optically tracked, wire-guided antitank weapon system

TRAM   target recognition attack multi-sensor

TRSB   time reference scanning beam

TST   Transonischer Tragflügel (transonic wing)

TTTS   tanker and transport training system

TV   television

UDF   unducted fan

UHB   ultra-high bypass

UKVG   United Kingdom variable-geometry

USAAC   U.S. Army Air Corps

USAAF   U.S. Army Air Force

USAAS   U.S. Army Air Service

USAF   U.S. Air Force

USAFE   USAF Europe

USB   upper surface blowing

USCG   U.S. Coast Guard

USMC   U.S. Marine Corps

UTTAS   utility tactical transport aircraft system

UTX   utility trainer experiment

V   engine with cylinders set at a V angle

VAX   navy attack experimental

V-STOL   vertical-short takeoff and landing

VTO   vertical takeoff

VTOL   vertical takeoff and landing

Wg. Comdr.   wing commander

VFX   navy fighter experimental

AIRCRAFT NAME INDEX

How To Use: This index is arranged in alphanumeric sequence. For example: Boeing aircraft series 777 is found under "*S*" and is followed by aircraft models SH-2 and SH-3A. The year, month and day in every index entry serves as the page locator. Asterisks * following the date indicate more than one text citation.

A

A-1 (Curtiss seaplane) 1911 Jun 30/Sep 7/Dec 20
A.I (Antoinette aircraft) 1906 Nov 19
AI (Morane Saulnier aircraft) 1913 Jul; 1917 Aug 7; 1920 May 26
A.I. (Fokker aircraft) 1914 Oct*/Dec 8
A-2 (Curtiss land/seaplane) 1911 Jul 13
A.II (Antoinette aircraft) 1908 Jul 22/Aug 21
AII (Morane Saulnier aircraft) 1913 Jul
A-3 (Curtiss seaplane) 1912 Nov 12
A-3/EA-3 Skywarrior (Douglas aircraft) 1952 Oct 28; 1959 Aug 25; 1967 May 31; 1972 Dec 18; 1975 Aug 1
A-3 Falcon (Curtiss aircraft) 1927 Feb 28/Jun 29
A-3J (North American aircraft) 1956 Jun 29
A.IV (Antoinette aircraft) 1908 Oct 9; 1909 Jul 25
A-4C (Douglas aircraft) 1967 Aug 30
A4N1 (Nakajima aircraft) 1932 Apr*
A-4 Skyhawk (Douglas aircraft) 1923 Jun 14; 1938 Feb 2; 1952 Jun 21; 1954 Jun 22; 1966 Apr 24/Jun 29; 1967 Mar 12; 1970 Apr 10; 1973 Oct 9/Oct 24; 1979 Feb 27; 1980 Jun 3; 1982 Apr 2/Sep 28; 1991 Feb 28*
A5M/ASM1 (Mitsubishi aircraft) 1932 Apr*; 1934 Feb; 1935 Feb 4/Jun; 1937 May 19/Aug 20*/Sept 4
A-5 Vigilante (North American aircraft) 1956 Jun 29; 1958 Aug 31; 1964 Aug 5; 1979 Sep 28
A-6/EA-6 Intruder (Grumman aircraft) 1960 Apr 19; 1966 Apr 24; 1967 Feb 26; 1968 May 25; 1971 Jan/Feb; 1972 May 9/Dec 18; 1974 Mar 22; 1976 Jun 5; 1983 Dec 4; 1986 Apr 14; 1987 Aug 25/Dec 23; 1989 Apr 3; 1990 Dec 31; 1991 Feb 24/Aug 28
A6M Reisen (Zero) (Mitsubishi aircraft) 1937 May 19; 1939 Apr 1*; 1940 Sep 13; 1941 Dec 7*/Dec 8; 1942 Jan 4/Jan 11/Apr 5/Jun 4*; 1943 Apr 7; 1944 Oct 19
A-7 (Vought aircraft) 1961 Feb 14; 1964 Feb 11; 1965 Sep 27; 1967 Dec 4; 1968 Apr 6; 1969 Jul 14; 1971 Jan/Feb; 1972 May 9; 1975 May 6; 1983 Dec 4; 1986 Apr 14
A.VII (Antoinette aircraft) 1909 Jul 27
A-8 Shrike (Curtiss aircraft) 1931 Sep 29
A-12 (McDonnell Douglas aircraft) 1987 Dec 23; 1991 Jan 7/Oct 29
A-12/YF-12 (Lockheed aircraft) 1959 Aug 29; 1962 Dec 27; 1964 Feb 29; 1965 May 1
A 16 (Focke-Wulf aircraft) 1924 Jun 23
A-20 (Douglas aircraft) 1938 Oct 26; 1944 Sep 14
A-22 (Lockheed aircraft) 1962 Apr 26
A-24 (North American aircraft) 1942 Feb 19
A-37 see T-37/A-37 (Cessna aircraft)
A-40 Albatross (Beriev aircraft) 1989 Aug 20
A 129 Manguster (Agusta aircraft) 1983 Sep 15
A.300 (Antoinette aircraft) 1923 Mar
A300 (Airbus aircraft) 1967 Jul 24; 1968 Dec 11; 1969 May 28; 1971 May 28*; 1972 Oct 18; 1974 May 23/Dec 26; 1976 Jun 27/Jul 3; 1977 Dec 13; 1978 Apr 4/Jul 10; 1983 Jul 8; 1984 Apr 12; 1987 Feb 1/Dec 9; 1988 Jul 3; 1991 Jul 5
A310 (Airbus aircraft) 1978 Oct 24; 1981 Oct 6; 1982 Feb 16; 1985 Jul 8
A320 (Airbus aircraft) 1984 Mar 12; 1987 Feb 22; 1989 Apr 18/May 20; 1991 Oct 25
A330 (Airbus aircraft) 1986 Jan 27; 1987 Jun 5; 1989 Apr 18; 1990 Oct 29
A340 (Airbus aircraft) 1986 Jan 27; 1987 Jun 5; 1989 Apr 18; 1991 Oct 25
AA-2 Atoll (Soviet missile) 1953 Sep 11; 1981 Aug 19
AA-5A Cheetah (Grumman aircraft) 1973 Oct 8
AB-1 (U.S. Navy aircraft) 1915 Nov 5
AB-2 (U.S. Navy aircraft) 1915 Apr 16/Nov 5
AB-3 (Curtiss aircraft) 1914 Apr 25
AB-5 (U.S. Navy aircraft) 1915 Nov 5
AB-6 see D-1 (AB-6/Model K) (Burgess aircraft)
AB-7 see D-2 (AB-7/Model H) (Burgess aircraft)
AC-130A (Lockheed aircraft) 1968 Feb 27/Dec 30
AD-1 (NASA research aircraft) 1979 Dec 21
AD-1/5 Skyraider (Douglas aircraft) 1945 Mar 18; 1951 May 1; 1951 Aug 17; 1954 Jul 26
AD-500 (Airship Industries aircraft) 1981 Sep 18
Ader flying machine (*Eole*) 1890 Oct 9; 1892 Feb 3
Aerodrome No.4 (Langley aircraft) 1893 Nov 16
Aerodrome No.5 (Langley aircraft) 1895 May 9; 1896 May 6; 1898 Mar 31; 1899
Aerodrome No.6 (Langley aircraft) 1898 Mar 31; 1899
AFVG (Anglo-French variable geometry fighter) 1965 May 17; 1968 Jul 17/Aug 23; 1969 Mar 26/Oct 1
Agile (balloon) 1794 Oct 31
AGM-62 Walleye (U.S. missile) 1967 Mar 12
AGM-65 Maverick (U.S. missile) 1980 Jun 3
AGM-69A SRAM (U.S. missile) 1972 Aug 4
AGM-86A/B ALCM (U.S. missile) 1976 Mar 5/Sep 9; 1978 Jun; 1979 Jul 17; 1980 Feb 8/Mar 25; 1981 Jan 11/Aug 15*/Sep 3; 1985 Feb 19; 1986 May 10/Oct 7
AGM-109 Altair (U.S. missile) 1985 Sep 17
AGM-109 ASAT (U.S. missile) 1985 Sep 17
AGM-109 AWG-9/AIM-54 Phoenix (U.S. missile) 1968 Mar 28; 1972 Apr 28; 1974 Mar 18; 1989 Jan 9
AGM-109 GAM-72A Quail (U.S. missile) 1961 Mar 7*
AGM-109 GAM-87 Skybolt (U.S. missile) 1960 Aug 2; 1961 Mar 6/Dec 9; 1962 Apr 19/Nov 7/Dec 21
AGM-109 Tomahawk (U.S. missile) 1976 Jun 5; 1978 Jun; 1979 Jul 17; 1980 Feb 8; 1991 Jan 17*/Feb 28*
AH-1 (McDonnell aircraft) 1954 Oct 18
AH-1 Cobra (Bell aircraft) 1965 Sep 7; 1966 Mar 11; 1967 Sep 1; 1976 Nov 5; 1977 Mar 16; 1979 Feb 5; 1983 Nov 16; 1989 Jan 24; 1991 Feb 24
AH-3 (Curtiss aircraft) 1914 May 6; 1916 Apr 2
AH-9 (U.S. Navy aircraft) 1916 Apr 2
AH-10 see Burgess-Dunne AH-10 (U.S. Navy aircraft)
AH-14 (U.S. Navy aircraft) 1916 Apr 2
AH-56 Cheyenne (Lockheed aircraft) 1965 Sep 7; 1966 Mar 11/Mar 23; 1967 Sep 21
AH-64 (McDonnell Douglas aircraft) 1991 Jan 17*/Feb 24

AH-64 Apache (Hughes aircraft) 1966 Mar 23; 1973 Jun 22; 1975 Sep 30; 1984 Jan 26
AIDC Chung-Kuo (Taiwan prototype fighter) 1989 May 28
AIM-54 see AGM-109 AWG-9/AIM-54 Phoenix (U.S. missile)
Airacobra see P-39 Airacobra (Bell aircraft)
Airacuda see FM-1 Airacuda (Bell aircraft)
Airbonita see XFL-1 Airbonita (Bell aircraft)
Aircar (Gwinn aircraft) 1938 Aug 23
Ajeet (Hindustin aircraft) 1976 Sep 30
AJ Savage (North American aircraft) 1946 Jun 24; 1951 Mar 6
AK-1 (Aleksandrov/Kalinin monoplane) 1924 Feb 8
Akron (U.S. Navy airship) 1921 Aug 10; 1924 Dec 15*; 1928 Nov 7; 1930 Jun 30; 1931 Mar 31/Oct 27/Nov 3; 1932 Jun 29; 1933 Apr 4; 1935 Feb 12
ALARM (British missile) 1985 Feb 13
Albatross (Beriev aircraft) see A-40 Albatross
Albatross (De Havilland aircraft) see D.H.91 Albatross
Albatross (Grumman aircraft) 1947 Oct 24; 1976 Aug 13*
ALCM see AGM-86A/B ALCM (U.S. missile)
Alizé see 1050 Alizé (Breguet aircraft)
Aloha (Breeze monoplane) 1927 Aug 17
Alouette see SE-3130 Alouette (Süd-Est aircraft)
Alpha-Jet (Franco-German aircraft) 1972 Feb 16; 1973 Oct 26; 1980 Dec 12
Alsace (French airship) 1915 Oct 2
Altair (Lockheed aircraft) 1934 Oct 22
Altair (U.S. missile) see AGM-109 Altair
Ambassador see A.S.57 Ambassador (Airspeed aircraft)
America (Model H) (Curtiss aircraft) 1916 Apr 6
AMX-T (AMX International aircraft) 1990 Mar 14
An-10 (Antonov aircraft) 1957 Mar 10
An-12 (Antonov aircraft) 1971 Mar 25; 1973 Oct 9; 1979 Dec 22
An-22 (Antonov aircraft) 1965 Feb 27; 1973 Oct 9; 1979 Dec 22
An-24 (Antonov aircraft) 1962 Oct 31
An-72 (Antonov aircraft) 1977 Dec 22
An-124 (Antonov aircraft) 1969 May 21; 1982 Dec 26; 1985 Jul 26; 1988 Dec 21*
An-225 (Antonov aircraft) 1969 May 21; 1988 Dec 21*; 1989 Mar 22/May13/Jun 5
ANF Les Mureaux 113 (French reconnaissance aircraft) 1938 Mar 9
Anson (Avro aircraft) 1935 Mar 24
ANT.1 (Tupolev aircraft) 1918 Dec 1; 1922 Aug
ANT.2 (Tupolev aircraft) 1922 Aug; 1924 May 26
ANT-4 (TB-1) (Tupolev aircraft) 1925 Nov 26; 1929 Aug 23/Sep 11; 1930 Dec 22; 1931 Dec 3
ANT-6 (TB-3) (Tupolev aircraft) 1930 Dec 22; 1931 Dec 3; 1941 Aug 25
ANT-7 (Tupolev aircraft) 1929 Sep 11
ANT-9 (Tupolev aircraft) 1929 May 7/May
ANT-14 (Tupolev aircraft) 1931 Aug 14
ANT-20 Maxim Gorky (Tupolev aircraft) 1934 Jun 15

G

G3M Nell (Mitsubishi aircraft) 1935 Jul; 1937 Aug 14/Sep*; 1939 Aug 26; 1940 Jan; 1941 Dec 8; 1942 Jan 11

G.IV (Caudron aircraft) 1916 Aug 2/Aug 6

G.IV (Gloster aircraft) 1927 Sep 26

G.IV (Gotha aircraft) 1917 May 25

G4M (Mitsubishi aircraft) 1937 Sep*; 1939 Oct 23; 1941 Dec 6/Dec 8; 1942 Feb 19; 1943 Apr 18/Sep 14/Oct 31

G.V (AEG aircraft) 1919 Jul 30

G.V (Gotha aircraft) 1918 Jan 28

G5N (Nakajima aircraft) 1941 Apr 10

G8N Renzan (Nakajima aircraft) 1944 Oct 23

G.12 (Fiat aircraft) 1940 Oct 15

G.18 (Fiat aircraft) 1935 Mar 18

G-21 Goose (Grumman aircraft) 1937 May 29; 1947 Oct 24

G.23 (Junker aircraft) 1925 May 15; 1926 Apr 6

G.24 (Junker aircraft) 1926 Apr 6/Jul 24; 1928 Mar

G.31 (Junker aircraft) 1928 Mar

G.38 (Junker aircraft) 1929 Nov 6; 1931 Sep 1

G.50 (Fiat aircraft) 1937 Feb 26; 1938 May 23; 1942 Apr 30

G.55 (Fiat aircraft) 1942 Apr 30

G.91 (Fiat aircraft) 1955 Jun 2; 1956 Jun 23/Aug 9

G.222 (Aeritalia aircraft) 1970 Jul 18; 1983 May 26*

GA-1 (U.S. military aircraft) 1920 Jun 7

Galaxy see C-5 Galaxy (Lockheed aircraft)

Gamecock (Gloster aircraft) 1917 Jun 5; 1925 Feb; 1929 Jan

Gamma (Northrop aircraft) 1932 Nov 29; 1933 Jun 2; 1934 Feb 19; 1935 Nov 22; 1936 Jan 13

Gannet (Fairey aircraft) 1949 Sep 19; 1957 Jun; 1961 Jun 30; 1970 Feb 24

GAR-9 Hughes (U.S. missile) 1963 Aug 16

G-ASCN see Skyvan (G-ASCN) (Short aircraft)

Gastambide-Mengin I (monoplane) 1908 Feb 8/Jul 22/Aug 21

Gates Learjet 1976 May 19; 1980 Mar 28; 1982 Jan 27; 1984 Mar 13; 1989 Aug 29; 1991 Jun 13

Gauntlet (Gloster aircraft) 1917 Jun 5; 1929 Jan; 1937 Dec

GAX (U.S. experimental aircraft project) 1920 Jun 7

GAZ-1 M-5 (Soviet aircraft) 1923 Aug 23

Gazelle (Westland aircraft) 1967 Apr 7

Gemini (Miles aircraft) 1948 Jan 13

Gemini (spacecraft) 1962 Mar 31/Jun 27

General Cambronne (balloon) 1871 Jan 28

General Myer (balloon) 1890 Oct 1; 1898 May 31

Genie see MB-1 Genie (U.S. missile)

George IV Coronation Balloon (balloon) 1821 Jul 19

Gerfaut see 1402 Gerfaut (Nord aircraft)

Gigant (Messerschmitt aircraft series) see Me 321 Gigant; Me 323 Gigant

GL40 (Levy aircraft) 1919 Nov 29

Gladiator (Gloster aircraft) 1917 Jun 5; 1931 Oct 1; 1934 Sep 12; 1935 Apr 12; 1937 Jul 29; 1939 Sep 22; 1940 Apr 24/Jun 11

Gladiator Charity (Gloster aircraft) 1940 Jun 11

Gladiator Faith (Gloster aircraft) 1940 Jun 11

Gladiator Hope (Gloster aircraft) 1940 Jun 11

Globemaster I see C-74 Globemaster I (Douglas aircraft)

Globemaster II see C-124 Globemaster II (Douglas aircraft)

Gnat (Folland aircraft) 1955 Jul 18; 1956 Sep 15; 1974 Aug 21; 1976 Sep 30

Goblin see XF-85 Goblin (McDonnell aircraft)

Gold Bug see Golden Flyer

Golden Flyer (Curtiss aircraft) 1909 Mar 2/Jun 26

Goliath see F.60 Goliath (Farman aircraft)

Goose see G-21 Goose (Grumman aircraft)

Gordon (Fairey aircraft) 1931 Mar 3; 1936 Feb*

Goshawk (Nieuport aircraft) 1921 Jul 12

Gouin (Blériot aircraft) 1914 Jun 6

Goupy I (triplane) 1908 Sep 5

Graf Zeppelin LZ 127 1928 Sep 18; 1928 Oct 11; 1929 Aug 1; 1931 Jun 23; 1932 Mar 20; 1937 May 8; 1986 Apr 23

Graf Zeppelin II LZ 128 1937 May 8

Great Aerodrome (Langley aircraft) 1898 Nov 3; 1899; 1901 Jun 19; 1903 Aug 8/Oct 7/Nov 28/Dec 8; 1905 Jan 3; 1907 Jul 11; 1914 May 28

Grebe (Gloster aircraft) 1923 May/May 7; 1924 Oct; 1926 Oct 21

Greyhound see C-2 Greyhound (Grumman aircraft)

Griffin see 1500 Griffin (Nord aircraft)

Gripen see JAS 39 Gripen (SAAB aircraft)

Ground Aircraft Experimental see GAX (U.S. experimental aircraft project)

G series (U.S. Navy airships) 1929

Guideline see SA-2 Guideline (Soviet missile)

Gulfstream II (Grumman aircraft) 1968 May 5; 1975 Sep 29; 1980 Mar 28; 1987 Mar 6; 1988 Feb 26

Gulfstream III (Grumman aircraft) 1982 Jan 10

Gulfstream/Sukhoi S-21G (U.S.-Soviet aircraft) 1989 Jun 13

Gull Six (Percival aircraft) 1980 Nov 21

Gunbus see F.B.5 Gunbus (Vickers aircraft)

H

H-1 (Hughes aircraft) 1935 Sep 13

H-2/SH-2 (Kaman aircraft) 1971 Mar 16

H-4 Hercules (Hughes aircraft) 1947 Nov 2

H-5 see R-5/H-5 (Sikorsky aircraft)

H6K (Kawanishi aircraft) 1936 Jul 14; 1942 Jan 4

H8K (Kawanishi aircraft) 1940 Dec 31; 1979 Apr 23

H-21 Workhorse (Piasecki aircraft) 1952 Apr 1*; 1956 Aug 23; 1961 Dec 11

H-43 Huskie (Kaman aircraft) 1958 Sep 19; 1962 Jun 13

H-46 see Model 107 (H-46) Sea Knight (Boeing-Vertol aircraft)

H-58 see OH-58/H-58 Kiowa (Bell aircraft)

H-75R (Curtiss aircraft) 1939 Jan 25*

Ha 139 (Blohm und Voss aircraft) 1937 Aug 15; 1938 Jul 21*/Oct 11

Ha 142/Bv 142 (Blohm und Voss aircraft) 1938 Oct 11

HA-3000 (Helwan aircraft) 1964 Mar 7*

Hadrian (Handley Page aircraft) 1931 Nov 9

Haefely DH 3 (Swiss aircraft) 1919 Jan 8

Halifax (Handley Page aircraft) 1909 Jun 17; 1936 Sep 8; 1938 Mar*; 1939 Oct 25; 1941 Jun 10; 1942 May 30; 1944 Mar 6*; 1945 Oct 9

Hampden (Handley Page aircraft) 1932 Sep; 1936 Feb*/Mar 17/Jun 21; 1940 Mar 19/Aug 25; 1941 Jul 9/Aug 12; 1942 May 30

Hannibal (Handley Page aircraft) 1931 Nov 9

Hanno (Handley Page aircraft) 1931 Nov 9

Hansa (LZ 13) (Zeppelin airship) 1912 Sep 19

Hansa Jet (MBB aircraft) 1980 Mar 28

Hardy (Hawker aircraft) 1934 Sep 7

Harrier (BAe aircraft) 1982 Apr 5; 1987 Jan 12/Jul 1; 1991 Jul 9

Harrier (Hawker Siddeley aircraft) 1967 Dec 28; 1968 May 11; 1969 Mar 19/Apr 24/Sep; 1970 Feb 16; 1973 Aug 17; 1975 Nov 6

Harrier, Advanced (Hawker Siddeley aircraft) 1973 Apr 12; 1976 Jul 27

Harrow (Handley Page aircraft) 1936 Oct 10; 1939 Aug 5

Hart (Hawker aircraft) 1925 Jan 3; 1928 Jun; 1931 Jun 22; 1932 Apr 20; 1934 Sep 12*; 1935 Jul 24; 1936 Feb*

Hart Trainer (Hawker aircraft) 1932 Apr 20

Harvard 1 see BC-1 (Harvard 1) (North American aircraft)

Hastings (Handley Page aircraft) 1956 Oct 11; Nov 5

Hawk (BAe aircraft) 1985 Sep 26; 1986 Feb 17/May 19; 1988 Apr 16; 1990 Jan 31

Hawk (Curtiss aircraft) see P-1 Hawk

Hawk (Hawker Siddeley aircraft) see HS Hawk

Hawk (Pilcher aircraft) 1896*; 1899 Sep 30

Hawk II/III (Model 75A) (Curtiss aircraft) 1937 Sep 4; 1939 Jan 23; 1942 Nov 8

Hawk 81-A (Curtiss aircraft) 1940 Apr 4

Hawkeye see E-2 Hawkeye (Grumman aircraft)

Hayabusa see Ki-43 Hayabusa (Nakajima aircraft)

HB-1 (Huff Daland aircraft) 1927 Feb

H biplane trainer (Burgess aircraft) 1912 Aug*; 1913 Jan 1*; 1914 Feb 14; 1915 Mar 12

HD 17 (Heinkel aircraft) 1926 May 21

He 12 (Heinkel aircraft) 1929 Jul 22

He 45 (Heinkel aircraft) 1937 Nov

He 50 (Heinkel aircraft) 1935 Oct*

He 51 (Heinkel aircraft) 1936 Jul 25/Nov 1; 1937 Apr 26

He 59 (Heinkel aircraft) 1931 Sep; 1937 Nov; 1940 May 10

He 70 (Heinkel aircraft) 1934 Feb 3/Jun 15/Dec 1; 1936 Nov 1/Dec 1

He 74 (Heinkel aircraft) 1933 Nov

He 100 (Heinkel aircraft) 1938 Jan 22/Jun 6; 1939 Mar 30

He 111 (Heinkel aircraft) 1935 Feb 24/Apr*; 1936 Jan 10; 1937 Apr 26/Nov*; 1938 Jul 8; 1939 Sep 1*/Oct 28; 1940 Feb 22*/Apr 24/Sep 22/Nov 14/Dec 21; 1941 May 20/Oct; 1942 Jun 2/Jul 5/Nov 25

He 112 (Heinkel aircraft) 1935 Oct; 1936 Nov 1; 1937 Apr; 1938 Jun 6

He 113 (Heinkel aircraft) 1938 Jan 22

He 115 (Heinkel aircraft) 1938 Mar 18; 1939 Nov 22; 1940 Apr 8*; 1942 Jul 5

He 132 (Heinkel aircraft) 1945 Mar

He 162 Salamander (Heinkel aircraft) 1944 Sep 8/Nov*/Dec 6

He 170 (Heinkel aircraft) 1939 Mar 23

He 176 (Heinkel aircraft) 1939 Jun 30

He 177 (Heinkel aircraft) 1936 Jun 3; 1937 Jun 2; 1938 Nov 7/Nov 12/Nov 19; 1944 Jul 20/Aug 16*; 1945 Mar 25

He 178 (Heinkel aircraft) 1939 Aug 27

He 219 Uhu (Heinkel aircraft) 1942 Nov 15; 1943 Jun 11*

He 277 (Heinkel aircraft) 1943 May 23

He 280 (Heinkel aircraft) 1940 Sep 22; 1941 Apr 2

Hector (Hawker aircraft) 1936 Jun 15*

Helena (Handley Page aircraft) 1931 Nov 9; 1932 Jan 20

Helistat (U.S. airship) 1986 Apr 26

Hellcat see F6F Hellcat (Grumman aircraft)

Helldiver (Curtiss aircraft) 1935 Dec 9; 1939 May 15

Hellfire (U.S. missile) 1991 Apr 5

Hendon (Fairey aircraft) 1930 Nov 25; 1934 Jul 23

Hengist (Handley Page aircraft) 1931 Nov 9

Heracles (Handley Page aircraft) 1931 Nov 9; 1938 Sep 23

Hercules see D.H.66 Hercules (De Havilland aircraft); H-4 Hercules (Hughes aircraft); Nike Hercules (U.S. missile)

Hermes (Handley Page aircraft) 1950 Nov 10

Heron see D.H.114 Heron (De Havilland aircraft)

Hewitt-Sperry biplane (Curtiss seaplane) 1916 Sep 12

Heyford (Handley Page aircraft) 1922 Nov 24; 1930 Jun 12; 1934 Jul 23; 1935 Feb 26; 1936 Mar 17

HF-24 Marut (Hindustin aircraft) 1961 Jun 17

HH-53 see CH-53/HH-53 (U.S. military aircraft)

HH-60 (U.S. military aircraft) 1984 Feb 4

Hien see Ki-61 Hien (Kawasaki aircraft)

High Altitude Monoplane see 138A High Altitude Monoplane (Bristol aircraft)

Hi-Hoe (air-launched anti-satellite missile) 1962 Jul 25

Hinaidi (Handley Page aircraft) 1927 Mar 26; 1928 Dec 23; 1930 Jun 12

Hind (Hawker aircraft) 1934 Sep 12*; 1936 Feb*

Hindenburg (LZ 129) (Zeppelin airship) 1936 Mar 4; 1937 May 6; May

Hiryu see Ki-67 Hiryu (Mitsubishi aircraft)

HL-10 (lifting body research vehicle) 1964 Jun 2; 1966 Jul 12; 1968 Nov 13; 1969 May 9; 1970 Jul 17

Ho I (Horten aircraft) 1938 Nov 12*

Ho II (Horten aircraft) 1938 Nov 12*

HO-4 (Bell aircraft) 1961 May 19; 1962 Dec 8

HO-5 (Hiller aircraft) 1961 May 19

Horatius (Handley Page aircraft) 1931 Nov 9

Hornet (De Havilland aircraft) see D.H.103 Hornet

Hornet (Hawker aircraft) 1931 Mar 25

Hornisse see Fa-266 Hornisse (Focke Achgelis aircraft)

Horsa (Handley Page aircraft) 1931 Nov 9; 1935 Aug 23

Horsley (Hawker aircraft) 1927 May 20*

HOS3 (U.S. military aircraft) 1950 Aug 3

Houston (U.S. Navy airship) 1934 Jul 19*

Hoverfly (Sikorsky helicopter) 1947 Aug 9

SUBJECT INDEX

How To Use: This index is arranged in letter-by-letter. The year, month and day in every index entry serves as the page locator. For example: Douglas Aircraft Co. 1928 Nov 30 takes you directly to the chronologically ordered text. Asterisks * following the date indicate more than one text citation.